Carl Schmitt

To Hans Gebhardt (1925–2013),
the only reader of Schmitt's shorthand

Carl Schmitt

A Biography

Reinhard Mehring

Translated by
Daniel Steuer

polity

First published in German as *Carl Schmitt* © Verlag C.H.Beck oHG, München 2009

This English edition © Polity Press, 2014

The translation of this work was funded by Geisteswissenschaften International – Translation Funding for Humanities and Social Sciences from Germany, a joint initiative of the Fritz Thyssen Foundation, the German Federal Foreign Office, the collecting society VG WORT and the Börsenverein des Deutschen Buchhandels (German Publishers & Booksellers Association).

Polity Press
65 Bridge Street
Cambridge CB2 1UR, UK

Polity Press
350 Main Street
Malden, MA 02148, USA

ISBN-13: 978-0-7456-5224-5

A catalogue record for this book is available from the British Library.

Library of Congress Cataloging-in-Publication Data

Mehring, Reinhard.
 [Carl Schmitt. English]
 Carl Schmitt : a biography / Reinhard Mehring.
    pages cm
 Translation of: Carl Schmitt : Aufstieg und Fall.
 Includes bibliographical references.
 ISBN 978-0-7456-5224-5 (hardcover) -- ISBN 0-7456-5224-7 (hardcover) 1. Schmitt, Carl, 1888-1985. 2. Political scientists--Germany--Biography. 3. Constitutional history--Germany. 4. Germany--History--20th century. I. Title.
 JC263.S34M43813 2014
 320.092--dc23
 [B]
                              2014011126

Typeset in 10 on 11pt Times New Roman MT by
Servis Filmsetting Limited, Stockport, Cheshire
Printed and bound in the United Kingdom by Clays Ltd, St Ives PLC

The publisher has used its best endeavours to ensure that the URLs for external websites referred to in this book are correct and active at the time of going to press. However, the publisher has no responsibility for the websites and can make no guarantee that a site will remain live or that the content is or will remain appropriate.

Every effort has been made to trace all copyright holders, but if any have been inadvertently overlooked the publisher will be pleased to include any necessary credits in any subsequent reprint or edition.

For further information on Polity, visit our website: politybooks.com

Contents

Abbreviations

List of archives

(Nachlass = posthumous papers; PA = personal files)
Archiv der Bayrischen Akademie der Wissenscgaften (Nachlass Johannes Winckelmann)
Archiv der Juristischen Fakultät der Universität Bonn (Berufungsakten der Fakultät [documents relating to appointments to the university])
Bayrisches Hauptstaatsarchiv (Akten der Handelshochschule München und Berufungsakten 1933 [documents relating to appointments to the university in 1933])
Bayrisches Wirtschaftsarchiv München (Akten der Handelshochschule München)
Bundesarchiv Koblenz (BAK) (Nachlass Ernst Rudolf Huber)
Deposit Jürgen Becker, now joined with Carl Schmitt's literary estate
Heinrich-Heine-Institut Düsseldorf (Nachlass Wilhelm Schäfer)
Historisches Archiv der Technischen Universität München (HATUM.PA Prof. van Calker)
Historisches Stadtarchiv Köln (HAStK, Nachlass Walter Warnach, Akten der Zentrumspartei [Files of the Zentrum party]) (Note: The archive was destroyed on 3 March 2009 when work on the Cologne Underground led to the collapse of the Stadtarchiv)
Landesarchiv NRW [Nordrhein-Westfalen], Abteilung Rheinland, Standort Düsseldorf (Nachlass Carl Schmitt RW 265, as well as other collections, e.g., RWN 260)
Niedersächsiche Staats- und Universitätsbibliothek Göttingen (Nachlass Rudolf Smend)
Staatsarchiv Hamburg (Einbürgerungsakten Heinrich, Fritz und Georg Eisler [documents on the naturalization of Fritz and Georg Eisler])
Universitätsarchiv Bonn (PA Schmitt, Friesenhahn, Vormfelde)
Universitätsarchiv Heidelberg (Nachfolge Anschütz, PA Lohmann)
Universitätsarchiv der Humboldt-Universität zu Berlin (among others: PA Carl Schmitt)
Universitätsarchiv Köln (among others: PA Carl Schmitt)

Universitätsarchiv Marburg (Dissertationsakte Kathleen Murray [file on Murray's doctoral examination])
Verlagsarchiv Duncker & Humblot (correspondence with Schmitt)

The most important works by Carl Schmitt (German edition followed by English translations)

AN	*Antworten in Nürnberg*, ed. with annotations by Helmut Quaritsch, Berlin, 2000
BP	*Der Begriff des Politischen, Text von 1932 mit einem Vorwort und drei Corollarien*, Berlin, 1963
BP 1933	*Der Begriff des Politischen*, Hamburg, 1933
CP	*The Concept of the Political*, trans. and with an introduction by George Schwab, expanded edn, Chicago, 2007
CPD	*The Crisis of Parliamentary Democracy*, trans. Ellen Kennedy, Cambridge, MA, and London, 1985
CT	*Constitutional Theory*, trans. and ed. Jeffrey Seitzer, Durham, NC, and London, 2008
D	*Die Diktatur: Von den Anfängen des modernen Souveränitätsgedankens bis zum proletarischen Klassenkampf* (1921), 4th edn, Berlin, 1978
D	*Dictatorship: From the Origin of the Modern Concept of Sovereignty to Proletarian Class Struggle*, trans. Michael Hoelzl and Graham Ward, Cambridge, 2014
DARD	*Über die drei Arten des rechtswissenschaftlichen Denkens* (1934), 2nd edn, Berlin, 1993
On the Three Types of Juristic Thought, trans. Joseph Bendersky, Westport, CT, and London, 2004
DC	*Donoso Cortés in gesamteuropäischer Interpretation: Vier Aufsätze*, Cologne, 1950
ECS	*Ex captivitate salus: Erfahrungen der Zeit 1945/47*, Cologne, 1950
FP	*Frieden oder Pazifismus? Arbeiten zum Völkerrecht und zur internationalen Politik 1924–1978*, ed. Günter Maschke, Berlin, 2005
GL	*Glossarium: Aufzeichnungen der Jahre 1947–1951*, ed. Eberhard von Medem, Berlin, 1991
GLP	*Die geistesgeschichtliche Lage des heutigen Parlamentarismus* (1923), 2nd edn, Munich and Leipzig, 1926
GM	*Gespräch über die Macht und den Zugang zum Machthaber*, Pfullingen, 1954
GU	*Gesetz und Urteil: Eine Untersuchung zum Problem der Rechtspraxis* (1921), 2nd edn, Munich, 1969
HdV	*Der Hüter der Verfassung*, Tübingen, 1931
HH	*Hamlet oder Hekuba: Der Einbruch der Zeit in das Spiel*, Düsseldorf, 1956

HH   *Hamlet or Hecuba: The Intrusion of the Time into the Play*, trans. David Pan and Jennifer Rust, New York, 2009

HP   *Hugo Preuß: Sein Staatsbegriff und seine Stellung in der deutschen Staatslehre*, Tübingen, 1930

ICWA   *Das internationalrechtliche Verbrechen des Angriffskrieges und der Grundsatz 'Nullum crimen, nulla poena sine lege'*, ed. Helmut Quaritsch, Berlin, 1994
'The International Crime of the War of Aggression and the Principle "Nullum crimen, nulla poena sine lege" (1945)', in *Writings on War*, trans and ed. Timothy Nunan, Cambridge 2011, pp. 125–97

L   *Der Leviathan in der Staatslehre des Thomas Hobbes: Sinn und Fehlschlag eines politischen Symbols* (1938), Cologne, 1982
The Leviathan in the State Theory of Thomas Hobbes: Meaning and Failure of a Political Symbol, trans. George Schwab and Erna Hilfstein, Chicago, 2008

LL   *Legality and Legitimacy*, trans. and ed. Jeffrey Seitzer, Durham, NC, and London 2004

LM   *Land und Meer: Eine weltgeschichtliche Betrachtung*, Leipzig, 1942

N   *Theodor Däublers 'Nordlicht': Drei Studien über die Elemente, den Geist und die Aktualität des Werkes* (1916), Berlin, 1991

NE   *Der Nomos der Erde im Völkerrecht des Jus Publicum Europaeum*, Cologne, 1950

NtE   *The Nomos of the Earth in the International Law of the Jus Publicum Europaeum*, trans. and annotated by G. L. Ulmen, New York, 2006

PB   *Positionen und Begriffe im Kampf mit Weimar – Genf – Versailles 1923–1939*, Hamburg, 1949

PR I   *Politische Romantik*, Munich and Leipzig, 1919

PR II   *Politische Romantik*, 2nd edn, Munich and Leipzig, 1925

PR   *Political Romanticism*, trans. Guy Oakes, new edn, New Brunswick, NJ, and London, 2011

PT   *Politische Theologie: Vier Kapitel zur Lehre von der Souveränität* (1922), 3rd edn, Berlin, 1979

PT   *Political Theology*, trans. George Schwab, Cambridge, MA, and London, 1985

PT II   *Politische Theologie II: Die Legende von der Erledigung jeder Politischen Theologie*, Berlin, 1970

PT II   *Political Theology II: The Myth of the Closure of any Political Theology*, trans. and introduced by Michael Hoelzl and Graham Ward, Cambridge, 2008

RK   *Römischer Katholizismus und politische Form*, 2nd edn, Munich, 1925
Roman Catholicism and Political Form, trans. G. L. Ulmen, Chicago, 2008

RSG   *Das Reichsstatthaltergesetz*, Berlin, 1933

SBV   *Staat, Bewegung, Volk: Die Dreigliederung der politischen Einheit*, Hamburg, 1933

SGN   *Staat, Großraum, Nomos: Arbeiten aus den Jahren 1916–1969*, ed. Günter Maschke, Berlin, 1995

SS   *Über Schuld und Schuldarten: Eine terminologische Untersuchung*, Breslau, 1910

SZZR   *Staatsgefüge und Zusammenbruch des zweiten Reiches: Der Sieg des Bürgers über den Soldaten*, Hamburg, 1934

TB I   *Carl Schmitt: Tagebücher Oktober 1912 bis Februar 1915*, ed. Ernst Hüsmert, Berlin, 2003

TB II   *Carl Schmitt: Die Militärzeit 1915–1919: Tagebuch Februar bis Dezember 1915: Aufsätze und Materialien*, ed. Ernst Hüsmert and Gerd Giesler, Berlin, 2005
          Carl Schmitt: Unpublished diaries 1922–1934 (provisionally transcribed), Nachlass Carl Schmitt, Hauptstaatsarchiv Düsseldorf; now Landesarchiv NRW, Abteilung Rheinland, Standort Düsseldorf

TDCW   'Die Wendung zum diskriminierenden Kriegsbegriff', in *Frieden oder Pazifismus?* (FP), pp. 518–97
          'The Turn to the Descrimination Concept of War (1937)', in *Writings on War*, trans. and ed. Timothy Nunan, Cambridge, 2011, pp. 30–74

TP63   *Theorie des Partisanen: Zwischenbemerkungen zum Begriff des Politischen*, Berlin, 1963

TP07   *Theory of the Partisan: Intermediate Commentary on the Concept of the Political*, trans. G. L. Ulmen, New York, 2007

TW   'Die Tyrannei der Werte', in *Säkularismus und Utopie: Ebracher Studien: Ernst Forsthoff zum 65. Geburtstag*, Stuttgart, 1967, pp. 37–62

VA   *Das internationalrechtliche Verbrechen des Angriffskrieges und der Grundsatz 'Nullum crimen, nulla poena sine lege'*, ed. Helmut Quaritsch, Berlin, 1994

VL   *Verfassungslehre*, Munich and Leipzig, 1928 (for English edn, see CT)

VRA   *Verfassungsrechtliche Aufsätze aus den Jahren 1924–1954: Materialien zu einer Verfassungslehre*, Berlin, 1958

VV   *Volksbegehren und Volksentscheid: Ein Beitrag zur Auslegung der Weimarer Verfassung und zur Lehre von der unmittelbaren Demokratie*, Berlin, 1927

WdS   *Der Wert des Staates und die Bedeutung des Einzelnen*, Tübingen, 1914

Correspondence

BS   *Carl Schmitt: Briefwechsel mit einem seiner Schüler*, ed. Armin Mohler, in collaboration with Irmgard Huhn and Piet Tommissen, Berlin, 1995

CSAD	*Carl Schmitt und Álvaro d'Ors: Briefwechsel*, ed. Montserrat Herrero, Berlin, 2004
CSLF	*Carl Schmitt/Ludwig Feuchtwanger: Briefwechsel 1918–1935*, ed. Rolf Rieß, Berlin, 2007
EFCS	*Briefwechsel Ernst Forsthoff/Carl Schmitt (1926–1974)*, ed. Dorothee Mußgnug, Reinhard Mußgnug and Angela Reinthal, Berlin, 2007
FBCS	*Franz Blei: Briefe an Carl Schmitt 1917–1933*, ed. Angela Reinthal, Heidelberg, 1995
GJCS	*Briefwechsel Gretha Jünger/Carl Schmitt (1934–1953)*, ed. Ingeborg Villinger and Alexander Jaser, Berlin, 2007
HBCS	*Hans Blumenberg/Carl Schmitt: Briefwechsel 1971–1978 und weitere Materialien*, ed. Marcel Lepper and Alexander Schmitz, Frankfurt, 2007
JB	*Carl Schmitt: Jugendbriefe: Briefschaften an seine Schwester Auguste 1905–1913*, ed. Ernst Hüsmert, Berlin, 2000
JS	*Ernst Jünger/Carl Schmitt: Briefwechsel 1930–1983*, ed. Helmuth Kiesel, Stuttgart, 1999
LMCS	*Luís Cabral de Moncada und Carl Schmitt: Briefwechsel 1943–1973*, ed. Erik Jayme, Heidelberg, 1997
SSA	*Carl Schmitt/Hans-Dietrich Sander: Werkstatt-Discorsi: Briefwechsel 1967–1981*, ed. Erik Lehnert and Günter Maschke, Schnellroda, 2008
WBCS	*Werner Becker: Briefe an Carl Schmitt.* ed. Piet Tommissen, Berlin, 1998

Translator's Preface

The Book

When Reinhard Mehring's biography of Carl Schmitt first appeared in German, one of its reviewers spoke of it as doing 'almost superhuman justice' to its subject. Indeed, one might be tempted to call the book a positivist biography, one that describes a life in the form of 'protocol sentences' (Rudolf Carnap). The 'case of Schmitt' is laid out in front of the reader; all the evidence is presented. However, the reader should not be misled by the style of the book. As in a good summation in court, all the descriptive detail serves the purpose of making the case clear and allowing for a proper sentence. In this way, Mehring's book carries out a difficult task: it analyses, even dissects, Schmitt's life and work without being tempted into shortcuts or hasty conclusions by the aversion that many of that life's deeds provoke.

If Schmitt's biography – even, and maybe especially, when viewed from the most factual and impartial perspective – proves one thing, it is that intelligence is neither a protection against delusion nor a guarantee of moral integrity. And, whereas we may assume that Hitler believed in his ideological constructs, at times not even that much is clear in the case of Schmitt. Rather, the 'case of Schmitt' is also the case of Germany, in that it raises the question of why there was so little solidarity with the victims, and how it was possible to install, practically overnight, an exclusionist and totalitarian regime that defied any legal or moral standard. These questions are still relevant today, not only in Germany.

Mehring's quasi-positivist biography again raises the question of whether it is possible to distinguish between someone's intellectual and scholarly work and his political and social behaviour and deeds. In the case of Schmitt, someone often said to have thought in terms of 'concrete' situations, the answer can only be a negative one. And this applies not only to the early National Socialist years. The subcutaneous effects of implicit ideology are always the greater danger, and anyone using Schmitt's work should think about the implications this may have. If Hitler's *Mein Kampf* is considered a dangerous book when published without commentary and explanation then this is true, perforce, of many of Schmitt's works. For here, force of (seeming) conviction and learnedness combine into a message whose effect may be, at times, as subcutaneous as that of *Mein Kampf*. For this reason, too, Mehring's biography is important.

The more the work on this translation progressed, hour by hour, the more often the translator's mind wandered off to the scenes where, as Georg Büchner put it in *Danton's Death*, 'what you see is what you've said – a precise translation of all your words', where the phrases become flesh and blood, and each word may be 'the death rattle of a victim'. This very factual story of a life, strangely, seemed all the more strongly to evoke the ghosts of these victims of delusional fanaticism, exaggerated self-importance and senseless and meaningless crimes. To these victims, the translation is dedicated.

Principles adopted in the translation

Often, the difficulty with translations from German, as all friends of Mark Twain know, is lengthy and convoluted sentences. Here, the opposite was the case. There are three-word sentences in the original. I have tried to maintain this paratactic style and brevity, as it is, in light of what has just been said, integral to the book's intention. As far as Carl Schmitt's use of the German language is concerned, it is often idiosyncratic, forcing a translator either to lose that idiosyncrasy in the translation or mildly to maltreat the target language. I have opted for a middle way, often 'normalizing' the formulations, and only in cases where matters of substance are concerned retaining the awkwardness of the original. In some of these latter cases, the original German has been added in brackets. For texts by Schmitt, the existing English translations have been consulted and used unless otherwise indicated. In the case of other German-language sources, the reverse is the case: translations are mine unless English editions are referenced in the notes. All footnotes are mine, endnotes are Mehring's. Where I have made additions to the latter, these are in brackets.

Many names of political, legal and other institutions and functions, especially from the National Socialist period, have no equivalents in English. I have retained these terms in German, adding explanatory footnotes where necessary. As in Tim Park's books on *Italian Neighbours* and *A Season with Verona*, which are interspersed with recurring Italian expressions, the hope is that the reader will easily pick up the meaning of these German terms.

No two legal systems are identical, and inevitably this holds for those that belong to the Anglo-Saxon case law system, on the one hand, and the continental civil law system (and German state law), on the other. Thus, legal terms, including certain types of courts, etc., are explained where they first occur, and sometimes the German original is added in brackets. Finally, the German distinguishes between Gesetz (law) and Recht (right), and, to make matters worse, the former can sometimes be used with a meaning very close to the latter. But, typically, an individual law is 'ein Gesetz', but a body of law is 'Recht' – e.g., public law is Öffentliches Recht, private law is Privatrecht. However, 'Recht' – and this is relevant for Schmitt – can also have an almost transcendent meaning, in which it refers to a right that should inform all individual laws and bodies of law. In order to avoid misunderstandings, the German has again been added in brackets in some passages.

I would like to thank the author, Reinhard Mehring, for always responding quickly to my many queries. Thanks are also due to Caroline Richmond for her excellent copyediting, to Sarah Lambert at Polity for her support throughout, to my friend Tim Carter for endless exciting discussions about the intricacies of the English language, and to the current students on the MA in Cultural and Critical Theory at the University of Brighton for their kindness, good humour and understanding (not all is lost as long as the next generation has such people in it). And more than thanks are due to my partner, Dr Birgit Illner, for her patience and support and for putting up with weeks without weekends.

Daniel Steuer
Brighton, March 2014

Foreword: A White Raven – The Strange Life of the German State Theorist Carl Schmitt

For me, it remains an open question: how was the 'case of Schmitt' possible? It is, after all, vital for us all, to understand the 'case of Germany' eventually.[1]

On the occasion of a Festschrift for Ernst Jünger, Carl Schmitt provided the following short note on himself as a contributor:

C. S., born 1888 in Plettenberg (Westphalia). Studied in Berlin, Munich and Strasbourg. Habilitation in 1916 at Strasbourg University. Lost his lectureship as a result of the outcome of the Great War. From 1921 to 1945, full professor of public law at Greifswald, Bonn, Cologne and Berlin. Became state councillor of Prussia in 1933. Lost his chair as a result of the outcome of the Second World War, and since 1947 has lived in Plettenberg (Westphalia). Three major works: *Dictatorship* (1921), *Constitutional Theory* (1928; reprinted 1954), *The Nomos of the Earth* (1950). (BS, p. 183)

'I think this should suffice', he added in his letter to the editor of the Festschrift, Armin Mohler. 'The three books may be left out, though I think it might be good to mention them. The identity with Germany's fate, the unity of scholarly profession and fate, becomes obvious enough in these details.' When Mohler requested a shortening of the biographical information, Schmitt replied: 'Ultimately, the following will do: C. S., born 1888, a white raven that can be found on every blacklist.' At that point, he was sixty-six years old and still had more than thirty years to live. He saw himself as someone 'defeated' and created a strong and beguiling legend of his 'identity with Germany's fate'.

The figure of the raven as someone who gives good advice appears in many legends and fables. A white raven is an innocent lamb and a black sheep. In claiming to be on every blacklist, Schmitt wanted to point to a discrepancy between reputation and character, as he did in the case of those authors who served him as intellectual points of reference: Donoso Cortés, Machiavelli and Hobbes. Schmitt countered legends in slightly ironic fashion with a counter-image. He proffered many means of interpretation and 'myths' for an understanding of his eventful and strange life[2] without resorting to the store of German myths.[3] He saw himself reflected in Don Quixote, Othello and Don Juan, in the Catholic counter-revolutionary Donoso Cortés, in Machiavelli, in Thomas Hobbes, or again in the fictional character Benito Cereno from Melville's novella of the same name. After 1945 he saw himself in the role of an intellectual who had failed, as a Hamlet or as the court theologian Eusebio. A biographer must cautiously pick up such ciphers and use them for a reconstruction of the protagonist's conception of himself. However, we should not hope to find a master key to this complex character. The following biography seeks to avoid strong judgments and retrospective projections and, instead, to present the open possibilities and contingencies of a life in, as it were, slow motion. Amid the wealth of material, the reader may from time to time miss a strong thesis. Roughly speaking, what the reader should expect is the old story of rise and fall: the biography of a social climber and outsider, who, with regard to power and law, chose as his theme the political conditions and foundations of constitutions and developed a new constitutional theory. With regard to power and spirit, Schmitt's life story is also a case study in the risks to which a committed constitutional lawyer exposes himself by becoming politically entangled. It is the story of the gradual descent of a highly talented and slightly extravagant intellectual to the depths of National Socialist and anti-Semitic delusion. Even after 1945, Schmitt never fully recovered from this. Nevertheless, he had important disciples in the Federal Republic who saved his work and gave it another lease of life under conditions of a liberal reception.

This biography historicizes the life and work of Schmitt. It does not give his work a place among the 'classical authors' of political thought or within the history of public law. It also does not discuss its actuality, which is often invoked with an alarming tone.[4] The constitution of the Federal Republic today no longer follows the script of the national state as Schmitt used it in his constitutional theory. Schmitt is certainly one of the fathers of the more recent statism and anti-liberalism. He legitimized the taking of exceptional actions and sometimes cloaked it in the guise of faith. But by now his immediate impact is a thing of the past. The dispute between Schmitt and his Weimar colleague Rudolf Smend over the antagonistic concepts of state and constitution, decision [Dezision] and integration, may have dominated the debates in German universities for a long time, and, 'surprisingly, many discussions in more recent times can be projected onto these fronts'.[5] But it seems almost unimaginable today that the high demands that Schmitt's thought placed on systematicity should be fulfilled.[6] His political views are thoroughly discredited. The statism, nationalism and anti-Semitism of Weimar no longer exist. And Schmitt made almost no attempt at characterizing even the old Federal Republic. He had only a vague premonition of the more recent Europeanization and internationalization of law.[7] Schmitt himself looked at his work in its historical context, and he understood it as a response to certain challenges and situations. There may be a world-wide reception of his views and concepts wherever an erosion of the constitutional state can be observed and universalist conceptions of law are attacked. However, in such cases a significant shift in meaning is involved. Thus, in the context of the development of the 'preventive state', we may currently experience a renewed politicization of law on a massive scale.[8] But Schmitt's work is firmly rooted in the interwar years and in the catastrophic national history of Germany after 1914. This biography puts the work into the context of the crisis of its times and reads it, in particular, autobiographically as a reflection of its author's life. The decline is manifest in his life, work and times.

Schmitt's biographical note, with which we began, points out a double 'loss' caused by the two lost wars. The 'councillor of the state' saw himself as someone who was 'defeated' in 1918 and 1945. To him, the 'fate of Germany' had been no success story. Nor, during thirty years of witnessing it, did he consider the Federal Republic to be a 'successful democracy'. He did not experience the 'long road West' from the vantage point of 1989–90, and hence did not see it as the resolution of the German tension between 'unity' and 'freedom'.[9] Rather, his life of almost a hundred years was a long story of disappointments. In his search for a fundamental order, Schmitt gradually had to abandon all political systems and alternatives: the Wilhelminian constitutional state and the Catholic Church, the parliamentary republic and the presidential system, the juridico-institutional foundation of meaning under National Socialism and the 'Reich' as the supranational model for political order, the legitimacy of individual resistance and the 'legal world revolution'. 'All this I went through, / and it all went through me', Schmitt remarked as early as 1948 (ECS, p. 92). This biography presents German history of the twentieth century as it is reflected in the life and work of an analytic mind and an active participant. At times coming close to a chronicle, it observes and records the sequence of events that made up Schmitt's problematic life, as well as his conscious attempts at finding normative orientation and stability.

As an author, Schmitt left behind a record of over seventy years. There are many specific studies today that argue at a high level and go into minute detail. However, the only existing biography is out of date.[10] Recently, a fictional biography has been published.[11] By contrast, this presentation of Schmitt's life attempts to be as factual as possible. Apart from published sources, it is based in particular on those of Schmitts's diaries from the Weimar period that have been transcribed so far and on the extensive posthumous papers in Düsseldorf.[12] Schmitt kept pretty much everything. Over long periods, his life can be reconstructed in detail, thanks to a lot of preliminary work that has already been done.[13] However, regarding the time before 1922 and after 1933 there are some significant gaps in the posthumous papers.[14] His reminiscences of his first wife, Pauline (Cari) Dorotić, as well as some sources from the National Socialist period, have been deleted from the record. Nevertheless, there is an abundance of documents. I was granted access to these sources in the most generous way. Schmitt's idiomatic shorthand notes, though, I could not read. To the present day, the burden of transcription rests with the stenographer Hans Gebhardt alone. Unfortunately, the pocket diaries and diaries after 1933 are not yet deciphered, and I could make only sporadic use of them. A lot of the information is not particularly important in itself. By contrast, important events sometimes are absent. The thrust of a restless life should nevertheless become visible. A puzzle of this magnitude will certainly not be free of factual errors and slips of the pen. Ultimately, Schmitt's life and work remains ambiguous and mysterious. Despite these limits, the biography you are about to read certainly does not lack substance or colour.

Part I

That 'False and Arrogant Idea "I am"': Schmitt's Rise in the Wilhelminian Era

1

An 'Obscure Young Man from a Modest Background'

The parents' ancestry from the Eifel

Carl Schmitt called himself time and again a Moselanian. However, even in the case of his parents this is not quite true. All relatives on his father's side[1] came from Bausendorf, a village on the Alfbach in the Eifel Mountains, about 6 kilometres as the crow flies from the Moselle. The distance to Bernkastel-Kues, the main place along the central part of the Moselle, is about 15 kilometres. After 1815, Bausendorf became part of Prussia. In the nineteenth century, the mostly Catholic population of about 500 lived off agriculture and the crafts. There was no viniculture. Bausendorf had its own parish building; close by was Heinzerath, a place of pilgrimage. Within the paternal line, we see a transition from agriculture to the crafts. One of the great-grandfathers was a baker, farmer and publican. The grandfather, Nikolaus Schmitt, had a bakery and public house, and he owned a barn and stables as well as a school and dance hall. In 1852, he married a certain Katharina Anna Franzen. The marriage produced nine children, of whom Carl's father, Johann Schmitt (1853–1945), was the eldest son. Thus, there were many uncles and aunts on his father's side alone. Carl never got to know his paternal grandparents.

At the age of five the father entered the boys' school in Bausendorf. At the age of fourteen he began training with the postal services in the nearby wine-producing municipality of Kröv and was soon put in charge of the post office at Bleialf in the northern part of the Eifel Mountains. Later, he joined the better-paid railway services. In 1874, his post was moved to Siegen/Siegerland in Westphalia, and thereafter to Wedohl at the River Lenne. In September 1876, he came to Plettenberg-Eiringhausen in the Westphalian part of the Sauerland, where in 1878 he joined the nuts and bolts factory Graewe & Kaiser (Graeka) as a commercial clerk and accountant. The factory had been founded only in 1872, was expanding strongly, and shaped the structure of the neighbourhood. Johann Schmitt's business travels also took him abroad.

In 1872, he made the acquaintance of Maria Rehse (1850–1882), and they married in August 1879. Maria was evangelical, meaning that Johann crossed the denominational border in marrying her. They had two children: Ernst (1880–1919) and Maria (1881). The second child died at birth,

Left: the father, Johannes Schmitt: 'Throughout his life, he remained faithful to the Catholic cause in a diaspora, which was still very hard at the time' – Carl Schmitt in a letter to the historian Rudolf Morsey (9 September 1960). Right: the mother, Louise: Schmitt would sometimes speak about her in rather negative terms.

and after a prolonged illness her mother followed her in 1882. At Whitsun 1886, Johann met Louise (Luise) Steinlein (1863–1943), Carl's mother, on a journey. She had been born as an illegitimate child in 1863 in Blasweiler (district of Ahrweiler) in the Eifel Mountains. In 1865, her mother, Augusta Louise Bell, married the customs officer Franz Josef Anton Steinlein from Trier. Franz is said to have been her father. But it is likely that his brother Nikolaus, a priest, was actually her biological father, which is why Louise was legitimated only in 1865, after the birth of a son, Andreas. Following Louise and Andreas, the Steinleins, Carl's grandparents, had another five children. Thus, Schmitt also had many relatives on his mother's side, some of whom lived in Lorraine where his mother grew up.

After a short acquaintance, Johann Schmitt and Louise married in September 1887. On 11 July 1888, the Year of the Three Emperors,[*] Carl was born in Plettenberg.[2] His siblings Auguste (1891–1992), Joseph (1893–1970) and Anna Margarethe (1902–1954) followed. Neither of the two sisters had children or married. His brother Joseph (Jupp) did marry and had three daughters (Claire-Louise, Auguste, Paula). He practised medicine in Cologne. Another half-brother, Ernst, became a butcher; he had six

---

[*] After Wilhelm I had died in 1888, his son Frederick III reigned for ninety-nine days. However, he had terminal cancer of the throat and was, in turn, succeeded by Wilhelm II in the same year.

children. Carl Schmitt himself married twice and had a daughter from his second marriage, Anima Louise (1931–1983). She married a Spanish man with whom she had four children (Beatriz, Carlos, Jorge, Álvaro). Thus, all in all Carl had many relatives. He got to know only one of his grandpas, but that was presumably not his real grandfather. Throughout his life, Carl remained in close touch with his family. Plettenberg, where his parents lived to a very old age, he often visited for longer periods of time. He also stayed in close contact with his siblings. Schmitt's father retired in 1928, at the age of seventy-five, after fifty years as a commercial clerk at Graeka. For the times, his rise had been remarkable.

At school in Plettenberg and Attendorn

Plettenberg is situated in the southern corner of the 'Märkisches Sauerland'. 'This meant: belonging to a confessional minority in an intensely evangelical environment, an environment partly even of protestant sectarianism.'[3] At the end of the nineteenth century, Plettenberg had already taken on the character of a small-scale industrial town. Between 1880 and 1900 its population increased to just about 5,000. Thus, Schmitt came from an expanding small town, situated in the valley of the little River Lenne, flowing through the wet, cold and hilly landscape of a low mountain range. At the beginning, the family rented a place in a more rural part of the town. In the summer of 1901, they moved into a semi-detached house in the Bahnhofstrasse in Eiringhausen. Nearby were a wire works, a sawmill and a forge, and a narrow-gauge railway passed directly in front of the house. In the beginning was the railway: Schmitt grew up next to a small marshalling yard. Only a few steps away are the Lenne and the surrounding landscape, through which Schmitt would later go hiking with great passion time and time again.

At Easter 1894, Schmitt entered school. He attended the Catholic Jüttenschule, first in the town centre, then in the Eiringhausen part of town. The average mark on his leaving certificate of 11 April 1900 was a 'good'.[4] His father was a member of the parish council and active in the society of stenographers at Gabelsberg. He taught him short-hand writing, which Carl would use intensely throughout his life. From his mother, who had been educated at a convent in Lorraine, he learnt the French language and to play the piano. Anna Margarethe, the younger sister, would later become a music teacher. Carl, too, played the piano to an old age. When he was eleven, he joined year three of the municipal secondary school (founded in 1515) in Attendorn. It lies about 15 kilometres away from Plettenberg, and, as it was not easy to get there, Schmitt entered the Catholic seminary Collegium Bernardinum. Thus, at age eleven he was sent to a strict boarding school, leaving a life in the Catholic diaspora for life in a dominant Catholic atmosphere. He spent his holidays with relatives in the Eifel Mountains, at the Moselle or with his French-speaking relatives in Lorraine, where one of his maternal uncles, André Steinlein, had become rich by selling plots of land to the mining industry. The son of this uncle, also called André Steinlein, formed a close friendship with his older cousin, and occasionally visited Plettenberg during the holidays. At the time, there were seventeen pupils in the third class, of whom thirteen were Catholic, three evangelical, and one Jewish. The main focus of the curriculum was on languages. In year seven Carl had seven hours of Latin and four hours of French per week. Later, he had eight hours of Latin, six hours of Greek, and in addition two hours of French. In the Oberstufe,* he had a choice between two hours of Hebrew or English and opted for English. The natural sciences played only a minor role, and there were also just two hours of religious studies. His mother wanted Carl to study theology and become a priest or monk. But for that he would have needed to opt for Hebrew. His decision against theology was final. Only later did he decide to study law, a decision he never regretted. There are very few informative sources on his childhood and schooldays. We do not learn about any key events or about any stories from boarding school life.

At secondary school, Carl got to know Carl Franz Kluxen, whose father owned a large department store for clothes at the Prinzipalmarkt in Münster. Franz soon left the school, but both met again while studying in Strasbourg. Kluxen had strong interests in the arts. At the young age of nineteen, he published a piece on 'Das "deutsche Drama" Richard Wagners als künstlerisches Ideal und schöpferische Tat' [The German drama of Richard Wagner as an artistic ideal and a creative act].[5] Later, he became a collector of modern paintings. Through Kluxen, Schmitt became acquainted with bourgeois wealth and the artistic avant-garde. Schmitt later noted down that it was Kluxen 'who initiated me into the thoroughgoing ingenious intellectuality of the nineteenth century, into R. Wagner and Otto Weininger' (GL, p. 151). Schmitt puts the date of his first acquaintance with Max Stirner, the author of the German Vormärz,[†] in year eight of secondary school. He mentions a disciplinary incident, namely having been caught reading David Friedrich Strauß. At the beginning of his last year at secondary school [Oberprima], on 3 August 1906, Schmitt was punished, together with twelve of his peers, 'with one hour of after school detention for breaking the rules and visiting a public house'. Presumably this was the reason why he had to leave the seminary in September. Thus, in the last months before his final examinations [Abitur], he had to commute as a 'train-farer' (JB, p. 58) between Attendorn and Plettenberg.

On 18 December 1906, he handed in his application for the examination. Due to his excellent performance so far, he was exempted from the oral examination. On 28 January, the written examinations began. Carl wrote a German composition on a maxim from Schiller's *Wallenstein*. Further subjects were mathematics, a Latin piece on Cicero and a Greek piece on Thucydides. He was happy with the results, writing to his sister at the beginning of February: 'The written exam is done, and it all went exceptionally well' (JB, p. 61). In physical education he got only a 'satisfactory';

---

*   In the German system, the last three years of secondary school.
†   Time between the Vienna Congress in 1815 and the March revolution of 1848; sometimes referred to as the Age of Metternich.

all else was 'good'. On 2 March 1907, he received his leaving certificate [Abiturzeugnis]. As a 'good' wasn't awarded as often then as it is now, it is justified to say that Carl was a remarkably good pupil throughout his time at school. He himself later called his leaving certificate 'a nice Abitur'.[6] In his application for the school-leaving examination, he wrote: 'I intend to study philology.' On the leaving certificate itself it says that Schmitt intended to study 'the subject of philology', which, in the context of a classical secondary school [Humanistisches Gymnasium], meant primarily classical philology.

University years in Berlin, Munich and Strasbourg

Carl Schmitt was only 1.60 metres in height and by conventional criteria not a beau. Photos from his youth show him with rather sharply edged jug ears, quite narrow almond-shaped eyes, a thin nose with a sharp line, thin lips, a prominent notched chin, striking gaunt wrinkles and light rimless glasses. Always noticeable are the large, dark eyes and the alert gaze. In some photographs Schmitt is all eyes. Franz Blei remembers 'a face in which every nerve is tense, illuminated by powerful eyes, with a mouth that seemed to contain the smile of a young boy.'[7] The young Schmitt looked very slim and ascetic. Later he became more rotund. In school photographs we find him in the centre. In one group photograph, he seems to tower over his classmates with folded arms and a domineering expression.

Carl was a good pupil, and yet his decision to study was not a foregone conclusion. 'The son of such modest people would not normally study at a university in these days, and certainly not law',[8] Schmitt would later remember. The mother insisted on him taking up his university studies. Financial help from the wider family was mobilized. Schmitt's younger brother Jupp later also went to university and studied medicine. Only the older half-brother, Ernst, learned a craft and became a butcher. Carl studied in Berlin, Munich and Strasbourg. Thus, he left his immediate vicinity and became familiar with important large cities. His uncle André advised him to study law. 'Thus, I travelled to Berlin', Schmitt remembered.

> In the university I read a note saying registration will take place on such and such a day. I can still see myself climbing up the steps of the Humboldt (then, of course, still Friedrich-Wilhelms) University, together with hundreds of people. I can still today see the sign in front of me: 'Faculty of Law'. I pondered for a moment, then I simply went into the section 'Faculty of Law' and stayed there. I thought the study of law was wonderful because it began straight away with Roman law in the first term. That was a joy for me: Latin – an enormous pleasure.[9]

The conflict over which subject to study, philology or law, was thus resolved by the fact that philology was useful for law.

Carl was able to stay with a relative of his father in a tenement in Lichtenberg (Wartenbergstraße). Berlin was 'a new world' to him, the

'Everything falls into place so that I climb higher up' – Schmitt in his diary, 22 September 1914

university 'a temple of a higher intellectuality' [Geistigkeit].[10] On 25 April 1907, he signed up for law. As was usual at the time, he also attended lectures and seminars from other disciplines. According to his official transcripts [Studienbuch], he took the following courses in the summer term of 1907: Einführung in die Rechtswissenschaft [Introduction to law] with Conrad Bornhak, Geschichte des Römischen Reiches [History of the Roman Empire] with Wilhelm von Seeler, System des römischen Privatrechts [The system of Roman civil law] with Theodor Kipp[11] and Kultur des Hellenismus [The culture of Hellenism] with Ulrich Wilamowitz-Moellendorff. At no point did he join a students' fraternity. Carl spent the summer-term break with his rich uncle in Bussingen (Lorraine) and returned to Berlin for the winter term 1907–8. In the meantime, his sister Auguste had also arrived there. He now took Deutsche Rechtsgeschichte [German legal history] with the Privatdozent* Ernst von Moeller,[12] Grundzüge des deutschen Privatrechts [The foundations of German private law] with Otto von Gierke,[13] a lecture and tutorial Einführung in die Rechtswissenschaft [Introduction to law] with Joseph Kohler,[14] courses on state law with Adolph Wagner and the Privatdozent Robert Wilbrandt, again System des römischen Privatrechts with von Seeler, and a lecture course on Bürgerliches Recht [Civil law] with Konrad Hellwig. The final transcript for his transfer to Munich is dated 7 March

---

* In the German university system, a lecturer who does not hold a permanent position and does not receive a proper salary.

1908. The professor extraordinarius von Seeler was the only one whose courses Schmitt took over both terms. But it seems that Kipp's Roman law also did not disappoint him.

After 1945, Schmitt wrote a memoir of this time as a student in Berlin, in which he compared the scholarly habitus of the two academic Großordinarien* Kohler and Wilamowitz-Moellendorff. Schmitt attended their courses in different terms. The contrast he saw between the legal scholar and the classical philologist shows that he was still in two minds with regard to the question of whether to study law or philology. In retrospect, he provided a physiognomy of these two grand figures, in order to 'present a picture of the question of the ego at the time'.[15] He described neither of them in particularly complimentary terms, criticizing them instead for their attitude towards their own selves. He sets Kohler's 'aestheticist unleashing of the self' in contrast to the northern German and Protestant 'ethicist armored self' of Wilamowitz. Schmitt emphasizes the 'existential inconsistency' between the habitus of these two mandarins and the political situation at the eve of the Great War, seeing himself as an eccentric observer: 'I was an obscure young man from a modest background. Neither the ruling elite nor an oppositional side had seized hold of me. I did not join any fraternity, political party or circle, and nor was I sought after by anyone.'[16] Schmitt claims to have had early on 'a distance from the myths of the German Reich under Bismarck and from the national-liberal atmosphere at Berlin University'.[17] He felt his whole life as if he were an intellectually superior social climber and outsider, an underdog who does not belong and is not shown enough respect, and who, in response, looks down on the 'bourgeois' world around him.

With the summer term 1908, Schmitt continued his studies in Munich. He took the following courses: Sachenrecht und Urheberrecht [Property law and copyright law] with Friedrich Hellmann, Familienrecht und Erbrecht [Family law and inheritance law] with Karl von Amira, Strafrecht [Criminal law] with Karl Ritter von Birkmeyer,[18] Allgemeine Volkswirtschaftslehre [General political economy] with the national economist Walter Lotz, Konkursrecht und Konkursprozess [Bankrutpcy law and bankruptcy procedure] as well as a seminar on Digesten-Exegese [Exegesis of the *digesta*]† with Lothar Ritter von Seuffert, Grundzüge der Sozialpolitik [Principles of social policy] with Karl Wasserrab, and, in the philosophical faculty, Geschichte Frankreichs im 19. Jahrhundert [The history of France in the nineteenth century] with the Privatdozent Theodor Bitterauf. The short term he spent at the university did not have any lasting influence on Schmitt, but he became familiar with the city in which he would later live for more than six years after 1915. Berlin and Munich became the two central places in his life. He was attracted by big cities.

---

* Plural of 'Großordinarius'. Before the reform of the universities in the 1960s, the 'Ordinarius' was the full professor who held the chair of a particular discipline or subdiscipline. The prefix 'grand' is often used to emphasize the power associated with that position in the old German university system.

† The *digesta* are an important collection of works by Roman legal scholars. They were declared established law by the emperor Justinian in 533 AD.

Given that, then, why did he change university again and go to Strasbourg? Although the faculty at Strasbourg had a good reputation, it is more likely that financial problems caused him to move to the border territory. Schmitt had relatives in Lorraine. His uncle André in particular was able to support him.

Thus, Schmitt continued his studies in the winter term 1908–9 at Strasbourg, where he quickly felt at home. On 10 January 1909, he wrote to his sister: 'If you could see my bright room with its solid stove, the high windows and heart-lifting views of the Black Forest, you would well understand why I feel so cosy and comfortable' (JB, p. 77). Soon he assured her: 'I feel very well at Strasbourg, much better, for instance, than exactly a year ago in Munich' (JB, p. 82). Schmitt lived together with his younger cousin André[19] at Ludwigshafener Straße 15 (today: rue de Reims). André remained one of his closest friends beyond Schmitt's time in Bonn. In Strasbourg he spent a considerable amount of time with his mother's side of the family. He established contact with Fritz van Calker, who would later become his mentor and doctoral supervisor. And he attended lectures and tutorials with the political economist Georg Friedrich Knapp.[20] He pushed ahead with his studies very fast; it took him only seven terms to complete them, including his doctoral thesis. He passed the first state examination in the spring of 1910.

For a long time, Alsace had been one of the most contested border territories in Central Europe. Goethe had been a student of law at Strasbourg when he revolutionized the German language. The university[21] had been founded in the spirit of humanism. Having flourished in the eighteenth century, it became French under Napoleon and diminished in significance. After the Franco-Prussian War, Alsace became German again and was

The Reichsuniversität Straßburg: Schmitt was a student and lecturer here between 1908 and 1910, and between 1916 and 1918.

given a special status[*] within the constitution of the Reich.[22] Nationalist tensions were mollified by regionalism and the federalist character of the Reich's traditionalism. Alsace saw itself not only from the perspective of either Germany or France but also as an independent culture and region within the context of the Upper Rhine. For reasons of regional traditions, authors from Alsace, such as René Schickele, were inclined towards universalist solutions. It is no coincidence that today Strasbourg is a capital of the European Union. The city symbolizes a transnational unity of origin and a common future. Although the Wilheminian Reich aimed at a 'Germanicization', the French tendencies could not simply be ignored or repressed. Thus, the teaching of state law at Strasbourg had as its peculiar theme the 'problem of autonomy', as can be seen in particular in the works of Paul Laband and Hermann Rehm.[23] Schmitt hardly ever referred to these tensions, either before or after 1918. However, they were his first experiences with border territories and sensitized him to nationalistic perspectives.

In 1871, Strasbourg had just about 80,000 inhabitants. At the end of 1905, the figure had risen to more than 150,000. The musical life of the city was cultivated to a high degree. From 1907, Hans Pfitzner was the director of the municipal conservatory. Otto Klemperer became his successor. Named the Kaiser Wilhelm University (Reichs University), the university was reopened as a bulwark of German culture and scholarship in 1872. Its architecture programmatically followed the style typical of the German Reich at the time. Important scholars, such as Karl Binding, Heinrich Brunner, Rudolph Sohm and Paul Laband, were appointed to the faculty of law. In 1844, the faculty moved into grand new buildings. Sohm wrote his *Institutes of Roman Law* in Strasbourg. Binding worked out his *Normen*[24] [Norms] and Mayer developed his administrative law. Strasbourg soon became one of the larger universities. By the time Schmitt completed his degree, it had around 2,000 students. The outstanding star in the Faculty of Law was Paul Laband – Strasbourg and Laband: they were one and the same thing. From the beginning to the end of his career, he never taught anywhere else. The great positivist *Staatsrecht des deutschen Reiches*[25] [State law of the German Reich], which Schmitt rejected, had been formulated at Strasbourg. As a Privatdozent, Schmitt became a 'colleague' of Laband's for a short time.

Until 1918, the composition of the faculty remained more or less constant. When he became a Privatdozent, Schmitt met almost all of the Ordinarien [full professors] with whom he had studied from the winter term of 1908–9 onwards. Apart from Laband and Hermann Rehm, there were, among others, Andreas von Tuhr, Wilhelm Kisch, Fritz van Calker and Wilhelm Sickel. The Privatdozent Max Ernst Mayer[26] was a significant intellectual figure with a strong presence. He was friendly with Gustav Radbruch and Emil Lask and is the only one who can be seen as belonging

---

[*] The so-called Reichsland Elsass-Lothringen did not enjoy the same rights as the other parts of the Wilheliminian Reich. Rather, it was governed externally by the administration of Prussia and the Reich.

to the 'südwestdeutsche Wertphilosophie' [Southwest German school of the philosophy of value]. In 1900, Mayer, who was a christened Jew, completed his Habilitation, titled *Die schuldhafte Handlung und ihre Arten im Strafrecht* [Culpable behaviour and types of it in criminal law], under the supervision of van Calker. It is likely that Schmitt knew Mayer more closely. Apart from Knapp, state law was taught by the professor extraordinarius Werner Wittich, whom Schmitt later befriended. Philosophy was represented by Theobald Ziegler, Clemens Baeumker and the Privatdozent Max Wundt. Among the historians were Martin Spahn, Georg Dehio and Harry Breslau.

Schmitt's mentor: Fritz van Calker (1864–1957)

Schmitt's teacher at Strasbourg, Fritz van Calker,[27] was more than a doctoral supervisor. As early as 1912 he offered Schmitt a lectureship. At the beginning of 1915, he extracted Schmitt from his marital crisis in Düsseldorf by getting him to Munich, where he was the major of an infantry regiment at the time. Once in Munich, van Calker saved him from military service at the front by finding him a position in the military administration. He soon gave Schmitt the opportunity to write his Habilitation, and later he was instrumental in Schmitt being offered a chair in Berlin. Schmitt dedicated his second monograph, *Gesetz und Urteil* [Law and judgment], to him, saying that he owed to him 'a strong need for methodological clarity and the orientation of his interests towards the realities of legal life' (GU, p. viii). Calker is one of the few people that Schmitt saw almost exclusively in a positive light. He virtually acted as his guardian angel. Despite all this, van Calker's name is practically absent from Schmitt's published works and posthumous papers. Schmitt almost never mentions him in his writings, and he probably did not meet him again after 1945. In Schmitt's library there is not a single publication by van Calker. Only two letters have been preserved. Calker is also forgotten in the historiography of law. Only in Schmitt's diaries do we come across him.

During Schmitt's four terms at Strasbourg, beginning with the winter term 1908–9 and ending with the summer term 1910, van Calker offered courses almost exclusively on Strafrecht [criminal law]. In the winter term 1908–9 he gave a lecture course, Einführung in die Rechtswissenschaft [Introduction to law], and a tutorial on criminal law. Schmitt probably took the seminar and met Fritz Eisler there. Calker gave lecture courses in the summer terms of 1909 and 1910 on criminal law and in the winter term 1909–10 on Strafprozessrecht mit besonderer Berücksichtigung einer neuen Strafprozessordnung [Criminal procedure law with particular reference to a new code of criminal procedure]. In the summer term 1910 he offered Wissenschaftliche Übungen im Strafrecht für Vorgerückte [Practical tutorial in criminal law for advanced students]. It is very likely that Schmitt took part in the latter, as he wrote his doctoral thesis on criminal law under the supervision of van Calker at that time. After the appointment to the faculty of Eduard Kohlrausch, another criminal law

'Calker is a genuinely good person, and he has diligently looked after me' – Carl in a letter to his sister Auguste, 19 February 1912

scholar, van Calker moved more towards the subject of legal policy. His work was characterized by an orientation towards political-pragmatic questions of legislative policy. In 1927, he published an Einführung in die Politik [Introduction to politics], which was explicitly said to have grown out of his 'practical experiences'.[28] Schmitt's political perspective on law can already be found in van Calker in the form of a legal perspective on politics. In the preface to his *Introduction*, van Calker defined politics as 'taking influence on the organization of communal life'. In his *Grundriss des Strafrechts* [Foundations of criminal law], van Calker thanked Schmitt for his suggestions.[29] In 1922, he reminded him of 'very nice notes', and asked him 'to provide' him with a copy of his notes on the *Grundrisse* for his work on the *Einführung in die Politik*, as his personal copy of the book had been 'stolen in the military barracks during the revolution'.[30] Calker's *Einführung* of 1927 was certainly no 'parallel campaign'.[*] It was not a version of Schmitt's notes, much less of his *Concept of the Political*. More interesting than the traces of Schmitt one may find in the writings of van Calker is the influence which his Strasbourg teacher exerted on Schmitt. Without a doubt, he introduced Schmitt to a political perspective on law. Schmitt repeatedly called him a 'friend'. As early as 1912, he wrote: 'Calker is a genuinely good person, and he has diligently looked after me' (TB I, p. 317).

---

[*] The reference is to Robert Musil's *The Man without Qualities*, in which Austria plans a 'parallel campaign' to celebrate the seventieth anniversary of the reign of the Emperor Franz Joseph in 1918, the same year the German Emperor Wilhem II celebrated his fortieth year on the throne.

Schmitt's friend: Fritz Eisler (1887–1914)

Hans Friedrich (Fritz) Eisler was born on 18 June 1887, the son of the Jewish publisher Heinrich (Henrick) Ludwig Eisler, in Hamburg. He had an older sister, Julie, and a younger brother, Bernhard Georg. The brother would also be a close friend of Schmitt's after 1914. Eisler's father was born in Budapest in 1853 and lived in Hamburg from 1877. His mother, Ida Ernstine, was from Vienna. Heinrich Eisler built up a rather large publishing company with more than 100 employees (1913) in Hamburg (Am Steinweg 23/25) and Berlin (Friedrichstraße 245). He started out trading advertisements ('Annoncen-Expedition')* and later founded journals and newspapers: *Küche und Keller* [Kitchen and cellar], the *Hamburger Woche* [Hamburg weekly] and the *Afrikanische Bord-Zeitung* [African on-board newspaper].† Soon he was considered the market leader in the advertisement trade. In 1922, he fused *Küche und Keller* with the *Deutsche Hotel-Nachrichten* [German hotel news] to form the official organ of the Reich association of the gastronomy industry. In 1914, he owned several properties in the Alter Steinweg and in the Benediktstraße, in the Schlüterstraße and the Düsterngasse, as well as having substantial assets. Yet, in 1908 his application for naturalization failed because of several previous convictions (twice in 1878, in Hamburg and Bremen, he had been sentenced to four months in prison for fraud, and in 1904 and 1907 he had been given fines and several days under arrest for lottery offences and violating the privacy of post).

Fritz grew up in Hamburg as a Hungarian national. From the winter term 1905–6 he studied in Lausanne, Munich and Kiel and from the summer term 1908 in Strasbourg. In the winter term 1908 he got to know Schmitt in Strasbourg. Eisler also took his doctorate with van Calker and completed it in 1910 *summa cum laude*. Afterwards, he again lived in Hamburg and worked in his father's business. His thesis, *Rechtsgut und Erfolg bei Beleidigung und Kreditgefährdung* [The legal interest and success in cases of defamation and injury to reputation], was published in the same series as Schmitt's in 1911. The winter term of 1912–13 Eisler spent as van Calker's assistant in Strasbourg 'for studies'. He then worked as an 'authorized representative' in his father's business again and probably also wrote articles in his papers. He repeatedly visited Schmitt during the latter's time as a legal trainee in Düsseldorf. They often wrote to each other. Their common work on the satire *Schattenrisse* [Silhouettes] and the meeting with the poet Theodor Däubler, but also Schmitt's lack of money, were more than enough to form a bond between them. The Eisler family supported Schmitt.

In 1912, Fritz was faced with the alternatives of working in his father's business or aspiring to an academic career. Before becoming van Calker's assistant, he handed in an application for naturalization. As a foreigner

---

* Companies that acted as agents between advertisers and newspapers. Precursors of advertising agencies.
† Newspaper for the ships of the Reich's postal service and the Woermann shipping line.

'For more than six years, we had been united in a friendship of a kind that can only be the result of many years of hours shared together and of common intellectual interests and aims'– Carl Schmitt about Fritz Eisler in his diary (8 October 1914)

he was not entitled to take state examinations, and with just a doctorate, without a first and second state examination in law, an academic career was almost impossible. The police authorities in Hamburg, however, caused difficulties, and Eisler had to involve a lawyer. His father provided comprehensive financial guarantees. Calker and others testified to his good reputation. Despite all this, the chief of police in Hamburg wrote in 1913: 'Nevertheless, due to the Hungarian-Jewish descent of the applicant . . . as well as the repeated criminal convictions of the father, I cannot endorse the application.'[31] In response, Fritz Eisler sent a letter to the authorities in Hamburg, in which he formally renounced the right to take the state examination and declared his willingness to do military service in Germany. At the same time he sorted out the question of his military service in Hungary. Thus, he gave up the possibility of an academic career while taking on all the responsibilities of a citizen. The authorities stressed yet again 'that the applicant does not acquire a right to be admitted to the first state examination in law through his naturalization'. On 24 February 1914, the chief of police in proxy finally approved the naturalization, 'after the applicant has declared that he does not intend to enter the civil service in Hamburg, but the large business of his well-to-do father'.[32] The certificate of naturalization is dated 29 May 1914.

Upon the outbreak of war, Fritz volunteered for military service and joined the field artillery regiment no. 9 in Itzehoe. Early on, on 27 September 1914, he was fatally hit by shrapnel. An obituary in the *Hamburger Woche*, his father's newspaper, said 'a colleague and advisor' and a 'friend' had

Strasbourg Cathedral: Ecclesia proudly lifts her head; Synagoga turns away.

been lost, whose 'preparations for a career as a university teacher of law had come close to their long-awaited end', and who lay buried 'now in foreign soil . . . as one of thousands and thousands who had to give their lives for the greatness and freedom of Germany'.[33] Schmitt was deeply moved by this untimely death. As a last favour to his friend, he edited one of Eisler's posthumous papers, 'Einleitung zu einer Untersuchung der Bedeutung des Gewohnheitsrechts im Strafrecht'[34] [Introduction to an investigation into the role of common law in criminal law]. Through Eisler, Schmitt for the first time came into a more intense contact with Jewish people and with Judaism. At the south portal of Strasbourg Cathedral, there is a sculptural representation of the relationship between Synagoga and Ecclesia. An older depiction comments on the figures as follows:

> Proudly, Ecclesia, the visible representation of the new covenant, of Christianity, lifts her head, holding in her right hand the flag of the victorious Church and in her left hand the chalice filled with the blood of the saviour. Synagoga, the personification of the old covenant and of Judaism, turns away from her, as if blinded by the radiance of the victorious power. A veil covers her eyes; she cannot endure the view of salvation and truth.[35]

With the Eisler family, Schmitt met the central theme of his life: the relationship between Christianity and Judaism.

'Guilt' at the beginning of the oeuvre

In 1910, Schmitt published his first article, 'Über Tatbestandsmäßigkeit und Rechtswidrigkeit des kunstgerechten operativen Eingriffs'[36] [On the elements constituting an offence and unlawfulness with regard to proficient surgery]. Why are medical interventions not treated as bodily harm? In this question we can already recognize Schmitt's inclination towards paradox and extreme points. Schmitt received his doctorate on 24 June 1910 for a monograph in criminal law with the title *Über Schuld und Schuldarten: Eine terminologische Untersuchung* [On guilt and types of guilt: a terminological investigation]. The theme of 'guilt' stood at the beginning of his work, a fact not without interest in the case of someone who became implicated in guilt and was later hardly ever able to admit it.

The thesis must have been written within a short period of time, as Schmitt completed his first degree quickly and, after the minimum required time of six terms, took the first state examination, which was immediately followed by the completion of the doctorate. During this time, he twice changed his place of study. Schmitt attended the courses of academic dignitaries such as Gierke, Kohler, Wilamowitz and Amira, but also of Privatdozenten and academic outsiders. His choice of courses reveals a focus on the study of criminal law and a strong interest in political economy and political science, as well as classical philology. By contrast, it seems that he did not manage to find space for any philosophical or theological courses in his dense programme of study. Apart from Calker,

Birkmeyer and Max Ernst Mayer were also teachers of criminal law. Mayer, in particular, looked for maximum theoretical sharpness. In addition, there were the discussions with Eisler. In Schmitt's thesis, the critical engagement with his own teachers, and with von Liszt and his pupil Radbruch, played an important role. He attempts a terminological clarification of established law. What he requires of a legal terminology is directed against 'any philosophical ambitions' and 'considerations of criminal justice policy'. Rather, his central point is that, in contrast to the ideas prevailing in the wake of Franz von Liszt, criminal law doctrine should be based not on the concept of 'types of guilt', comprised of 'premeditation' and 'negligence', but, even more fundamentally, on the 'concept of guilt'.

His study has two parts. The first one develops a 'definition of penal offence',[*] while the second one offers a discussion of 'the logical relationship between the concepts of premeditation and negligence, on the one hand, and guilt, on the other', which amounts to a critical revision of the prevailing legal theory. In it, Schmitt considers 'clarity regarding the concept of guilt' as a 'necessary condition' for a treatment of the 'actual topic' – i.e., for the 'consideration of the mutual relationships between the concepts of guilt, premeditation and negligence' (SS, p. 74). In his introductory discussion of Radbruch, he demonstrates how Radbruch was inconsistent in the way he took the 'types of guilt' as his point of departure. As a pupil of Liszt, Radbruch represented the liberal and psychologizing consequences of the prevailing theory. Thus, Schmitt's text must be seen in the context of the neo-Kantian critique of psychologism, which was also the starting point for the philosophers Edmund Husserl and Martin Heidegger. Schmitt examines Radbruch's 'premises' and then takes another route:

> It is a methodological mistake to set out from the so-called types of guilt in order to develop the concept of a penal offence. . . . It is not premeditation and negligence that should be the point of departure . . . but, on the contrary: it is necessary first to provide a conceptual definition of 'guilt' without recourse to the term 'types of guilt'. (SS, p. 14)

Setting out from a 'nominal definition', Schmitt wants to 'find the concept of guilt used in established law' (SS, p. 20). An action is only culpable, Schmitt argues, if it can be shown that the perpetrator acted in premeditated fashion or with negligence. He demands a strict 'separation of guilt from causality'. As an 'instance of inner life', guilt does not concern the causality of an action. A perpetrator is made responsible only for individual 'acts'. Schmitt rejects the idea of a 'character's guilt' [Charakterschuld] as the basis for establishing culpability, without denying that such a thing exists. 'Every human being', he says, 'had daily first-hand experience of the fact that we suffer retribution on account of our character' (SS, p. 47). Schmitt also does not deny that a 'character's guilt' is relevant for legal

---

[*] The German for 'penal offence' is 'Strafschuld', literally 'punishable *guilt*'. It may be useful to keep this in mind for the following discussion of Schmitt's argument.

judgments. However, it was only to be taken into the equation at the point of 'deciding the heaviness of the sentence'. Only once someone had been found 'guilty' of committing a specific crime could an evaluation of the perpetrator's character become relevant for determining the sentence. With this bracketing of 'character', the whole philosophical problem of 'freedom of the will' and the 'battle over determinism and indeterminism' (SS, p. 45) remains excluded from the discussion. Seen from the perspective of the state and the lawyer, guilt appears as 'the pursuance of purposes which do not correspond to the purposes of the law'. 'The intentions of the individual are meant to coincide with the intentions of the punitive state' (SS, p. 55), Schmitt wrote. 'The individual intentions of a person are measured and evaluated against the intentions of the state' (SS, p. 58).

The second part examines the contemporary use of the term 'types of guilt'. 'Premeditation' and 'negligence' are seen as 'types of evil will' (SS, p. 94). Schmitt clarifies that both 'types', in essence, apply to any kind of act which deserves the name. Hence, premeditation and negligence are 'not types of guilt' but 'preconditions for guilt': 'preconditions for the imputability' of guilt. Otherwise, 'anyone who acts intentionally would act culpably' (SS, p. 105). With this, Schmitt's thesis is complete: the usual parlance of 'types of guilt' is actually no more than a 'convenient and vague expression which isn't quite taken seriously' (SS, p. 132). Whoever wanted to base a doctrine of guilt on this expression, Schmitt says, would 'give up having a system in order to save a terminology' (SS, p. 123). Thus, Schmitt's 'terminological investigation' ultimately is interested not in terminology but in systematic unity, which, he holds, is made impossible by the ambivalent talk about types of guilt. If we apply to it Schmitt's later distinction between 'positivism' and 'normativism', then it presents not a 'positivist' argument on the basis of the established 'terminology' but a 'normativist' argument on the basis of 'systematic' rigour.

Schmitt's thesis was a daring proof of talent. A 21-year-old author courageously stood up to established doctrine and the legislator. In the 'types of guilt' he pushed aside a central concept of contemporary criminal law by analytically going back to the concept of guilt. His thesis got to the root of established law. Several of its characteristics point towards his future work: striking features are the 'purely' juridical way of proceeding, the terminological and systematic interest, the fact that he takes tensions and conceptual inconsistencies within a given system as his point of departure, and the critique of 'terminology' in the interest of the 'system'. Also noticeable is also the radical exclusion of philosophical, political and moral considerations, the exclusion of a 'character's guilt' and the orientation towards the state. Schmitt did not equate 'guilt' with 'legal guilt', as is shown by his acknowledgement of the possibility of a 'character's guilt' independent of any legal judgment. However, in 1910 he clearly put moral evaluations in second place behind legal judgments and viewed individual guilt solely from the perspective of state law. This approach he would continue to pursue. Thus, in his following monograph, *Gesetz und Urteil* [Law and judgment], he would limit the space left to a judge in making a decision by introducing a hermeneutical maxim. He had already hinted at the problem in 1910 (SS, p. 130). In his later monograph, and Habilitation thesis, on the philosophy of the state [Staatsphilosophie],* *Der Wert des Staates und die Bedeutung des Einzelnen* [The value of the state and the significance of the individual], the normative construction of the category of the individual by the state became an explicit topic.

A purely juridical perspective on the question of guilt comes naturally to a lawyer. The implications of such an approach for the identification of responsibilities can, for instance, be seen in Ernst Rudolf Huber's *Verfassungsgeschichte* [Constitutional history]. Huber talks of 'objective responsibility' rather than 'subjective guilt'.[37] In a similar vein, Schmitt distinguished between moral guilt and legal 'symptoms of guilt' ['Schuldsymptomen']. His analysis served the critical intention of distinguishing between law and morality. Schmitt bracketed the use of the concept of guilt altogether. In contrast to a moral thinker, he argued, a lawyer did not deal with 'guilt' at all. Judging 'events of inner life' was none of his business. 'Guilt is something internal to subjectivity', Schmitt wrote. 'For established law, only such guilt that has become manifest on the level of sensual phenomena is relevant: whatever remains hidden in the soul is of no concern to the law; cogitationis poenam nemo patitur;[†] thus, the manifestation of guilt in an external event must be part of its legal definition' (SS, p. 28). With all this the later Schmitt would still have agreed. His early juridical considerations regarding 'guilt' also illuminate his later reservations regarding meta-juridical judgments of guilt. At no point did Schmitt discuss the specificity of moral judgments in any depth. He did not assume that 'morality' was 'autonomous' in the Kantian sense or in the sense of today's secular ethics. He would always consider himself to be a collectively – politically or religiously – determined 'participant', and refer to his 'situation'. 'I haven't decided anything, Hitler decided', he once remarked in retrospect.[38] At times, reference to the 'situation' served as an alibi or excuse for him. Whenever Schmitt admitted 'guilt', his language took on religious forms, and he spoke in terms of 'sin' and 'penance'. The moral substance of such confessions is easily overlooked today, because such language has become alien to us. This makes his doctoral thesis all the more important, as it provides the juridical reasons for which Schmitt subordinated moral assessments to established law. The priority of the juridical perspective suggests a fundamental assumption regarding the philosophy of the state: it seems that Schmitt was already at that time inclined towards the view that moral norms are bound by established law. The anti-individualist starting point of his early work is already visible here. Thus, his doctoral thesis already hit some of the notes which would characterize his work as a whole. It displayed the ethos of the jurist. Criminal law, however, would only occasionally be considered in his publications from then on.

---

* The German term 'Staatsphilosophie' refers to questions at the crossroads of what in English would be political, social and religious philosophy. There is no strict equivalent in English.
† 'No one suffers punishment for mere intent.'

A few weeks before his twenty-second birthday, on 24 June 1910, Schmitt received his doctorate *summa cum laude*. On the recommendation of Calker, the thesis appeared in the same year as part of a series with the title *Strafrechtliche Abhandlungen* [Treatises in criminal law] in Breslau.[39] Finding the money for publication was difficult. The manufacturer Arthur Lambert helped out. Schmitt later worked for a short time as an apprentice for his brother, Hugo Lambert, who was a lawyer. In 1911, Schmitt justified this to his parents as follows: if

> I would have had any idea how expensive this would be, I wouldn't have done the doctorate in the first place. But now that I have done it, and seeing that the title is not altogether without significance, we'll just have to console ourselves. Fortunately, there is the help of Mr Lambert. I have been ill rewarded for my diligence. If the thesis had been half as long [it comes to 155 pages], the whole thing would have been half as expensive, and I still would have gotten my doctorate. But who knows what good may come of it.[40]

Undoubtedly, a shorter thesis would have sufficed for him to be awarded the doctorate. Schmitt wrote a remarkable thesis. However, towards his parents he only hinted at the possibility of an academic career. And to his sister Auguste he also spoke rather of a career as a lawyer during the years to come. Thus, in the summer of 1910, he went to the Higher Regional Court at Düsseldorf as a legal trainee.

2

The Law of Practice

A legal trainee in the district of Düsseldorf

In the sixteenth century, Düsseldorf became the capital of the duchies of Jülich, Kleve and Berg. In 1614, it fell to the aristocratic line of Pfalz-Neuburg. It saw a rise in prosperity at the end of the seventeenth century, when the Prince-Elector Jan Wellem (Johann Wilhelm von Pfalz-Neuburg), after the destruction of Heidelberg, ruled from Düsseldorf. Following the defeat of Napoleon and the Vienna Congress, the western provinces of Prussia expanded as bulwarks against France, and thus, in 1815, Düsseldorf became Prussian. From this point onwards, the ultra-Catholic Cologne was culturally in the firm grip of Düsseldorf and Bonn, with the latter being given its university in 1818 and the former its academy of art in 1819. There was a lively cultural exchange with Berlin. Peter Cornelius and Wilhelm von Schadow had a decisive influence on the academy; Immermann and Grabbe laid the foundations for a strong theatrical tradition; and for several years Felix Mendelssohn-Bartholdy and Robert Schumann acted as musical directors in Heinrich Heine's birthplace. The western provinces of the Rhineland experienced a rapid economic rise in the nineteenth century. Düsseldorf acquired a stock exchange, and it became an important industrial location as well as the 'office desk of the Ruhr area'.* In 1871 was founded the 'Langnam-Verein',† an association which represented the interests of industrialists in the Rhineland. Other industrial associations followed. While Düsseldorf had just 20,000 inhabitants in 1815, it had become a large city of 100,000 by 1881. In 1910, there were already more than 360,000 inhabitants. This enormous development was reflected in the lofty sense of self-confidence displayed by Düsseldorf's middle classes.

For a long time, the Higher Regional Court in Cologne was responsible

---

* 'Schreibtisch des Ruhrgebiets' – a colloquial expression for Düsseldorf as a centre of industrial and state bureaucracy.
† Founded on the initiative of the Irish industrialist William Thomas Mulvany, its full name was 'Verein zur Wahrung der gemeinsamen wirtschaftlichen Interessen in Rheinland und Westfalen' [Association for the protection of common economic interests in the Rhineland and Westphalia]. Bismarck, who considered this to be a rather long name – a 'lang[er] Nam[e]' – coined the phrase 'Langnam'.

for Düsseldorf, until the economic expansion and increasing population of Düsseldorf made it necessary to ease the court's workload. In 1906, the Higher Regional Court of Düsseldorf opened, at first sitting in provisional premises. It had six regional court districts and forty-two local courts under it. At the point of its inception, more than 2.2 million citizens were under its jurisdiction. In April 1910, shortly before Schmitt's arrival, the court moved into a new Wilhelminian building on Cecilianallee, where it still resides today. It was situated right on the Rhine, at the edge of the Hofgarten,* within a few minutes' walking distance of the academy of art. On average, there were about 750 legal trainees. The training took place within the individual sections, chambers and benches, and for each of its parts the trainee was assigned to a particular judge or public prosecutor.[1] It lasted five years altogether. 'The hardest of work is required, if the training is meant to be fully successful within such a short period of time', an anniversary publication tells us.[2] In 1911, there was a total of 11,800 accredited lawyers in the German Reich.[3] Even though their average income was higher than that of medical doctors, there were already complaints about oversubscription to the profession.

In July 1910, Schmitt arrived in Düsseldorf. On 25 August, he began his preparatory service at the local court in Lobberich, where he also took residence. From May 1911 onwards, he lived in Düsseldorf. After Berlin, Munich and Strasbourg it was the fourth major city Schmitt got to know. Between 1908 and 1933 he lived for about thirteen years in the Rhenish metropolitan cities of Strasbourg, Düsseldorf, Bonn and Cologne. The crisis years in Düsseldorf would make a lasting impression on him. First, he lived in the Kapellstraße, later in the Steinstraße. He was visited by Fritz Eisler, as well as Eduard Rosenbaum[4] from Hamburg, whom he had known since his student days (in Berlin or Strasbourg). On 27 October, he told his sister that he had completed a preliminary version of *Law and Judgment* [*Gesetz und Urteil*]. His personal copy is dated 'June 1912'. His contact with his uncle in Lorraine ceased at that time. As early as 4 February 1912, Carl wrote: 'For a whole year, I haven't seen or heard from Uncle André' (JB, p. 131). Several times, he had to move house within the city centre due to a lack of money. Together with Kluxen, Eisler and Rosenbaum he planned a 'Schnekkeroman',† but instead of this literary joke he completed a satirical text called *Schattenrisse* [Silhouettes] with Eisler. At that time, he made the acquaintance of the poet Theodor Däubler. He met regularly with two Jewish sisters, Marta and Helene Bernstein. He wanted to marry Helene, but, if only for a lack of money, it never happened. A possible return to Strasbourg also failed because of lack of money. In June 1912, Carl wrote to his sister:

> My new book [*Law and Judgment*] has already had great success, insofar as I have had an offer from Strasbourg to give lectures there on penal law and the philosophy of law. Therefore, your brother could now become a Privatdozent

---

* The court gardens.
† Literally, 'snail novel'.

if he wished to do so. But for financial reasons (the remuneration [reimburse-ment] was only 1,000 Marks per year), I had to decline. [. . .] Well, something similar will surely come along, and after all, I am still young. (JB, p. 153)

The Theory of Practice: *Law and Judgment* [*Gesetz und Urteil*]

No sooner did Schmitt, the legal trainee, become familiar with legal practice than he began to seek out its 'inherent standards'. With *Law and Judgment*[5] he wrote a significant study which, following his self-interpretation, is usually seen as the 'beginning' of his decisionist 'reflec-tions on the intrinsic meaning of the decision'.[6] *Law and Judgment* opens with the 'problem' that the ruling of the judge is not sufficiently deter-mined by the letter of the law: 'The idea of the "legality" of all decisions can be considered as obsolete today' (GU, p. 11). Such a theory, he said, constructs a 'will' of the law and the legislator. Using the philosophy of Hans Vaihinger, Schmitt deconstructs this 'dogma' as a 'fiction'. 'The leg-islator is being constructed, not reconstructed' (GU, p. 33). The common hermeneutic methods are only practical 'means'. Thus, Schmitt suggested nothing less than a paradigm shift. Legal theory should 'consciously' choose to be the 'servant of practice' (GU, p. 59). Unfortunately, Schmitt wrote, the opposite is often the case. 'But, fortunately, the method of prac-tice is better than what practice takes to be its method' (GU, p. 45).

Schmitt's analysis begins with the 'postulate of legal determinacy [Rechtsbestimmtheit]'. All aleatory elements are nothing but attempts at achieving legal determinacy. Primarily, the legal system strives not for 'substantive justice' (GU, p. 51) but for a degree of legal determinacy which exceeds the liberal demand for 'legal certainty [Rechtssicherheit]'. Schmitt sees his suggestion as being based on a 'normative perspective' (GU, p. 63) and distances himself from the sociological perspective and that of legal theory. In doing so he formulates for the first time his opposition to a legal theory which proceeds analytically and descriptively. Even though Hans Kelsen, 'with impressive clarity', has formulated the 'ideal of a theory of positive law' (GU, p. 58), the 'method of applying the law' is nonetheless something other than that theory. Legal practice is altogether 'something other than legal science'. Only practice creates law. The legal system [Recht] becomes a 'consistent living force' (GU, p. 27) not by way of its laws but only by way of concrete judgments.

In the final chapter, 'The Right Decision', Schmitt explains how judicial practice fulfils the 'postulate of legal determinacy'. He begins with a defini-tion: 'Today, a judicial decision is correct, if we may assume that another judge would have decided in the same way. In this context, "another judge" denotes the empirical type of the modern scholarly trained judge' (GU, p. 71). Schmitt refers especially to the 'principle of collegiality' and the doctrine of judicial precedent [Präjudizienpraxis]. He sets out from the 'addressee' of the reasons given for a judgment [Urteilsbegründung] and differentiates between a theoretical 'explanation' and a practical 'justifica-tion' given for it. Why do judges justify their decisions at all? Whom do they want to convince? According to Schmitt, it is not the legal parties who are the addressees of the justification, but 'learned jurists' and 'colleagues'. Accordingly, Schmitt writes: 'The practice justifies, and is justified, by itself.' And for the same reason he writes in the preface: 'This book addresses the practice which is at the same time its subject' (GU, p. viii). It is in legal practice, he claims, that 'objective criteria' (GU, p. 103) for legal determinacy have been developed. Schmitt's aim is to analyse these criteria, and thus to tie the judicial decision [Dezision] to the 'empirical type' of the judge. He demands a rational standard for professional practice without, however, making practical suggestions for the training of jurists.

This paradigm shift from legal theory to judicial practice had substantial consequences for the understanding of law. Schmitt sharply rebuffs legal positivism and moves from positive law to a 'law' which is grounded not in theoretical models of 'substantive justice', neither in 'natural law' nor in objective 'cultural norms', but in the collegiality and professional expectations of the judges. The law is what is accepted by judges as a justified judgment. That this approach must end up being critical of positivism is expressed with complete clarity by Schmitt when he finally asks 'whether a judge is allowed to decide against the literal meaning of the law' (GU, p. 111). Within the framework of his 'formula', he explicitly approves that possibility. In this case, too, the judgment of legal practice is what counts. In a footnote he refers to Shakespeare's *The Merchant of Venice*, calling Shylock's behaviour, which is often interpreted in anti-Semitic terms, 'wilful rabulism' (GU, p. 112). It is the paradigm shift from theory to practice in this early text by Schmitt that makes it ground-breaking. It already shows an orientation in the politics of law towards a guild of judges and a 'living law' of the future.

The brother as mentor

Schmitt's early postcards and letters to his younger sister Auguste provide us with information on the relationships within the family. Many of them are co-authored, so that almost all close relatives, including Schmitt's first wife, are present in the form of at least a few hand-written lines. Schmitt wrote because he wanted, or was supposed, to keep his sister's spirits up, and to let her know about family matters. Until her secondary school leaving certificate [Mittlere Reife], Auguste ('Üssi') attended the girl's high school [Lyzeum] in Plettenberg. From autumn 1905 onwards, she attended the secondary school of the convent of the 'Arme Schulschwestern' in Arnsberg. Then from 1908, having completed secondary school, she studied at the teacher training seminary of the 'Ursulinen' in Berlin. For a short period of time, as mentioned before, brother and sister both stayed with relatives in Lichtenberg. In spring 1911, Auguste passed the final state examination for teachers, after which she spent two years as a private teacher in Portugal. For eight years, Carl's letters were an important link home. They were partly pedagogical in tone, and not only contained information on what happened back home but also tried to stimulate, encourage and give advice to Auguste.

Music and poetry played an important role in their correspondence. Carl reported on visits to the opera and on his piano playing. Mozart and Wagner were his guiding stars, along with Richard Strauss. Books and sheet music were sent back and forth between the two siblings. Again and again, Carl comforted his sister and promised her a brighter future. 'All you need to do is pass your examination' (JB, p. 69), he wrote. 'So don't let it get you down' (JB, p. 71). He sent her books by Raabe and Möricke and a pre-published 'fragment from a novel by Thomas Mann which has not come out yet' (JB, p. 110) – i.e., a passage from *Felix Krull* which, he felt, reflected Auguste's 'homesickness': 'Whoever had a childhood like ours will from time to time suffer bouts of longing for small and narrow spaces, for a small and withdrawn life in an attic room' (JB, p. 110). Felix Krull rests only in order to step out into the glory of the world. Schmitt ended his communications of news with little self-composed poems, with longer excerpts, or with fictional letters. 'Keep on going, in another ten years we may well have become rich people' (JB, p. 99), he wrote in response to Auguste's despondence, and he sent her longer excerpts from the 'showman's exclamations' in Georg Büchner's *Woyzeck*: 'Ladies and Gentlemen. Roll up and see here the astronomical horse and the geographical ass. Consider the creature as God first made it: nothing, just nothing. Add civilization and see this ape here: walks upright, wears trousers and carries a sword'* (JB, p. 103). Soon afterwards, he sent her an example of a similar kind of anthropological scepticism in the form of writings by Christian Dietrich Grabbe, the poet who led a debauched life as a drunkard in Düsseldorf (JB, p. 103). Carl made Auguste part of his 'Schnekkeroman'. But, in the end, such literary amusements no longer came easily to him either. The complications in his private life and financial worries weighed down on him too heavily. Increasingly, he began, discreetly, to mention his own situation.

The central message to his sister was the necessity of a proper education. As early as 1908, Schmitt wrote to her: 'However, with regard to the financial side of things, we both haven't been very careful in the choice of our parents' (JB, p. 71). Later, he complained bitterly about social injustices and the conceit of 'rich people'. 'This is what makes our times so dreadful, that the individual person, what he is and what he can do, never matters, but only the role he plays within society' (JB, p. 167). At a time when he was already deeply entangled in private passions, he advised her to exercise the utmost caution in dealing with men. 'Don't trust these Portuguese happy-go-lucky windbags an inch. Do not even begin anything with them' (JB, p. 148). 'Every person is vehemently egotistic', he wrote, 'and it is a miracle that they do not murder and poison each other, but inquire about the weather instead. [. . .] The Germans are in no way better, but less polite, than the Portuguese' (JB, pp. 116f.). The anthropological scepticism which Schmitt extracted from the literature was pragmatically related to the possibility of social advancement. The ironic style and the literary detachment

---

* Schmitt quotes from one of the fragments of *Woyzeck*, which is not, in this form, part of the English edition. My translation draws on John Reddick, *Georg Büchner: Complete Plays, Lenz and Other Writings*, London: Penguin 1993, pp. 115f.

of the letters, however, already gave a first lively indication of an exit from dependency and the prospect of a better future.

Critical attempts: the 'foundation of normal common sense'

Between 1910 and 1916, Schmitt published five monographs. As soon as he had completed a book, he would begin the next one. His numerous legal reports and exam papers are probably lost. But at the time he published a series of brief texts in which he experimented with the literary form of the review and short miscellaneous writings, and expressed in more detail his position towards philosophy and the arts. In this, Schmitt retained his 'terminological' approach and judged the works under consideration pragmatically on the basis of the effect they had on the 'addressee'. While in his early books he limited the juridical discourse to the theory of 'practice', with these occasional texts he left the sphere of juridical discourse and hinted at the philosophical implications of his 'practical' approach. The first forum he found for this was the cultural journal *Die Rheinlande*, in which he published no fewer than six smaller articles between 1911 and 1913. The journal pursued an anti-modern, German nationalist, 'educational' agenda.[7] Schmitt's 'Drei Tischgespräche' [Three dinner table conversations] opened the door to the editor, Wilhelm Schäfer, as they belonged to the literary form of the anecdote for which Schäfer had a particular appreciation. A long letter exists in Schäfer's literary estate in which Schmitt makes negative comments on Sigmund Freud and psychoanalysis, promises one review, considers another, explains the juridical concept of 'specification'*, and ends on a note almost of astonishment: 'Why are you friendly and benevolent towards me? After all, I am nothing. A broad-shouldered dreamer. An arrogant lamb. A yearning good-for-nothing.'[8] At the same time, he makes fun of Schäfer's anecdotes in letters to his sister. In his diary he writes: 'Schäfer: scribbled down trifles' (TB I, p. 125).

The three pieces in 'Drei Tischgespräche'[9] are based on autobiographical details, and each ends with a surprising turn. An 'elder' brother converses with a 'sister, seventeen years of age' and a 'little sister of seven years'. In 1909 – the text was published in 1911 – this would have corresponded to the respective ages of Auguste and Anna. It is the little sister who produces the punchline at the end. The second conversation is between a 'stolid musician' and a 'witty journalist'; the punchline falls to a 'naïve dilettante'. The third conversation is held by a 'philosopher of art' and an 'aesthete'. However, it is 'a man with common sense' who has the last word. Moving from family, via culture, to scholarship, each of these pieces touches upon an intellectualization which, every time, is undone by the punchline. A literary form and an overall meaning are visible. 'Common sense' is proved right.

However, far more interesting is another text, written in the style of a novella, 'Der Spiegel'.[10] A 'first-person narrator' wants to support 'some

---

* Treatment of a question or matter in such a way that it is substantially modified.

strange theories' with 'a true story'. The issue in question is the philosophical assumption of 'the identity of the so-called mental world with so-called reality'. Franz Morphenius 'was frequently beaten as a child'. He wanted to please everyone. But, when he falls in love with a certain Rosalie Blöing, he ends up in 'conflict' with his mother. Body and soul fall apart. The soul is 'stuck inside a mirror', and all it can do now is reflect. However, when Rosalie steps in front of the mirror and a young man wants to kiss her, the mirror becomes 'agitated' with jealousy. The young man kicks the mirror, which scatters into many pieces. The parts take the 'path of normal development', they recognize the 'nullity of the world' and renounce 'the false self-conceit of "I am"'. Identity is shattered. The beaten child becomes an unhappy lover and destroys himself. Schmitt thus sketches a bitter anti-educational novella* with autobiographical undertones. Rosalie, from Saarburg, was the object of a flirtatious relationship during his student days. Schmitt thought of her repeatedly, and dreamt of her.

In his dissertation, Schmitt had distinguished between a 'terminological' and a 'systematic' approach. His review of Fritz Mauthner's *Wörterbuch der Philosophie* [Dictionary of philosophy] predominantly discusses the relationship between the critique of language and philosophy. Mauthner identifies everyday language as the medium of philosophy. However, Schmitt considers it an exaggeration to present this 'jumble of words' as a 'dictionary of philosophy'. 'For Mauthner, all critique of language amounts to a critique of knowledge.'[11] Schmitt does not identify the critique of language with philosophical 'truth' and thus does not push aside Plato's position. Rather, he is of the opinion that 'the problem of truth and of objectivity is not identical with the problem of intersubjectivity', and he suggests that there is 'a correctness other than' linguistic correctness. Schmitt considers Mauthner's reduction of philosophy to a critique of language insufficient. The 'systematic' aim of Schmitt's dissertation had already exceeded the task of pure 'terminological' clarification.

Still, what are the implications of the philosophical critique of language for everyday practice? Schmitt examines Hans Vaihinger's *The Philosophy of 'As if'*[12] [Die Philosophie des Als Ob] in several texts. Vaihinger was one of the main representatives of contemporary neo-Kantianism. He taught in Halle and founded the Kant-Gesellschaft [Kant Society] and *Kant-Studien* [Kant Studies]. Vaihinger had drawn a line under the epistemological discussions of the nineteenth century by using Nietzsche for interpreting Kant 'fictionally' and pragmatically, and thus bringing Kant up-to-date with contemporary perspectives. Schmitt's short review in *Die Rheinlande* begins by underlining as one of Vaihinger's results 'how fictions and hypothesis (the latter must be distinguished from the former) [. . .] are turned into dogmas by taking the "as if" to be a "because".'[13] His review is designed as application and a proof. The practical value of the book, he claims, is demonstrated by its success. Schmitt then publishes a

---

* The German neologism is 'Entbildungsnovelle'. Mehring's coinage alludes to the term 'Bildungsroman' [educational novel]. The prefix 'Ent-' indicates that it is not a case of formation, but 'de-'formation, loss of form, which is described by the text.

more extensive review of the voluminous book under the title *Juristische Fiktionen* [Juridical fictions] in the *Deutsche Juristen-Zeitung* [German Journal for Jurists]. In it, he expresses the hope that Vaihinger's philosophy would bring about a turn 'within the whole discussion surrounding legal science and legal practice'. Vaihinger has recognized, he writes, that what matters is 'not the reality of something conceived in thought, but the practical usefulness of a fiction'. The dogmatic attitude takes an 'as if' for a 'because'. Schmitt demonstrates this point, using 'the will of the law' as his example.[14] For a third time, he examines the 'philosophy of the as if' in a miscellany titled 'Richard Wagner und eine neue "Lehre vom Wahn"'[15] [Richard Wagner and a new 'theory of madness'],* which appears in the in-house publication of the Wagnerians, the *Bayreuther Blätter*, in 1912. Here, he begins with general hermeneutical reflections, sketches the task of finding a general perspective on Wagner, and exemplifies the latter with reference to Hans Sachs's 'madness monologue' in *The Mastersingers*. Schmitt uses this example to demonstrate how 'resignation' can make possible a 'moral' stance: a 'new participation in life' by virtue of 'a recognition of the usefulness and applicability of madness, of the fact that madness is practically unavoidable'. Following Vaihinger, Schmitt develops a critical concept of myth in the wake of Nietzsche which he sets against 'religious dogmas'. The latter 'usually turn an "as if" into a "because"'.

The question of the 'results' which a work effects for the 'addressee' further exercises Schmitt in his work on Cervantes. In his article 'Don Quijote und das Publikum'[16] [Don Quixote and the audience], he raises fundamental questions of poetics and hermeneutics. With regard to aesthetic effects, he asks who the 'addressees' of a text actually are, distinguishing, in principle, between 'understanding' [Deutung] and 'evaluation' [Bewertung]. Understanding marks the position of the audience, the 'ground of common sense', which Schmitt puts in contrast to learned 'interpretation'. The audience, as 'the myth-creating subject', has 'found the right understanding once and for all'. The position of the audience is also the 'ground' on which Cervantes stands. 'For Cervantes, the artist, remains with remarkable sureness on the ground of common sense.' Cervantes provides the right understanding: Don Quixote is mad and obsessed with an idea. Actually, the audience agrees with this, but its false theory of practice makes it impossible for the audience to reach a just evaluation. In contrast to the audience, Cervantes recognizes the 'human greatness' in the foolishness of the hero. As we shall see, Schmitt at the time experiences something similar with his first wife, Cari. This miscellany anticipates his later positive 'evaluation' of the passion for† which he would be mocked by his readers. In his *Political Romanticism* of 1919, Schmitt incidentally returns to Don Quixote, adopting, in essence, his earlier reading of 1912. He considers

---

* 'Wahn' carries the meaning of 'delusion'. But, as Schmitt refers to the third act of *The Mastersingers of Nuremberg* – 'Wahn, Wahn, überall Wahn' – the translation follows the established rendering of 'Wahn' in this passage as 'madness'.
† Presumably a reference to Carl Theodor Dreyer's silent movie *The Passion of Joan of Arc*, which Schmitt allegedly watched numerous times in the late 1920s.

Cervantes to be a great popular and epic poet. Similar approaches are familiar from aesthetic discussions after 1900,[17] in which the hope was expressed that the 'realist' and 'naturalist' novel would by itself dissolve into a new form of epic literature. Such hopes were mainly bound up with Russian literature, Dostoevsky and Tolstoy in particular. Schmitt, however, in those days considers Theodor Däubler's *Nordlicht* poem [*The Northern Lights*] to be an 'epic work of art' (TB I, p. 359) displaying 'absolute totality'. As his oeuvre progressed, he later addressed his longing for the restoration of a closed worldview, for a new 'totality of life' (Georg Lukács), primarily in the field of politics.

In a long letter of 12 April 1912 to Walther Rathenau, Schmitt referred to the epic *The Northern Lights*.[18] Rathenau replied to this peculiar letter from a young legal trainee to one of the most powerful industrialists and intellectuals at the time, whereupon Schmitt introduced himself in more detail on 24 April. His tone oscillates between devotion, presumption and the polemical. Schmitt offers 'profession', 'request' and 'confession'. He wants to tell Rathenau 'his very own thoughts' on Rathenau's critique of the age – not as a 'scholar', however, something which his character would not allow him to be. Yet, he could also no longer write 'as an innocent, naïve individual': 'This has become impossible to me due to the irritating witticisms of Jewesses, all of them such knowers of the human heart. Because Düsseldorf and its surroundings abound with Rahels, Lilliput-Rahels', Schmitt writes to Rathenau, whom he would soon categorize under the rubric of 'Non-Germans' in the *Schattenrisse*. He twists and turns in verbose negations: 'I am too much in awe of you to become witty. You were friendly enough to inquire about my own person, and I am grateful for that. But I do not yet think enough of myself to be able to answer you without being ashamed. But in a few years' time I shall be able to do so. At my age one is nothing.'[19]

Schmitt immediately published a cutting review of Rathenau's *Kritik der Zeit* [Critique of the age] in *Die Rheinlande*,[20] in which he once again poses the question of the critical viewpoint. From which 'perspective' does the critic argue? Every viewpoint refers 'to something historical, sociological, something which concerns the human being as a political being'. Some critics pretend to argue from a religious point of view, some from a scientific one. Rathenau's critique of the 'mechanical age' is led by the 'fundamental idea' of the 'soul'. However, this foundation of the critique is invoked only negatively, as a counter-image to the contemporary age. Rathenau's 'soul' is mystical and transcendent. There is no clarification of the criteria being applied. Hence, his study actually isn't a scholarly 'critique' at all, but only a 'lament', a modern, moralistic version of a 'sermon', such as 'many' – those with 'normal common sense' – commonly suspect to be lurking behind any 'critique of the age'. 'Rathenau = imprecise',[21] Schmitt would later note down sarcastically.* In Kantian terms, he raised the objection of a lack of transcendentalism against Rathenau's 'critique' and demanded a clearer explanation of the critical viewpoint. A jurist argues within the

---

* The sarcasm lies in the fact that the German – 'Rathenau = ungenau' – rhymes.

framework of the established legal system and criticizes inconsistencies in that system. Thus, he does not need to establish an external point of view. But someone holding up the 'soul' against his 'age' incurs a greater need for justification. Thus, Schmitt pulled the rug from under the feet of Rathenau's fundamental critique and went on, in his *Schattenrisse*, mercilessly to make him the subject of his satirical mocking, just as he did with Wilhelm Schäfer and Fritz Mauthner. Instead of a 'critique' in terms of moral philosophy, Schmitt opted for political satire. He included his critique of Rathenau also in his monographs *Wert des Staates* and *Theodor Däubler's 'Nordlicht'* [Theodor Däubler's 'The Northern Lights'], and he later repeated it in a review.[22] An interest in Rathenau remained. 'After reading Walter Rathenau: the scoundrel knows everything', he noted in his diary (TB I, p. 261). The murder of Rathenau would later touch him very much. 'Terrible shock. Fear, the feeling of fate. So, this was to be his fate, this is how he was meant to die, this educated, beautiful, [. . .] human being, superior in his weakness' (TB, 24 June 1922).

These short texts of 1914 are, of course, occasional writings. Schmitt was practising various literary forms, and he was seeking contacts. He had the courage to write about Cervantes and Wagner while under the impression of his meeting with Theodor Däubler, which we shall discuss later. Nevertheless, his writings also had a unifying philosophical topic: the discussion of the critical viewpoint, as it had been carried to its Nietzschean extreme by Vaihinger. Like Hegel before him, Schmitt considered the rational viewpoint [Vernunftstandpunkt] of the 'audience' as critically justified, and he polemically shuffled off abstract 'rational philosophy' [Verstandesphilosophie] (Hegel) to the learned 'interpretation' of romantic intellectuals. He took 'normal common sense' – the 'audience' as 'addressee' – as his guideline but also laid claim to a higher viewpoint. The overall result was a pragmatic diffusion of criticism [Kritizismus].*

---

* 'Criticism', in this context, refers to any philosophical attitude which, following Kant, asks for the conditions of the possibility of knowledge before trying to establish any empirical knowledge.

3

Apotheosis of the Poet, Rant against Literary Figures: The 'Untimely Poet' and the 'Received Wisdom of the Educated'

Retrospective perception of an epochal change

Although there was a long phase of preparation to the beginning of the twentieth century, the time after 1900 was generally perceived as an epochal change in Germany. The technological and economic development effected massive social transformations. The balance between 'education and wealth' no longer held. The citizen became a bourgeois, the peasant disappeared from the cities altogether, and the labourers developed consciousness as a class. The cities became electrified, bicycles and cars emerged. Technical universities were given the right to award doctoral degrees, women were admitted to universities, and new professions were created.

The year 1900 is, we can say, the date after which the artistic avant-garde took off. Cézanne and Picasso, Mahler and Schoenberg, Thomas Mann, Franz Kafka and Joyce, Max Reinhardt, Chaplin and Murnau are just some of its main representatives. This classical modernity was probably superseded only by the new technological revolution caused by the age of the computer in the 1980s.[1] Schmitt's lifetime covered this age of classical cultural modernity. He still sensed the coming of its end in his wariness of the new means of mass communication and his horror of all-pervasive electrical 'radiation'. Schmitt had an acute sense for the twilight of the 'long' bourgeois age and of the national liberal nineteenth century. 'Goethe' was seen as a 'representative of the bourgeois age' (Thomas Mann). Schmitt could only remember this 'Goethe mask' of the educated bourgeoisie with dismay when, in 1946–7, he wrote about his time as a student in Berlin:

> Originally, the podium was a pulpit and stood in a Christian church. The pulpit became a lectern for the delivery of philosophical and moral lectures. Then, the lectern turned into a stage, as the stage became a moral institution.*
> The transformations of the podium became visible in the physiognomy of the times. Three bourgeois faces met in the face of the intellectual type of these days: that of a preacher, that of a professor, and that of an actor. . . .

---

* Schmitt's term, 'moralische Anstalt', may be an allusion to Friedrich Schiller's *Die Schaubühne als moralische Anstalt betrachtet* [The stage as a moral institution], 1784.

The overall result was the tendency towards the 'Goethe mask'. The 'Goethe mask' was the worst evil of the time. With its help, the souls of thousands of enthusiastic youth were impregnated with the mirage of a *potestas spiritualis*.[2]

In this passage, Schmitt sees the turning away from Christianity and the transition towards an 'aesthetic phase' in a negative light. Little can be seen of this attitude in earlier testimonials. Only after 1914 do we come across signs of a decision in favour of religion and against a secular orientation. However, in his turn towards a 'tragic' literary history we can also sense a religious mood. In retrospection, Schmitt explained the path he took with reference to the Hölderlin cult that grew out of the George circle in particular. Stefan George had canonized and historicized[3] *Das Jahrhundert Goethes* [The century of Goethe],[*] and he had reintroduced a liturgical understanding of poetry which culminated in the cult around the young Maximilian Kronberger, who had died at an early age.[†] Sexuality was sublimated into eroticism; homoeroticism was refined into 'pedagogic eros'.[4] The George circle, held together by charismatic forces, was a laboratory of intellectual history from which a new understanding of Plato, of Nietzsche and of Hölderlin emerged. On 17 May 1948, Schmitt noted: 'The decisive step around 1900 was the transition from Goethe's to Hölderlin's ingenuity [Genialismus].' A day later, he wrote:

> 'Jugend ohne Goethe'[‡] [Youth without Goethe] (Max Kommerell), that meant for us, from 1910, *in concreto* a youth with Hölderlin[5] – i.e., the transition from an optimistic, ironic and neutralizing ingenuity to a pessimistic, active and tragic one. Everything remained within the cult of ingenuity, though; it even deepened it to unfathomable depths. Norbert von Hellingrath was more important than Stefan George or Rilke.

The year 1910 marked an epochal change within the George circle. Norbert von Hellingrath published Hölderlin's translations of Pindar in the *Blätter für die Kunst* [Journal for the arts], and the first volume of the *Jahrbuch für die geistige Bewegung*[§] [Yearbook for spiritual movement] appeared. Friedrich Wolters proclaimed *Herrschaft und Dienst* [Rule and duty] and Karl Wolfskehl announced the 'Geheime Deutschland'[¶] [Secret Germany]. The George circle stepped out of the confines of lyricism and

---

[*] An anthology of poems written in the age of Goethe, edited by Stefan George (1868–1933) in 1902.

[†] Maximilian Kronberger (1888–1904). George had met Kronberger, probably in 1902, and upon his death created the so-called Maximin cult, ascribing a god-like quality to Kronberger. This coincides with George's turn from *l'art pour l'art* towards the religious-metaphysical outlook of his later work.

[‡] Max Kommerell, *Jugend ohne Goethe*, Frankfurt, 1931.

[§] *Jahrbuch für die geistige Bewegung*, edited by Friedrich Wolters and Friedrich Gundolf between 1910 and 1912. An anti-modern, highly polemical yearbook representing the positions of the George circle.

[¶] Phrase first used by Wolfskehl in an article of the first *Yearbook* (1910), where it relates to George and a vision of an inner essence of Germanness that was opposed to the 'official' culture of the Kaiserreich at the time.

onto the general stage of intellectual historiography, offering its ideology of spiritual revival as a dogma. Plato and Hölderlin became ciphers for the circle. Schmitt associated the 'transition' towards a pessimistic interpretation of the cult of ingenuity with Europe's descent into the Great War. His basic rejection of the 'cult of ingenuity' [Genialismus] took place in the form of a farewell to Romanticism, but he set his general rejection of it at the later time of the existentialism of the Weimar Republic, which caused a counter-movement and a return to Christian ideas. After 1945, Schmitt would criticize the tragic 'cult of ingenuity' and demand a theocentric turn from the human individual towards God. His reference to von Hellingrath may originate from Heidegger.[6] It is meant to say: Stefan George's lasting importance lay in the first place in the impulses he gave for the rediscovery of the later Hölderlin that was initiated by von Hellingrath under the influence of George.

Schmitt could personally identify with von Hellingrath, who was stationed as an army volunteer in Munich and Amberg when he arrived in Munich at the end of February 1915. Schmitt could even conceivably have attended von Hellingrath's lecture on 'Hölderlins Wahnsinn' [Hölderlin's madness], a lecture of epochal significance for a war generation, including Heidegger, that was inspired by the youth movement and participated in a Hölderlin cult. Von Hellingrath also spoke of the 'secret Germany'[7] in these days, and he substituted Hölderlin for Goethe as the poet of the 'Germans'. The affinities even go further: von Hellingrath gave his lectures in Ludwigstraße 4, a building of the Business College at which Schmitt would later teach; von Hellingrath's edition of Hölderlin was published by Karl Müller, and the 'decisive' volume with Hölderlin's late poetry appeared in the same year in which Schmitt published his Däubler studies with the same publishing house. As late as September 1916, Schmitt still could have met von Hellingrath in Munich.[8] Such affinities were important to Schmitt, and thus he also identified with his generation as the one that had rediscovered Hölderlin and had idealized him as a hero.

However, in contrast to Heidegger, Schmitt went back beyond Hölderlin to Christianity and ultimately rejected the more recent 'philosophy of the I' [Ich-Philosophie] and the 'cult of ingenuity' [Genialismus] altogether. He placed the responsibility for the age of 'total' wars with the more recent history of education in Germany after 1945. Only the posthumous *Glossarium* [Glossary] mentions, several times, that his intentionally 'esoteric' references to poets such as Theodor Däubler and Konrad Weiß were secondary to his reception of Hölderlin and the George circle, the typical points of reference for his generation. Against the bourgeois educational canon he constructs an anti-canon informed by the anti-modernism of the youth movement and expressionism; and he even exceeds this canon, creating a calculated distance from Heidegger, with the adoption of his 'untimely' poets. From his faithful friend Ernst Hüsmert we know of a late dictum, dating from 1984: "'Yes", he said, "remember one last word from me. If Heidegger had come across Däubler instead of Hölderlin, he would have become the greatest German philosopher of language.'"[9] Schmitt followed up on Heidegger's Hölderlin in order to make his move towards Däubler plausible. He incorporated Däubler into a tragic literary history.

From Richard Wagner to Theodor Däubler (1876–1934)

Schmitt's retrospective sketches do not reflect his first contacts with the literary avant-garde correctly in every detail. Thus, Christian reservations about secular art can hardly be found in his early work. But a striking fact is that the humanistic canon of the age of Goethe played almost no role at all. Schmitt looked at the history of music along the axis from Mozart to Wagner. He did not go further back than Mozart, and hardly further on than Wagner, Richard Strauss and Hans Pfitzner. He rarely mentioned Mahler, Schoenberg and the Second Viennese School, who developed on the broad ground prepared by Wagner. But Schmitt had a fine sense for the artistic conditions during the 'Vormärz', out of which the avant-garde, including Wagner, emerged, and early on he refers to Büchner, Grabbe and Hebbel. Thus, Schmitt early on showed an inclination towards 'tragic' literary history. For him, too, Wagner was the epitome of the modern. However, he saw him with Nietzsche's eyes, and thus in a perpetually ambivalent light. By understanding Wagner's music (in accordance with Wagner's own theory) as poetry, Schmitt was able to set up the relationship between Wagner and Däubler as one of alternative choices. He not only carved out the alternatives Goethe or Hölderlin and Mozart or Wagner, but also the alternative Wagner or Däubler, taking a decision in favour of Däubler and, hence, in favour of poetry as the authentic expression of the avant-garde. The same turn from Wagner's great monumental music to lyricism can also be found in the George circle and in Heidegger at the time. The same can be said even of Thomas Mann, whose early work is suffused with lyrical elements. In his *Science as a Vocation*, Max Weber expressed it pointedly, against Wagner, saying that the greatest contemporary art was 'intimate rather than monumental',[10] and that art had retreated into 'the smallest intimate circles', such as the George circle. Schmitt's reception of the artistic avant-garde focused on the engagement with his poet friend.

Schmitt first met Däubler in 1912, possibly through Eisler. In January, Schmitt wrote to his sister: 'Soon I shall have a visit from Eisler and then from Däubler. I am particularly curious about the latter. He is almost 2 metres tall, fat, has a long black beard and is constantly talking and gesticulating' (JB, p. 127). In the summer of 1912, Schmitt and Däubler got to know each other well. In June, Schmitt wrote to his sister that Däubler was visiting again and that he had 'become a famous man' (JB, p. 153). In August, he tells her in retrospect that Däubler had stayed for six weeks; he is, Schmitt added, 'the greatest living poet . . . Eisler and I shall write about him, and we shall soon have completed an altogether witty book' (JB, p. 157). Thus, it appears that the Däubler studies were first intended as a parallel campaign to the *Schattenrisse*. In October, Schmitt then seems to have taken the project on by himself. In his diary, he noted down a passage from a draft letter to Däubler: 'I hate every book that I have not either

The poet and friend Theodor Däubler: 'He is almost 2 metres tall, fat, has a long black beard and is constantly talking and gesticulating.'

written myself or must admire to the highest degree. In writing learned books, I have nothing in mind but a prank'* (TB I, p. 27). This expresses a strong ironic reservation towards self-praise. At the time of writing this, Schmitt was probably already working on his study, which appreciates only the poet, not the pioneer of expressionist art.[11] Soon he would send his interpretation to the journal *Der Brenner*, in which Däubler had published several pieces. Hence, the first version was already meant for publication, but the attempt failed, whereupon Däubler suggested a publication in a '*Zeitschrift für religiöse Kultur*' [Journal for Religious Culture] (TB I, p. 231). Schmitt was pleased about this and made a note about the letter of acceptance from the editorial office: 'My essay on Däubler will be printed, will be read' (TB I, p. 234). However, this project also failed. For a third attempt, Schmitt reworked the introductory essay into a small monograph with the help of Däubler.

Thus, he did not aim at a monograph from the beginning, and later he was not always happy about having written it. He knew very well that his eulogy fell outside the scope of publications to be expected from a future state theorist, and therefore originally had opted for the more modest form of a literary essay. However, the outbreak of the Great War gave him a renewed opportunity for publishing this confessional piece on principles of poetry and on the philosophy of history. And despite the fact that Schmitt's later relationship with Däubler was from time to time also marked by ambivalences, and that he would revise his interpretation in

---

* Schmitt uses the term 'Eulenspiegelei', from the mediaeval figure of the trickster Till Eulenspiegel.

some respects, he nevertheless maintained his high esteem for the *Nordlicht* epic throughout his life. Eisler's part in all this was very important. When Däubler visited Düsseldorf again for a week in June 1913, Fritz accompanied him once more. After written examinations, Schmitt then met Däubler in Berlin in 1914.[12] Despite the fact that the history of literary criticism counts Schmitt as the first interpreter of Däubler, he nevertheless discovered Däubler together with Eisler. Schmitt's interpretation of Däubler is without doubt the affirmative and emphatic counterpart to the satirical *Schattenrisse*. The satire can only be understood in opposition to the high ideal of the task of the poet.

Schmitt's version of 1912 discusses the 'artistic urge' of the *Nordlicht* epic under three aspects: language, form and epos. It praises Däubler as an untimely poet who, in a 'time of mediacy', has 'no relationship with an audience' at all (TB I, p. 349), who makes no concessions to the taste of an audience because he has transformed language from a pure 'means for communication' into a purely aesthetic medium. Schmitt compares Däubler's artistic relationship with language, his aesthetic emancipation of language from practical use, with Wagner's: 'Richard Wagner had a special relationship with language. He felt the need for original creation, for a radical transformation. He saw the essence of his art in language, which is why he always put poetry first and wanted to subordinate the music to it' (ibid.). However, while Wagner understood music as poetry, Däubler wanted to transform language into music. 'Wagner's violence is actually directed . . . against music, which he brings close to language in order to subdue it. Däubler, in contrast, moves fully into language in order to unfold music out of it' (TB I, p. 350). The structure of his colossal poem describes the way and 'victory of spirit', its path towards the Northern Lights – i.e., the 'light of the earth itself' (TB I, p. 353).[13] Thus, the poem contains elements of a philosophy of history – i.e., the conception of Europe's historical path as the movement of 'spirit' from the Mediterranean region towards the North. Däubler tells the story of the 'destiny' of Europe, of mankind and of the earth. Schmitt compares Däubler's achievement to that of 'Hegel or Schelling'; he emphasizes the intellectual coherence of the work, the artistic idea and orientation around a 'central point'. Therefore, Schmitt says, the poem should 'be seen not as a lyrical work' but as 'an epic work of art' which represents a 'closed totality' (TB I, p. 359): as a work of 'great fulfilment, yet of even greater promise' (TB I, p. 362).

Schmitt's endorsement of Däubler was, then as now, little understood. His interpretation was limited to the theme of a philosophy of history and to Däubler's creative use of words as his material. The comparison with Wagner's 'Gesamtkunstwerk' might be daring, but its aim is plausible. Schmitt sets Däubler's intentions in contrast to the most recent bourgeois metaphysics of art. He wants to elevate Däubler to the highest ranks by measuring him against Wagner. In this context, the different attitudes towards the synthesis of word and sound make an interesting point of comparison. Schmitt's aesthetic axiom is to be taken seriously. It says that the language of poetry makes words ring out and that it brings about the unity of word and sound in the most concentrated and dense fashion. The fact that the young author, just about twenty-four years old, was proud to be friendly with an artist of the avant-garde is also understandable.

The dispute over the relative rank of poetry and music in the arts, the claim of lyrical art to be the highest form of art, is pervasive in art history. At least since Hegel such questions have been framed within large universal conceptions of history. Hegel himself put romantic poetry as the most recent formation of 'spirit' above music. Wagner took up these questions with great intensity. The revolution in modern arts at the time continued the legacy of the French avant-garde and, in the persons of Stefan George, Hofmannsthal, Rilke, Trakl and others, aimed at an artificial intensification of artistic expression. The more recent history of literary modernism began with lyric poetry. This was the context in which Hölderlin was rediscovered, and afterwards he was declared the father of the new lyrical movement and of 'tragic' literary history, as Schmitt expressed it in his later notes. However, Schmitt did not need George or Hölderlin as points of reference, because he had already found his poet in Däubler. Benn, Döblin and Brecht represent later, aesthetically more sophisticated developments.[14] It is surprising that Schmitt tied the possibility of artistic creativity to a break with linguistic conventions, because the 'audience' and the 'ground of common sense' were central categories in his shorter miscellaneous writings. But now he declared a decisive break with the audience as the condition of the possibility for artistic work. He stated that modern art had become esoteric because a common public or epic totality no longer existed. He drew a radical line between the 'received wisdom of the educated' and the truly artistic comprehension of the present.

Religious pathos and secular dogmas

After their Däubler summer journey, Schmitt and Eisler first wrote the *Schattenrisse* as a 'Bierzeitung'* [beer journal] during various meetings. The form of the 'silhouettes', a gallery of portraits of contemporary cultural figures, was taken from Herbert Eulenberg,[15] a successful contemporary author who was in charge of the 'matinees with poets and music poets' at the theatre in Düsseldorf. Eulenberg had published his introductions to these 'morning celebrations' in 1910 under the title *Schattenbilder* [Shadow images] with the aim in mind 'of providing the people with a substitute for Sunday services'.[16] Schäfer's *Anekdoten* bore a semblance to this literary form. The ironic subversion of these models can be seen as the literary starting point of the *Schattenrisse* project, in which both Eulenberg and Schäfer are the objects of satirical treatment. The close connection with Schmitt's own situation at the time also shows in the incorporation of portraits of Walther Rathenau and Fritz Mauthner. Schmitt had written reviews of works by both these men. Put differently, Schmitt transformed his occasional contributions to Schäfer's journal into a general day of reckoning with the 'received wisdom of the educated'.

---

* Name for a journal edited by pupils upon finishing school.

According to the preface, the *Schattenrisse* want to show that 'relativism' is not dead, and that 'naturalism' is still alive. In a first approximation, we may say that they set out to do precisely the opposite, while the keywords in the preface do not fully reflect the actual content of the satires: the grotesquely sketched portraits of the *Schattenrisse* take issue not with 'naturalistic' art in the narrower sense (which Schmitt, incidentally, in the case of Ibsen and others knew very well how to value) but with more recent literary attempts at 'overcoming' naturalism by figures such as Richard Dehmel and Thomas Mann. The naturalist-'monistic' programme of Wilhelm Ostwald, subject of the first of the *Schattenrisse*, can hardly be called relativist. The fact that they nevertheless emphasize this common denominator foreshadows a philosophical position that Schmitt would take in other contexts. Even though this first series of 'silhouettes' does not quite fit under the rubric of a relativist 'naturalism', Schmitt actually did see the modern era as such in these terms.

The text opens with a monistic Sunday sermon by Ostwald, introducing the philosophical tone of the satires. The philosophical, and overall anti-Christian, perspective of the secular 'received wisdom' can then be felt in the 'silhouette' on Elisabeth Förster-Nietzsche. It is not Nietzsche himself who is the model for the modern worldviews [Weltanschauungen] of which the *Schattenrisse* are parodies, but the contemporary Nietzsche cult in the naturalist interpretation that Elisabeth Förster-Nietzsche publicized and organized in a more limited parallel campaign to Cosima Wagner's activities. 'Pippin der Kleine' [Little Pippin] represents the discussions surrounding the naturalist cultural history of Karl Lamprecht, and Gottfried von Bouillon is the imperialist, and fond traveller, Kaiser Wilhelm II.[17] The fictional character Eberhardt Niegeburth* embodies the essence of all modern tendencies. Anatol France represents the Epicurean attitude towards life. Thus, taken together, the *Schattenrisse* are a general reckoning with Wilhelminian culture. A further theological detail is hinted at in the treatment of religion: those sharing the 'received wisdom of the educated' deceive themselves over the religious pathos of their convictions and cultural customs. They do not see themselves as the secular heirs of a Christian culture. This general diagnosis is already declared in the introductory chorus of the monist congregation. The satirical means serve the purpose of laying open the contradiction between religious pathos and 'naturalist' dogmas. Those sharing the 'received wisdom of the educated' misunderstand themselves, and thus the various characters that are the subject of parody also suffer from self-deception.

Schmitt never stopped liking this text, with its rich allusions, and he continued to read aloud from it in smaller gatherings even after 1945. The overall composition of the work would deserve a more detailed analysis. The text, for instance, associates the 'received wisdom of the educated' with the 'Schiller Prize', anticipating later polemics against candidates for the Nobel Prize and other laureates. The conclusion anticipates the

---

* The surname translates as 'never born'; nie = never, Geburt = birth. Thanks to Reinhard Mehring for pointing this out to me.

literary satire *Die Buribunken* by providing 'proof of the immortality of the species' (p. 51). The appendix offers an 'authentic interpretation' that deconstructs the text's populist aim to become the 'received wisdom for all educated people', and adds some 'Notes for the Uneducated', further confusing the reader by satirical means. 'Statutes of the Silhouettes Academy' present the economic and legal basis of culture and the arts. Finally, a prize competition invites the reader to participate in the production of silhouettes. Responses are to be sent *poste restante* to a certain Johannes Negelinus in Breslau, the pseudonym under which Johannes Reuchlin published his *Dunkelmännerbriefe* [Letters from shady characters] in 1515, in the context of the religious disputes at the time. Satire is meant to show an 'upside-down world', a practice well established in the Rhenish carnival. Only he who stands behind the mirror can hold up the mirror to others. With his reception of Däubler and his avant-gardism, Schmitt took up a position behind the mirror of conventional opinion. Thus, his meeting with the untimely poet is one of the conditions for his satire concerning 'received wisdom'.

4

On the Eve of the Great War: State, Church and Individual as Points of Reference

The dancer at the 'Tingel-Tangel':*
Carita (von) Dorotić (1883–1968)

Schmitt experienced the years after 1912 as a time of dramatic crisis and felt close to suicide and madness. One of the reasons for this was financial hardship: legal trainees did not receive any salary. But his problems were also of his own making. The crisis had a colourful name: Pauline (Pabla) Carita Maria Isabella (von) Dorotić (18 July 1883–28 August 1968) – Carl's Cari, his first passionate love and his first wife.

In April 1912, Schmitt still wanted to marry Helene Bernstein; however, this was soon a thing of the past after scenes of jealousy [involving Helene's sister] and after the parents forbade Schmitt from entering their house. In May 1912, Schmitt met Cari as a Spanish dancer in a vaudeville theatre, just at the right moment for her to free him from the love triangle. Carl wrote to his sister: 'I now have a delightful friendship with a Spanish dancer. You would like her, too' (JB, p. 151). There was no clear separation between stage and real life. Cari was not Spanish, though her German was not entirely fluent. She presented herself as a young, aristocratic and unhappy girl, just the type some men liked at the time. Soon after they met, she suddenly claimed to be the daughter of an aristocratic Croatian lord of a manor, Johann Franz von Dorotić, and to have been born in 1888, a week after Carl. After the early death of her parents, her story continued, she had been sent to an aunt in Munich who had treated her so badly that she fled and joined a theatre as a dancer. It was only in connection with his divorce proceedings in 1922 that Schmitt learned that Cari was actually born in 1883 as the illegitimate child of Augusta Maria Franziska Schachner in Gumpendorf, Vienna, and that she later became legitimized when her mother married the journeyman (plumber) Johann Dorotić from Agram (Zagreb). She was Protestant. In 1889, she came to Munich and lived in the Maximilianstraße, where her adoptive father worked. We know nothing about her youth. In 1907, she went to Vienna for more than a year, returning to Munich at the end of 1908. At the end of 1909, she gave notice of her departure to Prague for a couple of days, using a passport issued in

---

* Old-fashioned expression for a second-rate cabaret or nightclub.

Königsberg. Thereafter, she lived again in Munich for a couple of months, before her files finally slipped through the cracks in the city's administration. She was actually from Munich.

When Carl met her, she was twenty-eight years of age. She told him fantastical stories in order to prove her descent. It is hard to believe, but Carl fell for it. Years later, the great passion would turn out to have been a 'delusion'. Cari's life had the quality of a performance on stage; whether her stage performances had quality is less certain. In any case, she gave guest performances in Görlitz when Schmitt met her. Later, she had another contract in Wiesbaden. After the two had become engaged, work was a thing of the past for her. Schmitt's mentor at the time, Hugo am Zehnhoff, despite being positively disposed towards her, occasionally tried to talk Schmitt out of the relationship by mentioning the word 'Tingel-Tangel' (TB I, p. 296), knowing very well that this was a term rich in allusions. Schmitt married a dancer: a demi-monde, a femme fatale and an impostor. It was a daring feat to base his life on a relationship with Cari. However, passion follows its own laws. It is difficult to judge what Schmitt owed to Cari. The women of men of genius are often surprising choices. For a long time, no justice was done to Goethe's Christiane Vulpius, Wagner's Minna Planer or Nora Barnacle Joyce. Schmitt's great love was the beginning of a story with many twists and turns. The hurt of his disappointment never fully healed. Nevertheless, Schmitt went through these years without suffering any professional damage. His nervous tension predated his acquaintance with Cari. To speak the language of Thomas Mann's *Doktor Faustus*, maybe he was driven by an 'urge to take god-tempting risks', by the 'most secret desire for demonic conception'.[1] Cari became his 'Hetaera esmeralda',[*] his poisonous butterfly.

The contact with the Bernsteins ended at once. 'Praise and thanks to God' (JB, p. 153), were Schmitt's final words about this flirtatious episode. In the summer of 1912, Däubler, Kluxen and Eisler came to Düsseldorf. Schmitt travelled through the Rhineland and Alsace with Däubler and the patron of the arts Albert Kollmann. At that point, Cari may still have presented herself as a Spanish dancer, as Schmitt's sister was urged to get hold of a Spanish 'shawl' at all costs. From October 1912, the diary contains passionate love letters and an ecstatic philosophy of love that aims to base love on permanence and to 'enforce faithfulness' by idealizing love as 'devotion to an idea'. With, as well as against, Weininger and Strindberg, Schmitt constantly thought about the morality of love. With Weininger, he assumed that 'the one who loves wants to return to the motherly womb' (TB I, p. 27). However, while Weininger had a 'characterization of men' in mind, Schmitt was looking for a 'characterization of women' (TB I, p. 38). Schmitt wanted to conceive of his love from the perspective of eternity, a perspective in which 'Cari', then, had 'no predecessor and no successor' (TB I, p. 43). Schmitt saw himself as an 'advocate' who was 'devoted to an idea'. He declared the relationship with Helene Bernstein to have been

---

[*]   Figure in Mann's novel: a prostitute who warns Adrian Leverkühn that she has a venereal disease.

an error. He now felt that he had been 'painfully ambushed by a vain, common, ugly and arrogant virago who is now in possession of love letters from me' (TB I, p. 42). 'She has foisted herself on me as an addressee', Schmitt noted:

> Thus, I spit out her whole person; I have no more to do with her; I wash my hands clean; I took excrement for gold without letting slip from my fingers the pure gold that I now hold in my hands. Oh Cari, you appear so pure to me; you have no predecessor and no successor, and this hideous beast is as little your predecessor as an ape, cloaked in the robe of a king and successfully deceiving the people for a minute, thereby becomes a predecessor of the king. (TB I, p. 43)

Schmitt wanted to cleanse the idea of love from any historical impurities, he wanted to conceive of his passion in idealist fashion as absolutely unique. His thoughts on 'devotion to an idea' he at once used for academic purposes by transposing the idea of love to the idea of right, and writing down his conclusions regarding a philosophy of the state with utmost concentration. The diary fell silent in favour of this work.

In the summer of 1912, Schmitt was completely broke, and he established contact again with Uncle André in Bussingen. From October onwards, he began a placement with the judicial councillor Hugo Lambert in Mönchengladbach. He worked off his debts and hoped for further support. He rented a cheap room in Mönchengladbach for several weeks and complained bitterly about the fact that the lawyer earns a lot and the trainee nothing. The shortage of money became a permanent topic. Schmitt consoled himself and his sister with hopes for a better future: 'Hopefully, I shall be a rich man in a couple of years and then can help you all. But right now I am still a little ragamuffin who is just muddling through' (JB, p. 166). At that time Cari had her engagement in Wiesbaden, from where Carl picked her up in mid-December, and they spent Christmas together in Cologne. Afterwards, Carl went to Plettenberg for a couple of days. Between January and May 1913, he wrote *Wert des Staates* [Value of the state] in his 'chamber' in Mönchengladbach. The location helps to explain the limited apparatus of the work.

While *Über Schuld und Schuldarten* [On guilt and types of guilt] had set limits to juridical thought, *Gesetz und Urteil* [Law and judgment] proclaimed a turn towards practice: the law is what professional judges, in concrete cases and making a claim for acceptance by their colleagues, declare to be the law. The law only comes into existence with judgments. In *Wert des Staates* Schmitt held on to these ideas. However, the place of the judge who passes law in his judgments is now taken by the state, which realizes the law (see the full discussion of the text below). Not only the judges but every 'individual' is given a significance for the state as a 'servant of the law'. Schmitt takes the individual into the 'service' of the state in order to ascribe an ethos, a supra-individual significance to it. At the same time, he published a biting critique, 'Schopenhauers Rechtsphilosophie außerhalb seines philosophischen Systems'[2] [Schopenhauer's philosophy of right

considered outside his philosophical system]. While the monograph constitutes a critique of any methodology that starts out from the individual, the
note on Schopenhauer demonstrates in exemplary fashion the necessary
failure of such a way of proceeding.

Schopenhauer's methodological individualism, Schmitt wrote, is forced
to begin with the individual 'right to exist and not be negated' and with
'self-defence'. But, according to Schmitt, Schopenhauer does not make
this clear, and anyhow his approach leads to absurd consequences. 'Strictly
speaking, [in Schopenhauer] only a person whose will is negated in a concrete case has the right to a negation of the negation. In the case of murder,
that would be the person that has been killed.'[3] No 'justification for the
authority of the state' could be established on such grounds. In conclusion, Schmitt denies the possibility of 'taking Schopenhauer's philosophy
of right as the foundation for a systematic philosophy of right'.[4] At one
fell swoop he rejected the 'general view that everything positive is the
negation of a negation' along with the metaphysics of pessimism. Schmitt
denied the individual all the exaltations in which he privately indulged. His
experiences of dependency showed him that the individual is more or less
powerless against social attributions. Schmitt's juridical anti-individualism
is a constant feature of his early work. First, he reflected systematically
on the juridical 'significance of the individual', then, at the level of intellectual history, he criticized the Romantic 'invention' of the modern individual, and finally he drew the political conclusions from this in the form
of a critique of parliamentarism and liberalism. Thus, the foundations for
Schmitt's critique of liberalism were already established before 1914, in his
earliest works. A clear line runs from his dissertation to his Habilitation,
and on to his critique of intellectual history and of constitutional law.

The 'dignity' of the individual in the 'service' of the law

Schmitt's diary contains first thoughts on *Wert des Staates* at the end of
1912, in between reflections on the philosophy of love. In these remarks,
Schmitt sees his own character as that of an 'advocate':

> In terms of character, I am an advocate. I promote only other people's inter-
> ests. They are the only ones I can work for and pursue without suffering pangs
> of conscience. Lawyers are probably all people with a guilty conscience. My
> whole theory of devotion to an idea relies on this characterological trait of
> being devoted to a matter, an idea, whose advocate one becomes by giving up
> one's own personality. (TB I, p. 42)

Schmitt wanted to commit his 'queen' to love and faithfulness. And of
the state, in a parallel move, he expected 'devotion to the idea' of right.
Schmitt's position was that of an advocate for love and right. He idealized
the powers under which he lived. He now distinguished between the fictional 'will of the law' and the law as 'norm' and 'commandment' [Gebot].
'First there is commandment, the people are later', is his motto taken from

Däubler.[5] In detailed discussions of Kant and more recent philosophy of law (Stammler, Cohen), Schmitt again distinguished between morality and law, and rejected an ethical perspective on law that would set out from social 'mores'. He declared the question of the origin of law a taboo, and instead analysed the factually given legal system in its ambiguous position between power and right [Macht und Recht]. The existence of the state is a fact. If it is meant to be a legitimate state, it must be a state based on the rule of law [Rechsstaat]. A constitutional state institutionalizes the connection between power and right. Only as a means of right is power legitimate. The constitutional state confers rights on the individual and, thus, the individual acquires a meta-factual 'dignity'.

Schmitt did not argue on the level of state law but on the level of a 'philosophy of law'. He did not describe the actual constitutional situation; rather, he identified the basic conditions for any possible legitimate state, without any reference to established law at the time. A state can only be legitimate if it is a constitutional state. Any state under the rule of law constitutionalizes the distinction between power and right and assigns a normative significance to the individual. In this way, Schmitt also argued independently of the concrete form a state takes. His position was already that of an anthropological pessimism for which he would later enlist authors such as Donoso Cortés and Hobbes as alleged sources. 'If our considerations do not move beyond the material body, then the concrete physical individual is nothing but a wholly arbitrary entity', Schmitt writes in *Wert des Staates*, 'a drift of atoms whose form, individuality and uniqueness does not differ from that of dust that is blown into the shape of a pillar by a whirlwind' (WdS, p. 101). Schmitt's intention was to guarantee the metaphysical 'significance' of the 'individual' with the help of the law, without having to formulate a 'system of subjective rights' or fundamental rights for this. He had in mind the even more general question of the legal constitution of the 'person' [Persönlichkeit]: 'Whatever it is that makes a person is determined by the legal system itself' (TB I, p. 63). Schmitt also sketched a version of his thoughts critical of the times. At the end of this he said:

> The law is norm, beyond the world, before and after the world. The purpose of law is the realization of the norm. The result to be achieved is not law but a condition that corresponds to the norm; hence, law itself can never be the purpose to be achieved, only a condition corresponding to the law, a reality corresponding to the norm, can be that purpose. . . . We shall have to distinguish between two types of law. The essential law and accidental law. . . . Positive law deserves to be called 'law' only in a derivative sense. (TB I, p. 66)

Thus, Schmitt used his distinction between 'substantial justice' and positive 'law' in order to formulate an eschatological proviso, and he tied state law to the 'times of mediacy'; later he would talk about the 'normal condition' [Normalzustand] and the 'normal' situation in this context. He also talked about a 'ius divinum' and a 'natural law without naturalism'.

The short text of *Wert des Staates* consists of an introduction and three chapters. The introduction answers the 'objection of untimeliness', which claims that the study has anti-individualist consequences because it ties the significance of the individual to its value for the state. With reference to Rathenau, Schmitt emphasizes that the 'contemporary individualism' is in contradiction to the 'mechanical age': 'A time that calls itself sceptical and exact cannot in the same breath claim to be individualistic; neither scepticism nor the exact natural sciences provide possible foundations for individuality' (WdS, p. 4). Schmitt is of the opinion that an acknowledgement of the individuality (of 'modern man') can only rest on a 'constitution of individuality' within a philosophy of law. He directs the objections made by 'modern man' against modern man himself. However, with the newest 'works by Stammler and Cohen', the philosophy of law, Schmitt says, is still only at the very beginning of its task, because the 'question of the conditions of the possibility of jurisprudence as a science' (WdS, p. 12) has been addressed only insufficiently. In his first chapter, Schmitt provides the necessary conditions for jurisprudence as a science by way of a critique of theories of law based on power. Such theories of power [Machttheorien] had been advocated in various forms throughout the long nineteenth century. Thus, Schmitt says, it is possible to distinguish between power-based theories of law that make philosophically strong foundational claims and variants of such theories that, rather, abstain from making strong foundational claims – such as the one by Hans Kelsen, in which the question of the 'right law' (Rudolf Stammler)[6] is excluded as belonging to the 'ideology' of natural law. However, in this case, and in contrast to his later works, Schmitt does not argue historically. He is interested less in disproving, on their own grounds, positions that have historically been held than in an external critique that uncovers the implicit assumptions made by any theory of power.

Schmitt assumes that any 'power-based theory' of law [Machttheorie vom Recht] is an expression of a positive 'evaluation' of power and of 'trust in the ordinary run of things and in the justice of history' (WdS, p. 23). The truth, he suggests, is contained in the 'reversal of the antithesis': 'law is not based on power, power is based on law' (WdS, p. 24). Schmitt extracts a quasi-religious 'confession of the highest faith' in history from theories of power. He sets his own 'radical scepticism' in opposition to a time 'that calls itself sceptical and exact' (WdS, p. 24). This turning of theories of power against themselves is enough for Schmitt to claim the independence of law from power. 'If there is to be a law', he holds, 'then it cannot be derived from power' (WdS, p. 29). In truth, he adds, no one attempts to do that. A system of law can only exist if it cannot be affected by power. Thus, Schmitt separates the 'final purpose' of the law from any utilitarian means–ends relations, understands legal norms as 'commandments' (following the Däubler motto), and takes the state as the legal subject that mediates between norm and reality.

The second chapter, titled 'Der Staat' [The state], limits the definition of the state to the 'ideal' state, or 'the state understood as the idea of the state'. As theories of power see the state as the lawgiver by virtue of being the highest power [Macht], they once again imply a right based on power [Macht]:

The highest power [Gewalt] that characterizes the state is, in essence, a unity that results only from the application of evaluative criteria. The claim that the law could only be derived from the highest power [Gewalt] therefore turns against the very theories of power themselves and now says that the highest power [Gewalt] can only be what is derived from the law. Law does not exist in the state, but the state exists in law. (WdS, pp. 47f.)

Thus, we arrive at the following definition of the state: 'The state . . . is a legal entity whose sole purpose is the realization of right' (WdS, p. 52). The state is given 'legitimacy' as the 'foundation' for the realization of right. Only with the state does the law become positive, and with the state the distinction between the ideal and the actual law enters the world. The 'abstract' idea of legality [Rechtsgedanke] only acquires a 'shape in the form of the positive laws of a state': 'The idea of legality which is meant to provide guiding principles for the transformation of reality must become positive – i.e., its content is posited in an act of sovereign decision; the idea becomes statutory law and is given a concrete form' (WdS, p. 78). With this move the critique of power-based theories takes a new turn. Schmitt now assumes the state to be a mediator which, at one and the same time, posits power and law in the form of positive law. At this point, he also refers to the alternative solutions offered by Catholicism and Protestantism, taking up a contemporary debate between the two great theologians and canonists Rudolph Sohm and Adolf Harnack regarding the legal structure of the Church. Did the charisma of original Christianity have a legal form? And so, is there a divine canon law? Schmitt sides with Harnack[7] against Sohm, and he transfers the idea of an original canon law from the Church onto the state. He takes seriously, however, Sohm's reservations regarding the institutionalization of Christianity by the Church and retains them in the form of an eschatological proviso. With this, Schmitt has reached his concluding chapter, 'Der Einzelne' [The individual].

In this chapter, Schmitt discusses some consequences of his arguments for the 'significance of the individual'. He forcefully suggests that the individual only gains significance as a 'civil servant', as a 'servant' who is 'devoted' to the tasks of the state. Schmitt talks about a 'remelting' [Umschmelzung] and reshaping, referring to the concept of an office in the Catholic Church. At the same time, he again takes up his initial thought that an individual only acquires a legal value within the system of norms provided by a state: 'The derivation of the value of the individual from its task and from the fulfilment of that task does . . . not destroy the dignity of the individual. Rather, it opens up the possibility of a justified dignity in the first place' (WdS, p. 108). In conclusion, Schmitt formulates an eschatological proviso: 'There are times of mediacy [Zeiten des Mittels] and times of immediacy [Zeiten der Unmittelbarkeit]. During the latter, individuals are devoted to the idea as a matter of course' (WdS, p. 108). Schmitt links up this distinction with the 'opposition between intuitive and discursive thought', hinting at the fact that in apocalyptic times the individual relates intuitively, and outside the spheres of the Church or state, to the idea of legality. With this, Schmitt puts the 'example' of the Church into the context of his later programmatic 'Political Theology'. Schmitt's whole attitude towards the state is characterized by the assumption that the state decides the state of exception, creates order, is a stabilizing force in 'times of mediacy' and of institutional mediation, and provides a 'relation of protection and obligation'. If the state does not do these things, 'times of immediacy' ensue. Then, the individual's duty of loyalty no longer exists, and the individual is free to interpret the political chaos 'eschatologically' as something to which he or she bears an 'immediate' relationship.

Law [Recht]	State	The individual
Idea (commandment)	Power [Macht]	Person (not individual) Mediator
Ius divinum	Law	Servant, civil servant
[Church]	Authority	[Pope]

Der Wert des Staates is an extraordinarily important foundational text. In his later works Schmitt no longer argued at the same level of detail. Here, he formulates his anti-individualist credo that the individual only has normative significance and 'dignity' within a constitutional state. The constitutional state as such is simply considered a given social fact. There is a religious alternative to the normative proviso. Canon law figures as the school of all law. Schmitt constructs a wide concept of law in the classical tradition, rejecting modern contractualism as well as German idealism as anthropocentric theories of legitimation. On 19 July 1913, he informed his sister of the completion of his study in the 'philosophy of law'. In mid-September, he sent the manuscript to the publisher Mohr. It is dedicated to his 'Pabla von Dorotić'. At the beginning of October, he received a letter of acceptance from the publisher, and soon he would sit over the proofs. On 11 December, he received his author's copies.[8] Schmitt made various efforts to have the book reviewed. Thus, he sent a copy to Georg Lukács, whose works would interest Schmitt throughout his life. Schmitt's book had some success and was also positively received by the school of Kelsen. Alfred Verdross sent Schmitt a review (TB II, p. 498),[9] saying that he had 'presented the book in Kelsen's seminar on the philosophy of law', and that it had 'been met with great approval . . . in this small Viennese circle that is interested in the theory of norms'.[10] From then on, Schmitt's relationship with Kelsen was not just a negative one. Carl Brinkmann[11] also reviewed the work in positive terms and stayed in touch ever after.

Schmitt followed this up with a short author's announcement, which he published via Bruno Bauch in the *Kant-Studien* [Kant studies].[12] This announcement is interesting in two respects: on the one hand it illustrates the intended anti-individualist impetus; on the other it comments directly on the outbreak of the war. Schmitt writes: 'The great antithesis which moves all human history is not the one between state and individual, but the one between state (= power [Macht]) and right [Recht]. The individual plays no role at all. Its significance is only of derivative nature' (TB I, p. 346).[13] In October, only a few days before the death of Eisler, Schmitt wrote: 'The book was written in 1913, and published in early 1914. Today, anyone who has remained calm enough to reflect on the enormous events within their historical and cultural context will be shocked by the force [Gewalt] of the impersonal that may be seen as the sign of these great times' (TB I, p. 347). The 'ideas of 1914' are here exposed as the 'force of the impersonal'. It does not sound very much like euphoria.

5

Düsseldorf:
Living in a State of Exception

The 'privy councillor' Hugo am Zehnhoff (1855–1930)

Hugo am Zehnhoff grew up in Cologne, where after having finished his studies he was a lawyer at the Higher Regional Court. When the Higher Regional Court in Düsseldorf opened, he followed his clients to the new location. From 1898 he was a member of the state parliament for the Centre Party and from 1899 he was also a member of the Reichstag. In 1906, he moved to the Higher Regional Court in Düsseldorf and became a judicial privy councillor. From 1908 he was the deputy chief executive of the bar association. From 1913 he was the president of the bar association, until he became the first parliamentary minister of justice for Prussia in 1919. In 1920, he saw through the Adelsgesetz [nobility law] and arranged the entails [Fideikommisse], and he was also very influential regarding the penal system and the right to grant pardon. Zehnhoff was a devout Catholic from the Rhineland, with a universal education of heart and mind. He shaped the collaboration between the lawyers and the Higher Regional Court in the initial phase following its inception. In 1931, a commemorative publication by the Higher Regional Court reminisced:

> Among those who left the Court, Dr am Zehnhoff, whose death recently was mourned in the world of law and in state-minded circles of the public, deserves a special mention. His life combined a fruitful activity as a lawyer, in particular in the areas of commercial and inheritance law and the law of entails, with influential parliamentary work. The legal realization of the Mittelland Canal,* one of the greatest tasks in legislation regarding waterways, must be credited to him. His work as the Prussian minister of justice is in everyone's memory.[1]

From 1913, Schmitt was in close contact with the 'privy councillor'. He saw him almost daily, was frequently invited for dinner, and drank whole nights with the much older man, who was almost sixty. The asymmetry of their relationship is obvious. Schmitt needed the assignments to write legal opinions, an atmosphere in which he was paid generously for them

---

* Some 325 kilometres in length, the Mittelland Canal is still the main east–west waterway in Germany. Construction began in 1906.

(and often voluntarily more than required), and the connection for his professional career. However, the nocturnal feasts put a strain on him. By the time of the outbreak of the war his dependency on am Zehnhoff had become too much for him: 'My socializing with the privy councillor is a grave, a sin' (TB I, p. 183). Schmitt found a lasting image for the situation: The 'privy councillor has stretched out on my soul like a hippopotamus on a flowery meadow' (TB I, p. 184). In Schmitt's descriptions, am Zehnhoff seems like a pan-demonic spectre from a novel by Franz Kafka. Schmitt's diaries at the time read altogether like a subtext to Kafka's *The Trial*. But behind the grotesque, almost surreal, characterization appears a mentor who, though perhaps imperious at times, was after all jovial, caring and worldly-wise. Underneath the outward signs of Wilhelminian authoritarianism, he was a fatherly friend. Zehnhoff must have recognized the exceptional talent of Schmitt, and must have liked him despite his ambivalences and escapades. Although he interfered in Schmitt's private life from time to time and tried to protect him from a looming disaster, he even accepted Schmitt's engagement and only urged 'that [the Protestant] Cari becomes Catholic' (TB I, p. 106). His patience never ran out entirely. When Schmitt formally announced the end of their relationship, he gave in. Later, upon Schmitt's appointment to a chair in Greifswald, he confirmed that Schmitt had been employed part-time in his office between 1 May 1913 and 1 February 1915, and that he had worked in particular on matters relating to the law of entails and property assets, themes which, apart from questions of expropriation, played hardly any role in Schmitt's later work, but which helped to consolidate the foundations of his thinking as a lawyer. After 1919, Schmitt once again had close friendly relations with am Zehnhoff. Later, he would refer to their acquaintance as the 'most important' meeting in his life: 'It was only then that I really became a jurist.'[2]

Entails were family estates which had special stipulations attached regarding inheritance. They were bequeathed on a fiduciary basis only in the form of 'subsidiary ownership' ['Untereigentum'], while the full ownership ['Obereigentum'] remained with the patrilinear family ['Agnatenfamilie'] in order to keep the family fortune together. Within the region of the Upper Regional Court in Düsseldorf there were fifteen such large family estates. 57 per cent of the area belonging to the estates was forest land. Thus, in the first place the entails concerned special stipulations regarding the inheritance of forest estates. About 2.7 per cent of the total area of the Rhine provinces formed part of such estates, whereas the proportion in Silesia was the highest of all provinces, with 13 per cent. These arrangements also ended after 1918. The Weimar constitution [Weimarer Reichsverfassung], in article 155, incorporated an old demand first made in the constitution of the national assembly in the Paulskirche:* 'The entails

---

* The first German national assembly, which met in the Paulskirche in Frankfurt between 18 May 1848 and 31 May 1849, following the March revolution. It passed the so-called Frankfurt Constitution (Paulskirchenverfassung). The title of the document is actually *Verfassung des deutschen Reiches*. After the departure of the Austrian and Prussian parliamentarians in April and May 1849, the rump parliament and revolutionary forces in the German states failed in their attempts to implement the constitution.

'It was only then that I really became a jurist' – Schmitt about Hugo am Zehnhoff

are to be repealed.' The appointment of am Zehnhoff as Prussian minister of justice was closely connected with this task. Zehnhoff initiated the so-called Adelsgesetz [nobility law] of 23 June 1920 and thereby shaped the approach taken during the Weimar Republic in dealing with the legacy of the Prussian 'squirearchy' ['Junkertum'].* In the course of dealing with entail cases, involving family disputes, Schmitt came into contact with aristocratic circles. He noted with sarcasm the discrepancy between his own personal situation and that of his clients. While Schmitt could hardly pay his rent, he sometimes stayed overnight in the castles owned by the clients of the privy councillor. His obsession with nobility, for which he paid a price in the form of Pabla, may have had to do with this. The Higher Regional Court of Düsseldorf had a separate senate for the entails commissions. Zehnhoff worked closely with this senate.[3]

A complicated engagement

In June 1913, Theodor Däubler visited Schmitt for a week. Then, Schmitt once again spent some time in Strasbourg. In July the *Schattenrisse* appeared. In October 1913, Schmitt was engaged to Cari. He bought a ring, went to the consulate in order to arrange a date for the wedding and, in anticipation of an early wedding, took an apartment with Cari

---

* The word 'Junkertum' was first coined by liberal political forces in the time leading up to 1848. It was used as a polemical term meant to emphasize the arrogance of the Prussian aristocracy.

next to the Academy of Fine Arts, near the court. In his diary, Schmitt calls himself 'a married bachelor' (TB I, p. 108). However, the next day there were already ominous signs: one of Hugo Lambert's employees, the lawyer Friedrich Schneider, had 'gone wild' (ibid.). Schmitt tried to calm him down. On 20 October, Schmitt was shocked himself: Cari had 'lost her passport' (TB I, p. 110). She was not allowed to stay in the new apartment. She immediately had to go to Schmitt's parents in Plettenberg, and the wedding was postponed for a year. Was this planned by Cari? Did she 'lose' her passport in order to gain time? Did she try to gain time because her papers were not in order, but had wanted to get out of the 'Tingel-Tangel' and into the safe haven of the engagement? Only under the exceptional circumstances of wartime could the marriage finally go ahead.

Cari in Plettenberg

On 22 October, Cari travelled to Plettenberg. Schmitt and Eisler followed later. Schmitt had to pay for Cari's stay with the family. At first, Cari liked it there, but Schmitt had premonitions: 'In Plettenberg she is in the company of my hateful, mean and vicious mother and my spoiled little sister Anna. Only father makes life easy for her. I don't know what will become of me' (TB I, p. 114). Schmitt did not always talk about his parents in this tone, but he always preferred his father. In the ensuing time, he was in Plettenberg as much as possible. Throughout November all was well. There were daily exchanges of letters. Then, Carl suffered again from his 'Schmitt affects' (TB I, p. 124) – anxiety attacks and nightmares which also had an anti-Semitic layer to them. At that time, even Eisler was no longer excluded from this. 'Saw the two Jews Jakobson and Lessing bickering and was glad that I no longer have anything to do with [Eduard] Rosenbaum. I don't want contact with Eisler any more either' (ibid.). He dreamt: 'Cari dances with Eisler' (TB I, p. 125). Over the Christmas period it came to quarrels with the family in Plettenberg. Schmitt's sister Üssi was scheming against Cari, talking badly about her to the mother, practising 'Ohrenbläserei'.* Schmitt's brother Jupp and his father calmed things down. On 29 December, a conversation was meant to clear the air: 'Met with Cari, spoke to father in serious terms. However, in the long run Cari will be driven away nevertheless. But I would rather leave my parents and forsake becoming a lawyer than make her worry in the least or allow her to be insulted' (TB I, p. 132). At the beginning of January, Schmitt returned to Düsseldorf and soon received an express letter from Cari. 'Mother meanly accused her of being pregnant. . . . This is the end now. I have no money, and we have to linger around for another whole year until I have become an assessor' (TB I, p. 136). The whole episode demonstrates the awkward situation of a couple in times when marriage, according to custom, was

---

* Literally: the act of blowing into the ears of someone. An old-fashioned expression, occurring in some translations of the Bible (at Rom 1:30), for denunciation and defamation.

allowed only once a professional future was secured. It also demonstrates the worries associated with sexuality due to the fear of pregnancy. Carl and Cari behaved in conformity with the customs at the time. They wanted a bourgeois relationship. Only the question of the papers lurked in the background. Schmitt at once sought help from am Zehnhoff, who showed an 'interest' in the matter but did not provide any financial support. The situation in Plettenberg calmed down and for the time being Cari was able to stay on. 'Then we dreamt of our first child, whom we want to call Johann Nikolaus, and who is meant to become a cardinal' (TB I, p. 137). Schmitt resumed his ordinary life in Düsseldorf. The privy councillor used his influence at the Reichsgericht* in Leipzig and in Düsseldorf to support Schmitt. He suggested that the two of them should write 'a commentary on the law covering entails. Excellent!' Schmitt also considered entering the world of business. 'Plans: want to become a politician and influential man' (TB I, p. 151). At that time he at last moved to the Higher Regional Court and wrote the thesis for his first degree. Cari found a place in a convent in Cologne; Schmitt commuted between attic and Cari, court and privy councillor. The diary ends in mid-February with notes on a dispute with the landlady.

The outbreak of war and the death of a friend

In June 1914, Schmitt took up his diary again, with some dark reflections. He accused himself of wrongdoing and felt as if he was Cari's 'murderer': 'I am a murderer. I am destroyed, have turned into nothing, and have murdered the soul of a child. Where should I seek refuge; in the Catholic Church. But I can't. I might as well go to the great Dalai Lama of Tibet or to some Mexican God.' He cried 'for advice and help from the quiet, unknown gods' (TB I, p. 158). Schmitt saw himself as a 'gnostic' (TB I, p. 167), and at best he believed in a 'malicious creator of this world'. He visited his dying friend Wülfing in hospital, and the same evening he learned about the assassination in Sarajevo. Schmitt rushed to the privy councillor, wrote to Cari, and occupied himself 'with the last concerns of human beings' (TB I, p. 163).† The next day Wülfing died. The death of his friend became the harbinger of war.

Europe drifted into the Great War. Germany guaranteed Austria a loyalty in the alliance between the two countries that would have been worthy of the Nibelungen saga. At that time Schmitt felt 'fear in the face of the marriage with Cari': 'In life, you can't do without objectivity and common sense. You can in philosophy, also in love, but not in marriage' (TB I, p. 167). He felt the 'awakening of a misogynist complex' in him, and thanked his philosophical influences: 'Perhaps Weininger and Strindberg have sharpened my senses' (TB I, p. 169). On 23 July, Austria delivered an

---

*   Supreme court at the national level, as opposed to regional courts.
†   A possible reference to Otto Weininger, *On Last Things* [Über die letzten Dinge, 1904], trans. Steven Burns, Lewiston, NY, 2001.

ultimatum to Serbia. Schmitt visited Uncle André in Lorraine in order to ask him for money for the time of his examination. Together with his cousin André he travelled on to Strasbourg, reliving student memories. He visited 'Calker in college, together with Eisler', went to Colmar to see the altar by Grünewald, and had made to him, on the day of the Austrian declaration of war, the 'suprising suggestion' by van Calker of coming 'to Strasbourg as regional judge and lecturer' (TB I, p. 171). Calker opened up opportunities for the time after Schmitt's exam as an assessor, despite the fact that two years previously Schmitt had rejected similar plans. A few days before the outbreak of war, Schmitt was in Alsace, a potential region of conflict.

On 1 August, Schmitt commented on German mobilization as follows:

Perhaps the Slavs will be victorious because the Germanic people rendered the area east of the Elbe Germanic, upon which the Slavs became part of the Germanic people and turned into Prussians. They subdued the rest of Germany, and the Prussian spirit, this rattling and brisk machinery without any intellect or emotion, will see to it that the Germans will not be able to deal with the Russians. That would also be a kind of metaphysical justice. (TB I, p. 173)

He dissected the pathos of a 'rise' [Erhebung]* in psychological terms. 'When I see the masses of soldiers marching past and think that one day I shall be one of them, I feel a strong excitement, even elation [Erhebung]. But the individual soldiers are all repugnant to me, and as a mass they are equally disgusting' (TB I, p. 175). On 4 August, Schmitt noted in lapidary terms: 'The war has begun. We fear a siege of Cologne.' In these days he talked a lot about politics with the privy councillor. Schmitt had to register with the Landsturm,† stayed overnight in Weeze Castle and felt like a 'pleb' without any possessions. He hoped for a victory by the Austrians and thought in terms of a decisive battle. On 9 September he met Eisler, who was a gunner by then, in Dülmen. Eisler explained the 'workings of a gun' to him. Schmitt was worried about his assessor's exam. On 11 September, he was given the topic for the thesis he had to write for it. Fears about the exam and about the war now ran in parallel. 'Often afraid of the horrible war. Who knows how it is going to end. The war is conducted like pure genocide' (TB I, p. 198). 'I can decidedly feel the hand of fate', Schmitt wrote. And he is worried about Eisler: 'I have received a postcard from Eisler from Naumur. If only he is not killed in action, the dear old fellow' (TB I, p. 200).

Schmitt had just begun to work on his exam thesis when the news about Eisler's death reached him. A splinter from a grenade had hit him in the head. Proof, once again, 'that all sense of continuity is fake'. Why not me?, Schmitt asked: 'I am the only survivor. It is maddening. I can't just go on living. How ridiculous to be alive' (TB I, p. 221). The next day he

---

* The term 'Erhebung' can also mean 'elation'.
† A reserve force intended as replacement for front-line units.

experienced an air raid on Düsseldorf: 'Then there appeared an enemy plane dropping bombs on the Zeppelinhalle, which burst into flames. A sign!' Schmitt sought and found comfort in Kierkegaard. In his diary, he noted:

> On 27 September, my friend Eisler died in action. At midday, a splinter from a grenade hit him in the head. He died instantly, and his comrades buried him the very same evening. For more than six years we had been united in a friendship of a kind that can only be the result of many years of hours shared together and of common interests and aims. I have now lost my two friends in the course of a quarter of a year, and nothing seems more natural to me, in my present bewildered mood, than the thought that I shall be the next. (TB I, p. 222)

Schmitt journeyed to Eisler's brother Georg in Frankfurt, and they both travelled on to Strasbourg. Carl took care of Eisler's estate, inherited his books on the philosophy of law, and arranged for Eisler to be added to the list of fallen soldiers.[4] As a last service to his friend, Schmitt published the Introduction to Eisler's planned Habilitation.

Georg Eisler (1892–1983) now also formed an intense friendship with Schmitt, and until 1933 he was his closest friend. He was born and grew up in Hamburg, with the exception of seven months which he spent in Vienna, probably staying with relatives of his mother, for the purpose of passing his school leaving certificates. At the time, Georg was a 'commercial assistant' in the company of his father. Because at the beginning of August he had been assigned to the second reserve of the Landsturm [Landsturm zweiten Aufgebots] only when taking his physical with the Austrian army, he applied for naturalization in Germany on 7 August, so that he might fulfil his patriotic 'duty'.[5] He was immediately naturalized on the explicit condition that 'he will be taken into active service with the forces'.[6] The naturalization document is dated 2 September 1914. On 18 September, Georg received his notice as a volunteer, only days before the death of his brother, and he was at once drafted into a field artillery regiment. After the death of Fritz, in October 1914 the father renewed his application for naturalization. It was first turned down, but was finally accepted, with the documents dated 28 May 1915. In the decision, the fact that Eisler ran his paper, the *Hamburger Woche*, 'in a thoroughly German national spirit' had been taken into consideration.[7] Fritz and Georg's sister, Julie, was now also naturalized. With the death of Fritz the family paid a high price for their naturalization. In 1933, they were robbed of their flourishing company.

Fortunate interim solutions

Despite complications and stressful situations, some positive solutions began to emerge within the first weeks of the war. Cari's situation at the convent in Cologne became increasingly untenable. Schmitt reacted by drafting a sketch for a one-act play in which Cari, despite her grammatical deficiencies, triumphs over the young nuns at the convent (TB I, p. 215). The problems regarding the marriage papers were taken up again. On her own initiative, Cari wrote to the Austrian emperor. Carl paid a visit to a prostitute. 'Went home chastened. But never again!' (TB I, p. 194). The privy councillor covered the fee for the assessor examination using copyright money for the thesis. Although Schmitt mocked his fatherly care and 'unrestrained carnality', he admitted to himself at one point: 'The fact that I have come to know the privy councillor (as I came to know Calker before becoming a legal trainee) is excellent. Everything falls into place so that I can climb higher up' (TB I, p. 205). The written assignment gained momentum only slowly, but by mid-October Schmitt was working diligently on it. However, upon wanting to show the privy councillor a draft of it and not being admitted directly to his office, Schmitt wrote a formal letter of separation. The privy councillor at once declared this to have been a 'misunderstanding'. Nevertheless, Schmitt felt 'like Odysseus after having escaped the cyclop, Polyphem, the privy councillor' (TB I, p. 232). On 23 October, the thesis was completed. Only on 24 October did Schmitt have the courage to visit the privy councillor again, but not without having at once 'an awful feeling of trepidation and lack of freedom' (TB I, p. 234). Now the events dramatically came to a head.

Friedrich Wülfing senior, the father of Schmitt's deceased friend and owner of a tailoring business in Düsseldorf producing uniforms, suggested a substantial commission business that would have relieved all of Schmitt's financial worries at a stroke. Schmitt was given the topic of his second examination, 'the Relation'.* On 30 October, he drove to Cologne because Cari had been accused of theft and the police had found two shirts and a pair of trousers. 'We thought that Cari had to leave immediately. I have to find some money today, from the privy councillor and from Wülfing' (TB I, p. 239). Cari moved from the convent into Kardinalstraße. Carl wrote a petition for the police. The commission business threatened to go sour, but went ahead on more modest terms after all. At first, Schmitt had no success with the police. 'They are still establishing the facts. Who knows what will be the result' (TB I, p. 247). A lawyer by the name of Hüsgen made some helpful comments on the examination paper. At the same time, Schmitt helped his friend Heinrich Gross with his paper. 'The truth is, I dictated the whole work to him; but it seems he is grateful for it' (TB I, p. 257). He slightly regretted his efforts: 'In the meantime, I have helped someone to an excellent examination paper; my own one is not as good, and I get no thanks for it' (TB I, p. 259). In the end, as Gross fell ill, Schmitt brought his own work to a successful conclusion.[8]

On 5 December, Schmitt was given the date for his final written examination at the Kammergericht [Upper Regional Court] in Berlin. Only shortly before the journey was he able to organize the money necessary to make it. On 16 December, he travelled to Berlin, read up for a day in the university library, and then sat his three exams at the Kammergericht. Five hours

---

* Within civil law, a report on a lawsuit, prior to trial and judgment, in which a judge analyses the legal significance and validity of the claims made by plaintiff and defendant.

on 'BGB'* and three hours on criminal law were obligatory. In addition, there was another three-hour exam on another area of law.[9] Regarding the topic on criminal law, he was 'obviously lucky' (TB I, p. 276). For a couple of days after the exam, Schmitt roamed the streets of Berlin with Däubler and Moeller van den Bruck.[10] He also met the literary critic Julius Bab. Afterwards, Schmitt visited Georg Eisler in Hamburg. He was not only thinking of the deceased Fritz but also seeking a conversation with the parents over his 'future'. Schmitt spent the Christmas days with the rich Jewish family, which exercised him emotionally. His 'Jewish complex' (TB I, p. 226) was stirred again. After conversations on theology, Schmitt noted on Christmas Day: 'I begin to respect the Jews' (TB I, p. 282). About meeting the mother, he wrote: 'She is a proper housewife, economically thrifty, easily moved, but altogether cold and indifferent towards strangers. I can see that there isn't much to hope for from her' (ibid.). On his departure he noted: 'I had already fully resigned myself to not receiving anything, when later Georg told me that his father had asked him whether he should give me any money. I didn't take anything then, because Georg promised me something. The old man is a great chap' (ibid.). On 6 January, Schmitt received a 'letter from Georg Eisler, asking me to name a sum that his father would send me. How nice' (TB I, p. 290).

The months since the outbreak of war resembled a roller-coaster ride through hell. There was the conflict with the privy councillor, the death of Fritz Eisler and the meeting with his family, renewed plans for the wedding, the scandal around the theft, Schmitt's thesis and written exams – no easy times. Schmitt felt drained: 'I am at the end of my tether. All I am able to do is write in my diary' (TB I, p. 286). The same day, 2 January 1915, Schmitt rented an expensive apartment in Grünstraße, into which he moved with Cari on 5 January 1915, and which he furnished extravagantly, in the expectation of soon having passed his exams. For the first time, the couple lived in their own apartment. Until then, they had had a discreet long-distance relationship. The privy councillor regretted the decision. 'He said, if only I had never met . . . Cari!' Cari, meanwhile, had 'immediately received a positive reply to her letter to the king from the minister of justice' (TB I, p. 296). Carl went to see the privy councillor, who waived his debts, 500 Marks, and presented him with the 'bill' for his mistakes. 'About Cari, he said that she had been in a "Tingel-Tangel"' (ibid.). Schmitt called this 'hideous banality', but without actually being surprised. Eisler came to visit. 'Georg is a great chap, a clever, intelligent, decent Jew. They can, after all, be incredible fellows, something I never expected' (TB I, p. 304). Schmitt separated the 'incredible fellow' from his abstract anti-Jewish impulse. The oral assessor's exam was set for 25 February at the Higher Regional Court in Cologne. With difficulty Schmitt forced himself to do the necessary revision for it. At the beginning of February, he received the draft order for the army. His brother Jupp had already been drafted. From Munich, Eisler wrote that van Calker wanted 'to organize a post at the Leibregiment' (TB I, p. 311). Schmitt immediately travelled to

---

* 'Bürgerliches Gesetzbuch' = German civil law.

the Türkenkaserne (Maxvorstadt) in Munich. The infantry Leibregiment stationed there was the personal regiment of the Bavarian king. During the war it suffered substantial losses of more than 3,000 soldiers in Verdun and other places. Major van Calker reassured Schmitt that he was taken on as a volunteer who was fit for service only within the garrison. 'At Calker's place, deeply sad that I probably will have to become a soldier after all' (TB I, p. 314).

On 10 February, Schmitt was back in Düsseldorf, where Cari had, in the meantime, got hold of a fake birth certificate and had arranged the civil ceremony. There was another incident involving the privy councillor, who, in connection with the matter of the theft, had refused to provide the public prosecutor with 'reliable information' on Cari's former life. In other words, the 'Tingel-Tangel' got in the way again. Zehnhoff gave the advice to postpone the wedding until the matter of the theft was resolved, and probably hoped that Schmitt would break off the engagement before that. But, on 13 February, Carl and Cari were at the registry office. 'Finally, it was our turn; strangely, it all went smoothly. The registrar went through the procedure without hesitations. Two old invalids were present. Thus, we were married' (TB I, p. 317). Already the next morning, Schmitt had to return to the army barracks in Munich but was given a couple of days off for the church ceremony and his oral exam. 'I would never have thought that Calker would once more do so much for me' (TB I, p. 318). On 20 February, Schmitt passed his oral exam. 'I didn't do particularly well' (TB II, p. 21). His mark, unusual for him, was a 'satisfactory'. The same night he returned to the barracks.

Insufficient interim reflections

If we recapitulate the tensions of Schmitt's years in Düsseldorf, it seems unlikely that anyone would have wanted to be in his shoes. The way he laid the foundations for an academic and legal career may be impressive. And it may also be amazing how blindly, determinedly and doggedly he held on to his love for Cari and carried his passion into a marriage that must have appeared legally dubious to him. But how are we to evaluate his nervous tensions, swings of mood, suspiciousness and distrust? Schmitt himself offered an interpretation that was based on the psychology of resentment: he referred to his family background and his troubled relationship with his mother, while at the same time rejecting psychoanalytic interpretations in favour of those representatives of philosophical pessimism that he used as his points of reference. Even though time and time again he felt at home in Plettenberg, his family's milieu scared him, a fact that also impacted on his relationship with the Catholic Church. He hardly appears as a pious Christian. The fact that he was so easily irritated was the reverse side of his sensitivity, intellectuality and also morality. The fact that he was ready to be alarmed at any time was the consequence of a kind of permanent attentiveness. In a state of the highest tension, Schmitt perceived everything around him in a hypercritical fashion. His ambition was bourgeois wealth and independence, freedom from the depressing dependencies under which he suffered. The latter were still a burden on the relationship with the privy councillor. Who would criticize the fatherly mentor for advising against the relationship with Cari? The whole ambivalence in Schmitt's attitudes was condensed in the 'Jewish complex', where philo-Semitic and anti-Semitic inclinations were in conflict with each other. Even in his relationship with the brothers Eisler, Schmitt could not get over his resentment. Within the context of academic competition during the Weimar era, the anti-Semitic affect would later be victorious. And the poison of this affect remained active into his old age. Only Schmitt's relationship with Fritz van Calker was entirely unclouded. There is no bad word to be found about him; however, there is no unconditional trust either. Rather, what we find again and again are expressions of astonishment over the fact that such kindness can exist in this world at all.

6

World War and Defeatism:
Carl Schmitt in Munich

Carl Schmitt, the soldier

On 26 February 1915, Schmitt arrived in Munich and received his uniform. From the very beginning, military service appeared as 'slavery' to him, 'a spooky nightmare'. But already on 2 March, Cari visited him for three days on her way to Vienna. 'Life in the barracks', the marching and the drill, the stench of the 'plebs', nevertheless remained terrible to Schmitt; it was 'hell'. Carl experienced his service as 'coercion',* the barracks as a 'prison'. He was disgusted by the military jargon. On 11 March, he wrote: 'How will the world war end? Germany is becoming the country of justice, of the destruction of the individual. Germany realizes precisely what I postulated as the ideal state in my book on the state' (TB II, p. 24). The anti-individualism of Schmitt's early work now appeared to be a negative utopia, and he reinterpreted its categories in religious terms: the 'god of law' was abruptly juxtaposed to the 'god of love', and the old distinction between law and justice thus connected to the distinction between state and Church. Thus, Schmitt moved away from his earlier preference for state because he experienced the 'god of this world, the law' (TB II, pp. 28ff.) in terms of the 'destruction of the individual' (TB II, p. 64; cf. p. 130).

Through the agency of van Calker, on 23 March Schmitt was moved to the office of the deputy general command [Stellvertretendes Generalkommando].† He was now allowed to leave the barracks and slept in his own apartment in Gabelsberger Straße again. His basic military service did not last even a month. As mentioned before, Schmitt could theoretically have attended Hellingrath's lectures on Hölderlin, which he gave in Munich at the time. These lectures discussed the 'tragic genius' of the youth movement whose members went to war with Hölderlin in their knapsacks. 'Norbert' [Hellingrath] fell in battle in 1916 in Verdun. Schmitt

---

*   The German used by Schmitt – 'Vergewaltigung' – translates literally as 'rape'. It can, however, also be used metaphorically in the sense of 'coercion'.
†   Under the organization of the German military between 1871 and 1918, the 'Generalkommando' was a regional army corps with an administration of its own. It was headed by a general as commander in chief. The qualification 'stellvertretend' indicates that, at times of war, the administration remained immobile and deputized for the general who was moving around with the army.

did not credit the war with any heroic meaning. He sharply rebuffed the 'service' for the state that his earlier monograph appeared to have praised. He considered his time to be one of those exceptional 'times of immediacy' in which the individual is suspended from his or her 'duty of service'. His diary contains only entries expressing his yearning for peace and none expressing a hope for victory. 'Read in French newspapers again, feeling a strange kind of joy when the enemy is victorious. Expect the worst', runs one of his notes (TB II, p. 81). He 'would like to write a satire. The day of the last judgment dawns. The Prussians arrange it' (TB II, p. 144). During the world war, Schmitt fundamentally rejected the idea of service to the state because he considered the war unjust. In one passage of his diary, he is even critical of van Calker's 'pact with this world': 'In the course of a day, I remember often how van Calker after a good lunch explained to me with a twinkle in his eye: It is war, and minor illegalities do not matter right now. He has become unfaithful to himself; he acquires the meanness and hypocrisy of this world' (TB II, p. 34). Schmitt did not want to become part of this. Because he considered the war unjust, he also saw his activity in the general command in a negative light. After a trip to Dachau, he wrote: 'I was mad with anger about the Prussians, about militarism; I felt like committing the most ostentatious insubordinations. How ghastly for an individual to be sitting in such a prison' (TB II, p. 77).

Daily life in the general command

From 31 July 1914, Germany was at war. The Kriegs-Ermächtigungsgesetz [Enabling Act] of 4 August 1914 granted the executive a far-reaching right to pass emergency decrees.[1] Political power was transferred to the military commanders, who were given the right to pass legislative decrees and to decide whether the rules for the 'normal' or 'heightened' state of war applied. In the case of the heightened state of war, a number of fundamental rights were suspended. Important and controversial was the power to decide on protective custody [Schutzhaft] and restrictions on residence, limitations on the freedom of association and assembly, and censorship of the press and of letters. Though the emperor had the power of command, he had no central administration at his disposal. The individual deputy general commands were under his direct command, and they jealously protected their immediate relation to the emperor. Thus, unified military leadership became problematic, especially in the case of Bavaria, as the constitution granted Bavaria a special status of military autonomy from the Reich. 'The independent power of military command' was protected 'as the last bastion of the constitutional system'.[2] There were three deputy general commands in Bavaria, one in Würzburg, one in Nürnberg and one in Munich, which took on the executive power.

Schmitt worked in section P 6 of the Maxburg, Pfandhausstraße 2, in the heart of Munich. The head of the section was Captain Christian Roth. At first, Schmitt's characterizations of him were quite ambivalent. He saw parallels to the privy councillor and feared similar affects. Further physicals and possible fitness for active service were looming. On 18 April, Schmitt was again lucky. 'Thank God. I felt like being executed. I put on my act of being miserable, the doctors felt pity: general physical weakness, fit for service in the garrison' (TB II, p. 50). In July, another physical. 'I found out in the office that another physical examination of those fit for service in the garrison was due on Monday. I was struck with terror. I could no longer work, the skies darkened' (TB II, p. 95). Soon afterwards, he wrote: 'Heard in the morning that the examination will take place only on 15 August. It felt like a gift' (TB II, p. 96). At the beginning of August, he noted down anxiously: 'Slowly the day of the next examination to see whether I am fit for active service is coming closer. The *cauchemar* [nightmare] is weighing heavily on me. If only we had peace yet.' The examination with the result that Schmitt dreaded took place on 7 September. 'Fit for active service; a pleb of a medical officer. I am a poor sod' (TB II, p. 125). Schmitt had back problems (osteomyelitis – i.e., inflammation of the bone marrow) causing recurrent sciatic pain.[3] He lived in permanent fear of having to join the theatre of war. August Schätz, a new colleague from August 1915, suffered that fate. He was drafted and fell in battle on 28 August 1917. Schmitt later dedicated his *Concept of the Political* to Schätz. He himself wanted to escape the same fate. With his career at the general command, Schmitt ensured that he would remain at the 'home front'. At the same time, Max Weber, in his 'Intermediary Reflection' on the *Sociology of Religion*, wrote about the military meaning of the meaningless, a 'theodicy of death', 'integration of death into the series of meaningful and sacred events': 'As in the times of bondage, the community of the army at war today considers itself a community into death: the greatest of its kind.'[4] The interpretation of the 'new nationalism' (Stefan Breuer) following Versailles turned the military defeat into a regeneration and mobilization of the nation.[5] No such noises can yet be found in Schmitt before Versailles. In 1917, Stefan George wrote in a poem: 'no jubilations are due; no triumph will be, / just many undignified extinctions.'[6]

'Will I ever have a morning to myself again?', Schmitt asked himself.

> I was terrified by the horrible mechanism of daily professional life into which one is pressed. Will I have the force just to control myself? But the secret is always to keep silent on the side, to say nothing, and yet to want to determine the course of events. To make oneself inconspicuous. At the general command, deeply sad that I keep so much to the sidelines. (TB II, p. 64)

Schmitt suffered on the 'treadmill' and remembered his time at school: 'Extremely childish and degrading affects are aroused. One feels like a boy at school or in the seminary' (TB II, p. 94). For a long time, Schmitt couldn't settle in properly, and he ranted about his colleagues and the 'miserable role' he played at the 'general command'. Memories of the privy councillor also returned. The contact with him had been completely broken off. 'It was stupid that I dropped him and yet altogether the right thing to do' (TB II, p. 48). 'Have at times thought with disgust and horror of the time with the privy councillor. Cannot understand how I physically

'Roth's section was no office for hard-line propaganda and Dr Roth anything but a narrow-minded militarist.'

endured the atmosphere' (TB II, p. 88). Occasionally, Schmitt felt remorse: 'Thought often about the privy councillor, count the months that I haven't been in touch with him. . . . I have left him in such a mean way' (TB II, p. 107). Cari advised him to establish contact again, but Schmitt shied away from it, being mindful of the parallels with the captain.

Schmitt wasn't made for the daily routine of military service. However, there was often not much to do and Schmitt strolled around in the city. At the general command, he made himself familiar with typewriters. He wrote legal opinions and police orders on curfews. One entry summed it up thus: 'Office, transit passes, transfer of corpses, confiscation of books, consular letters' (TB II, p. 150). An edict on food-related crimes was a first success for Schmitt: 'Calker was at the general command. He spoke to Wilhelm II and told him that I drafted the famous edict on food' (TB II, p. 103). There were repeated conflicts between Schmitt's duties in service and his private convictions. When the correspondence of the literary author Wilhelm Herzog was confiscated, Schmitt was ashamed of his curiosity. Nevertheless, he wrote a report which lead to the closure of Herzog's journal, the *Forum*. Later he would comfort himself with the thought that Herzog was a 'shirker' (TB II, p. 141). Schmitt read *J'accuse*[7] with great interest and then went on to write the 'order of confiscation' [Beschlagnahmeverfügung] for it. Another 'order of confiscation' Schmitt cautiously repressed because he thought the publication might be a 'pan-German affair'. He applied double standards. On aphorisms by Rudolf Leonhard he remarked: 'A clever and intelligent Jew. I'll send him my book on the state via Georg Eisler' (TB II, p. 88). In these cases, Schmitt denied his duties in favour of his personal interests. Staff at the general command read out their horoscopes to each other. Schmitt came to appreciate Captain Roth, and became friendly with Georg von Schnitzler and his wife Lilly, with Alexander Münch and the 'sergeant [Feldwebel] and assessor Schätz'. At first, Schmitt had been suspicious of the latter due to his ambitiousness.

On the 'lead' of marriage

A reader of the diaries does not get the impression that Schmitt was actually caught on the 'treadmill'. He was permanently on the go, and he tended to his cultural interests and his private life. In 1915, at Easter, he went on holiday for three days and met Georg Eisler and his sister in Murnau. He was still plagued by financial worries. He received a monthly draft from the Eisler family, but that was dependent on his friendship with Georg. Dependency and friendship go ill together. One day, Georg would 'no longer see why we should receive 200 Marks each month' (TB II, p. 52). On 24 April, Cari moved to Munich, where she had spent her childhood and youth. One should have expected that the fake aristocratic lady feared being found out. Schmitt would soon afterwards note down the idea of writing reports on French newspapers. He wrote to Alexander Zinn, the editor of the *Hamburger Woche*, which belonged to the Eisler family, about this idea, and thus offered a service in return for the money he received. This, however, was in violation of his duties, as he used service-related tasks for generating a journalistic income. For this reason, his articles had to appear under a pseudonym, and Schmitt was constantly worried that he might be uncovered as the author.

On 1 May, the Schmitt-Dorotićs moved into a new apartment. Until autumn 1921, Schmitt lived at Schraudolphstraße 5, a small street that runs parallel to Barerstraße at the corner of Schellingstraße, behind the Pinakothek. (Cari stayed there until the beginning of 1923.) On 14 May, he received his appointment as a private from van Calker. Cari whiled the time away; a lot of it was spent with Eisler, who frequently travelled down from Hamburg to Dachau. She met Carl for lunch, visited the Zoological Garden or indulged in shopping. Carl and Cari quarrelled all the time. On the one hand Carl was still charmed by Cari's beauty, femininity and sly naivety, but on the other the egocentricity of the 'child-like girl' often got mightily on his nerves. The charisma of love dissolved in the daily routine of marital life. Schmitt satirized the old engagement phrase: 'I am me and you are you, / therefore don't disturb my peace'* (TB II, 68). Schmitt now suffered from the 'contrast between the general command and Cari'. 'The military and marriage; two nice institutions', he ironically remarked (TB II, p. 90), and took flight into work, rethinking his study of Däubler. Only

---

* 'Ich bin ich und du bist du, / also lass mir meine Ruh.' The original lines are from an old *Minnesang* text by an unknown author: 'Du bist mein, ich bin dein / dessen sollst du gewiß sein.' [You are mine, I am yours, / of that you may be sure.]

in October was the story of Cari's theft finally resolved. 'All went smoothly and I am very content and relieved' (TB II, p. 142).

Schmitt received news that Cousin André, his old friend from his days in Strasbourg, was experiencing difficulties with his dissertation. On 24 July, Schmitt's uncle André and the cousin came to Munich on this matter. Schmitt at first did not like the idea of a common meeting with Eisler, because he received money from both of them. 'I was scared that Georg Eisler might notice that I have a rich uncle' (TB II, p. 98). However, in the end they spent a lot of time together. At the end of August, Carl and Cari went on a hiking tour with Cousin André in Upper Bavaria and met with Eisler in Rosenheim. Regarding his cousin's examination, Schmitt finally wrote a 'fine, but slightly risky letter' (TB II, p. 121) to the jurist Max Ernst Mayer in Strasbourg. For years, he had been in the debt of his rich relatives, and now it was time that he did something in return. He probably helped André with his dissertation.[8] Later, Schmitt's brother Jupp spent ten days of holiday in Munich, following a stay in a military hospital. The anniversary of Fritz Eisler's death fell into those days. Schmitt associated the worries about his brother closely with the death of his friend, and he continued to see Georg Eisler all the time. Cari made scenes because of this.

Jewish friends and anti-Semitic affects

Anti-Semitism is a dark theme and casts a permanent shadow over Schmitt's oeuvre. In his published writings it emerges only after 1933, but his diaries and other evidence document life-long anti-Semitic attitudes and affects. Schmitt himself spoke of his 'Jewish complex'. Only through his diaries have we learned how intense his friendships with Jews were before 1933. He spoke fairly openly with the brothers Eisler about the 'Jewish question'. His friendship with Georg lasted until 1933. From 1918, he also had friendly contacts with Ludwig Feuchtwanger, the editor and managing director of Duncker & Humblot in Munich. The relationship with Jacob Taubes, late in life, still lived off the open discussion of political-theological differences between someone with a Jewish and someone with a Catholic-Christian identity. Schmitt never argued in biological terms, even if there are some mild notes of 'Blut und Boden' [blood and soil]. But he didn't argue on strictly confessional and assimilatory grounds either, as conversion, baptism and confession were no decisive criteria for him. A baptized Jew to him was still a Jew. In the context of his 'Political Theology', Schmitt saw the Jewish identity not least in terms of a common political fate. However, before 1918, his thinking about these questions was not yet rigid, and his reflections about Judaism aimed less at an anti-Semitic separation than an identification of his own problematic character. He saw in Judaism 'his own question as form' [die 'eigne Frage als Gestalt']. Social ambition and the psychological disposition to see oneself through the eyes of others, and to make oneself dependent on their judgment, were very important to him in this context. He deeply loathed this attitude.

Schmitt was permanently brooding over the question of his problematic character. He felt that he was a 'pleb' and planned to write a book: 'The pleb, or: the plebeian. . . . His instinct: to duck and dive as necessary. He is *ad alterum*' (TB II, p. 124). What he observed about himself, he again and again imputed to Richard Wagner and to Judaism: the 'dependence on the opinion of others' (TB II, p. 173). In his early diaries, Schmitt pushed his battle in a hall of mirrors around his hatred of himself and others to the point of self-parody. Like Otto Weininger[9] before him, he calls Wagner, the father of modern, post-Christian anti-Semitism, a 'Jew' (TB II, p. 115) and 'a purely intra-Jewish matter' (TB II, p. 164). But he is afraid of an 'intellectual Germany without Jews': the 'publisher Lehmann, a few major generals and university professors, mining directors as the heralds of intellectual Germany' (TB II, p. 178). Schmitt's anti-Semitism contained a lot of rhetoric; it was a kind of shadow boxing in the tradition of Heine, Wagner, Nietzsche and Weininger. Schmitt did not reach a clear understanding of his anti-Semitic affects. They fed not least off his resentment of his own background, a permanent source of suffering for the social climber. He was hardly able to think about, never mind to resolve, the wild mix of his philo-Semitic and anti-Semitic affects and the discrepancies between his personal friendships and his abstract and diffuse anti-Semitism. Out of his hermeneutic entanglement he fled into the arms of Catholicism. His diaries were already a means of distancing himself gradually from his suffering. For the time being, the psychological charting of his confusion ended in a reflexive objectification of his own situation and problems, namely in a critique of Romanticism.

An answer with Däubler

Compared to the time before 1914, the light of Munich as a city of the arts no longer shone quite as brightly during the Great War.[10] But the bohemian world does not live on bread alone, and the war also sparked new artistic energies. Schmitt lived and worked in the city centre, near Schwabing. By the time of his arrival, he was already an experienced author and he knew the scene. In his essay on *The Northern Lights* and in the *Silhouettes* he had made his aesthetic convictions and dislikes explicit; the friendly social intercourse with Däubler opened new doors to him, and his position at the general command also gave him a certain social status in artistic circles. Schmitt was an established authority who had something to say. Social meetings took place in cafes and restaurants, as Cari didn't cook. Schmitt visited the opera house, exhibitions and theatre performances. He met the painter Hugo Troendle and his circle of artistic friends, the publisher Wilhelm Hausenstein,[11] the author Alice Berend[12] and some other members of Schwabing's bohemian circles. However, his closest contact was Georg Eisler. Schmitt's relationship with the artistic circles changed as a consequence of his tasks at the general command. While earlier he had pursued his daily life as a jurist and his artistic inclinations in parallel, now the observation of certain circles of artists and authors became part of his official duties. Schmitt was living a double life as a sympathizer and at the same time a censor. He looked into the innermost details of the correspondence within literary circles and was ashamed of it.

Schmitt's acquaintance with Theodor Däubler continued, especially as Däubler often visited his sisters in Munich. After the second attempt at publishing his essay on *The Northern Lights* also failed, Schmitt began to turn it into a monograph. From mid-May onwards, both at the general command and during the night, he worked on his *Nordlicht* study which – according to the dedication – was written 'in memory of Fritz Eisler'. He wrote down the manuscript within ten days (14–23 July 1915) and at the end of July sent it first to Diederichs, a publishing house known for its critical attitude to contemporary culture and for having issued Kierkegaard's works, then to the Munich publisher Georg Müller. On 25 September, Schmitt received a letter saying that Müller wanted to publish the study. The negotiation of fees went well, not least because the publishing house was interested in good relations with the general command. From 7 October, Däubler was again in Munich for some time, together with his patron and lover Ina Bienert. First he stayed with the Schmitts, and they reworked the manuscript together.[13] Schmitt now expressed himself in ambivalent, even negative, terms about Däubler, and felt that he was abused as an 'advertiser' of his work. He began to regret the lofty tone of his study and considered retracting it. However, Mrs Bienert and Däubler valued the work. Though the study did not contribute to Schmitt's reputation as a theorist of state law, it brought a long intellectual preoccupation to a close and consolidated his contacts with literary circles.

The unpublished essay of 1912 formed part of the small book. Schmitt analysed the text again with regard to its 'elements', its 'spirit' and its 'actuality', going into more detail with respect to its historical and aesthetic elements. He explained with more clarity how Däubler's epic presents the movement of 'spirit' from the Orient to the Occident, and from South to North, and how it lets world history conclude with 'Germany'. There is no mention of a future beyond Europe. Schmitt now also discussed Däubler's 'relationship with language' (N, p. 40) as a form of emancipation from the pragmatic context of linguistic 'intercourse'. He put more stress on the religious 'spirit' of the poem and on the 'actuality' of the way it 'compensates for an age without spirit' [Kompensation des Zeitalters der Geistlosigkeit] (N, p. 64). Thus, the study was a response to the events of the Great War, which are also explicitly mentioned. The study's character as such a response was probably one of Schmitt's main motivations in taking it up again.

Schmitt's deliberations on the Christian 'spirit' amounted to a personal confession. In the wake of Eisler's death, he 'suddenly' found comfort in Kierkegaard (TB I, p. 222). The Däubler study marks the moment Schmitt stepped into Christianity. He found in Däubler a 'cosmic ethics' (N, p. 12) and a transfiguration of the cultural process on the basis of a philosophy of history. For Schmitt, the Northern Lights were a symbol for the earth's 'own light' [Eigenlicht]: for the transfiguration of history through its 'completion'. Schmitt put Däubler next to Hegel. In his view, both represent a 'belief' in 'spirit', and Däubler expresses the mystical 'secret' that 'nature is good and the human being is also "by its nature" good' (N, p. 53). Däubler's work, Schmitt writes, is a mystical 'revelation, gift, grace'. The present Schmitt considered in categories taken from Rathenau. The capitalist age of mechanism inverts the relation between means and ends. The 'antichrist' (N, p. 61) reigns. 'Many people had been seized by an eschatological horror before the horrors of the Great War became reality' (N, p. 64). In light of this, Däubler represents a moment of compensatory 'balancing'. His 'actuality' consists in his inner 'negation' of the present. In his study, Schmitt says farewell to his metaphysical 'doubts'. He presents a Christian interpretation and discards pessimism. Is his position one of a religion of the as if? Does he turn a Christian 'fiction' into his dogma, an as if into a because? In any case, he mobilizes an apocalyptic rhetoric against capitalism and the Great War. Religious love and grace judges the present to be the work of the devil. Throughout history, Christian theology again and again stepped up as a critic of the present and opposed the idea of the Church and the final judgment to the states' rapacious and devilish deeds. With his study, Schmitt joined this tradition. This was probably the central motivation for taking it up again and publishing it.

In Schmitt's literary estate there are numerous personal copies as well as letters from Däubler, covering the years between 1920 and 1926. Däubler was living in Athens at the time and was plagued by financial difficulties. In March 1920, he lamented his situation.[14] Soon afterwards,[15] he wrote to Schmitt saying that he had been successful in securing a new edition of the *Northern Lights* poem and Schmitt's *Northern Lights* study. At the same time, he sent him *Die Treppe zum Nordlicht*[16] [Steps towards the Northern Lights]. 'Frenchmen, save a poet!', Schmitt commented, somewhat sarcastically, in his notes about it. Däubler requested Schmitt's permission for a republication of his study. But Schmitt did not want a new edition, which would only have interfered with his academic career. Soon afterwards, Däubler congratulated Schmitt on his appointment to a chair in Greifswald. In July 1922, he announced a revised version of *The Northern Lights*.

Satirical enemy observations

The Däubler study looks at the Great War as an apocalyptic event. But what about the anonymous newspaper articles which Schmitt published at the same time? On 5 May 1915, he sent his first article to Alexander Zinn, the chief editor of the *Hamburger Woche*. The paper was an up-market boulevard magazine, richly illustrated and consisting of only a few pages. It was published weekly and contained mostly reports on the social and cultural life in Hamburg, but also a serial novel, humorous caricatures and many job advertisements. Theatre and the opera were given plenty of space. The reporting on the war was patriotic. Each week, a commemorative plaque showed pictures of soldiers from Hamburg who had died. In the middle of May there appeared the first of over twenty anonymous articles, which Schmitt wrote hastily and on the side. Schmitt wanted to justify his monthly draft in this way. The articles' casualness and banality are surprising. They make no attempt to get to the bottom of military and political questions regarding the war, do not engage with the discussion of war aims and strategies for peace, and do not reflect on the structural changes taking place within 'Wilhelminianism' and on the future. Compared to Max Weber's public interventions at the time they even appear pathetic. It is hard to believe that Schmitt was their author. Should one even speak of authorship? They are no more than translations of randomly selected articles with scant commentary! Schmitt translated from French and English newspapers. Instead of large lines of political argument he offered individual voices to the public. If one wanted to be bold one might speak of a subversion of the great questions through the satirical lens of the foreign press. All one would need to do is take the foreign countries for one's own, and the texts put the finger on the wounds caused by German censorship.

One of the articles discusses linguistic policies and mocks this serious topic. The absurd contrast between the theme and the way it is treated gives the reader pause. Another text talks about the 'threat of Zeppelins' and 'motorcar spies' in England. A third one discusses how these threats were banished with irony and 'English gallows humour'. Schmitt had personally experienced an air raid on Düsseldorf at the beginning of the war, and thus was aware of the military significance of the new weapon. One of the texts has the 'decline of the population' (TB II, p. 410) in France as a topic. In this case, too, a reader would need to be entirely mindless not to notice that, behind the triumphant tone, the actual message is about the destruction caused. The 'shirkers' are also mentioned; Schmitt quotes a 'horror story' (TB II, p. 412) about a soldier who was caught in women's clothes. The problem was not unknown to Schmitt. He had experienced it with his friend from school, Kluxen, who had asked him how one might dodge military service. Almost any family could have provided examples. Another text speaks of the English 'distrust of their own reports' (TB II, p. 415), a phenomenon which the censor Schmitt knew only too well applied also to the situation in Germany. Yet another text covers methods of recruitment and the insincere talk about 'voluntariness'. Schmitt himself only pre-empted his recruitment by volunteering.

All in all, the articles are more a satirical unmasking than defamations of the enemy. Under the rubric *Aus dem Lager des Feindes* [From the enemy's camp], Schmitt held up a mirror to the Germans. Yet again, he took revenge on the structures under which he suffered. The censor disclaims censorship with the help of foreign press reports. The general command offered Schmitt the possibility of learning about such strategies of political subversion. Thus, the literary genre to which Schmitt's articles should be compared is not so much Max Weber's journalistic analyses as political anecdotes in the style of a Heinrich von Kleist. Kleist used similar forms in the not very successful journals that he launched during the Napoleonic wars. He wrote a nationalistic *Katechismus der Deutschen* [Catechism of the Germans] and a satirical *Lehrbuch der französischen*

Journalistik [Textbook of French journalism], arranged in paragraphs, which expressed the principles of the press policies with complete clarity. French journalism he defined as 'the art of making the people believe what the government considers to be good'.[17] Schmitt opposed this situation by presenting individual voices.

7

Strasbourg, the State of Siege and a Decision in Favour of Catholicism

A new theme

On 6 September, Schmitt noted in his diary:

> At 8 o'clock I was ready to commit suicide, to sink into the world of night and silence, calm and collected; then, all I thought about was making a career in this world. A few hours later, I was indifferent towards everything and I didn't mind becoming a soldier – this disjointedness is maddening; what should I do? In an hour I shall shoot myself out of anger over my nullity. (TB II, p. 125)

The next day he wrote: 'Afternoon: write a report on the law of the state of siege [Belagerungszustands-Gesetz]. Give a justification for why the state of siege is to continue for several years after the war. Me, of all people! What else may providence have in hand for me' (ibid.). The theme of the state of siege suited Schmitt. He was meant to argue that the state of war required an exceptional extension of the executive's authority – a kind of 'Patriot Act', so to speak – in order to be able to take measures even after the war had ended. This would become a central theme in his later work. His constitutional theory entirely pleads the case that the liberal system of the separation of powers is no longer tenable and that the executive needs to be given the right to take exceptional measures – i.e., he makes the case for the extension of executive power at the expense of the legislature, classical parliamentarism and jurisdiction. In 1915, however, in the middle of the war, Schmitt was astonished to be given this task. 'Me, of all people! What else may providence have in hand for me.' Schmitt's remark was ironic as, of course, he knew that his superiors were responsible for handing the task to him. He hinted at the fact that he was not inclined to argue against the liberal separation of powers, and he did not affirm the renunciation of the rule of law [Rechtsstaatlichkeit], just as he did not affirm the war. Yet, he already felt that the theme of dictatorship, the expansion of the executive state, would stay with him, because the future tended towards it. Thus, his talk of 'providence' was not only meant ironically. It also contained a premonition of future developments that gave him a point of reference for orientation.

At once, he wanted to deal with the theme in the form of a 'book'. First, he wrote his 'report on the law of the state of siege'. Schmitt saw very well the difficulty in this legal instrument. He did not want to see the expansion of dictatorial powers. 'But there is no rescue from, and no help against, militarism; after the war, it will become increasingly worse. The individual counts for nothing; gruesome' (TB II, p. 130). Schmitt saw 'how right it is to be afraid of the military regime, and to introduce a separation of powers which mutually control each other. But all this is useless resentment' (TB II, p. 135). Schmitt talked to van Calker about his new project, 'that I am writing a book on the state of siege, asked him, why I had not yet been made a sergeant [Unteroffizier]' (TB II, p. 136).

Back in Strasbourg: the state of siege as a legal relationship

And, again, van Calker got the hint. Soon he would open up the hopeful prospect of a Habilitation in Strasbourg. Following the outbreak of the war, the number of students had taken a deep drop. Many of the members of staff had joined the army. The remaining lecturers were asked to make donations and to give patriotic talks in military hospitals and on the front line.[1] But, in 1915, only a few expected a catastrophic end to the war and the loss of Alsace. On 19 November, van Calker suggested 'sending an application for Habilitation to Strasbourg'. Schmitt was excited about the idea. 'How wonderful. The dream of a lovely time, when we shall live in Strasbourg and shall have our furniture back' (TB II, p. 157). He at once sent the 'application to Strasbourg'. Only a few days later he received a request from Hermann Rehm, asking him for an 'addition' to his application, which was then approved within the same term. At the time, Schmitt had 'great hope and joy of teaching and philosophizing again'. 'That is the real life' (TB II, p. 162), he noted down with unusual euphoria. However, he was still afraid of 'the privy councillor and his intrigues'. On 19 December he wrote: 'No news from Strasbourg. This is getting uncanny. Suspect the privy councillor am Zehnhoff is behind it.' But, yet again, Schmitt's worries were unfounded. Already on 16 February 1916, still within the winter term, Schmitt gave his trial lecture, 'Die Einwirkung des Kriegszustands auf das ordentliche strafprozessuale Verfahren' [The influence of the state of war on the due legal process in criminal proceedings]. A revised version of the lecture was published the same year.[2]

Schmitt begins his lecture by listing the rights that a military commander can suspend. Then he discusses in more detail how the principle of an independent judiciary is threatened by the 'transposition' of executive authority [vollziehende Gewalt] to the military commander. He discusses which consequences extended military powers have for the system of the separation of powers and mentions the resulting pressures on jurisdiction. Even though he ends on a comforting note as far as the rule of law is concerned, saying that the executive 'influence ends at the independence of judicial power', a warning regarding legal policy can hardly be missed. Schmitt holds that the military commander, 'despite his far-reaching authority, does not have the right of the state to inflict punishment at his disposal, but may only intensify or inhibit its execution' (TB II, p. 429). The limiting 'only' sounds like rhetorical appeasement. In actual fact, Schmitt draws attention to the opposite phenomenon, to a change in the attitude informing legal policies. This description of the status quo is the beginning of his studies of the development of 'commissary dictatorship'.

Schmitt was given leave to spend the summer term in Strasbourg, where he gave a lecture course on criminal law. In the faculty, he met almost all of his old teachers again: Paul Laband, Wilhelm Kisch, Hermann Rehm, Andreas von Tuhr, Wilhelm Sickel, Erich Jung, Georg Friedrich Knapp, Werner Wittich and Fritz van Calker. Georg Simmel was now teaching philosophy. As Eduard Kohlrausch had taken charge of criminal law by then, van Calker had more time to dedicate to 'legal policies'. Schmitt had to find a modus vivendi with Kohlrausch. He lived at Sternwartestraße 4 (today: rue de l'Observatoire), often without Cari, and, according to the *Vorlesungsverzeichnis*,* he lectured almost daily. Because Kohlrausch offered criminal law in the winter term 1916–17, Schmitt taught criminal procedure law instead. In the summer term of 1917, Kohlrausch ceded the criminal law lecture to Schmitt and only gave tutorials. Schmitt began working on a larger study of dictatorship.

At the end of 1916, 'Diktatur und Belagerungszustand: Eine staatsrechtliche Studie' [Dictatorship and the state of siege: a study in state law] appeared in the *Zeitschrift für die gesamte Strafrechtswissenschaft* [Journal for Studies in Criminal Law], in which all of Schmitt's early juridical articles appeared. This study is Schmitt's main work in state law during his time of military service in Munich, and the first larger work dealing with concrete questions of state law in the comparative context of constitutional history. Schmitt analyses the development of the concept of the state of siege starting out from French history after 1789, highlighting 1848 as the turning point in constitutional history. The year 1848 was about 'rebellion within the state'. The separation of powers had turned from a practical and technical means into an 'absolute axiom' (SGN, p. 5) that was upheld with 'doctrinal pathos'. Schmitt distinguishes between the state of siege as serving a 'military purpose' and as being an 'institution of security policy'. He establishes the expansion of exceptional measures from the 'area of the jurisdiction' to the 'area of administration, and on to 'legislature' and administration.

Schmitt writes that the 'exception is rather the acknowledgement of the principle, not its suspension' (SGN, p. 16). A temporary suspension of constitutional provisions, he says, does not render the constitution inoperative, and thus dictatorship does not negate the principle of the division of power. However, his central point in 1916 is another one: Schmitt goes back in time beyond the modern separation of powers and finds administration to be the core of a state's activities. He writes: 'The beginning of all of a state's activities is administration' (SGN, p. 17).[3] Administration is the 'primordial condition' [Urzustand] of state activities, and 'more than a pure application of positive legal provisions'. Thus, Schmitt distinguishes

* Booklet which, at German universities, lists all courses taught in a given term.

sharply between the concepts of dictatorship and the state of siege. He highlights in italics:

> This is where the decisive legal difference between the state of siege (or war) and dictatorship is to be found: *in the case of the state of siege, the separation of legislature and judicature remains in place and we have a concentration of power within the executive; in the case of a dictatorship, while the distinction between legislature and judicature continues to exist, their separation is abolished because the same authority is responsible for passing and applying laws.* (SGN, p. 16)

Schmitt formulates the same idea even more sharply and starkly at the end of his piece, writing that, under the state of siege, a 'return to the primordial condition' of state activity as it exists 'before the separation of powers' takes place. 'In that sense, the separation of powers no longer exists; the legal situation within the room for manoeuvre given to the military commander is as if the division of power had never existed. But, in the case of dictatorship, the division remains in place' (SGN, p. 19). Thus, Schmitt discreetly re-evaluates the two concepts by handing back the rule of law to dictatorship and taking it away from the state of siege. In contrast to his Habilitation lecture, he now states unambiguously that the state of siege cancels the liberal separation of powers. His attitude towards these developments, however, does not become clear. Later, he will drop his strict distinction between dictatorship and the state of siege and argue in favour of dictatorship as an institution that is subject to the rule of law. That he later tried to combine rule of law and dictatorship may point to the fact that his interpretation of the state of siege as extra-constitutional had been intended in 1916 as a subtle criticism. It makes clear that, during the Great War, Germany no longer acted as a liberal state under the rule of law, but as an executive administrative state. When read along these lines, Schmitt's first large 'study in state law' was more critical than those to follow.

Schmitt probably considered the study to be the 'book' that he had originally planned, because his next monograph was dedicated to another topic, *Political Romanticism*. Nevertheless, he may well have had an idea of the scope of the subject. One could speak of the sudden recognition of a theme that would continue to exercise Schmitt all his life. All of a sudden, on 7 September 1915, he knew what he had to do as a theorist of state law. He, of all people! However, the legal difficulty of the topic was hardly resolved yet. The dialectical trick of taking the exception as the confirmation of the legal principle was not wholly convincing, because his central thesis was another one: Schmitt denied that the state of siege falls under the rule of law. Could it be made to accord with legal concepts at all? Would Schmitt be able to see the state of siege as an institution that legitimizes the activity of the state as being at the 'service' of the idea of law? In 1916, he again returned to the characteristics of 'practice'. He did not offer a clear legal evaluation of the state of siege, but only pointed out that the categories of a constitutional state under the rule of law are not able to capture this type of state activity with precision. If that was the foundation of his thought at the time, then it denied the legality of the situation that existed in Germany. In that case, his argument would be in line with the apocalyptic tenor of his journalistic pieces on the war, which discreetly pointed out that Germany lived no longer in 'times of mediacy' but in apocalyptic times, in which every individual must find their own relationship to the idea of a reconciliation between God, man and world. It is also possible that Schmitt's differentiation between the state of siege and dictatorship was meant to mark the 'zero hour' of legal thought, from which he wanted to develop new reflections on state theory. In that sense, the study of 1916 constitutes an important point of departure; it brings the difficulties in thinking the present in terms of legal process to a head.

Schmitt gave out offprints of his article to some of the professors in Strasbourg. Paul Laband responded on 6 January 1917: 'The presentation of the opposition between dictatorship and the state of siege, and of the confusion of the two concepts in legislature and legal practice, is lucid and convincing' (TB II, p. 501). Thus, Schmitt was still given the honour of being addressed as a 'colleague' by Laband, the main representative of Wilheminian state-will-based legal positivism [Wilhelminischen Staatswillenspositivismus], a position Schmitt later attacked. Laband sent Schmitt his best wishes for his teaching: 'May you return soon and take up your academic activities again. Though the number of students attending lectures is of course not high at the moment.' The lecture halls were practically 'empty'[4] at the time. Most of those attending were wounded soldiers or soldiers on home leave. Schmitt was obviously not in Strasbourg, despite the fact that the *Vorlesungsverzeichnis* for the winter term 1916–17 announced him as lecturing on criminal procedural law from Monday to Friday, between 8 and 9. Around the same time, Schmitt's cousin André finally completed his doctorate with Rehm on 'Die Form der Kriegserklärung' [The form of declarations of war]. Schmitt is not mentioned in the list of courses for the winter term 1917–18. For the summer term 1918, he offered criminal law from Monday to Friday, between 5 and 6 o'clock. Later, he developed friendly relationships with the political economist Werner Wittich and with the philologist Friedrich Kiener.[5] Occasionally, he continued to be occupied with questions regarding state boundaries in the southwest of Germany.[6] Strasbourg remained lodged in his memory as an important place. His pupil Ernst Rudolf Huber met him there by coincidence at the end of 1944, bidding farewell to the burning city.[7]

Between Munich and Strasbourg

Upon his application of 17 March 1917, Schmitt was made a senior military civil servant (assessor) at the general command, his appointment taking effect from 1 October and being 'limited to the period of the war'. He now was head of his own unit responsible for the surveillance of the peace movement, the USPD* and the pan-German movement, for the import of printed media (including foreign newspapers), for enemy propaganda material, for the export of printed media and for granting permissions for lectures and meetings taking place outside Munich. The surveillance of mail was no longer one of his main tasks. He was in closer collegial contact with the assessors Schachinger, Dr Georg Schnitzler and Dr Alexander Münch. Schachinger was responsible for the surveillance of mail, Schnitzler for the press and Münch for the surveillance of foreigners. When Captain Roth was later, after having become the Bavarian minister of justice for the DNVP[†] on 16 June 1920, attacked for his activities at the general command, both Schnitzler and Schmitt[8] publicly defended him. Roth, they said, was 'the incarnation of common sense':

> Roth's section was no office for hard-line propaganda and Dr Roth anything but a narrow-minded militarist. ... The section had openly democratic members of staff, a fact known to Dr Roth without his trying to limit their independence. One of them, a notorious pacifist, published an extremely pacifistic article in the 'Münchner Post' in 1917, for which any superior with a remotely hard-line attitude would have reprimanded him. (TB II, p. 519)

Schmitt himself had published writings and anonymous articles that were not altogether loyal and patriotic, and that contained subversive opinions of which Roth was, at least to a certain extent, probably aware. A social democratic lawyer such as Philipp Loewenfeld, who had also been found a place at the general command by van Calker,[9] took a very different view. He made Roth primarily responsible for the anti-revolutionary practice of summary court-martialling after 1919, and still saw in Roth, the minister of justice, the 'habitual breaker of the law' who would later also take part in Hitler's failed Beer Hall Putsch.[10]

Franz Blei (1871–1942) and Schmitt's contributions to the journal *Summa*

During those days, Franz Blei became a close friend. Born in 1871 in Vienna, he was considerably older than Schmitt. In 1888, the year Schmitt was born, Blei had left the Catholic Church. He studied in Zurich and Geneva, wrote his doctorate in political economy, moved in leftist circles and got personally to know Lenin. From the 1890s onwards, he was active in publishing, working for the *Neue Rundschau* from 1901 and as a lector

---

* Unabhängige Sozialdemokratische Partei Deutschlands = Independent Social Democratic Party of Germany, established in 1917 by a left-wing group of the Social Democrats opposed to the war. In the early 1920s, the party became divided, with some members joining the SPD, others the Communist Party, and in the parliamentary elections of 1924 the USPD received only less than 1 per cent of the vote.

† Deutschnationale Volkspartei = German National People's Party, founded in December 1918. A national conservative party, it dissolved itself in 1933, and the members of the Reichstag joined the parliamentary group of the National Socialists.

for the Munich publisher Albert Langen from 1911. Blei was continuously editing short-lived journals, such as the *Zwiebelfisch*, in which a review of the *Silhouettes* appeared in 1913. At the outbreak of war, the *Weißen Blätter*, co-founded by Blei, had to close down. In 1915, Blei published *Menschliche Betrachtungen zur Politik*[11] [Human reflections on politics], a radical critique from a Christian perspective, which aimed to settle scores with democracy and political parties, with the Catholic Church and 'Jesuitism'. Blei was drafted into the Austrian army and joined the military's press office [Kriegspresseamt] in Vienna. For some time, he was sent to the Viennese 'Palais' of the industrialist Josef Kranz to serve as his secretary. Kranz's secret lover, Gina Kaus, officially his adopted daughter, began an affair with Blei and persuaded Kranz to act as a patron and finance the bibliophile journal *Summa*. It was edited by Blei, with Kaus taking care of the editorial work, and appeared in four volumes per year with the publishing house of Jakob Hegner.[12] Schmitt contributed to *Summa*. Blei's social contacts at the time included Jakob Hegner, Robert Musil, Hermann Broch, Franz Werfel and many other artists. However, after a while Kranz sacked him, and in 1917 Blei had to return to his less well-paid job at the press office. Soon afterwards, he closed down his journal *Die Rettung*.[13] In 1919, Blei joined the Catholic Church again and moved back to Munich, where he remained in close contact with Schmitt.

Blei enjoyed socializing. As a real womanizer, he was always surrounded by young ladies. He was habitually dressed in black and wore a big hat. Blei used up his inheritance and meanwhile caused intrigues and gave rise to gossip. At the time, he published *Das große Bestiarium der Literatur* [The great bestiary of literature], in which various literary authors were satirically portrayed as animals. Schmitt contributed anonymously with an entry on the creature 'Fackelkraus' [The torchkraus].[14] Blei wrote *Leben und Traum der Frauen* [The life and dreams of women] and produced a large edition of Stendhal's works. His life was focused on personal encounters and he wrote innumerable character portraits. He took human individuals as 'gestures of an idea'[15] and Catholicism as a supra-moral understanding of good and evil, of 'heavenly and earthly love'. Among others, Blei introduced Schmitt to his artist friends Albert Paris Gütersloh and, later, Robert Musil. Between 1923 and 1931 he lived in Berlin. For fifteen years he was one of Schmitt's closest friends. In 1931, Schmitt published an article on the occasion of Blei's birthday in which he called Blei a 'secularized cleric': 'Of significance, however, is that he nevertheless did not join any of the secularized church substitutes, neither that of militarism nor that of pacifism.' Blei, Schmitt wrote, was also no romantic occasionalist, but a 'gnostic' who did not follow any school of thought and who was not 'under the rule' of any authority. Schmitt compared him to Kierkegaard. 'God is mute silence. Nature is mute speaking. But great authors are speaking silence.'[16] Blei dedicated his next book, *Talleyrand*, 'in friendship and veneration', to Schmitt.[17] Blei's letters were very personal in tone, and he expressed himself freely on confessional topics such as Catholicism, alcohol and women. In the autumn of 1931, Blei moved to Mallorca for financial reasons. In 1933, the contact with Schmitt broke off on account

'He is certain to be a secularized cleric. Really an individuum ineffabile' – Carl
Schmitt about Franz Blei

of the political differences between the two. After the beginning of the
Spanish civil war Blei had to leave Mallorca. He returned to Vienna, where
he lived in conditions of severe financial difficulty. Following the outbreak
of World War II, he moved to Nizza and was still able to emigrate to the
USA via Lisbon in 1941. A year later he died, forgotten and impoverished,
in the USA. His last book, *Zeitgenössische Bildnisse* [Contemporary por-
traits], contains a rejection of Schmitt. 'How could this Roman, Rhenish,
wholly a-romantic Catholic . . . succumb to the Leviathan of the state?'[18]
    The contact between Schmitt and Blei probably came about as a result
of the publication of Schmitt's Däubler study. In the four volumes of
Blei's journal *Summa*, Schmitt published three larger contributions which
formed a triptych. The first postcard from Blei that still exists, dated 2
January, confirmed that the theme was to be 'visib[ility] of the Church'. It
seems that Schmitt's only explicitly theological publication was about to be
written. Schmitt was no faithful son of the Church. Although he occasionally went to church and celebrated the important holy days, the everyday
rituals of religion did not mean much to him. He was without a doubt a
religious person, but one who claimed the right to a sovereign definition of
his own Christianity.
    In abstract terms, religiosity may be defined as 'a way of coming
to terms with contingency' [Kontingenzbewältigungspraxis] (Hermann
Lübbe), as a relationship with the 'uncontrollable', or as an awareness
of the 'transcendent conditions for the meaning of human existence'.[19]
Experiences of the negative provoke religious questions. Philosophical
metaphysics establishes the border between 'faith and knowledge' by
defining the range of possible knowledge. Religiosity, in contrast, takes

a legitimate space of 'faith' as its point of departure and relates it in a movement of religious egocentrism to the individual's 'salvation'. Why me? Why, of all people, me? Clerical phraseology and the dogmatic answers of the Church could hardly pique Schmitt's interest at this point. Rather, his religious reflections concentrated on literature and poetry. Däubler was one of the authors who shaped his overall religious assessment of God, man and the world. But Dostoevsky and other 'tragic' authors also influenced his views. His encounter with Kierkegaard was highly important. Before 1914, Schmitt had vacillated between a dogmatic rejection of pessimism and his personal inclination towards a pessimism he found in Wagner, Schopenhauer, Strindberg and Weininger. Schmitt also considered this ambivalence in his studies of ecclesiastical history and his references to gnosis. Schmitt read Harnack, Troeltsch and older ecclesiastical authors. With the help of Kierkegaard, he finally left his religious pessimism behind. In 1915, he read the edition of Kierkegaard by Theodor Haecker, who lived in Munich at the time, and got in touch with him. Haecker's intention was to use 'satire and polemics', also biting anti-Semitism, in order to be a thorn in the flesh of the present.[20] Kierkegaard convinced Schmitt that piety also included doubt. What we see is a double escape – an escape from the present times and an escape into the present times. Schmitt fled into the present by subscribing to the counter-revolutionary state, and he fled out of time into the arms of Catholicism, a movement also described by Hugo Ball in his diaries *Flight out of Time: A Dada Diary*.[21]

For Schmitt, the 'leap' of faith was a permanent task. The key event in this context was the death of Fritz Eisler. The radical rejection of God, man and the world, drastically expressed in his diaries, is taken back and turned into a positive evaluation of God and man in his study of *The Northern Lights*. While Schmitt never doubted that the world was 'sinful', and while he asked himself continually whether human beings, as sinners, were not, after all, 'evil by nature', in his published writings he did not accept the most extreme doubts about God as expressed in the gnostic idea of a deceiving God playing wicked games with men. Faith in a 'good' God constituted the limit of his anthropological scepticism. He continued to expect the worst possible evil to be committed by concrete individuals and he also castigated himself as a 'sinner', using the full register of the Christian rhetoric of humility. But, in principle, he thought that God guarantees that human beings are good 'by nature', as made explicit by the Christian faith in the 'incarnation of God'. Schmitt had already referred to this article of faith in his study of *The Northern Lights*, and now in his 'scholastic reflection' on 'Die Sichtbarkeit der Kirche' [The visibility of the Church] he wrote: 'No matter how deeply we become aware of the sinfulness of human beings, the incarnation of God compels us back into believing that man and the world are "good by nature". Because God does not want anything that is evil' (TB II, p. 451). Schmitt made this religious turn under the influence of the Great War and his meeting with authors such as Theodor Haecker and Franz Blei.

In his contributions to the journal *Summa*, Schmitt juxtaposed a satirical 'historiographical essay' on 'Die Buribunken'* with the theologically sophisticated 'scholastic reflections' on 'Die Sichtbarkeit der Kirche'. At the time, Schmitt already worked within a normative framework which he had developed in his reflections on the philosophy of law. Thus, he was able to link the philosophy of history and scholasticism via the relation between power and law [Macht und Recht]. He now transposed the dialectic between power and law onto the form of the Church. He introduced the further category of the 'concrete', or 'official', Church into the controversy between the Protestant theologians Sohm and Harnack about the relationship between the 'invisible' and the 'visible' Church. Sohm saw the 'invisible' Church of love and faith historically realized in early Christianity, prior to any legal form. He held that God's spirit pneumatically brings the faithful together, whereas Harnack saw this as already the effect of a 'canonical law of God', which pushes for the Catholic form of organization. Schmitt agreed with Harnack, but further stressed that, within the Church, the difference between law and power also establishes itself as the 'distinction between genuine visibility and purely factual concreteness' (TB II, p. 449). In his scholastic reflection Schmitt took as his point of departure early Christianity's expectation that the world would end. He subscribed to the Catholic view that there is only one unique and universal 'visible' Church – one God, one Church! – and based the Church on Christus as a mediator. As long as there is a Church, he held, we live in times of 'mediacy'. With this argument, Schmitt shifted the role of the guarantor for upholding 'times of mediacy', of which he had already spoken in *Der Wert des Staates* [The value of the state], from the state to the Church, thereby making the Church an opponent to the state. It was the first time that Schmitt formulated an institutional dichotomy between state and Church, emphasizing the Church's 'reservations' vis-à-vis the state. 'When a Christian obeys the authorities because – as foundation and limit – they are God's work, he actually obeys God and not the authorities. This is the only revolution in world history that deserves to be called great: by acknowledging the worldly authorities, Christianity has imperceptibly based the authorities on a new foundation' (TB II, p. 447). Blei wrote at the same time: 'The Church has its life in Christianity, not vice versa, because Christianity existed in Jesus Christ before the Church existed, and love existed before words and doctrines.'[22] This Christian legitimation, Schmitt wrote, is an 'enormous proviso' (TB II, p. 447). Because of Christ's incarnation, humans live in community. The Church is this community. However, this 'mediation' of Christianity with the world leads to an uncanny blending of God and world, power and law. There erupts an 'incongruence between the concrete and the visible Church' (TB II, p. 450), an incongruence which makes critique legitimate and opens up the possibility of Protestantism as a religion. In the worst case, the Antichrist becomes pope. The Christian 'proviso' therefore is valid not only for the Church vis-à-vis the state but also for the individual vis-à-vis the Church. Schmitt assumed the right to criticize the state and the Church.

---

* A phantasy name.

Table 7.1 Schmitt's response to Sohm and Harnack

Sohm	Harnack	Schmitt
Invisible Church	Visible Church	Concrete (official) Church
Pneuma, love	Legal form, *ius divinum*	Forms of power
God	Christ	Devil, Antichrist
Early Christianity	Catholic Church	Religious individualism

In his tryptich, Schmitt juxtaposed this *scholastic reflection* with a jaunty satire on 'Die Buribunken', while 'Macht und Recht', the first chapter from his *Der Wert des Staates*, held the pieces together.[23] 'Die Buribunken', which he calls an *essay in the philosophy of history*, is primarily a satire on scholarship. Schmitt starts out from 'Buribunkology as a science' and mocks a self-referential scholarly machinery in which everything and everyone is researched. He then goes on to present a short history of the Buribunks: the typical modern man who turns life into autobiography. By introducing a fictional historical narrative, Schmitt offers a parody of the history of autobiography which was just emerging at the time through the efforts of Georg Misch. Schmitt is serious, though, about the 'historico-philosophical' approach and aim. He begins with Don Juan and Leporello. While Don Juan lives only for the erotic moment and shows no ambition to 'historicize himself' (TB II, p. 457), his servant Leporello becomes a chronicler and thus 'historian'. But even he is not yet a proper Buribunk. 'He lacked the awareness for the higher consciousness of the one who writes, is the author of a piece of world history, and thus assessor at the court where the world is tried, nay, who is even conscious that the verdict of this court lies in his hands' (TB II, p. 458). Leporello remains the servant of his master; he does not attempt to become master and 'hero' of the story himself. Schmitt mocks the 'insufficient register-keeping of Leporello'[24] and then draws a sketch of two fictional Buribunks who represent the ideal Buribunk type: Ferker* and Schnekke.† Ferker enjoys 'the right of primogeniture within the realm of the Buribunks' (TB II, p. 460). He has understood that his task is to lead a life dedicated to the idea of historicizing himself, and to switch from religious responsibility towards God to a profane 'afterlife in the memory of mankind' (TB II, p. 461). He has also recognized the consequences for the organization of science and understands the 'idea of the modern large-scale enterprise'.[25] However, as a nineteenth-century hero he has not yet fully substituted his life with narratives, and thus he is only a 'Moses' of Buribunkology. The real 'hero', who represents the ideal type, finally enters the scene in the form of Schnekke, the figure from Schmitt's co-authored novel. 'He is nothing but the keeper of a diary, he lives for his diary' (TB II, pp. 464ff.). Thus, he has erected the pure 'realm of Buribunkerism'. This realm is an institution such as the deputy general command in Munich, one that could be taken from a novel

---

* 'Ferker' suggests 'Ferkel' = piglet.
† 'Schnekke' suggests 'Schnecke' = snail.

by Kafka. The 'duty to keep a diary' is the absolute order. Any refusal to do so must also be recorded and justified. Whoever interprets 'freedom of mind' as a right to refuse 'will be eradicated because of his anti-social attitude' (TB II, p. 467).

The concluding 'Grundriss einer Philosophie der Buribunken' [Foundations for a philosophy of the Buribunks] makes explicit their anti-Christian impetus against an eschatological 'expectancy of the future' (TB II, p. 429). A Buribunk negates the possibility of a contingent future with his recording of history. He substitutes real life, practice, with imaginary memories, and holds: 'Knowing that actual reality can only be found in history, we seek real immortality in history, and not in some transcendent realm' (TB II, p. 470). With these ideas, Schmitt offers a variation on Nietzsche's *On the Uses and Disadvantages of History for Life*. Schmitt highlights the sterility of the Buribunks' attempts at escaping from the contingencies of life by fleeing into some metaphysical premises. The Buribunks delegate the opposite attitude to the footnotes in which a certain 'Schmitt' represents the scholastic counter-position – i.e., a theocentric attitude towards history which experiences the present with the idea of a contingent future in mind. The Buribunks' perspective is this: 'Christianity had "twisted" people's minds in the most proper sense of the word . . . for it had directed their view away from the factual past towards a transcendent future' (ibid.). In contrast, Schmitt followed the Christian perspective. There may be hints of an existentialist pathos, along the lines of Heidegger's 'care' about finitude and 'forerunning' into one's death. However, Schmitt's care, his opening of the present towards a contingent future, links openness to a rejection of exact predictability in connection with the ideas of 'eternity' and 'judgment'. This shift in the way the present is perceived, from an orientation towards the past to an orientation towards the future, would have consequences for Schmitt's thinking about legal policy in the years to come. He would later denounce the position of positive law as a striving for security that takes its orientation from the past, and he would liquidize legalism in the name of the political 'future'. However, his contributions to *Summa* still expressed a religious credo. They interpret the ambivalence of man between God and the world, between power and law, as two mental poles: a Christian expectancy of the future, on the one hand, and a secular fixation with the past that is averse to life, on the other. The contributions' religious 'reservations' against the Church and the state are also of great significance. While Schmitt insisted on the Catholic Church's claim to universality, he also considered criticism of the Church legitimate. His Christian credo negated metaphysical pessimism and Gnosticism. Schmitt demonstrated the consequences which the latter have for the conduct of life in the figure of the Buribunks. He also drew personal consequences from his reflections: for a while, he stopped keeping a diary.

8

Political Romanticists 1815, 1919

Romantic subjectivity

In the last years of the war, Schmitt wrote his first major monograph, *Political Romanticism*. At the time, the political prospects for Germany were not yet catastrophic. The American President Wilson promised a tolerable peace treaty. The Russian Revolution brought respite at the Eastern front in the form of the peace treaty of Brest-Litovsk in March 1918. However, the German spring offensive on the Western front was not successful.

On 16 July 1918, Schmitt offered his manuscript to the publisher Duncker & Humblot, and in August the book went to press. It appeared at the beginning of 1919, at a time that saw the political transformation of Germany take place. The book marked the beginning of the close but often fraught cooperation between Schmitt and Duncker & Humblot which would end, for the time being, in 1933. It also marked the beginning of the close friendship with the publisher's company lawyer and lector Ludwig Feuchtwanger, who belonged to an old Jewish family from Munich.[1] The author Lion Feuchtwanger was his elder brother. Ludwig Feuchtwanger, a student of the political economist Gustav von Schmoller in Berlin, joined the publishing company as a lawyer in 1914, giving up his scholarly activities for a couple of years. However, in his function as a publisher he had a formative influence on debates in legal and political science, and in the mid-1920s he took up his scholarly work again, among other activities as the editor of the *Bayerische Israelitische Gemeindezeitung* [Newspaper of the Israelite Community in Bavaria]. Feuchtwanger was one of the most important Jewish intellectuals of the Weimar Republic. In 1933, Schmitt abruptly ended his relationship with him.

In mid-August 1918, the military command (Hindenburg, Ludendorff) suddenly demanded an immediate ceasefire. In early October, the new German government offered a ceasefire on the basis of Wilson's agenda. The end of October saw the first mutinies among the soldiers. On 9 November, it was announced that the emperor had renounced his throne and the republic was declared. Prince Max von Baden handed the chancellorship to Friedrich Ebert. At the same time Schmitt was – probably not in Munich – going through the proofs of his *Political Romanticism*.[2] Thus, he did not for the time being continue with his study of dictatorship but abandoned the contemporary issue of questions regarding constitutional law in favour of pursuing his older, continuing interest in a critique of individualism, and bringing this work in intellectual history to completion. Even before 1914 he had already settled the question of the 'significance of the individual' in his own mind. Then he had moved from a systematic critique to reflections within the framework of intellectual history. In his study of *The Northern Lights* and in his 'scholastic deliberations' he had granted the individual the freedom of the Christian – i.e., an immediate relationship to God ['Unmittelbarkeit' zu Gott]. However, he saw this freedom being negated in the Romantic construction of individuality, which is why he now separated the possibility of the Christian decision from any moulding by Romanticism. Schmitt's edition, at the same time, of a short autobiographical story of conversion also served the purpose of drawing attention to the Christian alternative. Its author, Johann Arnold Kanne, 'experienced . . . three times [in his life] that being a follower of Christ and living for the pursuit of knowledge [den Wissenschaften leben] means serving two masters at the same time.'[3] According to Schmitt's short introductory remarks, Kanne tells the story of how his life was waning on account of his sins, how Christ saved him 'at a stroke', and how he dared to take the 'leap into the paradox of Christianity'. However, Kanne had nothing more than premonitions of the 'great confrontation with the demonic spirit of the nineteenth century'. It was only Kierkegaard who had to enter into these discussions as a 'new Church Father' in secular times (TB II, pp. 474f.). The Kanne edition recalled Schmitt from his youthful confusion to Christianity and hinted at his political-theological

'Is there a possibility of turning one's fate from suffering to an active conquering of the Jewish fate?' (Ludwig Feuchtwanger, *Die Gestalt des 'verworfenen Juden':* *Ein Versuch über Mythenbildung* [The figure of the 'rejected Jew': an essay on myth formation], 1933)

project. In his 'counter-revolutionary philosophy of the state' and his writings on Donoso Cortés, Schmitt finally fully established his counter-revolutionary position in the early 1920s.

The aim of 'Die Buribunken' had already been a critique of modern subjectivity; *Political Romanticism* now carried it out. The central part of the study is an analysis of the 'structure of the Romantic spirit', which is flanked by two chapters on political Romanticism. Schmitt approaches the 'structure' via the 'outward situation', which he sketches using the political biography of Adam Müller as an example. However, his aim is less the historical diagnosis of an epoch and more a typological critique. With this, he continues the tradition of Hegel's critique of Romanticism. However, while Hegel, following Fichte, dismissed Romanticism as 'subjective idealism', Schmitt goes back to Descartes and Malebranche and defines the Romantic attitude as 'subjectified occasionalism'. He views Romanticism in the context of the philosophical critique of early modern rationalism. Within the history of philosophy, the 'Lebensphilosophie' [philosophy of life] of Schmitt's time is usually seen as an answer to neo-Kantianism, an answer which resolves the opposition of 'thinking and being' on the basis of 'life'. 'Life', after 1900, was the all-encompassing metaphysical category.[4] In contrast, Schmitt goes back beyond the problem of rationalism in early modern philosophy and returns to 'God' as the 'highest reality of the old metaphysics'. From this perspective, the philosophy of Romanticism is a failed attempt at escaping the original faith. Schmitt talks of a Romantic 'substitution' of the old God 'with two new realities: the people and history'. Thus, he concedes to Romanticism a genuine 'search' for an absolute ground, but holds that it tries to evade the 'irrationality of the real' by adopting new 'demiurges'. Schmitt calls the latter, with juridical succinctness, the 'point of legitimation' (PR, p. 58). He assumes that God is 'irrational'. Apart from that he joins the critique of Romanticism by Hegel and the Hegelians, whom he mentions approvingly.[5] However, in contrast to Hegel, Schmitt shapes his critique of Romanticism along the lines of the Catholic counter-revolution.

Schmitt suggests a political interpretation of Romanticism: by answering the French Revolution with a turn to 'history', the Romantics adopted the revolutionary assumptions of their opponents, thus remaining negatively tied to them. The Romantic attempt to put the 'genial subject' in the place of God could only lead to fanciful 'constructions'. The Romantic ego could maintain itself against reality only with 'irony and intrigue'. 'The will to reality ended in the will to semblance' (PR, p. 78). Nevertheless, the Romantic movement did not end with social disaster. It found a broad resonance in the bourgeois age. Derisively, Schmitt remarks: 'The Romantic hated the philistine. But it turned out that the philistine loved the Romantic' (PR, p. 93; translation modified). In other words, the Romantic movement ended 'in the Biedermeier'. Schmitt did not dogmatically push aside modern subjectivity but looked for metaphysical problems that resulted from early theoretical decisions. He identified problems and debates at the origin of the Romantic movement, in a constellation which he would later also find in early modern philosophy (Hobbes), on the one hand, and in the intellectual history of the Vormärz (Cortés), on the other. The 'structure of the Romantic spirit' provided the perspective from which he tried to understand political views and attitudes. The last part, titled 'Political Romanticism', polemically goes through the writings of Adam Müller. Schmitt does not take them seriously because, he says, they lack 'belief in the law'. 'Müller's arguments can be judged only as an oratorical performance' (PR, p. 137), he writes, and, indeed, he analyses Müller's style rather than his views on the state. Schmitt ends with a discussion of David Friedrich Strauß, looking at a less well-known book of 1847 on the Roman emperor Julian, which had Frederick Wilhelm IV, the 'Romantic on the throne', in mind.[6] Schmitt shows that Strauß read Julian's politics of religion on the basis of his own Romantic conceptions, turning Julian into a Romantic (which he wasn't), because he wanted to damage the Prussian king by associating him with a simplistic notion of Romanticism. Schmitt does not unambiguously side against Julian. Rather, he argues that Strauß's critique, based on Romantic assumptions, was weaker than it could have been. Thus, Strauß played only a minor role in Schmitt's various historical projections of the intellectual constellation around 1848. With his monograph on *Political Romanticism*, he laid down the tracks for his future engagement with the 'metaphysical decision' of early modern times. With it, Schmitt also attacked the Romantics of the turning point 1918–19 and distanced himself from the older conservatism following 1789.

The end of the war and revolutionary turmoil: The Romantics' seizing of power

The years after 1916 remain mostly hidden in the dark, biographically speaking. There are only very few sources from the period before 1922 in Schmitt's literary estate. It is almost impossible to reconstruct Schmitt's life between Munich and Strasbourg with any degree of accuracy. We also know almost nothing about the state his marriage was in at the time. But in 1919 at the latest, it was in a state of crisis. At that time, Schmitt's literary friend Alice Berend published a *roman à clef* about his marriage. *Der Glückspilz* [The lucky devil] tells the story of a certain Professor Martin Böckelmann, who lives in an ivory tower and, as a naturalist, idealizes and naively believes all life to be 'good'. With the active help of her matchmaking mother, he marries a young girl called Marianne who, soon after their wedding, cheats on him, as he is only interested in his research on ants. A childhood friend of Marianne brings back a monkey from India which now receives Böckelmann's exclusive attention. In a manner of speaking, Böckelmann turns into a monkey* and freezes to death with the monkey in a park, while Marianne returns to her childhood friend. A friend of the professor asks himself 'why it is that someone who considers all human

---

* The German 'macht sich . . . zum Affen' is also an idiomatic expression for 'to make a fool of oneself'.

beings to be good, and the whole world to be beautiful, must give the impression of a jackass'.[7] Berend presents a caricature of the ivory tower professor who is cheated on by the whole world.

From 1916–17 onwards, Schmitt very likely spent a lot of time in Strasbourg. However, Munich probably remained the centre of his life. The *Vorlesungsverzeichnis* for the summer term 1918 still listed Schmitt's lectures on criminal law. Teaching at the university continued in a much reduced form until the end of the war. It was the Reichsuniversität's [University of the Reich's] 'mission to conquer the land intellectually and to strengthen its attachment to the Reich'.[8] The juridical faculty at the university, in particular, held strictly conservative views with regard to the Reich and also to the university's 'contributions to the war' [Kriegseinsatz], a 'Reichskonservatismus' (Schlüter) represented especially by Laband and Rehm. In 1917, the university sent encouraging 'Easter greetings', together with an appeal to hold out, to its members 'in battle'.[9] Even at the end of September 1918, the military still requested lectures to be given at the front. The armistice of 11 November included a retreat of the German groups. The annexation of Alsace–Lorraine was one of France's most important war aims. On 11 November, the Reichsuniversität closed, and on 30 November its president was removed from office. The members of the university fled over a bridge near Kehl. At a later point, they were allowed to fetch their furniture.[10] 'The end came suddenly and violently', it says in a contemporary retrospective. 'As once before on the occasion of the first defeat [by Napoleon], the will of destruction directed itself first against the German university. It was at once closed down. The war was over. But after only a few days, the first expulsions occurred under the most brutal and humiliating circumstances.'[11] However, these expulsions were soon used as an argument for re-employment. A 'central office of the University of Strasbourg' was formed in Freiburg and acted as an employment agency for the lecturers.

> The lecturers from Strasbourg succeeded in making the dissolution of Strasbourg University, and the way in which its lecturers had been expelled, a matter of national concern. For one last time, the characteristic bond between nationalist ideology and scholarship appeared in connection with the Kaiser-Wilhelms-Universität in an appeal to help the 'martyrs of German science'. As a result, posts for sixty ordinary professors [Ordinarien], and thirty-three Privatdozenten and honorary professors, were already found by the end of 1920.[12]

Calker and Schmitt were appointed to posts in Munich.

Presumably, Schmitt experienced the end of the war in Bad Tölz. His friend Alexander Krause had offered him 'a true refuge'[13] in the spa town, where Schmitt was able to recover. Munich, in contrast, became a laboratory for the revolution. Despite the fact that King Ludwig III had introduced a parliamentary system of government by edict of 2 November, a revolutionary coup took place, which had been instigated primarily by the Independent Socialists, led by Kurt Eisner, and by anarchist groups in which

Gustav Landauer and Erich Mühsam were active. Eisner was the motor of the revolution. When the regional parliament declared the abolition of the monarchy on 7 November, Ludwig III went to Austria and Eisner became the prime minister of a revolutionary cabinet that was also joined by members of the majority socialists [Mehrheitssozialisten].* The revolution had a tinge of Schwabing and carnival. 'If the fire brigade had been called in good time, their hoses would have washed them away', Moritz Julius Bonn says in his reminiscences.[14] On 15 November, Eisner announced his government programme. One of his most important actions was the publication of files regarding the question of responsibility for the war. The publication incriminated the German Reich heavily and attracted world-wide attention. The rejection of Eisner's action was universal. From then on, not even the Social Democratic Party dared to bring up the question of responsibility for the war in public, and instead a 'Kriegsunschuldslegende'[15] [myth of innocence regarding the outbreak of the war] prevailed.

Eisner followed a separatist course. He claimed Bavaria's independence as a state, in particular with respect to the power of military command. For some months, Bavaria was on the brink of a civil war. On 12 January, elections for the regional parliament took place. The Bayerische Volkspartei [Bavarian People's Party] emerged from the elections as the strongest party, with the majority socialists and independent socialists gaining only 35.5 per cent of the votes between them. On 19 January, elections for the national assembly followed. From 6 February the national assembly met in Weimar, and Ebert was elected provisional president of the Reich. Within the Reich, the 'Weimar coalition' of SPD, Zentrumspartei† and DDP‡ was formed. In Bavaria, Eisner played for time by postponing the date for the opening session of the regional parliament to 21 February. Before that meeting, on the way to the parliament building, he was shot dead by Count Arco-Valley – the first of a series of politically motivated murders that weighed heavily on the Weimar Republic from the very beginning. The murder led to tumultuous scenes in the parliament's opening session. The deputy prime minister, Erhard Auer, was seriously wounded by shots fired by a 'member of the workers' council'. More people were killed. The Independent Socialists of Munich then called a general strike. A 'Rätekongress' [soviet congress] and 'Zentralrat' [central committee] chaired by Ernst Niekisch,[16] Fritz Sauber and Karl Gandorfer eliminated the parliament and seized power. In contrast, the Independent Socialists pushed for a democratic government formed by the parliament. 'The local political situation is tolerably calm, thanks to the fact that the communists have been shaken off', Thomas Mann noted in his diary at the time: 'Thank God, the majority of the military opposes the despicable alliance of the radical literati and the rabble.'[17]

On 17 March, the regional parliament elected an interim minority government led by the majority socialist Johannes Hoffmann. However,

---

*   The main faction of the SPD after the Independent Social Democratic Party had split off.
†   Centre party – a right-wing liberal Christian party.
‡   Deutsche Demokratische Partei = German Democratic Party – a left-wing liberal party.

in defiance of this, the 'central committee' of the soviet congress declared the Räterepublik [Bavarian soviet republic] on 7 April 1919, and a few days later the rule of purely communist soviets, chaired by Eugen Leviné, was proclaimed. This was followed by an intervention in Bavaria by the Reich. The Hoffmann government set its hopes on Reichswehrminister [Reich's minister of war] Noske, but in addition sought the help of para-military Freikorps [free corps] hostile to the Republic and introduced a brutal policy of counter-revolutionary court martial. Captain Roth and the general command were centrally involved in this. But the soviets were equally militant.[18] The peak of their anarchist excesses was the taking and executing of hostages on 30 April in Munich. At the beginning of May, Munich was taken by government troops and free corps. Schmitt was moved to the Munich garrison headquarters at that point and ran into personal danger. On 1 May, Thomas Mann wrote in his diary: 'The communist episode in Munich is over; there will be little appetite for a repeat. As for my own person, I can also not help but feel released and exhilarated. The pressure was abominable.' At the same time, Oswald Spengler drew up the plan for his *Preußentum und Sozialismus* [Prussianism and socialism].* His *Decline of the West* had its finger on the pulse of the times.[19] Johannes Hoffmann was reinstated as prime minister. Numerous of the leaders of the Bavarian soviet republic were arrested and shot or summarily sentenced. Gustav Landauer, without a trial, was brutally murdered by soldiers; Eugen Leviné was executed. Ernst Niekisch, Erich Mühsam, Ernst Toller, Otto Neurath and others were sentenced to imprisonment in a fortress, some for long terms. 'They carry their cells with them in their dull eyes / and stumble, pilgrims no longer used to light, along the square.'[20] The confusion and turmoil of the time speaks from many sources – e.g., Thomas Mann's diaries, Moritz Julius Bonn's *Bilanz eines Lebens* [Taking stock of a life] or Oskar Maria Graf's memoirs *Wir sind Gefangene* [We are prisoners]. The memoirs of the social democratic politician and lawyer Philipp Loewenfeld are particularly detailed. The experiences of the revolution were clearly trau-matic. The policy of special courts remained in place. After the revolu-tion, Bavaria became a counter-revolutionary bulwark. Anti-Semitism was strongly on the rise. That was the milieu out of which the NSDAP[†] emerged. 'The trauma of the rule of the Räte was the fertile ground for Hitler's early successes.'[21]

If one elucidates the situation from this perspective,[22] the enemy obser-vations of the general command appear in a different light. It becomes clear that some of the pacifist and literary circles had energetic members with very concrete revolutionary plans, and with an urge towards violence and domination, aiming at a dictatorial revolt. Contemporaries such as

---

* An English translation of this text is available on the internet at: https://archive.org/details/ PrussianismAndSocialism (accessed 2 April 2014).
† The DAP, Deutsche Arbeiter Partei = German Workers' Party, was founded in 1919 and was renamed Nationalsozialistische Deutsche Arbeiterpartei = National Socialist German Workers' Party in 1920.

Max Weber or Thomas Mann agreed in their rejection of such plans. Weber knew some of the actors, such as Jaffé and Toller, and had some sympathy for motives that came out of ethical conviction. In contrast, Thomas Mann despised the revolutionary politicians and ethically motivated dictators but tended to accept the objective reasons for a revolution.[23] Mann shared the conviction that substantial change was needed. Weber placed his bet on the selection of leaders through democratization and parliamentarism. Schmitt rejected these early on as illusions and opted rather for the continuation of a commissary dictatorship and for the military of the Reich as the force maintaining law and order. However, we do not have any direct comments from Schmitt on developments in 1919. In any case, the uncertainty of his professional future would hardly have allowed for such statements.

Table 8.1 Against ideological politics

Immanuel Kant	Moral politician vs. political moralist
Georg W. F. Hegel	Virtue = terror: against Jacobins and Romantics
Max Weber	Ethics of responsibility vs. ethics of conviction [Gesinnungsethiker]
Carl Schmitt	Counter-revolution vs. restorative Romanticism

Political Romanticism contains some interesting remarks on the murder of the writer Kotzebue by the student Karl Ludwig Sand (PR, pp. 146ff.) – the classical case of a foolish murder out of conviction [Gesinnungsmord] that could serve as a model for the murder of Eisner. A presentation given at a press conference in May 1918 demonstrates Schmitt's evaluation of pacifist circles at the time. He did not deny that some members acted out of noble motives, but rather saw 'radical rebels shoulder to shoulder with bourgeois middle-class pacifists' (TB II, p. 394). However, he insinuated that the 'propaganda' pursued a stab-in-the-back strategy that was adopted from the myth of the Nibelungen: a strategy of 'spoiling the mood at home and causing inner turmoil, in order to achieve behind the front what one tried in vain to achieve at the front' (TB II, p. 395). The propaganda bet on a 'shift in the mood' and a 'sudden moral failing of the German people' (ibid.). Schmitt looked at the pacifist propaganda from the point of view of its political function and ignored the personal motivations behind it. Whereas Weber was more interested in the 'attitudes' [Gesinnungen], Schmitt was more inclined to take a sober professional look at the consequences. And he saw that the propaganda was effective. Schmitt had focused on at least one of the players in the revolution of the Bavarian soviets even before 1918: Friedrich Wilhelm Förster, whose name was also mentioned by Weber. With Förster in mind, Schmitt said it was 'sad to see how German pacifists, some of whom are exceptional men' (TB II, p. 398), were made use of as comrades-in-arms. In light of the events after November 1918, Schmitt's activities at the general command appear less politically negligible than some of the documents that have been preserved. And *Political Romanticism* had a finger right on the pulse of the times in 1919.

General tendencies in Schmitt's early work and life

In a late letter, an almost ninety-year-old Schmitt thanked his pupil Huber for sending him a volume of his *Verfassungsgeschichte* [Constitutional history] and recapitulated:

> You are right in assuming that I can read the history of the First World War with autobiographical interest as contemporary history because for four years I was the legal secretary [Referent] for martial law (according to the Bavarian KI law) in section P at the deputy general command I.b.AK in the Herzog-Max-Burg in Munich, later subjected to the rule of the Eisner- and Niekisch-Republic, then again member of the military staff of the government troops (under Captain Roth, the later Bavarian minister of justice) – these are all stages in your presentation of constitutional history that I can personally verify.[24]

If we look back at Schmitt's early work overall, we can see some striking and clearly articulated lines emerging, despite the biographical upheavals and difficult situations in which he often found himself. Schmitt was an exceptional pupil and student, and he finished his studies in a very short period of time. Afterwards, during his legal training, which he also completed in the shortest possible time, he wrote some substantial juridical works that remained foundational in his later thought. During his study and training he received continual and formative support. As early as 1912, van Calker offered him the opportunity of embarking on an academic career. However, Schmitt decided to lay the foundations for a career as a lawyer. He not only passed his examination as an assessor but also gained the friendly patronage of Hugo am Zehnhoff. Schmitt became an expert in a lucrative area of the legal profession: the law governing entails. In this connection he gained insight into the higher echelons of society. Thus, at the beginning of the Great War, a career both as a lawyer and as a university lecturer were open to him. Besides this, he also married and moved in literary circles. In Munich, he rose within the general command and gained a good position as a provisional civil servant. From 1917 at the latest, his position was practically secure. His prospects at the beginning of the Weimar Republic were excellent. Calker continued to be well disposed towards him. Schmitt made up again with am Zehnhoff, who became Prussia's minister of justice. Captain Roth became justice minister in Bavaria. Schmitt was an established author by then, and his talent as a jurist was plain to see.

Schmitt was no adherent of the 'ideas of 1914', of the authoritarian military state or of political Catholicism. In private, he tended intellectually towards an individualism which he publicly exorcised. The two great early studies in 'intellectual history', *Political Romanticism* of 1919 and the 1921 *Dictatorship*, were rooted in early formative experiences. In *Political Romanticism*, Schmitt generalized his critique of individualism, rejected altogether the bourgeois mentality as it had emerged out of Romanticism and, given his own highly strung sensitivity and subjectivity, implicitly condemned himself as well in doing so. In *Dictatorship*, he no longer criticized the subjective side of the bourgeois world but its objective political form. With this, Schmitt had found his proper theme. On the basis of his experiences in military service, he believed that the mentality and political form of the bourgeois world could not survive much longer. At the transitional point from the constitutional monarchy to the first German democracy, Schmitt already possessed a sharpened perception and a conceptual apparatus that made him realize how threatened the 'bourgeois rule of law' [bürgerliche Rechtsstaat] was.

Part II

Beyond Bourgeois Existence: Schmitt's Life and Work during the Weimar Republic

9

A Permanent Position?
The Handelshochschule[*]
in Munich

State of exception in Bavaria

Until the beginning of May 1919, revolutionary conditions prevailed in Bavaria. Following his deployment to the army's municipal headquarters [Stadtkommandantur], Schmitt witnessed the bloodiest days of the revolutionary dictatorship – the Reichsexekution[†] and the military resistance by the revolutionary government. What he had been spared during the war – scenes of military fighting – he now saw in Munich. The course of events affected his health. On 4 June he was given leave in order to restore his health, and on 30 June he was discharged. The situation had hardly calmed down at this point. The state of siege effectively remained in place.[1] Although the separatist path of the radical left had been defeated, the new governments still insisted on the essential independence of the state from the Reich. Bavaria's military sovereignty before 1914 provided a reference point for this demand. During peace time, the Bavarian troops were under the command not of the Reich but of the Bavarian government. Eisner had already invoked this fact, and his successors continued to use it as an argument. Even after the Weimar Constitution had taken effect, on 14 August 1919, Bavaria still insisted on having sovereign power over its military, over calling a state of emergency, and over the protection of the constitution. Bavaria turned into a counter-revolutionary enclave. The atmosphere was dominated by a politically tendentious judiciary and violence. After the swift failure of the Kapp Putsch in March 1920, Gustav von Kahr took over from Hoffmann as prime minister and formed an irregular militia. Only after Kahr's resignation in September 1921 did the new prime minister, Hugo Graf Lerchenfeld, repeal the state of exception. Following the murder of Rathenau in 1922, emergency regulations were in force for several months, and in September 1923 a state of exception was once more declared. Kahr gained executive power again by being made 'chief state commissioner' [Generalstaatskommissar]. He expelled the so-called Ostjuden [Eastern Jews], who were objects of hatred

---

[*] Graduate School of Economics.
[†] Term denoting the, if necessary, military intervention against a single state in order to enforce imperial – i.e., Reich's – law.

within anti-Semitic circles; and he assumed powers of military command and used paramilitary units. Huber called the Bavarian presumption of military powers independent of the Reich an unparalleled case of 'high treason'.[2] Kahr was later involved in the Munich Putsch, if, perhaps, only for tactical reasons.[3] He criticized the putschists for being dilettantes but pursued his own anti-democratic and separatist agenda. It was only after the putsch that the primacy of the Reich was effectively asserted. The state of exception was formally repealed only on 14 February 1925. The institution of the state of siege was not only used by the Bavarians as a means of calming down the situation. It also enabled them to set themselves on a collision course with the Reich, which contributed to the instability of the Weimar Republic. The almost continuous state of exception in Bavaria lasted not only four, but ten years. The relevance of the task Schmitt had been given in 1915, of constructing a justification for the extension of the state of exception beyond the end of the war, was fully confirmed by Bavaria's actual history. Schmitt's views on the state of exception were determined by these experiences.

A permanent lectureship at the Handelshochschule in Munich

Although Schmitt's post in the general command had been provisional until further notice, he did not find himself wholly without professional prospects in 1919. He renewed his contacts with the privy councillor Hugo am Zehnhoff, who had by then become the Prussian minister of justice. Upon Zehnhoff's intervention, Schmitt was offered a promising post as a senior civil servant [Regierungsrat] in the Ministry for Social Affairs [Volkswohlfahrtsministerium] soon after his release from active military service.[4] In addition, the privy councillor had plans for him involving a post in Cologne. At the same time, Schmitt was made a firm offer of a lectureship at the Handelshochschule in Munich by its director, Moritz Julius Bonn. Even am Zehnhoff advised Schmitt to accept the offer: 'I agree with you that a professorship would be better for you than a post in the ministry.'[5] Thereupon, Schmitt turned down the offer from the Ministry for Social Affairs, citing poor health as the reason. On 23 August, Moritz Bonn wrote to the ministry: 'The Council [Kuratorium] of the Handelshochschule Munich would like to inform the Ministry for Culture and Education [Staatsministerium für Unterricht und Kultus] that Dr Carl Schmitt, Privatdozent at the University Strasbourg has been appointed as full university lecturer for public law.'[6] To begin with, between 1 September 1919 and 30 September 1921, Schmitt formally continued as a Privatdozent, with an initial annual salary of 6,000 Reichsmark,[7] teaching at the Handelshochschule. Hence, almost without any interruption, he moved from his temporary post as a civil servant in the general command to a permanent lectureship, compensating him for the loss of his lectureship in Strasbourg. Schmitt was able to remain resident in Munich and, at only thirty-one years of age was established in an academic position. In February 1920, he and Cari assumed Bavarian citizenship. Following the 'König Ludwig-Kreuz', he was also awarded the 'Eiserne Kreuz, II. Klasse'. Considering the turmoil of war, Schmitt's professional career followed a comparatively stable path. However, looking back, Schmitt spoke of an 'unhappy time' in Munich (TB, 18 August 1927), during which his first marriage fell apart.

In Germany, Handelshochschulen, graduate schools of economics, developed around the turn of the century as further education colleges for merchants. They were cradles for the emerging economic sciences and models for private universities. One example they followed was the London School of Economics, which had been founded in 1895. Within the system of further education, the Handelshochschulen were responsible for teaching 'the management of large-scale enterprises and those business leaders who need a theoretical economic education'.[8] Hence, they were early forms of management school, whose graduates had good professional prospects. 'Where should the business leaders come from?'[9] The initiative to found Handelshochschulen was the answer to that question at the time. The Hochschulen awarded a business diploma and trained practitioners; they produced 'educated, not scholarly merchants'.[10] Handelshochschulen, of different designs and under different types of aegis,[11] were founded in Leipzig and Aachen (1898), Cologne and Frankfurt (1901), Berlin (1906), Mannheim (1908), Munich (1910), Königsberg (1915) and Nuremberg (1919). The schools in Frankfurt and Cologne soon merged with the newly founded universities. As early as 1922, the Handelshochschule in Munich, situated at Ludwigstraße 4, was also integrated into the already existing department of business economics at the Technische Hochschule [technical university], where van Calker had been in charge of jurisprudence since 1920.

The political economist Moritz Julius Bonn was the descendant of an old Jewish banking family from Frankfurt and a disciple of one of the founding fathers of the Hochschule, Professor Lujo Brentano. In 1910, Bonn became its first 'director'. In his memoirs, he reports that the city of Munich and the chamber of commerce founded the Hochschule in a race against Nuremberg, hoping that the Bavarian state would contribute to the financing of the project.[12] In mildly ironic fashion, Bonn mentions that the Hochschule in Munich was not taken completely seriously. The decision to found it was made in 1908, and upon its opening in 1910 it had about 130 students. External students and 'visitors' ['Hospitanten'] from the university and the technical university were allowed to attend. The 'commercially assiduous' students came with the equivalent of A-levels, or an intermediate school leaving certificate, and three years of professional experience. The degree programme took four terms and led to a business diploma. In the initial years of the Hochschule, questions of appointment policies and plans for a new building were dominant themes. The first jurists appointed, who later became renowned, were Claudius von Schwerin (full-time) and Karl Rothenbücher (in a secondary role). When Schwerin was appointed to a post at the university in Berlin, in the summer term of 1914 Friedrich Klausing took on responsibility for jurisprudence.[13] The appointment of Edgar Jaffé turned out to be a 'complete success' that contributed to the 'improving reputation of the Handelshochschule'.[14] However, in 1913 endeavours were already being made to close the Hochschule. Bonn was on leave in the USA at the time (between 1913 and 1917), and the lecturer Leo Jordan acted as provisional director. Teaching activities were much reduced during wartime. Some of the lecturers were at the front. Klausing was also drafted, and as a consequence Heinrich Frankenburger received a teaching contract and soon afterwards took on an (unpaid) lectureship in jurisprudence as a secondary job. In the autumn of 1917, Bonn took over the directorship again; in an advisory function he was also involved in the decisions about the general design of the Treaty of Versailles and the Weimar Constitution. In spring 1920 he moved to Berlin. Bonn left under acrimonious circumstances, and the new director, Klausing, did not even invite him to the celebrations of the tenth anniversary of the Hochschule in autumn 1920. At that time, the chamber of commerce withdrew its financial support. After Klausing left, Felix Werner took on the directorship in April 1921. The short history of the Hochschule in Munich ended soon after that. In Berlin, by contrast, the Handelshochschule continued to exist with the support of business and industry.

Schmitt was appointed to the Hochschule in Munich within that short time frame in which it was facing an uncertain future and seeking orientation after the turmoil of war. In Bonn, it had an urbane and flexible director, with some sympathy for a non-bourgeois life-style and intellectual habitus. Bonn also later supported Schmitt's appointment to the Handelshochschule in Berlin. In this connection, he writes in his memoirs:

> The most talented of my colleagues was without a doubt Dr Carl Schmitt. He was generally considered the most capable representative of the new type of political scientist. During my days in Munich, I had helped to start his career – he was a Privatdozent in Strasbourg and professionally stranded after the cession of Alsace–Lorraine. . . . Eventually, I managed to bring him to Berlin. I knew of his imbalanced character, but I trusted his strong talent.[15]

Before 1933, Bonn was on friendly terms with Schmitt; after 1933, this was also one of the relationships that broke down.

In 1920, the Hochschule in Munich had just eight full-time lecturers. Schmitt acted as 'lecturer in jurisprudence' at the side of Klausing. The other full-time lecturers were the economist Werner Mahlberg, the insurance expert Hanns Dorn, the Viennese practitioner Arthur Weiss, the economist Felix Werner, the teacher of French Leo Jordan, and the teacher of English Wilfried H. Wells. Thus, the subjects taught were economics, law and the usual languages of commerce. Dorn and Jordan were at the same time teachers at the technical university and the university, respectively. Heinrich Frankenburger and Heinrich Rheinstrom were part-time jurists, and other part-time members of staff were the political economist Wilhelm Morgenroth and the banker Siegfried Buff. Frankenburger later died, deprived of his rights, in Munich; Rheinstrom emigrated to France and then the USA. The editor of Max Weber's works, Melchior Palyi, had a teaching contract from the winter term 1918–19 onwards.[16] Schmitt later met him again at the Handelshochschule in Berlin. Palyi was also forced to emigrate. The Handelshochschule in Munich cooperated with the technical university and the university and employed several practitioners as teachers or part-time members of staff.[17] At this Hochschule Schmitt taught jurisprudence within the context of other 'political sciences' ['Staatswissenschaften'], something he shared with Weber, whose famous lectures on 'Science as a Vocation' (7 November 1917) and 'Politics as a Vocation' (28 January 1919), as well as the lecture 'Abriss der universalen Sozial- und Wirtschaftsgeschichte' [Sketch of a universal social and economic history], Schmitt attended. He also took part in Weber's seminar for lecturers, which was held fortnightly on Saturdays. Schmitt thus actually met Weber in person.[18] As stimulating as the new professional context was, the Hochschule nevertheless could not offer the same possibilities in teaching and research as a proper university. It did not have the right to make doctoral awards or to award a Habilitation. Whereas van Calker, given his mature age, could be content with his integration into the technical university, and was also given a teaching contract at the university, Schmitt, naturally, hatched further plans.

The lecture Schmitt developed at the time was already aimed at academically ambitious students. From October 1919, Schmitt gave lectures on the history of political ideas since the Reformation. For the first time, he treated the modern 'idea of the unitary state' on the basis of the classical authors from Bodin to Montesquieu and Rousseau. This material was entered into his first major work, *Dictatorship*, which Schmitt completed in the summer of 1920. This work would earn him his first appointment to a university. Apart from that, he published little in those days. In the summer term 1920 he lectured on 'Verfassung des Deutschen Reiches' [The constitution of the German Reich], the 'Betriebsrätegesetz' [Workers' Council Act], 'Grundzüge der Sozialversicherung' [Foundations of social insurance] and 'Politische Ideen seit 1789' [Political ideas since 1789]. For the winter term 1920–1, he announced 'Besprechungen aus dem Gebiet des öffentlichhen Rechts' [Discussion of themes from public law], a course on the foundations of 'Arbeitsrecht und Sozialversicherung' [Labour law and social insurance], and again one on the 'Betriebsrätegesetz', as well as 'Lektüre politischer Schriften' [Readings of political texts]. In the summer term 1921, he offered an 'Einführung in das öffentliche Recht' [Introduction to public law], 'Besprechungen aus dem Gebiet des Arbeitsrechts' [Discussion of themes from labour law], 'Rechtsformen der wirtschaftlichen Selbstverwaltung' [The legal structures of economic self-management] and 'Politische Ideen des 19. Jahrhunderts' [Political ideas of the nineteenth century].

In 1921, an article appeared in the *Historische Zeitschrift*[19] titled 'Politische Theorie und Romantik' [Political theory and Romanticism]. It makes use of Schmitt's engagement with the modern theory of the state. Spinoza and Rousseau are treated for the first time. At that point, Schmitt still intended to write a 'detailed account of the historical connection between occasionalism and Romanticism',[20] which, however, never happened after his appointment to professorships in Greifswald and Bonn. But in 1924 Schmitt integrated the article into the second edition of *Political Romanticism*, and thus emphasized the special nature of the path taken by Romanticism. He also had a contract with a publisher for a volume on *Liberalismus* [Liberalism] for the series *Der Deutsche Staatsgedanke* [The German idea of the state].[21] Apparently, Schmitt already had a critique of liberalism in mind at the time.

In spring 1920, several charges were pending against Cari; one for theft according to §49a of the StGB* – i.e., violent theft – was dropped. But another one for forgery of documents probably went to trial. Schmitt took the Jewish lawyer Dr Max Hirschberg as Cari's defendant.[22] She had again come to the attention of the police. Schmitt also began to doubt her aristocratic descent at that time.

As early as August 1920, the ideas about a possible dissolution of the Handelshochschule had an impact on working conditions.[23] With van Calker's support, Schmitt tried to get a teaching contract at Munich University, but encountered resistance from the director, Klausing.[24] Schmitt visited am Zehnhoff in Berlin[25] and entered into a close correspondence with the state theorist Kurt Wolzendorff in Halle.[26] Wolzendorff read the proofs for *Dictatorship* and brought Schmitt to the attention of his colleague Otto Koellreutter,[27] who would become a life-long acquaintance, sometimes as friend, sometimes as foe. Despite his difficult private situation, Schmitt had great success as a teacher at the Handelshochschule. The trustee effusively thanked him upon his departure, saying that the 'large gap' it left could 'not be filled': 'During your time at the Handelshochschule, you increased and maintained the interest of the students in those subjects you taught to such a degree that we must express our deepest gratitude to you. We infinitely regret that the difficult situation of the Handelshochschule does not allow us to secure your valued contributions for the future.'[28] Schmitt left on 1 October.[29] His teacher at Strasbourg, van Calker, took on his commitments.[30] The last lecturers were given their notice with effect in autumn 1922.

'The execution almost precedes the sentence': *Dictatorship*

Schmitt wrote *Dictatorship* during the chaotic times of revolution and civil war in Munich, on the one hand, and his private marital crisis, on the other. In the summer of 1919, the Versailles Treaty and the Weimar Constitution came into effect. The Kapp Putsch in March 1920 failed because of the general strike, and there were communist uprisings in the Ruhr area. In the first general elections of the Reich, the Weimar coalition lost its majority, making clear on what weak foundations the Weimar Republic rested. In October 1920, *Dictatorship* went to press at the same time that Schmitt was in Hamburg with Eisler for a couple of days and, by coincidence, also met Theodor Däubler. He kept in continuous close contact with Eisler by letter.[31] Eisler was travelling for quite some time in 1920 before taking

---

* Strafgesetzbuch = penal code.

up his studies in Freiburg, where he also attended lectures by Husserl and Heidegger.[32] In December, Eisler proofread *Dictatorship*. The book appeared at the beginning of 1921.[33] It was based on extensive study of sources from the history of ideas and legal history. Its conceptual distinction between 'commissary' and 'sovereign' dictatorship was later never questioned by Schmitt from the perspective of legal history.[34]

How can a dictatorial suspension of law still be lawful? Schmitt this time approaches the question from a different angle than he had in 1916. He sets aside the old terminological distinction between *dictatorship* and *state of siege* but retains the central intuition on which it was based. In 1916, the distinction served the purpose of conceiving the military state of siege as the 'originary mode' [Urzustand] (SGN, p. 19) of activity of the modern state 'before the separation of powers'. Schmitt holds on to this view, but he now reconstructs the concept of dictatorship, taking the state theory of early modern times and the 'practice' of the commissars as his point of departure. He establishes the primacy of practice by looking at the classicist late Renaissance and at Roman history and literature. State theory in the late Renaissance made use of classical concepts for an early modern and technical understanding of the organization of the state. Hobbes's system was based 'on the axiom that there is no law prior to the state and outside of it, and that the value of the state resides precisely in the fact that it creates the law by settling the dispute over what is right' (D, p. 16). The state posits the difference between power and right rhetorically and dictatorially as right. According to Hobbes, the state qua state is a dictator. Schmitt already uses some formulations that will become central in later work: 'The decision contained in law is, from a normative perspective, borne [*sic*] out of nothing' (D, p. 17). As in his lectures, he takes the early modern idea of a 'unitary state' [Einheitsstaat] as his point of departure in *Dictatorship* and begins to investigate in more detail how this idea prevailed in practice.

Dictatorship is temporally limited rule. The civil servant is bound by the law; the commissar is bound by his mandate. Schmitt categorizes the different types of commissars he comes across and introduces the concept of a 'commissar of action' [Aktionskommissar] (D, p. 31) for a commissar with especially far-reaching powers. He sees the Church as the model and motor for the formation of the early modern territorially bound state. Out of the 'primacy of the pope' rose the 'monarchical character of the Church' (D, p. 35). The pope appointed commissars, whose role was based on the 'idea of personal representation and authority by proxy' (D, p. 39; trans. modified). 'The idea of Christ's personhood is therefore the ultimate pinnacle of this conception of the law' (D, p. 39), Schmitt writes, and thus takes up central ideas from his 'scholastic reflections'. His whole 'personalism' is based on this 'Christian' approach.

The struggle between Church and state required a 'number of exceptional measures'. With the beginning of the early modern period, the commissars became commissars of the princes and the front lines changed. Commissars became 'commissars of service' [Dienstkommissare] (D, p. 61) within a bureaucratic organization. State bureaucracy grew out of this development. In Germany, the monarchical 'unitary state' emerged belatedly because the Reich could not assert itself against the princes. Schmitt shows in detail how Wallenstein, as 'commissary', remained bound by the emperor's supreme command. He then goes on to discuss the 'transition to sovereign dictatorship in eighteenth-century state theory': Montesquieu's 'doctrine of balance' was no 'doctrinal construct' (D, p. 85), but a historically saturated and politically wise conception. Only in Le Mercier's and Mably's[35] philosophy of history did the 'dictatorship of enlightened reason' (D, p. 90; trans. modified) fully break through. According to Schmitt, Rousseau forced the individual into general freedom. 'With respect to the state', an individual has 'only duties and no rights' (D, p. 107). The 'absolutism of the state' (D, p. 109) is practised by way of unlimited commission. The executioners of the *volonté générale* have 'omnipotence without law [Gesetz]' (D, p. 110). Schmitt very subtly analyses this shift from the executive to legislature, and from 'commissary' to 'sovereign dictatorship' (D, p. 111), before returning to constitutional history. Cromwell still legitimized his sovereign dictatorship with 'God' (D, p. 113). Sieyès, by contrast, proclaimed the sovereign nation. In the course of the French Revolution, the National Convention then suspended the separation of powers and political agency was handed over to the revolutionary people's commissars. The result was the emergence of 'an abstract apparatus of government and administration' (D, p. 143). Napoleon, finally, completed the bureaucratic system of modern administration.

The last chapter discusses the state of siege 'in contemporary law and order' (D, p. 148). In the nineteenth century, to begin with, martial law was 'a kind of situation outside the law'. Schmitt describes military action as exercising a 'right to self-defence' [Notwehrrecht] and situations in which 'the deed itself' decides 'whether the conditions for self-defence obtain or not' (D, p. 154). The one who acts, in such cases, is at once judge and executor. The communist revolutionaries had also claimed such a right to self-defence. Schmitt quotes a remark by the Reich's minister of defence regarding a proclamation by communist leaders of the revolution in 1920: '"Here you can see the new constitutional law": "one might think that in this case the execution almost precedes the sentence"' (D, p. 290, fn. 16; trans. modified).[36] Thus, Schmitt places the right to self-defence in the dubious context of the revolution.* On the counter-revolutionary use of court martial, as practised by the general command, he remains silent, and refers rather to the critical situation after 1918 and defends the efforts towards limiting such measures through the rule of law. At the time, universal authorization was 'replaced by a number of circumscribed powers' (D, p. 173). However, the impression given of a limitation of powers by the rule of law, Schmitt says, is deceptive. Even Article 48 of the Weimar Constitution still contains 'the authorization for a commission of action

---

* In the proclamation it says: 'The maintenance of order and security is conducted by the revolutionary people's militia [Volkswehr]. Whoever is seen engaged in activities such as robbery, looting, theft, or usury will be sentenced by being court-martialled and shot' (D, p. 290, fn. 16).

unlimited by law' (D, p. 175). He calls it 'a peculiar regulation' (D, p. 177), which hides the possibilities it allows behind an abundance of limitations: 'The right over life and death is *implicite* [implicit], the right to suspend the freedom of the press is *explicite* [spelled out]' (D, p. 177). Schmitt warns against the possibilities opened up by the article and calls for its strict limitation to executive measures. If Article 48 would provide the Reichspräsident with legislative authority as well, Schmitt argues, it would make him a sovereign dictator and the Weimar Constitution 'a precarious and provisional arrangement' (D, p. 176). Schmitt, at the end, hints at the fact that the construction of the state of siege in the Weimar Constitution may have been done with a bourgeois situation in mind, in which the 'solidary unity of the state' (D, p. 178; trans. modified) was ultimately not at stake. However, this condition no longer applies. After the revolutions of 1830 and 1848, 'questions arose simultaneously whether the political organization of the proletariat and the counteraction to it had not created a completely new political situation and, together with it, new concepts in constitutional law' [neue staatsrechtliche Begriffe] (D, p. 179). The dictatorship of the proletariat replaces the state of siege with a 'sovereign dictatorship'.

There can be no doubt that Schmitt wanted to warn against the development of a sovereign dictatorship, and that he saw the Marxist movements as heirs to the dictatorship of the Jacobins. In his lengthy preliminary remarks of summer 1920, he refers to the socialist discussions and criticizes their 'historical-philosophical' (D, p. xlii) justification of a dictatorship of the proletariat. Schmitt's decision in favour of the executive as the organ of a 'commissary' dictatorship results from the analysis of the historical shift of dictatorial powers from the executive to the legislature. In this context, he locates the transformation from an executive to a sovereign dictatorship in the state theory of the eighteenth century. Thus, he announces at the same time further studies on 'the philosophy of the nineteenth century' (D, p. 179), which will soon follow in the form of *Political Theology* and *The Crisis of Parliamentary Democracy*. Thus *Dictatorship*, we may say, prepared the ground thematically for the programmatic works of the Bonn years. In it, Schmitt investigates for the first time the emergence of the modern unitary state. Although he does still consider even martial law as a legal relationship, he does not push the argument for an extension of dictatorial powers. And although he questions the conditions for the validity of the 'bourgeois Rechtsstaat' towards the end, the study is not a sharp intervention against Weimar on the grounds of legal policies. Rather, it expresses worries over an understanding of revolutionary developments as still constituting legal relationships.

This was the first publication by Schmitt that intervened in contemporary discussions regarding the principles used in the interpretation of law, and thus qualified him for a juridical chair. It convinced Rudolf Smend immediately of the high rank of the author. He recommended Schmitt for a post in Greifswald and wanted to meet him in Munich. However, Schmitt was in hospital at the time and regretted that he missed 'being given the rare opportunity to talk to an expert in the history of German state law'.[37]

Smend continued to support his appointment to a chair in Greifswald and later in Bonn. On 23 August, he learned about Schmitt's appointment to the chair in Greifswald.

Farewell to Munich:
Schmitt's contribution to the *Erinnerungsgabe für Max Weber*[*]

The first three chapters of Schmitt's programmatic text *Political Theology* appeared in December 1922 in the second volume of the *Erinnerungsgabe für Max Weber*. Schmitt knew the editor, Melchior Palyi, from the Handelshochschule. At that time, *Political Theology* had already been published, and Schmitt was by then teaching in Bonn. As a partial reprint, the version published in the *Erinnerungsgabe*[38] did not receive any particular attention. In terms of the history of the work, the first three chapters were older than the last; as an answer to Weber, they belong to the Munich period. The fourth chapter, 'On the Counter-Revolutionary Philosophy of the State (de Maistre, Bonald, Donoso Cortés)', was written only in the summer of 1922. The differences between the two published versions of the first three chapters indicate an ambiguity in Schmitt's 'political theology' – using Jan Assmann's terminology,[39] that between a historically 'descriptive' and a politically 'active' political theology. In the *Erinnerungsgabe* Schmitt explains what he has learned from Weber and how he wants to make fruitful scientific use of Weber's 'hermeneutic sociology'; in his programmatic monograph, he indicates that he is giving up the observer perspective and instead is going to put his position and concepts to practical political use, 'bringing them to bear on the issues of the times' (VRA, p. 8). The two versions send out different signals.

Schmitt's contribution to the *Erinnerungsgabe* is limited to a scholarly response to Weber. Opening the second volume, it gives a sharp 'definition of sovereignty'. The second chapter, 'The Problem of Sovereignty as the Problem of the Legal Form and of the Decision', then goes on to confront the two ideal types of answer given in legal theory, that of juristic 'normativism' and that of personal 'decisionism' – i.e., the answers given by the dominant theory of public law (Kelsen) and by classical state theory (Hobbes). The third chapter, 'Political Theology', presents a sketch of Schmitt's view of these questions as belonging to a process of secularization[40] and as arising out of 'theological ideas' and 'metaphysical' assumptions. The title of the *Erinnerungsgabe* is *Soziologie des Souveränitätsbegriffs und politische Theologie* [Sociology of the concept of sovereignty and political theology]. 'Sociology of the concept of sovereignty', in this context, denotes the method and 'political theology' the research project.[41]

In *Wert des Staates* [Value of the state], Schmitt had described the disintegration of the state as an apocalyptic time of 'immediacy', in which, instead of a universally binding law, nothing but an immediate and individual religious commitment exists. Since 1914, Schmitt had seen himself

---

[*] A commemorative publication in honour of Max Weber, who had died on 14 June 1920.

as living in such a time. Even the end of the war did not bring peace or an end to the state of exception. Thus, Schmitt continued living in the early Christian 'expectation' of the end of the world, and he had to accommodate the 'delay of the Second Coming' in conceptual terms; he was forced to look at pure factual power, the chaos of the state of exception, as a legal process, and to identify the fundamental difference between power and right [Macht und Recht] displayed by the state of exception. In *Dictatorship* he refers to the 'act' of self-defence for that purpose, claiming that even martial law constitutes a 'return to legal form' (D, p. 175); the 'nature' of the right to self-defence consists in the fact 'that the act itself decides on the existence of its own prerequisites' (D, p. 179). The person acting in self-defence thereby assumes the right to act in this way. This realization, based on Schmitt's experiences during the revolutionary time in Munich, upsets his earlier distinction between power and right. Now, Schmitt sets himself the task of 'distinguishing between norms of law and norms of the application of law', taking the 'problem of the concrete exception' (D, pp. vif.) as his starting point. And he ends up suspending the distinction itself, because he reconstructs the norms of law on the basis of 'practice'. In conceptual terms, the conclusion drawn in *Political Theology* is this: the 'norms' must be understood on the basis of the 'exception'; at the core of right [Recht] is the 'decision'; 'the rule actually lives altogether off the exception' (PT, p. 15; trans. modified).

Schmitt introduces sovereignty as a 'limit concept'. *Political Theology* opens with the fomulaic: 'Sovereign is he who decides on the exception.' Whoever decides to act in self-defence is caught 'in' a situation. However, by making a distinction between power and right a person also puts him- or herself 'above' the pure factuality of the situation and evaluates it in legal terms. As a matter of fact, the person decides 'within' the state of exception 'upon' what constitutes right. In the development of modern legal thought, Schmitt argues, this right is negated, and thus it cannot capture the 'extreme case'. In the exceptional case, the fundamental elements of the legal system, the norms and decisions, are separated out. 'The exception reveals most clearly the essence of the state's authority. The decision parts here from the legal norm' (PT, p. 13). The 'essence of the state's sovereignty' therefore does not appear, as Max Weber claimed, 'as the monopoly to coerce or to rule, but as the monopoly to decide' (ibid.). The innermost core of the state, according to Schmitt, is executive authority. The norms of a state must be understood on the basis of 'fundamental decisions' taken on the political level. Schmitt also formulates this thought in terms of a sociology of law, writing: 'The norm requires a homogeneous medium. . . . For a legal order to make sense, a normal situation must exist. A normal situation must be established . . . All law is "situational law"' (ibid.).[42]

Schmitt presents his concept of sovereignty in contrast to the positions of the main representatives of Weimar normativism and positivism, the Viennese scholar of legal theory, Hans Kelsen, and Gerhard Anschütz in Heidelberg. Anschütz considers the 'gap in the law' as a 'gap in right' and rejects the distinction between law and right on positivist principles, in order clearly to distinguish right from politics. Where the text of the law falls silent, the space of political decisions begins. Kelsen, in this context, speaks of the 'face of Gorgo',* the reality of power which a jurist must be prepared to face up to. Schmitt does not reject such distinctions between power and right. He also wants clearly to separate out these two dimensions. But he refuses to identify the question of right with state law and to acknowledge a state of exception that would be outside the legal realm. For his take on the exception he invokes 'theological reflection' and quotes from Kierkegaard (PT, p. 15), indicating that a theological perspective on right beyond state law is possible. In a situation where the state is no longer able legally to contain the state of exception, theological reflection still guarantees the possibility of legally evaluating it. Beyond the state exists a right of God.

The second chapter, 'The Problem of Sovereignty as the Problem of the Legal Form and of the Decision', differentiates historically between a 'normativist' and a 'decisionist' understanding of sovereignty. The sketch ends by contrasting two ideal types, 'two types of juristic scientific thought'. Schmitt juxtaposes juristic 'normativism', taking Hans Kelsen to be its main representative, with Thomas Hobbes as the 'classical representative' of the 'decisionist type' who conceived of right, on the basis of the authoritarian decision, as command: 'Autoritas, non veritas facit legem'.[43] Schmitt emphasizes the connection of 'this type of decisionism with personalism' (PT, p. 33) and holds that a juristic decisionism can only be justified within a 'personalistic' view of the world. He is of the opinion that modern metaphysics, along with theism, has destroyed the metaphysical prerequisites for personalism, which alone could give personal 'authority' and 'dignity' to an individual decision.

The programmatic third chapter, 'Political Theology', then starts out from a strong thesis: 'All significant concepts of the modern theory of the state are secularized theological concepts' (PT, p. 36). Schmitt sees a family resemblance between absolutism and theism and between the 'idea of the modern constitutional state' and deism (PT, pp. 36f.) and awards Kelsen the 'merit' of having recognized these connections.[44] He ridicules the reductionist perspectives taken by 'spiritualist' and 'materialist' explanations' and praises Max Weber's sociological method of understanding certain ideas on the basis of their social 'bearers' and representatives. However, he does not want to follow that method either. And he holds that 'in its consequent manner this type of sociology is best assigned to belles-lettres' (PT, p. 45). Schmitt's own intentions aim not at the personal representatives and bearers of certain ideas but at a transpersonal 'sociology of concepts' (ibid.), which looks for analogies between the semantic fields of the individual sciences and establishes the 'basic, radically systematic structure' (ibid.) and conceptual form that they share: 'The metaphysical image that a particular epoch forges of the world has the same structure as what the epoch immediately understands to be appropriate as a form of

---

* Gorgo was a powerful Spartan queen, the daughter of a Spartan king, married to another king, and mother to a third.

its political organization. The determination of such an identity is the sociology of the concept of sovereignty' (PT, p. 46; trans. modified). In these words, Schmitt formulates an ambiguous programme for a conceptual history. It can be carried out as a diagnosis of epochs, as political theory, or as a history of metaphysics. Schmitt aims in particular at a critical history of the repression of the theoretical personalism that is a prerequisite of 'decisionist' legal thought.

Hobbes still defied the tendency towards normativism on account of a 'methodical and systematic necessity in his juristic thinking' (PT, p. 47; trans. modified). Since the Enlightenment, however, 'the consistency of exclusively scientific thinking has also permeated political ideas, replacing the essentially juristic-ethical thinking' (PT, p. 48; trans. modified). Schmitt notes a general transformation from transcendent to 'immanent conceptions'. In this context, the modern 'national consciousness' [Nationalbewußtsein] marked a transition from absolutism to democracy: to an 'organic' metaphysics and an organic conception of the state. The 'left-Hegelians' used the 'immanence philosophy' (PT, p. 50) in order to create an ideology of humanity, which, for Schmitt, is the foundation of modern democracy. In the Spanish critic of liberalism Donoso Cortés he saw a counter-movement which set theology and theism against this modern movement, and thus 'first [represented] a political theology', in the sense of an intentional politicization of theology. Cortés, Schmitt writes, was 'a Catholic philosopher of the state, one who was intensely conscious of the metaphysical kernel of all politics'. He concluded 'in light of the revolution of 1848 that '[r]oyalism is no longer because there are no longer any kings' (PT, p. 51; trans. modified), and as a consequence he declared himself openly in favour of 'dictatorship'. In the version of the *Erinnerungsgabe*, the reference to Cortés reads as a rejection of legitimacy based on dynasty. After all, the dynasty of the Wittelsbacher had also pathetically relinquished its rule during the November revolution.[45] Moritz Julius Bonn later recounted sneeringly: 'The king accepted his unexpected removal as a trial imposed on him by God, and did not consider for one moment defending his throne. He packed his family and went to the countryside.'[46]

As late as 1974 (SSA, pp. 319f.) Schmitt was of the opinion that '[t]he topic "Max Weber" is still far from obsolete; it is the topic "Political Theology"' – no more and no less.' To what extent, then, is Schmitt's contribution to the *Erinnerungsgabe* a response to Weber? What Schmitt owes to Weber is mainly the overcoming of a purely juristic concept of the state. The sociology of law, as a 'hermeneutic sociology', leads to a rejection of 'materialist explanations' and to a deeper analysis of the hermeneutical horizon of meanings within which actions take place. Weber's hermeneutic sociology had already focused on the sociology of religion by analysing meaningful social action on the basis of the religious character that it displays. In contrast to Weber and his universal history, Schmitt concentrates on the constellation of religious denominations in Germany, on Judaism and Christianity, but he shares with Weber the hermeneutical space that characterizes the position he took in relation to the world and from there looks at the influence of religious denominations and backgrounds in a genealogical perspective, seeing them, despite all modernization and secularization, as an indispensable resource for meaning and orientation in our actions. For Schmitt, there is no 'abstract' humanity and no 'neutral' position beyond cultural traditions. The philosophical sharpening of this approach in the form of the question of the relation between 'form of the state and worldview' [Staatsform und Weltanschauung] (Hans Kelsen) he owes explicitly to Kelsen, but he takes the opposite position to him. Kelsen ties the possibility of democracy to a relativist worldview. 'If I make a decision in favour of democracy', Kelsen writes, 'then solely for the reasons set out in the final chapter of this work: because of the relation between the democratic form of the state and a relativist world view'.[47] Schmitt agrees with this analysis. Like Kelsen, he is also of the opinion that the relativist worldview is inclined towards liberal democracy. But, unlike Kelsen, he believes that political authority is secure only within the framework of a theistic and personalistic worldview. This turns Kelsen into Schmitt's scientific antipode and his opponent with regard to legal policy; and later, for Schmitt, Kelsen also represented the essence of the 'Jewish spirit' against which he fought.[48] Schmitt's contribution to the *Erinnerungsgabe* for Weber confronted him with a decision to be taken: should he now become a historian of the relation between 'state form and worldview' and concentrate on a purely descriptive 'Political Theology' – a path later taken by Eric Voegelin in the wake of Kelsen and Schmitt – or should he concentrate on a 'Political Theology' as active intervention, one which uses 'theology' for political argument? The period of crisis caused by hyperinflation took the decision away from him. In the state of exception, a legal scholar had to intervene and insist on upholding the law. Schmitt opts for the counter-revolutionary philosophy of the state. But his analysis of the 'metaphysical' prerequisites of personalism, sovereignty and legitimacy reveals at the same time the fragility of his position.

10

A 'Faithful Gipsy' in Greifswald

A short appearance

With the beginning of the winter term 1921–2, Schmitt moved from the Handelshochschule in Munich to Greifswald, the smallest of the Prussian universities. In 1914 it had 1,456 students, in the summer term 1927 even fewer than that.[1] Of these, about 200 studied law. Schmitt's whole university career took place between 1921 and 1945 in Prussia, where he moved from Greifswald to Bonn, thence to Berlin, Cologne, and then back to Berlin. Therefore, his short intermezzo in Greifswald was not insignificant for his career. The first position at a university opens up paths for an academic career, while the last positions are its high point and end point.[2] In Greifswald Schmitt set his foot on the first step of his Prussian career ladder. For this reason alone, he could hardly have rejected the offer. The circumstances of his appointment were fairly confused.[3] After Erwin Jacobi had moved to Leipzig there was a vacancy for a personal professorship [persönliches Ordinariat] in public law, which was quickly filled by Erhard Neuwiem. Soon afterwards, Eduard Hubrich, who held the full professorship (chair) and also taught Protestant canon law, passed away. At that point, Neuwiem hoped to take the chair, rendering both professorships potentially available. Rudolf Smend, without having met Schmitt in person before, threw the latter's hat into the ring and recommended him in a letter of 16 March 1921. In his letter, Smend also referred to discussions with his colleague Erich Kaufmann (Bonn). Smend wrote: 'His three books on the individual and the state, Polit. Romanticism, and Dictatorship (1914, 1919, 1921) place him among the best of German state theorists. As someone from Strasbourg, he should be looked after . . . You would be making an excellent choice.' Did Smend not know that Schmitt was teaching in Munich? Did he assume that, in some way, he had to be 'looked after'?

The future of the Handelshochschule was uncertain at that time, and it was only in Greifswald that Schmitt would become a full professor. In addition, his marriage was breaking down and Schmitt wanted to get away. Smend was genuinely impressed by the recently published *Dictatorship*, and soon he would also recommend Schmitt as his successor in Bonn. His recommendation for Greifswald, however, at first fell flat. The professor of penal law, Albert Coenders, pushed through his candidate, Ludwig von Köhler. Schmitt was not on the first list of faculty, dating from March 1921, to be appointed. However, Köhler turned down the offer because he was moving to Tübingen, whereupon the ministry requested a new list. The faculty suggested Neuwiem for the full chair and Schmitt for the personal chair. But the ministry appointed Schmitt to the full chair in September 1921 and made him the director of the juridical department, with an annual salary of 14,100 Reichsmark.[4] It is hard to say what decided the course of events in the end. What we do know for certain is that it was Smend who made Schmitt part of the deliberations, and that both entities involved in taking the decision, the juridical faculty and the ministry, were in favour of appointing Schmitt to Greifswald. Schmitt was not forced upon the university, but he was being helped in getting the full chair.

Däubler congratulated Schmitt from Athens: 'I know Greifswald. It has many beautiful spots, especially the surroundings and neighbourhood. Strictly Protestant, though.'[5] A little later, he probed the point again: 'How do you like Protestant Pommerania?'[6] Not very much, would have been the answer! From August 1921, Schmitt was involved in a love affair with an Irish-Australian student, Kathleen Murray. He read Ovid's *Tristia*, the oldest poem written in exile, elegiac couplets from the time of his banishment to the Black Sea, and sent Franz Blei Latin quotations from it. Upon Schmitt's officially taking up his post, Blei sent him comforting words: 'Greifswald. It won't be for long. And you are living in the symbolically charged Bahnhofstrasse [station road]. See it as a trial.'[7] And, in even more drastic terms, he wrote: 'Just see Greifswald as a pre-hell', adding in late November: 'The stupidity of life can clearly be seen in the fact that you have to sit in Greifswald.'[8] The philologist of Romance literature Ernst Robert Curtius wrote: 'I can vividly identify with your situation in Greifswald.' At the time, Curtius was teaching in Marburg, in 'Greifswald upon the Lahn'.* 'Hopefully, this is a short-lived exile, a penitence which expiates us of much. The precept "one should have hard times" is part of German ethics.'[9] From Munich, Flora Klee-Pahlyi wrote, still referring to the 'pleasant company' of Schmitt's 'Frau Gemahlin' [wife], 'I am very sorry that the climate in Greifswald is so bad for you, and I hope soon to hear better news through your wife.'[10] Schmitt's acquaintance Heinrich Merk hoped for his speedy return: 'If one day a chair for the defence of the Spanish Inquisition is created in Munich, you will have to be its holder, and I shall be your most faithful listener.'[11] The philologist from Strasbourg Friedrich Kiener wrote:

> My dear colleague, with all my heart I would have hoped for a friendlier beginning at your new professional home. I would be very pleased to hear that you are better again. As little as you may like Greifswald, you will certainly not regret having moved from the south up north. Because wherever one can find disciples and sees them at work, and where one can live for one's studies, one will never feel like a stranger.[12]

---

*   Marburg is situated on the River Lahn.

With these words, Kiener emphasized the advantages of the university compared with the Handelshochschule. Schmitt was obviously not excited about Greifswald and intended it to be only an intermezzo. He had great plans with Kathleen Murray.

Kathleen Murray, Ernst Robert Curtius and the Greifswald doctorate

Kathleen Murray was born on 16 January 1895 as an Irish citizen in Sydney.[13] Her father was a journalist. In 1911, she left school and studied modern languages at the University of Sydney. In December 1914, she was awarded her Bachelor of Arts. Between April 1915 and July 1919 she worked as a teacher in Australia. She received a scholarship for doctoral study in Europe which, however, she could only take up in August 1919 because of the war. For the winter term 1919–20 she was enrolled at Bonn, and then she went to the newly reopened French university at Strasbourg for two terms. She first met Schmitt on 17 August 1921 in Strasbourg, probably through the Romance philologist Kiener. Murray wanted to do her doctorate in Bonn, where Schmitt was already being discussed as a candidate for a post, and to subscribe at the university there for the winter term 1921–2.[14] Schmitt met her in September in Cologne and went to the Mosel with her for a couple of days. In Trier and Alf, they conjured up a common future and made plans for a wedding. At the end of October, Schmitt travelled slowly, via Hamburg and Stralsund, to Greifswald. At this point, he separated from his first wife. On 5 November 1921, he still signed his name Schmitt-Dorotić, but then gave up the double-barrelled

DR. KATHLEEN MURRAY.

'There is after all only one woman for me, Kathleen' – Carl Schmitt about Kathleen Murray in his diary

name he had used since 1915 without ever having changed it officially. Soon he would say: 'There are innumerable Dorotics in Agram, the name is very common there, like Müller is here. What a disaster' (TB, 3 July 1922).

At that time, no one in Bonn was prepared to supervise Murray. Schmitt therefore wrote to Erich Kaufmann. On 8 November 1921,[15] Murray wrote from Cologne saying that the Bonn Anglicist Wilhelm Dibelius had refused her admission as a doctoral student in English on the grounds that the French faculty was responsible for her; Dibelius recommended a move to Ernst Robert Curtius. Schmitt then established contact with Curtius, who had taken up a chair at Marburg in 1920, referring to their common years in Strasbourg.[16] Curtius replied with extensive autobiographical references, promising to get in touch with Murray. In mid-November Murray arrived in Marburg. Between November and May, Schmitt sent numerous letters and cards to Curtius, and via Franz Blei he also made himself familiar with Curtius's writings. The issue of Murray's doctorate appears again and again in the background of their exchanges on Catholicism, German identity and Romanticism, and it is, in fact, the actual purpose of this correspondence.

However, the arrangement of the doctorate was not at all the only thing that Murray requested from Schmitt. He was also expected to help her with the actual work. A letter that has been preserved[17] allows us to guess the extent of that help:

> This morning I copied up the notes on Keats. Did you write another conclusion? You said the one you sent me is sketchy. There is nothing on Taine here. Neither the literary nor correspondence is in the seminar. I have not yet tried the Stadtbibliothek. I believe it is very hard to get any book you want. Carl, shall I send you my Taine et les Lokistes so that you can formulate that part of the business for me in German? Then we shall have finished with the middle chapter. Curtius says the Arbeit must be handed in in January. Will you make out the chapters and headings for me in German, as You* think it ought to be? The translation of Baldensperger's dispositions is somewhere in a letter. I have all your letters here, tied up together, and I don't like disturbing them while we are within reach of each other. Am I asking you to do too much, Carl dear? . . . Shall I use your translation of Baldensperger's dispositions or will you make me another index? When I have written all I can for the first two chapters will you formulate them for me in German, and add and alter what you think? . . . I believe all depends on the Arbeit. I have an idea that Curtius will not be hard in the oral, and that Deutschbein[18] will be easy because of Curtius' influence on him.

There are notes and manuscript pages in Schmitt's posthumous papers[19] which can be found practically verbatim in the monograph; an authorial influence by Schmitt is certain. However, from Munich came some news that caused a dramatic turn. Schmitt now considered Murray to be unfaithful and renounced the relationship. He was plagued by heart problems. For

---

* Capitalized in the original.

some time he stayed with am Zehnhoff in Berlin. In his diary, he noted: 'I am in a relationship with a woman for the second time and see how everything repeats itself, down to such a level of detail that I often feel I am sitting the same exam for the second time.' Schmitt constructed a strange alternative between God and Woman: 'But a Christian will understand when I say: the point of that exam is to fail it. If I pass it, if I even get a prize for it, I am done in the eyes of God' (TB, 3 December 1921). 'No one can serve two masters', he concludes, and signs, following the Bible (Psalm 121: 5–6), as 'the shadow of God'.* The next day he wrote a formal farewell letter in which he offered Murray his support as a 'second' and promised to set himself to work immediately. Schmitt was used to the practice of co-authorship from the 'Schnekkeroman' and the *Silhouettes* [Schattenrisse]. The joint writing of a dissertation represented a more intense *mise en scène*, in which the idea of co-authorship was led back to its erotic origins. Schmitt, the critic of Romanticism, acted as a Romantic author. The renunciation of love out of love, however, appears strange. Schmitt saw himself as a 'second' and assured Kathleen: 'From now on, you have only rights against me, I have only duties towards you.' It is hardly astonishing that Curtius promptly had the following news to report to Greifswald on 6 December: 'Yesterday, a crying Miss Murray came to me. She had received a piece of bad news (not from home) about which she did not want to say any more. She seemed completely bewildered, and I pitied her very much.' On 8 December, Schmitt assured Kathleen once more that he would meet her in Berlin at Christmas and sent her instructions for the exam. Thus Curtius was able to report that she had calmed down slightly. Schmitt apparently helped her diligently with the dissertation, and only a little later Curtius wrote to him: 'The other day, Miss Murray brought me fragments of her work which, to my joyful surprise, were excellent.' Schmitt was in Munich and Berlin for a short time in mid-December and then over Christmas again in Berlin for a couple of days, where he and Murray both stayed with Hugo am Zehnhoff. This arrangement required some delicacy as the old am Zehnhoff knew Cari from the time in Düsseldorf, and he was now again involved in Schmitt's private life.

At that time, Schmitt complained to Blei and Moritz Bonn over his lot in Greifswald.[20] Bonn, who was teaching at the Handelshochschule in Berlin by then, comforted him: 'I think it will not be difficult to release you from Greifswald. There is the prospect of four full professorships being established at the Hochschule here, one of which would be for the history of political ideas and problems of constitutional law. This professorship is intended mainly with your person in mind.'[21] Georg Eisler was at once happy about this 'release' from Greifswald. However, Schmitt was also discussed for a post in Bonn, where he had been third on the list of candidates since November. Eisler warned Schmitt of renewed romantic confusion: 'You had better not travel to Marburg for Miss M's exam; it is enough that

---

* 'The LORD *is* thy keeper: the LORD *is* thy shade upon thy right hand' (King James Bible). 'Der HERR behütet dich; / der HERR ist dein Schatten/über der rechten Hand' (Luther's translation).

you did the written work. I am sure the work will be good enough, so that there is no reason for you to worry.'[22] At the end of January, Curtius envisaged 1 March as a date for the viva, and assured Schmitt: 'I shall award the highest grade to her work.'

Smend expected Schmitt's appointment to the chair in Bonn as early as 1 March.[23] At the end of the term, Schmitt knew that his 'short-lived exile' would soon be over, and he spent hardly any more time in Greifswald. Taking into consideration his restless life of travelling, he perhaps stayed there overnight for little more than a month overall. What he achieved in terms of teaching and research during this short span of time can hardly be credited to Greifswald as an academic space. Nevertheless, Schmitt became friendly with the philosopher Heinrich Pichler, who asked him in May: 'How is the faithful gipsy coming along? And the volume on Max Weber?'[24] In a preliminary remark to the first edition of *Political Theology*, Schmitt remarked that he had written the booklet, together with a study on *Die politische Idee des Katholizismus* [The political idea of Catholicism], in March 1922. At that time he was in Marburg with Kathleen and was writing parts of her dissertation. The writing of the last chapter of *Political Theology*, and the revision of the essay on Catholicism, already fell, however, into his time in Bonn. The date of March 1922 relates more to the decision to compose these works and marks the prospective move to the Catholic Bonn as the result of Schmitt's term in Greifswald. The Privatdozent Günther Holstein, a disciple of Erich Kaufmann, became the substitute for Schmitt in Greifswald. Neuwiem nominally reached his goal later by taking up the chair, while Holstein remained on a personal professorship [Extraordinarius] in Greifswald, where he developed a Protestant canon law.[25] Schmitt fought vehemently in order to prevent his move to Bonn as the successor to Kaufmann.[26]

During early 1922, Murray's doctorate continued to cause difficulties. Curtius faced two main objections from the faculty, to which he replied in detail in a letter to the dean:[27] doubts were expressed, firstly, over the 'equal academic standing of the University of Sydney' and, secondly, regarding the willingness of the Australian university to grant German students the same 'academic citizenship' as Australians. Behind these points lay the political suspicion that, as an Anglo-Saxon, Murray belonged to the party of the enemy. Curtius picked up and reacted to these insinuations: Marburg had to counter the enemy's 'campaign of lies' with 'enlightenment and instruction'. With regard to politics, Curtius argued, Murray, as an Irish citizen, shared the 'stance of the Irish against English imperialism',[28] which was also the reason why she studied in Germany. Once her travelling visa had run out, she would return to Australia. 'If it were to be made impossible for her to conclude her doctorate, it would damage our German interests in terms of cultural politics, and the responsibility for this would lie with the faculty.' Apart from that, he added, the dissertation was an exceptional achievement.

Curtius promised the faculty an exposition by Dibelius on Australian procedures regarding doctorates as well as Australian documents. In response, the dean, in the first instance, asked the 'examiners' only for an 'unofficial report and judgment on the dissertation',[29] whereupon Curtius wrote an extensive report in which he attests that the work, among other things, is 'a completely mature perspective on intellectual history' and shows 'great intellectual independence': 'I do not hesitate to declare that this is the best piece of work that I had to examine so far.' Dibelius immediately sent his report from Bonn, and Murray organized the promised documents. Thereupon, the dean declared the examination procedure formally opened. On 20 February, Curtius informed Schmitt: 'Difficulties regarding Murray's doctorate resolved.' At that time, he told Murray that he was 'extremely content' with her work. Only 'a few minor improvements' were still needed. 'Then you may submit the work straightaway and ask the dean for a quick date for the examination.'[30] Curtius's colleagues, Deutschbein and Elster, shared his positive assessment of the work. At the end of February, numerous members of faculty, including Paul Natorp, confirmed the assessment. On 8 February, the faculty received permission from Berlin to open the examination procedure. Only the classical philologist Ernst Maaß, who had political reservations, declared himself to be 'against granting permission'.

Murray passed her viva, with French as the main subject and German and English as subsidiary subjects, on 15 March. Elster and Deutschbein gave her a 'very good', Curtius 'good'. Schmitt travelled to Marburg for the occasion and also visited nearby Wetzlar, which was attractive on account, among other things, of its links to Goethe's *Werther*.* Stendhal's *De l'amour* ends with a juxtaposition of the figures of Don Juan and Werther: 'What makes me believe that a Werther is the happier man is that Don Juan reduces love to nothing but an ordinary matter.'[31] Schmitt oscillated between these alternatives. At that time, Georg Eisler sent 2,000 Marks to Murray yet also beseeched Schmitt not to take her with him to Bonn and 'live with her', but to put the relationship to the test with a period of separation.[32] This is what the couple did, at least in purely spatial terms. On 16 August there was a meeting with Curtius. Although in April they still spent some time together in Bonn, Schmitt then travelled with Kathleen via Heidelberg and Kehl to Strasbourg, and there, on 4 May, put her on a train to Toulon. Via Naples, Port Said and Colombo, Kathleen returned to Australia. Numerous love letters and 'weekly reports' now crossed the sea. Soon after her return, Murray sent a long travel diary 'in remembrance of happy days and glorious hopes'.†

In early May, Schmitt began lecturing in Bonn. The first weekend without 'K', he fled with Eisler via Frankfurt into the Taunus Mountains, where he visited the Saalburg, an old Roman castle, and indulged in 'Roman reminiscences' (TB, 14 May 1922). Back in Marburg, the procedures regarding the PhD examination were not yet closed. Murray had not

---

* Goethe's semi-autobiographical epistolary novel *The Sorrows of Young Werther* (1774) is set partly in Wetzlar, partly in a fictional village – Wahlheim – nearby. J. W. Goethe, *The Sorrows of Young Werther*, trans. Thomas Carlyle and R. D. Boylan, Newton Abbott: Dover, 2002.
† English in the original.

returned some of the books she had taken out from the library (for which Curtius vouched), and she had to implement some amendments that had been requested. Curtius wrote to Schmitt: 'I had no opportunity of seeing Miss Murray again, since the feast with you following the viva, and neither have I heard anything from her. Thus, I would be very grateful for some expert advice from you on how to proceed further in this matter.'[33] A few days later, Curtius wrote again: 'At the same time as your letter, for which many thanks, a few lines from Miss Murray arrived, which, however, did not touch upon the library matter. Meanwhile, I am inquiring at Miss M.'s apartment, and hope to achieve a "mediation", à la Adam Müller, of Celtic genius and German sense of order.'[34] The books, indeed, appeared again. Schmitt now set upon revising the dissertation and dictated changes in the university's typing department. He was immediately annoyed 'that so much good work was done for nothing' (TB, 19 May 1922). On 22 May he had a rather reserved meeting with Curtius in Bonn. The same evening, he took up Kathleen's dissertation again: 'Read in it, how beautiful and decent it is, every word is mine' (TB, 22 May 1922). Only after all this could the examination process be brought to a conclusion. The PhD certificate is dated 26 May. Murray was awarded the title of 'Doctor of Philosophy', with the dissertation being graded 'excellent' and the viva passed with a 'very good'. At that time, she was still at sea, arriving in Sydney only on 10 June. Schmitt's intense correspondence with Curtius now came to an almost complete end. The only later item in the posthumous papers is a postcard from Curtius to Schmitt dating, according to the stamp, from January 1924.[35]

Murray's dissertation, which she dedicated to Schmitt, appeared in November 1924 with Duncker & Humblot. Schmitt took care of the correspondence with the publishers, revised the text once again in April 1923 and also corrected the proofs. The study bears his mark, showing analytically that very diverse 'aspects' and 'ideals' served as guiding lines in Taine's representation of the complex topic 'English Romanticism'. Taine, in his contradictory manner, appears as 'one of the great symbolic and representative men of the nineteenth century'.[36] The preliminary remark is dated 'Sydney, October 1922'. At that point, the two active researchers of Romanticism already lived worlds apart.

The novella of the 'faithful gipsy'

In the past, Alice Berend had characterized Schmitt's role in his marriage with Cari as that of an absent-minded professor and a 'lucky devil' blinded by love. Now Schmitt digested his trials and tribulations in matters of love in the form of a draft for a novella titled *Der treue Zigeuner* [The faithful gipsy]. Here is the plot: a woman wants to seek absolution for her sins by going on a pilgrimage. Her husband, the faithful gipsy, has to carry her. During their journey various men fall for her gracefulness. Both man and woman die. After their deaths, all the world debates whether the charming lady should be 'canonized'. The draft, which was already completed in Marburg in April 1922, presents Schmitt as a gipsy in the role of the betrayed pack mule and also provides a caricature of the public debate over his personal story from the perspective of an 'advocatus diaboli' for the woman, while the idealization of the woman is explained with her hypocritical naivety and attractiveness. Thomas Mann's character Tonio Kröger (1903), as an 'aberrant citizen', longed for the 'gypsies in a blue carriage'. Schmitt no longer longed for gipsies, but saw himself as one. If we read the draft as an autobiographical reflection, it is first and foremost a paradox of faithfulness which Schmitt talks about – the possibility of a faithful gipsy and unfaithful innocence.

At that time, Franz Blei was looking for contributions to his journal. On 10 April 1922 he asked for the novella, a version of which Schmitt had read out to him at the end of February:[37] 'Dearest Doctor, dearest Professor, what is the matter with you? You wanted to send me your story of the gipsy, make me curious about it, but the story doesn't arrive.' The faithful gipsy sent the text, but wanted to give it to another journal via Pichler. Blei put some pressure on Schmitt: 'Dearest Doctor and Professor Schmitt, the unwaveringly faithful gipsy is a magnificent story, or rather the skeleton of a story. . . . I ask you, and implore you, deploy yourself to it and execute it, the way the matter requires.' Blei made concrete suggestions for its publication. 'You must set yourself to work, must put some flesh on it.'[38] Blei insistently pursued the matter: 'It is a pity that you retain such comfortable repose regarding the gipsy.'[39] Schmitt now demanded the draft be returned. Blei assured him: 'The gipsy, I see from my notes, I returned to your address at Bonn University weeks ago. What do you intend to do with it?'

The draft ends in satirical fashion with a disputation over the correct way of how to interpret the female figure and the novella overall, in the literary tradition of the conversation framing a series of novellas. Schmitt writes:

Unfortunately, I couldn't tell the story to Franz Blei. But I have no doubt that he would interpret it as presenting the relationship between the official Church and heresy which continues to drag the Church along, and nevertheless leads to hell. By contrast, an Irish woman, Kathleen Murray, personally assured me that she never read a more beautiful apologia of Roman Catholicism. After the perfidious profundity of Franz Blei's take on the story, this was a great relief. And yet, I would like to tell the story once again.[40]

The passage is, of course, ironic. After all, Schmitt had sent the draft to Blei, asking for his opinion. And the canonization of an unfaithful woman hardly corresponds to the Catholic spirit. Rather, it would be a compensation of 'soullessness' (RK, p. 16), something the novella mocks. Thus, in fact, Schmitt makes slight fun of Murray.

However, over the summer term of 1922, Schmitt constantly thought of 'K'. He sent her 'weekly reports' and reminisced about their time together. He was told irritating stories about orgies in Bonn by Kathleen's fellow student Miss Baumeister. He sought conversation with two Irish women, and he intended to work on Irish questions and to edit Irish songs. In every letter he expressed his willingness to get divorced and marry again. From August 1922, inspired by Kathleen's travel diary, he kept a love diary, 'The Shadow of God'.[41] He noted down drafts of his letters in a book and interspersed them with various notes and reflections. The book begins with vows of love and marriage and soon develops into a book of separation. 'Crazy world', it says. What you will! Cosi fan tutte! Thus do they all! Schmitt interpreted his confusion in religious terms. Like the Romantic fleeing God, he saw himself torn between the idolatry of women and 'the shadow of God' and as someone floating on a 'melting ice floe', looking out for the next one on which to jump. God throws a shadow because he has 'substance'. God's pneumatic 'shadow is proof of a substance'. But Schmitt lived in a state of 'dependence' on women. Christianity had 'dealt him a blow' so that now he wavered between God and world.

After a disappointing affair with the physician Carola (Lolo) Sauer, the 'faithful gipsy' soon ruefully remembered his relationship with Murray and was embarrassed about his 'unfaithfulness' (TB, 14 January 1923). He continued to see himself as a 'faithful gipsy', a Don Quixote, an Othello or a Bluebeard. 'There is after all only one woman for me, Kathleen' (7 February 1923), he noted down, full of 'longing', and he wanted to travel to Marburg, the place of remembrance, or to Australia. Later, he would make inquiries about the 'requirements for a departure to Australia' (9 May 1923). He seriously considered marrying Kathleen. Even after he had met his future wife, Duška Todorović, he again and again yearningly remembered 'K'. As late as August 1923, an Australian priest visited Schmitt as Kathleen's 'messenger'. By then, however, Carl had made a decision in favour of Duška. There must have been a deep attachment between Schmitt and Murray, on both sides. In December 1938, she met Schmitt again in Berlin and afterwards wrote a love letter to him. After Duška's death she again sought contact with him. We have letters and postcards that refer to memories and 'vows'.[42] Murray asks for a meeting in Germany or Australia. As late as 20 December 1960, she wrote: 'Do you want to see me again in this life, Carl? . . . If your reply to this letter does not mention anything about it, I shall see from this that my visit would not give you any pleasure, and I shall accept that.' Apparently, Schmitt did not answer this letter, because on 23 December 1971, fifty years after their liaison, Murray wrote to the vicarage in Plettenberg, inquiring whether 'a Professor emeritus, Dr Carl Schmitt, is still among your parishioners', from whom she had not heard for fourteen years. The late letters sound as if Murray had been waiting all her life. The impression of an early strategic relationship with her academic ghost writer is thus dispelled.

11

Arrival in Bonn? Schmitt's Turn
towards the Catholic Church

Become who you are!

Schmitt's move to Bonn took place under extreme time constraints. By a
decree of 25 March, his new post was confirmed, and on 30 March the
faculty learned about his move to Bonn, to take place on 1 April.[1] At the
time of his arrival, Schmitt had not yet really gained a name for himself
as a theorist of state law in the narrower sense – i.e., as an interpreter of
established law – apart from a succinct warning against an extension of
dictatorship. Schmitt had declared himself to be against a 'dictatorship
of the proletariat' and against an expansion of exceptional powers in the
direction of a 'sovereign' dictatorship. Although it was clear that he did
not identify 'right' with state 'law' in positivist fashion, what use he would
make of the fundamental premises of his philosophy of law was still an
open question. At the time, there were little more than fifty professors of
public law. An 'unpolitical' attitude of restraint was common among them.
And such an attitude was tactically to be recommended, especially in the
case of an uncalled-for newcomer. It was common to distinguish between
political opinion on the one hand and legal analysis on the other. However,
the guild of lawyers soon engaged with the controversial issues. Germany,
in the wake of Versailles, was drifting towards a political and economic
crisis. There was a 'general nationalization in the way questions were
posed'.[2] It was only during his time in Bonn that Schmitt's convictions as
a jurist became visible. Only then did he become the political author we
know today. And only with his appointment to the University of Bonn did
he achieve a permanent position at a large university which allowed him to
show his true colours. And finally, only because of the dramatic crisis of
1923 did he feel forced to make an intervention. It is therefore not incorrect
when he later said that his battle with Versailles, Geneva and Weimar did
not begin before 1923.

At the University of Bonn

At the time of Schmitt's arrival in 1922 there were more than 140,000
people living within the area of today's city limits. More than 3,000 had

fallen during the war. The city turned into a large hospital. At the end of 1920, the French took over from the English as the occupying force. The university had been founded in 1818 as a Prussian bulwark in the Western Rhenish provinces. From the smallest of the Prussian universities, Schmitt moved to the second largest,[3] attended by 4,285 students in the summer term 1922, the term Schmitt took up his post. There were 365 male students and four female students studying law.[4] In May, Schmitt began lecturing. Student numbers rose in the following years.

Before 1918, Ernst Landsberg, Ernst Zitelmann, Karl Bergbohm and the young Rudolf Smend were the stars of the law faculty. Schmitt became the successor to Smend, who took up a chair in Berlin at the beginning of the summer term 1922. By a decree of 28 June, Schmitt became a member of the examination committee at the Higher Regional Court in Cologne. The juridical faculty resided on the ground floor of the castle at Franziskanerstraße 13 at the Stockentor. The resources weren't ample; there was just one shared room for all lecturers, and there were few assistants and aides.[5] To begin with, the institute had three departments. Zitelmann's 'Institut für internationales Privatrecht' [Institute for international private law] continued to exist. Erich Kaufmann directed a 'Seminar für wissenschaftliche Politik' [Seminar for political science] and Schmitt founded a 'Politisches Seminar' [Political science seminar]. A provisional

'Maybe it is just Protestant theology' – Carl Schmitt about Rudolf Smend's constitutional theory in a letter to Feuchtwanger (4 June 1928)

solution was found, according to which Kaufmann and Schmitt agreed to have a common 'Seminar für wissenschaftliche Politik', or an 'Institut für internationales Recht und Politik' [Institute of international law and politics], from the summer term 1923 onwards. For the winter term 1923–4, Schmitt was the director for the whole juridical seminar.

Schmitt taught state law, administrative law and international law, as well as politics and the history of political ideas. His announcements in the *Vorlesungsverzeichnis* were very vaguely formulated. The standard curriculum was taught in turns, and hence the course descriptions showed little about the individual academic profile of the teacher.[6] The membership of the faculty fluctuated greatly. From 1922, Erich Kaufmann was almost continuously on leave, a fact that put a strain on the whole faculty.[7] He continued to show a lively interest in questions regarding appointments. Professors declined, substitutes had to be found. Ernst Landsberg, Hans Schreuer, Heinrich Göppert and Fritz Schulz – the latter moved to Bonn in 1923 – were permanent figures at Bonn who taught alongside Schmitt. Ernst Isay was a Privatdozent. Schreuer was the second examiner of some of the early dissertations that Schmitt supervised. During the summer term 1922, Schmitt acquainted himself with the faculty. At the beginning, Erich Kaufmann and Ernst Landsberg were his closest colleagues. Schmitt socialized with them, and occasionally they attended each other's lectures. Schmitt also established a relationship with Landsberg's son, Paul Ludwig, a young philosopher who had just completed his doctorate with Max Scheler. Paul Ludwig Landsberg had enthusiastically read *Political Romanticism* and had had a hand in Schmitt's appointment. In the summer term 1922, Schmitt also had close social contacts with the expert in civil law Josef Partsch, who then moved to Berlin. Then there was Albert Hensel. Schmitt's remarks on him, however, were frequently ambivalent. Hensel had completed his doctorate with Triepel in Berlin in 1920.[8] Kaufmann brought him to Bonn as a 'faculty assistant'. In 1922, Hensel obtained his *venia legendi*, and in May the same year had already received a teaching assignment for administrative law with Schmitt's placet; he went on to substitute for Kaufmann and, with Schmitt's support, became an extraordinary professor with effect from 1 July 1923.[9] The speed of his career progression annoyed Schmitt so much that he even considered initiating 'disciplinary procedures'.[10] As a party member, Hensel was for some time active on the city council for the DVP.* In 1929, he moved to Königsberg as a pioneer in fiscal law. During Schmitt's early years in Bonn, Joseph Heimberger and Gerhart Husserl, the philosopher's son who had returned as an invalid from the war, were also on the teaching faculty. From the winter term 1926–7, Alexander Graf zu Dohna taught penal law and philosophy of law.

---

* Deutsche Volkspartei = German People's Party, a national liberal party in the Weimar Republic.

Catholicism as a political creed

Schmitt's years in Bonn are generally considered to have been his best. He was part of an important faculty and, together with colleagues, worked on questions regarding the 'dispute over the direction' to be taken in the field of legal methodology [Richtungsstreit]; it was here that he developed his constitutional theory, and it was here that he formed a seminar that produced notable disciples. In Bonn, Schmitt decisively took sides in matters of constitutional policy for the first time and presented himself explicitly as a Catholic thinker. Like his acquaintances from Munich, Theodor Haecker, Franz Blei, Konrad Weiß and others, Schmitt, under the influence of Kierkegaard, wanted to leave aestheticism behind and aimed for a renewal of religious commitment. This turn corresponded to a broad movement in the published literature stretching beyond Germany. At stake was a new definition of the relationship between Catholicism and modernity and the creation of a new Catholic intellectuality through the reception of literary modernism. Word went around of a 'rebirth of poetry out of religious experience'.[11] Religiosity was sought outside of forms of clerical organization. The phenomenology of religion discovered 'the holy' in moments of epiphany. The theology of history became devoutness in the face of fate [Schicksalsfrömmigkeit].

Baudelaire and Dostoevsky, Paul Claudel, Léon Bloy and Georges Bernanos were some of the authors who presented a radical interpretation of the difference between religion and morality. They pushed the difference to the point where morality and religion became antitheses and where Satanism became a religious attitude. Bloy met a prostitute and tried to save her by marrying her. The prostitute transformed into a saint

'I do not belong with these people' – Carl Schmitt in his diary after a meeting with Erich Kaufmann (13 February 1924)

and became mad.[12] Wilhelm Neuß told Schmitt 'stories about young girls who sacrifice themselves' (TB, 1 July 1922). That is what Schmitt wanted from the women he met. He intensely read Charles Maurras and Cardinal Newman – a book he had received as a birthday present from Cari (TB, 10 July 1922).[13] Schmitt read Stendhal's *Le Rouge et le noir*, edited by Franz Blei, as part of an edition of Stendhal's oeuvre. And he identified with Julien Sorel, the intellectually talented, poor and proud soldier of fortune for whom the clerical milieu of post-Napoleonic times was only a vehicle for his social climbing, and who ended up spectacularly under the guillotine. French Catholicism exerted some influence on the discussions in Germany. Schmitt called the *Action française* 'the most interesting newspaper available at present' (CSLF, p. 89). Between 1928 and 1939 it was on the index of the Church. Its anti-Semitic orientation influenced the Vichy government.[14] Carl Muth and the newspaper *Hochland* became the moderate vanguard of a revival in Catholic literature at the time. Hermann Platz,[15] in reaction to French nationalism, formulated a Catholic critique of nationalism. Ernst Robert Curtius[16] made more recent French literature known in Germany. In Bonn, Schmitt was in close contact with Hermann Platz, who suggested a joint edition of a collection of work on recent French intellectual history [Geistesgeschichte].[17] Schmitt was also somewhat in contact with Victor Klemperer[18] and became friendly with the theologians Wilhelm Neuß, Erik Peterson and Karl Eschweiler. At the time, Eschweiler was working through the recent history of theology and had read Jacques Maritain, a neo-Thomist who had taken on board the French avant-garde.[19] From his early days, Schmitt's French had been near native, and he read the literature in the original. He regularly talked about French literature with Franz Blei, who was one of its main popularizers.[20] George Bernanos[21] and Léon Bloy were among his staple authors. For some time, Schmitt was also in closer contact with Jacques Maritain.

Within the broad stream of Catholic literature at the time, various positions were represented: lay religion and mysticism at the outer edge of the Church as well as aestheticism, authoritarian statism and anarchism. Protestant theology also became more radical during these times. Adolf von Harnack moved from an interest in St Paul to Marcion,[22] bringing the Pauline oppositions between Judaism and Christianity, a religion of laws and Christian charity, Old and New Testament, to a head in Marcion's new gospel of the 'alien God'. On the basis of the opposition between a Christian God as the unknown redeemer and a Judaeo-Christian God as the known creator of the world, Marcion had reconstructed the gospel as a biblical theology. He made 'soteriology the centre of his teachings' and provided the 'decisive impulse for the creation of the Old Catholic Church'.[23] Even Harnack, a representative of Wilhelminian erudition, went beyond St Paul and Luther in order to make a 'clean sweep'[24] and discarded the Old Testament as the 'book of the inferior Jewish God'[25] in favour of the love of early Christianity. Tolstoy and Maxim Gorki appeared to him as contemporary examples of a Christianity in the spirit of Marcion. Karl Barth pushed the idea of the gospel of an 'alien God' to the paradoxical extreme of a 'negative theology'.[26] The dismissal of the 'just' God of the Old Testament was also interpreted in anti-Semitic terms at the time. Although Carl Schmitt was no follower of Marcion and did not dismiss history or argue exegetically, he nevertheless was very preoccupied with the antithetical version of Christianity as it was also formulated by Rudolph Sohm in his *Kirchenrecht* [Canon law]. In the 'shadow of God', Schmitt at the time experienced the alternative between God and world as an idolatrous fallenness and 'dependence' on the female sex. The negativistic or dialectical creation of a paradoxical God led him to a renewed affirmation of the Church as an institution. If the gospel is not of this world, then the Church need not be embarrassed about becoming a worldly institution. Religion and Church are meant to heal the state. Early on in Bonn, Schmitt realized: 'I really do not belong to this "Zentrum" culture'* (TB, 11 June 1922). He even spoke of 'atheism' (TB, 15 May 1922). Charles Maurras formulated the well-known phrase: 'Je suis athée, mais je suis catholique.' Franz Blei also applied it to himself: 'What is called salvation does not mean anything to me, and I take the claim that Christ had to die "for us" on the cross as an ordinary priestly trick in order to shirk responsibility for this mean deed of executing him. . . . Hence, I am a Godless cleric. Just like yourself, dear friend.'[27] These words are somewhat surprising because rather the opposite applied to Schmitt's 'scholastic deliberations' – i.e., Christian reservations against the Church. Blei did not fully believe in Schmitt's Christian creed. And Schmitt's acquaintance Heinrich Merk, as the reader may remember, had remarked not entirely without irony: 'If one day a chair for the defence of the Spanish Inquisition is created in Munich, you will have to be its holder, and I shall be your most faithful listener.'[28]

Schmitt came from Munich to Bonn with *Dictatorship* and his contribution for the *Erinnerungsgabe für Max Weber*. He used the phenomenon of dictatorship to establish that the distinction between power and right is created by elementary 'decisions' and that legal norms are determined by fundamental decisions. In his contribution to the *Erinnerungsgabe*, Schmitt asked the question of the 'metaphysical' prerequisites of personalism and decisionism. The contribution concluded with discussions of Donoso Cortés, who, 'in reference to the revolution of 1848' (PT, p. 51), broke with the principle of dynastic legitimacy and demanded open dictatorship. In the last paragraph, Schmitt wrote: 'A detailed presentation of this kind of decisionism and a thorough appreciation of Donoso Cortés are not yet available' (PT, p. 52). Thus, we may conclude that he originally intended the last chapter of *Political Theology* as a study of Cortés. In June 1922, shortly after Kathleen's departure, Schmitt began his work on Cortés by writing a sketch of the overall development of the *Counter-Revolutionary Philosophy of the State* from Maistre, via Bonald, to Cortés, a sketch that shows the development 'from legitimacy to dictatorship' (PT, p. 56). Schmitt had already prepared the ground for linking up his work

---

*   'Zentrumsmilieu' – an expression for the characteristic social and political attitudes associated with the *Zentrumspartei* which, during the Weimar Republic, represented a political Catholicism that was loyal to the constitution. Bonn and Cologne belong to a predominantly Catholic area of Germany.

with this philosophy of the state in his *Political Romanticism*, where the authors of the counter-revolution figured as an alternative to romantic Catholicism. Schmitt had discarded political Romanticism in order to present the counter-revolutionary philosophy of the state in a positive light.[29] His critique of Romanticism was 'only a prelude' (CSLF, p. 151). Only in the fourth chapter does Schmitt openly commit himself to an interventionist political theology, to the counter-revolutionary philosophy of the state and to a dictatorship that has broken with the tradition of dynastic legitimacy. To that end, he emphasizes the opposition between the Romantics and the Catholic philosophers of the state. 'Dictatorship is the opposite of discussion' (PT, p. 63). Schmitt revels in anthropological pessimism and 'outbursts' against the anarchist 'axiom of the good man' (PT, p. 57). His studies of Cortés are not least a stylized portrait of himself. Following Cortés, he saw anarchism as the worst enemy[30] because, in contrast to Marx, Schmitt says, Bakunin took theology seriously and realized that it was the foundation of the 'idea of the political'.[31] Following Cortés, Schmitt mobilized the intensity of the 'decision' and the reduction of the state to its dictatorial core. And also following Cortés, he conceived of political theology as a political programme to be actively pursued. For Schmitt, in Cortés's step from legality to dictatorship lay his 'actuality'. With these points, Schmitt went beyond the analytic approach he had taken in his contribution to the *Erinnerungsgabe*. The historical parallels were so obvious, for a contemporary reader, that almost all of them would have read this historical study as also an immediate intervention and a plea for dictatorship. Schmitt's study was first published in the autumn of 1922 in a special issue of *Archiv für Rechts- und Wirtschaftsphilosophie* on *Kirchliche Rechtphilosophie* [Ecclesiastical philosophy of law], and then as the final chapter to the programmatic *Political Theology* at the end of 1922. Once in Bonn, Schmitt declared his commitment to a politically committed Catholicism.

Table 11.1 Polarizations 1919–1923

Liberalism/Romanticism	Revolution	Counter-revolution
Guizot, Adam Müller	Proudhon, Bakunin	Donoso Cortés
	Marx, Lasalle	

A 'concrete' Church without reservations?

After the study of the counter-revolutionary philosophy of the state, Schmitt worked on his famous essay *Roman Catholicism and Political Form* while staying with Georg Eisler in Hamburg in the late summer of 1922. Kathleen Murray was the biographical background to this. 'The LORD is thy shade', he read in the Psalms (Ps. 121: 5–6), so that '[t]he sun shall not smite thee by day.' God's pneuma covers man like a shadow;[32] it darkens human reason and effects an 'ecstasy of the soul'. Schmitt tried to come to a religious understanding of his confusion in matters of love but remained silent on this in his essay on the 'political idea' of Catholicism.

He distinguished, so to speak, between private faith, which he confided to his love diary, and public confession – the essay is a piece with a strong narrative voice, and it sees things through the eyes of a counter-revolutionary. But precisely whose eyes are they? If those of Cortés, he would have to plead for 'dictatorship' and adopt an anthropological pessimism. But in 1922–3, rather than doing that, he followed de Maistre and his praise of the 'stately authority' ['obrigkeitlicher Autorität'] of the Church. Schmitt sang a song of praise for the 'political form' of the Church and for its idea of 'representation'.[33]

Schmitt assumed an 'anti-Roman affect' in his opponents, a fear of the power of the Church, of historical 'continuity' and political flexibility. The Church, as a 'complexio oppositorum' (here Schmitt implicitly quotes Adolf von Harnack),[34] unites all sorts of tendencies and inclinations under its form. In doing so, it stands in opposition to the capitalist 'operation' and the dominant 'economic thinking'. As successor to Christ, the Church transforms 'priesthood into an office' (RK, pp. 19f.) and gives individual human beings a 'personal mission' and 'dignity'. The Church is the 'true heir to Roman jurisprudence' (RK, p. 26). Schmitt praises the Church's 'strength in producing three great forms: the aesthetic form of the arts, the juridical form of the law and, finally, the glorious splendour of a world historical form of power' (RK, p. 30). By contrast, he denies liberalism and capitalism any form. He sharply juxtaposes the great 'rhetoric' of the Church, which he also finds embodied in the counter-revolutionary 'image' of dictatorship and of the final judgment, and parliamentary representation, identifying the current enemy less in Protestantism, liberalism or Marxism than in anarchism. In political terms, he is afraid of an alliance between the proletariat and its class struggle and the 'Russian culture which turns away from Europe' (RK, p. 51). Again, Schmitt singles out Bakunin as the enemy. In his hands, Marxism had become dangerous once again, because he had mobilized the 'lumpenproletariat'. What Schmitt has in mind is the situation of a revolutionary civil war after 1918 and a certain analogy between Bakunin and contemporary anarchists. The opposition between 'normativism' and 'decisionism' he now translates into the distinction between state and Church. ·

Schmitt ties the 'political form' of the Church to its 'invocation of the idea' (RK, p. 37), to authoritarian hierarchy and the identification of the theological enemy, where the enemy is the anarchist battle (of Bakunin) against the Christian 'idea'. At the same time as Schmitt was working on his essay, the second volume of Sohm's *Kirchenrecht* was published.[35] However, Schmitt rejects, in passing, Sohm's Protestant critique of the Church as an establishment, because he makes the possibility of following Christ conditional upon institutional continuity. He silently drops his previous thoughts about an early Christian apocalyptic 'proviso' and no longer makes any use of the distinction between a 'visible' and a 'concrete' Church. Rather, he speaks about the 'concrete' Church as a 'political form' without again entering into any 'scholastic reflections'. The rhetoric of the essay drowns out Schmitt's previous theological differentiations and reservations. He constructs the Church as an authoritarian bastion without offering a model of canon law that would establish the relation between the 'Church of the spirit and the Church of the law' ['Geistkirche und Rechtskirche']. At the end of the essay, the reader has not been told what Schmitt's opting for the form of the Church will mean for the actual relationship to the state. Does he praise the Church as a centre of order and guarantor of stability for the overall constitution? Or does he unmask it as a worldly power?

The Catholicism essay was written in 1922 in two stages. Franz Blei was one of Schmitt's closest partners in dialogue about Catholicism at that time. As early as the middle of 1922, Blei expected the printed version of the essay to appear. Moritz Julius Bonn read the 'brilliant piece'[36] in October. Schmitt later saw Blei again in Berlin, where he also met the Catholic-Jewish publisher Jakob Hegner.[37] After an intensive discussion, Schmitt made known his surprise about the latter's 'capacity for metaphysics' [metaphysische Möglichkeiten]. Schmitt retracted the essay from the journal *Dioskuren*[38] and in November 1922[39] gave it to the innovative publishing house of Hegner in Hellerau, which had once also published the journal *Summa* and was known for its editions for bibliophiles. Schmitt decided on the new title for the essay on 22 January 1923, the same day he met Duška Todorović for the first time. The essay only appeared at the end of April 1923. A 'beautiful book', Schmitt noted. 'Dear Doctor Schmitt', Blei wrote, 'many thanks for the magnificent publication that Hegner has now sent me – it has grown very much beyond its inner and outer volume in comparison to the first manuscript that I read at that time.' 'Sohm should still have met you', he continued, 'so that he would have had what he didn't have [Harnack?!], an enemy of proper rank. However, subtract from "enemy" any too strong emphasis, as, after all, you are not altogether opposed.'[40] Blei here referred to the following passage: 'Rudolf Sohm believed he had found the Fall [of the Church] in the juridical; others saw it, grander and deeper, in the will to dominate the world' (RK, pp. 43ff.). Blei's point is reminiscent of the early Christian 'proviso' that Schmitt introduced with his distinction between the 'concrete' and the 'visible' Church. The intellectual approach of the eulogy of 1923 is actually simpler than that of the 'scholastic reflection' of 1917. It is that of a secular apotheosis of 'Roman' Catholicism that 'brackets the religious in Catholicism'[41] and refers to other dimensions of the Church – i.e., its aesthetic, legal and political forms. With his essay, Schmitt positioned himself on the side of efforts at a renewal of an intellectual Catholicism, of an anti-romantic, Catholic 'classicism' (Carl Muth, Hermann Hefele), of the defence of the 'West' [des 'Abendlandes'] and of a limitation of capitalism. At the same time he established his distance from various other notions such as 'natural law' and the Catholic revocation of the idea of the Reich.[42] Hence, representatives of the Catholic left at once registered their opposition.[43] Waldemar Gurian brought the essay to the attention of Werner Becker, who, in 1923, joined Schmitt in Bonn and straightaway began work on his dissertation on Hobbes, 'because Hobbes, with his new concept of order, created a complete counter-system to the (medieval-)Christian one'.[44] Hans Barion would later also find his way to Schmitt through the essay.

The favourable conditions of the contract for the Catholicism essay were intended by the publisher as an advance on a 'series of treatises' that Schmitt had promised. Instead, he soon withdrew it, being dissatisfied with the sales. Despite all the old 'friendship', this led to some tensions in the relationship. Hegner asked Schmitt: 'Where is the new treatise? The nice beginning of your "Roman Catholicism" – should it all be over already? Two or three treatises per year were intended.'[45] This would have made Schmitt a Catholic in-house author, such as Haecker and then Josef Pieper later became. But after the quarrels surrounding Schmitt's divorce this was no longer an option. Hegner wanted a lecture given in Cologne on 'Romanticism and Politics' for the series,[46] but he soon wrote to Schmitt, not without irritation: 'Back then, we had agreed that you would publish a series of treatises with me. This was, after all, my main interest. You must admit that I have fulfilled all your wishes.'[47] Hegner assured Schmitt: 'Your booklet "Roman Catholicism" sells well'; he continued to follow up on the 'idea of a series of treatises' and wanted an expanded version of the *Summa* essay 'Über die Unsichtbarkeit der Kirche' [On the invisibility of the Church] to follow the Catholicism title in the same layout and format.[48] In the autumn of 1924, Hegner envisaged a second edition[49] but later wrote with resignation: 'I forego, forego, forego!'[50] At the end of May 1925, the Verein katholischer Akademiker[51] [Association of Catholic academics] requested the Catholicism essay, and at once transferred an honorarium of 500 Reichsmark. Soon afterwards the Theatiner publishing house confirmed the receipt of stylistic improvements[52] and Schmitt received the proofs.[53] And yet, on 10 August 1925,[54] Hegner once more picked up the old plan of a 'series of treatises': 'Now, I would like suggest that you let me have an expanded version of "Schicksal des Politischen"[55] [Fate of the political], to be published as a book and a companion piece to the "Idee" [Idea]. I would give it a similarly attractive layout as the "Idee".' Hegner wanted to keep the brochure as part of his programme, but Schmitt published it, with slight stylistic revisions and in an edition of 3,000 copies, as part of the series of the Association of Catholic Academics, alongside texts by theologians such as Grabmann, Przywara, Ildefons Herwegen and Mausbach. It may be that he was looking, with his divorce proceedings in mind, for the imprimatur of the Church. After these had failed, he did not publish any more theological treatises.

12

Schmitt as a Teacher in Bonn

Changing affections: Duška

In Bonn, Schmitt had to arrange his life on a new basis. His everyday life continued to be restless. His landlady, Mrs von Wandel,[1] took some care of him; yet he was now living on his own, was permanently visiting restaurants, in particular in the cultural centre 'Bürgerverein' in the Poppelsdorfer Allee, and was meeting with acquaintances. For the first months, settling down and the new teaching post took centre stage. After having revised Murray's dissertation, Schmitt wrote a review of a book on issues regarding the property of the Wittelsbach family – i.e., regarding the liquidation of 'dynastic legitimacy' – for an acquaintance from Munich, Konrad Beyerle.[2] At the end of July, Feuchtwanger came to Bonn for a weekend in order to make arrangements for an honorary doctorate to be awarded to Carl Geibel, the owner of the publishing house Duncker & Humblot.[3] Schmitt told Feuchtwanger the story of the 'faithful gipsy' and of his marriage (diary entries for 28 and 29 July 1922). The publication of *Political Theology* was most likely decided on that occasion. Schmitt constantly had to correspond with 'the lady' in Munich about the proportion of the rent and the subsistence he had to pay her. Cari was not yet completely written out of the picture. Schmitt spoke of 'bigamy' (27 May 1922). Although he was again in contact with Dr Max Hirschberg, who had represented him in the case of Cari's legal affairs in 1920, he did not yet formally open the divorce proceedings and actually looked for another lawyer. On the one hand, definite evidence for Cari's imposture was still missing, which is why Schmitt was making inquiries in Croatia. On the other hand, he observed the development of the relationship with Kathleen. At that point, there was a clear connection between divorce proceedings and marriage plans. Schmitt wanted to get divorced so that he could marry Kathleen, although he had not entirely decided that he would do so. His brother Jupp, his cousin André and Georg Eisler, who all knew Kathleen, advised him not to marry her. And Kathleen could also not shake off her Catholic reservations altogether, nor entirely convince her mother. Only in the autumn of 1922 did Schmitt learn officially that he had married a confidence trickster who had faked her date of birth and her descent. It is astounding that he did not notice this for ten whole years, in particular as Cari had also conjured up for herself a good education and a large family. Now Schmitt wanted to enter into divorce proceedings.

In the documents, Schmitt declares that he gradually developed 'grounds for suspicion' after his marriage. Cari had repeatedly become criminally conspicuous. In the spring of 1920, at the latest, Schmitt should have begun to have had thoughts about the suspected forgery of documents. Upon his move to Greifswald and falling in love with Kathleen Murray, he dropped the 'Dorotić' from his name. Back then, he had already asked his cousin to give evidence, and André had been prepared to do that.[4] But only in 1922, after his arrival in Bonn, did Schmitt have the academic standing that allowed him to survive a scandal. Before that, the story of Cari could have cost him his chances of being appointed. His marriage plans with Murray meant that Schmitt was looking not only for a divorce but also for an annulment of his first marriage, which would have allowed him to marry again with a religious blessing. For Murray was Irish, and it was above all the religious ceremony that counted for her. Schmitt pleaded for 'fraud in the strict criminal sense'. The fraud as such annuls the marriage! However, the divorce trial made the question of marriage fraud dependent on whether or not the promise to marry Cari had been linked to her aristocratic descent. Would a common descent have been an obstacle to the marriage? Did Schmitt want only to marry an aristocrat? His initial time in Bonn was heavily burdened by these questions. The trial dragged on, with jurisdiction for it moving from Munich to Bonn at the beginning of 1923. Schmitt changed his lawyer, dropping Hirschberg in favour of a Dr Meyer I. Schmitt now referred to Cari only pejoratively as 'the lady'; mentioning her name would remain a life-long taboo in his house.

From the very beginning, Schmitt was seeking to establish contacts in Bonn beyond the law faculty. He was acquainted with the classical philologist Rudolf Thurneysen and the historian Aloys Schulte. Already in May, through a friend of am Zehnhoff, Wilhelm Kisky,[5] he got to know Wilhelm Neuß, who was working on the early history of Catholicism in the Rhineland from the perspective of art history.[6] Schmitt met Karl Heinrich Vormfelde, who had held the chair for agricultural machinery and applied physics since 1920. Whitsun 1922 he spent with his parents in Plettenberg. In mid-June he met the musicologist Arnold Schmitz,[7] who was writing a book on *Das romantische Beethovenbild* [The Romantic image of Beethoven]. The book distinguished Beethoven from Romanticism and, according to the preface, was 'particularly indebted to' Schmitt.[8] Schmitz became a friend for life, whereas Schmitt's relationship with Vormfelde later became more distant. Schmitt was more closely associated with Neuß, even beyond his years in Bonn, just as this period in his life was in general characterized by conversations with theologians. His social networks reaching into Catholic circles were so close-knit that Andreas Koenen,[9] in his pioneering work, so rich in sources, identifies him as a source of inspiration for a strategically operating group of 'Reichstheologen' [theologians of the Reich]. However, Schmitt was not dedicated to a particular group; rather, he sought influence in various circles.

Schmitt's first doctoral students introduced themselves: Dr phil.

Bernhard Braubach and Anton Betz. The assassination of Rathenau occupied Schmitt a great deal. He was horrified by it, but then, after the 'suicide of Rathenau's murderers'* (TB, 19 July 1922), also felt pity for the perpetrators. Old relationships were revitalized in Bonn, such as the contact with am Zehnhoff, now no longer characterized by ambivalence, and the familial contact with his brother Jupp, who practised medicine close by in Cologne. Schmitt also maintained some of his friendships in Munich. Several times, for instance, he met with his military comrade Georg von Schnitzler and his wife Lilly. Schnitzler was now living in Frankfurt as a successful industrialist. Schmitt's cousin André appeared frequently; after the end of term, he visited Bonn for a couple of weeks, and Schmitt provided him with ideas for a book project. In mid-August, they both travelled along the Mosel to Trier, where Schmitt vividly recalled the trip he had undertaken with Kathleen in April, and from where he again sent the promises he had made to Australia. Afterwards, he went to visit Eisler for a couple of weeks in Hamburg. Eisler was by then working in the advertisement trade ['Annoncen-Expedition'] of his father. Schmitt provided some legal advice. For a few days in mid-September, he travelled to Heligoland with his cousin André. In Hamburg, Schmitt renewed the old friendship from his student days with Eduard Rosenbaum,[10] who had become the general counsel to the chamber of commerce and director of the famous Commerzbibliothek† in 1919. He met the editor Kurt Singer, the Oberregierungsrat [senior government adviser] Alfred Bertram[11] and the theorist of state law Albrecht Mendelssohn-Bartholdy. Through his contact with Singer,[12] an important Jewish economist and a member of the Jünger circle, Schmitt published several reviews in the *Wirtschaftsdienst* in the following years.

In the late summer of 1922, Schmitt was still very much yearning for Kathleen Murray and mourning her departure; he talked himself into believing in an idealism of love. But soon he was to meet the young medical doctor Ella Carola (Lolo) Sauer. Lolo was from Hamburg and had studied in Kiel and Munich from 1915. In 1921 she passed her state examination in Munich and then did her year of practical training. From September 1921 she worked in the polyclinic of Munich University, where she also received her doctorate in 1922. Schmitt's love diary on 'God's shadow' now mutated into a book describing his affections changing and moving to focus on a new woman. In mid-October, Schmitt travelled to Berlin to attend the first congress of state law theorists and then on to see Lolo in Munich. In mid-November, he again travelled to Lo. In December his contribution to the Weber *Erinnerungsgabe* appeared.[13] At that point, Schmitt spent a couple of days in Berlin, giving a lecture, possibly in connection with the prospect of an appointment there. He also met Franz Blei on this occasion. He pushed on with his divorce. Schmitt spent the Christmas break with Lolo, first in Hamburg, then in Munich. During that time, he said

---

* Only one of the assassins committed suicide, during a stand-off with the police.
† Founded in 1735, this is the oldest library specializing in economics. It is a part of the Hamburg chamber of commerce.

farewell to the 'lady' Cari, not without gratefulness and regret (TB, 2 and 3 January 1923). 'Helpless, who knows what will become of her', he on one occasion noted in his diary (TB, 6 May 1923).[14] January 1923 might have been the last time he saw her. Hugo am Zehnhoff inquired about the state of 'the matter',[15] just when Schmitt was bringing the case to Bonn. With Lolo Sauer, Schmitt was disappointed. As a 'denizen of Schwabing'* she led an easy and relaxed life, and her replies to his letters were too distanced for his liking. Nevertheless, Carl made efforts, contacting the psychiatrist Gustav Aschaffenburg, the director of the 'mental asylum' in Lindenthal, Cologne,[16] to find her a position as an assistant. However, he quickly began to see her as a 'pathetic carousel lady' (TB, 20 February 1923) and parted with her.[17]

At that time, Schmitt got to know Dušanka (Duška) Todorović (13 February 1903–3 December 1950), who would later become his second wife. She was born in Grozdanska (Grizanska), a few kilometres to the east of Agram (Zagreb), the daughter of Vasilije Todorović and his wife, Julijana, née Belajević.[18] The grandparents on her father's side were from Skenderovći (just under 100 kilometres to the south-east of Zagreb); on her mother's side they were from Voćin, about 20 kilometres east of Daruvar. Duška had (at least) one sister, of roughly the same age, and a brother. She did not have an easy childhood. She was frequently ill. In 1910, the parents divorced, whereupon her mother returned with her to Daruvar, from where her father 'kidnapped' her back to Agram. For Duška, Agram and Daruvar remained the two most important places in her homeland, which belonged to an area with a Serbian Orthodox minority within the Croatian region. Until 1918, it belonged to the multi-ethnic Austro-Hungarian state; after 1918 it became part of the newly created Kingdom of the Serbs, Croats and Slovenians.[19] At the beginning, there were border disputes with Austria; later, the national conflict between Croats and Serbs, which was primarily religious in character, erupted.

On 3 November 1922, Duška arrived from Agram and registered as a student of philosophy in Bonn. Schmitt met her for the first time on 22 January 1923 in her capacity as a translator in his divorce proceedings. The very next evening he met her again: 'The date of her birthday is the same as that of my marriage. Uncanny' (TB, 23 January 1923). Schmitt now definitely parted with Lolo. At the end of January he found a couple of days' rest, staying with the Schnitzlers in Frankfurt. The relationship with Duška, who was almost fifteen years his junior and only nineteen years of age, was restrained at first, with walks on the Rhine. However, Schmitt noted in his diary: 'Uncanny silence. I presume the catastrophe is approaching. I feel a strange kind of confidence. The same as in February 1915 [the time of his marriage to Cari]. So Duška tonight' (TB, 31 January 1923). Yet Schmitt compared her again and again with Murray, and for some time continued saying: 'There is after all only one woman for me, Kathleen.' On 10 February, Schmitt visited the Wallraf Richartz Museum in Cologne with Duška. A little later they went to see 'a wonderful per-

---

* Schwabing: a part of Munich renowned for its Bohemian life-style.

formance of Don Giovanni' in Cologne together. After three weeks, the
intimacy of the relationship became fairly apparent: 'I was amazed about
Duška's self-assurance. When I asked: Now, do you believe that Elvira
is being betrayed by Don Juan, she answered: It is she who has betrayed
herself' (TB, 16 February 1923). Was this a reassuring *carte blanche* for
Schmitt? He noted down: 'In the course of watching the opera, a wild
desire to hold life with both hands, then again worries about the devaluation of the [Reichs]Mark, finally cheerful, inspired by Mozart's music and
the beautiful evening with the intelligent, good girl Duška.' As she was
apparently not strikingly beautiful, he praised her 'delicate' – later actually
rather portly – figure and elegant demeanour. He wrote a review of Leo
Wittmayer's book *Reichsverfassung und Politik* [The Reich's constitution
and politics] in one day. But when he was told by a 'cleric from Sydney' that
Kathleen wasn't well, Schmitt was tortured by his conscience. With Lo he
was 'done' (TB, 26 February 1923). But in his love diary on 'God's shadow'
he renewed his decision to enter into marriage with Murray. Numerous
love letters now crossed the sea between Australia and Europe. On the
anniversary of Murray's viva in Marburg, Schmitt was again faced with
the question of whether or not he should marry.

Schmitt's socializing with Arnold Schmitz deepened his relationship
with music. He had Mozart and Chopin played to him and visited concerts
and the opera. Otto Klemperer had moved from Strasbourg to Cologne
and directed the opera (until 1924) in an avant-garde spirit. Schmitt talked
with Duška about Russian literature, and he gradually gained the impression 'that she gets used to me' and has 'great interest' (TB, 23 March
1923) in him. On 27 March he drove to Munich, where he was horrified
to find that Cari had sold his furniture and was gone. Even at the very
last moment he fell for her tricks. He soon found out that, in the words of
am Zehnhoff, 'the accused has sold the household furnishings and left the
country.'[20] Schmitt travelled on to his friend Krause in Bad Tölz, where
he took hiking tours in the mountains and also wrote a report on a book
by Günther Holstein,[21] the Protestant theorist of state law and disciple of
Kaufmann, who was now his substitute at Greifswald and later obtained a
personal chair there. The report caused Schmitt some headaches, as he was
indebted to Kaufmann but rejected Holstein's work on Schleiermacher.
He revised Murray's dissertation for publication. The Catholicism essay
appeared. Schmitt spent almost three weeks in Bad Tölz. During that time,
he became so friendly with Krause's young daughter Iser that Mrs Krause
suggested half-seriously that he could 'marry her and take her to Bonn with
him' (TB, 12 April 1923). From 16 April he spent some days in Munich,
where he followed the political crisis intently. Iser came along, and Schmitt
met her again and again, such that Duška became pretty much forgotten.
In Munich, Schmitt also saw his colleague Wilhelm Neuß and brought him
together with another friend of his, the art historian and librarian Hans
Rupé, in order to help with Neuß's studies on early Christian art. He met
Feuchtwanger and his old captain, Roth.

For his treatise on parliamentarism, Schmitt read speeches by Mussolini.
In Bad Tölz he had a political argument with an Oberregierungsrat [senior

government advisor]: Schmitt was afraid of 'the possibility of a division' of the Reich, of a triumph of separatism, as a result of which, together with the 'left government', 'the National Socialists' would rise' (15 April 1923). In this mood he again met Captain Roth, who was an important organizer of National Socialist alliances at the time. A few days later the two met once more. 'The talk was about the National Socialists; was surprised (harmless all that, probably) at the legal-mindedness of the Bavarian civil servants' (TB, 20 April 1923). The perspective of Schmitt's early view of National Socialism was determined by his knowledge of his fellow officers at the general command. Roth was a member of the associations of the radical right [rechtsextreme Bünde] and later, in 1923, became involved in Hitler's attempted putsch. As an officer who had experienced the revolutionary period, Schmitt placed his bet on the functional elite of civil servants as a stabilizing power. The belief that the nationalist movement would re-establish state 'authority' was also expressed fairly clearly at the end of the treatise *The Crisis of Parliamentary Democracy*,* which Schmitt began to write in May, immediately after his travels. His Bavarian experiences and the conversations he had in the spring of 1923 were important for Schmitt's critical view of parliamentarism. His diary provides evidence that in the background to his reference to Mussolini (GLP, p. 89; CPD, p. 18) stood a particular evaluation of the German radical right. Schmitt expected that this movement would remain within the bounds of state 'authority', and that it could have a beneficial effect as a counterbalance to the failure of parliamentarism to fulfil the fundamental task of forming a government.

On 22 April, Schmitt went to Berlin with Feuchtwanger. He stayed with am Zehnhoff and met with Franz Blei. On 26 April he travelled to his family in Plettenberg and soon after on to Bonn, where he found bound copies of his Catholicism essay upon arrival. He dedicated a copy to Kathleen 'as a memory of every day in April 1922 – Marburg, Wetzlar, Bonn, Heidelberg – April 1923'.[22] He took care of his correspondence and began to write *The Crisis of Parliamentary Democracy*. At short notice, he had to take over Kaufmann's lecture on international law. His affection for Duška, it seems, cooled at that point. Not until 7 May did he meet her, 'by coincidence, at the notice board' in the university. This first crisis in their relationship was certainly also caused by Murray's condition and by Schmitt seriously considering whether he should fulfil old promises by marrying her. Schmitt inquired about the 'requirements for a departure to Australia' and found out that there were formal hurdles. He also did not feel well. At the same time, he learned that Murray 'would like to come back'. However, in mid-May he once again bought roses for Duška, who attended his lecture. 'But she is always indifferent, and doesn't show the least interest in me' (TB, 14 May 1923). Schmitt received another letter from the cleric in Australia,

---

*   The German title is actually *Die geistesgeschichtliche Lage des heutigen Parlamentarismus* [The intellectual-historical situation of today's parliamentarism]. For the translator's very sound reasons for opting for a different title in English, see Ellen Kennedy, 'A Note on the Text and Translation', in *The Crisis of Parliamentary Democracy*, pp. ix–xi.

who asked 'questions regarding K'. Then, in Cologne, the journalist and expert on Russia Paul Scheffer explained to Schmitt how 'Russian women wait with noble passivity and let themselves be wooed'. Duška told him that he 'must only ever be her intellectual father and professor, never more than that' (TB, 24 May 1923). At that point, he completed his 'essay on parliamentarism', which had taken him no more than a month to write. On 30 May, he again spent an afternoon with Duška. She translated poems by the Serbian writer Milutin Bojić for him. They ate together in a restaurant, and Duška told him about her homeland. By then, Schmitt was wholly infatuated with her. In the evening of that day he went to Schmitz, made him play some Chopin for him, and regained some 'self-control'. The next day, he talked again with Duška about the poems by Bojić and straightaway wrote to 'Däubler about Bojić'. On this day, the Feast of Corpus Christi, he made a preliminary decision in favour of Duška. Lolo Sauer had long since been left behind and his sense of his Australian commitments also faded away. Schmitt put Kathleen under the rubric of *sexus*. On Duška, his diary has the following to say: 'I love her very much, but without sexuality playing any role. Often horny, but hot for this woman or that, for K' (31 May 1923).[23] At the end of July he probably spent the night with Duška for the first time. He emphasized the decisive character of the Serbian afternoon with Bojić later in *Hochland*. His 'Notizen von einer dalmatinischen Reise' [Notes on a journey to Dalmatia] indicate a space beyond Romanticism and conclude with Bojić.

From parliamentarism to a 'national myth'

1923 was one of the worst of Weimar's crisis years. In January, French and Belgian troops occupied the Ruhr area in order to make sure that the agreed war compensation was forthcoming. Germany reacted with passive resistance, which was supported by all bourgeois parties as well as a large proportion of the Social Democrats. Only the left wing of the SPD and the communists rejected it. On 22 February, the Reich's cabinet declared a general prohibition to obey orders from the occupiers' administration. This form of resistance was the final push towards full-blown economic disaster. Inflation became hyperinflation, and in the summer of 1923 Germany faced complete ruin. The coalition government reacted to the SPD's tendencies towards internal division by taking the DVP into the government and making Gustav Stresemann (DVP) chancellor. Stresemann proclaimed a 'dictatorship' to save the country. The Reichstag was no longer able to form a government according to parliamentary rules. A new Enabling Act led to intense crises in government and repeated cabinet reshuffles. Finally, the SPD left the government. It was the first major crisis of the Weimar Republic.[24] The president of the Reich, Ebert, supported Stresemann's line, whereas the head of the military command, Hans von Seeckt, planned a fundamental revision of the constitution. The ideas for a constitutional reform focusing on the role of the president that were discussed in the final years of the Republic, and which were juridically supported by

Schmitt, already had their prelude in 1923. The year not only saw Hitler's attempted putsch in Munich; everywhere political radicalism smelled an opportunity for success. The separatist movement in the Rhineland, supported by France, raised its head again. In October 1923 a 'Rheinische Republik' [Republic of the Rhineland] was declared in Aachen, only for the separatist movement to be crushed violently in November. Stresemann was toppled on 23 November by a vote of no confidence. On this Huber remarks: 'The overthrow of Stresemann was the work of a majority composed of heterogeneous forces. There is no better example for a destructive withdrawal of confidence.'[25] Stresemann, nevertheless, had achieved a certain stability. The end of hyperinflation and the crisis of 1923 took place during his period as chancellor, and he later continued to exert a stabilizing influence as foreign minister.

Schmitt's critique of parliamentarism was written in the midst of this time of crisis. His old hatred of Prussian militarism he now projected onto the French. In May, he completed the study under great time constraints and initially published it in the *Festgabe der Bonner Juristenfakultät* [Commemorative publication of the juridical faculty of Bonn University] on the occasion of the fiftieth anniversary of Ernst Zitelmann's doctorate. Zitelmann, after his retirement, still taught at the same time as Schmitt in the winter term 1922–3.[26] He died in November 1923.[27] Schmitt contributed to the *Festgabe* as a colleague in Bonn. This initial version later also appeared, with only minor revisions,[28] as a separate brochure. A preliminary note on Georg Lukács[29] and Ricarda Huch[30] was taken out at the last moment. The brochure quickly sold out, leading for the first time to disagreements with the publishers. Schmitt chronically suspected that his works were not adequately advertised and quoted.

Schmitt's treatise was a reaction to a contribution which his predecessor, Rudolf Smend, had made to another *Festgabe* at Bonn in 1919.[31] At that time, Smend had already claimed that the rationalist 'belief' in the 'dialectic' of parliamentary procedures was exhausted, that the parliament was deteriorating into a façade for the individual party factions, and that there was a need for a 'substitute'. Schmitt's treatise of 1923 begins by simply listing the then current 'deficiencies and faults of the parliamentary system' (CPD, p. 18; trans. modified) and then presents an argument at the level of 'intellectual history' [ein 'geistesgeschichtliches' Vorgehen] in order to 'find the ultimate core of the institution' (CPD, p. 20). Schmitt explicates how parliamentarism's metaphysical precondition of a 'belief' in public discussion, in discussion and a public sphere as the way towards political truth, is antiquated. This belief had lived off parliamentarism's enemy, monarchical rule, and lost its persuasiveness when this enemy became less important. Schmitt's *Crisis of Parliamentary Democracy* is a first historical sketch of the 'Political Theology' of parliamentarism and democracy. In it, he defines democracy formally as an identity that is produced through the 'identification' of those ruled and the rulers, whereas: 'A distance always remains between real equality and the results of identification. . . . Everything depends on how the will of the people is formed' (CPD, p. 27). In practice, a 'question' arises as to 'who has control over the means with which the will of the people is to be constructed' (CPD, p. 29). This is why Schmitt writes: 'Democracy seems fated then to destroy itself in the problem of the formation of a will' (CPD, p. 28). 'The development from 1815 until 1918 could be depicted as the development of a concept of legitimacy: from dynastic to democratic legitimacy' (CPD, p. 30; cf. D, p. xliv). This is the historical trajectory sketched by the treatise. Later, Schmitt also interpreted democratic identity and 'identification', following Rousseau, as social 'homogeneity' (CPD, p. 11) and unity, or agreement within a nation regarding the fundamental decisions on which it rests. For Schmitt, the formal principle of 'identitarian' democracy, independent of any procedures forming a representative will, is a legitimizing consensus on the fundamental principles of political unity.

In his monograph on *Dictatorship*, Schmitt had already emphasized the political function and role of the philosophy of history in the transformation of a 'relative' into an 'absolute rationalism'. In a long footnote (D, pp. 278–80), the arguments of the booklets of 1922 and 1923 were in part anticipated. Now, Schmitt characterizes parliamentarism as an ideal type defined by a 'belief' in the possibility of establishing 'correctness or truth' [Richtigkeit oder Wahrheit] through public discussion, a belief which institutionalizes the 'eternal conversation' between the political powers. Hegel's philosophy of history marks a transformation towards the 'organic' liberalism of the Vormärz,[32] on the one hand, and the adoption of the philosophy of history by Marxism, on the other. Schmitt diagnoses a revolutionary sublation by which 'relative rationalism' transforms itself into an 'absolute rationalism'. This move 'suspends democracy in the name of a true democracy that is still to be created' (CPD, p. 28) and sublates the 'relative rationalism' of a division and balance of powers into an 'absolute rationalism' (CPD, p. 46) of an educational dictatorship (cf. CPD, p. 28) based on a philosophy of history. Marx put the idea of class struggle in its most extreme form as the 'tension' between bourgeoisie and proletariat, but along with his claim to be 'scientific' (CPD, p. 54) he also adopted more reflective strands from Hegel's thought (cf. CPD, pp. 54f.). Marx knew 'coming things' only in the form of a negation of what is now, and he was not 'a Jewish prophet' (CPD, p. 61). Only a more recent irrationalism was able to answer the question of 'why battle at all?' with a 'philosophy of material life' (CPD, p. 64). Thus, the thesis of the transformation of rationalism into a new 'irrationalism' adds a new dimension to Schmitt's earlier discussions of 'dictatorship in Marxist thought' (CPD, p. 51; cf. CPD, pp. 51–64).

Under the title 'Irrationalist Theories of the Direct Use of Force', the fourth chapter of the treatise on parliamentarism offers mainly an interpretation of George Sorel's 'theory of unmediated real life' (CPD, p. 67) within the anarchist tradition. Schmitt considers this theory to be irrational because it links the relevance of historical evidence not to a construction of a necessary historical process but to the 'ability to act and the capacity of heroism' (CPD, p. 68) in the form of the general strike. What makes this a 'philosophy of material life' [Philosophie konkreten Lebens] (CPD, p. 64) is the fact that, following Bergson, it celebrates action as an enthusiastic unleashing of new potentialities of existence [Dasein]. Schmitt draws a sharp distinction between the rationalist preconditions of Marxism and the anarchist and irrationalist 'myths' in Bolshevism, taking Sorel as an heir to Bakunin who combines the Marxist 'image' of the bourgeois with the 'myth' of the 'general strike' (CPD, p. 68). Schmitt wants to demonstrate that, compared to classical Marxism, revolutionary Bolshevism, in the form in which it emerged after the November revolution, was particularly dangerous because it had new motivations, energies and legitimations at its disposal. Bolshevism solved the problem of a lack of legitimacy simply through the experience of 'creative force' (CPD, p. 71). The dialectical concentration of world history into the critical moment of the decision to be taken here and now is, by the myth of class struggle and of the decisive battle, turned into an irrationalist 'theory of the direct use of force' (CPD, p. 65) and direct action (cf. CPD, pp. 65–76). In conclusion, Schmitt refers to Mussolini's 'national myth' as the 'stronger myth' (CPD, p. 75).[33] Without a doubt he preferred Italian fascism as the 'foundation of a new form of authority . . ., an authority based on the new feeling for order, discipline, and hierarchy' (CPD, p. 76; trans. modified). At the same time, however, he stresses the 'abstract [ideelle] danger this kind of irrationalism poses' – i.e., the danger of 'polytheism' (CPD, p. 76).

Political Theology diagnoses a transformation within the history of metaphysics, from transcendent to immanent ideas and from theism to atheism. It makes the authority of personal decisions dependent on a theistic worldview and brings juridical thought into a tense relationship with modernity. *The Crisis of Parliamentary Democracy* also links the plausibility of the formation of a political will with metaphysical preconditions and diagnoses a historical trajectory from rationalism to irrationalism, from liberalism to democracy. The time for liberal debate, Schmitt thought, appeared to be over. But strong self-legitimizations on the basis of a philosophy of history are also obsolete in a time of irrationalist myths. Modern democracy finds new forms of staging political identification. Although Feuchtwanger wanted to see a stronger separation of 'the critique of the parliamentary idea from the critique of parliamentary technique' (CSLF, p. 34), and suggested as a title: 'Die moralische Lage des heutigen Parlamentarismus' [The moral situation of parlimentarism today],[34] he approvingly wrote that Schmitt had finally taken off 'the heavy armour of evidence': 'In *Political Romanticism*, and now in your critique of parliamentarism, you have thrown off the heavy coat of mail and present yourself like David with his slingshot' (CSLF, p. 35).

Was this history of legitimacy an example of 'descriptive' or of 'intervening' political theology? Did Schmitt affirm Italian fascism? Did he commit himself to nationalism or to Mussolini? Before committing *The Crisis of Parliamentary Democracy* to paper, Schmitt had visited Captain Roth, who at the time was in charge of the political coordination of the 'working community' [Arbeitsgemeinschaft] of the radical right-wing fighting associations [Kampfverbände] in Bavaria.[35] Did Schmitt reckon with a march on Berlin by the right? Whatever the answers to these questions, he was looking for a new 'authority'.

Table 12.1 Metaphysical or intellectual [geistesgeschichtliche] situation regarding the formation of political will

Liberalism	⟶	Democracy
'Relative rationalism'	'Absolute rationalism'	Irrationalism
Classical parliamentarism	Educational dictatorship	Violent revolution
Discussion/public sphere	Dictatorship of philosophical reason	Myth of violence
Guizot, Bentham	Condorcet, Hegel, Marx	Proudhon, Bakunin, Sorel, Lenin, Mussolini

After the first night they spent together, Duška went to her Serbo-Croatian homeland for the summer break. In August, the Australian cleric visited Bonn for a fortnight as Kathleen's 'messenger'. Schmitt felt ill and had to go to hospital for a couple of days. Over the summer, however, he was mostly in Plettenberg. He fell down a steep slope, and 'for weeks' could not 'show up in human company'. Schmitt sank into religious meditations on his love. Duška meanwhile was back home, and during the month of October even travelled as far as Romania and Macedonia. Schmitt went to Munich, where he stayed with his Jewish publisher and friend Feuchtwanger for a couple of weeks. (Duška joined him between 10 and 21 October. Of all places, Munich, the city associated with Cari, was the location for their 'honeymoon'.) Schmitt was in Munich only a few weeks before the putsch. With these events in mind, he says it is 'a sensational situation to be the professional observer of today's political spectacle' (CSLF, p. 46). Some chapters in Hobbes's *Leviathan* appeared to him at the time 'as relevant as an article by Radek' (CSLF, p. 45). Soon, he would also emphatically raise the question of authority in a small review, 'Eine französische Kritik der Zeit'[36] [A French critique of our times], in which he compared the French critique with the German crisis literature before and after 1918, referring to Rathenau's *Kritik der Zeit* [Critique of our times].[37] Rathenau had demanded more 'soul', while the French critique after 1918 called in more concrete terms for a new 'authority'. However, according to Schmitt, it did not ask the question of social domination and of elites – i.e., of the social stratum that would be the bearer of the new 'authority' – with enough clarity. Schmitt hints at the fact that the old social elites had abdicated after 1914, and that there is not really any new 'authority' anywhere in sight. He asks the question of new social strata that could fulfil this function in the German case and looks for forces outside of the battle between parliamentary parties. It seems that he had already at this point begun to turn away from the Catholic Church as a power providing stability. And he was also increasingly sceptical about the parliamentary course steered by the Zentrumspartei, which represented political Catholicism.

Schmitt quickly established the failure of Weimar parliamentarism to form a government, a point he made in two articles which later opened his volume of *Verfassungsrechtliche Aufsätze* [Essays on constitutional law]. He opted for the right of the president of the Reich to dissolve parliament in order to 'create the precondition in the first place which the Weimar

Constitution as such, and also art. 25, requires: i.e., a parliament with the power to act and a majority capable of forming a government' (VRA, p. 15).* In an article he wrote upon the request of the *Kölnische Volkszeitung* on the occasion of presidential elections, 'Reichspräsident und Weimarer Verfassung'[38] [The Reichspräsident and the Weimar Constitution], he warns against the 'great power' [Machtfülle] and 'concentration of power, that would be almost impossible in a constitutional monarchy' (SGN, p. 25) – in short, he warns against a 'constitutional dictatorship'. 'Showing great sagacity', the late Ebert had limited his role as president to that of a *pouvoir neutre* [neutral power] and thus had created a new 'type of president of a republican state' (SGN, p. 26), one who acts as a balancing power. But Schmitt emphasizes: 'With a new president, the Weimar Republic may acquire an entirely different face' (SGN, p. 27). He does not want to encourage the emergence of a dictator, he continues, but rather wants to warn of the constitutional possibility of one emerging.

1924: an incubatory period

The *Crisis* treatise appeared at the end of October 1923. At the same time, Schmitt pursued further his divorce proceedings, in which he was represented by Dr Meyer I. On 12 October, an oral hearing took place at the fourth civil chamber of the Regional Court in Bonn, in which Cari's criminal record was also taken into consideration. The accused was still missing. Erich Kaufmann was again on leave for the winter term, and Schmitt had to cover all courses on public law by himself. Kaufmann commented on this in a letter to Schmitt: 'In all nations it is the case that some professors, from time to time, have to privilege their other public responsibilities over their teaching.'[39] Schmitt was considering writing a textbook on international law. In November, Duška was back in Bonn, living in a guest house. Schmitt now clearly made a decision in favour of her. He wrote glowing love letters to her and thought about their relationship in religious terms. Schmitt expressed himself critically about capitalism, hyperinflation and those profiting from it. On one occasion he wrote: 'Hitler is a hysteric' (11 December 1923) and: '"Germany is Hamlet" – unfortunately for a long time no more' (1 and 2 December 1923). The turn of the year 1923 he spent with Duška. His relationships with Landsberg and Kaufmann were cooling off at the time, and his contacts with Vormfelde became more distant. By contrast, he continued to see Wilhelm Neuß regularly. Quite frequently he also met with the teacher and translator Karl Rick,[40] who soon moved to Aachen. However, the most intimate relationship was that with Arnold Schmitz, whom he visited frequently and who played music for him. He also remained in close contact with his brother Jupp. The matter

---

*   Article 25 of the Weimar Constitution reads: 'The Reich President can dissolve the Reichstag, but only once for the same reason. The new election takes place on the seventeenth day after the dissolution' (*Constitutional Theory*, 'Appendix: The Weimar Constitution', pp. 409–40; here: p. 413).

closest to his heart, however, was Duška. The relationship developed in an unexpected and ambiguous way. Schmitt sought and found 'support and a sense of direction' in her love, but at that time Duška had already developed a dangerous case of tuberculosis. On 11 December, Schmitt made a note about a secret 'engagement' in his diary. On 3 January 1924, Duška travelled to Agram and Daruvar to visit her divorced parents; she returned only at the beginning of May, at which point she was already seriously ill.

At the beginning of 1924, Schmitt made notes – sparked by a Chaplin movie – about his growing distance from Ernst Landsberg: 'After dinner to the cinema with Vormfelde to watch *The Kid* because Landsberg had praised the film so highly; rubbish, Jewish sentimentality. Realized my distance from these people' (TB, 17 January 1924).[41] From then on, Schmitt would note down similar thoughts again and again. On his social interaction with Kaufmann, he now also remarked: 'I do not belong to that kind of people' (13 February 1924). Duška was far away. Every positive letter she wrote comforted him, every little delay in their exchange of letters threw him into despair and doubt. 'I am under an illusion', he wrote (19 January 1924) – the *Lucky Devil**– a 'man under pathetic illusions', who was prone to imagined romance and again and again repressed the fact of her illness. Schmitt was 'afraid of the tuberculosis' and read Gide's *L'Immoraliste* as an antidote. On 18 January the Regional Court in Bonn sat on the matter 'Schmitt vs. Schmitt' again, and on 21 January Schmitt received the good news that his marriage with Cari had been 'annulled' by the state authorities because of wilful deceit. The verdict became legally binding on 2 March. 'The plaintiff believed that he was marrying the daughter of an aristocratic landowner, hence a woman from the highest circles of society, while in truth she was the illegitimate child of a man who was a craftsman', was the court's opinion. Schmitt at once wanted an annulment of the marriage by the Church as well. A priest who was knowledgeable about canon law provided help with the line of argument he should take. Two central points were to be considered: Cari's false declaration of identity and the fact that an aristocratic descent had been a *conditio sine qua non* for their marriage. In his request of 31 July 1924, presented to the Offizialat (the Church's judicial body) of the archbishop in Cologne, Schmitt emphasized the fraudulent basis on which the marriage had rested. He had trusted Cari so much, he said, that he had seen no reason for questioning her aristocratic background. The Church's court did not accept this argument. Even with the support of his two witnesses (his brother Jupp and his cousin André), Schmitt was not able to prove the essential point in a way that would have persuaded the Church authorities.[42]

At the end of January, Schmitt wrote a response to Richard Thomas's *Der Begriff der modernen Demokratie in seinem Verhältnis zum Staatsbegriff* [The concept of a modern democracy and its relation to the concept of the state]. Around the same time, he fell out with his oldest disciple at Bonn, Braubach. At the beginning of February, Schmitt was angered by a critical review of his *Crisis* treatise by Fritz Stier-Somlo, an expert in public law

---

* Reference to the *roman à clef Der Glückspilz* [The lucky devil] by Alice Berend; see p. 87.

from Cologne. This led to polemical exchanges which lasted the whole year. On 4 February Schmitt received news, by 'express letter from Triepel,'[43] that he was invited to give a talk at the meeting of the Association of State Theorists [Staatsrechtslehrertagung] in Jena. It was still term time. Schmitt's diaries repeatedly mention a 'National Socialist student, named Schnors', who gave a presentation on Oswald Spengler and National Socialism in February. At this time, Schmitt became interested in National Socialism and also in the Munich trials against Kahr[44] and Ludendorff.

His relationship with Duška strained him. He read Villiers de l'Isle-Adam,[45] used Othello to think about his suspiciousness and jealousy and, through the lens of Shakespeare's *The Merchant of Venice*, considered the possibility of being deceived again. He used his suspiciousness in order to legitimize his own unfaithfulness. Schmitt regularly met a friend of Duška's, Miss Tadic, once a dancer with the name of Sonninghaus, who reminded him of Cari. Many love letters to Duška at that time were written down in his 'God's shadow'. When at the beginning of March he was discussed as a possible candidate for the Reichstag for the Zentrumspartei,[46] he spoke with Wilhelm Neuß about the 'dissolution of the old centre, the absence of a leader' (TB, 7 March 1924). But when a safe seat was in fact offered to him, on 11 March, he declined without regret. He did not feel comfortable with the party's parliamentary politics. As the 'essential constitutional party'[47] of the Weimar Republic, the Zentrum was looking for parliamentary compromise.

Schmitt spent a weekend with Kiener and Wittich, friends from Strasbourg, in Mainz. He finally found his own place, at Endenicher Straße 20, examined his first doctoral candidate at Bonn (vom Dahl), and travelled to Bremen, Hamburg and Berlin. In Hamburg, he stayed with Eisler and got to know Eisler's young cousin Annie Kraus, who would later play a role in his life in Berlin. Georg Eisler was about to marry Käte Basseches; they would go on to have four children in the following years. At that time, Schmitt had news from Croatia saying that Duška had 'coughed up blood again' (18 March 1924) and that her condition was critical. Schmitt met with Alfred Bertram, Rosenbaum and Kurt Singer; he attended a performance of *Othello* and was reminded of Duška: 'She saved me from the fate of Othello; she is my only support' (TB, 22 March 1924). Only now did he begin to think about a paper for Jena. He travelled to Berlin and was able to breathe again in the big city. He stayed with his old patron am Zehnhoff, enjoyed the glory of his protection and worked out his paper at the library of the Ministry of Justice. Schmitt met Rudolf Smend and Heinrich Triepel, whom he soon suspected to be 'the worst kind of schemer[s]' (CSLF, p. 125). Together with Franz Blei, he dived into Berlin's nightlife and enjoyed a passionate affair with a 'countess' by the name of Hella Ehrik, who quickly kindled Schmitt's 'Othello affect' by renting herself a 'Russian' for five Marks. Those days Schmitt spent in Berlin before the Jena meeting were extreme in more than one respect. His friendships with Franz Blei, with am Zehnhoff and with Rudolf Smend were strong at the time. Out of his worry for Duška, Schmitt fled into a sobering erotic adventure.

Addressing the 'Association':
'The Dictatorship of the President of the Reich'

The 'primal catastrophe' of the Great War was also of epochal significance for the sciences. German historians were confronted with a
new topic that exercised them intensely – the question of war guilt
[Kriegsschuldfrage]. Philosophy moved from neo-Kantianism to neo-
Hegelianism. Whereas neo-Kantianism had formulated practical moral
postulates [Sollenspostulate] and had been inclined towards an 'ethical
socialism', neo-Hegelianism tied individual 'morals' back to collective
'ethical life'; it argued on the basis of the actual constitution and opened
itself up to debates in the social sciences and politics.[48] At the same time,
neo-Hegelianism increasingly interpreted 'morality' in nationalist and
anti-universalist terms. In those years, Max Weber's collected works were
published posthumously. They went beyond the economic paradigm that
also made Marxism attractive and developed a perspective that included
religious aspects and the sociology of domination. Weber asked the question of the 'legitimacy' and the 'motivation behind obedience': Why did
people obey? Which are the processes that create authority? Where the
'monopoly of legitimate violence' (Max Weber) was shaken, the state could
hardly remain an effective and legitimate authority. The legal system of the
state lagged behind dramatic historical developments and lost its position
as the regulatory power. In jurisprudence, the mode of legitimacy became
questionable at the same time as the discipline had to accommodate to the
conditions of a liberal democracy.

The consequence was a debate within the profession on the direction
jurisprudence should take, the so-called Richtungsstreit, a debate which
also had some characteristics of a generational conflict.[49] Hans Kelsen
in particular, in a kind of pre-emptive attack, tried both to seal off the
specifically legal form from 'meta-juridical' and 'natural law' influences
from politics, moral theory or religion and to strengthen the democratic
constitutional state as the bearer of peace in a pluralist and 'agnostic' community that entailed heterogenous 'worldviews'.[50] Against this position
there formed a heterogeneous group of 'anti-positivists', who rediscovered
the difference between right and justice, legality and legitimacy. Within
Marxism, following the division of the left into SPD and KPD, there also
emerged a new and constructive discussion of the roles of right and state.
Julius Binder and Erich Kaufmann, in their different ways, reformulated
legal philosophical arguments. Rudolf Smend, Carl Schmitt and Hermann
Heller, finally, despite the significant differences between them, were
generally seen as main representatives of an 'intellectual' turn [geisteswis-
senschaftliche Wende] that was critical of positivism and designed a new
form of theory which no longer argued on the basis of the theological or
philosophical tradition of a 'natural law'.

Via the notions of common law and 'unwritten constitutional law',[51]
Smend worked his way towards his constitutional theory, known as an
'Integrationslehre' [integration theory]. His theory of the formation of
a political will within the state and of decision-making by the executive

emphasized very strongly the 'purpose' [Sinn] of 'integration'. Heller, who was politically close to the Social Democrats, set out from a critique of the 'idea of national power' as an ideology and then moved from the statist core of 'sovereignty' to a 'theory of the state'.[52] Whereas Kelsen developed a 'pure' theory of law, Heller freed the theory of the state from the burden of a contemporary 'circle of ideas': the idea of national power, nationalism and fascism.[53] We might say that what united the critics of positivism was the attempt to discuss the difference between right and law, and between legality and legitimacy, without reference to prescriptive theological or philosophical arguments but, rather, solely on the basis of a political theory of the state.

Schmitt, however, often felt himself an 'outsider'[54] among his colleagues: as a social climber and non-dogmatic Catholic. During his time in Bonn he already felt surrounded by Jewish cliques, and he considered himself to be intellectually superior to and not respected by his colleagues. He suffered from a discrepancy between, as he saw it, his importance and his social status. In Bonn, he had made occasional remarks such as: 'I feel as if I was chased by a malicious gang and was outlawed.'[55] The disastrous 'stupidity' of his failed marriage kept nagging at him. At the same time, he did not want to accustom himself to a bourgeois life. Mostly, he knew well how to keep his negative impulses and opinions hidden from those around him; but in private he twisted the facts to his liking in the fashion of an advocate. Whereas with Smend he remained in friendly contact until 1933, he entered into increasingly sharp disputes with Kaufmann and Heller, and his relationship with them became more and more hostile.

During the Weimar Republic, the Staatsrechtslehre [theory of state law] was faced with the major task of leaving the framework of a constitutional monarchy behind and embracing the structures of a parliamentary democracy that placed a strong emphasis on the role of the president. The highly respected Berlin professor [Ordinarius] Heinrich Triepel responded to this challenge by founding the Vereinigung der Deutschen Staatsrechtslehrer[56] [Association of German State Theorists], which is still of outstanding importance today. In a circular sent out in September 1922, he invited all German-speaking colleagues, including those beyond the country's borders[57] in Austria, Switzerland and Prague to the association's first meeting in mid-October 1922 in Berlin.[58] The second meeting then took place in Jena in April 1924. The first theme to be discussed was 'Der deutsche Föderalismus in Vergangenheit, Gegenwart und Zukunft' [German federalism in the past, present and future]. Gerhard Anschütz and Carl Bilfinger presented on this topic. The second theme was 'Die Diktaturgewalt des Reichspräsidenten nach Art. 48 der Reichsverfassung' [The dictatorial power of the president of the Reich according to Art. 48 of the constitution]. The president's dictatorial powers had proved, during the revolutionary period after 1918,* to be one of the most important means

---

* Article 48 contains the emergency provision in the Weimar Constitution. It says that the president 'may provisionally suspend, in whole or in part, the basic rights established in Articles 114, 115, 117, 118, 124, 153' if 'in the German Reich the public security and order

by which the unity of the Reich could be defended against separatist tendencies. The 'dictatorial powers' could therefore also be seen as a response to federalism.

Schmitt's early work on dictatorship provisionally came to an end with the 'Bericht' [report] he presented in Jena.[59] This report was an inaugural statement made to the guild of legal scholars. Although his monograph on *Dictatorship* showed that Schmitt was qualified to talk about the topic, he had so far hardly any credentials as an expert in constitutional law. And his theory of dictatorship, to begin with, was also conceived on the basis of a conceptual history. At one moment he used it as a 'counter-revolutionary' argument against radicalism from both left and right, the next he set it up as a response to the crisis of Weimar parliamentarism. In addition to the formation of a government by parliament, the Weimar Constitution contained provisions for a formation of the government by the president. In the case of the latter, the chancellor was appointed by the directly elected Reichspräsident.* This 'dual system' allowed for a flight from parliamentarism into the presidential system. Only in Jena did Schmitt begin to intervene significantly in the constitutional debate over the presidential right to dissolve parliament. He argued for extensive presidential powers to dissolve parliament because he expected to see parliamentarism fail on account of its incapacity to guarantee the fundamental function of forming viable majority governments.

On 12 April, Schmitt travelled with Hella Ehrik to Leipzig. The following day, Hella left without a farewell. Schmitt travelled on to Jena, visited Naumburg,† and on 14 April presented his opening paper to forty-three theorists of state law [Staatsrechtslehrer]. He presented the tools of his trade in more detail than usual. The paper emphasizes the '[d]ifficiencies in the prevailing interpretation of the practice of the state of exception' (D, p. 183) and dissects the wording of the article and its history. Schmitt distinguishes between a 'general authorization' [allgemeine Befugnis] and a 'specific authorization' [besondere Befugnis] (D, p. 194) to suspend specific basic rights. He does not directly attack the limitation of dictatorial powers by the Rechtsstaat, but wants only to provide a critique of the way this limitation is justified. '[B]ecause some limitation of the authority of the president must be established. The question is whether this limitation should be established on the basis of a pseudo-argument or in full juridical awareness of the particularity and difficulty of Article 48, § 2' (D, p. 199; trans. modified). Schmitt points out that the limitations originally referred only to a 'provisional arrangement' (D, p. 208), and that a more

---

are significantly disturbed or endangered' (Weimar Constitution, p. 417). See also George Schwab's discussion of Schmitt's interpretation of the article in Schwab's introduction to PT, pp. xi–xxvi; here: pp. xix–xxiii.

* Article 41 states: 'The president is elected by the entire German people. Any German over the age of thirty-five is eligible for election' (Weimar Constitution, p. 416).

† Friedrich Nietzsche spent his childhood and youth in Naumburg, where he also attended secondary school. However, as Reinhard Mehring pointed out to me, more important to Schmitt was probably Naumburg Cathedral with its famous mediaeval sculpture of Uta, an icon of German nationalist legend.

detailed regulation had been intended. He blames the condition of parliamentarism for the fact that this further regulation did not come forth, and demands a regulation that would both be appropriate for the requirements of legal practice and make a debate on the adequate interpretation of the article superfluous. He emphasizes the necessity for any regulation to be based on the rule of law, to follow the formal legislative procedure, and to limit the powers of the Reichspräsident in accordance with the separation of powers under the rule of law. 'The president of the Reich is not a legislator' (D, p. 217), Schmitt writes. He does not have the right to pass a 'general Enabling Act' [allgemeinen Notverordnungsakt].

Schmitt's interest was clearly in establishing a categorical regulation on the basis of the rule of law rather than on the need for interpretation. And without a doubt he also, in terms of constitutional policies, argued for a regulation that would give more consideration to the reality and demands of legal practice. It is difficult to say whether reservations about basic rights provisos were an influence in the position he took. What is certain is that Schmitt argued on the basis of the principles of the rule of law for a limitation of dictatorial powers and for procedures based on the rule of law. 'The paper is of great political significance', he wrote to Feuchtwanger, 'without, I hope, giving up the objective and reserved position of the jurist' (CSLF, p. 64). His co-referent Erwin Jacobi agreed with Schmitt and argued in favour of more far-reaching limitations to the judicial review of parliamentary laws.[60] Objections were voiced in the discussion. 'By far the largest number of contributors took a different position', it says in an account of the discussion, whose author is not named,[61] pointing out that Article 48, paragraph 2, was not a 'provisional arrangement'. Schmitt himself was not entirely satisfied with his performance. '[S]poke well at first, later badly, disappointed and annoyed, it wasn't a failure, but no resounding success either', his diary says. 'Jacobi was the livelier speaker . . . Anschütz's presentation was bad, Bilfinger's even worse. Very disappointed. Relaxed after lunch, the discussions in the afternoon were disgusting' (TB, 14 April 1924). Schmitt continued to feel like an outsider, and for that reason did not regularly participate in the meetings during the following years. However, he did attend the meetings in Münster (1926) and Halle (1931). At the latter, there were yet again controversial discussions of the extensive interpretation of Article 48 of the Weimar Constitution. Only at that time, under conditions of rule by presidential decree – the so-called Präsidialsystem – did the article's practical impact become fully visible. Carl Bilfinger and Erwin Jacobi remained important allies at that point.

Hugo Ball's 'really quite beautiful' *Hochland* essay

After the Meeting in Jena, Schmitt and Smend visited the castles of Dornburg, where the tsarina Catherine had grown up and Goethe liked to spend some of his time. Over Easter, Schmitt went to Plettenberg. 'I am really not a Christian' (21 April 1924), he remarked in his diary on this occasion. He revised his Jena presentation for publication. At least his call for an implementation act found broad acceptance. Schmitt later repeated it in the *Kölnische Volkszeitung*,[62] but the corresponding legislation never came to pass. After his return to Bonn on 22 April, with his abode now at Endenicher Straße 20, Schmitt exchanged a few more letters with Hella. Shortly before Duška's return, he was surprised to receive a 'touching letter from Kathleen' (TB, 6 May 1924). Moritz Bonn wrote in a letter to Schmitt that the Germans at that time imagined 'the Messiah wearing the boots of a cuirassier and a twisted moustache'. The advocates of dictatorship, he said, did 'not get beyond the Old Testament in their anti-Semitism'. 'Their Wotan godfather, in essence, is nothing but Jehovah with a blond beard.'[63] On 6 May, Duška finally returned after four months' absence. At first she lived in the Heisterbach Convent, situated below the Petersberg in Bonn, which was led by Cellitinnen* at the time. Schmitt now needed a lot of money and forcefully demanded the payment of honoraria, which led to severe differences with Feuchtwanger and to Schmitt threatening to change publisher. He let out his anger over Stier-Somlo in a harsh review, which he discussed with friends and then sent to the *Frankfurter Zeitung*, where it was forgotten, so that it actually appeared only some months later in Singer's *Wirtschaftsdienst*. Carl Bilfinger was at this time interim professor at Bonn, covering for Kaufmann in his absence, and Schmitt befriended him. Schmitt was not fully convinced of Bilfinger's talents as a teacher,[64] but he also did not want 'public law in Bonn to be represented only by Hensel and Isay'.[65] For the same reason, he rejected Gerhard Lassar standing in for Kaufmann during his leave. 'Lassar will not work; one Christian against 3 Jews (Hensel, Isay, Lassar) is not an acceptable situation for me.'[66]

In the weeks following Duška's return, Schmitt spent a lot of time with her in Heisterbach. At the end of May, he read Hugo Ball's long essay 'Carl Schmitts Politische Theologie'[67] [Carl Schmitt's political theology] in the journal *Hochland* and found it 'really quite beautiful' (TB, 28 May 1924): 'a wonderful achievement, a masterpiece of German prose' (CSLF, p 60). Duška's health was critical; X-rays showed a 'horrific picture of the tuberculosis' (21 June 1924), and she had to move to the small village of Ruppichteroth, about 30 kilometres to the east of Bonn in the Bergisches Land. Schmitt considered a 'stay in Davos' – it was the year in which Thomas Mann's *Zauberberg* was published.

On 14 July, Heinrich Eisler, the father of Georg and Fritz, died after having suffered a stroke.[68] Georg, who had long since acted as the junior director, now took over the publishing enterprise as a personally liable partner. He closed down the *Hamburger Woche* and reduced the *Deutschen Hotel-Nachrichten* to two editions per week.[69]

At the time, Duška wrote: 'Carl, dear Carl, I wish I really was your joy, and not just your worry.' And in an almost beseeching tone: 'I am with

---

* The female equivalent of the Alexianer, a religious order which emerged during the Middle Ages, based on the principles of St Augustine. The order traditionally cares for the sick. Today, the Cellitinnen operate several hospitals and care homes in the area around Cologne.

The Bonn years: living in a Catholic environment

you and I shall never go away.'[70] The two Schmitts would retain the formal
address of 'Sie' throughout their life together. At the beginning of July,
the printed version appeared of Schmitt's presentation at the meeting of
the Association of State Theorists. 'We have no house, we have no home,
we travel to this place and that, and are like cats who make their nest one
moment here and another there', Schmitt noted (5 July 1924) in 'God's
shadow'. In August, they both travelled to Upper Bavaria and Munich,
where Duška was medically examined. On the spur of the moment, they
decided to continue on to Switzerland (on 19 August 1924), where Duška
went to a sanatorium in Lugano, while Schmitt met repeatedly with Hugo
Ball. Together with Ball, he also visited Hermann Hesse. On 9 September,
Schmitt journeyed to Stuttgart and visited Bilfinger; Duška remained
in Switzerland, where she wanted to translate Ranke's *Die serbische
Revolution* [The Serbian Revolution].[71] She intermitted at Bonn University
for the winter term 1924–5 and then gave up her studies. Via Frankfurt
and Darmstadt, Schmitt returned to Bonn, where he completed a new
preface for *Political Romanticism* and undertook a decisive 'revision'[72]
of the overall work, in which he emphasized the problem of rationality
and the European dimension. In November, he wrote an article on the

'A new type of confessor' – Hugo Ball about Carl Schmitt

'Reichtstagsauflösung nach Art. 25 der Reichsverfassung' [The dissolution of the parliament in accordance with Art. 25 of the constitution], and in December, under enormous time constraints, a review article on 'Die Kernfrage des Völkerbundes' [The core question regarding the League of Nations]. The encounter with Ball would remain important for Schmitt.

Hugo Ball came from those circles which had been enemies and under Schmitt's surveillance during his time at the general command. Ball was a poet and journalist, socialist and anarchist, and was deeply interested in Bakunin. He lived in Munich when Schmitt arrived there in 1915 but then emigrated to Switzerland, where he propagated Dadaism in the Cabaret Voltaire. From Dada he turned to the *Corpus Areopagiticum* of Pseudo-Dionysius, looking for the leap from aesthetics to faith. 'There is only one power that can stand up to the dissolution of tradition: that is Catholicism. But not the Catholicism of the time before the war, or that of war time, but a new, deeper, an integral Catholicism', Ball noted in his diary on 9 August 1920.[73] *Critique of the German Intelligentsia* had already appeared.[*] The de- and reconstructive intention of that work is encapsulated in the following diary entry of 10 August 1917:

A master of clear prose style such as Heine could not come to terms with Germany; neither could a deeply probing spirit such as Nietzsche. Neither a Jew nor a Protestant was able to do that. It is necessary to get an overview of the whole tradition and to have a sense for all of its paths. Only a Catholic could possibly do that. There are three German traditions: the strongest is

[*] Hugo Ball, *Critique of the German Intelligentsia*, New York, 1993. The German original was published in 1919.

the hieratic tradition of the Holy Roman Empire. The second tradition is the individualist one of the Reformation. The third one is that of the natural philosophy of socialism.[74]

Ball wanted to undo the tradition of the Reformation in order to uncover a Catholic socialism, and thus also to overcome nationalism.

As early as spring 1919, Ball and Schmitt met for the first time in Munich and discussed the French neo-Catholics (E. Hello, L. Bloy). But their relationship became more intense only after the *Hochland* asked Ball to write an essay on Schmitt's work. Schmitt was in contact at the time with the journal's editor, Carl Muth,[75] whose connections with the peace movement he had observed in Munich only a short while ago, in 1917. Schmitt agreed the publication of the new preface for the *Romanticism* book with Muth, and Muth requested further contributions on 'Ultramontanism' and on Donoso Cortés. A request for a contribution on Judaism Schmitt later cautiously rejected.[76] He engaged with the *Hochland* not least in order to have a standing within Catholicism. Muth pressed Schmitt to take up a position within the landscape of Catholic literature. Thus, he suggested that Schmitt should write an 'open letter'[77] to Romano Guardini. Schmitt's diary notes: 'Have sketched a letter to Guardini on Rome' (24 May 1924). But only a day later he noted down: 'Depressions at night. This letter to Guardini on Rome is pathetic.' Such a letter would have made Schmitt's 'Roman' understanding of the Church clearer. But Schmitt no longer wanted to present himself too much as a Catholic author. Muth commissioned Ball to write the review article on Schmitt. Schmitt knew about this and was happy with it.

Ball's excellently written essay covers the development from *Political Romanticism* to the Catholicism essay. He reads Schmitt's work as a method of 'testing' one's own 'basis'. He calls Schmitt the 'new type of German scholar', a 'confessor', who works on the assumption 'that ideas rule over life'. He sees *Political Romanticism* as an attempt to protect the counter-revolutionary 'role models' against Romantic 'misrecognition' and monopolization. According to Ball, the central motif is the distinction between the rational and the irrational, between 'reason and unreason'. Like Pseudo-Dionysius the Areopagite, Ball knows about the transcendence of faith, and he implies, not without justification, that Schmitt also tries to distinguish the sphere of faith from that of the state. He sees him as 'a rationalist with regard to the state, but an irrationalist with regard to theology'.[78] Ball's original and searching reading of *Dictatorship* takes it as an attempt at providing a personalist foundation for 'sovereign dictatorship', a reading he supports in particular with the picture being painted of Cromwell. A dictator such as Cromwell, he says, would be 'outside the Church', would be a 'rebel', 'heretic' or 'saint'. Here, Ball brings into his interpretation his own question of the type of the 'saint', and he senses the danger that an individual as sovereign may give up any ties to the Church. 'In *Dictatorship*, his personalism becomes a danger for Schmitt', Ball writes. Schmitt, he continues, did recognize this danger himself, and therefore recently brought the sovereign dictator back into the folds of the

Church. Schmitt's method of a sociology of concepts led him back to the Church as the foundation. Thus, Ball writes: 'The unity of Schmitt's work lies in the illumination of the relationships between reason and the supra-rational [Erhellung der Vernunftbeziehungen zum Übervernünftigen] as the principle of its form. However, these relationships are precisely those of jurisprudence to theology, and not, as in *Dictatorship*, the relationship of jurisprudence to an arbitrary usurpation.'[79] Schmitt, Ball says, recognized the danger inherent in a dictatorial usurpation of power. Almost inevitably, 'his sociological stringency led him to Roman Catholicism'.[80] Schmitt was compelled to recognize Catholicism as the 'basis' and to find the link that encompasses both state and Church in the question of 'representation'. Ball's essay is a brilliant feat in conceptual history. Perceptively, he recognizes a problematic that runs through Schmitt's work: the emancipation of an individual dictator from all commitments. He could not have found higher praise for Schmitt than to say that he took Catholicism seriously, and that he sees it as the result of a theoretical struggle. Ball's essay is free of any polemic or dogmatism and concentrates on the strengths in Schmitt's work by focusing on his theoretical stringency and by seeing a tendency towards the Church in it.

The controversy over *The Consequences of the Reformation*

After the essay had been published, Schmitt, as mentioned before, sought at once to make contact with Ball.[81] He used Duška's Swiss journey into the world of *The Magic Mountain* in order to get to know him more closely, and he tried to talk him out of writing a shorter version of the *Critique of the German Intelligentsia*. Only once he was in Lugano did Schmitt read the proofs of the latter. He wanted to save Ball from a public scandal and regretted the 'incongruent treatment' (CSLF, p. 70) of this important theme. But soon he wrote to Feuchtwanger: 'I have talked to Ball a great deal. Minor improvements would not change the overall impression a lot' (CSLF, p. 75). At the end of September, Schmitt offered Ball financial support and established some personal contacts for him. Ball softened his stance slightly: 'The conversations with Prof. Schmitt made me read the text once more very carefully and render some points more precise', he wrote with regard to the proofs.[82] The first author's copies he sent to Blei and Schmitt.[83] But when the book appeared at the end of 1924, with the title *Die Folgen der Reformation* [The consequences of the Reformation], Ball and Schmitt fell out with each other. Schmitt repeatedly hinted at his critique of Romanticism. On 7 December he told Ball that he had read the text and promised a review by his disciple Gurian as well as further comments. Schmitt repeatedly met Gurian in Cologne at that time.

From these days we have some short letters and many drafted letters in 'God's shadow' to Duška, who was in a hospital at Monte Brè. 'As soon as you are well again, you must come here', Schmitt wrote. 'However, the months between January and March are too dangerous.'[84] Over Christmas, Carl again travelled to Lugano. In January 1925, Ball still expected a positive review, but at the beginning of February he wrote to Carl Muth: 'It now turns out that Dr Gurian from Carl Schmitt's historical seminar, a young man lacking in independence, was allowed to write about my *Consequences of the Reformation* in the *Kölnische Volkszeitung*, and the result is that my sense of responsibility is made to look questionable.'[85] The draft of a letter Ball ended up not sending blames Schmitt for Gurian's review. Ball complained: 'My "Consequences of the Reformation" has been met with a hailstorm, and those who once reached for the highest notes when singing my praise now opt for the most dreadful dissonances. I lack a "sense of responsibility", they say, and that I have sunk to the level of the worst kind of "polemical pamphlets".'[86] To Feuchtwanger, Ball wrote:

> I am very disappointed by Schmitt's attitude. I admit, from the beginning he did not hold back his judgment of me. But he also knows that my publication is that of a convert and that, having been in companionable correspondence with him, I did not expect the deviousness of being judged by a seminarist. After Gurian's review, Schmitt has so far broken off our correspondence. But as this review contains many points that I have already heard from Schmitt in Agnuzzo, I must assume that he is silent out of embarrassment.[87]

This letter was an indirect prompt aimed at Schmitt. But Schmitt did not seek contact with him, which very much hurt Ball.[88] To Gurian, Schmitt remarked: 'I was a little surprised by Ball's letter. You seem to have touched a sensitive point in him.'[89] Feuchtwanger's succinct answer to Ball was: 'Your "Consequences" have unleashed the reaction that was to be expected.'[90]

Schmitt was not alone in rejecting *The Consequences of the Reformation*. On 25 November, Feuchtwanger had to tell Ball that, in the *Deutsche Literaturzeitung*, he was 'downright slaughtered by the most important living professor of theology, apart from Harnack, the present vice-chancellor of Berlin University, the Geh. Konsistorialrat* Karl Holl'.[91] The devastating review by Gerhard Ritter in the *Historische Zeitschrift*, for instance, also reads like a realization of Ball's worst fears. Ritter's opening sentence makes his position clear: 'The author of this book will not expect a scholarly journal to give his pamphlet the honour of a scholarly review.' In a sweeping blow, Ritter holds Ball's overall oeuvre to account. The fact that a 'political pamphlet of such intellectually low quality' is published by the same house as Ranke's *History of the Reformation* 'should be pilloried by German historians', writes Ritter,[92] who later would become a doyen of the historical sciences in the Federal Republic. Thus, Schmitt's concerns over Ball's reputation had been all too justified. Schmitt also suggested to Kurt Singer, his friend and editor at the *Wirtschaftsdienst*, that he might review Ball's book. Signed K.S., a short, sharp rebuff of *The Consequences of the Reformation*, not lagging behind Ritter's polemic in its sharpness,

---

* Karl Holl (1866–1926), an important Protestant church historian. Holl was privy councillor to the Church's governing body [Geheimer Konsitorialrat].

did indeed appear in the *Wirtschaftsdienst*. The initials stand for Kurt Singer; the review was printed next to another one by Carl Schmitt. Singer wrote to Schmitt: 'Dear Mr Schmitt, many thanks for your letter. I am delighted that you thought the "environment" of your review was very fitting. It was a difficult task, but I must admit that I am quite pleased with the solution myself.'[93] The text runs:

> Contemporary German literature is poor in intellectual-political pamphlets that show the power of originality and are of exceptional quality. It is even rarer that Protestantism, in the foundational role it played in the German state, faith and education over the last centuries, is made the object of a passionate and serious attack. The present pamphlet engages in such an attack with esprit and diligence, erudition and linguistic virtuosity, but wholly without measure or substance in its judgments, not only blind and unjust in its love and hate, but also deeply unbalanced and without any sense of orientation. Even its style is a caricature of *Ecce homo*, and hence probably the expression of a sick and rebellious soul seeking refuge.[94]

In its wording, characteristic style and intellectual orientation, this text could be by Schmitt, who, around the same time, made a similar reference to Nietzsche towards the end of his preface to the extended edition of *Political Romanticism*: 'The ultimate roots of romanticism and the romantic phenomenon lie in the private priesthood', he says. 'We must see three persons whose deformed visages penetrate the colourful romantic veil: Byron, Baudelaire, and Nietzsche, the three high priests, and at the same time the three sacrificial victims, of this private priesthood' (PR, p. 20).[95] Ball was another such victim for Schmitt, and he agitated against him at the time. He was certainly annoyed that Ball, after his Schmitt essay and his commitment to the Church 'hierarchy', took up early Christian and anarchic motifs of the revolutionary period again, thus disclaiming Schmitt's plea for the 'political form' of the Church. In the first place, however, he yet again condemned Romanticism in the form manifested by Ball. After the latter's death in November 1927, Schmitt received a long letter from Muth, in which he says: 'It always caused me pain that Hugo Ball, who was without a doubt a man of honest character, never understood your behaviour towards him with regard to the *Reformation* pamphlet. Without a doubt, he left this world feeling that he had been persecuted by you.'[96] In his reply, Schmitt wrote:

> I don't want to write much about Dr Gurian. It seems to be his fate to cause grief and confusion. I have a lot of pity for him; he has great journalistic intelligence; you know that I would like to help him, because he is not doing well. But he makes it very difficult for anyone to help him. Since I must fear that he contributed to the fact that Hugo Ball misunderstood me so terribly, I try to avoid any personal contact with Gurian.[97]

Schmitt always denied that he initiated Gurian's negative review. It could be that Gurian acted independently. But it was a lot to ask of Ball that he should accept Schmitt's accusation of Romanticism. Schmitt replied to Muth, saying that he saw a 'brother' in Ball, even claiming: 'Every line of my *Concept of the Political* is directed at him.'[98] Schmitt did not deny that theirs was a polemical relationship. He again fought his 'own Question as form'.[99] He mobilized his negative energies against what was closest to him.

The famous seminar

Schmitt was without a doubt a charismatic fisher of men. In Munich he was already very successful as a teacher. But only in Bonn could he work on founding a 'school'. Here, he created a seminar which produced important jurists. One of the criteria for calling someone a Schmitt disciple is a doctorate supervised by him. But not all of his doctoral students were disciples in the narrower sense. And not all of his disciples wrote their doctoral theses with Schmitt. Thus, other criteria are close academic contact, a certain thematic and methodical orientation, and intellectual positions taken under Schmitt's influence. During his time in Bonn, Schmitt was the first examiner and supervisor of the following students (listed according to the date of the viva voce examination): Dr phil. Bernhard Braubach (1923),[100] Mitchell Benedict Caroll (1923), Walter vom Dahl (1924),[101] Aloys Zimmer (1924),[102] Anton Betz (1924),[103] Carl Weber (1924),[104] Ewald Bergmann (1924),[105] Dr phil. Felix Schneider (1925),[106] Werner Becker (1925),[107] Ernst Forsthoff (1925),[108] Joseph Willms (1925), Karl Lohmann, Dr phil. Joseph Schlosser (1926),[109] Fritz Wiese (1926),[110] Heinrich Lenz (1926),[111] Josef Stein (1927),[112] Hermann Reiners (1927),[113] Ernst Rudolf Huber (1927),[114] Carl Georg Hirsch (1928),[115] Werner Weber (1928),[116] Ernst Friesenhahn (1928),[117] Otto Kirchheimer (1928),[118] Wilhelm Daniels (1928),[119] Johann Heinrich Wilckens (1928)[120] and Emil Gerber (1929).[121] Forsthoff, Schlosser, Huber, Friesenhahn, Lohmann, Zimmer and Kirchheimer were awarded a 'very good', Braubach, Becker and Weber an 'excellent'. Not all of these doctoral students are known as disciples of Schmitt today. Gurian's doctorate was examined by Scheler; Werner Becker came from Guardini. Hans Barion and Hubertus Bung, who were both later very close to Schmitt, were already students at Bonn. However, no one wrote a Habilitation with Schmitt.

Ernst Rudolf Huber recalls joining Schmitt's seminar in spring 1924; according to his memory, there were at the time 'the brothers Adams,[122] Waldemar Gurian, Werner Becker, Ernst Friesenhahn, Ernst Forsthoff and Karl Lohmann, later also Otto Kirchheimer and Werner Weber.'[123] In the preface to his doctoral thesis, which had developed out of a final paper written in the winter term 1925–6, he thanks Schmitt for the 'insight into the spirit of public law'. In those days, students who became assistants did so after their first state examination, and in most cases they did their legal training at the same time. Kurt Aschenberg, a seasoned soldier, was formally Schmitt's assistant.[124] He was succeeded by Ernst Friesenhahn, who would later become an influential university professor and judge at

Germany's Federal Constitutional Court. Friesenhahn studied in Bonn from 1920 and passed his first state examination in June 1924. During his legal training, he was Schmitt's assistant from the winter term 1924–5 onwards. Between 1 April 1925 and 31 March 1928 (i.e., until Schmitt's move to Berlin) he was again his permanent assistant.[125] On 15 February 1927 he passed his doctorate *summa cum laude*. Following his second state examination, he again became an assistant in Bonn in 1929, and after a while he was sent to join Schmitt in Berlin. Braubach, Schneider and Schlosser came from the philosophical faculty and were slightly older. Paul Adams[126] and Waldemar Gurian joined the seminar from the humanities and already held PhDs. Werner Becker was also a member of the seminar and was rather an 'outsider to the profession', although Schmitt took on the role of first examiner for his dissertation. In addition Duška participated in the seminars from time to time. Huber emphasizes in particular Schmitt's 'challenging way of asking questions', his turn towards the 'real' constitution, the 'culture of open discussion' and the social evenings spent together in the Weinhaus Streng, a wine bar.[127] Huber was very friendly with Karl Lohmann, the son of a priest from Koblenz, who studied law from 1922, after four terms of chemistry. Lohmann had come to Bonn in the winter term 1923–4, passed his first state examination in December 1925, and also passed his doctorate.[128] For two years he worked as the head of a factory's legal department before continuing his academic career from 1928–9 as a faculty assistant. Later he worked in the research division of the Deutsche Hochschule für Politik [German University for Political Sciences] in Berlin. After 1933, he again became a close collaborator of Schmitt.

There are dozens of letters from Schmitt's former students which mention a conversation, an encounter or a relationship that is 'unforgettable', or that was 'decisive' or 'formative'. Lohmann thanks him for the friendly 'interest that [he] always took also in those of his former students who were not famous'.[129] Forsthoff remembers: 'I took your tutorial in public law, and I admit that your name did not yet mean much to me at the time. I had not read any of your books. But this tutorial became a decisive event in my life. For the first time, I met with the spirit of law and of jurisprudence. In that summer of 1923, I became a jurist' (EFCS, pp. 397f.). Schmitt, at that time, gave Forsthoff the theme for his doctoral thesis. In June 1924, Forsthoff passed his first state examination and began his legal training. As early as January 1925 he handed in his thesis, and on 27 February he passed his viva. Again and again, Forsthoff recalled his moment of epiphany. Thus, he would later write:

> I realize that it is now thirty-five years since I first sat at your feet in the summer term of 1923 and learned only through you, in my fifth term, hence pretty late, but not too late, what it means to be a jurist – or rather, at that time, what it means to become one. The fact that you soon afterwards accepted me as your pupil was the turning point and piece of luck in my life, and what the later years comprise in terms of encouragement and the way I profited from you can hardly be put into words. (EFCS, p. 137)

Werner Becker[130] introduced himself on 24 April 1923 as Guardini's 'secretary'. 'Like Saul was looking for an ass, I was looking for an examiner, and found a teacher',[131] he wrote at once. In connection with his study of Hobbes, Becker went to England for a couple of months at the end of 1924 but resumed close contact with Schmitt after his return. As the editor of Guardini's journal *Abendland* [Occident], Becker promoted Schmitt's work. In 1975, he recalled: 'Fifty years ago today, you met me in the streets in Bonn and said: "Mr Becker, you are not looking well. In examinations, I wish to see well-rested candidates in front of me. Promise me: you will not touch a book again."' Becker thanked Schmitt that he 'was allowed to be one of [his] favourite pupils'.[132] Later, he would be even more precise: 'In your famous seminar in Bonn you handed the final presentation on 'Definition der Demokratie nach Schmitt' [Definition of democracy according to Schmitt] to me. In that presentation, I tried to argue independently of you and Hobbes with the help of the holy Thomas Aquinas – and remarkably you accepted that from the very beginning.'[133] There are many more testimonies to the fact that Schmitt was a charismatic teacher and a generous examiner. His examiner's reports on doctoral theses are an important source. However, some of his disciples later parted with Schmitt: Gurian as early as 1927, Friesenhahn later in 1934. And Becker also remembers: 'In 1933, I fell out with him [Schmitt] over the question of anti-Semitism, and only in 1940 did we accidentally meet again in the streets in Berlin.'[134] Only much later did Becker reconcile himself with Schmitt. Huber as well as Lohmann kept a personal distance after 1945. Of Schmitt's students during his time in Bonn, Forsthoff and Werner Weber became the strongest advocates of his work after 1945.

A difficult student: Waldemar Gurian (1902–1954)

Waldemar Gurian was born in 1902 in St Petersburg, grew up in St Petersburg and Moscow, and in 1911 moved with his mother to Berlin. He came from a Jewish family. In Germany, his mother converted to Catholicism, and her son was christened in 1914. After the outbreak of war Gurian lived in the Netherlands for some time. He passed his school leaving certificate [Abitur] in 1920 in Düsseldorf. In 1923 he completed his doctorate with Max Scheler in Cologne; the topic of his thesis was 'Die deutsche Jugendbewegung'. After the doctorate, he joined the editorial staff of the *Kölnische Volkszeitung*, a leading Catholic daily newspaper which repeatedly published pieces by Schmitt. Gurian soon changed his relationship with the paper into that of a freelancer, and in November 1924 he moved to Godesberg.

Gurian dated the period of his closer connections with Schmitt to the years 1924 to 1926. But, on 14 March 1923, Schmitt already had a note in his diary about 'a Russian Jew from Cologne'. Their close contact began at that time. As one of Schmitt's first students in Bonn, Gurian adopted the suggestion of distinguishing between a counter-revolutionary Catholic philosophy of the state and Romanticism and of representing the Catholic

position publicly. The dispute over his slating of Ball clouded their relationship. Further indiscretions and polemics put a strain on it. But during
all of 1927, Schmitt and Gurian still met frequently. Through Jacques
Maritain, Gurian[135] organized the translation of *Political Romanticism* by
Pierre Linn, who then became one of Schmitt's closer friends. In December
1927, an 'incident'[136] between Gurian and Eschweiler occurred in which
Schmitt took Eschweiler's side. At the beginning of 1928, the relationship
between Gurian and Schmitt ended completely. Schmitt wanted Gurian
'on no account' (CSLF, p. 251) to receive a copy of his *Constitutional
Theory*. However, some correspondence between them still took place until
1932. After 1933, Gurian emigrated to Switzerland, from where he heavily
attacked his former teacher in Bonn.[137] Gurian's biographer speaks of a
'peculiar attachment' and 'love–hate relationship'.[138] Hannah Arendt, in
retrospection, praises Gurian's exceptional talent and capacity for 'friendship' and 'faithfulness', his 'unfailing sense for quality and relevance', and
his 'quality of human greatness'.[139] She compares him to Dostoevsky's
'idiot' and uses him as an example of 'men in dark times'. If Gurian had
not been the highly talented and 'peculiar' character that Arendt depicts,
Schmitt would not have associated himself with him.

In his publications, Gurian pushed Schmitt's view of a Catholic literature to the limit. He saw himself as a decidedly 'Catholic writer'
[katholischer Publizist] and tried to create a new type of author, one
who would prove the 'possibility' of being a Catholic intellectual who
intervenes 'actively in the present crisis of the European spirit'. 'The task
of a Catholic author [Publizist] today is to have a missionary influence
on the modern world, not just to battle as a soldier against the modern
world.'[140] Gurian scorned the 'pragmatism' of everyday journalism and
in this respect saw himself as being in line with Theodor Haecker and
Hugo Ball, although he attacked them at times. He sought the 'connection
with scholarship' and a standing in the Church, sounded out the Catholic
terrain with a sharp pen, and continued Schmitt's critique of Romanticism
and his history of the counter-revolutionary philosophy of the state. In
this way, he picked up the impulse provided by *Political Romanticism*. His
interventions lived off the discussions he had with Schmitt, Eschweiler,
Peterson and others in Bonn.

The fact that Gurian pushed Schmitt's polemical views to the limit
already showed in his attacks on Ball[141] and also on Ernst Robert
Curtius.[142] The polemic against Curtius, behind which the latter suspected
Schmitt himself, closed the doors to a Habilitation for Gurian in Bonn.[143]
As a polemic against a 'secularized Catholicism', it was also in part a
hypercritical jab at Schmitt. Gurian polemicized against a 'certain circle
which admires the Church as a haven for spirit and political order, without
acknowledging its divine foundation', against those who pay homage to
a 'secularized Catholicism . . . which reveres a Church without Christ'
and sees 'the greatness of the Church in having tamed Christianity with
a Roman regime'.[144] Some of Schmitt's ideas went in similar directions.
Gurian soon turned against Bolshevism in his literary battle [publizis-
tischen Kampf];[145] he analysed the new nationalism,[146] criticized the

National Socialist struggle with the Church[147] and became a pioneer of a comparative critique of totalitarianism.[148] However, before 1933 his particular achievement was the creation of a combative type of 'Catholic author' [des katholischen Publizisten].

'What is Theology?' Erik Peterson (1890–1960)

Hugo Ball, Werner Becker and Waldemar Gurian were only three of Schmitt's early companions to interpret his *Political Romanticism* in a Catholic vein. Whoever sought Schmitt's company at the time needed to position himself accordingly. The theologian Wilhelm Neuß was Schmitt's oldest friend in Bonn. The Protestant theologian Erik Peterson, who had met Schmitt even before 1920, in Haecker's Munich circles,[149] came to Bonn in 1924 as professor for early Church history and the New Testament. He soon was one of Schmitt's closest partners in conversation. Whereas Schmitt, in particular in his correspondence with Smend, interpreted his disputes with Kaufmann, Hensel and others in the faculty in anti-Semitic terms and expressed himself very polemically, he noted in his diary what a 'great relief'[150] it was to have Peterson in Bonn as a partner in theological conversations. The two met almost daily. Soon, Schmitt would call him his 'best friend'.[151] In 1925, Peterson presented an outline of his approach in a lecture titled 'Was ist Theologie?' [What is theology?]. In it, he took up a stance against the dialectical theology of Karl Barth and Rudolf Bultmann and distanced himself clearly from 'theological journalism'[152] in the wake of Kierkegaard. With Barth, he shared the question of how one may speak of God. He tied the possibility to do so strictly to 'the fact [Punktum] of faith' in the revelation. Theology lives through 'obedient faith' in revelation. Only Christ was able to talk of God. Theology has only a 'derivative authority'. 'There is no theology among Jews and heathens', Peterson claimed. 'Theology only exists within Christianity, and only on the premise that the word made flesh spoke of God.'[153] Dogma and the sacrament, he said, are the 'continuation of the incarnation of logos and of its speaking of God'.[154] At that time, the dogma, for Peterson, also existed outside of the Church. Schmitt agreed with him on the rejection of dialectical theology and in the emphasis on the authoritarian and dogmatic core of Christianity, without his ever having practised dogmatic theology. However, Schmitt did not limit the possibility of theology to Christianity as strictly as Peterson. He also shared Peterson's reservations about religious journalism and protected the 'great scholar' against the accusation of producing journalistic 'exercises in beautiful writing'.[155] Whereof the juridical Political Theology, whose business was clarification, remains silent – i.e., the religious substance matter – thereof theological dogmatism must necessarily speak. Thus, it is hardly surprising that Schmitt, as a jurist, was also interested in the alternative of theological dogmatism.

Schmitt spent a lot of time, and went through many bottles of wine, with Peterson. He agreed with his return to the authoritative and positively

'Let the last act begin' – Erik Peterson in his diary on 17 July 1918

given 'actuality [Realcharakter] of revelation'. Peterson was an extraordinarily erudite person. As a 'theologian of jurisprudence' (Barbara
Nichtweiß), he understood the Christian concepts in a Roman context
and restored to them their theological dimension as well as giving them
an apocalyptic twist. Peterson wished for the appearance of the Antichrist
for the sake of bringing about the end. During the last weeks of the war,
he had already noted in his diary: 'The *katechon* . . . may stop his delaying work. Let the last act begin.'[156] Peterson did not restrict dogmatics to
a biblical foundation. He perceived the position of the Protestant Church
as altogether weakened after the 'end of sovereign episcopacy'. In 1928, he
discussed with Adolf von Harnack the danger of the 'Church becoming a
sect'[157] and of the 'history of the Church in Germany thus taking the same
path as the Anglo-Saxon Church'.[158] Peterson took a decision in favour of
a 'return to the Catholic tradition'[159] and converted to Catholicism in 1930.
On the level of theology, his 'dogmatic' approach pushed him in that direction; on the level of politics it was his search for a public appearance and
legal form for the Church. The understanding of the Church that Peterson
sketched in a short booklet in 1929 limited the Church as a 'visible'
'heathen Church' to its opposition to Judaism, and assigned to Judaism
the rather questionable role of being the 'delayer', which guaranteed the
interim existence of the Church. 'We may even claim', Peterson wrote,
'that the Jews delay the return of Christ through their disbelief.'[160] In 1933,
he took a less extreme stance and declared his opposition to National
Socialism. In this context, he attacked Schmitt as a heathen representative
of Caesarism. Between 1935 and 1951, Peterson and Schmitt again met
each other and exchanged letters, until their relationship was finally broken
off for good.

The mood changes

During his time in Bonn, Schmitt did not unambiguously opt for the Church as an alternative to the state. His Catholicism essay, not least, was blowing his own trumpet. On 18 January 1924, the Regional Court in Bonn annulled his first marriage because of wilful deception. Schmitt's attempt also to have the marriage annulled by the Church, however, failed. On 4 November, the Offizialat (the Church's judicial body) of the archbishop in Cologne questioned Schmitt on the matter: 'In great detail, with great decency, yet full of revulsion at my stupidity and ridiculousness. Feel deep shame and anger at being cheated' (TB, 4 November 1924). But, on 18 June, Schmitt's request for an annulment was rejected. By Easter 1925, Schmitt had already become engaged to Duška, and on 8 February they married in a civil ceremony without first waiting for the judgment on the appeal, which also turned out to be negative (9 July 1926). His remarriage meant that Schmitt was formally excommunicated and so no longer allowed to receive the holy sacraments. In addition, Duška was of Catholic Orthodox faith. Schmitt's reputation as a 'Catholic' theorist of the state was much diminished by this.[161] He considered the failure of his attempts to have his first marriage declared invalid as an injustice, something for which he would not forgive the Church. At that time, Schmitt changed his orientation yet again. There was no longer an alternative to the option of state authority, and his path towards the 'total' state slowly became visible.

At the beginning of 1926, Schmitt discussed the relationship between Christianity and the Roman Empire with Feuchtwanger. He wondered 'whether Christianity had destroyed or corrupted [gefälscht] this beautiful state, or whether it had rather saved it in the form of the Catholic Church' (CSLF, p. 155). Feuchtwanger responded, referring to oriental studies, that St Paul 'had founded the Christian Church, and that the principles and events which gave that foundation stability had been non-Christian and "non-religious" to the highest degree' (CSLF, p. 160). To Blei, Schmitt made negative remarks at that time, saying that 'the eon of Rome [has] ended'. Blei reacted by inviting Schmitt to co-author an anonymous publication with him:

This, and related issues, I would like to present in a (fictional) biography of Pope Boniface the Tenth (pope between 1927 and 1938): power and means of the Church then and now, futile attempts at restoration by precisely this Boniface, and why he failed, despite his enormous efforts as an important Christian character. But you must contribute to this work. As you can see from the dates, it is not meant to be a utopia. Everything that calls itself a statesman today will have a place in it. And the *homines novi* are nothing but living persons who have been transposed into the Church and inaugurated by the pope, persons such as, for instance, Prof. Dr Carl Schmitt . . . However, an important bit of preliminary work, which has never been undertaken so far, would be a description of the Church as an economic body, of its self-interest as an organized body of civil servants . . . Should we not secretly (for it would be published very anonymously) join forces for this biography?[162]

Blei took a certain preparedness for such serious jokes on Schmitt's part for granted. The eulogy on the 'political form' of the Church turned into the sharpest critique of her 'concrete' shape. In 1930, Blei wrote at the end of his autobiography:

> This, however, is the purpose of war: to demonstrate to a Christianity which only presumes it is Christian that the Christian eon has reached its end and that the Antichrist has been victorious and established his intermediate realm . . . Because the Church no longer spoke the word and could no longer speak because it did not have the word any more. What the Church spoke and did was secular throughout. What it spoke and did was not of Christ, but of the Antichrist.[163]

Did Schmitt also think along these lines? We cannot altogether rule out this possibility, although he reacted with complete outrage to any suggestion that he might be a godless advocate of the Church. His reservations about the modern state and his apocalyptic perception of the Great War drove him back to the alternative of the Church for some time. But the Church could hardly fulfil his high expectations. Schmitt was bound to be disappointed, with or without the divorce procedure. At the end of 1924 he had already fallen out with the Catholic milieu and clericalism. In addition, there were the dissonances with his 'Jewish' colleagues. Schmitt concentrated on his private life, on the contact with his students, and on colleagues from neighbouring disciplines whom he befriended. His arrival in Bonn did not give him a firm ground on which to stand.

13

From Status Quo to Democratic 'Myth'

The standards of a reviewer

Schmitt preferred small formats; he never wrote any doorstoppers. Only his *Constitutional Theory* is a solid textbook. Schmitt was a master of the short booklet of the type he wrote during his time in Bonn. For an author of his importance, he also wrote – from his youth right to mature old age – a surprising number of reviews and review articles. In Bonn he positioned himself against some great names of the Weimar period. One of his topoi was that the aim must be the 'concept'. From the time of his doctoral thesis, Schmitt distinguishes sharply between the 'terminological' approach and the 'systematic' and 'conceptual' aim. A French study he calls a 'likeable document of female enthusiasm' that would look better in a 'dress of free rhapsodic rhythms'.[1] He denies elementary knowledge of the problems of state theory and the 'capacity for the conceptual understanding of the material' to the philologist of German Paul Kluckhohn.[2] In a review of Charles Edwyn Vaughan's 'history of political ideas', he takes issue with forms of presentation that focus on individuals and with the 'compendia industry'. By contrast, the review praises the dialectical perspective of the 'Hegelians'. Schmitt establishes that Vaughan, with 'Victorian noblesse', conceives the fundamental question of 'how to construct the relationship between individual and state' in liberal terms, and that his book thus belongs to the pre-1914 'atmosphere'.[3] In a German edition of a book by Hobhouse, he criticizes mistakes made in the translation as well as its deceptive neutrality, which covered up the fact that it was actually 'propaganda literature'.[4] Schmitt praises Rudolf Kjellén's *Der Staat als Lebensform* [The state as a form of life] as an 'anti-liberal' book that reminds the reader of the 'geopolitical' foundations and the 'organic' unity of the state, and thus 'breathes new life into the great myth of the "state"'.[5] The miscellaneous text 'Eine französische Kritik der Zeit' [A French critique of the times] distinguishes the French analysis of the problem of 'authority' as preferable to Rathenau's 'lament' over contemporary times. Schmitt situates the books he reviews within the context in which they emerged and thus uncovers their hidden political agenda. And he holds up a mirror to German scholarship by contrasting it with foreign publications.

In the mid-1920s, Schmitt developed his critique of legal positivism, in particular in his engagement with the works of Richard Thoma, Leo Wittmayer and Gerhard Anschütz. At the end of January 1924 he wrote an analysis of Thoma's concept of democracy. Both Schmitt and Thoma, his later successor in Bonn, took Max Weber as their point of departure, but Schmitt criticized Thoma's contribution to the Weber *Erinnerungsgabe*[6] for being based on 'current linguistic usage' and demanded sharper 'conceptual definitions'. Thoma, he says, simply takes his understanding of 'democracy as self-government' (PB, p. 23) from vague everyday language, without clarifying the ideological assumptions this understanding contains. 'Kelsen's claim that the idea of democracy required a relativist worldview' (PB, p. 24), in any case, was not refuted by Thoma's arguments. Schmitt shifted the discussion onto the plane of 'metaphysical' conceptual definitions. Thoma's objections against his *Crisis* booklet Schmitt later countered with a detailed defence of his approach based on 'principles', juxtaposing his own concept of democracy to the 'illusion of the lively flame' (PB, p. 57) of parliamentary discussion. He demonstrated to Thoma how the concept of democracy had to be developed – i.e. by going systematically beyond the existing terminology.

With Leo Wittmayer, Schmitt entered into a proper battle of reviews. He explained to Wittmayer that his 'rejection of the political is a very special kind of politics'[7]: namely, the legitimation of the status quo. In response, Wittmayer wrote a negative review of the *Crisis* booklet and replicated critical remarks.[8] Gerhard Anschütz's standard commentary on the constitution Schmitt later also accused of a lack of 'fundamental concepts' and 'fundamental systematics':

It is part of what was called 'positivism' before the war to avoid the discussion of fundamental constitutional concepts in order to be able to interpret the constitution in the manner of civil law, and apart from that to point to the 'lawgiver' whenever a real problem occurs. But what may have been permissible under the stable conditions during the years from 1871 to 1914 is no longer possible and fails in the face of the real problems of today's state law.[9]

Schmitt's distinction between a 'terminological' and a 'systematic' investigation assumes a sharp demarcation line between a 'positivist' commentary and his own 'attempt at a system', later presented in the form of his *Constitutional Theory*.

Schmitt's works were again and again accused of polemical intensification, exaggeration and distortion, and so were his reviews. They were not free of rage. Schmitt smelled intrigue and deception everywhere. He perceived a 'Meinecke clique' and a 'Spann gang' (CSLF, p. 146), as well as a general positivistic delusion, to be at work. His personal dissonances with the theorist of state law Fritz Stier-Somlo, his (Jewish) colleague in nearby Cologne, he pursued in the form of pieces published throughout the whole of 1924. Schmitt was angered by a negative review which Stier-Somlo had published in the *Kölner Zeitung* (2 February 1924). Stier-Somlo contradicted Schmitt at the Jena meeting of state theorists and also wrote a report both on the discussions and on the meeting, neither of which made Schmitt look good. Schmitt reacted by writing a sharp review in which he picked the Hobhouse translation, for which he held Stier-Somlo responsible, to pieces. At the time, he was interested in questions of translation due to his personal contacts with the translator Karl Rick.[10] Schmitt wrote his scathing review immediately after the meeting in Jena, showed it to people he trusted, such as Bilfinger and Schmitz, in order to get their reactions, and then sent it to the *Frankfurter Zeitung*. Later, he asked for it to be returned[11] and gave it to Singer's *Wirtschaftsdienst*, where it appeared at the end of July in the *Kritischen Blättern* [Critical notes], a monthly literary supplement which was discontinued in 1926. Kurt Singer wrote to Schmitt: 'You will have received the author's copies by now. I particularly enjoyed seeing that this volume was made up almost exclusively of contributions by you, by Rosenbaum or by me. I hope it can be sensed that this journal is edited in the place where the *Hamburg Dramaturgy***** was written.'[12] The review sparked off biting interventions, which Schmitt recorded in his diary. The Meiner publishing house requested the right to a reply, which was published at the end of November.[13] Schmitt spoke of 'intrigues' (TB, 4 December 1924). Further to the publisher's protestations, Stier-Somlo clarified that he was not, as Schmitt had claimed, the editor of the work.[14] Schmitt considered the publication of a dossier on 'Der Fall Hobhouse–Stier-Somlo: Dokumente zur Soziologie der Wissenschaft' [The case of Hobhouse–Stier-Somlo: documents on the sociology of scholarship] (CSLF, p. 120). Feuchtwanger put him in his place: 'Such a publication on this matter might harm the author rather than the individuals concerned, because there is no need to prove general human and professorial weaknesses' (CSLF, p. 127). Despite this, Schmitt wrote to Smend with open anti-Semitism: 'I feel isolated in my profession, for someone who is orthodox in all his instincts this is a terrible situation ... the ridiculous situation that Wittmayer, Stier-Somlo, Mendelssohn-Bartholdy and Nawiasky – four Jews against one Christian – attack me in all of the journals, and no one notices what is going on.'[15] These polemics already displayed Schmitt's inclination to engage in friend–enemy relations and his capacity to polarize opinion. In the mid-1920s, he wielded his reviewer's sword against more of his liberal colleagues. Slowly, he worked his way towards an analysis of contemporary constitutional law. Although in his *Political Theology* he had already formulated the points of a fundamental critique of positivism and normativism, and of their main representatives Anschütz and Kelsen, the full force of his short remarks was hardly visible at that time.

---

* Gotthold Ephraim Lessing's *Hamburger Dramaturgie* was written between 1767 and 1769, while Lessing was Dramaturg [dramatic adviser] at the German National Theatre in Hamburg. It is not written as a systematic work, but consists of a series of critical notes on plays and productions containing fundamental observations on poetical and dramatic theory. English edition: *Hamburg Dramaturgy*, New York, 1962.

The principle of law versus Geneva: legitimate homogeneity?

Schmitt's constitutional theory was a result of his reflections on Versailles and Geneva. But in the background stood also a certain understanding of the problem of federalism within the Reich. Schmitt experienced, first, the situation in Alsace and Lorraine, later, the separatist crisis in Bavaria and the threat of annexation in the Rhinelands. The special problem of Alsace was characterized by the attempt of the state to stabilize a reconquered 'Reichsland' [a territory of the Reich] as a state within the federation [Bundesland]. Even more difficult was the situation of Lorraine,[16] torn between France and Germany; it obviously interested Schmitt also because of his family ties to the region. After 1918, there was a real danger that Bavaria would not remain a part of Germany. The extremist revolutionaries hoped to gain more freedom from the 'Reich' by pursuing a separatist course and a rapprochement with Austria. By contrast, the Rhineland was threatened primarily by French foreign policy after Versailles. The crisis of 1923, which saw the military occupation of the Rhine and Ruhr areas, politicized Schmitt's work. Schmitt now saw as his task a conceptual clarification of power relations and the principle of law. His 'battle' against Versailles and Geneva began at the end of 1924 with a review article on 'Die Kernfrage des Völkerbundes' [The core question regarding the League of Nations]. He took for granted that systems of international law reflected political power relations and were upheld by major powers. Loss of power, he assumed, led to reduced sovereignty. He also accepted as a given point of departure that a country that had lost a war became an 'object of international politics'. His 'core question', however, was whether the post-war order was able to develop into a legal order securing peace.

In order to answer this question it is first necessary to draw a distinction between a 'normal' and an 'abnormal' situation. Someone who considers the existing status quo, the contingent power relations after 1918, as a 'normal' situation confuses power and right and forsakes the chance of developing the legal foundation of the League of Nations. This is why Schmitt writes: 'The actual problem with the League of Nations is not the guarantee of the territorial status quo, but the guarantee of the legitimacy of today's status quo' (FP, p. 12). Starting out from the concept of 'federation' [Bund], he seeks to establish the legal justification of the League of Nations on grounds of principle. As his historical example he uses the Holy Alliance after 1815. However, Schmitt adopts from this example only the idea of legitimacy through homogeneity. The legitimacy of a 'real federation is based on a minimum of guarantees and on homogeneity' (FP, p. 4), he writes. The 'guarantee' is the result of homogeneity within the federation: of the common responsibility for shared constitutional standards. Schmitt discusses possibilities for further legal developments and ties the legitimacy of a federation to the existence of a homogeneous standard. Within the framework of his review article he presents various possible options, but ends inconclusively and avoids giving final answers. With reference to Soviet Russia, he only demonstrates that fundamental commonalities must be a precondition for joining. He does not conclusively answer the question of whether or not Germany should join the League of Nations, but only makes a plea against accepting the Soviet Union into it. On the question of the League's homogeneity, he only points to its controversial practices.

Schmitt wrote his review article in December 1924, under extreme time constraints, for *Schmollers Jahrbuch*. Later, in January 1926, he developed it into the monograph of the same title, and following Germany's request to be admitted into the League of Nations it was soon published, in the spring of the same year. His analysis identifies as 'the characteristic of a true federation' a 'minimum of guarantees and homogeneity'. And it investigates the 'object protected by guarantees' in order to warn against possible strategies of legal legitimization of political ends, which brings Schmitt to the 'guarantee of Art. 10' as an 'instrument for the protection of the victorious parties at Versailles and for the legalization of their bounty' (FP, p. 97). He explains the 'lack of any concrete' principle of legitimacy with reference to the historical failure of monarchist legitimacy and the recent principle of nationality. Schmitt now explains, more explicitly than he had in 1924, how the federal legitimacy of homogeneity is based on the requirement of common constitutional standards, using the Holy Alliance and the Monroe Doctrine as illustrations. 'No inter-state order without inner-state order' (FP, p. 118), he claims, and plays off the example of the Monroe Doctrine, the American practice, against the 'dogma on non-intervention'. Schmitt does not dogmatically reject the possibility of intervention, but rather accepts it as a necessary tool in order to guarantee federal homogeneity. The members of a federation guarantee mutual support for the sake of their shared constitutional standard. Finally, Schmitt uses the discussion of these questions against Soviet Russia and registers his reservations against a membership for 'Bolshevist Russia'. He does not argue against Germany joining the League of Nations in principle, but only warns against the dangers of political abuse and further legalization of interventions. The 'touchstone' (FP, p. 125) regarding his doubts about the homogeneity of the League of Nations is a clear stance against Soviet Russia. What holds the federation together and where does it end? (Today, such questions are also asked with respect to the EU.)

In a lecture in Bonn, Schmitt later explained that the 'Völkerbund und Europa' [The League of Nations and Europe] are two very different 'points of orientation' (FP, p. 241). The attitude of the United States alone, a 'mixture of absence and presence', is enough reason, Schmitt argues, not to equate the League of Nations with the homogeneity of the European tradition. A political unity of Europe would be 'a true miracle' (FP, p. 247). In another lecture, Schmitt compares the difficulties involved in the fiction of equality to the fable of 'the storks and the frogs', in which both are given equal rights to look for nourishment (FP, p. 262), and invokes the friend–enemy distinction in this context. Schmitt asks the 'question of the political existence of the German people' and, like Max Weber[17] before him, sees the danger of Germany 'turning into a kind of Switzerland' [Verschweizerung], of Germany, as a power in the middle of Europe, falling by the wayside and dreaming dreams 'of happiness without problems, without having to defend itself, and without history' (FP, p. 264).[18] Schmitt's strongest objection is directed against the legitimization of the status quo. If Versailles is considered as representing normalcy and not in need of revisions, then Germany deprives itself of its rights. Schmitt's horror in the face of such a fiction of normalcy was great. He expressed the 'moral' dimension of this horror very clearly in his lecture on 'The Rhinelands as an Object of International Politics'. In the journal *Hochland*, he also suggested that the present status quo did not guarantee peace, for the sole reason that it was upheld by heterogeneous interests.[19] The present times, he said, were characterized by 'strife' [Friedlosigkeit] and threatened to lead to the 'legalization of an unbearable condition between war and peace' (FP, p. 59).

From the 'injustice of foreign rule' to the 'deception of anonymity'

At the beginning of March 1924, Schmitt was offered a secure seat in the national elections by the Zentrumspartei of the Rhineland. Although he rejected the offer, the party remained interested in him as a speaker. Upon being contacted by the general secretary Wilhelm Hamacher, Schmitt, at short notice, agreed to give a lecture on 'Romanticism and Politics' at the Ursuline convent in Cologne on 19 May 1924. In November, he agreed to give another lecture, which first had to be cancelled, but apparently then took place in December.[20] On 14 April 1925, Schmitt again gave a lecture on the topic of 'The Rhinelands as an Object of International Politics' at the 'millennium celebration' of the Rhenish Zentrumspartei in Cologne. This was his first major political appearance. Schmitt immediately dictated the text for publication. Soon he would say: 'My lecture on the Rhinelands has been entirely ignored, probably because no one wants to have anything to do with a lecture that was given at an event of the Zentrum.'[21] A large exhibition had been organized at the event in Cologne. The cause of the celebration was not the treaty of Verdun which, in 843, divided the Carolingian Empire into three parts – i.e., a West and an East Franconia and Lorraine[22] – but rather the duchy of Lorraine's becoming part of the German kingdom in 925, hence the accession of a region that had subsequently been lost again to France. The date suggested itself solely on the grounds of the contemporary opposition to France. Schmitt's lecture marked the beginning of his engagement with the question of Versailles. In it, Schmitt does not claim that the Rhinelands were already nothing but an 'object', but he maintains that a process is under way that will 'turn the Rhinelands into an object of international politics and that organizes and legalizes their character as an object' (FP, p. 27). The lecture begins by presenting the transformations of imperial 'forms of rule'. Schmitt registers a turn away from open annexation and a transitional rule by protectorates and mandates. He asks the valid question of what the interest 'that makes the dominating power refrain from annexation' may be (FP, p. 30). He realizes that imperial powers want to minimize the costs of political rule and therefore adopt forms of indirect rule. The practice of annexation had the 'advantage of being out in the open and visible' and of clearly articulated relations of protection and obedience. By contrast, Germany today, he says, is ruled by a series of vague legal concepts that are capable of being 'interpreted in unpredictable ways' (FP, p. 32). However, Schmitt sees the greatest threat posed by vague legal concepts in the 'moral' confusion of the vocabulary, as a result of which 'words such as independence, freedom, self-determination, sovereignty [lose] their old meaning' (FP, p. 30).

Schmitt explains to his listeners, and hence to the Zentrumspartei, the moral advantages of clear power relations [Herrschaftsverhältnisse], using the Christian concept of authority [Obrigkeit]. He explains that the duty to obey was tied to the framework of the mediaeval order.[23] But he does not side emphatically with the concept of authority; rather, he only refers to the fact that the moral demand for clear power relations and loyal duties was widespread in the Christian tradition. The reasons why modern imperialism adds to the 'injustice of foreign rule the deception of anonymity' (FP, p. 36), he argues, have more to do with political and economic interests. The aims are political advantages and high economic profit and low cost. Ultimately, Schmitt claims, modern forms of rule destroy the 'possibility of leading an honest and decent life' (FP, p. 38). For this reason he adds to his demand for freedom and right the demand for 'truth' and juxtaposes the 'simple and elementary concepts' of 'truth, freedom and right' to the modern 'conceptual confusion'. Schmitt considers 'truth' to be the first and foremost condition of freedom. Only by systematically resolving the 'conceptual confusion', he holds, will it be possible to achieve the 'freedom' of a political self-determination that will restore 'right'.

Schmitt saw modern imperialism as the age of ideologies. He knew that the vocabulary used was a battle tool and had to be understood politically. On closer inspection, even his reference to the concept of authority [Obrigkeit] was intended to be critical rather than affirmative.

'Stupidity' and 'redemption': Duška and Magda

From August 1924, Duška was living in a sanatorium. Schmitt visited her over Christmas in Lugano. After her return to Bonn, Schmitt and Duška got engaged, during a journey along the Mosel with the Eislers during Easter 1925. Three years earlier, Schmitt had promised to marry Kathleen at the Mosel. Now he consciously repeated the same tour, so that this time all would turn out fine. That was the moment when he discontinued the love diary about 'the shadow of God'. From Kathleen, via Lola, Schmitt's path had found its destination: Duška. However, on 18 June 1925, the judicial court [Offizialat] of the archbishop of Cologne, chaired by the canon Dr Ott, decided against an annulment of his first marriage by the Church. Though the court accepted that Cari was an impostor, it was not convinced that her aristocratic descent had been a *conditio sine qua non* for the marriage. Schmitt appealed against the decision. At that time, he wrote a legal opinion on a dispute over the electoral law in Saarlouis for the Zentrumspartei.[24] On 22 July, he completed the opinion. Stier-Somlo

wrote a second opinion, prompting Schmitt to produce yet another legal
opinion on the matter.

Schmitt continued his diary again at the time of the 'Dalmatian
journey', a journey Schmitt and Duška undertook upon their engagement, setting out from Munich and Bad Tölz (TB, 18 August to 25
September 1925). They travelled via Salzburg and Trieste, the contested
territory of Istria, and along the Adriatic coast of Croatia to Split, Ragusa
(Dubrovnik), Kupari, Cavtat,[25] and the green island of Korčula. Carl met
Duška's father in Agram (Zagreb), in order to alleviate the worries of
the family, while Duška remained with her mother in Daruvar. Having
returned to Bonn without Duška, Schmitt took care of the appeal against
the judgment of the Offizialat in Cologne and took it to the higher court in
Münster. His cousin André warned him forcefully against a marriage with
Duška. Schmitt frequently met with his old friends Eisler, Rosenbaum and
Kluxen. In Münster, he gave a lecture on the Church to the Association of
Catholic Academics as an advocate for peace, probably also with his trial in
mind.[26] He wrote reflections on his Illyrian travels, which Kaufmann called
an 'engagement announcement' (TB, 11 November 1925). In the faculty
at that time there were serious conflicts over the appointment of Albrecht
Mendelssohn-Bartholdy. Kaufmann and Landsberg wanted him; Schmitt
was strictly against his acquaintance from Hamburg. Kaufmann assured
him that 'Mendelssohn-Bartholdy [was] no Jew' (TB, 9 November 1925).
Schmitt wrote a 'special report against the appointment', dug up an old
dispute in which this 'disgusting, craven, dilettante Jew' (TB, 24 November
1925) and 'aesthete' had been involved, and was delighted 'over his discov-
ery' or unmasking. Following a hotly contested vote, Alexander Graf zu
Dohna was appointed instead.[27]

Schmitt spent a lot of time with Peterson, Adams and Gurian.
Occasionally, he met Alois Dempf from the *Abendland*. Theodor Haecker
came to Bonn. Ernst Rudolf Huber, Karl Lohmann and Joseph Schlosser
completed their doctorates. Schmitt continued meeting Arnold Schmitz
and Wilhelm Neuß, but now saw Vormfelde only much more rarely. He
frequently met with the economists Edgar Sahn, Joseph Schumpeter and
Erwin Beckerath. Throughout his whole time in Bonn, he had an intense
relationship with his brother Jupp in Cologne as well as with his younger
sister, little Anna. He was terrified by assassination attempts on Mussolini
(TB, 30 November 1925). Huber recalls that, at the time, Schmitt spoke of
an assassination of Mussolini as 'the greatest disaster conceivable within
the realm of politics'.[28] Wilhelm Neuß tried to talk him out of marrying
Duška; Schmitt read *Othello*. After three months, Duška returned to Bonn
(on 12 December) and, to begin with, lived in a guest house. By that time,
Schmitt's appeal procedure looked 'pretty hopeless'. Over the Christmas
period, Cousin André visited, 'urged caution' (TB, 27 December 1925)
and advised Schmitt against the marriage. Schmitt spent New Year's Eve
on his own. The assignment (28 December 1925) of a legal opinion on the
expropriation of princes, given to him by his old friend from the general
command Alexander Münch, was very welcome for financial reasons. In
it, Schmitt argues on the basis of normal conditions under existing law

against the 'communist' and 'democratic' proposals. 'Today, the revolutionary conditions of the months from November 1918 to February 1919 no longer apply', he concludes. 'Neither does the sovereign dictatorship of a constituent national assembly still exist. For almost seven years now, the Weimar Constitution has been in effect in Germany.'[29] After a week, the opinion was completed and Schmitt sent it off. Peterson told him stories about Karl Barth's private life that he found 'disgusting'. 'I am completely done with Christianity', he noted in his diary (9 January 1926), and began to write his booklet on the League of Nations, as well as setting out to find accommodation. In mid-January, the printed version of the legal opinion arrived. Schmitt attended a lecture by Erwin von Beckerath 'on fascism, nothing new, but I still found it very interesting' (TB, 21 January 1926). Later, Schmitt reviewed Becker's monograph on *Wesen und Werden des fascistischen Staates* [The nature and development of the fascist state].

At the registry office, Schmitt inquired about the necessary marriage documents. On 29 January and 5 February he gave lectures in Recklinghausen. From 31 January he began dictating the booklet on the League of Nations.[30] On 3 February he informed his parents and Eisler about the forthcoming wedding. A Catholic priest from the parish of St Martin in Godesberg warned Schmitt against this final 'break with the Church' (TB, 6 February 1926): 'It is very fortunate that I am getting away from the parsons [Pfaffen]',* Schmitt commented. As a wedding present for himself, he bought, fittingly, 'the collected works of Macchiavelli'. Only a few people were present at the wedding: little Anna, who was living in Bonn at the time, and Peterson and Vormfelde as witnesses. Georg Eisler was slightly taken by surprise and congratulated Schmitt rather reservedly by letter.[31]

There were no wedding celebrations. In the afternoon of his wedding day, Schmitt prepared a lecture on demilitarized zones, which he gave in the evening to the Rhein-Rappoltstein Association of Catholic students in Cologne.[32] Already the next day another catastrophe loomed: Duška had 'coughed up blood again' (TB, 9 February 1926). This was followed by a 'horrible dream' a few days later, in which Duška suddenly, like Cari before her, wanted 'to learn how to dance and to become a stage artist'. 'Fear of her Slavonic face, of her Slavonic cleverness.' Via Munich, Duška returned to Croatia again. The duties of term time put strong demands on Schmitt. The term break he spent relatively calmly, at first, with smaller outings in Bonn, before travelling to Berlin and then Hamburg, visiting his old friends am Zehnhoff and Eisler. On 22 March he received a 'telegram from Duška, saying that she had severe bleedings of the lung'. Another 'terrible time' began. Schmitt made short notes on a visit to Bilfinger and on the negative impression (TB, 30 March 1926) he had of the meeting of the Association of State Theorists in Münster, which is today considered one of the crucial moments in the so-called Richtungsstreit, the debate on the question of the methodical direction jurisprudence should take; he noted: 'indifferent

---

*   The term 'Pfaffe' originally denoted a priest as opposed to a monk. After Luther, and certainly by the time Schmitt wrote this remark, it was a derogatory term.

and bad presentation by Kaufmann,[33] anger over the priests [Pfaffen], who treat me badly'. Schmitt was waiting for his trial. In May, he gave a lecture on the situation of the Saargebiet with regard to international law.[34] Duška returned from Croatia and at first stayed at Ruppichteroth, despite the fact that the two were now a married couple. At the end of June she had to go to the hospital of the Johanniter in Bonn with pleurisy. She stayed there for five months, until the end of October. Schmitt had permanent financial difficulties again, and, as had once been the case in Düsseldorf and Munich, he asked Eisler for support. On 10 July, the Offizialat [judicial court] of the archbishop in Münster, chaired by the prelate Dr Dr Bernhard Dörholt, confirmed the negative verdict of the first instance. Cari, in the court's opinion, was a 'forger and a fraud', but Schmitt had not proved that he had only been prepared to marry her because he believed her to be an aristocrat. An implicit assumption was not sufficient. It was actually a statement made by Cousin André that proved fatal for Schmitt. He did not confirm that Schmitt had ever said that he would only marry an aristocrat. The Church did not annul the marriage with Cari. Thus, from a Catholic perspective, Schmitt, having married Duška, lived in 'concubinage' and was thus excommunicated. He was no longer allowed to take part in the Eucharist or to go to confession.

Finally, Schmitt found a house of his own in Friesdorf, Bonn. Every day he visited Duška in hospital. The medical bills scared him. He had fits of rage and ranted all the time. On 10 August he got to know a certain 'Miss Lizzi' while Duška was 'critically ill in hospital'. 'This woman will kill me', Schmitt repeatedly noted in his diary. He spent almost two weeks with the Eislers in Blankenese, Hamburg, and then travelled for a few days to Berlin, while an acquaintance of Duška's took care of the 'whole move' to Friesdorf. The 'feeling of horrible betrayal' (TB, 20 August 1926) again took hold of Schmitt around that time. He registered his lecherousness and 'greed for life'. Amid severe disputes and against the advice of those around him, he had married another Serbo-Croatian, who was now critically ill with tuberculosis. On 1 September, he moved into the large and beautiful house in Friesdorf. On the same day he met Miss Lizzi again, and a passionate affair began which would last until the end of Schmitt's time in Bonn. Lizzi worked as a saleswoman. Schmitt saw her almost daily. From 6 September onwards he called her Magda. It was a solid relationship. They did it during train journeys or on a 'secluded path' (TB, 27 September 1926) in Mehlem on the Rhine. The great theorist of state law noted down his arousals and 'ejaculations' in semi-public spaces and was surprised by his 'deranged sexuality' (14 September 1926). His diary records day by day, openly and irrefutably, what by bourgeois moral standards might only be understood as an expression of despair over his renewed marital trauma.

Dr Heinrich Rommen[35] introduced himself (TB, 6 September 1926) and became a pivotal figure in the seminar. However, Schmitt found his Catholic thesis on Suarez 'disgusting'. Schmitt began work on his essay 'Der unbekannte Donoso Cortés'[36] [The unknown Donoso Cortés], which was intended for Carl Muth's *Hochland*. At the end of October he sent the typescript to the editor, Friedrich Fuchs. At the same time, Schmitt's devastating critique of Friedrich Meinecke's *Idee der Staatsräson* [The idea of the *raison d'état*] was published in the *Archiv für Sozialwissenschaft und Sozialpolitik*. Schmitt sent the review, together 'with a polite letter' (TB, 11 September 1926), to the important historian and later colleague of his. The review was his revenge for the alleged silence of the Meinecke school of thought over his *Political Romanticism*. In reality, Meinecke had reviewed the book and recommended Schmitt to the Berliner Hochschule für Politik [Berlin Academy for Political Science]. Schmitt bought a guard dog for his house, which he diligently took for walks. He was in despair over his debts and financial problems, and happy that he owned a revolver that gave him the opportunity 'to commit suicide one day'. Schmitt visited von Schnitzler, or rather Schnitzler's wife, in Frankfurt, and met Prince Karl Anton Rohan, the editor of the *Europäische Revue*. His passion for Magda became more intense. He dropped 'money as printed matter in her letter box' (TB, 29 September 1926). At the beginning of October he spent a few days with Bilfinger, who was by now his closest ally in the profession. Schmitt cursed the 'dreadful stupidity of [his] second marriage' (TB, 8 October 1926). Bilfinger came to visit for a couple of days. Duška's health gradually improved, while Schmitt's affair with Magda continued in train compartments or under open skies.

Otto Kirchheimer joined the seminar at that point and became a close student. Even before 1933, he founded something like a Marxist 'left-wing Schmittianism'. The historian Hans Rothfels arrived for a visit from Königsberg. Uncle André suffered the 'Steinlein's fate' of a failed marriage. Magda was 'lovely and devoted, but often rough' (TB, 19 October 1926). The temperatures at the Rhine began to feel chilly, which is why Carl and Magda opted for the railway or the empty and available house, where only Ms Webers, the maid, would occasionally be in the way. Schmitt read *Othello* again. He wrote an article on 'Das Ausführungsgesetz zu Art. 48' [The Implementation Act regarding Art. 48],[37] read doctoral theses and was delighted with the work of Ernst Rudolf Huber.[38] The night before Duška's release from hospital, there was an 'intruder in the garden'. A policeman was called. 'Strange feeling, that there is a woman in the house' (TB, 1 November 1926). Schmitt moved 'into bed with Duška' and for a short moment had 'the feeling that it [is] over' (TB, 3 November 1926) with Magda. However, sex with Duška did not work well. 'Ejaculation. But it wasn't a release. No release without conquest.' Soon he met with Magda again, and throughout 1927 their relationship remained as solid as before. Term began and, at the recently founded Mittelrheinischen Verwaltungs- und Wirtschaftsakademie, Schmitt gave the weekly 'university courses for civil servants'[39] which were organized by Schmitt's colleagues and 'directors of study' in Bonn, Albert Hensel and Hans Dölle (later organized, in fact, by Friesenhahn). For financial reasons, Schmitt continued to teach such training courses from time to time. On 19 November he travelled to Berlin to discuss with am Zehnhoff what prospects he might have there. On 29 November he gave a lecture in Aachen. He then began with the preparation for a lecture on 'Volksentscheid und Volksbegehren' [Referenda and petitions for referenda], which he gave on 11 December at the invitation of the Berliner Juristische Gesellschaft [Juridical Society], in the hall of the Oberverwaltungsgericht [Upper Administrative Court] in the Hardenbergstraße.

1926 was a very difficult year for Schmitt. After the quarrels around his marriage, it was dominated by Duška's critical and chronic tuberculosis and his flight into the passionate affair with Magda. Yet, despite all these worries, he had now found a comparatively stable arrangement with Magda and Duška by separating out Eros and Caritas.

The 'myth' of direct democracy

After his *Crisis* treatise, Schmitt turned mainly to questions of international law. Only after completing his booklet *The Core Question Regarding the League of Nations* did he return to the theory of democracy in order to prepare the foundations for his constitutional theory. In the battle with Versailles and Geneva, he considered a strong political will to be a necessary condition if the German people wanted to assert themselves. From now on his work on constitutional theory had the purpose of dismantling the liberal elements and of constructively demonstrating the possibility of a democratic will formation beyond liberalism. Is an anti-liberal democracy possible at all? Schmitt's analysis of constitutional questions increasingly deepened the distinction between liberalism and democracy. As a first contribution to the 'theory of direct democracy', he developed fully, in his Berlin lecture on 'Referenda and Petitions for Referenda', a concept of the national 'myth' (to which he had referred first in 1923 in connection with Mussolini). The 'myth' of 'direct democracy' he identified with the possibility of an 'exceptional lawgiver' [außerordentlichen Gesetzgebers]. In the lecture, Schmitt first distinguishes the two concepts 'referendum' and 'petition for a referendum' and then analyses their possible interaction as a particular 'process of popular legislature' [Volksgesetzgebungsverfahren], which he also calls an 'exceptional process of legislature'. At the end, he discusses the 'natural limits of direct democracy'. He derives the concept of a people characteristic of direct democracy from the opposition between 'people and magistrate' as it is found in Roman state law, and he quotes research by Peterson on the concept of acclamation. Within the context of modern 'mass democracies' the process of acclamation depends on given questions. The people themselves cannot ask questions, but can answer simple questions only with 'yes' or 'no'. A 'pure' direct democracy is an anarchistic utopia. 'The directness of democracy cannot be organized without ceasing to be direct' (VV, p. 49). It can only be organized in the form of an 'exceptional' process. However, a 'people who are fully formalized' lose 'their vital greatness and force'.

Schmitt discovered a 'rift between liberalism and democracy', between force and form within the process of legislation, which, in his following works, he would describe in terms of the tension between 'legality and legitimacy' with increasing intensity and as increasingly dramatic. At the outset of his *Constitutional Theory*, he ties the 'myth' of a national movement, which had been introduced in the *Crisis* treatise, to an exceptional process. Schmitt – inspired by Rousseau and Sorel – links 'myth' to the classical model of the Roman tradition, without any reference to Greek democracy. He observed Italian fascism, discussed its development with Michels, von Beckerath and others, evoked the possibility of an 'exceptional process of legislature', and was actively committed to the important referenda which the political right used to organize and mobilize itself against the Weimar Republic. Although he described alternative democratic forms as possible under the Weimar Constitution, at the same time he demonstrated that they belonged to the enemy; with liberalism, democracy also had to go. His critique of Versailles and Geneva led him to make a sharp distinction between liberalism and democracy and to the adoption of an analytical strategy that played 'democracy' off against liberalism.

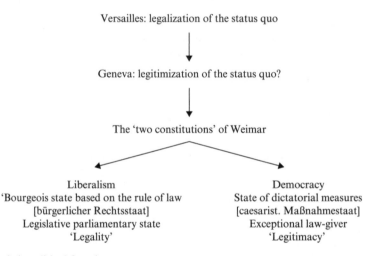

Versailles: legalization of the status quo

Geneva: legitimization of the status quo?

The 'two constitutions' of Weimar

Liberalism	Democracy
'Bourgeois state based on the rule of law	State of dictatorial measures
[bürgerlicher Rechtsstaat]	[caesarist. Maßnahmestaat]
Legislative parliamentary state	Exceptional law-giver
'Legality'	'Legitimacy'

Schmitt's political frontiers

14

The Yield of the Bonn Years: The Concept of the Political *and* Constitutional Theory

Sexus and system

At the beginning of 1927, Franz Blei was agonizing over how to give to his autobiography a form that would hide his 'complete indifference'[1] to his own person, and finally decided to dissolve the 'novel' describing his life into a series of portraits of his encounters with other people. Friendship alone, he said, was what kept him alive.[2] In contrast, Schmitt's diaries confront us with cascades of intimate passions and tragedies. Why, the rather irritated reader asks, did he do these things? Why did he hurl himself with open eyes into chaotic situations and catastrophes? Cari's dubious background was not wholly unknown to him. He married her despite the Tingel-Tangel, the suspicion of her being a thief and her disorderly papers. He also knew about Duška's health, and married her despite her illness and despite the breaks with the Church, the Zentrumspartei and the Catholic circles that it was likely to cause. Schmitt found many expressions for his 'stupidities', one of which was 'Unglücksrabe'.* One could also casually call him a 'Bruchpilot'.†

Dramatists pick their tragedies. Psychologists like to interpret a 'despite' as a 'because'. Sigmund Freud[3] saw people 'fail over their success' and choose their demise in a kind of 'theodicy of death' (Max Weber). Once all goals have been achieved, the guilty 'conscience' begins to nag in the form of 'inner renunciation'. At the beginning of the play, Othello can hardly believe his luck. Happiness has to be 'legitimate', has to be earned. Difficult characters cannot simply live their lives. For Schmitt, the tragic tensions in his private life were a condition of his creativity and productivity. His new marital disaster opened the way towards 'redemption'‡ by Magda and pushed him to leave Bonn. The precarious arrangement of a double life with Duška and Magda mobilized enormous energies for the writing of *The Concept of the Political* and *Constitutional Theory*.

---

* Literally: 'unlucky raven', a colloquial expression for someone attracting bad luck and disasters.
† Literally: 'crash pilot'.
‡ The German term 'Erlösung', as used by Schmitt in his diary, can mean both 'release' and 'redemption'. See his diary entries quoted in the previous chapter.

Heinrich Oberheid (dressed as a 'German bishop'; photograph taken after 1933): 'As a German, he has to study Protestant theology; that is the whole point of Germanness' – Schmitt's diary (22 March 1927)

1927 was taken up by Duška, Duška's illness and the liaison with Magda, as well as the production of magisterial works. The disputes surrounding Schmitt's appointment in Berlin went on for a long time before the decision was finally made.[4] After the departure of Walther Schücking, the chair of state law [staatsrechtlicher Lehrstuhl], which Hugo Preuß had previously held until 1921, became vacant. At the end of January, Schmitt gave lectures 'on fascism' and 'on sanctions' in Karlsruhe, Bonn, Recklinghausen und Buer (Essen). Newspaper articles published in Karlsruhe emphasize that, following Sorel, Schmitt spoke only about the fascist 'myth'.[5] On 20 January, Schmitt received a confidential inquiry from his old mentor, Moritz Julius Bonn in Berlin,[6] and on 28 January he travelled from Essen to Berlin in order to discuss the matter with Bonn and the Ministry of Culture. In early February he was back in Bonn but soon travelled again to Berlin, where he met Bonn as well as am Zehnhoff. Because of bad health, the latter retired from his post as Prussian minister of justice on 3 March 1927 and moved back to Düsseldorf. One last time, am Zehnhoff used his influence to help Schmitt. He spoke repeatedly to Bonn in order to find out 'whether the Hochschule is thinking about you'. To Schmitt, am Zehnhoff stressed the enormous importance which 'a move to Berlin would have for [him] as a state theorist'.[7] Moritz Bonn tried to make the Hochschule für Politik [Academy of Political Science] look attractive to Schmitt by mentioning the possibilities it offered for arranging lectures and training courses.[8] However, unauthorized initial negotiations with the ministry caused irritation,[9] and as a consequence Rothenbücher, as the first choice, was again ranked above Schmitt. Schmitt tried to explain his actions to Bonn in a letter:

I promised, if possible, to clarify the matter in advance – i.e., before you would begin to support my appointment. That is all I did. How should I otherwise be able to tell you that I would accept the appointment which I have not yet been offered. The amount of gossip in Berlin is incredible, and my only wish is to live in a matter-of-fact atmosphere such as objective people produce.[10]

Bonn's reply was sceptical: 'That academic life is full of gossip is not news to me. That you are astonished about it explains why you weren't more cautious in Berlin.'[11] At that point in time, Schmitt did not feel very optimistic about his chances.

However, around mid-February, all was still up in the air. Schmitt completed his 'university lectures for civil servants' at the Mittelrheinische Verwaltungsakademie in Breuel, Bonn. Theodor Däubler came to Bonn for a couple of days and gave lectures. Then, in March, Duška had to go to hospital for her first major lung operation. Schmitt registered this not without anger. 'Fit of rage because of all the costs, have to tap Eisler for money again' (TB, 27 March 1927). At the same time, he received an invitation from the Hochschule für Politik to join a 'discussion evening' on problems of politics. Continuing the theme from the winter term, the intended topics and problems to be discussed were from the 'area of domestic politics'.[12] Schmitt wrote down his *Concept of the Political*, which at first he called a 'state history' and 'state theory'. The text was quickly dictated (between 31 March and 4 April 1927) yet 'carefully formulated, and tried out in long seminar sessions and tutorials'.[13] Carl read it out to Duška in hospital, and her reaction was 'enthusiastic'. Between 5 and 10 April, Hermann Heller was in Bonn. Schmitt met him on friendly terms and gave him Bernano's text on the 'saint' as a present.[14] Soon afterwards, Schmitt submitted the text of *The Concept of the Political* for a fair copy to be produced.

In mid-April, Duška was released from hospital. Schmitt was very relieved about this, despite the fact that he continued to visit Magda and to keep an exact diary on his 'ejaculations'. After the completion of *The Concept of the Political*, he regularly practised shooting with a pistol and a rifle. Otto Kirchheimer, Heinrich Rommen and Carl Hirsch were by now the stars in the seminar. The close contact with Werner Becker continued, and the relationship with Heinrich Oberheid intensified into a close, family-like friendship.[15] Oberheid was a highly decorated volunteer. After the war, he studied political economy and soon became the confidant of the industrialist Hugo Stinnes. Following Stinnes's death, he unexpectedly took up the study of theology. Schmitt understood his move: 'As a German, he has to study Protestant theology; that is the whole point of Germanness' (TB, 22 March 1927). This would make Protestantism primarily a theology of nationalism. Oberheid, at that time, joined the SA* and the NSDAP, and in 1933 became a central figure in the 'German Christians', the political faction of Protestantism which followed National Socialism.

---

* SA = Sturmabteilung [attack division], the original paramilitary wing of the NSDAP, later replaced by the so-called SS = Saalschutz [security guards].

Schmitt received the fair copy of *The Concept of the Political*, tried out the text in his lectures, and then went to Berlin, in order to present it (on 20 May 1927) at the Hochschule für Politik.[16] Moritz Bonn, unfortunately, could not attend.[17] Schmitt was not happy with the event. 'Quickly changed dress; tired and nervous on the way to the Hochschule, red suitcase (Sombart was there, Blei accompanied by a beautiful woman), lost orientation, no good lecture, depressed. Awful discussion (Sombart's assistant Bloch, Paul Landsberg[18] very nice, touching how Heller defended me)' (TB, 20 May 1927). Schmitt's definition of the concept was met with strong opposition. Heller also soon formulated critical objections.[19] However, when the text was published in September, there were also many positive responses to it.

The next day, Schmitt attended Smend's lecture and went to the Kaiser-Friedrich-Gemäldesammlung [portrait gallery] with him. He then travelled to Halle and met with Bilfinger, before returning to Bonn on 22 May. On Ascension Day, Eisler arrived and stopped over for a couple of days. On 11 June, Schmitt wrote in his diary: 'want to write a constitutional theory. Often plan it, then again all in despair.' The same day he wrote to Feuchtwanger. In return, he immediately received a long 'letter from Feuchtwanger, that [he] should write the constitutional theory, although Smend is also working on one' (TB, 15 June 1927; cf. CSLF, pp. 207f.). The parallel publication of the two Weimar constitutional theories was no coincidence. Feuchtwanger was aware of the competition and fuelled it in the interest of both works.

Schmitt quickly thrashed out an article on Macchiavelli,[20] in which he praised the latter's sober 'humanity' (SGN, p. 104). At the same time he noted: 'Thought about the constitutional theory all the time with Eisler' (17 June 1927). Schmitt remembered old resolutions, when he finally took the decision to write it. On 25 June (CSLF, pp. 211f.) he received a 'nice letter from Feuchtwanger: I must write the constitutional theory.' In the coming days Schmitt would work very diligently. *Volksentscheid und Volksbegehren* appeared. Schmitt met with Leopold von Wiese in Cologne, where he regularly had to examine legal trainees, and he visited the ailing am Zehnhoff in Düsseldorf. His diary notes for the first time: 'Worked well on my constitutional theory the whole day. Read up in my diaries of 1920, seven years ago, when I was writing *Dictatorship*. That gave me courage. What an awful situation at the time. Grateful to Georg Eisler and Duška' (TB, 10 July 1927). In mid-July Schmitt was working diligently on the new work. Besides that, he corrected the proofs for *The Concept of the Political*. His notes on the concept of 'federation' he found 'very good'. With this, the rough outline was completed. On 21 July he gave a lecture on international law at the Geffrub[21] in Bonn. At an academic dinner in Cologne he met Max Scheler and Nicolai Hartmann. At the end of July, Schmitt noted in his diary: 'Have begun to write the constitutional theory, a couple of pages.' Throughout the term break, he would now work with great intensity on *Constitutional Theory*, without giving up his lively contacts and regular rendezvous with Magda. The French translator of *Political Romanticism*, Pierre Linn, came for a two-week visit. They frequently met during this time, discussed the translation (which had already been agreed in February 1926) and went on shorter excursions into the landscape of the Catholic Rhineland, visiting churches and monasteries. Schmitt visited am Zehnhoff in Düsseldorf. Occasionally, he made a remark in his diary about 'his fear of the enormous task of writing a constitutional theory' (TB, 5 September 1927).

Schmitt's appointment to the Handelshochschule came about only as the consequence of a fortuitous series of withdrawals. After Gustav Radbruch declined the offer of the chair in June 1927, Schmitt was listed in second place. But there were strongly diverging opinions on Schmitt within the Hochschule. Paul Eltzbacher mobilized the greatest possible resistance against him, while Moritz Bonn and Franz Eulenburg were in favour of his appointment. In the course of the discussions, a number of famous state theorists gave their opinions. Erwin Jacobi and Rudolf Smend declared their support for Schmitt. In response, Eltzbacher wrote an excoriating report against him, which openly declared its 'antipathy against the author' solely on the basis of the 'character' of his works. After Radbruch had turned down the offer, Kelsen, Koellreutter and Rothenbücher all declined as well. At that point, the Handelshochschule finally decided to enter into negotiations with Schmitt, and he was made a first offer. Schmitt's diaries do not mention any political motivation for moving to the capital. But important was the considerably higher salary as well as the 'joy of the big city' (TB, 16 September 1927). Later, he would write that he 'accepted the appointment to a full professorship at the Handelshochschule Berlin only out of scholarly interest, so that [he] could become familiar with the object of his discipline, namely the state, at close range.'[22] In Bonn, Schmitt felt trapped by the divorce disputes and the Catholic atmosphere, and he longed for a new sphere of activity. He did negotiate with the university councillor [Kurator] in Bonn, but wrote: 'They want to remove me from Bonn, so that they can mould the whole discipline according to their confession' (TB, 17 September 1927). He conferred with friends about the decision, went to see am Zehnhoff, who advised him to go to Berlin, and on 22 September, during a walk with Duška, he decided 'to go to Berlin and accept the offer from the Handelshochschule'. On 5 October, he communicated his acceptance to the Handelshochschule.[23] He took up a 'professorship for state law' [Professur für Staatsrecht], with a teaching assignment of eight hours per week and a guaranteed salary of 30,000 Reichsmark. Administrative law was to be covered by the former chancellor of the Reich, Hans Luther, in the form of a teaching contract.[24] On 26 October, Schmitt was appointed by the Ministry of Culture.[25] His contract, however, was with the Chamber of Industry and Commerce. The decision accelerated the completion of his *Constitutional Theory*. Schmitt wanted to start in Berlin with the completed work under his belt. He increased his work on the text, while at the same time writing a longer introduction to the new edition of *Dictatorship*.

Around the same time, the sociologist Carl Brinkmann from Heidelberg was in Bonn for a short period. Paul Landsberg died; Schmitt stayed in touch with his wife and his son Paul, a student of Scheler's, who was working on his Habilitation at the time.[26] Eugen Rosenstock came to visit, and Schmitt was troubled by his 'fear of this Jew'. On other encounters with Jewish scholars, such as, for instance, Julius Löwenstein,[27] he remarked in positive terms. At the beginning of the winter term, *Constitutional Theory* was essentially completed. Schmitt prepared a lecture on 'Völkerbund und Europa' [The League of Nations and Europe], which he presented on 29 October in Bonn.[28] On 1 November he gave another lecture for the Verwaltungsakademie on the topic 'Beamter und Völkerrecht' [The civil servant and international law],[29] after which he returned to the proofs of *Constitutional Theory*.

On 2 November, Schmitt received his certificate of appointment from Berlin and immediately told Bonn about his move.[30] The faculty tried to appoint Richard Thoma as his successor. Schmitt declared he would 'agree' to everything.[31] At the beginning of December he was 'exhausted' from his work.[32] Santa Claus brought him 'a marzipan book: *Constitutional Theory* by Carl Schmitt'. At that time, Schmitt fell out with Gurian for good. The death of Hugo Ball and his correspondence with Carl Muth occupied his mind. The second edition of *Dictatorship* appeared. His cousin André stayed with him for several weeks: 'André distracts me a bit, but he is modest and quiet.' Schmitt gave two lectures at the Verwaltungsakademie in Koblenz (9 and 16 December 1927). In Cologne, he attended a lecture by Jacques Maritain[33] and spent three days with this 'saint-like man'.[34] Schmitt rejected the offer of writing an article for *Hochland* for 'reasons of health': 'I am completely exhausted from writing the book on constitutional theory, and not even capable of reading the proofs.'[35] On Christmas Day, he received the last pages of proofs and passed them on to Friesenhahn as well as Albert Hensel, who also wrote a review of the work.[36] Schmitt's summary verdict on the year 1927 expresses contentment: 'very happy about the nice house, the satisfaction of my sexuality, the nice book that I have completed' (TB, 27 December 1927). On 31 December he sent off the proofs for *Constitutional Theory*, 'which to me appears dreadful, amateurish, ephemeral and superficial'. Although the preface is dated December 1927, Schmitt wrote it only in January. The index was sent off in mid-January.

The competition from Smend and the appointment to Berlin were two reasons why Schmitt completed the magisterial work with such speed, even if all of the intellectual work of his years in Bonn went into it. He wrote *Constitutional Theory* in just over four months, with the core effort taking place during the summer break 1927. *The Concept of the Political* took him not even a month. The definition of the concept given in it was used at once for the *magnum opus* on constitutional theory. At no point did Schmitt give up his social life. There was no question of a monastic retreat; only a small proportion of his social encounters have been mentioned here. Magda required his attention almost daily throughout the year. His contact with Heinrich Oberheid, which turned into a close friendship, also demanded more and more time. After Duška's release from hospital, Schmitt again and again registered his contentment with his marriage in his diary, and 'without any moral scruples' (TB, 15 June 1927). The women's roles were clear. 'Duška is sweet and friendly . . . I am very fond of her, and I feel completely indifferent towards Magda, although my sexuality is again very strong and I want to be with her. Strange. Fear of the Christian confusion of all instincts and concepts' (TB, 27 December 1927) – i.e., fear of the Christian separation of Eros and Caritas.

Core propositions of a foundation for the theory of the state: *The Concept of the Political* (1927)

Schmitt began his work on the foundations of his theory in 'intermittent' fashion with several short books. In *Political Theology* (1922) he formulated a concept of sovereignty, *Roman Catholicism and Political Form* (1923) introduced a concept of 'representation', and *The Crisis of Parliamentary Democracy* (1923) explained the decline of liberalism by looking at the changing forms of the formation of political will. *The Core Question Regarding the League of Nations* (1926) developed a concept of 'federation', and *Referenda and Petitions for Referenda* (1927) rendered the concept of democracy more precise. All of these writings are of fundamental importance for the magnum opus, *Constitutional Theory*. Just as Schmitt's overall oeuvre cannot be reduced to a theory of the friend–enemy relation, the overall process of theory formation is incompletely captured if one looks only at *The Concept of the Political*.[37] Although the *Concept* treatise is a 'key' (Ernst-Wolfgang Böckenförde) to *Constitutional Theory*, it is not a universal key from which the whole theoretical edifice can be deduced. If we compare *Constitutional Theory* with the Catholicism essay, we can already see a limitation in the textbook. Complex arguments regarding Staatskirchenrecht [Church constitutional law]* are absent from it. *Constitutional Theory* also fails to describe in any detail what it programmatically declares to be necessary to consider: the 'absolute' constitution, the historical and socio-moral 'status' of a 'people'.[38]

The normative and practical demands placed on theory by philosophers can be conceptually distinguished from the analytic and descriptive demands other disciplines place on theory. Philosophy aims at an argument-based justification of a normative practice, whereas analytic-descriptive theories are limited to an observer perspective. Schmitt's constitutional theory is analytic. Nor does *The Concept of the Political* develop a political philosophy.

The text of the *Concept* book exists in several versions. Emil Lederer[39] had requested a contribution for his *Archiv der Sozialwissenschaften* from Schmitt. The text was also published – with Lederer's permission[40] and with a preface by Arnold Wolfers, in which he distanced himself from the text – in the *Schriftenreihe der Hochschule für Politik* [series of the Academy of Political Science].[41] An extended 'edition' followed in November 1931 (though it was dated 1932) as a booklet with Duncker & Humblot, and a shorter version, with National Socialist inflections, in 1933 with the Hanseatische Verlagsanstalt. At the same time as his *Theory of*

---

* Law regulating the relationship between state and Christian Churches.

the Partisan, a reprint of the 1932 version, with some added 'corollaries', a new preface and some further notes and references, was published in 1963. Finally, in 1971 Schmitt wrote another retrospective preface for the Italian edition. *The Concept of the Political* is therefore not only a foundational text but also a summing-up of Schmitt's work. However, the systematic structure of the argument can already be extracted in the form of a few core propositions from the version of 1927.

1 *Core proposition*: 'The concept of the state presupposes the concept of the political' (CP, p. 19). Schmitt's introductory formula is intended as both a historical and a systematic statement. The 1927 version empha-sizes the formula's significance primarily for the theory of the state. Only after Schmitt had sketched the beginnings of a history of 'German state theory' in his short book on Hugo Preuß did he also emphasize the for-mula's relevance for constitutional history: it marks the beginning and the end of the modern 'epoch of statehood' ['Epoche der Staatlichkeit'; BP, p. 10]. Schmitt claims that the modern state, in particular the German state, has lost its political monopoly, and that a development can be seen 'from the absolute state of the eighteenth century via the neutral (non-interventionist) state of the nineteenth to the total state of the twentieth' (CP, pp. 22f.). This is Schmitt's response to the discussions of state theory in the Wilhelminian era and to the *Allgemeine Staatslehre* [General theory of the state] of Georg Jellinek and Max Weber. He is sharp in his criticism, claiming that the normative demand of a political monopoly of the state is factually obsolete in view of the 'identity of state and society'. Any 'theory of the state' therefore has to take an independent 'definition' of the politi-cal as its 'starting point'. Ultimately, Schmitt does not drop the concept of the state; rather, he points out conditions of its existence and makes a 'statist' appeal for a 'strong', politically determined state that defends its political monopoly by distinguishing clearly between friend and enemy.

2 *Core proposition*: 'The specific political distinction to which political actions and motives can be reduced is that between friend and enemy' (CP, p. 26). Schmitt asks the systematic question of the 'specifically political categories' (CP, p. 25) and presents his 'criterion' (CP, p. 26) of the distinc-tion between friend and enemy. In analogy with a personal relationship, he speaks of a dual relation which can be judged only from the participant perspective, by an existential 'partaking and participating' (BP, p. 27; but cf. CP, p. 27), not from the 'neutral' perspective of international law. Schmitt plays the dual relation off against norms that would be provided by a third party.

3 *Core proposition*: 'War follows from enmity, because enmity is the existen-tial negation of another being' (CP, p. 33; trans. modified).* Schmitt starts out by distinguishing his criterion from other categories. Then he speaks

---

* 'Der Krieg folgt aus der Feindschaft, denn diese ist die seinsmäßige Negierung eines anderen Seins' (BP, p. 33). On this occasion, the meaning of the existing English translation deviates in an important respect from that of the original: 'War follows from enmity. War is the existential negation of the enemy' (CP, p. 33).

of 'war as a manifestation of enmity'.* He makes an appeal to the German 'people', reminding it of war as a political means. He defends the right to declare wars and the pathos of a state's right 'to demand from its own members the readiness to die and to kill' (CP, p. 46; trans. modified) for reasons of 'self-determination', and in order to maintain political 'unity' and 'existence'. Schmitt argues in nationalistic terms against Versailles and Geneva. From 1927, the Weimar crisis and conditions resembling civil war became ever more pressing in Schmitt's mind, which is why he introduces numerous changes in the 1931 version of the text.

Schmitt defends the *ius ad bellum* for 'existential' reasons. He postulates enmity as the ultimate reason for war and interprets enmity as such (not only war) as an 'existential negation' and 'negation of one's own form of existence' (CP, p. 27; trans. modified), which justifies the 'existential defence of one's own form of life' (CP, p. 49; trans. modified†).[42] Schmitt suggested an analysis of political existence – a companion piece, so to speak, to Heidegger's main work *Being and Time*, which was also published in 1927 – which promises to explicate the self of self-determination, political identity, from the participant's perspective of a collective understanding of one's self and its borders. However, he did not pursue this path of an analysis of political identity and constitution any further. Instead of a positive explication of the characteristics of political identity, he chose the route of abstraction from other categories and defined it solely in terms of a formal and abstract criterion.

Schmitt does not say which existential characteristics can cause enmity and war. The political is 'total'. It could be anything and nothing. A philosophical and political analysis of existence would need to take the path of establishing the fundamental characteristics of identity from the participant's perspective and of clarifying what constitutes the inviolable core of political identity. But all Schmitt does is hint at the fact that this core is discovered only in the case of conflict. He is of the opinion that the exception has a 'decisive meaning which exposes the core of the matter' [enthüllende Bedeutung] (CP, p. 35). In the *Concept* treatise, Schmitt explicates existential characteristics only in the abstract and in an analytical perspective: political reasons are not moral, juridical, religious or economic reasons. Each type of reason is used differently by agents and observers. Schmitt systematically credits any agent with the arbitrary power to provide defining criteria: each participant can and must decide on his or her own whether his or her existence is threatened.

---

* My translation of *Der Krieg als Erscheinungsform der Feindschaft* (BP, p. 7), the title of the third section of the text in the German table of contents, which is not translated in the English edition.
† 'Wenn eine solche physische Vernichtung menschlichen Lebens nicht aus der seinsmäßige Behauptung der eigenen Existenzform gegenüber einer ebenso seinsmäßigen Verneinung dieser Form geschieht, so läßt sie sich eben nicht rechtfertigen' (BP, p. 50) – 'If such physical destruction of human life does not happen in the context of an existential defence of one's own form of life against an equally existential negation of that form, then it cannot be justified.' The existing English translation opts for a freer, more elegant solution, but loses the existentialist tone and the aspect of two radically incompatible 'existentialities' confronting each other.

On the one hand, Schmitt suggests a philosophical and sociological reflection on the constitutive significance of 'the alien' in order to define the enemy without any recourse to non-political categories, without recourse to 'the morally good, aesthetically beautiful, and economically profitable' (CP, p. 27). On the other hand, he switches to an observer's perspective and asks what constitutes an abuse of justificatory reasons, a question belonging to the analysis of power and the critique of ideology. Like Max Weber before him, Schmitt emphasizes the 'real' and 'ever present possibility of combat' (CP, p. 32): the possibility of a 'case of emergency' [Ernstfall] or the 'exceptional case' (BP, p. 35; CP, p. 35; trans. modified). On the one hand, Schmitt suggests that 'a world without politics' (CP, p. 35) would lack moral seriousness.[43] On the other hand, he argues from an observer's perspective against 'senseless' wars that are fought 'purely' (CP, p. 36) for religious, moral, juridical or economic reasons. The example he uses is the pacifists leading a 'war against war' (ibid.): a morally motivated war in the name of 'humanity' (ibid.). The sentence that he will quote later, in 1963, as proof that 'the concept of "enemy", as it is used here, aims not at the destruction of the enemy, but at self-defence, at the mutual measure of force, and at establishing common borders' (BP, p. 119) refers also to the example of the pacifists' war. It says:

> Such a war is necessarily unusually intense and inhumane because, *by transcending the limits of the political*, it simultaneously is forced to use moral and other categories in order to degrade the enemy and turn him into a monster that must not only be defeated but also utterly *destroyed, someone, in other words, who is no longer just an enemy that needs to be compelled to retreat into his own borders.* (CP, p. 36, trans. modified)

Schmitt's conceptual definition can hardly be separated from the context of his overall body of work; its aims were limited to the construction of a theory with a practical purpose and to being a tool in political battle. Thus, it opens itself up to criticism in several ways. As a strictly normative theory, it rules out any analytical application, because who is an enemy to whom and wars can no longer be explained on the basis of motivations and reasons.[44] It would be 'senseless' to explain them with reference to economic, juridical or moral motivations. Schmitt does not offer any unambiguous criterion for 'setting limits' to, say, religious or economic wars. His concept of existence remains vague because he analyses moral language only for the purpose of ideology critique, assuming throughout a conventional morality with universal validity claims, which he interprets as a rhetorical veil for economic interests and political aims. A polemical separation and juxtaposition of morality and politics can be found throughout his work.

4 *Core proposition*: '. . . that grouping is always political which orients itself towards the case of emergency' [Ernstfall] (CP, p. 39). Schmitt now begins to draw some consequences for the theory of the state. In this context, he talks a lot about enmity and war, and little about friendship and peace.[45] One often gets the impression that he makes the possibility of friendship

dependent on the existence of enmity, that only those who are challenged by enemies are associated with each other and experience their political 'tensions' with intensity. In any case, he strongly emphasizes the fact that political identity can also exist without a state. As human individuals can argue over anything and form new groupings as a result, the political (in the 1931 version of the text) refers to no more than 'the degree of intensity of an association or dissociation of human individuals'. One might object that economic, aesthetic or juridical categories are also 'total', that warfare, too, can be considered from an economic, juridical or aesthetic perspective. However, they are not total in the same way in which the political is. Any attempt at totalizing them confirms at the same time the specific 'totality' of the political. Wherever a problem leads to enmity and war, the political arises. Thus, an economic war ultimately follows the logic of war, not of economics. At this point, Schmitt's definition of the concept turns into a new foundation of the state. Where the 'point of the political' that leads to 'the readiness to die and unhesitatingly to kill' [Todesbereitschaft und Tötungsbereitschaft] (CP, p. 46) is reached, there is a 'state'. Schmitt calls it a core function of statehood to determine friendship and enmity. The isolation of the criterion of the political allows him to recognize this core of statehood more clearly and once more to tie a 'reasonable concept of sovereignty and political entity' (CP, p. 43; trans. modified) to the concept of the state.

5 *Core proposition*: 'The state as the decisive political entity possesses an enormous power: the possibility of waging war and thereby publicly disposing of the lives of men' (CP, p. 46). In chapter 5, Schmitt renders his criterion more concrete and talks about the institutionally organized 'state' as a 'people' that is organized and exists politically. His definition of the concept of the political had this interpretation in mind from the very beginning. The aim was a mobilization of the German nation for the battle against Weimar, Geneva and Versailles. The criterion could, of course, also be applied to other political subjects. But *The Concept of the Political* takes a politically existing people as the decisive political subject. *Constitutional Theory* defines it as the 'nation' and assigns it the right to self-organization as a state. Without mentioning the German people explicitly, Schmitt refers to its situation at the time and argues against extensive international integration by entering into contractual obligations. The cost of voluntarily entering into such obligations on the basis of international law, Schmitt expresses, with reference to the 'eternal connection between *protection* and *obedience*' (CP, p. 52; trans. modified; cf. BP, p. 53), in drastic terms: a people hand themselves over to a 'protector'.

6 *Core proposition*: 'From the criterion of the concept of the political follows the existence of a plurality of states.'* Schmitt argues against the idea of a universalist League of Nations and defends the existing political 'pluriverse' (CP, p. 53) of individual sovereign states.[46] A world state would 'altogether lose its political character' (CP, p. 57), because, in the absence of a sovereign determination of the enemy, genuine constitutional alternatives

---

* This sentence is omitted in the existing English translation (see CP, p. 53; BP, p. 54).

would also disappear. A sovereignty limited by international law, Schmitt holds, is no longer genuine freedom. If war is not accepted as a means of politics, there is actually no longer any genuine politics – i.e., no politics free of moral or juridical distortions.

7 *Core proposition*: 'One could test all theories of state and political ideas according to their anthropology and thereby classify these as to whether they consciously or unconsciously presuppose man to be by nature evil or by nature good' (CP, p. 58). Having presented the foundation of the state, Schmitt, in a chapter on method, suddenly asks the question of the anthropological presuppositions of political theories. He distinguishes between optimists and pessimists and analyses the range of theories in terms of the history of ideas as well as systematically. Educators, he says, are mostly anthropological optimists. Theologians, by contrast, assume the 'sinfulness of the world and man' (CP, p. 65; trans. modified). Political theorists, finally, believe in the 'real possibility' of enmity and war. A political theorist argues from the observer perspective. He considers validity claims in political terms and realizes that men fight for their ideas and ideologies. Hobbes in particular, Schmitt says, taught us that claims made on the basis of natural law often had the effect of a 'rallying cry for civil war'. Schmitt does not opt clearly for a position of his own. A more detailed discussion of his implicit philosophical premises would have been very interesting, but the *Concept* treatise brackets an explication of its philosophical presuppositions with reference to political consequences. Schmitt shifts to the observer perspective and criticizes moral claims on political grounds. Thus, in the chapter on method, the philosophical deficit of the *Concept* treatise, the fact that it forsakes the possibility of an existential analysis from the participant perspective, becomes visible. The chapter concludes the presentation of the treatise's foundations.

Schmitt considers philosophy to be a confessional discourse which legitimizes subjective commitments and can therefore be politically subversive. He does not sign up to any particular philosophy, although some preferences for Hegel and Hobbes are visible. Rather, he neutralizes philosophical validity claims and evaluates them, from the perspective of political theory, on the sole criterion of their anthropological beliefs. Any philosophy that affirms an 'anthropological pessimism' is acceptable for the purposes of Schmitt's theory. From the point of view of this theory it would be a strategic mistake to commit oneself to one of the philosophies from the range of anthropological pessimisms. Whether Hobbes, Hegel or Donoso Cortés, the only point of importance is that there is an anthropological pessimism that supports Schmitt's theory and acknowledges man's need to be governed.

8 *Core proposition*: 'The liberalism of the previous century has changed and debased all political ideas in a peculiar and systematic fashion.'*

---

* The existing English translation omits part of the sentence: 'Liberalism has changed all political conceptions in a peculiar and systematic way' (CP, p. 69). 'Durch den Liberalismus des letzten Jahrhunderts sind alle politischen Vorstellungen in einer eigenartigen und systematischen Weise verändert und denaturiert worden' BP, p. 68).

Schmitt ends with a sharp criticism of liberalism, which is his real opponent because he derives the political difficulties, the Weimar 'situation', from the liberal delusion of the political agents. The individualist basis, Schmitt holds, negates the 'political idea'; the 'system of liberal thought' dissolves all political thought into the two poles of 'ethics and economics' (CP, p. 70). Schmitt hints at the fact that economic interests are the driving forces: liberals fight for their economic interests in the form of ethical rhetoric. In this respect, Schmitt argues purely in terms of an ideology critique. He does not put individual freedom into a positive and constitutive relationship to the state and does not make it the basis of political rule. The developments which have shaped modern times Schmitt presents more systematically, and in more detail, in his lecture 'The Age of Neutralizations and Depoliticizations' of 1929, which ends the book version of the treatise.

Schmitt's political ethics concentrate on the 'self-assertion' of collective 'existence'. Political 'existence', here, does not mean simply the sheer fact of survival but also the battle to maintain one's identity and 'dignity'. Schmitt's treatise immediately attracted great interest. The 'friend–enemy criterion' especially was seen as a daring thesis, and it divided opinions. Schmitt himself repeated again and again: 'I consider my essay on the political to be my best work.'[47] Georg Eisler agreed: 'Your essay on the nature of politics is the greatest work you have written so far'.[48] However, Schmitt's 'existentialist' pathos also triggered manifold objections. Jurists were irritated by the abstract approach and the primary focus on foreign policy,[49] as well as by the power-political anti-universalism [machtstaatlicher Anti-Universalismus], philosophers by the absence of normative justifications, theologians by the weakening of the importance of the Church and of 'neighbourly love'.[50] Werner Becker wanted to set the criterion of the political in relation to the 'classificatory term' [Ordnungsbegriff] war and peace.[51] Ernst Michel, who belonged to the Catholic left, wrote: 'I am mostly in agreement with your understanding of the political, but not with your evaluation and prognosis. From a Christian standpoint, the state is an institution of relative natural law and has no place in the proclamation of God's kingdom.'[52] Hermann Heller, based on an inaccurate quotation, found an inclination towards the destruction of the enemy in the text. Schmitt confronted Heller in a letter[53] and assures him that, 'in the intellectual sphere [Sphäre des Geistes]', he 'cannot conceive of existence and destruction as ontologically identical'.[54]

It is possible to appreciate Schmitt's insistence on enmity and war as an existential doubt about the euphemistic 'attachment of meaning to the meaningless'. Ultimately 'liberalism' is presented as the essence of all ideological and strategic distortions of political conflicts, enmities and battles. Schmitt accuses liberal thought of hypocritically distorting the world of politics, of a veiling of economic interests with ethical rhetoric. The philosophical discussion of Schmitt's thought could begin at this point: Does a political anti-universalism necessarily imply an ethical anti-universalism?[55] Can the position be defended at all? *The Concept of the Political* ends with a very fundamental critique of liberalism. In it, Schmitt hints at the philosophical dimension of his critique for the first time. Regarding

Constitutional Theory, it is important to note that the structure of *The Concept of the Political* also relies on a radical distinction between liberalism and democracy.

Rough sketch of the 'system': the antithesis of liberalism and democracy in *Constitutional Theory*

A fortuitous constellation was needed to elicit *Constitutional Theory* from Schmitt. Soon after his arrival in Bonn, Schmitt intended to write a textbook. He spoke of a textbook of 'international law', considered a 'philosophy of the state', planned collections of works on international law, and confronted Duncker & Humblot with the option either to outdo an offer from another publisher or to lose him as an author. Feuchtwanger accepted Schmitt's plans and, in June 1926, sent him a publishing contract for a 'textbook on international law'. However, six weeks later Schmitt still hadn't signed the contract. The time frame, he said, was too narrow; he 'had a reputation to lose' (CSLF, p. 179). Cunningly, Feuchtwanger asked Schmitt whether he could think of an author for an 'outline of the state law of the German Reich', an assignment which Anschütz had handed back to the publisher (CSLF, p. 178). However, Schmitt did not jump at it, but kept talking about international law, without signing the contract. On 24 December, Feuchtwanger sent a reminder and tried to entice Schmitt with a second edition of *Dictatorship*. After that, their correspondence ceased for a while. Later, Feuchtwanger again reminded Schmitt of the book on international law. Out of the blue, Schmitt suggested, in June 1927, writing a constitutional theory, which would be 'practically more valuable', under the same contractual conditions, by the autumn. Feuchtwanger agreed straightaway and emphasized the importance of the work: 'I also wanted . . . to tell you, how much you owe the public, in particular the discipline of state law, a fundamental publication, because your books so far have been generally perceived as promises in the neutral sense: not that you would have promised anything, but your arguments promised a fully fledged theory' (CSLF, p. 207).

At the end of June, Feuchtwanger sent the contracts for *Constitutional Theory* and *Dictatorship*. Schmitt signed them and remarked: 'I am particularly looking forward to writing "Constitutional Theory", and I am genuinely grateful for your encouragement. Many nice individual parts for it are already done. . . . "Positive" state law in Anschütz's sense no longer suffices; a general theory of the state today is useless because there is no longer any state' (CSLF, p. 213). During the following months a flood of letters went to and fro, discussing the second edition of *Dictatorship*, the fee, the progress of the work and the race with Smend. Schmitt complained about the labour of correcting the text, found a lot of it 'very nice', and emphasized the 'systematic' character of *Constitutional Theory*. On 5 December he put the manuscript in the post. Feuchtwanger explained the details of the text going to press to Schmitt and set the work above Smend's: 'I am personally of the opinion that, of the two books which will be published about the same time and which, after all, have the principles of constitutional theory as their common subject, yours is far superior and better founded. I think I can say that without causing a dispute with anyone' (CSLF, p. 238). Schmitt wanted 'to inaugurate a new discipline of public law in Germany' (ibid., p. 241).

Constitutional Theory is divided into four parts: 'Concept of the Constitution', 'The Rechtsstaat Component of the Modern Constitution', 'The Political Component of the Modern Constitution' and 'Constitutional Theory of the Federation'. What is striking in the first place is the limitation to the 'modern constitution'. Schmitt distinguishes between the modern period and modernity. The modern period he defines by the emancipation of the secular state from the Christian framework. Modernity he lets begin after 1789, with the emergence of democratic 'legitimacy'. In a sense, *Constitutional Theory* is conceived backwards: within the context of the work, the 'theory of the federation', developed on the basis of international law, takes on a federalist aspect. The political components of the modern constitution Schmitt had already developed with his concepts of representation, parliamentarism and democracy. The Rechtsstaat components he had so far not developed in detail; his distinction between just two of its principles – a 'principle of distribution' of basic rights and the 'organizational principle' of the separation of powers – is new. Schmitt had never discussed basic rights in detail before. Also new is the thesis that the effective validity of the general concept of law on which the Rechtsstaat is based is linked to the existence of a 'normal situation' [Normallage]. In addition, Schmitt reformulates the 'concept of the constitution' which opens *Constitutional Theory*. However, his 'positive' concept of the constitution is informed by a concept of 'democratic legitimacy' and a theory of the constitution-making power which, within the context of the history of ideas, had already been discussed in some detail in *Dictatorship*. Thus, even beyond his lecture notes, Schmitt can make use of material from previous work, which he rearranges into a new system. The foundation now is the distinction between an 'absolute' and the 'positive' constitution of a people: between the 'concrete' present condition of the constitution [Verfassungszustand] and the existing constitutional laws.

Schmitt defines the state as the 'political unity' of a people and interprets the 'positive' constitution as the 'complete decision over the form and type of the political unity' (CT, p. 75). Every people with a political will decides for itself about its 'form of existence' and gives itself a legal constitution. A people with a political will (to the 'self-assertion' of its 'political unity') Schmitt calls a 'nation'. A nation makes a 'state'. This concept of the constitution aims at the 'homogeneous' national state. The sum of all 'fundamental political decisions', or constitutional decisions, Schmitt calls the 'substance' of a constitution, and distinguishes this substance from individual constitutional norms. He calls for an interpretation of individual constitutional laws according to the complete decision [Gesamtentscheidung] and argues that individual norms merely have relative legal validity on the basis of the complete decision. This distinction within constitutional theory between the 'substance' and the relative validity of individual laws is

Schmitt's tool for the affirmation and critique of constitutional policy. This tool allows him both to defend the 'substance' and to qualify the relevance of constitutional law as opposed to the hermeneutic construct of a fundamental political decision and substance. The 'absolute' politically existing 'form of forms', which interprets the 'constitution as the complete condition of concrete unity and order, as the form of the state', precedes the positive decision over the constitution as the 'norm of norms', providing basic laws.

Thus, *Constitutional Theory* sets out from the formation of the constitution-making power of the nation, which, in Weimar, was still governed by the ideal type [Idealbegriff] of the constitution of a bourgeois Rechtsstaat. This ideal type is explicated in the work's second part. In this context, Schmitt presents a fresh discussion of the principles of parliamentarism and explains the principles of the bourgeois Rechtsstaat: 'The Basic Rights' and the 'Separation (so-called Division) of Powers' as the 'principle of distribution' and the 'organizational principle' respectively. He conceives liberalism and democracy as political components of a Rechtsstaat, and in a chapter on the 'Bourgeois Rechtsstaat and Political Form' goes as far as to claim that the constitution of a Rechsstaat is 'no state form' but only a constitutional limitation. Schmitt will later also find this thesis confirmed in his reading of the constitutional history of Germany.[56] In terms of constitutional policy, this thesis allows for a reduction in the number of limitations that a Rechtsstaat sets on the power of the executive, thus enabling a 'strong' executive state.

The third part develops the formal political principles of 'identity' and 'representation' in the form of a 'theory of democracy' and a 'theory of monarchy'. With this move, Schmitt modifies the classical theory of state forms, replaces the qualitative criterion of the common good with the aspect of legitimacy, and understands parliamentarism as a 'mixed constitution' (*status mixtus*) made up of identity and representation: as a modern form of aristocracy. His presentation of the parliamentary system ends, coming close to prophecy, with a discussion of the 'dissolution of parliament' through the 'president's dissolution authority'. The fourth part, finally, presents the 'Constitutional Theory of the Federation': in its federal constitution, Schmitt says, Germany 'is no longer a federation' (CT, p. 394). And this is also the reason why Germany retained its sovereignty, even as a member of a federation (such as the League of Nations). Within a federation, Schmitt says, 'the question of sovereignty between federation and member states always remains open' (CT, p. 390).

The fourfold approach to the dismantling of the 'bourgeois' Rechtsstaat

During the writing of *Constitutional Theory*, Schmitt was fully engrossed in the task of 'taking off the death mask of liberalism'.[57] He could hardly have expressed with more clarity that the overall design of the book implements the distinction between liberalism and democracy. As a jurist, he criticized inconsistencies and contradictions as 'fractures' caused by self-dissolution. His principled approach gave him the possibility of further theoretical development and critique of the executive state. His concept of the political and constitutional theory determined the relationship between power and right in a new way, which sharpened the perspective on the politics of right. With the 'Rechtsstaat components of the modern constitution', Schmitt identified three principles, which, one by one, he would analyse more closely in three stages even before 1933. In each case, he would point to erosions which led to auto-destructive processes. *Constitutional Theory* emphasized the 'organizational principle' of the separation of powers, the 'principle of distribution' of basic rights, and the foundational role which the general concept of law plays for the Rechtsstaat. In *Der Hüter der Verfassung* [The guardian of the constitution], Schmitt described the erosion of the organizational principle. Then he went on to analyse the 'principle of distribution' in his works on the basic laws. And finally, in *Legality and Legitimacy*, he highlights the weakening of the general concept of law through 'exceptional' lawgivers. Thus, the concise explications of *Constitutional Theory* determined the general direction Schmitt's work would take until 1933. From providing conceptual definitions he changed to a more detailed observation and analysis of the material inconsistencies and contradictions within the 'liberal' constitution. With his twin book publications of 1927–8 and his move to Berlin, Schmitt was now academically fully established. He occupied a place at the heart of his discipline, and his personality and work divided opinion, with the reception of his work being polarized into friend and foe reactions. Friends and acquaintances reviewed *Constitutional Theory* – e.g., Alfred Bertram,[58] Albert Hensel and also Franz Blei.[59] Established names (such as Otto Hintze and Fritz Hartung) as well as the up and coming (such as Karl Larenz and Eric Voegelin) put pen to paper.[60] *Constitutional Theory* would, as foreseen by Feuchtwanger, play 'a major role also for [Schmitt's] external fate' in Berlin.

15

From 'Ice Floe to Ice Floe': Signals in the Berlin Maelstrom

Transitional times

Schmitt's early work used three anchoring institutions and points of reference, each of which, at specific times – in normal situations of order or chaotic times of immediacy – had a function and justification of their own: Church, state and the individual. Before the caesura of the Great War, Schmitt had opted for the state as the 'servant' of right. He then found himself thrown back to an apocalyptic immediacy during the war, which is the reason he began to think about the Church. In the atmosphere in Bonn, the Catholic alternative vanished again, in part as a result of the experience of his lost divorce trial. Schmitt's private life became confused. Beyond Church and 'bourgeois Rechtsstaat', Schmitt was now almost inclined to follow Franz Blei and Hugo Ball in their radical critique of the state and the Church. A move towards religious individualism and anarchism, even towards a Gnostic dismissal of his whole approach to Church, state and institutions, seemed possible. Although Schmitt never abandoned the state altogether, he also never opted for Weimar parliamentarism and liberalism. The fundamental distinction between liberalism and democracy then provided the basis for an anti-liberal interpretation of the constitution. Politically, Schmitt jumped, as he put it, 'from ice floe to ice floe' (PB, p. 138). In Berlin, he formulated a new option for the state: he reconstructed statehood on the basis of the 'dualism' between state and society and interpreted the constitution as an 'authoritarian' presidential system legitimated by plebiscite. Instead of the dualism between state and Church, the one between state and society now became the guiding distinction.

Schmitt moved to Berlin in 1928, a year that was politically calm rather than 'golden'. The Weimar Republic was having its best time, comparatively speaking. The government led by Wilhelm Marx, a bourgeois nationalist coalition, failed over a federal law on schools [Reichsschulgesetz]; however, in the early elections for the fourth Reichstag in May 1928, the DNVP suffered a heavy defeat and the SPD celebrated a great victory. This meant a moderate shift to the left and a difficult situation with respect to the formation of a government. The result was a return to the Great Coalition

(SPD, DDP,* DVP, BVP† and Zentrum), with Hermann Müller (SPD) as chancellor. He enjoyed a relatively stable twenty-one months in government. The death of the long-serving foreign minister Gustav Stresemann on 3 October 1929 then seemed to many like the death knell for Weimar.[1] 'Stresemann's death was an irreplaceable loss for the system of the great coalition, for the integration of the bourgeois nationalist middle ground, for the idea of German nationalism as well as for the idea of a unified Europe. It marked the conclusion of the period of consolidation and the beginning of the final crisis of the Weimar Republic.'[2] In 1929, the economic and political foundations of the Republic received heavy blows from which they never recovered. The unemployment figures rose dramatically, and the Weimar state entered the global economic crisis burdened with the liabilities of the post-war period. Given the level of mass unemployment, unemployment insurance could hardly be financed any longer. The simmering dispute over the principal question – market economy or social economy – escalated with the contested issue of whether to raise social security contributions or reduce benefits. The Zentrum, led by Brüning, used the dispute over financial policy to put pressure on the coalition. In March 1930, the SPD refused to support the compromise suggested by its own chancellor, Müller, and thereby not only caused the end of the Great Coalition but also squandered the last opportunity, for the foreseeable future, for parliament to form a government. The bourgeois centre parties sought this dispute, fully aware of their weakness in parliament. All sides were responsible for this end of parliamentary government, which was now replaced with presidential rule. In this situation, the SPD, in order to avoid a possible seizure of power from the right or left, followed a course of toleration of rule by presidential degree as the lesser evil.[3] The Reich's chancellor was appointed by and dependent on the Reich's president (Art. 53 of the Weimar Constitution) and ruled by emergency decree, according to Article 48 of the constitution. The president's authority to dissolve parliament, in practice, took the sting out of the parliament's authority to bring about the dissolution of the government by a vote of no confidence (Art. 54 of the Weimar Constitution). The economic and financial crisis continued to wreak havoc. In 1930–1, Brüning was not able to push through his budget and, in a move that Schmitt supported,[4] responded with a controversial emergency decree on financial stipulations and the dissolution of parliament. Next, the elections in September brought about the 'destruction of parliamentary democracy',[5] an explosive rise in national socialist votes from 2.6 per cent to 18.3 per cent, and strong gains for the KPD.‡ As early as 1930, the opponents of the constitution were in the majority. The only comparatively stable parties were those of political Catholicism.

Rule by presidential decree was made possible by the two distinct

---

* Deutsche Demokratische Partei = German Democratic Party.
† Bayerische Volkspartei = Bavarian People's Party – the Bavarian branch of the Zentrum, which broke off in 1919 and pursued a more conservative, monarchist and particularist course of Bavarian independence.
‡ Kommunistische Partei Deutschlands = Communist Party of Germany.

ways in which a government could be formed, which – in contrast to the Federal Republic's Grundgesetz[6] [Basic Law] – meant that the Weimar Constitution did not guarantee that the chancellor would be elected by parliament. At the time of the foundation of the Republic, those who designed the constitution, Hugo Preuß[7] and Max Weber,[8] for instance, were afraid of a kind of 'parliamentary absolutism' and thought that the young German parliamentarism needed a strong Reichspräsident, a 'substitute Emperor', as a counterweight. The intention was to incorporate some of the advantages of a constitutional monarchy into the parliamentary system in the form of a strong, directly elected president. In 1925, following the death of Ebert, Schmitt had already warned against the enormous 'concentration of power' in the Reichspräsident. 'A new president may change the face of the Weimar Constitution completely.' 'We may say that no other constitution on earth makes a legal *coup d'état* as easy as the Weimar Constitution' (SGN, p. 25). After 1925, Hindenburg stood for a conservative 'refoundation' [Umgründung] (Heinrich August Winkler) of the Republic.[9] Under Hindenburg's rule, many became active in an 'authoritarian' transformation of the system. Schmitt could also no longer think of another alternative to the paralysed parliamentarism and, until January 1933, opted for rule by presidential decree. This system, as Huber suggested retrospectively, had several different functions. It was an 'interim state of emergency', a means for guaranteeing 'governability', a means for preserving the 'unity of the state', a route to 'authoritarian democracy', the 'reconstitution' of the Reich, conservative reform of the state and a 'defence against totalitarian dictatorship'.[10] Although Schmitt shared several of these goals, for a long time he continued to consider a functioning parliamentary system as desirable.

The months before his first summer term in Berlin in 1928 were a transitional time for Schmitt. Tasks that had been left undone required attention, and his departure from Bonn needed to be organized. Travels to Paris, where he studied Sieyès in the Bibliothèque Nationale, and to Davos marked the break between Bonn and Berlin. For the first few days in January 1928, Schmitt was at a Catholic congress in Boppard on the Middle Rhine, where he gave a 'presentation on the bourgeois Rechtsstaat' (TB, 3 January 1928).[11] The text, transcribed by Werner Becker, was soon published in the Catholic journals *Die Schildgenossen* and *Abendland*.[12] It was a constitutional credo. Schmitt strongly emphasizes the dependence of the Weimar Constitution on Versailles and the 'posthumous' character of Weimar liberalism and parliamentarism, whose political purpose – i.e., the integration of the bourgeoisie into the state – Schmitt says, had long since been achieved. The actual contemporary task he sees as the integration of the proletariat (SGN, p. 49) into the forms of an anti-liberal, plebiscitary mass democracy. He writes: 'What is important for the development of the constitution in the near future is to save democracy from its liberal veil' (SGN, p. 47). In Boppard, Schmitt met Heinrich Brüning, the future chancellor under rule by presidential decree, and was looking forward to having 'the opportunity to see [him] in Berlin' (TB, 3 January 1928).

The last weeks of term in Bonn were very hectic. Schmitt examined legal trainees in Cologne, read doctoral theses and saw through their examination. Slowly his farewell to Magda approached. Schmitt handed her 'an envelope with 100 Marks' and summed up the situation thus: 'It is actually a wonderful combination: a clear-minded, beautiful, presentable wife, and a lover with whom one cannot be seen publicly' (TB, 18 January 1928). At the beginning of February he went to Berlin, staying with Smend. On 2 February, he gave a lecture on 'Die Krise des Parlamentarismus und Diktatur' [The crisis of parliamentarism and dictatorship]. This was the concluding session of a lecture course on 'Italien und seine Stellung im Mittelmeer' [Italy and its position within the Mediterranean], which paid particular attention to fascist Italy. Schmitt did not publish his lecture.

In Berlin, Schmitt looked at several apartments before Georg Eisler, together with a certain Dr Jacoby from the Chamber of Industry and Commerce, continued the search for accommodation for him.[13] However, Schmitt postponed the actual move until the autumn. At that time, his anti-Semitism became more radical and was also directed at Eisler. He wanted to get rid of 'the Jews' and lead a 'clean life' (TB, 6 February 1928). Smend and Schmitt first read their parallel campaigns on constitutional theory with mutual respect. But, soon, Schmitt expressed some scepticism regarding Smend's 'theory of integration': 'Maybe it is nothing but Protestant theology' (CSLF, p. 269). He declined to write a review of Kelsen's critique of Smend.[14]

Back in Bonn, his anti-Semitic impulses showed again. He got to know Kaufmann's successor there, Johannes Heckel, more closely, completed reports on doctoral theses (Daniels, Kirchheimer, Hirsch, Friesenhahn, Wilckens, Weber),[15] gave his last lecture and tutorial in Bonn, was given his farewell party by the faculty (24 February 1928), and conducted doctoral examinations (10 February and 24 February 1928). In mid-March, Schmitt travelled to Paris for ten days, where he worked in the national library, spent time with Pierre Linn, the translator of *Political Romanticism*,[16] and also met Maritain and some others. Upon his return, he found that the first bound copies of *Constitutional Theory* had arrived. He had to deal emotionally with the farewell to Magda. In mid-February, she already appeared 'no longer beautiful' to him. But then he was plagued again by a 'brothel dream with Magda', and it all began anew. Schmitt gave her 'fifty Marks and a box of pralines' for their farewell (TB, 29 March 1928).

In Siegburg, Schmitt gave another lecture in front of industrialists (30 March 1928) before travelling via Basel and Zurich to the first Hochschulwochen [university study weeks] in Davos. They were organized by Gottfried Salomon-Delatour,[17] whom Schmitt had met in Munich through Blei. On 2 April he lectured on 'Moderne Verfassungslehre' [Modern constitutional theory].[18] Schmitt criticized the 'bourgeois Rechtsstaat' yet again for lacking a principal political form, and saw the task of constitutional policy in finding a 'system of genuine representation' that constitutes a state. In Davos he met, among others, the French sociologist Marcel Mauss, the Jesuit priest Erich Przywara, Carl Brinkmann and Gustav Radbruch. He flirted with a dancer named Georgette and made wishful plans for a 'journey with Magda' (TB, 7 April 1928), which he would abandon only months later. The Hochschullehrertage [university lecturer days] in Davos were great events – 'half a seasonal university and half a meeting of scholars'.[19] In particular, the discussions between Ernst Cassirer and Martin Heidegger in 1929 are legendary. At the end of April there followed the meeting of state theorists in Vienna, where Heinrich Triepel and Hans Kelsen gave lectures, from opposite perspectives, on 'Wesen und Entwicklung der Staatsgerichtsbarkeit' [Nature and development of state jurisdiction]. But, although this would be his next planned project, Schmitt did not attend.

Masked as Cortés

From 29 April Schmitt was in Berlin. In the beginning, he stayed at the Hotel Continental near the Friedrichstraße train station.[20] Not only did he take up his post with *Constitutional Theory* under his belt, he also published his conclusions regarding constitutional policy as *Der bürgerliche Rechtsstaat* [The bourgeois Rechtsstaat] and excerpts from *The Concept of the Political* in the journals *Germania* and *Der Ring*. These efforts at increasing his visibility through publications show that Schmitt now wanted to play a political role. However, he brought with him an even older statement of intent: *Donoso Cortés in Berlin*. It has often been noted that Schmitt identified with the counter-revolutionary Spanish diplomat and critic of liberalism. For Schmitt, Cortés served as an autobiographical mask[21] and a reflection of his political self in the historical mirror of 1848. *Donoso Cortés in Berlin* was published in October 1927 in the *Festgabe* for Carl Muth,[22] the editor of *Hochland*, who represented the renewal of a Catholic literature. Schmitt had already promised to contribute in the summer of 1926[23] and immediately wrote the piece, but the actual publication was delayed. Only at the end of May 1927 did Fuchs send the volume to the printer. In the summer of 1926, Schmitt was already under consideration for the chair in Berlin. In January 1927 he received a first inquiry. Hence, he wrote the piece during a time of ongoing negotiations. Its title might as well be 'Carl Schmitt in Berlin'.

Let us remind ourselves: Schmitt took up his post in Bonn already having published *Political Theology* and *Roman Catholicism* – i.e., having expressed an open commitment to the Church and to a strategic alliance with the Zentrumspartei. Now he put on the mask of Donoso Cortés, took up his post – with Catholic reservations against the Protestant 'atmosphere' of Berlin – and explained the necessity of forming strategic alliances. What is arguably the most important sentence in the text claims: 'There is so far no European conservatism' (PB, p. 85). Schmitt knew Berlin from his early terms as a student. As many documents show, he did not feel it was his adopted home. Initial remarks to Feuchtwanger also show his reserve regarding the place. Although Schmitt soon moved temporarily into the villa of the 'famous architect [Muthesius], very nice and quiet' (CSLF, p. 269), which was situated at Potsdamer Chaussee 49, near the Wannsee, he did not feel at home. 'The city is very interesting', he wrote, 'but it is not in Europe. As someone from the Mosel, I cannot get over that fact' (CSLF, p. 273). He was glad, after an exhausting summer term in Berlin, to be back in his house in Bonn. As late as January 1933, in his last letter to Franz Blei, he wrote: 'This Berlin is a vacuum between East and West, a terribly draughty passageway. The people of Berlin take this draught to be the breath of the world spirit.'[24] Schmitt would later compare Berlin to the maelstrom of Edgar Allan Poe's novella *A Descent into the Maelström*.[25] 'For forty years a strong current has pulled me again and again from the west of Germany to Berlin, and has kept me there against all my inclinations and instincts, against all plans and resolutions, until the present day' (ECS, p. 35), Schmitt wrote in retrospect. He was more attracted to Munich, which he viewed as more of an adopted home. However, at the time, this European city of the arts increasingly closed itself off and became more provincial.[26] The maelstrom which pulled Schmitt to Berlin was politics, and he could best take up his position as a participant in politics here. A strict division between scholarship and politics as a profession does not apply to Schmitt's oeuvre.

It was certainly a stylization on Schmitt's part to compare his arrival in Berlin with that of Cortés in 1848 after the revolution. However, his text is meant to be very autobiographical. Schmitt begins with a discussion of the Spanish Catholic's 'aversion' (PB, p. 76) to the Protestant atmosphere of Berlin. He emphasizes the differences within Catholicism at the time but also insights of Prussian politics and the strategic necessity of an alliance across nations and confessions in the interest of 'joint conservative action in Europe' against Russia. Schmitt acquits the core of the Prussian monarchy of political Romanticism. By this, he meant – as Ernst Rudolf Huber would later also claim[27] – that the Prussian king, as he was in command of the army, retained sovereignty and the possibility of dictatorship. Schmitt writes that Cortés, with 'the way he constructed his political judgments', anticipated a 'much later situation', namely the 'idea of an imminent final and catastrophic battle between Catholicism and atheistic socialism' (PB, p. 81), the necessity for a dictatorship and 'joint European action' against Russia. The task, in Schmitt's view, was 'to save Europe from the Russian danger' (PB, p. 83) and to form, despite all inner differences, a unifying European alliance against the 'enemy of European civilization'. This position distanced Schmitt from the anti-Roman impulse of Bismarck as much as from the politics of the Vatican, which were averse to Protestantism.

Of course, we cannot read every statement about Cortés as a part of Schmitt's political programme; and yet the similarities are striking and the programmatic resonances can hardly be denied. This applies not only to the critique of liberalism and the way Cortés and Schmitt deal with their negative affects against Protestantism and Prussia, but also to the strong similarities between their views on the *Core Question Regarding the League of Nations* and on the need for an alliance against Russia as the legitimization of the federation. If we take this seriously and read the text as an analysis of the difficult situation in which conservatism finds itself, then we must probably also take the reference to dictatorship seriously as a comment on constitutional policy. Behind the mask of Cortés, and reflected in the historical moment of 1848, Schmitt formulated his own ideas about constitutional policy. He would soon make this even more apparent in an article for *Hochland*, 'Der unbekannte Donoso Cortés' [The unknown Donoso Cortés], which amounted to a first apologia for himself. The original title, still in the proofs, had been 'Der Misserfolg des Donoso Cortés' [The failure of Donoso Cortés].[28] The change of title probably reflects the unexpected success of his move to Berlin, which Schmitt expresses in the article.

Almost every word refers to Schmitt's own work: the interpretation of Cortés as a 'convert', who 'began as a liberal theorist of the state and ended as the theoretical herald of a conservative dictatorship' (PB, p. 115); the role of rhetoric; the attitude towards Christian dogma; and, finally, a parallel anthropological pessimism. Schmitt points out historical differences between the two counter-revolutionary situations. About Cortés, he says: 'His great theoretical importance for the history of counter-revolutionary theory consists in the fact that he abandoned the argument regarding legitimacy and no longer postulates a philosophy of the state for the Restoration, but a theory of dictatorship.' Something similar applies to Schmitt. He hints at historical differences, writing: 'Napoleon III, Bismarck and Mussolini found different answers to the question of an executive that is able to govern' (PB, p. 119. Schmitt ends with an apologia for the 'unknown' Donoso and his 'humanity'. 'In his private character, Donoso has something liberal in the best possible sense of the word; he is even better and more genuinely liberal compared to the humanitarian moralizing of his opponents', Schmitt thinks. 'It would be about time to recognize this unusual and sympathetic individual, in its purity and greatness, as a significant figure of European intellectual history [Geistesgeschichte] and, rather than to concentrate on the faults and deficiencies in his demonstration, to concentrate on the rare phenomenon of a political intuition practised within secular horizons' (PB, p. 120). Schmitt is also thinking of his own work when writing this. His Cortés essays are statements about himself, holding up a critical and slightly ironic mirror to their author. It is no coincidence that they were written as a prelude to his years in Berlin, which, apart from a short intermezzo in Cologne, lasted until after 1945. There is no need for the arduous task of extracting Schmitt's programme of constitutional policy from *Constitutional Theory*; he expressed it quite clearly in his Cortés studies at the time.

The Handelshochschule in Berlin

The Handelshochschule in Berlin was a product of late Wilhelminianism. Its foundation was an initiative of industry. Berlin was still an important industrial location at the time. In 1903, the Kaufmannschaft [merchants' association] decided to found it and acquired a piece of land in the Mitte district of Berlin, close to the stock exchange, at Spandauer Straße 1, between Heiliggeiststraße and Neuer Friedrichstraße (today named Burgstraße). The location was close to the university, behind the

Museumsinsel [Museum Island]. The imposing building was built as an annex to the Heiliggeistkapelle [Chapel of the Holy Spirit], which was thereby transformed into a lecture hall. 'Instructions on balances, book-keeping, and banking rise to the vaulted Gothic ceilings.'[29] Today, the building is part of Humboldt University. In 1904 the first statutes were formulated, which said that the school should foster 'the sciences that are necessary and useful for the commercial professions through teaching and research'. As it was a private foundation, its constitution differed significantly from that of a university. An 'Ältestenkollegium' [council of elders], comprised of members of the Kaufmannschaft, had a say in the decision-making. The pay was good, and by 1906 important figures such as Werner Sombart and Hugo Preuß had already been appointed.[30] At the beginning there were eight seminars, among them the 'Handelshochschulseminar für fremde Sprachen' [seminar for foreign languages] and a seminar for the training of teachers of business studies. Physics, chemistry and geography were also taught. Jurisprudence and political economy were taught together in a 'Volkswirtschaftlich-juristisches Seminar'. At first, a degree took four terms. In the winter term 1908–9 there were 402 registered students; in the winter term 1913–14 that figure had risen to 590. In 1928 the institution had 1,800 students, of whom almost 10 per cent were women. There was also a high proportion of foreign students and many guest students [Gasthörer].* In 1926, the school became a full higher education institution with the right to award doctoral degrees. Although it continued to be supported by industry and commerce in Berlin, it was now publicly governed. The length of the degree was extended to six terms, at the end of which students took the examination for a diploma in business studies or the teaching of business studies. Many merchants left without a diploma. Only very few students went on to do doctoral work.

As mentioned above, the carousel of negotiations around Schmitt's appointment was difficult.[31] Schmitt was ranked only fourth out of five in the list of candidates. The negotiations dragged on from summer 1926 to summer 1927. Franz Eulenburg and Moritz Julius Bonn supported Schmitt. They saw him as a new star in the sky of state theory who would be able to stand his ground against the university, and thus would help the Handelshochschule to strengthen its reputation. The high salary attracted Schmitt, but in the final analysis it was probably the 'maelstrom' of politics that brought him to Berlin. For the time being, he had done his theoretical work; *Constitutional Theory* was out. Now his task was to defend his concepts and to practise political state theory from the position of a participant. With effect from the summer term 1928, Schmitt was appointed to the 'chair in state theory' [Lehrstuhl in Staatsrecht] as the successor to Schücking.

It seems he did not have a fixed assistant at first. But, soon, Ernst Friesenhahn was seconded from Bonn to the Handelshochschule 'with a teaching appointment in civic education [Staatsbürgerkunde] and as

---

* Participants in an academic course or degree who do not take part in the examination process.

At the Handelshochschule, Berlin, 1928–1933

assistant to Professor Carl Schmitt'.[32] In July 1929, Werner Weber got in touch with Schmitt again. He was a teacher's son and had studied from 1923 in Marburg and Berlin and then from the summer term 1926 in Bonn. He passed his first state examination in December 1926, continued to participate in Schmitt's seminar while doing his legal training, and passed his doctoral examination on 25 February 1928 as one of Schmitt's last pupils in Bonn. Now he was overworked as an assessor at the regional court, was afraid of having to work in a law firm as he was financially insecure, and did not know what to do with his dissertation.[33] Schmitt offered him a post as his assistant.[34] Weber completed his assessor assignment[35] and published his dissertation in the *Archiv des Öffentlichen Rechts*.[36] In 1930 he became Schmitt's assistant on a teaching assignment until he moved as an 'auxiliary' to the Ministry of Culture, where he quickly moved up the ranks. Then in 1935 he became Schmitt's successor at the Handelshochschule. Later, he also held an important position as a secretary in Hans Frank's 'Akademie für Deutsches Recht' [Academy for German Right]. Weber was the only student from the Bonn period who continued to work with Schmitt throughout his life without any apparent interruptions or quarrels. After Weber had moved to the Ministry of Culture, Friesenhahn again supported Schmitt from Bonn. Tula Simons (later Mrs Hubers), the daughter of Walter Simons, who was president of the Reichsgericht [Supreme Court of the Reich][37] at the time, helped Schmitt out and took over a tutorial in the summer term 1931, after she had passed her doctorate in Bonn 'with distinction'. Werner Weber returned from the ministry. However, in the summer of 1932, Schmitt was again looking for an assistant. With the winter term 1932–3, Karl Schilling, who would continue after 1933 as Schmitt's assistant,[38] followed Weber. Again and again Schmitt used students, and male and female doctoral students, for support work and for dictating his work to them. For the chronicle of the Handelshochschule he wrote the following report:

> During the time covered by this report, tutorials and seminars were not taught, following the departure of Prof. Schücking, until I continued them again in the winter term 1928–9. All teaching of public law is done with the aim of combining strict juridical methods with the recognition of the realities of economic and social life. In accordance with this, the tutorials follow on from lectures, and seminars from tutorials, in a continuous sequence. The seminar in the winter term 1928–9 dealt with the problem of the inner political neutrality of the state and of the neutral entities within the state. Presentations were given on the president of the Reich, on the Reichsbank [central bank of the Reich] and the railway of the Reich, on Gneist's theory of self-administration, on the party-political neutrality of the radio broadcasting and the expert commissions, on the neutralizing effect of coalition governments, and on the neutrality of the state towards the sciences (Art. 142 of the Reich's Constitution).* In the summer term 1929, the topic was the problem of constitutional amendments (Art. 76 of the Reich's Constitution),† with presentations on the practice of constitutional amendments so far and on individual articles of the Reich's Constitution (Articles 127, 153, 165).‡ In the winter term 1929–30, the topic was the political relationship between the economy and the state, with presentations on economic incompatibilities, economic neutrality of the state, the form of government and economic order, and the state theory of Hugo Preuß. In the summer term 1930: agreements between that state and other domestic entities, contracts between the state

---

* Art. 142 reads: 'There is freedom of art, scholarship, and its teachings. The state ensures their protection and participates in their cultivation' (CT, p. 432).
† The article allows for amendments of the constitution 'via legislation', requiring a two-thirds majority 'of those present' in the Reichstag. Decisions on amendments taken in the Reichstag also required a two-thirds majority. A referendum on constitutional amendments required the 'majority of enfranchised voters'. And, finally: 'If the Reichstag passes a constitutional change against the objection of the Reichsrat, the president is not permitted to promulgate this statute if the Reichstag demands a referendum within two weeks' (CT, p. 421).
‡ Art. 127 relates to the right of self-government of local communities and associations (CT, p. 429); Art. 153 to property and expropriation (CT, p. 434); and Art. 165 to the rights of workers and employees and to workers' and economic councils (CT, p. 436).

and Churches, agreements between political parties, the corporative state [Ständestaat], and reservations in public law contracts.[39]

Within a relatively small circle of colleagues, there was close cooperation at the Handelshochschule between practitioners from the field of politics and the economy and academics. Teaching appointments were of great importance. Lines of political tension were tangible within the faculty. Within jurisprudence, the expert in commercial law, Paul Gieseke, became the successor to the late Eltzbacher. Karl August Eckhardt was given the newly created chair for traffic law in 1930, but soon moved to Bonn. In 1931 he joined the SA and in 1932 the NSDAP. He later became one of the leading SS jurists and a dangerous opponent for Schmitt. Other important jurists held teaching appointments at the Handelshochschule – for instance, the star lawyer Max Alsberg and the president of the Senate Hermann Dersch. Herbert Dorn, the president of the Reichsfinanzhof,* was an honorary professor. Political economy was taught by Franz Eulenburg and Moritz Julius Bonn. Friedrich Leitner and Heinrich Niklisch represented economics. Alfred Manes taught insurance studies. Philosophy was represented by pupils of Dilthey, for a long time by Max Frischeisen-Köhler and Max Dessoir. Later, Arthur Liebert was appointed to the Philosophy Faculty. Heinrich Spiess and Anton Palme represented languages. In addition, there were some natural scientists. Schmitt had many Jewish colleagues who would later lose their chairs. Hirsch, Bonn, Manes, Liebert,[40] Dorn, Melchior Palyi and others, all emigrated. Franz Eulenburg died on 28 December 1943 while in custody of the Gestapo.

Many of the students had professional experience, and from practitioners Schmitt could still learn something. The emphasis on practice had many advantages, but the study regulations did not allow the raising of students as one's pupils, and their training and preparation for an academic career, to the same extent as in a university. Schmitt, therefore, appreciated it when his collaborators and former pupils, or established jurists such as Werner Weber, Otto Kirchheimer and Franz Neumann,[41] took part in his seminar on 'constitutional theory'. Schmitt liked to give his lectures in the evening, even on Fridays. He got to know Günther Krauss, the son of a notary from Cologne, who studied at the university in Berlin from the summer term 1929 and would play a role after 1933. Schmitt frequently quoted from the works of his pupils. Of the Marxist pupils, Otto Kirchheimer was particularly close to him.[42] As first examiner, Schmitt was involved in the completion of only four doctoral theses at the Handelshochschule:[43] those of Wilhelm Haubold, Karl Scheidemann, Ruth Büttner and Johanna Kendziora. The dissertation by Kendziora, *Der Begriff der politischen Partei im System des politischen Liberalismus* [The concept of the political party in the system of political liberalism] Schmitt still valued later in life. Another doctoral student was called Arthur Nehrig. Wolfgang Dietl completed his doctorate only in 1936.[44] Dr Friedrich Dorn remained in touch as a grateful student after 1945.[45] Decades later, Dr Hans Wecke still kept in his possession 'three

---

* The supreme court for fiscal matters.

Carl Schmitt next to Moritz Julius Bonn during an examination

lecture notebooks from the years 1930 to 1932, containing your [Schmitt's] lectures on state and administrative theory, state law and administrative law'.[46] However, none of his students at the Handelshochschule is today closely associated with Schmitt's name. Schmitt, at that time, shifted his attention to gaining influence in the sphere of politics. The determination of the relationship between Church and state receded into the background, and the relationship between state and society became his central focus. Schmitt sought to establish a 'strong' state as the 'superior third party', in particular with regard to the economy, and to safeguard the 'neutral entities' as 'stabilizing powers' [haltende Mächte].

Permanent abode?
Biographical sketch of Schmitt's life until summer 1929

Schmitt's diary breaks off in April 1928 and continues again only with the move to Berlin in October. From the end of July, he was in Bonn and wrote on the 'Reichsgericht als Hüter der Verfassung' [The Reich's Supreme Court as the guardian of the constitution]. The evening of his fortieth birthday he spent in the house of Smend in Berlin, where he met for the first time the young Ulrich Scheuner, a pupil of Smend and Triepel. Schmitt and Scheuner remained in permanent contact from then on.[47] The author Alice Berend, who in 1919 had written the *roman à clef Der Glückspilz* [The lucky devil] came to Bonn. In mid-September, Duška went to take the waters in San Remo. At the beginning of October, Schmitt was in Berlin for a couple of days looking for accommodation. Afterwards he gave a lecture on 'Völkerrechtliche Probleme im Rheingebiet' [Problems of internation law regarding the Rhine area] at a conference of history teachers in Heppenheim. Back in Bonn, his meetings with Magda slowly came to a definite end. On the day of his move he went to see her one last time: 'She cried; I gave her 110 Marks, that soothed her, because what matters to her is the money' (TB, 20 October 1928). Schmitt said farewell to his brother in Bonn, to Karl Lambert in Mönchengladbach and to am Zehnhoff in Düsseldorf. He went to Plettenberg for a couple of days. On 29 October he slept in his new apartment, Klopstockstraße 48/I, next to the Tiergarten, for the first time. It was the former apartment of the painter Lovis Corinth.[48] Thus, Schmitt lived close to the government and with an underground connection from Tiergarten to Mitte. Frequently, he took his dog, Olaf, for a walk in the Tiergarten. Schmitt had two maids, Hanna and Elli. And, while Duška was away, Annie Kraus, Eisler's cousin, also looked after him. Schmitt dictated his correspondence and his texts daily to her. He also spent a lot of private time with her, without the relationship becoming intimate. For the course of a year, she was a source of stability and calm in his life.

Only now did the Berlin adventure begin in earnest. Schmitt continually picked up prostitutes at the Tiergarten and on the Kurfürstendamm, Unter den Linden or Potsdamer Platz. In cooperation with the Hochschule für Politik, he regularly gave juridical training lectures at the Foreign Ministry. His social contacts with Franz Blei were revived. He took walks in the Tiergarten with Alice Berend. Some pupils from Bonn were there – e.g., Kirchheimer and Oberheid. Schmitt paid his colleagues initial visits to introduce himself. Together with Karl Eschweiler, he watched the silent movie classic *The Passion of Joan of Arc*,[49] which impressed him so much – he remarked on the magic of the 'cinematic art' (VRA, p. 369) – that he talked about it for days. The film concentrates on the tension between religious calling and condemnation by the Church, on the martyrdom of a lay religiosity that faces the secular Church. Apart from the aspect of Saint Joan as a fighter for national liberation, Schmitt probably saw reflected in the film his trial with the Church, the unjust condemnation by the secular Church. Throughout the following months, he dragged various acquaintances and female friends, and also prostitutes, along to screenings of the film. Within the space of six months, he watched it more than ten times.

Schmitt met Gerhard Leibholz and Siegfried Landshut. Leibholz had already contacted Schmitt by letter in June 1926.[50] Schmitt met him frequently and read the proofs of his Habilitation, *Das Wesen der Repräsentation* [The nature of representation],[51] which may be seen as the first work that was inspired by the time in Berlin. Schmitt's report on Landshut's work was positive.[52] On 12 December, Schmitt gave a lecture for the 'Staatspolitischer Kursus' [course on state politics] of the General Association of Christian Trade Unions[53] in Königswinter, and went on to visit am Zehnhoff as well as his parents in Plettenberg. Back in Berlin, he felt 'happiness that I have left Bonn' (TB, 16 December 1928). He spent the time over Christmas with Bilfinger in Halle. Duška was far away –

throughout all of 1928 Schmitt had hardly seen her – and yet he wished to have 'a child with her' (29 December 1928). At that time, he wrote his 'essay on Beckerath' and a 'theatre review', probably of a performance at the Schiller Theater of an apocryphal play by Shakespeare on the parable of the prodigal son.[54]

In the following weeks, old friends, such as Eduard Rosenbaum, Erik Peterson and Wilhelm Neuß, came to visit. Schmitt was in closer contact with colleagues, such as Moritz Julius Bonn, Götz Briefs, Werner Sombart, Herbert Dorn, Smend and the philosopher Eduard Spranger. And he often saw the notary Heinrich Wimpfheimer, who wanted to become an honorary professor at the Handelshochschule. The colleague most esteemed by Schmitt at the time was Smend, despite the fact that he felt a certain reserve on Smend's part, which he interpreted in confessional terms: 'Am afraid of him and his indirect manner [Hintergründigkeit], etc.; he obviously hates me as a Catholic' (TB, 11 January 1929). Schmitt met Paul Landsberg again and got to know the young Reinhard Höhn, who would later become a dangerous opponent. Several times, Schmitt attended social gatherings at the home of Arnold Wolfers, who was at the Hochschule für Politik. Schmitt became friendly with the Russian dancer Koschwenikoff, whom he frequently met together with Paul Adams.[55] He saw in the dancer the 'misfortune of the emigrant' (TB, 15 May 1929). Occasionally, he attended functions and lectures organized by conservative clubs (Deutsche Gesellschaft, Herrenhaus), and he gradually deepened his acquaintance with Johannes Popitz,[*] who soon retired from his post as state secretary in the Ministry of Finance, but would go on to become Reichsminister at the end of 1932 and then Prussian Minister of Finance in April 1933, a function he held until his execution after the events of 20 July 1944.[†] Erich Zweigert, state secretary of the Ministry of the Interior, asked Schmitt to prepare a legal opinion on the rules for compensation in cases of expropriation (TB, 8 February 1929). Schmitt quickly wrote down an article on 'Die Auflösung des Enteignungsbegriffs' [The liquidation of the concept of expropriation] for the *Juristische Wochenschrift*[56] and then set to work on the legal opinion (15–18 February 1929).[57] As a second legal opinion to that of Erich Kaufmann, it argues 'in every respect' in favour of a planned law on compensation, as it does not count the introduction of a monopoly on the production of spirits as a case of expropriation. It was Schmitt's first public appearance as the antipode to Kaufmann with regard to questions of constitutional law. However, until early March, he worked mainly on an article on 'Der Reichspräsident als Hüter der Verfassung' [The Reich's president as the guardian of the constitution], which appeared in the *Archiv des öffentlichen Rechts*.

---

[*] Johannes Popitz (1884–1945) was part of the resistance circle. He offered Hitler his resignation after the pogroms of 9 November 1938, but it was not accepted. Popitz tried to win Himmler for a *coup d'état* and prepared a provisional constitution for a post-Hitler Germany. He did not take part in the events of 20 July 1944 but, like other members of the resistance, was arrested immediately after the failed assassination and executed on 2 February 1945.

[†] The date of the failed assassination of Hitler.

From the beginning of 1929, Schmitt was engaged in an intense affair with Margot von Quednow,[58] an acquaintance of Moritz Bonn and the psychiatrist Viktor von Gelbsattel. It was a serious liaison, though Schmitt was not altogether on fire. She did not give him the peace he found with Duška. What Margot was missing was 'eternity. She has no soul' (TB, 5 March 1929). But Duška was ill. Margot was well meaning towards Carl and told him to go and see his wife in San Remo. Schmitt thanked her with a typescript of *The Faithful Gipsy* and set off. He found Duška very ill and was full of remorse. 'Maybe this journey was my salvation' (TB, 10 March 1929). Duška did not want to be operated on and expected to die. Carl made preparations for a funeral and wrote to numerous friends. Eisler again helped out with money. Alice Berend arrived in San Remo. When Wilhelm Neuß used the situation for an 'attempt at conversion', Schmitt was very annoyed about this 'tactless apologetics at a deathbed' (TB, 16 March 1929) and inwardly broke with his friend from Bonn. There were several temptations in San Remo as well. Schmitt made an excursion to Monte Carlo and Nizza, visiting the grave of the French national hero Gambetta. At the beginning of April he sent out copies of his treatise on the Reichspräsident. On 9 April, after a month in San Remo, he travelled on to Rome, where he admired in particular 'the heathen Rome', picked up a prostitute and watched the film on Saint Joan with her; he also established contacts with Gaetano Mosca and Giorgio Del Vecchio.

On 17 April, Schmitt returned to Berlin, where he met his friend vom Tölz, Krause and his daughter Iser, as well as Feuchtwanger. On 22 April he gave a lecture in front of 'Highnesses' and got to know the young Theodor Eschenburg.[59] At the end of April he stayed with Eisler in Hamburg. His debts weighed down on him: 'Fear of the Jews, fear of my debts' (29 April 1929). In the summer term, Schmitt lectured on state theory, jurisprudence and international law. He suffered under his sexuality and frequented prostitutes because he wanted to avoid taking up his relationship with Margot again. He began to study 'pluralism' and dictated his lecture on 'Staatsethik und pluralistischer Staat' [The ethics of the state and the pluralist state] for a meeting of the Kant Society in Halle to Annie Kraus.[60] Schmitt got to know the sociologist Hans Freyer, with whom he would henceforth be connected. Over Pentecost, he travelled to Plettenberg and selected a grave for Duška. He then returned to Halle, where he stayed with Bilfinger and gave his opening address on the topic of the conference, 'Staat und Sittlichkeit' [State and morality], in the university's assembly hall. It was the Kant Society's twenty-fifth anniversary celebration of its foundation in Halle in 1904.[61] At the festive ceremony, Schmitt sat next to Rudolf Stammler, the doyen of the modern philosophy of right, then seventy-three years of age.

At the same time Duška went from San Remo to the Kantonsspital [county hospital] in St Gallen, where she was to undergo several severe operations during the next few weeks. Schmitt was very worried. He revised his pluralism text and wrote a legal opinion on 'The Exterritoriality of the Soviet Union' for Wimpfheimer,[62] who assured Schmitt of his 'admiration . . ., of the concise way in which you have touched upon and solved a plethora of problems of the greatest interest. I am genuinely amazed how quickly and thoroughly you have familiarized yourself with Russian law, a matter that is after all far from your own work.'[63] During June, Schmitt frequently met with Gerhard Leibholz. Inspired by a seminar presentation, he wrote an article on Egmont Zechlin's book on Bismarck.[64] And he made the acquaintance of the young Carl Joachim Friedrich,[65] who taught at Harvard. He repeatedly met Margot, but did not take up the relationship again with the same intensity as before. Schmitt wanted to remain faithful to Duška and therefore was more inclined to visit prostitutes. However, he had a crush on a student, Ruth Büttner – 'who looks so much like Duška', he wrote – and met several times with her.[66] On 28 June he dictated a lecture on 'Der Mangel eines *pouvoir neutre* im neuen Deutschland' [The lack of a neutral power in the new Germany] and the very same day gave it at one of the 'debating evenings' on 'Probleme der Koalitionspolitik'[67] [Problems of coalition politics] at the Hochschule für Politik. He now clearly made advances to 'Miss Büttner', had a short 'adventure' with Elfriede, the 'wife of a Stahlhelmführer' [leader of the Steel Helmet],* and continually looked for his favourite prostitute. His relationship with Annie Kraus also became ambivalent and critical at that time.

In mid-July, Eisler came from Hamburg and visited for a couple of days. Dr Max Clauss, who belonged to the circles around the *Europäische Revue*, invited Schmitt to a conference on 'Le problem social de la vulgarisation de la culture' [The social problem of the vulgarisation of culture] in Barcelona. The journey was organized at very short notice by Paul Adams.[68] Schmitt accepted 'purely out of weakness'. But maybe he also wanted to pull himself out of another affair, as he was increasingly drawn into a relationship with Miss Büttner. She is, 'however, cold and hard' and 'wimpy'.[69] Schmitt very quickly wrote an article on 'Zehn Jahre Reichsverfassung' [Ten years of the Weimar Constitution]. Then, in August, Duška had to be operated on for a fifth time in St Gallen. Carl was with her and wrote his lectures for Spain. 'The unknown Donoso Cortés' appeared even before the journey to Spain in *Hochland*, and the famous speech on 'Die europäische Kultur im Zwischenstadium der Neutralisierung' [European culture at the intermediary stage of neutralization] followed in the *Europäische Revue*. However, the main results of Schmitt's work at the time were, without a doubt, the two articles on 'The Guardian of the Constitution', which delineated Schmitt's position. On 15 October, Schmitt travelled to Barcelona and soon on to Madrid. He gave his lecture in French under the title 'L'état actuel de la culture européenne' [The state in today's European culture][70] and on 23 October also talked about Donoso Cortés's role within German state theory. He wrote enthusiastically to Smend about bullfights and the Escorial.[71] Schmitt's return journey at the end of October led him to Paris, where he visited Pierre Linn, a member of the circle around Maritain. Back in Germany, he spoke at the Übersee-Klub in Hamburg. On 29 November he gave a lecture on 'Parteienstaat und authoritärer

---

* The Stahlhelm, Bund der Frontsoldaten [Steel Helmet, League of Front-Line Soldiers] was a nationalistic paramilitary organization after 1918.

Staat' [The party state and the authoritarian state][72] and then worked on a major speech on Hugo Preuß. At the end of 1929, Schmitt formulated the following résumé in a letter to Feuchtwanger: 'In the last year, I have completed a few articles and lectures, which are good as they are and, much more importantly, do not block the way towards a systematic summary. The volume of material and experiences that Berlin offers is so vast that so far I have reacted to it only in the fragmentary form of articles and lectures' (CSLF, p. 311).

Living in an erotic state of exception

In 1929, Schmitt lived in a kind of erotic state of exception. While still in Bonn, he had made a clear distinction between love and sexuality, Duška and Magda. Now, the arrangement became more complex. Annie Kraus came around every day. Then there were the maids. In addition, there were countless prostitutes, some affairs and a more serious liaison with Margot, which Schmitt, after Duška's operation, abandoned only at the cost of renewed visits to prostitutes and a fling with a student. Other women, for instance Corina Sombart, came dangerously close to him. Close male friendships, such as the one with Arnold Schmitz in Bonn, which had provided stability, were missing. Instead, others, such as Paul Adams and Koschwenikoff, became members of Schmitt's closer circle of friends. The network of relationships became more complex and diffuse. Schmitt's sphere of interactions widened. He drifted into the world of hustlers and described himself like a sexual maniac who was straying around in his hunting area, until hit by the electrifying 'impact' of 'long legs' and 'white flesh'. These passages of his diary read less like literature and more like a medical report.

In his relationships with women, Schmitt vacillated from the very beginning between an idealization of love and a metaphysical gender battle à la Weininger, Strindberg and Kleist. His marriage to Cari was almost an attempt at providing proof that love is blind. But Schmitt not only increasingly lost himself in an idealism of love, he also developed more and more into a questionable Don Juan, rushing from conquest to conquest. In his satire *Die Buribunken*, he had already called Don Juan a man of the 'immediate present' (TB II, p. 457). His ironic remarks on 'Leporello's wholly inadequate keeping of a register' (TB II, p. 458) increasingly also applied to his novel of love. 'We sense no attempt at a demonstration of law-like regularity, . . . no aesthetic observations . . . There is even less of an effort at providing reliable detail, nowhere does he follow the deeper connections between the individual cases of seduction, nowhere do we find information on the status, background, age, etc., of Don Juan's victims that would be sociologically useful' (TB II, p. 459). Stendhal's *De l'amour* ends with a juxtaposition of Don Juan and Werther. Stendhal calls Werther the 'happier' character. After his more philosophical and high-minded existential experiment with Murray, at the end even, of all places, in Wetzlar, it seems that Schmitt made a practical decision in favour of Don Juan.

The impression one gets is that his *sexus* vehemently won the upper hand after Cari, Kathleen and Lolo, and in the absence of Duška. Schmitt freed himself from personal commitments and looked for fleeting encounters. He turned away from the precarious 'fusion of love and marriage',[73] which Mozart's operas present in all its variations, and kept *sexus* separate from commitment and relationships. Schmitt tested the bourgeois possibilities of a relationship with Murray, and he decided once more in favour of a love marriage with Duška. But this marriage also turned out to have been an economic and sexual 'stupidity', and Schmitt descended into darker regions.

Prostitution was widespread in previous times. Together with the contrast between bourgeoisie and proletariat it dominated the picture presented by cities. Stefan Zweig describes it in *The World of Yesterday*. Heinrich Mann's *Small Town Tyrant** was based on close observation. In July 1918, the young, and at the time also notoriously unfaithful, Martin Heidegger reported to his wife 'with disgust' from Berlin: 'Such an atmosphere of highly developed, most vulgar and shrewd sexuality I wouldn't have believed possible. However, I already understand Berlin better now – the character of Friedrichstraße has rubbed off on the whole city . . . the people here have lost their soul.'[74] After 1918, libertinage and prostitution were part of the new democratic start. There were about 24,000 prostitutes and 8,000 to 10,000 pimps in Berlin at the time. Centres of prostitution were the Friedrichstraße and Oranienburgerstraße, right next to the university. In Döblin's *Berlin Alexanderplatz* or Kästner's *Fabian* the prostitute becomes the allegorical figure for the whole city. Walter Benjamin found it in Baudelaire. Expressionist painting presents the milieu in garish colours. Kirchner and Beckmann, Dix and Grosz formed the picture of the time. Franz Blei was a more subtle eroticist who insisted on the 'myth of love for justification';[75] he asked Schmitt for advice when writing about female figures.[76] Schmitt distinguished between Eros and Caritas, love and marriage. At times, he described his erotic excitations in almost uncanny fashion as an animalistic fixation which he could not escape. 'In the tramway next to a woman. Suddenly the electric impact again. I followed her as if hypnotized' (TB, 30 January 1933). It was no casual, shabby and embarrassing libertinage on the side, no luxury of the socially privileged, but rather an anarchic passion which suffused everyday life like an 'affliction' [Heimsuchung] (Thomas Mann).

Schmitt used a whole canon of literature in order to reflect upon his relationship with women. He liked the 'tragic' authors, identified with Shakespeare's *Othello*, studied the literary motif of Don Juan from Mozart to Grabbe's tragi-comical adaptation of the theme and to the novel *The Girls* by Henry de Montherlant, which he took to be the last example of its treatment in literature, and which he recommended to others. Grabbe's Faust wishes to end up in hell; he is in competition with Don Juan and is the victim of his philosophical sentimentality, until both characters are

---

* Title of the English translation of Heinrich Mann's *Professor Unrat* (1905), the novel on which the famous film *The Blue Angel* was based.

finally caught by the devil. A hundred years later, the novel by Montherlant discusses the self-mortification of the 'hunt for women' through misogyny and takes the position of a strict disjunction between love and marriage. Published in the late 1930s, but set in the Paris of the 1920s, it tells the story of Pierre Costals, a Catholic Romantic author and avoider of marriage. He is confronted with the demand of marriage by Solange, whom he draws into an affair and turns into literature. Costals constructs a novel out of romantic encounters, is permanently on the 'hunt for women', and is even prepared to contract leprosy in order to escape the promises he makes out of self-interest. He shows fluctuating 'mercy for the women',[77] because he responds only occasionally to the demand for personal love and feels a supra-personal dependency on sexual adventure. The novel interprets men's love of women as a form of 'pity' and 'mercy'. This ambivalent form of mercy is also applied to Don Juan, who makes himself dependent on casual conquests and is hardly able to experience the happiness in love that requires symmetric gender relations. Schmitt's love life was a passion story. Before 1930, with Cari or Duška, there was hardly any quiet living together. The failing attempt at a fusion of love and marriage also meant the failing of bourgeois fulfilment, and Schmitt became dependent on his intimate conflicts. Whatever it was that attracted him to a Don Juan life-style, even the old Schmitt was still inclined towards a 'dualist' metaphysics of gender in the wake of Nietzsche, Strindberg, Ibsen and Weininger, a metaphysics according to which men and women are 'lepers' to each other. He hardly had an understanding of love and marriage as a sacrament, even if he thought about his love again and again as the pneumatic 'shadow of God', and even if he was afraid of sexual passion as an anti-Christian sanctification of life.

A new theme: 'The Guardian of the Constitution'

In Berlin, until 1933, Schmitt looked at the elements of the Weimar Rechstsstaat one after another. First, he analysed the principle of the separation of powers, then the principle of distribution of basic rights, and finally the foundational concept of law.

Table 15.1 Analysis and critique of the 'bourgeois Rechtsstaat'

Principle of organization Separation of powers	Principle of distribution Basic rights	Foundational concept of law
The Guardian of the Constitution	Civil rights and institutional guarantees; basic rights and duties	*Legality and Legitimacy*

The first longer work Schmitt wrote in Berlin was the treatise on the 'Das Reichsgericht als Hüter der Verfassung' [The Reich's Supreme Court as the guardian of the constitution]. At the end of August, he handed the manuscript to the publisher. It appeared on 1 October 1929 in a commemorative publication on the fiftieth anniversary of the Reichsgericht in Leipzig and was a response to the meeting of the State Theorists in April 1928 in Vienna. Schmitt asked the question of who the guardian of the constitution is, on the basis of his concept of the separation of powers as a 'principle of organization' and his distinction between politics and right. He had already formulated his understanding of the dictatorial powers of the president at that point. All he needed to do now was to render his old ideas regarding the 'independence' of jurisdiction by virtue of the rule of law more precise by applying his concept of the political, and the skeleton of 'The Guardian of the Constitution' was complete. Thus, Schmitt's positive understanding soon followed in a second treatise (published in the *Archiv für öffentliches Recht*), and the general lines of his application of *Constitutional Theory* to constitutional policy were already there in 1929. Schmitt answered the question of who the guardian of the constitution is with his distinction between executive and jurisdiction. He rightly considered the politicization of the constitutional court as a threat, which is why he assigned authority and political responsibility to the executive.

The treatise on 'The Reich's Supreme Court as the Guardian of the Constitution' circumvents dogmatic positions by asking after the direction 'from which a danger may threaten' (VRA, p. 66). At the moment of the birth of modern times, we find the absolutist executive state, against which there formed an opposition from the estates and the legislature. A more recent experience was the 'protection of the constitution against the legislature' (VRA, p. 67), which provided reasons for a turn towards jurisdiction. However, Schmitt argues, this conflictual constellation was also already a thing of the past. He spells out that a formulation of this idea of balance depends on the 'contractual' nature of the constitution and that there exists no 'general jurisdiction or constitutional judiciary' in Germany. The Reich's Supreme Court [Reichsgericht] is only one among many institutions. The constitutional judiciary competes with the legislature and can easily become a 'lawgiver with a highly political function' (VRA, p. 82). Especially in 'critical and turbulent times, the judiciary should not attempt to decide social and political conflicts' (VRA, p. 89). Following on from a judgment of the Staatsgerichtshof [Constitutional Court],[*] Schmitt therefore limits the right to judicial review: Article 76 of the Weimar Constitution, he said, was an 'absolute limit' (VRA, p. 94).

In the commemorative publication, Schmitt saw the judiciary as being in competition with the Reichstag. He did not take into consideration that the Reich's president could also act as an extraordinary lawgiver. It seems that he ignored the actually existing threat of a turn towards an executive state, which he continually talked about elsewhere. We may suspect some strategic calculations behind the fact that here he did not want to see the

---

[*] The Staatsgerichtshof was founded in 1921. It was not a standing court and dealt exclusively with questions regarding state institutions. Seated in Leipzig, the president of the Reichsgerichtshof was at the same time president of the Staatsgerichtshof. In 1927 the Staatsgerichtshof, in one of its decisions, had referred to itself as the 'guardian of the constitution'.

question of who was the guardian of the constitution against the backdrop of the tension between constitutional judiciary and presidential executive. Schmitt concludes with a synopsis of the 'centres of gravity in the respective concrete existence of states' (VRA, p. 99), and in this context considers Weimar to be primarily a legislative state. In footnotes, he marks his own position against those of Kelsen and also Smend. Kelsen quickly spelled out his understanding, antipodal to that of Schmitt, in a polemic.[78]

Schmitt thought that his text 'came out very well' (CSLF, p. 311). At the beginning of 1929, he added the longer treatise on 'Der Reichspräsident als Hüter der Verfassung' [The Reich's president as the guardian of the constitution], which makes reference to historical experiences and extends the engagement with Kelsen, but most importantly develops the position of the guardian of the constitution 'according to the positive sense given in the Weimar Constitution' [nach dem positive Sinn der Weimarer Verfassung].[79] For tactical reasons, Schmitt temporarily takes up Benjamin Constant's theory of the head of state as a 'neutral power' and sees the Reichspräsident as a 'neutral third party' who can play the role of a 'mediator' in the social conflicts within 'industrial nations'. He approvingly refers to Ebert and relies on the Reichspräsident as the democratically elected 'representative' of the 'unity of state and constitution'[80] and the 'centre' of an entire 'system of neutrality and independence, on which the political system of the state of today's German Reich depends'.[81] Schmitt frees his emphasis on the role of the Reichspräsident from the suspicion of dictatorship, distances himself from the monarchist theory of a 'higher third party', and gives an answer in particular to Smend with his reference to static and stabilizing powers within the state. 'Integration is not a type of state', he says; 'every state is "integrated" that does not say anything specific about a state' (CSLF, p. 230). In contrast to Smend, he wants to hold on to the view 'that there is no state without static elements' (VRA, p. 68). He gives a more detailed account of this view for the first time and offers his theory of a state-supporting 'neutral third party' as a relatively unproblematic, attractive argumentative tool.

A light shining from Italy? How to save democracy from its 'disguise'

Style and tone in the 'maelstrom' of Berlin, however, were different compared to Bonn. Schmitt felt this very keenly. After he had done his systematic work, he pushed the academic apparatus slightly to one side. His publisher was not happy about this at all. When Feuchtwanger, in 1928, once again argued for the scholarly 'path of science', Schmitt countered him emphatically, saying 'that there is no such thing as "being scientific" in matters pertaining to intellectual history [geistesgeschichtlichen Fragen]. That was only a happy moment in the context of bourgeois liberalism' (CSLF, pp. 272f.). Feuchtwanger did not accept that and insisted on solid 'criteria'.[82] But Schmitt gave second place to the 'habitus of science', privileging political controversy.

The state theory of the Federal Republic of Germany took the Anglo-

Saxon understanding of a 'representative' democracy as its point of reference.[83] Rousseauism was charged with responsibility for the 'total people's state'.[84] The classical nation-state put the discriminatory logic of its urge for homogeneity into practice and became discredited as nationalistic and racist. Large numbers of state theorists in the Weimar Republic took a different approach. They witnessed the 'dissolution of liberal democracy'[85] and saw Anglo-Saxon liberalism and parliamentarism as partly responsible for the Weimar crises. They did not look to the West so much, felt threatened from the East, and looked expectantly towards Mussolini. Schmitt explicitly rejected American constitutional thought as a point of reference.[86] Still, his interest in Italian fascism before 1933 should not be confused with a commitment to a 'total' Führer state.[87] At the time, many people who later had to flee from Hitler's Germany looked towards Italy with curiosity.[88]

In his *Crisis* treatise, Schmitt already had an inkling about a front of global civil war from Moscow to Rome as a possible future scenario and, faced with the alternative between 'anarchy' and 'authority', had opted for a plebiscitary nationalism and Caesarism. He then declared the need to take a stance against Soviet Russia to be the 'core question' regarding the League of Nations. He gave lectures on fascism, but expressed himself only rarely and cautiously in writing about it. Thus, he rejected an offer to write an article on fascism and neo-romanticism for the journal *Dioskuren*.[89] In the preface to the second edition of *Dictatorship*, Schmitt made reference to the contrary prognoses by von Beckerath and Nawiaski, and explicitly declared that he 'refrained from attempting one' (D, p. xxxv). Erwin von Beckerath, a colleague and friend, had made the prognosis that the 'authoritarian state' would gain 'territory' in ideological terms. Schmitt had already read his book, *Wesen und Werden des fascistischen Staates* [The nature and development of the fascist state] in 1927.[*] Another expert of the constitution of fascist Italy was Gerhard Leibholz, with whom Schmitt was in close contact in Berlin. Leibholz proofread a review of Beckerath's book by Schmitt, which was written around the turn from 1927 to 1928 and published in *Schmollers Jahrbuch* in February 1929. It summed up the discussions about Italian fascism in Bonn. According to Feuchtwanger, Schmitt, at the time, was 'probably the scholar best placed to judge fascism'.[90] However, for the moment all he published on it was the Beckerath review.

Despite its laudatory tone, the review is critical in substance. Although Schmitt had himself previously used an 'intellectual-historical' approach [geistesgeschichtliches Vorgehen], he now criticized von Beckerath's focus on the 'opposition between fascist ideology, on the one hand, and democratic and parliamentary ideology, on the other' (PB, p. 110). He approves of the 'democratic' character of Mussolini's rule legitimized by 'plebiscite' (PB, p. 111) – his colleague Moritz Bonn spoke of 'militarism' in this context,[91] Waldemar Gurian[92] of the fiction of a 'charismatic democracy' – and relies on the expectation that the fascist constitution will reconstitute

---

[*] The German text of this section, hereafter, partly retains the Italianized spelling 'fascistisch/ Fascismus', rather than 'faschistisch/Faschismus'.

the 'supremacy of the state' over the economy, and that Caesarism 'will benefit the employees in the long run' (PB, p. 113). Thus, Schmitt opposes the Marxist critique of the fascist 'class-based state', quoting Otto Bauer and Otto Kirchheimer respectfully as representatives of it and, given the economic crisis and the class struggle afflicting the Weimar Republic, seems to see a lot of attractive aspects in a state-run 'planned economy'.

His Catholicism essay had already criticized the primacy of 'economic thought'. Now Schmitt assigned the task of a political limitation of economics and capitalism to a fascist 'democracy' interpreted in anti-liberal terms. Regarding constitutional policies, the task for Schmitt was the integration of the 'proletariat' within the forms of an anti-liberal, plebiscitary mass democracy; regarding the question of legitimacy, he relied on the tools of acclamation and plebiscite, which were also the basis of Mussolini's legitimacy. Thus, for Schmitt, Italian fascism was a model for constitutional policies that would reconstitute statehood. He established a 'connection with the classical age', invoked Caesarism, and wrote: 'The fascist state, with the honesty of the classical age, wants to be a state again' (PB, p. 114). Schmitt did not reject von Beckerath's prognosis, but rather provided a sharper justification for it in the form of his separation of liberalism from democracy. His concept of fascism was clearly more anti-liberal than that of von Beckerath. For Schmitt, Italian fascism was proof that it might also be possible to save democracy in Weimar from its 'disguise by liberal characteristics'. Schmitt's earlier companions and critics, such as Hermann Heller[93] and Waldemar Gurian,[94] took this review seriously as a cautious approval of fascism. In retrospect, Wilhelm Neuß[95] and Ernst Rudolf Huber bore witness to Schmitt's early sympathies for Mussolini. However, probably no other of his companions followed his political biography during the Weimar period more closely than Ludwig Feuchtwanger, his lector and syndic at Duncker & Humblot.

Feuchtwanger's response

Schmitt and Feuchtwanger's professional and personal relationships with each other deteriorated. In the mid-1920s, Schmitt had already threatened to change his publisher, but the large textbook project calmed down the situation again. After the publication of *Constitutional Theory*, Feuchtwanger suggested a further project, for instance a 'work on the Reichsreform' (CSLF, p. 294) – i.e., the contemporary debate about constitutional reform, and in particular the dualism and imbalance between the powerful Prussian state and the rest of the Reich. Schmitt was thinking about a 'history of German state law since 1848' (CSLF, p. 318) but shelved the idea in favour of his 'present tasks'. He was under the impression that Feuchtwanger did not like the fact that his writing now turned towards the political battles of the day. Again and again, he accused Feuchtwanger of neglecting their correspondence and of not marketing his books with sufficient energy. With faint irony, he remarked 'that the relationship of publishers and authors conforms to the state of nature' (CSLF, p. 325). Back in 1926, he did not publish *The Core Question Regarding the League of Nations* with Duncker & Humblot, out of annoyance. In 1930–1, for two publications, he chose the Mohr publishing house, where his Habilitation had appeared. On the business side of things, Feuchtwanger accepted all of Schmitt's suggestions, and Schmitt assured him that he 'disliked any kind of discontinuity and defecting' (CSLF, p. 334), and that he did not want 'to continue fragmenting his work across several publishers' (CSLF, p. 346). However, at that point Feuchtwanger already felt a 'deep antipathy' (CSLF, p. 329) towards the popularization and politicization of Schmitt's writings. In the face of the general developments at the time, he increasingly turned towards studies of orientalism and of legal history, becoming a central figure in raising the awareness in German Jewry of its history and current situation.

As a pupil of Gustav Schmoller, Feuchtwanger took studies of economic history as his point of departure. The works on Judaism by Werner Sombart and Max Weber in particular were points of reference for him. Feuchtwanger's published texts took the form mainly of reviews. Once he began to work for Duncker & Humblot in 1914, he ceased to publish on the side and came to public notice again only from 1928 onwards, with critical revisions of the history of Judaism. In 1929 he became the editor of the *Bayerische Israelitische Gemeindezeitung* [Newspaper of the Israelite community of Bavaria] in Munich, and he wrote numerous articles for other Jewish organs. That year, in *Der Morgen* [Morning], the *Monatsschrift der deutschen Juden* [Monthly Journal of the German Jews], Feuchtwanger, like Leo Strauss, revised the 'Bible study' method based on Spinoza and Abraham Geiger and took sides against 'liberal' and theologically dogmatic limitations in favour of a broader-based study of antiquity.[96] He programmatically declared his support for 'Martin Buber's Erneuerung der Bibel aus dem Geist des Judentums' [Martin Buber's regeneration of the Bible out of the spirit of Judaism].[97] In 1929, the 200th anniversary of Moses Mendelssohn's birth, he published several shorter texts on him, which bore some similarities to Schmitt's studies on Cortés. Feuchtwanger distinguished between philosophy and confession; he looked at Mendelssohn as a pious 'Jew'[98] who considered himself bound by the 'ceremonial law'; Mendelssohn thus was misunderstood if he was taken as a representative of philosophical enlightenment when looked at from a Christian perspective. Mendelssohn and Herder, he wrote, were 'two people living on different planets'.[99] For Mendelssohn, the ancient Jewish doctrine of duties was the 'centre of his idea of religion'. He used philosophy only 'in order to prevent the dissolution of the religious forms of Judaism'. However, the delayer became, in Schmittian terminology, an 'accelerator against his will'. Involuntarily, he prepared 'a change of the religious substance'[100] and became a 'trailblazer for emancipation'.[101] How problematic that emancipation would prove to be was already made evident in the case of Mendelssohn's daughters.[102] Mendelssohn, as someone paving the way for emancipation, was still wholly immersed in 'Jewish customs [Volkstum]' and, contrary to his daughters, was under no 'illusions' regarding emancipation's possible success. His daughters, however, dissolved their 'Jewish character' through the act of conversion.

Feuchtwanger viewed the categories of emancipation and assimilation with scepticism. At that time he already found public debate of these problems 'simply hopeless'[103] and studied the roots of the hatred for Jews in Nietzsche, Dostoevsky and many contemporary authors.

Even before 1933, Feuchtwanger more or less agreed with Schmitt on the failure of assimilation.[104] And, like Schmitt, he considered Judaism as a 'manner of life' [Lebensordnung] and 'specific form' [Sonderart], declared the near complete failure of the liberal project of emancipation, and rejected assimilation as an attempt 'to dissolve the Jewish specificity'.[105] In splendid short reviews, Feuchtwanger referred to the continuous practice of Jewish self-organization in Germany since the early Middle Ages and to the fact that the 'autonomy and separation',[106] before the age of emancipation, had offered 'comparatively good opportunities for development'. Throughout the Weimar period, Feuchtwanger was one of Schmitt's closest companions and friends, someone who looked at his development with concern and also knew his peculiarities and kinks from very close at hand. The collapse of this friendship was one of the saddest personal break-ups in Schmitt's life.

Wearing Bismarck's mask

Of course, Schmitt's interest in Italian fascism should not be confused with him opting in favour of National Socialism. Even Feuchtwanger did not do that. But he realized that Schmitt sacrificed the part of his thought that was critical of the state in favour of an allegiance to the Leviathan, noticed the rising tension within the overall climate, and was worried about the German Jews. Schmitt briefly comments on this: 'I also believe that the Jews "of the tribe" are not liberal; but their concrete situation among the other peoples forces them nevertheless to declare the ideas of 1789 as sacrosanct. Any minority must insist on the sanctity of liberal principles' (CSLF, p. 276). Schmitt's reflections on constitutional matters at that time relied less on moral terms. There was no 'infinity clause' [Ewigkeitsklausel]. Rather, he considered the constitution more pragmatically as an instrument. As a jurist, Schmitt tried to argue on the basis of the existing constitution. In 1929, he still spoke about constitutional matters using masks: that of Donoso Cortés or that of books that he critically evaluated. Because he no longer offered an alternative to the state, he used other means of distancing himself from it in order to maintain the distinction between the legal and the political perspectives. Through the mirror of constitutional history he looked at a 'highly political and topical theme' (VRA, p. 29). Schmitt subsequently underlined the importance of his short essay on 'Staatsstreichpläne Bismarcks und Verfassungslehre' [Bismarck's plans for a *coup d'état* and constitutional theory], a review of the book by Egmont Zechlin bearing the same title, by incorporating it in his *Verfassungsrechtliche Aufsätze* [Essays on constitutional law]. Today we know better than his contemporaries that Schmitt, in the dying days of the Weimar Republic, was, indeed, involved in such plans as a legal advisor. 'Plans for a *coup d'état*' was not just a phrase to him, nor did he use it naively in 1929. The reference to Bismarck was meant to render the notion respectable in the eyes of the contemporary public by associating it with a national conservative attitude. Schmitt pointed to the 'double structure of a dynastic and democratic principle' (VRA, p. 31), which Bismarck used in order to play the princes off against the Reichstag, relying on the Länder as stabilizing factors. Schmitt took the federal organization into account as a political factor. His review proves once more that he took not least the problems of federalism as his point of departure. In any case, at the time of Schmitt's move from Bonn to Berlin he was not only occupied with the theory of the 'neutral third party' but also interested in Donoso Cortés, in Italian fascism and in Bismarck's pragmatic attitude towards plans for a *coup d'état*.

The 'spirit' of technology and the 'new elite'

The attention Schmitt paid to foreign countries was at first determined by the proximity of France. *Romantisme politique*, published at the end of 1927, was the first significant translation of one of his works. In the figure of Kathleen Murray, he encountered the Anglo-Saxon world through an Irish-Catholic lens. With Duška he also became familiar with Illyria and orthodox Catholicism. Then followed his interest in fascist Italy. With his journey to Spain in 1929, he expanded his 'Roman' excursion into the Mediterranean. After 1933, Schmitt would become a magnet for European fascism and would have a broad international impact. Today his work is the subject of global discussion.[107]

In October 1929, Schmitt travelled to Madrid and Barcelona for lectures. It was his first international lecture tour. On 23 October he gave his lecture on 'The Unknown Donoso Cortés' in Madrid. Before that, he spent a couple of days in Barcelona and presented his talk on 'European Culture at the Intermediary Stage of Neutralization'. Under the title 'The Age of Neutralizations and Depoliticizations', he also included the text in *The Concept of the Political*. It represents his first coherent account of the age and dynamic of the early modern period. The title is slightly ironic, because in the text Schmitt demonstrates the failure of all attempts at neutralizations and depoliticizations. Schmitt politicizes the picture of history by connecting the stages of secularization and 'central domains' of the early modern period – moving 'from the theological to the metaphysical domain, from there to the humanitarian-moral, and, finally, to the economic domain' (CP, p. 82) and to technology – with the respective 'active elites' (ibid.). He thus argues on the level of a sociology of power, and finally demands that a new elite should take control of technology. Schmitt aims at establishing a political 'awareness' [Vergegenwärtigung] of the situation in Europe and sees that situation as characterized by Europe's living 'in the eye of the more radical brother', the Soviet Union, which succeeded in gaining control of the economy and in building an 'economic state'. However, beyond this, the task of the present, Schmitt argues, is to banish the 'spirit of technology' and to gain control over modern technology (CP, p. 94).

Schmitt hopes that a new elite, which carries out a kind of 'rebirth' (CP, p. 94) of the initial early Christian moment, may be able to achieve this. His hints at a return to the time before the early modern period are in contradiction to his courageous politicization of technology. It is noteworthy that Schmitt does not mention Italian fascism and that he replaces the utopia of a sovereign 'economic state' with the challenge posed by modern technology. He illustrates this using the example of technological mass media, and in particular looks at radio as a powerful institution that can be used by the state in order to prove that it is the sovereign Leviathan.

Schmitt's lecture has a great ease and flow to it. Its substance could also be explicated further.[108] However, it is disappointing as far as the fundamental approach and the development of its thesis are concerned. The politicization of the image of history is too limited. The inner dynamic of the development of the sciences, for instance, is not even mentioned as an important factor. In *Political Theology*, Schmitt had ridiculed the reductionism of the sociology of knowledge. Now he himself offers a re-reading of the philosophy of history on the basis of a sociology of domination and of elites, without even mentioning the names of those who produced the discourses concerned. And he also pretty much leaves in the dark the question of who the coming masters of technology will be. What is left as the core claim of the text is the ironic prognosis of a sudden transition from depoliticization into excessive politicization. Or does he, after all, give us some hints as to what distinguishes the new elite from the false neutralizations? Is the reference to 'early Christianity', to a 'return to pure, uncorrupted nature', such a hint? Does 'nature' enable an adequate [sachgerechte] politicization, one that does not immediately turn into further new politicizations? Does he hint at something like a natural law?

At the end of the text, Schmitt quotes for the first time from Virgil's fourth eclogue ('Ab integro nascitur ordo'). The background to this is partly his reading of Eduard Norden's study *Die Geburt des Kindes* [The birth of the child],[109] which he discussed in his correspondence with Ludwig Feuchtwanger, his expert on questions of classical philology. Did Schmitt have in mind the birth of a new elite? In the works of Max Weber, Robert Michels and Gaetano Mosca, the question of the political elite emerged from the more recent sociology of power. The politicization of the sociology of elites led to a literary elitism.[110] Marginal forces imagined they were the masters to come. The 'young conservative' Ring-Bewegung [Ring movement][111] wrote 'elite' on its banners. Schmitt integrated his hopes for a new, extra-parliamentary authority into a picture of the historical dynamic of the early modern period. At the threshold of Schmitt taking up an active role, we find his call for a new elite who will take control of technology by virtue of being 'spiritually' superior. At that time, Schmitt on the one hand relied on the old elite of the Prussian civil service; on the other hand he saw himself involved in a literary battle for a new elite and demanded of his pupils an almost military discipline in fighting for the success of his 'positions and concepts'.

16

Reconstructing the 'Strong' State

From constitutional theory to state theory

In the 'maelstrom' of Berlin, Schmitt immediately changed gear, putting the question of who was the 'guardian of the constitution' into the context of dictatorship and fascism, plans for a *coup d'état* and the call for a new elite. With his move from Bonn to Berlin, he also changed his themes and categories. Versailles and Geneva were now less important; 'Weimar' came to the forefront. At the Handelshochschule, Schmitt moved from the theme of 'religion' towards the theme of the 'economy'. However, he did not specialize in a new area of law, unlike for instance Albert Hensel, who concentrated on fiscal law, or Ernst Rudolf Huber, who concentrated on economic administrative law [Wirtschaftsverwaltungsrecht], but led specialized questions back to more general ones. We might say that Schmitt, after 1928, turned his attention from constitutional theory to state theory. On the level of constitutional theory, this shift seems to be related to the legitimization of rule by presidential decree. However, independent of this context, Schmitt's reflections should also be considered from a systematic perspective. What characterizes a state theory in contrast to a constitutional theory?

Schmitt used the term constitutional theory in two ways: in the sociological wider sense of a comprehensive description of the 'absolute' constitution and in the juridically narrower sense of an analysis of constitutional law as it is given in a 'positive' legal form [Rechtsverfassung]. Schmitt based the interpretation of law on an 'absolute' constitution, whose elements he did not further analyse. 'State theory' discusses the state theoretical preconditions of a legal form. It may be constructed as a general or a 'concrete' theory of the state. The authors involved in the 'Richtungsstreit', the debate on the question of which methodical direction jurisprudence should take, were no longer interested in a general theory of the state of the kind formulated in exemplary fashion by Georg Jellinek, but in a politically 'concrete' theory of the state, which would describe in detail the general conditions of a legal framework and its relation to the extra-legal sphere. Schmitt distinguished between state and constitution. For him, the social conditions, for instance, which were historically necessary for the emergence of the 'bourgeois Rechtsstaat' did not form part of a constitutional theory – i.e., of a theory of constitutional law – but belonged to state theory. The necessary social and moral character of citizens, of a nation, for instance, was not a subject of constitutional theory, but it was a subject of a 'concrete' theory of the state. Schmitt considered the distinction between state and society, in particular, as a general condition for a 'modern' legal form.[1] In contrast, he did not discuss the older distinction between Church and state in any great detail, because in the early modern period, the age of privatizations, the Church was relegated to the social space of society. Schmitt saw the distinction between state and society primarily as a problem of state theory, because it required fundamental decisions which could not be provided by constitutional law itself. Only political decisions made constitutional stability possible. In this context, Schmitt saw a contemporary tendency towards the absorption of state sovereignty by society. He talked of a shift towards a 'self-organization' of society and detected a turn towards a universally responsible and overstrained 'weak' state. 'Neutrality' and 'totality' became key terms in his endeavour to determine the relationship between state and society. His attempts at conceptual clarification were not without deeper political significance. However, it is important to note that Schmitt did not substitute talk about the state with talk about the constitution, but distinguished between constitutional theory and state theory in a novel way, and he thus prepared his interventions in questions of constitutional policy with reflections on state theory.

A new state theory after Hugo Preuß

At the beginning of January 1930, Schmitt worked on a speech on Hugo Preuß,[2] the father of the Weimar Constitution, to be given at the 'Reichsgründungsfeier' [celebratory event on the occasion of the foundation of the Reich].[3] On 18 January he delivered the speech in the auditorium of the Handelshochschule 'with great success' (TB, 18 January 1930). Schmitt first gave the speech to the *Neue Rundschau* and then spoke to the publisher Siebeck about a separate publication. At the end of March he completed the corrections. The speech sketches a short history of the political bourgeoisie from Hegel to Hugo Preuß. Schmitt reconstructs this history politically and genealogically as a prehistory to the present time. He discusses Preuß in his *Hugo Preuss: His Concept of the State and his Position in German State Theory*, taking Wilhelmianism to be an intermediary stage between monarchic and democratic legitimacy, and establishing that the bourgeoisie arranged itself with the monarchy in order to gain economic freedom. The 'organic' state theory thus expressed the compromise of the bourgeoisie with the monarchic state. Preuß, Schmitt claims, translated the 'organic' solution into the democratic offering of 'equal chances' within 'class peace' between the bourgeoisie and the working class. Schmitt criticizes this solution for leading to the 'extreme case of an agnostic state that does not know anything and cannot make any distinctions' (HP, p. 19). The state, he says, increasingly becomes identical with the 'self-organization' of society, and this is the reason why Smend allocates to state theory the 'task of the self-integration of society' (HP, p. 21). In contrast, Schmitt takes his cue from older residues of statehood: from the tradition of the Prussian civil service, which still influenced Preuß, and which Hegel, Schmitt says, had explained in conceptual terms. After the triumph of Laband's 'formalistic' school, the theoretical interest in the state had moved into the discipline of political economy in the tradition of Gustav Schmoller, which had still been the starting point for Max Weber, and then died out altogether after 1914 and 1918. Schmitt is looking for a positive 'kind of neutrality' in which the state would find a new 'connection between state and spirit [Geist]' beyond the political parties; it seems that he is again thinking of a 'new elite' beyond the party political state and beyond the 'little belligerent myths of everyday polemics' (HP, p. 7). However, Schmitt does not yet offer a 'new state theory' (HP, p. 17); he only emphasizes the need for the development of a positive doctrine of the 'neutrality' of the state and thus recommends himself as a theorist of the state in the tradition of Hugo Preuß. Schmitt only talks about the theoretical task of the development of a new state theory. His speech found broad approval across party political boundaries.[4] The Marxist mayor of Kreuzberg, Carl Herz, however, contradicted Schmitt forcefully and also expressed his reservations in a letter to him. Schmitt responded by sending him some of his writings, whereupon the mayor concedes: 'You are, at least, one of the few bourgeois state theorists who, outside of Marxism, understands that all political concepts are embedded in constellations of political interests, and that they are nothing other than the ideological formulation of those interests.'[5]

Even decades later, Schmitt referred to this Preuß text as 'very important', and he considered its republication in a volume together with 'The Guardian of the Constitution'.[6] In 1930, Schmitt presented the text as announcing a 'scientific history [Wissenschaftsgeschichte] of German state law',[7] and thus tried to attract the interest of the Mohr publishing house. In his correspondence with Feuchtwanger he simultaneously mentioned a 'history of German state law since 1848', which he would sketch in a different guise after 1933. However, he presented the task of a new 'state theory' only in a few sketches. An offer by de Gruyter to write 'a booklet on state theory' for the Göschen series he rejected on grounds of being 'overworked'.[8] His unvarying schema of the history of science can be represented roughly as in figure 16.1. Of particular importance here is the sharp polarization between two lines of development and their political-theological interpretation.

The 'duty to the state' [Pflicht zum Staat]

Schmitt worked his way through the constitutional elements of the modern Rechtsstaat (until 1933) one by one: from the separation of powers, via basic rights, to the concept of law. He characterized the 'concrete constitutional situation' by a threefold turn away from political unity in the

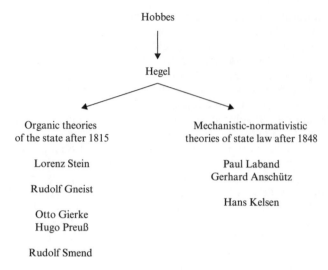

Figure 16.1   Constitutionalization of the state ('taming of the Leviathan')

form of pluralism, polycracy and federalism, and he also worked his way through these three keywords. First, he criticized the pluralist theory of the state in his lecture on 'Staatsethik und pluralistischer Staat' [State ethics and the pluralist state], published at the beginning of July 1930. The 'Vienna School' of Kelsen in particular referred explicitly to Kant, and Erich Kaufmann started the 'Richtungsstreit' with his *Kritik der neu-kantianischen Rechtsphilosophie* [Critique of neo-Kantian philosophy of right].[9] Thus, an engagement with Kant was long overdue. But Schmitt, in his lecture, did not talk about Kant in any detail; rather, he immediately claimed an ethics of duty for a 'state ethics' and sketched a 'short synopsis' of its 'intellectual situation' [geistesgeschichtliche Lage].

The core of Schmitt's lecture is a critical discussion of George Douglas Howard Cole and Harold Joseph Laski's pluralist theories of the state. Schmitt approaches his questions on a fundamental level and brings them into the context of 'political theology'. His answer to the philo-sophical task is a 'political theology'. He assumes that the 'pluralist' view of the state uses arguments from the Catholic social doctrine and from Bismarck's battle against the Catholic Church [Kirchenkampf]. He then repeats some thoughts on the individualist and religious relativization of the state. Schmitt once more expresses his idea that the citizen's duty of loyalty towards the state applies only in 'normal situations'; he quotes the Aristotelian 'critique of monistic exaggerations' (PB, p. 137), and he even justifies individualism on moral grounds: 'Maybe some quick and flexible individuals will succeed in performing the trick of preserving their freedom between the many powerful groups, the way one jumps from one ice floe to the next' (PB, p. 138). However, Schmitt sees at work in the plu-ralist theory of the state an unholy 'alliance between the Roman Catholic

Church and the federalism of the trade unions' (PB, p. 137), and rejects it politically.

At this point, he moves from political philosophy to a consideration of state theory. He does not pursue the question of whether there has been a failure of the state, such that a critique of the state is therefore justified, but rather puts the 'pluralist' theory of the state in place with the help of his concept of the political. The pluralist theory, Schmitt argues, in political – not moral or legal – terms, is right to say that social groups and not individuals are the relevant political powers. And he agrees that the 'unity of a state', looked at from the perspective of the sociology of power, is never based only on 'power' but also on 'consensus'. However, what matters in systematic terms, he holds, is to 'put pluralism in the right place' (PB, p. 141) and to situate it in the political pluriverse of the realm of states. The plurality of democratic nation-states is the 'expression of pluralism rightly understood' (PB, p. 142) – i.e., it is the expression of a political theology of the democratic nation-states as it can be found in William James. Thus, Schmitt beats pluralism with its own tools. Whoever takes 'pluralism' philosophically seriously, he thinks, is forced to abandon universalism and instead take the position of a 'political theology' of pluralism, which leads to a pluralism in the realm of states. This 'political theology' means, in particular, a 'duty to the state' (PB, p. 145), which Schmitt towards the end plays off against Kant's 'duty of the state' to 'submission under ethical norms' and against the liberal duties of the individual.

Schmitt's lecture is idiosyncratic and awkward. Again, he presents an immanent critique of a theory. He displays what a pluralist theory of the state might sensibly mean, reading its philosophical claims as a 'political theology' and thus linking Cole and Laski to William James. This radicalization leads Schmitt to draw conclusions different to those of pluralist theory. He could very well agree with pluralism's critique of the state and grant it the trick of jumping 'from one ice floe to the next'; after all, he often doubts the existence of a 'normal situation' himself. But Schmitt is of the opinion that the pluralism in the realm of states takes the form of radical alternatives. This intensification of the thesis of pluralism is at the core of his lecture. But it is presumably one of Schmitt's argumentative tactics, as a lawyer, to prove his opponent wrong rather than to justify his own position; after all, Schmitt did not sign up to the ideas of William James or of Spinoza, whom he quoted in *Constitutional Theory* as a proponent of the metaphysics of nationalism (CT, p. 128). Rather, he formulates his ethical approach with reference to the 'relation between protection and obedience' and takes a clear counter-position to Kant. In passing, he distances himself from 'left' interpretations of Catholic social doctrine.

After Duška's return

The diaries also allow us to provide a sketch of Schmitt's life in the early 1930s. At the beginning of 1930, Schmitt was completing his lecture on Hugo Preuß. At the end of January, he was asked to write a legal opinion (against Triepel and Kaufmann) by the Ministry of Finance, a task he dealt with quickly.[10] At that time, he still gave his weekly educational lectures for 'attachés' at the Foreign Ministry. On 7 February he travelled to Breslau (Wrocław) for a lecture on international law and met his old friend Arnold Schmitz, who had moved to a post at the University of Breslau. During the weeks in February he met with Gustav Steinbömer, Franz Blei and the Russian Koschwenikoff, Romano Guardini, and Kurt Singer. Although Ms Büttner continued to interest Schmitt erotically, she would become the successor to Annie Kraus only as his permanent shorthand typist. On 19 February, Schmitt spoke at the Kammergericht [Upper Regional Court] in Berlin. At the beginning of March he concluded his lectures for the civil servants, though for three weeks he continued to give daily lectures to jurists who had completed their legal training in the new Reichspostzentralamt [central office of the Reich's postal service] in Tempelhof.[11] He met Hans Lipps, Albert Mirgeler and Prince Rohan. Again and again he weighed the possibility of seductions against his faith to Duška and remained steadfast in the latter. Together with Paul Adams he attended the performance of a Shakespeare play. Peterson was in Berlin for a couple of days, and on 25 March Schmitt spent a long evening with him, Paul Adams, Franz Blei and Margot von Quednow. Schmitt expanded his Preuß article for the *Rundschau* into a short booklet and then went on to write a large lecture for the German Chamber of Commerce and Industry. On 3 April, Helmuth Plessner came to visit. On 8 April, Schmitt spoke on the 'neutrality' of the state with regard to 'domestic politics' in front of an audience of 700 people in the hall of the Kroll opera house at the meeting of the Chamber of Commerce and Industry.[12] He dictated the text for publication soon after the event. In mid-April, he travelled to Munich.

In June, he was in Plettenberg. In July 1930, he published a short article on 'Die politische Lage der entmilitarisierten Rheinlande' [The political situation in the demilitarized Rhinelands] in the journal *Abendland*, occasioned by the evacuation of troops from the second and third occupied zones.[13] Another article, on 'Die Einberufung des vertagten Reichstags' [The recall of the adjourned Reichstag] appeared in the *Kölnischen Volkszeitung*. On 25 August, Hugo am Zehnhoff, now old, died. Schmitt went to Düsseldorf for the funeral and on to Plettenberg, where he was visited by Georg Eisler. In mid-September, Schmitt returned to Berlin. He next gave a short presentation at a meeting of sociologists.[14] Soon afterwards he travelled to Breslau, where he gave an introductory lecture on 'Der Völkerbund' [The League of Nations] in connection with a training course on 'Staatsbürgerkunde' [civic education]. While in Breslau, Schmitt deepened his acquaintance with Hans Rothfels and came into closer contact with Arnold Brecht, whom he would later meet again at the trial 'Prussia vs. the Reich' at the Staatsgerichtshof [constitutional court]. He tried a new type of publication, a documentation of sources with commentary, with his 'Der Völkerbund und das politische Problem der Friedenssicherung' [The League of Nations and the political problem of securing peace], which collects central texts in a kind of 'secular argument and counter-argument' (FP, p. 281), as well as providing some annotations.[15] After Germany had left the League of Nations, a second extended edition appeared in 1934 under the shorter title 'Das politische Problem der Friedenssicherung' [The political problem of securing peace]. This version presented Germany's exit as the solution to the problem. Then, in 1935, Ernst Forsthoff published a volume in the Kröner series, titled *Deutsche Geschichte seit 1918 in Dokumenten* [Documents on German history since 1918],[16] as part of the preparations for his *Deutsche Verfassungsgeschichte der Neuzeit* [German constitutional history of the modern period]. Such collections of sources highlighted certain historical-political aspects and were aimed at a larger audience. With his collection, Schmitt continued a thread of his work so far, the critique of the League of Nations, without repeating himself.

At the beginning of October, an unpleasant encounter between Schmitt and Smend took place: 'finally done with him; disgusting impression' (TB, 7 October 1930). On 14 October, Schmitt made the acquaintance of Ernst Niekisch, a nationalist Bolshevist. A paper on Article 24 of the constitution appeared, which is important for understanding Schmitt's political position.[17] Schmitt was seeking to establish contact with Ernst Jünger. He met Karl Eschweiler, Georg Eisler and Carl Bilfinger, and he introduced Oberheid to Jünger. He then travelled to Plettenberg for a funeral and on to Düsseldorf, where, on 4 November, he spoke at the Langnam-Verein in front of '1,500 people'.[18] Once back in Berlin, he wrote a 'legal opinion on the question of whether the trade mission of the Soviet Union in Berlin is obliged to arrange a workers' council for its German employees'. Schmitt answered in the negative. He soon submitted the legal opinion,[19] but was unhappy with the fee. On 8 October he spent an evening with the two Jünger brothers and Veit Rosskopf. 'Sad and sceptical on the way home. They are all gentrified [verbürgerlicht] and belong to the declining class [Schicht]' (TB, 8 November 1930).

In the winter term 1930–1, Schmitt continued to give regular lectures to trainees of the postal service at the Reichspostzentralamt. In mid-November he travelled to Hamburg, reading Musil's *The Man without Qualities* on the journey. At the Überseeklub he gave a lecture on the state of exception.[20] Eisler, Rosenbaum and Alfred Bertram, who were in the audience, were 'apparently disappointed'. The next day Schmitt spent with Eisler, before returning to Berlin. At the end of November he spoke with Jünger about the figure of the worker: 'Impression of dilettantism' (TB, 26 November 1930).* Schmitt wrote an essay on the reform of the Reich's constitution[21] and worked on a lecture on 'Die Frau im Staat' [Women within the state], which he delivered, upon an invitation by the German Association of Catholic Women, on 5 December at the Reichswirtschaftsamt [the Reich's ministry of the economy]. The lecture was simultaneously broadcast on the radio. Schmitt appeals to women to become politically active and ends with two examples where women 'brought an order with female naturalness

---

* A few years later, in 1932, Ernst Jünger published a study entitled *Der Arbeiter: Herrschaft und Gestalt* [The worker: rule and type], Stuttgart, 2007.

[frauenhafter Selbstverständlichkeit] onto the political stage': Catherine of Siena, who brought the papacy back to Rome from Avignon, and

> St Joan, who led her people out of a desperate military situation . . . Almost any sentence from the mouth of this saint is an answer that any nation may give itself. When this saint answered the question of whether she wanted to claim that God hated the English, saying that she did not know whether that was the case, but she knew that the English had to leave France, she thereby gave an answer that every people must give their oppressors and exploiters through the mouth of this saint. (See also TP, p. 92)

Schmitt is here quoting from the classic silent movie on Jeanne d'Arc which he went to watch all the time, and he thus reveals a nationalist theme as the key to his fascination with the film. At the end of the lecture, he confesses his hope 'that hundreds of thousands of German women will keep alive this knowledge of natural order',[22] and he quotes the motto he used in the *Concept of the Political*: 'Ab integro nascitur ordo'.

At that time, Schmitt's friendship with Ernst Jünger became closer: 'I love him a lot, I like every one of his answers, wonderful chap' (TB, 6 December 1930). Jünger introduced Schmitt to Albrecht Erich Günther, the national traditional publicist [Volkstum-Publizist], on whom Schmitt noted: 'very interesting fellow'. The film based on Remarque's *All Quiet on the Western Front* divided opinion. Once, Robert Musil visited 'with his dreadful wife'. Then, Cousin André and his Swiss fiancée were in Berlin for a couple of days. Schmitt wrote a lecture for a radio broadcast and gave it at once in the Oberverwaltungsgericht [Higher Administrative Court], located in Hardenbergstraße, in the presence of the president of the Supreme Court of the Reich, Walter Simons, Karl Lohmann and Ernst Niekisch. Erik Peterson wrote about his conversion to Catholicism. Schmitt noted in his diary: 'No nice impression, nevertheless deeply moved; my Catholicism was awakened' (TB, 20 December 1930). Schmitt got to know Karl Schilling, who would later become his assistant. On 23 December he had an intense conversation with Rosskopf on Hölderlin and Däubler. Schmitt spent Christmas at his home. 'Duška was ill in the evening; she thought she was pregnant' (TB, 26 December 1930). New Year's Eve he spent with Eschweiler and Paul Adams, also at home.

Schmitt worked on the book version of *The Guardian of the Constitution*, and until 13 January he gave almost daily lectures in the Reichspostzentralamt. He also wrote another four radio broadcasts for Deutsche Welle, which he read out himself.[23] Duška was, indeed, pregnant. On 15 January, Schmitt spoke at the Philosophische Gesellschaft [Philosophical Society] in Berlin, and on 20 January, in front of an audience of about 100, at the Verwaltungsakademie [civil service academy] (Dorotheenstraße), on the significance of the emergency decree of 1 December in terms of state law.[24] Schmitt was discussed as a possible successor to Kelsen in Vienna around that time. The faculty in Vienna formally ranked him first on the list.[25] A newspaper in Vienna commented on this, saying it was a 'plan for making the University of Vienna fascist'.[26]

In a dissenting vote, Othmar Spann declared his opposition to Schmitt's appointment. In the end, the chair was not filled, and other Viennese scholars gradually moved up.

At the end of January 1931, Schmitt met with Ernst Jünger and the nationalist author Arnolt Bronnen. Soon after that, he met Eugen Rosenstock, Franz Blei and Margot von Quednow. On 4 February 1931 he spoke in the Berlin Hochschule für Politik [Berlin Academy for Political Science] on 'Recht im 20. Jahrhundert' [Law in the twentieth century and was 'very disappointed, a very small audience'. At that point, Schmitt became curious about National Socialism: 'The National Socialists left the Reichstag. Marvellous [Großartig]' (TB, 9 February 1931).[27] The National Socialists' retreat from parliament made rule by presidential decree more dependent on the SPD and forced the latter to adopt a more tolerant stance. Weimar drifted further away from an elected parliamentary government and further into rule by presidential decree. Schmitt met with the historian Horst Michael and Major Erich Marck's junior and completed a lecture for the Verwaltungsakademie. He frequently met with Johannes Popitz and Werner Weber, with Ernst Jünger, Paul Adams and Veit Rosskopf. Popitz, in a manner of speaking, served for Schmitt as a counterweight to the circle around Jünger. At the beginning of March, Schmitt completed the corrections for his *The Guardian of the Constitution*. On 18 March he spoke in Berlin at the spring course of the 'Deutsche Vereinigung für Staatswissenschaftliche Fortbildung' [German Association for Education in Political Science] on the topic 'Staatsideologie und Staatsrealität in Deutschland und Westeuropa' [The ideology and the reality of the state in Germany and Western Europe].[28] On 23 March, Schmitt spoke about 'Staat und Staatstheorien der Gegenwart' [The contemporary state and contemporary theories of the state] at the Kant Society in Halberstadt, then visited Quedlinburg and travelled on to Halle, Merseburg and Magdeburg. On 27 March he was back in Berlin. Duška told him 'that Georg Eisler has called his son Carl, very touched'.[29] The first copies of *The Guardian of the Constitution* arrived. Over Easter, Schmitt went to Plettenberg. In Cologne, he met Huber and Tula Simons, Ernst Friesenhahn and Werner Becker, and in Bonn there was a reunion with Wilhelm Neuß. On 20 April, Schmitt returned to Berlin, where Franz Blei thanked him for his birthday article.[30] Schmitt attended a lecture by Ernst Niekisch and met with Eugen Rosenstock, who handed him the proofs for his 'Constitutional History'.[31] Ernst Fraenkel came to Schmitt's seminar. A student, Kendziora, 'told me about her dissertation, the concept of elections, she is amazing, was very much in love, for a second' (TB, 12 May 1931). Schmitt would later consider Kendziora's dissertation the best examination thesis of his time at the Handelshochschule. He met Karl Mannheim – 'horrible, wretched Eastern Jew' (14 May 1931). Werner Weber was Ministerialrat [assistant secretary] in the Ministry of Culture by then. Throughout the summer term 1931, Tula Simons assisted Schmitt and also gave one of the tutorials. Weber then took on a tutorial in the following winter term. Schmitt travelled to Southern Germany and spoke on the 'Staat des 20. Jahrhunderts' [The state of the twentieth century] in Freiburg and either on 'Demokratie und

Diktatur' [Democracy and dictatorship] or 'Das Problem der Diktatur' [The problem of dictatorship] in the Uhlandsaal of Tübingen Museum, upon an invitation by the AstA.* At the beginning of July he was back in Berlin. He again met Hella Ehrik, with whom he had had an affair in Berlin in 1924, and was 'lustful and lecherous' for her. Meanwhile, Duška, heavily pregnant, rented a new apartment. On 8 July, Schmitt gave a presentation on 'Staatstheoretische Fragen der Politik' [State theoretical questions of politics] at the Philosophische Gesellschaft [Philosophical Society] in Leipzig. Hugo Fischer, a friend of Jünger and editor of the *Blätter für deutsche Philosophie* [Journal of German Philosophy], looked after him, and Alfred Bäumler, Schmitt's National Socialist colleague in philosophy in Berlin from 1933, was in the audience – 'an extremely clever and smart fellow'. The day after the event Schmitt spent with Erwin Jacobi, and then travelled back to Berlin in the evening. In the collapse of a bank (Danatbank)[32] he lost some money. He now met regularly with Hella and apparently manoeuvred himself into new difficulties in the weeks leading up to the birth of Anima.

'Mistake' as 'remedy': the Reichspräsident as the 'central point'

In May 1930, Schmitt considered a separate publication of his treatise on the Reichspräsident, but the publisher, Siebeck, rejected the idea of individual publication.[33] The 'cunning' of this deed was that it led to a larger work. At the end of 1929, Schmitt had already mentioned a systematic synopsis, and by the end of November 1930 an expanded edition to be published in book form was agreed. Schmitt emphasized the systematic significance of the new work and regretted, in a letter to Feuchtwanger, that this definitive summary of his thoughts was not published by Duncker & Humblot. 'I have by now finished the revision of "The Guardian of the Constitution"; the book will probably be published soon. May I tell you on this occasion that it pained me very much not to see this work, which is an important and, I hope, mature continuation of my books on *Dictatorship* and *Constitutional Theory*, published in your house. It is, however, not my fault' (CSLF, p. 334). As a first result of his years in Berlin, *Der Hüter der Verfassung* [The guardian of the constitution] appeared in May 1931, soon followed by a Spanish translation. 'Guardian against whom?', Schmitt noted on the cover of his copy.[34] At the end of May, he wrote to Feuchtwanger: 'My longing for a slow revision and shaping of the insights I have gained is growing ever stronger, but also more and more utopian. Did you receive "The Guardian of the Constitution"? The middle part "Die konkrete Verfassungslage der Gegenwart" [The concrete situation of the constitution today] would have been a particularly nice text for you, which would have done your publishing house and my name proud.'[35] In his response, Feuchtwanger called the book a 'work of art' (CSLF, p. 340).

Schmitt places the middle part between revised versions of his analyses of the judiciary and the Reichspräsident. The first part on the judiciary

---

* AstA = Allgemeiner Studentenausschuß, the German term for 'Students' Union'.

is substantially expanded. Schmitt clarifies in particular how federalism and party political pluralism are inclined towards an understanding of the judiciary as the guardian of the constitution, thus making the constitution a compromise and a contract. The 'short exposition' (HdV, p. 100) of the 'concrete situation of the constitution today' is new and emphasizes the politicization of the judiciary.[36] Schmitt holds on to his 'state ethical' [staatsethischen] perspective. Starting out from the 'turn towards the economic state', he describes the development towards a pluralist party political state, in which the 'transformation and recasting' of the party political will into a uniform 'will of the state' and a 'state ethos' [Staatsgesinnung] is no longer given, and obedience to the party takes the place of 'allegiance to the state and its constitution' (HdV, p. 90). Under the keyword 'polycracy', Schmitt presents a brief diagnosis which shows that the numerous economic actors cannot be subsumed under a state 'plan' and that parliamentarism as a steering medium is incompatible with an economic state.[37] He rejects the idea of the state providing an 'economic constitution' and explicitly takes up a position against the fascist solution (HdV, p. 100), for which he had shown some sympathy in his review of Beckerath in 1929.

Schmitt explores possible 'remedies and counter-movements'. He asks which elements, under conditions of a party politics state, might represent 'neutrality within domestic politics', and opts for the traditions of a state's civil service [Traditionen des 'Beamtenstaates']. In this context, he again takes up Max Weber's[38] sharp distinction between bureaucratic rule and political leadership and re-evaluates the civil service in positive terms. A systematic synopsis of the 'ambiguity in the concepts of neutrality and depoliticization' demonstrates in broad outline that Schmitt rejects liberal solutions (neutrality as passive tolerance, instrumental limitations, maintaining 'equal chances' and enabling 'parity') and that he sees Germany as facing the alternatives of either developing a 'state ethos' or accepting foreign 'rule by a protector state' [Schutzherrn]. He explicitly rejects the existing interpretation of Article 76 of the Weimar Constitution.[*] In this context, he also refers to National Socialism, reminds the reader of the need to preserve the 'political substance' of the Weimar Constitution by constitutional means, and argues for the setting of legal limits to constitutional amendments. Then, he moves on to Article 48 of the Weimar Constitution and to the Reichspräsident as the 'guardian of the constitution'.

Schmitt's nuanced discussion of the elements of 'neutrality in domestic politics' shows that he conceives the Reichspräsident as the 'central point' within a whole system of stabilizing institutions that are, to a certain extent, outside the reach of the party political state. He wants to demonstrate that political remedies cannot be plucked out of the air but must be structurally supported by tendencies and counter-movements in society. The limitations with which Schmitt qualifies his acceptance of law-representing decrees by the Reichspräsident are especially interesting. So far, Schmitt had limited the rights of the Reichspräsident through the organizational principle of the separation of powers and by withholding

---

[*] Article 76 concerns amendments to the constitution (see CT, p. 421).

legislative power from him. In *The Guardian of the Constitution* he now grants him that power on the basis of ten years of actual practice and the customary law that has emerged. But he continues to call the 'non-distinction' between exceptional measures and laws a 'mistake in the theory of law', a mistake which, however, has prevailed. 'The limitation of exceptional powers, constituted by their restriction, within the Rechtsstaat, to measures, now no longer exists', he writes. 'It would be pointless if the dominant legal doctrine would now try to reverse a development of the law [Rechtsbildung] that has been completed as the result of its own teachings, as soon as, in hindsight, it realizes the theoretical mistake it has made' (HdV, p. 126). Thus, Schmitt holds the 'dominant legal doctrine' responsible for the risks of rule by presidential decree. He unmistakably declares that he does not want to continue in his role of a Cassandra of legal theory who reminds the bourgeois Rechtsstaat that it has betrayed its principles.

Schmitt is of the opinion that it is politically dangerous to grant the Reichspräsident legislative authority. However, the responsibility for this abolition of the separation of powers he thinks lies ultimately with the Reichstag, which can and should retain its controlling power.

> The existing constitution grants the Reichstag, if it is capable of forming a majority and is functional, all rights and possibilities a parliament needs in order to assert itself as the decisive factor in the process of political will formation. If a parliament that has become the stage of the pluralist system is incapable of doing so, it does not therefore have the right to demand of all other institutional authorities that they should become incapable of acting as well. (HdV, p. 131)

This passage can hardly be interpreted as a direct push for the extension of presidential powers. The young conservative Storm and Stress characters close to the journal *Der Ring*, for instance, desired a far greater abandonment of juridical reserve at that time.[39] Schmitt's treatise unequivocally calls rule by presidential decree a break with the organizational principles of the bourgeois Rechtsstaat and a 'mistake of legal theory' that may lead to dangerous 'effects'. It is the middle part of the book that goes beyond Schmitt's articles of 1928.

Schmitt puts the question of the protection of the constitution into the broad framework of a typological characterization of the possible centres of a state. He diagnoses a general transformation from the legislative towards the executive state and shows how much the common idea of the 'judiciary as the guardian of the constitution' has been discredited by the dynamic of historical development regarding the constitution and by the erosion of the concept of law. In principle, it can hardly be doubted that Schmitt argued on the basis of the existing constitution. He was rather sceptical at the time about the possibilities for a reform of the Reich and the constitution[40] and opted for the alternative of crisis management. Talking at the Langnam Club in 1930, he said:

I feel . . . like a technician who warns against taking out a part of the car and replacing it with another while driving. As a jurist, I do not want to lay myself open to the criticism that I overestimate the constitution; thus, I am cautious and do not say that the constitution is, in fact, the engine of the car. But it is a very important and indispensable part, and it is better left in peace, if one does not want to embark on unpredictable and dangerous experiments.[41]

From classical civil rights [Freiheitsrecht] towards institutional guarantees?

Schmitt worked through the principles of the bourgeois Rechtsstaat one by one. After the 'organizational principle' of the separation of powers, he discussed the 'principle of distribution' of the basic rights. He remarked on the 'advance [in importance] of the second principle' (VRA, p. 34) of the constitution as early as 1929 in a short overview of 'Zehn Jahre Reichsverfassung' [Ten years of the Reich's Constitution]. He blamed the judiciary for false legal 'over-regulations and exaggerations' [Positivierungen und Überspannungen] and illustrated this practice using the example of the 'Auflösung des Enteignunsgbegriffs' [Dissolution of the concept of expropriation]. After his revision of the principle of the separation of powers, he now took on the analysis of basic rights provisions. First, he wrote an appreciative review of Nipperdey's 'Kollektivkommentar'.[42] On 2 August he wrote to Feuchtwanger:

I have completed a nice essay on basic rights for Thoma's Handbuch des Staatsrechts [Handbook of state law], which hopefully Thoma will not like so that I can then retract it and use it for the *Festschrift* [of the Handelshochschule], thus saving my holidays. I would like all too much to turn the thoughts I had during my lectures in Freiburg, Tübingen and Leipzig into a coherent text, but I do not yet know what will become of my holidays. (CSLF, p. 346)

However, Thoma accepted Schmitt's essay,[43] and Schmitt had to write another text – 'Freiheitsrechte und institutionelle Garantien der Reichsverfassung' [Civil rights and institutional guarantees in the constitution of the Reich] – as his contribution to the *Festschrift*; it was published immediately in October 1931. Soon after completing the *Festschrift* contribution, Schmitt edited the book version of his *Concept of the Political*. On 20 August, his daughter and only child, Anima-Louise, was born in Berlin. This meant that it was only in the following year that he was able to prepare his desired next *summa, Legality and Legitimacy*, which also contained his critique of basic rights.

In his article for Thoma's *Handbook*, Schmitt analyses the systematic possibilities of basic rights and their heterogeneous reality in constitutional law. In principle, he assumes that 'any concrete type of state [has] very specific basic rights' (VRA, p. 190). This, he says, shows in particular in the 'relation of basic rights to the organizational part of the constitution'.

If a state is stringently organized, it will rigorously implement its 'fundamental decision' regarding the 'types of basic rights'. However, pre-state 'civil rights [Freiheitsrechte] of individuals' in the sense of 'freedom from state intervention' [Freiheit vom Staat] and of classical 'basic rights in the narrower sense of the bourgeois Rechtsstaat', Schmitt says, would easily end up 'idling' within the 'alternative: programme – positive law' (VRA, p. 199) – i.e., they are either programmatic provisions that are not sufficiently implemented or superfluous because they are already part of positive law. Apart from such basic rights, the second part of the constitution also contains diverse other provisions, and it is therefore, Schmitt claims, used as an 'arsenal for advocates' and interpreted in all sorts of ways. Friedrich Naumann's efforts at creating a 'catechism for the people'[44] and 'peace between capitalism and socialism based on understanding' (VRA, p. 195) he sees as having failed. Scholarship interprets the text of the constitution in every possible direction, but legal practice takes the direction towards a 'decision for the liberal Rechtsstaat' (VRA, p. 198).

Schmitt does not stop at a hint towards the heterogeneity of the provisions and the lack of a fundamental decision, but analyses a multitude of relevant aspects. Thus, he finds diverse 'institutional guarantees' in the text of the constitution. He also finds various 'kinds of positivity' below the level of the formulation of strict laws – e.g., general legal reservations and legal assumptions that are to be taken into consideration in the practice of constitutional law. Schmitt argues 'against the elimination [Ausschaltung] of the lawgiver' (VRA, p. 224) and hopes that the tendency towards a judiciary state will resolve itself in the process of legal practice: although the multitude of 'formal' basic rights provisions opens the floodgates for interpretations of the constitution along the lines of a judiciary state, this may nevertheless result – and here lies the 'cunning' of the idea or institution – in a rationalization of the system. 'It leads to an inconspicuous growth on the one hand, to tacit repressions on the other, and may in this way bring about the overall decision which cannot readily be found in the content of the text of the second principal part' (VRA, p. 230).

In a second line of argument, Schmitt goes on to concentrate on the 'institutional guarantees', rendering more precise his conceptual objection to status quo guarantees: the existence of an institution does not yet guarantee its status quo. But Schmitt's main question concerns the relation between classic civil rights and institutional guarantees. 'Freedom is not an institute' [kein Institut] (VRA, p. 166), he says. Because liberal civil rights are practically idling within the 'dilemma' between a programmatic agenda [Programmatik] and positive law, the bourgeois Rechtsstaat protects freedom through 'new guarantees' and protective norms. This makes institutional guarantees into 'contextual and complementary guarantees' (VRA, p. 171) of liberal basic rights. The status of basic rights is transformed. They lose their character as pre-state rights and become rights guaranteed by the state. Schmitt ends with a pointed remark: 'The way from general freedom to a privilege is often very short; special guarantees and measures protecting freedom lie along this way' (VRA, p. 171). In these words, Schmitt hints at a tendency of the bourgeois Rechtsstaat to return to feudal structures, which also is in line with his critique of plural-ism. And yet, for systematic reasons, he sees it as necessary to move from pre-state freedom to 'institutional guarantees' and to consider 'subjective' rights as guarantees given by the state, which are subject to political provi-sos. Schmitt's two more substantial analyses of basic rights in the Weimar Constitution are cautiously formulated as regards legal policy. They do not bluntly call for the dismantling of classical civil rights; they do, however, suggest something like a shift in perspective from rights to duties and to the definition of basic rights by the state.

The end of theoretical endeavour?

Today, we usually analyse authors on the basis of their published works and not on the basis of their intentions and plans. Even Plato we rarely read against the background of his 'unwritten theory'. Thus, to us, Rudolf Smend is above all the author of *Verfassung und Verfassungsrecht* [Constitution and constitutional law], although he had plans for further works. Schmitt is read, with regard to politics, mostly on the basis of *The Concept of the Political*, in legal terms on the basis of *Constitutional Theory*. However, both approaches unduly limit his authorship. *Constitutional Theory* was not a final definitive statement. It only made 'positive' law dependent on an assumed 'absolute' constitution, the precise description of which would have been the task of a state theory. The companions in the Richtungsstreit also took such a path. Smend wanted to follow up his propaedeutical constitutional theory with a state theory. Hermann Heller wrote a *Staatslehre* [State theory], which was published posthumously.[45] Occasionally, Schmitt spoke about a history of German state science, state philosophy or state theory. His small book on Hugo Preuß can be seen as a first sign of such a project, which, however, the booklets to follow did not realize. Did he want to write a state theory? Did he have one in mind? Would it have been the logical consequence of his theoretical approach, or is Schmitt's intervention designed to deal only with what is required by rule by presidential decree? His works converging towards a state theory are factually related to the justification of rule by presidential decree and concentrate fully on the reconstruction of the distinction between state and society. Schmitt did not want to turn back the clock of modern constitutional history. He avoided spelling out the structures of a 'strong' state, which, in the open crisis of the Weimar Republic, would have been nothing but dreams of a possible future. He concentrated on the principles of the Rechtsstaat, put questions regarding state structures into the wide context of constitutional history, and hoped that the tendency towards an executive state would turn into 'strong' statehood ['starke' Staatlichkeit].

17

Within the Journalistic Circles of Weimar's Last Days

The faithful adjutant: Ernst Rudolf Huber (1903–1990)

Schmitt was never really satisfied with the impact of his publications. Often he complained that he was not appropriately quoted and acknowledged. This perception was also the reason why, during his time in Bonn, he became involved in feuds, played out in reviews, and wished for a formal process for settling matters of academic honour.[1] His *Crisis* treatise was in part received very critically. The essay on Catholicism found broader public resonance. However, his Catholic signal was soon contradicted by his personal life and his scholastically unreliable *Concept of the Political*. For a long time, Hugo Ball stood alone in his great appreciation of Schmitt's work as a whole. Only with *Constitutional Theory* did Schmitt finally receive widespread attention and the professional recognition that he sought. The further development of his work was now watched closely within the discipline. Schmitt was accepted as a voice within the Richtungsstreit, the debate over which direction jurisprudence should take. His interpretation of the Reichspräsident as 'The Guardian of the Constitution' caused controversy.[2] The 'Catholic' reception of his work to a certain degree broke off at that time. Some early respondents to his work disappeared. Other pupils of his were not yet mature enough and not yet positioned to contribute to the distribution of Schmitt's thought. Schmitt liked to quote from the writings of his pupils. Otto Kirchheimer was an important connection to socialist debates. Among his pupils in Bonn, Ernst Forsthoff, Karl Lohmann and Ernst Rudolf Huber belonged to those who were bustling around in the journalistic circles of the young conservatives, often publishing anonymously.

Huber's work represented the most important appropriation of Schmitt's thought at the time. He was altogether his closest, most independent and most important pupil. He figures only rarely in Schmitt's Bonn diaries. Huber was a Protestant, did not live in Bonn permanently, and did not seek to be close to Schmitt. Their correspondence on Huber's project for a dissertation began in May 1926. At that time, Huber was already doing his legal training, but met repeatedly with Schmitt in Bonn. In March 1927, Schmitt placed the dissertation with the publisher, and on 27 May 1927 Huber passed his viva. Having completed his legal training, he became the assistant of the business lawyer Heinrich Göppert in Bonn.[3] This allowed him to be part of Schmitt's base within the faculty as well. Huber now became increasingly productive in his publications. Within a short period of time he completed a wide-ranging exposition of the *Verträge zwischen Staat und Kirche* [Contracts between state and Church] and his path-breaking Habilitation on *Wirtschaftsverwaltungsrecht* [Business administration law]. In addition, he published numerous articles in the journals of the young conservatives, mostly under pseudonyms. From spring 1930 onwards, the contact between Schmitt and Huber intensified again. Huber read the proofs of *The Guardian of the Constitution*, which gave him the idea for a more extensive review essay. At first, Schmitt rather advised him against this plan[4] but, when he met Huber in April 1931 in Cologne, later encouraged him: 'I am looking forward very much to your report on the "Guardian of the Constitution", especially to your critical comments. There is nothing that would be more valuable and more motivating for me than such a critique, and as it cannot be expected to come from colleagues, who are older or the same age as me, I am wholly dependent on you and very few other young jurists in that respect.'[5] Huber's review would be the starting point for a comprehensive engagement with Schmitt's work.

While Ball wrote an initial overall appreciation from the perspective of *Political Theology* and Schmitt's turn towards Catholicism, Huber first wrote a review of *The Guardian of the Constitution*,[6] published under a pseudonym, and then an initial overall appreciation under the title 'Verfassung und Verfassungswirklichkeit bei Carl Schmitt' [Constitution and constitutional reality in Carl Schmitt]. This was followed soon afterwards by further substantial discussions by Leo Strauss, Otto Kirchheimer, Helmut Kuhn, Herbert Marcuse and Karl Löwith, which laid down the tracks for later scholarship on Schmitt. Heinrich Wohlgemuth wrote the first dissertation on Schmitt.[7] However, Huber's evaluation with regard to constitutional theory remained particularly important. The text was published in Hugo Fischer's *Blättern für deutsche Philosophie*. Huber does not get lost in detail, but rather asks what progress there is from *Constitutional Theory* to *The Guardian of the Constitution*. What is the significance of the analysis of the 'concrete constitutional situation', in terms of legal validity or the philosophy of law,[8] for the approach taken in *Constitutional Theory*? Huber finds in *The Guardian of the Constitution* an important further specification of the relationship between 'absolute' and 'positive' constitution. He does not shy away from further clarifying Schmitt's approach: is it possible to speak in 'decisionist' terms of a 'positive' constitutional decision [Verfassungsentscheidung] when a constitution is given in 'absolute' terms? The absolute constitution is not fully at the disposal of the constitutional legislature. A 'minimum of immediately given form' is always presupposed.[9] Huber illustrates this point with the constitution-making power of a national assembly. He draws the conclusion that one must 'stop considering the "conscious configuration" [bewußte Gestaltung] by the body given constitution-making power as its [i.e., the constitution's] decisive foundation.'[10] He therefore makes the terminological suggestion of substituting the concept of 'decision' with that of 'configuration' [Gestaltung].

'Constitutional legislature is, rather, conscious overall configuration',[11] 'constitutional configuration'. In this way, Huber introduces the terminological differentiation between 'decisionism' and the concrete 'intellectual ordering and configuring' [Ordnungs- und Gestaltungsdenken], which Schmitt, in 1934,[12] would present as an essential further development of his *Political Theology*. And Huber draws a further consequence: he considers the debate over the opposition between a 'static' and a 'dynamic' theory of the constitution, which Schmitt takes to be the point where he differs from Smend, to be wrong-headed. The clean separation between 'decision' and 'integration', which still dominated the front lines between the schools of legal thought after 1945,[13] Huber says, is mistaken. As a ruling order [Herrschaftsordnung], the constitution is 'a fact which can lay claim to validity on its own grounds' and which directs the developmental dynamic. Schmitt, Huber says, has recognized this 'tension between immediately given reality and normative validity'.[14] Along with his diagnosis of a 'turn towards the total state', Schmitt draws the conclusion that, under conditions of rule by presidential decree, the tension between the constitutional situation and constitutional law, between 'absolute' and 'positive' constitution, can have delegitimizing consequences. These can reach the point where the concrete constitutional situation gives birth to an alternative 'political idea', and a 'new constitution emerges'[15] which negates the existing constitutional law at its core – i.e., the constitutional decision. At this point, a 'dynamic' exists which requires a new 'coordination of rulers and people'.[16] Although Schmitt has not openly drawn such radical consequences, Huber continues, he has provided the tools for an understanding of how positively given constitutional law is dynamically supported by the 'political idea' inherent in a concrete constitutional situation.

Schmitt praised Huber's review for correcting the 'misinterpretations of "decisionism"' and added the proofs for *The Concept of the Political* to his letter.[17] Huber replied to Schmitt in the suave and obliged tone characteristic of his writing: 'When reading your letter I feel, and for this I thank you particularly, an immediate agreement in some fundamental categories, and your letter showed me with particular clarity how much I have become your pupil, just during those years that I have been externally separated from you.'[18] Straightaway he offered to follow up on his review with an essay on *The Concept of the Political*, addressing matters of principle, for Stapel's *Deutsches Volkstum*.[19] But Schmitt replied that, 'expediently' [zweckmäßigerweise], Albrecht Erich Günther wrote in this journal,[20] and Huber should not feel further obliged.

Huber's early review essay shows very clearly the significance that the determination of the 'absolute' constitution through the 'concrete constitutional situation' has for constitutional law. Huber emphasizes the light shed on *Constitutional Theory* by *The Guardian of the Constitution*. This light concerns the relationship between the 'absolute' and the 'positive' concept of the constitution: once the 'absolute' constitution is analysed more closely in its given form as the 'concrete constitutional situation', the 'positive' constitutional decision appears no longer as a contingent voluntary act but as a differentiated configurational complex and volatile basis. During the following years, Huber's work related to Schmitt's the way an explication relates to a thesis: whatever Schmitt quickly churned out in the form of 'positions and concepts', Huber thoroughly thought through in detail. His *Business Administration Law*,[21] which appeared in February 1932,[22] and his concept of the 'economic state', which Schmitt adopted with appreciation and discussed in the seminar,[23] read like an application of Schmitt's keywords to material questions. Again and again, Huber would probe the approach to constitutional theory with great intensity, modifying it with the help of Hegel and contrasting it with Schmitt's. His own constitutional theory finally turned out to be a strongly idealizing exposition of the national socialist 'constitution',[24] which seems to discredit the whole approach. And it is beyond any doubt that the fundamental distinction between an 'absolute' and a 'positive' constitution, between constitutional situation and constitutional law, provides a dangerous instrument for the politicization and legal legitimization of various forms of rule. However, the theoretical foundation does not determine a specific interpretation. Huber demonstrates clearly that the approach aims not at the political liquidation of right but at a differentiated expression of the tension between constitutional reality and constitutional law.

Mobilization of the 'new elite'

In terms of literary history, Schmitt rejected the romantic 'Genieästhetik'* from the very beginning and chose the 'effects' caused by a work, and hence its 'audience', as his point of orientation. He already reflected on the dependence of literary forms and rhetorical strategies on the addressee in his early reviews. He sought to adapt his various statements and texts to his respective audiences, and as a scholar of state law he strictly adhered to the forms of accepted discourse in the field for a couple of years. Excursion into 'intellectual history' he put on the back burner. Only after the completion of *Constitutional Theory* and his arrival in Berlin did Schmitt venture into areas beyond juridical publishing. But now it was no longer the literary discourse, or the discourse of cultural criticism, that he was interested in, and nor was it the Catholic context, but the journalistic area of daily politics. Blei regretted this turn.[25] Feuchtwanger was worried by it. Schmitt now was a legal advisor and political journalist. To a certain extent, these roles were in tension with each other. Someone who exposes himself to the public in journalistic publications can no longer play the impartial and unassailable role of a discreet and purely observing expert and advisor. The fact that Schmitt, after 1930, pushed into the field of political journalism may mean that behind the scenes he did not, or did not want to, play a central role.

The tendency of Schmitt's interventions can be deduced from his

---

* Aesthetic theories that concentrate on the subject's abilities and control over artistic production, as opposed to 'Wirkungsästhetik', which concentrates on the reception of the artwork and the effects it has.

choice of journalistic fora for them. Even early on Schmitt was spoilt for choice. He could hardly save himself from requests for articles from newspapers. Thus, for instance, the *Kölnische Volkszeitung*[26] repeatedly requested contributions from him. The *Vossische Zeitung*, the *Frankfurter Zeitung*[27] and many others requested contributions, in particular on Article 48 of the constitution and on the role of the Reichspräsident. Even the *Burschenschaftlichen Blätter* occasionally wanted contributions from Schmitt, though he had never been a member of a student fraternity.[28] Apart from specialist juridical journals, Schmitt, during his time in Bonn, concentrated especially on the Catholic press. The *Hochland* paid good money, had a good reputation, was politically open and reached a wider audience. In addition, Schmitt published in journals that were more programmatic and esoteric, such as Guardini's *Schildgenossen* and the *Abendland*. He became increasingly disappointed with the *Hochland*. 'But where should I go instead if I want to publish an article?' (CSLF, p. 163), he repeatedly asked Feuchtwanger imploringly. Feuchtwanger's answer was clear: 'In comparison, the *Hochland* is by far the best journal in which you could publish' (CSLF, p. 165). However, Schmitt had fallen out with the Catholic Church, and thus he also turned away from the Catholic press. As early as 1925, he had written to Prince Rohan of the *Europäische Revue*: 'As a category the journal belongs to the liberal era, a time that believes in discussion and conversation, hence to a Romantic age.'[29] Despite repeated requests, he published only one article, his lecture on Hugo Preuß on the occasion of the anniversary of the Reich's foundation, in the liberal *Neue Rundschau*.[30] He increasingly preferred to place his shorter texts with the 'national conservative' or 'national revolutionary' press.

Prince Rohan's *Europäische Revue* was politically still relatively tolerant. Towards the end of the Weimar Republic, Schmitt positioned himself more clearly with contributions in the young conservative *Ring* and in *Deutsches Volkstum*. With these publications, he reacted to the resonance that his writings had found in these circles. Formulaic talk of the 'Reich' and of the 'authoritarian' or 'total' state provided keywords in the efforts and hopes involved in constitutional policies. Schmitt had manifold links in this field. Andreas Koenen[31] has reconstructed these networks from the archives and puts Schmitt's aims regarding constitutional policies into the politico-theological framework of a 'Theology of the Reich'. For Schmitt, the 'Reich' was not only a political form but also a Christian 'idea'. He saw his intentions within a speculative or 'salvation historical' context of a counter-revolutionary battle against the modern age of secularizations, neutralizations and depoliticizations. His pupils played an important role in this, introducing him to a social environment and providing him with the opportunity to exert influence, something Schmitt had long been looking for. Stimulation and seduction were mutual. However, the influence his juridical work could have on a wider audience was limited. Hence, *The Concept of the Political* played a key role in Schmitt's career as a phrase that caught the attention of a more general public. It was also the text which brought him into closer contact with Ernst Jünger, which, in turn, opened up wider circles to him.

Schmitt had wanted to establish contact with Jünger since the summer of 1930 and sent him his lecture on state ethics and *Political Romanticism.* However, Jünger still reacted rather reservedly to this. Only when Schmitt sent *The Concept of the Political* did he win him over. In his famous response of 14 October, Jünger wrote:

> I have too much respect for the word not to appreciate the perfect certainty, cold-bloodedness and malice of your blow, which cuts through all parries. The rank of a mind [Geistes] is today determined by its relation to armament. You have succeeded with a special invention in war technology: a mine which explodes without a sound. . . . It is my intention to provide you with some of those readers who are, today, as rare as books. (JS, p. 7)[32]

Schmitt could not resist this accolade. Here, he had found the 'soldier' that his critique of Romanticism had been looking for. Now, the nationalistic circles around Jünger and his journalistic assault squads were open to him. He had finally found an anti-bourgeois environment in which he could figure as the avant-garde of world spirit and a 'Gestalt' [figure] of the twentieth century.

In 1928, Schmitt had already said that 'there is no such thing as "being scientific" in matters pertaining to intellectual history [geistesgeschichtlichen Fragen].' In 1930 he was unhappy with Duncker & Humblot. On 19 October 1930 he suggested to Feuchtwanger an expansion of 'The Concept of the Political' into a brochure, but the tension in their correspondence remained. Feuchtwanger confessed his 'deep antipathy' towards the fact that Schmitt's writings were 'used and popularized and turned into *belles lettres*' by the 'circles of the radical right' around Niekisch's *Widerstand* and Stapel's *Volkstum.* 'Maybe you do not feel quite at ease either', he hopefully suggested (CSLF, p. 329), with authors such as Ernst Jünger and Ernst Niekisch of the *Widerstand,* Hugo Fischer of the *Blätter für Deutsche Philosophie,* Wilhelm Stapel[33] and Albrecht Erich Günther[34] of the *Deutsches Volkstum* in mind. Further names could be added: for instance, Karl Anton Rohan of the *Europäische Revue,* Paul Adams of the *Germania,* Friedrich Vorwerk of the *Ring,* and Veit Rosskopf[35] of the radio station Deutsche Welle and of *Deutsches Volkstum.* Rosskopf, who had been part of the march to the Feldherrnhalle, introduced Schmitt to Hölderlin. Schmitt had only loose contacts with Hans Zehrer and the *Tat* circle. Stapel acquainted Schmitt with the Protestant 'theology of nationalism', a nationalist interpretation of Christianity, which the journal *Deutsches Volkstum* also suffused with anti-Semitism. These circles compensated their uncertain standing as political parties with self-legitimizations based on speculative theologies of history.

The Concept of the Political and the game of the Antichrist

During his time in Munich, Schmitt had led a kind of double life as a jurist and bohemian. In Bonn, he limited himself to juridical discourse and kept a cautious balance between closeness to and distance from the Catholic press. Now, in Berlin, he entered politicized circles of literary authors, and, in his eyes, esoteric circles were transfigured into the 'new elite'. He rejected parliamentarism as a method for selecting leaders. All the more he should have scorned journalistic circles as Romantic 'intellectual circles'. But he was now seeking to have an impact on young revolutionaries, for which purpose a new and expanded edition of *The Concept of the Political* was particularly important. Feuchtwanger did not like these ambitions of Schmitt, but neither did he want to lose him as an author of Duncker & Humblot. In June 1931, the publication was agreed. In August, Schmitt spoke of a revision that would integrate the 'further development' (CSLF, p. 349) of his ideas. He called the text his 'most important publication'. By combining it with the presentation he gave in Spain, he put the *Concept* treatise into the framework of an analysis of an epoch. Schmitt expanded the core text, in particular, with remarks on the domestic political situation and thereby made his analysis suitable as a legitimization of rule by presidential decree.[36] He distinguished between 'primary' and 'secondary' concepts of the political and argued in favour of a 'primacy of foreign policy'. The nation closes ranks against an 'external' enemy. With the insight into the necessity of such politicizations through the identification of enemies, modern times seem to approach their secular end.

The revision of the *Concept* treatise did not take Schmitt long. He was working on his contribution on basic rights for Thoma's *Handbook* at that time. In the seminar he met Franz Neumann and Otto Kirchheimer. Privately, he now enjoyed socializing with the Jünger circle. He entered into intimate relations with Hella Ehrik again. On 8 August he spoke at the Hochschule für Politik [Academy for Political Science] on 'Die Reichsverfassung in Wortlaut und Wirklichkeit' [Text and reality of the

'I am with you and shall never leave' – Duška to Carl, 25 July 1924

Reich's constitution]. Soon after, he travelled to Plettenberg, while Duška, heavily pregnant, remained in Berlin. Carl was longing for Hella. On 20 August he received news of the birth of his daughter, Anima-Louise. But Schmitt stayed on in Plettenberg, made excursions with his brother Jupp, and spent a couple of days with Georg Eisler before travelling to Goslar at the beginning of September, and then on to Berlin. On 5 September he saw his child for the first time and soon pushed her pram through the Tiergarten. 'Feeling of responsibility towards the poor little daughter, helplessness of human beings in general. Horrible world', he noted in his diary (TB, 7 September 1931). The Schmitt family now moved into a larger apartment (Flotowstr. 5, Tiergarten) and were annoyed about the noisy 'Jewish' tenants in the flat above them. Schmitt's former lover, Margot von Quednow, congratulated Schmitt on the birth of the child: 'Especially someone like you will certainly be infinitely happy with a daughter – because you can fall in love with her and spoil her.'[37] On 2 January the christening took place in the Clemenskirche in Berlin. In the evening there was a celebration with Popitz, Eschweiler[38] and also Guardini.

Mid-September saw Schmitt working on his essay on 'institutional guarantees'. He re-entered his Berlin life, met with Popitz and Jünger, and made corrections to *The Concept of the Political*. On 20 September he went, together with Werner Becker, to Lobeda Castle in Thuringia for a meeting also attended by Wilhelm Stapel, Paul Althaus, Albert Mirgeler and other theologians of nationalism. Schmitt spoke about the 'total state' and then travelled on to Naumburg and Halle. At the beginning of October he submitted the proofs of the *Concept* treatise. Schmitt wanted it to be distributed widely. 'How much will the booklet cost?', he asked. 'I want to give away a large number as presents' (CSLF, p. 351). 'I am looking forward very much to the publication of my treatise. It is surely a different and more dignified matter than the juridical bickering of advocates and the pseudo-scientific business of legal opinions today' (CSLF, p. 358). 'This "Concept of the Political" is my greatest achievement. The peculiar momentum necessary in order to capture such an intellectual space [geistigen Raum] with a few strokes is absolute and nothing but a fortuitous moment and not repeatable. This may explain my interest in this little brochure to you; and also my joy about its imminent publication' (CSLF, p. 366).

In mid-October, Schmitt travelled for the first time to Siedlinghausen, where the physician Dr Franz Schranz, over several decades, organized a sophisticated literary circle, of which the Catholic journalist and lyricist Konrad Weiß was also a member. On 13 October, Schmitt was in Plettenberg, reading the final proofs for *The Concept of the Political*. A week later he went to see Eisler in Hamburg, where he also met with Eduard Rosenbaum and Alfred Bertram. On 26 October he spoke to a small audience at the Hotel Kaiserhof in Berlin on 'Parlamentarische und außerparlamentarische Methoden der Willensbildung' [Parliamentary and extra-parliamentary methods of will formation]. The next day, the Handelshochschule celebrated its twenty-fifth anniversary; the *Festschrift* containing Schmitt's treatise on institutions was presented. Then Schmitt visited the meeting of state theorists in Halle. Huber and Forsthoff attended for the first time. The opening theme relating to civil service law [Beamtenrecht] was a reaction to incisive measures that were being taken under rule by presidential decree: the Reichspräsident, with some economic measures, had hit the state theorists where it hurt: cuts to civil service salaries! Schmitt was also affected by this and protested heavily in a letter to the university administration.[39] However, he then publicly defended the cuts[40] and ended up in a conflict with the association of civil servants [Beamtenbund]. Adolf Merkl and Hans Gerber gave two very different presentations. Schmitt's theory of 'institutional guarantees' was a hot topic of debate. The second theme was the reform of the electoral law. Leibholz's responding note was particularly controversial. The floor demanded a discussion of the 'use made in practice of the so-called right to pass emergency decrees [Notverordnungsrecht]'. Regarding a press release, Schmitt, Bilfinger and Erwin Jacobi, later the representatives of the Reich in the case *Preussen contra Reich*, were outvoted: the majority of the state theorists were of the opinion that the government should exercise stricter control in making sure 'that the tool of emergency decrees is not abused'.[41] Thus, the polarization within the discipline became public. 'Several intense discussions about our resolution and (along with Bilfinger and others) outvoted', Schmitt noted in his diary on 29 October. 'Saw the meanness and maliciousness of Rothenbücher, Kaufmann and Smend.' And he noted: 'Bought national socialist literature' (TB, 30 October 1931). The meeting of the state theorists in Halle was the last in the Weimar Republic. The annual meeting in 1932 was cancelled on account of the crisis situation. And in 1933 the time of discussions ended abruptly as a result of National Socialist censorship. Schmitt would now take his revenge on the discipline.

On 4 November, Schmitt gave a radio talk for the Deutsche Welle on 'Verfassungsstaat und Staatsnotstand' [Constitutional state and national state of emergency].[42] Afterwards, he attended Smend's lecture. 'Lousy' (TB, 5 November 1931). In mid-November, on the occasion of the centenary of Hegel's death, he gave a lecture on 'Hegel and Marx' on the radio.[43] At that time, the new edition of *The Concept of the Political* was published. Schmitt was nonetheless in an irritable mood and now entered fully into the affair with Hella. After Duška's recovery, Schmitt tried to stay faithful despite continual temptations. During the pregnancy and birth, the old arrangement we know from Bonn, the separation of sexuality and caritas, returned for a stormy six months. 'Revulsed and ashamed because of Hella', Schmitt noted down (22 November 1931). Duška knew Hella and suspected what was going on. 'Completely distraught by this dualism', Schmitt wrote on 20 December 1931, 'just as in Greifswald or Marburg [Murray] or Munich with Lola [Sauer]. What a fate; and in all this, love and admiration for Duška.' The expression of his discontent is permanently mixed with anti-Semitic remarks.

On 3 December, Schmitt travelled to Bremerhaven for a lecture on 'Diktatur und Wirtschaftsstaat' [Dictatorship and the economic state], which he repeated the following day in Bremen.[44] Thus, he inspected the city in which Cari was now living. Numerous letters arrived in reaction to *The Concept of the Political*. Schmitt celebrated his steps into the world of political journalism as if he was liberated from the academic corset. His list of recipients of free and review copies shows how much he was already established in right-wing intellectual circles at that time. Apart from the important specialist journals, review copies were sent, for instance, to Forsthoff of the *Ring*, Günther of the *Volkstum*, Zehrer of the *Tat*, Lohmann of the *Stahlhelm*,[45] Grewe[46] of *Die junge Mannschaft* and Max Hildebert Boehm of the *Baltische Monatshefte*. Günther Krauss wrote a longer review.[47] Reinhard Höhn[48] renewed his contact with Schmitt, writing a review and visiting him. The socialist and the Christian press also received many free copies of the book. Numerous key positions in the press of the young conservatives were at that time already held by former pupils. Schmitt sent Vorwerk to see Feuchtwanger and have the circulation list extended into right-wing intellectual circles. A particular focus on the Christian press was no longer discernible.[49] When compared with the dedicatory list of *Constitutional Theory*, which was led by Smend and Triepel, the shift in the group of addressees becomes obvious. And Schmitt aimed not only at the nationalist base but also at the presidential top. He specifically targeted and sent the treatise, via Lohmann and the historian Horst Michael,[50] to the circle around Schleicher and the antechambers of Hindenburg.

During the last days of Weimar, Schmitt liked to speculate on the process of history. *The Concept of the Political* ends with the quotation of a hermetic watchword from Virgil's fourth eclogue: 'Ab integro nascitur ordo.' The fuller passage actually runs: 'Ultima Cumaei venit iam carminis aetas: / magnus ab integro saeclorum nascitur ordo.' Eduard Norden,[51] who wrote a scholarly interpretation of the eclogue, read by Schmitt, translates this as: 'Auf die Endzeit folgt wieder die Urzeit mit ihrem Segen, und ein neues Geschlecht wird vom Himmel herabgesandt' [The last days are followed by a return of primordial times and their blessings, and a new race [Geschlecht] is sent down from the heavens].* As early as the time of the Emperor Constantine, Virgil's anticipation of a new ruler of the world was often given a Christian interpretation. Theodor Haecker popularized it in Schmitt's times.[52] The Roman idea of the Occident was also directed against Protestantism. Norden referred to the origin of eon mysticism and the idea of a saviour in the notion of the child prodigy in ancient Egypt. Outside Greek and Jewish mythology, Virgil's association of the turning of the times with the myth of the divine child or the coming ruler of the world can also be found in ancient Egypt. 'Christology', Norden writes, 'is religiously reinterpreted Graeco-Egyptian gnosis' and goes on to talk about a 'process of transposition'.[53] Virgil associated Horus, the divine child of Isis, with Cleopatra. Cleopatra gave birth to a son not only of Caesar but also of Antonius. A son of Isis, Augustus,[54] fulfilled what Virgil foresaw. Schmitt's contemporaries were familiar with Virgil's 'annunciation'. Ernst

---

* More conventional translations of the passage quoted in abbreviated form by Schmitt are: 'a new world order is born' or 'a great order of the ages is born anew'. The translator of CP remarks: 'In the context of Schmitt's remarks here, the abridgement could be interpreted to mean, "from integrity order is born" or "an order is born from renewal"' (CP, p. 96).

Kantorowicz[55] linked it to the Emperor Frederick II of Hohenstaufen, whom he saw as the prototypical dictator. Stefan George, by contrast, in 1928 propagated the 'secret Germany' as the 'new Reich' of poetry.[56] In the autumn of 1931, when his *Concept* treatise appeared, Schmitt quoted from Virgil's eclogue primarily for family reasons: the birth of his only daughter, Anima. The daughter – in Virgil's case it is a boy – also represented the hope of overcoming a time of crisis and the hope for a fresh future for the coming generation, as in Thomas Mann's 1919 *Gesang vom Kindchen* [Song about a newborn]. In terms of the sociology of domination, Schmitt again referred to a 'new elite' beyond any parliamentary or party political selection of leaders, not least with his own pupils in mind. In this context, he took his cue from the ideas on salvific history to be found in monastic traditions, and which were extended by Joachim von Fiore into the proclamation of a new and third gospel and 'Reich'. Political theology in the age of the Hohenstaufen had already combined such speculations with ideas about the Antichrist.[57] At the time, Wilhelm Stapel and the *Deutsches Volkstum* rediscovered the 'theology of nationalism' and the 'Ludus de Antichristo' of the age of the Emperor Frederick Barbarossa. Gottfried Hasenkamp, the translator of the Antichrist play, which was also performed in Berlin, sent Schmitt a copy of the text.[58] The play emphasized the role of the Reich as a counter-power and obstacle to the Antichrist and contained in condensed form some of Schmitt's speculations on the history of theology.

In the Ludus play, the Emperor, to begin with, submits all earthly powers to the one Reich. He gains victory over the kings of the Francs and Greeks and of Jerusalem and, with God's help, conquers Babylon. But when the victorious Emperor voluntarily hands over his power to the Church in the Temple in Jerusalem, heathen heresy appears and the Antichrist emerges 'from the womb of the Church'. The Church falls prey to worldly forces ('matrem ecclesiam vanitas occupavit'). The renunciation of power by the Emperor is presented as 'apostasy'. Next, the Antichrist, wearing the mask of the Good, gains entry by means of hypocrisy and submits the earthly powers to his rule. Only the king of the Germans offers resistance at first and triumphs over the armies of the Antichrist. But, in the end, the Antichrist deceives him as well. Only the synagogue resists. The prophets Elias and Enoch unmask the Antichrist and call on the members of the synagogue to stand by their faith again, whereupon they are brought in front of the Antichrist and executed. At that moment, divine thunder can be heard and the Church returns to its true faith.

The Crusades and the Hohenstaufer's idea of the Reich form the background to the play, which interprets the renunciation of power by the Emperor as the moment of the emergence of the Antichrist and the beginning of the fall from God. The circles around the *Volkstum* stressed the 'nationalist' tone of the play and the special role of the German emperor, and in their anti-Semitic way of reading the 'occidental' salvific history they liked to overlook the role played by the Jewish prophets, as martyrs, and the synagogue. The Jewish prophets save their Church by uncovering the Antichrist. In contrast, the German emperor ultimately does not play the decisive part in the salvific history. In the play, the Antichrist is not a Jew but a lapsed Christian.[59] The idea of the katechon as expressed in the second letter to the Thessalonians, with its positive reinterpretation and integration of the (Roman) Reich into salvific history, forms the 'nucleus' (Gerhard Günther) of this play. Jewish prophets are the last opponents and martyrs in the fight against the Antichrist. The discussions around this play and similar texts formed a good part of Schmitt's very vague and flexible speculations on the 'delayer' of the end of world history. Schmitt himself gave the year 1932 as the date when he formulated his idea of the katechon. With it, he put his extensive interpretation of dictatorial powers into the context of salvific history. But only in 1942, in the face of the coming defeat of the 'Reich', did he make public his concept of the kat-echon – as the salvific core of his idea of the Reich –and begin to look for new 'delayers', 'retarders and accelerators'.

Schmitt's take on the katechon was neither politically nor theologically unambiguous. The mediaeval play allows for various readings relating it to the present. What is important, however, is that, for Schmitt, the 'theologi-cal' justification of battle filled the gap left by constitutional law. At the limits of right, the theological perspective on history legitimized the nor-mative approach, because beyond the text of the law it is not chaos and an anarchic state of nature that rule, but a religious order and meaning. It is also striking that the play's text deviates from the traditional anti-Judaism of the Antichrist plays and resists anti-Semitic interpretations. Schmitt nevertheless associated the 'masks' of 'hypocrisy' with Judaism, for which there is hardly any evidence in the text. But for the time being he kept his 'katechontic' justification of dictatorial powers under rule by presiden-tial decree within the confines of his 'esoteric' private discourse and was careful not to criticize Weimar's radicalism from the left and right – KPD and NSDAP – directly and openly as expressions of the power of the Antichrist. In this way, Schmitt justified to himself his support for execu-tive dictatorial powers in terms of a theology of history, also drawing on earlier conversations with, and the ideas of, Peterson from his time in Bonn. These speculations led, via the time of the Hohenstaufer, back to early justifications of dictatorial powers for the emperor in Hellenistic times. In these early reflections, Schmitt's key concept of 'nomos' already took a prominent place. This is why Erik Peterson,[60] in 1933, compared Schmitt to the Caesaro-papist court theologian Eusebius and looked at his 'political theology' as an abuse of theological keywords for political and apologetic purposes. Schmitt's speculations seem, indeed, extremely 'occa-sional'.[61] Apart from the practical motive of forming elitist circles, they express his desire for a meta-juridical justification of his own commitments and a post-liberal understanding of the way political elites should form.

Feuchtwanger's reaction to Schmitt's *Concept* treatise was negative. He openly told Schmitt: 'I am now very curious as to the reactions the "Concept of the Political" will cause. I have spent a lot of time on this subject, especially the epistemological aspect. I disagree with your basic assumptions and methods' (CSLF, p. 369). The reception of the booklet took place in a different climate compared to that of the first version of

1927. It was no longer seen primarily as a 'Catholic' text but as the radicalization of the position of a prominent constitutional theorist in the last days of Weimar. Georg Eisler now also expressed reservations. '*The Concept of the Political* is certainly the most exciting text you have written so far', he said, but added his concerns over 'the existential partaking and taking part [Teilhaben und Teilnehmen]'.[62] Eugen Rosenstock, who was in touch with Schmitt from the latter's time in Bonn, criticized the 'civil war ideology'.[63] Willy Haas, in the *Literarische Welt*, remarked appropriately 'that Carl Schmitt has become the disciple of his disciples'.[64] Around the same time,[65] Carl Joachim Friedrich sent Schmitt the draft for an open letter against Ernst von Salomon, who had been involved in the assassination of Rathenau and was now starting a new nationalistic offensive in his book *Die Geächteten* [The outlaws]. Schmitt advised against the publication of such a letter of protest, and Friedrich followed his advice. In this context, Friedrich referred to his own engagement in the Freikorps.[66] Even as a Jew, he did not yet count Schmitt as a member of the extreme right. The most diverse readers reacted enthusiastically to the *Concept* treatise. Schmitt's brother Jupp agreed with the book.[67] Ernst Krieck thanked Schmitt for sending him the book and expressed his hope for a 'political science' 'of the kind already represented by Carl Schmitt'.[68] Ulrich Scheuner's endorsement was more differentiated, saying that 'the contrast [Gegensatz] to one's political opponent . . . belongs to the nature of politics.'[69] Wilhelm Herschel criticized the circular argumentation.[70] It was not only Christian authors who formulated their objections.[71] The criticism also came from nationalist circles. Leo Strauss,[72] however, elevated Schmitt to the rank of a classical author alongside Hobbes and associated the critique of liberalism with Hobbes in order to gain Schmitt's interest in his own Hobbes studies.

On 27 November 1931, Strauss introduced himself to Schmitt, presenting the work on Hobbes he intended to undertake and asking him the favour of supporting him with a reference. 'Dr Strauss announced himself, came at five, a fine Jew, learned, works on Hobbes, liked his thesis' (TB, 27 November 1931). On 21 December, Strauss brought his manuscript to Schmitt and soon afterwards asked him for a reference for the Rockefeller Foundation.[73] Strauss's 'Anmerkungen' ['Notes' on *The Concept of the Political*; see CP, pp. 97–122], sent to Schmitt only after the Rockefeller reference had been supplied, were a deal based on reciprocity. Schmitt read the typescript and arranged their publication in *Lederers Archiv*.[74] Lederer published them, though not without reservations, as they were arranged through Schmitt. In 1933, Schmitt broke off his contact with Strauss. To Schmitt's expressed joy over the 'Notes', Feuchtwanger responded by sending Jewish literature from his 'second life' and promised him philological material on 'love of the enemy' (CSLF, p. 378). He called Strauss's remarks a case of Jewish 'love of the enemy'.

On similar grounds, the Privatdozent Helmut Kuhn[75] in Berlin – an acquaintance of Strauss and of partly Jewish descent, who was strongly impressed by Heidegger but took Plato as his point of reference – criticized, in a review in *Kant-Studien*, the lack of philosophical rigour in the execution of Schmitt's 'existentialist' approach. Kuhn accepted his results. He, too, saw the moral pathos of Schmitt's 'decisionism' and saw the question of human 'nature' as fundamental. In contrast to Strauss, however, he no longer followed any strategic objectives in April 1933.[76] He sent Schmitt a 'copy' of his review together with an accompanying letter, in which he radicalized the critical aspects only hinted at in the review. Although Schmitt, the review says, assumes an existential 'pre-order of the political',[77] he does not offer a comprehensive interpretation of it along the lines of Plato, but only explicates it altogether insufficiently and within the confines of his polemic against liberalism. Schmitt's remarks on anthropology were enough to show this. The reference to Hobbes, which Strauss had emphasized, Kuhn sees as only secondary. Schmitt, he holds, is a 'Romantic of the state of nature', an 'inverted Rousseau', in whom the 'pastoral idyll' has mutated into a 'predator idyll'. With enmity as the 'test of existentiality' and 'genuineness' [Echtheit], Schmitt actually captures only a 'marginal phenomenon',[78] only one aspect of the Socratic question of the nature of the 'Good', which Kuhn himself detaches from Plato's ontological self-misunderstandings.[79] In the accompanying letter, Kuhn wrote:

Allow me to go just one step further than is permitted by the restraint required in a review. . . . I try to uncover the 'nihilism' hidden in your treatise . . . to bring it to itself, to a philosophical consciousness of itself, and to show how the radical question of a substance [Inhalt] as such – which is ultimately identical with Socrates's question of ἀγαθόν – emerges from it. This question, in fact the unavoidable precondition of any philosophy and any philosophy of the state, is the only positive assumption in my criticism. . . . Your treatise seems important to me because it leads precisely to the point where this kind of honesty can no longer be avoided.[80]

Schmitt wrote in his diary: 'Stupid article by a Jew in *Kant-Studien* on my Concept of the Political; cheeky and impertinent' (20 April 1933). However, his annotations in the margins of the review are often affirmative. Schmitt in particular thought that the 'ethos' of the 'pre-order' of the political was 'right'. He also thought it was 'right' when Kuhn wrote on the 'consequences' of this: 'But in the end this theory does not help nationalism, nor liberalism, nor socialism, nor any other political position.'[81] Decades later, Kuhn republished his critique of Schmitt as an appendix to his Platonic *magnum opus Der Staat* [The state],[82] thus indicating that his engagement with Schmitt was one of the impulses for developing a Platonic political philosophy which distances itself from the anthropological limitations that characterized the intellectual atmosphere of Weimar.

It is noteworthy that the more recent turn in the political philosophy of Jewish pupils of Heidegger towards Plato began with the reception of Schmitt. Heidegger himself did not take that turn, nor did his non-Jewish pupils. But Leo Strauss and Helmut Kuhn did. And, with Karl Löwith, who was also in conversation with Strauss, another close pupil of Heidegger formulated his objections to his teacher through a reception of Schmitt. Herbert Marcuse was also a pupil of Heidegger and engaged critically with Schmitt after 1933. Heidegger's Jewish pupils saw Schmitt as the main representative of a political existentialism whose extremist conclusions affected Heidegger's fundamental assumptions. Schmitt's nationalism showed them that something must be wrong with Heidegger's existentialist approach, although Schmitt himself did not share that approach. The significance of Kuhn's short critique, which went beyond Leo Strauss, lies in the fact that, in 1933, it meant a step out of political and philosophical restraint in asking for a systematic justification of his concept of the political, which Schmitt, on account of his polemical intention, had failed to provide. Although a 'systematic' interpretation was not what Schmitt himself wanted, Kuhn's objections to the polemical focus on the liberalist 'enemy' are worthy of consideration. The philosophical ennobling of Schmitt's definition of the concept of the political was, by and large, begun by 'Jewish' pupils of Heidegger. It is these pupils, in the first instance, whom Schmitt had to thank for his being received philosophically. In 1933, there was an attempt at a political closing of ranks between Heidegger and Schmitt. Heidegger sent Schmitt a copy with dedication of his *Rectoral Address*, and Schmitt thanked him by sending the revised edition of *The Concept of the Political* in the summer of 1933. Rector Heidegger sent a friendly reply, saying that the treatise contained 'an approach of far-reaching consequence',[83] but he remarked on it only in passing in his lectures, and never developed a political philosophy that would remotely satisfy Kuhn's expectations regarding systematic rigour.

The philosophical significance of the *Concept* treatise was only gradually recognized. At first, the response it found was rather fleeting. On 13 June 1932, Feuchtwanger wrote: 'What a stir and what grandiose misunderstandings your "Concept of the Political" has caused. Among the about 100 reviews, often of substantial length, there is almost only chaff' (CSLF, p. 379).[84] On the occasion of a pre-publication of a passage from *Legality and Legitimacy*, Feuchtwanger reacted almost with horror:

> Mr Vorwerk sent me the volume of 'Deutsches Volkstum' which contains your article. Although I knew about the pre-publication in this place, I must admit that I was pretty shocked when I actually saw the volume with your lead article in it, because I am used to seeing your publications in the best possible company. And, for me, by far the best place is an academic publisher. But I don't think, to be honest, that Stapel is the right editor for you. The volume on state law itself is admittedly very interesting and of high quality. But 'Tat' and 'Deutsches Volkstum' represent a type of journalism for which I have little sympathy: an anti-literary literary world [ein anti-literarisches Literatentum]. (CSLF, p. 384)[85]

Legality and Legitimacy was published in mid-August 1932. Otto Kirchheimer criticized – also in *Lederers Archiv* – its historico-philosophical exuberance and the idealism of its 'conceptual realism'.[86] Ernst Jünger, in contrast, appreciated the text and was almost exhilarated: 'As I can see in all journals, you shake up the situation enormously with your concepts and thus contribute substantially to the fact that German politics is gradually turning into a spectacle that can be of interest again' (JS, p. 15). All later criticism of the book in Germany was done under the auspices of National Socialism and purported to be a discussion of what constituted 'genuine' National Socialism. A free debate was no longer possible. Apart from these distortions, Schmitt paid a high price for the politicization of his legal thought. His life remained hectic and frenzied; his texts became ever shorter and more polemical. After *The Guardian of the Constitution*, he did not write a longer book for almost twenty years. He moved further and further away from the nineteenth-century ideal of objective scholarship to which Feuchtwanger remained committed. The fall in his life, which we mentioned in the preface, was already visible in 1932, if not before. Schmitt had not established a settled family life. Close friendships fell apart. He had distanced himself from the environment of the Church and Catholicism. In the face of the political developments at the time, he increasingly abandoned his commitment to the principles of a Rechtsstaat [seine rechtsstaatlichen Überzeugungen], became more radically anti-Semitic and, with no alternative left to him, moved slowly ever closer to the option of a 'total state'.

18

Carl Schmitt as an Actor during the Rule by Presidential Decree

In the antechambers of power

Jurisprudence is a practical discipline. As lawyers, jurists argue on the basis of a legal system and develop their line of argument strategically in order to find solutions for certain legal tasks. Schmitt always claimed in his work the perspective of someone active within the legal system. As a participant, he sought to get close to the centre of decision-making within the state, limiting his role, however, mostly to that of an advisor and provider of legal opinions. He rejected the possibility of taking up a parliamentary seat. He has often been called the 'crown jurist' during the rule by presidential decree and during National Socialism.[1] In the first place, this term refers to no more than an important role as an advisor. However, the title is used with the critical intention of highlighting Schmitt's abrupt turn from supporting rule by presidential decree to supporting National Socialism, as well as the role he played in National Socialism.[2] The role of an advisor is not to be condemned as such. It can easily be interpreted as a responsible activity. Whoever is influential as a jurist should also take the risks and responsibilities associated with assuming legal tasks. Especially in a situation of crisis it is almost a civic duty to take on such a role. And Schmitt's work can be understood from the perspective of the political vocation of the jurist. But, in contrast to his mentors van Calker and am Zehnhoff, Schmitt did not become an influential politician. And compared to those of his colleagues, such as Erich Kaufmann, his activities as an advisor and author of legal opinions also remained within rather moderate dimensions. The distance between jurisprudence and politics was fairly short in those days. Through his renewed friendship with am Zehnhoff, Schmitt came into contact with the ministerial bureaucracy in Berlin. In 1928 he made the acquaintance of Brüning, who became the first chancellor of the Reich under the rule by presidential decree, in 1930. As he was based in Berlin from 1928 onwards, it is no surprise that, as an expert in state law, he also moved in the circles of the political elite and was asked to provide legal opinions. However, he gained access to the circles of power only slowly.[3] He sent his publications to the antechambers of power, but until the autumn of 1932 he had comparatively little influence as an advisor.

In 1929, the state secretary Otto Meissner[4] thanked Schmitt for sending him *The Guardian of the Constitution*. Johannes Popitz[5] invited Schmitt to the Gesellschaft für antike Kultur [Society for Ancient Culture]; the invitation marked the beginning of a close friendship between the two. Soon, Schmitt got to know Erich Zweigert, state secretary in the Ministry of the Interior. In January 1930, Zweigert asked Schmitt to write a legal opinion for the government led by Hermann Müller, which was followed by a legal opinion on the question as to whether emergency decrees overruling fiscal laws were legally permissible,[6] in which Schmitt revised his earlier view that dictatorial measures should be limited to the organizational principle of the separation of powers. Closer contacts with Brüning did not develop. The historian Horst Michael, an assistant of the Bismarck expert Erich Marcks and a visitor to Schmitt's seminar, became a middle man. It was Michael who established contact with the circles around the influential Reichswehrminister [defence minister] General Kurt von Schleicher. Through Michael, Schmitt came to know Schleicher's close collaborators Major Erich Marcks junior[7] and Major Eugen Ott. These two remained Schmitt's most important connections to the later chancellors of the Reich Franz von Papen and Schleicher. Marcks was the head of the press office of the Reich's Ministry of Defence at the time and had access to Hindenburg. Ott was Schleicher's 'adjutant' and after 1933 became the German ambassador to Japan. Schmitt nurtured these connections. But for a long time Schleicher did not involve Schmitt in his plans. Schmitt learned only through the press about the Preußenschlag* of 20 July.[8] Schmitt did not have closer personal relationships with Brüning, von Papen, Schleicher or Hindenburg. In the end, he hated the Zentrum circles. He moved only in the 'antechambers' of power.

'From legality to legitimacy'

Schmitt had completed his analysis of the organizational principle and the principle of distribution by 1931. What remained was an analysis of the fundamental 'Rechtsstaat concept of law'. The function of this concept was to guarantee the standard of justice that basic rights and the separation of powers then put into practice. Schmitt had for a long time noted the erosion of the 'general' law. His analysis of the part of the constitution that covers basic rights also showed that there were different 'kinds of positivity' below the level of the laws of the Rechtsstaat. In *The Guardian of the Constitution*, Schmitt still declared himself explicitly to be in favour of the separation of powers but noticed that legal 'practice' had eroded the principle. He said clearly that he saw the abandonment of the distinction between law and measure as a 'mistake in the theory of law'. 'The limitation of exceptional powers constituted by their restriction, within the Rechtsstaat, to measures now no longer exists', Schmitt wrote. 'It would be pointless if the dominant legal doctrine now tried to reverse a development

---

* An emergency decree issued by Hindenburg which dismissed the Prussian government and placed the state under the direct administrative rule of the Reich.

of the law [Rechtsbildung] that has been completed as the result of its own teachings, as soon as, in hindsight, it realizes the theoretical mistake it has made' (HdV, p. 126).

The economic crisis was getting dramatically worse at the time, and the presidential government reacted with emergency decrees. At the end of 1931, the unemployment figure in Germany stood at 5.5 million. Under the rule by presidential decree, there were cautious attempts at accommodating Hitler, and on 10 October Hindenburg spoke with him for the first time. The following day, the 'Harzburg Front' was formed.* In January 1932, Brüning was in negotiations with Hindenburg over an extension of his time as president. Next, Hitler succeeded in gaining German citizenship with the help of a legal trick – i.e., his appointment as a civil servant in Braunschweig – and stood as a candidate against Hindenburg. Duesterberg was the candidate of the Stahlhelm. The Social Democrats supported Hindenburg as the lesser evil, in order to prevent a Hitler victory. The first round of the election on 13 March did not produce the necessary absolute majority for Hindenburg, his result falling just short of it at 49.6 per cent. Only in the second round on 16 April did Hindenburg beat Hitler, with 53 per cent compared to the latter's 36.8 per cent. In the course of 1932, a year that saw an election marathon, the National Socialists everywhere dangerously threatened to win more power. The elections in the states of Prussia and Bavaria were of 'national' importance. Schleicher and Papen held various talks with Hitler discussing their further rapprochement and integration with the aim of toppling Brüning. In the end, Brüning resigned and von Papen became chancellor.†

At the beginning of January 1932, Schmitt's affair with Hella was still ongoing. In mid-January he travelled to Heidelberg, where he met Walter Jellinek, Carl Brinkmann and Gerhard Anschütz, as well as giving a lecture. Around that time he was discussing the 'concepts of legality and illegality' in his seminar and also intended to give a radio talk on that topic. He visited a prostitute, in order to reduce his 'dependency' on Hella. The pressures of motherhood and Schmitt's infidelity contributed to Duška becoming ill. Duška and Hella had an open conversation, but nevertheless there was a 'big scene with Duška because of Hella' (TB, 3 February 1932). Schmitt increasingly saw Hella as a 'cocotte'. Ernst Forsthoff was working on a treatise which anticipated the core argument of Schmitt's *Legality and Legitimacy* regarding constitutional theory. Forsthoff wrote to Schmitt, saying that today everything depended 'not on legality, but only on legitimacy, the political attitude towards the foundations of the constitution [Fundamentalverfassung]' (EFCS, p. 40). Schmitt would push this point to its limits in 1933: the concept opposed to legality is legitimacy. Gaps in the law do not produce lawless situations. The law must be constructed on the basis of the 'sense' of the constitution, on the basis of the funda-

---

* At a rally of nationalist opposition forces at Bad Harzburg. Hitler attended for opportunistic reasons but also distanced himself by leaving before the march-past of the Stahlhelm, the organization of war veterans, and refusing to take part in the joint lunch of the nationalist leaders.
† Brüning and his cabinet resigned over Hindenburg's refusal to sign further emergency decrees in response to Brüning's plans for distributing land to unemployed workers.

mental decisions. State law has no end. Schmitt drafted his radio talk 'Was ist legal?' [What is legal?], then travelled to Hamburg and gave a lecture at the university on Article 48. Eduard Rosenbaum was in the audience.[9] The next day, Georg Eisler brought Schmitt to the train station. Schmitt dictated the lecture and published it at once in the *Reichsverwaltungsblatt* with the title 'Grundsätzliches zur heutigen Notverordnungspraxis' [Some fundamental points about the practice of emergency decrees today].[10] The article begins with a survey of the development of emergency decrees, and then identifies the rise of the Reich's president to the 'new lawgiver' and the abandonment of the distinction between 'law and measure' as the 'fundamental' changes. Schmitt talks about a turn away from the judiciary state and pejoratively calls the new 'administrative state' a 'business managing state' [Geschäftsbesorgungsstaat].

The affair with Hella continued. Duška said Carl needed 'three ways to retreat [Rückwege]: back to the university, to the Church, and to a bachelor's love life [Junggesellenliebe]' (TB, 16 February 1932). Schmitt travelled to Königsberg, where he met Albert Hensel again[11] and, upon an invitation from Hans Rothenfels, gave a major lecture[12] on 'Die USA und die völkerrechtlichen Formen des modernen Imperialismus' [The USA and the forms of international law of modern imperialism]. Karl Eschweiler wanted to lure him to 'Prussian Siberia';[13] he met with him in Marienburg and accompanied him to Elbing and Stuhm and the Weichsel. On 22 February, Schmitt was back in Berlin. He then gave his radio talk on legality. Eisler, Oberheid and, soon, also Arnold Schmitz came to visit him. In mid-March, Schmitt travelled to Munich and met with Peterson, Eisler and Krause. Together with Peterson, he travelled on to Bolzano, Bologna and Rome, where he wanted to free his thoughts of Hella. On Easter Sunday he attended High Mass in St Peter's Basilica. Schmitt spent all of the days with Peterson. At the end of March, he went to Milan and then via Frankfurt to Plettenberg. He returned to Berlin on 7 April and on 22 April received an initial inquiry from the University of Cologne. On the elections in Prussia he remarked: 'Great success for the Nazis, but no absolute majority' (TB, 25 April 1932). At the end of April he 'broke up with Hella, on the telephone, it was tolerable, thanks to God' (29 April 1932). Schmitt stuck with it. After Magda, Margot and Hella, the time of longer affairs was now probably over.[14] After 1929, Schmitt had also kept his distance from the prostitution scene. But he now increasingly had to battle his inclination towards alcohol and nocturnal drinking sessions. In mid-May he went to Würzburg, Tübingen and Stuttgart and visited the monastery in Maulbronn. After his return to Berlin he collected his ideas for *Legality and Legitimacy*. On 2 June, he gave a lecture on 'Die konkrete Verfassungslage der Gegenwart' [The concrete situation of the constitution at present] in the assembly hall of the University of Frankfurt.[15] Soon after that, he met his young conservative pupils Huber, Forsthoff, Lohmann and Wilhelm Grewe at a 'Reich's theological' [reichstheologischen] conference in Lobeda, Jena.[16] A few days after the appointment of von Papen as chancellor, on 1 June 1932, Schmitt gave a lecture at a private venue (in Nikolassee, Berlin) and then, out of the blue, offered the manuscript of *Legality and Legitimacy* to Feuchtwanger. He said he had 'finished a treatise, five to six print sheets in length, which treats the system of legality in today's state. The title is not decided yet. In substance, the text is about the transition from legality to legitimacy!' (CSLF, p. 376). This formulation is of interest as Schmitt does not talk here about the legitimacy of legality, but rather signals the 'legitimacy' of the transition to a different type of order. Such a tension was politically given with the change from Brüning to Papen as chancellor. It was controversial as to whether von Papen still acted on the basis of the constitution and whether his 'authoritarian' turn in the rule by presidential decree had a return to Weimar parliamentarism as its goal.

Legality and Legitimacy is a companion piece to the 1923 *The Crisis of Parliamentary Democracy*.[17] While the latter describes the process of self-dissolution of the classical principles, *Legality and Legitimacy* analyses the practical 'posthumous' consequences of parliamentarism for the Weimar 'legislative state'. The treatise is divided into two main parts: 'The System of Legality of the Parliamentary Legislative State' and 'The Three Extraordinary Lawgivers of the Weimar Constitution'. This division follows the distinction between liberalism and democracy. Liberalism was the realization of the 'bourgeois Rechtsstaat' in Germany as a 'legislative state'. The parliamentary lawgiver had held a 'monopoly' on legality. Schmitt explicates how liberalism suffered deadly inconsistencies on account of the loss of the relativist-rational foundations of its convictions and principles. The legislative state is incapable of guaranteeing the ethos which supports it and which it presupposes. The principle of majority rule requires a 'legal disposition' [legale Gesinnung] (LL, p. 34) – i.e., the willingness to renounce the 'political premium' (LL, p. 32) of being in power for the sake of preserving an 'equal chance for gaining political power' (LL, p. 27; trans. modified) also for one's opponent. The majority is asked not to make use of its power over minorities. 'Preserving the availability of the principle of equal chances' is the 'principle of justice' (LL, p. 29) of the legislative state. Schmitt warns against the possibility of a 'legal revolution' (LL, p. 95) – i.e., the possibility that parties that are enemies of the constitution gain the power to exclude their opponents by legal means and close 'the door of legality' (ibid.) behind them. Schmitt's example of this is the trick used by the Prussian government on 12 April 1932 of changing the standing orders (§ 20) to the disadvantage of the National Socialists (cf. LL, p. 35). This critique of the self-dissolution of a value-neutral constitution has been called the 'strict refutation of the main ideological point of state law during the Weimar period',[18] and it has earned Schmitt the title of mastermind of the 'constructive vote of no confidence',[19] even of a 'father of the fathers of the constitution',* which thus emphasizes his 'continuing influence on the state law of the Federal Republic'.[20] However, what precisely Schmitt saw as the 'substance' of the Weimar Constitution that he wanted to be preserved is highly controversial.

The second part of *Legality and Legitimacy*, in any case, demonstrates

---

* I.e. the *Grundgesetz* [Basic Law] of the Federal Republic of Germany of 23 May 1949.

that the Weimar legislative state 'represents the clearest case of suicide in constitutional history' (BS p. 103) – suicide, that is, by accepting constitutional compromises. The constitution knew 'three extraordinary lawgivers', whose effects combined with one another in the process of its dissolution: a part on basic rights (*ratione materiae*), which could be used for ideological purposes; the legal possibility of referenda and for petitions for referenda (*ratione supremitatis*), which brought plebiscitary legitimacy into opposition with legislative state legality; and extraordinary presidential powers for decreeing measures (*ratione necessitatis*). Schmitt explicates how the introduction of quantitative majorities and of plebiscitary possibilities delegitimized the parliamentary legislative state's idea of representation. Invoking the difference between formal and substantive laws, he speaks of a 'contradiction between the value commitments and value neutrality', of a 'counterconstitution' (LL, p. 53) represented by the Second Principal Part of the Weimar Constitution and of a 'struggle between two forms of law' (LL, p. 66). Schmitt's analysis shows that the dissolution of the Weimar Republic was already contained in the 'alternative' between the 'two constitutions' (LL, p. 94). Retrospectively, he called his treatise a 'despairing attempt to safeguard the last hope of the Weimar Constitution, the presidential system, from a form of jurisprudence that refused to pose the question of the friend and enemy of the constitution' (LL, p. 95). However, in the end, any 'plan for a reshaping of the German constitutional system' (LL, p. 93) is faced with an – ultimately rhetorical – alternative between two possible decisions:

> Now, if in the knowledge that the Weimar Constitution is two constitutions, one chooses between them, then the decision must be for the principle of the second constitution and its attempt to establish a substantive order. The core of the Second Principal Part of the Weimar Constitution deserves to be liberated from the self-contradictions and deficiencies resulting from the compromises [Kompromissmängeln] it contains, and to be developed according to its inner logical consistency. Achieve this goal and the idea of a German constitutional work is saved. Otherwise, it will meet a quick end along with the fictions of neutral majority functionalism that are pitted against value and truth. Then, the truth will have its revenge. (LL, p. 94)

Schmitt's diagnosis of the autodestruction of parliamentarism is clear. Less clear is what Schmitt took to be the 'core' of the Second Principal Part of the constitution, other than a combination of the extraordinary lawgivers into one, and thus a new 'democratic' constitution which asserts itself against the 'system of legality of the parliamentary legislative state' (LL, p. 15). Schmitt used catchwords such as 'German constitutional work' and 'substantive order' and spoke of a 'reshaping'. His thesis of the 'two constitutions' rules out the possibility that all he wanted to do was to remind the reader of the one fundamental decision and substance of the Weimar Constitution. In June 1932, Schmitt no longer believed that a reconstitution of the parliamentary legislative state was possible. At best, he had in mind a focusing on the 'core' of the Second Principal Part.

Feuchtwanger sent Schmitt the publisher's contract for *Legality and Legitimacy*. At the end of June, Schmitt travelled to Leipzig and then on to Munich, where he gave a talk on 'Demokratie und autoritärer Staat' [Democracy and the authoritarian state] at the 'Club of Young Academics'. At that time, the University of Cologne wanted Schmitt as the successor to Stier-Somlo, and Schmitt sounded out the mood through Erwin von Beckerath.[21] Schmitt and Kelsen as members of the same faculty would have been a spectacular experiment. Hans Carl Nipperdey in particular pursued it.[22] The young Karl August Eckhardt supported Schmitt. Kelsen mentioned 'his name first in the faculty meeting'.[23] At the beginning of June, Schmitt's name stood next to those of Walter Jellinek and Karl Rothenbücher on the faculty's list of candidates, which was sent to Lord Mayor Adenauer.[24] However, Adenauer had concerns about Schmitt's 'difficult character'. Nevertheless, the university's board of trustees ranked Schmitt first.[25] At the beginning of August, Schmitt received the offer of appointment, whereupon he sought a personal conversation with Adenauer in order to dispel the latter's doubts. Schmitt wanted to go on leave in the winter term 1932–3, and he asked Huber if he wanted to stand in for him.[26] Having finally arrived at the centre of presidential power, Schmitt was given the opportunity to return to a university.

Schmitt was not particularly optimistic about German politics at the time. Koschwenikoff reported to Count Kessler that Schmitt had resigned himself to a Nazi victory.[27] Feuchtwanger was worried about Schmitt's development. On 20 July, the day of the so-called Preußenschlag, Feuchtwanger, as already mentioned, expressed his dismay over the pre-publication of an excerpt from *Legality and Legitimacy* in the *Deutsches Volkstum*, and said:

> I could imagine that the events in Prussia, which have become public here this noon, may still be mentioned in your new treatise . . . I also think you should date the work 30 July [Feuchtwanger probably meant June], or with the day when you give the imprimatur for the final print sheet. For in the case of no other book is the date of publication is as important as in this one. (CSLF, p. 385)

Schmitt took this advice on board and dated the completion of the work 10 July. 'I hope the book will now soon come out. It is a good moment' (CSLF, p. 387). The booklet was published in mid-August. Schmitt was again not satisfied with the distribution and dissemination. He put plans for a new edition of *Constitutional Theory* on the back burner. 'In principle, the task would very much appeal to me, but the situation is uncertain and everything is in flux' (CSLF, p. 390).

Preußenschlag and emergency plan [Notstandsplan]

The crisis of the Reich could not be seen in isolation from the situation in the individual states at the time. For a long time, Prussia was ruled by a coalition between SPD and Zentrum, with Otto Braun of the SPD as prime minister.[28] In return, at the Reich level, the SPD tolerated Brüning. In Berlin, two large parliaments practised different politics in close proximity to each other. At the beginning of 1932, the Prussian coalition had eroded. Ahead of the state elections, it created an obstacle to the threat of a National Socialist seizure of power by changing the standing orders, making an absolute rather than a relative majority necessary for the election of the prime minister in the second round of voting. The elections on 24 April did not see any great successes for the NSDAP, but they did see a dramatic loss of votes for the DNVP, the DVP and also the SPD. Only the Zentrum maintained its position. Otto Braun's government no longer held a majority and acted only as a caretaker government until after the following national elections. At first, the Prussian government was not averse to help offered by the Reich. This changed, however, once Hindenburg withdrew his confidence in Brüning – for no compelling reason – and on 1 June appointed the widely unknown Franz von Papen as chancellor instead. Papen belonged to the right wing of the Zentrum, but in the course of events left the party on 3 June 1932.* His cabinet had hardly any parliamentary support. The Reichspräsident therefore immediately dissolved the Reichstag, and von Papen was given a free hand until after new elections. 'The overthrow of Brüning was a deep historical watershed', according to Heinrich August Winkler's judgment. 'On 30 May 1932, the first, moderate, parliamentarily tolerated phase of the presidential system came to an end, and a second, authoritarian, openly anti-parliamentary phase began.'[29]

Papen wanted a refoundation of Weimar as an 'authoritarian' state. The fluidity of the situation required that any 'reform of the Reich' should start out with the dualism between Prussia and the Reich. After the elections to the Reichstag, victory by the NSDAP in the Prussian state elections loomed, in which case the country would have been brought to the brink of civil war. The Prussian government was right to see the change from Brüning to Papen as a sign of a reorientation. While at first the actions of the Reich were directed only against the National Socialists taking hold of power, the threat of its interventions was now directed also against Otto Braun and social democracy. The summer of 1932 was characterized by a 'latent civil war situation'. There were permanent riots with casualties. And it was not just the NSDAP and the KPD who fought each other openly in the streets; the Reichswehr [Reich's army] and the Reich's police were also involved in battles. Had the NSDAP seized power in Prussia, it might well have led to a confrontation between the Prussian police and the Reichswehr. Thus, the Reich's intervention in Prussia had the immediate aim of preventing the National Socialists seizing power and thus preventing an open civil war. However, in addition it also pursued the aim of weakening the SPD and reforming the Reich in the direction of an 'authoritarian state'.[30] Drawing

---

* A day before being appointed chancellor, von Papen promised the party chairman Ludwig Kaas that he would not accept such an appointment. Being taking to task by Kaas over this, von Papen effectively pre-empted being expelled from the party.

on his dictatorial powers, Hindenburg dismissed the government of Otto Braun and on 20 July appointed the chancellor, von Papen, as the Reich commissar for Prussia. Severing, the Prussian minister of the interior, in particular resisted that move. As a result, a military state of exception for Berlin and Brandenburg was declared. The SPD forsook the possibility of mobilizing for a general strike at the time, as it would have further intensified the crisis, and instead opted for seeking legal clarification and set its hopes on the forthcoming elections to the Reichstag.

Schmitt learned of the Preußenschlag only through the press. 'Announcement that Papen has been appointed the Reich commissar for Prussia. Excited . . . Sad that I was not there' (TB, 20 July 1932). At the Handelshochschule, Schmitt immediately set about defending the move to his colleagues. Otto Liebmann asked him for an article for his *Deutsche Juristen-Zeitung*. Schmitt established contact with the circle around Schleicher and discussed the article with Ott, Marcks and Zweigert. On 22 July he was given the unofficial task, as 'chairman' [Obmann],[31] of putting together a legal team for the preparation of the trial. Schmitt was now the 'crown jurist' of the Reich in front of the Staatsgerichtshof [constitutional court]. Schmitt did not want to have Smend, who had been suggested by Ott, as part of the team. Carl Bilfinger and Erwin Jabobi, in contrast, had also argued in favour of the permissibility of rule by emergency decrees at the meeting in Halle. Schmitt agreed with their views. Thus, there was 'a very clear line'[32] and a triumvirate of defence lawyers after the 1924 conference in Jena, where Schmitt had presented his wide interpretation of Article 48 for the first time and the apologists of a dictatorship of the Reichspräsident had their first public appearance. The preliminary proceedings at the Staatsgerichtshof ended with a preliminary success for the Reich's government. Schmitt was now in constant consultation with Bilfinger and Jacobi. On 1 August his article on 'Die Verfassungsgemäßheit der Bestellung eines Reichskommissars für das Land Preußen' [The constitutionality of appointing a Reich commissar for the state of Prussia] was published.[33] In it, Schmitt mobilizes two arguments in favour of the Preußenschlag: first, he doubts the legality of the dismissed Braun caretaker government, which had been able to stay in power only with the help of a change in the standing orders. In this context, Schmitt speaks of a political abuse of the premium associated with being in power and of a 'process resembling a *coup d'état*'.[34] And, second, referring to Thuringia, a state held by the National Socialists, he emphasizes the duty of the Reich to act against parties that are enemies of the state and to prevent an 'outbreak of open civil war'.[35] What Schmitt denies to Prussia, the employment of dubious legal means in order to prevent the seizure of power by the National Socialists, he justifies in the case of the Reich. The argument regarding the prevention of a National Socialist seizure of power plays a central role in the article. While von Papen stressed the aim of a comprehensive reform of the constitution, the argument about keeping the National Socialists from gaining power became more and more important for Schleicher and the Reich. On 19 July, a day before the Preußenschlag, the *Tägliche Rundschau* had already published an excerpt from *Legality and Legitimacy*, together with a preliminary editorial note: 'Who provides a majority for National Socialism on 31 July . . . puts Germany entirely at the mercy of this group.'[36]

The elections on 31 July resulted in a catastrophic outcome for both the parliamentary system and rule by presidential decree. The NSDAP doubled its share of the vote. The right-wing parties of the 'Harzburger Front' gained 44 per cent of the vote. The KPD also increased its share, but its hopes for a shift to the left were disappointed. The parliament was again unable to form a government. But rule by presidential decree had also lost its feeble supporting base. Retrospectively, Huber wrote that the concentration of the forces in favour of reform around the 'idea of a "New State"', Schmitt's 'new elite', had now definitively lost the political battle, and the 'forces of youth' took the 'path into extremism'.[37] Schmitt continued to set his hopes on rule by presidential decree, although he was aware of its precarious situation.

On 9 August, von Papen passed a decree against political terror. Hitler insisted on becoming chancellor and radicalized the NSDAP with his message of solidarity with the SA murderers of Potempa. A group of SA members had brutally beaten to death Konrad Pietrzuch, a worker in Upper Silesia with communist leanings, and Hitler had sent a telegram expressing his 'unbounded loyalty' to the condemned murderers in prison.* Despite this turn away from the 'course of legality', there were serious negotiations between Zentrum and NSDAP regarding a possible coalition. Papen responded to the crisis with an economic and social programme, as well as a plan for a national state of emergency [Staatsnotstandsplan]; Schmitt and Huber were involved in the legal formulation of the latter. In mid-August, Schmitt brought his family to Plettenberg, but returned straightaway to Berlin in order to work with Bilfinger and Jacobi on the 'statement of defence'. It was dictated to Miss Büttner. On 23 August there was a meeting in the Ministry of the Interior. *Legality and Legitimacy* was published. Schmitt went to Plettenberg again. He summoned Ernst Rudolf Huber and sent him to Berlin[38] in order to meet with three high-ranking officers (Ott, Böhme and Carlowitz) and agree with them the legal-technical formulation of presidential emergency decrees and the wording of a justificatory appeal to the nation. Huber notified Schmitt by letter about the completion of the task.[39] Schmitt revised the drafts in Plettenberg. The fact that he left it to Huber to be present in person, and himself withdrew to Plettenberg, can be interpreted as an unreasonable demand placed on Huber, as caution on his part, or as paralysis.[40] The legally problematic core of the plan for a state of emergency was that it provided arguments that justified another dissolution of the Reichstag and so provided a justification for 'new elections to the Reichstag to be postponed beyond

---

* See the account in Ian Kershaw, *Hitler: Hubris 1889–1936*, London, 1998, pp. 381–3. The murders happened one and a half hours after the emergency decree had been passed. Papen eventually caved in to National Socialist pressure and turned the death penalties for five members of the group that had carried out the attack into life imprisonment. They were released under a Nazi amnesty in March 1933.

the constitutionally stipulated two months for an indefinite period of time'.[41] The plan contained a centralization of police powers as well as a possible prohibition of the NSDAP and KPD.[42] This state of emergency plan received its placet on Hindenburg's country estate, Neudeck, on 30 August. The same day, Schmitt went to Berlin again. Huber continued to stay with him, and soon Bilfinger would join them. Schmitt formulated five alternative justifications for the dissolution of the Reichstag. However, von Papen did not implement the plan immediately. The efforts to form a coalition between the Zentrum and the NSDAP failed, but the meeting of the Reichstag on 12 September took an unexpected turn. Strategic deviations from the standing orders and the cooperation of KPD and NSDAP led to a clear vote of no confidence by which the Reichstag wanted to avoid its dissolution. 'Ott came around afterwards, very agitated. Anger over the stupid Papen', Schmitt noted in his diary (12 September 1932).[43] Rule by presidential decree urgently needed some success at that point. In a long letter about *Legality and Legitimacy*, Ulrich Scheuner wrote: 'The authority of a government is either based on plebiscite or on a big success. . . . This is ultimately the issue today as well, no matter whether the letter of the constitutional law is adhered to or not. . . . When mistakes are made in this respect, or success doesn't come, a new legitimacy will form: that of a revolutionary uprising of the masses.'[44] The legally controversial vote in the Reichstag meant a loss of authority for Papen, which put him on the defensive and forced him to abandon the plan for a state of emergency. With this course of events, Schmitt's efforts had also failed.

In mid-September, Schmitt spoke with Adenauer about his appointment in the city hall at Cologne and quickly returned to Berlin. The *Münchener Neueste Nachrichten* (Rosskopf) claimed that he had been ordered to work out a new constitution.[45] Schmitt noted in his diary: 'At 7 Ott arrived, meant to come to Papen on Tuesday, wants draft for a constitution, I was scared by the task, but felt secure and competent in matters of state law' (25 September 1932). Soon he spoke with Papen in the Reich's Chancellery. 'Papen friendly, polite, modest, agreeable, Gayl and Kettner are meant to be involved after all. I was inwardly completely indifferent' (28 September 1932). With Minister of the Interior Gayl, the plans for a new constitution were in the hands of someone representing restorative ideologies that Schmitt rejected. He set to work only hesitatingly. 'An hour at my desk, but in despair and tired, ridiculous that I am meant to construct a new constitution, then more hopeful again' (29 September 1932). The new constitution was an impossible project because the dissolution of the Reichstag triggered new elections. Because of the trial at the Staatsgerichtshof [constitutional court], von Papen had to give up the idea of postponing new elections envisaged by the state of emergency plan, as well as his plans for constitutional reform which, after all, had been his central project. Schmitt's great plans – the state of emergency plan and the new constitution – had run aground on the Märkischer Sand.[*]

---

[*] Sandy areas of the Mark Brandenburg. The German formulation is 'verlaufen im märkischen Sand', playing on the German for 'to fizzle out' = im Sand verlaufen.

At the Staatsgerichtshof

After 20 July, Schmitt ascended to the role of Weimar's 'crown jurist' during the rule by presidential decree. Who else would have argued for years consistently in favour of the dictatorial powers of the Reichspräsident? Schmitt was now in permanent discussions with Bilfinger and Jacobi regarding the line of defence to be taken at the trial,[46] and he also continued to involve the young Huber.[47] Until September, the Reich's lawyers were occupied with developing a strategy for the trial. The original 'system-destroying intentions',[48] which came close to a *coup d'état*, had to be denied, and those aspects in line with the constitution had to be emphasized. The defence also had to follow von Papen's weak line of argument and to strengthen it. Despite this, the defendants saw the prospects for the trial in a positive light. However, von Papen's defeat of 12 September had changed the mood in the Reichstag.[49]

On 9 October, Schmitt travelled to Leipzig. The trial 'Prussia vs. the Reich' took place at the Staatsgerichtshof between 10 and 17 October. Schmitt was now the most important lawyer of the Reich in the most important political trial to take place in the Weimar Republic. It was the peak of his public influence before 1933. The protocols of the proceedings display a tension between collegial politeness and the partiality and polemics of an advocate. The conflict over the substance of the matter was contained by the dignity of the court, the importance of the trial and the role of the lawyer as a legal expert. Schmitt's pleas began with the 'declaration of illegality' [Illegalitätserklärung]: the battle against the 'National Socialist movement' had not been intended as an 'insulting equation with the Communist Party'.[50] His various statements emphasized again and again the priority of the Reich and the role and size of Prussia within it, the special dangers of 'divergent politics',[51] the Prussian state's 'duty of loyalty' and the 'spirit [Sinn] of the constitution'.[52] Schmitt invoked a potential confrontation 'where the Schupo* shoots at the Reichswehr'.[53] The fathers of the constitution, Schmitt declared, had 'intentionally created the exceptional degree of power [Machtfülle] inherent in Article 48';[54] its positivist interpretation was too narrow. The gaps in the law were no space outside the law;[55] in terms of constitutional theory, the 'spirit' [Sinn] of the constitution constituted the law. The federation and the states were not on an equal footing because a state was only a 'member' of the German Reich. The 'mutual penetration of the powers of the Reich and the states'[56] had to be understood in proper terms. The Reich depended on the executive of the states. With the 'creation of a substitute organization [Ersatzorganisation]',[57] the Reich had selected a soft variant from the available possibilities of how to take commissary power, one that did not abolish the state along with the government. On the contrary: Prussia's existence, Schmitt argued, was better secured through the Reich's intervention against a legally questionable caretaker government which

---

* Schupo = Schutzpolizei. Literally 'protection police'. Expression for the police units under state, rather than the Reich's, control.

was burdened with the 'odium of 12 April' [i.e., the devious use of the standing orders of parliament].[58] Huber spoke of an 'illegal caretaker government'.[59] In his closing argument, Schmitt brought the military myth surrounding the Reichspräsident into play:

> What happened in 1866? A military intervention [Bundesexekution] of the German Confederation against Prussia. And our Reichspräsident stood on the side of Prussia as a Prussian officer and fought against this military intervention. If that very same man, who defended Prussia against an intervention back then, now is forced to take the decision in favour of an intervention by the Reich against that same Prussia, this must be seen as an important and astounding fact.[60]

The Reichspräsident's act of the Preußenschlag had also been a means of preserving 'the dignity and honour of Prussia'. On 20 July, the Reich, Schmitt said, had acted as 'the custodian and the guardian' of Prussia's honour, defending it against the party political state.[61]

Schmitt's diary entries show vast mood swings.[62] He was angry about Hermann Heller.[63] He was plagued by nightmares and wanted to give up his mandate. 'Honour and burden of the Reich, ridiculous such a trial, shameful for myself' (15 October 1932). Schmitt was not satisfied with his closing argument either. 'Heller ran riot, protested against the insults from Braun and Severing, shouting hysterically, etc. Depressed and sad, full of nausea, feeling of being the defeated' (17 October 1932). On 19 October, a debriefing took place in Berlin. Schmitt agreed a substantial fee. There was a reception at Hindenburg's Chancellery. Schmitt then travelled to

'Hermann Heller sends his congratulations on the more than deserved honour bestowed on you by Minister Göring' – postcard from Hermann Heller sent from his Spanish exile, 17 July 1933

Braunschweig and Hildesheim, spoke with Hans Kelsen in Cologne (who agreed with the 'Reich')[64] about the planned appointment of Schmitt (22 October 1932), and also met with Günther Krauss and Huber. On 24 October he was back in Berlin, and the following day he travelled to Leipzig for the pronouncement. 'We were very sad.' 'Triumphant cries of the Jewish press' (26 October 1932). In Berlin, opinions were different. Schmitt had fulfilled expectations and continued to be in demand as a constitutional advisor. The judgment of 25 October meant a 'division' of Prussian state power and a significant paralysis of the reinstated Prussian government, but also a weakening of the rule by presidential decree in the form of the recognition, in principle, of the right of judicial review. From now on, dictatorial power could no longer be exercised in as unlimited and unrestrained a fashion as before. The Reichspräsident now had to reckon with a judicial discussion of his actions, and as a consequence Hindenburg increasingly returned to the principle of 'formal legality'.[65]

After the court's ruling in Leipzig

After the ruling of the court in Leipzig, Schmitt found himself in an extremely strange situation. On the one hand, he had finally found 'access to the powers that be' and had been able publicly to satisfy his great ambitions. On the other hand, he experienced defeats and was faced with the question of whether he should just, at that moment, at the high point of his influence, leave the capital of the Reich in order to return to the Rhineland and take up a post at the University of Cologne. Why had he come to Berlin in the first place? Had it not been the maelstrom of politics that had tempted him to apply his constitutional theory in practice? Should he just abandon the networks which he had established with so much effort from 1928 onwards? Did his political consciousness allow him to do that? The offer of a chair in Cologne had already been made in August.[66] 'Duška thinks I should stay in Berlin' (TB, 7 August 1932). Schmitt negotiated the salary for the post in Cologne with the Prussian Ministry of Culture: 'Excellent offer (similar to Kelsen), one obviously wants me to leave Berlin' (8 August 1932). His former lover, Margot, did not want to see him leave Berlin. 'As far as I can see, you should not give in and leave [das Feld räumen]. Who would then draft the new constitution?',[67] she writes with some irony, later hinting at reservations she had regarding Schmitt's political ambitions. A quick move in time for the winter term was out of the question because of the trial, which is why Schmitt also spoke, in Cologne, to Adenauer about delaying his move until the summer term 1933. On 5 October, Schmitt signed an agreement on his acceptance of the appointment. Kelsen and Schmitt, the two theoretical antipodes, assured each other of their mutual cooperation: 'I am hopeful and optimistic', Kelsen wrote, 'that our meeting will have the effect of making you accept the offer from Cologne. I am convinced that we can get on very well with each other on a personal level, despite all scholarly differences.'[68] Schmitt replied immediately, saying that he would strive to do the faculty 'proud and to work together with the faculty and each and every of its members in all collegiality and harmony'.[69] After the trial in Leipzig had ended, he told the undersecretary [Ministerialrat] Windelband[70] and the university that he had accepted the offer from Cologne.[71] Kelsen, as dean of the faculty, thanked Schmitt immediately.[72] Schmitt's letter of appointment from Cologne is dated 6 December, meaning that it was impossible to find a replacement for him in Berlin for the winter term. Thus, he continued teaching at the Handelshochschule during the winter term 1932–3: Monday to Friday state law, as well as a 'tutorial in international law' and a 'seminar on constitutional theory'.[73] The trustee of the Hochschule thanked Schmitt: 'We are aware that your teaching has furthered the reputation of the Handelshochschule immensely.'[74] Schmitt was attracted to Cologne by the salary (15,000 Reichsmark basic salary plus 12,000 Reichsmark 'Kolleggarantie'),* the university as such, the competition with Kelsen, academic leisure, renewed influence as a teacher and the prospect of gaining distance from his chaotic years in the 'maelstrom' of Berlin. He probably also had in mind that this could be a stepping stone towards a post at the university in Berlin, the final goal of every 'crown jurist'. However, the move to Cologne distanced Schmitt from politics. If he had been nothing but a 'crown jurist', he would never have moved to Cologne, despite the higher salary. On 21 November, Hensel congratulated him on the appointment:[75] 'In the long term, you are meant to be at a large university and must have pupils.' Nevertheless, the decision is a surprise, despite Schmitt's roots in the Rhineland. Bonn had been the more important university. Wasn't this a step backwards?

The trial in Leipzig attracted enormous attention. For the reputation of the government, its interpretation for propaganda purposes was also important. However, as one of the lawyers of the Reich's defence, Schmitt had to hold back in public. He therefore left the publication of a booklet on the trial to Huber.[76] By telephone, he again asked him to come to Berlin. Huber, at first, feared severe difficulties regarding his faculty position in Bonn. However, on Schmitt's initiative, the State Ministry requested that Huber be placed temporarily in Berlin and also paid him for that period of time, so that he could write his booklet *Reichsgewalt und Staatsgerichtshof* in close vicinity to the government. Schmitt observed all this not entirely without envy. In his diary, he noted: 'Again and again the same fate. Others publish my books.' From Düsseldorf, he would soon confirm to Huber by post that his treatise was 'absolutely brilliant'.[77] Huber thanked Schmitt for the time in Berlin and for his support in writing the treatise,[78] which had been produced upon Schmitt's initiative and in close cooperation with him; it carries signs of co-authorship. Schmitt noted in his diary: 'Sad that Huber publishes the treatise on Leipzig. It is good and will be effective' (3 December 1932). Bilfinger wrote to Schmitt that Huber had 'solved the difficult task in an incredibly short span of time and in almost exemplary fashion. Of all your pupils, he really is the pick of the litter.'[79]

---

* Additional payment for teaching duties, etc. Such additional payments for full professors were common practice.

'I am convinced that we can get on very well with each other on a personal level, despite all scholarly differences' – Hans Kelsen to Carl Schmitt in a letter of 7 October 1932

Huber's short treatise is a fundamental critique of the Leipzig ruling. It emphasizes, in 'state ethical' terms, the basic point that the 'front of the political parties of the federal state' had neglected the duties of the state, and that the Staatsgerichtshof had practised 'politics in judiciary form' while under pressure from the side of 'radically federalist' ideologies and the ideology of a judiciary state, and had arrogated the role of the 'guardian of the constitution' to itself. Using Schmitt's categories, Huber's analysis, moving beyond the scope of the individual trial in Leipzig, aims at the tension within constitutional theory between the Reich's powers and the Staatsgerichtshof. He fundamentally denies the Staatsgerichtshof any competence in such political questions.

Schmitt gave three lectures in November – during the time that Huber was working on his treatise – which touched upon the most recent events. On 4 November he spoke, together with his friend von Schnitzler, at the general meeting of the Verein zur Wahrung der Interessen der chemischen Industrie [Association for the Protection of the Interests of the Chemical Industry] on the topic of 'Konstruktive Verfassungsprobleme' [Problems in the construction of the constitution]. In accordance with the impression left by the Leipzig trial, he painted a stark picture of a 'party-political federal state', for which the 'federal independence of the individual states is to a large extent no more than a base' (SGN, p. 59) for party politics, and in which the distinction between state and society, this 'precondition for any reasonable order and freedom', vanishes in the general process of politicization. As in 1930,[80] Schmitt argues against fundamental constitutional reform and defends the extensive 'exploitation of the legal possibilities' of

Article 48 as a form of 'loyal resistance and an indispensable adjustment to what the state necessarily had to do' (SGN, p. 63). In the evening of the day of the speech, he had discussions in a restaurant with Jünger and Popitz. Then, on 10 November, Schmitt gave a talk on 'Das Leipziger Urteil' [The Leipzig ruling] in front of many prominent figures at the Deutsche Gesellschaft 1914 e.V.* According to a newspaper report, the talk criticized the 'swarms of enemies' of the Reich within the 'party-political federal state' and the argumentative 'arsenal of Bavarian federalism'. The fact that the Staatsgerichtshof awarded 'the moral high ground to Prussia' ['Preußen moralisch recht' gab] was merely proof that it arrogated to itself a political function and judiciary power which belonged only to the Reichspräsident. Schmitt presented theses from Huber's treatise. Heinrich Triepel and Hans Peters contradicted Schmitt in the ensuing discussion.[81] Smend left before the discussion, but announced that he would send a letter with his 'objections'.[82]

On 17 November von Papen resigned as chancellor but continued in office in an executive function. The reform of the constitution had been his central aim. Schmitt was now able to declare himself more openly in favour of a pragmatic 'crisis management without constitutional reform'.[83] He discussed Huber's treatise with him, read Jünger's *The Adventurous Heart*, and travelled to Düsseldorf, where, on 23 November, he gave a talk titled 'Gesunde Wirtschaft im starken Staat' [A healthy economy in a strong state] at the members' meeting of the Langnamverein. This talk praised the Preußenschlag, in glowing terms, as the first measure taken against the faulty design of the Weimar Constitution, and it argued explicitly against a 'confusion of economy and politics' (SGN, p. 80)† and for the political handling of the new 'means of power and possibilities'. Schmitt declared his opposition to a comprehensive reform of the constitution at that point in time. 'First of all, we need a strong state that is in a position to act and is up to the great tasks it needs to face. Once we have such a state, we can create new organizations, new institutions, new constitutions' (SGN, p. 83).

On 26 November, Schmitt was welcomed by the caretaker chancellor von Papen in his office. Schleicher and Gayl, Ott and Marcks were also present. Papen asked for an 'exposé on the situation of constitutional law [über die verfassungsrechtliche Lage]'. Schmitt conferred with Jünger regarding the Reichswehr [the Reich's army] and corrected his Langnam talk. For the time being, he did not publish his views on the Leipzig ruling. However, some points he integrated into an article on 'Die Weiterentwicklung des totalen Staats in Deutschland' [The further development of the total state in Germany], which he wrote at the end of the year in order to support Schleicher and to prepare for the 'renewed dissolution of the Reichstag'. Schmitt juxtaposed the pluralist and 'total' party-political

---

* Political club, founded in 1915, which aimed to promote the spirit of 1914 – i.e., a kind of truce across political and ideological divides.
† But see 'Strong State and Sound Economy: An Address to Business Leaders', in Renato Cristi, *Carl Schmitt and Authoritarian Liberalism: Strong State, Free Economy*, Cardiff, 1998, pp. 212–32.

state to the 'qualitatively' total state, which takes hold of film and radio for the purpose of propaganda. These new, technical Machtpositionen des modernen Staates [Power centres of the modern state] he would discuss in more detail in February 1933 in light of the 'new situation'. Schmitt then would argue in favour of the possibility of controlling 'radio broadcasting and cinema' through either a 'monopoly' or 'censorship' (VRA, p. 369), and thus of homogenizing the population politically. In the modern mass media, Schmitt recognized instruments of power that are easier to use than the economy or the constitution for the purpose of the reconstitution of statehood. However, at the end of December his critique of the pluralist party-political state still aimed entirely at a critique of the Reichstag.

Weimar's last chance

The national elections on 6 November 1932 brought significant losses for the NSDAP, but confirmed yet again that the parliamentary system of the Reich was unable to form a government. In addition, a rise in votes for the KPD made the party a strong junior partner on the road to destruction. At that point, Hindenburg spoke with the parties about the NSDAP participating in government. Against the rule by presidential decree, the Zentrum declared its support for such a participation and for Hitler becoming chancellor. However, Hitler demanded an enabling act and rejected the formation of a majority government, causing Hindenburg to decide against him again. Horst Michael made Hitler's correspondence with Hindenburg available to Schmitt at the time.[84] Papen considered a second plan for a state of emergency; however, it was turned down at the planning stage as impossible to execute by the Reichswehr. In the absence of any parliamentary alternatives, Hindenburg ordered von Papen to put together a cabinet once more. Schmitt was invited for breakfast with Papen.[85] However, Papen's ministers now sided with General Kurt von Schleicher, the Reich's minister of defence and a strategic eminence in the background, whereupon the latter was appointed as chancellor by Hindenburg on 2 December. Schmitt, together with Ott, drew up a proclamation for the Reichspräsident, which in the event, however, was not used. Suddenly, Schmitt was no longer 'in demand by the chancellor-general',[86] and was banished from the innermost circle of power.

Schleicher emerged from Papen's shadow with a plan for a coalition government that would cut across all parties and be based on a majority gained through mutual tolerance. The plan aimed specifically at dividing the NSDAP, and in particular wanted to win both the party's Strasser wing and the trade unions for rule by presidential decree. But at that moment, Strasser, because of conflicts with Hitler, suddenly resigned all his offices, and the rapprochement with the trade unions failed on account of the oppositional course taken by the SPD. The Reichstag decided against the chancellor and for the president of the Reichsgericht [Supreme Court of the Reich] as the 'deputy' [Stellvertretung] of the Reichspräsident, a fact which Schmitt[87] interpreted as another symptom of the self-abolition of parliamentarism and called a bad step towards the 'de-militarization of the executive top'.[88] Papen undermined Schleicher's efforts by seeking an understanding with Hitler by himself and agreeing a 'duumvirate' with him. Papen had Hindenburg's support for the further elaboration of such a system with two chancellors. The Reichspräsident shifted his allegiance once more to Papen's side. At the same time, Schleicher was seeking Hindenburg's support for a third state of emergency plan, including the dissolution of the Reichstag and the delay of new elections.[89]

After 3 December, Schmitt found himself in an astounding situation. He was the confidant of the confidants (Marcks, Ott); a moment ago, von Papen had entrusted him with representing the Reich at the Leipzig trial and with drafting a new constitution, and now, with Schleicher becoming chancellor, he was excluded from the corridors of power. Even more humiliating was the fact that Schleicher simply did not contact Schmitt, despite the fact that the latter believed he had the instruments with which one could fight extremist parties and negative majorities! One of the reasons for this sudden fall from grace, or temporary farewell to power, might have been a disapproval of Schmitt's draft by Hindenburg. Schmitt simply noted in his diary: 'Completely through with Hindenburg' (7 December 1933). The sudden downfall proves how weak the position of the 'crown jurist' was, even with Schleicher. He was enlisted and needed only 'occasionally'. Schmitt found it hard to assess his future options and was depressed.

On 23 December he travelled to Plettenberg. He went on excursions and spent New Year's Eve with Dr Schranz in Siedlingshausen. At the beginning of January he went to visit Koellreutter in Jena and then, back in Berlin, plunged himself further 'into the battle'.[90] He provided the minister of the interior, Franz Bracht, with 'valuable material'[91] for a speech and again gave talks at the Reichspostzentralamt [central administrative office of the postal service]. In mid-January he met with some high-ranking officers: 'Very nice conversation about the humanity of the soldier with Blomberg', his diary says (15 January 1933). On 18 January he presented the quickly drafted lecture on the occasion of the annual celebration of the foundation of the Reich, which bore the title 'Bund und Reich als Probleme des öffentlichen Rechts' [The federation and the Reich as problems of public law]. The ceremonial address at the Handelshochschule was framed by the overture from an opera by Gluck, the national anthem [Deutschlandlied] and the Hohenfriedberger military march. While Smend,[92] speaking at the university next door and arguing explicitly against Schmitt, defended the political traditions of bourgeois citizens [Bürgertum] against the bourgeois, Schmitt criticized the burden of the states [Länder] on the state and the federation and defended the primacy of the 'Reich'. At that point in time, he was trying to gain direct influence once more. When Schleicher made a final attempt at implementing the state of emergency plan and thus at preventing the appointment of Hitler, Schmitt tried to convince him, by means of a 'paper' he sent indirectly through Horst Michael and Bracht, to choose a juridically less controversial way of proceeding – i.e., non-acceptance of a vote of no confidence and confirmation of his government by the Reichspräsident. As an alternative to the plan for a national state of emergency, this option would have had the advantage of smelling less of a breach of the constitution and thus of taking into account Hindenburg's worry about a possible indictment of the president.[93] But Schleicher held on to the old state of emergency plan. Now, Schmitt also felt 'side-lined' (26 January 1933) by Ott.[94]

Schleicher's plan, probably the last chance for survival for the Weimar Republic,[95] met with broad opposition from the parties, among the public, and from Hindenburg. Following some preliminary talks, Hindenburg refused to support the plan on 28 January, and thus the last presidential regime had failed. With Hindenburg's shift towards Papen, Hitler now also became acceptable to him. In negotiations with von Papen, Hitler succeeded in securing the Prussian Ministry of the Interior, to be given to Göring, and on 30 January he also blackmailed Hindenburg into agreeing to another dissolution of the Reichstag. With the appointment of Hitler, Hindenburg handed the office of chancellor to a declared enemy of the constitution. Schmitt took note of that fact in his diary, quoting Erich Marcks:[96] 'The myth of Hindenburg has come to an end. Horrible situation. Schleicher steps down; Papen or Hitler will be next. The old man has gone mad.' The entry also referred to Schmitt himself, because he had banked on this 'myth', although he recognized the 'wealth of power' [Machtfülle] associated with the office.

Today we can be almost certain that Schmitt rejected the handing over of power to Hitler, or his 'Machtergreifung' [seizing of power], and that he wanted to prevent it. Before 1933 he did not opt for the 'total state of the Führer', although he certainly did not opt for Weimar's liberalism and parliamentarism either. The political evaluation of the rule by presidential degree is a large question. Was it, to use Schmitt's words, a 'delayer' or an 'unintentional accelerator'? This question needs to be discussed separately for the various chancellors. Alternatives, such as Papen or Schleicher, reform of the Reich or plan for a national state of emergency, are too simple. Schmitt supported all of the chancellors under the rule by presidential decree. However, he had fallen out with the Zentrum, and hence Brüning and the leader of the parliamentary faction, the Prelate Kaas, were dismissive towards him. On many questions, Schmitt was politically closer to Schleicher than to Papen. He shared, for instance, the former's reservations about comprehensive constitutional reform and his preference for a national state of emergency plan in the crisis of 1932. But personally he was closer to Papen. He kept an open mind about the possibility of a comprehensive reconstruction of the constitution. The role Schmitt played in the context of the Preußenschlag practically forced him into the direction of a reform of the Reich. Although he was a kind of 'crown jurist' for Papen, he no longer played a role among the actors in the last battle against the looming seizure of power by the National Socialists. His plan for a state of emergency was not implemented. With Schleicher as chancellor, he was in the end no longer in demand. These deep disappointments and personal wounds are not to be neglected as psychological reasons for his jumping ship to Hitler. The most influence he exerted in connection with the Leipzig trial. Only there did he play a prominent role. It would be wrong to claim that he was a heroic 'delayer' of National Socialism,[97] if for no other reason than he lacked the influence for that. His whole constitutional theory aimed at a justification of the rule by presidential decree. But the 'authoritarian state' at the time had neither the force nor the form that would have allowed it to become established as the normal constitution. The authoritarian state was at best a strategic tool for fending off a 'legal revolution'. And with Schleicher, the last of the 'delayers', Schmitt was never in close personal contact. The handing over of power to Hitler was done under the rule by presidential decree. Schleicher paid with his life for his attempts at salvaging the situation. In an article of 1934, Schmitt provided a conditional justification for his murder.

Part III

In the Belly of the Leviathan: Schmitt's Involvement in National Socialism

19

After 30 January 1933

One myth exchanged for another?

At the end of January 1933, Schmitt was faced with a political landscape in ruins. 'The myth of Hindenburg is over', he wrote. He had been disappointed by Schleicher, too. Hitler did not appear a 'charismatic' leader to Schmitt, while the Zentrum wanted to integrate Hitler into a coalition government. Schmitt was publicly attacked by the parliamentary leader of the Zentrum party, Prelate Kaas,[1] for having given juridical support to the rule by presidential decree. On 30 January, Schmitt responded in an open letter, declaring his continuing commitment to the 'spirit' [Sinn] of the constitution; he did not, he claimed, 'relativize state law, but [fought] an abuse which destroys state and constitution'.[2] In the evening of 30 January he was in bed with influenza. He asked Wilhelm Stapel to visit and discussed Prussia with him over some red wine. It was a 'very inspiring conversation'.[3] Schmitt was very depressed in these days. His personal defeat and the defeat of Schleicher both contributed to this. The battle against Hitler had failed. And what kind of future did he have under Hitler?

Schmitt's first reaction to the appointment of Hitler was a radio conversation on 1 February with Veit Rosskopf, which was recorded that evening at Schmitt's home. Schmitt emphasized his role as a theoretician. 'I am a theoretician, dear Doctor Rosskopf, a pure academic [Wissenschaftler] and nothing but a scholar.'[4] The positivist doctrine, Schmitt said, was wrong. Right was founded on a meta-positive plane. He himself was nothing but 'an organ of this substantive right [substanzhaften Rechtes] of the concrete people'.[5] As a theoretician, he was seeking the 'connectedness with his own people, the partaking, the participation in the last and most subtle manifestations of its intellectual life [geistigen Lebens]'.[6] In the conversation, Schmitt also referred to his critique of party politics and mentioned that the central problem was a reform of the Reich.

The teaching term was still not over, and Schmitt continued to give his weekly presentations at the Reichspostzentralamt [central office of the postal service]. Before his move to Cologne, his pupils Karl Scheidemann, Ruth Büttner and Johann Kendziora did their viva voce examinations with him in February. In the preliminary remark to the published version of Kendziora's thesis, on *Der Begriff der politischen Partei im System des politischen Liberalismus* [The concept of a political party in the system of political liberalism], it says: 'In the meantime, the political reality in Germany has drawn the consequences from the theses on political parties and the party state expounded in this work.'[7] The trust of the council of the Handelshochschule thanked Schmitt for his 'excellent teaching over many years'. Schmitt replied, saying 'how extraordinarily difficult' it was for him to leave.[8] In those days, he frequently met with Ernst Jünger and his circle – e.g., Ott, Popitz and the painter Werner Gilles. At Marcks's he made the acquaintance of Colonel-General Hammerstein, who told him about the sequence of events at the appointment of Hitler. Schmitt dictated work to Miss Büttner. At that point, Schmitt had not decided to back National Socialism. However, his article on 'Weiterentwicklung des totalen Staates in Deutschland' [The further development of the total state in Germany], which appeared in the February edition of the *Europäische Revue*, was at once interpreted and criticized by the Catholic *Hochland* as expressing support for the 'Leviathan' state.[9] At a farewell celebration held at the Politische Gesellschaft [Association for Politics] in Berlin, Schmitt gave a lecture on 'Bund, Staat, Reich' [Federation, state, Reich], in which he criticized the initiators of the Preußenschlag, von Papen and Schleicher. The lecture shows that Schmitt was at that point already moving away from Weimar. The principle of the federal state, he said, had made the dualism between Prussia and the Reich foundational and had threatened the unity of the state. In light of this, the statist attack on Prussia had been justified, but Schmitt now added a further question: 'Who actually is this Reich which takes hold of Prussia?'[10] Essentially, it had only been Prussian statism that had tried to defend the state – i.e., the Reich – against Prussia – i.e., one of its federal states. But this, by itself, was not enough to provide integration for a national state. 'This Schleicher–Papen experiment quite simply did not succeed',[11] was now, somewhat surprisingly, Schmitt's conclusion on 22 February 1933, and he emphasized: 'The Reich exists as a postulate.'[12] But whether the NSDAP would succeed in realizing it in the form of a one-party state remained an open question. On 22 February, just one month before the Enabling Act, Schmitt, it seems, would not have had any objections to the NSDAP's success in this.

Schmitt gave a radio talk on *Machtpositionen des modernen Staates* [Positions of power of the modern state] (6 March 1933). The looming move to Cologne alone would have accounted for his ambivalent mood at the time.

The National Socialists were quick at establishing facts. Hitler obtained the dissolution of the Reichstag, and new elections were to take place in March. Further decrees produced an atmosphere of repression and fear. After the Reichstag fire in the evening of 28 February the decree 'For the Protection of People and State' created a state of emergency and effectively led to the prohibition of the KPD and the SPD press. At the elections for the Reichstag on 5 March, in which Schmitt did not cast his vote,[13] the NSDAP gained only 43.9 per cent of the vote, despite various manipulations. However, the result was, together with that for the 'Kampffront

21 March 1933, 'Day of Potsdam': to the left of Hindenburg, wearing an SA uniform, is Herbert Gutjahr, one of the activists in the book burning and later Schmitt's assistant.

Schwarz–Weiß–Rot',* just about good enough to create an absolute majority. Schmitt spoke at the Leuna factory in front of executive personnel. His judgment of Hitler was ambiguous. It was, he said, as if one were in the jungle: 'You don't know whether he is a dove or a snake' (TB, 20 February 1933). On the 'Day of Potsdam', on 21 March, a false reconciliation with the bourgeoisie was staged.† On 23 March, as expected, the Enabling Act followed. All members of the Reichstag, except for those from the SPD (and, of course, those of the already crushed KPD, whose members had been excluded or imprisoned), voted in favour. It was a second 'legal revolution'. Following the executive, the parliament now also gave Hitler dictatorial powers. In response, Schmitt immediately agreed with Otto Liebmann to produce an article for the *Deutsche Juristen-Zeitung*, which he wrote the following day; it highlights the revolutionary significance of the law.[14]

Schmitt's article does not mention any legal reservations and expresses in all clarity that the government is now installed as the new legislature,

---

* Electoral alliance of DNVP, Stahlhelm (the organization of soldiers who fought in the Great War) and the Landbund (farmers' organization). It was founded on 11 February 1933, and this was the only election in which it took part.
† The ceremonial opening of the Reichstag, in the presence of Hindenburg, on the same day that Bismarck had opened the first Reichstag after his foundation of the Reich.

and that it is legitimate as the 'expression of the victory of the national revolution'.[15] But Schmitt also detects an institutional guarantee for the Reichstag in the law, and he asks the question of the 'identity of the current government'.[16] With this, he has in mind on the one hand Hitler's victory over Papen, on the other the 'collaboration of expert ministers' (such as Popitz) who are meant to safeguard the non-party-political and national character of the government. 'Let us make sure', Schmitt concludes, 'that, in the course of abolishing the sophistry of the old party-political state, we do not undermine the legal basis of the new state. Along with the state, state law and the theory of state law will also have to be cleansed and renewed.'[17] The article demonstrates that Schmitt fully recognized the revolutionary character of the developments. Only after the Enabling Act did he take his position on the new ground of legitimacy established by the National Socialists.

Around that time, Schmitt was invited at short notice to the spring meeting of the Vereinigung für Staatswissenschaftliche Forschung [Association for Research in State Theory] in Weimar as a substitute for two other speakers.[18] He was interested in presenting because it allowed him to collect his thoughts. On 27 March, Schmitt travelled to Weimar and gave the opening lecture, on 'Das Staatsnotrecht im modernen Verfassungsleben' [National state of emergency law within the context of the modern constitution]. His formulations were now more clearly intended to make the case for the 'recognition of the national revolution'; he spoke of the 'national state of emergency law'* and a 'jump beyond the limits of legality'. In Weimar, Schmitt declared the Weimar Constitution to be a thing of the past. 'By now we have entered, in legal fashion, the sphere of supra-legality [Überlegalität].'[19] Erwin Jacobi, Johannes Popitz and the Austrian minister of justice, and later chancellor, Kurt Schuschnigg also gave lectures. Schmitt went on a 'Goethe pilgrimage' with Popitz, visiting the Goethe Haus, and at a reception held by the lord mayor he had 'a nice conversation about Jewish university professors with a Nazi' (28 March 1933). He felt a strong tension between the old and new faith, between the ages of Goethe and National Socialism. Schmitt recognized that he would be able to continue in his old role as a theorist of state law only within the parameters of National Socialism. And from Popitz especially he learned a lot about the new masters and the new politics, without yet being fully decided on where he stood. His diary contains increasingly sharp anti-Semitic passages. Former companions, such as the Reich Minister Bracht, invited him to become actively involved in politics as a legal advisor.[20] On a stopover in Jena, Schmitt discussed the situation with Koellreutter. He then travelled on to Munich and sounded out his 'chances for an appointment in Munich' with his old acquaintances Konrad Beyerle and Fritz van

---

* The compound noun 'Staatsnotrecht' implies both 1) 'national state of emergency law' – i.e., the statutes which determine the legal mechanisms under a state of emergency and the conditions under which it can be called – and 2) a reading as 'the right of the state to take emergency measures if necessary', independent of any existing law. In the most general sense, the term denotes the right of the state to use emergency powers independently of the legislature and, if necessary, against existing law.

Calker. In his diary, he noted: 'The lawyer Frank II was an assistant' of Calker (31 March 1933). He was considering which of his contacts might be useful in the new situation. Schmitt's mentor van Calker established his contact with Hans Frank. Thus, his very first contacts with National Socialism were already associated with hopes for an appointment. Hans Frank* was called 'Frank II' because he bore the same name as his father, who had been a lawyer in Munich with a botched professional life. Schmitt met again his old friend Captain Roth,[21] who was a member of one of the extreme right-wing 'bündisch' organizations of soldiers that formed after the Great War. During these days, a fundamental 'change of perception and attitude [Perzeptions- und Gesinnungswandel]'[22] took place in Schmitt. He now concentrated on his affinities rather than his differences with National Socialism. He decided that, as a 'Märzgefallener',† he would now accept the new situation, and do in Rome as the Romans do. He did not have to do this: as a renowned conservative professor, he could have lived relatively undisturbed under National Socialism. But even his article on the Enabling Act was not yet a clear vote for National Socialism. He still argued on the juridical level, without emphatically supporting the developments that took place.

Next, on 31 March, the Preliminary Law for the Coordination of the Federal States [Länder] with the Reich was passed. Schmitt recognized the revolutionary change in the basis of legitimacy that had taken place, and now a new task lay ahead for him. The very same day he received a telegram sent by Popitz from Munich: 'Tomorrow afternoon, five o'clock, meeting at the Ministry [Staatsministerium].' Schmitt also received an official letter from Papen[23] saying that he had been appointed to the commission which was meant to work out the Reich Governors Law. If he wanted to play a role, then now was the time to join in. His unfulfilled ambitions from the period of rule by presidential decree were now combined with new hopes. Schmitt cancelled a planned trip to Rome and returned to Berlin. The 'boycott of the Jews' was already in place at that time. The resulting atmosphere and its effects are described in Lion Feuchtwanger's novel *The Oppermanns*.[24] Schmitt held sharply anti-Semitic views by now, with his friends around the *Deutsches Volkstum* and his hate of Erich Kaufmann being a factor in the equation. Duška also expressed anti-Semitic views. On the morning of 1 April, Schmitt arrived in Berlin from Munich and on the same day spoke with Popitz and Papen, who wanted the Reichsstatthalter [Reich governors] to be placeholders for the monarchy. On 2 April he was already working on a first draft for the Reichsstatthaltergesetz [Reich Governors Law]. Schmitt did not commit himself without reservations: in the evening, he had a conversation with Rosskopf 'on the problem

---

* Hitler's personal legal adviser, even before 1933. Elected to the Reichstag in 1930, later governor-general of Poland. Sentenced at the Nuremberg trials for war crimes and crimes against humanity, he was executed on 16 October 1946.
† 'Märzgefallene', literally: those who fell in March. The expression originally referred to those who died in the March Revolution of 1848 and in the Kapp Putsch of 1920. It was used ironically by the National Socialists for those who joined the NSDAP in 1933 for opportunistic reasons (allegedly) after the March elections.

of Ugolino[25] – the character from Dante's hell – who eats his children'. His concerns were all too justified: the revolution eats its children! Now Schmitt was working with Popitz on the second law. On 3 April, he dictated his draft. He met with Popitz, Frick, Papen, Göring and others in the Ministry of the Interior. 'Frick, the bureaucrat, had concerns, bad impression, craven and knavish. Göring, by contrast, dynamic. Dealt with the matter within a few minutes.' Schmitt was 'inebriated' [berauscht] by the habitus of the soldier: 'maybe the right type for these times' (3 April 1933). Göring's proposal, however, was not accepted, and Schmitt dictated a new draft straightaway. 'The spook of Leipzig is over, . . . Prussia will continue to be an administrative unit' (5 April 1933).

Schmitt moved from Flotowstraße into the Hotel Bristol, Unter den Linden, to stay for a few days. In the evening of 6 April he attended a press reception held by Hitler and Goebbels. 'Looked carefully at both. Hitler like a raging [gierige] bull in the ring. Shocked by his gaze' (6 April 1933). Later, he would remember that Hitler's rhetoric, tried and tested with 'mass audiences', fell to pieces in front of this elite group. 'He simply couldn't reach them, no sparks were flying.'[26] Within the space of three days, Schmitt dictated a booklet, *Das Reichsstatthaltergesetz* [The Reich Governors Law], as part of his work for the commission, and then travelled to Bilfinger and on to Koellreutter. Around the same time he withdrew *The Concept of the Political* from Duncker & Humblot and became an author of the Hanseatische Verlagsanstalt, which had a nationalistic profile.

Schmitt then travelled to the monastery of the Benedictines in Herstelle, visited Romanic churches, finally arriving on 18 April in Cologne, where soon the first copies of his *Das Reichstatthaltergesetz* were delivered. The regime's anti-Semitic intent was already obvious even in those early days. On 1 April, Jewish shops were boycotted. On 7 April, the Law for the Restoration of the Professional Civil Service was passed, in which Frick[27] was also involved. The expulsions and the cut and thrust over university positions began, with an avalanche of appointments and staffing changes.[28] Over the following years, the number of students (in particular of female students) decreased significantly. Although he had not yet joined the party himself, Schmitt now coordinated the party members. Huber practically delivered formal reports to Schmitt: he had explained to Koellreutter that he should join the NSDAP and leave the Staatsrechtslehrervereinigung [Association of State Law Theorists]. Stapel and Günther were on board. Vorwerk and Lohmann were, 'however, still very hesitant', he said.[29] Werner Weber informed Schmitt that he had joined the party and offered to support Schmitt in his plans.[30]

In Cologne, Schmitt met with old friends and disciples, such as Heinrich Oberheid and Günther Krauss. He talked about the 'Judengesetze' [Laws against the Jews] of 7 April with Ernst Forsthoff and Krauss. At one stroke, Schmitt lost all his Jewish colleagues, some of whom he hated, some of whom he personally appreciated. A halt to new party memberships was announced by the Nazis. Schmitt's brother Jupp advised him to join the party. It is difficult for us to say what should be judged more negatively, early or late party membership. Schmitt knew what he was letting himself

'Maybe the right type for these times' – Schmitt about Göring in his diary, 3 April 1933

in for; he saw the National Socialist state as also an anti-Semitic state. He joined the party on 27 April, with effect from 1 May (party member no. 2098860). His increasingly radical views now clearly came to the fore. Werner Becker, one of his closest disciples from his time in Bonn, came to visit from Aachen.[31] 'Big disappointment. He has become a priest in Marburg, told me about the Rabbi, whose beard they cut off, and whom, as a Catholic priest, he wanted to protect. We laughed at him' (26 April 1933). Becker later remembered: 'In 1933, I fell out with him [Schmitt] over the question of anti-Semitism.'[32]

Schmitt attended a 'Führertagung'* at Maria Laach Abbey, where the topic of the discussion was the relationship between German Catholicism and National Socialism. The conference took place under the patronage of Franz von Papen; hence Schmitt's participation did not compromise his work for the commission. It was time for an interpretation of the changeover of power in terms of a 'Reich theology'.[33] During the Weimar Republic, Abbot Ildefons Herwegen and the Maria Laach Abbey were already politically situated to the right of the Zentrum, and they now sounded out possible affinities with the new rulers.[34] However, Herwegen, in 1933–4, also gave shelter to Konrad Adenauer for more than a year. Around the same time, Schmitt began to revise *The Concept of the Political*. This text became his inaugural speech as a party member, while his juridical work for the Reichsstatthaltergesetz [Reich Governors Law]

---

* Conference attended by party leaders. The 'Führertagung' of the NSDAP on 14 Feburary 1926 in Bamberg is often mentioned as the occasion on which Hitler affirmed his authority over the party.

was still a consequence of his involvement in the Preußenschlag and the Leipzig trial. Schmitt at once made his decision to back National Socialism known through articles in National Socialist newspapers and started his new career.

The topography of reasons for Schmitt's decision to back National Socialism

Schmitt's decision to opt for National Socialism was preceded by a loss of alternatives. His Habilitation, *Der Wert des Staates* [The value of the state], mentioned the state, the Church and the individual as possible points of orientation. Romantic subjectivity Schmitt pushed aside. He then constructed religiosity and Church as an alternative to the state, in order soon to relativize and bid farewell to them again while living in a Catholic atmosphere during his time in Bonn. During his years in Berlin, before 1933, the distinction between state and society moved to the foreground. Schmitt now tried to safeguard 'neutral' areas against the pluralist 'party-political federal state'. Faced with the alternatives of the state understood as the 'self-organization of society' or a 'qualitative', 'strong' state, he opted for the latter: the Leviathan or Behemoth. After January 1933, Schmitt was struggling with a decision. What exactly it was that tipped the scales after 23 March cannot be said with certainty. But various motives and reasons can be established, though Schmitt was not necessarily aware of all of these as influencing his course of action. For some time he certainly wavered in his decision, and on occasion he had reservations about it and regretted it. What influenced his deliberations? We can identify some of his motives and reasons, which are listed below in no particular order:

1 *The argument regarding social history*: The time of the bourgeoisie and its political form is past! The 'state of the twentieth century' has to be constituted differently!

2 *The anti-liberal argument*: National Socialism puts into practice my concept of an authoritarian, anti-liberal leader democracy [Führerdemokratie], which openly distinguishes between friend and enemy.

3 *The nationalist argument*: As a 'national revolution', National Socialism has the legitimacy of 'German' resistance to the 'victorious parties' of 1918 on its side!

4 *The critique of pluralism*: The 'party-political state' divides the 'unity' of the people's will!

5 *The critique of federalism* ('*Preußenschlag argument*'): The independence of the federal states, and in particular the dualism between Prussia and the Reich, weakens the unity of the Reich to the extent that it becomes ungovernable!

6 *The argument of order*: Today, a civil war can only be avoided with the help of National Socialism! National Socialism no longer represents a party-political force favouring civil war!

7 *The patriotism argument*: We must present a picture of national loyalty to the world!
8 *The argument of legality*: National Socialism gained power in a legal way! Hitler was appointed by the Reichspräsident and given emergency powers by the Reichstag!
9 *The argument of legitimacy*: The National Socialist leader state [Führerstaat] has democratic and plebiscitary legitimacy! It is my duty to represent it as its advocate!
10 *His personal disappointment*: Hindenburg failed! We need another myth!
11 *Personal revenge*: Schleicher dropped me in the end! Papen was more faithful and called on me again! He should be in charge!
12 *The aspect of charisma*: Hitler is a charismatic leader! So are Göring and Frank!
13 *The social argument*: Hitler will create a welfare state which has plebiscitary legitimacy!
14 *The argument of the economy state*: We need a new state socialism! Only a fascist state will assert the primacy of politics over the economy!
15 *The taming argument*: I must help to avoid what would be worse!
16 *The argument for reform*: I have ideas for legal policies for a one-party state!
17 *The romanticist utopia of homogeneity*: Germany must become one great community again!
18 *The attitude of the Zentrum party*: Prelate Kaas and the Zentrum have arranged themselves with the National Socialist situation for the sake of the Reich Concordat* and have granted emergency powers to Hitler!
19 *The argument regarding Church politics*: The Church must protect its institutions and find a modus vivendi!
20 *The argument of authority*: As a functional elite, jurists must support the state and be loyal to it!
21 *The opportunistic argument*: It isn't all that bad! The others go along with it as well!
22 *The career argument*: I want to climb higher!
23 *The missing alternative*: As a German jurist, I can only work in Germany! I cannot emigrate!
24 *The argument of curiosity*: Curiosity is legitimate! I want to see firsthand what is going to happen!
25 *The argument of hubris*: I am a (great, irreplaceable) German jurist! Only I will be able to sort things out!
26 *The Kairos or Fortuna argument*: The situation is as it is! And now one must act upon it!
27 *The Picaro argument*:[35] I am an 'intellectual adventurer', an ironic player! The tedium of life is only endurable if one elevates it to the status of a play!

---

* The Reich Concordat between the Holy See and the Third Reich was signed on 20 July 1933 and was meant to protect the rights of the Catholic Church in Germany. It was, however, soon violated by the Third Reich.

28 *The narcissistic argument*: I am the greatest! All the world should see it and say it!
29 *The feeling of resentment*: Everyone disregards and betrays me! Now I shall fight back!
30 *The argument of foresight*: My wife is ill! I need a higher income for myself and my family!
31 *The argument of friendship*: Friends, such as Oberheid and Popitz, have asked me to collaborate!
32 *The paternalistic argument*: I need more influence within the discipline in order to promote my disciples!
33 *The revisionist argument*: Only National Socialism can effectively undo Versailles and Geneva!
34 *The pan-German idea*: Hitler stands for Austria as a part of the German nation!
35 *The geopolitical argument regarding Central Europe*: We need a reorganization of the larger European space [des Großraums Europa]* under German leadership.
36 *The Machiavellian argument*: In politics, moral inhibitions have only detrimental effects! We are in a state of nature!
37 *The cynical and nihilist argument*: I have tried everything. We did not have the Nazis before! Why not try them?
38 *The argument of prevention*: The world of politics lies in ruins. Run for protection! The evil neighbours are not idling!
39 *The argument of the katechon*: I try to be a delayer of the 'end of politics' and history and to act against those who accelerate the neutralizations and depoliticizations!
40 *The apocalyptic (anti-katechontic) argument*: The world is accursed! Let us accelerate its demise!
41 *The anti-Semitic argument*: The Jews are our misfortune!† One way or another, assimilation must be reversed!
42 *The eschatological argument*: We have to enter into the decisive religious battle at last!

Schmitt had further arguments up his sleeve. On some of them, he remained silent. The religious perspective on National Socialism played hardly any role for him in 1933 when he had to make his decision. Other arguments he ranked very clearly: for instance, he put the 'legitimacy' of the 'Machtergreifung' [seizure of power] above its 'legality'. Schmitt felt that he was living at the turning point between two epochs and opted for an authoritarian reform of the Reich. However, at no point did he fall for Hitler's charisma. The urge for recognition and the curiosity of the lawyer played a role. In 1947, while imprisoned in Nuremberg, he described

---

*   'Großraum' denotes a larger geographical and at the same time hegemonial political unit. In Schmitt's works it is usually not translated, and that practice will be adopted here.
†   'The Jews are our misfortune' was a phrase coined by the historian Heinrich von Treitschke in 1879 in the *Preussische Jahrbücher*. The national socialist weekly newspaper *Der Stürmer*, founded in 1923, printed it at the bottom of the front page of each issue.

himself as 'an intellectual adventurer' (AN, p. 60) who wanted to give 'meaning to phrases' (AN, p. 54), and who had no other stage but the Nazi Reich.[36] He struggled with his resentment: he had fallen out with the 'bourgeois' world. He felt like an outsider and wanted to be an insider for once. He stressed some arguments again and again: thus, he gave great weight to the reform and friendship arguments. In a radio conversation in 1972, he retrospectively analysed his decision to become involved in National Socialism. There, he stressed the significance of the conversations with Popitz, who was a member of the Reich cabinet, as well as the concrete collaboration with Popitz as the result of his legal policy efforts in the service of the 'Reich'. With hindsight, he said: 'Popitz had been my tried and tested friend, over years – a very close friend. And when he telegraphed me: "Tomorrow afternoon, five o'clock, Berlin, State Ministry", I simply followed. But that also was already collaboration with Hitler.'[37] This argument is weak, because Schmitt recognized at once that National Socialism was a 'revolution', and identified it as a kind of caesura even before the Reich Governors Law. With this in mind, the discussion regarding continuities and ruptures is settled: all continuities must be seen within the horizon of a fundamental caesura in the basis of legitimacy. Schmitt put his collaboration into the context of a general decision and general responsibility; he did not delude himself over the fact that he had crossed the Rubicon, leaving the bourgeois Rechtsstaat behind, and he knew that there was no way back into bourgeois scholarship [bürgerliche Wissenschaft]. From the very beginning, Schmitt saw the National Socialist state as also an anti-Semitic state. There were very few others who saw politics from the perspective of fundamental conflicts and battles to quite the same degree. That Schmitt had entered the 'Reich of the nether demons', as Ernst Niekisch put it, and cooperated with a gang of vandals, robbers, murderers and madmen, would soon become apparent.

Changes in Schmitt's personal relationships

Schmitt's relationships with Hugo Ball and Waldemar Gurian, Ernst Robert Curtius, Erich Kaufmann and Hermann Heller ended even before 1933. After 1933, many more paths parted. Eduard Rosenbaum and Kurt Singer, Moritz Julius Bonn and many others had to emigrate. Georg Eisler, Franz Blei and Ludwig Feuchtwanger were the closest of Schmitt's friends whom he lost as a result of his decision in favour of National Socialism, but he also lost his Jewish disciples Albert Hensel, Otto Kirchheimer, Franz Neumann and some others. His pupil from Bonn, Heinrich Rommen, asked Schmitt for advice as to whether he 'still saw possibilities for [him] to work scientifically in Germany'.[38] After two requests from Erwin Jacobi, Schmitt wrote a strongly positive reference for him,[39] and as late as summer 1933 he recommended Albert Hensel, upon his request,[40] albeit with reservations, as his successor to the post at the Handelshochschule in Berlin.[41] Erich Kaufmann, by contrast, he fought relentlessly. Thus, he deleted all references to his work from the 1933 edition of *Political Theology*. Schmitt was heavily involved in Kaufmann's expulsion from the University of Berlin, and on 14 December 1934 he sent a hate-filled and scornful letter against Kaufmann to the Ministry of Culture.[42] At that time, Schmitt's assistant for many years, Ernst Friesenhahn, broke with him.[43] The Protestant theologians Wilhelm Neuß, Erik Peterson and Werner Becker also distanced themselves from Schmitt, as did, more or less, Rudolf Smend, to whom Schmitt had been close for a long time. He even lost many companions in nationalist circles. Wilhelm Stapel remained reserved; Ernst Jünger observed him from a distance for a while, until their friendship was renewed in 1936. Ernst Niekisch became an opponent. Even Schmitt's closest disciple, Ernst Rudolf Huber, broke temporarily (between the end of 1935 and 1938) with him, and kept his distance after 1945. The list goes on. When looking at Schmitt's personal relationships, it becomes clear that he lost many old and close relationships because of National Socialism. He betrayed his former life. An atmosphere of distrustfulness, suspicion and discrimination poisoned his social inter-actions. Along with his friends, Schmitt lost certain options. Plato already considered the correlation between the individual man and the state from the perspective of the formation or deformation of character. For him, the just and the good coincided. The tyrant, ultimately, was an unhappy man. However, worse than the barbarization of the tyrants' own 'souls' is the fate of the persecuted.[44]

The destinies and responses of the victims

Many people broke with Schmitt for political, religious or moral reasons. Wilhelm Neuß and Erik Peterson, for instance, now saw him as an advo-cate of the totalitarian Leviathan and as someone who had done away with the distinction between Church and state. With requests for support, Neuß intentionally tested whether Schmitt was still prepared to distinguish between political and moral reasons and to help persecuted individuals. He first asked Schmitt to help a Jewish art historian.[45] He then sought help for a 'German' acquaintance.[46] Schmitt did not react. In the last letter we have from Konrad Weiß, he also asked Schmitt for support for an acquaint-ance.[47] Franz Blei at first continued to send diplomatically exploring letters from Mallorca, before returning to Vienna and then emigrating to Italy, France, Lisbon and, in 1941, finally the USA, where he died in 1942. Schmitt's last letter is dated 13 January 1933. Blei's last letter to Schmitt, on 17 August 1933, asked, in slightly disrespectful terms: 'What is Jünger up to, and this other bundle of nerves whose name I can't remember right now? . . . Now the name comes back to me: Günther. What is he up to?'[48] In 1940, Blei nevertheless published a portrait of Schmitt, in which he asked almost with amazement:

> How was it possible that this Roman, Rhinelandish, wholly un-Romantic Catholic author of the classical text *Roman Catholicism and Political Form* could succumb to the Leviathan called the state? How could this opponent

of political Romanticism succumb to the political sensationalist story of the frightened petit bourgeois? How could this contemplative, quiet man, who enjoyed his wine and saw humanism realized in the Roman and Christian tradition of his Rhenish homeland, succumb to such noisy rowdyism of Germanness [Berserker-Deutschtum]?[49]

In his attempts to find an answer to these questions, Blei was looking at 'private and personal reasons', at the feeling of being 'disrespected as a person' and at a contempt for the 'mass', at unsatisfied political ambitions and at the seductive influence of the nationalist circles around Ernst Jünger and Albrecht Erich Günther.[50] Blei considered Schmitt's publishing activities from 1933 onwards as a 'sacrifice of intellect' despite his better conscience: 'The man who wrote in *Dictatorship*: "Under the pretext of re-establishing order, unlimited acts of violence are carried out, and what hitherto had been called freedom is now being called revolt", cannot now write in good faith about "the species identity of the German people at one with itself [Artgleichheit des mit sich einigen deutschen Volkes]".'[51] Blei had left Germany early in the summer of 1932. He did not witness Schmitt's leap to National Socialism but had experienced his resentment first-hand. He knew that Schmitt could not possibly have a genuine belief in the National Socialist phrases he used or fail to see their terroristic tendencies.

German Jews had no choice. Many scientists found a home elsewhere, in particular in the USA. Erich Kaufmann and Hans Kelsen were internationally renowned and welcome. Waldemar Gurian, Helmut Kuhn, Otto Kirchheimer and Franz Neumann became pioneers of political science, and were able to use their analyses of the National Socialist dictatorship in comparative research on totalitarianism.[52] Moritz Julius Bonn and Eduard Rosenbaum moved to the London School of Economics. As a 'non-Aryan', Heinrich Göppert was affected by the Nazi policies and Erwin Jacobi lost his chair in Leipzig. The fate of the Landsberg family was particularly tragic. One of the sons died fighting in the Great War. Ernst Landsberg passed away in 1927. Anna, the mother, committed suicide in 1938. Paul, the son, emigrated to Switzerland and later held a professorship in Spain, which he lost in the Civil War, then moved to the Sorbonne in Paris, where, as a German, he was interned by the French at the beginning of the Second World War; he tried to save his wife, but was revealed to the Gestapo and died in Sachsenhausen concentration camp in 1944. Franz Eulenburg, who had brought Schmitt to the Handelshochschule in Berlin, died in Gestapo custody. Georg Eisler emigrated with his family to London in 1934, and then to New York in 1940. In the 1950s he returned to Hamburg. In the summer of 1983, fifty years after Schmitt and Eisler's ways had parted, a telephone conversation took place between them which had a touch of reconciliation about it. Ludwig Feuchtwanger also went into exile. Schmitt's termination of relationships and betrayal of friendships, when it came to his Jewish friends and acquaintances, is striking.

At the turn of 1932, Schmitt still sent his best New Year's wishes to Feuchtwanger. On 12 April 1933 he withdrew *The Concept of the Political* from Duncker & Humblot. 'Between Arnold Bergsträsser and Gerhard Leibholz [two Jewish authors], it [the *Concept* treatise] appears in a false, distorting light' (CSLF, p. 393). Feuchtwanger raised the point that such '"coordination" [Gleichschaltung]' did away with 'the concept of scholarship' (CSLF, p. 394). Soon afterwards, Feuchtwanger had to leave Duncker & Humblot and took up a teaching post and worked as a librarian at the Jewish Lehrhaus [house of teaching] in Munich. In November 1933, Feuchtwanger surprisingly still suggested to Schmitt that he might act as a point of contact in endeavours to secure a new 'status' for Feuchtwanger's 'comrades in faith and race, these sadly divine unlucky fellows punished by God': 'A Reich commissar working with an absolutely reliable Jewish expert and middle man would be needed for the introduction of such a regulation and as the person responsible for it' (CSLF, p. 395). He hoped for Schmitt's support, but enclosed an article on the formation of anti-Semitic myths, which described the image of the Jew as the enemy as a dangerous intellectual primitivization and 'limitation'. Feuchtwanger's only hope for an end to false mythifications lay in the discussions within the Jewish community. 'Can the power of the genuine myths of Ahasverus and Judas be broken?', he asked. 'Is there a force that can turn our fate from one of suffering to one of overcoming the Jewish fate?'[53] Schmitt did not respond to Feuchtwanger's suggestion, nor did he answer a later letter of request.

Even before 1933, Feuchtwanger and Schmitt more or less agreed about the failure of assimilation.[54] Feuchtwanger, like Schmitt, looked at Judaism also as a national identity: as a 'national law' (Heinrich Graetz), a 'manner of life' and a 'specific form' [Sonderart]. He took the position of Jewish 'autonomy',[55] and rejected assimilation as an attempt at 'dissolving the particular nature of Judaism'.[56] After 1933 he expressed his pessimism: 'The events following the Great War, between 1918 and today, not to say anything about those after 1933, deprived the Jews more and more of the possibilities for free initiatives and activities.'[57] Feuchtwanger began to 'search for the nature of Judaism' – for its 'undistorted face' as opposed to the anti-Semitic distortions; he sketched a plan for a 'contemporary account' and 'sociology of modern Jewry' and asked the question of an 'independent Jewish culture' and of 'being able to have an independent culture'[58] [Eigenkulturfähigkeit] under the conditions of National Socialism in Germany. One of his models was Eastern Jewry around 1600. He took a critical view of the process of 'transformations', of 'emancipation and secularization'.[59] However, he also considered a return to the status quo ante as impossible. Rather, the task was a 'purposeful transformation' of Judaism and the protection of its 'future existence' [Zukunftsmöglichkeit] with the help of – and here he followed Buber and Rosenzweig[60] – the 'building blocks' of religion and language.[61] After 1935, Feuchtwanger worked on a comprehensive Jewish history for the Schocken publishing house, which, however, was published only recently, seventy-five years after its author stopped working on it.[62]

In the context of the November pogrom of 1938, Feuchwanger was imprisoned for six weeks in Dachau as a 'protected Jew' [Schutzjude]. He immediately organized his emigration to England and was able to leave

Germany before the outbreak of the war. He stopped publishing at that point. At the end of the war he returned to Germany as a translator for the American army and wrote long letters to his brother Lion, in which he describes his encounters and observations in Bavaria.[63] For some time he also taught re-education courses to German prisoners of war in England, where he died on 17 July 1947 in depressing circumstances. A sad lecture on 'Jüdische Vergangenheit in England und Deutschland' [The Jewish past in England and Germany], which he gave in London in 1942, ended:

> Today, words would still be inappropriate; the events which suffocate our hearts are much too close for us to give a dispassionate account of the collapse of Jewry in Central Europe, which is without parallel. I tend not to explain this catastrophe organically – that is, not to deduce it as a necessary outcome of the development which the coexistence of Judaism and Germanic culture [Deutschtum] took. Most of the Jews in Germany did not really know what they died for. They were the pointless victims of a gruesome and inescapable Moloch.[64]

As to the history of Judaism, on which Feuchtwanger, in a 'reawakening' of Heinrich Graetz,[65] was working at the time, words failed him: the project got stuck in the early mediaeval period.

Fritz Pringsheim, a brother in law of Thomas Mann, once inquired, as a 'Jewish' historian of law, about Schmitt's polemical distortions. Schmitt replied: 'I do not wish to be interrogated by you. My publications provide information on my scholarly views.'[66] Alice Berend wrote to Duška: 'May I ask where C.S. will now be living in Berlin? Maybe I could get the chance to talk to him for five minutes there. I would be very glad.'[67] Berend emigrated to Italy in 1935 and died in Florence in 1938. Her last book was a history of the German 'philistine' [Spießbürger] up to the present day, the manuscript of which Schmitt had once read in draft form in 1929.[68] Another Jewish female friend had a narrow escape and survived.[69] Annie Kraus, a cousin of Eisler, continued to live in Berlin and made do with publications and translations. After she received the request to report for a transport 'to the East' in January 1942, she went into hiding in various locations. In June 1942 she let herself be christened by her helpers, and in spring 1943 she went to the Allgäu, where, suffering from ill health, she experienced the end of the war in a hideout. In the 1950s she entered the circles in Innsbruck around Karl Rahner, with whom she wrote her doctorate on Thomas Aquinas. While Feuchtwanger declared assimilation to be an experiment that had failed and concentrated on Jewish identity and history again, Kraus held on to the distinction between nation and religion and converted from Judaism to Catholicism. She insisted on her Christianity and, after 1945, published Catholic treatises. In a moving letter which she wrote to Waldemar Gurian in the summer of 1947, she called the 'physically and mentally [seelisch] hardest – unimaginably hard – years of [her] life at the same time those most filled with mercy and with blessings': 'In those years, the "other Germany" became so apparent and gleamed so brightly that I dare say: it offsets the horror of all else.'[70] In

1948 she published an intelligent essay, *Über die Dummheit* [On stupidity], which, following Thomas Aquinas, interprets stupidity as 'dullness of the heart'.[71] This was her response to National Socialism and to Carl Schmitt, who was 'genuinely pained' by this. In his *Glossarium* [Glossary], he noted: 'She acts like a little Angel of Death and yet does not belong to the society of prosecutors and accusers, and if I was responsible for, and have contributed to, the fact that she now ended up [in such company] after all, I regret this' (GL, p. 205). Such formulations still sound inappropriate. The settling of accounts, however, which was personally aimed at Schmitt, could hardly have been more confident and hitting: stupidity as a dullness of the heart! Kraus took up the Christian critique of Schmitt's 'existentialist' concept of the political, which Helmut Kuhn had formulated in 1933, and sharpened it into the diagnosis of a dullness of the heart. How was Schmitt able to live with his decision to side with National Socialism? 'Are you ashamed', he was asked at Nuremberg, 'that you wrote these things back then?' 'It is gruesome, of course', he answered in April 1947: 'There are no words to speak of it'* (AN, p. 66). Beyond his silence, he was looking for discreet ways of expressing himself about it. But such 'stupidity', such a failing, could not be dealt with. This is also demonstrated by the simplifications and falsifications, the hardening of his attitudes and the prosecutions, which he displayed in word and deed during National Socialism.

---

* Schmitt's formulation – 'Es gibt kein Wort darüber zu reden' – is mildly ambiguous and could also be rendered: 'Nothing needs to be said about it', or 'There is nothing to be said about it'.

20

Schmitt's Resistible Rise to the Position of 'Crown Jurist'

Revenge for Leipzig

Today, we see National Socialism as a 'totalitarian' Leviathan which swallowed up the institutions of civil society. Beyond the terror of the state, there was some economic consolidation in the context of the world economic crisis. Up until the early years of the war National Socialism acquired mass loyalty with the help of welfare state measures, financed with profits from 'Aryanization'. Large parts of the population were therefore happy to ignore the fate of the victims of discrimination and the murderous telos of the 'nihilistic revolution' (Hermann Rauschning) right up to the point of impending military defeat.[1] For a long time, the apologia of National Socialism on the basis of a nationalist attitude was common among national conservative circles in academic scholarship as well. However, from the very beginning Schmitt harboured comparatively few illusions. His *Concept of the Political* had already established the connection between integrative achievements and the identification of enemies. In contrast to Huber, for example, he did not really play the nationalistic card.

First, Schmitt dealt with the notion of the 'total state'. Before 1933, he had emphasized an ambiguity in the term and distinguished between a 'quantitative' and a 'qualitative' total state – i.e., between a negative and a positive politicization – which posits distinctions and creates structures. He considered the situation in 1933 as a turning point but also as open, and as one that required the creation of new structures and distinctions. His work on the Reich Governors Law then led him to National Socialism. At that point, in April 1933, Schmitt was not yet a party member, but he saw the law as the fulfilment of his wishes from the summer of 1932, and the negative references to the Leipzig trial form a basic theme in his comments. His concise commentary[2] was already published in April in an official series titled *Das Recht der nationalen Revolution* [The right of the national revolution]. The first edition of the *Reich Governors Law* soon sold out. An expanded edition (from which we quote here) appeared as soon as May, bringing the total number of copies to 4,000. Schmitt's commentary is based on the Preußenschlag and the Leipzig trial, as well as the Enabling Act, which is now called the 'provisional constitution of the German revolution' (RSG, p. 9). The big central term of the text is 'coordination' [Gleichschaltung]. The Reich governor's task is the enforcement of the 'Reich's rule' [Reichsgewalt] through the coordination of the federal states. In cases of conflict the Reich decides. The states are 'politically coordinated by the Reich' (RSG, p. 12). There is no guarantee for a preservation of the territorial status quo. What is important is the personal enforcement of the Reich's rule. The governor, as opposed to a commissar, is a 'permanent' organ and 'means for political coordination' (RSG, p. 16), with personal responsibility towards the Reich chancellor. As the governor he is an *ex officio* member of the federal state's government and appoints civil servants upon suggestion by the state. Only Prussia does not have a governor. Here, the Reich chancellor has at the same time the rights of the governor, which he may confer on the Prussian prime minister, as Hitler did on 25 April with Göring, who thus knew that he held a special relationship with Hitler. The Reich Governors Law creates a 'new constitutional law' beyond the Weimar Constitution and must be interpreted in the 'spirit of the new order of the Reich' (RSG, p. 24).

These reflections found a conclusive formulation in Schmitt's inaugural lecture at the University of Cologne on 16 June, which had been widely publicized. It had to be moved from an overcrowded assembly hall to a larger lecture hall.[3] Schmitt had already presented his theses in his speech at the event commemorating the foundation of the Reich,[4] which Moritz Julius Bonn had requested and which was at the same time Schmitt's farewell lecture in Berlin. The title, 'Reich – Staat – Bund' [Reich – state – federation], had also been mentioned before as a working title in a radio talk. On that occasion, Schmitt had simply said: 'I do not believe that the German Reich of today is a federal state.'[5] On 22 February he spoke again about the topic in Berlin. Now, in his Cologne speech, he demonstrated, in conceptual terms and in terms of constitutional history, the origin of the interpretation of the Reich as a federal state. The conception, he argued, originated in the fact that the old Reich was split into the dualism between Austria and Prussia, as well as several other states, and that the notion of a federation became 'the ally of the concept of a state against the concept of a Reich' (PB, p. 193). It mobilized the political independence of the states, which the reform of the Reich was meant to abolish. The danger of such an alliance of the idea of a federation with the concept of the state, he said, could still be seen at the Leipzig trial. There, under the 'impression of a certain constitutional theory and within the conceptual framework of a federal law' (PB, p. 195), Prussia had been confirmed in its 'right to an independent politics'. Huber, in his booklet, had spoken of an '*interpretatio bajuvarica*' of the Reich's constitution: of the influence of a 'radically federalist' Bavarian theory of the federal state.[6] Great concepts are mythical 'bearers of political energy' (PB, p. 198). Schmitt deployed Heraclitus against the concept of a federation and, in June 1933, fought against an enemy that had mostly been defeated already.

As the inaugural lecture of a 'crown jurist', Schmitt's revision of the Leipzig ruling on the basis of constitutional history and his critique of Prussia's position as an independent state appears strangely retrospective and '*post festum*'. Schmitt published it only in 1940. On 22 February he had said: 'The Reich exists as a postulate.'[7] But in 1933 he did not use the concept of the Reich in a positive and constructive way. Thus, he did not, as requested, write a contribution on 'Das Reich als Rechtsbegriff' [The Reich as a legal concept] for the journal *Deutsch Europa*, which stood for the ideology of the Reich.[8] While everywhere else Schmitt argued programmatically and wanted to construct the 'spirit' of the new state law, in his inaugural lecture he was looking back. This can only be understood as a sign of how painful the sting of the Leipzig trial had been. Schmitt was no stranger to feelings of resentment. Together with the National Socialists, he wanted to take revenge for his defeat in 1932. In an article in the *Westdeutscher Beobachter*, titled '1 Jahr deutsche Politik' [one year of German politics],[9] he stressed the continuity of that politics with the Preußenschlag, giving the latter the sole meaning of putting the Prussian government, as the 'main bastion' of Weimar, in its place. However, he says, the battle of the German 'military and civil service state' against the liberal constitutional state had only been decided by National Socialism. Hitler had found the proper middle ground between a 'pathological need for legality' and a National Socialist radicalism of 'illegality' in the 'German sense of order'. The article is a rejection of the radicality of 'illegality' and tries to reposition National Socialism in the context of national conservative 'German politics', against the opposition of many fellow party members. It is a testament to Schmitt's central desire to view National Socialism as on a continuum with the Preußenschlag. Schmitt would soon be forced to give up this perspective. There was no way of celebrating National Socialism as the restoration of the 'German military and civil service state'. And yet, the link to traditions represented by the name of Hegel remained a central motif in Schmitt's programmatic writings, with their emphasis on constitutional history.

Zero hour and first involvement

Schmitt's work on the Reich Governors Law was immensely important for his decision to side with National Socialism. Even before he joined the party, he was active as 'crown jurist'. It was a temptation to which he succumbed – he wanted to continue playing this role. At that point, he could not know that the legislative work would be done mainly within the ministerial bureaucracy, and that his work on the Reich Governors Law would remain his main involvement. Schmitt continued to have a strong influence on appointments, on the training of jurists and on questions of juridical hermeneutics. But the centre of legal power under National Socialism remained the legislative work done in the ministries,[10] and Schmitt had less and less access to this centre. He soon began to feel this tension between his ideological activity and the lack of actual influence.

Schmitt now lived with his family and two maids in a quiet street in Cologne – Pfarriusstraße 6 in the Lindenthal part of town, near the university. He took on the commissary directorship of the Institute for International Law and the Politics Seminar,[11] and he became a member of the Juridical Examination Office and the Examination Office for Political Economy in Cologne and Düsseldorf. The move to Cologne was a courageous experiment: Schmitt wanted to teach next to his antipode Kelsen and to confront the positivist 'pure theory of law' with his own politically based constitutional theory. However, upon his arrival, Kelsen had already been sent 'on leave'.[12] Nipperdey initiated a declaration of solidarity, which Schmitt did not sign.[13] The revised *Concept of the Political* appeared with the Hanseatische Verlagsanstalt, where Ernst Jünger, Wilhelm Stapel and many other right-wing intellectuals were also published. The Verlagsanstalt became Schmitt's personal publishing house and also a base for his pupils.[14] Thus, it published, for instance, Forsthoff's decidedly anti-Semitic programmatic text *Der totale Staat* [The total state]. Schmitt published his most important works of that time with the 'HVA' and also edited a series for it titled *Der deutsche Staat der Gegenwart* [The contemporary German state].

Schmitt's revision of the *Concept* treatise involved some conceptual clarifications and the introduction of some associations to National Socialism. But mainly he deleted all historicizing aspects of his conceptual definitions. The opening chapter and the reference to the lecture on 'The Age of Neutralization and Depoliticization' were omitted. Helmut Kuhn, in a letter to Schmitt, expressed his Socratic distance from Schmitt's 'nihilism' and political 'existentialism'. There was no mention of these revisions in the book. Responses from Herbert Marcuse[15] and Karl Löwith set out critically from these adjustments. Hans Bogner, in contrast, stressed the fact that: 'As attractive as it might be to consider the minor additions, cuts and changes in comparison to the second edition, it is clear that the essential content of the treatise did not require any rearrangement or reorientation.'[16] The text was more compact. Schmitt now started out from the fundamental 'distinction between friend and enemy'. He took an entirely fresh approach, reserving the concept of the political for National Socialism. The revision of the text stages the pathos of a new departure, as we know it from many rhetorically charged inaugural declarations at the beginning of National Socialist rule – e.g., from Heidegger's inaugural speech as pro-vice-chancellor of the University of Freiburg. Heidegger sent Schmitt his speech 'with German greetings' [Mit deutschem Gruß].[17] Schmitt sent Heidegger the revised version of the *Concept* treatise, for which Heidegger thanked him, asking for Schmitt's 'cooperation'.[18] Schmitt replied affirmatively, sent his inaugural lecture, which was unpublished at the time, and expressed his 'willingness for any kind of cooperation'.[19] Ernst Jünger, in contrast, warned against National Socialist activism.

Schmitt welcomed the revision of the *Concept* treatise for two reasons: on the one hand, a version cleared of the ballast of the Weimar years was more appealing; on the other hand, he needed to rewrite the constitutional prehistory and to reinterpret his earlier history of decline into a history of regeneration and final victory. Although he continued to view National Socialism in the context of German constitutional history, he now needed a new story line, which he elaborated further in his programmatic writings.

At the end of 1932, Schmitt had still agreed with Dean Kelsen to teach Reich and federal state law, tutorials in international law, as well as a seminar on the theory of the state and constitutional theory (*privatissime et gratis*).* But now, the short term in Cologne became a test run for his role as 'crown jurist'. On his arrival, Schmitt was already greeted as a leading National Socialist state theorist. At the beginning of May he gave his first lecture. The *Westdeutsche Beobachter* in Cologne boasted the headline: 'The great national state theorist Professor Dr Carl Schmitt appointed to Cologne University!' The pro-vice-chancellor and the dean congratulated him. Schmitt met regularly with Günther Krauss and also got to know the National Socialist student leader Ernst Hermann Bockhoff, who passed his doctorate in Cologne at the end of 1934[20] and then taught at the Hochschule für Politik [Academy for Politics] in Berlin. Schmitt's assistant was a certain Karl Pathe.[21] 'Burning of trash literature [Schundbücher]', Schmitt noted in his diary (17 May 1933).† On 18 May he visited a party event in the Gürzenich‡ before travelling to Plettenberg, for his mother's seventieth birthday, and on to Berlin, where he spoke to Achelis, the ministerial secretary responsible for academic appointments. The headline of the *Westdeutscher Beobachter* on the occasion of the Juridical Faculty's welcome evening was: 'A New Spirit at Cologne University'.[22] Schmitt gave a speech to the faculty which was critical of positivism and referred to 'existential' commitment in the 'political age':

> Jurisprudential insights only exist where one belongs existentially to the object of that science, where one partakes of the life of the people as a member of the people, and therefore also partakes in the community of right [Rechtsgemeinschaft], which creates and bears the right. He who does not belong to it is blind and without a relation to it; he may otherwise be as critical and sharp-witted as he likes.

Schmitt supported this claim also with a reference to the head of the University of Cologne's council [Universitätskurator] and 'state commissar' Dr Winkelnkemper and his 'great speech of 17 May on the occasion of the burning of un-German writings in front of our University in Cologne'. The world of the spirit [des Geistes], he said, was 'a battle-filled world': 'Here in the Rhineland we are in the deployment zone of the French.'[23] Schmitt played the apologetic card with great verve. Positions of power and privileges had to be secured before others got hold of them. Schmitt gave a number of lectures and in quick succession published articles in party papers, such as the *Westdeutsche Beobachter* and *Völkische Beobachter*, in which he unmistakably propagated his belief in National Socialism. He praised the 'spirit' of the German revolution and 'The

---

* Term for private seminars to which selected students and colleagues were invited.
† The burning of books considered to be against the German spirit took place in several places during May and June. On 16 May, a blacklist of such books was published by the *Börsenblatt des deutschen Buchhandels*.
‡ A dance hall in Cologne.

Proper Right of the German Revolution',[24] celebrated the 'transition to the one-party state' as a step towards the 'state of the twentieth century',[25] gave an interpretation of the 'new state council [Staatsrat]',[26] in which he ignored, in grotesque fashion, the political decapitation of the federal states, and justified the beginnings of National Socialism with the 'reform of the Reich' in the tradition of the Preußenschlag.[27] Were it not for the polemical tone, one might see an ironic programme of depoliticization in all of this.

Almost impossible to surpass in terms of its polemicism is, in particular, an article in the *Westdeutscher Beobachter* of 31 May 1933, the day of the faculty gathering, titled 'Die deutschen Intellektuellen' [The German intellectuals]. This article is clearly Schmitt's masterpiece, allowing him to be counted as a member of the NSDAP clique. In it, he anticipates a legal framework for forced expatriation [Strafexpatriation].[28] About German intellectuals, he says: 'They never belonged to the German people. And also not to the German spirit. [. . .] Germany has spat them out for all time.' Schmitt affirms the burning of books, reacts to first comments made by emigrants, considers the withdrawal of citizenship, and hints at further measures. He mentions by name Albert Einstein, who – next to Thomas Mann – was high up on the National Socialists' list of individuals to be stripped of their citizenship. Schmitt juxtaposed Annette von Droste-Hülshoff with Heinrich Heine, Hölderlin with Julius Stahl, understands 'spirit' [Geist] on the basis of 'attachment to the people' [Volksgebundenheit], and distinguishes between 'scholars' and 'intellectuals'. The article is among the worst excesses Schmitt ever published. One need only remind oneself of his former circle of friends and acquaintances to see how he draws a line under his previous life in this piece. He burns all his bridges, betrays his closest relationships, and engages in self-denial. This article was his journeyman's, or rather villain's, piece, proving that he was one of the National Socialists. With this drawing of a line, Schmitt also wanted to forget his own past. Only a little later he expressed his disgust at a postcard that Hermann Heller sent from his emigration in Spain, congratulating Schmitt on the conferral of the title of state councillor [Staatsrat]: 'Hermann Heller sends his congratulation on the more than deserved honour bestowed on you by Minister Göring.'[29] Schmitt called this the 'bluster of a parasite that has been shaken off', and angrily remarked: and the 'Juridical Faculty of Frankfurt University actively supports Heller; he continues to receive his salary!'[30] How could Schmitt consider the ironic telegram to be worse than his article? What did he expect? Had he forgotten the 'risk of the political'? His own polemics backfired.

Hans Frank (1900–1946) and the 'Akademie für Deutsches Recht'*

In spring 1933, the guild of jurists entered a new state of exception. 'Ideas of 1933' were being propagated. The age of programmatic texts returned,

*   Academy for German Right.

inaugural lectures were used for marking one's ideological point of departure. Many people realized the destructive aspect of National Socialism.
But many also liked to deceive themselves over the future of 'right' as a
'functional mode' [Funktionsmodus] under National Socialism. Their
'creation frenzy' [Schöpfungsrausch] (Stolleis) had the useful side effect
of fostering their careers. From April onwards, Schmitt was busy constructing positions of power for himself and practising National Socialist
politics. His access point was his involvement in the Preußenschlag. One
individual in particular now became important for his further rise: the
'party jurist' Hans Frank. Up to that point, Schmitt had always been lucky
with his mentors. Fritz van Calker, Hugo am Zehnhoff, Moritz Julius Bonn
and Rudolf Smend all steered him in positive directions. It would have
been better, however, if Schmitt had never met Hans Frank,[31] despite the
fact that Frank was a pupil of van Calker. Calker used Frank in order to
promote Schmitt's appointment in Munich. This was how the two of them
met.

In October 1939, Hans Frank became the 'general governor' of Poland,
and his name is therefore irrevocably linked to National Socialist politics regarding Poland and to the Holocaust. In contrast to Schmitt, he
was a long-serving party member. He grew up as the son of a lawyer in
Munich and took his school leaving certificate at the time of the Munich
revolution, which he actively opposed. He was a good pupil and a diligent
student. In 1923 he passed his first state examination in Munich, and in
1924 he completed his doctorate with Walter Jellinek in Kiel. For some
time he was van Calker's assistant in Munich before passing his assessor's
examination there in 1927. Early on, Frank became a member of the Thule
Society,* to which Hitler also belonged. Even before the 'Hitler Putsch', he
joined the NSDAP, on 3 October 1923; he took part in the 'march towards
the Feldherrnhalle', and thus was one of the old party allies on whom
Hitler set his hopes. Frank moved to fascist Italy in order to avoid legal
prosecution. In protest against the NSDAP's policies regarding Italy, he
temporarily left the party in 1926, though the reason for this may also have
been related to his career. He rejoined the party in September 1927 and
took on numerous representations at court. He lived for the party, but he
also lived off the party. Frank was notorious for his long-winded and vague
pleas at court, where Philipp Loewenfeld, the social democratic lawyer,
met him several times as an opponent. 'When he met with a Jewish lawyer
at the judge's bench', Loewenfeld remembered, 'he would, for instance,
for minutes silently murmur to himself: "Jew, Jew, Jew, Jew, Jew, Jew . . ."
And when the lawyer would then say: "Your Honour, can you hear what
that man is whispering?", he would rise to his full "height" and shout
with a stentorian voice: "Jewish defamation!"'[32] That was the character

---

* The Thule Society emerged in Munich in 1918 out of the 'Germanic Order'. It believed
in the purity of the Aryan race, whose homeland was said to be the mythical 'Thule', a
lost landmass in the North Atlantic. The Thule Society bought the *Münchner Beobachter*,
which later became the *Völkischer Beobachter*, the main National Socialist newspaper, and
it sponsored the DAP, the precursor to the NSDAP.

'My position depended entirely and exclusively on the personal interest shown in me, often very demonstratively, by Frank' – Schmitt about Hans Frank at Nuremberg, 1947

with whom Schmitt now cooperated. Frank was centrally responsible for the foundation of the Bund Nationalsozialistischer Deutscher Juristen (BNSDJ) [Association of National Socialist German Jurists], and at the end of 1928 he became the 'legal advisor to the party leadership', the party's chief jurist. Following the elections on 14 September 1930, he became a member of the Reichstag. His office was in the Braune Haus [Brown House] in Brienner Straße; he was blindly loyal to the 'Führer' and a member of the party leadership, although he was never among Hitler's closest confidants. In 1930, Frank prompted Hitler's so-called Legalitätseid [oath of legality] in the Ulmer Reichswehrprozeß,* which would be of significant strategic importance. He had an extravagant life-style and a chaotic private life, being married to an unfaithful wife who was herself drawn to pomp and splendour. Frank was a mixed-up aesthete and blusterer, a bragger and a characterless glutton.

Frank was not given the position of minister of justice in 1933 because Hitler left the ministry to the DNVP and Franz Gürtner.[33] Instead, in March he became the Bavarian minister of justice and distinguished himself at once through anti-Semitic activities. On the initiative of Gürtner, on 22 April 1933 Frank was appointed as the 'Reich commissar (Reich commissar of justice) for the coordination [Gleichschaltung] of the judiciary in the federal states and for the renewal of the legal system'. In June he proclaimed a 'German legal front', and soon afterwards he

---

* Trial against officers of the Reichswehr, in which Hitler, called as a witness, swore under oath that the NSDAP would use only legal means in trying to come to power.

founded the 'Academy for German Right', of which Wilhelm Kisch, an old teacher from Strasbourg who had already been involved in Schmitt's doctoral examination, became vice-president.[34] The task of the academy was 'to promote the reorganization of German legal life'.[35] It was not only an academy of scholars. Many political notables, and also industrialists, were members. In January, the academy moved into its 'Berlin offices' in the former Preußenhaus [House of Prussia]. With means provided by industry, Frank then acquired for it a magnificent building, Leipziger Platz 15, and later also opened a large 'Haus des Rechts' [House of Right] in the Ludwigstraße in Munich, in addition to the smaller 'Munich office'. The academy organized 'plenary sessions' and 'workshops', mostly in Berlin, as well as prestigious annual conferences in Munich. It published a yearbook and a series, as well as the *Zeitschrift der Akademie für Deutsches Recht* [Journal of the Academy for German Right] and the *Deutsches Recht* [German Right], in which Schmitt published numerous articles. However, along with jurisprudence itself, the academy became more and more a pure façade, as far as scholarship is concerned, and a backdrop for the National Socialist agenda. When the federal states' ministries of justice were put under the authority of the Reichsleitung [Reich leadership], Frank became a Reich minister without portfolio. However, the title was mostly *pro forma*. Hitler did not govern through the cabinet. Frank attended its meetings only rarely. His hopes, in particular, of gaining legislative influence through the academy failed. The decisions continued to be taken primarily within the ministry. There was some indirect influence that the academy exerted through its discussions, drafts and reports; however, this external advisory influence remained mostly marginal. Schmitt's initial hopes of significant involvement in the legislature, fuelled by his work on the Reich Governors Law, were disappointed. Frank increasingly compensated for his disappointment by celebrating a personal cult.

The year 1937 saw organizational changes. Carl August Emge took up the office of vice-president.[36] When Frank became governor-general of Poland at the beginning of the war, Emge was given presidential powers on a commissary basis. Frank now held court in lavish style at the old Königsburg in Kraków. Like Göring, he was an unscrupulous robber of art works and developed a broad 'artistic life'. Leonardo da Vinci's *Lady with an Ermine* – the original, let us note – hung on the wall of his castle. He was permanently on the go. Despite his central role in the Holocaust as governor-general of occupied Poland, he liked to see himself as someone who cultivated the concept of right. He had to share the power within the government general with the SS. In 1942, Himmler almost toppled him over his mismanagement and corruption. Hitler left him in the office of governor-general, but took the presidency of the academy away from him in August 1942. Thierack became his successor, whereupon Emge stepped down as deputy. The academy reduced its activism[37] massively at that point and became altogether insignificant. Frank experienced the end of the war at his country residence in Bavaria, a place Schmitt had visited repeatedly. Imprisoned in Nuremberg, Frank wrote a mendacious self-apology – *Im Angesicht des Galgens*[38] [Faced with the gallows] – converted to Catholicism, and was hung on 16 October 1946. This man was Schmitt's most important National Socialist mentor until the end of 1936. Not only did Schmitt become an accomplice of an unscrupulous National Socialist, he also backed the wrong horse. His 'statism' could have told him that the power would remain within the Reich ministries. But maybe he was no 'statist' during the time of National Socialism.

Summer 1933: 'And then this man appeared'

For a long time, Schmitt suffered from his resentment, from the feeling that he was not appropriately recognized. Now he saw the opportunity to assert his views and concepts. Did he want to be the juridical 'leader of the leader'? Was that a possibility at all? Were there any opportunities for shaping constitutional policies? Schmitt acted on several stages: at the university and at the academy. From May 1933, he was a member of the BNSDJ and later of the NSD-Dozentenbund.* His sphere of influence was determined by his membership in the Association of National Socialist German Jurists.

By the end of May, Schmitt had already received an inquiry from Heidelberg regarding the succession of Anschütz.[39] Walter Jellinek was interested in Schmitt being appointed. However, the faculty at Heidelberg doubted from the very beginning that the 'exceptional man' would be inclined to accept.[40] Thus, Schmitt's name was listed ahead of the usual three candidates, and he declared that he was prepared to move to Heidelberg. His dean at Cologne, Nipperdey, had already asked the university council at the end of May 'to do everything in order to ensure that Professor Schmitt will stay in Cologne'.[41] He bent the facts, inaccurately claiming in a letter to Vice-Chancellor Leupold that the faculty had already tried to recruit Schmitt in May 1932 as the 'representative of *völkisch*-national jurisprudence for the West Mark'.[42] At the same time, the University of Munich was looking for a successor to the late Rothenbücher. The faculty, led by the dean, Wilhelm Kisch, wanted Smend. Half of the faculty placed Schmitt second, jointly with Koellreutter. 'Canon law is far from Carl Schmitt's interests', the faculty accurately remarked. However, as early as 3 June the newly appointed Bavarian minister of justice, Frank, intervened in the appointment process and forcefully recommended Schmitt.[43] Immediately, plans were made for a double appointment of Koellreutter and Schmitt on the basis of two newly defined chairs. Then on 12 June, the Bavarian State Ministry informed Prussia of the intention to appoint Schmitt. Calker wrote to Schmitt:

> Yesterday, I had a very thorough conversation with Minister Frank. I had heard that he was inclined to suggest Koellreutter for the juridical chair [Rechtsstelle]. As much as I value our colleague K., I could not help mainly

* Nationalsozialistischer Deutscher Dozentenbund = National Socialist German Lecturers' Association.

drawing attention to you, which was all the easier as Frank, when he was still a member of my seminar, had had the opportunity to get to know your books in detail. And my impression was that Frank has, indeed, now made a decision in your favour.[44]

At that point, Schmitt's appointment had already been decided. Calker was given a chair at the Ludwig Maximilian Universität and, throughout the 1930s, continued to teach into his old age at the Technische Universität. On 10 June, Schmitt spoke at the Verwaltungsakademie [Academy for Administration] in Hamburg about the Enabling Act and the National Socialist Rechtsstaat.[45] In the evening he met with Erich Günther and Georg Eisler, and the following day still discussed the contemporary situation with Eisler, his closest Jewish friend.[46] On 13 June, Schmitt spoke at the Verwaltung-Akademie Berlin on the 'Geist des neuen Staatsrechts' [Spirit of the new state law].[47] A few days later he met Wilhelm Neuß, a strict opponent of National Socialism, in Bonn: 'Ghastly, never again these priests [Pfaffen]', he noted in his diary (18 June 1933). Schmitt was seeking to enter into conversation with Eisler and Neuß. On 17 June, the Bavarian State Ministry sent an official request regarding his appointment. Simultaneously, he received an initial inquiry from Achelis, the ministerial secretary in Berlin. In response, Schmitt told Achelis about the intention to appoint him in Munich. He had, Schmitt wrote, 'learned through the privy councillor van Calker, an old friend from my time in Strasbourg, that the minister of justice, Frank, has made a decision in favour of me'.[48] On 30 June, Schmitt spoke to the Association of Jurists in the Gürzenich in Cologne. On 4 July he spoke in Aachen, and on 6 July he spoke at the Juridical Faculty of Heidelberg University. The next day he sounded out the situation regarding his appointment with Anschütz and Jellinek, as well as with the minister of culture. Anschütz had given up his professorship, Radbruch had been sacked, and Jellinek was in the midst of a fight lasting several years, which was ultimately in vain, to have his Aryan descent approved.[49] Schmitt met with the vice-chancellor at Heidelberg, Ernst Krieck, a self-confessed National Socialist, and then travelled on to Koblenz. He did not accept the offer of appointment at Heidelberg, and only a few days later Koellreutter also declined.[50] Around the same time, Schmitt became a member of the examination board at the Higher Regional Court in Düsseldorf,[51] where he had once been a legal trainee. The Prussian State Council was newly constituted. Konrad Adenauer, who had been lord mayor of Cologne and president of the old State Council for many years, was kicked out, and the state theorist Schmitt, who had just taken up his post in Cologne, was appointed to Göring's State Council. The *Westdeutsche Beobachter* reported both pieces of news on the front page and printed Göring's letter of appointment, dated 11 July – as it happens, Schmitt's birthday – into the bargain.[52] The University of Cologne wanted to keep Schmitt at all costs. 'In academic and political respects, your work is indispensable for the West', wrote Nipperdey.[53] On 14 July, Schmitt gave a lecture in Münster. On 17 July he received the letter of appointment from the Bavarian Ministry.[54] On 21 July, at a lecture in Cologne, he met

Hans Frank for the first time and talked about the matter of the Munich appointment with him. In retrospect, Schmitt said: 'And then this man appeared in Cologne, not the Gauleiter himself, another one, in short, this is how it began.'[55] After their separation, Cari was only ever referred to as 'the lady'. 'The man' was now the second major 'stupidity' in Schmitt's life. At that point, he told Achelis of his appointment in Munich[56] and also informed the University of Cologne.

Schmitt went to Maria Laach one more time and attended the third sociological conference of the Association of Catholic Academics, which had as its theme 'The National Problem within Catholicism', and which brought together the Reich theologians.[57] The climax was an appearance of the vice-chancellor, Franz von Papen, who informed the gathering about the signing of the Reichskonkordat. Edgar J. Jung also spoke at the conference.[58] Schmitt behaved with restraint and did not further clarify his concept of the 'total state', even when asked to do so. He met Prince Rohan and Oberheid, but left before Papen arrived. He would soon break off his contacts with Catholic circles.[59] In the context of the discussions within Catholicism regarding its attitude to National Socialism, Schmitt joined Karl Eschweiler and Hans Barion in taking sides against the Zentrum, the official Church and Catholic dogmatics. He opted against political Catholicism.

The faculty at Cologne implored Schmitt to stay. The students published a letter in the press requesting Schmitt to remain with the 'borderland university' and the National Socialist student body. On 30 July, Schmitt gave a talk on 'Rechtspflege und Justiz im neuen Staat' [Jurisprudence and judiciary in the new state] for the BNSDJ in the Gürzenich in Cologne, in which he emphasized 'absolute species identity and attachment to the people' [unbedingte Artgleichheit und Volksverbundenheit].[60] The experience of the Leipzig trial resonated in this lecture as well. Schmitt now committed himself to an openly political judiciary. His 'Leitsätze für die Rechtspraxis' [Guiding principles for legal practice], which was published in several editions (and also as a small paperback), provides a formulaic summary of his position.[61] Schmitt took the common 'general clauses' as his point of departure, in order to align and commit the 'unlimited interpretation' (Bernd Rüthers)* to the 'principles of National Socialism'.[62] In his closing phrase he decreed: 'The National Socialist state is a just state.'

On 2 August, Schmitt had detailed negotiations regarding his appointment to the chair in Munich with the ministerial secretary Dr Müller in Munich. He declared that he was 'very inclined to accept the appointment to Munich University', but wanted to discuss the decision with Göring because of his involvement with the State Council.[63] Schmitt immediately went to Munich for further negotiations regarding his appointment, then spent a few days in Upper Bavaria before travelling on to Berlin for yet more negotiations. During a long evening in the Habel wine bar, Ernst Jünger

---

* The reference is to Rüther's classic analysis of private law in the Third Reich: *Die unbegrenzte Auslegung: Zum Wandel der Privatrechtsordnung im Nationalsozialismus* [Unlimited interpretation: on the transformation of private law under National Socialism], Tübingen, 1968; 7th edn, 2012).

warned Schmitt against his involvement with National Socialism.[64] On 9 August, Schmitt returned to Cologne. The state secretary to the Ministry of the Interior, Wilhelm Stuckart, wrote to Schmitt telling him that 'efforts' had 'begun' to keep him in Prussia. The irony of the appointment: Schmitt, who liquidated Prussia in terms of state theory, was meant to come to Berlin in the name of Prussia. In coordination with Schmitt, Frank wrote to Göring, saying that only the 'duty of gratitude'[65] towards Prussia kept Schmitt from accepting the appointment in Munich, thus suggesting an appointment for him in Berlin. Schmitt travelled to the Middle Rhine for a few days. At the end of August he went to Siedlinghausen. The firm offer of appointment from Munich was dated 31 August. But, on 1 September, Schmitt also received the offer of a chair in Berlin. He immediately wrote to Achelis: 'I feel that this offer of a chair in Berlin is the highest honour that I can receive in my profession.'[66] On 5 September he travelled to Berlin to negotiate his conditions of employment. After the negotiations he probably met with Heidegger, who had rejected the offer of a chair in Berlin. But on 1 October Schmitt accepted the offer, which included a 16,400 Reichsmark basic salary and a 7,000 Reichsmark stipend for teaching. The ministry told the faculty in Berlin that the state councillor Schmitt was to be appointed to a newly created chair 'for state political reasons'.[67] On 8 October, Schmitt spoke with the state secretary Achelis about his acceptance of the appointment. Only a few hours later, Heidegger, who had also been offered a chair for political reasons, spoke with Achelis. Schmitt and Heidegger probably met in Hitler's Hotel Kaiserhof. While Heidegger, on account of his excessive ambitions and dreams, declined the offer, Schmitt took up what would be his final university post in the winter term.[68] Only on 16 October did he decline the offer from Munich, whereupon Johannes Heckel was appointed in his stead.[69] The *Westdeutscher Beobachter* headline on 23 October was: 'A heavy loss for Cologne University'. Schmitt's was the first explicitly National Socialist appointment to the Juridical Faculty in Berlin. Soon Count Gleispach, Carl August Emge, Reinhard Höhn and Karl August Eckhardt would follow. By 1935 James Goldschmidt, Fritz Schulz, Erich Kaufmann, Ernst Rabel, Hermann Dersch and Martin Wolff had all been driven out.[70] Many more individuals were affected. According to the university's chronicle, Schmitt took up his post on 9 November. Otto Liebmann, in coordination with Popitz, asked him to become a co-editor of the *Deutsche Juristen-Zeitung*.[71] Schmitt also became a member of the examination board of the Kammergericht,* Berlin's Higher Regional Court.

The offer of chairs in Heidelberg, Munich and Berlin were all made within the same short period of time. Heidelberg hardly played a role, not even in Schmitt's negotiations with the other two places. Munich, in contrast, probably would have been attractive enough for him to leave Cologne. But the opportunity to move to Berlin arose almost at the same time as the offer from Munich, and Schmitt did not waver between the two for long. In

---

* When the higher regional courts were formed in 1877, the name was kept from the time when the court sat in the private chambers (=Kammern) of the prince-electors. It later housed the supreme courts of the territories ruled by the House of Hohenzollern.

Speech at the Neues Palais in Potsdam on the occasion of the first meeting of the Staatsrat [State Council] and in the presence of Göring, Himmler, Röhm and others

coordination with Frank, he used the Munich offer strategically from the very beginning in order to fulfil his ambition to move to Berlin. This was where he wanted to be, as he openly confessed in his letter to Achelis.

The formal celebration of the opening of the State Council took place in the Neue Aula of Berlin University on 15 September 1933. The orchestra of the State Opera played Bach and the overture to *Egmont* by Beethoven. Göring gave an address. The assembly moved outside to the monument of Fredrick the Great in front of the university, where Göring laid down a wreath. Then a Legion of Honour marched past.[72] Schmitt hoped to gain the greatest influence through the institution, and placed his bet on the possibility that the State Council would be the first step towards the establishment of a 'Führer Council', so that he might ultimately rise to being the 'Führer of the Führer'. The next day, in the presence of, among others, Göring, Himmler and Röhm, he presented a paper on 'Wesen und Gestaltung der kommunalen Selbstverwaltung im Nationalsozialismus' [The nature and shape of local government under National Socialism][73] at the first session of the State Council, which took place in the Neues Palais at Potsdam. He then returned to Cologne and began to prepare the annual conference of the jurists [Juristentag] and also finalized his report on the law governing the Prussian Municipal Constitution [Gemeindeverfassungsgesetz], which was passed on 15 December 1933.[74] At the end of September he travelled to Leipzig.

At the zenith: the Jurists' Convention

The old annual conferences of the jurists had been suspended at the end of April 1933.[75] The Convention of the Jurists from 30 September to 4 October

1933 was in actual fact the fourth national convention [Reichstagung] of the Bund nationalsozialistischer deutscher Juristen [Association of National Socialist German Jurists] (BNSDJ).[76] In 1936 and 1939 there were two more of these propaganda conferences [Schautagungen]. Founded in 1928, the BNSDJ had no more than 1,374 members on 1 January 1933. But the Jurists' Convention later that year nevertheless mobilized 20,000 participants. Hans Frank opened it to great applause and then introduced the Academy for German Right. Nicolai, Lange and Schmitt were the main academic speakers. On 3 October, at 10 a.m., Schmitt gave a lecture titled 'Neubau des Staats- und Verwaltungsrechts' [The new organization of state and administrative law], which he straightaway expanded into the small booklet *State, Movement, People*. At the Jurists' Convention, he pompously declared the 'will of the Führer' to be the 'nomos' and thus presented his new understanding of the concept of right. 'We are proven wrong', he explained,

> if we have no leaders, and we are victorious if we have great leaders. We have great leaders, and this is why I conclude my presentation today with the mention of two names: Adolf Hitler, the leader of the German people, whose will today is the nomos of the German people, and Hans Frank, the leader of our German legal front [Rechtsfront] and pioneering fighter for our proper German right, the model of a National Socialist German jurist.[77]

In the evening, Hitler gave the concluding speech at the exhibition hall. 'Wonderful speech by Hitler about the total state', Schmitt noted in his diary. 'Much consoled' (3 October 1933).

From 2 October, Schmitt was a member of the new Academy for German Right, and he became a member of its 'Führerrat' [Führer Council], which included many prominent National Socialists, as well as the chair of the committee for state and administrative law.[78] Schmitt travelled to Berlin for the second meeting of the State Council and then worked on the 'Bericht über die Selbstverwaltung' [Report on local government] in Cologne. On 20 October he spoke at a local group of the NSDAP in Cologne on 'Der Staatsrat und die Führerfrage im nationalsozialistischen Gemeinwesen' [The State Council and the question of the Führer in the context of the National Socialist polity].[79] Further speeches in Elberfeld and on Roman law at a 'Kulturbund' [cultural association] followed. Günther Krauss passed his examination at that time. Upon the initiative of the dean in Cologne, there was an 'Abschiedsschoppen' [farewell drinks] with the faculty on 31 October.[80] On 2 November, Duška had a miscarriage. Two days later Schmitt went to Berlin again and, on 5 November 1933, spoke at the first full conference and workshop of the academy in Berlin's town hall on 'Die Neugestaltung des öffentlichen Rechts' [The new organization of public law]. He presented his theses on the 'tripartite structure' of political unity and subordinated juridical tasks entirely to the 'political leadership'.[81] In later interventions, he explained in more detail how 'the logic of the new concepts leads to a plethora of tasks'. Now, all legal constructions were to be 'based on concrete order'.[82]

On 6 November, Schmitt gave his first lecture in Berlin. His old mentor, van Calker, accompanied him. Schmitt became academic advisor at the Kaiser-Wilhelm-Institut für ausländisches Recht und Völkerrecht [Kaiser Wilhelm Institute for Foreign and International Law], which was directed by Viktor Bruns. Schmitt declined a request from Cologne to fill the gap which his sudden departure had left with a 'larger lecture course on state law'.[83] He met Hans Frank again and had a 'very nice' conversation with the latter's wife, Brigitte. On 15 December he was appointed 'Reichsgruppenleiter' of the newly founded 'Fachgruppe Hochschullehrer' within the BNSDJ.[84] All professors, Privatdozenten and assistants at the faculty were members of this group. Schmitt became a member of the Hochschulkommission [commission for higher education establishments] of the deputy of the Führer, which was responsible for appointments. Later (from March 1936) this institution was called 'Rechtswahrerbund' [Association for the Preservation of Right]. Thus, for three years Schmitt held the most important position of power within the 'guild' of jurisprudence. At the end of November he moved house, from Pfarriusstraße 6 in Cologne, into a villa at Schillerstraße 2, in the Steglitz area of Berlin. His rental agreement in Cologne continued until 1 April; the rent was covered by the Ministry of Culture.[85]

Ahead of the national elections on 12 November, Schmitt published an article, 'Frieden oder Pazifismus?' [Peace or pacifism?], in which he called for plebiscitary support for an exit from the League of Nations. The 'pacifistic' conceptual universe of the League of Nations, he wrote, threw a veil over the actual power relations. It was only a 'surrogate of peace', a legitimization of the status quo. Why did Schmitt not call for participation in the national elections on that occasion? He had already interpreted the election on 5 March as a plebiscite and not as an election. After that, there was no further choice to be made. The national elections for the Reichstag in November were no longer free elections. '99% for Hitler', was Schmitt's terse remark in his diary (13 November 1933). The pace of change in the developing 'Führerstaat' [Führer state] at the time meant that all sketches and plans quickly become outdated. Schmitt therefore waited before publishing his programmatic text. Huber's booklet on economic law, *Die Gestalt des deutschen Sozialismus* [The shape of German socialism] was already outdated 'with regard to an important point at the moment of its publication'[86] at the beginning of 1934. Huber also was afraid of censorship.[87] In addition, there was the academic competition: 'Only in a few cases can we still assume a normal degree of decency', Schmitt wrote at the time.[88] In the form of the academy and the State Council, Schmitt sought alternatives to ministerial legislative work and was looking for power in new places. Although his expectation that the state of the new revolutionary movement would find new methods and institutions for legislating was not entirely unfounded, his plans did not work out. In retrospect, Hans Schneider wrote about the various attempts at 'reviving the State Council': 'It was not given any real chances to survive as an institution. Thus, the Prussian State Council had finished playing a role as a statutory body of the constitution [Verfassungskörperschaft] after 1848.'[89] Similar things could presumably be said about Frank's academy. However, it would be wholly mistaken to take Schmitt's understanding of his role as a 'state councillor' as merely symbolic. It was not only his desire for prestige but also strategic calculation which made Schmitt opt against the old ministerial bureaucracy and place his bets on the institutions of the State Council and the Academy for German Right.

First arguments about Schmitt's commitment to National Socialism

The discussion of Schmitt's work moved on from individual reviews to review essays and overall evaluations as early as 1930. In 1933, the Weimar work on constitutional theory all of a sudden became obsolete. New editions of older texts provide a 'reliable test'[90] for his political views [Gesinnungen]. Reprints raised sensitive questions regarding continuity and change, as exemplified by the new version of *The Concept of the Political*, which lays Schmitt open to criticism. Ernst Niekisch[91] distanced himself from Schmitt's commitment to National Socialism with a fairly critical review in *Widerstand*, a publication which would soon be prohibited. 'Those German intellectuals' who had emigrated fought back. Waldemar Gurian[92] reminded his readers of 'Carl Schmitt vs. Carl Schmitt' in Weimar. Karl Löwith discussed the *Concept* treatise in his seminar and – in line with Leo Strauss[93] – found that it lacked any 'justification of the friend–enemy distinction'. In 1935, Löwith's decisive critique of Schmitt's 'occasionalistic decisionism' appeared. Others also attacked Schmitt.

State theory within the Führer state was still a 'polycratic' discipline. The expulsion of Jewish colleagues alone did not suffice to produce its inner 'unity' and homogeneity. The 'line' of Triepel–Kaufmann–Smend was defeated. But Schmitt's leadership claim was still challenged even within the inner circle. No sooner did his pupils become colleagues than 'misunderstandings' began to arise. They suddenly affirmed a 'right to a politics of their own'. Schmitt was annoyed with Forsthoff even back then: 'Nasty fellow, disgust and anger', he noted about him in his diary (19 October 1933). The quick failure of his claim to leadership can be traced easily in his correspondence with Huber. One moment, Schmitt sang the highest praises of his work, but the next Huber was appointed to a chair in Kiel, married Tula Simons, and formed a kind of school of thought with his colleagues in Kiel, which complicated matters. A conference in Kassel and plans for a journal first caused Huber to explain himself to Schmitt and to declare his loyalty, which was a recurring feature of their correspondence from then on. Schmitt easily felt ignored and was suspicious when others followed their own paths. The title for the new journal was a point for controversy. It was meant to be a programmatic organ for the young revolution, based on an unusual principle: 'There is agreement that the publication of articles by members of our circle in competing journals requires the permission of the editors. Exceptions are publications in *Deutsches Volkstum* and in the *Blätter für deutsche Philosophie*.'[94] Schmitt had such academic 'incompatibilities' in mind when reconstructing the state. He pushed for the 'term

National Socialism' to appear in the title and impressed upon Huber 'that we do not have an easy task and cannot afford [to engage in] scholarly arguments with each other as before.'[95] Huber also strove for the 'unity' of the group. The series *Der deutsche Staat der Gegenwart* [The contemporary German state] was meant to be a forum. Schmitt took it to be a 'vanguard publication' [Stoßtrupp].[96] Huber had his booklet almost finished by the end of October; however, there were problems.

It seemed as if the plan for a journal would fail. Ritterbusch, the dean in Kiel, had violated the academic incompatibilities and had 'thrown in the towel'[97] by joining the *Zeitschrift für Politik* as co-editor, together with Koellreutter, the main enemy. At that time, the Catholic poet Konrad Weiß, in a poem called 'Justitia', still hoped that Schmitt would be a 'listener' for justice.[98] Some of the members of young conservative circles now switched from the 'theology of nationalism' to a 'theology of National Socialism'. Thus, Karl Eschweiler and Hans Barion, who knew each other from their time at the seminary in Cologne and now taught at the Braunsberg Academy in Eastern Prussia, committed themselves to National Socialism.[99] Eschweiler criticized the Reichskonkordat for giving up the Catholic claim to totality. In a long letter of 23 July 1933, he interpreted it as the 'formal relinquishment of the dogmatic totality and the Catholicism of the Church', and therefore made the 'decision theologically and philosophically to fight for National Socialism more than ever; because what is at stake is the reign of God and his anointed.'[100] For Eschweiler, Catholicism and National Socialism were not opposites, because he considered the latter as a means of Catholicization. He expected Catholic policies to come from Goebbels, the 'cath. Rhinelander', rather than from Papen and 'this stupid and presumptuous diplomacy of the Curia'.[101] He also justified National Socialism in his legal opinions. Braunsberg, at the time, became a thorn in the side of Catholicism, not least on account of Joseph Lortz. However, Eschweiler and Barion were looking to be appointed to chairs in Bavaria, got into trouble with Rome, and were suspended in the summer of 1934. Eschweiler felt that he was blackmailed: 'Either relinquishment of the teaching post and exit from the NSDAP – or immediate excommunication *propter obstinaciam*.'[102] With Barion, he thought he shared 'the fate of being the living illustration for the chapter on "Church and state"' and 'election propaganda for the "clerical" self-affirmation of the Church'.[103] At the end of 1935, following complicated negotiations, which on the side of the Ministry of Education were led by Werner Weber,[104] Eschweiler's suspension was revoked[105] and he was allowed to take up lecturing again. However, he died soon after, on 30 September 1936. Barion, after a confused interlude in Munich, moved to Bonn in 1939. Schmitt had made his acquaintance in 1932 at Eschweiler's home on the occasion of the celebration of the Reich anniversary. After 1945, Barion would become a close friend of Schmitt.

Another old friend registered his criticism: Erik Peterson. Even after Schmitt had left Bonn and after Peterson's conversion and move to Rome, the two had seen each other from time to time, and they had a quite lively correspondence. At Easter 1932, they went to Rome together and renewed their 'friendship'.[106] At the end of 1932, Peterson hinted at some political reservations he had,[107] but nevertheless he still sent greetings in old 'friendship' in February 1933.[108] Then, in July 1933, Peterson published an article in *Hochland*[109] in which he criticized the 'political theology' of National Socialism from the historical perspective of antiquity. Peterson saw two 'possibilities' for constructing a political theology from the New Testament: an apologia for or a critique of the Reich. With Eusebius, Peterson argued, the theological glorification of the Roman Empire, which took it as the framework for Christianization and saw Augustine as the emperor of peace, had declined into pure ideological legitimization. Peterson's article had Schmitt in mind, and Schmitt recognized the mirror image presented to him. He picked up the cue of 'Political Theology' and arranged a new edition of his 1922 booklet, which appeared in December. In a short preliminary remark, dated November 1933, he referred affirmatively to 'German Christians'. All 'abridgements' concerned passages which discussed Erich Kaufmann.[110] Schmitt accepted Peterson's claim that his interpretation of the 'Reich' was theological, but left the character of that theology open. He recapitulated the development of his work, using the concept of 'secularization' as his guiding thread. He referred positively to Heinrich Forsthoff,[111] Ernst Forsthoff's father, and to Friedrich Gogarten, while distancing himself from the 'dialectical theology' of Karl Barth. With the new edition of *Political Theology* Schmitt opened up his decision to back National Socialism to a 'religious' interpretation, without positioning himself clearly on the side of either politics or theology. In response, Peterson extended his view into a critique in terms of conceptual history. His scholarly study *Monotheism as a Political Problem* (1935)[112] sets out from the philosophical alliance of metaphysics and monarchy and moves, via the initial arrangement of Christianity with the Roman Empire, to the theological differentiation of the realms through the dogma of the trinity. Peterson distinguished between the glorification of the Reich by the theology of the court (Eusebius) and the critique of the Roman Empire (Gregor von Nazianz), juxtaposing his own theology to Schmitt's apology for National Socialism.

Throughout all of 1933, *Hochland*[113] criticized the 'Political Theology' of National Socialism, the situation of Catholicism and the emergence of the 'German Christians', who formed an organization after March 1933 and chose their representatives in the autumn. Erik Peterson immediately wrote an exact account of their emergence and a theological critique of them.[114] In October 1933, Schmitt's close friend Heinrich Oberheid, a member of the NSDAP from 1928, became a 'German' bishop of this 'Church', which had National Socialist affinities, and soon was active in Berlin.[115] The 'coordination' of the federal states was now meant to be followed by a 'coordination' of the Churches. In January 1934, Heinrich Forsthoff became Oberheid's deputy.[116] In his preliminary remarks, Schmitt hinted at these developments but did not say anything further about theological questions or questions of constitutional law on state–Church relations [Staatskirchenrecht]. Rather, he treated 'theology' from the perspective of the philosophy of law and positioned his more recent works within the process of the 'secularization' of law: where the positivist theory of state law could observe only a gap, a theory of sovereignty informed by the theory of secularization could still find an 'institutionally' formed right. Anschütz's theorem about the limits of right ('Here, state law ends'), Schmitt said, had 'backfired on' the positivist theory of state law 'itself': it now had to remain silent. Schmitt republished his *Political Theology* with Duncker & Humblot[117] in order to refresh the memory of the meta-positivist foundations of his work. This led to new criticisms.

Within the context of National Socialist 'polycracy', the act of critically distancing oneself from other positions was part of the battle for resources for academic work. Whoever wanted to make a bid for power in these days had to measure up to Schmitt. Among the older generation, Otto Koellreutter,[118] who had followed Schmitt's work for a long time, now emerged as a critic from the National Socialist side. He was also one of those who profited from the events of 1933: he moved to Munich, the 'capital of the movement', and secured positions as an editor with several major journals. Thus, Koellreutter reviewed practically all of Schmitt's texts. Even before 1933, he had missed the 'nationalistic' concretization of the 'formal' concept of the political, with its emphasis on foreign policy.[119] In 1933 he made a surprise return and challenged Schmitt as a serious contender for the title of 'crown jurist' and the power that came with it. Koellreutter thought that he could lay claim to older rights and attacked Schmitt's conception of the 'total' state. In response, Schmitt characterized Koellreutter's 'Rechtsstaat' as 'liberal'. Koellreutter countered by bringing 'völkisch' vocabulary into play. He referred to the lowest ranks, to Otto Dietrich and Alfred Rosenberg, as interpreters of the 'völkisch' ideology and presented Schmitt's 'Political Theology' as being in 'liberal' contradiction to it.[120] When Schmitt got his pupil Günther Krauss to write a polemical article on Koellreutter, Koellreutter involved the state secretary Lammers and warned him in strong terms against the new 'juridical pope' [Rechstpapst] and 'Fouché of the national revolution'.[121] As crude as it was, and although it naively separated out 'theology' and National Socialism, the argument worked. If there was such a thing as 'völkisch' philosophy, then Schmitt's conception of 'theology', based on a theory of secularization, could not be its authentic foundation, even if the ideological fixation on the 'völkisch' approach did nothing but stab around in the dark. National Socialism did not bother about academic philosophy. It tried to support its anti-Semitic and racist ideology with scientific paradigms, yet considered its 'Weltanschauung' as a 'faith' and did not seriously seek scientifically to treat and 'imbue with meaning what is meaningless'. Even the chief ideologists, such as Alfred Baeumler and Alfred Rosenberg, enjoyed more of a jester's privilege. Hitler's *Mein Kampf* was almost taboo as an authoritative text on questions of 'philosophy'. The Führer, after all, could not be pinned down to a fixed 'programme'![122] Younger SS jurists would soon appear on the scene as competitors. Karl August Eckhardt, Reinhard Höhn and Werner Best became dangerous rivals. Abroad, however, Schmitt was clearly seen as the 'crown jurist'. After 1933, it was essentially only Huber who was able to detect a serious theoretical effort in Schmitt's work. Otherwise, the discussions and responses remained at the level of catchphrases and were informed by polemical intentions.

21

The 'Year of Construction'? Beginning and End of the Juridico-Institutional Provision of Meaning*

Writings related to the provision of meaning

Under the conditions of the 'party political federal state' [Parteien-bundesstaat] before 1933, Schmitt had been cautious regarding fundamental constitutional reform. In times of crisis, he doubted that he should engage in constitutional legislature, saying one should not change the engine while the vehicle is in motion. Nevertheless, he believed that there was a need for fundamental reform, and in the context of the Preußenschlag he actually put a piece of 'reform of the Reich' into practice. He saw his work on the Reich Governors Law and the Municipal Constitution as continuous with these activities. With the Enabling Act, he lost his reservations regarding constitutional reform. Now, the task was to mould the practical work on reforms of the Reich into a constitution, and thus to give National Socialism its own constitution. Following the so-called seizure of power and the securing of that power, juridification was the next step. The juridico-institutional provision of meaning went into legal antics and overdrive in those days.[1] Schmitt did not yet suspect the extent to which National Socialism would simply ignore it. He did not know that his role would be almost exhausted as early as the end of 1933, and that he would no longer be needed. In retrospect, he had already fulfilled his transitional role for National Socialism by propagating its ideology and helping in the 'coordination' [Gleichschaltung] of jurisprudence.

Schmitt sensed some of the risks involved in intervening in constitutional policies. However, he believed that in 1933 the stage of 'coordination' had already been superseded by his own 'formal principles'.[2] He did not present his 'ideas of 1933' in an open forum straightaway, but waited for the first legislation to appear and the Jurists' Convention to have passed. Schmitt's programmatic text *State, Movement, People* took into account the developments up to December 1933.[3] The booklet opened his important series *Der deutsche Staat der Gegenwart* [The contemporary German

---

* 'Provision of meaning' translates 'Sinngebung', a term built on analogy with 'Gesetzgebung' = legislature – i.e., there is a parallel between the giving of laws and the giving, or constitution, of meaning at play here.

state]. It was important to Schmitt that the individual publications would quickly follow one another. By way of introduction, his hastily written text emphasizes the revolutionary character of the situation after the Enabling Act ('The Weimar Constitution is no longer in force') and the suspension of the separation of powers in the executive state. He then goes on to celebrate the 'tripartite structure of political unity' in the form of the 'triad' of state, movement, people, in which the movement, he says, is the 'politically dynamic element' mediating between the state as the 'politically static element' and the 'unpolitical' people: 'Today, the political can no longer be determined on the basis of the state; the state must be determined on the basis of the political' (SBV, p. 15). The connection between state and party 'rests mainly on the combination of roles in the same person' (SBV, p. 20). Schmitt interprets the dictatorial one-party state as a homogenizing force, recapitulates in polemical, simplified terms his earlier criticism of the 'bipartite construction of the state of liberal democracy', and provides a wide-ranging sketch of the liberalization of the 'German civil service state' within constitutional history after 1848. Friedrich Julius Stahl marks the turning point in this process. In substance, Schmitt repeats his reflections from the piece on Hugo Preuß, with Max Weber's old question[4] regarding the political elite during times of bureaucratic rule in mind.

Under conditions of liberalism and of 'normativist thought', civil servants could not completely fulfil their leading role in supporting the state. With the events of 30 January 1933, 'the German Reich had a political leadership again' (SBV, p. 31). Schmitt identifies the history of the German civil service state with the history of Hegel's influence. Thus, on 30 January 1933, 'one might say, "Hegel died". This, however, does not mean that the work of the great German philosopher of the state would now be insignificant and that the idea of a political leadership which stands above the egotistic interests in society would be forfeited. What is timelessly great and German about Hegel's powerful intellectual edifice will continue to be effective under the new shape of things' (SBV, p. 32). Hegel now becomes Schmitt's most important philosophical point of reference. The references to the Prussian tradition remain vague. Schmitt establishes that National Socialism has taken up political leadership. He hints at the fact that the liberalization of juridical thought is partly to blame for this, because it has limited the concept of right to a legalistic 'functional mode' of bureaucratic rule, and he concludes by demonstrating the tensions between state and movement, civil servants and NSDAP, pointing to the 'Führer principle [Führertum] and species identity [Artgleichheit] as fundamental concepts of National Socialist right'. What provides legal orientation for the Führer principle, he asks, if not the legality of the state? In this context, Schmitt first emphasizes the 'introduction of a Führer Council' (SBV, p. 35). Such a council, he claims, has 'found its initial concrete and exemplary form in the Prussian State Council, the great constructive achievement of the Prussian Prime Minister Göring' (SVB, p. 36). This suggestion of establishing a certain institution is among the most concrete points the text makes. Schmitt knew that, after the introduction of the Reich Governors Law, the State Council could have only marginal influence, but he banked on the fact that a beginning had been made and that the State Council would become part of the Führer Council. Nowhere else did he formulate his ambitions to become a councillor, or a 'Führer of the Führer', as clearly as in this text. But, in this respect, Schmitt's statement that the political 'dynamic' was fully monopolized by the 'movement' also proved to be correct. Hitler relied on the old party comrades, Hans Frank among them, and did not like to take advice from the old elite of the civil service. He did not want a formalized Führer Council and did not want scholarly jurists at his side.

'To lead does not mean to command, to dictate, to rule in centralistic-bureaucratic fashion, or any other form of arbitrary ruling' (SBV, p. 41), Schmitt writes. Images of shepherds and helmsmen do not apply. Schmitt, in 1933, sees Hitler as the incarnation of a form of leadership that has emancipated itself from the purpose of 'control' [Aufsicht]. Leadership 'is a concept that relates to an immediate present and a real presence'. Rule becomes leadership through 'the absolute species identity [Artgleichheit] between leader and followers' (SBV, p. 42), Schmitt holds, and hints at connections with theorists of race. The formulation sounds utopian. Franz Blei, in 1936, commented on it: 'Schmitt would need to conclude: as long as the "species identity" of a German people at one with itself has not yet been established, the rule of the Führer must be tyranny and capriciousness ... Thus the National Socialist state does not yet exist.'[5] Occasionally, Schmitt probably thought that way and might have said so in private. Some contemporaries considered him to be an idealist salon Nazi, who was aware of the difference between ideal and reality and who was occasionally inclined towards ironical cynicism. However, in his political role, he presented himself as a dyed-in-the-wool Nazi who interpreted the great figures of National Socialism. Thus, in the figure of 'State Secretary Freisler', Schmitt refers to a thought that he will put at the centre of his efforts to create a 'class of protectors of right' [Rechtswahrerstand]: 'not reform of the judiciary, but reform of the jurists'. Everything depends 'on the species and the type'! Only his 'species identity' turns the dictator into a leader! State Secretary Roland Freisler, not surprisingly, immediately wrote a positive review of the article.[6] Schmitt adapted his older concept of democracy to National Socialism. Social 'homogeneity' and democratic 'identity' become 'species identity' – the 'existential bond' [Seinsgebundenheit] of 'belonging to a people and race' (SBV, p. 45). Schmitt concludes: all questions and answers lead 'to the requirement of species identity, without which a total Führer state cannot exist for a single day' (SBV, p. 46).

Schmitt's programmatic text added a few concrete points to his picture of the 'total' state: it demonstrated that in it the elite had changed, noted that the state apparatus had been taken over by the party, and ended by asking the question of the relationship between the total state and dictatorship. Only once political education or 'coordination' according to National Socialist principles had been completed would such a difference exist.

Schmitt sent ample copies of the booklet to political notables,[7] and he actively participated in the work of 'coordination' in multifarious ways. Thus, he presented his friend Werner Sombart with an ultimatum for 'coordinating' the Verein für Sozialpolitik [Association for Social

Policies].[8] At that time he was also very busy with the launch of his series. Ritterbusch, Schaffstein, Huber, Henkel and Lange sent their contributions straightaway; Forsthoff did not participate.[9] The titles of the series were published in large numbers of copies and at a low price, with a 10 per cent royalty for Schmitt. But, most importantly, Schmitt continued to elaborate on his ideas in further programmatic texts with regard to aspects of both constitutional history and the theory of law.

At the end of 1933, Schmitt was fairly exhausted. Over the Christmas period he was 'tired'. On New Year's Eve he received a 'friendly telegram from Göring, who thanked me for my loyal cooperation' (31 December 1933). At the beginning of January, Schmitt went to Magdeburg and Halberstadt, and paid the Jüngers a spontaneous visit, before travelling on to Duisburg and Bochum for lectures. Around that time, he began to think about a major lecture on constitutional history. He visited a local party meeting in Steglitz, Berlin. 'Very pleasant people', he noted. During these days he spoke a lot with Eugen Ott. On 24 January 1934, on the invitation of the 'Wehrgeistige Arbeitsgemeinschaft' [working group for military morale], headed by Alfred Bäumler and Walter Elze, he gave a lecture on 'Heerwesen und staatliche Gesamtstruktur' [The armed forces and the overall structure of the state] at the University of Berlin.[10] In the run-up to the lecture there were already some irritated reactions, because the relationship between the army and the state, between the Wehrmacht and the party, was a sensitive issue at the time. In addition, Schmitt was, in a manner of speaking, stepping into the lion's den, as his new place of employment, the University of Berlin, was a stronghold of constitutional history.[11] Hans Dehlbrück, Otto Hintze and Fritz Hartung worked on the relationship between army and state. Schmitt developed his lecture into the booklet *Staatsgefüge und Zusammenbruch des zweiten Reiches* [State structure and collapse of the Second Reich]. In it, he moves beyond the 'civil service state' and considers the Prussian 'military state' [Soldatenstaat], describing the 'logic' of constitutionalization as an 'irresolvable conflict between the military Führer state and the bourgeois Rechtsstaat'. The argument sets in at a late point. Schmitt does not consider the old Prussian situation but begins long after 1848, with the Prussian constitutional conflict of 1862 and the 'spiritual subjugation' of the military class [Soldatenstand] brought about by Bismarck's request for 'indemnity'. He explains how Wilhelm I and Bismarck tried to hold on to monarchical sovereignty within the constitutional state, and how the 'military class', as 'the state within the state' (SZZR, p. 12), was able to maintain itself to a certain extent with the help of the extra-constitutional military charter [Militärverfassung], but became increasingly moulded by the 'logic of bourgeois constitutionalism' after 1890. As a result, the Wilhelminian system experienced leadership crises. The battle for a three-year-long military service was lost. The Prussian minister of war found himself 'at the intersection of all battle lines within the state' and became a 'tragic figure' (SZZR, p. 34). The attempt at 'total mobilization' failed and the effects of the 'spiritual subjugation' showed in the Great War. The Weimar Constitution was born out of the battle against the military state, because it gave 'an answer to an obsolete question which was no longer being asked in the actual present' (SZZR, p. 43). However, the Reichswehr in Weimar still succeeded in 'upholding the German state'. The Preußenschlag 'remains a day of glory for the German Reichswehr'. But with the trial in Leipzig, Schmitt says, 'the will to political leadership' within constitutionalism had reached 'rock bottom': 'The rescue of Germany could not have come about through such a system of legality' (SZZR, p. 49), but only through the 'political soldier' Hitler.

Table 21.1 Schmitt's polarizations

Nineteenth century	Twentieth century
Citizen [Bürger]	Soldier
Philosophical Romanticism	Theism of lay religion
Discussion	Decision
Liberalism/parliamentarism	Caesaristic dictatorship

Schmitt styles the 'dualism between soldier and citizen' into a 'contradiction between two essentially different types of human beings' (SZZR, p. 13) and praises the army as the 'cultivating school of the nation' (SZZR, p. 23). He mobilizes the power of the Reichswehr as a resource and expands the legend of the 'stab in the back' [Dolchstoßlegende] into a 'system legend'[12] against the Kaiserreich, emphasizing the weakness of its leadership on account of constitutional 'dualism'. Does this mean that, to a certain extent, he plays the 'military state' off against the party? Does he, in terms of the dispute at the time between SA and Wehrmacht, take sides for the traditional 'military state'? Might he even justify a military dictatorship as opposed to that of the NSDAP? The booklet, published in May, reads like a justification *ex ante* of the Reichswehr in the conflict with the SA. The dismantling of constitutionalism is flanked with a constructive reference to 'military' traditions. Is Schmitt already postponing the question of a new constitution? In essence, his polarizations are the same from the early 1920s onwards (see table 21.1). Schmitt's historical narrative was highly controversial. While Johannes Heckel was enthusiastic about it,[13] Fritz Hartung defended the historical standards in the Berlin tradition.[14] But even here all spirit is 'present spirit': the booklet is tendentious historiography in the service of the present. It wants to be effective, to mobilize military traditions and to remind people of the pre-constitutional 'concrete order' of 'institutions'. Schmitt radicalizes his critique of constitutionalism. He would soon get to the heart of his decision [Option] against 'normativist' thinking in his programmatic text on legal theory *On the Three Types of Juristic Thought*.

On 28 January, Schmitt spoke at a conference of Gau* expert advisors [Gaufachberatertagung] in the Prussian parliament. This was followed the next day by the second 'full meeting' of the academy in

---

* A 'Gau' was an administrative region of the NSDAP, and all of Germany was divided into 'Gaue', while a range of areas annexed after 1938 were each called a 'Reichsgau'.

the town hall of Berlin, where Schmitt also took part in a 'Führer meeting' [Führerbesprechung]. In coordination with Popitz, who had first-hand information, Schmitt wrote two articles, on 'Neubau von Staat und Reich' [The new organization of state and Reich] and 'Das neue Verfassungsgesetz' [The new constitutional law], which were immediately published in the *Völkischer Beobachter*.[15] He then worked on his next lectures, later published as *On the Three Types of Juristic Thought*. Günther Krauss and Karl Schilling, Javier Conde and Delio Cantimori were pupils close to Schmitt at the time. Schmitt met with Reinhard Höhn and wrote a positive report for him on his Habilitation for the University of Heidelberg. He regularly dictated to a certain Miss Hammerstein. He spoke 'about spiritual submission' in Halle[16] and then gave 'a long lecture about the Rechtsstaat' at the Gürzenich in Cologne. The treatise *On the Three Types of Juristic Thought* developed out of two lectures that Schmitt gave on 21 February and 10 March 1934 in Berlin. A week later, the third 'full meeting' of the academy took place. Schmitt dictated the treatise, and it was published at the beginning of May.[17] The fact that it was based on two lectures explains its two-part structure: the first part provides a typology of 'juristic types of thought', the second contextualizes these types with the 'overall development of legal history'. Schmitt here complements his earlier distinction between decisionism and normativism with the 'thinking in terms of concrete order and form [Gestaltung]',* thus integrating Huber's further differentiations. He considers the term 'legal system' [Rechtsordnung] misleading. He distinguishes between norm and order and sociologically limits the norm to 'a certain regulating function with a comparatively small degree of validity of its own, independent of the factual situation' (DARD, p. 11). Normativism, he says, is the ideology of a 'transaction-based society' [Verkehrsgesellschaft] (DARD, p. 16), as opposed to the 'concrete order' which is the 'nomos' of a 'people': the 'Gestalt' of the 'living relationships' [der lebendigen Verhältnisse] in which 'a people encounters itself'. Schmitt adduces Hölderlin's translation of Pindar, thus evoking the heroic cult of ancient Greece once practised by the Hölderlin generation of the youth movement, which Heidegger also cultivated only after 1933. Here we find the beginnings of Schmitt's later speculations on the nomos. The quotation from Hölderlin's translation is a cipher in particular circles.[18] Schmitt considers the 'nomos' as a kind of 'primal word'† of right, which unites in itself all 'types of thought' and one-sided interpretations. In the text's second part, Schmitt categorizes the types of thought in terms of the history of legal thought and emphasizes a strong tradition of the paradigm of 'institutional' order [Ordnungsdenken] in Germany, referring to the notion of order [Ordnungsdenken] in Maurice Hauriou and Santi Romano[19] and associating it with National Socialism. The first doctoral theses supervised by Schmitt in Berlin would then investigate the tension between 'positiv-

---

*   The term 'Gestaltung' can mean both the act of shaping and the resulting form.
†   The German term 'Urwort' suggests associations to Goethe's well-known poem *Urworte. Orphisch* [Primal Words. Orphic].

ism' and the 'notion of order' [Ordnungsdenken] in exemplary fashion: Günther Krauss found it in the form of a 'paradox' in Rudolph Sohm, and Albrecht Wagner identified it with the 'battle' fought by the normativistic judiciary against the notion of order [Ordnungsdenken] informing the administration.[20]

Schmitt related 'decisionistic' Gestaltung [creation of legal form] to traditional concepts of order [traditionelle Ordnungen]; however, he also emphasized the political interpretation of the legal medium [Rechtsmodus].[21] The accusation he levelled against decisionism – that it politicizes legal thought – was also the end result of his treatise. This showed very quickly in his dismantling of the concept of the Rechtsstaat with which he began in a speech given on 17 February 1934 at a Gau conference of the BNSDJ in Cologne,[22] which bore the title 'Nationalsozialismus und Rechtsstaat' [National Socialism and Rechtsstaat]. Schmitt spoke after Hans Frank. A year after the Reichstag fire, he defended the abandonment of the Rechtsstaat principle of non-retroactivity as expressed in the 'legal maxim of *"nullum crimen sine poena"'*. His speech discussed the 'opposition between the just state and the formal legal state', using the Reichstag fire as an examplary case in which 'respect for the formal institutions of the Rechtsstaat' had bordered 'on the limits of open injustice'.[23] Once again, Schmitt committed legal interpretation to the 'spirit' of National Socialism and criticized previous stages of 'spiritual submission' under the legalist thought in jurisprudence. He wanted to dismantle legality and the belief in legality. The place of normativism was taken by a 'notion of concrete order' [konkretes Ordnungsdenken]; the rule of law was replaced with the education of a 'new type of German jurist'.[24] Schmitt's programmatic texts, written within the space of a few weeks, removed constitutional legal concepts and aimed at an instrumentalization of law. The Hanseatische Verlagsanstalt made substantial efforts to promote them. By the beginning of September, 7,780 copies of *State, Movement, People* and 1,722 copies of the *State Structure* text were sold.[25] The series was so well established that it even served as a cover for 'communist' foreign texts.[26] At the end of 1935, the series of programmatic texts was finally replaced with a series of more comprehensive 'introductions' into various areas of law.[27] However, Benno Ziegler, the head of the HVA, repeatedly assured Schmitt how pleased he was 'that we persevered with the series, despite occasional impulses to abandon it'.[28]

Farewell to international law?

The juridical-institutional provision of meaning of National Socialism was facing a paradox: it had to present the dismantling of legality as a constructive achievement. Schmitt carried out the same procedure for international law. In his battle against Versailles and the French policies regarding the Rhineland he once discovered the great importance of international law. He saw his distinction between legality and legitimacy as the 'core question' of the League of Nations – i.e., whether Geneva actually possessed a principle of legitimacy that would elevate it above Versailles and allow it to create peaceful possibilities for revisions. Following Schmitt's move to Berlin, questions of international law receded into the background and constitutional questions took centre stage. Upon his return to Berlin he took up a chair in state law but also became academic advisor to the Institute for International Law of the Kaiser Wilhelm Society and co-editor of the *Zeitschrift für ausländisches öffentliches Recht und Völkerrecht* [Journal for Foreign Public Law and International Law].

In November 1933, in an article titled 'Frieden oder Pazifismus?' [Peace or pacifism?], Schmitt called for Germany to leave the League of Nations. Following Germany's departure he published an extended edition of his annotated collection of sources with the title 'Das politische Problem der Friedenssicherung' [The political problem of securing peace]. Had international law become obsolete along with the League of Nations? Was peace only a political problem? After the matter of the constitution, Schmitt now engaged with the foundations of international law. In the summer term 1934 he gave lectures on 'Allgemeines Staatsrecht und Staatslehre' [General state law and state theory] and on 'Völkerrecht' [International law].[29] On 18 July 1934, shortly after the Night of the Long Knives,* Schmitt gave a lecture on 'Nationalsozialismus und Völkerrecht' [National Socialism and international law] at the Hochschule für Politik. It was published as a booklet – with a slight delay, due to the mechanisms of censorship[30] – in a run of 3,000 copies at the end of October[31] and can be considered Schmitt's fourth programmatic text. His BNSDJ adjutant at the time, Hubertus Bung, took care of its distribution among party circles.[32] The blurb, formulated by Schmitt, ran:

> This text presents a vivid picture of the illusory blossoming of international law and its activities as they developed after 1919. The discrepancy between the pacifistic bustle and the inner discord and injustice of today's international situation is unveiled with the clarity of jurisprudential thought. The fundamental right of nations to self-affirmation and self-defence is juxtaposed to a system of pacts and norms, which is hollowed out by thousands of caveats, and to a League of Nations incapable of any consistency. The entry of Bolshevist Russia to the League of Nations makes this text particularly relevant today.[33]

The booklet initially formulates a kind of 'primacy of domestic politics': 'For domestic order is the basis and precondition of inter-state order' (FP, p. 391). There are 'basic rights of states and peoples' (FP, p. 392). International law, Schmitt holds, must be built on the right to the existence of political unities. But more recent international law is based on the 'Kriegsschuldlüge' [lie about war guilt] (FP, p. 396) and on 'discord' and 'injustice'. It rests, Schmitt says, on the 'contradic-

---

* The murder of members of the left wing of the Nazi party, the leader of the SA, Ernst Röhm, and conservative opponents of the Nazi party which took place between 30 June and 2 July 1934 in order to stabilize Hitler's power.

tion between substantial injustice and an illusory juridical blossoming'. Despite having left the League of Nations, Germany still belongs to the 'legal community' of the European people, in contrast to Bolshevist Russia.[34] 'We belong to it with such necessity that without us, or even against us, no European international law exists' (FP, p. 399). However, the League of Nations in Geneva has squandered its chances of developing further. It has substituted its legal substance with juridical fictions and has granted 'existential and meaning-creating [sinngebende] caveats', which allow politics to enter and destroy 'continuity and identity' with various 'transformations'. 'Today, the legal substance of the idea of European international law has its home with us' (FP, p. 406), Schmitt writes, and refers to Germany's exit from the League and the German–Polish non-aggression pact of 26 January 1934, which marks the beginning of a return to a politics where states meet on 'an equal footing'* (ibid.), a politics of direct inter-state contracts.

Schmitt talked not about the end of international law or of the exit from the League as the solution, but rather about a politics of securing peace by introducing a new regulation of international relations. He would continue to follow the 'transformations' of the League of Nations in the years to come and to test the 'logic' of mutual pacts,[35] interpreting 'systems of pacts' as a 'preparation for war' [Kriegsrüstung] and demonstrating problems that are internal to the duties of mutual military assistance. He justified the entry of German troops into the de-militarized Rhineland and Hitler's breach of the Locarno treaties with an antecedent 'breaking-up [Sprengung] of the Locarno community through the inclusion of the Soviets'. He considered Italy's war in Abyssinia as another self-capitulation of the League of Nations. He then moved from the problem of securing peace in Europe to the development of his concept of war. He handed over the European 'legal substance' to Nazi Germany.

The themes of Schmitt's writings, in which he attempted to create a new cosmos of meaning [Sinnstiftungsschriften], published in quick succession from April 1933 onwards, can be characterized roughly as shown in table 21.2.

Table 21.2 The provision of National Socialist meaning

RSG	The task of coordination [Gleichschaltung]
BP 1933	Primacy of NS policies
SBV	The state structure of National Socialism
SZZR	Constitutional history
DARD	The concept of right [Rechtsbegriff]
NSVR	International law
Leviathan	The fiction of unity

---

* The German is 'Auge um Auge': 'an eye for an eye'. But the context suggests that he meant 'Auge in Auge': 'face to face', as equals.

The 'immediately just state' of Adolf Hitler and 30 June 1934

During spring 1934, Schmitt continued his industrious efforts at promoting his institutional interpretation of legal meaning. On 11 May he travelled to a 'Gautagung' [Gau conference] of the Jurists' Association, where he presented a sketch of the 'fundamental principles of National Socialist jurisprudence'. 'All participants met at the sacrificial altar of Albert Leo Schlageter on the Golzheimer Heide for a consecration gathering [Weihestunde] whose deep meaning [Sinngebung] was evoked in the words of the Reich commissar of justice, Dr Frank.'[36] Schmitt became godfather to Ernst Jünger's second son, Carl Alexander, and on 19 May he travelled to Goslar for his christening. At a workshop of the Academy for German Right (26 May 1934), in the presence of, for instance, Gürtner, Freisler, Thierack and Frank, Schmitt identified a number of tasks: the problem of corporations under public law, of jurisdiction and of administrative jurisdiction. Schmitt extended his critique of the judiciary. After the Staatsgerichtshof [constitutional court], the critique of the Reich Administrative Court was now 'due, so to speak' [sozusagen fällig]*.[37] With the help of his father, Schmitt collected together a substantial number of documents on the family's history for the 'Ariernachweis' [proof of Aryan descent]. He also needed to document Duška's descent over several generations.[38] Some projects for journals took on a more concrete shape. Huber told him that the Kiel School wanted to take on the editorship for the *Zeitschrift für die gesamten Staatswissenschaften* [General Journal for State Theory] 'on behalf of the Ministry'.[39] He asked Schmitt, the state councillor, for his support as a 'Führer', but at the same time side-tracked him to a certain extent. Schmitt's reply was relaxed, despite his 'distrust of coordinated publishing houses',[40] especially as he could – in Huber's words – report the recent 'conquest' of the *Deutsche Juristen-Zeitung* [Journal of German Jurists].[41] Schmitt, for his part, plotted and schemed, launching an article written by Günther Krauss. In response, after a meeting with Schmitt (1/2 June 1934), Ernst Friesenhahn rejected the offer of the editorship of the *Juristen-Zeitung*.[42] He wrote to Huber: 'I think the other day we were in agreement about the character of Carl Schmitt; I cannot make myself entirely dependent on someone like this.'[43] This is a forceful formulation from someone who was close to Schmitt as his assistant over many years. Koellreutter protested to Hans Frank and State Secretary Lammers about the polemical article by Krauss. Schmitt would not get rid of these opponents. His pupil from Bonn, Karl Lohmann, took on the editorship instead of Friesenhahn.[44] He had been a member of the party since 1 May 1933, an SA training instructor [Schulungsreferent] and 'Rottenführer' [pack leader] and an academic advisor at the Kommunalwissenschaftlichen Institut [Institute for Municipal Studies], and he also qualified as the author of a booklet on *Hitlers Staatsauffassung* [Hitler's understanding of the state] and of an *Einführung in die Reichskunde* [Introduction to the science of the Reich]. Schmitt introduced the first volume with a call for the

---

* The German expression suggests destruction as well as critique.

coordination of the judiciary.[45] His suggestions were put to the test with the events of 30 June.

After the first year of revolutionary change, a year of consolidation for the new state was needed. Which side would win out in the conflict between 'movement' and state was as yet undetermined. As early as the beginning of 1934, Hitler was put under pressure from two sides: from the revolutionary wing of the movement and from the national conservative camp which supported him. In June 1934 the leader of the SA, Ernst Röhm, demanded a 'second revolution'.[46] However, Hitler needed the elite of the state apparatus for his war preparations. When Franz von Papen gave a much noticed speech (17 June 1934) in Marburg, which had been written by Edgar Julius Jung and which roused the spirit of the national conservative forces, Hitler thought it was time to act. He went to Bad Wiessee and, on 30 June, personally arrested Röhm and other SA leaders. Some SA leaders he had shot immediately. To Röhm he granted the privilege of shooting himself. As the Bavarian minister of justice, Hans Frank had legal reservations and actually spoke with those taken into custody in Stadelheim Prison, Munich, but then tolerated the murders.[47] Because Röhm did not carry out the sentence on himself, he was shot by SS henchmen. Hitler also used the occasion to liquidate some old opponents, among them Gustav von Kahr, Gregor Strasser, General von Schleicher and Edgar Jung. More than 100 people were murdered, of whom only about fifty were members of the SA. The SA was certainly a threat, but no plans for a 'Röhm Putsch' existed. And there was no legal sentencing of responsible actors, but rather a quick settling of scores and revenge taken even on rivals who had lost all power. Hitler demonstrated in full public view how dangerous the old competitors had been to him. The SS proved its subservience.

The murders were carried out in full public view. Despite all propaganda efforts, they left a strong negative impression, both in Germany and abroad. The state of exception had a 'revealing' effect: Hitler had now shown his murderous and revengeful character. On 3 July he decreed a 'Gesetz über Maßnahmen der Staatsnotwehr' [Law regarding measures of state self-defence], which consisted of a single article: 'The measures carried out on 30 June, 1 and 2 July in order to quell attacks aiming at treason and high treason are legal as acts of state self-defence.' However, imprisonment would have sufficed for such self-defence.[48] At the time, Thomas Mann noted in his diary:

> I confessed my feelings of satisfaction, hope, relief, gratification, which fill me in light of the events in Germany, to K. [Katia Mann] today. All the time one was under the pressure of the enthusiastic belief of fools. Occasionally, one might have wavered in one's beliefs oneself. At least now, after little more than a year, Hitlerism begins to prove itself for what one has seen, recognized and deeply perceived it to be all along: the ultimate lowness, degenerate stupidity and a bloody disgrace – it becomes obvious that it will certainly and unfailingly continue to present itself in that vein.[49]

From this moment onwards, it was obvious to Thomas Mann and those in bourgeois circles, who kept their eyes open, who Hitler was and what he would bring. 30 June 1934 was a key moment in the history of National Socialism. It was a key moment for Schmitt as well: the counter-moment, so to speak, to 20 July 1932. He, too, now knew that he was in allegiance with a gang of murderers, but, sitting in the belly of the Leviathan, he chose a strategy of pre-emptive defence, which, in fact, added the betrayal of his old companions during the time of rule by presidential decree to the betrayal of his Jewish friends in 1933, even though there were some moderate limitations to this later betrayal.

This was the time when the Volksgerichtshof [people's court] was created. Göring instructed the public prosecutor's office. Hitler gave a justificatory speech in the Reichstag and, in a manner of speaking, obtained 'indemnity'.[50] Schmitt had meetings with, among others, Popitz and officers of the Reichswehr and wrote his first article as editor of the *Deutsche Juristen-Zeitung*, titled 'Der Führer schützt das Recht' [The Führer protects the law], which justified Hitler's way of proceeding with reference to a state of emergency and on the basis of historical experience. The operation, he wrote, was not 'the act of a republican dictator'; Hitler's right originated in the 'people's right to live' [Lebensrecht des Volkes]. 30 June had removed an 'old and sick age' (PB, p. 201), whose sickness had been weak leadership and a lack of 'unity of state power'. Hitler had identified 'enemies of the state' who had violated duties of loyalty. Schmitt did not mention the names of the victims, did not mention Schleicher.

The historico-philosophical justification provided in this text is striking. Schmitt characterizes the emergency law [Notrecht] as an entirely new kind of law, writing: 'The Führer protects the law against the worst forms of abuse when, in the moment of danger, he immediately creates law by force of his character as Führer [Führertum] as the supreme legal authority [oberster Gerichtsherr]' (PB, p. 200).[51] The expression 'immediately' points towards a momentary lawlessness. Schmitt describes an exceptional creation of law within a secular context. If he takes his concepts seriously, he cannot possibly claim that Hitler 'protects' the law, because he creates it in the first place.

After 23 March 1933, Schmitt considered 30 June as the second epochal act of National Socialism, as a second foundational moment, or 'refoundation' [Umgründung], creating an 'immediate' state of justice, in which legality had lost any secure validity. The first foundational moment had also been revolutionary and created a new situation, but it still left effective those 'laws not explicitly suspended', as Schmitt emphasized several times.[52] With 30 June, this remnant of legal security was also fundamentally delegitimized. The Führer state had said farewell to the principle of the separation of powers. Schmitt interpreted Hitler's law of 3 July as the direct transformation of the system's second revolutionary beginning into a new legally binding and normal situation.[53] He demanded a 'particularly severe prosecution' of unauthorized 'special actions' [Sonderaktionen] (PB, p. 202) and critically emphasized the semantic cynicism of the expression 'special actions'. And, indeed, the judiciary opened investigations, and Gürtner's initiatives led to a trial.[54]

In terms of legal policy, it might be possible to see the significance of

Schmitt's article in the limitations it sets to 'special actions', in the fact that it openly discusses the dialectic between state of exception and normal situation. From this perspective, Schmitt would have, on the one hand, unmasked National Socialism as a state of exception and, on the other, demanded a return to a normal situation. However, such hermeneutic attempts at saving Schmitt's good name can easily sound like sophistry once we look at the emphatic legitimizing gesture of the article. The strongest accent lies on the importance of the events in historico-philosophical terms and on the absolution of Hitler.

Schmitt's article was sharply rejected by many contemporaries[55] and, to the present day, is seen as a scandalous selling off of the principle of legality to the dictator. It offers a purely political justification: Hitler guarantees the 'unity of state power' against a second revolution by the SA. Schmitt thus defends the alleged historical task of National Socialism, namely to provide an answer to Versailles. Schmitt read Huber's articles with great enthusiasm at the time. Huber's 'Einheit der Staatsgewalt' [Unity of state power] had been written before 30 June; however, Schmitt thanked him again for the article: 'It is really excellent, and one should think that now every German jurist should understand what the heart of the matter is.'[56] This was an allusion to his own justification of the 30 June events: the operation was necessary in the interest of the 'unity of state power'; the mistakes of Wilhelminian times must be avoided. When Huber's next article, on 'Das Staatsoberhaupt des Deutschen Reiches' [The head of state of the German Reich], appeared in print,[57] Schmitt wrote in retrospect: 'Your article on the head of state is very good; however, I do not believe that Art. 48 can continue to be in force, or that the W.[eimar] Constitution] is still applicable. . . . The interpretation of 30 June 1934 in terms of state law is the touchstone of all state law today.'[58]

A few days after 30 June, Schmitt gave his lecture on 'Nationalsozialismus und Völkerrecht' [National Socialism and international law], in which he brushed aside the principle of legality [Legalitätssystem] and tried to provide a new basis for the 'legal substance' in the form of the 'basic right' to self-determination. Further articles on the concept of the Rechtsstaat and 'Die Rechtswissenschaft im Führerstaat' [Jurisprudence within the Führer state] followed. First, Schmitt wrote an introductory article for Hans Frank's *Nationalsozialistisches Handbuch für Recht und Gesetzgebung* [National Socialist handbook for right and legislature], in which he once more told the story of the formalization of law and how it led to the Rechtsstaat becoming 'the conceptual opposite of the state of justice [Gerechtigkeitsstaat]' (SGN, p. 112), and in which he also provided a short survey of the institutional state of affairs at the time.[59] Next, in the article 'Was bedeutet der Streit um den "Rechtsstaat"?' [What is the significance of the argument over the Rechtsstaat?], Schmitt formulated his strategic understanding of the concept of the Rechtsstaat: 'In fact, the Rechtsstaat is precisely the conceptual opposite to an immediately just state' (SGN, p. 121). Holding on to the Rechtsstaat can only be an 'intermediary stage' – the word 'Rechtsstaat' will become 'superfluous'; the 'adaptation and further development of the word' will be the sign of a 'mental conquest' [geistige Eroberung], will be the 'trophy of a victory in intellectual history' [eines geistesgeschichtlichen Sieges]' (SGN, p. 131). In this way, Schmitt marked the completion of the National Socialist revolution in the course of which the 'state of justice' became emancipated from the liberal Rechtsstaat. If we remind ourselves of the great significance Schmitt already attached in 1914 to the 'times of mediacy' and the 'times of immediacy', and if we pay attention to this inconspicuous word 'immediately', we can detect a historico-philosophical signal in the expression 'immediately just state'. This is the point at which the Führer state is given its apocalyptic consecration. With this, the juridico-institutional provision of meaning had reached an endpoint.

The Reichspräsident, Hindenburg, died on 2 August, marking the conclusive end of the transitional period of rule by presidential decree. Hitler also inherited Hindenburg's office. The *Deutsche Juristen-Zeitung* published a short note, 'Hindenburg zum Gedenken' [In memoriam Hindenburg],[60] probably written by Schmitt. Around the same time, he withdrew his offer to write a preface for an 'Allgemeine Theorie des faschistischen Staates' [General theory of the fascist state], telling the publisher: 'I am currently ill and unable to work for two months.'[61] His project for the provision of meaning [Sinngebungsunternehmen] was now in crisis. Schmitt no longer really believed that National Socialism was based on a relatively stable legal system [Rechtsverfassung]. In this situation, he was inclined to opt for a strategy of pre-emptive defence. His National Socialist euphoria had not yet subsided. On the contrary, Schmitt threw himself into the arms of the new rulers more and more recklessly. On 27 August he swore his official oath of loyalty to Hitler. At the beginning of September, he attended Frank's 'Gauführerkongreß der Deutschen Rechtsfront' [congress of Gau leaders of the German right-wing front].[62] He then went to the party congress in Nuremberg[63] before spending a few days 'as a guest of H. Frank'[64] at the Schliersee, where Frank owned a country house. On 12–13 October, he again met with Frank; Schmitt gave the keynote speech at a Gau conference of the Reichsfachgruppe Hochschullehrer [Association of the Reich's University Teachers], in which he defended 'the movement's species-specific concept of education'.[65] A 'Kameradschaftsabend'* was held in the Löwenbräu-Keller in Munich and ended with the ceremonious unveiling of a commemorative plaque in front of the Feldherrenhalle. The old warrior Frank celebrated Theodor von der Pforten as a 'hero of German legal life' 'in the face of the blood flag' of 9 November 1923. Schmitt joined these grotesque rituals. He had reached the very top – or, if you prefer, bottom – of the camarilla. From then on, he increasingly limited his activities to organizational matters and withdrew from the analysis and justification of the 'concrete constitutional situation'. As the editor of the series *Der deutsche Staat der Gegenwart* [The contemporary German state], Schmitt continued to play

---

* Old-fashioned term for social gathering of 'comrades'. The term is often associated with the military but may also relate to other – male – groups, such as fire brigades, sports clubs, etc.

his role of a creator of meaning [Sinnstiftungsrolle]. However, at the end of 1934 he already saw fairly clearly that the juridico-institutional analysis of the meaning of a National Socialist 'constitution' had failed on the grounds of the destructive dynamic of the Führer state and that National Socialism would bring about a state of exception.

Disputation über den Rechtsstaat [Disputation on the Rechtsstaat], the *viva voce* examination of one of Schmitt's doctoral students, Günther Krauss, published together with a preface and afterword by Schmitt himself as an 'experiment'[66] in his series, can be interpreted as an ambiguous and ironic Mephistophelian conclusion to his efforts at the provision of meaning. The 'disputation', which took place on 1 February 1935, was presented as a 'practical example',[67] as the simulation of a 'scholarly' debate among National Socialists about the concept of a Rechtsstaat. Schmitt knew that his debate over the concepts of 'Rechtsstaat and state of power [Machtstaat]' had already concluded. In his afterword, he somewhat cryptically hints at the fact that at stake was the question of 'humanity or bestiality'.[68] It is again incomprehensible why, given these alternatives, he would vehemently opt for the side of 'bestiality'. The bishop of the German Christians of Saxony joined Schmitt in his critique of the concept of the Rechtsstaat.[69] Huber, at the time, juxtaposed it with a 'struggle to overcome the antitheses', with a 'battle for a true synthesis'.[70]

The small troop of the remaining faithful

At the time, Schmitt saw himself as a Führer and expected obedience. He hardly distinguished between morality, politics and right. Ernst Jünger distanced himself, ostentatiously moved from Berlin to Goslar, and rejected Hitler's wooing. Jünger looked at the figure of the 'worker' within a wide historico-philosophical context and at his times as reflected in the paintings of Bosch and Breughel. In his correspondence with Schmitt, there is a considerable gap during 1933, despite continuing personal contact. Both increasingly concentrated on the neutral terrain of art in their letters. But Jünger kept in touch, despite the differences in their attitude. The friendship was kept afloat not least by their wives. An intensive correspondence began between Schmitt and Gretha Jünger. On the one hand, Jünger retreated to the position of an observer; on the other, he contradicted Schmitt very clearly on occasion. Jünger saw himself and Schmitt as belonging to the higher echelons. On 9 November 1934 the two met in Berlin.[71] Jünger commented on their meeting in a letter: 'As I felt that we parted at a moment of slight disagreement, allow me briefly to remark that our relationship probably rests on a shared ground, where such a difference is of no importance whatsoever. What interests me is the absolute and substantial greatness of man; in order to measure it, I have at my disposal entirely different criteria, compared to, for instance, the political' (JS, p. 42). Jünger also plays the role of a soldier in his correspondence, demanding a 'heroic realism', which soberly registers the political reality and measures human beings according to their 'greatness'. Compared to the hierarchical relationships, which the Führer ideology imposed on people, the relationship between Jünger and Schmitt was a free exchange between equals.

Schmitt could not communicate as freely with his colleagues and pupils. The group he trusted became smaller and smaller. Hardly any of the colleagues he valued still stood by him. The group of followers among his pupils also melted like ice in the sun. Forsthoff distanced himself, and there were tensions even with Huber, his most loyal and important colleague. At the end of August, Huber was in Berlin in connection with appointment matters; the faculty in Kiel was meant to become a 'wholly uniform body'.[72] Huber stayed with Schmitt and thanked him for the 'nice days'. A major project was the textbook or 'Grundriss* series'.[73] Huber was undecided between the Hanseatische Verlagsanstalt and Mohr as publishers, and he also worried about the homogeneous appearance of the 'group'.[74] Schmitt commented with light irony 'that all young professors are dependent up to their ears on the pluralism of publishers and are "bound"'.[75] He complained about his 'internal difficulties'[76] and was disgruntled when told of a remark by Huber about Fritz Schultz, a colleague who had been expelled. Everywhere the pressures of establishing a homogeneous jurisprudence led to quarrels. The principle of just one journal, one publisher, one faculty, one crown jurist had inevitably to lead to conflict!

At the end of the year, important decisions were taken. Karl August Eckhardt – Schmitt's former colleague at the Handelshochschule, a long-serving party comrade, a historian of law with a firm belief in the Germanic race, and an SS lawyer – had also become an advisor at the Reichsministerium für Wissenschaft, Erziehung und Volksbildung [Reich Ministry of Science, Education and National Education] in October 1934. Upon an invitation from Schmitt, the Reichsfachgruppe Hochschullehrer [Association of the Reich's University Teachers] of the BNSDJ held a conference on 20 and 21 December in order to discuss a new curriculum.[77] 'For the first time, it has been possible to bring together the leading lecturers from all German universities in order to work together on the question of university teaching.'[78] Schmitt gave a concluding address in which he summarized the proceedings. But Eckhardt had taken on the 'general supervision [Gesamtleitung] of papers',[79] and he did not follow the advice of the association's members. Already at the outset, he made it clear that all decisions were taken by the ministry. He met his colleagues in good spirits and did not mince his words: 'We do it anyway, no matter what will be said about it.'[80] 'Forgive me for saying this: many of you have honestly and sincerely gone along with the times, but many of you are wrong to think that they are National Socialists. It is possible to experience what National Socialism is – I do not want to say "only", but – almost only as a member of the SA.'[81] We may assume that it was not easy for Schmitt to accept Eckhardt's speech for his series.[82] The contributions from Schmitt's 'spearhead group' [Stoßtrupp] and Eckhardt's speech appeared in two separate volumes. The Hanseatische Verlagsanstalt had also caught on to the changing winds, distanced itself from Schmitt and handed the co-editorship of the textbook series to Eckhardt. The ministe-

---

* The term 'Grundriss' refers to works which set out the fundamental principles of a subject.

'Many of you have honestly and sincerely gone along with the times, but many of you are wrong to think that they are National Socialists' – Karl August Eckhardt to Schmitt's Hochschullehrergruppe, 20 December 1934

rial guidelines did not recommend Berlin as a place of study: 'First, give preference to the legal faculties in Kiel, Breslau and Königsberg, which have been chosen [ausersehen]* as political spearheads!'[83]

The new curriculum 'replaced free teaching and learning with the guiding model of studies committed to the ideal of community'.[84] Even in its terminology it pushed the concept of right into the background. Instead of 'state law', the 'constitution' was studied, instead of 'administrative law', simply 'administration'. And these were also the titles of Huber's and Maunz's next textbooks. Schmitt's last article on the Rechtsstaat was a reaction to these changes. The concept of a constitution lost its juridical relevance, and hence it was again more or less unproblematic to use it. 'The inner strain caused by the battle in Berlin is harder than it looks', Schmitt wrote at the end of 1934, and continued to hope that Huber would remain a good 'comrade and ally'.[85] In Huber's summary, 'a step forward ha[d] been taken in this year of construction'.[86] He was working on his textbook and 'ideal picture' [Wunschbild][87] of a constitution. In Schmitt's view, the situation looked much bleaker, and yet he did not dissociate himself from National Socialism. Rather, he replaced his efforts at a juridico-institutional apologia for National Socialism with institutional battles, and he intensified his polemical interventions in international law and his anti-Semitic polemics.

* The term 'ausersehen' has religious connotations. The 'Ausersehene' denotes the Messiah.

22

Anti-Semitic Provision of Meaning

New approaches to legal theory

At the beginning of 1934, Schmitt still looked back optimistically on the first year with a National Socialist constitution. But while Huber embarked on the development of a National Socialist constitutional theory – beginning with the 'head of state' and the 'meaning' of the constitution, down to the 'principles' [Grundriss][1] – Schmitt drove the distinction between the state of law and the state of justice to its extreme of an 'immediately just state'. This state was a totalitarian Leviathan. The dismantling of the Rechtsstaat was turned into a legal principle.[2] The point of crisis in Schmitt's work is usually associated with his precarious situation in 1936; however, signs of it can be detected even earlier, and with the notion of the 'immediately just state' it is clearly indicated as early as the end of 1934. The time of programmatic texts was over. Until 1938, Schmitt did not publish any further monographs, nor did he engage in the analysis of the 'constitutional situation' in the context of Germany's domestic politics. After 30 June 1934 would have been the right moment for him to say farewell to National Socialism. His hopes of gaining greater influence on constitutional matters in his role as 'state councillor' had ebbed away in the face of the realities of the State Council. His initiative for the creation of a 'Führer Council' had not even been discussed. In front of the whole world, National Socialism had presented itself as the rule of violence. The attempt at transforming its rule into a normal situation had failed. Schmitt, too, now doubted that National Socialism was capable of 'constitutionality' and withdrew from efforts at the juridico-institutional provision of meaning. But he drew the wrong conclusions. After his influence on Göring began to diminish, he could also have taken his leave of Hans Frank, and thus put an end to the evil nightmare of his engagement with National Socialism. His collaboration would still have lasted longer than, for instance, Heidegger's as the Rektor [vice-chancellor] of Freiburg University, but it would still visibly have been an error he regretted, and one that could be granted some originally good intentions. Although it is not possible to leave a band of criminals at will, a retreat to his role as a scholar would mostly likely still have been possible at that moment in time. Therefore, Schmitt's continued engagement after 30 June 1934, despite the fact that he now knew about the violent character of the 'system' and the fact that it was based on a continuous state of exception, is almost more significant than his initial decision to side with National Socialism after 23 March 1933. Schmitt saw himself as living outside any normal situation, a situation resembling the apocalyptic end of times, and moved from the juridico-institutional provision of meaning to an anti-Semitic justification of violence. He no longer fought his counter-revolutionary 'decisive battle' primarily against Marxism and anarchism, as he did during the time of the Weimar Republic; rather, he now interpreted the situation in openly anti-Semitic terms as a 'battle against the Jewish spirit'. The emphasis of his work lay entirely on interventions on behalf of the party organization. Until the end of 1936, he acted as an itinerant political speaker at the side of Hans Frank. Biographical information on those years is sparse. Schmitt's stenographic appointment calendars for the years 1934 to 1945 (and beyond that into the 1970s) still exist, but his diary breaks off.[3] His correspondence with Huber, Forsthoff and Jünger fizzles out. Schmitt disappeared from the university scene and plunged into the clique of functionaries.

Helmut Quaritsch offers two explanations for the astounding 'loss of quality' in Schmitt's work. Either

[t]he ideological convert Schmitt thought he had to outdo all other jurists with regard to 'loyalty to the Führer' and anti-Semitism. Or he intentionally loaded his confessions with so much byzantine exaggeration that the adepts, upon closer scrutiny, had to recognize that they were foolish jubilations [Narrenjubel] and nonsense-proskynesis . . . Such a play within a play, to the point of becoming a 'parody of himself', cannot be put beyond Schmitt.[4]

The ironic player acted like a Shakespearean figure. Waldemar Gurian suggested a third possibility and read it as a sign of complete 'cynicism'. Following the apotheosis of the Führer regarding 30 June, Gurian wrote: 'On the basis of his past, we may assume that the crown jurist of the Third Reich does not take National Socialism seriously, but uses it only as a means for his personal purposes.'[5] Caesarism creates diverse rituals and pathos formulas. In Schmitt's genuflexion before the Führer state, fear and ironic despair over the new form of 'stupidity' entered into a chaotic mixture. His cautious reserve against comprehensive accounts of the legal situation already shows that he had insight into the 'foolish jubila-tions' [Narrenjubel]. However, Schmitt did not create a clearly identifiable double authorship which would allow one to distinguish between esoteric critique and external apologia. Rather, his doubts about the 'constitu-tion' of National Socialism produced the most horrendous justifications. Schmitt had little belief left in the capacity of the system to create order, yet he threw himself into anti-Semitism and affirmed National Socialism as the anti-Semitic state. His anti-Semitism, long-standing and continuously visible since 1933, became his central justificatory ideology.

In terms of quantity, what Schmitt wrote after the articles on the Rechtsstaat up to 1938 he would at other times have produced very quickly.

A few articles on international law continued his critique of the League of Nations[6] and, via the *Begriff der Piraterie* [Concept of piracy], work their way towards the diagnosis of a *Turn to the Discriminating Concept of War*. Smaller reviews were done on the side.[7] Within the context of the reform of the university curriculum, he gave his opinion on the 'Aufgabe und Notwendigkeit des deutschen Rechtsstandes' [The task and necessity of the German legal profession] and 'Über die neuen Aufgaben der Verfassungsgeschichte' [On the new tasks of constitutional history]. The latter was also a response to Hartung's criticism and at the same time formulated a new area of research, which, however, Schmitt left to be developed by Forsthoff and Huber. He deepened his reflections on 'Die geschichtliche Lage der deutschen Rechtswissenschaft' [The historical situation of German jurisprudence] and characterized 'Die Rechtswissenschaft im Führerstaat' [Jurisprudence in the Führer state] with a political concept of law that stressed the aspect of planning. The title reflects the fact that, for Schmitt, talk about the 'Rechtsstaat' now gave way to talk about the 'Führer state'; 'The law is the plan and will of the Führer.'[8]

Schmitt analysed this concept of law again in terms of legal theory by rejecting the alternatives 'Kodifikation oder Novelle?' [Codification or amendment?] and by identifying two main formal elements of the plan within the practice of National Socialism: the 'practice of guiding principles' [Leitsatzpraxis][9] and the 'the new type of transformative laws [Umwandlungsgesetze]'.[10] He further elaborated this new descriptive approach to legal theory in a 'Vergleichendem Überblick über die neueste Entwicklung des Problems der gesetzgeberischen Ermächtigungen (Legislative Delegationen)' [Comparative survey over the most recent development of the problem of legislative authorization (delegation of legislature)],[11] a text which can be considered as the analytically most important publication until the *Leviathan* book, because it provides the justification for the apologia of the Führer state in terms of legal theory. Schmitt now set the end of the principle of the separation of powers and of constitutionalism at the time of the Great War and looked at the English, French and American practice of legislative authorization in order to relativize the liberal doctrine of the separation of powers: the concept of law in the 'parliamentary legislative state', Schmitt said, was obsolete, even in France. The term 'Rechtsstaat', as used in the constitutional model states, meant 'something fundamentally different' each time (PB, p. 228). Schmitt then went on to sketch the dissolution of the principle of the separation of powers and the development of legislative authorization into the 'new concept of law' of National Socialism. He called the contemporary 'practice of governmental legislature [Regierungsgesetze]' a return to the 'pre-constitutional tradition' (ibid.) and quoted Aristotle and Aquinas as authorities vouching for the 'practical reason' inherent in 'governmental legislature'. The great importance of these legal-theoretical texts of 1935–6 lies in their acceptance of the task defining the new concept of law analytically and descriptively. Their comparative perspective points towards Schmitt's future comprehensive look at 'European jurisprudence'. He takes a step back from providing apologias to the task of analysis and confirms the major caesura – his perception of the time after 30 June 1934 as an 'immediately just' state of exception – with his change of perspective. He again spoke as a jurist. However, at the very same time he wrote his most disastrous texts. He praised the Nuremberg Laws, calling them 'Die Verfassung der Freiheit' [The constitution of freedom], explained their consequences for marital law, distinguished between 'Faschistische und nationalsozialistische Rechtswissenschaft' [Fascist and National Socialist jurisprudence], not least on anti-Semitic grounds, and organized a conference on 'Das Judentum in der Rechtswissenschaft' [Judaism in jurisprudence], which threw a lasting shadow over his work. He continued his absurd 'scientification' [Verwissenschaftlichung] of anti-Semitism in the *Leviathan* book and also included his anti-Semitic polemics in his texts on international law.[12]

Dark years: Schmitt's pupils under National Socialism

At the end of 1934, Schmitt already thought that a juridico-institutional justification of National Socialism was no longer possible. However, by no means did he retreat from National Socialist jurisprudence. Rather, he concentrated on organizational activities, for which several platforms were at his disposal: the university, the academy and the BNSDJ. Thus, he was able to find positions for, and to promote, his pupils in various networks. By 1944 he had supervised four Habilitations (Daskalakis, Franzen, Suthoff-Groß, Maiwald) and more than twenty doctoral theses. At the university he kept a 'critical distance' from the 'Höhn School' and cooperated closely with the international lawyer Viktor Bruns.[13] Huber and Forsthoff occupied important chairs in 1933. In 1935, Werner Weber became Schmitt's successor at the Handelshochschule and stayed in close contact while in Berlin and also later, from 1942, in Leipzig.

Of the younger generation, Günther Krauss was now particularly keen to take up the role of the young conservative hopeful. From 1929 he had studied in Berlin, and with the winter term 1932–3 he returned to his home town, Cologne. Even before 1933 he published here and there in the journals of the young revolutionaries. In his correspondence with Schmitt, he expressed himself in a sharply anti-Semitic tone. Thus, on a review of *The Concept of the Political*, which had been published under a pseudonym, he remarked: 'The Jew is the actual enemy. The passage on metics in your "Concept of the Political" surely must be interpreted in that sense.'[14] Like Karl Eschweiler, Krauss belonged to the extreme right wing of Rhenish Catholicism. After a term in Cologne he followed Schmitt to Berlin as his doctoral student,[15] and passed his examination in January 1935 with a thesis on Rudolph Sohm. He saw Sohm's thought as tragically torn between the positivist concept of right and a religious insight into the 'divine nature of the Church': 'Sohm takes refuge in a paradox: the nature of canon law is in conflict with the nature of the Church.' According to Krauss, the paradox shows, after all, 'an attempt at transcending the limits of the positivist legal system'.[16] With his *Disputation über den Rechtsstaat* [Disputation on the

Rechtsstaat], Krauss positioned himself clearly as a pupil of Schmitt. His opponent in the disputation was Otto von Schweinichen, a pupil of Carl August Emge and also of Schmitt; in 1938, von Schweinichen committed suicide in somewhat mysterious circumstances.[17] The oral examination was a protracted and inward-looking discussion among members of the National Socialist circle who knew themselves protected by the ruling power. The preparation of the text for print then proved so troublesome that Schmitt handed the text to his 'adjutant', Bernhard Ludwig von Mutius, and asked him to shorten it.[18] The contribution from the second opponent, Ernst Hermann Bockhoff,[19] was left out of the printed version. Schmitt urged a speedy completion of the project and recommended 'more humour'[20] and sober distance. After his examination, Krauss, for financial reasons, returned to Cologne to do his legal training. However, he wanted to become Schmitt's assistant, and saw 'employment in the adjudancy of the group of university teachers in the BNSDJ only as a kind of interim measure'.[21] In October 1935 he was in Berlin for a couple of days, and together with Schmitt he also visited Brigitte Frank. At the end of 1935 he contemplated a 'transfer to Berlin'.[22] Schmitt had his work cut out with Krauss: Krauss resolutely insisted on keeping the unwieldy title of his thesis; he was annoyed about critical remarks on one of his presentations. Schmitt nevertheless praised the thesis and wanted to 'find a position' for Krauss.[23] From spring 1936, Krauss was Schmitt's advisor at the Reichsgeschäftsstelle [Reich bureau] of the BNSDJ. His plans to publish as Schmitt's pupil, however, went fundamentally wrong. When Schmitt caught the attention of the SD,* Krauss wanted to help his master with an article,[24] which actually only fanned the flames further. At the end of 1936 he was forced to ask for his dismissal.[25] The contact between Schmitt and Krauss was broken off until 1945.

Posts for university assistants were scarce. Members of the next generation, for the most part, worked with Schmitt only for shorter periods of time before or alongside their legal training. The regulations for 'legal trainees' [Gerichtsreferendar] (civil servant candidates) of July 1934 required, as part of the three-year preparatory service, a National Socialist attitude, military and work service, and a two-month participation in 'community camps' [Gemeinschaftslagern] (Jüterbog camps)[†], as well as a two-year participation in a 'working group'. In 1939 the regulations changed again. Despite these requirements, legal trainees had quite a lot of free time left to them,[26] and Schmitt was able to let younger scholars work for him. The employment prospects for legal trainees were not very good at the time, and Heydrich was therefore able to recruit some of them for the SD and the SS.[27] Until 1945, Schmitt had the following assistants at the university: Karl Schilling, Gustav von Schmoller, Herbert Gutjahr, Walter Golombek, Karl Lohmann, Werner Schulze-Thulin and Günter Wasse.[28]

For the winter term 1933–4, Karl Schilling, an assistant at the

---

* Sicherheitsdienst = secret service.
† Named after the town Jüterbog (Brandenburg), where these camps for the National Socialist education of jurists took place.

Handelshochschule, was Schmitt's 'adjutant'. On 1 May 1934 he was followed by Gustav von Schmoller, a nephew of the famous political economist,[29] who soon passed his second state examination and, at the end of 1935, became an advisor at the Reich Ministry of Economics. From 1941 he was a senior civil servant [Regierungsrat] in Prague.[30] In 1944 he passed his doctoral examination with a thesis titled *Die Neutralität im gegenwärtigen Strukturwandel des Völkerrechts* [Neutrality in the context of the current structural changes in international law]. He remained in regular contact with Schmitt throughout his life. For the summer term 1935, Schmitt was on leave. In the winter term 1935–6, Herbert Gutjahr joined the university staff. He was practically imposed on the faculty by the NS Dozentenbund [Association of University Teachers]. Born in Berlin, he had studied there from the summer term 1930 to the winter term 1934–5. He was a member of the NSDAP from 1 June 1931. As a leader of the National Socialist students, he was an activist in the 1934 burning of books. He was a member of the SA and from August 1933 also of the SS. In spring 1935 he passed his first state examination with an 'excellent' and then joined the preparatory service. Alongside this, he worked as a faculty assistant and also as a 'specialist advisor' [Sachbearbeiter] of the Wissenschaftliche Abteilung [academic section] of the NSRB (BNSDJ). From the autumn of 1935 he was the contact man [V-Mann]* of the SD. However, he stayed closely affiliated with Schmitt over several years and acted as a kind of mediator, or double agent, between the two NS competitors Schmitt and Höhn. In 1937 he continued to be a faculty assistant. For the winter term 1938–9 and the summer term 1939, he was again allocated to Schmitt.[31] Thus, most likely he was Schmitt's assistant for almost four years. In 1939 he passed his second state examination and then became an assessor in the international section of the Ministry of Economics. From 1939 he was at the front, becoming SS-Hauptsturmführer in 1943. On 12 March 1944 he died in the Ukraine after having been wounded. Almost all members of the SS of his calibre were involved in war crimes.

Within the BNSDJ, Hubertus Bung, Bernhard von Mutius, Eberhard von Medem and Günther Krauss assisted Schmitt. Hubertus Bung had studied with Schmitt from 1927 and was an adjutant in the Reichsfachgruppe Hochsschullehrer [Reich Association of University Teachers]. His aim was to 'pour "poison" into the Catholic people' with his publications. In the journal *Kreuzfeuer* [Cross-Fire] he wanted to propagate '"State – Movement – People" bit by bit, peppering it with Thomas Aquinas, the doctors of the Church, and papal encyclicals', and thus help to coordinate Catholicism.[32] Bung distinguished himself with sharp anti-Semitic articles in *Jugend und Recht*, but stopped being a collaborator of the journal over arguments at the end of 1934. The 'years of alienation'[33] from Schmitt lasted until 1939; only after 1947 did he have close contact with him again. Bernhard Ludwig von Mutius[34] was born in Constantinople, the son of a diplomat. From the winter term 1932 he studied at Berlin University. On 4

---

* Verbindungsmann = the secret service's connection to, and informant on, the faculty, a somewhat more sinister role than the term 'contact man' suggests.

November 1933 he became a member of the SS.[35] Between December 1934 and October 1935, he was the successor to Bung as Schmitt's 'adjutant' in the Fachgruppe Hochschullehrer, doing his legal training at the same time. He then went on a scholarship to Trinity College, Cambridge,[36] and later became an assistant at the Academy for German Right, where he continued to meet Schmitt frequently. After he had passed his second state examination, he was drafted into the army in 1939. Then he became the personal advisor of the 'Reichsleiter' Ritter von Epp[37] and for some time the personal advisor of a certain Ministerialdirektor [ministerial director] Illgner in the Reich Ministry of the Economy.[38] Following them, Eberhard von Medem, who studied in Berlin from summer term 1931, was Schmitt's secretary and adjutant from the end of 1935 onwards. He emphatically thanked Schmitt for what he had learned in the year 1936[39] and later for the way the time with Schmitt had 'shaped' him.[40] The time with Schmitt had been, he wrote, 'almost like a parental home'. When von Medem married at the outbreak of war, Schmitt was his best man.[41]

Someone Schmitt continued to work with very closely after 1933 was Karl Lohmann. Lohmann took over the editorship [Schriftleitung] of the *Deutsche Juristen-Zeitung* in the summer of 1934. After the journal was discontinued, he moved to the *Zeitschrift der Akademie für Deutsches Recht* and then to the *Deutsche Rechtswissenschaft*. In 1940 he unexpectedly became Schmitt's assistant for a year, before moving to Heidelberg. Another of Schmitt's co-workers at the time was Dr Helmut Pfeiffer. Born in Eiringhausen, Plettenberg, he passed his first state examination in 1931 in Cologne, then began legal training, passed his doctorate with Nipperdey in 1932,[42] and from March 1935, as 'Organisationsleiter' [organisational manager] for the convention of the Jurists' Association at the head office of the BNSDJ, worked closely together with Schmitt.[43] He later was a close assistant of Hans Frank in Poland. He became SS-Hauptsturmbannführer and died as a deserter in a Gestapo* prison in Copenhagen. Josef Kölble was another close pupil whose doctoral thesis Schmitt supervised.[44] Bung, Gutjahr, von Medem and Kölble all belonged to the body of collaborators of the journal for junior jurists *Jugend und Recht* [Youth and Right] and commented, not least, on questions regarding the reform of juridical training.[45]

One can hardly overlook the fact that the first pupils, in particular, of this period were all strident National Socialists. Almost all of them were Protestants (e.g., Lohmann, von Mutius, von Medem, Gutjahr). What is striking is Schmitt's inclination towards pupils who were of aristocratic descent and who came from military circles or from the area of his home town, Plettenberg. This generation of Schmitt's Berlin pupils was strongly shaped by the phase in which National Socialism began to take shape. Its members, therefore, did not become influential in the Federal Republic,[46] and they are hardly known today. However, there was a middle generation of students, between Bonn and Berlin, whom Schmitt influenced academically before and/or after 1933, and who went on to put their stamp on

---

* Geheime Staatspolizei = secret state police.

state theory in the Federal Republic: Gerhard Leibholz and Carl Joachim Friedrich, Ulrich Scheuner, Franz Wieacker and Theodor Maunz, Wilhelm Grewe, Herbert Krüger and some others: all, in different ways, had learned from Schmitt. After 1933 Berlin became the capital of European fascism, and in his role as 'crown jurist' Schmitt became a focus of international discussions. Numerous visiting students and scholars from neighbouring friendly states came to Berlin and sought contact with him. Schmitt always enjoyed conversations and inspiration from foreign influences. His focus and sphere of influence extended to South-Eastern Europe, as well as beyond Europe.

However, at the beginning of 1935, Schmitt felt somewhat exhausted from the failure of his attempts at a juridico-institutional provision of meaning and applied for a term's leave, which was immediately granted.[47] At that time, he began to plan the next Jurists' Convention. At the end of February, the 'sixth full meeting' of the academy took place. On 10 March, Schmitt went to Holland, and over the following days he gave talks on the 'Entwicklung der Begriffe Führerstaat und Rechtsstaat im verfassungsrechtlichen Denken der Gegenwart' [development of the concepts of the Führer state and Rechtsstaat in the current thought on constitutional theory] at the universities of Utrecht and Leiden, as well as at the Handelshochschule Rotterdam, partly upon invitation from the student organization.[48] On 1 April he spoke at the assembly hall in Mühlheim. Via Goslar, he returned to Berlin, where he gave the opening address at a large conference of the Reichsgruppe Hochschullehrer on the 'Reform des Studiums der Volkswirtschaft' [Curriculum reform for the study of political economy].[49] Around the same time, Hartung's critical review of Schmitt's *Staatsgefüge und Zusammenbruch des zweiten Reiches* [State structure and collapse of the Second Reich] was published. 'I am only amazed', Schmitt remarked to Huber about it,[50] 'about the perfect ignorance with which these historians voice and execute their own death penalty.' Schmitt responded to Hartung: 'My treatise looks at the development towards the state of Adolf Hitler from the perspective of my own historical perceptions and experiences.'[51] He did not deny the charge of politicization, but insisted on his view and claimed the right 'to remain silent on your essay'. Huber sounded notes of moderation: 'The second Reich was not bad enough not to have deserved better defendants!'[52] Huber was at that moment in time still holding on to the 'vision of an academic battle'; soon he too would use the interpretation of Wilhelminianism in order to argue his side in his differences with Schmitt and for his defence of constitutionalism.

Schmitt gave a talk on university curriculum reform at the Haus der Deutschen Rechtsfront [House of the German legal front].[53] On 12 April he travelled to Italy and visited a whole 'range of Italian cities': Bolzano, Verona, Ravenna and Padua.[54] He gave a talk in Rome, at the end of May he was in Zagreb,[55] and by mid-May he was back in Berlin, where a workshop of the Reichsfachgruppe Hochschullehrer on the theme of 'Eigentum und Enteignung' [Property and expropriation] took place. Werner Weber and Wieacker reported on it.[56] This was followed by the fifth meeting of the State Council before Schmitt travelled to Munich, where the second annual meeting of the Academy for German Right was held under the guiding motif 'Lebensrecht statt Formelrecht' [Living law instead of formulaic law]. Schmitt spoke about 'Die Rechtswissenschaft im Führerstaat' [Jurisprudence in the Führer state]; Hans Franck, Koellreutter and Hedemann also gave lectures. At the concluding session, the Führer was present in person.[57] Schmitt considered working his presentation into a small book.[58] Work on constitutional matters, however, now lay in Huber's hands. Schmitt reacted with high praise to the fact that Huber's position moved closer to that of his own textbook. Huber's *Wesen und Inhalt der Verfassung* [Nature and content of the constitution], he said, provided an 'almost perfect plan for a lecture course to be newly invented'.[59]

In his pocket diary, Schmitt noted the address (Schückertstr. 18) of his collaborator von Mutius, adding: 'very good for personal life, emotional things, love matters, talking'.[60]

Schmitt probably had not yet completely broken his habit of having affairs. At the Nuremberg Party Congress, the new racial laws were passed, and Schmitt immediately justified them in an article for the *Deutsche Juristen-Zeitung*. Between 7 and 12 October he directed a 'week of specialist training for civil servants in the judicial system' in the Berlin Academy, in which Gürtner, Schlegelberger and Freisler took part. Schmitt spoke about 'Das Gesetz als Plan und Wille des Führers' [The law as the plan and will of the Führer].[61] Another workshop of the Reichsfachgruppe Hochschullehrer, on 'Vereins- und Körperschaftsrecht' [Law governing associations and corporate law], followed straight afterwards. Four main guiding principles for the 'law governing communities and associations' were formulated in the discussion and deliberation, which corroded the legal concepts of 'human being' and 'person'. The legal concept of a 'human being', they said, veiled and distorted 'the difference between Volksgenosse [a fellow member of the German people], citizen of the Reich, foreigner, Jew, etc.'[62] This was the reaction of Schmitt's Hochschulgruppe to the Nuremberg Laws. Gurian, from his exile, commented sneeringly: 'Schmitt abolishes the human being . . .'

On 15 October, the new prestigious building of the Academy for German Right at Leipziger Platz 15 was opened.[63] The following day, Schmitt gave his talk on 'The Law as the Plan and Will of the Führer' in Kiel, and in November he gave two talks in Cologne on the subject of 'Faschistischer und nationalsozialististischer Verfassungstaat' [The fascist and the National Socialist constitutional state]. At the end of the month, he presented a paper on questions regarding the application of the Nuremberg Laws at the academy, on the occasion of the annual meeting of the German section of the International Law Association.[64] Regarding their anti-Semitism, Schmitt and Frank very firmly closed ranks at that point in time. Frank assigned the leading role in the newly formed academic and legal-political section of the BNSDJ to Schmitt. On 21 and 22 December, the third workshop of the Reichsfachgruppe Hochschullehrer, on 'Öffentliches und privates Recht' [Public and civil law], took place. After this workshop, there is a gap of two years in Huber's correspondence with Schmitt.

The moment that Huber distanced himself from Schmitt coincides with Schmitt's justification of the Nuremberg Laws. For the meeting of the Hochschullehrer in October 1936 – the theme was 'Das Judentum in der Rechtswissenschaft' [Judaism in jurisprudence] – Huber sent his apologies and declined to offer a paper,[65] giving 'active military service' as the reason. After a long silence he justified this decision, in January 1938, referring to his 'scholarly responsibility'.[66] This justification, of course, was a pointed remark as well; it implicitly questioned Schmitt's academic standards. However, although Huber clearly did not go along with Schmitt's intensified polemics – he never, for instance, engaged in anti-Semitic polemics himself – his own idealization of the National Socialist constitution in terms of 'constitutional law' was nevertheless also problematic.

To begin with, the Prussian Gestapo was under the control of Göring. Rudolf Diels was its first organizer. In the course of centralization and 'Verreichlichung' [transfer of powers to the Reich], Heinrich Himmler then took power as the 'inspector' of police forces. Following the 'Röhmputsch', the SD-Sicherheitsdienst [central security department] was established within the SS and took up residence in the Prinz-Albrecht-Palais in Wilhelmstraße. With the political parties having been destroyed, the ambitious members of the Sicherheitsdienst were looking for new fields of activity and soon found them in the nearby university. From the winter term 1935–6, Reinhard Höhn taught there. Smend had to move to Göttingen to make room for him.[67] Höhn was a member of the SS and the SD from 1932. He came from Heidelberg, moved the Institut für

'Höhn I saw occasionally as a colleague at the Juridical Faculty of Berlin University. I behaved in a polite and correct way towards him, as one reasonably does towards a member or associate of the secret police' – Schmitt about Reinhard Höhn at Nuremberg, 1947

Staatsforschung [Institute for State Research] from Kiel to the Wannsee in Berlin, and was also instrumental, to a certain extent, in the creation of the 'Auslandswissenschaftliche Fakultät' [Faculty for Research on Foreign Countries].[68] As a senior head of department at the SD-Sicherheitsdienst, he was working closely with Heydrich and developed versatile and expansive activities, with his doctoral factory being one of the more harmless examples. In 1940 he was made the holder of a chair [Ordinarius]. He was an SS-Standartenführer and gave his lectures in uniform. In 1944, he became SS-Oberführer.[69] Höhn dismantled the concept of the state. In his inaugural lecture on 6 December 1935, he settled scores with Otto von Gierke.[70] Schmitt distinguished two strands within more recent theories of the state: the 'positivist' line of development from Laband to Anschütz and Kelsen and the 'organic' from von Gierke to Preuß. Only the former was categorically rejected by Schmitt. Höhn, however, represented a second step in the dismantling of constitutionalism, marked also by a dismissal of the 'organic' line of von Gierke and the search for the 'Volksgemeinschaft' [the community of the people] in dark, prehistoric times. Such formulaic battles over theoretical positions were often politically rather than academically motivated. But Schmitt now had a strong opponent within the faculty.

At the beginning of 1936, a severe conflict occurred. Eckhardt had already ignored the suggestions made by Schmitt's Hochschulgruppe regarding the question of curriculum reforms. Now, on 18 January, a preparatory meeting took place in which the organization of the Jurists' Convention and the 'discussion of the effects of curriculum reform' were the topics.[71] Eckhardt protested to Schmitt about the list of speakers.[72] Six of the eight, he said, were not real National Socialists – e.g., Johannes Heckel and Werner Weber. Heinrich Lange,[73] in particular, he added, was entirely unacceptable. Eckhardt felt he had to report the matter to the minister, and explained to Dr Walter Raeke, who had been Frank's deputy since May 1935, that he could not join the BNSDJ because it would mean his 'political subordination to State Councillor Schmitt'.[74] On 1 and 2 February, a Gauführer conference of the BNSDJ and the Deutsche Rechtsfront, chaired by Frank, took place, at which Schmitt was one of the speakers.[75] Immediately after that conference, on 3 February, Eckhardt, in a letter to Minister Frank, formally 'drew a line between [himself] and State Councillor Schmitt'.[76] Schmitt, he wrote, was a political opportunist; he belonged to Catholic circles and as late as 1932 had spoken out against Hitler. Schmitt's appointment diary for these days contains numerous meetings with von Medem, Höhn, Raeke and Eckhardt.[77]

At the end of February, Schmitt spoke at a district meeting of the BNSDJ in Magdeburg on 'Die Nationalsozialistische Weltanschauung als Rechtsquelle der heutigen Rechtsprechung' [The National Socialist worldview as the legal source of today's jurisdiction]. Arnold J. Toynbee was speaking at the academy, in front of a host of key political figures, on 'Peaceful Change'* and on 'collective security'. Schmitt participated in the

---

* Title in English in the original.

discussion and got to know Toynbee,[78] who, together with the organizer of the event, Fritz Berber, had a longer private audience with Hitler.[79] On 5 March, the fifth and last meeting of the State Council took place. Two days later, Schmitt went to visit Ernst Jünger in Goslar. On 21 and 22 March he held a BNSDJ-Hochschullehrer conference on the 'Lage und Aufgaben der heutigen Rechtswissenschaft' [Situation and tasks of today's jurisprudence] in 'preparation' for the Jurists' Convention.[80] Ahead of the conference, he published an article on 'Die geschichtliche Lage der deutschen Rechtswissenschaft' [The historical situation of German jurisprudence].[81] The historical perspective and the 'corporative' [ständisch]* angle of the article met with quite some opposition. Schmitt then announced the next conference, on the theme of 'Das Judentum in der Rechtswissenschaft' [Judaism in jurisprudence].

At the beginning of April, Hans Frank travelled to Italy and had an audience with the king and *il Duce*.[82] Schmitt followed him, travelled to Rome and gave a talk in German on 'Die heutigen Theorien des Politischen' [Today's theories of the political]. Professor Costamagna arranged a private audience for him with Mussolini,[83] to whom, in the years to come, Schmitt sent his publications.[84] Schmitt later remembered:

> I had a longer conversation in private with Mussolini in the Palazzo Venezia on the evening of the Wednesday after Easter. We talked about the relationship between party and state. Mussolini said, with pride and clearly directed against national socialist Germany: 'The state is eternal, the party is transient; I am a Hegelian!' I remarked: 'Lenin was also a Hegelian, so that I have to allow myself the question: where does Hegel's world historical spirit reside today? In Rome, in Moscow, or maybe still in Berlin after all?' He answered with a sweet smile: 'I hand that question back to you', whereupon I said: 'In that case, of course I have to say: in Rome!', which he accepted with a charming, polite and ironic gesture. The conversation with him was a great intellectual pleasure and remains unforgettable for me in all its details. The purpose of the conversation was a warning to Hitler I was meant to pass on, which, very cautiously, I did, something that did me no good at all. (BS, p. 418)

Schmitt probably had in mind his report on 'Faschistische und Nationalsozialistische Rechtswissenschaft' [Fascist and National Socialist jurisprudence], which emphasizes the 'differences between the two worldviews'. In it, Schmitt mentions the 'battle over Hegel': Italian fascism had decided in favour of the 'primacy of the state over the party'. And: 'The problem of race is being ignored in Italy.'[85] One may see a preference for Mussolini's 'statism' in this; however, Schmitt's anti-Semitic remarks rather point towards a decision against Rome and for Berlin. He later, again and again, recounted various versions of his conversation with Mussolini which, in the interpretation of Schmitt's role at the time, led to

---

* The expression refers to the article's emphasis on the legal profession, the 'juristischen Berufsstand', as a guild.

its turning into a 'statist' legend. On 17 March, he travelled on to Milan, where he gave a talk on the constitution of one-party states.

In mid-May 1936 there appeared a special issue of the journal *Deutsches Recht* on the professional guild of jurists. Schmitt contributed an article on 'Aufgabe und Notwendigkeit des deutschen Rechtsstandes' [The task and necessity of German jurisprudence].[86] Between 16 and 19 May, the second major National Socialist convention of jurists took place in Leipzig.[87] Hans Frank, Rudolf Heß and Goebbels were prominent speakers. As the organizer, Schmitt did not give a long lecture, but on the Sunday (17 May) he introduced the 'meeting of the Gau representatives of the academic section' and provided a 'more extensive survey of the development of the Reichsgruppe so far, and of its position within jurisprudence'.[88] At the meeting of the sub-section on economics, he spoke about the relationship between economics and jurisprudence and reminded his audience of the tradition of a comprehensive science of the state [Staatswissenschaften].[89] Thus, he was still a centrally visible figure at this Jurists' Convention. In mid-July, he spoke on 'Nationalsozialismus und Recht' [National Socialism and right] at the Deutsche Hochschule für Politik in the context of a 'course for foreigners' in front of an audience of visitors to the Olympic Games.[90] Around that time, he intensified his preparations for the 'major conference on Judaism in jurisprudence'. He had a 'list of Jewish authors' checked at his university seminar.[91] In parallel, his opponents became active. A report by an informer contained critical remarks Schmitt made on the SS: 'Community of the people [Volksgemeinschaft] at the front, and Gestapo at the back.'[92]

There had been plans for a reform of the penal code for some time. In 1935, Frank became the chair of the planning group and also initiated a reform of the code for criminal proceedings. In the summer of 1936, Schmitt formulated a statement in which he opposed the commission in charge of the reform of criminal proceedings.[93] An interview he gave in the Berlin party newspaper *Der Angriff* caused some irritation,[94] prompting Schmitt to ask for a 'necessary clarification' – i.e., that he did not equate the political 'party trial' with a 'trial by the inquisition'.[95] In mid-September he submitted his statement, the fundamental claim of which was: 'The code for criminal proceedings is a part of constitutional law.'[96] Schmitt argued in favour of the introduction of the 'Führer principle' into the code for criminal proceedings. The idea of the Führer had to be implemented in the code for criminal proceedings in addition because the penal code was an 'element of the overall political constitution', and the 'unity of right'[97] had to be maintained. The Führer, Schmitt said, was the 'supreme legal authority', 'the Reich a Führerreich'.[98] Schmitt declared a substantial 'increase in the power of the public prosecutor' and interpreted the criminal deed as also a 'disloyalty'[99] towards the party, a fact that, he argued, had to be taken into consideration. In other words, Schmitt's statement undermined the established independence of the judge and of criminal proceedings from other political bodies. In terms of terminology, Schmitt now consistently spoke of a 'Führerreich'. As late as mid-September 1936, he thus explicitly positioned himself against the majority of his colleagues in the 'Rechtswahrerbund' [Association of the Protectors of Right] as a National Socialist agitator.

Providing meaning with the help of Richard Wagner: 'Judaism in Jurisprudence'

Anti-Semitism was a central element in the ideological programme of National Socialism. Hitler was first and foremost an anti-Semite. He believed in a 'redemptive anti-Semitism' (Saul Friedländer) and in the absurd scenario of a Jewish world conspiracy and an inevitable decisive battle against 'international world Jewry', a view which, apart from and independent of its biological and racist foundations, had historical roots in Christian anti-Judaism and in the pessimistic ideologies and 'worldviews' of the nineteenth century. From early on, Hitler's anti-Semitism became visible again and again. However, for tactical reasons he also sought political moderation, both before and after 1933. The 'final solution' was not part of his agenda from the beginning. To begin with, the politics of National Socialism aimed at exclusion, a phase which saw its completion in the Nuremberg Laws. Then, a strategy of emigration and expulsion was followed, which saw a radicalization and acceleration after the 'Anschluß' [annexation] of Austria in March 1938. It was only after the invasion of the Soviet Union, the radicalization of warfare and the likely defeat of Germany, which became apparent towards the end of 1941, that Hitler changed to a politics of extermination, which he had already publicly prophesied in 1939 – even if an actual 'order for the final solution' remains controversial among historians.[100]

Between 10 and 16 September 1935, the 'Reichsparteitag der Freiheit' [Reich party rally of freedom] took place in Nuremberg. At the very last moment, Hitler decided to introduce the Nuremberg Laws, which came as a surprise to most. Drafts of the Reich Flag Law, the Reich Citizenship Law and the 'Law for the Protection of German Blood and German Honour' were hastily improvised by the ministerial bureaucracy, in particular Wilhelm Stuckart, 'without any more detailed guidelines being given regarding content'.[101] Schmitt celebrated this Reich party rally at once as 'Die Verfassung der Freiheit' [The constitution of freedom]. 'The state is now a means for the people's force and unity. . . . The foundations of our people-based [völkische] order have now been firmly established.'[102] Schmitt assumed that the creation of a constitution was now completed, as hoped by many, and understood the party rally as a 'warning'.[103] He immediately explained the consequences of the Nuremberg Laws at the academy in Berlin. On 28 August, in front of an international audience, he spoke – following Hans Frank and Walter Simons – to the German section of the International Law Association on 'Die nationalsozialistische Gesetzgebung und der Vorbehalt des "ordre public" im Internationalen Privatrecht' [National Socialist legislation and the proviso of the 'ordre public' in international private law]. The 'biological' definition of the Aryan or Jew stopped at the level of the grandparents. Grandparents were factually considered Jewish if they belonged to a Jewish religious community.[104] This meant that the 'probing' [Erforschung] of the 'Jewish spirit' had been extended beyond the 'biologistic' paradigm to the field of the humanities. And, at the 'general assembly' of the academy, Hans Frank simply declared: 'No one but us decides what is German.'[105] Schmitt categorically and casuistically presented the racial laws, including their regulatory provisions and the 'Ehegesundheitsgesetz' [marriage health law] – the 'Law for the Protection of the Hereditary Health of the German People' of 18 October 1935 – as the core of the 'people's right' [völkischen Rechts], and discussed a number of consequences for international private law, using marital laws as an example. He argued against what he called 'an aggressive use' of NS laws by trying to avoid them – e.g., by marrying abroad – and emphasized the 'moderate restraint in our legal provisions'. Schmitt wanted to pre-empt the possibility of an interpretive circumvention of the laws. In a short article, 'Faschistisches und nationalsozialistisches Rechtsdenken' [Fascist and National Socialist juridical thought],[106] he called the 'problem of race', next to the primacy of the party, the most important point of difference between the National Socialist 'worldview' and fascism. Schmitt also made sharp anti-Semitic remarks in his lecture course on 'Verfassungsgeschichte der Neuzeit' [Modern constitutional history].[107] His conference on 'Judaism in Jurisprudence' would then provide the justification of his anti-Semitism in the form of a 'worldview'.

Following the Nuremberg Laws, anti-Semitism increasingly became a topic in academia. Under the guidance of Walter Frank, for instance, a 'Reich Institute for the History of the New Germany' was founded, which also created a 'Research Division on the Jewish Question'.[108] Many a scholar now presented studies in 'intellectual history' on the influence of Jewish legal theorists. Schmitt quoted Johannes Heckel[109] and Heinrich Lange.[110] He read vast amounts of Judaic[111] and anti-Semitic literature with the intention of taking the leading role in this debate as well, especially as his career had reached a turning point. There were manifold reasons for that. In addition to the power struggle between Gürtner and Frank, the Ministry of Justice and the Reich Führer of the Jurists, there was the rise of the ambitious SS jurists Eckhardt and Höhn. On the question of the curriculum reforms, Schmitt had already suffered a heavy defeat against Eckhardt. His audience with Mussolini was a symbolic pinnacle of his career, but his high-profile course of a radical dismantling of constitutional elements was risky in the face of the polycratic chaos of National Socialism. Schmitt's career depended on Frank. Worries that Gürtner might be deprived of his power by Frank and that Schmitt might climb further as a consequence – might, for instance, become a state secretary – formed one reason for Schmitt's downfall. His high-profile pamphlet on criminal law, which brought him into conflict with various sides, was another.[112] Schmitt had created many enemies for himself, and had put off even close confidants with his brusque behaviour and his Führer affectation. From several sides, his polemics now bounced back on him. External and internal critique by opponents as well as followers of the National

Socialist regime came together. At one point, Schmitt had analysed the dangers of negative majorities within the party political landscape. Now, he experienced a situation in which heterogeneous forces were united against him. The emigrants, who had been 'spat out' in 1933, provided the arguments for the SS. Otto Koellreutter, Reinhard Höhn and Karl August Eckhardt jointly brought about Schmitt's loss of power. Schmitt's conference on 'Judaism in Jurisprudence' at the beginning of 1936 was also, by integrating prominent National Socialists,[113] an attempt at demonstrating his loyalty to the party line. In addition, Schmitt gave a radio lecture on 'Recht und Judentum' [Right and Judaism] on the Deutschlandsender.[114] However, his NS competitors, each of whom would have liked to install himself as the chief ideologue, reacted with particular irritation to such obvious strategies. Looking back, Schmitt stressed the manifold opposition, from the office of Rosenberg, the ministry of Rust, the Church ministry of Kerrl, the Foreign Office and the party headquarters.[115] With his conference, Schmitt laid claim to a topic in which many others were also interested.[116] And it was an absurd topic.[117] It is not easy to establish Jewish descent. 'Jewish' authors represented the most varied positions within jurisprudence. And at the end of 1936, after Jewish colleagues had effectively been removed from their positions, the conference was of only 'marginal significance'.[118] However, Schmitt chose the topic not only for opportunistic reasons; he was also a fervent anti-Semite.

The title for Schmitt's conference, 'Judaism in Jurisprudence', was an allusion to Wagner's essay on 'Judaism in Music', in which Wagner denied and disowned his revolutionary past in the Vormärz and his modernity. Wagner was one of the fathers of modern anti-Semitism,[119] and via his wife, Cosima, and Bayreuth he influenced Hitler.[120] There are two versions of Wagner's 'Judaism in Music'. While in the background to the 1850 essay, published under a pseudonym, were humiliating experiences of artistic failure in Wagner's Parisian exile,[121] the extended text of 1869 was a response to his experiences in Munich. Wagner writes: 'The period of Judaism in modern music can only be described historically as one of complete unfruitfulness and of disappearing stability.'[122] Whoever does not have a mother tongue, Wagner holds, cannot find a musical language either.[123] In 1850, Wagner's essay ended with an expression of hope for the 'deliverance' of 'Ahasverus' through the 'Untergang'* of Judaism in 'true men' (pp. 49f.). Wagner thus renewed the revolutionary programme of an overcoming of national particularities within a universal humanity.[124] A similar idea of complete emancipation in the form of universal humanity, a 'deliverance' from Judaism, was around the same time also put forward by Bruno Bauer[125] and Karl Marx in their treatises *On the Jewish Question*, which made a strong impression on Schmitt. In 1869, Wagner assumed 'the complete triumph of Judaism in every sense' (p. 88),[126] concluding: 'Whether the decadence of our culture can be prevented by forcible

---

* The English translation leaves this term in German, adding a footnote suggesting that the 'inferno' is meant. The meaning of the term ranges from physical destruction to decline or disappearance, with a core meaning of 'final end and disappearance'.

expulsion of foreign elements of pernicious character I cannot say; as powers for this purpose are requisite, of the existence of which I am not aware' (p. 93).[127] At that moment in time, these very powers were beginning to form; eliminatory anti-Semitism began to raise its head. The 'second publication, driven by no external necessity',[128] exerted broad influence; however, it was also met with rejection, even in Wagner's closer circles, for instance, by Franz Liszt and Friedrich Nietzsche.

Wagner's essay was the model for Schmitt's conference; the conference, however, exceeded Wagner's essay in the radicalism of its tone, and, of course, it took place within a completely different political framework. 'Far more than a hundred university teachers of law and economics from all Gaue of the Reich, as well as a large number of guests', turned up,[129] but the Reich Führer of the Jurists Frank and Gauleiter Julius Streicher cancelled at short notice. Established authors, such as Johannes Heckel and Heinrich Lange, did not participate. Schmitt invited Rudolf Smend to give a presentation. 'Declined', Smend simply noted in the margin.[130] Theodor Maunz did not submit his contribution. None of Schmitt's close pupils wrote a contribution. No member of the 'Kiel School', no author from the 'Stoßtrupp' [vanguard] of *Der deutsche Staat der Gegenwart*, was there. Oberheid could not attend for health reasons, although he had been 'so much looking forward to the . . . conference on the Jews'.[131] Schmitt's 'followers' were absent.[132] At the beginning of the conference, an opening speech by Hans Frank was read out. Schmitt's opening speech followed, in which he quoted 'guiding principles' of Hitler and Hans Frank, as well as of the NS martyr Theodor von der Pfordten, and then sketched some of his own thoughts on the 'problem of the Jew'. Two short speeches by Gauführer Schroer and the Berlin university lecturer Falk Ruttke[133] attempted a theological and 'race theoretical' approach to the theme. The introductory booklet ends with Schmitt's concluding remarks and a solemn 'vow taken by the participants of the conference'.[134] As the vow was sent to the minister of science, Bernhard Rust, those who took it must have felt bound by their pledge.

Already in his opening speech, Schmitt alluded to Wagner by distinguishing between the influence of Italian music on German musicians and the 'Jewish infection', which 'spread from Heine and Marx'.[135] Wagner's essay resonates even more clearly in Schmitt's short introductory remark to Edgar Tatarin-Tarnheyden's contribution on 'Der Einfluss des Judentums in Staatsrecht und Staatslehre' [Influence of the Jews on state law and state theory].[136] In it, he suggests that 'the systematic hollowing out of the healthy völkisch-German thinking of the state [Staatsdenken]' should be seen in the 'overall context of the invasion [Einbruch] of the Jewish people'. Schmitt said: 'The totality of the Jewish invasion took hold of the literary-journalistic life (Heine, Börne, Harden etc.), musical life (Mendelssohn-Bartholdy, Meyerbeer), economic practice (Rothschild, Bleichröder, Rathenau), the theory of economics (Ricardo, Marx), as well as law [Recht].'[137] Schmitt started out from the authors Wagner had referred to and then extended the list to include Rathenau, Kaufmann and Kelsen. Thus, he complemented Wagner's list with his main opponents. It is almost surprising that he did not also mention composers of the 'new music', as Heinrich Berl had already reactivated the theorem of 'Jewish music' in his 1926 book on *Das Judentum in der Musik* [Judaism in music], which Schmitt had read approvingly.

Both Schmitt's opening address and his introductory remarks are of an aggressive sharpness which it is difficult to surpass. His concluding address, finally, defined the 'Jewish spirit' in political-theological terms as 'Jewish legal thought' [jüdisches Gesetzesdenken] and drew the foregone conclusion:

All lectures have shown that the Jewish law appears as deliverance from chaos. The polarity [*Deutsche Juristen-Zeitung*: strange polarity] between Jewish chaos and Jewish legality, between anarchic nihilism and positivist normativism, between a rough sensual materialism and an abstract moralism, now lies so plainly in our view that we may consider this fact to be a scientific insight of our conference, which is also decisive in the racial theory of mind [Rassenseelenkunde], and which we can use as the foundation of our future work in jurisprudence.

This fixation of polarities in the fashion of an 'ideal type' sounds enormously scientific, although its substance is almost non-existent. Such typological statements must apply at least roughly to some of the individuals they talk about. When Schmitt talked about 'positivist normativism', he was thinking in the first place of his antipode Kelsen, who systematically pursued the connection between 'state form and worldview'. However, Schmitt's characterization is bluntly polemical, because Kelsen did not take a materialist or a moralist position, still less an anarchic one. Which materialist would ever have been a representative of an abstract moralism? Why should normativism be a nihilism? In order to evoke the 'religious' meaning of his battle, Schmitt quoted Hitler: 'In fending off the Jew, I fight for the work of the Lord.'[138] Thus, Schmitt demolished his 'Political Theology' as a serious programme of research. His work had reached its nadir.

The pseudo-scientific summary legitimized brutal consequences. Schmitt quickly moved on to 'practical questions', which were also addressed by Hans Frank[139] and others. Schmitt demanded a bibliography of Jewish authors to be established, the 'purification of libraries', and a practice of referencing, according to which 'full Jews' were allowed to be quoted only as examples of Jews. 'For us, a Jewish author, if he is quoted at all, is a Jewish author.'* Schmitt's suggested lists and prohibitions regarding references proved to be impossible in practice. Thus, in March 1938, a decree of the Reichswissenschaftsministerium stipulated: 'A categorical prohibition for doctoral students to reference Jewish authors in their works is impossible.'[140] Schmitt assumed 'that the Jew is unproductive and sterile for the German kind of spirit'. Wagner had written: 'The period of Judaism in modern music can only be described historically as one

---

* This is not a mistranslation. The tautology is no less pronounced in the original German.

of complete unfruitfulness and of disappearing stability.' In the context of eliminatory anti-Semitism, Schmitt's adoption of Wagner's questions and approach implied far more forceful consequences. What both authors shared, however, was a personal feeling of resentment; like Wagner, Schmitt personalized his anti-Semitism; and, like Wagner, he assumed a sterile unproductivity of the 'Jewish spirit'. Both believed they could make out a strange discrepancy between achievement and success. In this context, it is possible to distinguish between an anti-Semitic paradox and an anti-Semitic argument. The anti-Semitic paradox – the thesis that there is a discrepancy between achievement and success – both shared in similar fashion, but within the framework of their own theories they justified their absurd belief in a 'sterile' 'unproductivity' in markedly different ways. Wagner, who considered music as a language, emphasized the mother tongue in Romantic fashion. Schmitt, who distinguished strictly between law and right and brought the 'state of justice', integrated by the person of the Führer, in opposition to the positivist 'state of law', dismissed legal thought altogether as unproductive. When Schmitt talks of a 'parasitic, tactical and commercial' relation towards the German state, this must be taken literally. Schmitt gave Hitler's parasitological metaphors the blessing of legal philosophy. He probably believed in what he wrote no less than Wagner. However, his theorem of the 'sterile' character of the 'Jewish spirit' is in contradiction to his permanent efforts (with dubious results)[141] at identifying Jewish authors acting at the 'turning points' in legal history as the nomothetic sources of false developments. Schmitt spoke less of Jewish 'economic imperialism'. In contrast to Wagner, he did not so much refer to economic power – over, for instance, the press – when trying to explain the 'domination' of Judaism, but rather sought his explanations in their 'susceptibility' to emancipatory and liberal attitudes in legal thought itself. He therefore probably took the domination of the 'Jewish spirit' even more seriously than Wagner. And hence, in comparison to Wagner's purely theoretical anti-Semitism, he pursued his programme of exclusion, his 'healing exorcism', backed by the Nazis, in the more concrete form of legal policy.

Schmitt's descent in the bureaucratic hierarchy

Around the same time that the conference took place, several of Schmitt's opponents were busy bringing about his fall. We know that the main characters responsible for it were the SS jurists Reinhard Höhn and Karl August Eckhardt, who were both close to Himmler and Heydrich. Koellreutter supported them with his earlier criticism of Schmitt. Herbert Gutjahr probably spied on Schmitt on behalf of the SD. And Waldemar Gurian also provided dangerous ammunition against him from his exile in Switzerland, reminding everyone of Schmitt's background in political Catholicism, his intellectual contacts with Jewish colleagues, and his efforts directed against National Socialism during the time of rule by presidential decree.[142] Repeatedly, Gurian mentioned Eschweiler as a seduced 'victim'[143] of Schmitt, recommended Schmitt to the SS-publication *Das Schwarze Korps* as a subject to be 'unmasked',[144] and – like Marcuse and Löwith – pointed out editorial touches Schmitt had made to his texts.[145] He observed Schmitt's anti-Semitic deliberations with particular care. Schmitt's adulation of the Nuremberg Laws he still read ironically. Probably, he says, Schmitt 'secretly laughs most about this' – i.e., his apologias.[146] Once Schmitt had announced the conference on the Jews, Gurian intensified his strategic efforts at playing off 'Carl Schmitt against Carl Schmitt'.[147] He now thought Schmitt was a completely amoral, nihilistic 'cynic', whose 'extreme formulations give away his inner lack of faith'.[148] Gurian saw his unmasking of Schmitt, in addition, as an application of Schmitt's discriminating principles of citation against Schmitt himself.[149]

Rather involuntarily, Günther Krauss provided further ammunition against Schmitt by publishing a sketch of the development of his work in the journal *Jugend und Recht*, in which he also mentioned Hitler's Catholic roots.[150] On 3 December, the SS publication *Das Schwarze Korps*,[151] which cooperated, not entirely without frictions, with the SD, picked up on this under the heading 'Eine peinliche Ehrenrettung' [An embarrassing saving of honour], adding the ironic sigh: 'Oh Lord, save me from my friends!' Under the headline 'Es wird immer noch peinlicher!' [It is getting even more embarrassing!], the journal followed this up on 10 December with a collection of allegedly incriminating passages from Schmitt's texts, denouncing him as a representative of a political Catholicism that was positively inclined towards the Jews. The articles were based on a dossier of the SD. It was a matter not of argumentation but of incrimination in order to increase the power of the attacking side. Whoever was attacked by an SS organ was at risk. The very same day, 10 December, Schmitt noted appointments with Frank and Göring in his calendar. 'Quod vestrum scelus est, meus somnus erit', he added, quoting from Book XVII of *De civitate Dei*: What is a crime to you, will be only sleep to me.[152]

After the publication of the articles, incidents occurred which caused the dean, Gleisspach,[153] to ask Schmitt to cancel his lectures. Palandt, the president of the Reichs-Justizprüfungsamt [Reich legal examination office] provisionally took him off the list of examiners.[154] And, with effect from 1 January, Hans Frank suspended him from all offices. The BNSDJ newsletter of 15 December explained this officially with reference to 'health reasons'. The newsletter of 15 January then referred to 'professional demands'.[155] Schmitt's successor as Hochschulgruppenleiter was Paul Ritterbusch, a radical ideologue of National Socialism. With effect from March 1937, Schmitt was reinstated as an examiner. The attacks on him were noted in his personnel file. The office of Rosenberg wrote a report.[156] An anonymous letter from a 'colleague' said:

Did you read the article in the '*Schwarze Korps*'? Right. Very good! At last you are uncovered as a first-rate bastard [Schweinehund I-Klasse]. . . . Now your time as a state councillor will soon be over. [. . .] In the Third Reich, bastards like you are eradicated. Then you've had it, because in civilized countries [Kulturstaaten] you are a nothing. You nothing, insulting great Jewish scholars [jüd-große Gelehrte] who are celebrated everywhere where there is culture. Now it's over, you nothing and bastard of the worst kind![157]

Gurian wrote about the attacks by the *Schwarze Korps* with great satisfaction.[158] Under the title 'Auf dem Weg in die Emigration oder ins Konzentrationslager' [On the way into exile or a concentration camp], he reminded his readers of Schmitt's presence at the academic conference in Maria Laach in April 1933. 'Edgar Jung dared publicly to ask the question: "Is Christianity compatible with the total state?" Carl Schmitt said under his breath, but audibly: "This man is ready for the concentration camp."'[159] Edgar Jung was actually one of those who were later murdered after 30 June. By publishing this at the time, Gurian more or less directly recommended that Schmitt should be imprisoned by the National Socialists. Franz Blei, who had a much closer and longer friendship with Schmitt, which lasted until 1933, commented almost with pity on 'The Case of Carl Schmitt': 'Schmitt's publications since 1933 are almost exclusively limited to doing all he can to defend his indefensible theorem of the total state. He can do this only by sacrificing his intellect to an incredible degree.' The scholar, he said, has been 'abandoned by his spirit'.[160] Gurian soon restricted himself to noting in passing that the 'dictatorship of the cynically coordinated Carl Schmitt [is] broken' and that Schmitt 'owed the fact that he is not completely wrecked only to certain personal relations'.[161] Apparently, Gurian knew about the personal intervention by Hermann Göring, who had prohibited the further public dismantling of his 'state councillor'. Hans Frank protested to Gunter d'Alquen, the founder of the *Schwarze Korps*: 'It deserves to be especially noted that essentially these attacks only repeat what has long since been said by Jewish emigrants in the inflammatory foreign press.'[162] Gurian's keyword was 'cynicism'. One might find it questionable that old companions sought Schmitt's downfall. But Schmitt had no right to complain about this. His descent down the bureaucratic ladder protected him from even worse consequences. What would have happened had Schmitt still been Hans Frank's confidant after 1939? 'Call yourself lucky that you are getting out of such company', was his brother Jupp's comment.[163] But, even after 1936, Schmitt occasionally socialized with members of the SS. Even after his fall he could not leave National Socialism behind.

23

A New Turn with Hobbes? Meaning and Failure of Schmitt's Commitment to National Socialism

After 1936, Schmitt's 'creative euphoria' and energetic efforts at the provision of meaning cooled down considerably. He had himself been affected by the discriminating logic of the Führer state. The only surprise is that he was astonished by this and saw himself as a victim. Jurisprudence was licking its wounds, retreating into the haven of its own history and reactivating an old debate from the transitional period between 1930 and 1933. The 'total state' returned as a buzzword. Schmitt once saw it as a chance for depoliticization. Now he discussed the possibility of constructing a 'total' state or of a regenerated political unity, triggering a new debate. Schmitt did not criticize National Socialism for being a totalitarian Leviathan, or – as Franz Neumann would soon do[1] – as a Behemoth; rather, he asked for a theory that would provide the foundations for a 'total' state.

Under conditions of 'total' politicization, all intellectual-historical debates were at the same time ciphers. The current state of affairs was discussed as reflected in the work of classical authors. Historical parallels became the background against which authors would take critical positions at times of political repression and censorship. However, the space for the direct expression of one's opinion was not that small either, and ambiguous esotericism was often just literary playfulness. Thus in the end Schmitt's analyses of the concept of the 'Führer's will' at the level of legal theory expressed the dictatorial character of National Socialism much more clearly than many of the 'esoteric' twists in the Hobbes debate. Thomas Mann was annoyed about the allusions in Stefan Zweig: 'I glanced through Zweig's book on Erasmus. The historical allusion and parallels are unacceptable, because they tender too much feeble virtue to the present. "Luther, the demonic man driven by inchoate German racial forces." Who can fail to recognize Hitler in this? But that is just the point – that the disgusting travesty, the abject, hysterical mimicry is taken to be mythical recapitulation. That is already submission.'[2] However, such historical reflections were not entirely without their risks. Schmitt, the former censor, knew this very well. 'What the censor does not understand – and that is true for all dictatorships – the people do not understand either.'[3] Hermann Oncken presented Hitler as reflected in Cromwell,[4] Hans Freyer[5] used Machiavelli and Borgia, René König soon saw Schmitt as Machiavelli.[6] Over the years, Schmitt developed a series of catchwords and images that reflected Hitler, National Socialism and his own role. Thus, he interpreted Max Kommerell's speech on 'Schiller als Gestalter des handelnden Menschen' [Schiller as the creator of acting men] as a reflection of the events of summer 1934 and found therein the striking comparison between Hitler and Schiller's Demetrius figure.[7] In 1935, Schmitt compared his situation to that of Wallenstein: 'Courageous were the words, because the deeds were not so / Now they will, what happened without plan, / tie into a farsighted plan for me.'[*]

In 1937, Schmitt started to approach the debate about state theory from a historical perspective. The 300th anniversary of Descartes' *Discours de la méthode* [Discourse on method] was celebrated widely in many countries. Attitudes to early modern rationalism were discussed. In this context, Schmitt gave a lecture on 'Der Staat als Mechanismus bei Hobbes und Descartes' [The state as a mechanism in Hobbes and Descartes] in Berlin, and he initiated a special issue of the *Archiv für Rechts- und Sozialphilosophie*,[8] edited by Carl August Emge and editorially overseen by Otto von Schweinichen, the disputant of the *Rechtsstaat* booklet. Emge was Schmitt's closest conversational partner and companion within the faculty in those days. Schmitt assured him of his 'friendship and admiration'[9] and thanked him for 'many conversations held in the brightest light'.[10] Schmitt had for a long time seen in Hobbes one of the fathers of the modern 'unitary state' [Einheitsstaat] and of 'decisionist' legal theory. Leo Strauss had brought him back to Hobbes again, and now Schmitt worked out Strauss's thesis that Hobbes was one of the fathers of liberalism, setting out from the counter-thesis of a French author that Hobbes was the father of 'today's totalism' (SGN, p. 140). Who was the philosopher of totalism? Was a 'total' state possible at all? Was there a philosophical theory of the total state? Was it possible to use Hobbes's 'mechanistic' thought as the foundation for a 'total' state? Or was an 'organic' approach of the kind elaborated in German state theory what was needed? From the winter term 1936–7, Schmitt repeatedly gave lectures on 'Volk und Staat' [People and state].[11] His argument was a sharp critique of 'mechanistic' thought. He explained how Hobbes had drawn the consequences of Descartes' 'metaphysical decision' for state theory and thus had also effected a 'return projection' of the mechanistic concept of the state onto the image of the human being. The human being was now also looked upon as a machine.

Apart from this systematic philosophical approach, Schmitt also took the 'mythic image of the Leviathan' and a 'juridical construction of the contract' from Hobbes. But Hobbes, Schmitt said, had picked up the mythic image only casually; it was 'no more than a half ironic literary idea born of

---

[*]   'Kühn war das Wort, weil es die Tat nicht war / Jetzt werden sie, was planlos ist geschehn, / Weitsehend, planvoll mir zusammenknüpfen' (Schiller, *Wallensteins Tod*, Act 2, scene 2).

the good sense of humour of the English' (SGN, p. 142). And the person-based idea of the contract was 'drawn into the process of mechanization' (SGN, p. 145). It was impossible to construct a 'total' state within the framework of mechanical thought. Thus, Hegel appeared as the 'organic' alternative to Hobbes. Schmitt referred to Carl August Emge, the editor of the special issue, but he might as well have used Ernst Rudolf Huber or Karl Larenz. His hope of being able to capture the notion of the 'total' state on a right-Hegelian basis may refer directly to Huber's *Grundriss* [Principles], which appeared in 1937. However, Schmitt did not follow Hegel systematically either; rather, he investigated the 'view expressed by E. Peterson according to which the "total" concepts of the modern age were not meant as concepts at all, but as myths, and that, hence, totaliza-tion meant mythologization [Mythisierung]' (SGN, p. 146). Therefore, deliberations on the 'mythic image' of the Leviathan already took up a lot of space in the lecture. Schmitt was looking for a philosophical foundation for 'totality' and dismissed the 'mechanist' worldview. He didn't identify with Hobbes; at best, he hinted at the fact that the National Socialist state could perhaps be justified with the help of mythic images. Schelsky, in his reply,[12] overlooked the fact that, because Schmitt aimed at a foundation for political totality in terms of 'mythologization', he fundamentally rejected Hobbes's thought. All he positively picked up from Hobbes were the begin-nings of a political myth. Schmitt interpreted philosophical justifications 'theologically' and considered them as mythical resources. Like National Socialism itself, he opted for political myth.[13] And, precisely in that respect, he thought Hobbes had failed, which is why he devoted his next book to the 'meaning' and 'failure' of the 'Leviathan' as a symbol.

When Schmitt's article for the special issue appeared, he felt that the discussion of the 'problem of totality' had essentially only just begun (JS, p. 66). The *Archiv* initiated a little controversy around Schmitt's contribu-tion. Georg Daskalakis,[14] a Habilitant of Schmitt, responded to Schelsky's objections with a review of previous discussions and the clarification that the 'total' state was a political moment – in Schmitt's terminology, a 'degree of intensity' – of the state. Numerous publications on the 'total state' followed. One of them was Hans Krupa's doctoral thesis (written in Hamburg and partly supervised by Joachim Ritter): *Carl Schmitts Theorie des 'Politischen'* [Carl Schmitt's theory of the 'political']. It demonstrated the development of Schmitt's thinking about the political, as Löwith and Krauss had done previously. The editorial supervisor of the *Archiv*, von Schweinichen, sent Schmitt his critical review and added a note on the typescript: 'Krupa's work is objectively unimportant, but is read a lot these days. Hence the long review.'[15] Schmitt continued to develop his interpre-tation of Hobbes. Two lectures, given in Leipzig and Kiel, he combined into a book. 'For months, I have been following a peculiar track', he wrote to Smend: 'Why has no one yet thought about what the Leviathan as a symbol and political myth actually means?'[16]

We have Schmitt's pocket diary for the year 1938.[17] Recurrent names are, for instance, those of his collaborators Eberhard von Medem, Bernhard von Mutius, Karl Lohmann and Herbert Gutjahr, the visiting lecturer from

Switzerland William Gueydan de Roussel,[18] and the deeply anti-Semitic author Johann von Leers. On 21 January, Schmitt, upon an invitation from Arnold Gehlen, gave a lecture on Hobbes at a meeting of the local section of the Philosophical Society in the Alte Handelsbörse [Old Trade Exchange] in Leipzig. On the occasion of the 350th anniversary of Hobbes's birth, on 5 April 1938, he published a letter to the Hobbes Society, in which he addressed Hobbes, the 'great political thinker', exclaiming: 'Non iam frustra doces, Thomas Hobbes!' [Thomas Hobbes, now you do not teach in vain!][19] These are also the words which end his book on Hobbes (L, p. 86).* On 28 April, Schmitt spoke at the Verwaltungsakademie [Academy for Public Administration] in Flensburg on 'Volksgruppenrecht' [Rights of ethnic groups].[20] The following day he gave his second lecture on Hobbes in Kiel.[21] On his return to Berlin he visited the *Volkstum* publicist Albrecht Erich Günther in Hamburg.[22] He straightaway worked on the compilation of his two lectures; the preface gives 11 July 1938 – his fiftieth birthday – as the date of completion. The publisher had already received the first part of the *Leviathan* book by mid-April, and in mid-May 1938 it was completed and went to press.[23]

Schmitt attended a meeting of the academy's section for international law. On 2 and 3 June he was at a conference on 'Diktatur und Demokratie' [Dictatorship and democracy] in Berlin, which was organized by the NSRB Hochschulgruppe, now under the leadership of Paul Ritterbusch.[24] He probably met Ernst Forsthoff again on this occasion. There were dinner parties with the ambassador General Ott, with Baron Evola, Gustav Steinbömer and Mrs Moeller van den Brueck. The conference was followed by the fifth annual meeting of the Academy for German Right, at which Hans Frank spoke about 'Die geistesgeschichtliche Lage der deutschen Rechtswissenschaft' [The situation of German jurisprudence in the context of intellectual history].[25] On 1 July the 'academic discussion' of Daskalakis's Habilitation took place. Schmitt and Emge were the examiners.[26] In early July, a few days before Schmitt's fiftieth birthday, the *Leviathan* book was sent out by the publisher. Clearly the intention was to mark his birthday. Schmitt saw the completion of the book as a birthday present from himself, to himself, and sent it to various places. He gave something to those congratulating him, not vice versa.[27] Smend's copy contained the dedication: 'To my best companion on the dangerous path of public law, Rudolf Smend, in loyal admiration and with grateful memories'. Smend did not attend the birthday party.[28] However, he wrote a detailed letter in response to the presentation copy as a 'birthday present'.[29]

Schmitt celebrated his fiftieth birthday with a series of meetings. On 10 July the oldest of his companions, Schnitzler, Krause, Oberheid and Popitz, were invited.[30] The actual birthday, 11 July, was marked with a lunch, followed by a large dinner the next day. On 13 July, Schmitt organized an evening with his pupils Hans Schneider,[31] Herbert Gutjahr, Werner Weber, Eberhard von Medem, Karl Lohmann, Otto von Schweinichen,

---

* All translations from the *Leviathan* book are mine.

Bernhard von Mutius, Helmut Pfeiffer[32] and Gustav von Schmoller. On other days, Emge, Mrs Sombart and others visited. In line with common practice at the time, half of the German jurists sent their congratulations. The letters he received on his round birthday say a lot about their authors' positions. Many of them responded to the *Leviathan* book. Thus, the letters cover the spectrum of possible positions within National Socialism at the time. Hans Frank and others also sent letters or telegrams. But, of Schmitt's pupils from his time in Bonn, only Werner Weber and Karl Lohmann were among those who congratulated him. Thus, Schmitt could hardly miss the painful ruptures in his biography.

The small book on the *Leviathan* concentrated wholly on the 'political symbol'. The cover text also emphasized the 'image of battle' [Kampfbild], the 'history of this symbol' and the 'substance of genuine emblems'. As the beginning of a political iconology, the book is still appreciated today.[33] It stands out from Schmitt's National Socialist writings through its scholarship and 'esotericism'. Schmitt demonstrated his qualities as an author again. The political tendency of the monograph – which at 132 pages is the longest of his writings after 1931 – remains, however, controversial. Schmitt would later understand it as a sign of 'inner resistance' and compare it to Ernst Jünger's *On the Marble Cliffs*. He wrote instructions on how to read the book, in which he warned against 'esotericism'. In fact, the monograph resembles Jünger's book insofar as its interest in mythology is concerned, rather than with respect to its political tendencies. Schmitt did not want to justify the 'ineradicable individualist proviso' (L, p. 84) in liberal terms; instead, he criticized it as the 'germ of death' (L, p. 88) within the liberalization of political 'unity'. The 'meaning' of the symbol is presented as the restoration of political unity. However, as a consequence of its instrumentalization, the symbol became a 'failure'. Can that failure be healed with the help of the symbol?

Schmitt reflects again on the legitimacy of legality and justified the state as political unity with the myth of the Leviathan. The Leviathan, however, can only be realized in a one-sided fashion. The 'mythic totality of God, man, animal and machine' (L, p. 31) cannot be realized in homogeneous fashion. The state may require the myth as a source for its legitimacy, but it cannot be founded equally on God, man, animal and machine. Hobbes was still aware of the mythical foundation of political unity, but, in line with the metaphysics of his times, he realized it only in the form of a constitutional machine. In scholarly excursions, Schmitt reminds his readers of the 'mythic' meaning of the symbol and demonstrates that Hobbes's attempt at hiding the limits of a rational construction of the state behind symbols categorically failed and turned into its opposite. Schmitt distinguishes 'two main lines of interpretation': 'Christian symbolization' and 'Jewish mythification' (L, pp. 14f.). Jewish mythification, understandable as a consequence of the 'Jewish existence' (L, p. 89), 'situation and attitude' (L, p. 16), led to a 'Jewish–Christian divide in the originary political unity' (L, p. 21) which, in turn, led to ultimate 'failure' as a result of the liberal interpretation of the schism, which Schmitt associates with a 'Jewish front' (L, p. 108) – i.e., Spinoza,

Table 23.1 Political-theological front lines

Hobbes/Donoso Cortés	Spinoza/Kelsen
Decisionism	Normativism
Personalism	Mechanism
Theism	Atheism
Christianity	'Jewish spirit'

Mendelssohn and Stahl. The 'Jewish interpretation had a retroactive effect on the Leviathan of Hobbes' (L, p. 124). Schmitt understands his book as part of a 'battle against the Jewish falsification of Christianity'.[34] He distinguishes between this interpretation and an original Christian symbolization and turns Hobbes into the tragic point where these discourses cross over and are articulated. In great detail, he again tells his story about the 'transition of legitimacy into legality' (L, p. 303), about liberalization and 'rationalization', 'mechanization', 'constitutionalization', 'neutralization', 'functionalization' and 'bureaucratization' of the modern state. He identifies Hobbes's distinction between private 'faith' and public 'creed' within a Christian state as a turning point, and he locates the conflict between Christianity and modernity in Hobbes's thought itself: Hobbes could not articulate his own 'piety' within the context of the modern paradigm and thus retreated to a form of 'agnosticism' (L, p. 126). If we draw further on Schmitt's *Political Theology* of 1922, we get roughly the picture shown in table 23.1.

This is not the place to discuss Schmitt's learned excursions beyond the creation of polemical confrontations. His manifold references to literature are also hard to disentangle. Thus, Schmitt probably also responded to the resumption of German whaling,[35] to Leo Strauss as well as to Helmut Schelsky, to Jewish as well as to National Socialist discussions. Schmitt responded to Peterson's criticism from the Catholic side, to the accusation that he had sacrificed the Christian distinction between Church and state on the altar of an ancient Caesarism. In his monograph *Monotheism as a Political Problem* [see Peterson, *Theological Tractates*, pp. 68–105], Peterson had distinguished between heathen and Christian approaches. Friendly postcards were still exchanged between Schmitt and Peterson in April and June 1938. But when Schmitt sent him the *Leviathan* book, Peterson rejected its anti-Semitic allusions in a short postcard and distinguished sharply between the Platonic and philosophical heritage and heathen mythologization. 'These are concepts from Plato's cosmology', he wrote, 'which do not prove that Hobbes had to turn the state into a God.' Schmitt's polemics against the *potestas indirecta* 'make sense only if you renounce being a Christian and decide in favour of heathenism.'[36] With these words, Peterson again denied Schmitt his Christianity. Gustav Steinbömer, by contrast, combined his Christian understanding of the *Leviathan* with a critique of Ernst Jünger.[37] Herbert Meyer, Eckhardt's successor in the faculty from the winter term 1937–8, wrote: 'The inner truthfulness of your account forces your reader to agree with you. Also harrowing is your demonstration of how the Jew twice spotted the point of least resistance in the edifice erected by H., in order to turn it upside-down and thus make it serviceable to his own purposes.'[38] Ulrich Scheuner welcomed the fact that the 'image of the Leviathan' figured as the opening to Schmitt's new cycle of writings:

> The problem of the relationship between political power and religious faith, the question of the domination of the body politics [sic!]* over true religion today, rises up with renewed force. And on a new basis, which is derived from its *völkisch* and historical mission, the state, as the expression of the community of a people, achieves the utmost power, a state, which rejects any argument over its legitimacy, even any thought of a limitation that would be imposed on it from outside.[39]

In a short time, Schmitt was able to collect numerous reviews as well. The Catholic press registered moderate reservations. Albrecht Erich Günther wrote an affirmative review for the *Deutsches Volkstum*. The *Neue Züricher Zeitung* reported in detail: 'It is not the Leviathan symbols which cast a shadow over the slim book, but rather Schmitt's past that makes some of its parts academically questionable and undignified in human terms.'[40]

What Schmitt has to say about the division between Christian faith and scholasticism – that the 'divide' within political unity, brought about by the distinction between Church, state and society, does not correspond to the original intention, and that Christian faith also was in favour of a mythological strengthening of political unity – may well be questionable. However, he clearly articulates, and conceptually identifies, this theological difference through his distinction between 'symbolization' and 'mythologi-zation'.[41] The whole point of his study, like that of Hobbes before him, is the 'restoration of the political unity' (L, p. 21), and it discusses the alter-native of a 'rational' or 'mythic' foundation for 'totality'. Schmitt is of the opinion that the possibility of creating unity symbolically has been lost in the modern age, and that the attempt to seize the profitable advantages of myth had to fail. He shows that, within the context of the modern age, the Leviathan, political unity, is no longer possible, either on 'mythic' or on 'rationalistic' grounds.

Schmitt did not share the liberal view that a 'total' Leviathan would be unjust. Factual political unity – in Hegel's words, the unity of morality and ethical life – continued to be Schmitt's goal. But within the modern context he understood this unity as a utopia, and thus held that 'mythic' homog-enization in the present must fail. Schmitt criticized political mythology as a vain attempt at stability and ended with a sketch of the 'failure' of 1933. And he meant failure in the full sense of the word. Again and again, Schmitt emphasized the final result of his study – i.e., that Hobbes 'made a mistake' in choosing his image and that his 'attempt at restoring natural unity' (L, p. 130) had failed. Bayonets make uncomfortable seats; a 'total'

---

* 'Body politics' in English in the original.

state cannot be established on the basis of the nightmare or horror scenario of the Leviathan image alone. National Socialism used its symbolic capital. 'Hitler, the creator of myths, feared nothing more than the mythic curse.'[42] Schmitt's book on Hobbes can therefore also be understood as a warning.

If, however, Schmitt had National Socialism in mind when he spoke about the instrumentalization of the 'symbol', then his description of a kind of 'double state', which forms mythic strategies on its bureaucratic foundations, amounts to a euphemistic characterization of the actual status quo. Schmitt would have been the first one to admit that the National Socialist Führer state had eliminated any legal security at the level of bureaucracy and had abolished right as a functional mode. He himself had described this in terms of legal theory. It would be misleading to say that the National Socialist 'Leviathan' was justified by the need to hold down the revolutionary 'Behemoth'. Schmitt's small book of 1938 continued the essay of 1937 by moving on from the critique of the 'mechanistic' approach to the more detailed investigation of the potential of the symbol. In the end, Schmitt considered the attempt to cover up the limits of the liberal state's power with political mythology, and thus to found an actual 'political unity', to have failed. The formation of unity, the construction of a 'total' state, continued to be his goal. But he was afraid of 'making a mistake' in the way that Hobbes had done. He moved the question of legitimacy and of the foundations of the state into the field of 'Political Theology' and ascribed the limits set to political unity to the 'Jewish' influence. This makes Schmitt's *Leviathan* book his most elaborate contribution to his 'battle against the Jewish spirit in jurisprudence'. What he had not presented in 1936, a larger study of intellectual history, he now provided. His Hobbes studies are anything but the expression of liberal reservations; rather, they are a critical diagnosis of the fact that the attempt at the mythic foundation of the 'total' state had failed. Schmitt blamed Judaism for this fact. Although the message of the Hobbes studies is one of resignation, and despite the fact that they are an 'epilogue to the state',[43] they nevertheless hold on to the utopia of a 'total' state or of a pre-constitutional political unity, and they use 'Political Theology' as a tool of intellectual history in order to do so. Schmitt was looking for another dimension in which he could give his anti-Semitism a scientific form, and – in 1938 – he presented his most substantial analysis of the 'meaning and failure' of the liberal state.

The *Leviathan* book remained of particular importance to Schmitt. It was his most ambitious response to the debates about the 'total' state. In it, he formulated paradoxical criteria for the formation of political unity: while the law establishes a difference between legality and morality, the myth pretends that there is consensual 'unity'. This tension can only be resolved in one-sided fashion. Thus, Schmitt brought the question of the legitimacy of legality to a head with the actualization of the Leviathan symbol in the constitutional state. The state, Schmitt thought, had to present itself in the form of a Leviathan. Under the conditions of modern metaphysics, however, this is not wholly possible. The constitutional state of the modern age embodies the 'meaning' [Sinn] of political unity only imperfectly. Schmitt's utopian idealization of the debates about the 'total' state moved beyond the modern constitutional state to the mythic beginnings of the symbol. If the *Leviathan* book, beyond being an intervention in contemporary debates, contains an answer to ultimate theoretical questions and a constitutional credo, then this lies beyond the modern age and modernity. The book thus relativizes the *Constitutional Theory* of the Weimar period. Schmitt's movement beyond modern ideas of a constitution to fundamental preconditions of statehood renders the legitimacy of the modern age problematic.

24

The Right to Power? Großraum Order and Empire Formation

Fictional or political peace?

In the summer of 1937, Schmitt again did not feel well. He spent a few days in bed, 'in the most miserable condition'. 'If only good friendships were half as loyal as bad illnesses!', he wrote to Smend.[1] On 24 September he celebrated his parents' golden wedding anniversary with them in Plettenberg. On the same day he was asked to stand in for Koellreutter, who was not available, and write a report on the concept of war in international law. He must have felt relieved about this readmittance to the echelons of academia; at least his loss of importance in the bureaucratic hierarchy did not exclude him from all areas of debate. On 20 October he presented his report on *The Turn to the Discriminating Concept of War*, which he had sent off just shortly before, to the section on international law at the fourth annual meeting of the academy. Werner Weber organized the publication of the report, with a print run of 1,000 copies, as part of the academy's series.[2] At the end of February the text went off to the publisher, at the beginning of April Schmitt corrected the proofs, and at the end of April 1938 the booklet was sent out by the publisher. The academy received fifty copies.

In the report, Schmitt does not analyse the practice, but rather the theory and system, of international law, beginning with the presentation of two works of international law by Georges Scelle and Hersch Lauterpacht. He reads both as typical representatives of more recent French and Anglo-Saxon thought in international law and counteracts the tendency towards universalism with this renationalization of legal thought. He acknowledges in particular Scelle's approach as the consequent idealization of a post-statist individualism and universalism. In Scelle, he says, the state is 'radically dethroned' (TDCW, p. 39), and the individual is elevated to the position of the only and 'immediate subject of international law' (TDCW, p. 40, trans. modified; FP, p. 529). War, Schmitt says, becomes 'intervention' and the classical war between states is transformed into a 'civil war' (TDCW, p. 44). The Geneva League of Nations announces an 'ecumenical global legal order' (TDCW, p. 48). Lauterpacht, Schmitt suggests, reaches similar conclusions. Schmitt's more recent articles clarified the consequences for the classical concept of 'neutrality' and the concept of war.

Towards the end, Schmitt explains that a turn towards a discriminating conception of 'just' 'wars of execution or sanction' already manifests itself. A 'denationalization' – today, we speak rather of 'Entstaatlichung'* (Münckler) – of war is taking place, which puts certain parties in the place of a collectively responsible people and which will end in 'civil war'. Schmitt attributes part of the blame for the 'mixing' (TDCW, p. 72) of League of Nations and international law to universalist theories. The literary review is interesting not only for its critical diagnosis of 'destatification' and 'denationalization' but also for its renationalization of legal thought and its idealist orientation towards theory and system. Schmitt's old friend from Strasbourg, Friedrich Kiener, doubted that the suggested developments were representative for the time: 'It is a pretty bleak diagnosis you offer regarding the prospects for a future transformation of international law', he wrote, 'but, given your sense for things to come and sharp formulations, how interesting all this is!'[3] As usual, Schmitt sent his treatise to members of the political circles. The foreign minister, Ribbentrop, thanked him in a personal letter.[4] On behalf of the supreme command of the navy, a ministerial secretary, Dr Eckhardt, welcomed the 'work of doing away with these erroneous foreign tendencies' in a letter to Werner Weber, but missed a positive answer to the question 'whether and to what extent a concept of war that would be closer to the true reality can be derived from his [Schmitt's] premise of total enmity'.[5] Schmitt deplored the state of his discipline and complained about the stupid and ugly way in which his diagnosis had been 'shot at'.[6]

Some shorter articles clarify the ramifications of Schmitt's argument. A survey, 'Über das Verhältnis der Begriffe Krieg und Feind' [On the relationship between the concept of war and the concept of enemy], works out the 'logic of the law of peace' according to which war and peace are seen as a simple 'disjunction' and as a pair of 'alternatives' (FP, p. 603), and international law, therefore, considers any condition in which open military actions are absent as peace. 'However, what does this mean for our question regarding the relationship between war and peace?', Schmitt asks. 'It shows that enmity, the *animus hostilis*, has become the primary concept' (ibid.). Schmitt had always been reproached for this primary orientation towards the concept of the enemy. Now, he claimed that the disjunctive logic of international law had forced this approach upon him. Within the context of a universalist international law, the 'just war' absorbs the *ius belli*. The sovereign right to declare war disappears. The 'just war', however, does not tolerate 'neutrality'; rather, it demands commitment.[7] Schmitt's argument is addressed to the neutral states, and it suggests that they should remain neutral. At the outbreak of war, on 1 September 1939, Schmitt published yet another powerful article,[8] which explained the difference between the fictional peace of Versailles and a 'genuinely peaceful order' (SGN, p. 633), using, inter alia, Czechoslovakia as an example. Schmitt wanted to show categorically that the wide and weak concept of

* This term would usually also be translated as 'denationalization' – 'destatification' would be a neologism formed in order to express the difference between the German terms.

peace used in international law was a euphemistic description of the inter-war period, which allowed the toleration of hostile behaviour below the threshold of outright war.

Reconstruction of the 'Reich'?

Carl Schmitt, a theoretician of political myths, invoked the 'force of genuine, mythical images' (L, p. 133), but was strangely reserved towards the typical German myths.[9] He did not talk in grandiose terms about Germanic myths and the loyalty of the Nibelungen, the myth of Barbarossa about the renewal of the Reich, the counter-myth of Henry the Lion prop-agated by Himmler, or other commonplaces of the nineteenth century, which was replete with myths. If he invoked myths at all, they were likely to be Prussian myths. Although Schmitt considered myths as symbolic capital and as resources providing legitimation, he cited them only discreetly, despite the rhetorical force with which he expressed himself. He was also aware of the compulsions to act and the traps implied in myths, and he was afraid of their 'curse'. He therefore added a warning against a 'false choice' to his concept of a mythical reconstruction of political unity. The story of decline presented in the *Leviathan* book ended before 1933; his review essay of 1939 entitled 'Neutralität und Neutralisierungen' [Neutrality and neutralizations] drew the consequences for the present. In it, the 'Reich' concept of international law took the position of the failed symbol of the Leviathan, without Schmitt referring to the old stories of the Reich at any great length. The Reich now became his symbol for the possibility of a pre-constitutional political unity and 'totality'. The comprehensive essay discusses Christoph Steding's book *Das Reich und die Krankheit der europäischen Kultur* [The Reich and the sickness of European culture]. Steding was a protégé of the NS court historian Walter Frank.[10] He had written his doctorate on Max Weber in 1931 and then, with support from the Rockefeller Foundation, embarked on carrying out the plan for a major history of the 'neutralization' of Germany. He became Frank's great hope. After Steding's early death in 1938, Walter Frank began to sift through the mountains of material and edited his historical-political legacy. Thus, with his review Schmitt also positioned himself with regard to Walter Frank, the leading National Socialist historian.

To begin with, Schmitt praises Steding in the most glowing terms, before continuing his thoughts from *Staatsgefüge und Zusammenbruch des zweiten Reiches* [State structure and collapse of the Second Reich]. The essay was also a reaction to Schmitt's renewed intensive discussion with Ernst Rudolf Huber about the evaluation of constitutionalism and Wilhelminianism. To Schmitt's view of the 'victory of the citizen over the soldier', Huber[11] added, in *Heer und Staat* [The army and the state], a wide-ranging and in-depth account of the 'state-constituting force of the army'. For both Schmitt and Huber, the 'soldier state' was a fundamental and stable core element of the National Socialist constitution. Both were now looking towards the nineteenth century in order to find the historical reasons for the absence of state unity. They no longer identified the November revolution or Versailles and Geneva as leading to the central constitutional problem in which Germany found itself, but rather the constitutional dualism that led to the crises in leadership during the Great War.[12] However, while Huber defended the constitutional compromise of Wilhelminianism, Schmitt rejected modern constitutionalism wholesale. For Schmitt, the fall from grace was first marked by the 'calamitous figure of Stahl-Johlson' (PB, p. 293), who recommended constitutionalism to the Prussian monarchy. But, following Steding, he also referred back to Hegel: although Hegel had saved the myth of the Reich in the form of the 'myth of the state', in doing so he nevertheless laid the 'foundations for the constitutional neutralization of the monarch' (PB, p. 292). The idea of the 'Reich' now symbolized for Schmitt the idea of an extra-constitutional political unity and 'totality'. In his review essay the idea of the Reich takes on the function of the failed symbol of the Leviathan. Thus, only by looking at the concept of the 'Reich' in the essay on Steding can the question be answered as to whether Schmitt wanted to reconstitute the Leviathan symbol as an image of terror constituting unity [einheitsstiftendes Schreckbild]. And the answer is negative. He did not need the Leviathan symbol, because he transferred the function of constituting symbolic unity to the concept of the Reich instead. He did not, with Hobbes and natural law, turn away from political 'totality', but wanted to see the formation of political unity on the basis of a new myth of the Reich. Schmitt straightaway translated the political symbol of the Reich into a legitimation, according to international law, for 'pan-German' expansion. He also emphasized the National Socialist character of his conception of the Reich in a review of Heinrich Triepel's magisterial work on *Hegemonie* [Hegemony].[13]

On 12 March, the German army had marched into Austria. The 'Sudetenland crisis' about the situation of Germans in Czechoslovakia followed. The question of 'German expatriates' was used to serve expansionist politics. At the end of September the Munich conference sanctioned Hitler's act of force and allowed the invasion of the Sudetenland, to be followed in November by the 'Reichskristallnacht', the Night of Broken Glass. In mid-March the German army marched into the 'Resttschechei', the other parts of Czechoslovakia, and on 23 March it occupied the Memel area. The 'Reich protectorate of Bohemia and Moravia' was founded. Duška's guest book lists Werner Weber, Gutjahr, von Mutius and Dr Pfeiffer as visitors on an evening with Schmitt's pupils on 19 March. Schmitt wrote a short preface for the Spanish edition of *Political Theology* and *The Concept of the Political*, edited by Francisco Javier Conde, in which he spoke of a 'bitter spiritual [geistigen] battle of universal significance' and of the 'appeal' for a 'front'.[14] Between 31 March and 3 April there was an anniversary celebration of Paul Ritterbusch's Institute for Politics and International Law in Kiel. In the context of the celebration, a meeting of the Reichsfachgruppe Hochschullehrer also took place, at which Schmitt, on 1 April, spoke about 'Völkerrechtliche Großraumordnung'

[Großraum order in international law]. The first edition of this speech was published the very same month. Gustav Adolf Walz judged the text to be moderate. 'I read it in the morning while waiting in anticipation of the Führer's speech', he wrote.[15] The publication found international attention because the idea of a 'German Monroe Doctrine' was also propounded by Hitler in a speech on 28 April. Hitler confronted Roosevelt's demand for peace with a reference to the Monroe Doctrine and its stipulation of non-intervention of powers 'from outside' ['raumfremde' Mächte] in a Großraum: 'We Germans assume exactly the same doctrine for Europe, certainly with regard to the area and the concerns of the pan-German Reich'.[16] It was too late, of course, for Schmitt to react to this speech in his publication. Thus, his reference to the 'deed of the Führer' (SGN, p. 306) referred not to Hitler's response to Roosevelt but to 'pan-German' expansion.[17] Schmitt's text appeared only months before the war broke out. Expanded editions followed in 1941.

Schmitt switched at a stroke from a critique of the League of Nations to a critique of the Monroe Doctrine, interpreting the latter as the counterpart to the idea of the German Großraum and Reich. In the past, he had established that the possibility of a peaceful revision of the status quo was at the heart of the legitimacy of the League of Nations: the League of Nations is legitimate if it establishes homogeneity within the alliance through peaceful revisions of Versailles. Looking at various 'transformations' of the League of Nations, Schmitt had demonstrated the erosion of its identity and substance. Now he wanted to enlist the legitimacy at the heart of the Monroe Doctrine for the 'Reich'. In other words, Schmitt was looking for a legal principle that the USA had to accept because they claimed it for themselves. The text from spring 1939 therefore was directed in particular at the United States.

In his text, Schmitt assumes that there are economic and technological tendencies which lead to Großraum formations, mentions 'examples of false and obsolete spatial principles' – such as the principle of 'natural borders' – and then discusses the Monroe Doctrine as a 'precedent for a Großraum principle in international law'. His point of departure is the 'precedent' as it occurs in legal practice, something Anglo-Saxon legal thought cannot but accept. International law, he says, is a 'law of provisos' (SGN, p. 279). The political provisos are more interesting than the legal norms. The USA adopted the Monroe Doctrine in the nineteenth century as a 'defence' (SGN, p. 280) against British pretensions to the right of intervention. However, it gradually experienced an 'imperialist-capitalist reinterpretation' (SGN, p. 284), which was politicized by Wilson and in the context of the Geneva League of Nations turned into a 'pan-interventionist world ideology'. Schmitt illustrates this shift in meaning from 'defensive' non-interventionism to 'aggressive' pan-interventionism through a comparison with the British 'principle of security for transport routes'. He then contrasts these capitalist forms of thinking about space with the 'volkliche' [people-based] way of thinking about space in National Socialism.

When Germany as a major power claims the Central and Eastern

European Großraum as a 'performance space' [Leistungsraum],* it does so not out of 'capitalist' interests, Schmitt claims, but in the interest of the 'volkliche' order. He distinguishes between the liberal 'minority right' of the Geneva League of Nations and a National Socialist 'right of ethnic groups' [Volksgruppenrecht];[18] to the latter he attributes a 'principle of mutual recognition of all ethnic groups [jeden Volkstums]' (SGN, p. 294). The 'protection rights of ethnic German groups of foreign nationality' alone demand an active conduct from Germany as a Reich. Schmitt does not discuss in detail which consequences for the 'ethnic groups' he has in mind. Huber, in his writings up until the summer of 1939, presents them in the form of the 'establishment of a pan-German people's Reich [Großdeutschen Volksreichs]',[19] and thus provides a nationalist justification for expansion before the outbreak of war. Schmitt hints at specific consequences for Jewry, which he considers an 'alien' [artfremde] ethnic group in Central and Eastern Europe (ibid.), and thus – in the more extreme terms of the 1941 version of the text (SGN, pp. 317f.) – he provides a justification for resettlements and deportations.

Schmitt's speech ends with remarks on the 'concept of the Reich in international law'. The concept of the Reich is presented as the 'new concept of order'. The fiction of the equality of sovereign states under international law has come to an end. International law should recognize the formation of superpowers as the basis of law and carry out a 'ranking of the subjects of international law', in which only Reich formations have the *ius belli*. However, to some extent Schmitt, it seems, reserves the hallowed title of 'Reich' for Germany, and he singles out the 'concept of a people' (SGN, p. 306) as a special 'political idea'. In a letter to his French friend Pierre Linn, he intimated: 'In my opinion, the fact that today Großräume form, and battles break out over them, is no worse and no more terrible than other effects of modern technology and other landslides in previous centuries. . . . La mer contre la terre. Until Christ appears again, the world will not be in order.'[20] In the following years Schmitt also gave his 'concept of the Reich' a theological-historical interpretation. However, of primary importance is that he developed 'new ideas which [went] beyond the pure interests of an advocate',[21] and that he pushed international law aside in order to reserve the 'Central and Eastern European' Großraum for National Socialist Germany, flanked by a 'prohibition of intervention for powers from other spaces'. Schmitt justified the Reich as a power upholding order within the context of a 'global civil war' [Weltbürgerkriegslage] following 1918, with its manifold crisis zones and aggressors. He did not define its right to expansion in strictly nationalist terms, and he also left the limits of the claim to expansion broad and vague. The extent of the anti-universalist approach remained equally vague. Had a Reich within its Großraum the right to posit 'international law' at will and to do whatever it

---

* The term as used by Schmitt is a neologism, which blurs the distinction between two possible meanings: a space *for which* something is done (e.g., the area for which a particular service is offered) and a space that does something for you (i.e., whose resources are being utilized).

likes? Soon afterwards, in another article, Schmitt analysed the American opposition to a Japanese Monroe Doctrine.[22]

In the context of Hitler's 'German Monroe Doctrine', Schmitt's speech caused widespread debate both in and outside Germany.[23] An Italian translation soon appeared.[24] Huber at once recognized the connection between the text and the Steding review and praised Schmitt's anticipation of future developments.[25] The speech had an impact even in the highest circles. Almost all German scholars of international law gave their opinion on the legal questions involved in the formation of a Reich. Major discussions of Schmitt's text were published by Erich Wolgast, Hermann Jahrreiß, Herbert Krüger, Reinhard Höhn and Hans Spanner.[26] Some National Socialist authors found fault with the missing 'biological' or racial foundation of the argument.[27] The SS jurist Werner Best demanded a 'völkisch' foundation rather than one 'in terms of international law'.[28] Schmitt reacted to these criticisms with an expansion of the text. Hans Grimm, author of *Volk ohne Raum* [A people without space], and a colonialist and expansionist, received a copy of the text with dedication in exchange for a volume with novellas.[29] Schmitt propagated his ideas in numerous lectures, both in Germany and abroad. Thus, on 4 May 1939 he spoke in Lychen and Rostock. At that point in time he probably did not go to the 'I. Großdeutschen Rechtswahrertag' [First Pan-German Convention of the Protectors of Right] in Leipzig, the smaller successor event to the Jurists' Convention. However, on 7 June he was at a meeting of the academy's section on international law. In July 1939, Duška travelled to Yugoslavia. In August, Schmitt spent a fortnight in Plettenberg. His diary shows several meetings with Popitz, Jessen and Ahlmann for a period after 1 September; the reason for these meetings, however, is not clear.[30]

To begin with, Schmitt used the legitimating title of 'Reich' only very cautiously. Only with the booklet of 1939 did he present his concept in print. His inaugural lecture in Cologne, 'Reich – Staat – Bund' [Reich – state – federation], had at that point not yet been published. Schmitt emphatically introduced the concept at the end of the speech: in the autumn of 1937, he says, he had been asked on the occasion of his critical report on the 'concept of war' what 'novel structure he could actually put in the place of the old order of states' (SGN, p. 306). 'Today, I can give the answer', Schmitt said on 1 April 1939. 'The deed of the Führer' has 'given the idea of our Reich [Gedanken unseres Reiches] political reality, historical truth and a great future in the context of international law' (ibid.). After the war had broken out, these words had to be understood as a justification of hostilities, a fact underlined by the republication of the text at the end of the collection *Positionen und Begriffe* [Positions and concepts], where Schmitt added his Virgil motto at the end: *Ab integro nascitur ordo*.

The other texts of *Positions and Concepts*, which appeared in December 1939, had also all been completed before the outbreak of war. Bernhard von Mutius on one occasion expressed his hope 'that the social and religious revolution will find its most conducive conditions behind the Chinese walls of the great empires [Großreiche], under the thin layer of imperial leadership and state religion, and in the pregnant soil of the broad and forlorn masses.'[31] Schmitt probably thought and spoke in similar terms. In 1941, he repeated his motto – *Ab integro nascitur ordo* – one last time. The association of a dawning new age with the hope for a new ruler of the world, here, it seems, legitimized National Socialism. However, Schmitt spoke of the Reich as a legal concept. The 'Reich', for him, was more than an entitlement to expansion. He also associated it with a level of order that 'leaves the elements of order contained in the concept of the state quite intact' (FP, p. 306). After the outbreak of war, Schmitt continued to give numerous lectures on the question of Großraum order, often under the title 'Europäische Ordnung und europäischer Friede' [European order and European peace].[32] But after 1941 he spoke about the 'Reich' in less affirmative terms, and referred rather more ambiguously to the 'nomos of the earth'. The expanded editions of the Großraum text already render the title of Reich problematic. At the end of July 1941 – a few weeks after the invasion of the Soviet Union – Schmitt gave the published text the status only of a 'document. It does not try to keep pace with the course of events' (SGN, p. 269). Its republication also signalled a farewell to the text.

25

The Captain Held Hostage?
Carl Schmitt's Farewell to the
'Reich'

A professor again

After his fall in the bureaucratic hierarchy, Schmitt turned once again to the university as his stage and slowly found his way back to the role of professor, which, in fact, he had never completely abandoned. There were a few changes in the faculty. In contrast to the confusion of the times, something like business as usual established itself, at least temporarily. However, student numbers dropped sharply. After the outbreak of war, the proportion of female students rose because the men were drafted into the army.[1] The universities received only marginal attention from the National Socialists and the solidarity among colleagues improved slightly. Schmitt's fall was no individual case. Within the totalitarian state no one was safe. Eckhardt also lost his position of power and moved to Bonn. Even in his dealings with Reinhard Höhn, Schmitt found a professional modus vivendi, though the ideological lines of demarcation remained visible.

Schmitt did not create a large pool of doctoral students. Nevertheless, he was extensively involved in examination processes, especially as he also had to examine the political economists in public law,[2] and from the end of 1933[3] he was again a member (with the exception of a three-month break after December 1936)[4] of Palandt's state examination board at the Supreme Court [Kammergericht],[5] which was sometimes also chaired by Freisler. Dozens of examiner's reports written by Schmitt relate to this second state examination. His doctoral students were often extreme National Socialists, some of whom made it into the 'chancellery of the Führer'.[6] Among those taking university courses there was a strikingly high number of foreign students.[7] This also had a thematic impact, in particular in the context of Schmitt's cooperation with Viktor Bruns: many of the students' works were on geopolitical topics or topics to do with foreign countries. Some of the foreign doctoral students were diplomats. One of them, Mladen Lorković, for instance, would later become the minister of the interior in the fascist Ustahe regime in Croatia.

Eckhardt's reforms of university degrees had reorganized the curriculum, putting it on 'völkische foundations'.[8] Race, ethnic groups and folk traditions [Volkstum] were obligatory topics. The standard courses were on constitutional and administrative law as well as international law.[9]

At the end of 1934, Schmitt had already declared that he would also be prepared to teach again at his old place, the Handelshochschule, and so he did, most likely for the first time and 'free of charge', in the winter term 1935–6, when he gave a lecture course on international law. From the winter term 1936–7 onwards, this became a permanent teaching contract.[10] Schmitt promoted the introduction of 'Verfassungsgeschichte der Neuzeit' [Constitutional history of the modern age] as a subject.[11] However, the only lecture course under that title he announced was for the summer term 1936. In the winter term 1936–7 and the summer terms 1938 and 1939 he lectured on 'Rechtsentwicklung der Neuzeit' [The development of right in the modern age], and thus put the focus on constitutional history as the history of right. After 1936 there was a clear preponderance of courses on international law. In the winter term 1939–40, Schmitt offered a 'Seminar über den deutschen Rechtswahrerstand' [Seminar on the German protectors of right], a seminar he would offer only once. In 1940 and 1941, the academic year was divided into three terms. In the first term of 1941, Schmitt taught a 'Seminar über den Strukturzusammenhang von Völkerrecht und Verfassungsrecht' [Seminar on the structural connection between international law and constitutional law].[12] After the war had started he announced further courses on 'Verfassung' [Constitution][13], and thus actively pursued the question of the constitution even after his farewell to the 'concept of the Reich'. In the end, he held his tutorials in private in his own apartment. It seems that at that time his charisma once again showed in his lectures and seminars. Even decades later, his students remembered them:

> I can still see you in front of me, as if I had left the large lecture hall in the Friedrich-Wilhelms-Universität only yesterday; you were always leaning forward towards the auditorium, standing to the left of the lectern. Your right arm was leaning on it, and friendly eyes looked through sharp spectacle lenses at the rest of the lecture hall, which attentively received what was presented to its ears in an explanatory conversational style: state, administrative and international law.[14]

During the time of National Socialism, nineteen Habilitation theses were successfully completed at the Berlin faculty, most of them on public law.[15] What is striking is that not one of Schmitt's assistants or collaborators was among the candidates. His own Habilitanden formed a rather eccentric group: Georg D. Daskalakis (*Das Gesetz als konkrete Seinsordnung und Planverwirklichung* [The law as a concrete order of being and realization of a plan], 1938),[16] Hans Franzen (*Ireland und Großbritannien seit 1919* [Ireland and Great Britain since 1919], 1939), Rudolf Suthoff-Groß (*Die Rechtsstellung des Bürgermeisters in seinem Verhältnis zum Staat und zu den übrigen Beamten der Gemeinde* [The legal position of the mayor in his relation to the state and to the other civil servants in the municipality], 1943), Serge Maiwald (*Die Staatsfreiheit des Seehandels als Kardinalprinzip des bisherigen Völkerrechts* [The independence of maritime trade from the state as the cardinal principle of international law to date], 1944).

Daskalakis came to Berlin, already a lawyer, in the winter term 1935–6. After his successful Habilitation he returned to Athens, became a soldier and in 1941 was appointed professor for politics and state theory at an academy for political science in Athens.[17] He later became an influential advisor. Schmitt's daughter, Anima, visited him in Greece in 1954. In 1950 and 1959, Schmitt and Daskalakis met again.[18]

Hans Franzen, Schmitt's second Habilitand in Berlin, was a member of the NSDAP from 1931, had worked on his doctoral thesis in Berlin since autumn 1933, and had visited two of Schmitt's seminars; but then, in 1935, he completed his doctorate in Bonn.[19] Franzen remembered the seminar thus: 'In truth, he [Schmitt] held discussions, which were marked by sovereign command of the material and brilliant elegance, with himself. In this way, the problem became transparent. The play with thoughts and the people who seemed to articulate them was breath-taking at times, often also uncanny.'[20] Franz passed his second state examination in 1937 and then received a scholarship to go to Dublin as an exchange student of the German Academic Exchange Service. From Dublin he sent a report to Schmitt. He initially wanted to obtain his PhD from Dublin. But Schmitt, in the summer of 1939, accepted the proofs of the German version as Franzen's Habilitation without any further ado. Franzen later recalled that his Habilitation 'fell into his lap as a result of a retroactive initiative of Carl Schmitt'.[21] Schmitt's examiner's report[22] shows his interest in the Irish battle for independence from England as a model for a 'legal revolution'. We may presume that Schmitt accepted this work as a Habilitation in part because of his memories of Kathleen Murray, his former Irish lover. Franzen took part in the war at both the Western and the Eastern fronts; he reported on his experiences in letters. After the war, Schmitt advised Franzen against an academic career,[23] and he became a very successful lawyer in Wiesbaden; they stayed loosely in touch.

The third Habilitand, Rudolf Suthoff-Groß, was the NSDAP mayor of the Wedding district of Berlin from March 1933. He should also not be called a real pupil of Schmitt.[24] In 1938 he published a commentary on the *Verfassung und Verwaltung der Reichshauptstadt Berlin* [Constitution and administration of the Reich capital Berlin]. His Habilitation on *The Legal Position of the Mayor* also deals with municipal law, which Schmitt had helped to reform in 1933. Schmitt published his examiner's report almost verbatim as a review.[25] The disputation took place on 24 July 1941. Suthoff-Groß did not receive a lectureship.

Of the four Habilitanden, Serge (Sergius) Maiwald was probably the pupil closest to Schmitt. He was born in Russia but had a German father. He also developed a close acquaintance with Duška. From 1935 he studied in Berlin, and in 1938 he passed his first state examination, after which he spent a year in Lausanne and Geneva. In September 1939, while a legal trainee, he asked for a topic from international law for his doctoral thesis, and in 1942 he submitted his dissertation on *Die völkerrechtliche Stellung der Staatshandelsschiffe* [The legal position of state trading merchant vessels in international law].[26] He later worked on his Habilitation in Paris.[27] Although he submitted it in 1943 and an academic colloquium about it took place on 29 November 1944, the process of his Habilitation did not reach a positive conclusion in time before the end of the war. In contrast to Schmitt, Maiwald considered 'the maritime world in essence to be a better guarantor of individual freedom' (FP, p. 873). After 1945, he made efforts in his journal *Universitas* to revive Schmitt's prospects as an author. He was the only one of all his pupils for whom Schmitt wrote an obituary.

At the Handelshochschule, Schmitt sponsored very few doctoral theses. His intermezzo in Cologne brought only Günther Krauss and Ernst Bockhoff to Berlin. Only after 1936 was Schmitt able properly to reap the fruits of his teaching.[28] He took care of his relationship with his pupils, many of whom he met again after 1945. He developed a particularly close friendship with the Serb Sava Kličković, who had been in Berlin since 1935.[29] He praised Kličković's dissertation on *Der Begriff der Enteignung* [The concept of expropriation] in glowing terms as an 'advance' and an 'overcoming of the so-called classical concept of expropriation', an overcoming which 'today no longer identifies the purpose [Sinn] of the legal operation of expropriation in a negative, defensive and individual-ist fashion as a removal of property, but in a positive fashion as serving the idea of spatial ordering [dem Raumordnungsgedanken]'. Although the work of a foreigner, Kličković's dissertation, Schmitt said, was 'informed by the German spirit to an exceptional degree'.[30] After the viva voce examination in February 1940, Schmitt organized a celebratory dinner [Doktoressen] for Kličković, who had defended his work against Karl Lohmann and Josef Kölble as his opponents. Kličković went on to work on a Habilitation, which, however, he would not be able to submit.

Before 1939, Krauss, Lohmann, von Schmoller, von Medem, von Mutius and Gutjahr were probably Schmitt's closest collaborators. In addition, there were his doctoral students and Habilitanden. But some visiting students and lecturers were also important. Schmitt frequently met with Gueyedan de Roussel and Julius Evola. Von Mutius and von Medem were drafted into the army soon after the outbreak of war. New names appear in Schmitt's appointment calendar, people who assisted him in various ways. Correspondence within the faculty was purely aca-demic; Schmitt expressed his praise and professorial approval and only hinted at critique. In addition to the award of the *venia legendi*, the right to teach at universities, the Reich regulations for a Habilitation at the time required the attendance at a 'Reich camp for civil servants' and a teach-ing examination. In the context of the latter, Hans Peter Ipsen[31] came to Berlin for his demonstration lecture. Schmitt's response to the Habilitation of Höhn's pupil Herbert Lemmel, who argued on the basis of the 'truth of race' [Rassewahrheit], was pointed: 'This is not the place for a counter-critique.'[32] Some Habilitation works Schmitt rejected. Others he approved as external examiner. His report on Hans Schneider's, in the context of his appointment to a chair in Tübingen, was very positive.[33] He also consid-ered Ernst Wilhelm Eschmann as worthy of an appointment to a chair.

For the summer term 1939, Walter Golombek and Werner Schulze-Thulin were assigned to Schmitt as his assistants.[34] In 1940 his old pupil from Bonn, Karl Lohmann, returned unexpectedly.[35] Lohmann had changing professional fortunes. Between 1933 and 1936 he worked as an academic advisor at the Kommunalwissenschaftliches Institut [Institute for Municipal Science] of the University of Berlin. He became the copyeditor [Schriftleiter] of the *Deutsche Juristen-Zeitung* and then of the *Zeitschrift der Akademie für Deutsches Recht*, and even later of the *Deutsche Rechtswissenschaft*. Lohmann was married with three children. After the outbreak of war, 'upon the urgent request of State Councillor Prof. Dr Carl Schmitt', he declared his 'willingness to take on the role of an assistant at the Rechts- und Staatswissenschaftlichen Fakultät [the Faculty of Jurisprudence and State Theory] of Berlin University in addition to his function as copyeditor'.[36] In 1941 he moved to Heidelberg, where he joined Schmitt's old companion Bilfinger and received his Habilitation with a work on *Die Auflösung des Aufopferungsanspruchs* [The abolition of the Aufopferungsanspruch]* in March 1943.[37]

Schmitt did not always have an assistant during those days. In 1943, however, Erland Weber-Schumburg[38] helped him in various ways. On 17 April 1943, Schmitt brought Günter Wasse, a friend of Maiwald, to the attention of the dean.[39] Wasse had joined the NSDAP in the autumn of 1938 and studied in Berlin from the winter term 1938–9. He had passed his first state examination, was a legal trainee at the court and gave 'university career' as his professional goal. For the summer term 1943 and the winter term 1943–4, he was assigned as an assistant to Schmitt.[40] However, his attempts at writing his doctorate dissipated in the confusions of wartime. After 1945 he continued his legal training in Göttingen and applied to Smend for a fellowship.[41] He completed his doctorate in Göttingen only in 1954.[42] In 1938, Johannes Winckelmann, later the editor of Weber's works, met Schmitt by coincidence in the Schlosscafé Unter den Linden[43] and enthusiastically picked up on his remarks on 'spatial revolution' as an 'obliteration of scientific concepts and the scientific way of thinking'.[44] A long and close friendship ensued; after 1945, Schmitt established the contact between Winckelmann and Joachim Ritter, which would become very important after 1945. As the editor of Max Weber's works, Winckelmann, in academic terms, probably became the most important of all of Schmitt's Berlin pupils.

The beginning of the Second World War also caused a change of attitude in Schmitt. He no longer supported the swastika unequivocally. Numerous students who attended his lectures mention political hints he made in that direction; Schmitt could never quite control his loose tongue and sparkling ideas. On one occasion, at the end of 1942, he summarized the situation in a letter: Golombek is still a legal trainee; von Mutius is in a field hospital in Cologne; Gutjahr is back at the front; Kölble has become a senior civil servant, 'Medem is still in Cracow'.[45] Schmitt would also supervise a student who was under political pressure, Ferdinand Friedensburg,

---

* *Aufopferungsanspruch*: a claim to financial compensation for the violation of rights, such as the right to life, health, physical integrity, freedom of movement, etc., by the state which leads to loss of property or assets.

who wrote on the topic of the 'theatre of war' and whose father had been removed from his post as head of a regional council [Regierungspräsident] in 1933.[46] Friedensburg moved to Freiburg, where Maunz took on his supervision. However, Friedensburg still wanted to have the 'honour' of doing his doctorate with Schmitt.[47] In return, he received a 'fantastically good political reference' from the NS students' association and was left to pursue his work in peace for two and a half years. In 1944 he sent his thesis to Schmitt. Some doctoral students weren't able to complete their work because they were drafted into the army.[48] At the beginning of 1944 there were already more women than men in the seminars.[49] Many doctoral students had incredible difficulties. In 1941, Werner Haseroth deplored the state of his project after he had been drafted. In 1942, however, he successfully completed the examination. Almost forty years later, in 1980, Haseroth wrote:

> My dear old academic teacher and doctoral supervisor! It was a moving moment for me to stand in front of you again on 6 November 1980 in your home! ... After the campaign in Poland you gave me 'Die treaty-making power und die Bedeutung der Ratifikation in der Sowjetunion' [The treaty-making power and the significance of ratification in the Soviet Union] as the topic for my doctoral thesis. I wrote it during the campaigns of 1939, 1940 and 1941, and passed my oral examination on 20 May 1942, with yourself, Kohlrausch and Gieseke being the examiners.[50]

In 1943, Haseroth was taken as a prisoner of war in Stalingrad and returned from captivity only in December 1955: 'In 1960, at the age of forty-six and after twenty-one years as a legal trainee, I passed my second state examination in Düsseldorf. Since then, I have been working as a historian/jurist for the Bundeswehr.'[51] Walter Golombek wrote in similar terms from the front and later assured Schmitt, as a former 'assistant' of his, that:

> Each one of us was too much caught up in the situation at the time; it was too much a question of naked survival for anyone to reflect and keep a distance from the immediate events. And, apart from that, all non-material values and criteria seemed to have become unsettled. But I realized one thing especially during those times: how much fundamental – in the first place – human and moral values emanated from your work in jurisprudence, also where it touched upon the level of politics.[52]

Such extreme conditions produce emotional attachments and solidarities beyond political differences and the space of academic work.

The situation of the 'protector of right' [Rechtswahrer] at the beginning of the war

On 23 August 1939, the Hitler–Stalin Pact was agreed. On 1 September, German troops marched into Poland. After this 'Blitzkrieg', the 'General

Government' was established, on 12 October 1939, and Hans Frank now resided as the general governor on the old Königsburg in Krakow. In April 1940, Germany attacked Denmark and Norway, and on 10 May the Western offensive began. Rotterdam was bombarded and the Dutch army capitulated. Eupen and Malmedy fell to the Reich. At the end of May, Belgium capitulated. Soon, the 'Axis power' Italy joined the war, and German troops marched into Paris without encountering any resistance. On 22 June the German–French armistice was signed in the forest of Compiègne. As an officer, Eberhard von Medem was involved in the war from the very beginning and kept Schmitt informed through his letters. He did not 'believe' in the 'battle against France', and yet he was involved in it. Along the way, he saw 'the large cemeteries, which are gracefully laid out'. He explained the military success with his observation that every single 'German soldier was mentally superior to the Frenchmen'.[53]

In contrast to 1914, the general mood in the population after the attack on Poland was not euphoric, but after the capitulation of France it was momentarily lifted by revanchist feelings. It seemed as if the revenge for Versailles had been the aim of the Führer, in his great wisdom, and the nationalistic meaning of the war. France seemed to accept its defeat. Parliamentary democracy had been eroded there as well, and the collaborating Vichy government – as an 'authoritarian' constitutional experiment – had some legitimacy in the remaining 'free' part of France.[54] However, the emerging 'world war' further required a battle against England. Italy attacked Greece, and Germany 'help[ed] out' in Northern Africa and in the Balkans. In Galicia, von Medem felt at the end of 1940 'that great decisions are in the air'.[55] On 22 June 1941, the Russian campaign began, which was again based on the strategy of the 'Blitzkrieg', but it ran into the ground in the Russian winter before reaching Moscow. At the beginning of December 1941, Japan attacked Pearl Harbor and the USA joined the war. Almost everyone now expected that Germany would be defeated. Hitler reacted by declaring war against the USA and intensifying anti-Semitic activities. On 20 January 1942, at the 'Wannsee Conference', and in the shadow of the war of annihilation, the 'final solution' was organized.

Schmitt continued to propagate his Großraum doctrine in numerous lectures. In spring 1940, for instance, he spoke in Bremen, Kiel and Rostock, in the summer in Halle, Naumburg and Cologne, in the autumn in Kiel and Berlin. In the summer, he had his physical examination and received a 'Wehrpass' [military ID card] which gave 'Landwehr'* as his degree of fitness for military service.[56] Schmitt concentrated during that time mainly on historical-scientific self-reflection. He had pushed forward the dismantling of constitutionalism with all the strength he could muster. He had moved from legality to 'ethical life' [Sittlichkeit] and put the 'corporative' [ständische] control of the 'protector of right' in the place of legal security guaranteed by the rule of law. 'Reform of the jurists' had

---

* The 'Landwehr' was formed in 1935 and comprised all men between the age of 35 and 45 that were fit for military service. However, they were used mainly at the 'home front' for guard duties, etc., or to supplement infantry divisions.

been the motto. His attempts at defining his position were associated with reflection on the past history of the discipline. Schmitt's conference on 'Die geschichtliche Lage der deutschen Rechtswissenschaft' [The historical situation of German jurisprudence], took aim against the constitutional 'triumph of jurisprudence over the lawgiver'. In 1936, he had still called the 'Allgemeine Deutsche Staatsrecht' [General German state law] a 'liberal "Rezeptionsrecht"'* of Western constitutionalism'.[57] With the outbreak of the world war, Schmitt now turned from 'German' to 'European' jurisprudence. He wrote four larger texts, in which he formulated his stock-taking of the historical situation.

In Schmitt's history of legal science, Lorenz von Stein marks the transition from a philosophical perspective to a science of the state [Staatswissenschaften]. The short text 'Die Stellung Lorenz von Steins in der Gesetzgebung des 19. Jahrhunderts' [The position of Lorenz von Stein within nineteenth-century legislature], which was also published, with minor changes,[58] as an afterword to an edition of von Stein's text on the 'Preußische Verfassungsfrage' [Question of the Prussian Constitution], asked the question of the 'preparedness for a constitution': 'Only once all of Germany has a constitution will it become possible to solve the problem of the Prussian Constitution' (SGN, p. 156). Schmitt reminded his reader of Stein's political biography and compared him to Bruno Bauer: Bauer saw the development towards Caesarism, in a 'parallel' (SGN, p. 158) to antiquity, as a chance for Christianity to expand. After 1848, Stein was disappointed and went to Vienna, where he was not able to continue with his theoretical endeavours. However, had he stayed in Berlin, he would have 'probably gone along with Bismarck's compromise with the national liberals in 1866, and thus the overall line of his development would not have differed from that of his generation in general' (SGN, p. 159). Bauer and Stein were two figures with whom Schmitt identified in his own work; due to historical parallels with 1848, they reflected his own path and existence. In 1919, Schmitt's analysis in *Political Romanticism* was at the same time an autobiographical confession (J. E. Kanne). In similar confessional fashion, Schmitt now aligned himself with Stein's attitude towards the constitutional question with his little booklet. Just like Donoso Cortés, Bruno Bauer, Thomas Hobbes and others, Lorenz von Stein was an autobiographical point of reference for Schmitt. Thus, the edition of 1940 was also a statement about his view on the contemporary constitutional situation.

Another scholarly article of programmatic importance was Schmitt's 'Das "allgemeine deutsche Staatsrecht" als Beispiel rechtswissenschaftlicher Systembildung' ['General German state law' as an example of system building in jurisprudence]. It was a companion piece to Huber's programmatic declaration 'Die deutsche Staatswissenschaft' [German science of the state] of 1935 and opened the 100th edition of the journal of the same title with a call for renewed efforts at carrying legal theory forward. Schmitt moved away from his rejection of 'received' laws and acknowledged the systematic contribution of jurisprudence to the creation of a 'German

---

* A law, or set of laws, taken over from another country or culture.

general law' [deutschen Gemeinrechts].[59] After the decline of the old Reich,* German jurisprudence had been faced with the task of assuming the national unity of right in its academic work. After 1848, this attempt faced the pressure of constitutionalism. A national liberal legal science transformed 'the political defeat of the liberal movement in 1848 and the victory of the conservative reaction into a triumph for constitutional law'† (SGN, p. 173). Schmitt now tried to reorganize the 'overall achievement of German jurisprudence', the creation of a 'German general law', from the perspective of 'concrete order formation' [konkreten Ordnungsdenken]. 'As soon as the concept of the Reich has been restored', he wrote, the 'concept of a German general law [must] be purified of all after-effects and residues of the development so far' (SGN, p. 180). The task was a new 'system formation' and 'formation' of 'spirit' [des Geistes]. The German 'protectors of right' have to prove their superiority in their 'war deployment'. Schmitt participated in the 'war effort' of German scholarship and gave many talks at the German cultural institutes in France, Hungary and Romania, in Spain and Portugal.

Even before the outbreak of war, Schmitt had presented a paper on the French legist in Leipzig. His high-spirited scholarly treatise on 'Die Formung des französischen Geistes durch den Legisten' [The formation of the French spirit by the legist] appeared in August 1942 in the journal *Deutschland–Frankreich*, published by the German Cultural Institute in Paris. It was a 'contribution to the theory of national characters on the basis of intellectual history' and, in the words of one of its readers, a eulogy on the 'legist' as a heroic type of the French national character.[60] Schmitt spoke of the 'shaping' and 'forming' of the French 'spirit' and 'national character' by 'juridical-legist education'. He particularly stressed the importance of the 'political legists' and concentrated especially on Jean Bodin. Schmitt praised the ethos of the jurist without any reservations. However, he also emphasized that the European order at present 'will be established through Germany and the Reich' (SGN, p. 210). For this, a strong philosophical and systematic orientation was necessary. In *Land and Sea*, Schmitt followed this history of the formation of the 'French spirit' with a genealogy of the English 'spirit'. He tried to understand the respective political styles of the two countries, but, in similar fashion to Eugen Rosenstock before him,[61] in the first place he produced a typological comparison of the history of the formation of two nations. Schmitt's professional self-reflection on the type of the jurist also found expression in a long birthday letter to Rudolf Smend. Schmitt now praised Smend in the most glowing terms for the fact that he represented being a 'professor as a form of life' and that 'intellectually' he had had a 'command of the overall situation', contrasting this to his own position as a 'lone wolf'.[62] *Land and Sea*, in 1942, then represented his literary distancing from National Socialism. In his correspondence with Ernst Jünger and Ernst Rudolf Huber, further revisions and a further distancing set in.

---

* The reference is to the Holy Roman Empire of German Nations.
† The original has the somewhat pleonastic 'des konstitutionellen Verfassungsrechts'.

The 'symbolism of the situation':
Schmitt's identification with the figure of Benito Cereno

To begin with, Schmitt's relationship with Jünger suffered after 1933 because of their differing attitudes to National Socialism. But after 1936 there was again a greater closeness on both sides. They shared an inclination towards metaphor and associations, towards literature, esotericism and elitism. Jünger's hints at the 'beds of Procrustes' (JS, p. 68) – i.e., censorship – Schmitt did not want to follow. He did not feel, he said, like a 'Hercules, who slays this Procrustes, but I do feel like a radiologist who accompanies this Procrustes without him noticing it' (JS, p. 70). When, in April 1939, Jünger moved to Kirchhorst, in the vicinity of Hannover, he came closer to Schmitt again, whose travel route from Berlin to Plettenberg and the Rhineland passed by Jünger's new home. Now the two families met more frequently again.[63] During wartime, Schmitt and Jünger appreciated each other as congenial observers and as analysts of events.

Schmitt's book on the Leviathan was an attempt at understanding the situation 'symbolically'. Jünger encouraged him to continue in that direction. On the *Leviathan* book, he remarked: 'You know that I have a preference for big fish. . . . I feel that you should on occasion write a work without the academic apparatus of footnotes, with a second naivety, so to speak, which, I think, would suit you well' (JS, pp. 77f.). With *Land and Sea*, which in many ways continued the Leviathan study, Schmitt would follow this advice. Jünger, in 1939, aimed at a 'secret look at our times' with his *On the Marble Cliffs*. He rejected the idea of a direct literary reflection on National Socialism. Poetry [Dichtung] should in his view not be allegorical, but symbolic. Jünger did not take '[him]self seriously in the realm of science' (JS, pp. 71f.) and rather sought to capture the events of the world war by literary means. In contrast to Schmitt, he served as an officer in the Second World War. 'I have seen a great deal in France, but haven't digested it all yet', he wrote. 'At times I felt like Scipio on the rubble of Carthage. How is one to start again when the war has ended?' (JS, p. 99).[64] With his *Gärten und Straßen* [Gardens and streets], Jünger distanced himself from the war by means of literature. Schmitt read the manuscript of the text and situated it between moralist reflection and painting (JS, p. 133). In the Great War, Jünger, the Stoßtruppführer [spearhead leader] had always been right at the front. Now he was lagging behind and appreciated the streets as providing access to the gardens.

Schmitt accompanied an invitation to visit him in January 1941 with a mild warning about the air raids: 'The fervent howling with which the Behemoth greets the big bird Zitz at night will not disturb you' (JS, p. 107). The first British attacks were, indeed, not very effective. On 9 April 1941 the state opera burned down. But the bombardments truly intensified only from the end of January 1943.[65] Schmitt corrected Hobbes's erroneous choice by calling the 'Reich' the Behemoth (cf. SGN, p. 417). On 25 January 1941 he spoke on the Großraumordnung at the Verwaltungsakademie [School of Administration] in Dortmund. At the beginning of February he had 'late-night conversations' with Jünger. On 8 February he spoke at the annual meeting of the historians in Nuremberg on 'Staatliche Souveränität und freies Meer' [State sovereignty and the free sea]. He turned down an invitation to Romania. At that time, Hermann Melville's novella *Benito Cereno* became, for him, the most important reflection of his situation within National Socialism. He wrote to Jünger: 'I am completely overwhelmed by the altogether involuntary, hidden symbolism of the situation in itself' (JS, p. 115). At the end of March, Schmitt spoke in Bremen. At the beginning of April he asked again: 'Have you read B. Cereno by now? Very important.' Melville's greatness, Schmitt said, lay in the 'capacity to create objective, elementary and concrete situations'. 'This makes Benito Cereno greater than the Russians and all other narrators of the nineteenth century, so that next to him even Poe seems anecdotal, and Moby Dick, as an epic of the sea, can only be compared to the Odyssey' (JS, p. 121).*

Jünger continued to be interested in Bosch and Poe, as impressively documented in letters from the Eastern front:

> It is a shame that Bosch cannot paint what I saw yesterday, from the tiny cabin of a cable car, in which I swayed suspended over a river, while beneath me in the valley, swarms of captivated bearers slowly moved along, wounded were disembarked, horses fell into the river and the lightning fire of heavy artillery tore through the air. An artillery soldier peered out from the destroyed pillar of a bridge in order to shout out the command to fire to those below, just like one of those characters you see in Breughel paintings look out of tents or egg-shells. At the same time, over the chaos [Tohuwabohu] in the valley basin you could hear 'Silent night, starry night' coming from the loudspeakers of a lorry belonging to a propaganda company. This kind of thing far exceeds the best inventions of the early utopians. (JS, pp. 152f.)

The description of a battle is no more than 'episodic narration';[66] it no longer presents an overall picture, provides no strategic insights and no political evaluation; it does not judge about friend and enemy, but rather, through its impressive subjectivity, points to the moral integrity and 'authenticity of the limited experience of an eyewitness'.[67] Jünger presented himself as a moral observer by clearing his perspective of any serviceable provision of meaning. Only art is able to capture the absurdity and contingency of events. It foregoes any great instigation of meaning and makes it aesthetically possible to keep one's distance. The turn towards art was far more than political esotericism and aestheticist justification. It was also an opposition to the meaning provided by the 'propaganda companies'.

What did Benito Cereno symbolize for Schmitt? The historical background to Melville's novella, set in 1799, was the issue of slavery in America.[68] A large sealer and general trader lies at anchor in the harbour of St Maria. On the second day, the captain, Amasa Delano, is told about another ship approaching the harbour, which is hardly able to navigate and

---

* Schmitt apparently uses the story's title as a *pars pro toto* for its author. I have retained this in the translation, despite the resulting incongruous comparisons.

is apparently in some distress. The captain boards the ship in order to help guide her into the harbour. It turns out to be a Spanish merchant vessel, and its load consists of black slaves. The crew is heavily decimated, starved and ill. The Spanish captain, Benito Cereno, appears peculiar, vague and disturbed. His authority, it seems, has suffered. A black servant by the name of Babo does not move from his side. Melville describes in detail how Captain Delano wavers between pity, rejection and suspicion in the face of the disintegration of authority and the lack of order on the ship. Soon he feels like a prisoner of the crew he had wanted to save. He fears that Cereno is double-crossing him, but again and again overcomes his doubts. Sudden violent moments occur. Cereno tells his story on a barber's chair under the razor of Babo. When the ship finally arrives at the harbour and is moored next to the sealer, there are some strange moments when Cereno and Delano are saying farewell. Suddenly, 'Don Benito' jumps across to the sealer. At first, Delano fears that this is an attack, before he understands that Benito Cereno and the Spanish crew had been hostages of the slaves. Delano arranges for the fleeing ship to be pursued and brings the mutineers, the slaves, before the 'vice-regal courts'. The wondrous rescue appears like an act of 'providence'. The ringleader Babo had forced Cereno to behave in such strange ways in order to get into the harbour. As punishment, he is 'dragged to the gibbet at the tail of a mule'. Benito Cereno dies three months after the end of the trial.

The novella shows an ambiguous sequence of events and explains it through the trial. The slaves are described in very negative terms. Their perspective, their right as slaves to mutiny, is nowhere mentioned. Schmitt drew a parallel between the slaves and the National Socialists, at the same time parodying the latter's racism – he will later refer again and again to Shakespeare's Caliban – and compared himself to the mildly mad, near-dead captive captain, who had let himself in for the journey and had become a victim of the mutiny. Schmitt is especially interested in the ambiguity in Benito Cereno's situation: seen from the external perspective of Delano, he appears as a weak commander, a madman, or a criminal and a con-man; from the internal perspective of the actual events, he is a hostage of the mutineers and is forced to play a role just in order to survive, running a high risk and also endangering the life of Delano and his crew in the process. 'The pirate is, according to an old interpretation, the ship as a whole' (ICWA p. 178), Schmitt wrote in 1945. 'Everyone who is found aboard the pirate ship is treated as a pirate if it is not obvious that he was there as a prisoner or as a victim of the pirates' (ICWA, p. 178f.). The normative questions raised by the novella can be pushed further: Is Benito Cereno really an innocent victim, given that he engaged in slave trade? Did he have the right to endanger the crew of the sealer in the way that he did? Such possible guilt was not what interested Schmitt. His Cereno was a poor, pitiable victim. Even when jumping onto the ship and into safety, he is hardly an actor. His partial guilt is touched upon only at the very end, when the watchword of the mutineers – 'Follow your leader' – is quoted to describe the captain's end: 'Benito Cereno, borne on the bier, did, indeed, follow his leader.' In this respect, Ernst Jünger gave Schmitt's comparison a different slant: rather than 'Don Benito', he liked to call him 'Don Capisco', without entirely agreeing with him politically.

'As long as the wine cellar is not empty': life during the war

Schmitt had already complained about supply shortages at the beginning of the war. 'Otherwise, life in black-out Berlin is not uncomfortable, as long as the wine cellar is not empty; a lot of superfluous sociability has ended' (GJCS, p. 33). In Dahlem, the Schmitts had a maid and a cook. Anni Stand joined the household, stayed on after the end of the war, and continued to be in charge of it from the early 1950s onwards. By then, 1939, Schmitt had felt disappointed with National Socialism for some time. From November 1939 the painter Werner Gilles lived in their house for a couple of months. The closest conversations Schmitt had during this period were those with Ernst Jünger. Maria Hasbach, an acquaintance from Bonn, also stayed as a 'refugee' with the Schmitts for a while.[69] His pupils were, among others, Walter Golombek, Moritz von Bethmann, Johannes Winckelmann and Egon Vietta. In the summer of 1941, Gilles was again 'lodging' with the Schmitts for two months.[70] Schmitt repeatedly went to the quieter Plettenberg for some relaxation. 'My longing for the Sauerland / suddenly gets out of hand', he rhymed jocularly (GJCS, p. 50).

The friendship with the Jüngers had reached its high point when Gretha Jünger, at short notice, arranged an invitation to the German Institute in Paris, directed by Karl Epting.[71] Schmitt set off on 15 October, giving a talk on 'La mer contre la terre' [The sea against the land] the following day. He met with Pierre Linn, Gueydan de Roussel and Colonel Hans Speidel, and he went on an excursion to Port Royal, Rambouillet and Chartres

'Upon the ascent of illegitimate powers, the position of the crown jurist becomes vacuous, and the attempt at filling it is made at the expense of one's good reputation. That's just how the misfortunes of the profession would have it' – Ernst Jünger in his *Strahlungen* (diaries), 14 December 1943

with Jünger and Captain Grüninger.[72] He encountered Drieu la Rochelle, Friedrich Sieburg and the poet Montherlant, and met again with Speidel. On 23 October he returned via Strasbourg, where he met with Huber (who had just moved there) and his old cousin André Steinlein, who worked as a notary in Vic-sur-Seille in Lorraine. Paris felt like a 'fairy-tale island' to Schmitt; he compared his situation to that of Benito Cereno.[73] He thanked Jünger poste-haste and then began to prepare his next talk in Leipzig, where he spoke on Tocqueville's 'great prognosis' on 5 December.[74] Shortly before Christmas 1941, he met Jünger for two days in Kirchhorst.[75] In the following years, he again and again had the opportunity to give presentations in friendly or occupied neighbouring countries, as a travelling cadre of the party, so to speak. Thus, he went to France, Hungary, Romania, Spain and Portugal. Schmitt had to submit meticulous reports on his journeys; thus we are well informed about his itineraries and about the people he met.[76]

In mid-January 1942 he once again attended a concert of the philharmonic orchestra. At the end of February, Gretha Jünger came for a visit. At the beginning of March 1942, Schmitt travelled to Plettenberg. In Cologne he visited his brother Jupp as well as his pupil Herbert Gremmels in the field hospital. On 19 March, Schmitt spoke in Bremen. Back in Berlin he complained about the 'desertedness' of the city and the 'art of forming psychological masks' (GJCS, p. 57) – i.e., the adaptation to political threats. Duška was planning a journey to Croatia in order to free her Serbian brother from imprisonment there. After the invasion of German troops, a brutal civil war between Croatia and Serbia had broken out in 1941. Members of the Ustashe had massacred many Serbs. Schmitt was reluctant to let Duška travel to this 'robbers' den'. In mid-April she set off and in mid-May she returned, having successfully carried out her mission, probably with the help of Schmitt's former pupil Lorković, a politician of the Ustashe.[77] On 30 April, Schmitt took the night train to Budapest, where, upon an invitation by Hans Freyer, he gave talks about 'Verwaltung und Verwaltungsrecht' [Administration and administrative law] and 'Völkerrechtliche Großraumordnung' [Großraum order in international law] at the Deutsches Wissenschaftliches Institut [German Academic Institute].[78] According to the reports on these talks, Schmitt's aim was to fight the 'legal nihilism which informs the development of administration today'. Schmitt returned on 8 May.[79] As Berlin was by now permanently threatened by air raids, at the beginning of June Duška brought Anima to Cloppenburg, where she lived, together with her cousin Claire-Louise, with a family by the name of Weßling. Anima also went to school there and saw her parents only occasionally until Easter 1948. Even during holidays she rarely came to Berlin; the family met more often, though, in Plettenberg. On 9 July, Schmitt travelled to Königsberg for a talk. At the end of July the Schmitts went to Plettenberg, and in mid-August they went to visit Anima in Cloppenburg. By mid-August they were back in Berlin, and on 25 August Schmitt spoke on the topic of 'Der gegenwärtige Krieg und das Völkerrecht' [The present war and international law] within the festive surroundings of the Brandenburg town hall.[80] On 27 October he travelled to Hamburg and celebrated Wilhelm Stapel's sixtieth birthday with him in the Hotel Atlantic.[81] He also spoke with Hans Schomerus about the 'katechon' on that occasion.[82] On 30 October, Schmitt travelled again to France, where – 'with perfect culinary support' – he gave talks at the German Institute in Paris as part of the support for the troops [Wehrmachtsbetreuung]. On 3 November he visited Napoleon's grave in the Invalides,[83] and the following day he travelled to Lilles and Brussels for further talks. Altogether, he gave four talks on 'Neues Staatsrecht' [New state law].[84] Ernst Jünger was no longer residing on the 'fairy-tale island' at that point, but visited the Schmitts on a stopover in Dahlem with Gretha in mid-November.[85] Schmitt sent *Land and Sea* to him at the Eastern front. The book, he said, showed that the 'history of mankind is, in accordance with the teachings of antiquity, a journey through the four elements. We are now in fire. . . . From the ashes, Phoenix, the bird, will rise – i.e., an empire [Reich] of the air' (JS, p. 151). Schmitt thus shifted all hope towards a future time. He now took more notice of Jünger's references to Bosch. In Berlin, he was in conversation about the painter with the art historian Wilhelm Fraenger.[86] Fraenger interpreted Bosch's vision of the 'thousand-year Reich' within the tradition of the Joachimite annunciation as an 'anthropogeny'.[87] A new vision of man corresponds to the visions of hell.

At the end of January 1943 the Jüngers were in Berlin. At the beginning of February their eighteen-year old daughter, Veronica Schranz, came to visit. As she remembered later:

> It was a magnificent event. C. S. had put together a proper programme for me. Apart from the visits to museums and galleries, where he accompanied me in the mornings before pursuing his own activities, because I was not used to travelling on the underground and tramway, I was one evening[88] allowed to sit in Hermann Göring's box at the opera and listen to 'Fidelio' and the next evening to watch 'The Taming of the Shrew'. A concert with Wilhelm Furtwängler and the Philharmonic Orchestra was also part of the planned activities. I spent two evenings in the presence of very noble company in his apartment in Dahlem. Among others, there were the Prussian Minister of Finance Johannes Popitz and his son Heinrich and daughter Conny, Dr Wilhelm Ahlmann, who impressed me very much because of his blindness, which I almost did not notice, and the couple Privy Councillor Werner Sombart and his wife Corina. C. S. accompanied a singer on the grand piano; I unfortunately have forgotten her name.[89]

Schmitt socialized with many artists at the time, such as, for instance, Werner Gilles, Werner Heldt and Ernst Wilhelm Nay,[90] the harpsichordist Eta Harich-Schneider,[91] and also the writer Ivo Andrić.

On 13 February, Schmitt travelled to Romania and gave talks in Jassy and Bucharest on 'Der Einfluss des Juristen auf die Formung des europäischen Geistes' [The influence of the jurists on the formation of the European spirit] and on the relationship between land and sea. The high point was a conversation with the deputy prime minister and minister of justice, Mihai Antonescu,[92] whose legislature applied the National Socialist theory of race to the 'Slavonic people'. All in all, Schmitt was rather critical of the situation in Romania. The French exerted great influence, but he stood at the 'gateway' in order to 'break through the power of this French tradition for the first time'.[93]

At the beginning of March, Schmitt celebrated his father's ninetieth birthday with him in Plettenberg. Soon afterwards, on 27 March 1943, his mother died of pneumonia. In mid-May, Schmitt gave a talk on international law to officers.[94] Gottfried Benn sat for an 'extremely fascinating hour' in one of Schmitt's lectures.[95] Between 28 May and 11 June, Schmitt travelled in Spain, giving talks on structural changes in international law in Madrid[96] and Salamanca; he was also shown paintings by Hieronymus Bosch at the Prado. By mid-June he had returned from his 'full and rich, but also very exhausting journey',[97] 'which had been almost paradisiac' (GJCS, p. 78). Schmitt emphasized that he had 'broken through the circle of free-masonic pacifism' in his talk on Francesco de Vitoria.[98] Back in Berlin, he wrote to Gretha Jünger: 'In our home, one day follows the other, with a feeling of a last respite. Frau Schmitt invests a lot of effort in her poor protégés [Serbian forced labourers]. Anima will soon have holidays and does not know where to go. The news from the West, Cologne and Westphalia, is awful' (GJCS, pp. 78ff.). Schmitt now anticipated an imminent defeat. 'At the moment, I am sitting here alone at home, with our fearful cook Anne. All of Berlin is fleeing. Tens of thousands of flats are simply left empty, the slogan "first be victorious, then travel" seems to have been turned upside-down. I cannot bring myself to flee as well, and enjoy the loneliness at my desk' (GJCS, p. 80).

On 23 August the Schmitts were bombed out of Kaiserswerthstraße 17 by an aerial mine. They just managed to escape through the laundry room. The house was destroyed; paintings, books and manuscripts, however, mostly survived. The Schmitts went to Plettenberg straightaway and stayed there for a few months. Carl applied for leave in the winter term; however, the request was turned down by the faculty.[99] Erland Weber-Schumburg stored 250 valuable books safely in a dry cellar[100] and sent a full report on his operation. He rescued books, manuscripts and documents. 'I took the Latin copy of Leviathan with me. Grotius, I had already brought to Amselstrasse on an earlier occasion.' A volume of poetry by Konrad Weiß he could not find.[101] Johannes Popitz helped Schmitt, even in practical tasks such as the restoration of a valuable book, and offered accommodation in his own house.[102] Schmitt went back to Berlin for a couple of days at the end of September in order to take care of a few matters, staying temporarily with Popitz. Colonel-General Oskar von Niedermeyer, a friend of Schmitt, reported from the front that the enemy had 'underestimated our power of resistance': 'Otherwise, however, the air war and partisan warfare are exceptionally effective military means employed by the opponent, whom we have underrated for so long.'[103] Captain Hans Schneider also reported from the front that he was 'leading a beautiful and (first and foremost!) complete and well-armed unit'.[104] Schmitt's doctoral student Günther Schwarz wrote that the war would probably 'end soon'. One was living 'like a wild animal. It is terrible.'[105] Schwarz finished his doctorate, and he survived the war. Schmitt replied to him from Plettenberg:

'My ministry is one of the few that are still there. The opera and theatre are still there. Many other *signa Borussiae* [Prussian landmarks] are missing' – Johannes Popitz in a letter to Schmitt, 4 December 1943

> From the end of August I have been living without a fixed abode as one of those who have been 'bombed out'. . . . The situation of the totally bombed-out civilian is very interesting and possibly more important for the problem of total war than the situation of the soldier who has lost his weapons. Because the soldier is at once carried along by a powerful organization and receives new weapons; the civilian receives a ration coupon. (FP, p. 590)

At the beginning of November, Duška returned to Berlin and rented a villa in Schlachtensee (Schönerzeile 19) from 1 December. She fell ill due to her exertions. Schmitt was granted additional living space for his library.[106] He compared his 'life of a vagabond' to the 'life of a refugee' (JS, p. 17).

From 5 to 13 November, Schmitt was again in Budapest. Having been invited by Freyer,[107] he spoke at the German Institute about the transformations on the concept of war in international law, and then at the university about 'Die heutige Lage der europäischen Rechtswissenschaft' [The situation of European jurisprudence today].[108] Weber-Schumburg, who had just saved Schmitt's belongings, wrote laconically about the complete loss of his flat in Wilhelmstraße:

> My situation is very uncomfortable now, as I have lost all my clothes and do not even have a spare shirt. But that can be overcome as well. What is worse is that the Kaiserhof, with its whole stock of wine, has been destroyed. How nice it would have been, at least, to be able to seek comfort over a good bottle

of wine. – The fire at Pompei cannot have been more effective than the two attacks on 22 and 23 November. . . . Consider yourself lucky that you are in safety in Westphalia.[109]

The Wirtschafts-Hochschule was also badly hit and had to cancel all courses. At the end of November, Schmitt once again found safety and 'distraction'[110] in the form of a journey. He flew to Barcelona and spoke about Donoso Cortés. Around that time, Popitz dropped hints about his political worries: 'I do not want to go into further details about the situation in Berlin. My ministry is one of the few that are still there. The opera and theatre are still there. Many other *signa Borussiae* [Prussian landmarks] are missing . . . What will things look like next year?'[111] Cousin André, who was a notary in Lorraine, sent a 'rabbit by express mail'.[112] Duška took care of the move. In January 1944, Schmitt gave a talk at Berlin University[113] that would lead to his last wartime publication: 'Die letzte globale Linie' [The last global line].

Ernst Jünger came to Berlin because one of his sons had been arrested and imprisoned for making critical remarks about the regime. Only in mid-September was Ernstl released on probation at the front; he fell in Italy at the end of November. Schmitt compared his situation in Berlin at the time 'with that of the Anabaptists during the siege'.[114] Due to his widespread contacts he received a lot of information about the war events. His pupils also kept him up to date. Because the mail was censored, these reports read almost comically at times. Herbert Gremmels wrote from the Eastern front:

As regards the general situation, we soldiers in the East wait calmly for the things to come. We are – I saw that once again – infinitely superior to the Russians. The closer we can move the front to the General Government, the more advantageous the general strategic situation gets, in particular with respect to the invasion from the West that is to be expected. . . . The Russians have ground to a halt in the East; the English and Americans are busy in Italy as well as with their air war.[115]

Schmitt was of a different opinion. He had for quite some time been expecting an imminent defeat. On 17 March he repeated his talk on 'The Last Global Line' one more time at the Rechts- und Staatswissenschaftliche Vereinigung [Association for Jurisprudence and State Science] in Bremen.[116] At the end of March he was meant to speak about 'Land and Sea' in Hamburg upon an invitation from Rear Admiral Claussen. And his talk on 'The Situation of European Jurisprudence' was also planned to be given in Paris, for which the German Institute provided him with a French translation. Ernst Jünger sent 'cordial greetings'.[117] In April 1944, Schmitt was in Prague.[118] Sava Kličković came for a visit from Vienna. As a Serb, he had political problems; Duška tried to help him.[119] Between 4 May and 9 June 1944, Schmitt again travelled in Spain and Portugal. The travel dates, controversially, fell into term time. He gave talks about the situation of jurisprudence, on Francisco de Vitoria, on Donoso Cortés and on 'Land and Sea' in Madrid, Coimbra, Lisbon, Granada and Barcelona.

'I feel that this offer of a chair in Berlin is the highest honour that I can receive in my profession' – Carl Schmitt, 4 September 1933

In Lisbon he made the acquaintance of José Ortega y Gasset and of the Romanian theologian Mircea Eliade. In his report, however, he particularly emphasized his meeting in Granada with Álvaro d'Ors, with whom he later formed a close friendship. The travel report highlighted the 'many possibilities' for cooperation: 'Here, the German spirit still has a wide, entirely open field in front of it, in which it can have the strongest effects.'[120] In contrast to his colleagues and friends Popitz and Jessen, Schmitt was not involved at the time in the plans for resistance in connection with 20 July. It is possible that he did not appear trustworthy or important enough. After the failed assassination and attempt at a putsch, 'Operation Valkyrie', Wilhelm Ahlmann committed suicide in order to avoid arrest. Popitz and Jessen were executed. 'There may be times when madness rules. / In those it is the best heads that roll.'[121] But we have no evidence for the way in which Schmitt perceived the events of 20 July at the time. Later, Schmitt dedicated his 'Verfassungsrechtliche Aufsätze' [Essays on constitutional law] to Popitz, but he never claimed any political closeness to the resistance.

Between 26 September and 27 October, Schmitt gave additional lectures on the topic of 'Constitution' for a 'holiday course for participants in the war'.[122] On 1 December he was with Werner Weber in Leipzig for a talk on the situation of jurisprudence. At the end of 1944, Erna, the maid, was still in the house. Schmitt pursued the 'eviction' of a lodger, Frau Hädicke.[123] Schmitt's Saint's Day was celebrated with a goose and four bottles of wine. Weber came from Leipzig for the occasion. There were still some rabbits held in reserve. Schmitt, then, had to attend a military exercise of the

Volkssturm. On 21 December, Anima arrived from Cloppenburg. On New Year's Day, Schmitt wrote to Karl Lohmann: 'In the terrible year 1944, I have lost so many close friends, making the remaining ones invaluable. It began with the loss of Gutjahr in March 1944, and it ended with the sad death of poor Dr Ahlmann in Kiel.'[124] On 11 January, Schmitt gave a lecture in Hamburg.[125] Duška brought Anima back to Cloppenburg, returning to Berlin on 27 January. Carl reported to the Volkssturm on 28 January, but was released again as soon as 8 February.[126] His friend the physician Siebeck then wrote him a medical note for his chronic sciatic pains.[127] At that point, the Schmitts decided to stay in Berlin. Anni Stand, the maid, however, still considered a journey to Cloppenburg.

In mid-February, Schmitt wrote a six-page typewritten examiner's report for Ernst Riekmann, who had written his doctorate with Höhn on 'Der Ausnahmezustand und seine geistigen Grundlagen' [The state of exception and its spiritual foundations]. Schmitt was obviously very interested in the topic. He had numerous reservations, criticized the fact that it only examined the period up to 1914, and would have expected a deeper discussion of the 'spiritual foundations' with regard to his *Political Theology*. Schmitt hinted at the fact that the 'collapse of the system of legitimacy of the bourgeois Rechtsstaat' after 1914

> had created a new kind of exceptional lawgiver with the help of the state of exception. Right up to the present day, there are still important legally binding decrees which were passed on the basis of Art. 48. Even in the area of police law this connection still exists. One look at the most recent account of today's police law by Th. Maunz (Gestalt und Recht der Polizei [Form and right of the police], p. 23), published in 1943, suffices to show how this kind of positivist significance of Art. 48 still haunts us today.[128]

The report points towards sovereign acts 'beyond the judiciary' ['justizfreie' Hoheitsakte], and demonstrates the interest in National Socialist jurisprudence in dissolving the legal form. That aside, the pretence of normal academic work at the end of February 1945 is surprising. Duška told Anima about heavy bombardments, as a consequence of which Marlies Hasbach and Blischkes were now permanent lodgers.[129] They would stay on beyond the end of the war. In mid-March, Schmitt congratulated Ernst Jünger on his fiftieth birthday and mentioned, as a truth which they both recognized, 'that a man knows no more about his next day than he knows about life after death' (JS, p. 191).

A look back at constitutional history: 'the questionability of total nationalization'

Schmitt reflected on the catastrophe of National Socialism from the perspective of constitutional history, in particular in his correspondence with Ernst Rudolf Huber. After the completion of his textbook *Constitution*, Huber increasingly set himself the task of a nationalistic revision of constitutional history.[130] For two years, the conversation between the two had ceased altogether. Then, on 11 March 1938, Schmitt wrote to Huber on the occasion of the birth of the latter's third son. When Huber replied, Schmitt addressed their conflicts and expressed his hope that Huber would 'be spared the worst' of what he had to endure in terms of internal attacks.[131] In response, Huber wrote a long, reconciliatory letter for Schmitt's fiftieth birthday on 11 July, in which he praised Schmitt's life's work in high terms and added a 'personal word': 'Due to a chain of misunderstandings and uncontrollable, indirect communications, the clear and unambiguous relationship which existed between you and me has been disturbed in the last years.' His congratulations should not be 'tinged' by this. Huber enclosed *Heer und Staat* [Army and state], perhaps his best book, as a 'humble present'.[132] Schmitt thanked him extensively and emotionally, spoke of 'friendship', and wanted to renew their 'conversation'. In December, a meeting between the two took place in Berlin, after which their contact continued seemingly undisturbed until the end of the war. From 1937, Huber was in Leipzig, and he invited Schmitt for a talk on 'Die Gestalt des französischen Juristen' [The type of the French jurist], from which the important treatise on the 'Legisten' [Legists] emerged.[133] Schmitt sent Huber 'Völkerrechtliche Großraumordnung' [Großraum order in international law] and the review article on 'Neutralität und Neutralisierungen' [Neutrality and neutralizations]. Huber understood at once the 'deep and characteristic inner connection'[134] of the two texts with regard to the 'concept of the Reich', and he emphasized how much he was reminded 'of the function of [Schmitt's] earlier writings by these works from the past two years. You determine the inner situation of the time at a moment when the true structure is still covered by rubble and residues'.[135] Huber took Schmitt seriously again as a scholar and began a new discussion with him, which is reflected in important letters during the following months. Huber asked the 'question of the constitution' with regard to the 'path from the people to the Reich' and thought that the 'inner constitution' and the 'outer' were inseparable. The National Socialist revolution could not be brought to completion before the revision of Versailles has led to the 'creation of the pan-German people's Reich' [Errichtung des Großdeutschen Volksreichs]. Huber described this process in the introductory preamble[136] on constitutional history that opened the reprint of his *Constitution*, up to the point of 'the affiliation' of the Sudentenland, the 'integration' of Moravia and the 'reunification' of the Memel area with the Reich. He called the people 'home into the Reich' [Heim ins Reich].

On 2 June 1939, Schmitt gave his talk on the 'Legists' in Leipzig. Next, he published his programmatic article on 'Das Allgemeine Deutsche Staatsrecht' [General German state law] in Huber's journal. At the end of 1939 his *Positionen und Begriffe* [Positions and concepts] appeared, in a print run of 1,500 copies. Huber praised the collection emphatically and appreciated the ethos of academic struggle.

> By committing yourself to positions and concepts, you have shown yourself to be prepared for battle – and you have, and it couldn't be otherwise, pro-

'Of all your pupils, he really is the pick of the litter' – Carl Bilfinger about Ernst
Rudolf Huber in a letter to Schmitt, 15 December 1932

voked opposition and enmity. It always appeared to me as a questionable
decay of scholarly standards [Wissenschaftlichkeit] that you used to have
more open opponents and fewer secret enemies compared to later times. But
maybe it was just the glory of your many victories, which more and more
prevented your enemies from taking up their positions openly.[137]

Schmitt and Huber now entered into intense discussions about constitutional history in the Reich of Bismarck. Huber invited Schmitt for a talk
again in July 1940.[138] For an edited volume on *Idee und Ordnung des Reichs*
[Idea and order of the Reich], which was published in 1941 as part of
the 'Ritterbusch campaign', he requested a contribution on fundamental
questions from Schmitt. Schmitt hesitated; with his article on 'Reich und
Großraum', he felt he had already 'leaned himself out of the window' quite
far.[139] He feared renewed attacks. Soon, Huber sent the manuscript of his
long review article on *Positions and Concepts*, to which Schmitt reacted
with praise.[140]

Huber worked out the negative polemical structure of the work, correcting Schmitt's views of Hobbes and Hegel at certain points. As a
matter of course, he stressed that the work argued 'against liberalism
and democracy' and 'against neutralization and pacifism'; he contradicted only Schmitt's assumption of an 'identity of constitutionalism
and parliamentarism'.[141] Huber agreed with the critique of parliamentarism but defended Prussian constitutionalism, as he had done in *Heer
und Staat* [Army and state]. He juxtaposed the 'new theoretical edifice
of international law' to Schmitt's dismantling of state theory. In addition to *Positions and Concepts*, Huber referred to more recent treatises

by Schmitt. It is all the more striking that he did not mention Schmitt's earlier attempts at a juridico-institutional provision of meaning, and thus did not credit them with making any positive contribution to the creation of the state. He did, however, acknowledge that Schmitt had identified modern 'hegemonial imperialism' as a political fact, and that he had achieved the 'conception of a new international law', in which only the great powers [Großmächte] were given the *ius belli* and which raised 'the decisive question' of what elevates power into being right, what effects the 'dialectical transformation of the distribution of power into the legal status quo'.[142] Huber remarked that there had to be a principle of justice. 'It is not the possession of power, but the rule of power [das Walten der Macht] that decides': 'The just rule of power will provide the distinguishing criterion for the opposition between the old imperialism and a genuine Großraum order based on international law.'[143] A 'system of direct and open rule' had a lot going for it, he said. In mid-1940, Huber probably did not write this without it causing him some headache. Even his account of the 'creation of the pan-German people's Reich' was not covered by these formulations. In letters from that time, he criticized the misuse of the expression 'concrete order formation' [konkretes Ordnungsdenken].[144] His edited volume slipped into the Procrustean bed of the 'Ritterbusch campaign'.[145] 'I assume', Huber wrote, 'that the whole conference is still at a very vague stage of planning and that the original programme will be subject to major changes.' Schmitt pointed out that he already had contributed two articles to the war efforts of Ritterbusch[146] but considered a retrospective look at the Preußenschlag. Huber pushed Schmitt for at least some kind of contribution to the edited volume. 'Without you in it, it would not have succeeded.'[147]

Immediately after the victory over France, the decision was taken to reopen Strasbourg University. In May 1941, Huber was appointed to a chair there. Around the same time he enthusiastically welcomed Schmitt's beautiful edition of Lorenz Stein's *Zur Preußischen Verfassungsfrage* [On the question of the Prussian Constitution].[148] In Strasbourg he could vividly experience the constitutional history of the old Reich. Huber worked on a history of the German idea of the state, which would have been a companion piece, in intellectual history, to *Army and State*; however, it remained unpublished, though some preparatory texts appeared before the end of the war. Schmitt announced his visit to Strasbourg, on the way back from Paris, for the end of October.[149] Afterwards he thanked Huber for the stay, during which he also had met with Cousin Steinlein. In the end he did not contribute to the Ritterbusch volume, and Huber completed the project in September 1941.[150] At the end of November, Strasbourg University was reopened. Apart from Huber, Ulrich Scheuner and Herbert Krüger were meant to teach public law, but they were drafted into the army at that time. At the end of 1941 the edited volume appeared as the 'common work of German state theorists' under the title *Idee und Ordnung des Reiches* [Idea and order of the Reich]. Huber's opening article, on 'Bau und Gefüge des Reiches' [Edifice and structure of the Reich], again mentioned the difference between power and right. If the Reich openly pursued an imperialist policy of leadership, he said, the Großraum would be turned into a legal concept. Huber forcefully demonstrated the discriminating consequences for civil rights in the Reich [im Reichsbürgergesetz]. He very openly discussed the 'authority of the Reich' [Reichsgewalt] in times of war.[151]

At that point in time, Huber was convinced that all dreams of a constitution had come to an end. 'The last years have demonstrated to us in all clarity the questionability of total nationalization [Verstaatlichung] of the Volkstum, which is only very provisionally covered up with the help of völkisch ideologies', he wrote. '[A]t the same time, though, [they demonstrated] the inevitability of this historical process.'[152] Huber now went back beyond the nineteenth century to the older 'consciousness of a people' [Volksbewusstsein] and the old Prussian 'state patriotism',[153] to a time before the population was mobilized by the state for nationalistic purposes. He hinted briefly at his reservations: 'Now we have ended up deep in the development of a "feudal dukedom" [Stammesherzogtum] and a "feudal kingdom" [Stammeskönigtum]. Are we meant to lose the state as the base of German unity again on the way towards the Reich and Großraum?'[154] With these words, Huber criticized the polycratic tendencies in National Socialism. But he was still far from a general reckoning, although he was full of critical reservations. What he still did not question was the national right to self-determination, which he believed, after Versailles, could not be accomplished without corrections in the direction of a 'pan-Germany' and the formation of a new major power [Großmachtbildung]. But Huber carried out a historical revision of the fundamental categories. He went beyond the Romantic formation of the 'nation'[155] and the opposition between 'power state' and 'cultural nation' [Machtstaat und Kulturnation] to the eighteenth century, because the problems in Germany's development towards becoming a national state originated in the 'nationalistically' connoted and polemically laden concept of a nation as it emerged in the wars of liberation against Napoleon. The return to the older 'consciousness of a people', as experienced by Herder and Goethe in the border region of Strasbourg, Huber thought, might provide an alternative foundation. Huber presented a programmatic sketch of this general revision in his essay 'Reich, Volk und Staat in der Reichsrechtswissenschaft des 17. und 18. Jahrhunderts' [Reich, people and the state in Reich jurisprudence of the 17th and 18th centuries],[156] in which Leibniz provided the point of departure for a 'Reich mentality' [Reichsgesinnung].

Schmitt's substantial response[157] to this essay took its cue from 20 July 1932 and referred the origins of the problem to before 1848. Huber and Schmitt agreed on the obvious fact that their attempts at constitutional policies under National Socialism had failed. However, while Schmitt looked for the causes of that failure in the nation-state agenda of the period before 1848, Huber, in his search for a solution, went even further back in time to more ancient roots. Schmitt now openly distanced himself from Hans Frank and from the 'sacrificium intellectus' in National Socialism. In the context of the constitutional crises of the old Reich, he pointed Huber to Franz Grillparzer's tragic drama *Ein Bruderzwist im*

Hause Habsburg [A fraternal strife in the Habsburg dynasty].[158] The play, completed in 1848, deals with struggles surrounding the succession to the throne in the old Reich. The peace-loving Rudolf II of Habsburg abdicates in favour of his brother Matthias. But then his nephew Ferdinand, later to become emperor, and Colonel Wallenstein appear as harbingers of the Thirty Years' War. Schmitt saw the polycratic struggles around successions in the Third Reich reflected in Grillparzer's play. Huber responded in detail that 'the nature of the Reich was precisely that its problems were irresolvable', and asked rather rhetorically 'whether we do not all, because of our premature and glib watchwords, carry responsibility for a development that is going awry, and which we have fostered in its beginnings, without fully grasping its tendencies and dynamic.'[159] The German jurists had become not proper legists but, rather, civil servants; they did not constitute a 'class that would be necessarily associated with the right by virtue of its existence'.[160] These reflections ended Schmitt and Huber's theoretical discussions for the time being. Huber reacted with resignation to *Land and Sea*.[161] At around the same time he made exonerating statements at the trial at the People's Court [Volksgerichtshof] of two female students who had been accused of high treason.[162] At the turn of the year 1944, he sent Schmitt the second edition of *Heer und Staat* [Army and state], writing: 'Second editions are probably always a problem. . . . In this particular case, the gap of five years, which separates the first from the second edition, is especially deep, and it goes without saying that it would no longer be possible to maintain the thesis of the state-forming force of the army with the same kind of optimism as before an onslaught.'[163] Thus, Huber now hinted at the fact that German warfare in the Second World War had had no positive effect on the 'formation of a constitution'. His thesis, he said, had been a 'demand'. Huber's words sound cautious and euphemistic. Every soldier would have had a clear opinion on that matter. Huber knew that he was still comparatively safe in his 'provisional situation' in Strasbourg, but he expected an invasion by the Allies and said: 'Maybe for the future everything depends on whether we shall find the way from the citizens, from the worker, from the soldier to the human being.'[164] Huber was working on a history of political ideas at the time (which remained unpublished but is among his posthumous papers). In April 1944,[165] he had reached the chapter on Hegel. He asked Schmitt for contributions to his journal. But, at that point, Schmitt had not sought publicity in Germany for some time.

As far as Schmitt's correspondence shows, Jünger and Huber were his two closest and most important conversational partners at the time. Both had their reservations towards him. To put it simply, Jünger's reservations were more of a political nature, Huber's more moral. Both, however, knew that Schmitt was moving away from National Socialism, as expressed in his restraint regarding publications, his literary references and historical reflections. As his conclusion concerning Schmitt's 'case and fall', Ernst Jünger noted in his diary:

> Of all the minds [Geistern] I got to know, C. S. is the one most able to define things. As a classical legal thinker, he is associated with the crown, and his

situation must necessarily become skewed when one set of the demos replaces another. Upon the ascent of illegitimate powers, the position of the crown jurist becomes vacuous, and the attempt at filling it is made at the expense of one's good reputation. That's just how the misfortunes of the profession would have it.[166]

Schmitt later accepted this sober analysis.

26

Last Writings under National Socialism

The literary staging of an exit

The coming military defeat was common knowledge, also among National Socialists. The USA's entrance into the war on land – if, in fact, only quite late on, with D-Day – was generally considered as the turning point. Even Hitler suspected the defeat at times and began to concentrate on the hellish scenario of a 'great' downfall. History was meant to be staged 'according to the model of the Nibelungen myth'.[1] Authors could still react to the events of the war; despite a lack of paper, the publishing world remained surprisingly active until the end of the war. There was still 'bourgeois' scholarship taking place. Even within the framework of the 'Ritterbusch campaign' – i.e., the 'war effort' made by German scholarship in the humanities (Geisteswissenschaften) under the leadership of Paul Ritterbusch[2] – the spectrum of political opinion was relatively broad. Thus, Erik Wolf,[3] for instance, was allowed to publish alongside Karl Larenz, despite being active in the Confessing Church. Scholarship threatened to deteriorate into an intellectual façade that provided justifications, but it was nevertheless still possible to make some critical noises.

With the publication of his *Positionen und Begriffe* [Positions and concepts], Schmitt marked the outbreak of war as a turning point. The collection of papers documented a successful battle 'with' Weimar 'against'[4] Geneva and Versailles. Schmitt dismantled the 'fictions' of right in order to make the political core of Versailles more visible. The collection begins with the nationalistic 'theory of myth' and ends with the 'concept of the Reich', and thus documents the successful battle to get from myth to Reich. 'Becoming a Reich' is presented as the 'goal'.[5] This was also the way Wilhelm Grewe[6] understood the papers in an anonymous review, which Schmitt stuck to the inside cover of his personal copy at Christmas 1939. But, apart from this triumphant structure of the book, there are also contrary tendencies. The preface of 20 August 1939, dated a few days before the outbreak of war, speaks in a rather resigned tone of the 'professional hazard' of being misunderstood. It is not surprising that the texts on constitutional law from the period of the Weimar Republic are absent from the collection. But it is striking that almost all texts on a National Socialist 'constitution' are missing, and that texts which are sharply anti-Semitic have also been left out (see, however, PB, p. 316). The 'new construction' is mentioned only briefly,[7] and the 'concept of the Reich', at the very end, appears as a rather isolated demand. 'I read your "Positions and Concepts" every evening', Kličković wrote to Schmitt. 'I feel then as if I was with you and we were walking through the Grunewald. It is a peculiar, a lively book, which, like Dorian Gray, changes its face from day to day.'[8]

During 1940, Schmitt would still draw some conclusions regarding the relationship between international law and state law from the outbreak of war.[9] But, in the first place, the year was characterized by the keyword 'spatial revolution' [Raumrevolution]. At the end of September, Schmitt published a reminder in the weekly journal *Das Reich* that 'peace' was the 'purpose [Sinn] of war'.[10] And he published preparatory studies on the history of international law.[11] Ulrich Scheuner commented on these:

> Many thanks for kindly sending me your essay on the dissolution of the European order. . . . After this, I suppose what was called the European order is now firmly history, and this war probably pretty much destroys the last hopes of rebuilding a new order in Europe on the basis of that old idea of balance; whatever may emerge from this can rest only on the basis of domination or leadership, not on a delicate system of balance and 'order'.

Scheuner asked 'what the future foundation of order' would be, and wanted to see a 'genuine element of an ethical attitude' in it.[12] Schmitt did not discuss these matters openly, but indicated a 'shift in meaning' with a few additions in his *Großraum Order in International Law*. Only a few weeks before the invasion of the Soviet Union, his preliminary remark to the fourth and last edition, dated 28 July 1941, spoke of a 'document' that was not meant 'to keep pace with the course of events'. Newly emerging questions, he said, required a 'new approach'. Schmitt gave the publication a motto, which alluded to *Benito Cereno*: 'We are like sailors on a continuous journey, and no book can be more than a log book.' Even the edition of 1939 had not put imperial Germany on the throne of the 'Reich' completely without hesitation. Insertions into the pre-war text legitimated expansion through acts of war. But the additions, which had been published as separate articles in 1940, first and foremost clarified that the events of war exceeded the criteria for order which typify the Reich. The chapter on 'Reich und Raum' [Reich and space] emphasizes 'the spatial revolution caused by the airforce' (SGN, p. 307) and ties the possibility for a 'relativization of war' – a fundamental transformation of the relationship between man and space – to the presence of open spaces. The last chapter, 'Der Raumbegriff in der Rechtswissenschaft' [The concept of space in jurisprudence], justifies the biological 'performance space' [Leistungsraum] – and includes anti-Semitic rantings – with the 'connection between concrete order and location [Ortung]' (SGN, p. 319). Schmitt identified a tension between the concept of the Reich and the spatial revolution. He thought that the 'spatial revolution' brought about by the war of expansion made any political control or legal constitution impossible. On the one hand, he tied the order of the Reich to an open 'space of expansion' beyond the 'Central and Eastern European Großraum' but, on the other hand, the notion of the performance space, which he understood in biological terms, not only in terms of a people – thus probably also accommodating 'völkisch' critics such as the SS jurist Werner Best – remained an abstract formula shrouded in ambiguous debates about mediaeval legal history. Schmitt immediately started to undertake extensive historical studies, which led to *The Nomos of the Earth*.[13] His reflections on 'maritime' legal thought caught the interest of a different audience. Thus, Schmitt came into contact at that time with Rolf Stödter, a maritime law expert from Hamburg, a contact which would become important after 1945.

Between 1940 and the end of the war Schmitt did not publish much. He took a first step beyond the boundaries of the continental state in his talk on 'Staatliche Souveränität und freies Meer' [State sovereignty and the open sea], which he gave at the beginning of February 1941 at a conference of historians in Nuremberg. The text confronts the continental 'concept of order' – the state – with the 'spatial revolution' caused by the conquering of the seven seas in the early modern age. Schmitt aimed at a genealogical reconstruction of 'two entirely different orders of international law' (SGN, p. 407). At the end of the text, he expressed the expectation that the German people would take the 'lead' [die Führung] by conquering the air. One last time, he quoted his formula of hope: *Ab integro nascitur ordo*. On the sidelines of the conference, Schmitt spoke with Theodor Schieder and Gerhard Ritter, who would later become doyens of the historical sciences in the Federal Republic.[14] Gustav Steinböhmer responded enthusiastically to the text and asked Schmitt for a meeting.[15] Ernst Wolgast criticized some of the details, but praised the text as a whole: 'What you establish is of revolutionary importance: there are two kinds of international law.'[16]

Schmitt's Paris talk on 'Das Meer gegen das Land' [The sea against the land] was published in March 1941 in the journal *Das Reich*.[17] At the time it was of primary importance to understand why England was an enemy, and Schmitt thus turned towards 'England's decision' to pursue a 'maritime existence'. He concluded optimistically that, due to modern technological developments in warfare, the sea had turned from being an element to being purely 'space'; the 'time of the Leviathan' (SGN, p. 398), Schmitt thus claimed, was over, and England's advantage with regard to domination of the seas no longer existed. 'And we shall tell our grandchildren the tale about the empire of the Leviathan', Schmitt concluded, announcing the narrative form that *Land and Sea* would take. Reclam, the publishing house, explicitly wanted this 'world-historical reflection' as the continuation of the article.[18]

With *Land and Sea*, Schmitt realized the suggestion made by Ernst Jünger that he might write with a 'second naivety' (JS, p. 78) and without scholarly apparatus.[19] Smend called it a 'world-historical-cosmic symphony'.[20] The genre of idyllic literature presents private harmony against the backdrop of catastrophic events. Goethe wrote his epic poem *Hermann and Dorothea* at the time of the Napoleonic wars. Thomas Mann set his family idyll in contrast to the Great War and the revolutionary chaos of 1918–19.[21] The literary significance of such idyllic fiction lies in the contrast between private order and political disorder. A good idyll piece is not sentimental but uncanny; it makes the threat shine through. Schmitt's text also aims at the 'intrusion of the time into the play'.* It unmistakably signals a turn from reflections on 'international law' to reflections on 'world history', and from the concept of order of the 'Reich' to the chaotic 'elements'. From a world-historical perspective, and in a literary form, Schmitt interprets the war as an elementary event. He 'tells' his daughter Anima about the mythic elements and the historical 'possibilities of human existence', about the limits of Venetian rule of the sea and the conquering of the sea by whale hunters, pirates and corsairs, about England's decision for a 'maritime existence', its rise to the status of a world power, and about the planetary 'spatial revolution' that was caused by the conquest of the New World. He tells her about the 'world-wide battle between Catholicism and Protestantism' (LM, p. 55), between 'Jesuitism and Calvinism', about the 'contrast between land war and sea war' and about the 'world-wide battle' between England and Germany, which has intensified as a result of the industrial revolution, and which has been carried into the element of the air. With the 'age of electronics' a 'new, second spatial revolution' (LM, p. 73), a 'change in essence' [Wesenswandlung] and a new distribution of global spaces sets in, according to Schmitt. 'Even during the cruel war [edition of 1954: 'bitter struggle'] between old and new forces, just measures emerge and meaningful proportions form' (LM, p. 76). The text ends with a prognosis: the battle between the elements will be decided by the domination of the air. The war in the air leads to a collision of the elements. Flames rain down from the sky, and from the sea the enemy invades the country. Schmitt's contemporaries must have understood this turn away from the concept of the Reich and towards world-historical reflections, and the fact that the text addresses a member of the family, as a signal. At the end of 1942, Schmitt reacted to the fact that an analysis of power showed that the Reich was no longer a sovereign power providing order [souveräne Ordnungsmacht]. His text constitutes a very speculative beginning for a history of England's mentality and of the mentality that informed international law. What it was not was an active apologia or a detailed observation of the enemy in the style of the propagated 'foreign studies'.

The change in the course of the war was already visible at the end of 1941. The Russian campaign, which had been planned from the very beginning as a 'war of extermination', was forced to a halt outside Moscow by the Russian winter, and the USA entered the war after Pearl Harbor. Hitler held 'world Jewry' responsible for this turn in events and now called for its total extermination.[22] The Wannsee Conference, the assassination of Heydrich and the warning sign of Stalingrad soon followed. In the course of 1942, Schmitt, in a manner similar to his reaction during the Great War, developed an apocalyptic perspective on the course of events and again turned to the figure of the katechon in Paul's letter to the Thessalonians. In contrast to Romans 13, this figure integrated the (Roman) Empire

---

* Thus the subtitle of Schmitt's later *Hamlet or Hecuba*.

[Reich] into the divine plan of salvation, thus allowing Christianity to find an initial arrangement with the Reich. Schmitt's continual reference to this figure, which he frequently discussed in letters, thus shows that he was still playing with the idea of legitimizing the Reich. He interpreted the figure in various ways without committing himself to any one version. But, in any case, it signals a critical stage in the legitimation of Christianity. Schmitt summarized his normative plea for Ernst Jünger as follows:

> Shall I send you my short book on 'Land and Sea'? It says at the end that the history of mankind is, in accordance with the teachings of antiquity, a journey through the four elements. We are now in fire. What did Prometheus tell you in the Caucasus? What is called 'nihilism' is incineration in fire. The urge to be burnt in crematoria is 'nihilism'. The Russians have invented that word. From the ashes, Phoenix, the bird, will rise – i.e., an empire [Reich] of the air. (JS, p. 151)

Did Schmitt have only cremation in mind, or was he in some way alluding to the Holocaust when mentioning 'crematoria'? What did he know, and what did he suspect in the context of his reflections? As long as his wartime diaries remain untranscribed, we can only speculate on such questions. In any case, his analyses of the history of the war put an emphasis on the 'total' war of extermination, and because of his anti-Semitism he took Hitler seriously. Schmitt also had privileged access to insider information. Nevertheless, ideological differences – Schmitt did not agree with a radically biological racism, which considered man solely as an animal – also indicate limits of the imagination, a last barrier, maybe, which makes the Holocaust unthinkable. There is no doubt that Schmitt considered genocide and the Holocaust as crimes. But he would remain silent about it throughout his life. During the war he analysed the national characteristics of France, England and the USA. 'Die letzte globale Linie' [The last global line] criticized a change in American strategy from 'isolationism' to 'pan-interventionism'.[23] A publication in part in the *Deutsche Kolonialzeitung*[24] mentions the 'great bird', the griffin, in its title – indicating that Schmitt thought air superiority was the factor that would decide the outcome of the war.

Rise and fall of a Reich

After 1939, Schmitt staged a long literary farewell to the Third Reich as the realization of the idea of the 'Reich'. Ernst Forsthoff's Protestant end point to the Reich was his *Recht und Sprache* [Right and language].[25] Ernst Rudolf Huber retreated into intellectual history. As part of the 'Ritterbusch campaign', Theodor Maunz, as late as 1944, published a didactic text on the rise and fall of a Reich which was strongly influenced by Schmitt.[26] Maunz knew Schmitt from the Leipzig trial.[27] He then visited him at the Schliersee in 1934, and soon published in Schmitt's series. The two of them met quite often. Again and again, Maunz thanked Schmitt for having 'reached out his hand' in order 'to allow him to embark upon an academic career under the most difficult circumstances'.[28] Maunz very attentively followed the theory of the Großraum.[29] Towards the end of the war, in a monograph on *Das Reich der spanischen Großmachtzeit* [The Reich of Spain's empirical age], he supplemented Schmitt's distinction between land powers and sea powers with a 'third type of formation shown by history', speaking of a 'triad, land power – sea power – clerical power [Priestermacht]', within the picture presented by European history. Maunz considered the '*Reconquista* idea', the reconquering of Spain, as the root of faith in the Spanish Reich, and emphasized that 'Spain, at the beginning of the sixteenth century, came very close to that legal type we today call a state.'[30] Spain remained a 'land power'; it thought along 'terrestrial' lines. Maunz identified the high point of Spanish power with the reign of Karl V; Philipp II, he said, then began a 'complete transformation of the political constellation of forces'. The idea of a Reich had been associated with a 'claim to world hegemony'. However, the process of becoming a nation effected a secularization and an 'impoverishment of the substance of the Reich'. Maunz's sketch of the 'finale' to the Spanish Empire was brief:

Due to the earth's changing form, the association of faith and sword had lost its genuine meaning. The theocratic backbone of Spain's dominance, the power of the clergy, had been undermined by enlightenment and liberalism. And the consciousness of being the executors of a transcendental destiny, the faith in having a mission, had been lost. This had to lead to the end of Spain's old position in the world.[31]

Maunz divested the theory of the Reich of its missionary ideology, showed that there was a plurality of competing myths and relativized any exclusive faith in having a mission to fulfil. If we read his work as a reflection of the history of National Socialism from within, Maunz not only registered that the National Socialist ideology of a Reich was wearing out, but he also criticized the quasi-religious excesses of its imperial claims. Such writings are important as literary gestures. Schmitt registered an overstretching of the concept of the Reich in the course of the spatial revolution, a loss of sovereignty in National Socialism. Within the context of his theory, this implied a normative evaluation. Without effective control of its area of dominance [Machtraum], a power can no longer rightfully claim authority [Macht] and, because of the 'relation between protection and obedience', can no longer demand loyalty. This literary abandonment of the ideology of the Reich in 1942 did not yet mark a political turn. And yet it was a farewell and marked a transition in thought, which signals an understanding of what was happening. The authors at least did not want to look foolish at the end of the war.

Delayed harvest: an eschatology of international law?

Schmitt was still very productive during the last years of the war. His thoughts on 'spatial revolution' and 'spatial order' had now matured.

'Europe' was a keyword linking the two. Schmitt expanded his ideas into *The Nomos of the Earth*; he unified his perspective on 'European jurisprudence' and took up his Cortés studies again for a Spanish audience.

In 1943 one of his talks – 'Strukturwandel des Internationalen Rechts' [Structural transformations in international law] – appeared in Spanish translation. The text talks about a self-destruction of the political 'myth of the Western hemisphere' (FP, p. 669)[32] in the course of the transition from 'isolationism' to a 'pan-interventionism'. Already in 1939 an article by Hans Niedermayer suggested to Schmitt that he might take up his reflections on the nomos again.[33] Schmitt wrote to Niedermayer that the 'unfortunate division between juridical and philological-historical expertise' had so far kept him from further nomos studies. But maybe, he said, the strong impulse exerted by Niedermayer's article would now contribute to him 'making some free time in the next holidays, in order to approach the topic anew'.[34] From 1942, Schmitt no longer spoke of the 'Reich', but of the 'nomos'. As early as 1943 he announced a talk on the topic of 'The Nomos of the Earth'.[35]

The Nomos of the Earth in the International Law of the Jus Publicum Europaeum is a collection of studies on the emergence and dissolution of European international law in modern times. It stands to *Land and Sea* in the way an epic stands to idyllic literature. Its perspective takes a step back from the present, so to speak. It begins with 'five introductory corollaries', which briefly present, in a speculative way, the book's normative point of departure – i.e., 'land appropriation' as the 'unity of order and orientation'.* Schmitt then moves from the 'land appropriation of a new world' and the '*jus publicum Europaeum*' to the current 'question of a new Nomos of the Earth'. 'The restored nomos 1815–1918', Schmitt notes in his personal copy,[36] and criticizes the fact that an 'account of the Great European treaties' since the Westphalian Peace is missing. In quantitative terms, the book deals mainly with the present, which Schmitt presents as a time of crisis – as a time of 'dissolution' and of a 'reorientation' [Sinnwandel] in 'classical international law' which requires new solutions. The fundamental lines of argument of long passages of the second and fourth parts can already be found in Schmitt's pre-1945 work. The concept of the nomos itself had also already been introduced in 1934. After 1945, Schmitt gave the text to some readers he trusted. He incorporated his Vitoria interpretation and a legal opinion written in 1945, and completed the work on his last more substantial monograph in 1950 in somewhat improvised fashion and under difficult circumstances. The individual parts are slightly heterogeneous and imbalanced. Schmitt later wanted to

---

* 'Orientation' translates 'Ortung' in the English edition of *The Nomos of the Earth*. 'Ortung', the way Schmitt uses the term, is a neologism. In normal German usage, 'Ortung' and the substantivized noun 'Orten' refer to the act of identifying the location or position of an object or person. In Schmitt's usage it refers to a person or group of people taking a position, establishing themselves in a location. (The examples he gives are: 'appropriating land, founding cities, and establishing colonies'; NtE, p. 44.) While I therefore consider 'location' a better equivalent, I nevertheless follow the translator's choice when quoting from the English edition.

introduce significant changes to the text: the corollaries, for instance, he wanted extended and moved to a different position. A lot of the material after 1945 was new, in particular the summary view of the development of the nomos.

By way of introduction, Schmitt again defines right as the 'unity of order and orientation'. Orientation, with its military associations, refers to the spatial aspect of right: right is only valid within the framework of a spatially limited and effective 'spatial order'. The history of international law is political history, and it therefore seems right to distinguish the various epochs of international law according to the hegemonial power that supported them. In this way, Wilhelm Grewe, in his Berlin Habilitation, had distinguished between the mediaeval, the Spanish, the French and the English 'ages' in the orders of international law. In the summer term 1943, Schmitt let Grewe teach his tutorial in international law.[37] Because he had been bombed out, Grewe was unable to publish his Habilitation quickly,[38] but he did have 'some ready printed and bound copies' at the end of the war.[39] Soon, Ludwig Dehio would look at international orders from the perspective of 'balance or hegemony'.[40] Schmitt does not give a detailed account in terms of political science[41] but limits his role to that of an avant-garde juridical thinker with a speculative and esoteric touch. On the basis of the history of power in international law, he advocates a system of balance between several big powers. Beyond that, Schmitt writes a universal history about the rise and fall of European international law in the form of a critical history of international law's 'relativization' and 'disorientation' [Entortung] (NtE, p. 234).[42] Using international law as an example, Schmitt confronts jurisprudence with the 'question of its existence' and provides a negative answer: it is being 'crushed between theology and technology' (NtE, p. 6).

Schmitt starts out with a discussion of the 'de-theologization' of European international law during the transition from the mediaeval Church to the modern territorial state. In this context, he considers the land appropriation of a new world as the precondition for the relational order of the system of European states. Francisco de Vitoria, the Spanish representative of late scholasticism, Schmitt sees as a 'break point' [Einbruchstelle] (NtE, p. 84), as someone similar to Hobbes. Vitoria's 'theological arguments', Schmitt says, were neutralized, secularized and put to humanist use 'by Protestants' (NtE, p. 86). Schmitt changes the confessional aspect of his constitutional history. The place of the 'Jewish front' is now taken by Anglo-Saxon Protestantism. In this context, in the version of 1950, Schmitt speaks of a 'power of division inherent in humanitarian ideology' (NtE, p. 104) and in 'absolute humanity' which leads to the distinction between 'the *superhuman* and the *subhuman*' (ibid.). With these words, Schmitt also implicitly commented on National Socialism and made secular humanism responsible for its eliminatory racism.

Schmitt describes the decline of state-based international law in connection with the rise of the 'island of England' and the 'Western hemisphere', and he considers the enforcement of a universalist international law to be a triumph of the Anglo-Saxon concept of international law, modelled on maritime law. His account picks up on various questions of the time. In conclusion, Schmitt describes how the role of the supporting power shifts from the European system of balance to American hegemony, and he criticizes this process as the destruction of right and of jurisprudence altogether. Schmitt explains that 'maritime' legal thought, which developed out of the law of naval warfare, did not know of the 'bracketing' of the concept of enemy and of war that characterized conventional international law. The dissolution of the *jus publicum Europaeum* therefore led to a 'change of meaning' of war. The rise of the USA destroyed the system of balance and the common European 'constitutional standards' of the European order of states without establishing a new nomos. Schmitt interprets the discriminating concept of war as the return of the 'just war' under post-Christian conditions. 'Just war', for Schmitt, is an 'ideological phenomenon which accompanies the industrial-technological development'. All these developments he traces back to the 'Western hemisphere'. He does not talk explicitly about National Socialism, and he looks at the development of international law in the inter-war period not as a response to European totalitarianism but as the triumph of 'nihilism' (NtE, pp. 36, 159) implicit in 'maritime existence', a nihilism which cancels the 'unity of order and orientation'.

The individual lines of argument in *The Nomos of the Earth* cannot be disentangled. The theses on the connection between a 'maritime existence' and industrialization and the progressive development of technology in particular are very speculative in their normative implications – i.e., the reference to man as a 'land-roamer' [Landtreter] and 'son of the earth'. One possible misunderstanding would be to adopt a Christian framework for the interpretation of the text: Schmitt did not measure secular international law against the older concept of law of the imperial theology of the Middle Ages, although he did set up his question regarding the 'delayer' from a theological perspective even before 1945.[43] Another misunderstanding would be to assume that Schmitt saw land appropriation as absolutely the only form of legal title, and that he wrote a history of power and international law. Rather, he understood land-appropriation as only a 'provisional' (I. Kant) legal title and considered the mutual recognition of sovereign states as the genuine basis for legal titles. His earlier 'overcoming of the concept of the state in international law' (SGN, p. 300) seems to be forgotten here. If we look more carefully, however, Schmitt, in *The Nomos of the Earth*, has also only the great powers in mind when thinking about the entities that support the legal order in the form of a spatial order. Thus, there is a strong continuity between the Großraum order and its reformulation as a 'spatial order'. With the help of his concept of a union, Schmitt now interprets the Großraum order as a system of balance between great powers that recognize each other in reciprocal fashion. And the possibility of a bracketing of enmity and war he puts under the proviso of imperial land appropriation. After 1945, Schmitt established a problematic understanding of the *jus publicum Europaeum*, in which the principle of sovereignty was firmly embedded.[44]

An 'unfortunate figure' under National Socialism?

At the same time as he was writing the history of European international law, Schmitt revised 'Die Lage der europäischen Rechtswissenschaft' [The situation of European jurisprudence]. He spoke on the topic, sometimes in French,[45] in Bucharest and Budapest, Madrid, Coimbra, Barcelona and Leipzig, and published a part of the text in Hungarian. With Werner Weber, he discussed its possible publication in a Festschrift for Johannes Popitz,[46] which was also meant to contain an 'Introduction *ad personam*'.[47] Barion, Forsthoff, Huber, Koellreutter, Wieacker, Hans Schneider and others were intended contributors. On 22 December Weber thanked Schmitt for sending the manuscript, together with a short 'piece on the case of the Göttinger Sieben'.[48] With this piece, Schmitt alluded to the destiny of German resistance;[*] Weber mentioned the 'death' of Ahlmann 'with shock'. Popitz was executed on 2 February 1945. Instead of the planned Festschrift, Weber therefore suggested a special publication with the publishing house Koehler & Amelang in Leipzig, which was still printing at the time. However, the text, revised in its concluding section in particular, appeared only in 1950.

Schmitt reconstructed the unity of European jurisprudence on the basis of its reception of Roman law, shifting from the National Socialist fault-line to a positive view of Roman law as a case of a successful 'reception of a jurisprudence'.[49] Schmitt then jumped to the 'crisis in the legality of the state of law'; he once again reconstructed the dissolution of the liberal concept of law and emphasized the danger of the rationalizing effect of jurisprudence as an 'independent third entity' (VRA, p. 408) being crushed by the accelerated ('motorized') change of the form of 'law'. What was new was Schmitt's turn to 'Savigny as the paradigm provided by the first distancing from the legality of the state of law'. Savigny, according to Schmitt, made the 'astonishing attempt' of 'assigning jurisprudence the role of being the genuine protector of right' (VRA, p. 414). However, as the minister for legal reform, he betrayed his own theory of the 'Volksgeist' [people's spirit] and thus experienced failure. Schmitt described this 'unfortunate role' of Savigny clearly as a parallel to his own 'decline': 'Today, we know that Savigny, immediately before the outbreak of the revolution in 1848, organized in great haste a simplification and acceleration of the process of legislation, which was, in fact, at the expense of the powers of participation of the very same state council of which he was the president' (VRA, p. 418).

The text's 'glorification of Savigny' surprised even Werner Weber.[50] However, it was yet again the result of Schmitt's personal identification with the historical figure. Down to the expression 'state councillor', Schmitt saw his own 'failure' reflected in that of Savigny. He referred to

---

[*] The 'Göttinger Sieben' were seven professors at the University of Göttingen, among them Jakob and Wilhelm Grimm, who, in 1837, wrote and signed a letter of protest against the suspension of the constitution in the kingdom of Hanover; they were dismissed from their posts.

the 'overall catastrophe in intellectual history' which took place at the 'moment of the collapse of older and the rise of new forces', and did not omit to mention that Savigny soon 'found his way back to his true persona and to his European stature' (VRA, p. 419). There is no clear evidence for what exactly Schmitt said about the role of jurisprudence in his public lectures before 1945.[51]

Schmitt certainly was familiar with 'failure' in the context of active involvement, even if he had not succeeded in becoming the 'minister for legal reform'. Together with Hans Frank, he had failed outside the gates of the Ministry of Justice and did not actually gain 'access to the ruler'. Schmitt now suggested that his 'concrete order formation' had been meant to serve the purpose of a 'distancing' and a 'slow development' of a 'common law'. He placed the blame for its failure on the 'motorized lawgiver' and asked for an understanding of the dilemma in which he had found himself between distancing and involvement. One may concede to a certain extent that, in 1933, one of his reasons for getting involved had been the wish to resolve the 'crisis in the legality of the state of law'. That his motivation had been to protect the rationalizing role of jurisprudence caught 'between theology and technology' is somewhat harder to believe. One would have to understand 'theology' in a very wide sense for that.

Schmitt saw the 'unfortunate figure' (VRA, p. 418) as the representative of a global catastrophe, which is why he accompanied the reflection of his own failure as a 'crown jurist' with a final study of Donoso Cortés as a reflection of the 'catastrophe' of his own failure in the Third Reich through parallels with 1848.

Schmitt had used Donoso Cortés as a mirror of his own situation before, in the 1920s. To begin with he refrained from Catholic confessions during the time of National Socialism. Following his personal decline, he included his texts on Donoso Cortés in his *Positionen und Begriffe* [Positions and concepts]. In his talk on 'Donoso Cortés in gesamteuropäischer Interpretation' [Donoso Cortés interpreted in a pan-European perspective], which he gave in 1944 in Madrid, he juxtaposed the Marxist 'interpretations of the significance' [Sinndeutungen] of 1848 with a range of alternative approaches. He distinguished between three levels of establishing meaning with historical continuities: 'prognosis, diagnosis and historical parallels' (DC, p. 87). Prognosis and diagnosis he found to be very pronounced in Tocqueville, in his prognosis that the number of political actors on the world stage would diminish, and his diagnosis of a process of 'centralization', 'industrialization and the progress of technology', leading to a 'final situation', in which the state would become an enterprise. However, going beyond this, Donoso Cortés, Schmitt wrote, also saw his own time from the perspective of the 'great parallel' with the Christian turn of the ages, and thus he entered into the counter-revolutionary battle with socialism, declared to be the 'new religion' after Saint Simon. Schmitt contrasted Cortés's religious understanding of the parallel with the positions of Bruno Bauer[52] and Kierkegaard. For Cortés, 'the parallel melted in the immediacy of his faith' (DC, p. 104), which is why he led the 'most Christian battle against the Christian Church' (DC, p. 107). Schmitt described Cortés as an intuitive seer, who looked into the abyss of human nature' and captured the negative consequences of the humanist 'idea of absolute humanity' (DC, p. 110). He spoke of the discriminating split within the idea of humanity: who posits 'man' as the absolute measure, and does not relativize man with reference to God, ends up in a 'nihilistic' opposition between 'man and non-man', the 'superhuman and sub-human' (DC, p. 111). It is possible that Schmitt did not say this in quite this form before the end of the war, when giving the talk in Madrid. But he certainly wanted to point to the 'great parallel' and to the Christian interpretation of the meaning of the 'spatial revolution' within the present historical process. For this purpose, he constructed a 'small parallel' between 1848 and his own time, and was thus able to set up his autobiographical hall of mirrors. Schmitt identified with a whole range of authors around 1848 and used them to explicate his own views. With Savigny he played the game of 'failure' in constitutional policies; with Cortés he claimed a Christian interpretation of meaning [Sinndeutung] for himself.

One can follow these stylizations only with great reservations. In contrast to Savigny, Schmitt, in 1933, had only a marginal influence on legislation, even if he sought to gain such influence through Göring's State Council and Frank's academy. One can hardly say that he acted in a 'conservative' fashion. And, to the extent that Schmitt was right in claiming Christian motivations for his action, during National Socialism these were expressed mainly in the form of an aggressive and apocalyptic anti-Semitism. They were certainly not in line with the teachings of the Church. And they do not appear Christian to us today. Only after 1939 can signs of a cautious distancing be detected; from then on, Schmitt no longer acted in the way of a National Socialist zealot and apologist. His self-interpretation of his role in National Socialism presents, of course, a manicured picture. Ambition, opportunism, cynical arrangement with 'nether demons', the betrayal of friends, the destruction of legal certainty and of legal procedure, victims of discrimination – none of this appears in this picture of himself. One may just about credit Schmitt's juridico-institutional provision of meaning in 1933–4 with some moderating and constructive influence, although even there the meaning of the key concepts could be stretched to the point of complete opportunism. But his attempts in terms of academic policies and organization, which ended up facing opposition from many sides, aimed at a radical dismantling of the principles of the Rechtsstaat. Maybe Schmitt wanted to protect his own academic standards with his legal concepts. But, when he recognized the character of National Socialism as a state of exception and of terror, he responded with his anti-Semitic provision of meaning as a pre-emptive defence. Following the Enabling Act, he acted as a radical National Socialist until at least December 1936. He justified the 'pan-German' politics of expansion and probably felt that the victory over France was a just revenge for Versailles. He did, though, realize the catastrophic consequences of the National Socialist politics of expansion relatively early, and from 1942 he increasingly withdrew from actively providing legitimation for the Reich.

Part IV

'One Man Remains': Schmitt's Slow Retreat after 1945

27

Detention and 'Asylum'

After the storm

In October 1944, Allied troops captured Aachen. In December, the last counter-attack, the offensive in the Ardennes, failed. The concentration camps were evacuated and trails of KZ inmates were driven through the devastated landscape like 'stumbling columns of corpses'.[1] On 22 January, Duška brought Anima to Cloppenburg, herself arriving back in Berlin on 27 January.[2] On the same day, Auschwitz was liberated. Schmitt was briefly drafted into the Volkssturm at that point, but given leave 'for some time' on 8 February. Schmitt compared the situation to the plank of Carneades,* 'the primordial image for all morally irresolvable problems of so-called states of exception' (JS, p. 192). Everyone is just trying to save their lives; survival is all that matters. On 3 February, Berlin was heavily bombarded; between 13 and 15 February, Dresden was destroyed. Everywhere the German defences now broke down. The Americans crossed the Rhine at Rehmagen. At the beginning of March, Berlin was divided into three concentric defensive rings.[3] Hitler issued his so-called scorched earth decree and exhortations to hold out. The inferno produced an apocalyptic atmosphere. Churchill urged Roosevelt to occupy Berlin. However, Roosevelt died, leading Hitler to believe in a second miracle of Brandenburg.† Eastern Prussia was cut off. Terrible refugee tragedies took place. The Americans conquered Magdeburg and Leipzig, halting their campaign on the Elbe, as agreed among the Allies. By 25 April, Berlin was surrounded by the Russian army. The inner circle of the city was to be defended by SS and 'Werwolf' units until the very end. Hitler shifted imaginary armies across the board, had Göring arrested, dismissed Himmler, the 'traitor', and in his testament encouraged the German people to 'painstaking adherence to the racial laws'. He married Eva Braun a day before they both killed themselves on 30 April. The same day, Schmitt was temporarily arrested

---

* A moral thought experiment of the Greek philosopher Carneades: two survivors of a shipwreck see a plank that can carry only one of them. One of them pushes the other one off, leaving her to drown. Can this be justified, or is it murder? – Carneades taught only orally; the example is reported by Cicero in *De officiis*.

† In 1762, Frederick the Great was 'saved' by the death of Tsarina Elisabeth, following which Russia left the anti-Prussian coalition in the Seven Years' War.

and interrogated by Soviet troops in his house in Schlachtensee, Berlin. Mr and Mrs Goebbels poisoned their six children. On 2 May, Berlin capitulated. The new 'government' led by Dönitz still made an illusory attempt at negotiating a capitulation for the Western front only, while continuing the fight against 'Bolshevism' in the East. However, on 7 May the Wehrmacht capitulated, and on 8 May the unconditional surrender was signed at Karlshorst.

With the end of the war, the Americans discontinued their supply of aid to Russia. As early as May, Churchill spoke of an 'iron curtain'. For two months the Russians had Berlin to themselves. Waves of suicides swept through the noble suburbs; plundering and rape became everyday occurrences. Schmitt stayed in Berlin and experienced dramatic weeks of conquest and wilful violence. Berlin was also destroyed as an industrial location. Only towards the end of June did the situation quieten down somewhat. General Lucius Clay arrived as Eisenhower's deputy, and the first American and British troops moved into Berlin. Although they came as victorious enemies, compared to the Russians they were also seen as liberators. The 'Potsdam Conference' was held in Schloss Cecilienhof and various villas in Babelsberg. Stalin arrived by special train from Moscow; Churchill and Truman visited the completely destroyed Berlin. The conference began on 17 July, though Churchill lost the election in Britain that month and thus did not attend the final meetings. Truman informed Stalin about the development of the atomic bomb. On 30 July the Allied Control Council met for the first time. On 6 and 9 August the atomic bombs were dropped on Hiroshima and Nagasaki. The Grunewald became the preferred district of residence of the Americans. The time of 're-education',[*] of black markets and of cigarettes as currency began. Trails of refugees pushed into a completely bombed-out and overcrowded Berlin. There was an extreme shortage of accommodation.

What exactly Schmitt and Duška experienced during those weeks and months has not yet been established, as the preserved diaries still need to be decoded.[4] The general misery, in any case, was almost indescribable. At the beginning of May, Schmitt plunged himself into speculations on intellectual history and wrote an 'exposé' in English on his 'work with the Nazis'. He compared being 'betrayed' by Hitler to his first marriage. Duška spoke Russian, and thus was able more or less to 'protect' the house.[5] Schmitt was worried that the apartment might be confiscated and therefore made his library available to the public. Their daughter Anima, meanwhile, remained in Cloppenburg. Since April no news had arrived from there. It was, to begin with, almost impossible to travel; the mail did not work, the payment of salaries was stopped. According to a communication from the Wirtschafts-Hochschule, dated 4 June, 'all employment contracts and pension arrangements' were annulled by a resolution of the magistrate. Everyone had to make efforts to be re-employed. Schmitt reported monthly at the district's job centre[6] and, like Emge, Höhn and others, also directly to the university's Rektor [vice-chancellor] Spranger

---

[*] English in the original.

for duty.[7] He was annoyed by a questionnaire sent by the university, and later, as a form of revenge, he would publicly embarrass Spranger. Spranger replied: 'It was so far from me "to expect" Herr Prof. Schmitt "to fill in a questionnaire", that I actually advised him not to fill one in. Whoever no longer wanted anything from the university of Berlin was free not to fill it in.'[8] However, no one was quite sure about the exact formal significance of the questionnaires. Hans Schneider visited Schmitt on the occasion of his birthday, 11 July.[9] Schmitt's colleague from Berlin, Hans Peters, wrote a report counselling against Schmitt's continued employment by the university; Karl Löwenstein pursued Schmitt's arrest and also wanted him sentenced as a war criminal.[10] In August, Schmitt wrote a legal opinion on 'The International Crime of the War of Aggression', in consultation with the jurist Dr Konrad Kaletsch,[11] who worked for Friedrich Flick.* A two-page 'Conclusion of the Opinion'† is dated 28 August.[12] Thus, Schmitt's legal opinion was also addressed to the American victors. In September, US soldiers searched his flat. On 26 September, he was arrested by the Americans and brought initially to the detention camp at Wannsee. On 3 October, Schmitt reported to the 'Prüfungsstelle auf Antifaschismus' [Office for the Verification of Antifascism] of the district administration.[13] In a registered letter of 29 December he was informed that, as a member of the NSDAP, he was to be dismissed from university service with immediate effect.[14]

Crimes and responsibilities

In his legal opinion on *The International Crime of War of Aggression and the Principle 'Nullum crimen, nulla poena sine lege'*, Schmitt first excludes two types of war crimes from his approach: crimes committed during wartime – i.e., 'breaches against the so-called law *in* war' (ICWA, p. 126) – and 'inhuman atrocities' (ICWA, p. 127), whose bestiality turns the perpetrator into an 'outlaw'‡ (ICWA, p. 128). Such sadistic crimes characterized National Socialism. Schmitt wrote:

The atrocities§ in the special sense that were committed before the last world war and during this war must indeed be regarded as '*mala in se*'. Their inhumanity is so great and so evident that it suffices to establish the facts and their perpetrators in order to ground criminal liability without any regard for hitherto existing positive penal laws. Here, all arguments of natural sense, of

---

* Friedrich Flick (1883–1972), a German industrialist who acquired his fortune in the iron and steel industry during the Great War and in the Weimar Republic. He cooperated closely with the National Socialists and was sentenced to seven years in Nuremberg in 1947 for forced labour, plundering, expropriations and participation in SS crimes. After his early release in 1950, within five years he again became the richest person in Germany and one of the richest in the world.

† English in the original.
‡ English in the original.
§ English in the original.

human feeling, of reason, and of justice concur in a practically elemental way to justify a conviction that requires no positivistic norm in any formal sense. Nor must one enquire here as to the extent to which the perpetrators had a criminal intent. All of this goes without saying. Whoever raises the objection 'nullum crimen' in the face of such crimes, whoever would want to refer to the hitherto existing positivistic penal legal determinations would put himself in a suspicious light. (WA, p. 135)

This was written by Schmitt in the context of an unpublished legal opinion, which he produced as an advocate in the summer of 1945, hence at a point in time when the whole scale of National Socialist war crimes was only beginning to emerge. Later he would occasionally, for instance in reflections on de Sade, associate sadistic excesses with the situation of a state of exception.[15] People act sadistically when there is no yesterday and no tomorrow, no law and no judge, when the perpetrator turns himself into a judge, in order to experience his absolute power over his victim within a general situation characterized by chaos and powerlessness. When Schmitt later, again and again, felt persecuted as an 'outlaw',[*] he thought his case was subsumed under the category of such abnormal crimes. He reacted with outrage when he was lumped together with the worst of the perpetrators.

His legal opinion, however, investigates in more detail only a third kind of war crime: the case of a war that is in itself a crime, or the 'crime of war'. Had the criminalization of wars of aggression in international law proceeded far enough by 1939 that the citizens should have understood it to be a crime? Had a war of aggression (by Nazi Germany) to count as a war crime, such that an individual citizen would have to consider his or her economically motivated participation in it as a criminal act, and thus would have to face criminal proceedings? Schmitt argues on the basis of the very principle of non-retroactivity 'nullum crimen, nulla poena sine lege', whose validity he himself had limited under National Socialism.[16] Now he calls this principle of the Rechtsstaat 'a maxim of natural law and morality' (WA, p. 196) and comes to the conclusion that the penalization of wars of aggression had not yet developed to the point that one could speak of it as a maxim of valid positive international law. Hence, Schmitt rules out any criminal proceedings against an economically active 'ordinary business-man'.[†] Schmitt's legal opinion, unsurprisingly, argued against a prosecution of his client Friedrich Flick.

Apart from the strategic reference to the principle of non-retroactivity, the text suggests another interesting criterion for political responsibility. Schmitt identifies the circle of perpetrators on the basis of their having had 'access to the political leadership' (WA, p. 196) within the personal form of rule within the 'Hitler regime'. Whoever had access to the top was a perpetrator. All others were merely participants. According to this very wide criterion, having had the opportunity to communicate with the top suffices to make someone a perpetrator. If so, then the advisor of an advisor – a

---

[*]   English in the original.
[†]   English in the original.

Prussian state councillor, for instance – would also potentially be a perpetrator, on account of his indirect access to the top. Schmitt remained silent about this possibility. He did not see himself as a perpetrator. An economically interested participant, such as the industrialist Flick, he did not see as a perpetrator either. Rather, he was of the opinion that, under conditions of political 'totality', the 'total' state and 'total' war, no one had a chance to remain neutral. Schmitt argued that citizens were forced to make an assumption in favour of the reasonability of the public declaration of enmity and had to renounce personal declarations of enmity. As long as a political leadership is identifiable and the state effectively exists, the relation between 'protection and obedience' remains in force. Hence, loyalty had been required even towards National Socialism.

In the camp

Denazification began with a period of 'automatic detention'. About 200,000 people were interned. Soon the automatic procedure was replaced with individual procedures based on questionnaires and tribunals at courts with lay assessors, leading to the questionable practice of whitewashing.[17] Schmitt was not automatically detained, but was arrested on 26 September 1945 and brought to the American interrogation center at Wannsee, Berlin, on the initiative of Karl Löwenstein, who was a legal adviser to the military government. His library was inspected by Löwenstein, confiscated,[18] and then collected on 18 October. On the same day, Schmitt was interrogated. It is possible that Löwenstein already knew Schmitt from his time in Munich, and he had studied his constitutional theory intensely. Even in his letter setting out the reasons for Schmitt's arrest he called him 'a man of near-genius rating'.[19] Thus, it was personal outrage over Schmitt's turn to National Socialism which led to his detainment. It was his Jewish acquaintances from the Weimar period who made sure that Schmitt was considered and treated as a perpetrator after 1945. On 31 October he was taken to the detention camp in Lichterfelde-Süd, Berlin, and at the beginning of 1946 to a 'civilian detention camp' at the Wannsee. He was allowed to write to his wife only once a month,[20] received only very little news, but kept a pocket calendar and diary. From autumn 1945, Anima attended a Catholic secondary school for girls in Cloppenburg. For the first time she was not at home over Christmas.[21] Duška had some positive family news: Anima, the family in Cologne and Schmitt's very old father in Plettenberg were all well.[22] Duška could also work as an interpreter for Dr Ferdinand Friedensburg, who had important positions in the post-war administration and became deputy lord mayor of Greater Berlin in December 1946. Schmitt made several applications for release. Duška argued for his release on the basis of the illness and then death of Schmitt's father on 6 December 1945. On 11 November she was allowed to visit Carl for the first time.[23] After his father's death, she spoke about moving to Plettenberg, but then, together with Anni Stand, who worked as a housemaid for the family again, remained in Berlin after all. She wanted to stay close to Carl. On 19

November she spoke with Löwenstein about Carl's situation and his case. On 20 November the Nuremberg trials against the main war criminals began. Schmitt knew at least three of them closely: Göring, Frick and Frank. Franz Schlegelberger and Franz von Papen were later also tried. On 14 December, Duška was again allowed to visit Schmitt and reported about it to Rudolf Smend.[24] At Christmas, she wrote to Carl: 'The pain we have suffered will be our treasure.'[25] At the end of December she told him about visits to exhibitions. Anima had inherited her inclination towards painting. Duška sent Melville's *Benito Cereno* to Schmitt. For January she was not granted permission to visit him,[26] but passed on news regarding the whereabouts of friends. At the end of January she thanked him 'for the 20 blessed years' of their marriage.[27]

Mr and Mrs Schmitt often lived apart and wrote regularly to each other. The volume of their correspondence must have been enormous. However, there are only very few letters from the camp among the posthumous papers in the archive at Düsseldorf. Looking back, Schmitt noted: 'These letters belong to my personal posthumous papers.'[28] He added them more as a documentation of his situation at the time than as a reflection of his marriage. Schmitt felt like an innocent being persecuted and considered his internment to be an injustice.[29] Every day he wrote down remarks in narrow lines on bad paper. The uncertainties and the slowness of the mail often required clarification of the state of correspondence: Which parcel had actually arrived? Who had written? Carl wrote: 'The separation of these bad times has only tied us closer together. So far, we have not disgraced ourselves, or lost our soul, despite many sufferings. That is what is most important.'[30] He was not desperate, he said, but he had worries. 'You cannot imagine the state of the soul of the inmates of the camp, most of whom soon fall prey to a camp psychosis [Lagerpsychose] and speculate about their fate* day and night, whereby the self-obsession of the Germans comes to light to a fantastic extent.' 'Self-obsession' became an important category for Schmitt at that time. He soon explained it as the *wisdom of the cell* and used it for the description of academic teachers in his characterological sketch '1907 Berlin'. Schmitt came across 'self-obsession' as an aspect of camp psychosis.

In minute detail, Schmitt reported on matters of clothing and food; he asked about the situation at home and instructed Duška regarding his correspondence. A letter of 8 February 1946 enquired about the fate of his colleagues. 'I would like to hear more details about how Siebeck [the director of the Charité], Smend, Siebert, Huber, Forsthoff are doing; but maybe it is still too early for that.' Schmitt wanted to know 'who of our faculty was present at the opening of the new university'.[31] Duška told him in a letter. He replied reassuringly that journals and books were available, and that his encounters in the camp were often stimulating. Schmitt drafted a 'report on Benito Cereno in the context of intellectual history',[32] addressed to the theologian Erich Przywara, which put Bruno Bauer's 'writings on Jewry' at

---

* The German is 'Kombinationen schmieden' – however, we are not told of what the 'combinations' are combinations.

the centre. In the camp he studied Theodor Däubler again, together with his colleague from the Charité and former vice-chancellor of the university Lothar Kreuz.[33] To Duška he wrote: 'I think you would be happy with my condition . . . Soon the sixth month of my imprisonment will begin, and I am still not demoralized or dejected like so many of the others.'[34] As a surprise he could report: 'My old enemy Koellreutter sent me a long letter to the camp.'[35] None of the others, he added, had the idea of writing to him. Walz was sitting in Rottweil, Heckel had been acquitted by an American military court, Forsthoff was allegedly back in his post at Heidelberg; 'of Huber, I have not heard anything.' Schmitt went through almost all of the jurists in this fashion. He asked Duška to send Koellreutter his thanks. During the following years, Koellreutter's surprising initiative led to closer contacts between the two.

At that point, Schmitt did not yet think that he would be permanently excluded from working at universities, but he wrote: 'The whole bustle among colleagues has become alien to me, and I would find it humiliating to try and get a place from an alien conqueror.' Schmitt interpreted his situation in religious terms: 'Tout ce qui arrive est adorable',* he quoted from Léon Bloy. Duška, around that time, found some comfort in the Orthodox Church.[36] Schmitt's later letters from the camp sound more depressed. On a tiny piece of paper he wrote: 'Two lawyers, defence counsels, from Nuremberg were here and talked about the possibility that I may take part in the defence.'[37] In these words one can hear the faint hope that he might get another opportunity for a great appearance, this time as a lawyer for the defence at Nuremberg. What an absurd idea! Schmitt did not lament, but was glad to have survived the harsh winter of starvation. For a couple of months, Anni Stand was not in Berlin and regularly sent food parcels. Duška planted vegetables. The Schmitts' neighbours, the Blischke family and Marlies Rosenhahn, were still living in Schlachtensee. In a letter of 15 May,[38] Schmitt spoke in caustic terms about the next forthcoming interrogation: 'I look forward to the date without any great worries, insofar as the continuation of my present condition is concerned.' His persecutors would 'personally take care that I shall perish in a cold way. God has helped me again and, as during the Nazi period, has turned what was not evil anyhow towards the good.' Some of his colleagues, therefore, might as well display their hate, 'after they have breathed fire and brimstone for twelve years, like everyone else'. Schmitt developed an attitude of aggressive resentment that would not leave him in the coming years. Berlin was poisoned for him. He expressed only a 'longing for the Sauerland' and wanted to work academically again. 'Often I have bouts of productivity', he wrote. 'Then I feel a pain, as if an abyss had been ripped open, especially when I think of my readers. . . . Everything I have written, the *Concept of the Political*, etc., is given unexpected and new confirmation by our present situation.'

At the beginning of June he again made an application for release.[39] The attacks on him in *Das Schwarze Korps* now served as his central exculpatory material.[40] Ferdinand Friedensburg stood up for Schmitt; Hans Peters

---

* Whatever happens is admirable.

declared himself 'also to be in favour of your release'.[41] A whole string of supporting letters exists.[42] Some of the inmates wrote poems for Schmitt's birthday. Schmitt was summoned to Zehlendorf, where he defended himself skilfully. 'The investigating committee [Prüfungsausschuss] has unanimously suggested your release', Duška reported to Schmitt in the camp.[43] On 2 August, Schmitt's release was ordered, but he was not immediately set free. Duška wrote: 'In Plettenberg we are joyfully expected',[44] but on 4 September she still had to write: 'This morning I had a beautiful dream about you coming home.'[45] When the camp in Lichterfelde was closed, Schmitt was again brought to Wannsee, on 12 September. Because the sick were meant to be released first, Duška organized medical certificates.[46] On 10 October 1946, after more than a year, Schmitt was let out.[47]

'Letters from detention': the 'authentic case of a Christian Epimetheus'

Schmitt was banned from writing in the camp. Nevertheless, large parts of *Ex captivitate salus* were written there. A 'philanthropic American camp doctor . . . made it possible, to make notes and . . . to get letters and notes out of the camp without the camp's administration being involved.' The doctor had thus performed a 'providential task', Schmitt wrote in the preface to the Spanish edition in 1958.[48] Schmitt composed a 'number of letters' on the leaves of a prescription pad and later sent off transcripts of the individual parts. He told Ernst Jünger that the notes 'had come about driven by phonetically determined dreams, thus, for instance, a note on Tocqueville, another about two graves in Berlin (the grave of Kleist[49] and the grave of Däubler), about two professors from my first term at the university in Berlin, whose voices I can still hear' (JS, p. 195). The individual chapters are dated according to the time when they were written; their temporal sequence is evidenced by an extant manuscript.[50] The memoir '1907 Berlin' was not included in the small book. *Ex captivitate salus* is a response to the request of an 'accuser', 'discloser' [Durchleuchter] and 'know-all' – i.e., Spranger, the first post-war vice-chancellor of Berlin University,[51] with whom Schmitt had been in close contact until 1933 – to fill in a questionnaire. Instead of providing answers, however, Schmitt presents his 'case' in formulaic terms: 'It is the bad, undignified, and yet authentic case of a Christian Epimetheus' (ECS, p. 12).[52] In Greek mythology, Epimetheus did not listen to the warnings of his brother, Prometheus, and let in the beautiful Pandora, who was the bringer of all of the evils Zeus administered as revenge. If we read Schmitt's text as an explication of this formula, then, in the first place, it wants to indicate (in the form of a belated response to Karl Mannheim)[53] that curiosity and scholarship formed the basis of his work. Next, he compares himself to the historian Tocqueville. Like him, Schmitt had made his prognosis as someone 'defeated' and then raised the theme of the decline of the West. Schmitt reflects on the suicide epidemics and graves among the 'heap of rubble' that was Berlin, identifies with Kleist and Däubler, and characterizes the present as a time of civil war,

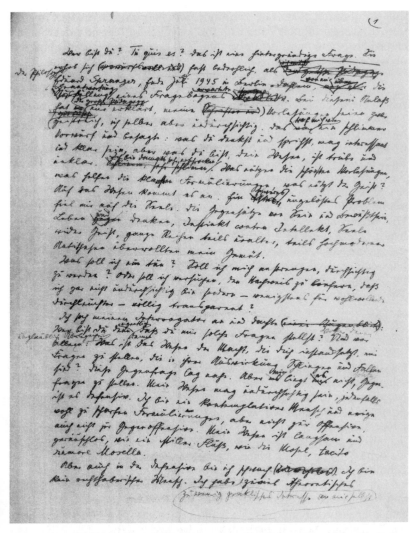

'Who are you?' Manuscript of Schmitt's reply to the Rektor [vice-chancellor] of
Berlin University, Eduard Spranger, in the summer of 1945

of the deprivation of rights [Entrechtung] and of political justice. He sees
his situation in parallel to that of Bodin and Hobbes, who were the first
representatives of the *jus publicum Europaeum*, while Schmitt sees himself
as its 'last teacher and scholar in an existential sense'. In the concluding
chapter, 'Wisdom of the Cell', written in spring 1947 while imprisoned in
Nuremberg, he criticizes the modern idea of 'mankind saving itself'. In
summary, his self-apology runs roughly like this: I am a scholar; in political
terms I am someone who has been defeated and who, in the context of a
situation of civil war at the end of the rule of European international law,

asks the question of the fate of Europe from the perspective of a Christian faith in 'salvific support', and with the 'katechontic' idea of a delay of the end of history in mind, and who thus opts against the Adamitic longings of Western civilization.

In *Ex captivitate salus*, Schmitt characterizes the enemy for the first time as his 'own question as form' [eigne Frage als Gestalt] (ECS, p. 90; TP, p. 85).* He would later repeat this formula again and again. In *Glossarium*, Schmitt quotes from a Däubler poem: 'The enemy is our own question as form. / And he will hound us, and we him, to the same end' [Der Feind ist unsere eigene Frage als Gestalt. / Und er wird uns, wir ihn, zum selben Ende hetzen.][54] Even meditation is seen as a way of becoming entangled in the snares of 'self-delusion', caused by the attempt to establish one's identity in the battle for recognition. Schmitt ends with an interpretation of autobiographical experience, a condensed piece of history in metric form. His 'Gesang eines Sechzigjährigen' [Song of a sexagenarian] is a religious hymn. 'Three times I sat in the belly of the fish', he wrote. 'Suicide by the hangman's hands, I looked it in the eye. / But the protective words of sibylline poets received me, / and a saint from the East, opening the doors, saved me.' Schmitt is referring here to the times of crisis in 1918–19, 1936–7 and 1945. The reference to the 'saint from the East' remains obscure.

'I am here as what?' Return and renewed arrest

On 10 October 1946, Schmitt was back from the camp. As a 'freelance scholar (provider of legal opinions)', he received category 3 ration cards.[55] But there was no way he would stay in the 'heap of rubble' that was Berlin. A return to the reopened, sovietized university was unlikely. Berlin was altogether unsafe. In this situation, Plettenberg offered an alternative. Schmitt's parents had died; his brother practised as a medical doctor in Cologne.[56] The parental home in Brockhauserweg had been inherited by Schmitt's sisters,[57] but there was enough space. His sister Anna sent a telegram: 'Come as soon as possible.'[58] Schmitt's former adjutant Bernhard von Mutius wrote from Munich: 'The fact that you have survived shows that your historical mission as a witness of events has not yet come to an end.'[59] Schmitt stayed in Berlin for another five months.

On 17 March 1947, Schmitt was summoned for an 'interrogation'[60] by Ossip K. Flechtheim, whose doctoral thesis Schmitt had once failed. The interrogation took place on 24 March, and on 29 March Schmitt was transported, 'strictly legally, by railway'[61] across the zonal border to the 'Palace of Justice' in Nuremberg. He remained in custody in Nuremberg

---

* The translator of *Theory of the Partisan* opted for a paraphrase of this expression – 'the enemy defines us' – and adds a useful footnote explaining Schmitt's meaning, quoting from the post-war notebooks *Glossarium*: '*Historia in nuce* [history in a nutshell]. Friend and enemy. The friend is he who affirms and confirms me. The enemy is he who challenges me (Nuremberg 1947). Who can challenge me? Basically only myself. The enemy is he who defines me. That means *in concreto*: only my brother can challenge me and only my brother can be my enemy' (TP, p. 85, fn. 89).

for five weeks and was interrogated four times by the chief prosecutor Robert Kempner. Neither the legal basis nor the purpose for the arrest was clear. Schmitt was called a 'possible defendant',* and there were plans to bring him before the court either as an accused or as a witness. Duška asked the jurist Hermann Jahrreiß to make enquiries.[62] Kempner requested written answers to a few questions from Schmitt. He wanted to win him, against his will, as an expert witness for the upcoming Wilhelmstraße trial against the state secretaries. Some letters to Duška that have been preserved point in that direction.

Kempner's interrogations touched upon various questions. In the first one, on 3 April, Schmitt called National Socialism his 'platform' [Tribüne]; he thought it possible at the time to give 'meaning to the phrases' of national socialism (AN, p. 54). Later, he called himself an 'intellectual adventurer' (AN, p. 60) and added: 'I wanted to give the term National Socialism my own meaning' (AN, p. 65). Schmitt asked bluntly: 'I am here as what? As an accused?' Kempner asked him to explain his contribution to the 'theoretical underpinning of Hitler's Großraum politics'. In the second interrogation, on 11 April, Kempner asked Schmitt about the connection between his texts from before and after 1933, and about the theoretical justification of wars of aggression.[63] For the third interrogation, on 21 April, Schmitt brought along his written answers. Kempner asked Schmitt, as an 'expert' in 'state law' (AN, p. 61), about his opinion regarding the responsibility of leading civil servants such as Lammers and Ernst von Weizsäcker, formulating a thesis in his question which partly anticipates the answer: 'Lammers held the handle to the door of the dictator' (ibid.). By the fourth interrogation, on 29 April, Schmitt had written down his answer, which he would later publish in revised form. 'I am glad to have found a reader again' (AN, p. 64), he said, thus redefining their roles: Kempner was now no longer an interrogator, but a reader and partner in discussion.

Until the third interrogation, Schmitt did not know what, exactly, Kempner wanted from him. During that time he wrote his meditation 'Weisheit der Zelle' [Wisdom of the Cell], the last chapter of his interpretation of his experiences in *Ex captivitate salus*. Letters to Duška from that period reflect his uncertainty.[64] Schmitt reassured her that he was having a nice Easter. 'In the morning I hear the Easter bells ringing from the churches of Nuremberg and the birds' song from the prison yard' (6 April 1947). He asked her to pray for him, and requested Latin texts. It was cold, he wrote, but the blankets were good. Schmitt reminisced about music, wanted a pair of glasses and some envelopes. He spent an hour every day in the prison yard, he said. On 20 April he thanked Duška for a parcel and assured her: 'I have kept up well so far and haven't lost courage. The psychological and moral resources I have collected in my life are very large, and loneliness was always my friend, one of whom you weren't even jealous, dear Duška.' He was not bored for a second in his solitary confinement, he assured her, and welcomed the fact that Duška planned to move to Plettenberg. Schmitt thought of Anima and his brother Jupp, remembered Strasbourg. 'I no

* English in the original.

longer make plans; God is better at that than us botchers.' Schmitt asked about relatives, and his thoughts went back to his time in Bonn. It was only after the third interrogation that he knew with more certainty that he would not be put on trial. He told Anima about reading a book from his youth again, remembered Berlin, sent greetings. Duška sent documents for his defence.[65] She was just moving into a two-room flat at that time.[66] On 4 May, Schmitt was still not able to say much about his situation, but reported a 'strange occurrence' [merkwürdige Begegnung] in church: 'A Palm Sunday poem by Konrad Weiß was written down on a worn-out page in an old newspaper' – 'I remembered his "Christian Epimetheus", the copy worn by many readings, which accompanied me for so long.' He again had the idea of seeing himself as a 'Christian Epimetheus'.

On 6 May, Schmitt was moved to a house 'for voluntary witnesses',[67] where he was able to move around the 'terribly destroyed' Nuremberg like a day-release prisoner but was not yet fully released. He soon found himself in the comfortable 'situation of a voluntary witness' who received 'witness money'. Schmitt met Jahrreiß and attended a talk by 'Professor Lortz from Münster, an acquaintance of Eschweiler from the time in Braunsberg'. The meeting had consequences: Lortz would later provide intermediate storage for Schmitt's library. On 13 May, after the interrogations had been completed, a final conversation with Kempner took place in the witness house. Schmitt was meant to write another statement on the question 'Why did the German state secretaries follow Hitler?' Schmitt was released the same day, and his travel expenses to Plettenberg were reimbursed. Duška was then busy with packing up the household. However, Schmitt told her not to waste too much time with the furniture. 'The most important thing is you yourself, beautiful Duška.' Schmitt was content. The detention had 'not so far [ended] badly' for him.

'I knew a few things about the legal, semi-legal and illegal means of power': Schmitt's statements in Nuremberg

Schmitt had to answer four questions while in detention: To what extent did he support the theoretical underpinning of Hitler's Großraum politics? Was he involved in a central position in the preparation of the war of aggression and the crimes associated with it? What was the position of the Reich minister and the chief of the Reich chancellery? Why did the German state secretaries follow Hitler? While the last two questions concern, rather, the analysis of the NS system, the first two concern Schmitt's personal contacts and situation within National Socialism, and his answers give us some information about those. Schmitt, on his own initiative, laid open his 'personal relationships' with central figures of National Socialism. And he referred to his 'financial situation' as key to an understanding of his situation: 'I was a state councillor, with no possessions worth plundering' (AN, p. 71).*

---

* The formulation is no less awkward in German.

Schmitt distinguished his Großraum theory from 'three types of theoretical underpinning': from party doctrine, from 'advocatory or apologetic statements', and from the approaches of the SS jurists Höhn and Best. His remarks on the SS are particularly enlightening:

> In 1936, I was publicly defamed by the SS. I knew a few things about the legal, semi-legal and illegal means of power employed by the SS and the circles around Himmler, and I had every reason to fear the interests of the new elite. This is why, with all due caution, I kept my distance. I avoided the political head of the group, Best. I never spoke a word with him or shook his hand. Prof. Höhn I saw occasionally as a colleague at the Juridical Faculty of Berlin University. I behaved in a polite and correct way towards him, as one reasonably does towards a member or associate of the secret police. (AN, pp. 76ff.)

Schmitt's statements are detailed and trustworthy.

Schmitt's second answer provides more detail, in particular on his relationship with Göring and Frank. It also contains interesting statements. Thus, for instance, he defends his interest in the institution of a state council, calling it a 'counter-balance to party activities' (AN, p. 86). However, it was also an alternative to the ministerial bureaucracy. Schmitt openly wrote: 'My position depended entirely and exclusively on the personal interest shown in me, often very demonstratively, by Frank . . . From the end of 1936, I no longer worked with Frank and there was also little private contact' (AN, pp. 86f.) The key role Frank played for Schmitt was thus identified by Schmitt himself, even if in slightly obscure and understated terms. He admitted that he might have some '"ideological" responsibility' (AN, p. 89) on account of his theories and ideas, but not in a sense that would be 'justiciable' in the sense of the charges brought forward at the Nuremberg trials (GL, p. 258). He was very cautious in his statements at Nuremberg, did not question the authority of the court, and carefully avoided giving any impression that charges could be pressed against him when expressing his expert opinion on the questions he was asked. In his third answer Schmitt explained how the Reich Chancellery was a centre of power. Access to the dictator was a key question in every case of a 'personal regime' [Regiment]. Hitler's methods of governing, he wrote, were in clear 'contradiction' to the principles of a civil service state. Hitler's system knew 'no binding forms or institutions' and replaced the bureaucratic mode of governing with an arbitrary 'entangled net' [Durch- und Nebeneinander] of orders and decrees. The system, Schmitt wrote, was characterized by the 'fundamental discrepancy between the omnipotence of the Führer and a state-based mechanism of legality [staatlicher Legalisierungsordnung]' (AN, p. 99). It was of 'fundamental abnormity'. The state secretaries, according to Schmitt, followed Hitler because they fell for 'Hitler's-legality-protestations' (AN, p. 103)[*] and, out of a traditional 'German urge for legality', confused the tyrannical system with a functioning civil service state. Schmitt analysed the system as a 'double state' of, on the one hand,

---

[*] I have retained the unusual hyphenation of the German: 'Hitlers-Legalitäts-Beteuerungen'.

chaotic tyranny and, on the other, slavish obedience. As for himself, he claimed that he did not fall for the façade of normality, which he had once helped to erect. Regarding his first years under the new regime, he spoke of a 'disgrace' [Blamage]. However, again and again he mentioned the key experience of 1936 and the threat which the SS posed for him. 'When did you disavow the devil?', Kempner asked him directly during the interrogation. '1936', was Schmitt's short answer (AN, p. 66). Kempner referred to the moral substance of the Faust legend, at the time applied to National Socialism by Thomas Mann in his *Doctor Faustus*. Schmitt avoided it,[68] because he rejected retrospective moral evaluations and preferred simply to analyse the political dealings of the past. In the following years he collected and annotated newspaper articles on various 'cases' to do with National Socialism – such as that of Veit Harlan, Werner Krauss, Schlegelberger and others – and added them to the notebook with his handwritten expert opinion.[69]

'Asylum' in Plettenberg

On 21 May, Schmitt was back in Plettenberg, Brockhauser Weg 10, near the train station and the river. There was little space for everyone. On the second floor, the house, which the parents had built with the help of their children in the 1930s, narrowed into an attic flat. Schmitt's sisters Anna and Auguste, one a piano teacher, one a primary school teacher, lived on the ground floor, Carl and Duška in the attic flat. To begin with, Anima still went to school in Cloppenburg and moved to Plettenberg only at Easter 1948. There was a piano room on the ground floor, occasionally also used by Schmitt. From the attic, he could overlook the valley. The house and garden were on a slightly sloping mountainside. Schmitt enjoyed his quiet room and, as a passionate walker, his hiking tours, especially to the top of the (about 500 metres high) Saley mountain, to the Bommecktal or along the River Lenne to the ruin of Schwarzenberg Castle. For a long time he avoided the telephone, radio and television. Living with his two sisters was not without conflict. In Berlin, Schmitt had maids and a cook. Only after Duška had died did Anni Stand join him again and take charge of the household.

Within months, acquaintances from close by showed signs of life. On 6 June 1947, Hans Barion got in touch.[70] He had lost his chair in Bonn, but continued to be a priest and representative of an 'authoritarian-institutional decisionism' (Thomas Marschler) within the Church. He, too, felt unjustly treated and excluded and, even after years of legal proceedings, did not return to a university. To no one else did Schmitt speak as intensely and openly about his involvement with National Socialism as with Barion. A theoretical point of reference was Rudolph Sohm, against whose Protestant separation of powers both Schmitt and Barion set their Catholic approach. Barion sent Schmitt books by Kafka and Melville, and Schmitt imagined a continuation of Melville's *Benito Cereno*: 'B. C. at a trial, accused of piracy' (30 November 1947; GL, p. 55). Barion responded:

'As far, however, as the "Benito Cereno situation" is concerned, I ended up in it only after the end of the war; before, I could find no Babo who would have been able to put his razor to my throat.'[71] Some of Schmitt's pupils got in touch again, such as Hans Schneider, Werner Weber, and many others.[72] In the following years, Schmitt met with Carl Bilfinger, Carl Brinkmann and other former colleagues. He also was in closer contact with Koellreutter now. Of the younger National Socialist jurists it was in particular Gottfried Neeße who sought a correspondence with Schmitt, which, however, turned out to be rather one-sided.[73] With Fraenger, Schmitt began to discuss Bosch again. Schmitt's Berlin pupil Herbert Gremmels visited him in Plettenberg, and Hubertus Bung[74] offered him a 'Persilschein'.* The furniture from Berlin arrived only in September 1947; the grand piano remained in Berlin for the time being.[75] From October 1947, Duška was permanently in Plettenberg, putting an end to the Berlin years. Schmitt would never again set foot in Berlin, where he had lived for nearly twenty years. The household had to be re-established in a makeshift way. In November, for instance, they had coal, but no oven. Nevertheless, in comparison to the 'heap of rubble' that was Berlin, Schmitt experienced Plettenberg as an asylum. At last he was back in his native landscape and was able to go hiking. Most importantly, he lived in a place where his biography was not known in any detail and where no one reproached him.

By the end of 1947, the household had consolidated itself. Schmitt wrote: 'Mrs Schmitt did really succeed in establishing a dwelling here. The Fish by Gilles, the Leviathan by Nay, the wonderful Diamant by Nay, everything surrounds me again. Like a U-boat that continuously rebuilds itself, I continue on my submarine, subterranean, sub-lunar voyage through fire and water' (GJCS, p. 100). For an article in *Merian*, Schmitt later wrote about his 'Welt großartigster Spannung' [World of most enormous tension]:[76]

We are pulled into an elementary course of events and are made participants in a process of creation. We do not see the first, but we do see the second day. Solid earth emerges from the sea. The mountainous tops slowly rise, in graceful beauty, like a Venus Anadyomene, from the waters. The division between the realm of the heavens and the dry land occurs . . . The mountains rest in firm earth, but they are veiled, often in rain, fog or snow, often in sunshine of crystal purity. At certain hours they lie there like turtles in their massive impact; at other hours, they become pale, as if they were a dream of the sea. Often their heavy massif turns into a silver-blue or into an unearthly deep patina blue. However, all is more radiance than colour. (SGN, p. 515)

Schmitt owed the 'elementary' perspective of his late work to the experience of this landscape, similar to the way that Heidegger referred to the 'creative landscape' of the Black Forest.

Schmitt's financial situation was difficult. But even his old Catholic friends offered him help. Wilhelm Neuß wrote a report in support of

---

* Colloquial expression after the war for a 'whitewash' of someone's National Socialist involvement in the form of a certificate.

Schmitt; Peterson sent money from Italy.[77] Some former students offered him 'Persilscheine'.[78] The financial difficulties contributed to the formation of solidarity. Schmitt considered this first time in Plettenberg as one of 'the best in [his] life'.[79] On 11 July 1948 he celebrated his sixtieth birthday with a small circle of friends. There were a few toasts, and Schmitt read out his 'Gesang eines Sechzigjährigen' [Song of a sexagenarian] (ECS, pp. 92f.). Ernst Forsthoff, Rolf Stödter[80] and Hans Peter Ipsen got in touch again.[81] Ulrich Scheuner remarked to Schmitt that he saw his work woven into the risks of politics and the 'dissolution of Europe'.[82] Werner Weber very much regretted that the Festschrift that he had planned years ago, together 'with Jens Jessen and other common friends', now could not be realized.[83] Schmitt's colleague from Berlin reminisced: 'Not least, generations of students will on this day gratefully remember their teacher. During my time in Berlin, I have often been told by your students how much you gave to them in your lectures, tutorials and seminars.' As the dean of many years, he thanked Schmitt for continuing until the end with his 'lectures with a sense of duty that was as joyful as it was tenacious'.[84]

Gremmels began publishing again. However, Schmitt agreed with his book *Der Leviathan und die totale Demobilmachung* [The Leviathan and total demobilization] only insofar as it was a very last 'sign that your generation is not dead and not only coordinated, but has a voice of its own'.[85] Schmitt's pupils from Berlin did have a tough time after 1945. In political terms, they no longer had a home. Their critique of the legal system was overtaken by historical developments. Those who stayed in opposition, such as Günther Krauss, marginalized themselves. In 1947, Schmitt's former assistant Gustav von Schmoller founded an 'Institut für Besatzungsfragen' [Institute for Matters of Occupation] in Tübingen, which, as the name suggests, remained limited to questions relevant during the transitional period.[86] In 1952 von Schmoller moved to the Foreign Office, and in 1964 he became the ambassador to Sweden; however, in 1968 his past caught up with him when he was publicly criticized in Sweden for his activities in Prague during the war, and he resigned from his post.[87] Another of Schmitt's pupils from Berlin, Helmut Rumpf, converted to Catholicism. Schmitt's comments on this were also rather pointed. He had experienced many conversions, 'beginning with Theodor Haecker in 1916 and ending with comrades in the camp in 1946'. He wouldn't want to intervene 'in the incomprehensibility of such mysterious individual events', however: 'I consider it of importance to tell you that you are now a Catholic but not a theologian. As far as I can see, you remain a jurist.'[88] For three years Schmitt met frequently with Gerhard Nebel, whom he had already encountered in 1943 in Berlin. Nebel belonged to the Jünger circle, was a friend of Gremmels, lived close by in Wuppertal, and was a soldier, a wanderer, a wine-lover and a man of letters.[89] Jünger supported their contact.[90] Schmitt and Nebel met for the first time in September 1947 in Wuppertal. Very soon, in April 1948, Nebel spoke of 'friendship',[91] but at the same time he reported to Jünger about Schmitt's resentment: 'He lives, while comparing himself to you; he almost suffers because of you, because you, rather than him, have become the German myth.'[92] Nebel was working on a biography of Jünger at the time and repeatedly met him in Wuppertal. Schmitt was sceptical about Nebel's approach. 'I am still thinking about the conversations with Ernst Jünger', he wrote to Gremmels in 1948: 'He really is a monad, and one should not expect more human warmth from him than he actually has. Maybe, in this respect, Gerhard Nebel expects too much of him.'[93] Nebel invited Schmitt to Wuppertal for a meeting with Jünger: 'We are planning a series of enormous celebrations.'[94] He very much regretted it when Schmitt could not attend: 'I hope there will be another opportunity.'[95] Nebel completed his biography in March 1949[96] and then spent three nice spring days visiting 'the old man from Plettenberg'.[97]

The ABC of the post-war situation

With the help of Hans Schneider, Schmitt, under a pseudonym, published a fairly extensive revision book on international law, in a print-run of 2,000 copies. 'The editor does not know the author.'[98] Barion wrote the companion volume on canon law, Schneider the one on constitutional and administrative law. The revision book was the longest legal text Schmitt wrote after 1945. Surprisingly, the work on it was not integrated into *The Nomos of the Earth*. However, before he bade farewell to the state, Schmitt had to come to terms with the post-war situation. As a prelude, in 1948, he mocked the ideology of the 'just war' and the 'Völkerrecht der Zukunft im Unterricht der Zukunft' [International law of the future in the education of the future] in a circular letter, whose form parodied Kleist's *Katechismus des Deutschen* [Catechism of the Germans].[99] His revision book, the 'ABC of International Law' (FP, p. 701), was a precise analysis of the post-war situation. Schmitt gave a detailed presentation of the inter-state character of international law following the foundation of the United Nations. Although there were 'inroads' towards a 'future primacy of international law' (FP, p. 709), the individual states still remained the legal subjects [tragende Subjekte]. For its implementation, international law continued to require the 'transformation' and 'intercalation' of the state. It was, however, Schmitt said, a very 'imperfect' right. A 'world state' was nowhere in sight. Schmitt discussed statehood in great detail, using historical examples. In this context, he also referred to Germany's legal situation after 1945.[100] He tested his central thesis of the inter-state character of international law and of the state as the 'protagonist of the great drama' (FP, p. 724) by looking at non-state subjects in international law. Schmitt discussed piracy as the 'primordial type of a so-called world crime' (FP, p. 765) and actually had the recent war crimes in mind when doing so.

In contrast to 1945, Schmitt now looked back on the great trials. His target was less the legal basis of the Nuremberg court: he granted victorious powers the right to military tribunals. Rather, he asked about the long-term consequences of the judgments passed at Nuremberg: the prosecution had drawn a small circle around potential perpetrators, a fact about which Schmitt seems almost astonished. But, using the punishable offence of a 'crime against peace', the Nuremberg trial treated the perpetrators as 'immediate' subjects of international law by putting them, like pirates, outside the legal order and ostracizing them as 'enemies of mankind'. Schmitt simply stated: 'Here, the state was successfully dethroned' (FP, p. 772). The end of state-centred international law had begun. The United Nations's declaration of human rights, however, only formulated 'a kind of moral codex'; it was not 'immediately valid law' (FP, p. 775) because a world citizen right as immediately valid international law had 'so far not been created' (FP, p. 776): 'The protection of every individual's human rights, offering the same efficacy as intra-state guarantees, would probably only be possible in a centralized world state with a world constitution. As long as states are recognized as the immediate subjects of international law, the individual citizen or person subjected to the state [staatsunterworfene Mensch] will be mediated by international law' (ibid.). The military tribunals, he wrote, assumed a new form of immediacy, but all in all the legal foundation of modern times remained in place: 'The state is still the legal subject [tragende Subjekt] of today's international legal order and decides its structure' (FP, p. 777). The occupation of Germany, therefore, could not be a 'permanent condition', and the occupation would have to end with a peace treaty. Thus, Schmitt identified points where 'classical' international law began to crumble, but he nevertheless still considered it valid. His later farewell to the concept of the state therefore comes as something of a surprise, especially as the situation did not really change after 1950. Nowhere else did Schmitt juridically analyse the post-war constellation in such detail. Very discreetly, the little word 'immediately' turned up again. Hans Schneider soon wanted a sequel to the revision book: 'The publisher has already sent his fourth reminder . . . I would be much obliged if you could send something off, no matter what the manuscript looks like.'[101] On 27 March 1951 he wrote again: 'Freymark is breathing down my neck. When will the next manuscript "International Law" arrive? How should I respond? I have to fulfil my contractual obligations somehow or cancel the contract.'[102] That, however, was not one of Schmitt's worries. After the publication of *The Nomos of the Earth*, the topic of international law was done and dusted for him.

'Quartered and trampled underfoot, but not destroyed': Schmitt's look back in *Glossarium*

From 1942, at the latest, until the 1980s, Schmitt again kept his stenographic diary, almost without interruption.[103] He also kept a diary in the camp and in Nuremberg. In Plettenberg, in 1947, he began a diary of intellectual reflections, the *Glossarium*, which he kept, with minor breaks and changes in form, until 1958. Even in their external appearance, the five volumes of the *Glossarium* differ from the other diaries; they are written in longhand, in heavy, black notebooks. Encounters and letters serve as impulses for their reflections. Schmitt noted down numerous replies to letters, so that the *Glossarium* oscillates between monologue and dialogue.

It almost overflows with different themes and references. In it, Schmitt developed the central categories of his late work.

Schmitt considered the 'destruction of asylum' [Asylzerstörung] – i.e., the impossibility to retreat into the private sphere – as the sign of the post-war era. Everywhere, he suspected victor's justice to be at work, and he criticized the idea of a 'just war' as a method of criminalization and discrimination. 'The victor of a just war turns himself into a judge' (GL, p. 70). Schmitt presented the resulting 'international law of the future' in a dialogical style, similar to that of Kleist, and distributed it among his circle. He also published an article on 'Amnestie' [Amnesty].[104] Again and again, he defended his engagement after the Preußenschlag. The 'great yes-men [Jasager]* of 1933' (GL, p. 197) were genuinely enthusiastic: 'How harmless were those who sensed the opportunity for intellectual change at the awakening [Aufbruch] in Germany in 1933, in comparison to those who took intellectual revenge on Germany in 1945' (GL, p. 216). In his 'cooperation with Frank', however, he had fallen prey to a 'self-delusion' (GL, p. 174); he had, he wrote, put 'the Caliban to the test', an attempt that was doomed to fail. After 1936 he had broken with National Socialism, and yet, he thought, he was being criminalized *ex post facto*.

Schmitt reflected intensely about a general return and restoration of Christian thought and ideas of natural law, and he reformulated the 'natural law' of theology on the basis of his juridical categories of legality and legitimacy. A novel idea was his critique of post-war concepts as ideology. The future appeared 'utopian' to him, and, within the context of intellectual history, the contemporary utopia, or rather dystopia, seemed represented by total planning. 'That is the logical consequence of Brave new World',† Schmitt wrote to the teacher Marie Stewens:

Look out for this aspect some time: the relationship between utopias and human nature (education, breeding, finally fabrication of the homunculus). In Morus still a classical humanist idea; in Defoe (Robinson) already a construction on the basis of the isolated individual; in Swift already a fantastic change of the human being itself (giants, dwarfs, horses); in Aldous Huxley the planned scientific production of standardized human beings. It is, in other words, total planning. (GL, p. 47)

– which, with Hitler, turned into total destruction. In this way, Schmitt made modern humanism partly responsible for National Socialism, and, in the face of the alternative between a theocentric or anthropocentric picture of the world, he opted for a sharp critique of humanism. He looked at the debates of the post-war era in the light of historical parallels: 'Should it be the case again', he wrote,

that we, in Germany, now suffer the communist revolution, which was due in 1918, miserably from foreign hands and posthumously, that we blindly repeat

---

* Schmitt's use of the term hints more at Nietzschean affirmation than at obedience.
† 'Brave new World' in English in the original.

[nachexerzieren], as we did when we realized the bourgeois revolution, which was due in 1848, during the collapse of 1918–19? Or shall we posthumously reproduce it in a wholly utopian-romantic fashion within the context of entirely different developments, the way we experienced the peasants' revolt of 1525 in the form of the 'Reich Food Estate' of 1933, or the thirty-year revolt of the Saxons against Charlemagne in the form of the Nordic Society in the Böttchergasse or the Anabaptists' scandal* of 1534 in the form of the defence of Berlin in 1945? (GL, p. 72)

In such notes Schmitt condensed his picture of history.

Schmitt reflected on the future of Germany by looking at the fate of Czechoslovakia. 'With Masaryk's suicide,[†] the epoch in which there was a third alternative to West and East has come to an end', he noted.

> Masaryk, the father, was a genuine European katechon, the katechon of European liberal democracy . . . The son . . . was the guarantor for this option for the West: with Benesch designated by Masaryk as his successor. And now this epoch ends with the son jumping out of the window of the Czernin Palais. That is more than the former defenestrations of Prague . . . Which wars will be caused by this third defenestration? (GL, pp. 113f.)

Schmitt thus buried any hopes for a 'third way' and concentrated on an intellectual understanding of the situation. 'We are defeated, have been thrown to the ground, subjugated, quartered and trampled underfoot, but we are in no essential respect destroyed, in particular not morally or juridically. We are occupied, but not conquered. Only he who knows his bounty better than himself is able to conquer' (GL, p. 115). Schmitt tied his 'mental self-affirmation' to his understanding of the Nuremberg trials, which he saw as victor's justice. 'The master of the Nuremberg trial was the Soviet Union', Schmitt wrote, 'which made good use of American moral outrage' (GL, p. 117). Wilhelm Grewe, he said, had recognized this,[105] and he, Schmitt himself, had, in his legal opinion of 1945, 'saved the honour of European jurisprudence' (GL, p. 143).

Schmitt's ideology critique always aimed at clarity; he emphasized that all political perception was generally distorted while remaining blind to his own obsessive prejudices. He looked at the historical forces, not least from the perspective of religious history, while rejecting, however, the dominant theological discourses as moralizing. At that time he discussed his ideas mostly in conversations with Barion, whom he considered to be a 'jurist of theology', in contrast to himself as a 'theologian of jurisprudence' (GL, p. 23). 'I have always spoken and written as a jurist, and, as a consequence, ultimately only to and for jurists. My misfortune

---

* Schmitt probably meant the so-called Münster Rebellion in which the Anabaptists took hold of the city and established an independent government, which, however, fell in 1535. The exact correspondences, as throughout this linguistically and – in a manner of speaking – intellectually catachretic passage, are not clear.

† There was widespread suspicion at the time that Jan Masaryk had been murdered, and a forensic investigation by the Prague police in 2004 concluded that this was, indeed, the case.

was that the jurists of my time had become positivist technological operators of laws [Gesetzeshandhabungstechniker], deeply ignorant and uneducated, in the best cases Goetheans and neutralized humanitarians' (GL, p. 17). Schmitt was no theologian in the sense of a historian of religion or a dogmatic exegete. As a 'theologian of jurisprudence', he described the historical conditions of legal validity and affirmed and interpreted it as a trans-individual and non-negotiable [unverfügbaren] 'sense' of history. The *Glossarium* expresses Schmitt's consciousness of the end of the Goethean era and of the disappointment of the hope placed on Hölderlin and Hegel. He suffered from the fact that he no longer belonged to the age of Goethe and not yet to that of technology, and that, as a 'theologian of jurisprudence' or, more precisely, as a 'Catholic layman of German citizenship and member of the German people' [katholischer Laie deutscher Volks- und Staatsangehörigkeit] (GL, p. 283), he was 'sundered between theology and technology' (NtE, p. 38). His hope that the 'self-dissolution of German idealism' would unleash new 'theurgical forces' (GL, p. 83) seems born of a certain helplessness. In his failure, Schmitt identified with Kleist, whose marriage to the Catholic poet Annette Droste-Hülshoff he imagined in a vision. But the truly tragic hero in all this is only one person – Carl Schmitt himself, 'the last conscious representative of the *jus publicum Europaeum* in an existential sense' (ECS, p. 75), who saved the 'honour' and provided an 'asylum' for European jurisprudence at all times. Schmitt asked the question of conservative forces within world history, forces which may be capable of halting 'the end of history':

> I believe in the katechon; it is the only possibility for me as a Christian to understand and find meaning in history. . . . Today's theologians do not know it and, ultimately, they do not want to know it either. Really, I wanted to know from them: who is the katechon today? It is, after all, hardly possible to think it is Churchill or John Foster Dulles . . . For every epoch of the past 1948 years, it must be possible to name the katechon. Its place was never unoccupied, otherwise we would no longer be here. . . . There are temporary, transient, splinter-like and fragmentary holders of this task. I am even certain that we could agree on many concrete names up to the present day, as soon as the concept itself is clear enough. Donoso Cortés failed in his theology because he did not know this concept. (GL, p. 63)

Schmitt was once again looking for 'Catholic intensification' (GL, p. 165). All his identifications of important figures in intellectual history became to him aspects of self-reflection – aspects of his 'own question'. The answer he gave relied not least on open anti-Semitism. Schmitt again tied his identity to the question of the 'Jewish spirit' and discussed his relationship to Judaism as the reverse side of his Christian self-understanding. He offered a fundamental myth which tied his various definitions of the enemy to anti-Semitism. Again and again he identified his counter-positions with his opposition to the 'Jewish spirit'. In doing so, he showed an inclination to let all concrete references evaporate: 'Because Jews always remain Jews.

While a communist may improve and change. That has nothing to do with the Nordic race, etc. The assimilated Jew, in particular, is the true enemy. There is no point in demonstrating that the slogans of the Elders of Zion[106] are fake' (GL, p. 18).

Schmitt's picture of Hitler after 1945

In his *Glossarium*, Schmitt reflects extensively on Hitler. He asked himself how it was possible that such an 'uneducated' individual could rise to become the 'Führer' of a cultured nation. He understood Hitler as an executioner of German history and saw him as reflected in numerous historical and literary characters, such as, for instance, Schiller's Demetrius and the Anabaptists of Münster. Schmitt had already come across Max Kommerell's idea that Hitler could be seen in the light of Schiller's Demetrius in 1935. Fritz Reck-Malleczewen's *Bockelson: Geschichte eines Massenwahns*, published in 1937 and immediately put on the index, also became important to him. In 1948, a noteworthy book on the *Vorläufer des Antichrist* [Precursor of the Antichrist] was published in Berlin; it contains various of Schmitt's interpretive approaches to the understanding of history.[107] His most important notes on Hitler can be found in the *Glossarium*:

> What happened in Germany after 1918? From the darkness of a social, moral and intellectual nothingness, from out of the pure lumpenproletariat, from the asylum of a homeless non-education, an entirely empty and unknown individual rose up. . . . Now Germany had someone who took things seriously, who got real, someone who did nothing but put things into practice, carried them out and executed them; a pure executor of the ideas that had been so pure until then, a pure henchman. . . . [Germany had] [t]hus the pure formula of the intellectual history of these seventeen years, the great comic opera of pure (i.e., nothing but) the execution of the pure German cult of genius [Genialismus]. Someone condemned by history to act, the great theme of Schiller and his concept of tragedy. (15 May 1948; GL, p. 149)

> We need to look in Schiller for the concepts of tragedy which give us the key to this criminal activism [Tätertum]. Every deed is already a crime, a betrayal of the idea. Every doer [Täter] is a tragic criminal and, ultimately, mystical to himself. The fake Demetrius as the primordial image of all doers [Täter]. The 'need for pretence of the one acting' (in Kommerell's words about Schiller's doers), the 'imposed life', the activity of semblance and the figure (of Demetrius) as someone condemned by history to do evil. (1 May 1949)*

---

* In Schiller's unfinished play, Demetrius gains access to the tzars' throne with the help of Poland, wrongly believing that he is the son of Ivan the Terrible. He reigns benevolently until his false identity is discovered: his alleged mother does not recognize him, and when Demetrius requests her to provide identification, and thus give him legitimacy,

He was meant to be the son taking their revenge for the lost First World War. This Kaspar Hauser and soldier *inconnu* was adopted as a fake Demetrius by mother Germania, who – between 1933 and 1941 – repeated again and again to herself:

And though he may not be my heart's son,
still he shall be the son of my revenge.

But the unfaithful mother Germania did not persevere in her role when she saw the abyss approaching. And he, he took the house down with him. (1 May 1949; GL, p. 239)

Why did the German bourgeoisie, of all people, choose Hitler as its 'executioner'? Schmitt's speculative answer is based on Schiller's play. He tries to understand the problem in literary terms and abstracts and idealizes the relation between idea and execution with the help of *Demetrius*. Part of his intention in 1949, the 200th anniversary of Goethe's birth, was also to subvert the dominant 'Goethe cult'. He also celebrated his own counter-perspective on intellectual history with renewed reflections on Theodor Däubler and Konrad Weiß. Together with local acquaintances Wilhelm Wessels and Peterheinrich Kirchhoff, as well as the Catholic philosopher of art Walter Warnach, he remembered Däubler. At Kirchhoff's home, a small conference discussing the 'problem of editing a selection of Däubler's works' took place on the fifteenth anniversary of the author's death. For Schmitt, it became 'less and less understandable that Däubler, after the Great War, from 1920 onwards discarded the Northern Lights without further ado and returned to the South' (BS, p. 155). After the poem's attitude to Christianity, its whole approach to history now became questionable for Schmitt. Friedhelm Kemp,[108] also an admirer and editor[109] of Konrad Weiß, commented on Schmitt's 'problem: Däubler probably did not drop the idea of the Northern Lights, but he did, it seems to me, move it away slightly from the centre of his worldview; the experience of Greece apparently brought the poet closer to an Apollonian Hermeticism and the Gnosis.'[110] In addition, the circle celebrated the twentieth anniversary of Däubler's death in 1954. Schmitt discussed Kemp's Däubler edition with him and praised in the most glowing terms it in a questionnaire on 'books of tomorrow'. As he had done forty years earlier, he again praised Däubler as the great 'untimely' figure who had stepped out of the 'shadow of contemporary celebrities' and had then put them 'in his shadow' (BS, p. 228).[111] Thus, Schmitt settled down in Plettenberg in part through the help of his old poet friends. The debates about Däubler and Weiß in Siedlinghausen Schmitt continued, in particular, in friendly conversations with Walter Warnach. At the beginning of the 1960s he moved away slightly from Walter Kemp, but thought to establish some connection

she nevertheless refuses. Of course, in this passage 'Täter' could equally be translated as 'perpetrator' or even 'criminal'. The passage is based on the universalized equivocation of 'acting' and 'incurring guilt'.

with the discussions going on in Catholicism via Warnach. With Konrad Weiß, the Siedlinghausen circle, Friedhelm Kemp, the university chaplain Wilhelm Nyssen and, in particular, Warnach, Schmitt's interpretations of the intellectual history of the Weimar period thus continued into his late work. Even after 1949, he again and again identified points of divergence with Catholicism, without, however, ever negating his Catholic self-understanding.

28

From Benito Cereno to Hamlet: The 'Comeback' of the Intellectual?

Schmitt's networks after 1949

Following the war, Schmitt again exerted a polarizing effect on people.[1] After 1945 he first collected his family and some old friends around him. The possibilities for him to visit friends were still fairly limited, but a few old acquaintances lived close enough to be reached. Schmitt's brother Jupp made Cologne a constant draw for him. Oberheid lived in Kaiserswerth, Düsseldorf, Barion in Bonn, and Krauss in Cologne. Through Ernst Jünger, new acquaintances were introduced into Schmitt's house, such as, for instance – in August 1948 – Armin Mohler, who, as a Swiss national, had once illegally entered the country in order to join the Waffen SS and take part in the battle against the Soviet Union. After a visit, Mohler thanked Schmitt, 'in memory of the four days in Plettenberg', with a watercolour drawing of Theodor Däubler.[2] Schmitt got to know some of his neighbours, for instance Emil Langenbach, the director of the local savings bank Gustav Wollenweber, the paediatrician Bakowski and the architect Hans de Fries. Schmitt became well acquainted with Peterheinrich Kirchhoff, a member of the Bundestag for the CDU. The 'Siedlinghausen circle' allowed him to make quite a few new contacts. From the end of 1948, Schmitt was in close contact with Walter Warnach. He again exchanged letters discussing Hieronymus Bosch with Wilhelm Fraenger. His Berlin pupils Hans Franzen, Gustav von Schmoller, Eberhard von Medem and Bernhard von Mutius, Helmut Gremmels and Helmut Rumpf, Sava Kličković and Ferdinand Friedensburg, as well as former students from Berlin, such as Rüdiger Altmann, Joseph H. Kaiser and many others, got in touch with Schmitt. (It seems that of his closer collaborators only Gutjahr and Pfeiffer fell in the war.) Hans Freyer moved from Leipzig to Wiesbaden. Ernst Forsthoff was in Heidelberg and played a key role in re-establishing Schmitt academically. Tübingen became a focal point for him, with Carl Brinkmann, Joseph H. Kaiser and Hans Schneider, as did Hamburg with Rolf Stödter and Hans Peter Ipsen. For the summer term 1949, Werner Weber, 'unnoticed',[3] crossed the border from Leipzig to Göttingen. Schmitt had friendly contacts with his old colleague Friedrich Giese. Theodor Maunz thanked Schmitt effusively for his 'support and stimulating suggestions'. The correspondence with Huber was revived, albeit in a more distanced way. Every year, until their contact ended in 1961, Schmitt exchanged formal birthday greetings with Smend. In April 1950, Schmitt wrote: 'At the lecterns of German universities, the third rank of scholars spreads itself out, which removed its rivals in 1945 and filled their posts. The best people in my discipline today are: Prof. Werner Weber (Göttingen), Prof. Dr Ernst Forsthoff (Frankfurt), Prof. Dr Hans P. Ipsen (Hamburg); in international law Prof. Dr Rolf Stödter (Hamburg) and Prof. Wilhelm Grewe (formerly Freiburg, now Heidelberg).'[4] Of his Jewish pupils, Otto Kirchheimer visited Schmitt repeatedly. Other former pupils, for instance Ernst Friesenhahn, did not get in touch again.

Schmitt's exchanges with Johannes Winckelmann at the time soon became more intense. Winckelmann had come to know Schmitt in 1938 and had enthusiastically picked up his keywords 'concrete order formation' [konkretes Ordnungsdenken] and 'spatial revolution'.[5] After the end of the war, Winckelmann was appointed by the British as head of the Hessische Landesbank [State Bank of Hesse], but he left with a good pension after only a couple of years in order to realize the dream of his life: an edition of the works of Max Weber. Early on, while still at the Landesbank, Winckelmann got in touch with Schmitt regarding his plan for a critical edition of *Society and Economy*.[6] In February 1948 he had already sent an 'Investigation into the intellectual structure of Max Weber's "Society and Economy"'.[7] He was especially interested in the concept of legitimacy. Winckelmann was in contact with Marianne Weber and drew Schmitt's attention to Joachim Ritter, who taught in Münster from 1946. In 1949, Winckelmann sent 'the winter lectures of my friend Joachim Ritter'.[8] Ritter then went to Istanbul as a visiting professor for the years 1953 to 1955, so that Schmitt met him in person only in 1956.

By the end of the 1950s, the third generation of Schmitt's pupils had formed in the Federal Republic: Nicolaus Sombart, Hanno Kesting and Reinhart Koselleck, Piet Tommissen and Roman Schnur, Dieter Groh, Peter Scheibert, Ernst-Wolfgang Böckenförde, Rainer Specht, Hans-Joachim Arndt and quite a few more. Through Rüdiger Altmann, Johannes Gross joined the circle. Ernst Hüsmert was present as a piano student and a childhood friend of Anima. Gerd Giesler grew up in the neighbourhood. From the early 1960s onwards he provided Schmitt with the latest information on academic and political life and later promoted his work in manifold ways. Through his father, Joachim, Henning Ritter[9] had also known Schmitt since his youth, and he helped him keep a public profile through the *Frankfurter Allgemeine Zeitung*.* Later, George Schwab, Julien Freund and others frequently came to visit. Schmitt continued to find new conversational partners throughout the 1960s. His academic influence after the war, the second lease of life for his work provided by its liberal reception, was already under way at that point. In the 1960s, the core group of pupils met again at Forsthoff's seminars in Ebrach;† its members became a core group of authors publishing in the journal *Der Staat* [The State].

---

*　Henning Ritter was one of the chief editors of the newspaper.
†　Regular seminar courses held by Forsthoff during the vacations in Ebrach in the Steigerwald.

The 'shadows of recent years':
quarrel with Jünger and the death of Schmitt's wife

At Christmas 1947 the family was finally reunited. During Easter 1948, Anima moved from the school in Cloppenburg to one in Plettenberg. At that point Gretha Jünger noticed an 'atmosphere of strangeness' [Geist der Fremdheit] (GJCS, p. 111) between the Schmitts and the Jüngers. The stable situation in Plettenberg then suddenly collapsed. In January 1949 there had already been signs of Duška falling ill again. At the same time, Schmitt's friendship with Ernst Jünger suffered serious upsets and crises. As he was in financial difficulties, Schmitt was urgently looking for work. Rolf Stödter, who was closely connected with shipping companies in Hamburg, arranged a meeting with a certain Dr Dörr.[10] Although in the end the meeting did not take place, a consultancy contract with the Phrix-Werke Aktiengesellschaft, dated 15 February, and with a monthly payable fee, resulted from Schrödter's initiative.[11] Hans Peter Ipsen looked after Schmitt while he was in Hamburg in March. A Däubler celebration took place in Kirchhoff's home.[12] Kaiser spent 'Russian Easter in Plettenberg'.[13] Gerhard Nebel put it to Jünger again that in Plettenberg he 'had fallen in disgrace, in particular with Mrs Duška'.[14] At first, Jünger was relaxed about it, and wanted to ask personally 'where the shoe pinches him [Schmitt] with regard to me'.[15] Nicolaus Sombart reported about a meeting with Gremmels and Nebel: 'It was exhilarating to learn some concrete news about the influence of the unique elite', he wrote, 'to which Gremmels and Nebel belong as entourage and in whose "lower ranks" I would like to claim a modest place as an adept for myself as well.' Sombart spoke of a 'powerful spiritual force of order' [Ordnungsfaktor] which had helped him, as a 'young German', in making his decision to return from Italy to Germany. However, he added, he looked at 'the "communities of heroic characters" by no means without concerns'.[16] Sombart had in mind here the circles around Jünger and other elitist circles outside National Socialism.

At the beginning of May 1949, Schmitt was again in Hamburg, where he met with Gerhard Günther, who belonged to the Stapel circle. At Whitsun he travelled to the Middle Rhine with Günther Krauss and Oberheid. During these months he was working on the completion of his first post-war books, often in the Dominican monastery Walberberg. Gremmels had political difficulties in his post as municipal director of Königslutter, a fact which Schmitt registered with 'nausea and outrage'.[17] In July, Nebel came to visit, together with Gebhard, who owned a factory, a friend of the Däubler circle from Iserlohn, Wessel, and the mayor Kirchhoff. Sombart also spent a couple of days in Plettenberg at that time, but wrote, 'sadly': 'I could not get rid of the feeling that you had somehow given up on me and had written me off; that I had lost a teacher.'[18] Schmitt reassured him straightaway:[19] 'My expectation to find in you a scholar of the Werner Sombart–Max Weber times was, after all, at bottom naïve.'* Schmitt did not want

---

* While Sombart uses the formal 'Sie' in this exchange, Schmitt addresses him informally with 'du', expressing the hierarchical relationship between the two generations.

any epigones, and he preferred intellectual independence. Mohler became Jünger's private secretary, and in early September a short meeting with Nebel and Mohler took place at which Schmitt found 'the conversation too tumultuous' (BS, p. 66). Schmitt, then, spent some time in the Walberberg monastery, where he also gave a talk on 'just war'. Warnach wrote in retrospect: 'The word thanks is actually quite insufficient for expressing what moves me about you.'[20] In Walberberg, Schmitt met Dr Kurt Zierold, a member of the Notgemeinschaft der deutschen Wissenschaft [Association for the Support of German Science],* whom he had known from 1930 onwards 'through many conversations'.[21] Zierold encouraged Schmitt to apply for a grant, because in the case of first-class scholars it would be possible, 'exceptionally', to support individuals who were not in the early stages of their careers. Schmitt applied.[22] Nebel invited Schmitt to a meeting with Jünger.[23] In mid-September, Rolf Stödter came to Plettenberg. At the same time, Duška had to go to hospital again. She went to Professor Siebeck in Heidelberg, Schmitt's friend and former colleague in Berlin. Siebeck diagnosed intestinal cancer and carried out an extensive operation at the end of October. Schmitt wrote to Heidelberg almost daily. Forsthoff offered him a 'room as a visiting lodger', and Anima and Schmitt stayed repeatedly in Forsthoff's mill in Schlierbach. A close and friendly relationship between Schmitt and Forsthoff dates from this time, which also led to a renewed contact with the younger generation through the vacation seminars in Ebrach. Forsthoff had lost his chair in Heidelberg in 1946. He shared the experience of exclusion and resentment with Schmitt. 'I am not tempted to return to the university of today', he repeatedly assured him (EFCS, p. 53). The 'ties of collegiality' had been 'severed' after 1945 (EFCS, p. 55). In the form of his *Lehrbuch des Verwaltungsrechts* [Textbook of Administrative Law],[24] Forsthoff would soon publish what was, according to Schmitt, 'a great achievement in jurisprudence'. The turn from the constitutional state to the executive-administrative state is taken on board in this book. The tendency of the time led from constitutional theory to administrative theory. From the constitutional perspective of Schmitt's school of thought, Forsthoff's systematic textbook was a congenial companion piece to Schmitt's *Constitutional Theory*, the masterpiece, so to speak, from the generation of Schmitt's pupils. With this achievement, Forsthoff's friendship with Schmitt was consolidated.

Anni Stand returned to the Schmitt household. Ernst and Gretha Jünger tried very much to help, and also saw a chance to remedy the simmering tensions with friendly gestures. Jünger wrote very matter-of-factly: 'My wife will visit yours in Heidelberg in the course of these days' (JS, p. 240). Soon afterwards, he sent greetings to Duška in hospital.[25] The meeting between Nebel, Jünger and Schmitt, which had been planned by Nebel for some time, had to be postponed for a couple of days. It was also affected by Duška's operation and a 'denunciatory inflammatory article'[26] which threatened Schmitt's literary comeback. Nevertheless, Schmitt was hopeful: 'Apart from that, tomorrow I expect to meet Ernst Jünger and

---

* Precursor organization of today's Deutsche Forschungsgemeinschaft.

Gerhard Nebel in Werdohl, where they have been invited by Peterheinrich Kirchhoff.'[27] Anima wrote a humorous and ironic letter to Duška, in which she poked fun at Jünger's northern German reserve and arrogance. 'You can imagine that I feel the urge (and Daddy urges me, too) to tell you about the important visitor. ... So, first of all: Jünger looks fantastic, is very well dressed. When he makes an effort at a kind smile (which happens only rarely), he can look charming for seconds.' This description is followed by a barrage of mocking remarks about Jünger's behaviour at the home of the painter Wilhelm Wessel. 'The most attractive aspect for me was my primitive and malicious enjoyment in sitting that close to a man, for being in whose presence hundreds of women would envy me. To me, someone of such self-assured arrogance appears unbearably absurd and nonsensical in our times.'[28] Schmitt also wrote acrimoniously: 'Jünger's egotism is grotesque. It seems he can only be social with billionaire women and female adorers of his.'[29] The visit contributed in no small measure to Schmitt's and Jünger's alienation from each other. Nevertheless, Jünger sent Duška a card from his visit.[30] However, Jünger's novel *Heliopolis* further estranged Schmitt from the author's mannerisms. 'The book is a master class in the complete exploitation of any idea whatsoever', he wrote to Duška in the Heidelberg clinic.[31]

At the beginning of December 1949, Duška was released from hospital and slowly made her way back to Plettenberg. The family was hopeful. Werner Weber wrote saying that Schmitt's application to the Notgemeinschaft was 'reasonably protected against attempts at throwing spanners in the works'.[32] But soon Zierold wrote to Schmitt: 'I have done a lot regarding your application that I do not want to put in writing here. I am no longer very optimistic; people are more narrow-minded and unforgiving than I thought.'[33] At the beginning of January 1950, Gretha Jünger came to visit and spoke of Duška's 'regained health' (GJCS, p. 125). The visit would have catastrophic consequences. Ernst Jünger was very annoyed about Schmitt's attempts at getting Gretha on his side by telling her indiscreet 'stories'.[34] Nebel had to apologize for his 'interest in gossip' [Klatsch-Neugier].[35] Gretha drew the conclusion that Nebel had to be 'banned from the inner circle forever' because of his false account of his conversations with Schmitt. 'I know only one thing', she wrote to Schmitt (GJCS, p. 129), 'that such a figure of secondary importance does not belong to the level of your relationship with E. J.'. What was at stake, she said, was 'the importance of spiritual [geistigen], political and human encounter'. Schmitt now also broke off his contacts with Nebel.[36] At the end of February, Schmitt travelled again to Hamburg, where Stödter, Ipsen and Karl Maria Hettlage[37] took care of him. However, the attempts at establishing a professional contact between Schmitt and Dr Dörr failed,[38] and as a consequence Schmitt's close relationship with Stödter cooled off.

The first more substantive publication after the war, *Die Lage der europäischen Rechtswissenschaft* [The situation of European jurisprudence], appeared in March. Sombart came to Plettenberg again, and this time his visit was a success.[39] On 12 April 1950, Duška had to be admitted to the hospital in Heidelberg again. On the way she stopped over in

Frankfurt.[40] On 26 April she was temporarily released, but by June, and again in July, she was back in the clinic. Schmitt stayed with Forsthoff again and told him about the dramatic deterioration of Duška's condition.[41] At that point in time he was not in a mood to resolve the conflict with Jünger. To Gretha, he wrote: 'I shall not respond to the accusations against me which you mention in your letter. Whoever wants to make accusations against me will easily find more than enough material and proofs and allies' (GJCS, p. 133). He now had to concentrate his energies in order to complete his monographs. Jünger wrote repeatedly to Duška while she was in hospital. Schmitt visited her in August, October and November, and reported on the progressive deterioration of her condition. He vehemently rejected Jünger's accusation. 'Ernst Jünger has enough to do looking after himself', he wrote to Jünger's wife. 'His capacity for altruism has not grown, but diminished, since 1945. Everyone who talks to him sees and feels this; and everyone says it as well, and that is where the great problem of the situation lies. It is not the year 1933, but the year 1945 that has made the decisive differences between people visible' [hat die Menschen entscheidend gruppiert] (GJCS, p. 137; cf. EFCS, p. 72). These comments were not particularly diplomatic. Schmitt insinuates resentment on the other side and praises his own 'politeness'. For the time being, the Jüngers ignored this. On 6 September they visited Duška in hospital. Duška asked them for financial support for the funeral and to comfort her two 'orphaned children' (JS, p. 682). Ernst Jünger straightaway told her 'not to worry about money':[42] 'Leave that to us.' In mid-September, Schmitt met Jünger again in Werdohl and in the Rhein-Ruhr Club in Düsseldorf. 'We had a very nice and open conversation', he wrote to Gretha, 'and I hope that our old friendship has recovered from the dark times of recent years' (GJCS, p. 141). Nicolaus Sombart wrote an elegiac letter to Duška: 'You know that the decisive encounter in my life was that with Carl Schmitt – a seducer, a magician, who cast a spell over my thought; . . . I think it is magic which opens up an access to the secrets.'[43] And, he added, she had been a part of that magic.

At the end of September, Duška told her 'dearest' Gretha about a visit from Carl. 'We said goodbye so merrily that I would like to go to sleep forever tonight' (JS, p. 685). Schmitt, however, did not react positively to Jünger's efforts regarding Duška. 'Jünger is an entomologist', he noted in his *Glossarium*, 'or not even that: he is a collector of beetles. He collects beetles and last words – insects and those dying' (GL, p. 311). Schmitt did not trust Jünger's humane motivation in his care for Duška. At that time, Siebeck, the physician in charge, asked Schmitt 'to come soon'.[44] Schmitt went to the clinic one more time. He put his *Nomos of the Earth* on her bed. As a dedication, he had written in it: 'Despite bombs and despite Morgenthau plan, / Despite terror and despite the theft of heroes, / Despite automatism and betrayal, / Despite Nuremberg and despite barbed wire, / Despite all this, this book emerged and a blessing grew out of the curse.'[45] Corina Sombart visited Duška 'as often as her physical and emotional condition would permit.'[46] Werner Weber said 'farewell'.[47] The Jüngers sent their greetings from a journey to Italy.[48] Carl wrote almost daily until the end. He sent[49] Duška an article[50] 'by Dr Rosenbaum . . . whom you met in April 1933 in Hamburg. Now he takes revenge for his fear back then.' Schmitt's last letter, of 2 December, responded in a 'profoundly shocked' way to photographs of the terminally ill Duška. 'You will always have to stay with us.' Duška died on 3 December at the age of forty-seven. Barion made it possible for Duška, who was Orthodox, to be buried in a Catholic cemetery and also held the funeral mass. On 7 December she was buried in the Eiringhausen Waldfriedhof. At the funeral, Schmitt looked as if he was 'running away from himself'.[51] According to the death announcement, 'The long and serious illness she had to suffer did not break the spirit of her soul.' Gretha Jünger attended the funeral; Ernst Jünger sent his commiserations. Nebel[52] also sent his commiserations 'across all graves'.* Wilhelm Grewe spoke of Duška's 'unique combination of unusual courage, composure, sense of reality and human warmth'.[53] Erik Peterson, who had been best man at the Schmitts' wedding, remembered her as a 'model of courage & spiritual strength'.[54] 'I have also lost one of those most dear to me on this earth', wrote her friend from Berlin, Heidi Hahn.[55] Schmitt quoted Konrad Weiß: 'So the sense, the more it seeks itself / is led out of dark captivity, the soul to the world / carry out what you need to do, it is always / already done and all you do is respond.'[56] 8 February 1951 would have been their silver wedding anniversary.

Father Eberhard Welty and the New Order

Until the foundation of the Federal Republic of Germany in 1949, Schmitt was officially not allowed to publish – or, as contemporary parlance would have it, he wasn't 'allowed to swim yet'.[57] But Schmitt was financially dependent on publications and so published under a pseudonym. He also took on smaller legal opinions and reports. Schmitt began a notebook at that time, in which he meticulously recorded the recipients of his typescripts and publications.[58] The list includes all post-war publications and, in addition, all invitations to give talks, a bibliography of his works, important letters and also, up to the treatise on Hobbes of 1965, poems. His close circle of addressees, and the way in which this circle changed, can be read off that one notebook.[59] The list shows, for instance, that Schmitt sent out, or lent out (the notebook had a list under the categories 'lent out/returned'), his unpublished legal opinion on 'The Crime of the War of Aggression' of 1945 to more than forty people, including all of his closest pupils. Typescripts of *Ex captivitate salus* he gave out over fifty times before its publication. He gave away more than two hundred copies of *The Nomos of the Earth* as presents before 1963. His publications under a pseudonym he called 'Apocrypha'.[60]

    With the help of Father Eberhard Welty, Schmitt, under a pseudonym, published two older studies, on Donoso Cortés and Francisco de

---

* 'über alle Gräber hinweg'. Nebel inverts Schmitt's earlier rhetorical progression from 'Gräben' to 'Grab' with which Schmitt had broken off their relationship (see note 36).

Vitoria, in the journal *Die neue Ordnung* [the New Order], which was edited by the Academy of the Dominicans at Walberberg, near Bonn. The academy played a significant role in the foundation of the CDU, the Christian Democratic Party. In 1933, Welty had attended some of Schmitt's lectures in Cologne[61] and thus also knew Günther Krauss. Welty persuaded Schmitt to give him the text on Cortés and 'cordially' invited him to spend a few weeks as a guest at the academy.[62] In February 1949 he invited him again, and wanted to discuss matters pertaining to the journal with him and Father Stratmann, as well as with the business economist [Betriebswirt] (and former colleague at the faculty in Berlin) Theodor Beste.[63] Schmitt sent him his manuscript on Vitoria; he experienced Walberberg as an 'asylum',[64] and also went repeatedly to the monastery in order to work in its quiet atmosphere. However, in the autumn appeared the 'inflammatory article' that incriminated Schmitt, a reply to his Vitoria essay by a former assistant of Kelsen, August von der Heydte. The reply speaks of an 'unknown author', but states very clearly: 'The spectacles of Carl Schmitt distort the image of the great Spaniard.' The essay, it further claims, perpetuates the 'the myth of a power that can create right'.[65] Welty at once began to think about possible countermeasures.[66] Schmitt, he suggested, should explain his position to the priest Laurentius Siemer in Cologne and write a short 'note' on it for the journal.[67] Schmitt went to see the Father but was terribly annoyed by this visit. To Forsthoff, he made the most extreme and presumptuous comments regarding this 'violation of asylum' [Asylschändung]: 'Never in the twelve years of Hitler's rule has a Jewish colleague been exposed to such infamous malice' (EFCS, p. 59). Just to remind the reader: in 1933, Schmitt 'spat them out' and in 1936 he prohibited them from publishing. The attack on him now made it Schmitt's 'duty . . . to move on and look for another asylum'.[68] When von der Heydte also was given space in the *New Order*, Schmitt no longer felt welcome there. He wrote at the time: 'That von der Heydte appears as an author in that place, straight after his attack, is actually incredible. It is probably for the best if I now leave quietly and discreetly.'[69] Schmitt still sent a contribution, which Welty accepted.[70] Schmitt's Nuremberg opinion on the *Problem der Legalität* [Problem of legality] appeared. Welty invited Schmitt to a discussion group,[71] and he asked him to come 'for a couple of weeks' in order to discuss questions 'regarding [his] professional activities'.[72] For autumn 1950 Schmitt, together with Krauss, still planned an international conference on Vitoria at Walberberg, but the relationship became increasingly difficult.[73] Schmitt yet again had the experience that his persona and his publications were controversial. His renewed attempt to associate with Catholic circles had thus failed. After 1951, Schmitt halted the re-Christianization of his work. Welty again asked him to come to Walberberg, and in May 1952 he was at the monastery once more.[74] But Schmitt did not meet a later request for a contribution to the journal.[75] The Dominicans' interest in Schmitt might be surprising, but the first three more substantial essays which Schmitt published after 1945 appeared in their journal upon the initiative of Father Welty.

Serge Maiwald and the Universitas

Schmitt's pupil from Berlin, Serge Maiwald, opened up a second 'asylum' in which Schmitt's publications could reach a wider public. As early as 8 May 1945, Maiwald got in touch with Schmitt from Tübingen and later told him about his newly founded monthly journal *Universitas*, which began to appear in April 1946.[76] Soon he offered Schmitt the opportunity to publish some pre-publications and reviews. *The Situation of European Jurisprudence* appeared in March 1950 in Maiwald's university press in Tübingen.[77] With this article, Schmitt presented himself again as a jurist within the 'European' tradition and gained legitimacy for his *Nomos of the Earth*. 'The come back* of Carl Schmitt has to take place purely in the field of jurisprudence and under no circumstances in the field of politics, if one wants to pull the rug from under the feet of any resistances and ugly attacks from the very beginning', Winckelmann wrote at the time.[78] He recommended that Schmitt write a study of John Locke, but earned Schmitt's 'scorn' for it.[79] On 22 February, after a long illness, Maiwald died suddenly of a stroke.[80] Schmitt wrote an obituary, and thereafter published nothing in *Universitas*. Despite assurances of continued interest in contributions from the editorial office,[81] Schmitt, after the *New Order*, also wrote off *Universitas*. From then on, he would publish only rarely in journals. From 1954, numerous short reviews appeared in the literary gazette *Das Historisch-politische Buch* [The Historical-political book].[82] But Schmitt no longer published anything in the great specialist journals of jurisprudence. Only with the foundation of the journal *Der Staat* [The State] did this change.

Carl Schmitt, No and Yes: publication campaign with the Greven publishing house

When Duška fell ill again, it caused severe financial difficulties for Schmitt. Friends helped him out and initiated a collection of donations. Schmitt now wanted and was forced to make the results of his wartime work public. Without the acute financial pressures, he probably would not have relaunched his career as a writer with four monographs within a year. At the same time, he made efforts to gain the rights for his *Land and Sea*,[83] and he offered *The Nomos of the Earth* to various publishers, many of which signalled their interest. On 27 July 1948, even before the licensing of publishers by the Allies, Benno Ziegler of the Hanseatische Verlagsanstalt re-established contact with Schmitt and expressed his hope for renewed cooperation.[84] However, Ziegler died soon afterwards, and the contact with the publishing house ended.[85] In 1948, Schmitt got in touch again with his old regular publisher Duncker & Humblot.[86] To Schmitt's anger and suspicion[87] that his relations with the publisher had probably expired, the head of the house, Johannes Broermann, replied with the positive news that he had not terminated the contracts. With some regret, he took

---

* English in the original; spelling as separate words also in the original.

note of Schmitt's choice of the Greven publishing house. These contacts were nevertheless the first step back to Duncker & Humblot, and in 1954 Schmitt's actual return to the publishing house began with a new edition of *Constitutional Theory*. Günther Neske was also interested in publishing Schmitt.[88] However, Schmitt opted for Greven, not least because Karl Epting, the former head of the German Institute in Paris, worked there.

At the end of October 1949, the publisher got in touch with Schmitt for the first time.[89] Then, on 25 January 1950, Epting wrote in order to discuss 'the question of the publishing of some of your writings with us'.[90] A meeting took place soon after, and Epting sent Schmitt an offer of a contract. However, even before the publication of his monographs, Schmitt was concerned about the reception of his work because of his negative 'experiences'[91] in the past. His 'spiritual path' [geistigen Weg][92] he described in his confessional text *Ex captivitate salus*. His collection of Cortés studies again showed him as a 'counter-revolutionary' author. Schmitt wrote a longer introduction to the book on Cortés, in which he described the contemporary 'mental situation' [Bewußtseinslage] as characterized by the opposition between 'anarchy and nihilism' (DC, p. 9). He worked on the proofs of the *Nomos* book and, at the very last moment, added substantial parts of his legal opinion of 1945. *Ex captivitate salus* appeared in mid-August. 'Letters from imprisonment' is what he called it in his personal copy.[93] At the end of October, 'A Pan-European Interpretation of Donoso Cortés' [Donoso Cortés in gesamteuropäischer Interpretation]* was sent out, and at the beginning of November *The Nomos of the Earth* appeared.

Schmitt's texts caused difficulties for the publisher. Greven, for instance, was threatened with the 'withdrawal of printing orders from the associations of Catholic academics'.[94] Epting reacted by planning a documentation of the 'case of Schmitt', intended as an advertising campaign. Schmitt wrote a small brochure, *Carl Schmitt Nein und Ja* [Carl Schmitt, no and yes], which was sent out to all juridical faculties and almost all lecturers, and which was meant to 'cause quite a stir'.[95] Schmitt's list records 270 recipients. Sombart disliked its having the 'character of a mock newspaper' [Bierzeitung].[96] When Epting was dismissed (and became a school teacher), Schmitt's relationship with the publisher deteriorated. Despite substantial marketing efforts, and the discussions and responses Schmitt's texts caused, sales were slow. Epting considered a 'sales plan' for mass orders,[97] but the publisher planned to liquidate its academic section, and in early 1953 there already loomed the threat of the shorter books being sold at fire sale prices [Verramschung].[98] After some negotiations, the plan was to give Schmitt's works to another publisher, which, however, proved difficult to realize. At that point Schmitt arranged for some of the copies to be bought up by Academia Moralis,[99] the association which supported him,† and he then generously gave them away to members of his circle. Simultaneously, he began looking for another pub-

---

*   Carl Schmitt, 'A Pan-European Interpretation of Donoso Cortes' (1950), trans. Mark Grzeskowiak, *Telos* 125 (2002), pp. 100–15.
†   This was a formally constituted group of friends; on the group's origin, see the section on 'The man who caught the whale', p. 462 below.

lisher for *The Nomos of the Earth*. He had to pay back part of the advance he had received from Greven.[100] *The Situation of European Jurisprudence* was sold at a discount in 1956.[101] Throughout the 1950s there were quarrels over accounts. In 1960 Greven offered to buy up the remaining copies.[102] In the end, Duncker & Humblot bought the remaining copies of *The Nomos of the Earth*,[103] and the publishing house and bookstore Otto Zeller took on the distribution of *Ex captivitate salus* and the book on Cortés.[104]

Following these events, Schmitt tried to do business with the Neske publishing house in 1952. Together with his daughter Anima, he prepared a German edition of Lilian Winstanley's *Hamlet and the Scottish Succession* and offered further editorial work.[105] In 1954, he published his *Gespräch über die Macht* [Conversation on power] with Neske, who, incidentally, was also the publisher of Heidegger. However, soon Schmitt was unhappy with Neske as well.[106] Reclam published another edition of *Land and Sea*, slightly revised as requested by the publisher.[107] And, in 1956, *Hamlet oder Hekuba* [Hamlet or Hecuba] appeared with Diederichs. Both publishers, though, at least in Schmitt's perception, 'politely, but determinedly, asked him to leave'.[108] In 1955, an *Einführung in die Rechtswissenschaft* [Introduction to Jurisprudence] for Bertelsmann, which had already been agreed, fell through on account of a political clause.[109] After all these experiences, it must have been a relief for Schmitt, when, with his *Constitutional Theory*, he was finally able to return to Duncker & Humblot, the publishing house he had left in 1933 for political reasons. In 1959 the rights for his works with the Mohr publishing house were also returned to him.[110]

'The dark sense of our history': a Christian image of history?

As a clever media strategist, Schmitt planned the effect his publications would have very carefully. He frequently sent out his writings, and made sure members of his circle wrote reviews. Early on, he began to make use of radio broadcasts. However, in 1950 his possibilities were still limited. The journal *Universitas* was the most important platform for his work at the time. Maiwald published pre-publications and reviews,[111] which Schmitt used in order to test the water with regard to Spain, Italy and Austria. But, through Hans Paeschke and Joachim Moras, Schmitt also had old contacts with the monthly *Merkur*. In June 1949, Paeschke visited Schmitt in Plettenberg and wondered 'in which way the "Merkur" might arrange a co-operation with [him] as an author right now'.[112] He sent Schmitt Karl Löwith's *Meaning in History*, requesting a review of it,[113] and arranged a translation of the book with Hanno Kesting. Schmitt responded by sending a short piece on Löwith, 'Drei Möglichkeiten eines christlichen Geschichtsbildes' [Three possible Christian images of history]. However, Paeschke was not happy with it. As a 'short summary and interpretation of the role of the philosophy of history', he wrote, it did show 'the lion's paw',* but it did not give enough paraphrase of the 'outline of Löwith's

---

* Play on Löwith's name: 'Löwe' = lion.

approach'.[114] Paeschke requested a substantial reworking of the piece, but Schmitt rejected being advised in this fashion and gave it to Maiwald's *Universitas*.[115] Although Paeschke continued to be interested in Schmitt, only one publication in the *Merkur*, as late as 1952, resulted from his efforts.

The short text emerged from the 'deposit' for Przywara and constitutes a very fundamental reply to one of the most important of Schmitt's critics. In 1935, Karl Löwith published a critique of Schmitt's 'occasionalist decisionism', which still impacts on today's scholarship on Schmitt. In his 1941 book *From Hegel to Nietzsche*, Löwith then diagnosed a 'revolutionary break' in the nineteenth century, and thus belonged to the small group of authors who had a perspective on 1848 similar to that of Schmitt. While Löwith concentrated on Left Hegelianism, Schmitt made polemical use of Donoso Cortés. Löwith's critical approach was informed by Left Hegelianism. His short history of the philosophy of history, *Meaning in History*, which was soon translated (by Kesting) and published (by Koselleck) under the title *Weltgeschichte und Heilsgeschehen* [World history and salvation], not only exposed the 'theological preconditions' of the modern philosophy of history by taking a critical 'step back' (Heidegger) to the beginnings, but also, with its use of Nietzsche and Burckhardt, aimed at a 'heathen' dismissal of teleological and finalist historiography. This step beyond the old eschatology Schmitt did not mention, or did not notice.[116]

Schmitt begins by characterizing modern philosophy of history as a political tool for 'planning', and he praises Löwith's 'path from the philosophy of history to a theology of history and to eschatology' as the 'path of initiation' into the recognition of the sublime 'meaning' of history. He also praises Löwith for his insight into the genealogy of the modern philosophy of history and ties his own 'comments immediately to the results and conclusions of the book'. Schmitt establishes 'three possible Christian images of history' and lists them as: 'the great parallel, the Kat-echon and the Christian Epimetheus' (HBCS, p. 166). These three possibilities correspond to central motifs and criteria of Schmitt's reflections on history, which he explicated at the same time in his monographs. He tied the possibility of historical prognoses to the Christian theology of the katechon and the 'great parallel'. The katechon he saw at the core of the religious consciousness of finitude, which founds political responsibility and care about the 'end of history'. Schmitt separated the figure of the katechon from the mediaeval idea of the Reich and defined it in terms of its function – i.e., to delay 'the end of history' in Christian piety. There are 'no entitlements [wohlerworbene Rechte] to the achievements of the katechon' (NtE, p. 33), he writes, and mentions very different 'delayers' – including Hegel – as belonging to various contexts; and he describes all of them as pushing against the neutralizing and secularizing tendencies with Christian piety. With his reference to the 'eschatological' roots, Löwith, Schmitt says, has pointed to the 'great historical parallel' between early Christianity and the present time. Schmitt claims: 'A Christian has to elevate the parallel and turn it into an identity, because to him the core events of the Christian aeon, the Son of Man descending to earth, his death on the cross and his rising from the dead, remain alive in an unchanging presence' (HBCS, pp. 163f.). Schmitt then stresses the point that the early Christian 'expectation' did not have to lead to an 'eschatological paralysis' because St Paul knew the idea of a force, the 'Kat-echon', who 'delays the end and holds down the evil person' [den Bösen] (HBCS, p. 164). Even Luther, he says, still saw that force in the old 'Reich'; only Calvin shifted it onto the mere 'preaching of the word of God'. In the context of modern conservatism, the 'idea of holding and delaying forces and powers' was then almost entirely secularized; however, it was still active at least as late as in Hans Freyer's *Weltgeschichte Europas* [World history of Europe].[117] As a third possibility, Schmitt found a truly Christian – Epimethean and Marian – view of history in the work of his Catholic poet Konrad Weiß.

Just once is Schmitt's formulation almost dogmatic:

> In its innermost essence, Christianity is not a form of morality and no doctrine, no penitential sermon and no religion in the sense of comparative religious studies, but a historical event of an infinite uniqueness, which cannot be possessed or occupied. It is the incarnation in the virgin. The Christian credo speaks of historical events. Pontius Pilate has his essential place in it, and is not just an unlucky character who, for some strange reason, ended up there. A Christian looks back at accomplished events and finds there a primordial foundation [Ingrund] and primordial image [Inbild], in which, when actively contemplated, the dark sense of our history continues to grow. (HBCS, p. 165)

Schmitt speaks of an 'integration [Einstückung] of the eternal into the passing of time'.

Nowhere else does Schmitt express himself in such decidedly Christian terms. His biography relates to these criteria in different ways. The presence of early Christianity is reflected in the apocalyptic state of exception. His 'katechontic' perspective on his engagement in matters of constitutional policy is questionable. Schmitt might not have denied that his justification of the rule by presidential decree and of National Socialism, looked at in hindsight, had an accelerating effect. But he would have vehemently insisted on the fact that such effects were not his intention. At best, he would have therefore accepted that he had made political mistakes, but not that he was morally culpable. The third criterion of the Christian image of history, the following of Christ, is hardly present in Schmitt's work in any explicit form. Schmitt suggests that Löwith takes an 'eschatological' perspective and saw him as a 'Jewish' eschatologist. However, he soon noticed that his Christian clarifications and characterizations were better addressed to the Jewish philosopher of religion Jacob Taubes,[118] because Löwith wanted to do away with all theological foundations and was seeking a 'stoic withdrawal' (Jürgen Habermas) from history into 'cyclical' nature. From autumn 1950, Löwith taught, like Hans-Georg Gadamer, in Heidelberg. The younger pupils of Schmitt were ambivalent towards him, though Koselleck later became friendly with him. Kesting made fun of the 'all-too long monologues of Löwith, his pale and expansive manner'.[119]

It was not only the programmatic text on the 'Christian image of history' that appeared in Maiwald's *Universitas*. In addition, Schmitt published some of the 'corollaries' to his *Nomos of the Earth* in the journal, as well as, in September 1951, a short text on 'Raum und Rom – zur Phonetik des Wortes Raum' [Space and Rome: on the phonetics of the word space]. Schmitt's reflections on 'phonetics' had their origins in conversations with Wilhelm Ahlmann, who committed suicide in 1944 in order to avoid arrest.* Schmitt also published the short text, together with his *Rechtsbegriff* [Concept of right], in a commemorative publication for Ahlmann which was initiated by Hans Freyer,[120] and thus emphasized its close connection with *The Nomos of the Earth*. Later, he added further corollaries, and thus turned his final work on international law into a work in progress. The expansions concern speculations on the theology of history.

Schmitt had long been interested in esoteric ideas. Conversations with Ernst Jünger touched upon horoscopes, graphology and other esoteric matters. He took seriously Jünger's 'Lob der Vokale' [Praise of the vowels]. He intentionally strayed from conventional academic standards and – already in *Land and Sea* – looked for a 'step beyond the mythological into the mythical proper' (GL, p. 141). Schmitt's hermeticism created a need for a hermeneutics. His phonetic speculations aimed at 'primal words' [Urworte] of a 'primal' and 'holy language' (SGN, p. 491). His initial idea was that linguistic meaning develops etymologically ('Language still knows it . . .'), and that phonetics therefore provides an access to the history of language beyond the family relationships between languages established by positivist linguistics. Thus, Schmitt was looking for the unity of world history in the unity of its language. The primal language guarantees the unity of mankind, which Schmitt identified [ortet] with Rome. In a confessional tone, he wrote: 'I am certain that space and Rome are the same word' (SGN, p. 491). Schmitt tried to establish the phonetic birth of the German 'Raum' [space] out of ancient 'Rome', in order to build a 'bridge' between Rome and 'Reich', and further speculated about the preservation of meaning. He pursued similar intentions when speculating on the etymology of 'nomos'. Of course, one may find such speculations absurd, but to Schmitt they were very important. They were the form in which he tried to perceive the 'earth's realm of meaning' [Sinnreich der Erde] in religious terms, beyond the descriptive historical sciences and philosophical conceit. These speculations are the language of his 'Christian image of history'. His private notes continually circle this 'esotericism'.

'A strong spirit of a satanic kind':
discussions surrounding Schmitt's comeback

After 1945, the Staatsrechtslehrervereinigung [Association of State Theorists] was established once more, and in 1950 the 'question of

---

* Wilhelm Ahlmann (1895–1944) was close to Johannes Popitz and Stauffenberg and involved in the failed attempt at assassinating Hitler.

membership' arose.[121] There were initiatives to include Koellreutter and Huber again, but there was bitter resistance against Schmitt rejoining. His comeback as an author was more important to him, but here, too, he stumbled across his past and met with a barrage of attacks. On 6 July 1950 the *Westfalenpost* still reported positively about a 'Besuch bei Prof. Carl Schmitt' [Visit to Prof. Carl Schmitt]. Ernst Jünger wrote to Duška at the hospital: 'I have read *Ex captivitate salus*, and I think only those of C. S.'s opponents who are completely incorrigible will not be touched by it.'[122] Then, as we saw, Friedrich von der Heydte wrote his 'Response' to the Vitoria essay. Other responses to Schmitt's re-emergence were titled 'Carl Schmitt redivivus?' [Carl Schmitt revived?] (Walter Lewald) or 'Carl Schmitt – Kein Bundesgenosse' [Carl Schmitt – not an ally] (Ludwig Raiser).* 'Not a noble spirit', Lewald wrote, 'but a strong spirit of a satanic kind'![123] In the daily newspaper *Die Welt*, Rudolf Pechel attacked Giselher Wirsing for including a contribution by Schmitt. Michael Freund promised Schmitt he would publish a more substantial discussion of his work – a plan which, however, fizzled out.[124] Karl Korn wrote a mildly elegiac, positive review of the 'Christian Epimetheus'.[125] Karl Thieme sounded a warning against 'Carl Schmitts Apologie' [Carl Schmitt's apologia].[126] In November 1950, the *Rheinische Merkur* published a critical review of *Ex captivitate salus* – 'Carl Schmitt vor den Toren' [Carl Schmitt before the gates] – in which a friend from his youth, Eduard Rosenbaum, warned against the possible effects of Schmitt's text.[127] 'But which effect does the book have on a prejudiced reader, someone who, for instance, shared the youthful days of brightly sparkling conversations with Schmitt?', Rosenbaum asked himself. A public reader at the time could hardly know what a long story was behind this settling of accounts, but Schmitt was cut to the quick, and all the more so as the article coincided with Duška falling terminally ill. He feared that 'Greven will panic' and called it shameful 'to subject a German Catholic to the categories of a Jewish emigrant'.[128] Even decades later, Schmitt would ask: 'Who threw the first stone?' His answer: 'The "Rheinische Merkur", the paper of Adenauer, at the end of November 1950, with the article by Eduard Rosenbaum "Carl Schmitt ante Portas?"'. This article, breathing fire, destroyed the attempt by the Greven publishing house to create an objective discussion through 3 publications' (SSA, p. 353). A number of positive reviews by respected authors followed.[129] Serge Maiwald reviewed *Die Lage der europäischen Rechtswissenschaft* [The situation of European jurisprudence] in *Universitas*,[130] and had the intention of further promoting Schmitt's work. However, it was Karl Thieme who expressed the public mood at the time with an 'appeal to resistance' – 'Gegen den Zynismus der Gestrigen' [Against the cynicism of yesterday's men] – which he published in a Catholic weekly. 'Impossible even just to hint at the richness of these pages', a reviewer of one of Schmitt's publications wrote in the *Mannheimer Morgen*.[131] 'But then the exposure of a well-known scholar is irritating, as is the dropping of various

---

* The German title, obviously, plays on the idea that Schmitt was not supporting the newly founded Bundesrepublik.

hints and various raisings of the eyebrow.' The publisher received angry letters. A notary asked: 'Do you not know what a characterless part this "scholar" has played over decades?'[132] Golo Mann reviewed *The Nomos of the Earth* in *Der Monat*, and called it 'juridical dabblings' [schlechte Juristerei].[133] With the prospectus *Carl Schmitt, No and Yes*, the publisher set its hopes fully on the interest in his 'controversial' case.

'To realize fully, at least subsequently', what the system of extermination was: estrangement from Huber

The difficult year 1950 not only cast a lasting shadow over Schmitt's relationship with Jünger; it also left a failure to clear the air with Huber. Both personal differences and differences in professional opinion were already visible during the time of National Socialism. To begin with, Huber was in the same situation as Schmitt after 1945. He had also lost his chair and returned to a university only at the end of the 1950s. However, in contrast to Forsthoff, Huber remained reserved on the personal level. He lived in the Black Forest with his family, wanted to communicate only by letter and avoided a personal encounter with Schmitt. Immediately after the latter's return from the detention camp, Huber enquired about his condition.[134] Only in June 1948 did he get in touch again. In the following months, the two exchanged frequent letters about the National Socialist time and the situation after Nuremberg.[135] Tula Huber was by then a successful lawyer in Freiburg, and Huber was working on his survey of constitutional history. He sent notes on Nuremberg, to which Schmitt responded by sending his legal opinion of 1945, at the same time also signalling some distance from Huber's writings.[136] In reaction to this, Huber's letter congratulating Schmitt on his sixtieth birthday mentioned the necessity of having an 'argument' [Streitgespräch].

> I think I see things somewhat differently to you, and what I would have to say about this would be a kind of debate [Streitgespräch] . . . However, I am also of the opinion that it is necessary to absorb the factual material which has been collected at Nuremberg in its entirety, and in this way to realize fully, at least subsequently, what, in its effects, the Third Reich, as a system of extermination, represented. For someone who knows how to read files, there is no more harrowing documentation than the bureaucratic record of terrorism contained in those files.[137]

Schmitt responded by evoking their old comradeship and said that an argument would 'rather [concern] two "types" of jurisprudential mentality [Geistigkeit]'.[138] He also referred to the old differences in opinion on matters of constitutional theory. A little later, he hinted at political differences, made sceptical remarks about the 'idealization' of the possibility of resistance to Hitler, and opposed a 'certain uncritical idealization of democracy' and Huber's nationalist trust in the 'people'. 'Hitler's power had all legality and even democratic legitimacy on its side', Schmitt wrote. 'But, in the Germany of the Hitler regime, there was not even a shadow of a counter-government! I hear the people around Goerdeler these days claim that they formed a government. I was able to observe some of this, as far as Popitz and Jessen were concerned, from very close by.' Schmitt mocked these 'heroes'.[139] In response to the difficulties of discussing their differences in writing, Schmitt increasingly expressed his wish to meet in person.

In February 1950, Huber sent Schmitt the typescript of his collection of sources on constitutional history,[140] shifting the ground on which to carry out their argument to that area. He also asked Schmitt directly whether '[his] kind of legal and state theory isn't ultimately an expression of an existentialist philosophy of right'.[141] Huber looked at the 'forms' of legal thought from the perspective of the difference between decisionism and order formation and, like Löwith, counted Schmitt's position as an existentialist decisionism. Schmitt admitted straightaway 'that the first existentialist category, which Heidegger's turn to "historicity" will encounter, as soon as it becomes concrete, will be the distinction between friend and enemy.'[142] He enclosed the newly published *Situation of European Jurisprudence* in his letter. Huber praised the 'masterly essay' in strong terms, but also formulated some objections. Thus, he criticized Schmitt's turn to Savigny and defended the power for reform and 'reality of law' [Gesetzeswirklichkeit] under Wilhelminianism. In Huber's reading, the central point of Schmitt's essay becomes the critique of legality, and Huber again referred unmistakably to National Socialism:

Notwithstanding all polemics against the instrumental use of legality, one should not forget that, during this final phase in the decomposition, not only the 'law' but also 'natural law' becomes a tool of arbitrariness, discrimination and terror. The reference to 'concrete order', to the 'healthy sense of justice and feeling of the people' [gesundes Rechts- und Volksempfinden], to irrational energies, to nature or reason, to justice and humanity, to Christian natural law and to a divine order of law [Rechtsgebot], all this, as much as 'law', becomes a weapon for strategic discrimination, deprivation of rights and extermination. Thus, the decomposition is only complete once the open brutality of pseudo-legalistic postulates [Setzungen] is joined by the poison of pseudo-legitimate assertions, and all this with the help of an assiduous jurisprudence. The question is where there could still be an asylum for an uncorrupted sense of right and wrong [Rechtsbewußtsein] in such a situation.[143]

Though Schmitt saw a similar dilemma of jurisprudence, as caught 'between theology and technology', he would not tolerate any allusions to his own role. Thus, Huber's next letter spoke of 'a certain estrangement'. Their relationship had been at the same tense point in the mid-1930s, which is why it did not sort itself out now either.

On 1 December 1950, two days before Duška's death, Schmitt asked Huber to be understanding of his sensitivity, but their contact after that was limited to polite reminiscences about the Weimar period. Huber wrote a touching letter of condolence, in which he remembered Duška as part of the seminar in Bonn, her 'hospitality' and her 'intrepidity', and reported a dream in which he 'gave [Schmitt his] hand as a symbol of empathy'.[144] Such a meeting of the two remained a dream. In forty years following the end of the war, Huber did not once meet his teacher again. He congratulated him, rather formally, on his sixtieth birthday, thanked him for the copy of *Constitutional Theory*, which Schmitt had sent him, sent Schmitt a copy of his inaugural lecture in Wilhelmshaven, congratulated him on his seventieth birthday, and on the occasion of his seventy-fifth birthday, with some delay, he invoked the 'tradition' which Schmitt had founded in the 'realm of the spirit' [Reich des Geistes].[145] After that, their correspondence fell almost completely silent. In 1976, Schmitt felt attacked by certain remarks made by Huber against political decisionism and Schmitt's occasionalism. When Huber sent the fifth volume of his *Constitutional History* as a document of lived history,[146] Schmitt was again moved and thanked him as a 'predestined reader and user of [his] work'.[147] In 1978, Huber sent a last long birthday letter, in which he reminisced about the seminar in Bonn in great detail.[148] But when, on 30 August 1981, Huber sent his last letter to Schmitt, enclosing the sixth volume of *Constitutional History* and an article on the Richtungsstreit,[149] Schmitt noted in the margin of the letter: 'poisoned'. Their ties, it seems, had been severed for good. And actually, after 1950, they had never properly formed again. Their correspondence lived off of the memory of the Weimar times. The experiences under National Socialism also led to a lasting separation of Huber from Schmitt.

Huber was seeking an open discussion of errors and lapses. But Schmitt did not show any regret towards his younger pupil. Of his pupils from Bonn, only Forsthoff and Werner Weber took his side. Schmitt remained completely silent towards his personal acquaintances [Mitwelt]. On occasion, he justified his silence on a 'decisionist' basis: together with the 'challenge'* or the situation of National Socialism, any answers were obsolete, and his decisions and attitude at the time could no longer be understood. He kept his silence with iron discipline. There was probably a confessional side to this. Schmitt himself distinguished a Protestant-'ethicist ego-armouring' from a Catholic-'aestheticist ego-unleashing'.[150] While Huber, the Protestant, demanded conscientious self-justification, Schmitt, the Catholic, at best confessed his lapses to a God. Guilt and atonement, confession and repentance, were part of his personal relationship with God. This was the reason why he was appalled by public rituals of confession and repentance.

Some people think to themselves: 'Maybe a genius, but no moral character.' The term character denotes a predictable consistency of attitude and behaviour. Schmitt hardly conformed to such a predictability based on rules or principles. Due to his exceptional talent (or, if you like, his narcissistic-egotistic character) he assumed special rights for himself, expected such rights to be respected and often ignored the rule of reciprocity. After 1933 he applied his theory of sovereignty to himself and at times acted like an occasionalist God of arbitrariness [okkasionalisticher

---

* 'Challenge' in English in the original.

Willkürgott]. His personal acquaintances [Mitwelt] forgave him quite a few of his antics, even thought of him – the *Lucky Devil* – as child-like and naive. But in 1933, at the latest, Schmitt lost his political innocence. The aggressive resentment with which, after 1945, he repressed and denied the role he had played put off many of his former companions. His self-pity and sometimes excessive insults did not match the ethos of the 'soldier', which he had invoked against the 'citizen'. Schmitt increasingly retreated into circles where no one would question the way in which he dealt with his past, and he developed iron-clad rituals for making certain questions taboo. He did read the research on the National Socialist time, and he realized what National Socialism, in Huber's words, 'in its effects, as a system of extermination', had been. But he continually relativized these crimes and glossed over his role. He tried to commit those around him to apologetic legends and interpretations (such as the legend of the 'statist', the katechon figure and critic of Hobbes), and he remained stubbornly silent especially on his cooperation with Hans Frank. He favoured indirect or 'esoteric' forms of expressing himself on these matters. He spun himself a hermetic interpretation of his role and tried to dictate the terms of the discussion. After 1945, Huber was probably the only one of his very close companions who tried to persuade him to undertake a full and open discussion of these matters and to accept the historical facts. And, on the basis of 'more than twenty years of companionship' [Weggenossenschaft], Schmitt explicitly granted Huber the right to ask for such a full and open discussion, but he wanted a personal conversation as the framework for it (which Huber wanted to avoid) and, as the final point of divergence between them, Schmitt referred to the types or 'forms' [Gestalten] of jurisprudential thought.[151] Within Schmitt's *Political Theology* there is no space for the morality of an individual. Nevertheless, it is difficult to comprehend how his religiosity should have affirmed National Socialism and remained silent on the Federal Republic. In hindsight, his reference to 'political theology' often appears as nothing but an ideological justification. In 1949, Hannah Arendt wrote to Jaspers about Heidegger: 'What you call impurity I would call lack of character – but in the sense that he literally has none and certainly not a particularly bad one. At the same time, he lives in depths and with a passionateness that one can't easily forget.' His distortion of the facts, she said, were 'intolerable'. His life in Todtnauberg was 'really a kind of mouse hole he has crawled back into because he rightly assumes that the only people he'll have to see there are the pilgrims who come full of admiration for him.'[152] With good reason, many people thought like this, or very similarly, about Schmitt in Plettenberg.

After Duška's death: 'wonderful welcome' and 'malicious persecution'

After Duška's death, Schmitt was in a very bad way; he urgently needed a new task. He stared at the bottom of many, maybe too many, bottles of his favourite wine, Amontillado, and perceived the double meaning in Edgar

Allan Poe's short story 'The Cask of Amontillado', where the wine also stands for the grave. Schmitt's first distraction was a journey to Hamburg, where, on 22 February 1951, he spoke on 'Das Problem des Friedens' [The problem of peace] at a private event.[153] At the end of February he continued with his entries in the *Glossarium*, which soon took on another form. The unpublished 'IV. book'[154] comments on contemporary events increasingly in the form of newspaper articles glued into the volume. Soon, Schmitt would also lose Anima's company. In mid-March she passed her oral school leaving examination and then went to Munich in order to study at the Academy of Art and become a stage designer. She was, however, worried about one point: 'Only in the case of creatures of above-average talent is a one-year period of practical training not required. Do you think I might be considered to fall into that category?'[155] On 5 April, Schmitt organized a small, 'somewhat improvised', private conference, 'Three Hundred Years of Leviathan', to which he unsuccessfully tried to invite Norberto Bobbio. Among others, Sombart, Winckelmann and Alfred Andersch (from Hessischer Rundfunk) took part. Winckelmann said: 'To me, a celebration of Thomas Hobbes feels like drinking a glass of sparkling wine to the health of the headsman.'[156] The contact with Andersch would prove useful in the future when Schmitt made various radio broadcasts. His short paper at the conference concentrated very much on the ostracism Hobbes suffered as a 'scapegoat', thus reflecting Schmitt's personal situation. The text, through the arrangement of the journalist Hans Fleig, was published on 5 April in the journal *Tat*.

Only with great difficulty did Anima find a room in Munich. She soon contemplated studying jurisprudence. 'It is nice at the academy, but the intellectual standards get on my nerves.'[157] In mid-April, upon an invitation from Rafael Calvo Serer, Schmitt travelled to Spain, where he gave his lecture on 'Die Einheit der Welt' [The unity of the world] several times.[158] He was met with a 'really wonderful welcome' and, after a long period, had success once more as a professor. He wrote to Carl Brinkmann:

> The journey to Spain (April to June) was a distraction, which, however, like every distraction, ended with a forceful reminder of my real situation: I am still as if numbed by the contrast between the truly wonderful, and also honourable, welcome in Spain and the malicious persecution in my fatherland. In Spain, I celebrated a glorious renewed encounter with jurisprudence and the juridical faculty, including the greatest possible public attention at the Ateneo in Madrid, in the overcrowded Aula Magna [main auditorium] in Barcelona, in the overcrowded Paradicho in Santiago, as well as in Murcia and very nicely in Seville;* not only the universities' officials, but also ministers and governors formally welcomed me.[159]

Universitas published a note on the trip to Spain,[160] and on 28 July Schmitt gave a report on it to the support association Academia Moralis in the Stadtgarten restaurant in Cologne. The event was the first highlight of

---

*   The German 'und sehr schön in Sevilla' is equally elliptical.

'Her father's house in Plettenberg is now only a petrol station and repair centre for her' – Schmitt about Anima in a letter to Armin Mohler (4 April 1955)

the association's activities, with around seventy people attending; Schmitt received a fee of 250 Deutschmarks.

Schmitt's reflections on the philosophy of history were the topic of the first radio conversation with Walter Warnach, which the Hessische Rundfunk broadcast on 19 June 1951. An unexpected letter reached Schmitt's house. Kathleen Murray, his former lover, reminded him of old 'vows' and asked to meet him again in Germany or Australia.[161] Sombart told Schmitt that he had a 'two-hour private weaning-off seminar on C. S.' with Waldemar Gurian in Frankfurt.[162] In September, Schmitt made an 'appeal to all well-meaning readers of historical works and lyrical poems', asking them to send him examples of 'counterfactual conditional clauses in works by historians' and 'unusual rhymes' (BS, p. 105), which he collected. The historical conditional seemed bad poetry to him.[163] Together with Anima, he visited the Jüngers in Wilflingen for the last time in December. To Carl August Emge he wrote: 'The many nice things they have to say about "humaneness" of course refer only to those approved, who include Tom, Dick and Harry but, by a long stretch, not me. Rather, the humanitarian syllogism, which applies to me, runs: I have sympathy for every human being, / For Carl Schmitt, I have no sympathy, / Therefore Carl Schmitt is not a human being.'[164]

In Munich, Anima spent a lot of time with her cousin Claire Louise. In the summer term 1952 she studied in Hamburg, and for the autumn she went to the Landestheater in Darmstadt as a trainee. Schmitt had established the contact through Egon Vietta, who was now the artistic advisor of the theatre's director, Gustav Sellner.[165] However, Anima soon dropped out of the practical training, changed her subject and began studying at the institute for translation and interpreting in Heidelberg. She completed her degree in 1952 with a translation of Lilian Winstanley's book on Hamlet. While she was working on it, Schmitt studied Shakespeare. At least the questions over his financial situation began to resolve themselves. A legal solution had to be found for those who left the civil service in 1945, and Schmitt now pursued his retirement (according to Article 131 of the Grundgesetz [Basic Law])* – but not his taking on emeritus status as a professor – with the Regierungspräsident [head of the regional government] of Arnsberg. He declared that he had 'voluntarily given up' his political offices 'in November 1936'.[166] With effect from 1 May he was retired and, to begin with, received a pension of just about 1,400 Deutschmarks. A legal opinion for the Buderus-Werke brought additional money into the household. Thus, Schmitt was able to use the money from an 'account initiative' by the support association Academia Moralis† for buying up some of his own works. Forsthoff finally regained his chair in Heidelberg. 'After all that has happened here, and partly is still happening, the break cannot be repaired' (EFCS, p. 89), he declared, and forthwith engaged in the 'expulsion of the Heidelberg spirit' (EFCS, p. 133) from the faculty. Anni Stand now returned for good as Schmitt's 'housekeeper'. Schmitt increasingly made contact with younger talents. Sombart introduced Hanno Kesting, who, in turn, brought along Reinhard Koselleck. Roman Schnut was in close contact from 1951 onwards. Heinrich Popitz, the son of Johannes Popitz, was at the Institut für Sozialforschung [Institute for Social Research] in Dortmund, where he wrote his doctoral thesis on the young Marx;[167] he frequently came to visit and soon established such a close rapport with Anima that Schmitt hoped for a lasting relationship. However, a trip to Paris with Anima led to tensions between them, and their relationship evaporated after Popitz moved to Freiburg.[168]

1953 became a turning point. With Anni Stand being there, with visitors staying several days, and with many excursions into the intellectual landscapes of his conversational partners, Schmitt's life in Plettenberg settled down. However, his friendship with the Jüngers ended when Jünger, from remarks made by Mohler, got the impression that Schmitt's resentment had solidified into enmity. A few days before Jünger's sixty-fifth birthday, the relationship manifestly broke down. Jünger cancelled Schmitt's invitation through Mohler. Schmitt felt that this was a massive 'insult' (GJCS, p. 182). Gretha invited him again 'as a guest, whenever you happen to come around' (GJCS, p. 185), but Schmitt did not reply to this and for a long time remained only in formal contact, which continued because of Schmitt's godchild, Carl Alexander. On 15 April 1954, Schmitt's younger sister Anna Margaretha Schmitt, the piano teacher, died after a short illness. 'Her love of music was a source of joy and cheerfulness for her',

---

* The article is part of the transitional and final provisions and refers to the rights of those who were in civil service on 8 May 1945, including refugees and the expelled, but were no longer used as civil servants and had left for reasons other than those covered by civil service law.
† See the section 'The man who caught the whale', p. 462 below.

Ernst Hüsmert, Carl Schmitt, Anni Stand and Sava Kličković on the platform of Finnentrop railway station in the 1960s

Schmitt wrote in the death notice. Only now did he inherit a small part of the house in Brockhauser Weg (about a third of Anna's half of it, with the other two halves owned by his surviving sister and his brother). His sister Üssi continued to live in the house. Anni Stand, the 'housekeeper', had a somewhat obscure but somehow familial position in the house. This was the situation in the Brockhauserweg until Schmitt, at the end of 1970, moved house one last time.

'I can well understand that you do not want to speak any more': quarrels over lectures

As soon as Schmitt had arrived in Plettenberg, he began to establish contacts with friends abroad again. He wrote to friends in Italy, Spain and Portugal. From March 1948 he was in lively correspondence with the Portuguese jurist Luís Cabral de Moncada. Through Moncada, Schmitt's contact with the Spanish scholar Álvaro d'Ors was renewed and continued throughout the remainder of his life. Schmitt was also in correspondence with Bobbio about questions regarding Hobbes editions.[169] However, when Bobbio declined the invitation to the Hobbes anniversary celebration, the contact was broken off. Other attempts at establishing contacts also failed. The vague connection over many years with Alessandro Passerin d'Entrèves ended with d'Entrèves's letter of 6 February 1949: 'I have not forgotten you. For me, it remains an open question: how was the "case of Schmitt" possible? It is, after all, vital for us all to understand the "case of Germany" eventually.'[170] Schmitt did not respond to such questions. Beyond taking care of friendly relationships, his correspondence was not entirely without hidden intentions. Schmitt was looking for responses, invitations, translations of his work, a professional future abroad. In 1949–50 he seriously considered emigrating to Argentina, the place to which his friend Gueydan de Roussel had absconded after having been sentenced to death as a collaborator in France. Schmitt had already acquired permission to enter the country and the assurance of receiving a visa.[171] However, an old acquaintance advised Schmitt against it.[172] Then Duška's illness intervened, and the final settlement of his rights to a pension made his emigration unnecessary.

In the 1950s, Schmitt gave numerous talks in semi-private circles. They represent a stage in the long history of a political public, of political clubs and associations.[173] Especially important to Schmitt was the Rhein-Ruhr Club, founded in 1948, an 'association for the study of political-economic-cultural questions', with its office in Gevelsberg. Schmitt gave his first major post-war talk on 13 December 1950, only a few days after Duška's death,[174] for the Rhein-Ruhr Club in the Düsseldorf restaurant Wolfsschlucht. The title was 'Die Einheit der Welt und die Einheit Europas' [The unity of the world and the unity of Europe]. He repeated the talk in January upon an invitation from Dr Schimpf[175] and the Gesellschaft für Wirtschaftsforschung [Society for Economic Research] in the Engelsburg in Recklinghausen. On 19 February 1951, Schmitt spoke 'Über den gerechten Krieg' [On just war] to the Auslandswissenschaftliche Gesellschaft [Society for foreign studies] in Hamburg, where he also met Hjalmar Schacht.[176] Another talk in Baden-Baden followed; a further talk in Hamburg was cancelled. In October he gave a talk on Spanish national character, on bull fights, and on the Spanish human type in Neheim-Hüsten, at the home of Theodor Beste.[177] On 20 November he spoke on 'Land and Sea' in Plettenberg to a group of 'Heimatfreunde' [friends of the homeland]. He explained how he had arrived at his topic 'from the specificity of the Sauerland soil'.[178] On 21 April 1952 he repeated his talk on 'The Unity of the World' at the 'Fourth Rhenish University Week' in the ballroom of the Duisburger Hof. The organizer was Dr Lottmann from the society at Duisburg University.[179] Heinrich Barth invited Schmitt to Bremen, where Heidegger also gave a talk.[180] The Grotius Society requested a celebratory lecture.[181] In August 1952, a symposium marking Hans Freyer's sixty-fifth birthday took place at the Eberbach monastery. Then Schmitt went to Frankfurt and Baden-Baden, where he came to 'know and love' (BS, p. 144) a certain Michelle Amédée Ponceau. On 23 October he spoke at a club in Bremen on 'The Nomos of the Earth'. Afterwards, he visited a conference of the Shakespeare society in Duisburg.

Hans Schomerus invited Schmitt to the Evangelische Akademie in Herrenalb for a conference on 'Conservatives and Reactionaries'. Remembering a conversation with Schomerus in 1942, Schmitt suggested as a topic 'Der Antichrist und die Schöpfung' [The Antichrist and creation] and expressed his wish for a critical discussion of 'one-sidedly eschatological Christianity', which often led to pure 'enthusiasm'. At the same time

Schomerus invited Schmitt to a conference about 'New Approaches to Shakespeare' on the Mainau,*[182] for which Schmitt announced a paper on 'Der Antichrist und was ihn aufhält' [The Antichrist and what delays him] as well as on 'Hamlet der Spieler Gottes' [Hamlet – God's player]. Apparently, Schmitt wanted to continue his speculations on the katechon and his reflections on the 'Christian image of history'.[183] However, his invitation caused Walter Strauß, then the state secretary in the Ministry of Justice, to protest to the bishop of Baden, Bender,[184] and the conference was threatened with cancellation. Schmitt received a telegram from Schomerus saying that both papers had been 'prohibited'.[185] In a letter of the same day, he also told Schmitt that he had offered his 'resignation'.[186] Schmitt experienced a similar cancellation of an invitation from the Evangelische Akademie in Rhineland-Westphalia.[187]

On 15 October 1953, Schmitt formulated a new 'point of view within the contemporary debate about the worth and worthlessness of modern technology' on the occasion of opening a working group on 'The Spirit of Our Age' in the assembly hall of a school in Iserlohn.[188] And on 20 October he spoke about 'Land and Sea' at the Kaufmännischen Verein [Association of Commerce] of Iserlohn. Despite ample opportunities for speaking, Schmitt was annoyed by the cancellation of these invitations. To Brinkmann he wrote:

This past year, 1953, was full of disappointments for me, apart from the one, admittedly very bright, spot of the celebration marking my sixty-fifth birthday and the wonderful Festschrift to which you have so courageously contributed with your very beautiful article. Apart from that, I am experiencing a novel and particularly infamous kind of persecution. No fewer than four times within the space of a year, I was eminently politely and formally invited and then, after a few months, the invitation was cancelled in a brusque and insulting manner. Two times, evangelical academies excelled in this method, once the Darmstädter conversations, and the last cancellation, exactly at Christmas time, came from the German mission in Mexico. I assume that Hallstein[189] is involved in this last case, because a year ago . . . he already made sure that the great invitation to the celebration of Donoso Cortés' hundredth birthday (3 May 1953) – an invitation I surely deserved and on which everyone on the Spanish side agreed – was not sent out. This kind of persecution by German authorities is part of their style.[190]

Nevertheless, in 1954 Schmitt also gave several talks. Upon an invitation from Erwin Hölzle of the Wissenschaftliche Vortragsgemeinschaft [Association for Academic Lectures], for instance, he spoke about 'Die Teilung der Erde' [The division of the earth] in the Bürgersaal [community centre] in Konstanz.[191] He took part in discussions at events organized by the Academia Moralis and the Rhein-Ruhr Club. His ideas at the time went into his contribution to a Festschrift for Ernst Jünger.[192] In 1955, an invitation from the 'Verwaltungshochschulwochen' [administrative

---

* An island on Lake Constance.

academy seminars] in Bad Meinberg was again cancelled,[193] and the same happened in autumn 1956 with an invitation to come to Mainz. On 11 February 1955, Schmitt spoke about the 'Gegensatz zwischen Land und Meer als weltgeschichtliches Problem' [The contrast between land and sea as a problem of world history] at the Volkshochschule [adult education centre] in Düsseldorf.[194] The organizer agreed a talk on Hamlet and urged Schmitt to give further presentations, but soon wrote to him: 'I can well understand that you do not want to speak any more.'[195] On 30 November 1957, Schmitt spoke again about 'Probleme des modernen Völkerrechts' [Problems of *Modern International Law*] in a hotel in Wuppertal, having been invited by the 'Round Table "Bergisch Land"'.[196] Later, to the list of 'invitations and cancellations'[197] was added a cancellation from the WDR [Westdeutscher Rundfunk] in the autumn of 1959 and from the Evangelische Akademie Loccum in May 1965. The cancellations were the reason for Schmitt's withdrawal from public speaking. The quarrels surrounding his lectures and publications showed him that his academic position and the circle of his addressees had changed completely. Thus, almost without exception, he now spoke only at colloquia of university teachers who were friends.

'Unity of the world' or post-war nomos?

The 'eschatological' aspect of Schmitt's late work does not quite fit together with the question of a post-war nomos. The fundamental political fact of the post-war era was the contrast between East and West in the form of the Cold War. Schmitt had to find a universalistic interpretation for this dualism in order to maintain his eschatological perspective. To that end, he distinguished between a normative dimension and a dimension of power analysis, between a factual description of the bloc formations and a critique of the ideologies which were meant to provide normative justifications of these blocs. Schmitt had already distinguished sharply between the philosophy of history and the theology of history in his discussion of Löwith and his introduction to the small book on Cortés. This disjunction now allowed him to assume an ideological unity underlying the dualism of the two blocs, to read a common 'philosophy of history' out of the situation and to paint a 'picture of the technical-industrial unity of the world' (SGN, p. 497). Against this background, Schmitt stipulates a third force in his lectures on 'The Unity of the World', which he published in *Der Merkur*[198] in 1952 as well as in an extended Spanish version. His argument is surprising because it juxtaposes the emphatic stress on the difference between the capitalist and communist systems with the assumption of their convergence in a 'general tendency towards the technical-industrial unity of the world' (SGN, p. 499) – a thesis that was increasingly argued for in the 1970s. Schmitt speaks of the 'unity in the self-interpretation' of East and West 'in terms of the philosophy of history' (SGN, p. 500). In order to make this claim he goes back to 'Saint-Simon's philosophy of history as industrial progress' (SGN, p. 502), to which, he says, both Marxism and more recent Western philosophies of history had succumbed. He understands the philosophy of history politically as an instrument of 'planning', and he registers a 'discrepancy between technical and moral progress' (SGN, p. 503). He adds his own religious alternative in the Spanish edition. Only within the 'Christian picture of history' does he find the 'possibility of a third force' (SGN, p. 500) and a 'new international law'.

Schmitt explained his cautious distinction between a philosophy and theology of history to d'Ors as follows:

> The point of my lecture is precisely to develop a picture of today's situation on the basis of a cold and matter-of-fact diagnosis, which leads up to the threshold of eschatology, but not a single step further. This is part of my style as a jurist, and my success as a jurist is based on the fact that I adhere strictly to this style; however, the hatred and the enmity of my opponents are also based on it. (CSAD, p. 120)

In April 1952, he asked: 'Is there still a German proviso? There is. However, it derives not from German maliciousness, but from a deeper view of the world' (SGN, pp. 511f.) Schmitt provided little evidence for his diagnosis of a unity of East and West from the perspective of a philosophy of history. Was the technological utopianism of early socialism really the driving force in Marxism? Did Lenin understand this correctly? Schmitt left it to the younger generation of his pupils to develop his theses academically. Nicolaus Sombart, Hanno Kesting and Reinhart Koselleck began to study the political function of the philosophy of history. Peter Scheibert and Dieter Groh described the self-understanding of Russia and the Soviet Union. Even more than Mohler's doctoral thesis on *Die konservative Revolution in Deutschland 1918–1932* [The conservative revolution in Germany, 1918–1932], Hanno Kesting's thesis on *Utopie und Eschatologie* [Utopia and eschatology] was the result of intensive discussions with Schmitt. Kesting called Schmitt 'the absolute centre' of his thinking and 'the real and only teacher'.[199] Schmitt also read a draft of Koselleck's thesis in 1953. Schmitt's central idea at the time was to use his distinction between the philosophy and theology of history for a critique of the utopian ideology of progress and thus to gain new territory for the critique of universalism.

However, in the 1950s Schmitt provided keywords more or less only in the form of short interventions. In a short text, 'Der neue Nomos der Erde' [The new nomos of the earth], which he wrote for a radio programme called 'Living Knowledge' upon an invitation from Heinz Friedrichs, Schmitt sketched only briefly 'three possibilities': a world state, hegemony of the USA or 'independent Großräume or blocs' (SGN, p. 521). Schmitt gave the most comprehensive account of his position in his contribution to the Jünger Festschrift, *Freundschaftliche Begegnungen* [Friendly encounters], with the title 'Die geschichtliche Struktur des heutigen Welt-Gegensatzes von Ost und West' [The historical structure of today's world opposition between East and West].[200] The editor of the Feschrift, Mohler, pursued the idea of a consolidation of right-wing intellectual masterminds. He repeatedly assured Schmitt that he did not need to fear any interventions: 'The only censorship lies within yourself' (BS, p. 157). By the end of August, Schmitt had completed the manuscript, but he feared that he would no longer be welcomed after his break with Gretha Jünger.[201] And his contribution was not free of provocation. It develops a counter-position to Jünger's *Der gordische Knoten* [The Gordian Knot] and its portrayal of East–West relations.[202] Schmitt agrees with Jünger that 'the question of the core and the structure of the dualist tension' must be investigated outside conventional positivist methods, but he distances himself from Jünger's 'intuitive' and mythic 'thinking in polarities' (SGN, p. 531) and instead looks for the 'historical structure' with the help of his elementary distinction between land and sea. He then goes on to set his position apart from the more recent 'Question-Answer-Logic'* of Collingwood and Toynbee. The 'call of history' [Ruf der Geschichte] is, he says, a 'calling' [Anruf] of history itself, based loosely on Heidegger: the nomos asks questions. Man only asks insofar as he hears the question. Schmitt again sketches his theses about the birth of the industrial revolution out of England's 'metaphysical' decision to adopt a maritime existence. He sees an elective affinity between 'maritime existence' and modern technology, which he ties to the choice between 'house or ship' (SGN, p. 542), and disputes Marxism's 'monopoly' on access to the meaning of history by beginning an ideational-political dispute over Hegel's heritage and what authentic 'Hegel appropriation' [Hegel-Nahme] is.† Schmitt juxtaposed left Hegelianism with 'another Hegel line'.[203] He grants Hans Freyer the honour of being the heir to Hegel's and Dilthey's philosophies of history and of having provided the 'first' answer to the post-war situation.

Schmitt defended his avoidance of a detailed answer of his own in his 'Gespräch über den Neuen Raum' [Conversation on the new space] as the 'question of the great question' (SGN, p. 559): a historical truth, he said, was 'true only once'. In light of the danger of pure 'repetition' (SGN, p. 567) of old answers, a lot was therefore already gained by asking the question of the momentary [aktuellen] 'calling' with clarity. It was at the time of writing this text that Schmitt entered into correspondence with the French Hegel scholar Alexandre Kojève.[204]

In the club in Bremen, Schmitt began a parallel campaign: 'In the summer, Heidegger gave a talk on "Logos – Heraclitus's key word" there. I would now like to give the immediately preceding talk on the NOMOS as a key word. I am, of course, very tempted to do that, especially as I have made some interesting philological discoveries regarding the NOMOS' (CSAD, p. 119). His talk 'Appropriation/Distribution/Production'[205] divides the nomos into the etymological components and meanings of 'appropriating', 'distributing' and 'producing'.[206] Schmitt emphasizes 'the fundamental precedence of appropriation before distribution and produc-

---

* English in the original.
† Schmitt's neologism is obviously meant to hint at a parallel to the arguments surrounding 'Landnahme' – the appropriation of land – in *The Nomos of the Earth*. Cf. also footnote in chapter 26, p. 398.

tion' (ADP, p. 329).* Appropriation, he says, is today frowned upon; even capitalism is striving towards the distributive justice of a social market economy and concentrates increasingly on 'Weiden' – i.e., on production and consumption. But this production is also based on a fundamental taking [Nahme], the great modern 'industry-appropriation [Industrie-Nahme]' (ADP, p. 334), which Schmitt takes to be a final stage:

> because what one today calls world history in the West and in the East is the history of development in the objects, means, and forms of appropriation interpreted as progress. This development proceeds from the *land-appropriations* of nomadic and agrarian-feudal times to the *sea-appropriations* of the 16th to the 19th century, over the *industry-appropriations* of the industrial-technical age and its distinction between developed and underdeveloped areas, and, finally, to the *air-appropriations* and *space-appropriations* of the present. (NE p. 347)

Schmitt presents the text as the seventh corollary of *The Nomos of the Earth*, which concludes the *Verfassungsrechtlichen Aufsätze* [Articles on Constitutional Law]. His speculative text on 'Nomos–Nahme–Name' was, then, his 'last essay' (CSAD, p. 191) from an overall legal-historical perspective on the 'nomos'.[207] Schmitt adds some philological reflections on the concept of nomos and refers to Greek history, criticizing the – since Philo, conventional – translation of nomos as 'law' and reminding the reader of appropriation as the first stage in the development of the relation between appropriation, distribution and production. He emphasizes the systematic 'connection between appropriation and name' (NNN, p. 348; trans. modified): the conclusion of appropriation in the decisive act of naming. This act, he says, overcomes 'the satanic temptation to keep power invisible, anonymous and secret' (NNN, p. 349). Only in the act of naming do the power relations assume 'visibility, publicity and ceremony [Krönung]' (ibid.). However, the present time hardly possessed the force any longer for such etymological argumentation. Schmitt had always criticized the concealment of actual power relations by juridical 'fictions', and he had always seen the present day and age as characterized by a decline in forms of ostentatious representation. Now he almost declared the positive act of naming to be creating a legal title.

Library matters

In October 1945, Schmitt's library was confiscated. Schmitt wrote: 'While I experienced the loss of other things more as a lightening of baggage,

---

* The English translator of this text has, for good reasons, rendered 'Nehmen/Teilen/Weiden' as 'appropriation/distribution/production'. It may be interesting, though, to point out that the German is more concrete than that. Hence, the translation could also be 'taking/dividing (or even sharing)/grazing (or pasturage). In Schmitt's text, this tension between the concrete and the abstract introduces a normative, and at the same time archaic, authority into what would otherwise be a purely descriptive account.

the removal of the library, which had grown over thirty years, felt to me like a mutilation.'[208] On the initiative of Eberhard von Medem[209] and Gisela von Busse, the Americans returned his books in September 1952. However, Plettenberg did not have enough space for them. Schmitt therefore had them sent to the Institut für Europäische Geschichte [Institute of European History] in Mainz,[210] which was led by the Church historian Joseph Lortz, a colleague of Eschweiler and Barion in Braunsberg. The young Roman Schnur, the cousin of a neighbour in Berlin,[211] helped with sorting the books. He was slightly disappointed with the content of the twenty-three boxes. He couldn't believe 'that you [Schmitt] did not own more major works'.[212] The first dispatch, he thought, was probably incomplete. Schmitt sent some more books from Plettenberg. The University of Mainz was not interested in buying any of them.[213] Thus, in December 1954 the library was sold to the antiquarian bookshop Kerst in Frankfurt.[214] Schmitt thanked Lortz for the 'accommodation' of the books over two years.[215] The philosopher Günter Patzig bought a first edition of Wittgenstein's *Tractatus* and asked Schmitt whether the sale was legal.[216] Schmitt confirmed this, adding that the book had been a present from Franz Blei. 'Only in about five cases, from a total of several thousand juridical books, did the two stamps by the American authorities lead to personal inquiries with me', he answered Patzig.[217] Later, Schmitt sold further parts of his library to the antiquarian bookshop Semmel in Bonn. Some catalogues of antiquarian books demonstrate just what a treasure was dissipated at the time.

Press contacts: 'Into hyenas countesses grow'

Schmitt knew the old leaders of German journalism and publishing. Many of them were still active in key roles after 1945. Thus, in the 1950s, Schmitt published in almost all major newspapers and publishing houses. There can be no talk of him having been boycotted. In fact, he rejected many requests. Sometimes, though, difficulties emerged.

Rudolf Fischer was an old acquaintance of Schmitt[218] who worked for the *Fortschritt*, a publication belonging to the circle around Stapel. Through Mohler, Schmitt came into contact with Hans Fleig and the Zurich-based *Tat*.[219] Through Klaus Mehnert and Giselher Wirsing, Schmitt was able to publish in *Christ und Welt*.[220] The latter did not want to publish the short text on Löwith, asking for a contribution on the nineteenth century instead.[221] Later, Schmitt followed a suggestion of the journal's editors and wrote a eulogy of Hans Freyer.[222] Smaller pieces on Herbert Nette and Karl Korn appeared in the *Frankfurter Allgemeine Zeitung*,[223] such as the small confessional fragment 'Weisheit der Zelle' [Wisdom of the prison cell] and a commentary on the critical situation of the bourgeoisie – the bourgeoise that Schmitt, in earlier days, had scorned.[224] *Die Welt* wanted his Iserlohn lecture on 'Wert und Unwert der Technik' [Worth and worthlessness of technology] and requested a further article on the Bundesverfassungsgericht [Federal Constitutional Court].[225]

As late as 1971, Günther Zehm asked Schmitt 'whether [he] had the time and felt like being an occasional contributor'.[226] Schmitt rejected the offer.

Schmitt was in correspondence with Margret Boveri, a journalist in Berlin, and he had closer contacts with Paul Weinreich, Richard Tüngel and the 'Illyrian' Walter Petwaidic of *Die Zeit*.[227] In 1956, Petwaidic moved to the *Deutsche Zeitung* and later worked for the Deutschlandfunk. When *Die Zeit* published an excerpt from *Gespräch über die Macht* [Conversation on power], Countess Dönhoff protested.[228] Tüngel was paid off as a co-owner and had to leave. Schmitt's mocking commentary was: 'Into hyenas countesses grow' (BS, p. 200).[229] Even in 1982, Ulrich Greiner still asked for Schmitt's participation in a survey on the question of the 'contemporary condition of conservatism'.[230]

Occasionally, Schmitt's work as an advisor earned him a case of wine.[231] However, in the 1950s Schmitt was not averse to more permanent work. Thus, efforts were made to establish him at the CDU paper *Wirtschaftsbild*.[232] Sepp Schelz, with whom Schmitt was friendly, asked him for an opinion piece on the topic of the 'national state of emergency' [Staatsnotstand] for the *Westdeutsche Rundschau*: 'I know that you have no intention of publishing officially. But maybe we could feature it under a pseudonym, or I could use your ideas as the basis for an article.'[233] Schmitt sent him a one-page exposition, in which he called the 'modern state of exception or of emergency' a 'problem of the economic and social constitution' and demanded the 'fast introduction of a regulation by federal law'.[234] Schmitt probably wrote such expositions more than once during this period. Nor can it be ruled out that he occasionally published under a pseudonym. However, in contrast to, for instance, Theodor Maunz or Hans Barion, he did not engage in substantial pseudonymous publishing. Had he done so, he would have entered this into his register of texts and publications.

In 1952, Rudolf Augstein considered a constitutional complaint in connection with a confiscation of an issue of *Der Spiegel*[235] and asked for a personal 'discussion' with Schmitt.[236] In mid-October, Augstein visited Schmitt in Plettenberg and remained loosely in touch after that. *Hamlet or Hecuba* he read approvingly: 'I almost like it better than previous discussions of the same theme.'[237] *Der Spiegel* published an article, 'Die Mutter ist tabu' [The mother is taboo].[238] Later, Augstein wanted an opinion piece on a series about the Reichstag fire.[239] However, he rejected suggestions to mark Schmitt's seventieth birthday in a more visible way. One of *Der Spiegel*'s editors, Dieter Brumm, wanted a conversation about Walter Benjamin, and, as late as 1982, Augstein had a request for an interview sent out.[240]

This rather accidental collection of press contacts nevertheless shows that Schmitt was not shy of looking for various contacts and that, beyond his publications, he performed advisory functions. He studied the journalistic contemporary commentary and critique of Margret Boveri, Winfried Martini, Mohler and others with the same seriousness as if it were specialist juridical literature. In the middle of the 1950s he formed especially close ties with Johannes Gross, whom he got to know through Rüdiger Altmann.

Altmann and Gross edited the RCDS* newspaper *Civis*, to which Schmitt contributed some satirical poems. Altman and Gross also incorporated the poems into their collection *Die neue Gesellschaft* [The new society], which is very telling regarding the mixture of restorative ideology and euphoria about the economic miracle within Adenauer's CDU. Schmitt remained in close contact with both Altmann and Gross. Even in the last newspaper picture, showing an alert Schmitt on his ninety-fifth birthday, the short Gross is standing next to the even shorter "great man" Schmitt (see the picture on p. 534).

'The man who caught the whale': Schmitt's sixty-fifth birthday, the zenith of his life

Until his retirement in 1952, Schmitt was financially insecure. Therefore, Peterheinrich Kirchhoff,[241] together with Forsthoff, made an appeal for help among his circle of friends. The initiative was formalized as the support association 'Academia Moralis'.[242] This 'academy' grew out of private meetings. Krauss and Barion were its driving forces; Oberheid made his office in Düsseldorf available. The statutes of 1 March formulated the purpose of the association in ironic terms: the association serves '1. to promote an international attitude, tolerance in all areas of culture, and the idea of understanding among peoples by cultivating the will to peace among them'.[243] In the summer of 1952 the association acquired the status of a registered society. It was very active organizing talks, but understood itself primarily as a support organization for Schmitt. Frequent meetings were held in the Stadtgarten restaurant in Cologne, where Schmitt first spoke about the historical-philosophical 'Unity of the World' and then about 'Eindrücke einer Spanien-Reise' [Impressions while travelling in Spain].[244] The association was a private circle of people close to Schmitt which increasingly sought to move into the public limelight between 1951 and 1954. After that, its activities slowly dwindled. The formal organization served the purpose not least of giving their association charitable status, so that donations were exempted from tax.

The highpoint of the association's activities consisted of the celebrations for Schmitt's sixty-fifth birthday, on 11 July 1953, in the Düsseldorfer Rheinterrassen restaurant. Barion and Krauss were in charge of the improvised organization of the event at short notice. The title for a Festschrift, 'Epirrhosis' [Encouragement], was decided, but only a bibliography of Schmitt's works was actually printed in the end. About 150 guests attended the reception. There were musical performances by a female pianist and a female singer. Forsthoff gave an 'unforgettable speech' (EFCS, p. 97), in which he recalled the epiphany of their first encounter ('In that summer of 1923, I became a jurist') and praised

---

* Ring Christlich-Demokratischer Studenten [Association of Christian Democrat Students], the student organization of the CDU.

Schmitt's 'restoration of state theory' as the 'renewal of the science of public law'. Under National Socialism, he said, Schmitt 'had looked into the very depths of war and civil war' (EFCS, p. 398); his life's work, he added, was 'by no means complete yet'. Schmitt gave a thank-you speech. The celebrations ended in the evening in Plettenberg, where the younger guests performed a sketch titled 'One Man Remains'.[245] Anima played the lead role of 'Nemesis', who gives a critical appreciation of Schmitt's achievements. The title alludes to the last 'scapegoat' (SSA, pp. 76f.), the one who evades adaptation. 'One man remained. Legal? Legitimate? A katechon is embodied in him.' Nemesis declares that Schmitt 'exposed celibate bureaucracy / made Bruno Bauer a genius / disintegrated Erich Kaufmann / . . . / revised political theology / predicted global civil war, / amoralized the friend–enemy relation / criminalized criminalization.' All this, and a lot more, is admitted. But, most of all, Nemesis recognizes a 'son' in Schmitt. '[B]ecause he is the man who caught a whale' – i.e., who harnessed a Leviathan by providing a conceptual definition of it. Was this Leviathan meant to stand for National Socialism? Many of the guests found the celebration 'wonderful'.[246] There also was a short note in the *Frankfurter Allgemeine Zeitung*.

'Intellectual radio plays'

Schmitt had frequently spoken on the radio, even before 1933. After the war he first found contacts at the Hessischer Rundfunk, where he was in touch with Alfred Andersch and then with his successor, Heinz Friedrich, of the 'Nachtstudio' [night-time radio]. On 19 June 1951, Hessischer Rundfunk broadcast a conversation between Walter Warnach and Carl Schmitt on the topic 'Hat Geschichtsphilosophie noch einen Sinn?' [Is philosophy of history still useful?].[247] In the autumn of 1953, Friedrich asked Schmitt for a further contribution for the series 'Hier spricht die Wissenschaft' [This is science calling].[248] Schmitt first suggested something on 'The Nomos of the Earth'. He then got to know Raymond Aron in Tübingen and suggested a conversation with him on the topic of power. However, Aron and, later, Schelsky and Arnold Gehlen declined, and Friedrich agreed to the idea of producing the conversation with a fixed text and professional speakers. Thus, the 'project "Principles of Power"' was originally planned as a genuine conversation and became a staged dialogue and 'intellectual radio play' (BS, p. 180) only as a result of the negative replies from Aron, Schelsky and Gehlen. It was recorded on 21 June at Hessische Rundfunk.

Schmitt explained the idea thus: 'The conversation is a kind of intellectual game insofar as its main part is centred on the opposition between moral and dialectical thought. Speaker X represents the moral standpoint, which immediately evaluates events instead of waiting and seeing.'[249] The conversation takes place between a 'boy', who asks questions, and 'C. S.', who gives answers. The speakers' roles are defined, while there is no mention of the location where the conversation is supposed to take place.

In contrast to, for instance, Heidegger's *Gelassenheit* [Releasement],* not to mention the Platonic dialogues,[250] the situation in which the conversation takes place, the objective 'situation' of the 'dialogue partners', is irrelevant with respect to the course it takes. C. S. leads the conversation in an authorial and doctrinal manner. He lectures on access to the ruler [Machthaber] and the ruler's dependence on the 'overall situation' and constellation. Halfway through the conversation, the boy has more or less fallen silent. In order to liven up the scene, there is an 'intermezzo'. In the second half, the boy asks the question of how to evaluate power, whether it is good or bad. In response, C. S. derives the answers given by Pope Gregory the Great and Jakob Burckhardt from their respective historical situations. In doing so, he exposes their knowledge as superficial and leads the boy to Hobbes. With reference to the Leviathan, C. S. points out the modern experience of powerlessness. He does this without philosophically discussing processes of legitimization. The boy asks: 'But man! Where is man in all this?' (GM, p. 29), whereupon C. S. ends the conversation in a not very satisfactory way: going back to man was 'not a solution, but only the beginning of the problem we discussed' (ibid.). The figure of C. S. is not a Socratic partner in dialogue but a lecturer in political science. As a model for the conversations that took place in Plettenberg, he would be a disappointment.

The programme was produced with professional speakers and broadcast on 22 June 1954 in the Abendstudio [evening programme] of the Hessischer Rundfunk under the title 'Prinzipien der Macht: Gespräch mit C. S.' [Principles of power: conversation with C. S.].[251] With Anima, Schmitt also recorded the text privately on a tape recorder, as part of his birthday.[252] On 22 November, the conversation was repeated on the nighttime programme of the WDR, with a vindicating preamble.[253] Schmitt thanked the radio station for the 'excellent reproduction and interpretation'.[254] In mid-September, the text appeared with Neske 'in the style of the small Heidegger volumes'.[255] To begin with, the title was left undecided. Neske did not like 'conversation with C. S.'. Schmitt suggested: 'Das Maß der Macht: Antwort eines Alten an einen Jungen' [The measure of power: answer of an old man to a young man].[256] He also considered: 'Der Zugang zur Macht oder: Raum und Vorraum menschlicher Macht' [The access to power, or: room [space]† and anteroom of human power].[257] In the publisher's contract, the title was still 'Gespräch über die Macht und den Zugang zur Spitze' [Conversation on power and access to the top].[258] The text was finally published as *Gespräch über die Macht und den Zugang zum Machthaber* [Conversation on power and access to the ruler].

Friedrich asked Schmitt to provide a further text 'for the programme of the coming winter'.[259] When Schmitt suggested something on 'just war', he found the topic 'a bit delicate'[260] and wanted a 'technology topic' instead.

---

* The reference is to 'Conversation on a Country Path about Thinking' [Zur Erörterung der Gelassenheit: Aus einem Feldweggespräch über das Denken] in Martin Heidegger, *Discourse on Thinking*, New York, 1966.
† The German glosses over the difference between 'room' and 'space'.

Schmitt sent the new edition of *Land and Sea* and Friedrich accepted the theme. At the end of 1954 he met with Schmitt in private. In February 1955, Schmitt, motivated by his talk at the adult education centre in Düsseldorf, developed his 'Gespräch zu Dritt' [Three-way conversation]. Around that time, Friedrich invited him as a contributor to the collected volume on *Lebendiges Wissen* [Living knowledge],[261] for which Schmitt sent him the conversation on which he had been working and which had transformed into a 'Gespräch über den neuen Raum' [Conversation on the new space]. It met with Friedrich's 'exceptional approval'.[262] It was broadcast on 12 April by the Hessischer Rundfunk in a 'gloriously presented' version (BS, p. 192) and was soon repeated. Giselher Wirsing published a shortened version in *Christ und Welt*.[263] Schmitt also considered publishing it with Diederichs.[264] The dramatic composition of this text is more complex. There are three characters, Altmann, Neumeyer and MacFuture. Heinz Friedrich spoke the part of Altmann. The positions of the speakers are determined by the generational gaps between them and by their attitude towards the future. There is no real 'Three-Way Conversation', though, as the title of the shortened version suggests. 'Altmann' presents his 'elementary' point of view and his 'conservative' principle of man as the 'son of the earth'. The 'departure into the cosmos', he says, will not be able to resolve the questions of contemporary politics. Rather, the 'harnessing of unleashed technology' (SGN, p. 568) is the immediate 'Challenge'.* But most of all it is important to put the 'question of the great question' (SGN, p. 559) in the right way and not to resort to antiquated answers prematurely. In the end, 'Altmann' turns out to be the genuine MacFuture.

Friedrich then left the Hessischer Rundfunk, and as a consequence an already suggested project regarding the Hamlet book, which Schmitt had just completed, was not realized. But, in July 1954, Sombart produced another broadcast, on 'Benito Cereno oder der Mythos Europas' [Benito Cereno or the myth of Europe],[265] which stimulated Schmitt to engage in intensive conversations, which in turn influenced his interpretation of Hamlet. There were further projects in the following years. The WDR, for instance, inquired about a radio conversation with Raymond Aron on 'Europäische Linke – heimatlos geworden?' [The European left – homeless by now?].[266] Schmitt accepted, but the cancellation soon followed.[267]

The 'disproportion between thinking and acting': Carl Schmitt as Hamlet

After 1945, Carl Schmitt saw himself 'as the King Lear of public law', whose realm was divided while he was still alive.[268] His studies of Shakespeare are, in fact, his major works of the 1950s. In his work on constitutional theory, he had been searching for the political foundations beneath the juridical 'fictions'. Now his reflections examined the seriousness behind the play, the historical foundations and 'taboos' around which

---

* In English and capitalized in the original.

Shakespeare's dramatic writings turn. *Land and Sea* had been a story he told Anima. His interpretation of Shakespeare he now developed together with her while she was studying to become a translator. In the 1960s, she would translate many of her father's works into Spanish. The Shakespeare project was the trial run.

Anima translated Lilian Winstanley's book on Hamlet in the spring of 1952. In July, Schmitt wrote a preface for it. He read a lot of literature on Shakespeare and had wide-ranging correspondence on him. And he considered writing a study on the word 'state'* in Shakespeare.[269] Such excursions into literary criticism are not uncommon among jurists. They like to solve legal cases in literature. 'Gesetz und Urteil' [Law and judgment] already contained an interesting footnote on *The Merchant of Venice*. At the Shakespeare conference in Duisburg, Schmitt got to know a certain Dr Giere, and later wrote a long letter to him.[270] Shylock, the letter says, does not embody the 'opposition of right and mercy' but 'an intensification of the *jus strictum*'. 'Shakespeare was a court poet, and the play "The Merchant of Venice" is delightful court poetry. Without this core of historical reality, the pure "fairy tale" would probably no longer interest us.' Schmitt thus substitutes his political interpretation for the conventional reference to Christian 'mercy'. In his preface to Anima's translation, Schmitt emphasizes Winstanley's thesis that the play has contemporary history at its core.[271] The drama tells a 'piece of family history of the Stuarts', only thinly 'veiled'. Jacob I is Hamlet. The baroque attitude towards life, he says, is inclined towards 'theatricalizing its own historical existence'. The play within the play stands for the art of bringing the real events onto the stage. Shakespeare staged the real events for his 'contemporaries'. Schmitt refers to the 'Berlin audience of 1934' and 'the Röhm affair'.[272] Back then, Schmitt had found the Röhm Putsch reflected in Max Komerell's piece of literary criticism on *Schiller als Gestalter des handelnden Menschen* [Schiller as the creator of acting men]. Now, he shifted the literary interpretation from Schiller to Shakespeare and emphasized that, with his negative figure of Hamlet, Shakespeare wanted to beseech the historical Jacob I not to undermine 'the divine right of the kings, the sacred substance of kingdom with reflections and discussions'. In February 1952, Neske began with the production of the book, which appeared the following year in October. When reading it, Gustav Steinbömer remembered conversations with Schmitt in Berlin with gratitude, but insisted on the autonomy of art: 'At the hand of the true poet, primordial images experience such a transformation that they become irrelevant for the reader or listener.'[273] The reception of the small Winstanley book '[set] in only slowly'.[274] The topic, however, continued to exercise Schmitt.

On 30 October 1955, Schmitt gave a talk on Hamlet at the adult education centre in Düsseldorf, which became the basis for his *Hamlet or Hecuba: The Intrusion of the Time into the Play*. That talk was very important to Schmitt,[275] but turning it into a book was difficult, in part because he was also dissatisfied with Neske as a publisher. Schmitt was 'sad' that his carefully crafted manuscript did 'not find a publisher'.[276] However, through

---

*   In English in the original.

Herbert Nette,[277] it finally ended up with Diederichs, and 1,000 copies were sent out to the bookshops at the end of April 1956. The title, which was not easily agreed,[278] refers to the play within the play. In Shakespeare's play, an actor weeps for Hecuba, the wife of Priam. Hamlet asks whether he should weep as well. Schmitt's essay suggests an interpretation based on an aesthetic of reception by analysing the effect of the play on the audience, thus rejecting aesthetic theories that understand the work of art as a subjective expression and production of a genius. Schmitt instead deciphers the historical content that Shakespeare put on stage for his 'contemporaries'. He distinguishes between mere 'allusions' (HH, p. 50) and 'true' 'intrusions of the time into the play'. The 'intrusion' of the time Schmitt calls the 'origin' [Ursprung] and the 'source of the tragic' (HH, p. 32). Such an 'intrusion takes place within a 'common public sphere' (HH, p. 35), shared by both the author and the audience as witnesses of history. According to Schmitt, Shakespeare's greatness consists precisely in the fact that 'he recognized and respected the tragic core' (HH, p. 51).

Schmitt's essay concerns the fate of Catholicism and the 'divine right of kingdom' ('dynastic legitimacy'). But there are also allusions and reflections that indicate the fact that Schmitt was here dealing with the time of National Socialism. He stresses two genuine intrusions of history which Shakespeare presents to his audience in literary form: Shakespeare makes the question of the queen's guilt a taboo and he gives the avenger the character of Hamlet. Schmitt hints at the fact that his own articles had been written for a 'common public sphere', 'not for some neutral or foreign audience, and also not for posterity, but for the contemporaries', who saw through the 'transparent *incognito*' (HH, p. 37). Through the mirror of literature, he points at the reason why, respecting certain taboos, he had published at all, and why he did not write a conservative critique of the events which would have been possible in the form of a transparent *incognito*.

Walter Benjamin once sent Schmitt his book *The Origin of German Tragic Drama*, together with a short letter of thanks. In light of Benjamin's later fame, this connection became interesting to Schmitt.[279] He rejected Benjamin's theological distinction between tragedy and mourning play. For him, it was not the relationship to Christianity but the contemporary substance, the 'intrusion of the time into the play', which raises a play to the status of a tragedy. Schmitt used Hamlet as a symbol for his own situation, as a model for the political public sphere in which he acted during National Socialism. In a manner of speaking, the essay on Hamlet is Schmitt's esoteric lecture on Melville, his own 'play within a play' in the context of his interpretation, through literature, of his situation during the time of National Socialism. Of course, the audience in the Federal Republic will hardly have understood this statement in the form of a cipher, and thus Schmitt was yet again dissatisfied with the responses. On 12 June 1956 he opened a discussion evening at the Diederichs publishing house with the somewhat grouchy introduction 'What did I do?'.[280] He did not drop all pretence, but rather analysed the negative reception of his text and emphasized the turn towards 'myth': 'Through the masks, the historical present becomes visible. That is what I call the intrusion of the time into the play'

(BS, p. 222). In this way, Schmitt said, he had violated 'the taboo of the autonomous work of art'. 'By talking about the taboo of Mary Queen of Scots, I have myself violated a taboo' (BS, p. 223). Schmitt's explanation, which was published upon the initiative of Tommissen,[281] veers into hermeneutic questions, while the actual esotericism of the text consists in its parallel to Schmitt's own situation in 1934. *Hamlet or Hecuba* marks the end of Schmitt's attempts at giving an esoteric account of National Socialism. Jünger remarked with slight irony: 'I think that in your case everyone always suspects ulterior motives, even when you write about a glass of water. To him who hath shall be given, and you receive additional astuteness' (JS, p. 308).

On 21 January, Schmitt gave a talk on Shakespeare's 'Hamlet als mythische Figur der Gegenwart' [Shakespeare's Hamlet as a contemporary mythical figure] at the Rheinland-Westfälische Technische Hochschule [Technical University of Rhineland-Westphalia].[282] In it, he calls Hamlet the 'mythical figure of the European intellectual', characterized by a 'disproportion between thinking and acting, by paralysis through reflection and self-observation'. The talk sets out from a conceptual distinction between the cleric and the mandarin and takes the Enlightenment as its historical starting point. Schmitt discusses Romanticism's picture of Hamlet and the 'political actualization of Hamlet by the liberal bourgeois revolution' (Heine, Börne, Freiligrath, Gervinus), his 'de-politicization' after 1848, and an 'act of separation [Lösungsakt] from the bourgeois myth of Hamlet' since the Great War. Schmitt explicates the 'identity crisis' of the myth in Paul Valéry and analyses the 'sharp distinction between bourgeois and Marxist intellectuals' following 1918. First, he criticizes the Marxist intellectuals as the bearers of 'progress'. Then, he moves on to the 'bourgeois countries' and analyses the development of the 'Hamlet image' in Germany, England and the USA. As the most recent political analysis, he mentions Raymond Aron's *The Opium of the Intellectuals*,[283] which had just come out in German translation. As the last stage of the development, he looks at 'today's condition of the world' and the 'nomos of the earth'. The 'intellectuals', he says, are 'fitted in' [eingepaßt]. 'Their old myth has reached its end', he claims. He wanted not to deprive the audience of 'the enjoyment of one of the greatest plays in world history', but to open the way for its 'contemplation free of self-delusion'.

Schmitt placed himself as a Hamlet figure within the history of the bourgeois intellectual and within the tension between 'spirit and power' [Geist und Macht]. His lecture analysed the situation for which Hamlet had become the 'symbol'. Schmitt liked to add as a note 'a hieroglyph of the Western world' in copies he gave away. Germany, Europe, the whole world is Hamlet! Even the Catholic Church he occasionally called Hamlet. At the time, the 'mythic figures' of the present interested him more than descriptions of constitutional law. He almost meticulously avoided a major juridical or political summary of the post-war situation and the era of Adenauer. Schmitt limited himself to cryptic allusions and threatened to become forgotten as an author.

29

Private Seminars in Plettenberg: Schmitt's Renewed Influence on Pupils in the Federal Republic

Did Schmitt ever arrive in the Federal Republic?

In the previous two chapters we looked in detail at the conditions, difficulties and worries that Schmitt experienced after 1945. His National Socialist past was not forgotten. He was not able to establish himself academically again, he had quite a few problems as an author, and as a speaker he no longer reached a large audience. Schmitt was enormously embittered about this, and he often assumed the right to act in ways he did not grant to others. He made hardly any connection between his behaviour after 1945 and that before 1945. He did not realize that he himself had engineered discrimination of an entirely different order compared to that he now suffered. He distorted the facts in order to create an apologia for himself. In terms of intellectual themes, he also appears paralysed after 1949. He drew some further conclusions from his theory of world historical forces and made some experiments with the form of the staged dialogue, but after the harvest of his thoughts in 1950, with four monographs coming out in one year, he did not publish any truly substantial work that would have compared to the class of his Weimar writings until the *Theory of the Partisan*, leaving aside, as a possible candidate, the small 'esoteric' book on *Hamlet*. The history of his political experiences and disappointments, it seems, had run its course. Schmitt's perspective was clouded by resentments, and the eschatological constraints of his theoretical thought darkened his vision of the most recent developments. Schmitt no longer wanted to publish as a juridical author; his search for new political subjects, orders and forms had exhausted itself. The Federal Republic of Germany, as a country without sovereignty, was no longer of interest to him. The German Democratic Republic appears little in his work. There is not the slightest trace of a 'nationalist' solidarity with the population of the GDR. With the book on Hamlet, at the latest, a phase of retrospection set in, which was, in effect, interrupted only by the *Theory of the Partisan*. Without the latter, Schmitt's late work during the time of the Federal Republic would barely deserve attention. And without the last generation of academic pupils, the old Schmitt would scarcely be visible as a political thinker.

Let us briefly remind ourselves: before the foundation of the Federal Republic, Germany was divided into occupation zones. At the end of 1947 the American and the British zones were joined into a dual zone. Under the sign of the 'Cold War', the Allied Control Council became dysfunctional in March 1948. In June 1948 new currencies were introduced in the Western and Eastern parts of Germany, and the blockade of Berlin began. From August, the constitutional convention met at Herrenchiemsee and began to work out a draft constitution in coordination with the Western military governors and on behalf of the prime ministers of the Länder. Then a parliamentary council was constituted, and constitutional consultations began. In 1949, NATO was founded. In May the blockade of Berlin ended and the parliaments of the Länder of the Western zones ratified the Basic Law [Grundgesetz]. On 14 August the first national parliament [Bundestag] was elected, and on 15 September Konrad Adenauer became the first federal chancellor.

In his *Glossarium*, Schmitt noted on 25 April 1949: 'Have they still not understood that today a basic law as such is something much more horrible than organizational statutes?' (GL, p. 233). He again feared that the status quo would be cast in legal form – i.e., that the fact of foreign rule would be veiled. On 20 July, the fifth anniversary of the attempt to assassinate Hitler, he wrote: 'Reading the Basic Law of the Bonn Republic, I am lightly amused like an all-knowing old man' [befällt mich die Heiterkeit eines allwissenden Greises] (GL, p. 259). Arranged by the expert in railway law and Schmitt's companion in internment Dr Werner Haustein,[1] and under Haustein's name as a pseudonym, Schmitt published a series of articles on the Basic Law in the *Eisenbahnerzeitung*, a journal for professional education, even before the Basic Law had come into force.[2] He again provided the 'ABCs' of constitutional law. His 'instructions' on the right way to read the constitution focused on two controversial questions to which a constitution must provide an answer: the 'electoral system' and the 'organization of political parties'. After the Basic Law had been ratified, Schmitt cursorily went through its text. He pointed out 'limitations and provisos', its 'intermediary character' between 'organizational statute and constitution', and named some fundamental features which are still being emphasized today: the central position of basic rights, the weakening of the role of the president, the 'constructive' vote of no confidence and the 'exceptional importance of the Federal Constitutional Court [Bundesverfassungsgericht]'. Less well known today are other aspects marked by Schmitt, such as the law's 'strong federalism' (more striking then), his legal-theoretical view on the 'simplification and acceleration of the formal legislative process', and his interest in the position of civil servants and in the rules for expropriation. The Basic Law, in Schmitt's eyes, confirmed his earlier prognosis of a development towards a judiciary state founded on basic rights. The 'question of the relationship between occupational statutes and democratic constitution' he set aside; this question was answered by the presence of the Allies. Thus, Schmitt did not ignore the new law, and so it is all the more striking that he remained silent about these publications, and that he did not publish any further analyses after 1949. In his bibliography of 1959 the revision book on international law is still not mentioned, and the short commentary on the Basic Law in the form of these articles is not mentioned even in the later bibliography of 1968. Only in a supplementary bibliography of 1975 does it suddenly appear. Schmitt clarified the new legal foundations for himself in order not to make any mistakes in his writings, but in public he no longer wanted to pose as a dogmatic scholar of right.

In 1952, in a legal opinion on 'Rechtststaatlicher Verfassungsvollzug' [Application of the constitution within the Rechtsstaat], Schmitt examined the legal process in the Rechtsstaat for the case of 'socialization'.* His work was 'an exceptional help' in the trial.³ However, the decision did not go the way of Schmitt's client, the Buderus iron works, and they considered an appeal to the Constitutional Court, so that the trial continued to exercise Schmitt. In June 1953 he travelled to Wetzlar in connection with the case. Occasionally, he was also involved in other legal cases. Thus, he worked together with the tax law specialist Carl Herrmann in Cologne and the lawyer Kurt Behling in Hamburg. Schmitt continued to provide legal opinions in later times. In 1956, for instance, he received more than 6,000 Deutschmarks in fees for advisory work from the Wuppertal lawyer Hermann Schroer, who was a 'pupil and friend'.⁴ The Verband der Weiterverarbeitenden Industrie [Association of the Manufacturing Industries] and the company Gloerfeld in Lüdenscheid consulted Schmitt about a constitutional complaint regarding competition law. The exact volume of Schmitt's work as a legal advisor is not quite clear, but on the whole it was probably rather modest. The legal opinion for Buderus is the only contribution on the Federal Republic's law that he included in his collection of *Verfassungsrechtliche Aufsätze* [Essays on constitutional law]. Schmitt liked to express his scorn in satirical form. A notebook titled 'Rhyming Exercises' contains dozens of poems and drafts.⁵ 'Rhyming as a safety valve', Schmitt noted in the book. He circulated only a few of his satirical poems among his group of friends. He also collected this short text under the pseudonym Erich Strauss and dedicated them to 'Carl Schmitt on 11 July, in adoration'.⁶ Schmitt did not become an advocate of the Federal Republic, and he avoided any positive reference to a system that reliably paid him a pension over thirty years; but he also did not – like, for instance, Werner Best – become actively involved in extreme right-wing circles. Rather, he retreated to the role of an inconspicuous observer and expressed his critical impulses only within his small group of friends. Schmitt neither committed himself emphatically to or against the Federal Republic and, mentally, he emigrated to his second homeland, the Spain of Franco.

The existence of the Federal Republic confronted Schmitt with the fact that the turn towards an economic and social constitution did not lead to a clear break with the 'bourgeois Rechtsstaat'.⁷ His legal opinion on the 'Application of the Constitution within the Rechtsstaat' discusses the 'problem of the compatibility of Rechtsstaat and socialization' (VRA, p. 452) in the case of a concrete example. Schmitt asks what the insistence

---

* The term here refers to the expropriation of private property on grounds of its use for the benefit of the public.

on the principles of the Rechtsstaat means for the legal principle of socialization, and argues against socialization by 'immediate application of the constitution'. Instead of such an application, which would turn individual constitutional provisions into levers and 'instruments of an automatic industry appropriation' (VRA, p. 488), he stresses the 'importance of intermediary laws in a Rechtsstaat' (ibid.). For strategic reasons, he argues with principles of the Rechtsstaat within the context of the trial. And he again refers to his central distinction between times of mediacy and of immediacy, demanding an intermediary legal regulation and the passing of a 'law on the process of socialization'.

Schmitt in particular puts his finger on one formulation. The Basic Law (Grundgesetz Art. 14, Abs. 3)* stipulates: '[Expropriation] may only be ordered *by* or *pursuant to a law* . . .'. Expropriation 'by law', Schmitt says, characterizes the 'immediate' application of the constitution, expropriation 'pursuant to a law', by contrast, the 'application of the constitution according to Rechtsstaat principles'. Schmitt now stressed the protective function of procedural principles. He discovered the liberal significance of the law, which he had often rebuked as a purely 'functional mode'. Only such an 'intercalation', Schmitt says, would guarantee the distinction between constitution and simple law. The 'immediate application of the constitution', by contrast, would lead to an executive and administrative state. The 'intercalation of a law' is 'the last bastion of Rechtsstaat principles' (VRA, p. 475). 'An expropriation through the immediate application of the constitution, by contrast, would mean an absolute removal of guarantees for proper process, and it would only be possible as an explicit exemption clause [Ausnahmebestimmung]' (VRA, p. 488). Schmitt saw the organizational principle of the bourgeois Rechtsstaat, the separation of powers, as still upheld by the constitution of the Federal Republic. But in the subtle difference in wording between expropriation 'by a law' or 'pursuant to a law' he thought he had discovered a lack of awareness of principle. After 1949, he suspected that the guardian of the Rechtsstaat constitution was rather to be found on the side of jurisdiction. What at first looks like a return to the bourgeois Rechtsstaat thus turns out to be in line with Schmitt's diagnosis of a constitutional transformation towards a judicial and administrative state under conditions of industrial society.

Around the same time, the 'classical' authors of the Weimar Richtungsstreit collected their fundamental writings. With the republica-

---

* Emphasis added. Full text: 'Eine Enteignung ist nur zum Wohle der Allgemeinheit zulässig. Sie darf nur durch Gesetz oder auf Grund eines Gesetzes erfolgen, das Art und Ausmaß der Entschädigung regelt. Die Entschädigung ist unter gerechter Abwägung der Interessen der Allgemeinheit und der Beteiligten zu bestimmen. Wegen der Höhe der Entschädigung steht im Streitfalle der Rechtsweg vor den ordentlichen Gerichten offen.' Official translation as: 'Expropriation shall only be permissible for the public good. It may only be ordered by or pursuant to a law that determines the nature and extent of compensation. Such compensation shall be determined by establishing an equitable balance between the public interest and the interests of those affected. In case of dispute concerning the amount of compensation, recourse may be had to the ordinary courts' (http://www.gesetze-im-internet.de/gg/art_14.html; accessed on 17 February 2014).

tion of his *Constitutional Theory*, Schmitt presented himself once more as a 'classical' author from that period and established his relationship with Duncker & Humblot again.[8] In a preface of March 1954, Schmitt justified the republication in terms of the perseverance of the form of the Rechtsstaat. The book came out in mid-May. From a textbook on constitutional law it was transformed into a textbook of constitutional theory. 'Constitutional law perishes, / constitutional theory persists' (JS, p. 279), Schmitt said in private. He asked the publisher to be cautious with sending out review copies, as he feared polemical reactions.[9] There was a strong demand for the reprinted book, causing Schmitt to be annoyed again with the publisher: 'Now he should slowly come to understand what he missed by letting five valuable years pass before finding the courage for a reprint.'[10] Ulrich Scheuner, showing his lasting loyalty, wrote a laudatory review.[11] Hans J. Wolff praised the book's limitation to pure 'description'. Schmitt did not consider the Federal Republic to be a sovereign state, and for that reason did not come forth with any pronouncements about its constitution. In the mid-1960s, he still wrote on one occasion: 'The situation regarding international law remains defined by the fact that we do not yet have a peace treaty and that the Potsdam Agreement remains the basis.' Karlsruhe, he said, dominates Bonn:* 'I find myself in a situation, however, where I am not allowed to open my mouth in order to intervene in the business of the Bonn professionals' (BS, p. 363).

Anima marries and moves to Spain

Throughout the 1950s Schmitt did plenty of travelling, and his daughter Anima hardly less. She did not pursue her studies with particular diligence, and preferred to travel around, especially to Southern Europe. In April 1954 she visited her grandfather in Serbia, and then travelled on to Athens and Italy. After her return she helped out as a secretary to Oberheid for a while. Her father's house became increasingly, in his words, only a 'petrol station and repair centre' (BS, p. 190). In May 1955, Anima travelled with her father and Forsthoff to Törwang, Reichenhall and Munich. The time between August 1955 and March 1956 she spent in Spain, first at the international summer school in Santander, and then in Cordoba and Granada, before returning by bus from Barcelona. Schmitt picked her up in Bonn. At the end of April, Anima went to Heidelberg again. She celebrated Schmitt's birthday in 1956 together with him in Plettenberg. In mid-September, Schmitt's Spanish friend Álvaro d'Ors visited Germany for a conference, together with his colleague the historian of law Alfonso Otero. Schmitt met Otero in Heidelberg and introduced him to Anima, who fell in love with him. She then visited Otero in Santiago de Compostela, the old pilgrim's destination at the front line of the Reconquista. At first, Schmitt was alarmed. At the end of January he wrote to Jünger: 'Anima wants to

---

* I.e., the Federal Constitutional Court (in Karlsruhe) dominates the government (at the time in Bonn).

travel to Spain again at the beginning of March. I hope she is not going to marry a Spaniard' (JS, p. 320). However, at the end of March they decided that they would become engaged. Anima was in Santiago, where she stayed with Álvaro d'Ors. She travelled through the country and to Paris with Alfonso. To her father she reported: 'After eight days in Paris, I love Spain and the Spanish, who have far more dignity, more than ever.'[12] On 9 April, Schmitt wrote to d'Ors about the forthcoming engagement: 'Since 1929, I have been friendly with your father Don Eugenio ... Now, in 1957, it so happens that you become the guardian spirit of my daughter' (CSAD, p. 173). Schmitt gave Anima a Volkswagen Beetle cabriolet as an engagement present. In May, Anima and Anni Stand travelled to England for a fortnight. Then, at the beginning of August, Otero formally asked Schmitt for permission to marry Anima. He did not speak a word of German. The civil ceremony took place at the beginning of December. Afterwards, on 13 December, Anima and Otero were married by Barion on a snowy day in the chapel of Heidelberg Castle. Álvaro d'Ors and Arnold Schmitz were the witnesses. Old friends, such as Frau von Schnitzler, Corina Sombart[13] and Oberheid, attended. D'Ors later became godfather to their first child, Beatrize. There were several further grandchildren, and until 1970 Schmitt frequently spent weeks and months in Spain.

'A generation lives off you': Schmitt's pupils in the 1950s

1953 was a crisis year and a turning point for Schmitt. He had settled into life in Plettenberg without Duška and Anima, and after his sixty-fifth birthday there was a possibility that he would live from now on just for his resentment. But a third generation of pupils began to form out of various focal points, with Heidelberg being the main centre. Some were 'grand-pupils', the pupils of his former pupils. Others, such as Nicolaus Sombart and Heinrich Popitz, were the sons of friends. Still others found Schmitt through his writings. While a certain discontent with the Adenauer era may well have played a role in this, this new generation was most definitely not attracted by National Socialism. They saw in Schmitt a contemporary witness and the 'crown jurist' of the rule by presidential decree, someone who allowed himself to be seduced in order to avoid something worse. This generation suspected little about the breadth and depth of Schmitt's involvement with National Socialism. Schmitt did not talk about it, and nor would he let himself be questioned about it. The initial historical research on the era, in the 1950s, concentrated first on the 'dissolution of the Weimar Republic' (Karl-Dietrich Bracher). The detailed description of National Socialism followed only later. In terms of political orientation, the 'third generation' of Schmitt's pupils in the Federal Republic stood firmly on the ground of liberalism. It was a generation of soldiers and Flakhelfer:* a 'sceptical generation' (Helmut Schelsky) which had no desire for great ideologies as a consequence of their experiences in the Hitler

---

* Mostly very young anti-aircraft gun operators during the Second World War.

Youth and the war. It was a 'generation in the shadow, always only the anvil, never the hammer'.[14]

Many contacts came about by spontaneous enquiries from students, to which Schmitt almost always responded. His friendship with Mohler began through the latter's research into the 'conservative revolution'. Schmitt sent him 'The old professor's sigh': / I often wonder anxiously: / How far progressed may Mohler's work now be?' (BS, p. 37). Schmitt had been in close contact with Winckelmann for a long time, and he discussed Winckelmann's publications on, and editions of, Weber in detail with him. The distinction between 'legality and legitimacy' was at the centre of their conversations. Winckelmann admitted to Schmitt: 'Of course you are absolutely right in saying that Schleicher was the last attempt and the last possibility to fight off Hitler.'[15] In political terms, dear 'Hannes' did not agree with Schmitt, yet he asked him again and again 'to help him with a few points in the final editing of Max Weber's "Economy and Society"'.[16] After some 'nice days' they had spent together, he sent a 'concluding report' to Schmitt, commenting that now there was 'reasonable success in turning the torso into a readable book'.[17] 'An amazing scandal', Schmitt wrote: 'Compared to previous editions . . . more than 1,000 textual corrections' (BS p. 212). It is indisputable that Schmitt played a part in Winckelmann's new edition of Weber's *Economy and Society*. Winckelmann then published a treatise 'closely connected with the reconstruction of Max Weber's great sociology';[18] Schmitt reviewed the treatise as well as the Weber edition and the collection of Weber's political writings.[19] The two had extensive discussions of problems to do with the production of books and quarrels with publishers. 'A generation lives off you',[20] Winckelmann wrote in a letter on Weber's *Sociology of the State*;[21] he continued to be close contact with Schmitt.

Nicolaus Sombart, after discussions in Plettenberg, sent Schmitt his doctoral thesis on Saint-Simon, which had been supervised by Alfred Weber: 'terribly curious what you will have to say'.[22] However, Schmitt missed him in Heidelberg; he suspected him of being 'unreliable', and his judgment of the thesis was negative. Their relationship remained ambivalent. From as early as 1948, Schmitt was in contact with Hanno Kesting.[23] In September 1951, Sombart and Kesting were in Plettenberg for 'intensive conversations on the philosophy of history' (BS, p. 102). Piet Tommissen made contact with Schmitt in August 1950 as a collector of 'material'[24] on Schmitt and from then on offered his services as a kind of Eckermann.* In January 1952, Tommissen was working on a bibliography and also considering a 'new C. S. monograph in Flemish'.[25] In May 1952 he was in Plettenberg for a first 'week of doing bibliography' (BS, p. 123). His efforts at collecting material, and his editorial efforts over decades, initiated the historical-biographical research on Schmitt.

Roman Schnur established contact with Schmitt at the beginning of

---

* Johann Peter Eckermann (1792–1854), a German poet and author, in close contact with Goethe during the last years of Goethe's life and best known for his *Conversations with Goethe*, covering the years 1822 to Goethe's death in 1832.

1951, then passed his first state examination in Mainz and began his legal training. He first considered writing a doctoral thesis on the 'legists', but then changed to the more confined topic of the *Rheinbund von 1658* [The League of the Rhine of 1658].[26] Schnur read the current authors such as Kojève, Maxim Leroy and Jouvenel; he lived in the world of books. In autumn 1952 he wrote to Schmitt: 'Your advice on some of the problems of my work is extremely valuable to me. By following it, the work will be able to present the larger context even more clearly. Unfortunately, I cannot altogether write the way I would like to, because I am writing for the faculty of Mainz.'[27] Sombart arranged a meeting in Heidelberg, where Schnur got to know 'such excellent minds as Kesting and Koselleck' and talked with them about 'ideology as a means for bringing about civil war'.[28] At the end of 1952, Schnur concentrated on his second state examination. He read Voegelin and Taubes and, in mid-1953, started out on an academic career as a 'Hilfsassistent' [auxiliary assistant] at the juridical seminar in Mainz, without clear prospects for the future. At the end of August he sent Schmitt his completed doctoral thesis, and at the beginning of 1955 he passed his second state examination. He then went to Paris again, where he also met with Kojève. He sent a detailed report on the meeting: 'Kojève appears exceptionally forceful, filled with immense energy.'[29] Through his work as an editor for the *Archiv für Rechts- und Sozialphilosophie*, Schnur established further contacts. The journal was not financially secure. 'For the editorial staff this means: publish as much official material as possible, so that we can also accommodate the other work.'[30] In 1956, Schnur became the assistant of Carl Herman Ule at the Verwaltungshochschule [Academy for Administrative Studies] in Speyer. In 1957 he agreed a topic for his Habilitation with Forsthoff.

At the end of 1952, Reinhart Koselleck came to Plettenberg and wrote a review of the small Winstanley book. The ensuing correspondence opened with a fierce critique of historicism by Koselleck:

> The reduction of all intellectual expression [aller geistigen Äußerungen] to the situation puts an absolute end to all further relativizing in relation to a before and after, or an above and below. The focus should therefore be on the finitude of the human being, not in the sense of an individual existence . . . but with respect to the perennial origin of history: i.e., with respect to the structures of a 'situation', without which something like history could not exist.[31]

Today, these lines read almost like the germ of Koselleck's research and his life-long theme. He thus distanced himself from Heidegger, whom he had met in Heidelberg through Löwith and Gadamer. At the end of 1953, Koselleck again came to Plettenberg, and informed Schmitt in detail about the progress of his doctoral work.[32] In an early review he already referred approvingly to Schmitt's notion of secularized modern times.[33] In January 1955 he sent him his doctoral thesis 'in grateful remembrance of the conversations, without which this work could never have been written'.[34] Koselleck then spent some time as a Lektor in Bristol (England), and returned to Heidelberg in the autumn of 1955 to become the assistant of

Johannes Kühn. In the following year he continually looked for scholarly conversations with Schmitt, without any hint of disharmony or the little jealousies of restless ambition.

Early on, the members of the network that formed around Plettenberg understood themselves as an elitist circle. Sombart inquired: 'Should we not edit a volume "Corresponence with Carl Schmitt", in which the letters to and from Altmann, Kesting, Koselleck, Scheibert, Schnur, Krauss, Warnach, etc., exchanged since the war would be published in chronological sequence? (Only the best, of course.) I think our circle would thus present itself to history as the most fruitful centre of German intellectual life after the war.'[35] A bold and presumptuous idea! Schmitt's influence at the time was only beginning to set in. Later, Sombart would remember the trio Sombart, Kesting and Koselleck in all modesty as 'Faust, Mephisto and Wagner', allocating himself the role of Faust and Koselleck that of Wagner.[36] To Schmitt, he would attribute a 'fundamentally paranoid character' [paranoide Grundstruktur] and an anti-Semitic 'pathology'.

Beginning in 1953, Schmitt closely supervised Ottmar Ballweg on his 'Natur der Sache' [Essence of the matter],[37] but in the 1960s they lost touch.[38] Werner Böckenförde wrote to Schmitt on 15 March 1953, also on behalf of his brother.[39] A meeting was agreed. Ernst-Wolfgang Böckenförde wrote that he had been very impressed by *Constitutional Theory*.[40] The brothers Böckenförde were from nearby Arnsberg and were about to pass their examinations in Münster. At their first meeting, Schmitt explained the 'automatism of the application of the constitution'. At the end of 1953, Ernst-Wolfgang passed his first state examination. He then became the assistant to Hans J. Wolff in Münster and embarked on his doctoral thesis. Christmas and Easter were convenient times for visits. In December 1954, Böckenförde again asked for a conversation with Schmitt, and after that their contact never ceased. During the following years and decades, he became Schmitt's most important post-war pupil, variously inspired by him, yet also being independent. At the end of January he invited Schmitt 'to a private juridical colloquium in Münster', which took place in the Ratsschänke.[41] Schmitt spoke on 'property and expropriation'. Böckenförde's thank-you letter called the meeting a 'genuine pleasure and a true experience'.[42] He would from then on frequently invite Schmitt to Münster.

On 18 July 1955, Schmitt talked about 'Die Teilung der Erde' [The division of the earth],[43] having been invited by the 'Politisches Forum' [Political Forum] of the student union at Tübingen University. On the suggestion of Winckelmann, Joachim Ritter[44] wrote an initial, 'wonderfully beautiful letter' to Schmitt.[45] On 23 February 1956, Schmitt spoke about the lessons learned from the Weimar Constitution to an audience of students at the historical colloquium in Göttingen.[46] Schmitt also spoke at a 'working group' organized by Böckenförde. He was never hesitant to speak to talented scholars of the next generation and did not think it below him to present papers to small groups.

In 1956, both of the Böckenfördes completed their juridical doctorates. Ernst-Wolfgang Böckenförde arranged for Martin Kriele and Robert

Spaemann[47] to visit Plettenberg. Schmitt discussed the topic of a doctoral thesis in history with the historian Franz Schnabel from Munich and moved to the city for some time. He established a very warm relationship with Rainer Specht, an outstanding expert on early modern philosophy. Böckenförde went through his dissertation with Schmitt at the beginning of the year before finalizing it for publication. Schmitt made some suggestions for cuts, which Böckenförde 'mostly' adopted.[48] His brother's thesis was already in print in April 1957. In January 1958, Böckenförde sent the published version of his juridical dissertation to Schmitt as a 'modest token of thanks for a great debt'; in the preface, he also mentioned 'decisive suggestions for the revision'.[49] Schmitt thanked him enthusiastically for the printed version and thought about ways of distributing it. He also wrote:[50] 'While reading your book, I frequently had the thought of whether a work on organizational power would not be a nice theme.'* This would later become the topic of Böckenförde's Habilitation.

Münster and Ebrach

In January 1956, Joachim Ritter wrote to Schmitt for the first time. In the summer of the same year, after having completed his work on *Hegel und die französische Revolution* [Hegel and the French Revolution], he suggested to Winckelmann that they might invite Schmitt to a colloquium,[51] and on 6 January 1957 they both asked Schmitt to come to Münster.[52] Winckelmann 'implored' Schmitt to attend,[53] and Schmitt thought the invitation was 'wonderful' and accepted it.[54] Around the same time, and at short notice, Schmitt arranged a talk by Alexander Kojève on 'Kolonialismus in europäischer Sicht' [Colonialism from a European perspective] for the Rhein-Ruhr Club.[55] On 16 January, Kojève spoke at the restaurant Wolfsschlucht in Düsseldorf. Schmitt talked to him until midnight and met him again the next day around midday.[56] Even more than Ritter's Hegel interpretation, Kojève's eschatological reading of Hegel within the contemporary context became a stimulus for Schmitt. Hanno Kesting was inspired by Kojève's talk to undertake a revision of his history of the modern philosophy of history.[57] Together with Winckelmann, Schmitt attended the 'anniversary meeting' on the occasion of ten years of the 'Collegium Philosophicum' on 9 March 1957 and spoke about 'Today's Nomos of the Earth'. His presentation of an 'overview of the concrete problem of today's nomos of the earth' (BS, pp. 235f.),[58] responding to Kojève, concentrated on the discrimination of imperialism by 'anti-colonialists'. Winckelmann extended his old ideas about the dialectic between land and sea, formulating the thesis that the one who brings about the decision in a certain situation is the one 'who can bring about the combination of the elements: fire, water, air and earth in the right moment and with the greatest effect'.[59] Thus, the colloquium witnessed

---

* Of course, a 'work' on something cannot be a 'theme' – i.e., that very something – but I have here retained the structure of the German sentence.

an intense conversation that Schmitt and Winckelmann had had before in the early 1940s. Winckelmann was irritated about the fact that his remarks caused 'political' disquiet. He published the talk he gave in Münster in an extended version as *Gesellschaft und Staat in der verstehenden Soziologie Max Webers* [Society and state in the hermeneutic sociology of Max Weber]. Odo Marquard presented a humorous 'Fundamentalkantate' [Fundamental cantata], to which Schmitt added his 'Die Sub-stanz und das Sub-jekt' [The sub-stance and the sub-ject] (BS, pp. 192–8), a revolutionary ballad in Hegelian style: the ballad of pure being, 'over which everyone started cheering'.[60] Schmitt emphatically thanked Winckelmann and Ritter for the invitation. Ritter wrote: 'Your visit has a lasting effect and bears fruit.'[61]

In March 1957, Forsthoff invited Schmitt to his first vacation seminar in Ebrach. It had originally been an idea of the students,[62] and the seminar was a genuine 'parallel campaign'* to Ritter's colloquium. Forsthoff wrote very explicitly 'that the aims of a *studium generale* today in [his] opinion' could only be reached 'outside the university': 'the aim is a gathering of at the most forty selected students for a fortnight',[63] who would discuss a different theme each year together with selected experts. Thus, from the very beginning Forsthoff designed Ebrach as a small-scale counter-university. He covered the costs out of his own pocket to a large degree. He very openly practised his counter-concepts: his counter-university, his opposition to the 'spirit of Heidelberg', his initiatives for commemorative publications and his journal projects. Forsthoff's three-year intermezzo as a constitutional judge in Cyprus, a role Forsthoff took on in addition to his professorship, was also an act directed against the Federal Republic, which Forsthoff 'in all likelihood' expected 'to die of its loyalty to the constitution' (EFCS, p. 60) because of its strong constitutional jurisdiction. The first Ebrach seminar had already generated very positive reactions, and the autumn meetings in the Gasthof Klosterbräu became a fixed institution. Between 1957 and 1967, Schmitt attended almost every year. On 23 September he spoke on 'The Nomos of the Earth' at the seminar.[64] One of the students wrote: 'Your papers, contributions to our discussions, and especially your conversations with participants in smaller circles, contributed essentially to the character of our meeting and guaranteed its success.'[65] These autumn seminars were the most important and the last forum in which Schmitt talked to the younger generation. There were strong personal overlaps with the Ritter circle.

At the end of May 1957, Böckenförde wrote from Munich: 'I am making quite good progress with my work. In order not to let it get out of hand, I shall limit it to the examination of research on constitutional history.'[66] In June 1957 he met the American doctoral student George Schwab in Plettenberg.[67] Schmitt was soon enthusiastic about Schwab, and

---

* The reference is to Robert Musil's *The Man without Qualities*, in which Austria plans a 'parallel campaign' to celebrate the seventieth anniversary of the reign of the Emperor Franz Joseph in 1918, the same year the German Emperor Wilhem II celebrated his fortieth year on the throne.

in September they went to Ebrach together. Through Schwab, Schmitt's old contact with Carl Joachim Friedrich was renewed. Schwab was particularly interested in Schmitt's commitment to National Socialism and in Weininger's anti-Semitism.[68] Bernhard von Mutius suspected that he was at least a 'half-Jew'.[69] In June 1959, he again came to Plettenberg for two months. Schmitt and Schwab would remain close friends.

Schmitt's seventieth birthday and a 'new type of book'

From the point of view of the publisher, *Constitutional Theory* was a success. From March 1957, plans for the edition of Schmitt's *Verfassungsrechtliche Aufsätze* [Essays on constitutional law] were being developed.[70] In July, Schmitt sent the publisher his preface and a draft of the book's intended structure. On 18 October the provisional manuscript followed. In mid-November, Schmitt still wanted to add 'occasional additions to the remarks', which actually turned into substantial glosses. In February he was working on the index. By that time Böckenförde was back in Münster and organized literature for Schmitt. He also proofread the manuscript, and – according to the list of recipients[71] – he was the first to be sent a copy of the book. In the following years Böckenförde continually tried to support Schmitt, and his great oeuvre represents the possibility of the liberal transformation of Schmitt's thought and its adaptation to the settled political situation of the Federal Republic. At the beginning of March, Schmitt visited Böckenförde in Arnsberg and also met his teachers Joachim Ritter and Hans J. Wolff there. Wolff wrote to Schmitt about the 'Laocoon-like situation' in which Schmitt had ended up 'due to his curiosity and . . . will to be influential [Wirkungswille]'.[72] On 31 March, Schmitt wrote to d'Ors:

> I had a lot of work in the last weeks and months, because I had to edit and 'annotate' a collection of twenty-one essays on constitutional law from the years between 1924 and 1954, as well as an extensive index, altogether a book of 517 pages. The publisher . . . wants to publish the book in May, to be followed by a volume of essays on international law and a third volume of essays on the philosophy of right, but I don't think that I shall have the energy to take on the substantial task of such a self-editing for a second time. (CSAD, p. 185)

When the *Essays on Constitutional Law* came out,[73] Schmitt remarked with satisfaction that 'a new type of book [had] emerged'.[74] The first copies arrived in mid-April.

Forsthoff compared the 'event' of the publication of the *Essays* to the publication of *Constitutional Theory*.[75] The pupils again and again demanded sequels to the volume. Thus, Böckenförde wrote: 'It seems to me that you should definitely do it, and again with annotations.'[76] However, Schmitt feared that the collection would 'bring only renewed persecution and viciousness' (BS, p. 243). 'My solitude grows and becomes ever greyer', he wrote on Easter Sunday.

The edition of the essays on constitutional law (with a well-thought-through subject index) was only a very external distraction . . . To find the right balance between the new 'annotations' and the old texts was a difficult problem, and I did not have a model for its resolution. It seems to me that, indeed, a new type of book has resulted. The light which is thrown on the days before Hitler's appointment as Reich chancellor (30/133) is sensational and will provoke my persecutors. (BS, p. 244)

To Huber, Schmitt emphasized the 'central importance of the year 1932 for constitutional history',[77] as highlighted by the collection.

The structure of the collection is such that it first takes a step back from the original situation with regard to constitutional law, moving to the question of who the 'guardian of the constitution' actually is, and then ending with the extreme question of constitutional law under conditions of civil war. In the first outline, Schmitt distinguished between 'state of exception and condition of civil war', on the one hand, and 'climax and turning point of the crisis in 1932/33', on the other.[78] The core elements were *Legality and Legitimacy* and *Die Lage der europäischen Rechtswissenschaft* [The situation of European jurisprudence]. At that point in time, Schmitt's intention was to present his justification of the rule by presidential decree as a defence of the Weimar Republic and to maintain his 'loyalty' (Kurt Sontheimer)[79] to Weimar. In the preface, he called his essays 'documents on the fate of the Weimar Constitution'. Some of the essays, he said, 'were written close to decisive events and were very consciously thrown onto the scales of time's balance'. They were only relevant as part of the 'unmastered history' of Weimar. Thus, they were not meant as material for a constitutional theory for the Bonn Republic. Again and again, Schmitt stressed the historicity of questions and answers concerning constitutional law. In the wake of his diagnosis of the self-dissolution of the bourgeois Rechtsstaat and the 'end of the epoch of statehood', he looked for the character of the Basic Law outside of the categories of his *Constitutional Theory*. Schmitt's overall oeuvre was a diagnosis of the constitutional transformations leading from the bourgeois Rechtsstaat to the 'total' economic and administrative state of the industrial society.

This also shows in his pointed short comments on the Federal Republic. Schmitt concentrated on the end of Weimar, but often ended with remarks on the Federal Republic and on the general development of the constitution. He confirmed that there was a tendency towards a judiciary state, criticized the 'dissolution of property into a general property law' (VRA, p. 118), considered as problematic the Federal Republic's adoption of welfare state principles, the role of values [Wertdenken] and the denial of imperial 'appropriation' [Nehmen], and he asked the question of the 'delayer' in the form of the alternative between 'Savigny and Hegel' (VRA, p. 427–9). Winckelmann remarked, 'slightly saddened', that Schmitt had decided against adopting the former's position within the controversy surrounding the concept of legitimacy, something he could not understand, 'because you [i.e., Schmitt] are the restorer of a material theory of constitutional law, and my emphasis on the structure of rational values as the one that is actually legitimate points in precisely the same direction.'[80] Around that time, a shadow was cast over Schmitt and Winckelmann's relationship. Winckelmann's remark shows the extent to which their discussions of Weber entered into Schmitt's critique of the 'tyranny of values'.

On 11 June 1958, Schmitt flew to Madrid and spent his seventieth birthday with Anima in Santiago. He seriously considered moving to Spain. Böckenförde's letter congratulating him on his birthday arrived with a memorable card from the Ritter colloquium enclosed.[81] The latter was signed by Joachim Ritter, Odo Marquard, Karfried Gründer, Hermann Lübbe, Jürgen Seifert, Reinhart Maurer, Günther Bien, Lothar Eley, Friedrich Kambartel, Böckenförde and others. One might speak of a 'Ritterschlag' [knightly accolade]. An unsigned article on his birthday, titled 'Der Umstrittene' [The controversial one], appeared in the *Frankfurter Allgemeine Zeitung*.[82] Forsthoff published an appreciation in *Christ und Welt*, titled 'Der Staatsrechtler im Bürgerkrieg – Carl Schmitt zum 70. Geburtstag' [The state theorist in civil war – for Carl Schmitt on his seventieth birthday],[83] which provoked a polemical reply from Erich Kaufmann.[84] Schmitt refrained from reacting to it, because he wanted 'to save the world the spectacle of a dispute between old men' (EFCS, p. 142). On 18 October a large gathering of friends took place at Oberheid's home in Düsseldorf.[85] Tommissen sent an exposition on 'Carl Schmitt und die Geschichte seines Ruhms' [Carl Schmitt and the history of his fame],[86] and thus secured the receipt of further *Schmittiana* by offering himself as the bibliographer of Schmitt's fame.

The Festschrift for Schmitt's seventieth birthday, for which Oberheid had organized the financial means, was published only after a substantial delay of almost a year.[87] Barion presented it to Schmitt a few days before his seventy-first birthday. It had already been in print with Kohlhammer when the publisher suddenly pulled out, and was now published by Duncker & Humblot in a lavish edition. Barion, Forsthoff and Werner Weber were the editors and also contributed articles of their own. Apart from them, the only old companion represented in the volume was Hans Freyer. Ernst Jünger was absent. Younger colleagues who contributed were Hans Schneider, Joseph Kaiser, Günther Krauss and Roman Schnur. In addition there were contributions from Spain, Anima's new home. On 19 December 1959 a meeting of the friends, at which all 'donors' were present, took place at Oberheid's home. Forsthoff anticipated 'that the publishing of a Festschrift will trigger very considerable emotions' (EFCS, p. 143). Adolf Schüle published a protest in the *Juristen-Zeitung*. Forsthoff reacted by referring to the concessions Schüle himself had made to National Socialism and initiated a counter-campaign. Schmitt wrote a mocking poem: 'What evil people's hate intended / to repress this book, no less / God Almighty then prevented / making the Festschrift a success' (BS, p. 267). Schmitt's juridical pupils were by now increasingly perceived once more as a school. The debates at the time were crucially characterized by the opposition between pupils of Smend and of Schmitt. The state-focused decisionism of the 'Schmittians' opposed the prevailing integrative theory of Smend.

The 'gum tree' of Karlsruhe: 'the tyranny of values'

At the beginning of 1958, Böckenförde sent a report on the annual meeting at Ebrach. Soon afterwards he also reported enthusiastically about the Ritter colloquium: 'The whole discussion highlights how much the jurists today practise their discipline without actually knowing what they are fundamentally doing.'[88] He again invited Schmitt to Ritter's colloquium, and Schmitt attended on 24 February 1959. In the evening he told the story 'of the concrete events in the winter of 1932–3' in the Rheinischer Hof.[89]

Anima came to Plettenberg with her husband and the first grandchild, Beatrize. An invitation for the Ebrach seminar of 1959 Schmitt at first rejected.[90] It took some persuasion to change his mind. In the end, Böckenförde drove Schmitt to Ebrach by car. The theme that year was 'Tugend und Wert in der Staatslehre' [Virtue and value in state theory]. The working title for the talk Schmitt gave on 23 October was 'Tugend–Wert–Surrogate' [Virtue–value–surrogates], later to become 'Die Tyrannei der Werte' [The tyranny of values].[91] This text represents Schmitt's intellectual engagement with, and fundamental stance towards, the order of values [Wertedenken] of the Federal Republic and the Federal Republic's points of reference in terms of intellectual history. Böckenförde therefore emphasized that Ebrach was, 'not least because of your presence, immensely inspiring and intellectually focused'.[92]

In his talk, Schmitt criticizes the moralization of right, which threatens a naive order of value when it falls for the apparent objectivity of values. 'The Tyranny of Values' looks at the logic of the order of value in the 'light of the application of the constitution in a Rechtsstaat' and criticizes the development of the role of the (constitutional) judge towards someone who is an 'immediate applier of values'. In the introductory section, the talk quotes from Heidegger's history of metaphysics in order to contextualize the order of values historically as the end-point of European Platonism and 'nihilism'.[93] Schmitt takes up in particular Heidegger's formulation about the philosophy of value [Wertphilosophie] as a 'positivist substitute for the metaphysical' (TW, p. 53). He then goes on to distinguish between the subjectivist theory of value of Max Weber and the objectivist philosophies of value of Max Scheler and Nicolai Hartmann. With regard to the validity of values, he agrees with Weber. We encounter values on an intersubjective level, as 'objective spirit', but they are valid only insofar as individuals hold them. In contrast, objective theories of value award values an appearance of validity that Schmitt finds problematic. They do not limit themselves to description, but rationalize values and introduce a hierarchy of values by attaching 'importance' [Stellenwert] to them within a 'system of values'. If this is done only descriptively, it is unproblematic. As long as the analysis of values does nothing but describe social practice, it does not impose its hierarchies on anyone. But Schmitt stresses, following Weber, that such ideal types are easily misunderstood as practical suggestions for a utopia. Schmitt is concerned about an appearance of objectivity and an 'urge for recognition' [Geltungsdrang] which, in the context of the 'battle of valuations', will lead to a 'value-destroying realization of values'

(TW, p. 57). 'Who posits values thus distances himself from non-values [Unwerte]', Schmitt says. 'A value's urge for recognition is irresistible and the conflict between valuers, de-valuers and revaluers [Aufwerter] unavoidable' (TW, p. 58). Nicolai Hartmann, Schmitt writes, already saw this and thus spoke of the 'tyranny of values'. 'The urge to assert values here becomes a compulsion to immediately apply values' (TW, p. 61). Against such an 'immediate' application of values, Schmitt once more demands a 'legally mediated application of values'. As in 1914, he again quotes

> what Goethe said about the idea: it always enters reality as a foreign guest. And a value can presumably not become real in any other way either. The idea requires mediation, and if it appears as a phenomenon in naked immediacy or in the form of automatic self-realization, terror results and the disaster is great. . . . In a community [Gemeinwesen] whose constitution knows a lawgiver and laws, it is the task of the lawgiver and of the laws he passes to determine the mediation in the form of predictable and enforceable rules, and to avoid the terror of the immediate and automatic application of values. (TW, p. 62)

Thus, Schmitt again argues for the intercalation of legal regulations, opposing the moralization and politicization of the constitution with his insistence on clear legal regulations.

Carl Schmitt and Ernst-Wolfgang Böckenförde in Ebrach

It is correct to say that a legal system is no system of strict rules. The analytic theory of right today speaks of a 'rule–principle model' (Robert Alexy). Whatever is not governed by clear rules is open to debate. However, the unity of any positive legal order has to be imagined 'normatively' on the basis of certain legal maxims and principles. Any meta-positive intervention has to be based on a discursive and procedural justification. In earlier days, Schmitt had himself argued for political interpretations according to the 'meaning' [Sinn] and 'spirit' of the constitution. Now he interpreted the philosophy of value with Weber as the reconstruction of an ideal type and pointed out the dangers of abuses. It is therefore always necessary to go beyond the values themselves and ask the question of who holds them.

Schmitt thinks that 'material value ethics' (Scheler, Hartmann), in particular, in fact only increases the conviction with which values are held by subjects and sparks off an aggressive 'urge for recognition' of one's own values. He hints at the fact that he does not consider the immediate application of the constitution and of values to be a specifically juridical mode of thought. The

> immediate value-application destroys the juridically meaningful application, which can only take place in a concrete order on the basis of fixed statutes and clear decisions. It is a fateful error to believe that the goods and interests, goals and ideals, in question could be saved from the absence of value [Wertfreiheit] of the modern scientific culture by being *turned into values* [Verwertung]. Values and theories of value are incapable of founding legitimacy; all they can ever do is precisely turn into value. (TW, p. 45)[*]

Schmitt thus allows us to draw the conclusion that he did not accept the constitutional theory and practice of the Federal Republic as a juridical mode of thought. As the 'intellectual scholarly orientation' [geisteswissenschaftliche Richtung] and school of Rudolf Smend dominated the interpretations of the constitution at the time, Schmitt's 'Tyranny of Values' was also a reaction to his old opponent from the Weimar days.

However, in the first instance the text was probably addressed to Winckelmann, who was trying both to preserve Schmitt's critique of normativism and his 'order formation' [Ordnungsdenken] with his Weber edition and to argue for a 'material' reception of Schmitt's work. Winckelmann was therefore fairly irritated by the fact that, in the debate over legality or legitimacy, 'formal' or 'material' legal theory, Schmitt suddenly shifted his position towards formality. 'Values', he responded,[94] 'are neither "fairies" [Wesen] nor ghosts, and thus also not the dreams of a spirit-seer [Geisterseher].'[†] Martin Kriele raised the question of the alternative between philosophy of value and Christianity, asking 'which possibilities

---

[*] In this passage, Schmitt plays with the ambiguity of the term 'Verwertung', which in the unusual way in which he uses it means 'to make something, or turn something, into a value' but may also mean 'utilization', even 'exploitation', thus implying that value theories do almost the exact opposite of what they pretend to do.

[†] The reference is to Immanuel Kant's *Dreams of a Spirit-Seer* (1766), in which he takes issue with Emanuel Swedenborg's religious mysticism.

and chances' Christianity would still have in the future.[95] Schmitt distanced himself from value-philosophical foundations. Moncada's polite reaction shows that Schmitt thus also put off followers of natural law: 'It appears to me as if your whole critique rests only on one fatal misunderstanding, that is, on the almost unconscious false substitution of the existential moment of valuing and life's valuations [des Wertens und Wertungslebens], as human beings do, indeed, experience them and carry them out, for the essential and ideal moments, for the values as such, if I may express myself in this way' (LMCS, pp. 38f.). Helmut Quaritsch read the text with the sharp mind of the jurist: 'When "values" were given exaggerated prominence in discussions of constitutional law I always had the uncomfortable feeling that knowledge and confession were being confused, the lectern was being mistaken for a pulpit.'[96] Schmitt argued on sober juridical grounds, not on deontological grounds; he stressed the role of the lawgiver and abstained from any moral or religious argument. Thus, the theoretician of law Karl Engisch could also agree with the 'rejection of the objectivist philosophy of value'.[97] However valid the main thrust of Schmitt's argument may be, he did not further elaborate the philosophy of right that underpinned his approach. His project of 'order formation' [Ordnungsdenken] ended at this point. His polemical attitude to the Federal Constitutional Court in Karlsruhe is expressed in a short poem of April 1964, in which those pursuing theories of value are compared to lemurs:

> In Karlsruhe, a gum tree they do raise
> Lemurs are walking through the space
> The dream of freedom for me and you
> They hang on the tree as a value
> Huh huh
> To this what say you?
> We say: shish – taboo![98]

30

The Partisan in Conversation

Changing categories after 1945?

Although it is astounding that the 'crown jurist' of the rule by presidential decree and of National Socialism again invoked the principles of the Rechtsstaat after 1945, as if he had never wanted anything else but the 'bourgeois Rechtsstaat', we must nevertheless assume that Schmitt was serious in arguing for the organizational principles of the liberal Rechtsstaat and didn't do so only because it was then a requirement for an advocate to argue on the basis of the proclaimed principles and of valid law. His rejection of a judiciary state in which Karlsruhe would dethrone Bonn was not off the point. His concerns that the reference to 'values' could lead to a pretence that the legal system had objective validity and a normativist coherence were thus justified. His reference to the presence of the Allies and the absent sovereignty of the Federal Republic was also appropriate. Schmitt did not present this fundamental fact about the post-war era nearly as forcefully as he had done in his 'battle' against 'Versailles'. Anyway, until well into the 1960s he expressed his critical view of the post-war situation almost exclusively in private circles. 'The Tyranny of Values' appeared only in private print. What appears strange is the selective limitation to a few sharp blows. Schmitt's critique no longer had the same quality it had had before 1933. The dialectic between state of exception and normal situation seems to have disappeared from his thought. A balanced general account that would acknowledge the achievement of rebuilding a legal system after National Socialism is missing. The place of the double perspective on the state of exception and the normal situation was taken by an oppositional attitude towards the legal system as a whole. The 'unity of the world' is presented as its final eschatological stage in the light of which Schmitt was looking for a political-theological alternative. He did not find one within the confines of the Federal Republic. To Schmitt, 'value theory' [Werttheorie] and 'turning into value' [Verwertung]* were subtle ciphers for metaphysical delusions. He expressed himself openly only to those he trusted, such as Álvaro d'Ors: 'The situation of Germany today is terrible, much worse than most people think, because they are blinded by the economic miracle. As an old man I suffer severely from this and have genuine Cassandra depressions' (CSAD, p. 200).

The old partisan:
the logic of condemnation and the legitimacy of resistance

A further talk by Schmitt at Joachim Ritter's colloquium was planned for February 1960. Martin Kriele was in charge of the organization.[1] On the day, Schmitt got to know Bernard Willms.[2] In mid-March, *The Tyranny of Values* appeared in a limited private edition of 150 copies. In April, Schmitt was in Heidelberg for Forsthoff's birthday. While there, he considered celebrating the fiftieth anniversary of his doctorate with the French sociologist Julien Freund, whom he had met for the first time in Colmar in 1959.[3] However, Schmitt cancelled the plan[4] and instead, at the beginning of May, drove by car via Versailles to Spain and celebrated the anniversary there. He returned at the end of July. The 'row of professors' in Ebrach that year was 'more brilliantly filled than ever. The student participants . . . were also very well chosen' (EFCS, p. 167). The general theme was 'Der Beitrag der Wissenschaften für die Erkenntnis unserer Zeit' [The contribution of the sciences to an understanding of our times].[5] Schmitt participated for a full two weeks and praised the 'wonderful' vacation seminar with forty 'selected' students (BS, p. 289).

Around that time, the president of the Federal Republic, Theodor Heuss, repeatedly mentioned Schmitt in negative terms. Schmitt responded with the 'lament of an old man in the Sauerland', a satirical poem on Heuss, which invokes 'old father Zeus' against the 'enabler' of 1933 (BS, p. 294). This was quickly followed by a 'romance in the style of Quevedos': 'I am not the great Ali-Baba / No, I am the tiny Ali-Bibi' (BS, p. 296), meaning the alibi which 'enablers' such as Heuss, allegedly, liked to 'install' for themselves. Schmitt thus produced another variation of his old schema of the 'scapegoat'. The Federal Republic he mocked as 'Persilien'.*

The third generation of pupils entered a phase of intensified productive transformation. Hermann Lübbe had only limited contact with Schmitt.[6] Roman Schnur[7] resigned as editor for the *Archiv* and also cast off other 'ballast' in order to concentrate on his Habilitation.[8] Together with Böckenförde and Spaemann, he discussed 'plans for a journal'[9] and agreed a series on 'political science' with the Luchterhand publishing house. Wilhelm Hennis, a pupil of Smend, became co-editor of this *Politica* series.[10] Then, at the beginning of January 1961, the journal *Der Staat* was founded. 'It goes without saying that your cooperation would be desirable to the highest degree', Schnur wrote to Schmitt.[11] The faculty at Heidelberg demanded a substantial 'reworking' of Schnur's Habilitation. Schnur reacted cynically: 'I am most grateful to the faculty

---

* The reference is to the contemporary colloquial expression 'Persilschein' for the certificate stating that one had not been a National Socialist, implying that whitewashing was common.

The Partisan in Conversation 489

(except Forsthoff) for having drawn my attention to a vital fact: that one must never deviate from the opinion of the faculty because other opinions cannot be entertained on scholarly grounds.'[12] After some quarrels, Schnur passed his Habilitation with *Studien zum Begriff des Gesetzes* [Studies on the concept of law][13] and then took on a teaching contract at the University of Saarbrücken. The journal *Der Staat* began to appear from early 1962 onwards. It was intended as a 'place for reflection on the state' [Stätte der Staatsbesinnung][14] and helped form the front lines between the legal schools in the early Federal Republic.[15] Böckenförde and Schnur were the chief editors. Forsthoff praised the 'monopoly-breaking effect' (EFCS, p. 185) of the journal as the counter-piece to the *Archiv des öffentlichen Rechts*, which was the organ of Smend's pupils. The 'so-called CS clique' had a pretty bad reputation.[16] However, the journal was also fairly successful abroad, and it stabilized the circle around Schmitt.

These impacts were not to everyone's liking. Jürgen Habermas wrote a critical review of Kesting and Koselleck.[17] Rudolf Smend, in his history of the Juridical Faculty in Berlin, called Schmitt a 'pacemaker of the National Socialist system of power [Gewaltsystem]'.[18] In response, Schmitt ended his formal correspondence with Smend.[19] Dolf Sternberger acted as an antipode in Heidelberg. His inaugural lecture of November 1960 played off peace against Schmitt's concept of the political: 'Peace is the political category par excellence. Or, to put it differently, peace is the base and the characteristic and the norm of the political, all this at once.'[20] Sternberg understood 'the political' in normative terms as the counter-concept to pure violence. Later, he would distinguish Aristotelian 'politology' from Machiavellian 'demonology' and Augustinian 'eschatology'. Sternberger, at the time, shared a building with Forsthoff. Their circles became ever more polarized. Koselleck and Böckenförde in Heidelberg were also to a certain extent branded as Schmittians. Forsthoff came under pressure in the course of the student movement on account of his support for the Greek junta and engagement in Cyprus.

In September 1960, the scholar of contemporary history Rudolf Morsey had a conversation with Schmitt on the role of the Zentrumspartei in the decline of Weimar.[21] At the beginning of October he visited Schmitt again. Böckenförde's article on 'Der deutsche Katholizismus im Jahre 1933' [German Catholicism in 1933] caused quite a stir at the time because it indirectly questioned the Catholic conscience of the Federal Republic. 'E. W. Böckenförde is infamously shot at', Schmitt wrote on this. 'Everyone who had constructed a new legend for himself under the pressure of finding an alibi screams with outrage' (BS, p. 303). In February 1961, Schmitt was in Spain. At the beginning of June he went with Anni Stand to England for a couple of days, and from there on to Anima by ship. He spent some time in Boiro (La Coruña), 'in the most Western corner of the European continent', and watched the Berlin crisis and the building of the Berlin wall from there. In mid-August he flew back from Madrid to Frankfurt with Anima. Around that time he summarized his reflections on the figure of the partisan.

The partisan was a central actor in the Second World War. After 1945,

Schmitt saw himself as an 'outlaw'* within a 'landscape of betraya
(Margret Boveri). Schmitt rejected the writings on the partisan by Jünge
and also Gerhard Nebel as either theological (Jünger) or, in the case c
Nebel, 'metaphysical spice' (TP, p. 19). However, from 1955 onward
he had intense conversations about the partisan with the publicist Rol
Schroers.[22] When Schroers sent his own manuscript on the partisan to th
publisher, he thanked Schmitt: 'Only the encounter with you and you
work has given me the categories that made my book possible, howeve
it may now have turned out.'[23] Schmitt, though, was disgruntled that th
book called him a 'historical accomplice'. Schroers apologized for the fac
that his 'offering for you [Schmitt] was poisoned',[24] but added: 'I did nc
formulate an accusation – who would I be to do so! But at best a tragedy.'
Schmitt relented and advertised the book in his circle.

In December 1961, Schmitt had to undergo a 'bad operation' of th
prostate. While in hospital, he wrote a satirical poem on Jünger's *Waldgan*
[Walk into the woods] (JS, p. 872). Shortly before Christmas he was allowe
home, where the brothers Böckenförde visited him. Schmitt wanted t
recover fully in order to be fit for lectures in Spain. At the beginning c
February, Anima received the lecture notes for translation. Schmitt trav
elled to Paris and from there, joined by Álvaro d'Ors, on to Spain. On 1
March he gave a lecture in Pamplona, and on 17 March he gave his tw
lectures on 'The Theory of the Partisan' in Zaragoza. On 21 March h
was elected an honorary member of the Instituto de Estudios Politicos i
Madrid, and gave a lecture titled 'El orden del mundo depués la segund
guerra mundial', which can be considered his most important answer t
the question of the 'new nomos'. Schmitt published only the Spanis
version of the lecture. Only in this version does he connect his ideas wit
the development of the United Nations. Around the same time he was als
very closely following the progress of Francis Rosenstiel's doctoral thesis
supervised by Julien Freund in Strasbourg – on 'supranationality';
Schmitt arranged the publication and even revised the translation himsel

The point of departure of Schmitt's Madrid lecture was the 'ant
colonialism' after 1945, which he considered a 'reflex' to the destructio
of the old, European spatial order. Schmitt distinguishes 'three stages c
the Cold War': the monist stage of the 'alliance between the states an
the Soviet Union' against the Germany of Hitler, the dualist and bipolɑ
stage of the first post-war years, and the contemporary 'pluralist stage' c
decolonization, in which a 'surprising number of new African and Asia
states' (SGN, p. 602) no longer defer to the East–West opposition and us
the United Nations in order to form a 'third front'. In 'The Theory of th
Partisan', Schmitt mentions Mao's 'pluralist image of a new nomos of th
earth' (TP, p. 62) in this context. And in 1978, he still claimed: 'The impul
towards the formation of supranational spaces provided by the industri
development so far has not led to the political unity of the earth, but onl
to the establishment of three Großräume: USA, USSR and China' (Fl
p. 927). The major importance of these remarks within Schmitt's oeuvɪ

---

*   In English in the original.

lies in the fact that in them Schmitt handed over the role of the opponents and guarantors of the pluriverse from Germany and Europe to other 'Großräume'. At the same time, he shifted the question of the new nomos of the earth – following Kojève – to the problem of development aid: 'If you now ... ask me what the nomos of the earth is today, I can clearly answer: it is the division of the earth into industrially developed and less developed zones, combined with the question, immediately raised by this, of who makes this division.* This distribution is today the real constitution of the earth' (SGN, p. 605). Whether the world still contains alternatives, accordingly, is decided by the attitude of developing countries towards aid: Will they let themselves be bought? Or will they develop the competence to use their significance within the East–West conflict in order to blackmail both East and West? With his reference to development aid, Schmitt identified a weak tool for economic intervention. He probably did not answer his question of the new nomos of the earth anywhere in more detail than in this lecture.

After the Madrid lecture, Schmitt stayed in Spain and spent Easter week in Santiago, where he gave an additional lecture on 4 April. To Giesler, he wrote: 'It was a piece of luck that I took the risk of the journey.'[27] At the end of May, Julien Freund gave a presentation at the Ritter colloquium, with Schmitt being present as a guest. In June the Berlin jurist Josef Hadrich visited him for the first time,[28] after they had been in frequent correspondence for many years. Next, Schmitt published a short article on Rousseau as a partisan in the *Zürcher Woche*. Again, there was a deluge of protests against the newspaper's acceptance of Schmitt as an author,[29] and Hans Fleig, Schmitt's friend over many years, was in considerable trouble over this. At the end of July, Schmitt travelled to his old cousin André Steinlein in Lorraine[30] and then on to Strasbourg to visit Julien Freund. Schmitt discussed the figure of the partisan with this former resistance fighter, and completed the manuscript on the partisan in mid-September. It is dedicated to Forsthoff on his sixtieth birthday: 'How far apart were our points of departure and backgrounds [Herkünfte] about forty years ago! And how close to each other do we stand today!' (EFCS, p. 186). Schmitt planned a triple whammy for his seventy-fifth birthday: the publication of the new editions of *The Concept of the Political* and of *Dictatorship*, and the publication of *The Theory of the Partisan*. At the beginning of October he met with Julien Freund and Francis Rosenstiel in Frankfurt, before travelling on to the annual seminar in Ebrach. At the beginning of 1963 the Spanish versions of the 'Partisan' lectures appeared. The German version Schmitt sent to the publisher in February, and it appeared on time for his seventy-fifth birthday.

After the introduction, *The Theory of the Partisan: Intermediate*

---

* Schmitt's formulation – 'verbunden mit der unmittelbar folgenden Frage nach demjenigen, der sie nimmt' – is strictly speaking ungrammatical. A 'Teilung' – division – 'wird vorgenommen', not 'genommen'. The point is relevant, as the grammatical deviation hints at his discussion of 'nehmen' and 'Nahme' (appropriating, appropriation) in *The Nomos of the Earth*.

Commentary on the Concept of the Political discusses, in two separate parts, the historical development of the theory of the partisan and then some analytical aspects and the concepts characterizing the last stage of the development. Schmitt stresses the 'sketch-like' character of the text. The more recent development began, according to Schmitt, with the Spanish war of liberation against Napoleon. Since those times, the practice of modern warfare 'moved away from the conventional enmity of controlled and bracketed war [gehegten Krieges]* and into the realm of another, real enmity' (TP, p. 11). The 'spark' of the national war of liberation caught on. The Prussian Landsturm edict† constituted a temporary 'legitimation of partisans for national defense' (TP, p. 44). In parallel, Clausewitz developed a theory of enmity, which gave the partisan a 'legitimation based on philosophy'. Two types of partisans developed: the original 'defensive autochthonous defenders of the homeland' were supplemented by the 'globally aggressive revolutionary activists' (TP, p. 30). In the context of the Cold War, Schmitt makes Marxism primarily responsible for the turn towards 'absolute' enmity. He describes the historical development of the theory and formulates the legal problem of an appropriate evaluation of the partisan.

The 'development of the theory' (TP, p. 33) he sketches by following the use made of the partisan for world revolutionary purposes, starting out from Clausewitz and moving on to Lenin and Mao Tse-tung. However, in his differentiating remarks on the relationship between the Prussian spirit and the spirit of the partisan, he also makes detailed comments on the German Wehrmacht. But Schmitt does not talk about discriminating warfare, the crimes of the Wehrmacht, or the Holocaust. He emphasizes the 'Prussian incompatibility with the partisan' (TP, p. 33), despite the fact that he sees an initial acceptance and legitimation in the edict of 1813, and thus seems to serve the myth of the 'pure Prussian spirit' [Preußentum] and the 'clean' Wehrmacht. Even the Volkssturm, to which Schmitt had belonged for a few days, he still counts as a regular militia. The victories of Stalin and Mao he explains as the result of a strategic connection of the world-revolutionary partisan with the nationalist, originally 'telluric' and 'autochthonous', defender of the 'homeland'. The revolution was victorious in the name of the people. Today, some historians make even stronger claims: 'The place of socialism was taken by patriotism once and for all.'[31] With these reflections, Schmitt saves his nationalism while at the same time acknowledging its defeat. However, Schmitt speaks not only of the Prussian 'incompatibility with the partisan' but also of the partisan as a 'Prussian ideal' (TP, p. 40). He wants to explore the precarious possibility of legitimate resistance and to determine the actors in historical terms. Although he seems to tie the legitimacy of the partisan to the 'telluric

---

* Schmitt's 'gehegt' is a neologism from 'einhegen' – 'to fence in', or 'hedge' – referring to a legally confined war between opponents who respect each other as legal entities. The term further suggests that in such wars there are also limits to physical destruction and cruelty.

† The edict of April 1813 obligated every citizen 'to resist the invading enemy with weapons of every type. Axes, pitchforks, scythes, and hammers are (in §43) expressly recommended' (TP, p. 43).

character' of the 'homeland' in nationalist fashion, he ends up questioning even this criterion.

Not without sympathy does Schmitt describe the example of the high-ranking French officer Raoul Salan, with whom he identifies to some extent. Salan, he says, had 'succumbed to the inexorable logic of partisan warfare' (TP, p. 63; trans. modified), defined the enemy himself and proceeded to attempt a putsch against his government. Schmitt discusses the logic of his sentencing without denying him respect for his courage and the claim to a 'higher type of legitimacy' (TP, p. 83): 'Salan's case demonstrates that even the legality that is challenged in the modern state is stronger than any other type of right' (TP, p. 84). Like Salan, Schmitt insists on the possibility of a different right. Within the contemporary context, he anticipates the emergence of an 'industrial partisan' (TP, p. 79; trans. modified), and explains that partisans within a world-political context 'must be legitimated by the regular' (TP, p. 75). In addition, Schmitt raises the philosophical questions of how it is at all possible for the 'real enemy' to mutate into the 'absolute enemy': 'Is it not a sign of inner conflict to have more than one real enemy? The enemy is our own question as form' (TP, p. 85; trans. modified).* The malleability in the formation of an identity only solidifies when confronted with the 'absolute enemy. Absolute enmity, however, creates an 'abyss of total devaluation' (TP, p. 94). Finally, Schmitt anticipates 'new types of absolute enmity'. Because war only acquires its humane 'meaning' [humanen 'Sinn'] through enmity, the development of war technology demands new determinations of the enemy. The possibility of legitimate resistance disappears in the course of its technical realization, because absolute means of destruction 'require an absolute enemy' (TP, p. 93). Resistance disintegrates into pure ideology and unleashed technology. Legitimacy dissolves into technology. To make this point, Schmitt quotes from Hegel: 'weapons are the essence of the fighter' (TP, p. 94). This production of enmity as a result of the need to give meaning to technology is one of Schmitt's most disturbing diagnoses. His late work, in fact, destroys his earlier hopes for a concept of the enemy that would be capable of supporting a *new nomos of the earth*.

Schmitt continued to exchange letters about the partisan with the former Wehrmacht officer Helmut Staedtke. Staedtke invited him to his home in Tübingen for a conversation on the partisan on 9 May 1964.[32] Schomerus, who is cited several times in *The Theory of the Partisan*, chaired the conversation. It served as a rehearsal for a radio conversation with Joachim Schickel, which was broadcast on 22 May 1969 by the Norddeutscher Rundfunk and also appeared in print.[33] The conversation with Schickel concentrates on Mao and his 'partisan army' (SGN, p. 360) and explores the mental or elementary aesthetics of the partisan: a Chinese partisan has a different conception of his space compared to an urban guerrilla.

---

* The existing translation paraphrases, or rather circumvents, the last, cryptic, sentence: 'Is it not a sign of inner conflict to have more than one real enemy? If the enemy defines us, and if our identity is unambiguous, then where does the doubling of the enemy come from?' (TP, p. 85) – See the illuminating footnote 89 (ibid.).

Schmitt was interested in China as a 'third' power and Großraum, and a an entity that was unlike the West or the East.

Böckenförde as the editor of Schmitt's late works

Schmitt usually wrote his texts in reaction to specific occasions and within short periods of time. However, after 1949 he did not very much like to publish any more. Following the disputes over his literary comeback one almost had to elicit the texts from him. From 1958, Ernst-Wolfgang Böckenförde became the most important editor of his works. Without him, Schmitt's late work would look significantly different. Supported by his secretary over many years, Hildegard Hirsch, Böckenförde took more and more interest in Schmitt's texts, and in the course of the 1960s he grew into the role of Schmitt's master pupil. His doctoral thesis in law, *Gesetz und gesetzgebende Gewalt* [Law and law-giving power] describes the history of the emergence of the positivist concept of law. In 1961, the political history of the historiography of constitutional law followed, in the development of which Schmitt was also involved.[34] Then, Böckenförde, in path breaking articles, pointed out how German Catholicism had temporarily arranged itself with National Socialism. At the time, Rolf Hochhuth' play *The Representative* (1963) caused heavy controversies over Pope Pius XII's attitude towards the Holocaust. Böckenförde spoke of the Church's unhistorical entanglement in natural law, of its anti-liberalism and 'affinity towards the 'authoritarian' system, of it failing to fulfil its 'mission', and of the overall responsibility of the Catholic 'citizen' for the common good. He spoke of the separation of the 'offices of the shepherd, the guardian and the custodian' [Hirten- und Hüter- und Wächteramt] in the modern state in which the political responsibility of the Christian stood over his concern for the Church. We do not find such a Christian critique of the authoritarian and anti-Judaic aberrations of the Church in Schmitt. Böckenförde also revised the 'historicity of right'.[35] Almost all of his early writings were independent continuations of Schmitt's work. Thus, in conversation with his brother, he continued to practise the cooperative relationship between the legist and the canonist.

Böckenförde had already helped Schmitt with his collected essays in 1958 and continued, again and again, to urge him to publish more such collections. On one occasion, Schmitt reacted to these attempts by quoting from the Bible:* 'Break up your fallow ground, and sow not among thorns.'[36] Böckenförde gave advice on *The Theory of the Partisan*. However, Schmitt at the time wanted in particular a 'definitive edition' [Ausgabe letzter Hand] of *The Concept of the Political*.[37] The new edition was also meant

---

* This is the King James version of Jeremiah 4:3. The German translation makes the quotation more poignant: 'Plough anew, and do not sow under the thorns' (Pflüget ein Neues und säet nicht unter den Dornen!'). Schmitt's wording differs slightly: 'Pflüget vor Neuem und säet nicht unter der Hecke [hedge]'. He may have quoted from memory or from a different translation.

as a point of orientation for the emerging secondary literature on Schmitt. A simple reprint would have been problematic. Schmitt wanted to make the link between *The Concept of the Political* and *The Theory of the Partisan* through 'corollaries', which would draw some consequences from both works. However, such a 'systematic' gesture, without any historical relativization, would also have been controversial. Böckenförde wrote to Schmitt:[38]

> As regards the new edition of the 'Concept of the Political', on second thoughts, I have doubts about the 'corollaries' after all. As these would not be new corollaries (as I at first erroneously believed), such as, for instance, the annotations to the collected essays on constitutional law, one has to consider very carefully if and what of the already published material would fit in there. . . . The best, in my mind, would probably be – even if it would mean more work for you – if you turned the preface into a longer foreword, or rather introduction.[39]

Schmitt took Böckenförde's suggestions seriously and followed them. He bracketed the text of 1932, as well as three corollaries, with an introduction on constitutional history and some rather cryptic 'Further Notes' [Hinweise], appended at the end, which contain comments on the history of the text's reception and contextualize the work with political theology through a so-called Hobbes crystal.* Böckenförde was full of praise: 'The preface is now fantastic, a genuine introduction, which is on a par with the two others (Pol. Rom.; Crisis of Parliamentary Dem.), and, most importantly: according to style and content a true C. S.'[40] Helmut Quaritsch joined Schmitt's circle around that time,[41] and Schmitt asked him to do the proofs.[42]

Initially, a great reception at Schloss Auel, near Siegburg, was planned for Schmitt's seventy-fifth birthday. A list of guests was prepared; the menu was already decided.[43] However, on the basis of their experiences with the Festschrift, Barion and Oberheid advised against holding the event, whereupon Schmitt cancelled all celebrations at short notice and spent the day at home with Anima and his grandchildren.[44]

The publications of 1963 again raised questions regarding the continuity in Schmitt's thought.[45] Karl-Heinz Ilting held a tutorial on the finally available *Concept of the Political* in his seminar and reported on it in person in Plettenberg. Robert Spaemann allocated to Schmitt the entry for 'peace' in Ritter's *Historisches Wörterbuch der Philosophie* [Historical dictionary of philosophy]. 'Your own contributions on the development of concepts in legal philosophy and of political concepts will be discussed by other authors in various contexts', he wrote, 'but if you would write especially

---

* The 'Hobbes crystal' is a schema in the shape of a hexagon which presents, in Schmitt's words, 'the fruit of life-long work on this major topic [the political] in general and on the work of Thomas Hobbes in particular' (*Der Begriff des Politischen*, p. 122). Unfortunately, it is not to be found in the English edition, which is based on the 1932 text and does not contain the later 'Hinweise'.

this article yourself, it would, in my mind, make visible what the actual scope of your political thought is. Only one who has thought as much as you about war and enmity understands anything about peace.'[46] But Schmitt no longer wanted to take on such work.

Final thoughts: Hobbes and Hegel

Schmitt worked on Hobbes all his life. But after 1938 he published only a few more pages about him. Incidentally, he once wrote: 'It would, by the way, be time to talk about Hobbes's position within the context of Luther's ideas.'[47] The Hobbes dissertation of the theologian from Basel and pupil of Karl Barth, Dietrich Braun, gave Schmitt the impulse for a far-reaching revision of his own interpretation of Hobbes. 'The book is very important', he wrote.[48] His review article concluded a life-long interest of his. He took from Barion the crucial question of whether Hobbes inverted the hierocratic Corpus system and discussed it first in a short review.[49]

Around 1964, Schmitt was also occupied with the events surrounding Max Weber's hundredth birthday. Wolfgang Mommsen's historicizing *Max Weber and German Politics, 1890–1920*, a piece of ideology critique, Schmitt considered the work of a pupil of Weber who was 'quick to learn'.[50] 'Thus, he too (M. W.) [*sic*!] a "pioneer". Club them to death, wherever you find them!', Schmitt scornfully remarked (EFCS, p. 157). Karl Löwenstein also contradicted Mommsen's view vehemently. Löwith underlined the illegitimacy of the comparison between Weber and Schmitt, which put Weber in the position of someone who helped prepare the way for the Führerstaat.[51] Winckelmann found a strong word for Mommsen: 'Idiot!'[52] He was saddened by the fact that Schmitt, in his review, certified 'the young oaf a great achievement'.[53] Winckelmann's contacts with Schmitt ended abruptly in 1963. Looking back, he wrote: 'Something, unbeknownst to me, then caused Carl Schmitt to end our relationship. I assume that he could not accept my deviating position.'[54]

Schmitt saw Weber's theory of 'charismatic legitimation' as an 'offspring' of Protestant theology (PT II, p. 66) and went beyond Weber to the scholar of canon law Rudolph Sohm. Schmitt was looking for a new theme at the time. 'A minor attempt at treating the topic of "charismatic legitimacy" led only to a renewed reading of Sohm, who astonished me ever more and without whom Max Weber cannot be understood', he wrote to Forsthoff (EFCS, p. 218). In a short review he published this thesis: 'Max Weber's "charismatic legitimacy" can only be unravelled with the help of Sohm.'[55] Moving on from Weber and Sohm, Schmitt finally ended up with Peterson. A request by the Peterson Institute to provide some information in writing he at first declined: 'For a responsible reconstruction and fixation in writing I would need more time and inner concentration than you can allow me.'[56] Schmitt was irritated by Peterson's neutralizing classifications, in which 'Adolf Hitler and Kurt Eisner' (PT II, p. 74) end up next to each other and 'Political Theology' becomes one with the 'spirit' of Max Weber. Max Weber and Thomas Hobbes were two ancestors of Schmitt's thought.

In *Political Theology II*, both these lines finally run together in Peterson. However, Schmitt's search for his concluding work lasted a decade.

'Back and rib-pain' (BS, p. 335) belatedly were diagnosed as a hernia, and Schmitt had an operation on 25 May. He had hardly recovered when he began to work on the review of Braun, which he developed further into a treatise which had a categorical point to make. Braun wrote to him: 'Only Leviathan is the expression of completed reformation.'[57] Schmitt underlined this sentence and used it as his title for a review essay on Hobbes in 1965 ('Die vollendete Reformation'). Braun tried to 'unmask the author of the Leviathan as a cynic' (L, p. 146). Schmitt thought that this 'cynical' interpretation of the esoteric play with masks was mistaken.[58] Although Hobbes was part of the movement of Protestant sects and argued 'on the basis of the individual', he still represented the 'core of the apostolic proclamation' (L, p. 164), and he wanted to found a genuinely Christian community. Schmitt quotes Barion in support of the central thesis of his review article – i.e., that Hobbes is the completion of the Reformation, because he unveiled the 'purely political meaning of the clerical claim of the right to make decisions' (L, p. 167). In theological terms, Schmitt seems to have welcomed this emancipation of the secular state from the Church as, at the same time, the emancipation of the Church from the secular state. However, his main intention was to point out the reason in intellectual history for the misjudgment of Hobbes's 'formal' rationality and practical philosophy. Hobbes formulated the 'concrete historical opposition between clerical and secular power' (L, pp. 174f.) in the interest of Christian piety. He was not a 'totalitarian' thinker. Schmitt supplemented and revised his earlier anti-Semitic interpretation of 1938 by concentrating on the Protestant context and the Protestant impulse.

Schmitt spent the summer of 1964 in Spain, where Böckenförde and Hüsmert visited him. He returned at the beginning of September and went to the seminar in Ebrach, which had 'secularization' as its theme that year. Karl-Heinz Ilting made comments on the proofs of the Hobbes article.[59] Bernard Willms denigrated Schmitt for his 'adoption of Braun's theses'.[60] When Schmitt's article finally appeared in *Der Staat*, Ilting was so 'unhappy'[61] about critical comments that he broke off contact with Schmitt for years. Rainer Specht reacted with slight irony to the hermetic character of the text: 'I do not say that I have understood the article, that would be difficult to prove, but I have read it several times, and your underlinings and annotations even more often. I think I have also understood one or two points.'[62]

With his *Glossarium*, Schmitt had created a new form of intellectual diary. In the 1960s, he again invented a new form. Since the 1930s he had received every year *Die täglichen Losungen und Lehrtexte der [Herrnhuter] Brüdergemeinde* [Daily watchwords and instructional texts of the [Herrnhut] Brethren] as a present from Margarete Oberheid. It contained a Christian motto for every day of the year. From 1965, one page is left blank for notes. In the first volume Schmitt noted down hermeneutic maxims which scorn any kind of exegesis: 'The three ways of reading the Bible: / Frottage of the word / Grating [Grattage] of the sentences /

Collating [Collage] of the sense.'[63] Thus, Schmitt let his reading be guided by almost Dadaist maxims. Over the years, his chaotic notes increasingly turned into biographical remarks, notes on dreams and memories. The watchwords Schmitt turned into doodles. The mottos became occasions for alliterations. The Herrnhut spirit was turned into the realm of the Buribunks.

For his birthday in 1965, Anima came to Plettenberg. Tommissen read out Schmitt's sketch '1907 Berlin'.[64] Mohler dedicated his book *Was wir Deutschen fürchten* [What we Germans fear] to Schmitt. Schmitt rightly remarked: 'You have now joined the four books dedicated to me, which are listed in the Tommissen bibliography, where – next to Australia (Kathleen Murray), Austria (Franz Blei), Arnold Schmitz (Federal Republic of Germany) and Spain (Álvaro d'Ors) – you represent your home country, Switzerland' (BS, p. 355). At the time, the 'total state' caught up with Forsthoff. His planned honorary doctorate from Vienna University 'has – for the time being, at least – fallen through' (EFCS, p. 209): 'Thus, the intended honour has turned into a disqualification', wrote an embittered Forsthoff. Only many years later was the honorary doctorate discreetly awarded. In the autumn of 1965, Schmitt set up his will.[65] Forsthoff was increasingly appalled by the chaotic situation at the universities. 'The political course points ever more clearly to the left. That is particularly true of the student body', he wrote (EFCS, p. 216). He wanted to resign from his professorship 'at the earliest possible date'; Ebrach, by contrast, was 'absolutely a special case' (EFCS, p. 220). It again took some persuasion to make Schmitt attend the seminar. In political terms, Schmitt was interested in the Second Vatican Council, whose 'breakthrough' to religious freedom Böckenförde interpreted as a liberation of the Church from the burdens of being a political party.[66] Schmitt, however, considered it an accommodation to 'little thought-through ideas of an American type' (CSAD, p. 242). Soon, he even suspected a 'co-existence of Roman Catholicism and Marxist communism' (CSAD, p. 250). At the Ebrach seminar of 1965, Schmitt declared his stance against Pope Paul VI, criticizing the 'moral acknowledgement of the UN by the pope', as well as the fact 'that the antiquated alliance of throne and altar is now followed by a progressive alliance of UN and altar' (EFCS, p. 463), which sets the seal on the 'unity of the world in the form of a world state. Within this context Schmitt revised his 'Political Theology'. The grateful participants at the seminar gave Schmitt a copy of Leo Strauss's *The Political Philosophy of Hobbes* as a present.[67]

Rainer Specht wrote his Habilitation in Hamburg.[68] For the *Politica* series, he translated a title by Díez del Corral.[69] Koselleck wrote his major book on Prussia.[70] Böckenförde worked on the *Organisationsgewalt im Bereich der Regierung* [Organizational powers within the sphere of the government],[71] Quaritsch wrote his Habilitation on the history of *Staat und Souveränität* [State and sovereignty].[72] This generation of Schmitt's pupils in the Federal Republic would soon be appointed to chairs. Master pupils such as Koselleck and Böckenförde immediately occupied 'leading positions' within their discipline.[73] After the 1967 Ebrach seminar, Schmitt developed a close contact with Christian Meier, a scholar of ancient history. Meier had just published his Habilitation on the crisis in the late Roman republic[74] and worked on a conceptual history of 'democracy' for Koselleck's dictionary. Through Meyer, Schmitt's thought gained access to new academic circles but, in its reception, was also synthesized with Hannah Arendt's work, a fact which disconcerted Schmitt at times. Meier himself also fell into disgrace with the 'intellectual magnate',[75] yet remained fascinated by Schmitt's ritualized culture of conversation. Schmitt prepared his meeting with others, gave the conversations a thematic focus, and the next morning, after a good night's drinking, straightaway confronted his partner with tough exercises in solving intellectual riddles and tasks. Schmitt did listen, cultivated his correspondence, and was stimulating in many ways.

The summer of 1966 Schmitt again spent in Spain with his family; by then, he had four grandchildren. In the autumn he was once again in Ebrach for ten days, where he heard presentations by, among others, Böckenförde, Koselleck and Forsthoff.[76] At the end of 1966, false rumours were circulating regarding Schmitt's influence on the new chancellor, Kurt-Georg Kiesinger, the only chancellor of the Federal Republic who had been a member of the NSDAP. In parliament, Thomas Dehler asked, with ironic despair: 'Who is actually the patron saint of this cabinet?'[77] Dehler referred to Schmitt as a symbol for National Socialism. The organ of the German Democratic Republic, *Das Neue Deutschland*, did not miss the opportunity and outed *Kiesingers braune Berater*[78] [Kiesinger's brown advisors].* During those days, Kličković, after a long period of time, visited Plettenberg again. Schmitt kept in close touch with all of his family, including those in Serbia. On 22 December 1966, the Westdeutscher Rundfunk interviewed him on the state of emergency article in the Weimar Constitution.[79] The programme was broadcast on 3 January 1967, and the editor Ansgar Skriver was so pleased with it that in 1973 he led another conversation with Schmitt, this time on Hitler's seizure of power.

Böckenförde wanted a few pages 'on the memory of Rudolph Sohm' for *Der Staat*.[80] His brother Werner was writing a theological dissertation on *Das Rechtsverständnis der neueren Kanonistik und die Kritik Rudolph Sohms* [The conception of right in more recent canon law and the critique of Rudolph Sohm].[81] This work, according to its preface, was also inspired by 'didactic conversations' with Schmitt. Schmitt replied to the request for an obituary: 'With Sohm you make my heart heavy. The theme is greater, more important and critical than the theme Max Weber.'[82] To *Der Staat*, Schmitt sent 'a preliminary remark on vol. 1 of Hahlweg's documentation on Clausewitz'. Böckenförde was 'exceptionally impressed' by this and suggested 'Clausewitz as a Political Thinker' for a title.[83] This stimulated Schmitt to extend his 'Hahlweg review',[84] in several attempts, into a longer treatise, which was completed by the end of 1967. This double character of the piece as a review and a treatise makes the text slightly opaque.

Schmitt begins by establishing the problem that the Prussian reformers

---

* The uniform of the National Socialists, of course, was brown.

risked the 'open collision between dynastic and national legitimacy' (FP, p. 892). He then widens the discussion into an analysis of the 'Prussian enmity against Napoleon', juxtaposing Clausewitz and Fichte with the admiration for Napoleon shown by Goethe and Hegel. The treatise, which appeared at the end of 1967, was the sum of many conversations about Prussianism and nationalism. It discusses central questions of post-war historiography: the turning point towards nationalism and the philosophical roots of its radicalization, as well as the relationship between Germany and France. Following Clausewitz, Schmitt defends the Prussian military state against Fichte, on the one hand, and against Hegel's justification of a constitutive constitutional compromise, on the other. With this stance, Schmitt also intervened in the debate about the role of Wilhelminianism in German constitutional history, which was triggered by Huber's monumental rehabilitation of Wilheminianism. But Schmitt also responded to Joachim Ritter's interpretation of Hegel, which had a strong impact within the circle of pupils. In the form of a review article, Schmitt presented parts of a critique of nationalism. In his two treatises on Hobbes and Clausewitz Schmitt revised his views on turning points in modern history and modernity, and on aspects of Hobbes and German idealism, in the light of more recent literature, and thus prepared for the completion of *Political Theology II*.

The commemorative publication for Ebrach

From 1957 onwards, Schmitt participated in the seminars at Ebrach. In 1967, an anniversary seminar was coming up, at which Schmitt's presence was a must. The themes of the previous years had been 'Secularization' (1964), 'Utopia' (1965) and 'Institutions and Ethics' (1966). The theme for the anniversary seminar was 'The Present Situation of the State'. The participants wanted to top it off with a commemorative publication, and Böckenförde therefore asked Schmitt early on for a contribution.[85] The commemorative publication was meant to document ten years of vacation seminars in the spirit of the *studium generale*, and thus the use of former presentations was explicitly welcome. Schmitt was grateful that his '1959 contribution to the discussions in Ebrach [did] not get lost in apocryphal writings',[86] and quickly wrote a 'preliminary remark' for it. At the end of May he sent off a revised version, which was longer than the original presentation and clarified the context of the argument's origin and its intention to attack the alliance between 'economic' thought and philosophy of life [Lebensphilosophie]. His explications of the 'simultaneity, osmosis and symbiosis of value philosophy and philosophy of life' (TW, p. 41) throw philosophical light on his ideas and point in the direction of an attack of the general tendency towards 'neutralization'. Within the context of his 'Political Theory', he presents value theories as accelerators of secularization and looks back at the 'revival of natural law' in the early Federal Republic. Böckenförde thanked Schmitt, saying: 'The preliminary remark turned out really excellently; it is indispensable in order to understand the full substance of the "tyranny of values", and thus it represents a truly original contribution to the commemorative publication.'[87] At the end of August, Schmitt again travelled to Madrid and on to Santiago for a couple of weeks, before attending the Ebrach seminar for one more time[88] 'as a birthday present for Forsthoff'.[89] Although he called himself 'an old man often requiring preferential treatment, half of the time lying in bed being tired' (BS, p. 358), he was nevertheless enthusiastic about the event. 'The days in Ebrach were so rich that I am still completely filled by it', he wrote to Böckenförde.[90] Ebrach was Schmitt's last forum as an academic teacher.

Schmitt's eightieth birthday

The celebration of Schmitt's eightieth birthday was meant to be in no way inferior to that of Forsthoff's seminar. Thus, Böckenförde again urged Schmitt to think about 'a second volume of "Collected Essays"'.[91] But Schmitt was at best prepared to consider a 'reader with shorter passages/corollaries under the title: Positions and Concepts II'.[92] However, Böckenförde warned against a simple reprint without new commentary: 'As far as your ideas about a further volume of essays are concerned, I am against lowering the project to the level of a reader or textbook.* It seems to me that a volume of collected essays with some further annotations at the end would be the right format. I also wouldn't readily use the title "Positions and Concepts" again.'[93] Forsthoff and Böckenförde were planning a large Festschrift as well.[94] Following the nuisances in 1959, Schmitt this time involved himself intensively in the preparations and sketched a preamble for the Festschrift, which he saw as a 'demonstration' of the continuing academic acknowledgement of himself.[95] In mid-March 1968 he spent some days at the Quellenhof in Aachen with Forsthoff, and Forsthoff then came with him to Plettenberg. Schmitt wanted to spend his eightieth birthday with Anima again, 'away from any form of manipulated public' (SSA, p. 42). Forsthoff accompanied him on the flight and insisted on congratulating Schmitt on the day and on giving a birthday speech. Hubertus Bung was also there. 'Forsthoff, the witness. Bung, the witness – i.e., witness of his political path', Schmitt noted in his watchword book on 11 July 1968. Böckenförde wrote: 'Across the vast distance in space, we shall be united with you on this day, and the great mediaeval pilgrim's route may symbolize the spirit and sense of that union.'[96]

The Festschrift *Epirrhosis* (Encouragement) was published in two parts.[97] The first volume was reserved for the older companions and also contained some contributions from the unpublished Festschrift of 1953. The second volume 'contains the contributions of those authors who entered into an academic or personal relationship after 1945'. Arnold Schmitz was the oldest companion of those who contributed. However, many of his master pupils from the time in Bonn were not represented in any of the Festschriften, such as Huber, Kirchheimer and Friesenhahn. Instead, there

---

* 'Textbook' in English in the original.

Schmitt with Anima's family in Spain

were Spanish friends. Many of the younger pupils from Heidelberg and Münster contributed – for instance, Koselleck, Böckenförde, Spaemann, Lübbe and Specht. Schwab and Julien Freund represented Schmitt's international links.

On 19 October 1968, the Festschrift was presented to Schmitt at the Industrie Club in Düsseldorf; a lunch followed, which was attended by twenty-four people. Forsthoff chaired the event. According to Barion's report, Schmitt had 'stylized' his concluding speech as a 'farewell speech'.[98] In the evening some wine was shared at Oberheid's house. The next day, Schmitt visited an exhibition of works by a friend from Berlin, the painter Werner Heldt, together with Mohler. On that occasion, Mohler later remembered that a 'disharmony' (BS, p. 396) between them was noticeable for the first time. Barion congratulated Schmitt, saying that 'hatred and vileness, which you have encountered so much, and still encounter, were never able to bend the direction your life took.'[99] Böckenförde kept pressing Schmitt: 'Could the Festschrift not be the motivation for you to complete the planned collection of essays – "Vom Begriff des Staates zum Begriff des Politischen" [From the concept of the state to the concept of the political], you've even got the title already – after all?'[100] Forsthoff said that the Festschrift had become a specific semi-public literary form 'in which our circle expresses itself from time to time' (EFCS, p. 273). Schmitt, in private notes, emphasized in particular the contributions of his by now closest friends Barion and Forsthoff. The second volume, he wrote to Böckenförde, appeared 'like a surprising new start'.[101] However, in his diary he also noted: 'At night 7.–8. November: depression because of some of the contributions in *Epirrhosis* (Freyer).[102] With Marianne Kesting, Schmitt entered

into a conversation about Benito Cereno. He soon suggested producing an
edition of the text, a suggestion Kesting turned into reality in 1972.[103]

'The first, original N.P., that is me': the consequences of 1968

Throughout the 1960s the institutional transformation of the universities
into 'mass universities' took place. The 'student movement' was also a reaction to this change. For the older generation the events were an almost trau-
matic experience. As early as 1967, Forsthoff wrote: 'The vulgarization has
reached a degree that is unbearable. This is what becomes of universities
when the state no longer exists' (EFCS, p. 242). He increasingly withdrew. 'I
never shied away from intellectual debates, but I avoid vulgar attacks – and
nothing else is to be expected' (EFCS, p. 255). In April 1969 he went as far
as to say: 'The university cannot be salvaged. What National Socialism did
not achieve – in the Federal Republic it will happen – the final destruction'
(EFCS, p. 282). The student movement, unexpectedly, led to a renewed
actuality of Schmitt's work. Memories of Weimar at the brink of civil war
returned. Theodor Maunz wrote: 'On you, as someone exceptionally familiar with pre-revolutionary developments, the political events in the Federal
Republic must have an oppressive effect.'[104] Schmitt applied the newly
coined phrase 'Notstandsprofessor' [emergency act professor] to himself.*
'I think, the first, original N.P., that is me; all those who followed were inaugurated and initiated by me' (EFCS, p. 261). Quaritsch moved to the Free
University of Berlin at the time: 'Five years ago, who would have thought',
he wrote, 'that the university, of all places, would be where the "Concept of
the Political" is confirmed?'[105] Rainer Specht reported that by now he had
'become a pimp of fascism and henchman, with professorial qualification,
of capitalism . . . If I had been appointed in 1966, I would at least have
experienced for one year what it means to hold a chair. What a shame.'[106]
'Left-wing' authors were quick to discover the usefulness of Schmitt's
work for their anti-liberal understanding of democracy. With Joachim
Schickel, a self-declared Maoist, Schmitt had a 'conversation on the partisan' and discussed the most recent metamorphoses of the 'figure' with
him.[107] Schmitt's presence in circles of left-wing theorists immediately
caused sharp reactions. Helmut Ridder, Jürgen Seifert and others sounded
warnings. Ingeborg Maus began a probing Marxist analysis and in the end
wrote a general reckoning. Schmitt was interested in the edition of posthumous papers by Bruno Bauer.[108] Eike Hennig, a doctoral student of Iring
Fetcher and Friedrich Kabermann,[109] who worked on Niekisch, found
their way to Plettenberg, as did Wolfgang Schieder, who had conversations
on Italian fascism and Mussolini with Schmitt.

---

* The term referred to those professors who supported the planned Emergency Act, which
was passed on 30 May 1968 under a Great Coalition, guaranteeing the two-thirds majority
necessary for this constitutional amendment of the Basic Law. There were widespread
protests against the Act, which many feared would create a legal situation in which
something like the Enabling Act of 1933 is again possible.

At the same time, Hans-Joachim Arndt in Heidelberg, who had been in close touch with Schmitt from 1955 onwards, became a central figure of the right-wing Schmittians.[110] Arndt had an unconventional career. He had close contacts with Jacob Taubes and George Schwab. For some time he lived in Düsseldorf, where he also attended Kojève's lecture at the Rhein-Ruhr Club. For a short period of time he gave a 'guest performance as a contract teacher' at the university in Heidelberg; from there, he reported on a lecture by Hannah Arendt in which she presented the theses of her later book on Eichmann.[111] In the mid-1960s Arndt was living in Cologne and often visited Schmitt. He published on *Politik und Sachverstand im Kreditwesen* [Politics and expert knowledge in lending] and then unexpectedly became the successor of the famous Carl Joachim Friedrich, who had already explicitly asked Schmitt for a 'reference on Dr Arndt' in the summer of 1959, and had received one.[112] In Heidelberg, Arndt soon complained about his political 'isolation': 'So many of my former "old friends" of my generation have become so very cautious . . .; only scarcely are there open discussions, not even with the likes of Koselleck, Böckenförde, Schnur; – I am reminded of the attitude of many Germans between 1943 and 1945, who buried their heads in the sand.'[113] Bernard Willms also associated himself with the generation of 1968 and criticized Schmitt as a 'late bourgeois' intellectual. Schmitt caustically remarked in the margin: 'Who would not feel pity with such a subject? Everyone shouts with Schmitt.'[114] Only in the 1970s did Willms ruefully return to Schmitt and to the 'nationalist' position and ask him for a meeting 'at a time convenient to you'; 'My first, and so far last, visit in Plettenberg was seventeen years ago.'[115] Arndt combined his letter congratulating Schmitt on his ninetieth birthday[116] with the announcement of a *Politologie für Deutsche* [Political science for Germans] – a critical history of political science in the Federal Republic, which would pick up Schmitt's old theorem of 'mental submission'.

Another 'nationalist' partner in the conversations of Schmitt's late years was, from 1967 onwards, the journalist Hans-Dietrich Sander. Sander went to East Berlin in 1952, returned to the Federal Republic in 1957, and then worked for some years for Hans Zehrer at the feuilleton of *Die Welt*. The contact with him was established through Mohler. In December 1969, Sander passed his doctorate with a thesis on *Marxistische Ideologie und allgemeine Kunsttheorie* [Marxist ideology and the general theory of art], which was supervised by Hans Joachim Schoeps in Erlangen. In his thesis, he published the letter which Walter Benjamin had sent to Schmitt on 9 December 1930;[117] Schmitt had placed the letter intentionally in order to irritate and attract the 'new left'. Sander then worked as a freelance journalist, but wanted to write a Habilitation. From the Volkswagen Foundation and the Deutsche Forschungsgemeinschaft he received scholarships for a project on the 'neutralization [Aufhebung] of the state in the party' (SSA, p. 325), hence on Schmitt's thesis that totalitarian tendencies have their origin in political parties. Sander took on temporary teaching posts in Hanover and at the Free University Berlin. He also practised his critique of Marxism in the form of literary criticism. He regularly visited Schmitt in Plettenberg, and they had extensive correspondence with each other. Sander attended the Ebrach seminar several times and was annoyed with the liberal statements coming from the participants. He rejected any form of accommodation to the Federal Republic. He did not find an academic home. He became an increasingly radical 'dissident',[118] in terms of his nationalist and also of his anti-Semitic leanings. In the context of the expanded edition of his doctoral thesis, he was trying to find 'access to Jewish intellectual history' (SSA, p. 309). Schmitt warned him 'against an excessive expansion [Ausuferung] of the book in the direction of the Jewish problem' (SSA, p. 313). But Sander insisted: 'Without the Jewish question the Frankfurt School cannot be dealt with' (SSA, p. 320). He was in friction with his academic teachers Löwith, Schoeps, Salin and Taubes. Schmitt wanted to turn Sander into a scholar. For the last time, he accompanied a difficult, and ultimately unsuccessful, academic career. In 1978, Schmitt ended his correspondence with Sander.

The emergence of secondary literature

Schmitt fuelled the review activities around his publications very well, and he also followed the doctoral work that was done on his work. In 1942, Gustav Schmoller gave him a bound copy of 'Discussions of Carl Schmitt' as a present.[119] After 1933 and 1945, many of his old companions and friends publicly distanced themselves from Schmitt.[120] Niekisch's characterization of him was particularly stark. 'The religious Catholic turned into a secular Catholic', Niekisch wrote, who 'understood the völkisch dogma almost exclusively as anti-Semitism'. Many other companions were estranged from Schmitt. Arnold Schmitz, Heinrich Oberheid and Werner Weber were probably the closest of the faithful. They knew Schmitt from his time in Bonn and kept friendly ties with him throughout all phases of his life. His relationship with Ernst Jünger remained troubled. Thus, despite some personal continuities, Schmitt's late social environment was, in the end, very different from earlier ones. His old companions were not responsible for the apologetic and hagiographical tendencies within the literature on Schmitt. Those close to him did not idealize him, in contrast to those who met him only after 1945 and fell for the myths he created about himself.

A first concise study on the *Niedergang des staatsrechtlichen Denkens im Faschismus* [The decline of state law theory under fascism] was 'written already in 1934 with only minor later supplements'.[121] For the emerging research on contemporary history after 1949, Schmitt was, to begin with, only a marginal figure. But again and again he mocked the standardized, ritual distancing and 'belated kicks' [Eselstritte]:* 'If ever an organization of animal lovers should take care of the donkeys and declare inalienable donkey rights, the basic right to such kicks surely would have to be one of them.'[122] At the end of the 1950s, a secondary literature on

---

* The German term 'Eselstritte', literally 'donkey kicks', refers to belated attacks on someone who has already lost in a fight or argument.

Schmitt began to emerge. Peter Schneider sent him the print version of his *Ausnahmezustand und Norm* [The state of exception and the norm];[123] Schmitt ironically rejected this weak Habilitation 'with all the mellowness' old age brings.[124] Christian von Krockow's doctoral thesis *Die Entscheidung* [The decision], Schmitt felt, was an 'echo' of Helmuth Plessner, whom Schmitt called a 'revengeful returned emigrant'.[125] Being compared to Jünger and Heidegger was enough to annoy Schmitt. In his personal copy,[126] he registered the official recognition of Heidegger and Jünger, and added: 'One man remained.' In his eyes, only he did not accommodate himself to the new situation. Schmitt placed great hopes on the doctoral thesis of Schwab. With Jünger he discussed the question of how to deal with secondary literature. Jünger counselled serenity: 'We both share the fate that a not always pleasant literature is spreading around us during our lifetime' (JS, pp. 336f.). 'Whether we like it or not, we are popular subjects for pamphletists' (JS, p. 364), Jünger remarked on the important work by von Krockow. In the following years, the doctoral theses of Jürgen Fijalkowski (1958),[127] Peter Paul Pattloch (1961),[128] Heinz Laufer (1961),[129] Hasso Hofmann (1964) and Mathias Schmitz (1965)[130] appeared.

Schmitt was always looking for exchanges with his interpreters. The early works (Ball, Huber, Strauss, Kirchheimer) were influenced by him. The first Schmitt bibliography by Tommissen renewed his interest in research on him – in, for instance, Heinrich Wohlgemuth's very early dissertation, which had already been completed in December 1931.[131] To Wohlgemuth's supervisor, Schmitt wrote: 'What shocked me most is that Herr Wohlgemuth never had the idea of talking to me. I do not even know whether he ever saw me in person. The diligence and dogged thoroughness of his dissertation suggests an exceptionally deep, almost fanatic opposition, and I have to ask myself where such an opposition comes from, and where it has its ultimate roots.'[132] Schmitt asked himself this question again and again. His reasons for wanting to engage in conversations were not only apologetic. He commented critically on weak work;[133] better work he praised, even if it presented views that were contrary to his.

As mentioned before, Schwab's dissertation was the one he followed most closely. Schwab reconstructed Schmitt's development up to 1936. He sent Schmitt a detailed report on a heated debate with Kirchheimer, who rejected in particular the distinction 'between racial theory and a Catholic anti-Semitism'.[134] Schwab submitted his thesis in October 1960 but had to revise his text. He considered a 'petition'[135] to the university's president, asking to exclude Kirchheimer from the examination process on grounds of bias. At the beginning of 1962 he submitted the revised version. The defence of his thesis ended in an éclat. Kirchheimer accused Schwab of being apologetic and polemical,[136] and Schwab had to write a new thesis. At that point, Schmitt ended all contacts with Kirchheimer and developed a close friendship with Schwab, who even considered moving to Europe. 'I am already prepared to give up my academic career now', he wrote at the beginning of 1965.[137] A publication with Princeton University Press failed as a result of a negative reader's report. Schwab now increasingly thought of publishing the text on the other side of the Atlantic. He repeatedly came to Plettenberg and asked Schmitt to intervene on his behalf at Duncker & Humblot, and in 1967 the publisher agreed to publish the original American version.[138] The printing took a long time. In August 1969, Schwab sent the corrected proofs. Schmitt wrote a long report on the book in which he reached the conclusion: 'This work is in no way an apology. It is extremely critical towards me and does not leave out anything that today might appear to incriminate me.'[139] At that time, Schwab finally established himself in a permanent university position. Gratefully, he wrote to Schmitt: 'Well, dear Herr Professor, I have not only won the battle but the war at the university.'[140] He was working on a translation of *The Concept of the Political*, which, in July 1972, brought him to Plettenberg for a longer period of time. In the following years he continued to keep Schmitt informed about his 'battles' and regularly came to Plettenberg. At the beginning of the 1980s, Schmitt still wrote the following dedication in a book for him: 'I cannot be denazified, / because I cannot be nazified.'[141] The controversies over Schwab's work confirmed Schmitt in his view on the politics of scholarship. Everywhere, he sensed resistance and 'donkey kicks'.*

With regard to the early literature on Schmitt, a friend–enemy polarization has often been observed. He was rejected as a representative of state law during the years of the Weimar crisis and as the 'crown jurist' of National Socialism. The focus was on the friend–enemy criterion as 'political theory', a link was established between his critique of Weimar and his apologia of National Socialism, and thus a 'prior opting' for the 'Führer state' was extracted from his work. In 1964, Hasso Hofmann's decisive dissertation appeared in the *Politica* series, after Schnur had left as editor.[142] Hofmann takes Schmitt's work seriously as asking fundamental questions regarding the philosophy of right and presents an immanent reconstruction of the historical problems it addresses. His work raises Schmitt's status from that of someone who exploited the latest intellectual fads [Zeitgeistsurfer] and was a turncoat [Wendehals] to that of a serious theorist and author dealing with the crises of the twentieth century.[143] In an 'effort at keeping a critical distance', Hofmann avoided making contact with Schmitt.[144] However, his editor Frank Benseler asked him for permission to send the book to Schmitt for inspection,[145] and did so as the basis for a conversation between Benseler and Schmitt. After a difficult meeting, Benseler diplomatically thanked Schmitt: 'You must have noticed how impressed I was by your reaction to the work of Hofmann.'[146] Böckenförde, and also Forsthoff, put in a good word for Hofmann's work. The book, Forsthoff said, 'was the most intelligent of all belonging to this genre' (EFCS, p. 206). Schmitt did not altogether deny this work, which is still of fundamental importance today, his respect.[147] Theodor Maunz, however, at the time still a minister in Bavaria, expressed his solidarity with Schmitt and identified with his position: 'What happens in these days and months with regard to "coming to terms with the past" is unspeakable and incomprehensible. I have read with outrage that a young man from

---

* See previous footnote.

Erlangen has insulted you in unheard of ways. I do not know him or his work. But he is in no way able to damage your reputation as a scholar.'[148]

In 1965, at a conference organized by the Evangelische Akademie Berlin [Evangelical Academy Berlin] on the theme of 'Feind – Gegner – Konkurrent: Antagonismen in Politik und Gesellschaft' [Enemy – opponent – competitor: antagonisms in politics and society], Hofmann presented a paper in a session on 'Feindschaft – Grundbegriff des Politischen?' [Enmity – a fundamental concept of the political?]. The title of Hofmann's paper was 'Carl Schmitt und das Freund–Feind-Modell' [Carl Schmitt and the friend–enemy model], and Schmitt had also been invited. However, his reply had erroneously been 'interpreted as declining the invitation'.[149] Schmitt filled the whole conference prospectus with comments; he wrote of a 'gutting of the crux of the matter by a de-materializing of the crux',[150] by which he meant the transformation of the 'criterion' into a 'model'.* His renewed publication of his early *Gesetz und Urteil* [Law and judgment][151] was also meant as a response to Hofmann as well as to Bernd Rüther's path-breaking work on the politicization of juridical hermeneutics under National Socialism.[152] Schmitt's republication was a reminder of the new methodological approach he had developed outside the sociology of right, neo-Kantianism and Freirechtslehre.† 'A reflection on this beginning', he wrote in his preface in 1968, 'could help to clarify a polemically confused discussion and to make it possible to lead it to acceptable conclusions.'

Otto Kirchheimer is the progenitor of all Marxist reception of Schmitt. Before 1933, he had a close relationship with Schmitt. The first time he came to Plettenberg again was in 1949. However, the difficult attempts at reconciliation failed with the events surrounding Schwab's doctorate in 1962. Jürgen Seifert made a fresh attempt at a left-Schmittian approach. Seifert met Schmitt at the Ritter colloquium and later invited him for a talk on behalf of the SDS‡ in Münster.[153] Schmitt feared adverse reactions and declined.[154] However, he reacted sympathetically to Seifert's review of *Constitutional Theory*. A talk by Schmitt in the Ritter colloquium then became for Seifert a stimulus for further engagement with Schmitt. He congratulated Schmitt on his seventy-fifth birthday in the name of the debate over one's 'own question as form'.[155] At the beginning of 1968 he sent Schmitt some texts, to which Schmitt reacted reservedly. He 'sensed' the same tendencies as those of his critic Helmut Ridder.[156] When Seifert

---

* The German plays on the proverbial 'des Pudels Kern' (from Goethe's *Faust*) as an expression for the crux of the matter: 'Entkernung des Pudels durch Entpudelung des Kerns'. The poodle in Faust turns out to be Mephistopheles.
† Legal theory developed in the early twentieth century by, among others, Kantorowicz, which argued that a judge is free in his interpretation of the law, and that the understanding of his role should not be based on the model of a 'decision-making machine'.
‡ Sozialistischer Deutscher Studentenbund [Socialist German Students' League], founded in 1946 as a branch of the Social Democratic Party. After tensions over policies, notably the rearmament of the Federal Republic, the SPD, in 1961, excluded all members of the SDS from the party. The SDS became an important part of the so-called extra-parliamentary opposition during the 1960s.

took the side of Ridder and inquired about Kirchheimer,[157] Schmitt sharply replied: 'I do not accept Herr Prof. Ridder, neither as persecutor nor as judge. . . . Kirchheimer prevented the acceptance of the work [of Schwab] in a fashion that made me realize a mistake I had made since 1927.'[158] He now had had enough of the older left-Schmittianism.

After 1968, a more detailed investigation of the legal history of National Socialism set in. Bernd Rüthers and Michael Stolleis[159] analysed the politicization of juridical hermeneutics in the form of the 'unlimited interpretation of law' and through 'reference to the common good' [Gemeinwohlformeln]. The first works on Schmitt's role within the rule by presidential decree appeared.[160] Schmitt remarked: 'Fairy tales through and through / Contemporary historians make them come true' (SSA, p. 178). In February 1969, Lutz-Arwed Bentin came to Plettenberg.[161] Schmitt wrote to Ernst Jünger: 'The book by Bentin (on Popitz and my own criminal self) shows you how the documents are blurred. One is not even allowed to die in peace' (JS, p. 386). Sander warned 'that these young people are even more dangerous than their masters', because they 'have no personal relationship' with the material any longer and distort it purely for 'reasons to do with their careers'. But he also thought 'that the anti-Schmitt literature [was] well on its way to mutual destruction' (SSA, p. 230). Schmitt still had an extensive correspondence with Ingeborg Maus. His reaction to her first publication on the '"Zäsur" von 1933' [The 'caesura' of 1933],[162] when he sent her a copy of *Law and Judgment*, marked the beginning of the most intensive phase in their exchange of letters. When the publisher sent her *Political Theology II*, Maus made some cautious comments. Later she adopted a more forthright strategy for defending her position: 'Especially here in Frankfurt/M. there exists a large circle of your "negative admirers", as someone recently expressed it. I would be happy if my little attempt could possibly find a bit of your negative approval.'[163] In July 1971 she sent Schmitt the typescript of her doctoral thesis. Schmitt thanked her as the 'victim of her vivisection' and invited her to Plettenberg; however, she did not come. Schmitt congratulated her on her doctorate and expressed his hope soon 'to be able to read the book in print'. Maus's book was a 'skilful frontal attack'.[164] Maus defended her 'thesis of the continuity with bourgeois legal thought' as an objection to the common 'confusion of personal polemics and theoretical discussion';[165] she sent the book, calling it a 'little wave in the still rising waters of literature on Carl Schmitt'. Schmitt also thanked her kindly for sending the printed book.[166] But to Mohler he wrote: 'A horse from the stable of Carlo Schmid-Count Krockow (Frankfurt) has stepped up, armed as heavy cavalry, in order to attack my unperson, which has already been destroyed twenty times over, for the twenty-first time' (BS, p. 410). Schmitt was very interested in this sharp critic and, despite her critique, congratulated her on her 'appointment to a chair'[167] – which, however, was in fact only a temporary professorship – and also sent her the new edition of *Land and Sea*.

Schmitt followed the international discussion of his work until the end with great attention. The books by his friends Schwab and Rumpf met with his approval. Kodalle's exposition he disliked.[168] Ruth Groh he knew for a long time.[169] With Heinrich Meyer he was in correspondence. Closer connections developed with Joseph Bendersky, who wrote his doctoral thesis on Schmitt and then embarked on a biography of him. As a pupil of Schwab, Bendersky stood outside the German party factions, and thus Schmitt granted him access to the posthumous papers. At the end of 1972, Bendersky came to Plettenberg for the first time and made 'a good impression' on Schmitt.[170] In August 1978 he visited Schmitt again and then worked at the archive in Düsseldorf. He completed the biography in 1980. At their annual meeting, the American Political Science Association organized a 'panel' on 'Carl Schmitt: The Modern Equivalent of Hobbes',[171] chaired by Schwab. Ellen Kennedy and Joseph Bendersky presented papers. Gary Ulmen was the respondent. Schmitt received and read Bendersky's biography. His copy contains a dedication, dated '30 January 1983'[172] – exactly fifty years after Hitler's appointment as chancellor. At that time, the volume of secondary literature produced began to decrease. The borders were drawn, the front lines established. Ellen Kennedy repeatedly visited Schmitt in Plettenberg and translated the treatise on *Parliamentary Democracy*.[173] In Freiburg, with the support of Wilhelm Hennis, she started a polemical attack on the left-Schmittianism in Frankfurt and drew attention to the 'expressionist' roots of Schmitt's early work. Schmitt's negative view of the discussions surrounding his work was mainly the result of two decisions: he rejected any suggestion of a continuity and insisted on the 'caesurae' of 1933 and 1936. And he limited his involvement with National Socialism to an episode of three years, denied that this time was in any way relevant for his theories, remained silent about Hans Frank, and did not see his critique of liberalism as scandalous.

31

Past Eighty:
A Look Back to Old Questions

The 'pseudo-religion of absolute humanity':
Schmitt's final work: *Political Theology II*

At the same time as the secondary literature on him emerged after
1945, Schmitt cultivated myths about his life and work which were
directed against that literature. He increasingly made instrumental use of
Benjamin's letter to him and of the essay by Hugo Ball. In comparison, his
close relationship with Franz Blei played a lesser role in Schmitt's politics
of his past. But then, for the Festschrift for Barion,[1] he engaged with a
legendary figure who was, indeed, important for his work: Erik Peterson.
As a student in Bonn, Barion had read Schmitt's essay on 'Catholicism
as a Political Form', while his own work later dealt with the challenges
of Protestantism. Whereas Sohm separated state and Church from a
Protestant perspective, Barion was looking for a clear Catholic separation of powers. These questions were raised again during the 1960s, in
the context of the Second Vatican Council. Schmitt described the situation with epigrammatic succinctness: 'In the battle for Rome, the victor
is Rudolf Sohm' (JS, p. 198).[2] While Böckenförde again and again praised
the Second Council as a 'breakthrough' for 'religious freedom', Barion
formulated a sharp critique of it. He published canonist commentaries on
the discussions, dismissed the social doctrine of the council as the 'utopia
of the council' and confronted it with Schmitt's Catholicism essay.

Barion spoke of a fundamental crisis that had taken place since the
appointment of Pope John XXIII and was sharply polemical about the
'progressivist party of the council'. Although it did not succeed in breaking
papal primacy, the process of the 'homogeneous formation of one will within
the Church' [homogene gesamtkirchliche Willensbildung], he claimed, had
been weakened. The strict distinction between the two realms, demanded
by Barion on theological grounds, had been 'neglected and missed'; the
'de-politicization of the Church' had failed. In the Festschrift for Schmitt,
Barion spoke of a humanist 'appeasement* of the Church' and of an epochal
break in its history. The 'triumphalism' of the Church, to which Schmitt had
paid homage, was now a thing of the past: 'The Vaticanum II has removed

---

* 'Appeasement' in English in the original.

the foundations of Schmitt's eulogies.'[3] However, the death of the historical 'reality' of this political theology did not mean, of course, the death of
its 'possibility'. Within the context of these discussions, Barion points to
Peterson's critique and to the need for a 'study of the doctrine of the Trinity
as a political problem'.[4] Thus, when Schmitt, after decades, picked up his
engagement with Peterson again, this was in direct response to Barion and
within the context of the debates about the Second Council. He laboured
over his text: 'I can unfortunately no longer make plans', he wrote to
Böckenförde. 'An attempt at an essay on "Political Theology", which I was
meant to submit in August, has failed.'[5] In his watchword book, he noted:
'Between 25 and 31 August struggled with Peterson's 1935 treatise political
monotheism; a bold, impertinent, superficial claim, disguised [verfremdet]
with scholarly specialist research. Outrageous insolence. Awful recognition
of a scandal; how could I engage with such a person?'[6]

Schmitt called this 'analysis of the substance of Peterson's treatise of
1935' merely a preparation for 'an energetic advance towards the treatment of the modern-scientific disbandment of any political theology (H.
Blumenberg, Die Legitimität der Neuzeit, Suhrkamp 1966) in a short,
but very dense "concluding remark"' (JS, p. 294). Schmitt had received
Blumenberg's book through Giesler in mid-August 1969.[7] 'There is a
bluff in the way Blumenberg argues which interests me', he wrote in his
thank-you letter to Giesler,[8] and immediately set himself to work on an
afterword. Werner Becker came to visit, and they spoke about the death
and funeral of Peterson. 'Agony over Peterson / God is dead; the theologian survives him', Schmitt noted down in his watchword book on 17
September 1969. His reply was also a burial. His treatise, written 'under
unspeakable agony and troubles' (JS, p. 297), was sent to Bielefeld at the
end of November. Hildegard Hirsch, Böckenförde's secretary, produced a
typed copy. *Political Theology II* was initially published on 16 December
1969, Barion's seventieth birthday, in the Festschrift *Eunomia*, which had a
preliminary binding and was not available from bookshops. Schmitt asked
Forsthoff to see whether it might appear in his *res publica* series. Until
mid-April, he revised the text, inquired with Koselleck about the history
of the concept of 'stasis',[9] and received important ideas for his 'political' interpretation of the Trinity in return.[10] His health was frail at the
time. Böckenförde's secretary produced another copy and also corrected
the proofs. Only thereafter did Schmitt offer the treatise to Duncker &
Humblot.[11] Sander read the galley proofs and remarked: 'That an author
enjoys disappearing behind vexing games is probably part of the immense
attraction of the mature style of old age' (SSA, p. 124). The first copies
were sent to Barion, Böckenförde, Oberheid and Forsthoff.[12] Regarding
the subtitle, Schmitt noted in his personal copy: 'The disbandment of what
was legendary puts an end to the great C'[13] – i.e., to the Christian self-
understanding of the party that had just lost the election.*

---

* After the federal elections on 28 September 1969, Willy Brandt (SPD) became chancellor
and the Christian Democrats were, for the first time after the war, not represented in
government.

This last, 'desperately hermetic' (JS, p. 379) *Political Theology II: The Myth of the Closure of any Political Theology* was often brushed aside as a cumbersome work of old age. Although Alois Dempf, Hans Maier and other theologians had taken up Peterson's 'myth', and the so-called liberation theology gave the 'closure myth' renewed relevance, Schmitt's rejection of Peterson's theological critique[14] nevertheless appeared all too self-centred. In a short review, Oswald von Nell-Breuning remarked on this: 'If Peterson's study was really the miserable piece of work it is presented as here, then it is not quite understandable why an author of the stature of Schm., thirty-five years after its publication, spends so much erudition, acumen and wrath on it.'[15] In *Hochland*, Gustav E. Kafka asked the question 'Who sorts out whom?'[16] However, on closer inspection, this late work is also very conspicuous and important.

Political Theology II first explains the content of the 'myth of the ultimate theological closure' (PT II, p. 37), the 'legendary document' (PT II, p. 60), and finally the 'legendary conclusion' (PT II, p. 103). In the first part, Schmitt rejects Peterson's critique as a typical product of the Protestant theology of crisis, which assumes a 'fiction of a "pure" and "clean" separation between religion and politics' (PT II, p. 44; trans. modified). In the second part, he examines how far the argument in 'the legendary document' actually carries. He reviews Peterson's relevant publications and demonstrates that he himself argued in political-theological terms.[17] Peterson investigates the political conditions for the development of monotheistic ideas, but – according to Schmitt – dogmatically avoids applying this procedure to the Christian realm. Instead, he consoles himself – against Eusebio – with the dogmatic formula of St Gregory of Nazianzus 'that in the Trinity *stasis* is no longer imaginable' (PT II, p. 75). Schmitt rejects this approach. He turns against Peterson's judgment of 'Eusebio as the prototype of a political theologian'.[18] One cannot, Schmitt thinks, deny a pious layman the interpretation of political events in terms of salvific history. Schmitt becomes even more explicit, saying that the 'Lateran treaties' – agreed between Mussolini and the pope in 1929 – 'were, for millions of pious Roman Catholic Christians, an event of providential significance' (PT II, p. 89). And Eusebio's stigma was Schmitt's: he celebrated the empire as the 'victory of the One* true faith in God over polytheism', without, however, confusing the emperor or leader with a transcendent God or with Christ. Schmitt claims that this was the way that he himself had interpreted the Third Reich. In the third part, which concentrates on the 'legendary conclusion', Schmitt juxtaposes Peterson's presumption with the division of labour between himself and Barion.

In the 'Postscript', Schmitt discusses Blumenberg's defence of the 'legitimacy of the modern age'. He confronts Blumenberg's thesis of the overcoming of the gnosis in modern times with his political interpretation of the Trinity, and thus holds on to the question of 'monotheism as a political problem'. Schmitt predicts that 'the new human being' of secularized, modern times will also develop new forms of enmity. His

---

* Capitalized in the original.

'counter-perspective' [Gegenbild] to that of Blumenberg is also meant as a last word and conclusion to his oeuvre.[19] He reflects on the relationship between state and society through Trinitarian speculations on the relationship between the 'creator God' and the 'God of salvation' (PT II, p. 124). He speaks of the 'Christologico-political conflict' (PT II, p. 125), the fact that father and son are, 'so to speak, *by definition enemies*' (ibid.); he looks at Christ as a 'Promethean' rebel against God, and calls it 'an example of Christological insight that it may not be wrong to raise the problem of political theology in terms of the enemy' (PT II, p. 127). Within the process that characterizes modern times, the primacy of political decision-taking, Schmitt says, moved from the Church and state to society. Hobbes was still able to recognize 'the state as a clear alternative' to the Church (PT II, p. 125). However, this completion of the Reformation, this separation of Church and state, did not last. Hegel was faced with the problem that the Protestant critique sparked revolutions. Thus, he undertook a second attempt at completing the Reformation, which, however, likewise caused the formation of counter-concepts. The reinterpretation of his Christology into a 'pseudo-religion of absolute humanity' by left Hegelianism ensued, which – according to Schmitt's dramatizing account – opened 'the way towards inhuman terror'. The political-theological problem thus expands into a 'modern Church–state–society problem', which Schmitt sees as characterized by the fact that the politicization of society empowers every individual to question authority. Schmitt understands this process of the individual's emancipation as the completion of the Reformation; and the completion of the Reformation in the form of political emancipation, according to him, determines the dynamic of modern times. The 'metaphysical formula' for this empowerment he names 'political Christology'. The consequence of the humanist inversion of Christology, says Schmitt, turns out to be a horrible '*homo–homini–homo* eschatology' (PT II, p. 54). In the final pages, Schmitt sketches a nightmare image of the self-destruction of modern man. He does not end with Hegel's Christology of 'reconciliation' but incorporates the more recent experience of self-destruction into his image of modern man. In contrast to Hegel, Schmitt emphasizes 'the non-identity of the Father with the Son' (PT II, p. 82) and the 'transcendence' of God.

The argument of *Political Theology II* is extremely hermetic and proceeds in three steps. It defends Schmitt's scholarly competence against Peterson, sketches a political interpretation of dogmatic development, and finally presents a theological concept of God's 'transcendence'. In contrast to Peterson, Schmitt does not simply assume the dogma but tries to capture it as a 'metaphysical formula'. Schmitt considers a religiously indifferent and scholarly theology possible and insists on his own position. Koselleck remarked on the text: 'The fundamental question, then, is: is a theology at all possible that would conclusively face the threshold beyond which political positions have to be called theological? You resolve this question into the situational question of how theology and politics appear to be related in each epoch.'[20]

On 13 March 1970, Schmitt went to the Aachener Quellenhof for

Barion's and Oberheid's birthday celebrations. Then, at the end of May, the 'private' Festschrift for Barion was ceremoniously presented to him at Forsthoff's home in Heidelberg. Oberheid wrote to Schmitt: 'It would be very sad if your health didn't allow you to travel to Heidelberg. After all, you are, and will remain, the master of the circle in the presence of which the Festschrift is meant to be presented to our friend Barion.'[21] When Schmitt, indeed, couldn't attend, the festive party sent him a postcard.[22] After the publication of Schmitt's last work, Barion thanked him with moving words: 'When I read something by you for the first time in 1923 at the seminary, namely your essay on Roman Catholicism, I could never have imagined, or would have dared to imagine, that the decisive effect which it had on me would, or could, lead to works of my own and, finally, the answer you have given now.'[23]

Schmitt's *Political Theology II* appeared in time for the annual seminar in Ebrach. Barion was responsible for its planning, and the theme of the year was 'Task and Position of Catholic Theology in the Present Time'. The topics of the presentations covered a wide range. Apart from Koselleck and Julien Freund, Karl Larenz and Niklas Luhmann also gave papers.[24] Given the chosen theme, why did Schmitt not attend? One reason may have been that, after his eightieth birthday, he had withdrawn himself even further. But Barion also discerned, quite rightly, a distancing tone in Schmitt's presentation of himself as the 'theologian of jurisprudence' in contrast to the canonist. After Barion's death, Hubertus Bung,[25] who was Barion's literary executor, wrote to Schmitt: 'In fact, Barion felt very affected by Pol. Theol. II. In the introduction, hidden behind the eulogies, he saw himself placed in the same category as Peterson . . . Thus, he felt that the destruction of Peterson was also an (intended) destruction of Barion.' Walter Warnach and Weiß's circle of admirers did not fully agree either.[26] Schmitt had once again put off the Catholic milieu. Bung and Forsthoff were planning an edition of collected essays by Barion. Forsthoff asked Schmitt for a 'friend's favour' (EFCS, p. 344) – editing them and writing a preface – but Schmitt declined. For financial reasons, the project could not be completed at that time. But, at Christmas 1984, Werner Böckenförde was still able to present the Barion volume to a Schmitt, who, by then, was suffering from dementia.

Legends of Weimar: Hugo Ball and Walter Benjamin

The topic of political theology was also echoed in the conversation on Hugo Ball that Schmitt had with Joachim Schickel in Plettenberg on 10 February 1970, and which was broadcast on 3 March 1970 by the Norddeutscher Rundfunk.[27] 'I was satisfied with the conversation', Schmitt wrote to Giesler, 'because – thanks to your help – I was well prepared and Joachim Schickel asked wonderful questions.'[28] In a manner similar to his treatment of Peterson, Schmitt criticized Ball as a theologically blinded convert, talked about his attempts at dissuading Ball from publishing *Kritik der deutschen Intelligenz* [Critique of the German intelligentsia] in the summer of 1924, and emphasized Ball's political blindness towards the consequences of his touched-up *Critique*: 'He did not see anything', 'was totally absent'. Emmy Ball, he said, was also against publishing it. 'Poor Picaro', Schmitt had written in his preparatory notes for the conversation: 'Hugo Ball ended up in the Ticino in the arms of the born Protestant and candidate for the Nobel Prize Hermann Hesse.'[29] Soon after the conversation, Schmitt was annoyed by a republication of the *Critique of the German Intelligentsia*. 'A comparison of the three costumes (of 1919, 1925 and 1970) shows the picture of a fantastic change of masks' (SSA, p. 128). The conversation's substance and importance lies for the most part in the parallels with the critique of Peterson; Schmitt immersed himself again in the political-theological front lines of the Weimar period and recapitulated the discussions he had had at the time. Whereas in earlier times he had actualized intellectual history, the present was an occasion for remembrance.

At the beginning of the 1950s, Walter Benjamin's legendary importance – fostered by Adorno – for 'Critical Theory' slowly became apparent. Schmitt had already reacted to this in his *Hamlet or Hecuba*,[*] but only in connection with the cult of Benjamin that began with the student movement did he engage fully with him. The student movement gained access to its ancestors through Benjamin. Schmitt now inserted the letter of 9 December 1930 intentionally into the debate, and many students found their way to Schmitt through Benjamin and Taubes. Schmitt and Forsthoff detected an erosion in the 'new left'. 'Taubes is once more proof that Marxism cannot come to terms with the realities', Forsthoff wrote to Schmitt: 'It finally takes refuge in the New Man [Neuen Menschen], which would certainly have amused Marx very much' (EFCS, p. 308). Schmitt claimed: 'The syndrome of German Hegelianism, English economics and French socialism, which make up the substance of Marxism, is beginning to unravel' (EFCS, p. 309). In this situation, some people defected to Schmitt's 'Political Theology'.

Marianne Kesting repeatedly visited Schmitt in Plettenberg. Melville and Poe were two foci in their conversations. Kesting told Schmitt about a meeting with Peterson. 'How can you possibly marry a manicurist from Trastevere', had been Schmitt's outraged reaction, apparently not remembering his Cari. Schmitt, Kesting wrote, was not in a good way. 'He also told me about heart problems and, when we said good-bye, he embraced a stack of wine boxes which reached to the ceiling, exclaiming: "My pillar!"'[30] In the summer of 1972, Kesting's edition of *Benito Cereno* came out, and Schmitt thanked her for it: 'I congratulate you on this altogether exceptional publication, which I shall immediately bring to the attention of all my friends.'[31] The 'case' of Peterson still occupied Schmitt in the mid-1970s. To his ultra-Catholic friend d'Ors, he wrote: 'Peterson is a scandalous case; his book of 1935 is a revocation of his lecture of 1925; it is a return to Protestantism, to its pietistic origins, and to Bultmanianism; it is

---

[*] *Hamlet or Hecuba* contains an appendix – 'On the Barbaric Character of Shakespearean Drama: A Response to Walter Benjamin's The Origin of German Tragic Drama' (pp. 59–65).

a declaration of peace with Karl Barth and "religious socialism"' (CSAD, pp. 277f.). All of the Catholic movement after 1918, he said, had already been a symptom of crisis.[32]

Quarrels among Schmittians

After 1968, Schmitt's pupils in the Federal Republic were academically established. Koselleck developed his theory of history; Böckenförde liberalized constitutional theory on the basis of 'religious freedom'; Schnur practised European administrative law as a model for communication and the formation of elites; Lübbe and Kriele provided a liberal interpretation of decisionism. Kriele also defended parliamentarism against the historical backdrop of its formation in early English history. He sent Schmitt his 'short book on Hobbes and the English jurists', with the assurance that 'contradictions with your ideas can simply be explained with reference to the different initial situations of my generation ... Please allow me to express my gratefulness and admiration despite my in many respects antithetical position.'[33] In this case, 'Hobbes' acts as a negative symbol for 'Schmitt'.

In the 1970s, the nationalist opposition to the system of the Federal Republic lost all power and influence, and the nationalist faction of Schmitt's pupils became divided over this. Hans-Dietrich Sander became even more right wing than Arndt and Mohler. Schmitt himself no longer believed in an extreme nationalism. In a conversation on television for the series 'Zeugen der Zeit' [Contemporary witnesses],[34] Schmitt drew 'a clear line of demarcation [between himself and], for instance, an Armin Mohler'.[35] Mohler confronted Altmann, who had been involved in the programme, and also wrote, with obvious anger, to Schmitt. He interpreted Schmitt's distancing as 'flirting with the "old sixty-eighters" [Altachtundsechziger]' (BS, p. 400). Oberheid went even further: 'I cannot understand that you now publicly call your joining of the NSDAP a "fall from grace", after you have remained steadfastly silent in the face of all attacks over twenty-five years. I cannot understand your reasons for now calling Adolf Hitler, using the jargon of the left, a "rabid private soldier".'[36] The letter demonstrates the serious disharmony within the circle, which subsided slightly only towards the end of the year. But, in November, Schmitt appeared on television with his critique of Mohler. Schmitt had always been sensitive and difficult, assuming special rights for himself and expecting to be courted. In his dealings with publishers, he was often unpredictable. From the 1960s he became increasingly incomprehensible even to his closest friends. In the end, the chain of estrangements also reached Barion and Oberheid, his oldest friends and the driving forces within the circle after 1945.

Nicolaus Sombart staged a radical break. From early childhood he had been able to get away with a lot. Now, he included Schmitt and also Ernst Jünger in his 'patricide' (SSA, p. 401). When Jünger complained about this, Schmitt replied, correctly, that he '[had had] no contact with

Nicolaus Sombart for years' (JS, pp. 374f.). A lot might be explained, he said, by the general 'uncertainty' after 1968. After a long silence, Sombart spoke about a 'renewed meeting with you [Schmitt], who is, from the days of my youth onwards, the intellectually decisive figure in my life'. Now he had found 'a piece of home' [Heimat] again.[37] However, Sombart went on to write an exceptionally charged article for *Der Merkur*,[38] in which he called Schmitt a companion in Hitler's Schwabing,[*] as well as sending Schmitt autobiographical reminiscences about walks in Berlin. In a letter to Schmitt, he called his contributions an antidote to the secondary literature.[39] Schmitt disliked this searching for home [Heimatsuche]. Sombart, he said, had become a 'Euro-Eurotic' [Euro-Erotiker] (BS, p. 416). 'What does Nicolaus want?',[40] Schnur asked in astonishment. Sombart then attended Schmitt's ninetieth birthday and was surprised by the latter's protest against being 'connected with the erotic movement in Munich'.[41] Sombart contextualized Schmitt's work with the theme of 'sexuality and politics', which occupied the '68 generation. Schmitt reacted calmly to these speculations and gave some supplementary hints, although he saw the validity claim of his work negated. Sombart admitted: 'I am aware that these obstinate incursions into the Wilhelminian era are part of the permanent conflict [Auseinandersetzung] with my father.'[42] Sombart later published his memoirs and wrote a speculative reckoning with Schmitt as an exemplar of 'German men'.[43] His books and letters he sold off to antiquarian bookshops.

The last station: Pasel, Plettenberg

Throughout the year 1970, Anni Stand was building a small, detached, one-storey house. At the beginning of August, Anima came to Plettenberg and then took her father to Spain. It would be his last major journey. At the end of September 1970 he returned to his now completed new home, Am Steimel 7, with Anima and his granddaughter Dusanka. At the time, Pasel was still a 'village in the vicinity of Plettenberg' (JS, p. 377). Schmitt felt comfortable in this quiet rural setting, near a river and at the edge of the forest. He called his small home San Casciano, had iron letters wrought by the smith in the village, and fixed them to the rear elevation facing the garden; in the autumn of 1972 he instructed Hans-Dietrich Sander to have picture postcards printed with the title San Casciano on them. The name was an allusion not only to Machiavelli's 'asylum' but also to the holy Saint Cassian, a martyr under Diocles, who was 'killed with a pen' by his pupils.[44]

Schmitt socialized with his neighbours. He often went to their houses, asking for some technical help or just making up some pretext in order to have a chat. He regularly walked along the Lenne from Pasel to Rönkhausen or up the gently rising path to the ruin of the Schwarzenburg.

---

[*]　Quarter of Munich associated with a Bohemian life-style.

When accompanied by guests he often did not get very far, because he liked to stop during conversations.

The autumn meeting in Ebrach in 1970 took place without Schmitt. Böckenförde still wanted to motivate him to publish further. Schmitt read Brüning's memoirs with great interest: 'One may well risk the predictions that, after the publication of these memoirs, the topic of "Carl Schmitt before 1933" will be discussed again.'[45] Böckenförde suggested making a start on the 'sifting and transcription of [his] diaries 1930–1933'. Schmitt then revised some diary excerpts from January 1933.[46] However, on 27 December 1970, he had a mild heart attack and had to rest for a couple of months. An autobiographical conversation, which had been planned, had to be cancelled.[47] Schickel then led a shorter 'conversation on the dialectic of enmity' with him.[48] Böckenförde initiated a review of *Political Theology II*. When Hans Maier declined,[49] Christian Meier took it on and visited Schmitt in May and October in Plettenberg.[50] In July 1971, Anima and the little granddaughter Dusanka visited for a couple of days. In August, Kličković and George Schwab visited, and they belatedly celebrated Schmitt's move to the new home. Böckenförde sent individual chapters for a textbook on 'institutions' of state law which he planned to write. He did not publish a major, systematic textbook, a new constitutional theory, which would have represented an alternative to, for instance, Konrad Hesse's *Gründzüge des Verfassungsrechts* [Fundamental principles of constitutional law].[51] Schmitt and Forsthoff had set such high standards for the tasks of a constitutional theory that not even Böckenförde dared to try to fulfil them. But throughout the 1970s he remained in the role of a Socratic helper, even if the letters and encounters now became more infrequent.

In 1971, Forsthoff organized the last seminar in Ebrach, on a much smaller scale.[52] The following year he cancelled it due to a shortage of speakers and participants. 'But maybe Ebrach no longer fits into these times', he wrote somewhat wistfully (JS, p. 334). On the suggestion of Johannes Gross and Wolf Jobst Siedler, Schmitt at the time considered publishing a collection of his texts for the publishing house Propyläen, which was to contain central texts such as *Political Theology*, the Catholicism essay, the *Leviathan* book and the 'Großraum Ordnung' text.[53] However, Siedler was particularly interested in the early texts, while Schmitt was more inclined towards his later works.[54] Thus, in September 1971, he more or less withdrew from the project: 'The "Political Writings", which have already been announced under my name, . . . are far from having matured into a manuscript ready for print' (EFCS, p. 322).

Dieter Groh and Klaus Figge carried out the plan for an autobiographical conversation. Schmitt had once attentively followed the development of Groh's doctoral thesis on the European image of Russia.[55] In September 1971, Groh established contact with Schmitt again,[56] and rather suddenly their reunion turned into an interview. Groh thanked Schmitt, writing: 'I, or rather we, enjoyed being able to have discussions with you over three days.'[57] On 5 and 6 February 1972 a further conversation with Groh and Figge took place, and on 5 March the Südwestfunk broadcast the revised conversation,[58] which – following some autobiographical details of Schmitt's background and university studies – concentrated fully on the situation in 1932–3. On 16 October it was repeated on the Deutschlandfunk. In his watchwords book, Schmitt noted: 'Saw myself (as if it was television) as an old, frail man, but this made my explications convincing; strange. Dieter Groh balanced the deficiencies with his interpolations, his references to contemporary history and his presence.'[59] In the conversation, Schmitt was looking for the key to the appointment of Hitler as chancellor in Hindenburg's need for legality: 'The trauma of the oath and an allergy against trials' made him suddenly see Hitler as the 'guardian of the constitution'.[60] Thus, Schmitt did not repeat the great myth of his own role as 'delayer' of the 'legal revolution'. He emphasized his 'private existence' after 30 January, as well as the importance of the Enabling Act, for his change of heart [Fahnenwechsel]. Schmitt gave the date the Act was passed, 24 March 1933, as the date of his decision to 'cooperate', and remained silent on his collaboration with Hans Frank. He saw himself in the role of the curious, intellectually seduced technician of law [Rechtstechniker], not that of the great saviour of constitutional policies. Schmitt also inserted these reflections into the preface – typed by Hildegard Hirsch[61] – for an Italian collection of his writings. At that time, Schmitt was also pursuing the translation of *The Concept of the Political* into English, French and Italian, perhaps with his upcoming eighty-fifth birthday in mind. Böckenförde used this as an occasion to remind him yet again of a possible publication on the situation in 1932–3.

   In the spring of 1972, Schmitt had pneumonia, and thus his meeting with the French translator Marie Luise Steinhauser had to be postponed.[62] At the beginning of May, Anima came from Santiago, and she visited again in October. Schmitt now increasingly adopted a 'wait-and-see' attitude to life; he no longer travelled longer distances on his own – at best he made it to Düsseldorf. After his heart attack, a certain fatigue in his old friendships set in. Academically ambitious visits became rarer, while the permanent contact with Ernst Hüsmert, Johannes Gross and Gerd Giesler was not burdened by a common past or by academic aims. Schmitt increasingly experienced his life as a 'reprise', 'repristination, palimpsest'.[63] His notes mention sleeping problems; he took sleeping pills and reached for the wine bottles. The fact that he was now hard of hearing made conversations more difficult. The telephone took the place of the letter. From 1974 onwards, Schmitt wrote the watchword book in shorthand. He kept his long list of visitors on the inside of the cover. To Koselleck he remarked about 'the total incapacity in old age of making decisions, a miserable condition:[64] Shall he go or shall he stay? / All his will is taken away; / Plumb on easy roads he gropes / Like the blind, he totters, creeps."* Schmitt also mentioned his tribulations more and more often to Jünger. 'We, who once made shadows into beings / Now see beings move away from us as

---

* Schmitt quotes from Goethe's *Faust*, Part II, ll. 11,471; here in the translation by David Constantine (London, 2009).

shadows' (JS, p. 390),* he quotes from Chamisso, and assures Jünger: 'The shadow lives' (JS, p. 391). Jünger had a clear criterion: 'Only once the hand-writing wobbles does the whole man wobble' (JS, p. 380). Whether or not this was the case now increasingly depended on the day.

Carl Schmitt and Hans Blumenberg: a conversation among equals

In *Political Theology II*, Schmitt concluded his oeuvre with a surpris-ing postscript on Blumenberg, who had defended *The Legitimacy of the Modern Age*. Against Peterson, Schmitt had insisted on the 'political' char-acter of his theology, and against Blumenberg he insisted on the impor-tance of theology as such. At first, it was not clear whether Blumenberg would react to the postscript, but he then opened their correspondence with a letter in which he admitted that his own critique of Schmitt's use of 'secularization' as 'implying illegitimacy' (HBCS, pp. 105f.) had referred more to the ordinary use of the word. He then mentioned his and Schmitt's interpretation of Goethe's motto 'nemo contra Deum nisi Deus ipse'† as a test of their mutual understanding.[65] Schmitt initially received this discreet offer of a discussion only politely, without responding directly to the argument. However, more than three years later, in October 1974, Blumenberg wrote again and sent the revised version of the first part of *The Legitimacy of the Modern Age*, in which he holds up anthropo-logical 'self-preservation' [Selbstbehauptung] against Schmitt's critique of 'self-legitimation' [Selbstermächtigung] in the modern age. Only now did Schmitt reply in more detail, referring to his age as an excuse and point-ing to the problem of the katechon. He then adds that his approach was concerned mainly with historical 'continuity' (HBCS, p. 125) and enclosed the new edition of *The Nomos of the Earth*. Around the same time, Schmitt drafted a lecture (which he probably did not give) on the 'de-arcanization of the katechon'.[66] This time it was Blumenberg who postponed writing a more detailed response until August 1975. Then, he said that the 'core of [their] differences' (HBCS, p. 131) could be captured in the question of 'whether eschatological faith and historical consciousness were compati-ble'. Blumenberg denied this, interpreted eschatology in Gnostic terms and criticized the attitude of religious expectation as a distortion of historical meaning. In the question of the critique of contemporary Christianity, however, he moved closer to Schmitt, speaking of the cheap 'reversal of the eschatological promise into the promise of a delay of the eschata [last things]' (HBCS, p. 132), and juxtaposing his approach to Löwith's inter-pretation of Goethe's motto. Löwith was the common opponent against whom both Schmitt and Blumenberg defined themselves as scholars.

---

* Schmitt quotes, not quite accurately, from Adalbert von Chamisso's poem *An meinen alten Freund Peter Schlemihl* [To my old friend Peter Schlemihl] (1834): 'Wir, die wir Schatten Wesen einst verliehen / Sehn Wesen jetzt als Schatten von uns ziehen'. Chamisso wrote: 'Die wir dem Schatten Wesen sonst verliehen / Sehn Wesen jetzt als Schatten sich verziehen' (*Peter Schlemihls wundersame Geschichte*, Berlin, 2013, p. 3).
† 'No one is/can do anything against God except God himself' (see PT II, p. 126).

Blumenberg set up a parallel between his defence of the intrinsic legitimacy [Eigenrecht] of the modern age and the possibility of a polytheistic interpretation of Goethe's motto. Should Goethe be read in heathen and polytheistic terms or as an immanent critic of Christianity? Schmitt's response was evasive and referred to the personal importance of the katechon problem. He also adduced the question of Löwith's position: Peterson, he said, was 'the mystagogue of Löwith' (HBCS, p. 128). Löwith could be subsumed under Schmitt's critique of Peterson. Thus, to begin with, Schmitt simply repeated his earlier answer (cf. PT II, p. 126ff.). Blumenberg probably did not expect much else from old Schmitt. However, Blumenberg's next book, *The Genesis of the Copernican World*, led to another, more accommodating answer. Schmitt now referred Blumenberg to Däubler's epic *The Northern Lights* as the poetic response to the revolution in the image of the world, and enclosed his *Ex captivitate salus*. Blumenberg's reaction was surprisingly positive. Although, with 'Masada and Warsaw',[67] he mentioned his own experiences of persecution, he nevertheless wrote that, while he had tried to work out the 'logic of [their] differences' in the revision of his *Legitimacy of the Modern Age*, Schmitt's little book had rather led him onto the 'track' of what they had 'in common' [auf die Spur des Gemeinsamen] (HBCS, p. 148). He had understood that Schmitt let the differences persist but valued what they had in common in their search for answers in intellectual history. Blumenberg sent Schmitt a preliminary study for *Das Lachen der Thrakerin* [The laughter of the Thracian woman],[68] which Schmitt read enthusiastically and called a 'true masterstroke' (HBCS, p. 151). While at first they both defined themselves as scholars in their opposition to Löwith, they now agreed in their opposition to the 'irrealists' of the academic world, on the one hand, and the ignorant rejection of true 'scholarship in the humanities' [Geisteswissenschaft], on the other. Their correspondence ended on a personal note, with Schmitt reminiscing about his defence of his Habilitation and his thanks for Blumenberg's congratulations on his ninetieth birthday. Their exchange retained intellectual concentration until the end. Two great scholars shook hands across generations, despite their differences.

Problem child: 'legal world revolution'

Ever since his book on the Leviathan, Schmitt had celebrated special birthdays with publications. His eighty-fifth birthday, however, passed by quietly. Sepp Schelz published a birthday article in the *Allgemeines Sonntagsblatt*. Rüdiger Altmann praised Schmitt as a 'Thinker of the State with Left-Wing Epigones' in the *Deutsche Zeitung*. Hans-Dietrich Sander celebrated Schmitt in *Die Welt* and heavily criticized the 'anti-Schmitt literature'.[69] Friedrich Karl Fromme acknowledged Schmitt in the *Frankurter Allgemeine Zeitung* as an important critic of liberalism.[70] Fromme's article provoked a sharp reply from Gerhard Leibholz, whose *Wesen der Repräsentation* [Nature of representation] Schmitt had once read at the proof stage.[71] Leibholz reminded his readers of Schmitt's anti-Semitism and considered the conference on 'Judaism in Jurisprudence' to be the 'consequence' of *The Concept of the Political*. Ernst J. Cohn also wrote a critical letter to the editor: Schmitt, he said, 'has forsaken any claim to be acknowledged as a genuine teacher of right either now or even by posterity.'[72] Thus, his status as a 'classical author' remained controversial.

The article in *Die Welt* led to some surprise mail for Schmitt: 'Lolo' Sauer, his lover between Kathleen and Duška, now a physician in Berlin, got in touch and wrote:

> You will hardly be able to remember me, as half a century has passed since our paths once crossed for a short time; it was in 1922–3. And I don't write to you today to congratulate you, though one could do that in your case. I want only to tell you that our acquaintance was the most fruitful event in my life, and that it had an impact that lasts still today.[73]

Wilhelm Grewe sent a telegram saying that Schmitt's work had had a 'decisive influence on [his] choice of profession'.[74] Arnold Schmitz also congratulated Schmitt: 'It is by now more or less exactly fifty years since you first visited us in Bonn, in Kronprinzenstraße 2. . . . For a lifetime, you have granted me, and upheld, your friendship, and for that I cannot thank you enough, of that I am proud.'[75]

Schmitt's ninetieth birthday was meant once more to be marked by a celebration. His pupils urged him to produce the volumes of collected essays.[76] Schmitt told his publisher about a conversation with Böckenförde: 'In terms of the principal structure – separation of works on state theory from those on constitutional law, international law and publications on the philosophy of law – the publication is clear to us both.'[77] But Schmitt first wanted a new edition of *The Nomos of the Earth*, 'with, for instance, rearranged corollaries'. Soon, he said that he did not want to edit 'another voluminous anthology', but rather unite several shorter texts under a 'topical title': 'Nomos and Value, as well as Hobbesiana'.[78] Böckenförde wrote: 'I am glad that you have now decided to do the second volume of essays.'[79] In March 1974 he asked Schmitt for a 'Festschrift contribution for François Perroux'.[80] Tommissen, and later Quaritsch, took care of the translation.[81] A manuscript in German, with the 'final title' 'Weltrevolutionäre Legalität' [World revolutionary legality], is dated 28 October 1975.[82] The further difficult story of the emergence of this last longer essay by Schmitt illustrates his diminishing strength. Böckenförde looked over various versions and fragments and returned the synoptic 'result' to Schmitt.[83] This difficult birth took place on Böckenförde's initiative so that Schmitt's ninetieth birthday would, after all, be marked by a new publication.

At that time, Schmitt started to speak of having 'one foot already in Charon's barque' (CSAD, p. 265). Compared to the '[s]uper-time, supersonic and super-human speeds' of the present day, he was crawling along, 'so that a racing competition between two snails is becoming more interesting to me than the competitive flight between two astronauts' (HBCS, p. 118). During those years, many of Schmitt's old companions and friends died. At the end of July 1974, Jünger met with Schmitt and still found him to have quite a 'presence' (JS, p. 405). But Schmitt found it increasingly difficult to keep up his correspondence.

In the summer term 1977, Böckenförde moved to the University of Freiburg; he kept urging Schmitt to have the collected volumes 'ready in time for the ninetieth birthday', and Schmitt continued to reply evasively. Böckenförde asked: 'Should such a day pass without any such presentation of parts of your work?'[84] He succeeded, at least, in pushing forward the problem child *Legal World Revolution*. The working titles for the collections of essays were 'Vom Staatsbegriff zum Begriff des Politischen' [From the concept of the state to the concept of the political] and 'Einheit der Welt gegen Nomos der Erde' [Unity of the world against nomos of the earth]. In November 1977, Böckenförde asked for clarification of a few questions in connection with the work on these volumes.[85] The editors still wanted to have them ready for Schmitt's ninetieth birthday. Böckenförde formulated as a criterion for selection 'that the purpose of these volumes is to make the lasting actuality and significance of your scholarly work also obvious in the present day, and thus to counter the tendency of historicizing you and your work by putting it under the rubric of "Weimar period".'[86] In mid-January, he vigorously inquired about the progress of the work again, but Schmitt remained hesitant. Finally, Böckenförde asked Schmitt, as a 'token' [Zeichen] of his continuing intellectual presence, at least to have the 'Legal World Revolution' ready for the ninetieth birthday.[87] Only as late as May 1978 did he finally receive this 'swansong on legality'.[88] However, the volumes of collected essays did not see publication. Despite his intense efforts, Böckenförde did not succeed in crowning Schmitt's ninetieth birthday with the momentous publication of two long-planned volumes of collected essays. But he dedicated his inaugural lecture in Freiburg – 'Der verdrängte Ausnahmezustand' [The repressed state of exception][89] – to Schmitt: 'I would be delighted', he wrote when sending Schmitt the lecture, 'if when reading the text you could reach the conclusion: doceo, sed non frustra [I do not teach in vain].'[90] Mohler organized a lecture series on 'Der Ernstfall' [The emergency] in the Siemens Stiftung [Siemens Foundation] in Munich, which 'was understood as a homage to Carl Schmitt' (BS, p. 422). In the winter term 1978–9, Böckenförde again taught a seminar on Schmitt's work, together with the political scientist Hennis.[91]

The Legal World Revolution accommodated Böckenförde's wish that Schmitt should discuss the break of 1932–3 again with the help of the categories of 'legality and legitimacy'. In his late texts, Schmitt reconsidered some of his central earlier texts, such as *The Concept of the Political*, his interpretation of Hobbes, the *Political Theology* and *Legality and Legitimacy*. His arguments were finally free of apologetic provisos and tit-for-tat responses. Schmitt explained that the Weimar Republic kept open the 'door of legality' for alternative legal systems. He emphasized that the 'legal revolution' could only succeed with the help of nationalism as a 'national revolution', and that nationalism and 'revanchism' were the 'real strength' and driving force used by Hitler (FP, p. 931). As late as 1981, he mentioned 'the monstrous stupidity of Versailles' (JS, p. 447) as his earlier point of reference. The will of the Basic Law to learn lessons and to eliminate the possibility of a 'repetition', he said, was 'more than understandable'. This also applied to the banning of parties. Schmitt was here talking in a new tone. After decades, he finally clearly expressed himself as opposed to National Socialism and as in favour of the Federal Republic. He, too, it seems, had made his peace.

However, he continued to see the unity of the world qua 'legal world revolution' in a negative light. He now actualized his critical reflections on 'legal revolution' in his critical analysis of a 'legal world revolution', by which he understood the revolutionary power of a legalist mode of right, which affirms itself and perseveres as the only source of legitimacy. Within the legal world revolution, the legitimacy of legality, the ideologically exaggerated faith in the procedural form of 'legality', becomes a revolutionary power. Schmitt understood the 'planetary industry-appropriation' as the end of all politics within a unified world without alternatives: 'World politics reaches its end and is turned into world police – a dubious kind of progress' (FP, p. 926). He spoke in detail about the failure of the European Union: 'The progress towards a legal world revolution has no parallel in a political will towards the political unity of Europe or even towards a European revolution', he said. 'Someone who delves into the more than a thousand pages . . . of the standard work "Europäisches Gemeinschaftsrecht" [European Union law] by H. P. Ipsen (Tübingen 1972)[92] . . . will fall into deep sadness. The world political forces and powers, which battle for the political unity of the world, are stronger than the European interest in the political unity of Europe' (FP, p. 932). Schmitt saw Europe decline due to the universalization of certain constitutional standards. Here, a clear rejection of the European Union as a motor for the formation of an alternative Großraum corresponds to his view of China as a third power. When Schmitt speaks with regret of a missing European revolution, he has in mind a constitutional decision that would not be corrupted by existing forms of legality. He sets up the 'super-legality' of the world revolution against 'another kind of legality', in which he still placed his hopes, but the possibility of which he saw threatened by the existing legitimacy of legality. Again and again he criticized the 'monopoly of legality of the state of law' (VRA, p. 412), the fact that the law-giving state had monopolized its legal form as the only source of legitimacy to such a degree that no other legitimacy could emerge. 'Legitimacy then appears as a kind of higher legality' (FP, p. 923). And portentously he wrote: 'Our present analysis of the possibility of a legal world revolution concerns only legality, not the legitimacy of a world revolution' (FP, p. 920).

Thus, Schmitt did not consider the project of the European Union after 1945 as a genuine option. After Germany's defeat, he no longer saw any entity with a strong political will to maintain Central Europe as a Großraum. Only the authoritarian Spain, he said, was still an heir and guardian of the 'historical legitimacy' and 'substance' of the old Europe. In terms of power politics, Europe no longer had a role to play because it did not offer any alternative to the system of economic-technological 'progress'. According to Schmitt, someone who accepts the existing legitimacy of legality as a means of revolution has already lost. This is also the reason why, after 1945, the old options of fascism and Marxism were no longer alternatives for him. Schmitt very radically analysed the process of the 'dethronement' of Europe;[93] the process of unification, which, in those days, was moving forward only slowly and often encountered obstacles, he did not consider a real force for an alternative configuration of the constitution. His expectations were of such a fundamental nature that even the alignment of the economic order to that of the West ruled out any oppositional system. Thus, his late work shows how fundamental a meaning he attached to the idea of an alternative constitution.[94]

Only rarely do we find political comments in his correspondence of that time, which was beginning to diminish. However, with Álvaro d'Ors, Schmitt exchanged letters on the transformation of Franco's Spain. D'Ors considered himself as a 'victor of 1939' against the communist revolution: 'The experience of those of my generation is that Spain was never better off (and the peseta was never worth more) than under the dictatorships of 1923 to 1930 and 1939 to 1975. Now, we live in a lamentable pornodemocracy' (CSAD, p. 276). He no longer saw any 'chance of a saving dictatorship'. Schmitt consoled him with his old categories of dictatorship and eschatology, which he otherwise hardly ever used after 1949: 'There is no reason for giving up hope; the state of power [Gewaltstaat] was never "normal", so let us remain "expectant"' (CSAD, p. 284). Schmitt here uses his old categories in quotation marks. He has become cautious and sceptical even towards his own thinking.

In the maze of the posthumous papers: Schmitt's last work

Early on, Schmitt was already convinced of his importance within the history of scholarship. In terms of a typology of literary estates, he was the paradoxical case of someone who was chaotic but who never threw anything away. In this respect, he too was one of his 'Buribunken'.* From his time in Bonn, he kept any notes – even if in no sort of order – and collected not only drafts, manuscripts and typescripts but also proofs, publisher's prospectuses and reviews, newspaper articles, excerpts, hotel reservations, invoices for beverages – quite simply everything. Various different ideas, types of writing and languages criss-crossed in his notes. He continually switched between stenographic and normal writing in all of the common academic languages. The only one of these languages he did not speak was Hebrew. Even in old age, he liked to have the occasional conversation in Latin. All this is preserved in the labyrinth of his posthumous papers.

As early as 1953, Schmitt got in touch with the Bundesarchiv Koblenz [Federal Archive of Koblenz]. At the same time he made efforts at selling his library. In his first will, of 24 November 1965, Anima was the sole heir, although it should also help 'to provide security for [his] faithful helper of many years, Anni Stand'. Hubertus Bung was named as the executor.[95]

---

* The characters from his early satire; see chapter 7.

In the early 1970s, Schmitt's negotiations with the Bundesarchiv Koblenz failed, and, supported by Böckenförde and Eberhard von Medem,[96] he began to negotiate with the Landesarchiv Nordrhein-Westfalen [Regional Archive for North Rhine-Westphalia] in Düsseldorf. The executive director of the state archive, Dr Wilhelm Janssen, got in touch and came to Plettenberg. An intensive process of building up trust was necessary in order to elicit the literary estate from Schmitt. Janssen assured Schmitt: 'As I already indicated when we spoke, it would be possible to formulate provisos and controls against unwelcome uses of the posthumous papers, which would be contractually fixed.'[97] The purchase of the papers was not cheap and the estate differed from the other main emphases of the archive. The archiving was no easy task either. Schmitt signed a 'depository agreement' [Hinterlegungsvertrag] with a right of first refusal. He now could put his literary estate piece by piece into archival boxes.[98] On 10 October 1975, he drafted a new 'last will and testament'.[99]

Over the coming years, Schmitt gradually gave a large part of his literary estate to the archive in Düsseldorf. He sifted through the material and developed a new form of self-commentary with the posthumous papers in mind. Employees from the archive, first Dr Rolf Nagel, then Dr Dieter Weber, put the piles of paper in boxes and brought them to Düsseldorf. The first delivery took place in spring 1976. 'The diaries are securely stored away', Nagel assured Schmitt.[100] In December another sixty boxes followed.[101] Then, in March 1977, Weber took care of another delivery. Schmitt was sketching a short history of this library, with its painful losses in 1921 (Cari), in 1943 (bombed out) and in 1945 (confiscated).[102] Nagel produced an edition of the correspondence with Curtius, which was the first publication of material from the posthumous papers.[103] Schmitt not only prepared the material for collection but also worked through it, and this sifting led to productive interpretations. It is difficult to estimate the proportion of his late work that lies hidden in the mountain of material that is his literary estate. No biographer can remotely disclose everything that may be contained in these boxes and files, hidden by the cryptic style of his late work and by the hieroglyphs of his idiomatic stenographic writing. Schmitt collected his thoughts and satirical ideas in *écriture automatique*. At the end, Expressionism and Dadaism seem to have triumphed over scholasticism. In the form of satirical nonsense poetry, Schmitt was trying creatively to approach new ideas.

Just one example: In a file 'Tu quis es?', Schmitt collected autobiographical reflections on his own 'case'.[104] He compared his situation as a 'scapegoat' with other 'cases': that of Papen, Schacht, Globke, Veit Harlan.[105] He came across a stamp on which Else Lasker-Schüler is pictured, critically eying the viewer. Schmitt glued the stamp onto a sheet of paper and wrote above it: 'Sous l'oeil des Juives'. He listed Jewish women who had eyed him critically over the years: a certain Aronstein from Lichtenberg, Berlin (during his time as a student), and Else Lasker-Schüler herself, who was part of the circle around Theodor Däubler. Below these two, he noted the names of Alice Berend, Annie Kraus and Käte Eisler.[106] The list provides new riddles: we know nothing about an acquaintance between Schmitt and

Else Lasker-Schüler, not even a fleeting one, but it is not unlikely that he knew her. Nothing is known about an acquaintance from his youth with the name Aronstein.

Another example: In 1963, Ernst Bloch published an article on 'Die sogenannte Judenfrage' [The so-called Jewish question] in the *Frankfurter Allgemeine Zeitung*, in which he criticized the philo-Semitism of the Federal Republic as an 'immanent piece of anti-Semitism' and as a failed attempt at coming to terms with the past.[107] Schmitt agreed with Bloch's critique, but found it to be a symptom in itself; and he began, in several notebooks under the title of Bloch's article, to collect newspaper articles on the debate about Hochhuth's *The Deputy*, on attitudes towards Judaism and Israel, and on Bloch and the student movement. The second of these notebooks, 'The So-Called Jewish Question II', also has the ironic heading 'Sozialismus ist nicht viel' [Socialism is not a lot].[108] For Schmitt, the 'so-called Jewish question' was the 'question of sacred places', by which he meant: for Ernst Bloch, the 'so-called Jewish question', the utopian question of the sacred place, is the actual question behind that of socialism. Schmitt denounced this question of religious truth as a Jewish 'distortion', taking as the point of departure for his view Bloch's book on Münzer, which he had once read during his time in Munich.[109] He found the new edition of it 'de-Christianized' and 'de-Münzered' [entmünzt]. 'Bloch has recast [umgemünzt] Münzer in a similar way to Ball's recasting of himself in the "Folgen" [Consequences]; interesting parallel', Schmitt wrote to Sander (SSA, pp. 114f.). In March 1970, he condensed his thoughts as follows: 'Ernst Bloch Münzer falsified / False Münzer, true Bloch, / Thomas retreats into the mouse-hole. / False-Bloch-Münzer gets serious in 1962.'[110] To Bloch's article, he responded: 'Mary really gave birth to God's child.' In this fashion, Schmitt continued his malicious and ironic dialogue between Christianity and Judaism.

In 1975, it was Thomas Mann's hundredth birthday. In his notebooks, Schmitt staged an imaginary private counter-event to the public celebrations.[111] Another of his folders pushed the Hitler–Demetrius identification to further extremes. There are dozens of such folders in his posthumous papers, which are often no less interesting than some of the published texts. Schmitt read various newspapers, including the *Nationalzeitung*, but also very attentively *Der Spiegel*, always with pen in hand, and he collected and amassed articles in his folders. Schmitt as a reader of newspapers would also be an interesting topic. Right into the 1980s, Schmitt kept a diary. In addition, there are the stenographic commentaries. For his diaries, he even created an alphabetic 'index of names' in the style of a critical edition.[112] Even at the age of ninety, he still wrote many pages of text every day. Some of it seems to have in mind a possible readership. Schmitt was probably never so close to the realm of the Buribunken.

'Ad multos annos!': Schmitt's ninetieth birthday

In May 1978, Anima wrote to Schmitt regarding the intended schedule for the celebrations:

After many ideas and suggestions were discarded, a simple but practical plan emerged: we shall organize a reception in a restaurant in the vicinity, at eleven in the morning (these Germans!) and all groups will straightaway come together: the office of the mayor and the official honouring, the neighbours from Pasel, the friends and pupils from out of town who want to come. Alfonso and I, with Dusanka and Carlos, will also be there. (CSAD, p. 286)

The official high point was the presentation of the 'ring of honour' of the city of Plettenberg to Schmitt by the mayor Dr Heinz Baberg. The celebration took place on 11 July in the Berggasthaus Tanneneck. Joseph Kaiser gave a welcoming speech[113] and Julien Freund and Tommissen presented Schmitt with a small Festschrift.[114] Offprints of *The Legal World Revolution* were available on time. The mayor presented the ring and spoke about the consultations in the city council: 'We reached the conclusion that Carl Schmitt was neither the crown jurist of Hitler, nor someone who paved the way for National Socialism or helped to destroy the Weimar Republic. On the contrary: today, we know that he was far removed from National Socialist ideology – even the National Socialists knew that from 1935 onwards, when Carl Schmitt ended up in their firing line.'[115] The award certificate acknowledged his 'great scholarly achievement'. Ernst Jünger gave an improvised celebratory speech, and Schmitt spoke some words of thanks.

There is a magnificent photograph of the celebratory party. In it, Schmitt is sitting – or rather is enthroned – on a chair, beneath some trees, surrounded by the large party. Two of his grandchildren kneel down at his feet, with Anima, Anni Stand and Hans Schneider next to them. Standing on his right is Ernst Jünger, looking to one side; behind Carl is his sister Auguste, who would survive him by a few years. The erudite assembly is grouped in the background. Johannes Gross looks cheerfully into the camera. Peter Scheibert talks to Piet Tommissen. Christian Meier, who had not been formally invited because of a slight tension between him and Schmitt, is deep in conversation with Böckenförde. Gustav von Schmoller is present, as he had been in 1938.[116] Rüdiger Altmann is part of a separate group on the side.[117] He, too, had just fallen into disgrace again on account of some critical remarks. 'Who are you?', Schmitt pointedly greeted his pupil from Berlin. A squadron of the air force was coincidentally flying overhead. 'That is the tribute of the air force on my birthday', Schmitt remarked to Christian Meier; it was not unambiguously clear whether this was meant to be ironic.[118]

This birthday was no longer marked by any serious disputes. Mountains of mail congratulating Schmitt arrived. Numerous pupils and former students got in touch.[119] Schmitt experienced that even companions with whom he had fallen out congratulated him: for instance – initiated by Isensee[120] – Ernst Friesenhahn, Ernst Rudolf Huber and Karl Lohmann.[121] Theodor Maunz wrote that Schmitt had 'given scholarship on state law in the twentieth century a new shape and a higher meaning'.[122] Scheuner also sent a long retrospection on fifty years of occasional encounters and inspirations, which also, however, pointed out 'deeper differences': 'Without denying

'That is the tribute of the air force on my birthday' – festive company with, among others, Ernst Jünger, Nicolaus Sombart, Joseph Kaiser, Johannes Gross, Christian Meier, Ernst-Wolfgang Böckenförde, Gerd Giesler and Rüdiger Altmann

that antagonism, the battle for power, is a part of the political, I would not call this the essential fundamental aspect but rather the founding of peace and order.'[123] The general objection was raised against Schmitt again and again over the course of fifty years. He nevertheless thanked Scheuner 'for the noble way in which you accept some aspects of my life's work without humiliating me straightaway'.[124] The 'Heimatkreis Plettenberg' [circle of the citizens of Plettenberg][125] congratulated the 'Faustian man' 'ad multos annos!'. Many relationships had ended and many themes were now exhausted. But Schmitt did not yet retreat into total reclusion.

'Precious days' with Jacob Taubes

One of Schmitt's old contacts only came properly alive in these late years, namely, that with Jacob Taubes. In 1952, Taubes had already written an affirmative letter about *Constitutional Theory* to Mohler. Schmitt glued it to the inside of his personal copy. Taubes's letter, from then on, played a similar mythical role to the letter from Benjamin. In 1955, Taubes wrote again, asking about a possible contribution from Schmitt.[126] Conversations with Mohler led to the occasional postcard. In the summer term of 1973, Taubes taught a seminar, 'Zur Gesellschaftstheorie Carl Schmitts und Walter Benjamins' [On Carl Schmitt's and Walter Benjamin's theory of society], to mark Schmitt's eighty-fifth birthday. But only very late did the two actually meet in person. In the summer of 1977, Taubes made the acquaintance of Hans-Dietrich Sander at Mohler's place. Their conversation led to a jointly written postcard to Schmitt (BS, p.414). Taubes invited Sander to the Free University in Berlin and opened up the prospect of a scholarship from the Deutsche Forschungsgemeinschaft [German Research Council] and a possible Habilitation. Taubes shared with Schmitt an interest in 'occidental eschatology': the retrograde orientation beyond more recent philosophy of history to the 'theological preconditions'. Within this context, Taubes, as a philosopher of religion, was mostly exercised by the fate of Judaism. What attracted him most in Schmitt was the politically 'concrete' interpretation of religion and theology. St Paul and Spinoza were two key authors for him, and Schmitt's late interpretation of Hobbes provided him with an impetus

Taubes wanted to secure Schmitt's cooperation for a new journal, 'Kassiber'.[127] Such a journal, Schmitt said, needed a 'motto'.[128] But Schmitt was a 'professional jurist and not a professional revolutionary'. Taubes then made the surprise suggestion of placing some text with the Suhrkamp publishing house – even in the face of the braying of the 'Habermasse'.* Initially, Taubes had a documentation of the Schmitt–Peterson controversy in mind, but then also considered an edition of Schmitt's 'materials on literature'. Around the same time, a volume on *Monotheismus als politisches Problem? Erik Peterson und die Kritik der politischen Theologie* [Monotheism as a political problem? Erik Peterson and the critique of political theology] was published.[129] Its editor, Alfred Schindler, son of the Swiss jurist Dietrich Schindler,[130] entered into correspondence with Schmitt about the book.[131] After having enquired about Schindler,[132] Schmitt expressed his reservations about it and spoke of a 'seminary-theological doing away with the doing away of Peterson's thesis of closure' (SSA, p.435). He rejected in particular the reconstruction of his theology.[133] Taubes now planned a similar venture but took Schmitt's side against Peterson, because he shared Schmitt's antipodal approach and did not keep theology and politics separate.

In response to Taubes's idea, Schmitt suggested a 'personal meeting'.[134] But when Taubes wrote to him about his plans, Schmitt was immediately irritated because he feared that Taubes wanted to squeeze their conversation into a 'complicatedly rushed (haste is the worst) travel itinerary'.[135] Taubes assured him that his trip was not a 'duty visit',[136] but that he wanted to risk a conversation 'face to face, also with regard to what remains unsaid' [Aug im Aug, auch im Ungesagten]. Sander made efforts to arrange the meeting. 'It is important to me to have seen and talked to Taubes personally at least once', Schmitt replied. 'If that can be arranged for the end of February, I shall be as ready as I can be, but only in private [unter vier Augen]' (SSA, p.429). The date in February could not be realized, and another attempt to bring about their meeting in May 1978 also

---

* Taubes plays on the fact that the plural form of Habermas's name produces the term 'mass', and thus can be read either as 'many people like Habermas' or as the 'Haber mass', suggesting that the braying is not based on independent reflection.

failed. Schmitt abruptly broke off his contact with Sander at the time, just as he had rejected Gerhard Nebel's role of intermediary in his dispute with Jünger. Sander experienced this as a 'nightmare' (SSA, p.450).

In the winter term, Taubes held a colloquium on 'political theology' at the Freie Universität Berlin, and in September 1978 their conversation finally took place. Taubes afterwards thanked him for the 'friendly welcome, for [his] patience and for [his] openness'; he referred back, beyond Hobbes, to St Paul: 'Not only the "first liberal Jew" discovered this "breaking point", but already the apostle Paul, to whom I turn in the changing fortunes of time' [an den ich mich wende in den Wenden der Zeit].[137] Schmitt received Taubes's remarks in the 'spirit of friendship'.[138] Taubes at once asked him for a second meeting, because he saw in Schmitt perhaps the only reader 'who can fathom the depths and breadth of the swansong that followed 1848'.[139] That second meeting took place on 23–4 November 1978.[140] The young comparatist Wolfgang Fietkau brought Taubes to Plettenberg by car and for one afternoon also took part in the conversation. Schmitt thanked Taubes for these 'precious days'.[141] Although he did not respond to Taubes's editorial plans, he suggested a review of the volume by Schindler.[142] Taubes discussed *Hamlet or Hecuba* in his seminar and wanted to see, at the very least, this text published by Suhrkamp.[143] Schmitt wrote to Unseld,* who, however, responded only belatedly,[144] such that Schmitt had 'lost interest'.[145] On 3 February 1980 a third meeting took place, at which Martin Kriele was also present.[146] Schmitt afterwards suggested 'speak[ing] about the fact that Fichte had awakened Moses Hess for himself, the way that Hegel had awakened a Marx for himself'.[147] And he continued to be interested in the religious motifs in National Socialism and socialism. But there were no more meetings after these three. The conversations with Taubes showed Schmitt once more in full force. For one last time, he focused his 'political theology' on the discussion of Judaism and Christianity. At no point did either of them ignore their antipodal positions.[148]

From the working group 'Poetics and Hermeneutics'† emerged the idea of applying hermeneutical methods to politics. Taubes organized a colloquium on 'Political Theology III', with well-known speakers. Schmitt read many of the papers in typescript. The first collected volume of the project 'Religionstheorie und politische Theorie' [Theory of religion and political theory], titled *Der Fürst dieser Welt* [The prince of this world], was then dedicated to Carl Schmitt's work and its consequences. In October 1980 a colloquium on Hobbes took place, in 1982 there was a follow-up conference on 'Gnosis und Politik' [Gnosis and politics] and, even later, another one on 'Theokratie' [Theocracy]. Schmitt received the first volume, with a slight delay, for his ninety-fifth birthday.[149] He still worked through some of the contributions. The discussions between Taubes and Schmitt were

---

*   Siegfried Unseld (1924–2002), one of the best-known publishers of the Federal Republic, led the Suhrkamp Verlag on his own after Peter Suhrkamp's death in 1959.
†   Group of scholars who met between 1963 and 1994; originally an initiative by Hans Blumenberg, Clemens Heselhaus and Hans Robert Jauß. Taubes belonged to this group.

completed, almost in the form of a legacy, in the lectures that the terminally ill Taubes gave in 1987 in Heidelberg.[150] Hans-Dietrich Sander, who at one point had been an intermediary in these conversations, further radicalized and isolated himself. He styled himself as a pamphleteering advocate of Schmitt.[151] But, in Plettenberg, Taubes would hardly have listened to his crude theses on the Federal Republic's repression of the 'national imperative' through an 'imitatio Ahasveri', and Schmitt was probably wise to take him out of the equation.

Last will and testament

From early on, Schmitt saw himself as an 'old man'. Even though he was in his tenth decade, he impressed visitors with his presence and carried them with him through his 'world of most amazing tensions'; yet, despite Sava Kličković finding him 'in the best possible health'[152] and Johannes Gross finding him in a 'splendid mood',[153] Schmitt himself increasingly felt that his 'new friend Charon, in his barque, [made him] hurry up' (BS, p.405). He looked upon himself as 'standing in the queue waiting for Charon's next barque' (JS, p.443). On occasion, he said: 'But my persecutors do not let me die' (CSAD, p.266). In his last essay, he concluded with the 'words of a dying ruler': 'I have no enemies, I have killed them all' (FP, p.936). He often quoted Goethe: 'An old person suffers the loss of one of the greatest human rights: he is no longer judged by his equals'* (CSAD, p.286). In 1979, Schmitt altered his will in order to transfer all assets and functions to Anima as his 'only legal heir' [einzigen Legalerben].[154] He probably did not want to threaten Böckenförde's chances of being appointed as one of the judges of the constitutional court by making him the executor.[155] Böckenförde commented: 'Your letter has affected me, in particular because of your efforts at removing any disadvantages, wherever possible, which your friends may suffer as a result of being connected with your name.'[156] Böckenförde respected this 'considerateness' without desiring it. In 1981, Schmitt entered into serious negotiations about moving his posthumous papers to the university library in Münster with Oberbibliotheksrat [senior library consultant] Dr Bertram Haller.[157] However, these negotiations became a long-drawn-out process, especially because Anima was meant to become part of them, and Schmitt finally ended them.

Schmitt kept a list of people who died before him. Franz Blei ends his *Erzählung eines Lebens* [Story of a life] with the image of friends who protect you from taking the step towards suicide. Schmitt now quoted Adalbert von Chamisso, who lets the figure of death answer the poet: 'Why, when now the world around you / shatters gently and mild like never before / do you not want to enter into the shadow of my tent / who are you, person I don't know?' (BS, p.427). Death was now luring him. His handwriting became shaky. But still Schmitt answered letters and looked

* Johann Wolfgang Goethe, *Maxims and Reflections*, London, 1998, p.43.

for new contacts, for instance with the French scholar André Doremus, with Angelo Bolaffi, Peter Koslowski and Herfried Münkler and others. On Schmitt's 'initiative',[158] a new edition of *Die Tyrannei der Werte* [The tyranny of values] 'in a Lutheran version',[159] with contributions from Eberhard Jüngel and Sepp Schelz, appeared in October 1979. Schmitt's text was followed by an affirmative piece on the Weimar theology of crisis by the Protestant theologian Jüngel. God, Jüngel wrote, was wholly different from conventional law. The religious experience was characterized by an 'interruption' of everything customary. The Christian experience of truth was therefore 'a radical putting into question of all talk about values and all thinking in terms of values'.[160] This edition strengthened the religious interpretation at the price of entering into an alliance with the Protestant theology of crisis, which Schmitt had once vehemently rejected. Thus, Schmitt once again increased his distance from Catholic natural law.

In 1980, Schmitt published a short letter to the editor of *Die Welt*.[161] Günter Maschke got in touch with a plan for an edition of Schmitt's work on literary criticism.[162] Schmitt was rather sceptical about this plan and wanted to save Maschke 'disappointment'.[163] At the end of June, Maschke came to Plettenberg, and a new edition of *Land and Sea* was agreed upon.[164] Supported in this by Anima, Maschke also urged Schmitt to publish a new edition of the *Leviathan* book. In April 1981, Schmitt wrote a short afterword to the new edition of *Land and Sea*, which was published at the end of September.[165] Maschke then took forward the republication of the *Leviathan* book. Schmitt selected a picture for the cover and had to dispel the political worries of the publisher with an 'afterword'

Schmitt on his ninety-fifth birthday, together with his grandchildren and Johannes Gross

[Nachspruch]. In mid-October the volume appeared with a very nice cover showing an old copper engraving of a stranded Leviathan.[166] The Maschke edition nevertheless ran into difficulties and had quickly to be discontinued. Thus, after Schmitt's hesitation over many years regarding volumes of collected essays, two monographs with a literary bent from the National Socialist period came out. Böckenförde, predictably, had some concerns over this new comeback.[167] Soon, the Klett publishing house took over both volumes and produced further editions. After Schmitt's death, his will came into effect, and his work remained mostly with Duncker & Humblot.

On his own initiative, in 1983 Ernst Hüsmert called Schmitt's old friend from his youth Georg Eisler in Hamburg. In his high old age, Eisler was still living as an active member of the Jewish community according to the maxim 'as long as I learn, I am alive'. Through Annie Kraus, he passed on his address to Schmitt.[168] Schmitt rang him twice and they had reconciliatory conversations. Schmitt's former assistant Günter Wasse met Schmitt in March 1983 in a 'lively' mood.[169] However, Anima was now diagnosed with cancer. On 17 June 1983, she died at the young age of fifty-two. Koselleck vividly remembered her 'cheerfulness and openness'.[170] Her death threw a shadow over Schmitt's ninety-fifth birthday. Nevertheless, a celebration took place, which was attended by, among others, Joseph Kaiser, Johannes Gross, Gerd Giesler, Günter Maschke and some of Schmitt's grandchildren. A stack of telegrams arrived.[171] Some newspapers mentioned the special birthday. The left-Schmittian Ulrich K. Preuss wrote an article in the *TAZ** with the title 'Die latente Diktatur im Verfassungsstaat' [Latent dictatorship in the constitutional state]. The *Süderländer Tageblatt* published a photograph of Schmitt, with Johannes Gross next to him, probably the last photograph of an alert Schmitt. The *Westfälische Rundschau*'s headline was 'Bedeutender Plettenberger: Carl Schmitt wird heute 95' [An important Plettenberger: Carl Schmitt is ninety-five today].[172] The *Frankfurter Allgemeine Zeitung* had a short note under 'Personalien' [People]. Walter Dirks, Schmitt's companion and member of the Catholic left, wrote in the *Badische Zeitung*: 'He may have despised the brown masses. But Hitler's *coup d'état* fitted his concept too well.'[173] From New York, Charles Wahl looked back over fifty years: 'I am particularly grateful to you for the open and clear warning to your "non-Aryan" pupils to take the dangers of National Socialism seriously. This meant that I left Berlin in good time.'[174]

From October 1982, if not before, Schmitt was a 'serious nursing case'.[175] He suffered from dementia and various other conditions. However, even after his ninety-fifth birthday, he remained responsive and able to take part in conversation. On 27 September 1983, the sixty-ninth anniversary of the death of his friend from his youth Fritz Eisler, he had his last telephone conversation with Georg Eisler. Christian Meier visited and brought along the new edition of the *Leviathan* book.[176] Böckenförde reported in detail about his election as a judge at the Constitutional Court.[177] It was a 'remarkable fact', he said, that he had been elected unanimously. Schmitt

* *Tageszeitung*, but better known as *TAZ*. A left-wing Berlin newspaper, also read nationally.

wrote his last lines around that time. Annie Kraus informed him of Georg Eisler's death:

> Each time you called, he rang me straightaway and told me about it, and after your first call he said that once he had regained his strength he would go and visit you. The second time, on the day of Fritz's death that is, he also rang me straightaway in Tyrolia and told me about it, but probably no longer expected his health to be restored . . . I was very grateful that you and Georgi did find each other again.[178]

Eisler is buried in the Jewish cemetery in Ohlsdorf, Hamburg. The late reconciliation with his oldest friend, not initiated by Schmitt, is of symbolic importance. With Eisler's death, Schmitt's energy also began to die out. He increasingly felt he was haunted [verfolgt] by radiation and spoke of invisible enemies. His delusions created the figure of 'a strong bloke with a bellowing voice, who organizes the terror but is himself only the executive organ of powerful, shady characters [Dunkelmänner]'. Schmitt called him 'Kra', quoting Däubler's *Northern Lights*.[179]

The grave of Carl Schmitt in 2005 with Ernst Hüsmert, his friend of many decades and executor of his private estate

Anima's death necessitated a last change of the will. Joseph H. Kaiser quickly took the initiative.[180] On 1 February 1984, the notary Werner Kessel certified a new last will and testament in Schmitt's house.[181] With a shaking hand, Schmitt, by now in very poor health, signed the document which made his four grandchildren his heirs. Kaiser became the executor for the scholarly posthumous papers and Ernst Hüsmert the executor for the personal papers.[182] There was a shadow over the remainder of the year 1984. Franzen, a former pupil from Berlin, came to visit and then thanked Schmitt: 'The late encounter is the most cordial.'[183] Schwab travelled to Plettenberg one more time. The former 'adjutant' von Medem arrived for Schmitt's birthday and thanked Schmitt, probably not just out of politeness, for the 'good conversations'.[184] On 31 December, Ernst Hüsmert and Werner Böckenförde were no longer able to communicate with Schmitt. In the evening, he had a fall in his room and broke his thigh. He was now bedridden, and he refused to eat. Occasionally, he came around and spoke a few words, without, however, responding to what others said. On Easter morning, 7 April 1985, he died in the Evangelisches Krankenhaus [Evangelical Hospital] in Plettenberg. The death notice from the family quoted lines from Konrad Weiß. Joseph Kaiser signed a separate notice in the *Frankfurter Allgemeine Zeitung* on behalf of 'friends and pupils'. The funeral service was held on 11 April in the Pfarrkirche [parish church] of Plettenberg-Eiringhausen. Werner Böckenförde gave the sermon, which was about Easter and resurrection. He quoted a late dedication of 11 July 1983, which Schmitt had written into the *Leviathan* book: 'Result: every old man becomes a King Lear.' The funeral on the Waldfriedhof was preceded by a macabre occurrence. Niklas Frank, the youngest son of Hans Frank, had the coffin opened for him in the chapel and thought that he recognized his biological father in Schmitt.[185] The late reconciliation with Eisler was thus flanked by a reminder of Schmitt's involvement in National Socialism. The large natural gravestone carries an orthodox cross and the Greek inscription καὶ νόμον ἔγνω. There are also longer quotations from the *Odyssey* in Schmitt's writings (NtE, p. 46): 'Sing to me of the man, Muse, the man of twists and turns / driven time and again off course, once he had plundered / the hallowed heights of Troy. / Many cities of men he saw and learned their minds, / many pains he suffered, heartsick on the open sea.'* Schmitt translated: 'The cities ἄστεα of many men he saw and recognized their *nomos*' (VRA, p. 490).

---

* Homer, *The Odyssey*, trans. Robert Fagles, London, 1996, ll. 1–5.

Afterword to the English Edition

The German edition of the present biography of Carl Schmitt appeared in the autumn of 2009.[1] It was based on many years of work on Schmitt and on numerous newly available sources. Schmitt's unpublished diaries from the time of the Weimar Republic, for instance, could be drawn on for the first time, which changed the perspective on his biography considerably. Many new names and relationships appeared, and it became possible to answer some central questions regarding Schmitt's life, such as that of the identity of Schmitt's first wife (Carita Dorotić), those surrounding his love affair with Kathleen Murray, those about the details of his sexual promiscuity, those concerning his formative friendship with Georg Eisler, and those concerning the central role of the National Socialist top-rank politician and mentor of Schmitt, Hans Frank. These themes were probably treated in detail for the first time in the 2009 biography.

The book you hold in your hands tells the scandalous story of a 'life lived in a state of exception', in which the experiences of political and personal crises are inextricably linked with one another. Schmitt's academic work is also discussed in detail and against its biographical context. His normative reflections on, and literary stylization of, both personal and historical crises provide the narrative thread of this biography. Schmitt's oeuvre was, so to speak, an attempt to pull himself out of these crises. His work combines sharpness and depth of thought but also includes nonsense and insanity.

The book discusses the 'case' of Schmitt in detail, and in all its complexity, on the basis of extensive archival research. Not all biographical questions could, by any means, be sufficiently investigated and resolved, and many of the references are meant to stimulate further work. Since the book's publication, further sources have been published,[2] which were already used in its writing: Schmitt's diaries between 1930 and 1934, a retrospective conversation from the 1970s, the correspondences with Rudolf Smend and Jacob Taubes, the material in *Schmittiana*, new series (2011) and (2014), and various other items. Other important sources are forthcoming, in particular the correspondence with Ernst Rudolf Huber (edited by Ewald Grothe), which contains the most important letters on constitutional policy from the 1930s and 1940s. Some sources were edited by myself, such as the correspondence with Smend and Waldemar Gurian, with Walter Jellinek and with university professors of philosophy during the Weimar period.

For some thirty years now I have studied Carl Schmitt. I first came across his work during my time as a student in Freiburg, in seminars taught by Friedrich Kittler, Ellen Kennedy and my doctoral supervisor Wilhelm Hennis. In 1988, I completed my doctorate on Schmitt. The discussions in Germany at the time were just shifting from the comprehensive philological reconstruction of his 'political theology' to the contextualization and historicization of Schmitt as a political actor.[3] Two long conversations I had with Ernst Rudolf Huber are firmly embedded in my memory. Huber's memoir on 'Carl Schmitt in der Reichskrise der Weimarer Endzeit' [Carl Schmitt during the crisis of the Reich in the last days of Weimar] marks for me the beginning of detailed research into Schmitt as a political actor. How should one interpret his apologia of the rule by presidential decree in political terms? This question of Schmitt as a historical actor Huber had put on the table. During the 1990s it was discussed in the form of the question of whether he had been a follower of Papen or rather of Schleicher. Wolfram Pyta, Lutz Berthold and Gabriel Seiberth argued in favour of Schleicher, while Andreas Koenen – probably more correctly – saw Schmitt as closer to Papen. As Schleicher's 'crown jurist', Schmitt would have been an opponent of Hitler until 1933 and a 'katechon' of Weimar; as an advocate of Papen, he would have been, rather, a supporter of an authoritarian third way. As a consequence of the publication of newly edited sources, the bases of this discussion kept shifting. But, in the diaries of the period from 1930 to 1934, we now have a central source at our disposal which provides a firm ground for an evaluation of Schmitt's position at the time. These diaries are not particularly sympathetic towards the idea of defending Weimar. Today, I see the 'crown jurist' of the rule by presidential decree rather as taking the distanced position of the advocate and of someone curious about possible new solutions. In his *Carl Schmitt im Kontext* [Carl Schmitt in context] (2012),[4] Stefan Breuer rightly emphasized that Schmitt's pupils and the younger authors of the 'conservative revolution', before and after 1933, were more nationalistic than Schmitt. But this is not enough reason for seeing Schmitt as an advocate of Weimar. Rather, his pronounced statism and anti-Semitism fitted National Socialism no less than the young conservatives' nationalism. More recent German publications that are important for the contextualization and historicization of Schmitt are, among others, the fourth volume of Michael Stolleis's major *Geschichte des öffentlichen Rechts* [History of public law] (2012)[5] and the new multi-volume history of the University of Berlin: *Geschichte der Universität Unter den Linden* [History of the university Unter den Linden] (ed. Rüdiger vom Bruch, Heinz Elmar Tenorth and Michael Grüttner). I would also like to mention the now completed multi-volume *Geschichte des politischen Denkens* [History of political thought] by Henning Ottmann, whose penultimate volume, *Der Totalitarismus und seine Überwindung* [Totalitarianism and its overcoming] (2010), contains an account of the 'conservative revolution' and of Carl Schmitt. For some years now, the continuously updated digital bibliography of the Carl Schmitt Gesellschaft e. V. allows one to orientate oneself within the mass of new publications.[6]

For the English edition, the German text has been revised and amended and some new material added. Some mistakes, no doubt, will remain, as is unavoidable in the case of a work of such tortuous dimensions. After the completion of this biography, I thoroughly revised and updated my older *Introduction* to Schmitt.[7] In the meantime, I have also, in separate publications, discussed some important aspects in more detail, in most cases on the basis of further archival work. These are worth mentioning here because they supplement and provide more detail on the following essential themes: Schmitt's apocalyptic religiosity;[8] his correspondence with university professors of philosophy in the Weimar period, where Eduard Spranger and Eric Voegelin are important figures while Leo Strauss is rather marginal;[9] his attitude towards legal positivism;[10] his views on constitutional policy in 1932–3[11] and the beginning of his commitment to National Socialism during the summer term 1933 in Cologne;[12] his personal relationships with the Eisler family,[13] publishers in Hamburg, and with his daughter Anima;[14] his reception of the 'classical' authors Rousseau,[15] Hegel and Bruno Bauer;[16] his political-theological understanding of anarchism;[17] the often tense correspondence with Rudolf Smend,[18] the congenial theorist of constitutional law; Schmitt's pupils in Bonn, Waldemar Gurian[19] and Otto Kirchheimer;[20] his reception of Karl Mannheim[21] and Helmuth Plessner;[22] his correspondence with the Heidelberg jurist of administrative law Walter Jellinek, which was quite intense, in 1932–3;[23] the failed National Socialist cooperation with Martin Heidegger in the autumn of 1933;[24] Schmitt's late instrumental use of Walter Benjamin to put a different slant on his past;[25] various phases in his relationship with Ernst Jünger;[26] his dealings with Arnold Gehlen;[27] the esoteric conversational culture of the old 'partisan' Schmitt in Plettenberg;[28] Schmitt's late reckoning with Erik Peterson,[29] his former companion in Bonn; and the transformation of his 'political theology' into Reinhard Koselleck's theory of history.[30] I have also been intensely interested in Schmitt's Jewish publisher Ludwig Feuchtwanger,[31] and I have discussed some systematic aspects of the revaluation of Schmitt's anti-liberal distinction between liberalism and democracy and his determination of their relation to each other.[32] (Revised versions of some of these studies are likely to appear soon in a collected volume entitled *Kriegstechniker des Begriffs: Biographische Studien zu Carl Schmitt* [A technician of conceptual warfare: biographical studies on Carl Schmitt].)

With Machiavelli, Hobbes and Hegel, authors who were central points of reference for him, Schmitt stood within the 'terrestrial', or rather continental European, tradition of conceptions of the state and discussions of sovereignty. Only from 1939 onwards did his interest in the 'maritime' thought of the Western hemisphere begin to grow, though his reception of Anglo-Saxon liberalism was at no point affirmative. However, at school he had already learned English to a quite acceptable standard, which was not yet a matter of course at the time. For his attitude towards the English language, his early and intense love affair with the Irish-Australian student Kathleen Murray was important; Schmitt had a hand in the writing of her doctoral thesis on Taine and English Romanticism.[33] From that time, Schmitt saw his life as reflected in the plays of Shakespeare: he looked at himself as an Othello, as a Hamlet and as a King Lear. In 1956 he published a concise hermetic text on *Hamlet*, which is key to understanding his thought. In old age he liked to quote Goethe: 'An old man is always a King Lear.'[34]

This hardly explains the interest that Schmitt provokes in the English-speaking academic world today. From a contemporary history perspective, one of the reasons for it is probably the continued interest in Schmitt as a National Socialist 'case'. Another reason is certainly the theoretical importance of his critique of liberalism. However, the surprising extent to which Schmitt is present within international debates is not further discussed here. As a biography, it is concerned only with the historical 'case', and it tells Schmitt's crisis-ridden life as a paradigmatic story from a crisis-ridden time. It lets the sources speak for themselves and mostly avoids strong evaluations. Many aspects of Schmitt's life conflict so violently with our contemporary standards that we obviously feel, in considering it, a certain distance and alienation. From that historical distance, both life and work, in all their radicality and eccentricity, can now be looked at with some serenity and be criticized on the basis of sound argumentation. The English-language literature on Schmitt, which contains excellent work on him by authors such as Joseph W. Bendersky, John P. McCormick and Gopal Balakrishnan, has unfortunately not been given the space it deserves. Some things I would see differently today; some points I would correct or add. The publication of such a biography, with its complex historical and theoretical context, and despite all the detail presented here, is always a risky business. I would like to thank the publisher and the translator, Dr Daniel Steuer, for making it possible for me to take that risk.

Reinhard Mehring
Düsseldorf, July 2013

Chronology

1888
Carl Schmitt born on 11 July in Plettenberg, Westphalia. His family belongs to a Catholic minority within a predominantly Protestant environment. Carl is a good pupil. He attends several schools, has far to travel to school at times, and for some time also attends a boarding school. Good school leaving certificate. Learns major languages at school but not Hebrew.

1907
Studies jurisprudence in Berlin, Munich and Strasbourg. Friendship with Fritz Eisler, the son of a wealthy Hungarian-Jewish publisher.

1910
Schmitt passes his first state examination and his doctorate in criminal law at the Alsatian 'Reichsuniversität' Strasbourg. Title of doctoral thesis: 'Über Schuld und Schuldarten' [On guilt and types of guilt]. His doctoral supervisor, Fritz van Calker, continues to support Schmitt as a mentor. Move to Düsseldorf for legal training at the Upper Regional Court in Düsseldorf. Permanent financial difficulties over the coming years of his unpaid training. First minor publications.

1912
First juridical experiences with case-oriented daily juridical practice, which Schmitt immediately reflects upon in theoretical terms: *Gesetz und Urteil* [Law and judgment]. Schmitt meets Carita (von) Dorotić, the 'privy councillor' Hugo am Zehnhoff, who would become another of his mentors, and the poet Theodor Däubler.

1914
Publication of the programmatic work on the philosophy of the state *Der Wert des Staates* [The value of the state], shortly before the outbreak of the Great War. Schmitt hates Prussian 'militarism'. Fritz Eisler dies in battle; beginning of Schmitt's close friendship with Fritz's brother Georg, which lasts until 1933.

1915

Schmitt passes his second juridical state examination. He marries the impostor Carita Dorotić in an improvised wedding due to wartime conditions. Schmitt informally adopts the double-barrelled name Schmitt-Dorotić. Fritz van Calker protects Schmitt from possible service at the front by requesting him for a post at the deputy general command of the military administration in Munich. Accommodation in Munich's Schwabing district. Double life between general command and Munich's bohemian circles.

1916

With Calker's support, Schmitt's *The Value of the State*, published in 1914, is accepted as his Habilitation in Strasbourg. Privatdozent with emphasis on criminal law. Commutes between Strasbourg and Munich. Writes treatise on *Theodor Däubler's Nordlicht* [Theodor Däubler's The Northern Lights]. Socializes with the important publicist Franz Blei.

1919

The end of the war is followed by a revolutionary situation close to civil war, especially in Munich: Räterepublik [Republic of Councils], assassination of the Bavarian prime minister Kurt Eisner and increasing radicalization of politics. Schmitt continues working at the general command as a soldier; he experiences the revolution from the perspective of the counter-revolutionary military as a personal threat. His superior, 'Captain Roth', later becomes the Bavarian minister of justice and is involved in Adolf Hitler's attempted *coup d'état* in 1923 (the March towards the Feldherrnhalle), as is Schmitt's later mentor under National Socialism, Hans Frank. Post-revolutionary Bavaria develops into a counter-revolutionary bastion over the coming years. As an ordinary member of the Reichswehr, Adolf Hitler forms his politics in the post-revolutionary climate of Munich. Rise of right-wing extremism. Schmitt studies the legal history of dictatorship as a political institution. Attends talks, lectures and the 'lecturer's seminar' of Max Weber. Schmitt's doctoral supervisor and mentor Fritz van Calker takes up a professorship at the Technische Hochschule in Munich. With the support of the polyglot Jewish political economist Moritz Julius Bonn (Frankfurt), Schmitt becomes a lecturer at the Handelshochschule in Munich from the winter term 1919–20. Beginning of his friendship with the Jewish publisher Ludwig Feuchtwanger, brother of the literary author Lion Feuchtwanger, who, along with the brothers Fritz and Georg Eisler and Eduard Rosenbaum, becomes an important Jewish intellectual partner in conversation for him. Publication of *Political Romanticism*, which is also a reckoning with the political ideology [Gesinnungspolitik] of the revolution of the councillors [Räterevolution]. Schmitt's marriage is now clearly breaking down.

1921

Dictatorship comes out. With the support of Rudolf Smend, Schmitt is appointed to his first full professorship for state law in Greifswald, requiring him to move from Bavaria to Prussia. From then on, until 1945, Schmitt teaches only at Prussian universities. Continued close contact with Ludwig Feuchtwanger. Separation from Carita Dorotić; Schmitt drops double-barrelled name. Intense love affair with the Irish-Australian and Catholic student of Romance literature Kathleen Murray, involving plans of their possible marriage. Schmitt has an input into the writing of Murray's doctoral thesis in Marburg.

1922
With support from Rudolf Smend and Erich Kaufmann, Schmitt is appointed to the University of Bonn, at the time a highly innovative Prussian university, in particular in the area of public law. Kathleen Murray returns to Australia. Schmitt's extraordinarily productive years in Bonn begin. *Political Theology* and *Roman Catholicism and Political Form* appear. Close collegiate contacts with Erich Kaufmann, Ernst Landsberg and his family, Albert Hensel. Beginning of his life-long friendship with the musicologist Wilhelm Neuss. Love affair with Lola Sauer, a medical doctor (1922–3). Schmitt develops a strong influence as an academic teacher. In the following years he supervises the doctoral theses of, among others, E. Forsthoff, E. Friesenhahn, E. R. Huber, O. Kirchheimer, W. Weber. The Weimar Republic destabilizes: inflation and hyper-inflation.

1923
Schmitt meets Duška Todorović. The Ruhr area is occupied by France. Beginning of Schmitt's battle against Weimar, Geneva, Versailles – i.e., parliamentarism, liberalism and the League of Nations: *Die geistesge-schichtliche Lage des heutigen Parlamentarismus* [published in English as *The Crisis of Parliamentary Democracy*].

1924
Schmitt's marriage with Cari is annulled by the civil authorities, but his attempts at also having it annulled by the Church finally fail the following year. Lecture on 'Die Diktatur des Reichspräsidenten' [The dictatorship of the Reich president] at the meeting of the Staatsrechtslehrervereinigung [Association of State Theorists] in Jena. The positions within the so-called Richtungsstreit (see chapter 12) begin to emerge. Alliance between Schmitt, Carl Bilfinger and Erwin Jacobi. Increasing tensions between Schmitt and Kaufmann. Duška develops life-threatening tuberculosis. Friendship with the theologian Erik Peterson.

1925
Battle with Versailles: *Die Rheinlande als Objekt internationaler Politik* [The Rhineland as an object in international politics].

1926
Battle with Geneva: *Die Kernfrage des Völkerbundes* [The core question regarding the League of Nations]. Schmitt marries Duška, whose illness is still life-threatening; excommunication from the Church. From September,

permanent affair with the shop assistant Magda. Beginning of Schmitt's double life and the division between 'Eros and Caritas', which lasts into the 1930s.

1927
The Concept of the Political. Lecture on 'Volksentscheid und Volksbegehren' [Referenda and petitions for referenda].

1928
Constitutional Theory. Provisional end of Schmitt's theoretical endeavours. Schmitt wants to escape the Catholic circles and moves to the centre of politics in Berlin, taking up a chair at the Handelshochschule. Multifarious contacts. Schmitt constantly frequents street prostitutes. Schmitt is very active giving lectures in many places; the envisaged audience of his political publications changes.

1930
Schmitt provides justification for the rule by presidential decree in the Weimar Republic. More serious affair with Margot von Quednow. Friendship with Ernst Jünger. Schmitt more and more becomes part of the circles around the 'new nationalism'. Duška recovers.

1931
Der Hüter der Verfassung [The guardian of the constitution]. Passionate affair with Hella Ehrik. Birth of Anima-Louise, Duška and Carl's only child.

1932
Legality and Legitimacy. Contacts with the chancellor, Franz von Papen. Legal representative for the Reich in the trial 'Prussia vs. the Reich'. Schmitt plays no role of comparable importance when Schleicher becomes the next chancellor.

1933
Schmitt faces a complex situation. After the Enabling Act of 24 March, he makes a clear decision to back National Socialism. He takes revenge for the Leipzig trial: cooperation in the legal-technical formulation of a draft for the 'Reichsstatthaltergesetz' [Reich Governors Law], which serves the purpose of coordinating the individual federal states [Gleichschaltung]. On 1 May, Schmitt joins the NSDAP [National Socialist German Workers Party]. Move to the University of Cologne. Schmitt meets and cooperates with Hermann Göring and then, in particular, with Hans Frank. Further contact with central figures of National Socialism, such as Wilhelm Frick and Roland Freisler. Schmitt breaks off many old contacts and friendships, among them those with Georg Eisler, Franz Blei and Ludwig Feuchtwanger. Beginning of the juridical-institutional interpretation of the meaning of National Socialism: *State, Movement, People.* A meeting with Heidegger fails to lead to further cooperation between them. With the

beginning of the winter term, Schmitt moves to the University of Berlin. Further offers of appointments to chairs in Leipzig, Heidelberg and Munich. Official functions, among others: Prussian state councillor (from July 1933), member of the Akademie für Deutsches Recht [Academy for German Right], member of the Bund Nationalsozialistischer Deutscher Juristen, BNSDJ [Association of National Socialist German Jurists], Reichsfachgruppenleiter Fachgruppe Hochschullehrer [Head of the University Teachers' Section of the Reich Association of Jurists]* (until 1936), member (1934–6) of the Commission for Universities subordinated to the deputy of the Führer, which was responsible for appointments, editor of the series 'Der deutsche Staat der Gegenwart' [The contemporary German state], editor of the *Deutsche Juristen-Zeitung* (1934–6). First attacks on Schmitt from inside National Socialist circles by Otto Koellreutter.

1934
Further programmatic National Socialist texts: *On the Three Types of Juristic Thought*; *Staatsgefüge und Zusammenbruch des zweiten Reiches* [State structure and collapse of the Second Reich]; *Nationalsozialismus und Völkerrecht* [National Socialism and international law]. Apologia for the murders on 30 June (the so-called Night of the Long Knives): 'Der Führer schützt das Recht' [The Führer protects the law]. Schmitt moves towards an anti-Semitic and apocalyptic provision of meaning by an 'immediate' (lawless) form of justice. Turn towards the apocalyptic perspective of the 'state of exception'. Close pupils increasingly distance themselves from Schmitt, for instance Friesenhahn, Werner Becker and, later, Forsthoff and Huber.

1935
Schmitt's cooperation with Hans Frank continues. Justification of the Nuremberg racial laws. Rivalry with Reinhard Höhn.

1936
Dispute with Karl August Eckhardt over the organization of the annual meeting of the jurists in 1936. Schmitt is granted a personal audience with Mussolini. Organization of the conference on 'Das Judentum in der Rechtswissenschaft' [Judaism in jurisprudence]. Decline in the bureaucratic hierarchy after attacks against Schmitt in the SS organ *Das Schwarze Korps*. Schmitt loses his party and honorary positions, but not his chair in Berlin or the title of Prussian state councillor. He increasingly turns towards studies in legal history and international law.

1938
Schmitt's fiftieth birthday: *The Leviathan in the State Theory of Thomas Hobbes*.

---

* There were Reichsfachgruppen for everything under the sun, including, for instance, beekeepers.

1939

Völkerrechtliche Großraumordnung [Großraum order in international law]. Schmitt again very active presenting lectures in various locations.

From 1940

Lecture tours to France, Hungary, Romania, Spain and Portugal.

1942

Land and Sea. Schmitt says farewell to the concept of the Reich. He begins work on *The Nomos of the Earth*.

1945

Survival in Berlin. *The International Crime of the War of Aggression and the Principle 'Nullum crimen, nulla poena sine lege'*. Schmitt interned in a detention camp between September 1945 and October 1946. He loses his chair in Berlin.

1947

Schmitt is again arrested. Interrogation in the context of the Nuremberg trials. Release and return to Plettenberg. Schmitt's social contacts re-emerge. He starts to note down his experiences and begins his *Glossarium*. First encounters with the younger generation of scholars. The following years marked by financial difficulties. Schmitt develops the resentments of an 'outlaw'. Close social contact with the theologian Hans Barion and the editor of Max Weber's works Johannes Winckelmann. Estrangement from Ernst Jünger and also from Ernst Rudolf Huber. Beginning of his close friendship with Ernst Forsthoff. Publishes partly under pseudonyms. Looks for other professional opportunities. Attempts a re-Catholicization of his work.

1950

Die Lage der europäischen Rechtswissenschaft [The situation of European jurisprudence]; *Ex captivitate salus*; *A Pan-European Interpretation of Donoso Cortés*; *The Nomos of the Earth*. Disputes over Schmitt's come-back as an author. His wife dies.

1951

Lectures in Spain. Schmitt becomes very active, travelling and giving lectures. The 'Plettenberg system': extensive national and international correspondence up to his old age, numerous visitors and lively contacts with various circles. Family life with his 'housemaid' Anni Stand and his daughter Anima. Shakespeare studies. A young generation of pupils emerges: Roman Schnur, Reinhart Koselleck, Ernst-Wolfgang Böckenförde. Contacts with the philosopher Joachim Ritter and Ritter's colloquium in Münster. At the end of **1957**, Schmitt's daughter Anima marries and moves to Spain, her husband's home country.

1958

Verfassungsrechtliche Aufsätze [Essays on constitutional law], a collection of old essays, with new critical annotations. Disputes over a Festschrift for his seventieth birthday. *The Tyranny of Values*. Schmitt's public appearances are limited to Forsthoff's 'Ebrach seminars'. Continued trips to Spain until 1970.

1963

Theory of the Partisan. New edition of *The Concept of the Political*.

1968

Second Festschrift. Schmitt now also withdraws from the Ebrach seminars. He is interested in the left Schmittians.

1970

Conclusion of his oevre with *Political Theology II*. Estrangement from old friends such as Hans Barion and Armin Mohler. Schmitt suffers a mild heart attack. New corresponding partners are Hans-Dietrich Sander, Hans Blumenberg, and later also Jacob Taubes. Further debates around 'political theology'. Schmitt begins to make arrangements regarding his literary estate. In his old age he continues to write down cryptic notes.

1978

Festive celebration of his ninetieth birthday. Last substantial publication: *Die legale Weltrevolution* [Legal world revolution]. The long-planned edition of collected juridical writings can no longer be realized. Conversations with Jacob Taubes; plans for a jointly written *Political Theology III*. Through the influence of Günter Maschke, the political audience for Schmitt's work shifts once again.

1982

First new edition of a work from the time of National Socialism: *The Leviathan in the State Theory of Thomas Hobbes*.

1983

Death of Schmitt's only child, Anima. Reconciliatory telephone conversations with Georg Eisler. At the end of the year, Schmitt, who now suffers from dementia, falls silent.

1985

On 7 April, Schmitt dies in Plettenberg.

Notes

Foreword

1 Allesandro Passerin d'Entrèves to Carl Schmitt, 6 February 1949 (RW 265-108620). Cf. also Franz Blei, 'Der Fall Carl Schmitt: Von einem der ihn kannte', *Der christliche Ständestaat* (25 December 1936), pp. 1217–20.
2 On this, cf. Reinhard Mehring, 'Wie fängt man ein Chamäleon? Probleme und Wege einer Carl Schmitt-Biographie', *Idee: Zeitschrift für Ideengeschichte* 2/3 (2009), pp. 71–86.
3 On this, cf. Herfried Münckler, *Die Deutschen und ihre Mythen*, Berlin, 2009.
4 On this, recently, to name but one author, Thomas Darnstädt, 'Der Mann der Stunde: Die unheimliche Wiederkehr Carl Schmitts', *Der Spiegel*, no. 39 (22 September 2008), pp. 160–1.
5 Christoph Möllers, *Der vermisste Leviathan, Staatstheorie in der Bundesrepublik*, Frankfurt, 2008, p. 97. Cf., recently, Günter Frankenberg, *Staatstechnik: Perspektiven auf Rechtsstaat und Ausnahmezustand*, Frankfurt, 2010.
6 As has been pointed out before by Ernst Forsthoff, 'Zur heutigen Situation einer Verfassungslehre', in *Epirrhosis: Festgabe für Carl Schmitt*, Berlin, 1968, pp. 185–211.
7 On this, see, for instance, Rainer Wahl, *Verfassungsstaat, Europäisierung, Internationalisierung*, Frankfurt, 2003; Christoph Schönberger, *Unionsbürger: Europas förderales Bürgerrecht in vergleichender Sicht*, Tübingen, 2006.
8 On this, e.g., Stefan Huster and Karsten Rudolph, *Vom Rechtsstaat zum Präventionsstaat*, Frankfurt, 2008.
9 Thus, Heinrich August Winkler, *Germany: The Long Road West*, vol. 1: *1789–1933*, Oxford: 2006; vol. 2: *1933–1990*, Oxford, 2007.
10 Paul Noack, *Carl Schmitt: Eine Biographie*, Berlin, 1993. Cf. also Joseph W. Bendersky, *Carl Schmitt: Theorist for the Reich*, Princeton, NJ, 1983, and the (not quite complete) bibliography by Alain de Benoist, *Carl Schmitt: Bibliographie seiner Schriften und Korrespondenzen*, Berlin, 2003.
11 Christian Linder, *Der Bahnhof von Finnentrop: Eine Reise ins Carl Schmitt Land*, Berlin, 2008.
12 Schmitt's library and posthumous papers are held in the Landesarchiv Düsseldorf.
13 The start was made by Piet Tommissen's efforts, over several decades, at collecting and editing material.
14 The files of the university archives at Strasbourg have been mostly destroyed or lost. No official records on Schmitt's studies, dissertation and Habilitation at Strasbourg are known to exist. There are also no documents on his time as

a legal trainee at the Upper Regional Court in Düsseldorf. We have no posthumous papers of Fritz van Calker.

Chapter 1   An 'Obscure Young Man from a Modest Background'

1 Gregor Brand, 'Non ignobili stirpe procreatum: Carl Schmitt und seine Herkunft', in *Schmittiana* 5, Berlin, 1996, pp. 225–98.
2 His birth certificate gives Carl (not Karl).
3 Carl Schmitt in conversation with Dieter Groh and Klaus Figge, 1971, in Piet Tommissen (ed.), *Over en in zake Carl Schmitt*, Brussels, 1975, pp. 89–109; here: p. 92.
4 In retrospect Schmitt emphasized the influence of his primary-school teachers Josef Wüst and Ernst Sommer. Some letters from Josef Wüst, dating from the time between July 1949 and 1958, are preserved (RW 265-18433/18442). Schmitt also advised Wüst in some legal matters. He repeatedly met with his old teacher in Frankfurt.
5 Franz Kluxen, *Das 'deutsche Drama' Richard Wagners als künstlerisches Ideal und schöpferische Tat*, Burgsteinfurt, 1906. The friendship with Kluxen more or less came to an end in the 1920s. And even though Kluxen was living in Berlin and Potsdam at the time, there were only a few meetings during Schmitt's years in Berlin. After 1945, Kluxen made negative remarks about the political role Schmitt had played (see the letters to Schmitt of 7 September 1948 [RW 265-7922] and 12 February 1958 [RW 265-7927]). In a response of 30 September 1948, which has been preserved, Schmitt ironically tries to explain to Kluxen the 'political theory of colours', of 'brown' and 'red', and remarks sharply: 'I feel today that the verses from your time in Florence and Strasbourg were better than the (artistically more elegant) ones of the time after 1912.' Kluxen remained a friend from school days, and they stayed somewhat in contact over fifty years.
6 Certified copy (RW 265-21561). Carl Schmitt in conversation with Dieter Groh and Klaus Figge, 1971, in Tommissen, *Over en in zake Carl Schmitt*, p. 94. Cf. Schmitt's letter of thanks of 3 March 1957 to the school's director, Schulte, on the occasion of the fiftieth anniversary of his Abitur (RW 265-13515).
7 Franz Blei, *Erzählung eines Lebens*, Leipzig, 1930, p. 494.
8 Carl Schmitt in conversation with Dieter Groh and Klaus Figge, 1971, in Tommissen, *Over en in zake Carl Schmitt*, p. 93.
9 Ibid., p. 94. On the Faculty of Law at the time, cf. Ernst Heymann, 'Hundert Jahre Berliner Juristenfakultät', in *Festgabe der Deutschen Juristen-Zeitung*, ed. Otto Liebmann, Berlin, 1910, pp. 3–63; here: pp. 47ff. On its modest facilities, cf. Brunner, Kahl and Hellwig, 'Das juristische Seminar', in Max Lenz, *Geschichte der königlichen Friedrich-Wilhelms-Universität zu Berlin*, vol. 3, Halle, 1910, pp. 25–8.
10 Carl Schmitt, '1907 Berlin', in *Schmittiana 1*, Berlin, 1988, pp. 13–21; here: p. 14.
11 On this, cf. Theodor Kipp, *Geschichte der Quellen des Römischen Rechts*, 2nd edn, Leipzig, 1903. Cf. also Martin Wolff, *Theodor Kipp: Ein Vortrag*, Berlin, 1932.
12 On this, cf. Ernst von Moeller, *Die Trennung der Deutschen und der Römischen Rechtsgeschichte*, Weimar, 1905.
13 On this, cf. Otto von Gierke, *Deutsches Privatrecht*, 3 vols, Leipzig, 1895–1917.
14 Cf. the introduction of the various legal disciplines in Joseph Kohler, *Einführung in die Rechtswissenschaft*, 2nd edn, Leipzig, 1905.

15 *Carl Schmitt*, '1907 Berlin', p. 15. In 1965, Schmitt gave the text to Tommissen for it to be published.

16 Ibid., p. 20.

17 Ibid., p. 21.

18 On this, cf. Karl Ritter von Birkmeyer, 'Strafrecht', in von Birkmeyer (ed.), *Enzyklopädie der Rechtswissenschaft*, Berlin, 1901, pp. 1025–92.

19 André Steinlein was born on 6 December 1891 in Diendenhofen. He attended secondary school [Lyzeum] at Strasbourg and Metz, and then studied in Paris, Munich, Berlin and Strasbourg. Later, he worked as a notary in Vic-sur-Seille (Lorraine).

20 On this, cf. Georg Friedrich Knapp, *Staatliche Theorie des Geldes*, Leipzig, 1905.

21 A brief contemporary portrait of the university can be found in Otto Mayer, *Die Kaiser-Wilhelm-Universität Straßburg und ihre Tätigkeit*, Halle, 1922. Ernst Anrich, 'Geschichte der deutschen Universität Straßburg', in *Festschrift aus Anlass der feierlichen Wiederaufnahme der Lehr- und Forschungstätigkeit an der Reichsuniversität Straßburg*, Strasbourg, 1941, pp. 9–148. On the cultural-political situation, cf. Werner Wittich, *Deutsche und französische Kultur im Elsass*, Strasbourg, 1909. Wittich talks about a 'mixed culture' and argues against political 'Germanization'.

22 Details on this can be found in Ernst Rudolf Huber, *Deutsche Verfassungsgeschichte seit 1789*, vol. 4: *Struktur und Krisen des Kaiserreichs*, Stuttgart, 1969.

23 Bernd Schlüter, *Reichswissenschaft, Staatsrechtslehre, Staatstheorie und Wissenschaftspolitik im Deutschen Kaiserreich am Beispiel der Reichsuniversität Straßburg*, Frankfurt, 2004. Unfortunately, Carl Schmitt and his teacher Fritz van Calker do not appear in Schlüter's excellent study, as he focuses on Laband and Rehm. Van Calker is mentioned only once in passing as a 'pan-German' professor (p. 335), despite the fact that he taught for twenty years as 'Ordinarius' in Strasbourg and was politically active as an expert on legislative policy.

24 Karl Binding, *Die Normen und ihre Übertretung: Eine Untersuchung über die rechtmäßige Handlung und die Arten des Delikts*, 4 vols, reprint of the 4th edn (Leipzig, 1922), Aalen, 1991.

25 Paul Laband, *Das Staatsrecht des deutschen Reiches*, 3 vols, Tübingen, 1876–1882.

26 Max Ernst Mayer, *Der Causalzusammenhang zwischen Handlung und Erfolg im Strafrecht: Eine rechtsphilosophische Untersuchung*, Strasbourg, 1898; *Die schuldhafte Handlung und ihre Arten im Strafrecht: Drei Begriffsbestimmungen*, Berlin, 1903; *Rechtsnormen und Kulturnormen*, Breslau, 1903; *Deutsches Militärstrafrecht*, 2 vols, Leipzig, 1907; *Der rechtswidrige Befehl des Vorgesetzten*, Tübingen, 1908; *Der allgemeine Teil des deutschen Strafrechts*, Heidelberg, 1915; *Rechtsphilosophie*, Berlin, 1922. In 1919, Mayer was appointed to a chair at the newly founded university at Frankfurt am Main.

27 Fritz van Calker was born in 1864 in Wesel on the Lower Rhine, the son of the local mayor. He studied law in Freiburg, Berlin and Munich. In 1888, he completed his doctorate in Munich and in 1891 his Habilitation with Franz von Liszt in Halle. His subjects were criminal law, criminal procedure and military criminal law. In 1896 he was appointed to an 'Ordinariat' [i.e., as professor ordinarius] at Strasbourg. He was married with four children. He was a long-standing member of the Strasbourg municipal council. From 1912 to 1918, he was a member of the Reichstag [parliament] for the Nationalliberale Partei

[National Liberal Party]. Until 1933, he was a member of the Deutschnationale Volkspartei [German National People's Party]. During the Second World War he served as commanding major in a Bavarian infantry regiment in Munich. After his removal from office in Strasbourg, he became an honorary professor at the University of Munich in 1920 and, on the basis of the Beamtenfürsorgegesetzes [Law on the welfare of civil servants], was at the same time given a teaching post with full salary, title and rank of a professor ordinarius at the Technische Universität [Technical University]. On 1 October 1922, he took over a full professorship for law at the latter. He became privy judicial councillor and privy councillor. In 1933, he was given a chair in criminal law and legislative policy at the University of Munich in addition to his professorship at the Technical University. Although he became emeritus as of the summer term 1934, he continued in his chair at the Technical University on full pay until 1936, and continued teaching there even until 1938, when an eye operation finally forced him to bid farewell. From 1933, van Calker was a member of the Akademie für deutsches Recht [Academy for German Right], where he was in charge of the committee for Rechtsfragen der Bevölkerungspolitik [Legal issues in population policy]. He spent his last years in Bad Wörishofen and on the family estate, 'Deinhofen', near Moosach in Upper Bavaria. Information compiled from the extensive personal file in HATUM.PA Prof. van Calker [Historisches Archiv Technische Universität München. Personalakten = Historical Archive of the Technical University Munich. Personal Files]. Publications (selection): *Das Recht des Militärs zum administrativen Waffengebrauch*, Munich, 1888; *Die strafrechtliche Verantwortlichkeit für auf Befehl begangene Handlungen*, Munich, 1891; *Die Delikte gegen das Urheberrecht*, Halle, 1894; *Strafrecht und Ethik*, Leipzig, 1897; *Vergeltungsidee und Zweckgedanke im System der Freiheitsstrafen*, Heidelberg, 1898; *Ethische Werte im Strafrecht*, Berlin, 1904; *Hochverrat und Landesverrat: Majestätsbeleidigung*, Berlin, 1906; *Gesetzgebungspolitik und Rechtsvergleichung*, Tübingen, 1908; *Die Reform der Gesetzgebung in Strafrecht und Strafprozess*, Leipzig, 1910; *Grundriss des Strafrechts*, Munich, 1916; *Recht und Weltanschauung*, Mannheim, 1924; *Bismarcks Verfassungspolitik*, Munich, 1924; *Grundzüge des deutschen Staatsrechts*, Munich, 1925; *Grundzüge des deutschen Verwaltungsrechts*, Munich, 1925; *Einführung in die Politik*, Munich, 1927; *Wesen und Sinn der politischen Parteien*, Tübingen, 1928.

28 Fritz van Calker, *Einführung in die Politik*, Munich, 1927, p. v. Cf. van Calker, 'Rechtspolitik', in Paul Laband et al. (eds), *Handbuch der Politik*, vol. 1: *Die Grundlagen der Politik*, Berlin, 1912, pp. 11–14; also *Politik als Funktion des Rechts*, Bad Wörishofen, 1950.

29 Fritz van Calker, *Grundriss des Strafrechts*, Munich, 1916, preface.

30 Letter of 30 October 1922 from van Calker to Schmitt (Posthumous papers of Schmitt, RW 265-2492).

31 Letter of 25 September 1913 from the chief of police in Hamburg to Hans Friedrich Eisler. No. 3848/13I2 (Staatsarchiv Hamburg, Staatsangehörigkeitsaufsicht B VI, no. 140). I also owe some of the information on the history of the Eisler family and business to the Hamburger Gesellschaft für jüdische Genealogie.

32 Letter of 24 February 1914 from the chief of police to Fritz Eisler. No. 7753/14I2 (Staatsarchiv Hamburg, Staatsangehörigkeitsaufsicht B VI, no. 140).

33 Obituary in *Hamburger Woche*, vol. 9, no. 42, 14 October 1914, p. 4.

34 Fritz Eisler, 'Einleitung zu einer Untersuchung der Bedeutung des Gewohnheitsrechts im Strafrecht', *Zeitschrift für die gesamte Strafrechtswissenschaft* 31 (1914–15), pp. 361–9.

35 Hans Weigert, *Das Straßburger Münster und seine Bildwerke*, Berlin, 1928, p. 61.

Cf. also the depiction given by the Strasbourg art historian Georg Dehio in *Das Straßburger Münster*, Munich, 1922, p. 28.

36 Carl Schmitt, 'Über Tatbestandsmäßigkeit und Rechtswidrigkeit des kunstgerechten operativen Eingriffs', *Zeitschrift für die gesamte Strafrechtswissenschaft* 31 (1910), pp. 467–79.

37 Ernst Rudolf Huber, *Deutsche Verfassungsgeschichte seit 1789*, vol. 7, Stuttgart, 1984, p. 1267. ('Instead of subjective guilt, we want to ask the question of objective responsibility. And we want to answer it with the cautiousness that is due, in particular in the eyes of someone who lived through and was involved in the problems of the Weimar Republic.')

38 In a conversation with Dieter Groh and Klaus Figge in 1971. Quoted after the unpublished transcription of the recording by Dimitrios Kisoudis (2010). I would like to thank Mr Kisoudis for kindly granting me access to this text. See Frank Hertweck and Dimitrios Kisoudis (eds) (2010) for the published version of the conversation.

39 Completion of the doctorate preceded Schmitt's time in Düsseldorf. This is why he dedicated a copy of it to the *Stadt- und Landesbibliothek* of the city of Düsseldorf 'with the assurance that it bears no responsibility for this book'. The presentation copy is now in the University Library, Düsseldorf.

40 Piet Tommissen, 'Bausteine zu einer wissenschaftlichen Biographie', in Helmut Quaritsch (ed.), *Complexio Oppositorum: Über Carl Schmitt*, Berlin, 1988, p. 75.

Chapter 2   The Law of Practice

1 Detailed information on this is in Adolf Wach, 'Reform des Rechtsunterrichts: Vorbildung des Juristenstandes', in Paul Laband et al. (eds), *Handbuch der Politik*, 2 vols, Berlin: 1911–12, vol. 2, pp. 594–600. Cf. Ernst Zitelmann, *Die Vorbildung des Juristen*, Leipzig, 1909; Erich Kaufmann, *Die juristischen Fakultäten und das Rechtsstudium*, Berlin, 1910; Leopold Wenger, *Das juristische Studium an den deutschen Universitäten*, Berlin; 1912. Topical issues at the time were the relationship between theory and practice, the role of practitioners, whether internships and traineeships should be brought forward, the relationship between lectures and practical exercises and between oral and written examinations, and the risks of the tutor system. Kaufmann, for instance, argued for a theoretical and scholarly orientation (through the medium of lectures), while others opted for a more practical orientation.

2 The President of the Senate Krey, 'Das Ausbildungs- und Fortbildungswesen', in Franz Schollen (ed.), *Blätter zur Erinnerung an das 25jährige Bestehen des Oberlandesgerichts Düsseldorf*, Anrath, 1931, pp. 105–13; here: p. 108.

3 Adolf Weissler, 'Die Rechtsanwaltschaft', in Laband et al. (eds), *Handbuch der Politik*, vol. 2, pp. 455–60.

4 The title of Eduard Rosenbaum's thesis was *Ferdinand Lasalle: Studien über den historischen und systematischen Zusammenhang seiner Lehre*, Weimar, 1911. Rosenbaum was the son of a merchant from Hamburg. From the summer term of 1906, he studied in Munich, Berlin, Strasbourg and Kiel. He received his doctorate from Kiel in 1911 and soon after joined the Chamber of Commerce in Hamburg. In 1919, he became the director of the Commerzbibliothek in Hamburg. Schmitt was in close contact with him again until 1933.

5 Carl Schmitt, *Gesetz und Urteil: Eine Untersuchung zum Problem der Rechtspraxis* [Law and judgment: an investigation into the problem of legal

practice], Berlin, 1912. There are numerous additional references to secondary literature in Schmitt's first personal copy (RW 265-28578). On the sleeve, Schmitt also listed the numerous reviews.

6 Thus, Schmitt in his preface of October 1968 to the (identical) reprint of 1969.

7 For extensive detail on this, see Ingeborg Villinger, *Carl Schmitts Kulturkritik der Moderne: Text, Kommentar und Analyse der 'Schattenrisse' des Johannes Negelinus*, Berlin, 1995, pp. 250ff. Cf. Sabine Brenner, *'Das Rheinland aus seinem Dornröschenschlaf wecken!' Das Profil der Kulturzeitschrift 'Die Rheinlande' (1900–1922)*, Düsseldorf, 2004.

8 Letter from Carl Schmitt to Wilhelm Schäfer, 13 February 1912 (Heinrich-Heine-Institut, Düsseldorf, literary estate of Wilhelm Schäfer).

9 Carl Schmitt, 'Drei Tischgespräche', *Die Rheinlande: Monatsschrift für deutsche Kunst und Dichtung* 21 (1911), p. 250. Cf. also Schmitt, 'Tischgespräch: Rosenkavalier', *Frankfurter Allgemeine Zeitung* (no. 236), 11 October 1993, p. 36.

10 Carl Schmitt, 'Der Spiegel', *Die Rheinlande* 12 (1912), pp. 61–2.

11 Carl Schmitt, 'Die Philosophie und ihre Resultate', *Die Rheinlande* 13 (1913), pp. 34–6; here: p. 36.

12 Hans Vaihinger, *The Philosophy of 'As If': A System of the Theoretical, Practical and Religious Fictions of Mankind*, New York, 1968 (German original published in 1911).

13 Carl Schmitt, 'Der Adressat', *Die Rheinlande* 11 (1911), pp. 429–30: here: p. 430.

14 Carl Schmitt, 'Juristische Fiktionen', *Deutsche Juristen-Zeitung* 17 (1913), cols. 804–6.

15 Carl Schmitt, 'Richard Wagner und eine neue "Lehre vom Wahn"', *Bayreuther Blätter* 35 (1912), pp. 239–41.

16 Carl Schmitt, 'Don Quijote und das Publikum', *Die Rheinlande* 12 (1912), pp. 348–50.

17 On this, see Georg Lukács, *Theory of the Novel: A Historico-Philosophical Essay on the Forms of Great Epic Literature*, London, 1978 (German original published in 1916).

18 Schmitt to Rathenau, 12 April 1912, quoted in Ernst Schulin, 'Carl Schmitt und Walther Rathenau', *Mitteilungen der Walther Rathenau-Gesellschaft*, no. 14 (2004), pp. 23–9; here: pp. 25–6.

19 Schmitt to Rathenau, 24 April 1912, ibid.

20 Carl Schmitt, 'Kritik der Zeit', *Die Rheinlande* 11 (1911), pp. 323–4.

21 Note on page 452 in Schmitt's personal copy of Franz Blei, *Erzählung eines Lebens*, Leipzig, 1930.

22 Carl Schmitt, 'Eine französische Kritik der Zeit', *Wirtschaftsdienst* 11 (1926), pp. 593–4.

Chapter 3   Apotheosis of the Poet, Rant against Literary Figures

1 According to the survey by Frank-Lothar Kroll, *Kultur, Bildung und Wissenschaft im 20. Jahrhundert*, Munich, 2003. Cf. also August Nitschke et al. (eds), *Jahrhundertwende: Der Aufbruch in die Moderne 1880–1930*, Reinbek, 1990. See also Friedrich A. Kittler's theoretical analysis of the *Discourse Networks 1800/1900 [Aufschreibesysteme 1800/1900]*, Stanford, CA, 1992, and his *Die Wahrheit der technischen Welt*, Frankfurt, 2013.

2 Carl Schmitt, '1907 Berlin', in *Schmittiana* 1, Berlin, 1988, pp. 13–21; here: p. 18. Later, on 6 February 1951 (CSAD, pp. 108f., cf. p. 113), he quoted: 'Goethe –

the world-famous, humane Goethe – did, indeed, say "Consolation is an absurd word; he who cannot despair, should not live either." [Schmitt misquotes slightly. Goethe's poem reads: 'Ja, schelte nur und fluche fort / Es wird sich Beßres nie ergeben; / Denn Trost ist ein absurdes Wort: / Wer nicht verzweifeln kann, / der muss nicht leben.' Schmitt quotes: 'Trost ist ein absurdes Wort; wer nicht verzweifeln kann, *soll* auch nicht leben.' However, Schmitt probably also read *Goethes Sprüche in Reimen*, ed. Max Huber, Leipzig, 1908, where (p. 26) the wording of the poem corresponds to Schmitt's version. Thanks to Reinhard Mehring for bringing this to my attention.] Such statements belong to the "other" Goethe and to the reverse side of absolute humanity.' Thus, Schmitt's criticism of the 'Goethe-mask' may have had 'another' Goethe in mind. Signs of a conception of such a different Goethe can be found at the time. In a later letter, Schmitt apologizes for his earlier distanced attitude: 'I may have sent you this quotation from the old Goethe before (this man really did know everything, but one must first become old oneself in order to understand this): "An old person (says the old Goethe) loses one of the most important human rights; he is no longer judged by his equals."' (Letter of 30 April 1963 to de Moncada, in Eric Jayme (ed.), *Luis Cabral de Moncada und Carl Schmitt: Briefwechsel 1943–1973*, Heidelberg, 1997, p. 47).

3 Cf. Thomas Karlauf, *Stefan George: Die Entdeckung des Charisma*, Munich, 2007, pp. 303ff., pp. 406ff.

4 On this, see ibid., pp. 342ff.

5 In the published letters and diaries from the time of his youth, as well as in the *Schattenrissen*, there are, however, no references of any kind to Hölderlin. Only from 1934, following conversations with Veit Rosskopf, did Schmitt explicitly refer to Hölderlin in connection with his translation of Pindar's *Nomos basileus* (DARD, p. 14; NtE, p. 73). Schmitt came into contact with Hölderlin, von Hellingrath and the – for Schmitt fundamental – term 'nomos', through his acquaintance with Edgar Salin, which began in 1923.

6 Cf. *Martin Heidegger–Imma von Bodmershof: Briefwechsel 1959–1976*, ed. Bruno Pieper, Stuttgart, 2000. On the great significance of von Hellingrath for Heidegger, a brief passage in Reinhard Mehring, *Heideggers Überlieferungsgeschick: Eine dionysische Selbstinszenierung*, Würzburg, 1992, pp. 90ff.

7 Norbert von Hellingrath, 'Hölderlin und die Deutschen', in von Hellingrath, *Hölderlin-Vermächtnis*, ed. Ludwig Pigenot, 2nd edn, Munich, 1944, pp. 119–50; here: p. 120: 'We call ourselves "the people of Goethe" . . . I call ourselves "the people of Hölderlin" because it is deeply rooted in the nature [Wesen] of the Germans that its innermost glowing core . . . comes to light only in the form of a secret Germany.'

8 Details on this can be found in Klaus E. Bohnekamp (ed.), *Rainer Maria Rilke/ Norbert von Hellingrath: Briefe und Dokumente*, Göttingen, 2008, pp. 106ff. Von Hellingrath's lecture on 'Hölderlin und die Deutschen' [Hölderlin and the Germans], which put 'Hölderlin in the place of Goethe' (p. 137), was given on 15 February 1915 in Ludwigstraße 4. On 27 February, he spoke on 'Hölderlins Wahnsinn' in the same place, with a repeat of the lecture on 6 April. Schmitt's civil marriage had taken place on 13 February in Düsseldorf, and on 14 February he began his military service in the Türkenkaserne in Munich. However, he was released from service for his church wedding and in order to take his oral exam as an assessor of law, and thus his continuous presence in Munich began only on 26 February 1915. On 23 March, he was moved to the deputy general headquarters [Stellvertretendes Generalkommando] and lived

outside the barracks in the city again. Thus he could, indeed, have attended von Hellingrath's lecture on 'Hölderlin's madness'; however, it is unlikely that he actually did.

9 Ernst Hüsmert, 'Die letzten Jahre von Carl Schmitt', in *Schmittiana* 1, pp. 40–54; here: p. 46.

10 Max Weber, 'Science as a Vocation', in David Owen and Tracy B. Strong (eds), *Max Weber: The Vocation Lectures: 'Science as a Vocation', 'Politics as a Vocation'*, trans. Rodney Livingstone, Indianapolis, 2004, p. 30.

11 See Theodor Däubler, *Im Kampf um die moderne Kunst und andere Schriften*, ed. Friedhelm Kemp and Friedrich Pfäfflin, Darmstadt, 1988.

12 Together with the publicist Arthur Moeller van den Bruck (1876–1925), who became a forerunner of right-wing intellectualism in the Weimar Republic, in particular through his books *Der preußische Stil* (1914) and *Das Dritte Reich* (1923).

13 The Northern Lights are the polar light caused by the earth's magnetic field.

14 See the impressive book by Helmuth Kiesel, *Geschichte der literarischen Moderne: Sprache, Ästhetik, Dichtung im zwanzigsten Jahrhundert*, Munich, 2004.

15 Herbert Eulenberg, *Schattenbilder*, Berlin, 1912.

16 Ingeborg Villinger, *Carl Schmitts Kulturkritik der Moderne*, Berlin, 1995, p. 235.

17 Ibid., pp. 201ff.

Chapter 4   On the Eve of the Great War

1 Thomas Mann, *Doktor Faustus: Das Leben des deutschen Tonsetzers Adrian Leverkühn erzählt von einem Freunde*, 1947, in *Gesammelte Werke in dreizehn Bänden*, Frankfurt, 1974, vol. 6, p. 206.

2 Carl Schmitt, 'Schopenhauers Rechtsphilosophie außerhalb seines philosophischen Systems', *Monatsschrift für Kriminalpsychologie* 10 (1913), pp. 27–31; cf. also Schmitt's negative review of Julius Binder in *Kritische Vierteljahresschrift für Gesetzgebung und Rechtswissenschaft* 18 (1916), pp. 431–40.

3 Carl Schmitt, 'Schopenhauers Rechtsphilosophie', p. 30.

4 Ibid., p. 31.

5 Theodor Däubler, *Das Nordlicht* [The Northern Lights], vol. 2: *Sahara*, Munich, 1910, p. 542.

6 Rudolf Stammler, *Die Lehre vom richtigen Rechte*, Berlin, 1902. Eng. edn: *The Theory of Justice*, trans. Isaac Husik, South Hackensack, NJ, 1969.

7 Adolf von Harnack, 'Urchristentum und Katholizismus', in von Harnack, *Entstehung und Entwicklung der Kirchenverfassung und des Kirchenrechts in den zwei ersten Jahrhunderten: Urchristentum und Katholizismus*, Leipzig, 1910.

8 Carl Schmitt, *Der Wert des Staates*, Tübingen, 1914. In his personal copy (RW 265-28399), he later made the following note: 'Attack from academic classroom lions [Seminar-Löwen-Hieb]: idea – concept/ typical objection from disputants versed in neo-Kantianism: it is nothing but Platonism, metaphysics of ideas. Note: the title of the work is Value of the State, not: Concept!!' A presentation copy, now in the library of Düsseldorf University, says: 'Presented to the Stadt- und Landesbibliothek Düsseldorf with kind regards', and is dated 5 January 1914. Even after his time in Munich, Schmitt still remained in touch with the director of the municipal library in Düsseldorf, Constantin Nörrenberger.

9 Verdross sent his review 'with the greatest admiration for the author' on 14 July

1914: 'Das Problem von Recht und Macht im Lichte der neueren rechtsphiloso-phischen Forschungen', *Wiener Reichspost*, 12 July 1914 (RW 265-16871).

10 Verdross to Schmitt, 29 July 1914 (RW 265-16872).

11 Carl Brinkmann, 'Review', *Deutsche Literaturzeitung* 36 (1915), pp. 520–3.

12 In 1916, Bruno Bauch retired from the co-editorship of the *Kant-Studien* because, in a letter to the editors, he had questioned whether Hermann Cohen belonged to the German nation on account of his Jewish descent. On the dispute surrounding this event, see the letter from Cassirer to Paul Natorp of 26 November 1916 (Ernst Cassirer, *Ausgewählter wissenschaftlicher Briefwechsel*, NWT, vol. 18, Hamburg, 2009, pp. 28f.) and Cassirer's reply (in Ernst Cassirer, *Zu Philosophie und Politik*, NMT, vol. 9, Hamburg, 2008, pp. 29–60).

13 These formulations probably reflect ideas from Schmitt's unpublished review of a book titled *Individuum und Staat*. Schmitt had sent the review to the *Deutsche Juristen-Zeitung*, but it had been rejected (TB I, p. 97). Most likely, the review contrasted his own approach with that of Chatterton-Hill (Georges Chatterton-Hill, *Individuum und Staat: Untersuchungen über die Grundlage der Kultur*, Tübingen, 1913).

Chapter 5 Düsseldorf

1 '25 Jahre Anwaltschaft beim Oberlandesgericht Düsseldorf', in Franz Schollen (ed.), *Blätter zur Erinnerung an das 25jährige Bestehen des Oberlandesgerichts Düsseldorf*, Anrath, 1931, pp. 126–30, here: p. 126. Biographical information on Zehnhoff can be found in an article on the occasion of his birthday in the *Kölnische Volkszeitung* (February 1925); in particular a long commemorative article by Wilhelm Kisky in RW 265-20539; and obituaries in the *Kölnische Volkszeitung*, nos. 465 and 488 (1930) and the *Frankfurter Zeitung*, no. 633 (1930).

2 Frank Hertweck and Dimitrios Kisoudis (eds), *'Solange das Imperium da ist': Carl Schmitt im Gespräch mit Klaus Figge und Dieter Groh 1971*, Berlin, 2010, p. 80.

3 Based on information in Lehmann, 'Fideikommissenat und Auflösungsamt für Familiengüter im Oberlandesgericht Düsseldorf', in *Blätter zur Erinnerung an das 25jährige Bestehen des Oberlandesgerichts Düsseldorf*, pp. 70–4.

4 In *Deutsche Juristen-Zeitung* 19 (1914), col. 1365: 'Dr Fritz Eisler, of Hamburg, for many years assistant to Prof. Dr. van Calker, 27 Sept. on the Oise.' Eisler was buried in a mass grave in France.

5 Letter of 7 August 1914 from Georg Eisler to the Hamburger Aufsichtsbehörde (Staatsarchiv Hamburg Staatsangehörigkeitsaufsicht B VI, no. 222).

6 Letter of 21 August 1914 from the chief of police for Hamburg, no. 6622/14.I.2, to Bernhard Georg Eisler (Staatsarchiv Hamburg Staatsangehörigkeitsaufsicht B VI, no. 222).

7 Files on the naturalization of Heinrich Eisler in the Staatsarchiv Hamburg, Staatsangehörigkeitsaufsicht, Bestand 352-7 B VI 457.

8 Of his fellow legal trainees at the time, Schmitt later stayed in touch with Walter Fuchs, whom he had met at the trial chamber through a certain Mr Clostermann. Fuchs led an adventurous life as a diplomat in Africa and Asia. Numerous of his later letters invoke the old times (RW 265-4586/05), especially one of 9 January 1952, sent to Schmitt from Bonn (RW 265-4598).

9 On the examination regulations, see Hans-Heinrich Jescheck, *Die juristische Ausbildung in Preussen und im Reich: Vergangenheit und Gegenwart*, Berlin, 1939.

10 On this, see the photographs of Däubler, notes and diary excerpts in RW 265-21551.

Chapter 6　World War and Defeatism

1 Ernst Rudolf Huber, *Deutsche Verfassungsgeschichte seit 1789*, vol. 5: *Weltkrieg: Revolution und Reichserneuerung 1914–1919*, Stuttgart, 1978, pp. 62ff.; cf. Christian Schudnagies, *Der Kriegs- oder Belagerungszustand im Deutschen Reich während des Ersten Weltkriegs: Eine Studie zur Entwicklung und Handhabung des deutschen Ausnahmezustands bis 1918*, Frankfurt, 1989.

2 Huber, *Deutsche Verfassungsgeschichte*, vol. 5, p. 600.

3 In a medical report of 14 June 1919 (RW 265-21285) by the chief medical officer [Oberstabsarzt] of the Kuranstalt Moorbad in Dachau, it says that Schmitt was 'for years in [his] medical care due to a vertebrae- and rib-related condition which required him to wear an orthopaedic corset. Longer periods of sitting or standing still are associated with pain.'

4 Max Weber, 'Zwischenbetrachtungen', in Weber, *Gesammelte Aufsätze zur Religionssoziologie*, vol. 1, Tübingen, 1920, pp. 548f.

5 On this, see also, for instance, Heidegger's speech at a class reunion '25 Jahre nach unserem Abiturium', in *Martin Heidegger-Gesamtausgabe*, vol. 16, Frankfurt, 2000, pp. 279–84.

6 Stefan George, 'Der Krieg', in George, *Das neue Reich, 1928* (*Gesamt-Ausgabe*, vol. 9), Düsseldorf, 1964, p. 30.

7 Probably Richard Grelling, *J'accuse! Von einem Deutschen*, Lausanne, 1915.

8 André Steinlein, *Die Form der Kriegserklärung: Eine völkerrechtliche Untersuchung*, Strasbourg and Munich, 1917; Schmitt quotes the last sentence of Steinlein's dissertation in *Dictatorship* (p. 291, fn. 17). The first examiner was Hermann Rehm. In a preliminary note, Steinlein says that the work was completed in 1916. The first sixty-eight pages, arranged according to the individual centuries, present the development of formal claims between the sixteenth and twentieth century on the basis of legal-historical sources. A separate chapter deals with the development up until 1914. Then, on the next forty-three pages, Steinlein analyses in detail the declarations of war since 1914. Finally, in a theoretical part, he formulates 'essential requirements for formal declarations of war'. The topical theme, the extensive consideration given to the 'classics' of early modern international law, and the special interest in the 'form' of law all carry the signature of Schmitt's intellectual style. The broad, additive and documentary style, however, do not point towards Schmitt's authorship or co-authorship. Nevertheless, his collaboration is likely. The dissertation also fell into Schmitt's time as a Privatdozent in Strasbourg. Thus, he might have exerted some local influence on the examination procedure as well.

9 Dieter Borchmeyer (*Richard Wagner: Ahasvers Wandlungen*, Frankfurt, 2002, pp. 378ff., pp. 458f.) mentions that the satirical suspicion that Wagner was a Jew was common in nineteenth-century caricatures, and that it can also be found in Gustav Freytag, Eugen Dühring, Friedrich Nietzsche and Weininger. The intention of these satires was to brush 'Wagner's unacknowledged modernism' against the grain of his anti-Semitism and anti-modernism. Weininger says in his revealing chapter on 'Judaism': 'The *aggressive* anti-Semite . . . always exhibits certain Jewish peculiarities.' Weininger distinguishes between an 'anti-semitism of *the Jew*' and an 'antisemitism of *the Aryan*', and says: 'But even the most profound anti-Semite – Richard Wagner himself – cannot be cleared of

having a Jewish element, even in his art' (Otto Weininger: *Sex and Character: An Investigation of Fundamental Principles*, Bloomington, IN, 2005, pp. 274f.). He also speaks of '*Judaism as a possibility*' and as a '*Platonic idea*' (p. 276). His aim is a '*rebirth of the human being*' (p. 297) through a 'deliverance from Judaism' that is achieved by Christianity as the '*absolute negation of Judaism*' (p. 298). Thus, he writes: 'the Christian is the purpose of the Jew' ['der Christ ist der Sinn der Juden'] (*Geschlecht und Charakter*, 26th edn, Vienna, 1926, p. 440). Weininger differs from Schmitt in his adoption of a general humanistic perspective in the tradition of the *Vormärz*: in his belief in the possibility of general emancipation from all particular forms of religiosity towards a universal humanity.

10 Cf. Thomas Mann, 'Musik in München', in Mann, *Gesammelte Werke in dreizehn Bänden*, Munich, 1974, vol. 11, pp. 339–50.
11 See Wilhelm Hausenstein's retrospection: *Die Welt um München*, Munich, 1929.
12 See Alice Berend's retrospective letter to Schmitt of 26 December 1919, in *Staat – Souveränität – Verfassung: Festschrift für Helmut Quaritsch*, ed. Dietrich Murswiek, Berlin, 2000, pp. 600ff. Schmitt later met Berend again in Berlin.
13 Material relating to this in RW 265-20114/5 and 20119.
14 Däubler to Schmitt, letter of 3 March 1920 (RW 265-18593).
15 Däubler to Schmitt, letter of 10 May 1920 (RW 265-2703). The new edition of *Das Nordlicht*, in two volumes, appeared in Leipzig in 1921–2.
16 Theodor Däubler, *Die Treppe zum Nordlicht*, Leipzig, 1920 (RW 265-22558).
17 Heinrich von Kleist, 'Lehrbuch der französischen Journalistik' (§ 2), in von Kleist, *Werke und Briefe in vier Bänden*, ed. Siegfried Streller, Berlin, 1995, vol. 3, p. 401.

Chapter 7 Strasbourg, the State of Siege and a Decision in Favour of Catholicism

1 See the rich detail in Bernd Schäfer, *Reichswissenschaft, Staatsrechtslehre, Staatstheorie und Wissenschaftspolitik im Deutschen Kaiserreich am Beispiel der Reichsuniversität Straßburg*, Franfurt, 2004, pp. 487ff.
2 Carl Schmitt, 'Die Einwirkung des Kriegszustands auf das ordentliche strafprozessuale Verfahren', *Zeitschrift für die gesamte Strafrechtswissenschaft* 38 (1916), pp. 783–97.
3 On the developments in administrative law at the time, cf. Michael Stolleis, *Geschichte des öffentlichen Rechts in Deutschland*, vol. 2, Munich, 1992, pp. 381ff.
4 According to Eduard Schwartz's retrospection, 'Die Kaiser-Wilhelms-Universität Straßburg und ihre Bedeutung für Deutschland', 1929, in Schwartz, *Gesammelte Schriften*, vol. 1, Berlin, 1938, pp. 266–77, here: p. 276.
5 As late as summer 1933, Schmitt invited Kiener for a couple of days to his house in Cologne (letter of 27 August 1933 to Kiener, RW 265-13164); cf. Friedrich Kiener, 'Werner Wittich und das Elsass', *Schweizer Monatshefte* 17 (1937), pp. 1–7.
6 Thus, on principles of legal doctrine he argued strongly for the legal validity of an old law and against the new (French) electoral regulations of 1920: Carl Schmitt, 'Die Wahlordnung für das Saargebiet vom 29. April 1920: Ein Beitrag zur Lehre von den Prinzipien rechtlicher Ordnung', *Niemeyers Zeitschrift für internationales Recht* 34 (1925), pp. 415–20.

7 Personal communication from Ernst Rudolf Huber in spring 1988. The meeting in Strasbourg was the last time Huber saw his teacher.

8 Letter to the editor in the *Frankfurter Zeitung* of 7 August 1920. Roth joined the second cabinet of Kahr as justice minister. When Kahr resigned, Roth, on 12 September 1921, also stepped down and joined the radical Deutschvölkische Freiheitspartei, of which Ludendorff was a member. Thus, at the beginning of the 1920s, Roth belonged to the extreme right (Ernst Rudolf Huber, *Deutsche Verfassungsgeschichte seit 1789*, vol. 6, p. 783, p. 284). Schnitzler and Schmitt received a long letter from a certain Dr Boerkner in response (letter of 12 August 1920 to Schmitt, RW 265-1914). In his function as a member of the Ministry of War, Dr Boerkner had cooperated with Schmitt, and he verified his account, saying that, as a disguise, the general command in part had to pretend to the Ministry of War that is was the 'lackey of the police'. Roth wrote a positive reference for Schmitt on his work at the general command, dated 2 March 1921 (RW 265-21565).

9 *Recht und Politik in Bayern zwischen Prinzregentenzeit und Nationalsozialismus: Die Erinnerungen von Philipp Loewenfeld*, ed. Peter Landau and Rolf Rieß, Ebelsbach, 2004, pp. 148ff.

10 Ibid., pp. 349ff., pp. 359ff., pp. 401f., pp. 521f.

11 Franz Blei, *Menschliche Betrachtungen zur Politik* (1915), 3rd edn, Berlin, 1916.

12 See Gina Kaus's colourful memoir, *Von Wien nach Hollywood*, Frankfurt, 1990, pp. 30ff.

13 Cf. Burkhard Dücker, '"Es lebe der Kommunismus und die katholische Kirche": Intellektuelle Selbstverständigung als gesellschaftliches Orientierungsangebot: Zu Franz Bleis Zeitschriften "Summa" und "Die Rettung"', in Dietrich Harth (ed.), *Franz Blei: Mittler der Literaturen*, Hamburg, 1997, pp. 82–105.

14 Stenographical manuscript in RW 265-19419.

15 Franz Blei, *Ungewöhnliche Menschen und Schicksale*, Berlin, 1929, p. 14.

16 Carl Schmitt, 'Franz Blei', *Frankfurter Zeitung*, 22 March 1931; quoted after Schmitt's typescript of 18 January 1931 (RW 265-19418).

17 Franz Blei, *Talleyrand*, Berlin, 1932 ('For Carl Schmitt, in friendship and veneration').

18 Franz Blei, 'Carl Schmitt', in Blei, *Zeitgenössische Bildnisse*, Amsterdam, 1940, pp. 21–9; here: pp. 21f.

19 Thomas Rentsch, 'Religion und Philosophie', in Birgit Weyl and Wilhelm Gräb (eds), *Religion in der modernen Lebenswelt: Erscheinungsformen und Reflexionsperspektiven*, Göttingen, 2006, pp. 315–34; here: p. 334; Thomas Rentsch, *Gott*, Berlin, 2005.

20 Theodor Haecker, *Satire und Polemik 1914–1920*, Innsbruck, 1922; cf. Haecker (ed.), *Kierkegaard: Der Pfahl im Fleische*, 2nd edn, Innsbruck, 1922; *Kritik der Gegenwart*, 2nd edn, Innsbruck, 1922. At the time, Haecker also wrote polemically (see his piece on 'Blei und Kierkegaard' in *Satire und Polemik*, pp. 19–27) about Blei's reception of Kierkegaard in order to distance himself, as a serious religious author, from the purely literary author.

21 Hugo Ball, *Flight out of Time: A Dada Diary*, trans. Ann Raimes, New York, 1974. See Helmuth Kiesel, *Geschichte der literarischen Moderne*, Munich, 2004. Cf. also Bernd Wacker, 'Die Zweideutigkeit der katholischen Verschärfung – Carl Schmitt und Hugo Ball', in Wacker (ed.), *Die eigentlich katholische Verschärfung … Konfession, Politik und Theologie im Werk Carl Schmitts*, Munich, 1994, pp. 123–45.

22 Blei, *Menschliche Betrachtungen zur Politik*, 3rd edn, p. 178.

23 In addition, there were plans for an advance publication of a passage from

Political Romanticism. Jakob Hegner asked Feuchtwanger on 9 January 1919 for the permission to print it, which Feuchtwanger granted on 13 January 1919 (Archive of Duncker & Humblot, file on 'Carl Schmitt, Politische Romantik').

24 Cf. Reinhart Koselleck, 'Die Verzeitlichung der Utopie', in Koselleck, *Zeitgeschichten: Studien zur Historik*, Frankfurt, 2000, pp. 131–49.

25 Cf. Adolf von Harnack, 'Der Großbetrieb der Wissenschaft' (1905), in von Harnack, *Wissenschaftspolitische Reden und Aufsätze*, ed. Bernhard Fabian, Hildesheim, 2001, pp. 3–9.

Chapter 8 Political Romanticists, 1815–1919

1 Cf. Heike Specht, *Die Feuchtwangers: Familie, Tradition und jüdisches Selbstverständnis im deutsch-jüdischen Bürgertum des 19. und 20. Jahrhunderts*, Göttingen, 2006.

2 Schmitt's personal copy of *Political Romanticism* (RW 265-28263) contains many supplementary annotations. On the contemporary debates regarding democracy, cf. Markus Llanque, *Demokratisches Denken im Krieg: Die deutsche Debatte im Ersten Weltkrieg*, Berlin, 2000.

3 *Aus meinem Leben: Aufzeichnungen des deutschen Pietisten Johann Arnold Kanne*, ed. Carl Schmitt-Dorotić, Berlin, 1919, p. 23. Typescript of Schmitt's preface: RW 265-21928.

4 Cf. Wilhelm Dilthey, *Weltanschauungslehre: Abhandlungen zur Philosophie der Philosophie*, Leipzig, 1931.

5 Cf. Karl-Heinz Bohrer, *Die Kritik der Romantik: Der Verdacht der Philosophie gegen die literarische Moderne*, Frankfurt, 1989. On the re-evaluation of the distinction between political Romanticism and counter-revolutionary philosophy of the state [Staatsphilosophie], cf. Henning Ottmann, *Geschichte des politischen Denkens*, vol. 3/3: *Die politischen Strömungen im 19. Jahrhundert*, Stuttgart, 2008.

6 David Friedrich Strauß, *Der Romantiker auf dem Thron der Caesaren, oder Julian der Abtrünnige*, Mannheim, 1847. Schmitt later also owned a copy of *Der Kaiser der Römer gegen den König der Juden: Aus den Schriften 'Julians des Abtrünnigen'*, Berlin, 1941.

7 Alice Berend, *Der Glückspilz: Roman*, Munich, 1919, p. 219.

8 Bernd Schlüter, *Reichswissenschaft: Staatsrechtslehre, Staatstheorie und Wissenschaftspolitik im Deutschen Kaiserreich am Beispiel der Reichsuniversität Straßburg*, Frankfurt, 2004, p. 483.

9 Ibid., pp. 493f.

10 Ibid., p. 497.

11 Johannes Ficker, *Die Kaiser-Wilhelm-Universität Straßburg und ihre Tätigkeit*, Halle, 1922, pp. 31f.

12 Schlüter, *Reichswissenschaft*, p. 499. Cf. Erich Klostermann, *Die Rückkehr der Straßburger Dozenten 1918/19 und ihre Aufnahme*, Halle, 1932; A. Dörner, 'Der Freiburger Universität unauslöschlichen Dank: Die Auflösung der Reichsuniversität Straßburg im November 1918 und ihre Aufnahme durch die Universität Freiburg', *Freiburger Universitätsblätter* 145 (1999), pp. 131–41. Schmitt established contact with the 'central office' by having a copy of his *Political Romanticism* sent to the Freiburg historian Heinrich Finke (CSLF, p. 19).

13 Carl Schmitt, 'Eine Tischrede' (1938), in *Schmittiana* 5, Berlin, 1996, pp. 10–11; here: p. 11. Cf. Wilhelm Hausenstein, 'Tölz', in Hausenstein, *Die Welt um München*, 1929, p. 173.

14 Moritz Julius Bonn, *So macht man Geschichte: Bilanz eines Lebens*, Munich, 1953, p. 192.
15 According to Heinrich August Winkler, 'Die verdrängte Schuld: Warum die Weimarer Sozialdemokraten auf den moralischen Bruch mit dem Kaiserreich verzichteten', in Winkler, *Auf ewig in Hitler's Schatten?*, Munich, 2007, pp. 58–71; here: pp. 70f. For a general history of political crisis, see Heinrich August Winkler, *Weimar 1918–1933: Die Geschichte der ersten deutschen Demokratie*, Munich, 1993.
16 Later, in Berlin, Schmitt was in closer contact with Niekisch, who was a close friend of Ernst Jünger.
17 Thomas Mann, *Tagebücher 1918–1921*, Frankfurt, 1979, p. 166.
18 At least according to Philipp Loewenfeld in his detailed memoirs of the revolution: *Recht und Politik in Bayern zwischen Prinzregentenzeit und Nationalsozialismus: Die Erinnerungen von Philipp Loewenfeld*, ed. Peter Landau and Rolf Rieß, Ebelsbach, 2004, pp. 310ff., 359ff., 401f.
19 Cf. Detlef Felken, *Oswald Spengler: Konservativer Denker zwischen Kaiserreich und Diktatur*, Munich, 1988, pp. 95ff.
20 Ernst Toller, 'Spaziergang der Häftlinge' [Walk of the prisoners] (1919), in *Lyrik des expressionistischen Jahrzehnts: Von den Wegbereitern bis zum Dada*, Wiesbaden, 1955, p. 266 [Sie schleppen ihre Zellen mit in stumpfen Augen / und stolpern, lichtentwöhnte Pilger, im Quadrat].
21 Heinrich August Winkler, 'Vom Kaiserreich zur Republik: Der historische Ort der Revolution von 1918/19', in Winkler, *Streitfragen der deutschen Geschichte: Essays zum 19. und 20. Jahrhundert*, Munich, 1997, pp. 52–70; here: p. 63. Cf. David Clay Large, *Where Ghosts Walked: Munich's Road to the Third Reich*, New York and London, 1997.
22 My presentation follows Ernst Rudolf Huber, *Deutsche Verfassungsgeschichte seit 1789*, vol. 5: *Weltkrieg: Revolution und Reichserneuerung 1914–1919*, Stuttgart, 1978, pp. 1014ff., 113ff.; cf. Winkler, *Weimar 1918–1933*, pp. 76ff.; an extensive discussion can be found in Allan Mitchel, *Revolution in Bavaria 1918–1919: The Eisner Regime and the Soviet Republic*, Princeton, NJ, 1965. On the revolutionary situation in Munich, see, in detail, Reinhard Mehring, 'Politische Theologie des Anarchismus: Fritz Mauthner und Gustav Landauer im Visier Carl Schmitts', in Gerald Hartung (ed.), *An den Grenzen der Sprachkritik*, Würzburg, 2013, pp. 85–111.
23 See Reinhard Mehring, *Thomas Mann: Künstler und Philosoph*, Munich, 2001, pp. 181ff.
24 Letter from Carl Schmitt to Huber, 10 March 1978 (BAK, N 1505, no. 198).

Chapter 9   A Permanent Position?

1 My presentation follows Ernst Rudolf Huber, 'Militärgewalt, Notstandsgewalt, Verfassungsschutzgewalt in den Konflikten zwischen Bayern und Reich', in Huber, *Bewahrung und Wandlung: Studien zur deutschen Staatstheorie und Verfassungstheorie*, Berlin, 1975, pp. 171–92.
2 Ibid., p. 186.
3 According to Huber, *Deutsche Verfassungsgeschichte*, vol. 7: *Ausbau, Schutz und Untergang der Weimarer Republik*, Stuttgart, 1984, pp. 402ff.
4 Documents in TB II, pp. 510ff. (RW 265-1975/78).
5 Zehnhoff to Schmitt, 23 August 1919 (TB II, p. 516). Schmitt's patron in Mönchengladbach, Arthur Lambert, also agreed: see his postcard to Schmitt of 8 September 1919 (RW 265-8607).

6 Moritz Julius Bonn, on behalf of the university council [Kuratorium], to the Ministry for Culture and Education, 23 August 1919, in Bayerisches Hauptstaatsarchiv MK 22 500. There are no documents relating to Schmitt's appointment in Bayerisches Wirtschaftsarchiv München K I/XIX 19, 4. Akt (June 1917 – June 1920). It seems only the correspondence between the Handelshochschule and the Bavarian Ministry and the chamber of commerce has been preserved.

7 Letter of 21 August 1919 from the director M. J. Bonn to Schmitt (RW 265-2971). Employment contract of 25 August 1919 (RW 265-21564). In 1920, Schmitt received an overall annual salary of 31,500 Reichsmark (finance department of the Handels-Hochschule, letter to Schmitt of 23 April 1921, RW 265-5687).

8 Frank Zschaler, *Vom Heilig-Geist-Spital zur Wirtschaftswissenschaftlichen Fakultät: 110 Jahre Staatswissenschaftlich-Statistisches Seminar an der vormals königlichen Friedrich-Wilhelms-Universität: 90 Jahre Handels-Hochschule Berlin*, Berlin, 1997, p. 19.

9 Moritz Julius Bonn, 'Die Aufgaben der Handelshochschule München', in *Die Aufgaben der Handelshochschule München: Reden und Begrüßungen anlässlich der feierlichen Eröffnung*, Munich, 1911, pp. 15–24, here: p. 21.

10 Ibid., p. 23.

11 Cf. Ignaz Jastrow, 'Handelshochschulen', in Paul Laband et al. (eds), *Handbuch der Politik*, Berlin, 1912–13, vol. 2, pp. 37–8.

12 Moritz Julius Bonn, *So macht man Geschichte: Bilanz eines Lebens*, Munich, 1953, p. 144. Cf. Herbert Zander, *Gründung der Handelshochschulen im deutschen Kaiserreich (1898–1919)*, dissertation, University of Cologne, 2004, pp. 175ff.

13 His son, Friedrich Karl Klausing (1920–1944), was closely involved with the resistance group of 20 June 1944 as the adjutant to Claus Schenck Graf von Stauffenberg. He was sentenced to death by the 'Volksgerichtshof' [People's Court] on 8 August 1944, and immediately executed in Plötzensee Prison, Berlin. His father, Friedrich Klausing, thereupon committed suicide.

14 Bonn, *So macht man Geschichte*, p. 182. On the founding members of the Hochschule, cf. Moritz Bonn, 'Vorläufiger Bericht über das Gründungsjahr 1910', in Bonn, *Die Aufgaben der Handelshochschule München*, pp. 39–42.

15 Bonn, *So macht man Geschichte*, p. 330.

16 Request of 4 December 1918, presented to the council [Kuratorium] of the Handelshochschule by Moritz Bonn (Bayerisches Hauptstaatsarchiv MK 22500).

17 Based on the information given in the *Vorlesungsverzeichnis* [listings of courses taught] for the winter term 1920–1.

18 Schmitt's calendar mentions a meeting with Weber on 24 January 1920. See also TB II, pp. 15f.

19 Carl Schmitt, 'Politische Theorie der Romantik', *Historische Zeitschrift* 123 (1921), pp. 377–97. The article was written before Schmitt took up his professorship and was originally planned to appear in the *Preußischen Jahrbücher* (letter of 9 October 1919 to the *Zeitschrift für öffentliches Recht*, RW 265-13588).

20 Schmitt, 'Politische Theorie der Romantik', p. 387 (foonote).

21 Letter of 13 April 19120 from the Drei Masken Verlag to Schmitt (RW 265-16955). Max Weber's *Gesammelte Politische Schriften* [Collected political writings] appeared with the same publisher at the time. Schmitt wanted to pass the project on to Wolzendorff (on this, see Wolzendorff to Schmitt, 21 February 1921, RW 265-18428).

22 Letters from Hirschberg (solicitors' office of Adolf Kaufmann, Max Hirschberg and Philip Loewenfeld) to Schmitt, 12 April 1920 and 16 May 1920. There are no surviving documents on this trial in Munich. Cf. Max Hirschberg, *Jude und Demokrat: Erinnerungen eines Münchner Rechtsanwalts 1883–1939*, Munich, 1998.

23 Letter of 13 August to Schmitt from the director, Klausing, regarding a new work contract (RW 265-2972).

24 Draft, dated 30 November 1920, for a letter to a professor at the University of Munich (RW 265–13431).

25 Hugo am Zehnhoff writing to Schmitt, 10 October 1920; also see his Christmas greetings of 22 December 1920 (RW 265-18480/1).

26 Correspondence published by Martin Otto (ed.), in *Schmittiana*, NF (new series) 2 (2013), pp. 53–86.

27 Numerous letters, with melancholic overtones, from Wolzendorff to Schmitt, written between 6 September 1920 and 6 March 1921 (RW 265-18421/29). Wolzendorff passed away soon afterwards.

28 Letter of 2 September 1921 from the trustee of the university to Schmitt (RW 265-8586).

29 Letter of 3 September 1921 (Bayerisches Hauptstaatsarchiv MK 22500). Schmitt had already announced labour law, economic self-administration and 'Lektüre politischer Schriften' [Readings of political texts] for the coming winter term, 1921–2.

30 Minutes of the meeting of the council [Kuratorium] of 8 September 1921 (Bayerisches Wirtschaftsarchiv Munich KI/XIX 19, 5. Akt).

31 From 1920 alone, we have more than twenty-five, mostly longer letters from Georg Eisler (RW 265-3095/3120).

32 On 10 November 1920, Eisler asked: 'Do you know a Privatdozent called Heidegger, who lectures on the phenomenology of religion?' (RW 265-3113). On 14 November 1920, Eisler wrote: 'The other day I attended one of the lectures by Heidegger on the phenomenology of religion. A younger man, and a Jew, it seems' (RW 265-3114).

33 Schmitt's personal copy (RW 265-28242), dated 1 February 1921.

34 See also Schmitt's lexicon definitions of 'dictatorship' (SGN, pp. 33–7) and of 'absolutism' (SGN, pp. 95–9) published in 1926.

35 On the formation of the philosophy of history, see the impressive account by Andreas Urs Sommer, *Sinnstiftung durch Geschichte?*, Basel, 2006. Cf. also Skadi Krause, *Die souveräne Nation: Zur Delegitimierung monarchischer Herrschaft in Frankreich 1788–1789*, Berlin, 2008.

36 On the riots along the Rhine and Ruhr, cf. Huber, *Deutsche Verfassungsgeschichte*, vol. 7, pp. 101ff.

37 Schmitt to Smend, 11 May 1921 (Niedersächsische Staats- und Universitätsbibliothek Göttingen, Cod Ms R. Smend, A 759).

38 Carl Schmitt, 'Soziologie des Souveränitätsbegriffs und politische Theologie', in *Hauptprobleme der Soziologie: Erinnerungsgabe für Max Weber*, ed. Melchior Palyi, Munich, 1923, vol. 2, pp. 3–35, here quoted following the widely used edition of the *Politische Theologie*. A detailed discussion of Schmitt's contribution can be found in Otto Koellreutter (*Archiv des öffentlichen Rechts* 46, 1924, pp. 365–8), who praises in particular Schmitt's 'courage to be metaphysical'.

39 Jan Assmann, *Herrschaft und Heil: Politische Theologie in Altägypten, Israel und Europa*, Munich, 2000, pp. 15ff. From the intensive discussions surrounding this question, cf. Ernst-Wolfgang Böckenförde, 'Politische Theorie und politische Theologie: Bemerkungen zu ihrem gegenseitigen Verhältnis', in

Böckenförde, *Kirchlicher Auftrag und politisches Handeln*, Freiburg, 1989, pp. 146–58; Henning Ottmann, 'Politische Theologie als Herrschaftskritik und Herrschaftsrelativierung', in Manfred Walther (ed.), *Religion und Politik: Zu Theorie und Praxis des theologisch-politischen Komplexes*, Baden-Baden, 2004, pp. 73–83; Heinrich Meier, *Was ist Politische Theologie? Einführende Bemerkungen zu einem umstrittenen Begriff* [1992], Munich, 2006; Jürgen Mannemann, *Carl Schmitt und die Politische Theologie: Politischer Anti-Monotheismus*, Münster, 2002. Heinrich Meier has reconstructed the consistency of Schmitt's political-theological perspective in great detail: *Die Lehre Carl Schmitts: Vier Kapitel zur Unterscheidung Politischer Theologie und Politischer Philosophie*, Stuttgart, 1994.

40 Schmitt emphasized this point in the preface to the second edition of 1934.

41 Hermann Lübbe in particular reads Schmitt's *Political Theology* as a descriptive project: 'Politische Theologie als Theologie repolitisierter Religion', in Jacob Taubes (ed.), *Der Fürst dieser Welt: Carl Schmitt und die Folgen*, Munich, 1983, pp. 45–56. Also Lübbe, 'Carl Schmitt liberal rezipiert', in Helmut Quaritsch (ed.), *Complexio Oppositorum: Über Carl Schmitt*, Berlin, 1988, pp. 427–46, and *Säkularisierung: Geschichte eines ideenpolitischen Begriffs*, 2nd edn, Freiburg, 1975.

42 On the validity conditions of social recognition set out by the sociology of law, cf. Robert Alexy, *Begriff und Geltung des Rechts*, Freiburg, 1992, pp. 139ff.

43 'Authority, not truth, makes law' (Hobbes, *Leviathan*). On this, see also the dissertation by Heinrich Lenz, *Autorität und Demokratie in der Staatslehre des Hans Kelsen* (University of Bonn), which was supervised by Schmitt.

44 See, e.g., Hans Kelsen, 'Gott und Staat', *Logos* 11 (1922–3), pp. 261–84.

45 See Carl Schmitt, 'Die Auseinandersetzung zwischen dem Hause Wittelsbach und dem Freistaat Bayern', *Kölnische Volkszeitung*, 436 (4 June 1922). Reprinted in *Schmittiana*, NF (new series) 1 (2011), pp. 11–12.

46 Bonn, *So macht man Geschichte*, p. 192; cf. Huber, *Deutsche Verfassungsgeschichte*, vol. 5, Stuttgart, 1978, pp. 1014ff.

47 Hans Kelsen, *Vom Wesen und Wert der Demokratie*, 2nd edn, Tübingen, 1929, p. 118. Cf. Kelsen, 'State-Form and World-Outlook' (1933), in Ota Weinberger (ed.), *Hans Kelsen: Essays in Legal and Moral Philosophy*, trans. Peter Heath, Dordrecht and Boston, 1973. Cf also Fritz van Calker, *Recht und Weltanschauung*, Mannheim, 1924.

48 See Reinhard Mehring, 'Antipodische Polemik: Zur Kontroverse zwischen Hans Kelsen und Carl Schmitt', in Manfred Walther (ed.), *Religion und Politik: Zu Theorie und Praxis des theologisch-politischen Komplexes*, Baden-Baden, 2004, pp. 265–72; Volker Neumann, 'Theologie als staatsrechtswissenschaftliches Argument: Hans Kelsen und Carl Schmitt', *Der Staat* 47 (2008), pp. 163–86.

Chapter 10   A 'Faithful Gipsy' in Greifswald

1 Adolf Hofmeister, *Die geschichtliche Stellung der Universität Greifswald*, Greifswald, 1932.

2 Cf. Marita Baumgartner, *Professoren und Universitäten im 19. Jahrhundert: Zur Sozialgeschichte deutscher Geistes- und Naturwissenschaftler*, Göttingen, 1997; Baumgartner, 'Berufungswandel und Universitätssystem im 19. Jahrhundert', in Werner Buchholz (ed.), *Die Universität Greifswald und die deutsche Hochschullandschaft im 19. und 20. Jahrhundert*, Stuttgart, 2004, pp. 87–116.

3 My presentation follows Matthias Miguel Braun and Volker Pesch, 'Die Umstände der Berufung Carl Schmitts nach Greifswald', in *Schmittiana* 7 (2001), pp. 195–206.
4 Letter of 9 September 1921 to Schmitt from the minister C. H. Becker. Employment contract of 30 August 1921 (RW 265-21564).
5 Theodor Däubler to Schmitt, 22 September 1921 (RW 265-2705).
6 Däubler to Schmitt, 20 January 1922 (RW 265-2706).
7 Franz Blei to Schmitt, 1 October 1921, in FBCS, p. 27.
8 Blei to Schmitt, 29 November 1921, ibid., p. 28.
9 Curtius to Schmitt, 25 November 1921, in Rolf Nagel (ed.), 'Briefe von Ernst Robert Curtius an Carl Schmitt', *Archiv für das Studium der Neueren Sprachen und Literatur* 133 (1981), pp. 1–15; here: p. 5.
10 Flora Klee-Pahlyi to Schmitt, 6 October 1921 (RW265-7657).
11 Heinrich Merk to Schmitt, 26 February 1922 (RW 265-9436).
12 Friedrich Kiener to Schmitt, 12 November 1921 (TB II, p. 508).
13 Information based on Murray's *curriculum vitae* in the still existing file on her doctorate [Promotionsakte] at the Universitätsarchiv Marburg (UniA 307d, no. 282). A report from the *Sydney Morning Herald*, 'Brilliant Student', which is among Schmitt's posthumous papers (RW 265-21295), contains slightly different information, mentioning Paris, Strasbourg, Bonn and Marburg as the steps in Murray's itinerary.
14 Admission offer according to a letter of the secretary's office of Bonn University, dated 12 November 1921 (UniA Marburg 307d, no. 282).
15 Kathleen Murray to Schmitt, 8 November 1921 (RW 265-10058).
16 See Nagel (ed.), 'Briefe von Ernst Robert Curtius an Carl Schmitt'. This edition is not complete. In Schmitt's posthumous papers, there are further letters and cards from Curtius, reaching up to 1924. These have been consulted here. On Curtius's biography, cf. Heinrich Lausberg, *Ernst Robert Curtius (1886–1956)*, Stuttgart, 1993.
17 Letter of 22 November 1921 from Murray to Schmitt [English in the original] (RW 265-10053).
18 Max Deutschbein (1876–1949), professor of English in Leipzig (1906), Halle (1910) and Marburg (1919–46).
19 The manuscript pages that have been preserved (RW 265-21295) refer to the chapter 'Burns', in Kathleen Murray, *Taine und die englische Romantik*, Munich, 1924, pp. 14–16.
20 Moritz Julius Bonn, *So macht man Geschichte: Bilanz eines Lebens*, Munich, 1953, p. 330: 'He then was appointed to a chair in Greifswald. In the Protestant atmosphere there, the Catholic from Westphalia felt rather unhappy. He often came to visit me in Berlin and lamented his situation.' See also Bonn's letter of 8 December 1921 to Schmitt (archive of Duncker & Humblot, file on 'Schmitt, *Dictatorship*').
21 Letter of 20 January 1922 from Bonn to Schmitt (RW 265-537). Cf. Theodor Heuss, *Erinnerungen 1905–1933*, Tübingen, 1964, pp. 302–4.
22 Letter of 25 January from Georg Eisler to Schmitt (RW 265-3128).
23 Letter of 1 March 1922 from Rudolf Smend to Schmitt (RW 265-15211).
24 Hans Pichler, 7 May 1922, to his 'dear friend' Schmitt (RW 265-11059).
25 Günther Holstein, *Die Grundlagen des evangelischen Kirchenrechts*, Tübingen, 1928.
26 See Schmitt's letters to Smend of 9 March 1922, 1 June 1927 and 17 October 1927 (Niedersächsische Staats- und Landesbibliothek Göttingen, Cod Ms. R. Smend, A 759).

27 Letter of 4 February 1922 from Curtius to the dean (file on Murray's doctorate, UniA Marburg 307d, no. 82).
28 Cf. Moritz Julius Bonn, *Irland und die irische Frage*, Munich, 1918, pp. 243ff.; Hans Franzen, 'Irland und Großbritannien since 1919: Ein Beitrag zur Verfassungslehre', *Jahrbuch des öffentlichen Rechts* 25 (1938), pp. 280–375, esp. pp. 289–92 (a Habilitation supervised by Schmitt).
29 Letter from the dean, dated 9 February 1922 (file on Murray's doctorate – UniA Marburg 307d, no. 282).
30 Letter from Curtius to Murray, February 1922 (RW 265-2680).
31 Stendal, *On Love* . . . ('Ce que me fait croire les Werther plus heureux, c'est que don Juan réduit l'amour à n'être qu'une affaire ordinaire').
32 Eisler to Schmitt, 7 April 1922 (RW 265-3130).
33 Curtius to Schmitt, 10 May 1922 (RW 265-2693).
34 Curtius to Schmitt, 14 May 1922 (RW 265-2693). On this, cf. also the letter by the chancellor of the university to Schmitt (RW 265-16701).
35 Postcard from Curtius to Schmitt (RW 265-2695).
36 Murray, *Taine und die europäische Romantik*, p. vi. Review by Waldemar Gurian, in the 'Literarische Beilage' [Literary supplement] of the *Kölnische Volkszeitung*, no. 1 (1 January 1925).
37 Carl Schmitt, 'Der treue Zigeuner', in *Schmittiana* 7 (2001), pp. 20–7; here: p. 26.
38 Blei to Schmitt, 19 April 1922, in FBCS, p. 42.
39 Blei to Schmitt, 7 May 1922, ibid.
40 Schmitt, 'Der treue Zigeuner', p. 27.
41 Carl Schmitt, 'Der Schatten Gottes: Tolle Wirklichkeit und was ihr wollt' (provisional transcription). These diaries will be published by Gerd Giesler in 2014.
42 Murray to Schmitt, 29 May 1951 (RW 265-10055).

Chapter 11   Arrival in Bonn?

1 Letter of 30 April 1922 from the university's trustee Norrenberg to Schmitt (Universitätsarchiv Bonn, personal file of Carl Schmitt, PA 8888). Schmitt to Smend, 9 March 1922 (Niedersächsische Staats- und Universitätsbibliothek Göttingen, Cod Ms R. Smend, A 759). No documents on Schmitt's appointment have been preserved in the files on 1918 at the faculty in Bonn.
2 Michael Stolleis, *Geschichte des öffentlichen Rechts*, vol. 3, Munich, 1999, p. 88.
3 Ernst Zitelmann, *Die Bonner Universität: Rede bei der Feier ihres hundertjährigen Bestehens*, Bonn, 1919, p. 10. Cf. Karl T. Schäfer, *Verfassungsgeschichte der Universität Bonn 1818 bis 1960*, Bonn, 1968, pp. 151ff.
4 Figures according to the *Vorlesungsverzeichnis*: in the summer term 1925 there were 412 students of law, in the summer term 1926 there were 592, and in the summer term 1927 there were 670.
5 Ernst Friesenhahn, 'Juristen an der Universität Bonn', in *Alma Mater: Beiträge zur Geschichte der Universität Bonn*, Bonn, 1970, pp. 21–48; here: pp. 44f. Friesenhahn remains silent on his doctoral supervisor Carl Schmitt.
6 In the summer term 1922, Schmitt lectured on state law and international law. In the winter term 1922–3, he lectured on 'Deutsches Reichs- und Landesstaatsrecht' [German national law and the law of the individual German states] and 'Politische Ideen' [Political ideas], as well as giving an 'Einführung in die Allgemeine Staatslehre (Politik)' [Introduction to the general theory of the state (politics)]. In the summer term 1923, he continued with his lecture

course on Staatslehre and 'Politische Ideen' and offered 'Staatsrechtliche Übungen' [Tutorial on state law]. For the summer term 1923 and the winter term 1923–4, he took over international law from Kaufmann. In the winter term 1923–4, he again lectured on 'Reichs- und Landesstaatsrecht' and offered both a 'Verwaltungsrechtspraktikum' [Practical exercises in administrative law] and a 'Staatsrechtlich-politisches Seminar' [Seminar on state law and politics]. In the summer term 1924, he gave an introductory lecture on 'Die deutsche Verfassung von 1919' [The German constitution of 1919], which was open to students from all disciplines. In addition he gave a large lecture on 'Völkerrecht' [International law] and 'Staatsrechtliche Übungen'. In the winter term 1924–5, Schmitt again lectured on international law and offered 'Verwaltungsrechtliche Übungen' and his 'Staatsrechtlich-politisches Seminar'. In the summer term 1925, he gave a lecture on 'Die Weimarer Verfassung' [The Weimar Constitution] and another one on 'Deutsches Reichs- und Landesstaatsrecht'. In addition he offered 'Staatsrechtliche Übungen'. In the winter term 1925–6, he lectured on 'Staatstheorien' [State theories], in the plural, as well as on 'Völkerrecht'. He also held 'Öffentlich-rechtliche Übungen' [a tutorial on public law] and a specialist 'Staatsphilosophisches Seminar' [Seminar on the philosophy of the state]. In 1926, he announced for the first time courses on 'Verwaltungsrecht' [Administrative law] and 'Grundsätzliche Fragen des modern Völkerrechts' [Fundamental issues in modern international law]. He also taught 'Staatsrechtliche Übungen'. In the winter term 1926–7, he lectured again on 'Völkerrecht' and gave 'Verwaltungsrechtliche Übungen' as well as a seminar on 'Staatstheorien'. In the summer term 1927, he lectured on 'Politik (Allgemeine Staatslehre)' [Politics (general theory of the state)] and on 'Deutsches Reichs- und Landesstaatsrecht'. In the winter term 1927–8, his last term in Bonn, he offered 'Einführung in die Allgemeine Staatslehre (Politik)', his lecture on 'Völkerrecht', tutorials in public law and a 'Staatsphilosophisches Seminar'. This information, culled from the *Vorlesungsverzeichnis*, does not always correspond to the courses that Schmitt actually taught.

7 See the indignant letter of 1 June 1923 from Kaufmann to Schmitt (RW 265-7314). On Kaufmann's influence, cf. Frank Degenhardt, *Zwischen Machtstaat und Völkerbund: Erich Kaufmann (1880–1972)*, Baden-Baden, 2008.
8 Hensel was of Jewish descent, but a Protestant. In the Great War, he had fought at the front. He had strong artistic interests and had come up with a book on Beethoven, but, under the influence of the war, decided to study jurisprudence. As a former front-line soldier he did not immediately lose his chair in 1933. He died while on a trip abroad. His wife committed suicide in a Gestapo prison in 1942 [Gestapo = Geheime Staatspolizei, the secret police under NS rule]. Cf. Ekkehart Renier and Christian Waldhoff, 'Zu Leben und Werk Albert Hensels (1895–1933)', in Albert Hensel, *System des Familiensteuerrechts und andere Schriften*, Cologne, 2000, pp. 1–124. Further publications by Hensel: *Der Finanzausgleich im Bundesstaat in seiner staatsrechtlichen Bedeutung*, Berlin, 1922; *Steuerrecht*, Berlin, 1924; *Kommunalrecht und Kommunalpolitik in Deutschland*, Breslau, 1928; *Grundrechte und politische Weltanschauung*, Tübingen, 1931.
9 Schmitt actually formulated the proposal to appoint Hensel, in Akten der Juristischen Fakultät der Universität zu Bonn, Fach 4, no. 1 (covering the period between 17 April 1918 and 2 February 1939 (Archiv der Juristischen Fakultät Bonn, 42).
10 Schmitt to Smend, 14 November 1924 (Niedersächsische Staats- und Universitätsbibliothek Göttingen, Cod Ms. R. Smend, A 759).

11 Karl Muth, *Die Wiedergeburt der Dichtung aus dem religiösen Erlebnis*, Kempten, 1909.
12 Léon Bloy, *Le Désespéré*, 1886. L. B., *Lettres à Véronique. (1877–1879)*, 1933 [2010].
13 Zehnhoff was of a different opinion; see Zehnhoff to Schmitt, 30 May 1920 (date of stamp) (RW 265-18479).
14 Saul Friedländer emphasizes this point in his *The Years of Extermination: Nazi Germany and the Jews, 1939–1945*, London: Phoenix, 2008, pp. 115f.
15 Hermann Platz, *Geistige Kämpfe im modernen Frankreich*, Munich, 1922. Platz, *Um Rhein und Abendland*, Burg Rothenfels, 1924; *Deutschland–Frankreich und die Idee des Abendlandes*, Cologne, 1924; *Der geistige Umbruch in Frankreich*, Breslau, 1932.
16 Ernst Robert Curtius, *Die literarischen Wegbereiter des neuen Frankreich*, Potsdam, 1919. Curtius, *Maurice Barrès und die geistigen Grundlagen des französischen Nationalismus*, Bonn, 1921. Cf. also Hugo Friedrich, *Das antiromantische Denken im modernen Frankreich*, Munich, 1936.
17 Letter of 23 January 1928 from Platz to Schmitt (RW 265-11094).
18 Among Schmitt's posthumous papers there are four postcards and letters from Klemperer, falling between 1922 and 1930 (RW 265-7674/77).
19 On this in particular, Karl Eschweiler, *Die zwei Wege der neueren Theologie: Georg Hermes – Matthias Scheeben: Eine kritische Untersuchung des Problems der theologischen Erkenntnis*, Augsburg, 1926. Eschweiler, *Johann Adam Möllers Kirchenbegriff: Das Hauptstück der Auseinandersetzung mit dem deutschen Idealismus*, Braunsberg, 1930. See more recently, Thomas Marschler, *Karl Eschweiler 1886–1936: Theologische Erkenntnislehre und nationalsozialistische Ideologie*, Regensburg, 2011.
20 Blei had translated Maurice Barrès, Claudel, Oscar Wilde and many others, as well as edited Stendhal and Casanova. He was one of the most knowledgeable experts on the erotic literature and culture of the Rococo.
21 George Bernanos, *Vorhut der Christenheit: Eine Auswahl aus den polemischen Schriften*, ed. Walter Warnach, Düsseldorf, 1950.
22 Adolf von Harnack, *Marcion: The Gospel of the Alien God*, Durham, NC, 1990. On the significance of Harnack's interpretation of Marcion within the contemporary debates, cf. Jakob Taubes, *The Political Theology of Paul*, Stanford, CA, 2004.
23 Harnack, *Marcion*, pp. 246f.
24 Ibid., p. 254.
25 Ibid., *Marcion*, p. 255.
26 Karl Barth, *The Epistle to the Romans*, Oxford, 1968 [1933]; *The Word of God and the Word of Man*, New York, 1957.
27 Franz Blei to Schmitt, 7 December 1921, in FBCS, p. 32.
28 Heinrich Merk to Schmitt, 26 February 1922 (RW 265-9436).
29 The sharp distinction drawn by Schmitt can also be seen in a review he wrote of an edition of de Maistre in the *Zeitschrift für die gesamte Strafrechtswissenschaft* 79 (1925), pp. 727–8. Schmitt's disciple Gurian later described the polarization within French Catholicism after 1914: Waldemar Gurian, *Die politischen und sozialen Ideen des französischen Katholizismus 1789/1914*, Gladbach, 1929. Gurian, *Der integrale Nationalismus in Frankreich: Charles Maurras und die Action française*, Frankfurt, 1931. Cf. also Gurian's review of *Political Theology*, published under a pseudonym, in *Kölnische Volkszeitung*, no. 343 (10 February 1925), pp. 2–3; Günter Maschke, 'Die Zweideutigeit der 'Entscheidung' – Thomas Hobbes und Juan Donoso Cortés im Werk Carl Schmitts', in Helmut

Quaritsch (ed.), *Complexio Oppositorum: Über Carl Schmitt*, Berlin, 1988, pp. 183–221.

30 Mentioning Otto Groß, Schmitt also referred to anarchism in Munich. On this, see the retrospective Hansjörg Viesel (ed.), *Jawohl, der Schmitt: Zehn Briefe aus Plettenberg*, Berlin, 1988.

31 Cf. Mikhail Bakunin, *God and the State*, New York, 1916. On secularized papism and on Bakunin's 'negative political theology', cf. Henning Ottmann, *Geschichte des politischen Denkens*, vol. 3/3: *Die politischen Strömungen im 19. Jahrhundert*, Stuttgart, 2008, pp. 32ff., 204ff., 216ff.

32 Eduard Norden, *Die Geburt des Kindes: Geschichte einer religiösen Idee*, Berlin, 1924, pp. 92f.

33 Notes on conceptual history in folder RW 265-20803.

34 Harnack, *Marcion*, pp. 6 and 11f.

35 Rudolph Sohm, *Kirchenrecht*, vol. 2: *Katholisches Kirchenrecht*, ed. Erwin Jacobi and Otto Mayer, Munich, 1923.

36 Bonn to Schmitt, 30 October 1922 (RW 265-16515).

37 In the mid-1970s, Schmitt, in the draft of a letter to the theologian Schwindler, recalled that Hegner had 'not yet been baptized' when his essay appeared (RW 265-19981, sheet 2). A vivid description of Hegner (from a later period) can be found in Josef Pieper, *Noch wusste es niemand: Autobiographische Aufzeichnungen 1904–1945*, Munich, 1976, pp. 125ff. Cf. also Peter de Mendelssohn, '"Einen Verlag muss man leben": Erinnerungen an Jakob Hegner', *Börsenblatt des deutschen Buchhandels* (18 January 1977), pp. 109–15.

38 The journal also later published a piece by Schmitt's disciple Bernhard Braubach, 'Der Bereich des Politischen im Katholizismus', *Die Dioskuren: Jahrbuch für Geisteswissenschaften* 3 (1924), pp. 216–44.

39 Letter of 22 November 1922 from Jakob Hegner to Schmitt (RW 265-5833).

40 Letter of 10 June 1923 from Blei to Schmitt, in FBCS, p. 55.

41 According to Josef Isensee, 'Aussprache zum Vortrag von Klaus Kröger', in Quaritsch (ed.), *Complexio Oppositorum*, p. 173.

42 The debates and the reception of Schmitt's essay are laid out in Manfred Dahlheimer, *Carl Schmitt und der deutsche Katholizismus 1888–1936*, Paderborn, 1998, pp. 56ff. and 82ff. Dahlheimer rightly emphasizes Schmitt's proximity to Carl Muth and Hermann Hefele, and he expresses doubts about the strong theses of Andreas Koenen – *Der Fall Carl Schmitt*, Darmstadt, 1995 – which situate Schmitt within the liturgical movement and the 'Theology of the Reich' associated with Maria Laach.

43 Ernst Michels, 5 October 1923, on the occasion of sending his review (RW 265-9488).

44 Werner Becker to Schmitt, 6 September 1923 (WBCS, p. 27). On their first contact in retrospect, see Becker to Schmitt, 10 July 1969 (WBCS, p. 81).

45 Hegner to Schmitt, 9 April 1924 (RW 265-18837).

46 Hegner to Schmitt, 21 May 1924 (RW 265-18838).

47 Hegner to Schmitt, 2 June 1924 (RW 265-18839).

48 Hegner to Schmitt, 18 August 1924 (RW 265-1141). Cf. also Hegner's interim statement of account of 3 May 1924 (RW 265-17142).

49 Hegner to Schmitt, 25 September 1924 (RW 265-18840).

50 Hegner to Schmitt, 21 April 1925 (RW 265-5836).

51 Letter of 23 May 1925 from the assocation to Schmitt (RW 265-16867).

52 Letter of 9 June 1925 from the Theatiner publishing house to Schmitt (RW 265-17231).

53 On this, see the letters of 24 June 1925 and 2 July 1925 from Maria Linke of the Catholic Association of Academics (RW 265-7293/4).
54 Hegner to Schmitt, 10 August 1925 (RW 265-5837).
55 Carl Schmitt, 'Um das Schicksal des Politischen', *Die Schildgenossen* 5 (1924–5), pp. 313–22. Separate publication of an extract from *Die Rheinlande als Objekt der internationaler Politik* [The Rhineland as an object in international politics], Cologne, 1925.

Chapter 12   Schmitt as a Teacher in Bonn

1 The landlady's daughter, Margarete von Wandel, passed her doctorate from the University of Bonn on 25 March 1923. The title of her dissertation was *Die Wirtschaftsräte des Artikel 165 der Reichsverfassung*. Schmitt wrote the second examiner's report on the dissertation.
2 Carl Schmitt, 'Die Auseinandersetzung zwischen dem Hause Wittelsbach und dem Freistaat Bayern', *Kölnische Volkszeitung*, no. 436 (6 June 1922). Review of Konrad Beyerle, *Die Rechtsansprüche des Hauses Wittelsbach*, Munich, 1922.
3 Letter of thanks of 20 December from Geibels to Schmitt (RW 265-4695).
4 Letter of 4 November from André Steinlein to Schmitt, in deposit of Jürgen Becker.
5 See Wilhelm Kisky to Schmitt, letter of 18 May 1922 (RW 265-7648).
6 Wilhelm Neuß (1880–1965), *Die Anfänge des Christentums im Rheinlande*, Bonn, 1923; *Die Kunst des alten Christen*, Augsburg, 1926. Retrospectively, Neuß, *Die Kirche der Neuzeit*, Bonn, 1954. Neuß's posthumous papers at the Universitätsbibliothek Bonn cannot yet be accessed.
7 Arnold Schmitz (1893–1980), PhD Bonn 1921, associate professor at Bonn 1928, full professor at Breslau 1929–45, full professor at Mainz 1946–61.
8 Arnold Schmitz, *Das romantische Beethovenbild: Darstellung und Kritik*, Berlin, 1927, pp. viif. Schmitz quotes various publications by Schmitt in various contexts. In particular, he gives him credit for 'having given the concept of secularization and its application to processes of intellectual history a concrete meaning and precision' (fn, p. 73). On 6 December 1978, Schmitz wrote to Schmitt (RW 265-13882).
9 Andreas Koenen, *Der Fall Carl Schmitt: Sein Aufstieg zum 'Kronjuristen des Dritten Reiches'*, Darmstadt, 1995.
10 Letters from Rosenbaum to Schmitt, 30 November 1922 and 13 December 1922 (RW 265-11744/5). Eduard Rosenbaum, *Der Vertrag von Versailles: Inhalt und Wirkung*, Leipzig, 1920; *Das Gesicht Hamburgs*, Hamburg, 1927.
11 Alfred Bertram (1890–1937), born in Hamburg, became assessor and senior civil servant [Regierungsrat] in 1920, chief senior civil servant [Oberregierungsrat] in 1922, chief councillor at the Higher Regional Court [Oberlandesgerichtsrat] in 1931, and government director [Regierungsdirektor] in the central administration of the regional department of justice [Landesjustizverwaltung] in 1931. Between 1929 and 1931 he was also associate judge at the Hanseatic Higher Administrative Court, and between 1928 and 1932 he was the head of the Juristische Gesellschaft Hamburg [Juridical Society of Hamburg]. (Information based on *Das Hanseatische Oberlandesgericht: Gedenkschrift zu seinem 60jährigen Bestehen*, Hamburg, 1939). Cf. Alfred Bertram, *Hamburgs Zivilrechtspflege im 19. Jahrhundert*, Hamburg, 1929.
12 It is possible that Schmitt already knew Kurt Singer (1886–1962) from

his time in Strasbourg, as the latter did his doctorate with the economist Georg Friedrich Knapp in Strasbourg in 1910. Schmitt also attended classes with Knapp. Between 1916 and 1928 Singer was the main editor of the *Wirtschaftsdienst*. In 1931 he went to Japan, and later spent two years in China. In 1939 he emigrated to Australia. On the important Jewish economists from the Jünger circle, Singer and Edgar Salin, both of whom Schmitt knew, see Korinna Schönhärl, *Wissen und Visionen*, Berlin, 2009.

13 Card of thanks of 28 December from Giorgio del Vecchio to Schmitt (RW 265-16857).

14 The following facts have emerged from various archives. From October 1925, Cari was commercially registered in the healthcare industry and the hairdressing business. From the summer of 1926, she lived with frequently changing addresses around the railway station in Munich (fifteen different addresses within three years). At that time, both her parents were already dead. In 1929, she had a hairdresser's shop in the Nymphenburger Straße for a couple of months, before, now registered as an Austrian national, she informed the authorities at the end of the year about moving to Bremerhaven. From January 1934, she lived in Bremerhaven under the name of 'Maria Büschen', and was married to Adolf Peter Büschen. Having lost their home in the bombing raids, she and her husband were registered as moving to Langeoog. In 1949, Cari applied for status as a victim of political persecution because she had been arrested for a couple of days in 1934. Büschen died in 1966 in Aurich and Cari died on 28 August 1968 in a hospital in Osnabrück.

15 Hugo am Zehnhoff to Schmitt, 7 February 1923 (RW 265-18483). In particular, Zehnhoff asks about an 'appointment' with the lawyer that had taken place on 23 December 1922.

16 Aschaffenburg (1866–1944) had studied psychiatry and criminal law. He wrote his Habilitation as a disciple of Emil Kraeplin in Heidelberg. From 1900 he was a professor in Cologne and from 1904 the editor of the *Monatsschrift für Kriminalpsychologie und Strafrechtsreform*, in which Schmitt's miscellaneous text on Schopenhauer appeared. In 1938 he emigrated to the United States. He died in Baltimore in 1944.

17 The title of her dissertation was *Über einen Fall von Rankenneurom des Oberlides*, Munich, 1922. Sauer (1895–1979) continued living in Munich (Landwehrstraße) before establishing herself as a general practitioner in Berlin in 1930. On 22 January 1930, she wrote to Schmitt from Berlin: 'Carl, may I ask you the favour of one more short meeting with you, and may I ask you not to turn down this request? I do not want to bring back anything that belongs to the past, nor do I wish to leave anything behind when I go. All I want is a quiet and concluding conversation with you. I am waiting for your reply' (RW 265-12250). Initially, Schmitt wanted to give her a ring, but then actually didn't (TB, 21 January 1930). Carola Sauer lived at Speyerer Straße 26 (in the district of Schöneberg). She married the lawyer Erwin Braune but was later divorced. After 1945, she continued to be listed as a general practitioner in the directory of medical doctors in Berlin, with Sybelstraße 66, in the district of Charlottenburg, as her address. On 11 July 1973 (RW 265-2002), his birthday, Dr Carola Braune, née Sauer, wrote one more letter to Schmitt: 'You will hardly be able to remember, as half a century has passed since our paths once crossed for a short time; it was in 1922–3. And I don't write to you today to congratulate you, though one could do that in your case. I only want to tell you that our acquaintance was the most fruitful event in my life, and that it had an impact that remains today.' She died on 13 January 1979. I owe

most of the biographical information on her to Jutta Buchin of the Charité in Berlin.

18 Information based on authenticated birth and marriage certificates which Duška requested from Zagreb in 1933 in the context of Schmitt's 'certificate of Aryan descent' [Ariernachweis]. In deposit on Jürgen Becker. Information provided by Duška in 1936 can also be found in Schmitt's personal file in Berlin (University archive of Humboldt University, PA Carl Schmitt 159/a Bl5). In that year Duška gave as the profession of both her father and her grandfather 'mayor and notary'. At the time of Duška's death, her father lived in Podravska Slatina in Croatia, a place at the River Drava not far from the border with Hungary, and her mother lived in Daruvar, a small town about 130 kilometres from Zagreb. Little is known about Duška's family background and youth. She had a brother with whom she remained in touch. After her parents' divorce, she may have grown up in Agram (Zagreb). This would be of interest, insofar as that place had a large Jewish community, and there are numerous reports that bear witness to Duška's anti-Semitism. The opposition between Croatia and Serbia found expression primarily in religious terms. While Christianity in the Roman world constituted itself against Rome, resulting in a dualism between Church and state, orthodox Christianity emerged as a state religion. Hence, the latter is based more on principles of political authority and piety, and liberalism is more alien to it (cf. Dimitrios Kisoudis, *Politische Theologie in der griechisch-orthodoxen Kirche*, Marburg, 2007). The same probably applied to Duška's attitude. After her death, there was only little contact with relatives in Yugoslavia. Schmitt did not visit them. Their daughter Anima visited some relatives in Yugoslavia on her way to Greece.

19 Cf. the dissertation by Karl Schilling, *Ist das Königreich Jugoslawien mit dem früheren Königreich Serbien völkerrechtlich identisch?*, Berlin, 1939. On the prehistory, see also Serge Maiwald, *Der Berliner Kongress 1878 und das Völkerrecht: Die Lösung des Balkanproblems im 19. Jahrhundert*, Stuttgart, 1948.

20 Zehnhoff to Schmitt, 1 April 1923 (RW 265-18484).

21 Günther Holstein, *Die Staatsphilosophie Schleiermachers*, Leipzig, 1923. Cf. Otto von Campenhausen, *Günther Holstein: Staatsrechtslehrer und Kirchenrechtler in der Weimarer Republik*, Pfaffenweiler, 1997.

22 Carl Schmitt, 'Der Schatten Gottes', diary entry, 30 April 1923.

23 The division between love and sexuality was common after 1900 and a position taken by various authors. See, e.g., Heinrich Scholz, *Eros und Caritas: Die platonische Liebe und die Liebe im Sinne des Christentums*, Halle, 1929; Ludwig Klages, *Vom kosmogonischen Eros*, Jena, 1930.

24 Ernst Rudolf Huber, *Deutsche Verfassungsgeschichte*, vol. 7: *Ausbau, Schutz und Untergang der Weimarer Republik*, Stuttgart, 1984, pp. 390ff.

25 Ibid., p. 431.

26 Cf. Ernst Zitelmann, *Lebenserinnerungen*, Bonn, 1924, p. 39.

27 Obituary, 'Ernst Landsberg', *Deutsche Juristen-Zeitung* 29 (1924), cols 41–2. Cf. also Heinrich Mitteis on the *Festgabe*, *Deutsche Literaturzeitung* 46 (1925), pp. 279–84. A dissertation by Aloys Zimmer analyses the weakening of parliamentarism through federalism: *Parlamentarismus und Föderalismus als verfassungspolitisches Problem in der deutschen Reichsverfassung*, Bonn, 1924.

28 The corrections are noted in Schmitt's personal copy of the Zitelmann *Festgabe* (RW 265-28267).

29 Georg Lukács, *History and Class Consciousness: Studies in Marxist Dialectics*, London, 1971.

30 Ricarda Huch, *Michael Bakunin und der Anarchismus*, Leipzig, 1923.
31 Rudolf Smend, 'Die Verschiebung der konstitutionellen Ordnung durch die Verhältniswahl', in *Festgabe der Bonner Juristischen Fakultät für Karl Bergbohm*, Bonn, 1919, 278–87. Cf. Smend's letter to Schmitt, 22 December 1923 (RW 265-15213).
32 Cf. Ernst Wolfgang Böckenförde, *Die deutsche verfassungsgeschichtliche Forschung im 19. Jahrhundert*, Berlin, 1961.
33 Schmitt also sent the treatise to Robert Michels, who picked up the reference to fascism. The correspondence between Schmitt and Michels can be found in Piet Tommissen, *In Sachen Carl Schmitt*, Vienna, 1987, pp. 85–9. 1928 was the year of Schmitt's first contact with Gaetano Mosca; see ibid., pp. 93–4. Waldemar Gurian took on board Schmitt's distinction in his 'Faschismus und Bolschewismus', *Heiliges Feuer* 16 (1927–8), pp. 507–18.
34 Letters from Feuchtwanger to Schmitt, dated 8 December 1925 and 6 May 1926 (CSLF, p. 34). Schmitt responded on 11 May 1926 (CSLF, p. 162) and sent a definite negative reply to Feuchtwanger on 19 July 1926 (CSLF, p. 179).
35 According to Huber, *Deutsche Verfassungsgeschichte*, vol. 7, p. 317.
36 Carl Schmitt, 'Eine französische Kritik der Zeit', *Wirtschaftsdienst* 11 (1926), pp. 593–4, review of Lucien Romier, *Explication de notre temps*, Paris, 1925.
37 Schmitt does not mention in his review the assassination of Rathenau on 24 June 1922. On the renewed interest in Rathenau, cf. Franz Blei, 'Walther Rathenau', in Blei, *Männer und Masken*, Berlin, 1930, pp. 257–76. Blei was a friend of Robert Musil, who painted a negative portrait of Rathenau in the form of Arnheim, one of the central characters in *The Man without Qualities* and based on the German politician.
38 Cf. Fritz Wiese's dissertation *Die parlamentsrechtliche Stellung des deutschen Reichspräsidenten*, Bonn, 1926.
39 Letter from Kaufmann to Schmitt, 1 June 1923 (RW 265-7314).
40 Karl Rick's letters of 19 January 1924 and 1 November 1931 (RW 265-11619/11623).
41 On the motif of Chaplin as a Jewish pariah-artist, cf. Hannah Arendt, *Die verborgene Tradition: Essays*, Frankfurt, 2000, pp. 64–7.
42 Copies of all decisions were kindly put at my disposal by the literary executer, Prof. Dr Jürgen Becker.
43 Triepel to Schmitt, 3 February 1924 (RW 265-16399).
44 Schmitt read Karl Rothenbücher's *Der Fall Kahr*, Tübingen, 1924. Rothenbücher presents a detailed reconstruction of the events in Munich's Bürgerbräukeller and pleads for a harsh punishment of Kahr. This booklet alone would have given Schmitt a comprehensive picture of Hitler's actions on the day.
45 Villiers de l'Isle-Adam, *Tomorrow's Eve*, trans. Robert Martin Adams, Urbana, IL, 2001 [1982].
46 Letter from the Zentrum's politician Hanns Schauff to Schmitt, 6 March 1924 (RW 265-12308). Request submitted to Reichsparteivorstand [national party executive] of the Zentrum by the Deutsche Windhorstbünde [youth organisation of the Zentrumspartei] and Jungakademiker [association of young academics]. 'Turned down 6/3' reads Schmitt's lapidary note on the letter (RW 265-21438).
47 According to Carl Schmitt, *The Concept of the Political*, preface to the Italian edition of 1971, in Quaritsch (ed.), *Complexio Oppositorum*, pp. 269–73; here: p. 270. See also Schmitt's letter of 9 September 1960 to Rudolf Morsey (RW 265-13298): 'As far as my background is concerned, I was unambiguously

associated with the Zentrum, and I tried for long enough to fulfil the expectations that went with it. My father, who died in 1945 at the age of ninety-two, was a prime example of a faithful adherent of the Zentrum; throughout his long life, he served the Catholic cause, living in the condition of a diaspora that was still very hard in those days.'

48 On this tendency, from a neo-Hegelian perspective, see especially Karl Larenz, *Die Rechts- und Staatsphilosophie des deutschen Idealismus und ihre Gegenwartsbedeutung*, Munich, 1933; *Rechts- und Staatsphilosophie der Gegenwart*, 2nd edn, Berlin, 1935. Cf. also Reinhard Mehring, 'Der sozialdemokratische Strafrechtsdiskurs in Weimar und seine Kritik: Gustav Radbruch, Erik Wolf and Karl Larenz', in Manfred Gangl (ed.), *Linke Juristen in der Weimarer Republik*, Frankfurt, 2003, pp. 169–87.

49 Retrospectively, Ulrich Scheuner, 'Die Vereinigung der Deutschen Staatsrechtslehrer in der Zeit der Weimarer Republik', *Archiv des öffentlichen Rechts* 97 (1972), pp. 349–74; Rudolf Smend, 'Die Vereinigung der deutschen Staatsrechtslehrer und der Richtungsstreit', in *Festschrift für Ulrich Scheuner zum 70. Geburtstag*, Berlin, 1973, pp. 575–89; Michael Stolleis, *Der Methodenstreit der Weimarer Staatsrechtslehrer – ein abgeschlossenes Kapitel der Wissenschaftsgeschichte?*, Stuttgart, 2001; Christoph Möllers, 'Der Methodenstreit als politischer Generationskonflikt: Ein Beitrag zum Verständnis der Weimarer Staatsrechtslehre', *Der Staat* 25 (2004), pp. 399–424.

50 Cf. the following works by Hans Kelsen: *Der soziologische und der juristische Staatsbegriff*, Tübingen, 1922; *Allgemeine Staatslehre*, Berlin, 1925; *Der Staat als Übermensch*, Berlin, 1926; *Die philosophischen Grundlagen der Naturrechtslehre und des Rechtspositivismus*, Berlin, 1928; *Vom Wesen und Wert der Demokratie*, 2nd edn, Tübingen, 1929; *Der Staat als Integration*, Vienna, 1930; *Wer soll Hüter der Verfassung sein?*, Berlin, 1931; *Staatsform und Weltanschauung*, Tübingen, 1933; *Reine Rechtslehre*, Vienna, 1934 [Eng. trans. as *Introduction to the Problems of Legal Theory*, Oxford, 1992].

51 Smend's works are collected in *Staatsrechtliche Abhandlungen und andere Aufsätze*, Berlin, 1955.

52 Hermann Heller, *Die Souveränität: Ein Beitrag zur Theorie des Staats- und Völkerrechts*, Berlin, 1927; *Staatslehre*, Leiden, 1934.

53 More substantial works of ideology critique by Hermann Heller are *Hegel und der nationale Machtgedanke in Deutschland*, Leipzig, 1921; *Sozialismus und Nation*, Berlin, 1925; *Die politischen Ideenkreise der Gegenwart*, Breslau, 1926; *Europa und der Fascimus*, Berlin, 1929.

54 See Schmitt's extensive remarks on this in a letter of 11 September 1928 to Smend (Niedersächsische Staats- und Universitätsbibliothek Göttingen, Cod Ms R. Smend, A 759).

55 Schmitt to Smend, 14 September 1925 (Niedersächsische Staats- und Universitätsbibliothek Göttingen, Cod Ms R. Smend, A 759).

56 Michael Stolleis emphasizes this as the motivation for founding the association in his *Geschichte des öffentlichen Rechts*, vol. 3, pp. 188ff. Cf. also Manfred Friedrich, *Geschichte der deutschen Staatsrechtswissenschaft*, Berlin, 1997, pp. 320ff.

57 A list of members for 1924 can be found in *Der deutsche Föderalismus: Die Diktatur des Reichspräsidenten: Veröffentlichung der Vereinigung der Deutschen Staatsrechtslehrer*, vol. 1, Berlin, 1924, pp. 140–4. List of participants at the 1924 meeting of the association in Fritz Stier-Somlo, 'Die zweite Tagung der Vereinigung der deutschen Staatsrechtslehrer', *Archiv des öffentlichen Rechts* 46 (1924), pp. 144–5.

58 See the statutes of the association in *Veröffentlichung der Vereinigung der Deutschen Staatsrechtslehrer*, vol. 1, pp. 144–5.

59 Schmitt considered the inclusion of the text of his presentation in *Dictatorship* early on (see his letter to Feuchtwanger of 20 June 1924; CSLF, p. 60). 'This presentation should, indeed, be part of the book; it is an example of the application of the theories developed in it', he later wrote to Feuchtwanger on 15 June 1927 (CSLF, p. 209). The text of 1927 is a slightly revised version, which does not contain the 'guiding principles of the commentator' that Schmitt had formulated for the presentation: *Veröffentlichung der Vereinigung der deutschen Staatsrechtslehrer*, vol. 1, pp. 103–4. The text of 1927 in D, pp. 180–226: 'The Dictatorship of the President of the Reich according to Article 48 of the Weimar Constitution'.

60 Erwin Jacobi, 'Leitsätze des Mitberichterstatters', in *Veröffentlichung der Vereinigung der deutschen Staatsrechtslehrer*, vol. 1, p. 136. Cf. Martin Otto, *Von der Eigenkirche zum Volkseigenen Betrieb: Erwin Jacobi (1884–1965)*, Tübingen, 2008. For Schmitt's correspondence with Jacobi, see Martin Ott (ed.), *Schmittiana*, NF (new series) 1 (2011), pp. 33–55.

61 Account of the discussion on 'dictatorship', in *Veröffentlichung der Vereinigung der deutschen Staatsrechtslehrer*, vol. 1, pp. 137–9. The state theorist Fitz Stier-Somlo (Cologne) provides a more detailed account of the proceedings of the meeting and discussions: 'Die zweite Tagung der Vereinigung der deutschen Staatsrechtslehrer', in *Archiv des öffentlichen Rechts* 46 (1924), pp. 88–105. There are identical formulations to be found in the two accounts, making it likely that Stier-Somlo was also the author of the one published in the association's proceedings. In his report on the meeting, Stier-Somlo writes (p. 95) that, together with others (such as Nawiaski, Triepel, Thoma, Anschütz), he had contradicted Schmitt. And he acknowledges at the end: 'So far my extremely short report. It was difficult for me to retain the pragmatic and objective perspective of the chronicler in it' (p. 104). From then on, Schmitt became very polemical about Stier-Somlo. In the context of Schmitt's appointment to the Handelshochschule [graduate school of economics] in Berlin in 1926, Stier-Somlo wrote an objective and respectful report on Schmitt, but did hint at their personal dispute (Christian Tilitzki, 'Carl Schmitt an der Handelshochschule Berlin 1928–1933', in *Schmittiana* 4, 1994, pp. 157–202; here: p. 170). Stier-Somlo also reviewed Schmitt's *Der Hüter der Verfassung* [The guardian of the constitution]), in *Archiv des öffentlichen Rechts* 21 (1932), pp. 447–53.

62 Carl Schmitt, 'Das Ausführungsgesetz zu Art. 48 (sog. Diktaturgesetz)', in SGN, pp. 38–41. The evidence provided by Maschke and his deliberations: SGN, pp. 42f.

63 Letter from Moritz Julius Bonn to Schmitt, 5 May 1924 (RW 265-1937).

64 Schmitt's evaluation of Bilfinger for Smend was rather negative: Schmitt to Smend, 27 June 1924 (Niedersächsische Staats- und Universitätsbibliothek Göttingen, Cod Ms R. Smend, A 759).

65 Schmitt to Smend, 25 May 1924 (Niedersächsische Staats- und Universitätsbibliothek Göttingen, Cod Ms R. Smend, A 759).

66 Schmitt to Smend, 21 July 1924 (Niedersächsische Staats- und Universitätsbibliothek Göttingen, Cod Ms R. Smend, A 759).

67 Hugo Ball, 'Carl Schmitt's Politische Theologie', *Hochland* 21 (1924), pp. 263–86.

68 Obituary on Heinrich Eisler (with photo) in *Deutsche Hotel-Nachrichten*, 28/25 (21 June 1924), p. 3.

69 See the editorial news of 20 September 1924 and 27 September 1924, and the article 'Die Entwicklung unserer Zeitschrift', *Deutsche Hotel-Nachrichten*, 28/40 (1 October 1924), p. 3.

70 Letter from Duška to Schmitt, 25 July 1924 (RW 265-13769).

71 Leopold von Ranke, *The History of Servia and the Servian Revolution*, trans. Mrs Alexander Kerr, London, 1853 (*Die serbische Revolution, Aus serbischen Papieren und Mittheilungen*, originally pubd 1929). Letters from Schmitt to Feuchtwanger of 21 August 1924 (CSLF, p. 67) and 28 August 1924 (CSLF, pp. 70f.). On 30 August 1924, Feuchtwanger formally granted the translation rights.

72 Letter to Feuchtwanger, 12 October 1924 (CSLF, p. 85). Cf. letter to Feuchtwanger of 18 January 1925 (CSLF, p. 112). On 2 February 1925, Schmitt considered 'a further [complementary] chapter on Chateaubriand' (CSLF, p. 115) as the 'counterpart to Adam Müller'. A reference to Josef Nadler finds its explanation in the correspondence of 1921–2 (letters from Nadler to Schmitt in RW 265-10127/31). Review by Hans Rothfels in *Deutsche Literaturzeitung* 47 (1926), pp. 432–7. The 'demarcation line' between Romanticism and Catholicism is considered by Alfred von Martin, 'Romantischer "Katholizismus" und katholische "Romantik"', *Hochland* 23 (1925), pp. 315–37. Further reviews by, among others, Carl Brinkmann, *Archiv für Sozialwissenschaften und Sozialpolitik* 54, pp. 530–6; Erich Przywara, *Stimmen der Zeit* 109 (1925), pp. 471–2; Gerhard Masur, *Historische Zeitschrift* 133 (1926), pp. 373–6.

73 Hugo Ball, *Die Flucht aus der Zeit*, Lucerne, 1956, p. 272 [*Flight out of Time: A Dada Diary*, Berkeley, CA, and London, 1996]. On Ball's development, cf. Kurt Flasch, *Die geistige Mobilmachung: Die deutschen Intellektuellen und der Erste Weltkrieg: Ein Versuch*, Berlin, 2000, pp. 202–23.

74 Hugo Ball, *Die Flucht aus der Zeit*, pp. 174f.

75 Carl Muth wrote a review of the Catholicism essay: 'Zeitgeschichte', *Hochland* 21 (1923–4), pp. 96–100.

76 Letter to Carl Muth dated 23 December 1927, in *Politisches Denken: Jahrbuch 1998*, pp. 146f.

77 Carl Muth to Schmitt, 2 May 1924, in *Politisches Denken: Jahrbuch 1998*, p. 133. Muth had in mind a response to Guardini's critique in *Schildgenossen* 1924. On this, see Schmitt to Smend, 25 May 1924 (Niedersächsische Staats- und Universitätsbibliothek Göttingen, Cod Ms R. Smend, A 759).

78 Hugo Ball, 'Carl Schmitt's Politische Theologie', *Hochland* 21 (1924), pp. 263–86, here: p. 276.

79 Ibid., p. 282.

80 Ibid., p. 284.

81 Correspondence as edited by Bernd Wacker, '"Vor einigen Jahren kam einmal ein Professor aus Bonn . . .": Der Briefwechsel Hugo Ball/Carl Schmitt', in *Dionysius DADA Areopagita: Hugo Ball und die Kritik der Moderne*, Munich, 1996, pp. 207–40. Cf. also Wacker, 'Die Zweideutigkeit der katholischen Verschärfung – Carl Schmitt und Hugo Ball', in Wacker (ed.), *Die eigentliche katholische Verschärfung . . . Konfession, Theologie und Politik im Werk Carl Schmitts*, Munich, 1994, pp. 123–45 (contains further interesting references).

82 Ball to Feuchtwanger, 17 September 1924 (Archive of Duncker & Humblot, folder on Ball, *Folgen der Reformation*).

83 Ball to Feuchtwanger, 12 November 1924 (Archive of Duncker & Humblot, folder on Ball, *Folgen der Reformation*).

84 Letter from Schmitt to Duška, 17 December 1924 (RW 579-671).

578   *Notes to pp. 154–6*

85 Ball to Carl Muth, 6 February 1925, in Hugo Ball, *Briefe 1911–1927*, ed. Annemarie Schütt-Hennings, Zurich, 1957, p. 199. Gurian ordered a review copy from the publisher on 26 November 1924 and sent his review to the publisher on 28 January 1925, together with a covering letter in which he referred to further versions of the review in the *Rhein-Mainische Volkszeitung*, the *Deutschen Reichszeitung* (published in Bonn) and *Hochland* (Archive of Duncker & Humblot, folder on Ball, *Folgen der Reformation*).

86 Draft of a letter to August Hofmann, dated 14 February 1925, in Emmy Ball-Hennings, *Hugo Ball: Sein Leben in Briefen und Gedichten*, Berlin, 1930, pp. 239f.

87 Letter of 25 March 1926 to Ludwig Feuchtwanger, in Ball, *Briefe 1911–1927*, p. 208. Cf. also Gurian's letters to the publisher in RWN 260-389 (also in Archive of Duncker & Humblot, folder on Ball, *Folgen der Reformation*). During that time Schmitt was in fact in frequent correspondence with Gurian, and in October 1924 he met him in Cologne (letters from Schmitt to Gurian, RW 579-477).

88 At least this is what Ball's daughter, Annemarie Schütt-Hennings, wrote to Schmitt on 5 July 1961 (RW 265-14676).

89 Schmitt to Gurian, 16 February 1925 (RW 579-477).

90 Feuchtwanger to Ball, 27 April 1925 (Archive of Duncker & Humblot, folder on Ball, *Folgen der Reformation*).

91 Feuchtwanger to Ball, 25 February 1924 (Archive of Duncker & Humblot, folder on Ball, *Folgen der Reformation*).

92 Gerhard Ritter, 'Rezension von Hugo Ball', *Historische Zeitschrift* 131 (1925), pp. 296–7, here: p. 297. Feuchtwanger had sent a review copy to the editor, Friedrich Meinecke, saying: 'The strong reservations which speak against the publication of the first book [Ball], reservations regarding its style, which at times resembles that of a pamphlet, and regarding some excessive claims, we decided should be ignored in the case of such a highly talented and exceptionally important author' (Archive of Duncker & Humblot, folder on Ball, *Folgen der Reformation*).

93 Letter of 28 June 1925 from Kurt Singer to Schmitt (RW 265-15181).

94 Kurt Singer, review of Hugo Ball, *Wirtschaftsdienst* 10 (1925), p. 1010.

95 Publication of parts of the text in *Germania* caused Schmitt to ask for an honorarium. Letter of 10 March 1925 from the editors of *Germania* rejecting the demand (RW 265-11434).

96 Ball-Hennings, *Hugo Ball*, p. 237. The complete letter can be found in *Politisches Denken: Jahrbuch 1998*, pp. 140–3. Schmitt then read Emmy Ball-Hennings, *Hugo Balls Weg zu Gott: Ein Buch der Erinnerung*, Munich, 1931. At the end of his personal copy of Ball's *Flucht aus der Zeit* [Flight out of Time] he placed the remark (p. 156 and on cover): 'On 8 February 1926, my flight *into* time began' – an allusion to his marriage and excommunication.

97 Letter from Carl Schmitt to Carl Muth, 15 November 1927, in *Politisches Denken: Jahrbuch 1998*, p. 144.

98 Bernd Wacker, '"Vor einigen Jahren kam einmal ein Professor aus Bonn . . ."', pp. 238f.

99 'The enemy is one's own question as form' ['Der Feind ist die eigne Frage als Gestalt'] was a key formulation of Schmitt's, which he often quoted after 1945 (cf. ECS, pp. 89f., FP, p. 903, TP, p. 87).

100 Bernhard Braubach passed his doctorate with Schmitt on 31 July 1923. The title of his thesis was *Zum Begriff des Abgeordneten: Ein ideengeschichtlicher Versuch zum festländischen Staatsrecht*. It was awarded the rare mark

'excellent'. Published version: 'Der Einfluss der Stoa auf das französische Staatsrecht der Revolution', *Schmollers Jahrbuch* 48 (1924), pp. 219–42; 'Stoa und Demokratie in der Ideenwelt der französischen Revolution (Condorcet)', *Schmollers Jahrbuch* 48 (1924), pp. 637–53. Cf. Braubach, 'Kant als Schöpfer einer neuen Metaphysik', *Philosophisches Jahrbuch* 39 (1926), pp. 419–34. See also Braubach's first thesis: *Die Einführung der Kantischen Philosophie in Frankreich durch Charles de Villiers*, Bonn, 1919.

101 Walter vom Dahl, *Über die Umwandlung der Stellung der Frau im öffentlichen Recht: Ein Versuch öffentlich-rechtlich-politischer Untersuchung*, Bonn, 1924 (the second examiner was Hans Schreuer).

102 Aloys Zimmer wrote his doctorate on *Parlamentarismus und Föderalismus als verfassungspolitisches Problem in der deutschen Reichsverfassung*, Bonn, 1924 (second examiner: Hans Schreuer). Zimmer (1896–1973) became Regierungspräsident [president of the district] of Montabaur in 1947. One of the co-founders of the CDU in Rhineland-Westphalia, he became minister of the interior and of social affairs in Rhineland-Westphalia in 1951 and was a member of the Bundestag [the lower house of parliament] between 1957 and 1965. His cautious attempts at helping Schmitt professionally had little success. There are a few letters to Schmitt, falling into the period between 30 October 1927 and 12 August 1953 (RW 18564/67), but no letters from Schmitt in Zimmer's literary estate in the Landesarchiv Koblenz.

103 Anton Betz, *Beiträge zur Ideengeschichte der Staats- und Finanzpolitik der deutschen Zentrumspartei von 1870–1918*, Saarlouis, 1924 (Second examiner: Hans Schreuer). Betz (1893–1984) describes the 'worldview' and development of the Zentrumspartei. He did a more or less cumulative doctorate on the basis of some articles that were already published in 1920–1, and was only in Bonn for a few weeks for his examination. His thesis also discussed 'the literary groundwork' of political Romanticism, and thus touched on Schmitt's interests. Betz stood in Catholic opposition to National Socialism and later became a successful publisher (among others, he founded the *Rheinische Post* in Düsseldorf) and politician. His memoirs do not mention Schmitt's name: Anton Betz, *Zeit und Zeitung: Notizen aus acht Jahrzehnten 1893–1973*, Düsseldorf, 1973, esp. p. 132.

104 Carl Weber, *Die Geschichte der rheinischen Gemeindeordnung vom 23. Juli 1845*, Müllenbach, 1924.

105 Ewald Bergmann, *Die Gesetzgebung im Saarland*, Mönchengladbach, 1924.

106 Felix Schneider, *Die deutschen Kolonien unter den Mandatsbestimmungen des Versailler Friedensvertrags: Eine völkerrechtliche Rechtsdarstellung*, Bonn, 1925 (second examiner: Heinrich Göppert). Schneider, born in 1873, held a doctorate in chemistry and for a long time worked in industry. In his *curriculum vitae*, he thanks Schmitt in detail.

107 Werner Becker, *Die politische Systematik der Staatslehre des Thomas Hobbes*, Cologne, 1928. Schmitt's important examiner's report on Becker's doctoral thesis, as well as further examiner's reports by Schmitt (on Braubach and Gerber) and further material on the Bonn faculty, in Reinhard Mehring (ed.), *'Auf der gefahrenvollen Strasse des öffentlichen Rechts': Briefwechsel Carl Schmitt–Rudolf Smend 1921–1961*, 2nd edn, Berlin, 2012, pp. 164–5.

108 Ernst Forsthoff, *Der Ausnahmezustand der Länder*, Bonn, 1925.

109 Studienrat [teacher's rank] Joseph Schlosser, *Die rechtliche Stellung der Religionsgesellschaften hinsichtlich des Religionsunterrichts nach der Reichsverfassung vom 11. August 1919*, Bonn, 1926 (second examiner: Heimberger). Schlosser, born in 1891, did his doctorate in history in 1914.

According to his *curriculum vitae*, he then volunteered and became an army officer, acting as liaison officer for Turkish divisions, and in 1919, as 'Turk.[ish] chief of military trains', was still involved in battles 'for Odessa and Nikolajew against the Bolshevists', until he ended up in French captivity, and finally began teacher training at the end of 1919. In 1921 he became Studienrat in Barmen (Wuppertal).

110 Fritz Wiese, *Die parlamentsrechtliche Stellung des deutschen Reichspräsidenten*, Bonn, 1926.

111 Heinrich Lenz, *Autorität und Demokratie in der Staatslehre von Hans Kelsen*, Bonn, 1926.

112 Josef Stein, *Die Teilnahme der Gewerkschaften an der Gesetzgebung*, Bonn, 1927.

113 Hermann Reiners, *Bolingbrokes politische Lehren*, Bonn, 1927; Cologne, 1932 (second examiner: Hans Schreuer). Reiners was born in 1900, the son of a priest. His thesis emerged from a seminar presentation. In his *curriculum vitae*, Reiners thanks Schmitt 'for his many stimulating suggestions'. He passed his first state examination in June 1924, followed by his *viva voce* examination on 29 July and the second state examination in January 1928. He then worked as a temporary judge [Hilfsrichter] and from 1930 was a judge at a magistrate's court.

114 Ernst Rudolf Huber, *Die Garantie der kirchlichen Vermögensrechte in der Weimarer Verfassung*, Tübingen, 1927.

115 Carl Georg Hirsch, *Die rechtliche Stellung der internationalen Beamten unter besonderer Berücksichtigung der Funktionäre des Völkerbundsekretariats in Genf*, Bonn, 1928 (contains 'heartfelt thanks' to Schmitt).

116 Werner Weber, *Parlamentarische Unvereinbarkeiten*, Bonn, 1930. Outline of the thesis in a letter by Weber to Schmitt, dated 5 March 1927 (RW 265-17728). Thank you letter from Weber to Schmitt, dated 22 February 1928 (RW 265-17791).

117 Ernst Friesenhahn, *Der Eid auf die Verfassung nach der Verordnung des Reichspräsidenten vom 14. August 1919*, Bonn, 1928. Extended edition: *Der politische Eid*, Bonn, 1928.

118 Otto Kirchheimer, *Zur Staatstheorie des Sozialismus und Bolschewismus*, Bonn, 1928. On Kirchheimer's doctoral studies in Bonn, see Reinhard Mehring, 'Ein typischer Fall jugendlicher Produktivität: Otto Kirchheimer's Bonner Promotionsakte', in Robert von Doyen and Frank Schale (eds), *Das Staatsverständnis von Otto Kirchheimer*, Baden-Baden, 2011, pp. 19–34. On other examiner's reports by Schmitt (on Lenz, Lohmann and Friesenhahn), cf. Reinhard Mehring, *Carl Schmitt zur Einführung*, Hamburg, 2011, pp. 117–21.

119 Wilhelm Daniels (1903–1977), *Der 'historische Begriff' der bürgerlichen Rechtstreitigkeit in der Rechtsprechung des Reichsgerichts*, Bonn, 1928 ('I owe the idea for the present work to Prof. Carl Schmitt, to whom I am also deeply indebted for his kind support.') Daniels later became lord mayor of Bonn.

120 Johann Heinrich Wilckens, *Die Entwicklung des Abrüstungsbegriffs*, Bonn, 1930.

121 Emil Gerber (born 1897), *Der staatstheoretische Begriff der Repräsentation in Deutschland zwischen Wiener Kongress und Märzrevolution*, Neunkirchen, 1929 (completed 'autumn 1926'). Correspondence with Schmitt until 1935 (RW 265-4712/4717). Gerber fell in battle in the Second World War.

122 Paul Adams (1894–1961). After his doctorate, from 1925 onwards, he was a freelance author in Bonn before moving to Berlin and joining the journal *Germania* in 1928 (folder: Adams RW 265-21589). Title of thesis: 'Das Weltbild

in Grabbes "Theodor Herzog von Gothland"', in *Literaturwissenschaftliches Jahrbuch der Görres-Gesellschaft* 2 (1927), pp. 103–35.

123 Ernst Rudolf Huber, 'Carl Schmitt in der Reichskrise der Weimarer Endzeit', in Helmut Quaritsch (ed.), *Complexio Oppositorum: Über Carl Schmitt*, Berlin, 1988, p. 35. Cf. Huber, 'Verfassungswirklichkeit und Verfassungswert im Staatsdenken der Weimarer Zeit', in *Arbeiten zur Rechtsgeschichte: Festschrift für Gustav Klemens Schmelzeisen*, Stuttgart, 1980, pp. 126–41.

124 Kurt Aschenberg was born on 20 June 1893 in München-Gladbach and grew up in Andernach. From the summer term 1912 he studied at various universities before volunteering for military service in August 1914. He quickly became a staff officer. After the war he was at the high command of a Landjägerkorps [military police corps] in Dresden, and left the army only in March 1921 in order again to take up the study of jurisprudence in Bonn. On 16 July he passed his first state examination and became a faculty assistant at Bonn for two years, while also doing his legal training. In 1927 he passed his doctorate with Fritz Schulz. Title of thesis: *Pacht an Renten und Rechtsgütern*, Bonn, 1927. In 1927, Aschenberg established a solicitor's office in Cologne which still exists today.

125 *Curriculum vitae* Friesenhahn of 20 February 1938, on the occasion of his appointment to a personal chair [Extraordinarius] (Universitätsarchiv Bonn, personal file of Friesenhahn, PA 2184). On his time as an assistant, see Friesenhahn's retrospection in his letter to Schmitt of 31 December 1976 (RW 265-4511). After Schmitt had left, the assistant post was extended. In this context, Friesenhahn, on 13 January 1929 (RW 265-4498), asked Schmitt whether he would advise him to write his Habilitation. In the spring of 1932, he completed his Habilitation in Bonn (see the letters to Schmitt of 26 March 1932 and 20 May 1932; RW 265-4505/6). Cf. Stefan Scholte, 'Ernst Friesenhahn: Wissen und Gewissen machen den Juristen', in Mathias Schmoeckel (ed.), *Die Juristen der Universität Bonn im 'Dritten Reich'*, Cologne, 2004, pp. 185–231.

126 In addition, his brother Alfons Adams, *Die Lehre von Verbrechen und Strafe im System Adolf Merkels*, diss., Bonn, 1928.

127 Letter of 8 June 1978 from Huber to Schmitt (RW 265-6290).

128 Karl Lohmann, *Die Delegation der Gesetzgebungsgewalt im Verfassungsstaat: Ein Beitrag insbesondere zum deutschen und französischen Staatsrecht*, Bonn, 1928. Schmitt agreed to be first examiner.

129 Letter of 10 July 1978 from Lohmann to Schmitt (RW 265-8910).

130 See especially the letter of thanks of 10 June 1969 (WBCS, pp. 81–2). Only a few letters from the time before 1957 have survived. Becker later lived as a priest in Leipzig but as a cleric also travelled to the Federal Republic. In 1973 there was a 'reunion' with Schmitt.

131 Werner Becker to Schmitt, 6 September 1923 (the correct date is probably 1924) (WBCS, p. 27).

132 Becker to Schmitt, 11 July 1975 (WBCS, p. 92; RW 265-1152). Becker passed his viva voce examination on 23 July 1925.

133 Becker to Schmitt, 10 October 1978 (WBCS, p. 101; RW 265-1157).

134 Letter of 8 October 1971 from Becker to Piet Tommissen (RW 265-1158).

135 According to Gurian in a letter to Schmitt, dated 22 June 1927 (RW 265-5510).

136 Gurian's formulation in a belated letter of apology to Schmitt, dated 7 June 1929 (RW 265-5511).

137 First under the pseudonym Paul Müller, 'Entscheidung und Ordnung: Zu den Schriften von Carl Schmitt', *Schweizerische Rundschau* 34 (1934–5), pp. 566–7.

582 *Notes to pp. 159–61*

138 Heinz Hürten, *Waldemar Gurian: Ein Zeuge der Krise unserer Welt in der ersten Hälfte des 20. Jahrhunderts*, Mainz, 1972, p. 13. Cf. Reinhard Mehring and Ellen Thümmler (eds), '"Machen Sie mir die Freude und erwähnen Sie die Negerplastik": Waldemar Gurian–Carl Schmitt: Briefwechsel 1924–1932', *Schmittiana*, NF (new series) 1 (2011), pp. 59–111.

139 See Hannah Arendt, 'Waldemar Gurian 1903–1954', in Arendt, *Men in Dark Times*, New York, 1955, pp. 251–62.

140 Waldemar Gurian, *Der katholische Publizist*, Augsburg, 1931, pp. 16f.

141 Waldemar Gurian, 'Die Folgen der Reformation', *Augsburger Postzeitung*, Sunday supplement of 30 January 1925. W. G., 'Hugo Ball', *Kölnische Volkszeitung*, no. 705 (25 September 1927).

142 Waldemar Gurian, 'Gegen die Diktatur der Zeit: Offener Brief an Herrn Prof. Ernst Robert Curtius', *Kölnische Volkszeitung*, Sunday supplement, no. 786 (24 October 1926), p. 1.

143 Curtius's intervention against Gurian is printed in Heinz Hürten, *Waldemar Gurian*, Mainz, 1972, pp. 45f. The documents can also be found among Schmitt's posthumous papers.

144 Gurian, *Der katholische Publizist*, pp. 14f.

145 Waldemar Gurian, *Der Bolschewismus: Einführung in Geschichte und Lehre*, Freiburg, 1931.

146 Walter Gerhart (pseudonym for Waldemar Gurian), *Um des Reiches Zukunft: Nationale Wiedergeburt oder politische Reaktion*, Freiburg, 1932.

147 Waldemar Gurian, *Der Kampf um die Kirche im Dritten Reich*, Lucerne, 1936.

148 Early work on this: Waldemar Gurian, *Bolschewismus als Weltgefahr*, Lucerne, 1935.

149 Barbara Nichtweiß, 'Apokalyptische Verfassungslehren: Carl Schmitt im Horizont der Theologie Erik Petersons', in Bernd Wacker (ed.), *Die eigentlich katholische Verschärfung ... Konfession, Theologie und Politik im Werk Carl Schmitts*, Munich, 1994, pp. 37–64; here: p. 40. For a general account, see Barbara Nichtweiß, *Erik Peterson: Neue Sicht auf Leben und Werk*, Freiburg, 1992, esp. pp. 727ff.

150 Schmitt to Smend, 27 November 1924 (Niedersächsische Staats- und Universitätsbibliothek Göttingen, Cod Ms R. Smend, A 759). Cf. also Schmitt's strong recommendation of Eschweiler in his letter to Smend of 15 January 1925 (Niedersächsische Staats- und Universitätsbibliothek Göttingen, Cod Ms R. Smend, A 759). On Peterson's Protestantism, see Schmitt's remarks in a letter to Salin of 26 August 1925 (RW 579-520).

151 Schmitt to Smend, 15 June 1925 (Niedersächsische Staats- und Universitätsbibliothek Göttingen, Cod Ms R. Smend, A 759).

152 Erik Peterson, 'Was ist Theologie?', in Peterson, *Ausgewählte Schriften*, vol. 1: *Theologische Traktate*, Würzburg, 1994, pp. 3–17, here: p. 8.

153 Ibid., p. 12.

154 Ibid., p. 14.

155 As levelled against Peterson by Feuchtwanger in a letter to Schmitt of 6 May 1926 (CSLF, p. 160).

156 Peterson, diary entry of 7 July 1918, quoted from Nichtweiß, 'Apokalyptische Verfassungslehren' (fn. 149), p. 61.

157 Erik Peterson, 'Briefwechsel mit Adolf von Harnack und ein Epilog', in Peterson, *Theologische Traktate*, pp. 177–94; here: p. 181.

158 Ibid., p. 180.

159 Ibid., p. 190.

160 Peterson, 'Die Kirche' (1929), in Peterson, *Theologische Traktate*, pp. 247–57; here: p. 248.
161 This follows Andreas Koenen, *Der Fall Carl Schmitt: Sein Aufstieg zum 'Kronjuristen des Dritten Reiches'*, Darmstadt, 1995, p. 867.
162 Letter from Blei to Schmitt of 1 July 1926, in *Briefe an Carl Schmitt 1917–1933*, Heidelberg, 1995, pp. 68f. Cf. also, for instance, Franz Blei, 'Schreiben an S. H. Papst Benedikt XV., eine europäische Verfassung betreffend', *Summa*, 2 (1917), pp. 1–7; 'Die Krise der Kirche', *Summa*, 4 (1918), pp. 171–82. On the difference between Schmitt's earlier apology and Blei's critique of the Church, cf. Manfred Dahlheimer, *Carl Schmitt und der deutsche Katholizismus 1888–1936*, Paderborn, 1990, pp. 109f.
163 Franz Blei, *Erzählung eines Lebens*, Leipzig, 1930, pp. 489f.

Chapter 13   From Status Quo to Democratic 'Myth'

1 Carl Schmitt, review of Marie-Anne Cochet, *Essai sur l'emploi du sentiment religieux comme base d'autorité politique*, Paris, 1925, in *Deutsche Literaturzeitung* 46 (1925), pp. 2308–10.
2 Carl Schmitt, review of Paul Kluckhohn, *Persönlichkeit und Gemeinschaft: Studien zur Staatsauffassung der deutschen Romantik*, Halle, 1925, *Deutsche Literaturzeitung* 47 (1926), pp. 1061–3, here: p. 1062.
3 Carl Schmitt, review of Charles Edwyn Vaughan, *Studies in the History of Political Philosophy before and after Rousseau*, London, 1925, in *Deutsche Literaturzeitung* 46 (1925), pp. 2086–90.
4 Carl Schmitt, review of the translation of Leonhard T. Hobhouse, *Die metaphysische Staatstheorie*, Leipzig, 1924, in *Wirtschaftsdienst* 9 (25 July 1924), pp. 986–7. Some sources related to the dispute over Hobhouse in Reinhard Mehring (ed.), *'Auf der gefahrenvollen Straße des öffenlichen Rechts': Briefwechsel Carl Schmitt–Rudolf Smend 1921–1961*, 2nd edn, Berlin, 2012, pp. 155–61.
5 Carl Schmitt, review of Rudolf Kjellén, *Der Staat als Lebensform*, 4th edn, Berlin, 1924, *Wirtschaftsdienst* 10 (1925), p. 1010.
6 Richard Thoma, 'Der Begriff der Demokratie in seinem Verhältnis zum Staatsbegriff', *Hauptprobleme der Soziologie: Erinnerungsgabe für Max Weber*, vol. 2, Munich, 1923, pp. 37–64.
7 Carl Schmitt, review of Leo Wittmayer, *Reichsverfassung und Politik*, Tübingen, 1923, *Schmollers Jahrbuch für Gesetzgebung, Verwaltung und Volkswirtschaft* 47 (1924), pp. 349–51. Cf. also Schmitt, 'Die Weimarer Reichsverfassung', *Literarische Beilage der Frankfurter Zeitung* (2 March 1923), p. 2. Schmitt's reviews of works on state law by Beyerle, Wittmayer, Kjellén, Anschütz and Nipperdey are reprinted in *Schmittiana*, NF (new series) 1 (2011), pp. 8–31.
8 Leo Wittmayer, in *Archiv des öffentlichen Rechts* 47 (1925), pp. 231–3, and 49 (1926), pp. 87–90.
9 Carl Schmitt, review of Gerhard Anschütz, *Die Verfassung des deutschen Reiches vom 11. August 1919: Ein Kommentar für Wissenschaft und Praxis*, 3rd edn, Berlin, 1926, *Juristische Wochenschrift* 55 (1926), pp. 2270–2.
10 The first translation of a work by Schmitt was done by Karl Rick: *The Rhinelands as an Object of International Politics*, Cologne, 1925.
11 Letter of 4 June 1924 from the *Frankfurter Zeitung* to Schmitt (RW 265-11428): 'We were about to tell you that we were happy to print your article on the book by Hobhouse when the letter arrived in which you request the return of the article.'

12 Letter of 8 August 1924 from Kurt Singer to Schmitt (RW 265-15179).
13 'Einige Feststellungen', *Wirtschaftsdienst* 9 (1924), p. 1680. Kurt Singer's replies of 23 September 1924 and 29 November 1924 to Meiner (RW 265-15185/6). On this, a letter, dated 9 September 1924, from Meiner to Schmitt (RW 265-17001).
14 Fritz Stier-Somlo, 'Zum Thema: Hobhouse', *Wirtschaftsdienst* 9 (1924), p. 1832. However, Stier-Somlo's preface to Hobhouse's book allows for Schmitt's interpretation.
15 Schmitt to Smend, 21 May 1925 (Niedersächsische Staats- und Universitätbibliothek Göttingen, Cod Ms Smend, A 759). On the Hobhouse dispute, see also Schmitt's letters to Smend of 25 May 1924, 11 June 1924, 27 June 1924, 10 July 1924 and 21 July 1924 (Niedersächsische Staats- und Universitätbibliothek Göttingen, Cod Ms Smend, A 759).
16 On this question, with overtones associated with connotations owed to the time it was written, see Max Hildebert Boehm, *Lothringerland: Anderthalb Jahrtausende Grenzlandschicksal zwischen Argonnen und Vogesen*, Munich, 1942. Also Raymond Poidevin and Jacques Bariéty, *Frankreich und Deutschland: Die Geschichte ihrer Beziehungen 1815–1975*, Munich, 1982.
17 Max Weber, 'Zwischen zwei Gesetzen', in Weber, *Gesammelte politische Schriften*, Munich, 1921, pp. 60–3. Cf. Weber, 'Deutschland unter den europäischen Weltmächten', ibid., pp. 78–93.
18 Carl Schmitt, 'Völkerrechtliche Probleme im Rheingebiet' (1928), in FP, pp. 255–65.
19 Carl Schmitt, 'Der Status quo und der Friede' (1925), ibid., p. 51.
20 Schmitt received another invitation from Hamacher on 9 December 1924 (RW 265-5682).
21 Schmitt to Smend, 5 June 1925 (Niedersächsische Staats- und Universitätbibliothek Göttingen, Cod Ms Smend, A 759).
22 Cf. Gerd Tellenbach, *Die Entstehung des Deutschen Reiches*, Munich, 1940. Dietmar Willoweit, *Deutsche Verfassungsgeschichte*, Munich, 1990, pp. 31ff.
23 Cf. Henning Ottmann, *Geschichte des politischen Denkens*, vol. 3/1, Stuttgart, 2006, pp. 64ff.
24 Carl Schmitt, legal opinion (dated 22 July 1925) on 'Die Frage der Anwendung der Wahlordnung für das Saargebiet vom 29. IV. 1920 auf die Gemeinde Saarlouis-Roden' [The question of the application of the electoral law for the Saargebiet of 29 April 1920 to the borough of Saarlouis-Roden], in Historisches Archiv of the city of Cologne, Best. 1111, No. 132–137. Schmitt argued that the electoral law of 1920 retained its legal force, despite an administrative act of 1906, and that an ordinance of 1923 was therefore 'legally invalid'.
25 See Schmitt's long and enthusiastic letter of 14 September to Smend (Niedersächsische Staats- und Universitätbibliothek Göttingen, Cod Ms Smend, A 759).
26 An article on the lecture, titled 'Weltfriedensidee' [Ideas of world peace], appeared in the *Kölnische Zeitung* on 2 November 1925 (RW 265-21317).
27 See the faculty's ranked list of candidates sent to the university trustee on 21 November 1925, in Akten der Juristischen Fakultät zu Bonn, Fach 4, no. 1, from 17 February to 2 February 1939 (Archiv der Juristischen Fakultät, no. 42).
28 Ernst Rudolf Huber, 'Aussprache zum Vortrag Tommissens', in Helmut Quaritsch (ed.), *Complexio Oppositorum: Über Carl Schmitt*, Berlin, 1988, pp. 71–100; here: p. 106. Tommissen's presentation, ibid., pp. 71–100. ('After one of the attempts to assassinate Mussolini had failed in 1926, Schmitt, whom I told the news upon visiting his home, said: for him, a successful assassination would have been the greatest disaster conceivable in the realm of politics.')

29 Carl Schmitt, *Unabhängigkeit der Richter, Gleichheit vor dem Gesetz und Gewährleistung des Privateigentums nach der Weimarer Verfassung* [Independence of the judges, equality before the law, and the guarantee of private property according to the Weimar Constitution], Berlin, 1926, p. 27.
30 The first edition was still available from the publisher in 1977. Hence Schmitt had to buy the remaining copies in order to acquire the copyright. (Correspondence in 1977–8 between Hubertus Bung at the publishing house and Schmitt, RW 265-18616).
31 Letter from Eisler to Schmitt, 8 February 1926 (RW 265-3155).
32 Article in *Kölnische Zeitung*, 16 February 1926 (RW 265-21522).
33 Erich Kaufmann, 'Die Gleichheit vor dem Gesetz im Sinne des Art. 109', *Veröffentlichungen der Vereinigung der Deutschen Staatsrechtslehrer* 3 (1927), pp. 3ff. Congress report by Günther Holstein, 'Von den Aufgaben und Zielen heutiger Staatsrechtswissenschaft', *Archiv des öffentlichen Rechts* 50 (1926), pp. 1–40.
34 Article in *Deutsche Reichs-Zeitung* (published in Bonn), 14 May 1926 (RW 265-21317). See the letter by the mayor of Saarlouis of 24 March 1926 (RW 265-2156).
35 Heinrich Rommen, *Die Staatslehre des Franz Suarez*, München-Gladbach, 1926 (RW 265-2156); *Grundrechte, Gesetz und Richter in den Vereinigten Staaten von Nordamerika: Ein Beitrag zur angelsächsisch-nordamerikanischen Staatsrechtskunde*, Münster, 1931; *Der Staat in der katholischen Gedankenwelt*, Paderborn, 1935; *Die ewige Wiederkehr des Naturrechts*, Leipzig, 1936. The preface to the book of 1931 thanks 'Prof. Dr Heckel and privy councillor Prof. Dr Thoma in Bonn for their valuable advice'.
36 Carl Schmitt, 'Der unbekannte Donoso Cortés', *Hochland* 27 (1928), pp. 491–6.
37 Carl Schmitt, 'Das Ausführungsgesetz zu Art. 48 (sog. Diktaturgesetz)', *Kölnische Zeitung*, 30 October 1926 (SGN, p. 38).
38 See Schmitt's examiner's report on Ernst Rudolf Huber's doctoral thesis, dated 28 November 1926 (RW 265-21670). Schmitt recommended the thesis to the publishing house Mohr; on this, see Siebeck's letter to Schmitt of 24 March 1927 (RW 265-15135).
39 Cf. Clemens Hürfeld, 'Aus der Geschichte der Mittelrhein. Verwaltungsakademie', in Ernst Friesenhahn (ed.), *Festschrift zum zehnjährigen Bestehen der Mittelrheinischen Verwaltungsakademie Bonn–Koblenz–Trier*, Bonn, 1935, pp. 17–29. From 1928, Friesenhahn offered repetition classes. (On this, Albert Hensel to Schmitt, 23 November 1928; RW 265-5953). Cf. also *Verwaltungsprobleme der Gegenwart: Festschrift zum zehnjährigen Bestehen der Verwaltungsakademie Berlin 1929*, Mannheim, 1929.

Chapter 14   The Yield of the Bonn Years

1 Letter of 1 January 1927 from Blei to Schmitt, in FBCS, p. 72.
2 Franz Blei, *Erzählung eines Lebens*, Leipzig, 1930.
3 Sigmund Freud, 'Some Character-Types Met with in Psychoanalytic Work' (1916), in *The Standard Edition of the Complete Works of Sigmund Freud*, vol. 14, London, 1957, pp. 309–34; 'The Theme of the Three Caskets' (1913), ibid., vol. 12, London, 1958, pp. 289–302.
4 Detailed account in Christian Tilitzki, 'Carl Schmitt an der Handels-Hochschule Berlin 1928–1933', in *Schmittiana* 4 (1994), pp. 157–202.
5 See 'Faszimus', in the *Badischer Beobachter* of 24 January 1927. 'Über

"Faszismus": Vortrag des Professors Carl Schmitt in der Gesellschaft für geistigen Aufbau', in *Karlsruher Tageblatt* of 28 January 1927 (RW 265-20105).

6   Letter of 19 January 1927 from Bonn to Schmitt (RW 265-1938).
7   Letter of 12 February 1927 from Zehnhoff to Schmitt (RW 265-18486).
8   Letter of 28 February 1927 from Bonn to Schmitt (RW 265-1939).
9   Letter of 1 March 1927 from Bonn to Schmitt (RW 265-1940).
10 Letter of 3 March from Schmitt to Moritz Julius Bonn, in Universitätsarchiv der HUB, PA Carl Schmitt, 159/a III Bl. 11.
11 Letter of 10 March 1927 from Bonn to Schmitt (RW 265-1941).
12 Invitation letter of 25 March 1927 from the director, Simons, and from Dr Wolfers to Schmitt (RW 265-18382). Hendrik de Man and Smend were also approached but did not participate.
13 Letter of 15 November 1927 from Carl Schmitt to Carl Muth, in *Politisches Denken: Jahrbuch 1998*, p. 145.
14 Letter of thanks from Heller to Schmitt, dated 17 April 1927 (RW 265-5872).
15 See the retrospection in Oberheid's birthday letter to Schmitt, dated 8 July 1968 (RW 265-10511).
16 Wilhelm Bleek, *Geschichte der Politikwissenschaft in Deutschland*, Munich, 2001, pp. 198ff., 214.
17 Letter of 19 May 1927 from Bonn to Schmitt (RW 265-1942).
18 Schmitt sent the book to Landsberg when it came out, and Landsberg replied extensively: letter of 25 November 1931 from Landsberg to Schmitt (RW 265-8628).
19 Hermann Heller, 'Politische Demokratie und soziale Homogenität', in *Probleme der Demokratie*, Berlin, 1928, pp. 35–47; here: pp. 37ff.
20 Carl Schmitt, 'Macchiavelli: Zum 22. Juni 1927', in SGN, pp. 102–5. On Macchiavelli's 'paradigm change' and break with the Christian tradition, cf. Henning Ottmann, *Geschichte des politischen Denkens*, vol. 3/1: *Neuzeit*, Stuttgart, 2006, pp. 11ff. Schmitt does not refer to the perspective of the history of metaphysics taken in his *Political Theology*.
21 On the 'Geffrub' [Gesellschaft von Freunden und Förderern der Universität Bonn], the society of friends and supporters of Bonn University, cf. Max Braubach, *Wege und Formen der Studienförderung*, Bonn, 1968, pp. 89ff.
22 Schmitt's carbon copy of a letter (dated 30 January 1933) to the journal *Beamtenbund* (RW 265-12807).
23 Letter of 5 October from Schmitt to the university councillor, privy councillor Demuth, in Universitätsarchiv der HUB, PA Carl Schmitt, 159/a III Bl. 30. Cf. letter of 17 October 1927 from Schmitt to Smend (Niedersächsische Staats- und Universitätbibliothek Göttingen, Cod Ms Smend, A 759).
24 See the letters of 13 September 1927 and 22 October 1927 from the university councillor Demuth to Schmitt (RW 265-8574/8585), and Schmitt's agreement of 22 October 1927, in Universitätsarchiv der HUB, PA Carl Schmitt, 159/a III Bl. 45. On their later political rivalry, cf. Hans Luther, *Vor dem Abgrund 1930–1933: Reichsbankpräsident in Krisenzeiten*, Berlin, 1964, pp. 271–2.
25 Employment contract of 17 October 1927 (including a guaranteed salary of 30,000 Reichsmark) and the certificate of appointment of 26 October 1927, in RW 265-21564.
26 Paul Ludwig Landsberg, *Die Welt des Mittelalters und wir*, Bonn, 1922; *Wesen und Bedeutung der platonischen Akademie*, Bonn, 1923; *Pascals Berufung*, Bonn, 1929; Paul Ludwig Landsberg and Heinrich Lützeler (eds), *Novalis: Religiöse Schriften*, Cologne, 1923. Schmitt's provisional reference for Landsberg, in *Schmittiana*, NF (new series) 2 (2014), pp. 161–8.

27 See letter of 9 August 1927 from Löwenstein to Schmitt, regarding the 'fundamental idea' of Löwenstein's interpretation of Hegel (RW 265-8897). Julius Löwenstein, *Hegel's Staatsidee: Ihr Doppelgesicht und ihr Einfluss im 19. Jahrhundert*, Berlin, 1927.

28 Outline of lecture, RW 20109 II. Published version: 'Der Völkerbund und Europa', FP, pp. 240–8; see also p. 249. Letter of thanks for the 'excellent lecture' from Carl Duisberg, the chairman of 'Geffrub', to Schmitt, dated 31 October 1927 (RW 265-3051).

29 Programme of the event in RW 265-21317.

30 Letter of 3 November 1927 from Schmitt to the vice-chancellor (Universitätsarchiv Bonn, personal file Carl Schmitt, PA 8888).

31 Schmitt's note of 6 November 1927 regarding the letter of 31 October 1927 from Kaufmann to Schmitt (Akten der Juristischen Fakultät Fach 4 Nr. 1, 17 February 1918 to 2 February 1939 – Archiv der Juristischen Fakultät Nr. 42).

32 Letter of 6 December 1927 from Carl Muth to Schmitt, in *Politisches Denken: Jahrbuch 1998*, p. 146.

33 See Karl Eschweiler (ed.), *Der Künstler und der Weise*, Augsburg, 1927. On Maritain's political development, cf. Jan Werner Müller, 'Katholische Entschärfung? Jacques Maritain und die christdemokratischen Fluchtwege aus dem Zeitalter der Extreme', *Idee: Zeitschrift für Ideengeschichte* 2/3 (2008), pp. 40–54.

34 Schmitt to Smend, 28 December 1927 (Niedersächsische Staats- und Universitätbibliothek Göttingen, Cod Ms Smend, A 759).

35 Letter of 23 December 1927 from Carl Schmitt to Carl Muth, in *Politisches Denken: Jahrbuch 1998*, p. 147.

36 Albert Hensel, *Archiv für Sozialwissenschaften und Sozialpolitik* 61 (1929), pp. 181–95.

37 On more recent discussions, cf. Reinhard Mehring (ed.), *Carl Schmitt, Der Begriff des Politischen: Ein kooperativer Kommentar*, Berlin, 2003.

38 This wide framework is adopted in Ernst-Wolfgang Böckenförde, *Schriften zu Staat – Gesellschaft – Kirche*, 3 vols, Freiburg, 1988–90. Schmitt kept a diary on the conceptual history of 'status' (RW 265-21698).

39 Letters of 14 November 1926 and 5 December 1926 from Lederer to Schmitt (RW 265-8663/4). See also Schumpeter to Schmitt, 23 November 1926 (RW 265-14794).

40 Lederer to Schmitt, 7 June 1927 (RW 265-8665).

41 The volume opens with Schmitt's contributions, followed by contributions from H. Heller, M. H. Boehm, E. Michel and F. Berber. After the concept of the political, other topics covered are 'social homogeneity', peoplehood [Volkstum] and democracy, rendering Schmitt's concept of the political more concrete.

42 On the social construction of the 'alien' as the enemy, cf. Herfried Münkler, 'Barbaren und Dämonen: Die Konstruktion des Fremden in imperialen Ordnungen', in Jörg Baberowski, Hartmut Kaelble and Jürgen Schriewer (eds), *Selbstbilder und Fremdbilder: Repräsentation sozialer Ordnung im Wandel*, Frankfurt, 2008, pp. 153–89. Cf. also Udo Tietz, *Die Grenzen des Wir: Eine Theorie der Gemeinschaft*, Frankfurt, 2002.

43 This point was already stressed by Leo Strauss, 'Notes on Carl Schmitt, *The Concept of the Political*', in CP, pp. 97–122.

44 See Volker Gerhardt, 'Politik als Ausnahme: Der Begriff des Politischen als dekontextualisierte Antitheorie', in Mehring (ed.), *Carl Schmitt, Der Begriff des Politischen*, pp. 205–18.

45 Theodor Haecker already remarked critically on this, in *Was ist der Mensch?* (1933), 3rd edn, Leipzig, 1935, pp. 71ff. Cf. also in particular Dolf Sternberger, *Die Politik und der Friede*, Frankfurt, 1986.

46 This is the starting point for Jürgen Habermas's discussion of Schmitt's 'nationalistic' approach and its anti-universalist consequences. See, in particular, Habermas, *The Inclusion of the Other: Studies in Political Theory*, Cambridge, MA, 1998, pp. 134–8, 141–2 and 181. See also his *The Divided West*, Cambridge, 2006, pp. 113–93.

47 Schmitt to Smend, 20 October 1927 (Niedersächsische Staats- und Universitätbibliothek Göttingen, Cod Ms Smend, A 759).

48 Georg Eisler to Schmitt, 25 September 1927 (RW 265-3158). Hermann Hefele to Schmitt, 9 September 1927 (RW 265-5827).

49 Otto Koellreutter, *Integrationslehre und Reichsreform*, Tübingen, 1929, pp. 6ff.; *Deutsches Verfassungsrecht: Ein Grundriss*, 2nd edn, Berlin, 1936, pp. 3f.

50 Cf. Erich Brock, 'Der Begriff des Politischen: Eine Auseinandersetzung mit Carl Schmitt', *Hochland* 29 (1932), pp. 394–404. Cf. Hermann Hefele, 'Zum Problem einer Politik aus katholischem Glauben', *Abendland* (1927), pp. 195–7. Franziskus Stratmann, 'Um eine christliche Außenpolitik', *Der Friedenskämpfer*, no. 4 (1928), pp. 1–7, and no. 6, pp. 1–7.

51 Becker to Schmitt, 1927 (no exact date) (RW 265-1131). See Becker's article 'Nochmals zu Carl Schmitts "Begriff des Politischen"', *Friedenswarte* 5/1 (1929) (the journal's editor was Walter Dirks). Becker sent the article to Schmitt in a letter of 6 September 1928 (RW 265-1136).

52 Ernst Michel, 10 May 1929, in response to Schmitt's having sent him his *Constitutional Theory* (RW 265-9489). Christoph Horn emphasizes that the Christian relativization of the state in St Augustine led to a pragmatic acknowledgement of it; in terms of moral judgment, the state was no longer judged as strictly as before. Christoph Horn, 'Augustinus', in *Hauptwerke des politischen Denkens*, ed. Manfred Brocker, Frankfurt, 2007, pp. 62–77.

53 Letter of 18 December 1928 from Carl Schmitt to Hermann Heller (RW 265-13078).

54 Letter of 22 December 1928 from Schmitt to Heller (RW 265-13079).

55 This critical route, setting out from Schmitt's anti-universalism, is taken by Matthias Kaufmann, *Recht ohne Regel? Die philosophischen Prinzipien in Carl Schmitts Staats- und Rechtslehre*, Freiburg, 1988.

56 Cf. Carl Schmitt, *Staatsgefüge und Zusammenbruch des zweiten Reiches: Der Sieg des Bürgers über den Soldaten*, Hamburg, 1934.

57 Schmitt to Smend, 17 October 1927 (Niedersächsische Staats- und Universitätbibliothek Göttingen, Cod Ms Smend, A 759).

58 Alfred Bertram, in *Wirtschaftsdienst* 35 (31 August 1928), 1449.

59 Franz Blei, in *Die literarische Welt*, no. 24 (1929), p. 4. Schmitt taped Blei's review to the back cover of his personal copy (RW 265-28281).

60 Peltastes (pseudonym of Waldemar Gurian), 'Die Zeit im Buch', in 'Literarische Blätter' of the *Kölnische Volkszeitung*, no. 144 (10 May 1928); Erich Eyck, *Vossische Zeitung*, no. 451 (23 September 1928); Hermann Jahrreiß, *Archiv des öffentlichen Rechts* 53 (1928), pp. 441–59; Otto Hintze, *Historische Zeitschrift* 139 (1929), pp. 562–68; Fritz Hartung, *Zeitschrift für die gesamte Strafrechtswissenschaft* 82 (1929), pp. 225–39; Albert Hensel, *Archiv für Sozialwissenschaften und Sozialpolitik* 61 (1929), pp. 181–95; Otto Koellreutter, *Deutsche Juristen-Zeitung* 34 (1929), col. 451; Karl Lohmann, *Die Schildgenossen* (1929), pp. 433–6; Justus Hashagen, *Schmollers Jahrbuch* 53 (1929), pp. 127–33; Margit Kraft-Fuchs, *Zeitschrift des öffentlichen Rechts*

9 (1930), pp. 511–41; Gottfried Salomon, *Weltwirtschaftliches Archiv* 34 (1930), p. 288; R. Fuchs, *Juristische Wochenschrift* 60 (1931), pp. 1659–64; Karl Larenz, *Blätter für deutsche Philosophie* 5 (1931), pp. 159–62; Eric Voegelin, *Zeitschrift für öffentliches Recht* 11 (1931), pp. 89–109; Reinhold Aris, *Neue Blätter für Sozialismus* 3 (1932), pp. 19–29.

Chapter 15 From 'Ice Floe to Ice Floe'

1 See, for instance, the emphatic reaction by Thomas Mann, 'Deutsche Ansprache: Ein Appell an die Vernunft' (1930), in Mann, *Gesammelte Werke*, vol. 11, Frankfurt, 1974, pp. 870–89; here: pp. 886ff.

2 Ernst Rudolf Huber, *Deutsche Verfassungsgeschichte seit 1789*, vol. 7, Stuttgart, 1984, p. 697.

3 Heinrich Winkler, *Germany: The Long Road West*, vol. 1: *1789–1933*, Oxford, 2006, pp. 441ff.

4 Carl Schmitt, 'Die Einberufung des vertagten Reichstags' [The recall of the adjourned Reichstag], *Kölnische Volkszeitung*, no. 542 (23 October 1930); 'Einberufung und Vertagung des Reichstags nach Art. 24 Reichsverfassung' [Recall and adjournment of the Reichstag according to Art. 24 of the Weimar Constitution], *Deutsche Juristische Zeitung* 35 (1930), col. 1285–9.

5 Huber, *Deutsche Verfassungsgeschichte*, vol. 7, pp. 778ff.

6 Cf. Friedrich Karl Fromme, *Von der Weimarer Verfassung zum Bonner Grundgesetz*, Tübingen, 1960.

7 Cf. Detlef Lehnert, *Verfassungsdemokratie als Bürgergenossenschaft: Politisches Denken, Öffentliches Recht und Geschichtsdeutungen bei Hugo Preuß*, Baden-Baden, 1998; Christoph Schönberger, *Das Parlament im Anstaltsstaat*, Frankfurt, 1997, pp. 367ff.

8 Cf. Wolfgang J. Mommsen, *Max Weber und die deutsche Politik 1890–1920*, 2nd edn, Tübingen, 1974, pp. 380ff.

9 See Winkler's concise account of this: 'Hindenburg, ein deutsches Verhängnis', in Heinrich Winkler, *Auf ewig in Hitlers Schatten?*, 2nd edn, Munich, 2008, pp. 85–92; here: p. 87.

10 See the introduction in Huber, *Deutsche Verfassungsgeschichte*, vol. 7, pp. 736ff.

11 Carl Schmitt, 'Der bürgerliche Rechtsstaat' [The bourgeois Rechtsstaat], SGN, pp. 44–50.

12 Letter of 26 June 1929 from the editor, Hermann Rinn, to Schmitt (RW 265-11372). Rinn introduces himself as a former member of one of Schmitt's seminars in Munich and calls himself 'a diligent reader'.

13 On this, see Schmitt's letter of 20 February 1928 to the university trustee Demuth, and the letter of 13 February 1928 from Georg Eisler to Dr Jacoby, in Universitätsarchiv der HUB, PA Carl Schmitt, 159/a III Bl. 109 and 97.

14 Inquiry, dated 20 October 1930, by Leopold von Wiese on behalf of the *Kölner Vierteljahreshefte für Soziologie* (RW 265-17989).

15 On this, looking back after fifty years, Friesenhahn to Schmitt, 15 March 1978 (RW 265-4513).

16 Carl Schmitt, *Romantisme Politique*, Paris, 1928. This much abbreviated version of the second edition in particular does not contain the passages on Adam Müller, and thus emphasizes the 'European' and philosophical perspective.

17 Salomon-Delatour was the editor of writings by, among others, Saint-Simon, Proudhon and Lorenz von Stein. Schmitt's encounter with him was probably

the reason why he took a closer interest in Lorenz von Stein. There is a magnificent *Vorlesungsverzeichnis* 'Davoser Hochschulkurse Frühjahr 1928' which contains photos and the bibliographies of the participating lecturers; Schmitt's are on p. 59 (in RW 579-671).

18 Outline of the lecture in RW 265-20109.

19 Constanze Glaser's words in her report on the congress, in *Archiv für Rechts- und Wirtschaftsphilosophie* 22 (1928–9), pp. 222–5; here: p. 222. The information on Schmitt's lecture contained in the report suggests that he essentially repeated the one on 'The bourgeois Rechtsstaat'.

20 Schmitt to Smend, 30 April 1928 (Niedersächsische Staats- und Universitätbibliothek Göttingen, Cod Ms Smend, A 759).

21 See Franz Blei, *Männer und Masken*, Berlin, 1930.

22 Stenographic manuscript (RW 265-20928). Schmitt entered into intensive correspondence with Hermann Hefele at the time. Hefele also thought that Muth was too liberal (see his letters to Schmitt, dated 9 September 1927 and 31 October 1927; RW 265-5827/8).

23 Letter of thanks from the editor, Dr Friedrich Fuchs, to Schmitt, dated 9 June 1926 (in *Politisches Denken: Jahrbuch 1998*, p. 159). On 30 October, Schmitt sent the text to Fuchs. At one point, Schmitt apparently wanted the text to appear in *Hochland* rather than the *Festgabe*, because on 17 May (RW 265-11442) Fuchs asked Schmitt to place the text in the *Festgabe*. At that point, the text was not yet in print.

24 Schmitt to Franz Blei, 13 January 1933; quoted from Blei, 'Der Fall Carl Schmitt: Von einem, der ihn kannte', *Der christliche Ständestaat* (25 December 1936), pp. 1217–20; here: p. 1217.

25 Carl Schmitt, '1907 Berlin', in *Schmittiana* 1 (1988), pp. 13–21; here: p. 13.

26 At the time, Schmitt's old acquaintance Wilhelm Hausenstein commented critically on this in his 'München – Sinn und Verhängnis einer Staat', in Hausenstein, *Die Welt um München*, Munich, 1929, pp. 70–104.

27 Ernst Rudolf Huber, *Heer und Staat in der deutschen Geschichte*, Hamburg, 1938, pp. 179ff. Huber wants to demonstrate throughout that the monarchy held on to sovereignty by retaining the power of command. He defends Wilhelminism and the legitimacy of monarchical sovereignty. In his large constitutional history, he later attenuates this point.

28 The proofs still exist (RW 265-21330).

29 Franz Hessel, *Spazieren in Berlin* (1929), Munich, 1968, p. 80.

30 Information on the Handelshochschule based on Frank Zschaler, *Vom Heilig-Geist-Spital zur Wirtschaftswissenschaftlichen Fakultät: 110 Jahre Staatswissenschaftlich-Statistisches Seminar an der vormaligen königlichen Friedrich-Wilhelms-Universität: 90 Jahre Handelshochschule Berlin*, Berlin, 1997, pp. 26f. Cf. also Paul Eltzbacher, *Handels-Hochschule Berlin: Bericht über die Rektoratsperiode Oktober 1913–1916*, Berlin, 1917; *Die Korporation der Kaufmannschaft von Berlin: Festschrift*, Berlin, 1920, pp. 379ff. Detailed information on the student body in *Chronik der Handels-Hochschule Berlin 1926–1930*, Berlin, 1930, pp. 100ff.; *25 Jahre Handels-Hochschule Berlin 1906–1931*, Berlin, 1931.

31 My presentation of the circumstances of Schmitt's appointment and his time at the Handelshochschule follows Christian Tilitzki, 'Carl Schmitt an der Handels-Hochschule Berlin 1928–1933', in *Schmittiana* 4 (1994), pp. 157–202.

32 Ernst Friesenhahn, in his *curriculum vitae* of 20 February 1938, in Universitätsarchiv Bonn, Personalakte Friesenhahn (PA 2184). He is listed

as a lecturer [Lehrbeauftragter] for the year 1930 in the chronicle *25 Jahre Handels-Hochschule Berlin*, Berlin, 1931, p. 53.

33 Werner Weber to Schmitt, 27 July 1929 (RW 265-17729). Letters by Schmitt to Weber in the latter's posthumous papers in the Bundesarchiv Koblenz begin only in 1950.

34 Weber to Schmitt, 7 June 1930 (RW265-17730).

35 Weber to Schmitt, 25 October 1930 (RW265-17731).

36 Werner Weber, 'Parlamentarische Unvereinbarkeiten (Inkompatibilitäten)', *Archiv des öffentlichen Rechts* 19 (1930), pp. 161–254.

37 Cf. Ernst Rudolf Huber, 'Walter Simons: Staatsmann und Richter in Kaiserreich und Republik', in Huber, *Bewahrung und Wandlung*, Berlin, 1975, pp. 152–70. Cf. Tula Simons, *Der Aufbau der Kohlewirtschaft nach dem Kohlewirtschaftsgesetz vom 23. März 1919*, Bonn, 1931.

38 Karl Schilling, *Der Versailler Vertrag und die Abrüstung: Deutschlands militärische Gleichberechtigung*, Berlin, 1933.

39 'Seminarbericht Rechtswissenschaft, Öffentlich-rechtliche Abteilung' [Seminar report for jurisprudence, division: public law], in *Chronik der Handels-Hochschule Berlin 1926–1930*, Berlin, 1930, p. 70. In the summer term 1930, Schmitt lectured on state theory and constitutional theory, in the winter term 1930–1 on state law. We have meticulous notes taken by Heinz Weckes on both (RWN 260-414).

40 On this, see Reinhard Mehring, 'Arthur Liebert: Ein Geschäftsführer des philosophischen Humanismus im Exil', in Gerald Hartung and Kay Schiller (eds), *Weltoffener Humanismus: Philosophie, Philologie und Geschichte in der deutsch-jüdischen Emigration*, transcript, Bielefeld, 2006, pp. 91–109.

41 At least in the winter term 1930–1 and the summer term 1931, Franz Neumann took part in Schmitt's seminar. In the first letter that has been preserved, dated 21 November 1930 (RW 265-10356), he registered for the seminar with a suggestion for a presentation. Schmitt mentions his participation in the summer term 1930 (VRA, p. 168). Most likely, Neumann also attended Schmitt's seminar in the winter term 1931–2, as he sent Schmitt a worked-out manuscript, asking him for his 'unreserved' comments, on 21 April 1932 (RW 265-10357).

42 Schmitt wrote a positive reference for Kirchheimer, dated 14 December 1930 (RW 265-13422), for the Rockefeller Foundation. However, Kirchheimer's application was not successful. See letters of 4 December 1930 and 3 March 1931 from A. W. Fehling to Schmitt (RW 265-11679). Between 1949 and 1961, Schmitt was again in touch with Kirchheimer, until he broke off contacts over his anger at the latter's rejection of George Schwab's doctoral thesis.

43 Wilhelm Haubold (1901–?), *Reichswirtschaftsrat und Reichsreform*, Berlin, 1933. Karl Scheidemann (1903–?), *Die Neutralität des Staates gegenüber der Tagespresse*, Uslar, 1933. Ruth Büttner (1907– after 1954), *Wirtschaftliche Inkompatibilitäten*, Berlin, 1933; examiner's report on the thesis in *Schmittiana* 4 (1994), pp. 201–2. Johanna Kendziora (born in 1903 in Kattowitz), *Der Begriff der politischen Partei im System des politischen Liberalismus*, Bottrop, 1935. On 30 January 1933, despite strong reservations, Schmitt passed a doctoral thesis by Fritz Müller (RW 265-21499).

44 Wolfgang Dietl (1905–?), *Die Organtheorie*, Berlin, 1936. Letter from Dietl to Schmitt (RW 265-2887/8).

45 Friedrich Dorn (1906–?), *Die Rentabilität der deutschen Zellstoffindustrie*, Berlin, 1934. Letters from Dorn to Schmitt (RW 265-3026/36).

46 Wecke to Schmitt, 22 May 1968 (RW 265-17808). On 11 July 1963, he

contacted Schmitt for the first time and wrote that he 'can confirm, as an opponent of National Socialism, that you mostly endeavoured to be objective in your lectures' (RW 265-17806). Doctoral thesis: Hans Wecke, *Die Neuregelung des deutschen Lagerscheinrechts*, Bottrop, 1934.

47 Letter of 10 July from Scheuner to Schmitt (RW 265-12434). Up to 1933, Scheuner, in long letters, commented in detail on Schmitt's Weimar writings (RW 265-12426/49).

48 It is possible that Schmitt got the apartment through his friend from his time in Munich, the author Alice Berend, whose sister Charlotte was married to Corinth.

49 Carl Theodor Dreyer (director), *La Passion de Jeanne d'Arc* (France, 1928), a dramatic silent movie which concentrates exclusively on the last days of Jeanne d'Arc – i.e., on her tragic trial and condemnation.

50 Leibholz to Schmitt, June 1926 (RW 265-8715).

51 Gerhard Leibholz, *Das Wesen der Repräsentation unter besonderer Berücksichtigung des Repräsentativsystems: Ein Beitrag zur allgemeinen Staats- und Verfassungslehre*, Berlin, 1929. A mention of Schmitt's name in the preface is missing in later editions: 'For this task, it was particularly valuable to find in the outstanding exposition by C. Schmitt also a detailed discussion of the problem of representation' (p. 8). Leibholz dated the completion of his work to before the publication of the works by Smend and Schmitt.

52 Inquiry of 20 June 1928 by Eduard Heimann to Schmitt (RW 265-5840). Schmitt wrote a report on two texts by Landshut on 25 June 1928, which were positive, but with some qualifications (copy in a letter of 25 June 1928 to Heimann; RW 265-13075). On Landshut's difficulties with his Habilitation, cf. Rainer Nicolaysen, *Siegfried Landshut: Die Wiederentdeckung der Politik: Eine Biographie*, Frankfurt, 1997, pp. 96ff.

53 Letter of thanks, dated 13 December 1928, from the West German branch of the General Association of Christian Trade Unions to Schmitt (RW 265-4734).

54 See Schmitt's letters to Smend of 10 December 1928 and 8 January 1949 (Niedersächsische Staats- und Universitätbibliothek Göttingen, Cod Ms Smend, A 759). The production in question was the 'London' prodigal son, which in 1928–9 was performed thirty-five times at the Schiller Theater in Berlin alone. The text was published as William Shakespeare, *Der verlorene Sohn*, ed. Ernst Kamnitzer, Hellerau, 1930. In a letter, Schmitt called the play 'a most instructive and important chapter of political theology. It is possible that the review appeared, perhaps in *Germania*, through the mediation of Franz Blei or Paul Adams.

55 Paul Adams, Blei, Eschweiler and, in particular, Koschwenikoff also frequented the house of Thea Sternheim, the wife of the dramatist and writer of short stories Carl Sternheim. In June, Schmitt met the Sternheims. See Thea Sternheim, *Tagebücher 1903–1971*, vol. 2: *1925–1936*, Göttingen, 2002, pp. 236ff.

56 Carl Schmitt, 'Die Auflösung des Enteignungsbegriffs', in VRA, pp. 110–18.

57 Carl Schmitt, 'Gutachten über die Frage, ob die gesetzliche Aufwertungsregelung des vorliegenden "Entwurfes eines Gesetzes über Entschädigung von Betrieben und Arbeitnehmern auf Grund der Einführung des Branntwein-Monopols" im Wege eines einfachen Reichsgesetzes verfassungsrechtlich zulässig ist' [Legal opinion on the question whether the introduction of the legal revaluation regulations in the 'Draft for a law on the compensation of companies and employees in the context of the introduction of a monopoly on the production

of spirit' by way of a simple Reichs law is in agreement with the constitution]. The document is dated 17 February 1929 (in RW 265-21691).

58 Among Schmitt's posthumous papers are a few mildly melancholic letters from Margot von Quednow expressing friendship; they cover the period until 1940 (RW 265-11280/7). Letters of 12 March 1928 (1929?) and of Palm Sunday 1929 contain best wishes for the outcome of the operation and recovery. On a card of 15 August (1929), she also sends her regards to Duška. A letter of 26 August 1931 (RW 265-11284) congratulates her on the birth of their daughter.

59 Theodor Eschenburg, *Also hören Sie mal zu: Geschichte und Geschichten 1904–1933*, Berlin, 1995, pp. 246f.

60 Corina Sombart translated the text into Romanian.

61 The invitation was probably made by Arthur Lieber, a colleague from the Handelshochschule.

62 Inquiry from Heinrich Wimpfheimer to Schmitt, 7 June 1929 (RW 265-18037).

63 Wimpfheimer to Schmitt, 10 June 1929 (RW 265-18038). Later, Wimpfheimer read another legal opinion by Schmitt on the 'Anwendung des Betriebsrätegesetzes auf die Handelsvertretung' [Application of the law on workers' councils to trade missions], about which he was enthusiastic; Wimpfheimer to Schmitt, 17 November 1930 (RW 265-18040).

64 Egmont Zechlin, *Staatsstreichpläne Bismarcks und Wilhelms II: 1890–1894*, Stuttgart, 1929. There is an emphatic thank you to Schmitt in Zechlin's letter to him of 20 July 1929 (RW 265-18458).

65 As early as 1927 Friedrich had requested a review copy of *Dictatorship* from the publisher (Friedrich to Feuchtwanger, 15 October 1927, in Verlagsarchiv D & H, Mappe Schmitt, Diktatur).

66 Büttner was born in 1907 and grew up in Upper Silesia. She registered as a student at the Handelshochschule in 1927 and she passed her Diploma in 1930. She then became a trainee [Hospitantin] and passed her examination as a doctor of economic sciences on 24 February 1933. Information based on the preface and *curriculum vitae* in Ruth Büttner's doctoral thesis, *Wirtschaftliche Inkompatibilitäten*, Berlin, 1933. In the preface, Büttner thanks her first examiner, Schmitt, for 'the wealth of suggestions'.

67 Programme of the talks in RW 265-20107. The presentation was published as Carl Schmitt, 'Die neutralen Größen im heutigen Verfassungsstaat' [The neutral entities in today's constutitional state], in *Politische Wissenschaft*, no. 10: *Probleme der Demokratie*, Berlin, 1931, pp. 48–56. In an afterword (pp. 69–72), Albert Salomon explicitly calls the series a sequel to the series of debating evenings in the summer term of the previous year, where Schmitt had given his talk on 'The Concept of the Political'. This time, Schmitt argued cautiously in favour of depoliticization; he gave 'only a very subtle analysis of possible neutral institutions' (according to Salomon in his afterword, p. 71).

68 Letter of 31 July 1929 from Prince Karl Anton Rohan to Schmitt (RW 265-11423).

69 In 1933 she completed her doctorate with Schmitt, and sometime in 1934 their contact ended. On 28 November 1954, Ruth Büttner, now Studienrätin [title of a secondary school teacher] in Hamburg, wrote him a cheerful letter which began: 'There are many reasons for writing this letter, and many for not writing it' (RW 265-2161). Schmitt replied on 5 December 1954 (RW 265-12851). A reunion in Hamburg was discussed.

70 Typescript and list of participants: RW 265-20039. Friends from the circle

around von Schnitzler in Frankfurt were also among the participants. The lecture in Barcelona 'went well', Schmitt wrote on 16 October to Duška.

71 Letters of 22 October 1929, 26 October 1929, and with no date to Smend (Niedersächsische Staats- und Universitätbibliothek Göttingen, Cod Ms Smend, A 759).

72 Different outlines for the presentation: RW 265-20109 II.

73 On the precarious 'fusion of love and marriage' in Mozart, cf. Dieter Borchmeyer, *Mozart oder die Entdeckung der Liebe*, Frankfurt, 2005.

74 Martin Heidegger, letter of 11 July 1918 to Elfride, in *'Mein liebes Seelchen!' Briefe Martin Heideggers an seine Frau Elfride 1915–1970*, Munich, 2005, pp. 72f. On the topography of Berlin's street prostitution, see David Clay Large, *Berlin*, New York, 2000, pp. 94f., 180.

75 See Franz Blei, *Das Lehrbuch der Liebe und Ehe*, Hellerau, 1928, p. 314; cf. p. 9: 'No act of human love comes about without phantasy, and where it is not love that gives that phantasy its drive and direction, it misleads into madness and despair.' Cf. Blei, *Himmlische und irdische Liebe in Frauengestalten*, Berlin, 1928.

76 Letter of 5 February 1931 from Franz Blei to Schmitt, in *Briefe an Carl Schmitt 1917–1933*, Heidelberg, 1995, p. 70. In a letter of 6 July 1926, Blei laments the loss of his girlfriend, of the 'ornament of the love of a woman', as consequence of his work on *Frauengestalten*.

77 Cf. Henry de Montherlant, *Erbarmen mit den Frauen*, Darmstadt, 1959, pp. 174, 715 [*The Girls*, London, 1969, pp. 242, 257 and passim. I owe the reference to the personal importance this book held for Schmitt to Ernst Hüsmert, who also received an offprint from Schmitt: Joachim Wach, 'Henri de Montherlant: Ein Dichter des heroischen Lebens', *Preußische Jahrbücher*, 209 (1927), pp. 196–200. Cf. also Gustav Steinbömer, 'Don Juans letzte Abenteuer', *Merkur* 13 (1959), pp. 890–3.

78 Hans Kelsen, *Wer soll der Hüter der Verfassung sein?*, Berlin, 1931. On commonalities between Schmitt and Kelsen, see Christoph Schönberger, 'Die Verfassungsgerichtsbarkeit bei Carl Schmitt und Hans Kelsen: Gemeinsamkeiten und Schwachstellen', in Olivier Beaud and Pasquale Pasquino (eds), *Der Weimarer Streit um den Hüter der Verfassung und die Verfassungsgerichtsbarkeit: Kelsen gegen Schmitt*, Paris, 2007, pp. 177–95.

79 Carl Schmitt, 'Der Hüter der Verfassung', *Archiv des öffentlichen Rechts* 55 (1929), pp. 161–237; here: p. 212.

80 Ibid., p. 237.

81 Ibid., p. 233. On the Reichspräsident as a 'symbol of unity', see also Albert Hensel, *Institution, Idee, Symbol*, Königsberg, 1929.

82 His reservations, especially regarding 'dialectical theology', Feuchtwanger explained in 'Grundsätzliches zur Leben-Jesu-Forschung', an introduction to Ditlef Nielsen, *Der geschichtliche Jesus*, Munich, 1928, pp. vii–xxvii.

83 See Ernst Fraenkel, *Deutschland und die westlichen Demokratien*, Stuttgart, 1964.

84 According to Gerhard Ritter, *Europa und die deutsche Frage: Betrachtungen über die geschichtliche Eigenart des deutschen Staatsdenkens*, Munich, 1948. On the negative picture of Rousseau in Germany, see Reinhard Mehring, 'Vordenker der souveränen Diktatur? Das antiliberale Rousseau-Bild und Carl Schmitt', in *Politisches Denken: Jahrbuch 2012*, pp. 129–44.

85 Cf. Gerhard Leibholz, *Die Auflösung der liberalen Demokratie in Deutschland und das autoritäre Staatsbild*, Munich, 1933. Cf. also Leibholz, *Zu den Problemen des faschistischen Verfassungsrechts*, Berlin, 1928.

86 At a seminar of the German Vereinigung für staatswissenschaftliche Fortbildung [Association of Further Education in State Theory] in spring 1931 in Berlin. Report on the seminar in *Deutsche Richterzeitung* 23 (1931), pp. 271–2.

87 As does Jürgen Fijalkowski in his otherwise very useful early book on Schmitt: *Die Wendung zum Führerstaat: Ideologische Komponenten in der politischen Philosophie Carl Schmitts*, Cologne, 1958.

88 See Wolfgang Schieder, 'Carl Schmitt und Italien', *Vierteljahresschrift für Zeitgeschichte* 37 (1989), pp. 1–21; 'Das italienische Experiment: Der Faschismus als Vorbild in der Krise der Weimarer Republik', *Historische Zeitschrift* 262 (1996), pp. 73–125. Cf. also Ilse Staff, *Staatsdenken im Italien des 20. Jahrhunderts: Ein Beitrag zur Carl Schmitt-Rezeption*, Baden-Baden, 1991.

89 Inquiry of 9 February made to Schmitt by Dr Karl Landauer from the editorial office of *Dioskuren* (RW 265-17181).

90 Feuchtwanger in a letter of reference of 13 March 1929 to the German consul in Italy Otto Carl (CSLF, p. 300). Eduard Rosenbaum, as early as 2 December 1924 (RW 265-15181), asked Schmitt for a review of Ludwig Bernhard, *Das System Mussolini*, Berlin, 1924, for *Wirtschaftsdienst*.

91 Cf. Moritz Julius Bonn, 'Schlusswort', in Carl Landauer and Hans Honegger (eds), *Internationaler Faschismus: Beiträge über Wesen und Stand der faschistischen Bewegung und über den Ursprung ihrer leitenden Ideen und Triebkräfte*, Karlsruhe, 1928, pp. 127–150; esp. pp. 142ff. Schmitt also discussed the alternative 'liberal or fascist state' in the seminar. See the letter of 30 December 1932 from the student Ludwig M. Lachmann to Schmitt (RW 265-8601).

92 Waldemar Gurian, *Der Faschismus*, Paderborn, 1930.

93 Hermann Heller, *Europa und der Fascismus*, Berlin, 1929.

94 Gurian, *Der Faschismus*. A careful comprehensive exposition of *Constitutional Theory*, taking the Beckerath review as a point of departure, can be found in Mila Radakovic, 'Carl Schmitt's Verfassungslehre', *Hochland* 26 (1929), pp. 534–41; see esp. p. 541. Schmitt read the piece in manuscript.

95 Wilhelm Neuß, report of 1 May 1947 on Schmitt, in Sammlung Tommissen [Tommissen collection], RW 579-677.

96 Ludwig Feuchtwanger, 'Grundsätzliches zur Forschung über das Alte Testament', *Der Morgen* 5 (1929), pp. 173–85, 264–79, 600–14. Republished in Feuchtwanger, *Auf der Suche nach dem Wesen des Judentums: Beiträge zur Grundlegung der jüdischen Geschichte*, Berlin, 2011, pp. 77–117.

97 Ludwig Feuchtwanger, '"Bibelforschung aus dem jüdischen Geist": Martin Bubers Erneuerung der Bibel aus dem Geist des Judentums', *Der Morgen* 8 (1932), pp. 209–24.

98 Ludwig Feuchtwanger, 'Das Bild Moses Mendelssohns bei seinen Gegern bis zum Tode Hegels' (1929), in Feuchtwanger, *Gesammelte Aufsätze zur jüdischen Geschichte*, ed. Rolf Rieß, Berlin, 2003.

99 Ibid., p. 27.

100 Ibid., p. 35.

101 Ludwig Feuchtwanger, 'Der Streit um den Geist Moses Mendelssohns: Anlässlich seines 150 Todestages 4 January 1936', in *Gesammelte Aufsätze zur jüdischen Geschichte*, p. 52.

102 Ludwig Feuchtwanger, 'Die Töchter Moses Mendelssohns' (1929), in *Gesammelte Aufsätze zur jüdischen Geschichte*, pp. 44–9.

103 Ludwig Feuchtwanger, 'Die Judenfrage' (1930), in *Gesammelte Aufsätze zur jüdischen Geschichte*, p. 113.

104 Early critical remarks on assimilation can be found in *Schmollers Jahrbuch* 36 (1912), pp. 954–7.
105 Ludwig Feuchtwanger, 'Der Streit um den Geist Moses Mendelssohns' (1936), p. 53. A critical exposition of the connection between assimilation and anti-Semitism can also be found in the historical novels of Ludwig's brother Lion Feuchtwanger, beginning with *Jud Süß* (1925) [*Jew Süss: A Historical Romance*, London, 1926].
106 Ludwig Feuchtwanger, 'Die Haltung des kurbayerischen Kanzlers Alois von Kreittmayer in Judensachen' (1930), in *Gesammelte Aufsätze zur jüdischen Geschichte*, p. 84.
107 On the reception history, see most recently Jan-Werner Müller, *A Dangerous Mind: Carl Schmitt in Post-War European Thought*, New Haven, CT, 2003; Rüdiger Voigt (ed.), *Der Staat des Dezisionismus: Carl Schmitt in der internationalen Debatte*, Baden-Baden, 2007.
108 A detailed analysis can be found in Henning Ottmann, '"Das Zeitalter der Neutralisierungen und Entpolitisierungen": Carl Schmitts Theorie der Neuzeit', in Reinhard Mehring (ed.), *Carl Schmitt, Der Begriff des Politischen: Ein kooperativer Kommentar*, Berlin, 2003, pp. 156–69.
109 Eduard Norden, *Die Geburt des Kindes: Geschichte einer religiösen Idee*, Leipzig, 1924.
110 E.g., Hans Bogner, *Die Bildung der politischen Eliten*, Oldenburg, 1932.
111 See Ferdinand Muralt's critical account 'Die "Ring"-Bewegung', *Hochland* 29 (1931), pp. 289–99. Cf. Yugi Ishida, *Jungkonservative in der Weimarer Republik: Der Ring-Kreis 1928–1933*, Frankfurt, 1988.

Chapter 16   Reconstructing the 'Strong' State

1 See Ernst-Wolfgang Böckenförde, *Die verfassungstheoretische Unterscheidung von Staat und Gesellschaft als Bedingung der individuellen Freiheit*, Opladen, 1973; Böckenförde (ed.), *Staat und Gesellschaft*, Darmstadt, 1976.
2 Important excerpts, materials and reviews, and in addition the list of recipients of the brochure, in RW 265-20831. The file also contains supplementary remarks in typescript which distinguish Preuss in positive terms from Friedrich Julius Stahl.
3 Cf. the report in the *Chronik der Handelshochschule Berlin 1926–1930*, Berlin, 1930, p. 28, which may have been written by Schmitt.
4 Including the approval of Theodor Heuss in a letter to Schmitt, dated 20 January 1930 (RW 265-6042).
5 Letter of 1 July 1930 from the mayor of Kreuzberg (Herz) to Schmitt (RW 265-7332). See also the letters of 29 January 1930 and 17 March 1930 (RW 265-7330/32).
6 Schmitt to Broermann on 25 May 1968 (Verlagsarchiv D & H, file: Schmitt, Legalität und Legitimität, reprint).
7 Letter of 15 March 1930 from the publisher Siebeck to Schmitt (RW 265-15137). The older standard work was written by Schmitt's colleague from Bonn Ernst Landsberg: *Geschichte der deutschen Rechtswissenschaft*, vol. 3/2: *19. Jahrhundert bis etwa 1870*, Munich, 1910.
8 Letter of inquiry of 26 August 1933 from the publishers to Schmitt (RW 265-17243). Letter of 5 September from Schmitt to de Gruyter publishing house (RW 265-13688).
9 Erich Kaufmann, *Kritik der neukantischen Rechtsphilosophie: Eine Betrachtung*

über die Beziehung zwischen Philosophie und Rechtswissenschaft, Tübingen, 1921.

10 Legal opinion (in printed form) of 30 January 1930 on the German–Polish agreement regarding damages caused by liquidations (VRA, pp. 124–36).

11 On the organization of precisely this course, see Postrat [councillor of the postal service] Lang, 'Das zentrale Unterrichtswesen bei der deutschen Reichspost einst und jetzt', in *Das Reichspostzentralamt: Ein Erinnerungsbuch*, Berlin, 1929, pp. 103–24, here: pp. 116–17.

12 On this, see the letter of 17 March 1930 from President Franz von Mendelssohn to Schmitt (RW 265-9419. Published as: 'Das Problem der innerpolitischen Neutralität des Staates', in *Mitteilungen der Industrie- und Handelskammer zu Berlin* 28 (1930), pp. 471–7 (VRA, pp. 41–58).

13 Concept for a presentation (RW 265-20109).

14 Carl Schmitt, 'Presse und öffentliche Meinung' [The press and public opinion], in *Schriften der deutschen Gesellschaft für Soziologie* 7 (1930), pp. 56–8.

15 Cf. Eduard Rosenbaum, *Der Vertrag von Versailles: Inhalt und Wirkung*, Leipzig, 1921.

16 Ernst Forsthoff (ed.), *Deutsche Geschichte seit 1918 in Dokumenten* (1935), 2nd edn, Stuttgart, 1938.

17 Carl Schmitt, 'Einberufung und Vertagung des Reichstags nach Art. 24 Reichsverfassung', *Deutsche Juristen-Zeitung* 35 (1930), cols 1285–9.

18 'Beitrag zur Aussprache über das Thema der deutschen Wirtschaftskrise' [Contribution to the discussion of the topic of the economic crisis in Germany], *Mitteilungen des Langnamvereins* 29 (1930), pp. 458–64.

19 Typescript of the legal opinion (RW 265-21521).

20 Report in a Hamburg daily newspaper of 15 November 1930 (RW 265-20105).

21 Carl Schmitt, 'Reichs- und Verwaltungsreform' [Reform of the Reich's constitution and administration], *Deutsche Juristen-Zeitung* 36 (1931), cols 5–11.

22 Carl Schmitt, 'Die Frau im Staat', lecture broadcast by the Deutsche Welle on 6 December 1930. Typescript: RW 265-20100, p. 14. Letter of thanks of 15 December 1930 from M. Hellweg to Schmitt (RW 265-7297). Report in *Germania*, no. 574 (10 December 1930). Cf. also the dissertation of Walther vom Dahl, *Über die Umwandlung der Stellung der Frau im öffentlichen Recht*, Bonn, 1924.

23 Concepts in: RW 265-20109 II.

24 Carl Schmitt, 'Die staatsrechtliche Bedeutung der Notverordnung, insbesondere ihre Rechtsgültigkeit' [On the significance of the emergency decree in terms of state law, especially its legal validity], in *Notverordnung und öffentliche Verwaltung*, Berlin, 1931 (VRA, pp. 235-60).

25 Letter of 8 February 1931 from the faculty to the Federal Ministry for Education (Tommissen RW 579-672).

26 Collected by Schmitt: RW 265-19898.

27 On this protest by the NSDAP, together with the DNVP and the KPD, against a reform of the standing orders, see Ernst Rudolf Huber, *Deutsche Verfassungsgeschichte seit 1789*, vol. 7, Stuttgart, 1984, pp. 813ff.

28 Carl Schmitt, 'Staatsideologie und Staatsrealität in Deutschland und Westeuropa', *Deutsche Richterzeitung* 23 (1931), pp. 271ff.

29 Colin Tobias Eisler, born 1931, later studied at Yale, Oxford and Harvard and became a well-known art historian at New York University.

30 Carl Schmitt, 'Franz Blei', *Frankfurter Zeitung*, no. 218 (22 March 1931), Literaturbeilage [literary supplement], pp. 2–3.

31 By 'Constitutional History', Schmitt is referring to Eugen Rosenstock, *Die*

europäischen Revolutionen: Volkscharaktere und Staatenbildung, Jena, 1931. The historians Hans-Ulrich Wehler and Heinrich August Winkler testify to the great significance of this book in *Ein Buch, das mein Leben verändert hat* [A book that changed my life], ed. Detlef Felken, Munich, 2007, pp. 445ff., 461ff.

32 See Huber, *Deutsche Verfassungsgeschichte*, vol. 7, pp. 852ff.

33 Siebeck to Schmitt, 31 May 1930 (RW 265-15138).

34 Schmitt's personal copy (RW 265-19280), p. 2. Only as late as November 1969 did an identical reprint appear with Duncker & Humblot. Schmitt considered an expanded version with his lecture on Preuß as a 'kind of corollary' (Schmitt to Broermann, 25 May 1968); Verlagsarchiv D & H, file: Schmitt, Legalität und Legitimität, Neudruck).

35 Letter of 30 May 1931 from Schmitt to Feuchtwanger (CSLF, p. 338). Reviews collected by Schmitt (RW 265-19281). An interesting list with names of individuals who received a copy of the book (RW 265-19280).

36 For a more detailed analysis of the culture of liberal parties, see the dissertation by Johanna Kendziora, supervised by Schmitt, *Der Begriff der politischen Partei im System des politischen Liberalismus*, Bottrop, 1935.

37 On this, in more detail, Ernst Rudolf Huber, *Wirtschaftsverwaltungsrecht*, Tübingen, 1932.

38 Max Weber, *Parlament und Regierung im neugeordneten Deutschland*, Munich, 1918.

39 See Manfred Wild (pseudonym of E. R. Huber), 'Der Hüter der Verfassung', *Der Ring*, 4/18 (1931), pp. 417–20.

40 See Carl Schmitt, 'Reichs- und Verfassungsreform', *Deutsche Juristen-Zeitung* 36 (1931), cols 5–11.

41 *Mitteilungen des Langnamvereins* 29 (1930), pp. 458–64; here: p. 464. Also Schmitt, 'Zur politischen Situation in Deutschland', *Der Kunstwart* 34 (1930–1), pp. 253–6; here: p. 256.

42 Carl Schmitt, 'Besprechung von Hans Carl Nipperdey (Hrsg.), *Die Grundrechte und Grundpflichten der Reichsverfassung: Kommentar zum zweiten Teil der Reichsverfassung*, 3 Bde., Berlin (Scriptor Verlag): 1929/30', *Juristische Wochenschrift* 60 (1931), pp. 1675–7.

43 Letter of 3 August 1931 from Thoma to Schmitt (RW 265-16008).

44 See Ernst Rudolf Huber, 'Friedrich Naumanns Weimarer Grundrechts-Entwurf: Versuch eines Modells der Grundwerte gegenwärtiger Daseins', in *Festschrift für Franz Wieacker*, Göttingen, 1978, pp. 384–98.

45 In preparation for this at the time: Hermann Heller, 'Bemerkungen zur staats- und rechtstheoretischen Problematik der Gegenwart', *Archiv des öffentlichen Rechts* 55 (1929), 321–54.

Chapter 17 Within the Journalistic Circles of Weimar's Last Days

1 See Schmitt's letter of 17 July 1925, in which he complained about the Privatdozent Heinz Marr in Frankfurt (RW 265-11391). See Rosenbaum's review in *Wirtschaftsdienst* (26 February 1926).

2 Cf. Hans Kelsen, *Wer soll der Hüter der Verfassung sein?*, Berlin, 1931.

3 Cf. Matthias Maeschke, 'Ernst Rudolf Huber', in Mathias Schmoeckel (ed.), *Die Juristen der Universität Bonn im 'Dritten Reich'*, Cologne, 2004, pp. 368–86.

4 Letter of 23 January 1931 from Schmitt to Huber (BAK, N 1505-198).

5 Letter of 2 May 1931 from Schmitt to Huber (BAK, N 1505-198).

6 *Der Ring*, 4/18 (1931), pp. 328–30.

7 Heinrich Wohlgemuth, *Das Wesen des Politischen in der heutigen neoroman-tischen Staatslehre*, Emmendingen, 1933. In 1933, Wohlgemuth emigrated to the USA and later could not be traced there by his family. Biographical information provided by Prof. Wenzel on 9 May 1953 to Prof. Dr Liermann, who had inquired on Schmitt's behalf. Copy in RW265-8761.

8 For a critique from the perspective of the philosophy of law, see Karl Larenz, 'Carl Schmitts Verfassungslehre', *Blätter für Deutsche Philosophie* 5 (1931), pp. 159–62.

9 Ernst Rudolf Huber, 'Verfassung und Verfassungswirklichkeit bei Carl Schmitt', *Blätter für deutsche Philosophie* 5 (1931), pp. 302ff.; quoted according to the reprint in Huber, *Bewahrung und Wandlung: Studien zur deutschen Staatstheorie und Verfassungsgeschichte*, Berlin, 1975, pp. 18–36; here: p. 23.

10 Ibid., p. 25.

11 Ibid., p. 22.

12 Carl Schmitt, *On the Three Types of Juristic Thought*, Westport, CT, 2004.

13 See the impressive Frieder Günther, *Denken vom Staat her: Die bundesdeutsche Staatsrechtslehre zwischen Dezision und Integration 1949–1970*, Munich, 2004.

14 Huber, 'Verfassung und Verfassungswirklichkeit bei Carl Schmitt', p. 29.

15 Ibid., p. 30.

16 Ibid., pp. 35f.

17 Schmitt to Huber, 15 October 1931 (BAK, N 1505-198).

18 Huber to Schmitt, 20 October 1931 (RW 265-6252).

19 Huber to Schmitt, 22 November 1931 (RW 265-6253).

20 Schmitt to Huber, 25 November 1931 (BAK, N 1505-198).

21 Letter of 18 February 1932 from Schmitt, congratulating Huber (BAK, N 1505-198).

22 Ernst Rudolf Huber, *Wirtschaftsverwaltungsrecht: Institutionen des öffentlichen Arbeits- und Unternehmensrechts*, Tübingen, 1932; *Das Deutsche Reich als Wirtschaftsstaat*, Tübingen, 1931; 'Bedeutungswandel der Grundrechte', *Archiv des öffentlichen Rechts* 59 (1933), pp. 1–98.

23 Schmitt to Huber, 25 November 1931 (BAK, N 1505-198).

24 Ernst Rudolf Huber, *Verfassung*, Hamburg, 1937; *Bau und Gefüge des Reiches*, Hamburg, 1941.

25 Franz Blei to Schmitt, 14 April 1931, in FBCS, p. 76.

26 There are letters dated 14 February 1925 and 13 June 1927 among the posthumous papers. The paper requested an article on the presidential elections in 1925 and also initiated the article on Macchiavelli (RW 265-11448/52). Gurian was a regular contributor at the time.

27 At the beginning of 1932, Hermann Herrigel requested a contribution for a series on 'Was will die antiliberale Jugend?' [What does the antiliberal youth want?'] (letters from Herrigel, dated 22 January 1932 and 29 February 1932: RW 265-11430/31).

28 Letter of 2 July 1926 from the editor, Edgar Steltzner, a public prosecutor, to Schmitt (RW 265-11346).

29 Letter of 8 July 1925 from Schmitt to Prince Rohan (RW 265-13423).

30 There had been repeated requests from the *Neue Rundschau* – e.g., on 16 October 1925 (RW 265-11403).

31 Andreas Koenen, *Der Fall Carl Schmitt: Sein Aufstieg zum 'Kronjuristen des Dritten Reiches'*, Darmstadt, 1995.

32 Cf. Helmuth Kiesel, *Ernst Jünger: Die Biographie*, Berlin, 2007, pp. 323ff. Apart from Jünger's brother Friedrich Georg, other members of his circle were, for instance, Hugo Fischer, Ernst Niekisch, Friedrich Hielscher, Valeriu Marcu,

Franz Schauwecker and Ernst von Salomon. Jünger also socialized with Wilhelm Stapel and Albrecht Erich Günther. Schmitt continued corresponding with Hugo Fischer for some time even after 1945.

33 Cf. Siegfried Lokatis (ed.), 'Wilhelm Stapel und Carl Schmitt: Ein Briefwechsel', in *Schmittiana* 5 (1996), pp. 27–108. Cf. Heinrich Kessler, *Wilhelm Stapel als politischer Publizist: Ein Beitrag zur Geschichte des konservativen Nationalismus zwischen beiden Weltkriegen*, Nürnberg, 1967. Gerhard Günther confirmed Stapel's sympathies for Hitler, which lasted 'into the beginnings of the war', to Schmitt on 25 September 1975 (RW 265-5429). Cf. Wilhelm Stapel, *Der christliche Staatsmann: Eine Theologie des Nationalismus*, Hamburg, 1932; *Sechs Kapitel über Christentum und Nationalsozialismus*, Hamburg, 1931; *Die Kirche Christi und der Staat Hitlers*, Hamburg,1934; *Die literarische Vorherrschaft der Juden in Deutschland 1918 bis 1933*, Hamburg, 1937.

34 Albrecht Erich Günther, 'Der Endkampf zwischen Autorität und Anarchie: Zu Carl Schmitts "Politischer Theologie"', *Deutsches Volkstum* 14 (1931), pp. 11f.; Günther (ed.), *Was wir vom Nationalsozialismus erwarten: Zwanzig Antworten*, Heilbronn, 1932; 'Die politische Seite der Judenfrage', *Europäische Revue* 8 (1932), pp. 489–97; 'Staat, Bewegung, Volk: Zur neuen Schrift Carl Schmitts', *Deutsches Volkstum* 16 (1933), pp. 940–5. On the reception and radicalization of Schmitt's work by young revolutionary circles, see Stefan Breuer, *Carl Schmitt im Kontext: Intellektuellenpolitik in der Weimarer Republik*, Berlin, 2012. On the development of Schmitt's relationship with Jünger, see Reinhard Mehring, 'Don Capisco und sein Soldat: Carl Schmitt und Ernst Jünger', in Stephan Müller-Doohm and Thomas Jung (eds), *Prekäre Freundschaften: Über geistige Nähe und Distanz*, Munich, 2011, pp.173–85.

35 Veit Rosskopf, *Der Titel des lyrischen Gedichts*, dissertation, Tübingen, 1927.

36 This point is stressed correctly in Wolfram Pyta, 'Schmitt's Begriffsbestimmung im politischen Kontext', in Reinhard Mehring (ed.), *Carl Schmitt: Der Begriff des Politischen: Ein kooperativer Kommentar*, Berlin, 2003, pp. 219–35.

37 Letter of 26 March 1931 from Margot von Quednow to Schmitt (RW 265-11284).

38 Thank you letter of 3 January 1932 from Eschweiler to Schmitt (RW 265-3362).

39 Schmitt to the university's board of trustees, 31 January 1931, in Universitätsarchiv der HUB, PA Carl Schmitt 159/a III Bl. 112.

40 Carl Schmitt, 'Wohlerworbene Beamtenrechte und Gehaltskürzungen' [Duly acquired rights of civil servants and salary reductions] (VRA, pp. 174–80).

41 'Eröffnung', in *Verhandlungen der Tagung der Deutschen Staatsrechtslehrer in Halle am 28. und 29. Oktober 1931*, Berlin, 1932. Arnold Köttgen, 'Die achte Tagung der Vereinigung der Deutschen Staatsrechtslehrer', *Archiv des öffentlichen Rechts* 60 (1932), pp. 404–31. The proceedings and Köttgen's report keep discreetly silent about the controversial discussions. On the meeting, cf. Friedrich Grüter (= Forsthoff), 'Krisis des Staatsdenkens', *Deutsches Volkstum* 14 (1931), pp. 169ff.; Michael Stolleis, *Geschichte des öffentlichen Rechts*, vol. 3, pp. 195ff.

42 Carl Schmitt, 'Verfassungsstaat und Staatsnotstand' (typescript: RW 265-20101/21444).

43 Letter of invitation from the Funkstunde [broadcast hour] Berlin, dated 23 October 1931 (RW 265-11433). The radio station asked Schmitt for the written version of his talk. Complete typescript: RW 265-20099. Cf. *Hegel-Feier der Friedrich-Wilhelms-Universität zu Berlin am 14 November 1931*, Berlin, 1932 (with speeches by Spranger, Erich Kaufmann and Reinhold Seeberg).

44 Outline of the speech: RW 265-20109.

45 Karl Lohmann, 'Rezension', *Reichsreform: Mitteilungen zur Erneuerung des Reiches* 3/11 (1931), pp. 226–7.

46 Wilhelm Grewe, 'Der Begriff des Politischen: Politik und Moral', *Die junge Mannschaft* 6 (1931), pp. 2–6.

47 Published under the pseudonym Clemens Lang, 'Die Ideologie des Widerstandes: Bemerkungen zu Carl Schmitts "Begriff des Politischen"', *Deutsches Volkstum* 15 (1932), pp. 732–49. Krauss was in lively correspondence with Schmitt even before 1933 and reviewed several of his works. On 18 May 1932 (RW 265-8229) he sent his text to Schmitt, adding, among other things, a sharp anti-Semitic remark: 'The Jew is the actual enemy. I assume your passage on the metics in the 'Concept of the Political' must be understood in this way.'

48 See the letters of 30 December 1931 (RW265-6159) and 2 May 1932 (265-6160) from Höhn to Schmitt.

49 Schmitt's revised list in Feuchtwanger's letter of 6 November 1931 (CSLF, p. 361–5).

50 Cf. Horst Michael and Karl Lohmann, *Der Reichspräsident ist Obrigkeit! Ein Mahnruf an die evangelische Kirche*, Hamburg, 1932.

51 Eduard Norden, *Die Geburt des Kindes*, Leipzig, 1924, p. 9 [*The Virgin Birth of Christ*, Watford, 1930].

52 Theodor Haecker, *Virgil: Father of the West*, London, 1934 [1931].

53 Eduard Norden, *Die Geburt des Kindes*, pp. 98, 165, 168: 'The story of immaculate conception has moved through the mediation of Graeco-Egyptian gnosis from the pneuma into the gospel.'

54 Ibid., pp. 140ff.

55 Ernst Kantorowicz, *Frederick the Second 1194–1250*, New York, 1937.

56 Stefan George, 'Geheimes Deutschland', in *Das neue Reich, 1928 (Gesamt-Ausgabe*, vol. 9), Düsseldorf, 1964, pp. 59ff. ['The Kingdom Come', in Stefan George, *Poems*, ed. and trans. Carol North Valhope and Ernst Morwitz, New York, 1946]. On the politicization of this Reich from Friedrich Wolters to Claus von Stauffenberg, see Thomas Karlauf, *Stefan George: Die Entdeckung des Charismas*, Munich, 2007, pp. 430ff., 577ff., 611ff.

57 See Henning Ottmann, *Geschichte des politischen Denkens*, vol. 2/2: *Das Mittelalter*, Stuttgart, 2004, pp. 118ff., 169ff.; *Geschichte des politischen Denkens*, vol. 2/1, *Die Römer*, Stuttgart, 2002, pp. 183ff., 337ff.

58 Gottfried Hasenkamp to Schmitt, 5 August 1932 (RW 265-5743). Gottfried Hasenkamp, *Das Spiel vom Antichrist: Mit einem Beitrag über den Ludus de Antichristo, seine Aufführung und Übersetzung*, Münster, 1932. Hasenkamp later (14 November 1949: RW 265-5744) sent Schmitt a copy of the new edition of his translation (Münster, 1949) and remained loosely in contact. For the contemporary discussion, also important were, among others, Alois Dempf, *Sacrum Imperium: Geschichts- und Staatsphilosophie des Mittelalters und der politischen Renaissance*, Munich, 1929. Albrecht Erich Günther, 'Das Spiel vom Antichrist', *Deutsches Volkstum* 11 (1928), pp. 267–73; Günther, 'Der Ludus de Antichristo, ein christlicher Mythos vom Reich und dem deutschen Herrscheramte', *Der fahrende Gesell* 20 (1932), pp. 67–75 (typescript of 1932 in RW 265-20025); Günther, 'Der Ludus de Antichristo, ein christlicher Mythos vom Reich und dem deutschen Herrscheramte', typescript of 1939 (RW 265-20025). Retrospective summary in the commentated edition of Hasenkamp's translation, edited by Gerhard Günther, *Der Antichrist: Der staufische Ludus de Antichristo*, Hamburg, 1970. Detailed comments also in Koenen, *Der Fall Carl Schmitt*, pp. 585ff.

59 These points are stressed in Gerhard Günther's commentary, which can be seen as a late self-criticism of the interpretation of the *Volkstum*.

60 Erik Peterson, 'Kaiser Augustus im Urteil des antiken Christentums', *Hochland* 30 (1933), pp. 289–99.

61 See Felix Grossheutschi, *Carl Schmitt und die Lehre vom Katechon*, Berlin 1996.

62 Eisler to Schmitt, 12 December 1931 (RW 265-3165).

63 The review is reprinted in *Schmittiana* 7 (2001), p. 338, along with the corre spondence of 1931, pp. 333–43.

64 Willy Haas, 'Eine neue politische Lehre', *Die literarische Welt*, no. 21 (20 May 1932) (RW 265-19068, Bl. 12). Further reviews by, among others, Hans Bogner, *Neue Literatur* 33 (1931), p. 495; Otto Hintze, *Historische Zeitschrif* 146 (1932), p. 589; Hans Speier, *Zeitschrift für Sozialforschung* 2 (1932), p. 203 Hans Liemann, *Archiv des öffentlichen Rechts* 23 (1932–3), pp. 353–4.

65 Letter of 18 January 1932 from Friedrich to Schmitt (RW 265-4422).

66 Letter of 15 February 1932 from Friedrich to Schmitt (RW 265-4424).

67 Jupp Schmitt to his brother Carl, 7 December 1931 (RW 265-13832).

68 Letter of 15 December 1931 from Ernst Krieck to Schmitt (RW 265-8447).

69 Ulrich Scheuner to Schmitt, 21 November 1931 (RW 265-12429). Cf. Ulrich Scheuner, 'Das Wesen des Staates und der Begriff des Politischen in der neuerer Staatslehre', in Scheuner, *Staatstheorie und Staatsrecht: Gesammelte Schriften* Berlin, 1978, pp. 45–79.

70 Wilhelm Herschel to Schmitt, 19 April 1932 (RW 265-6016). However, Herschel did not take that point of criticism, one still often made today, to be of great importance.

71 According to Erich Brock, 'Der Begriff des Politischen: Eine Auseinandersetzung mit Carl Schmitt', *Hochland* 29 (1932), pp. 394–404.

72 Leo Strauss, 'Notes on Carl Schmitt, *The Concept of the Political*', in CF pp. 97–122.

73 See the letter and remarks in Heinrich Meier, *Carl Schmitt, Leo Strauss und 'Der Begriff des Politischen': Zu einem Dialog unter Abwesenden*, enlarged edn Stuttgart, 1998, pp. 129ff., and the letters of 29 January 1932 and 11 March 1932 from Dr Fehling of the Berlin office of the Rockefeller Foundation (RW 265-11681/2), now published in *Schmittiana*, NF (new series) 2 (2014) pp. 170–6. At the same time, Schmitt wrote a reference for the (also successful application of Dr Hans Hermann Schüler. Strauss thanked Schmitt in a letter of 13 March 1932, sent some further comments on *The Concept of the Political* on 4 September 1932, and asked him for helpful information on 10 July 1933 The letters from Strauss, unusually for Schmitt, contain no comments added or passages underlined by Schmitt (RW 265-15910/2). The international discussion of Schmitt's relationship to philosophy focuses too much on Leo Strauss. More important than Strauss were, for instance, Eduard Spranger and Eric Voegelin. See my detailed documentation on this: Reinhard Mehring 'Carl Schmitt im Gespräch mit Philosophen: Korrespondenzen bis 1933', in *Schmittiana*, NF (new series) 2 (2014), pp. 110–99.

74 Letter of thanks from Emil Lederer to Schmitt, 24 June 1932 (RW 265-8669).

75 Helmut Kuhn, 'Carl Schmitt: Der Begriff des Politischen', *Kant-Studien* 3 (1933), pp. 190–6. Reprinted as an appendix in Kuhn, *Der Staat: Eine philoso phische Darstellung*, Munich, 1967.

76 On Kuhn's precarious situation in Berlin, see Volker Gerhardt, Reinhard Mehring and Jana Rindert, *Berliner Geist: Eine Geschichte der Berliner Universitätsphilosophie bis 1946*, Berlin, 1999, pp. 281–4. On the tenden

cies within the philosophy of history, see Reinhard Mehring, 'Weimarer Philosophie als Einwand? Von der Existentialismuskritik zur Autorität der Tradition in der bundesdeutschen Nachkriegsphilosophie', in Christoph Gusy (ed.), *Weimars langer Schatten: 'Weimar' als Argument nach 1945*, Baden-Baden, 2003, pp. 176–98.

77 Kuhn, 'Carl Schmitt: Der Begriff des Politischen', p. 191.
78 Ibid., p. 195.
79 Helmut Kuhn, *Sokrates: Ein Versuch über den Ursprung der Metaphysik*, Berlin, 1934.
80 Letter from Helmut Kuhn to Schmitt, 11 April 1933 (RW 265-8546), now published in *Schmittiana*, NF (new series) 2 (2014), pp. 177–8.
81 Notes made by Schmitt in the margin of his offprint of Kuhn's review in *Kant-Studien* (RW 265-22468).
82 Helmut Kuhn, *Der Staat*, Munich, 1967, pp. 447–58.
83 Letter of 22 August 1933 from Heidegger to Schmitt, in Martin Heidegger-Gesamtausgabe, vol. XVI, p. 156. Cf. Reinhard Mehring, 'Martin Heidegger und Carl Schmitt in Berlin', *Merkur* 67 (2013), vol. 764, pp. 73–8. Reinhard Mehring, 'Heidegger und Carl Schmitt. Verschärfer und Neutralisierer des Nationalsozialismus', in Dieter Thomae (ed.), *Heidegger-Handbuch*, 2nd edition, Stuttgart (Metzler): 2013, pp. 352–5.
84 Some newspaper reviews are collected in RW 265-19024 and in RW 265-19068.
85 The article in question is Carl Schmitt, 'Legalität und gleiche Chance politischer Machtgewinnung' [Legality and equal chances for gaining political power], *Deutsches Volkstum* 15 (1932), pp. 557–64. Feuchtwanger may have in mind in particular the contribution by Huber, which followed Schmitt's (*Deutsches Volkstum* 15 (1932), pp. 564–71). Huber, in a discussion of Wilhelm Ziegler, distinguishes the 'German concept of nation' from the French one and, to the advantage of the position of the Reichspräsident, sets the old concept of the Reich in contrast to 'national democratic' thought. Little is problematic about Huber's contribution. The critique of the French concept of a nation was still common after 1945.
86 Otto Kirchheimer and Nathan Leites, 'Bemerkungen zu Carl Schmitt's Legalität und Legitimität', *Archiv für Sozialwissenschaften und Sozialpolitik* 68 (1933), pp. 457–87. See Reinhard Mehring, 'Otto Kirchheimer und der Links-Schmittismus', in Rüdiger Voigt (ed.), *Der Staat des Dezisionismus: Carl Schmitt in der Diskussion*, Baden-Baden, 2007, pp. 60–82.

Chapter 18   Carl Schmitt as an Actor during the Rule by Presidential Decree

1 Wilhelm Stapel to the literary author E. Kolbenheyer, 11 June 1933: 'He is a kind of crown jurist of the Hitler government', in *Schmittiana* 5 (1996), p. 48.
2 Thus, based on detailed knowledge, Carl Hermann Ule, 'Zum Begriff des Kronjuristen', *Deutsches Verwaltungsblatt* 108 (1993), pp. 77–82.
3 See Gabriel Seiberth, *Anwalt des Reiches: Carl Schmitt und der Prozess 'Preußen contra Reich' vor dem Staatsgerichtshof*, Berlin, 2001, pp. 78ff.
4 Letter of 8 April 1929 from Otto Meissner to Schmitt (RW 265-2160). Meissner's memoirs: Otto Meissner, *Staatssekretär unter Ebert, Hindenburg, Hitler*, Hamburg, 1951.
5 Popitz to Schmitt, 21 August 1929 (RW 265-11160).
6 Carl Schmitt, 'Verfassungsrechtliches Gutachten über die Frage, ob der

Reichspräsident befugt ist, auf Grund des Art. 48 Abs. 2 RV finanzgesetzvertretende Verordnungen zu erlassen' (RW 265-18911).

7　Marcks to Schmitt, 11 May 1931 (RW 265-9024). Marcks was a general in the Second World War and died in battle on 19 January 1944 (see Schmitt's notes on this: RW 265-19502 and 19580). Schmitt also got to know the historian Walter Elze through Marcks (Elze to Schmitt, 11 March 1932; RW 265-16692). Schmitt remained in fairly close contact with Elze after 1945.

8　My account follows Wolfram Pyta and Gabriel Seibert, 'Die Staatskrise der Weimarer Republik im Spiegel des Tagebuchs von Carl Schmitt', *Der Staat* 38 (1999), pp. 423–48 and 594–610; here: pp. 429ff. Schmitt's diaries of 1930–4 have in the meantime been published by Wolfgang Schuller, *Carl Schmitt Tagebücher 1930–1934*, Berlin, 2010. See my review in *Göttingische Gelehrte Anzeigen* 263 (2011), pp. 57–72.

9　It appears there was some tension between Rosenbaum and Schmitt at the lecture. Rosenbaum formally retracted his 'objection' in a letter to Schmitt, dated 13 February 1932 (RW 265-11752), and later reacted with ostentatious positivity to *Legality and Legitimacy* (Rosenbaum to Schmitt, 22 September 1932; RW 265-11754).

10　Carl Schmitt, 'Grundsätzliches zur heutigen Notverordnungspraxis', *Reichsverwaltungsblatt und Preußisches Verwaltungsblatt* 53 (27 February 1932), pp. 161–5. The manuscript was requested for the *Reichsverwaltungsblatt* by the president of the Senate, Lindenau, in a letter to Schmitt of 5 February 1932 (RW 265-11472).

11　Letter from Hensel to Schmitt, 14 December 1931 (RW 265-5956).

12　See Schmitt's detailed hand-written outline (RW 265-19230) and the commentary by Maschke, in FP, pp. 376f.

13　Postcard from Eschweiler to Schmitt, sent from Braunsberg, 18 December 1928 (RW 265-3354).

14　This assumption is made with the caveat that it might be proven wrong once the diaries covering the years after 1934 have been transcribed. The possibility of further affairs cannot be ruled out. There were rumours in particular about an affair with Brigitte Frank, the wife of Hans Frank. However, it seems that Schmitt's marriage more or less settled down after Duška's recovery and the birth of their daughter, Anima.

15　Report in the *Rhein-Mainische Volkszeitung*, no. 127 (3 June 1932), p. 2.

16　Andreas Koenen, *Der Fall Carl Schmitt: Sein Aufstieg zum 'Kronjuristen des Dritten Reiches'*, Darmstadt, 1995, pp. 163ff., attaches 'central importance' for the formulation of a 'Reich's theological' basis for an 'authoritarian' constitutional reform to this conference (p. 170).

17　Ulrich Scheuner already realized this in his eleven-page letter to Schmitt on the treatise, dated 4 September 1932 (RW 265-12433).

18　Cf. Vittorio Hösle, 'Carl Schmitt's Kritik an der Selbstaufhebung einer wertneutralen Verfassung', *Deutsche Vierteljahresschrift für Literaturwissenschaft und Geistesgeschichte* 61 (1987), pp. 1–34. Heinrich August Winkler argued, along with Schmitt and Fraenkel, for the 'actual introduction' of a prohibition of negative majorities and a 'mild breach of the constitution' by declaring a national emergency in order to avoid Hitler. See Winkler, *Weimar 1918–1933: Die Geschichte der ersten deutschen Demokratie*, Munich, 1993, pp. 521ff., 577, 608; also *Germany: The Long Road West*, vol. 1: 1789–1933, Oxford, 2006, ch. 7, pp. 339–490.

19　Cf. Lutz Berthold, 'Das konstruktive Mißtrauensvotum und seine Ursprünge in der Weimarer Staatsrechtslehre', *Der Staat* 36 (1997), pp. 81–94.

20 Hans Lietzmann, 'Vater der Verfassungsväter? Carl Schmitt und die Verfassungsgründung in der Bundesrepublik Deutschland', in Klaus Hansen and Hans Lietzmann (eds), *Carl Schmitt und die Liberalismuskritik*, Opladen, 1988, pp. 107–18; Reinhard Mußgenug, 'Carl Schmitts verfassungsrechtliches Werk und sein Fortwirken im Staatsrecht der Bundesrepublik Deutschland', in Helmut Quaritsch (ed.), *Complexio Oppositorum: Über Carl Schmitt*, Berlin, 1988, pp. 517–28; Ulrich K. Preuß, 'Vater der Verfassungsväter? Carl Schmitt's Verfassungslehre und die verfassungspolitische Diskussion der Gegenwart', in *Politisches Denken: Jahrbuch 1993*, pp. 117–33.

21 Letters from Beckerath, dated 13 February 1932, 4 June 1932, 29 June 1932, 24 November 1932 (RW 265-1169/72). Letter of 4 June: 'Whether Kelse has enough greatness of soul is hard to tell. Personally, I do not consider it altogether impossible.'

22 Nipperdey's first inquiry to Schmitt is dated 7 April 1932 (RW 265-10404) and contains a reference to Kelsen's positive attitude.

23 Letter of 17 September from Albert Hensel to Schmitt (RW 265-5958).

24 Personal file Schmitt in the Universitätsarchiv Köln, Zugang 17/5273, Bl. 7.

25 Personal file Schmitt in the Universitätsarchiv Köln, Zugang 17/5273, decision of the board of trustees, 25 July 1932, Bl. 15.

26 Postcard to Huber, 9 July 1932 (BAK, N 1505-198).

27 Count Harry Kessler, 'Tagebücher 1918–1937, Eintrag vom 14.7.1932', *Die Welt*, no. 276 (27 November 1961) (with stenographical remarks by Schmitt in: RW 265-21242). Also in Kessler, *Tagebücher 1918–1937*, ed. Wolfgang Pfeiffer-Belli, Frankfurt, 1961, pp. 676f.

28 Hagen Schulze, *Otto Braun oder Preußens demokratische Sendung: Eine Biographie*, Tübingen, 1977.

29 Heinrich August Winkler, *The Long Road West*, vol. 1: *1789–1933*, Oxford, 2006, p. 454. Cf. also, concisely, Winkler, *Auf ewig in Hitlers Schatten?*, Munich, 2007, pp. 85–92.

30 My account follows Ernst Rudolf Huber, *Deutsche Verfassungsgeschichte seit 1789*, vol. 7, Stuttgart, 1984, pp. 973ff. On the catastrophic effects of Brüning's downfall and on the '*coup d'état* of 20 July 1932', see, in detail, Heinrich August Winkler, *Weimar 1918–1933: Die Geschichte der ersten deutschen Demokratie*, Munich, 1993, pp. 470ff., 498ff. For a short account, Winkler, 'Die abwendbare Katastrophe', in *Auf ewig in Hitlers Schatten?*, pp. 93–104.

31 Bilfinger's term in a letter of 6 August 1932 to Schmitt (RW 265-1364).

32 Letter of 6 August 1932 from Bilfinger to Schmitt (RW 265-1364). Schmitt took sides against Smend.

33 Carl Schmitt, 'Die Verfassungsgemäßheit der Bestellung eines Reichskommissars für das Land Preußen', *Deutsche Juristen-Zeitung* 37 (1932), cols 953–8. An earlier article on the question was 'Ist der Reichskommissar verfassungsmäßig?' [Is the Reich commissar constitutional?], *Deutsche Allgemeine Zeitung* 71 (29 July 1932). Long letter of 1 August from Scheuner to Schmitt in which he expressed his agreement (RW 265-12432).

34 Schmitt, 'Die Verfassungsgemäßheit der Bestellung eines Reichskommissars für das Land Preußen', col. 957.

35 Ibid., p. 958.

36 Carl Schmitt, 'Der Mißbrauch der Legalität' [The abuse of legality], *Tägliche Rundschau*, no. 167 (19 July 1932), p. 2. On the authorship of the editorial note, see Gabriel Seiberth, *Anwalt des Reiches*, Berlin, 2001, p. 94. It is not clear whether the editorial note had been discussed and agreed with Schmitt. Friesenhahn also read Schmitt's understanding of the 'vote of no confidence' as

directed against National Socialism (letter to Schmitt, 24 June 1932; RW 265-4508).

37 Huber, *Deutsche Verfassungsgeschichte*, vol. 7, pp. 1050f.
38 According to Ernst Rudolf Huber's recollections (which are confirmed by letters): 'Carl Schmitt in der Reichskrise der Weimarer Endzeit', in Quaritsch (ed.), *Complexio Oppositorum*, pp. 33–70. See also Huber, *Deutsche Verfassungsgeschichte*, vol. 7, pp. 1076ff.
39 Letter to Schmitt, 28 August 1932 (RW 265-6256). According to a letter by Liebmann to Schmitt, dated 19 September 1932 (RW 265-8754), Schmitt also placed an article by Huber with the *Deutsche Juristen-Zeitung* around that time.
40 Huber, 'Carl Schmitt in der Reichskrise der Weimarer Endzeit', pp. 62ff.
41 Ibid., p. 41.
42 Ibid., p. 57.
43 On this in detail, Winkler, *Weimar 1918–1933*, pp. 521ff.
44 Scheuner to Schmitt, 4 September 1932 (RW 265-12433, sheets 10f.).
45 Article collected by Schmitt: RW 265-19897.
46 Files relating to these discussions in RW 265-18908. Important collection of contemporary press reports in RW 265-19897/8.
47 Huber to Schmitt, 5 October 1932 (RW 265-6257).
48 On this change of strategy and 'retreat' of the Reich, and in general, see Gabriel Seiberth, *Anwalt des Reiches*, Berlin, 2001, pp. 97ff., 165ff.; here: p. 106 ('stranded *coup d'état*').
49 The account and quotations follow Wolfram Pyta and Gabriel Seiberth, 'Die Staatskrise der Weimarer Republik im Spiegel des Tagebuchs von Carl Schmitt', *Der Staat* 38 (1999), pp. 423–48; here: pp. 445ff.
50 *Preußen contra Reich vor dem Staatsgerichtshof*, Berlin, 1933, p. 39. The same qualification, which certainly was also strategically motivated, is made in more detail in Ernst Rudolf Huber, *Reichsgewalt und Staatsgerichtshof*, Oldenburg, 1932, pp. 32ff. Schmitt's defence against the assumption of equal treatment of NSDAP and KPD is worth noting, because all too often Papen and Schleicher are credited, in wholesale fashion, with the motive of wanting to prevent National Socialism, while their various attempts at a rapprochement and integration are happily overlooked. A (not only tactical) preparedness to meet the NSDAP halfway seemed almost unavoidable at the time, given the party's strength. However, on Papen's and Schleicher's inclinations against the NSDAP, see in detail Seiberth, *Anwalt des Reiches*, pp. 124ff.
51 *Preußen contra Reich vor dem Staatsgerichtshof*, p. 40.
52 Ibid., p. 177.
53 Ibid., p. 179.
54 Ibid., p. 181.
55 Ibid., pp. 316f.
56 Ibid., p. 318.
57 Ibid., p. 322.
58 Ibid., p. 468.
59 Huber, *Reichsgewalt und Staatsgerichtshof*, p. 50.
60 *Preußen contra Reich vor dem Staatsgerichtshof*, p. 469.
61 Ibid., p. 469. On the myth of Prussia, see Herfried Münckler, *Die Deutschen und ihre Mythen*, Berlin, 2009, pp. 213ff., 275ff.
62 The account and quotations follow Wolfram Pyta and Gabriel Seiberth, 'Die Staatskrise der Weimarer Republik im Spiegel des Tagebuchs von Carl Schmitt', pp. 445ff.; Seiberth, *Anwalt des Reiches*, pp. 179ff.

63 Theodor Maunz, a lawyer defending Prussia, by contrast, made a positive impression on Schmitt. See Schmitt's letter of 12 September 1934 to Christian Roth (RW 265-13427).

64 Kelsen was trying to find a possible date for their meeting – letters of 7 September 1932 and 14 September 1932 from Kelsen to Schmitt (RW 265-7337/8). 'With best wishes', Kelsen sent his article 'Das Urteil des Staatsgerichtshofs of 25 October 1932', *Die Justiz* 8 (1932), pp. 65–91.

65 According to Huber, *Deutsche Verfassungsgeschichte*, vol. 7, pp. 1129f. See also Carl Schmitt in conversation with Dieter Groh and Klaus Figge, 1971, in Piet Tommissen (ed.), *Over en in zake Carl Schmitt*, Brussels, 1975, pp. 89–109. Critical of the sanctioning of presidential powers is Hinnerk Wißmann, 'Verfassungsrechtsprechung im Übergang: Die Judikatur des StGH zu Notverordnungsrecht und Diktaturgewalt 1925–1932', *Der Staat* 47 (2008), pp. 187–211; esp. pp. 204ff. ('the appointment of Hitler on 30 January 1933 had to be seen almost as a return to a formally even more legitimate type of government').

66 See Nipperdey's letter to Schmitt, dated 11 August 1932 (RW 265-10406).

67 Margot von Quednow to Schmitt, 16 August 1932 (RW 265-11282). See also her letter to Schmitt regarding *Legality and Legitimacy*, dated 23 September 1932 (RW 265-11285).

68 Letter from Kelsen to Schmitt, 7 October 1932, sent from the Hotel Monte Verità (RW 265-7339).

69 Schmitt to the dean, Kelsen, 20 November 1932, in Universitätsarchiv Köln, Fakultätsakten, Zugang 598/204.

70 Letter of 1 November 1932 from Schmitt to a ministerial undersecretary (RW 265-13592).

71 Schmitt to Privy Councillor Eckert, 11 November 1932, in Universitätsarchiv Köln, Zugang 17/5273 Bl. 36.

72 Letter of 15 November 1932 from Kelsen to Schmitt (RW 265-7340). Until 10 December, Kelsen, in his function as dean, wrote Schmitt another three letters regarding the term times (RW 265-7341/7344). There are no further letters from Kelsen from the time after 1933 among Schmitt's posthumous papers. On 11 November, Schmitt informed the Handelshochschule of his acceptance of the offer from Cologne: Universitätsarchiv der HUB, PA Carl Schmitt, 159/a III Bl. 123.

73 See Schmitt's correspondence with Kelsen in December 1932, in Universitätsarchiv Köln, Fakultätsakten, Zugang 598/204.

74 Letter of 17 November 1932 from the university's trustee Demuth to Schmitt (RW 265-8582).

75 Hensel to Schmitt, 21 November 1932 (RW 265-5959).

76 Huber, *Reichsgewalt und Staatsgerichtshof*. The publisher had approached Schmitt first. See the letter from the publisher Gerhard Stalling to Schmitt, dated 26 September 1932 (RW 265-15650). Reviews of Huber's treatise (RW 265-20249).

77 Postcard of 23 November 1932 to Huber (BAK, N 1505-198).

78 Letter of 3 December 1932 from Huber to Schmitt (RW 265-6258).

79 Letter of 15 December 1932 from Bilfinger to Schmitt (RW 265-1376).

80 Carl Schmitt, 'Eine Warnung vor falschen politischen Fragestellungen' [A warning against asking the wrong political questions], *Der Ring* 3/48 (1930), pp. 844–5.

81 Announcement of the event (RW 265-20107). Newspaper report, titled 'Carl Schmitt's Epilog: Nach dem Leipziger Staatsprozess', *Vossische Zeitung*, 11 November 1932 (RW 265-21410).

82 Smend to Schmitt, 11 November 1932 (RW 265-15224).
83 According to Seiberth, *Anwalt des Reiches*, p. 239; cf. pp. 214ff.
84 In a letter by Horst Michael to Schmitt, dated 24 November 1932 (RW 265-18890).
85 Printed letter of invitation from the Reich's chancellor for 26 November (RW 265-18877).
86 The account mostly follows Pyta and Seiberth, 'Die Staatskrise der Weimarer Republik im Spiegel des Tagebuchs von Carl Schmitt', p. 607.
87 Carl Schmitt, 'Die Stellvertretung des Reichspräsidenten' [The deputy of the Reichspräsident], *Deutsche Juristen-Zeitung* 38 (1933), cols 27–31 (VRA, pp. 351–6).
88 Schmitt to a lieutenant-colonel [Oberstleutnant], 11 December 1932 (RW 265-13352).
89 Huber, *Deutsche Verfassungsgeschichte*, vol. 7, pp. 1243ff.
90 As announced in a letter of 31 December 1932 to Huber (BAK, N 1505, 198).
91 Letter of 17 January 1933 from Bracht to Schmitt (RW 265-1976).
92 Rudolf Smend, 'Bürger und Bourgeois im deutschen Strafrecht' (1933), in Smend, *Staatsrechtliche Abhandlungen*, Berlin, 1955, pp. 309–25.
93 According to Lutz Berthold, *Carl Schmitt und der Staatsnotstandsplan am Ende der Weimarer Republik*, Berlin, 1999; Seiberth, *Anwalt des Reiches*, pp. 248ff.
94 After 1933, Ott went to Japan as a diplomat. He kept in loose contact with Schmitt (letters between 1932 and 1951, in RW 265-10741/46).
95 According to, for instance, Winkler, *Weimar 1918–1933*, pp. 550ff.
96 We must take note of the fact that Schmitt, in a conversation in 1972, explicitly called this diary entry a quotation from the 'poet' Erich Marcks (Carl Schmitt in conversation with Dieter Groh and Klaus Figge, 1971, in Tommissen (ed.), *Over en in zake Carl Schmitt*, pp. 89–109; here: p. 102). In that case, Schmitt would have entered the dictum of Marcks into his diary without marking it as a quotation. The fact that this remark is a quotation is rarely considered in the scholarship. But it is unlikely that Schmitt should be tricked by his memory in that matter.
97 Scepticism regarding such a view has already been expressed by Wilhelm Hennis in the discussion of Huber, 'Carl Schmitt in der Reichskrise', in Quaritsch (ed.), *Complexio Oppositorum*, pp. 54ff. The clearest and most subtle discussion of the matter can be found in Seiberth, *Anwalt des Reiches*.

Chapter 19   After 30 January 1933

1 Kaas to Schleicher and Hindenburg: 'not for a national state of emergency [Staatsnotstand] but for a system of rule!', in *Germania* 63/29 (29 January 1933), p. 1. The letter was also reproduced in Koellreutter's *Jahrbuch des öffentlichen Rechts der Gegenwart* 21 (1933–4), pp. 141–2.
2 The full text of the letter can be found in 'Discussion of Ernst Rudolf Huber, Carl Schmitt in der Reichskrise der Weimarer Endzeit', in Helmut Qaritsch (ed.), *Complexio Oppositorum: Über Carl Schmitt*, Berlin, 1988, p. 53. Carl Schmitt's 'Recollections of 30 January 1933', in RW 265-19369. An examiner's report by Schmitt on Fritz Müller's *Die Beschränkung der politischen Rechte des Beamten*, awarding it a 'noch ausreichend' [pass], is also dated 30 January 1933 (RW 265-21499).
3 Letter of 4 February 1933 from Wilhelm Stapel to E. G. Kolbenheyer, in *Schmittiana* 5 (Berlin, 1996), p. 48.

4 Radio talk of 1 February 1933, in Piet Tommissen (ed.), *Over en in zake Carl Schmitt*, Brussels, 1975, pp. 113–19; here: p. 114.
5 Ibid., p. 115.
6 Ibid., p. 117.
7 Johanna Kendziora, *Der Begriff der politischen Partei im System des politischen Liberalismus*, Bottrop, 1935, 'Vorbemerkung' [Preliminary remark].
8 Excerpt from the council minutes, in Universitätsarchiv HUB, PA Carl Schmitt, 159/a III Bl. 129.
9 Friedrich Fuchs, 'Der totale Staat und seine Grenzen', *Hochland* 30 (1933), pp. 558–60.
10 Thomas Marschler (ed.), 'Carl Schmitt: Bund, Staat und Reich: Vortrag in Berlin am 22. Februar 1933', in *Schmittiana*, NF (new series) 2 (2014), pp. 7–41; here: p. 35.
11 Ibid., p. 39.
12 Ibid., p. 40.
13 According to Carl Schmitt himself, in his conversation with Dieter Groh and Klaus Figge, 1971, in Tommissen (ed.), *Over en in zake Carl Schmitt*, pp. 89–109; here: p. 104.
14 Carl Schmitt, 'Das Gesetz zur Behebung der Not von Volk und Reich' [The Act for the Removal of Distress from People and Reich], *Deutsche Juristen-Zeitung* 38 (1933), cols 455–8. See Hans Schneider, *Das Ermächtigungsgesetz vom 24. März 1933: Bericht über das Zustandekommen und die Anwendung des Gesetzes*, Bonn, 1961; Roman Schnur, *Die Ermächtigungsgesetze von Berlin 1933 und Vichy 1940 im Vergleich*, Tübingen, 1993.
15 Schmitt, 'Das Gesetz zur Behebung der Not von Volk und Reich', p. 456.
16 Ibid., p. 457.
17 Ibid., p. 458.
18 Letter of 9 March 1933 from the chairman, Saemisch, to Schmitt (RW 265-11990). Schmitt filled in for Bracht and Frick (acceptance letter dated 14 March 1933). Programme of the conference: RW 265-20107. On the conference and the contemporary discussions about a 'change of perception', see Andreas Koenen, *Der Fall Carl Schmitt: Sein Aufstieg zum 'Kronjuristen des Dritten Reiches'*, Darmstadt, 1995, pp. 241ff.
19 Carl Schmitt, 'Das Staatsnotrecht im modernen Verfassungsleben', *Deutsche Richterzeitung* 25 (1933), pp. 254–5; here: p. 254. The text was published only in the autumn. Schmitt himself authorized the stenographic record of Carl Theodor Brodführer (typescript RW 265-21489). An early detailed report on Schmitt's presentation by George Löning: *Deutsche Juristen-Zeitung* 38 (1933), cols 675–7.
20 Letter of 26 March 1933 from Bracht to Schmitt (RW 265-1978).
21 Draft for a letter from Schmitt to his son Heinz Roth, dated 6 November 1975 (RW 265-13428). The last time Schmitt met Captain Roth was in the summer of 1933 in Cologne. The posthumous papers contain a letter to Christian Roth, dated 12 September 1934 (RW 265-13427).
22 As pointed out by Koenen, *Der Fall Carl Schmitt*, p. 227; cf. pp. 227ff.
23 Letter of 31 March 1933 from Papen to Schmitt (Sammlung Tommissen, RW 579-672). The letter mentions Frick, Popitz, Schmitt and von Papen as members of the commission. However, a letter sent on behalf of the Prussian prime minister [Ministerpräsident] speaks only of the 'provision of a legal opinion'; letter of 12 May 1933 to the state secretary at the Chancellery of the Reich (RW 265-2159).
24 Lion Feuchtwanger, *The Oppermanns*, New York, 2001. Cf. also the documentation

Der gelbe Fleck: Die Ausrottung von 500,000 deutschen Juden [The yellow stain: the extermination of 500,000 German Jews], Paris, 1936, which was initiated by Lion Feuchtwanger.

25 Dante tells the story of Ugolino in his *Divine Comedy*.

26 Carl Schmitt in conversation with Dieter Groh and Klaus Figge, 1971, in Tommissen (ed.), *Over en in zake Carl Schmitt* (1972), pp. 89–109; here: p. 108. See Frank Hertweck and Dimitrios Kisoudis (eds), '*Solange das Imperium da ist': Carl Schmitt im Gespräch mit Klaus Figge und Dieter Groh 1971*, Berlin, 2010.

27 Saul Friedländer, *Nazi Germany and the Jews: The Years of Persecution 1933–1939*, London, 1997, p. 34.

28 Detailed summary in Michael Stolleis, *Geschichte des öffentlichen Rechts*, vol. 3, Munich, 1999, pp. 254ff. (gives further sources). On the situation of the student body, see Matthias Bühnen and Rebecca Schaarschmidt, 'Studierende als Täter und Opfer bei der NS-Machtübernahme an der Berliner Universität', in Rüdiger vom Bruch und Christoph Jahr (eds), *Die Berliner Universität in der NS-Zeit*, Stuttgart, 2005, vol. 2, pp. 143–57.

29 Postcard of 14 April from Huber to Schmitt (RWN 265-375).

30 Werner Weber to Schmitt, 3 May 1933 (RW 265-17732).

31 See the letter of Easter Sunday 1933 from Becker to Schmitt (RW 265-1138). However, Becker stayed in touch with Schmitt by correspondence.

32 Letter of 8 October 1971 from Becker to Tommissen (RW 265-1158).

33 In detail on this, see Koenen, *Der Fall Carl Schmitt*, pp. 263ff., 284ff.

34 See Marcel Albert, *Die Benediktinerabtei Maria Laach und der Nationalsozialismus*, Paderborn, 2004, pp. 37ff.

35 The old Carl Schmitt was very interested in the Spanish tradition of the picaresque novel (Quevedo), not least with reference to National Socialism.

36 In the second interrogation on 11 April 1947, which has recently been published in English by Bendersky, Schmitt's formulations put even more stress on the aspect of curiosity: 'Hiking is the miller's dream. That is in reality the satisfaction in the realization that one is experiencing something new. Like the satisfaction an ethnologist derives when he sees a new tribe of Kaffirs. In this respect I am guilty. Intellectual curiosity is a characteristic of my very essence': *Telos* no. 139 (2007), pp. 39–43; here p. 41.

37 Carl Schmitt in conversation with Dieter Groh und Klaus Figge, 1971, p. 107. In the longer version of the conversation (Hertweck and Kousidis (eds), '*Solange das Imperium da ist*', p. 102), the passage runs slightly differently: and when the tried and tested friend sent a telegraph, 'I simply followed. You ask me about "collaboration with Hitler" – that was collaboration with Hitler, but it is up to you to evaluate and to judge this.' In the conversation, Schmitt only dated – as a precise answer to the question – the beginning of his collaboration (giving 3 April 1933), and then talks simply about his involvement in the formulation of two draft laws (the Reich Governors Law and Prussian Municipal Law) in 1933. He only hinted at his further collaboration with Hans Frank: 'And then this man appeared in Cologne . . . that was the beginning . . . and then that continued' (p. 107).

38 Letter of 6 December 1933 from Heinrich Rommen to Schmitt (RW 265-11729).

39 Letter of recommendation of 26 October 1933 (RW 265-13132) to Jacobi. Jacobi had previously asked Schmitt for his support, on 7 May 1933 (RW 265-6486). The exceptional rules for civil servants and soldiers did not apply to Jacobi, as he had become a civil servant only in 1916 and was not

a volunteer during the Great War. He asked Schmitt to use his influence as a lawyer to bring about equal treatment of Privatdozenten and civil servants. On 16 September 1933 (RW 265-6487) Jacobi sent an ironic reminder: 'While you are creating world history, I have to pester you with my personal matters by asking you to clear up a misunderstanding. But I promise not to return!' Only after this letter, it seems, did Schmitt respond. The correspondence between Schmitt and Jacobi, in *Schmittiana*, NF (new series) 1 (2011), pp. 33–57.

40 Cautious plea for help in a letter from Hensel to Schmitt, dated 28 May 1933 (RW 265-9425).

41 Letter to Giesecke, dated 18 July 1933 (RW 265-13032). However, in his letter Schmitt drew Giesecke's attention in particular to the National Socialist Privatdozent Gustav Adolf Walz, whom Schmitt had just met in Marburg. In the end, Werner Weber became Schmitt's successor in 1935. See Weber's letter of thanks to Schmitt, dated 24 December 1934 (RW 265-17733).

42 The letter is printed in Anna-Maria von Lösch, *Der nackte Geist*, Tübingen, 1999, p. 207. On Kaufmann's dismissal, see ibid., pp. 201ff. Cf. also Helmut Quaritsch, 'Eine sonderbare Beziehung: Carl Schmitt und Erich Kaufmann', in *Bürgersinn und staatliche Macht in Antike und Gegenwart: Festschrift für Wolfgang Schuller*, Konstanz, 2000, pp. 71–87.

43 Friesenhahn retracted his application for party membership on 17 September 1934. Copy of the letter from the NSDAP in Bonn to Schmitt, dated 3 November 1934 (RW 265-10853).

44 General survey in Michael Grüttner and Sven Kinas, 'Die Vertreibung von Wissenschaftlern aus den deutschen Universitäten 1933–1945', *Vierteljahreshefte für Zeitgeschichte* 55 (2007), pp. 123–86.

45 Neuß to Schmitt, 5 July 1933 (Sammlung Tommissen, RW 579-672).

46 Neuß to Schmitt, 11 December 1933 (Sammlung Tommissen, RW 579-672).

47 Weiß to Schmitt, 22 September 1933 (RW 265-17877). There is only one later letter, from 'Frau Konrad Weiß' (dated 14 December 1948 – RW 265-17878), in the posthumous papers at Düsseldorf.

48 Letter of 17 August 1933 from Franz Blei, in FBCS, p. 84.

49 Franz Blei, *Zeitgenössische Bildnisse*, Amsterdam, 1940, pp. 21f. Cf. Franz Blei, 'Der Fall Carl Schmitt: Von einem, der ihn kannte', *Der christliche Ständestaat* (25 December 1936), pp. 1217–20.

50 Ibid., p. 25.

51 Ibid., p. 29.

52 See Alfons Söllner, *Fluchtpunkte: Studien zur politischen Ideengeschichte des 20. Jahrhunderts*, Baden-Baden, 2006.

53 Ludwig Feuchtwanger, 'Die Gestalt des "Verworfenen Juden": Ein Versuch über Mythenbildung' (1933), in Feuchtwanger, *Gesammelte Aufsätze zur jüdischen Geschichte*, ed. Rolf Rieß, Berlin, 2003, pp. 125–32; here: p. 132.

54 See Schmitt's early critical comments in *Schmollers Jahrbuch* 36 (1912), pp. 954–7.

55 This is also the position of Simon Dubnow, *Weltgeschichte des jüdischen Volkes*, vol. 3, Jerusalem, 1938, pp. 557f.

56 Ludwig Feuchtwanger, 'Der Streit um den Geist Moses Mendelssohns' (1936), in *Gesammelte Aufsätze zur jüdischen Geschichte*, p. 53.

57 Ludwig Feuchtwanger, 'Neuere Geschichte: Verwandlungen 1837–1887–1937', ibid., p. 96; cf. p. 49.

58 Ludwig Feuchtwanger, 'Gibt es eine eigenständige "jüdische Kultur"' (1938), ibid., p. 153.

59 Feuchtwanger, 'Neuere Geschichte: Verwandlungen 1837–1887–1937', p. 95; cf. p. 160.
60 Ludwig Feuchtwanger, 'Bibelforschung aus jüdischem Geist: Martin Bubers Erneuerung der Bibel aus dem Geist des Judentums', _Der Morgen_ 8 (1932), pp. 209–24; 'Zu Ehren Martin Bubers: Zu seinem 60. Geburtstag am 8 Februar', _Bayerische Israelitische Gemeindezeitung_ (1 February 1938), pp. 34–5.
61 Feuchtwanger, 'Gibt es eine eigenständige "jüdische Kultur"', p. 163.
62 Ludwig Feuchtwanger, _Der Gang der Juden durch die Weltgeschichte: Erstveröffentlichung eines Manuskripts von 1938_, ed. Reinhard Mehring and Rolf Rieß, Berlin, 2013.
63 Letters can be found ibid., pp. 319ff.
64 Ludwig Feuchtwanger, 'Jüdische Vergangenheit in England und Deutschland: Ein Vergleich und der Versuch einer Interpretation der neuesten jüdischen Geschichte' (1947), in _Gesammelte Aufsätze zur jüdischen Geschichte_, p. 108.
65 See Ludwig Feuchtwanger, 'Zur Geschichtstheorie des jungen Graetz', in Heinrich Graetz, _Die Konstruktion der jüdischen Geschichte: Eine Skizze_, Berlin, 1936, pp. 97–108.
66 Schmitt to Pringsheim, 4 December 1933, in Fritz Pringsheim, 'Die Haltung der Freiburger Studenten in den Jahren 1933–1935', _Die Sammlung_ 15 (1960), pp. 532–8; here: pp. 533–4.
67 Postcard of 11 September 1033 from Berend to Duška (RW 265-1260).
68 Alice Berend, _Die gute alte Zeit: Bürger und Spießbürger im 19. Jahrhundert_, Hamburg, 1962, pp. 249f.
69 My account follows Andreas Mix, 'Hilfe im katholischen Milieu: Das Überleben der Konvertitin Annie Kraus', in Wolfgang Benz (ed.), _Überleben im Dritten Reich: Juden im Untergrund und ihre Helfer_, Munich, 2003, pp. 131–42.
70 Letter of summer 1947 from Annie Kraus to Waldemar Gurian, reproduced in _Frankfurter Allgemeine Zeitung_, no. 166 (20 July 2007), p. 35.
71 Annie Kraus, _Über die Dummheit_, Frankfurt, 1948; rev. edn, _Vom Wesen und Ursprung der Dummheit_, Cologne, 1961.

Chapter 20 Schmitt's Resistible Rise to the Position of 'Crown Jurist'

1 On the destructive telos, see Thomas Mann, _Ein Briefwechsel_, Zurich, 1937; Hermann Rauschning, _Die Revolution des Nihilismus: Kulisse und Wirklichkeit im Dritten Reich_, Zurich, 1938. On the mobilization for war as the final aim, cf. Ludolf Herbst, _Das nationalsozialistische Deutschland 1933–1945: Die Entfesselung der Gewalt: Rassismus und Krieg_, Frankfurt, 1996. On the burden of the unfulfilled myth of the Reich, see Heinrich-August Winkler, _Germany: The Long Road West_, 2 vols, Oxford, 2006–7. On the welfare state as a bounty state, see Frank Bajohr, _Parvenüs und Profiteure: Korruption in der NS-Zeit_, Frankfurt, 2001; Götz Aly, _Hitler's Beneficiaries: Plunder, Racial War, and the Nazi Welfare State_, New York, 2005. On the general social history, see Hans-Ulrich Wehler, _Deutsche Gesellschaftsgeschichte_, vol. 4: _Vom Beginn des Ersten Weltkriegs bis zur Gründung der beiden deutschen Staaten 1914–1949_, Munich, 2003.
2 Carl Schmitt, _Das Reichsstatthaltergesetz_, Berlin, 1933. Cf. Carl Bilfinger, 'Das Reichsstatthaltergesetz', _Archiv des öffentlichen Rechts_ 24 (1933), pp. 161–254. The publisher was very satisfied with Schmitt's booklet; by the end of 1933, 8,000 copies had been sold (Heymanns-Verlag, 20 December 1933: RW 265-16907). As late as 12 February 1935, the publisher wanted a 'revised edition'

(RW 265-16909). Cf. also Ernst Rudolf Huber, 'Das Reichsstatthaltergesetz vom 30.1.1935', *Deutsche Juristen-Zeitung* 40 (1935), cols 257–64; Arnold Köttgen, 'Die Entwicklung des öffentlichen Rechts in Preußen vom 1. Mai 1930 bis zum 1. November 1934', *Jahrbuch des öffentlichen Rechts* 22 (1935), pp. 273–338. Legal texts and material relating to the transition to National Socialism in Fritz Poetzsch-Heffter, Carl-Hermann Ule and Carl Dernedde, 'Vom deutschen Staatsleben (vom 30. Januar bis 31. Dezember 1933)', *Jahrbuch des öffentlichen Rechts* 22 (1935), pp. 1–272. Cf. also the Berlin dissertation (with Schmitt as co-examiner) by Walter Lehder, *Die staatsrechtliche Stellung der Reichsstatthalter*, Greifswald, 1937.

3 Report in *Westdeutscher Beobachter*, no. 143 (20 June 1933).

4 As evinced clearly in Schmitt's letter of 23 January 1933 to Wilhelm Stapel, in *Schmittiana* 5 (1996), p. 47.

5 Carl Schmitt, 'Ein Rundfunkgespräch vom 1. Februar 1933' [A radio talk on 1 February 1933], in Piet Tommissen (ed.), *Over en in zake Carl Schmitt*, Brussels, 1975, pp. 113–19; here: p. 119.

6 Ernst Rudolf Huber, *Reichsgewalt und Staatsgerichtshof*, Oldenburg, 1932, pp. 20ff., 53f.

7 See Thomas Marschler (ed.), 'Carl Schmitt: Bund, Staat und Reich', in *Schmittiana*, NF (new series) 2 (2014), pp. 7–41; here: p. 40.

8 Letter of invitation of 15 October 1933 from H. Keller to Schmitt (RW 265-11399).

9 Carl Schmitt, '1 Jahr deutsche Politik: Rückblick vom 20. Juli 1932: Von Papen über Schleicher zum ersten deutschen Volkskanzler Adolf Hitler' [One year of German politics: retrospection on 20 July 1932: from Papen, via Schleicher, to the first German chancellor of the people Adolf Hitler], *Westdeutscher Beobachter* 9/176 (23 July 1933), p. 1.

10 This point is emphasized by Gerhard Otte, 'Die Rollen von Rechtswissenschaft, Rechtsprechung und Gesetzgebung im Nationalsozialismus', in Käte Meyer-Drawe and Kristin Platt (eds), *Wissenschaft im Einsatz*, Munich, 2007, pp. 128–33.

11 See the letter of 3 May 1933 from the trustee of the university [Universitätskurator] Eckert to Schmitt, in Universitätsarchiv Köln, Fakultätsakten, Zugang 598/204.

12 See Hans Kelsen, 'Autobiographie 1947', in *Hans Kelsens Werke*, vol. 1, Tübingen, 2007, pp. 30–91; here: pp. 79ff. Kelsen writes that he emigrated immediately in mid-April, in order not 'to be sent to a concentration camp'. He does not mention Schmitt. Cf. the letter of 7 April 1933 from the Swedish professor Nils Herlitz to Schmitt, asking him what Kelsen may have to fear (RW 265-6006).

13 Michael Stolleis, *Geschichte des öffentlichen Rechts*, vol. 3, Munich, 1999, p. 283. Cf. Frank Golczewski, *Kölner Universitätslehrer und der Nationalsozialismus*, Cologne, 1988, pp. 114ff., cf. pp. 298ff.

14 Cf. Siegfried Lokatis, *Hanseatische Verlagsanstalt: Politisches Buchmarketing im Dritten Reich*, Frankfurt, 1992.

15 Herbert Marcuse, in *Zeitschrift für Sozialforschung* 3 (1934), pp. 102–3.

16 Hans Bogner, 'Der Begriff des Politischen', *Münchner Neueste Nachrichten* (26 July 1933), in RW 265-19068, Bl. 21. Cf. also Karl Lohmann, in *Berliner Börsenzeitung* (30 July 1933).

17 The presentation copy is among Schmitt's posthumous papers.

18 Heidegger's letter to Schmitt, dated 22 August 1933 (RW 265-5839), can also be found in *Martin Heidegger-Gesamtausgabe*, vol. 16, Frankfurt, 2000, p. 156.

19 Schmitt's formulation in a stenographic note (dated 27 August 1933) for his response in the margin of Heidegger's letter (RW 265-5839).

20 Ernst Bockhoff, *Die Intervention im Völkerrecht*, Würzburg, 1935.

21 After 1945, Karl Pathe did his doctorate in Innsbruck and worked as an advisor [Referent] in the Ministry for Housing [Wohnungsbauministerium].

22 'Neuer Geist in der Kölner Hochschule', *Westdeutscher Beobachter*, no. 127 (1 June 1933). Report in the *Westdeutsche Akademische Rundschau*, no. 10 (1933), p. 6.

23 Carl Schmitt, 'Entwurf zur Ansprache beim "Begrüßungsabend der Juristischen Fachschaft am 31 Mai 1933"' [Draft for the address at the 'Welcome evening of the Juridical Faculty on 31 May 1933'], typescript (RW 265-21321).

24 Carl Schmitt, 'Das gute Recht der deutschen Revolution', *Westdeutscher Beobachter*, no. 108 (12 May 1933), pp. 1–2. Also printed in *Münchener Neueste Nachrichten*, no. 151 (3 June 1933).

25 Carl Schmitt, 'Der Staat des 20. Jahrhunderts', *Westdeutscher Beobachter*, no. 151 (28 June 1933), p. 1.

26 Carl Schmitt, 'Die Bedeutung des neuen Staatsrats' [The significance of the new state council], *Westdeutscher Beobachter*, no. 169 (16 July 1933), p. 1.

27 Carl Schmitt, '1 Jahr deutsche Politik', p. 1.

28 Carl Schmitt, 'Die deutschen Intellektuellen', *Westdeutscher Beobachter* (31 May 1933), p. 1. On the July regulations on denaturalization and expatriation, see the extensive discussion in Dieter Gosewinkel, *Einbürgern und Ausschließen: Die Nationalisierung der Staatsangehörigkeit vom Deutschen Bund bis zur Bundesrepublik Deutschland*, Göttingen, 2001, pp. 369ff.; esp. p. 376. It cannot be ruled out that Schmitt knew about ideas to change the law on citizenship from his cooperation with Wilhelm Frick on the Reich Governors Law. An impressive contemporary analysis of emigration (to France and Russia) can be found in Michael Berg (pseudonym?), 'Die Tragödie der Emigration', *Hochland* 31 (1934), pp. 333–49.

29 Hermann Heller to Schmitt, 17 July 1933 (RW 265-5874). Heller died soon afterwards, on 5 November 1933 in Madrid.

30 Letter of 1 September 1933 to Wilhelm Stapel, in *Schmittiana* 5 (1996), p. 55.

31 The biographical account follows the slightly sensationalist depiction by Dieter Schenk, *Hans Frank: Hitlers Kronjurist und Generalgouverneur*, Frankfurt, 2006. Cf. also Christian Schudnagies, *Hans Frank: Aufstieg und Fall des NS-Juristen und Generalgouverneurs*, Frankfurt, 1988.

32 Philipp Loewenfeld, *Recht und Politik in Bayern zwischen Prinzregentenzeit und Nationalsozialismus: Die Erinnerungen von Philipp Loewenfeld*, ed. Peter Landau and Rolf Rieß, Ebelsbach, 2004, p. 562.

33 See the magisterial work by Lothar Gruchmann, *Justiz im Dritten Reich: Anpassung und Unterwerfung in der Ära Gürtner* (1988), 3rd edn, Munich, 2001.

34 See the letter of 18 December 1934 from Wilhelm Kisch to Schmitt (RW 265-7645). See also Susanne Adlberger, *Wilhelm Kisch: Leben und Werk (1874–1952): Von der Kaiser-Wilhelms-Universität Straßburg bis zur national-sozialistischen Akademie für Deutsches Recht*, Frankfurt, 2007.

35 Charter of the 'Akademie für Deutsches Recht', §2, in *Jahrbuch der Akademie für Deutsches Recht* 1 (1933–4), p. 249. For a detailed study of the academy, see Hans Rainer Pichinot, *Die Akademie für Deutsches Recht: Aufbau und Entwicklung einer öffentlich-rechtlichen Körperschaft des Dritten Reiches*, Kiel, 1981; Hans Hattenhauer, 'Die Akademie für Deutsches Recht (1933–1944)', *Juristische Schulung* 26 (1986), pp. 680–4.

36 See Stefan K. Pinter, *Zwischen Anhängerschaft und Kritik: Der Rechtsphilosoph C. A. Emge im Nationalsozialismus*, Berlin, 1996.

37 See O. Thierack, 'Zehn Jahre Akademie für Deutsches Recht', *Zeitschrift der Akademie für Deutsches Recht* 10 (1943), pp. 121f.

38 Hans Frank, *Im Angesicht des Galgens: Deutung Hitlers und seiner Zeit aufgrund eigener Erkenntnisse und Erlebnisse*, Munich, 1953.

39 Files in Universitätsarchiv Heidelberg (B-7200/1, Lehrstühle der Juristenfakultät; H-II 563/3 Lehrstuhl für öffentliches Recht/Nachfolge Anschütz). Walter Jellinek supported Schmitt's appointment (letters of 24 May and 28 May 1933 to Schmitt, RW 265-6537/8). Correspondence between Schmitt and Jellinek, in *Schmittiana*, NF (new series) 2 (2014).

40 Files of the Juridical Faculty, Nachfolge Anschütz (Universitätsarchiv Heidelberg, H-II 563/3).

41 Nipperdey to the chair of council, Privy Councillor Eckert, 29 May 1933, in Carl Schmitt's personnel file at the Universitätsarchiv Köln, Zugang 17/5273, Bl. 78.

42 Dean Nipperdey to Vice-Chancellor Leupold, 27 July 1933, in Universitätsarchiv Köln, Fakultätsakten, Zugang 598/204.

43 Excerpts in Bayerisches Hauptstaatsarchiv MK 69287 (Akten des Staatsministeriums für Unterricht und Kultus). See Helmut Böhm, *Von der Selbstverwaltung zum Führerprinzip: Die Universität München in den ersten Jahren des Dritten Reiches (1933–1936)*, Berlin, 1995, pp. 454–7.

44 Letter of 14 June 1933 from Fritz van Calker to Schmitt (RW 265-398).

45 Factual report: 'Die staatsrechtlichen Grundlagen des neuen Reiches', *Hamburger Fremdenblatt*, no. 159 (11 June 1933), p. 5 (RW 265-20105).

46 In 1932, Georg Eisler transformed the 'Heinrich Eisler Annoncen-Expedition' into a joint stock company. As early as 5 April 1933, the co-owner Rudolf Sylvester Fastnacht left the company. On 20 May 1933 the company changed its legal form. In June a certain Hans Crampe, as well as the co-owner Ludwig Schilling, joined the board of directors. New Articles of Association followed in October. Eisler's 'initial capital' [Stammeinlage] was now considered as 'fully repaid', and one of the associates, Hartung, took over his share. Together with Crampe, Georg Eisler left the company's board of directors on 13 December 1933. In August 1934, Ludwig Schilling became the company's sole representative. In 1935 it was transformed into an oHG [Offene Handelsgesellschaft = general commercial partnership; in an oHG, each partner has unlimited liability], and in 1936 the Fachverband GMBH [Gesellschaft mit beschränker Haftung = limited liability company] was incorporated. The branches in Hamburg and Berlin (at Friedrichstraße 43) went through the same changes. Upon urgent advice from a former employee, Georg Eisler, with wife and his five children, emigrated via Switzerland and London to New York at the beginning of 1934. His elderly mother, Ida Ernestine, emigrated in 1937. After the end of the war, Schmitt immediately wrote to Eisler in New York. Georg Eisler was later a witness in Germany against the possible denazification of Schmitt.

47 Summary in *Germania*, no. 165 (18 June 1933).

48 Letter of 25 June 1933 from Schmitt to Achelis (RW 265-12766).

49 See the vivid account in Klaus Kempter, 'Ein Rechtsprofessor im Konflikt mit der NS-Rassegesetzgebung: Der Fall Walter Jellinek', *Zeitschrift für Geschichtswissenschaft* 46 (1998), pp. 305–19. In mid-1934, Jellinek was forced into retirement as a 'Volljude' [100 per cent Jewish]. However, he continued to fight for proof of the 'non-Jewish descent' of the Jellineks until 1941. He

considered himself to be a 'Christian German'. Seen in the context of his efforts, it is particularly pertinent that Schmitt gave a lecture in 1936 which was titled 'Walter Jellinek als Jude' [Walter Jellinek as a Jew] (see Andreas Koenen, *Der Fall Carl Schmitt: Sein Aufstieg zum 'Kronjuristen des Dritten Reiches'*, Darmstadt, 1995, p. 696). Hans Frank had done his doctorate with Jellinek. According to Kempter, only Frank's protection saved Jellinek from being deported.

50 Koellreutter to the Hochschulministerium [Ministry for Universities] in Karlsruhe, 19 July 1933 (Universitätsarchiv Heidelberg, Juristische Fakultät, Nachfolge Anschütz, H-II-563/3).

51 Letter of 21 July 1933 from the president of the Upper Regional Court in Düsseldorf to Schmitt (RW 265-21545 Bl. 270).

52 *Westdeutscher Beobachter*, no. 165, 12 July 1933 (RW 265-18895).

53 Letter of 26 July 1933 from Nipperdey to Schmitt (RW 265-10409). Cf. Nipperdey's earlier letter of 29 May 1933 in the wake of the inquiry from Heidelberg (RW 265-10408).

54 The ministerial secretary Müller to Schmitt, 19 July 1933 (RW 265-1121).

55 Frank Hertweck and Dimitrios Kisoudis (eds), *'Solange das Imperium da ist': Carl Schmitt im Gespräch mit Dieter Groh and Klaus Figge 1971*, Berlin, 2010, p. 107.

56 Letter of 22 July 1933 from Schmitt to Ahlmann (RW 265-12767). The University of Cologne continued its efforts to keep Schmitt (letters of 23 June 1933 and 6 July 1933 from the trustee of the university [Universitätskurator]: RW 265-8592/93).

57 Letters of invitation of 17 and 19 June 1933 from the general secretary, Dr Landmesser, to Schmitt (RW 265-7295/6). On Schmitt distancing himself from Papen and on the 'schism' within Catholicism, see Koenen, *Der Fall Carl Schmitt*, pp. 419ff.

58 Report by F. von der Heydte, 'Die Katholiken im neuen Deutschland', *Schönere Zukunft*, no. 47 (20 August 1933), pp. 1131–3. Cf. Marcel Albert, *Die Benediktinerabtei Maria Laach und der Nationalsozialismus*, Paderborn, 2004, pp. 71ff.

59 In a letter of 5 September 1933 he declared his exit from the Görres Society (reply from the society, expressing regret, dated 7 September 1933: RW 265-5060).

60 Report: 'Rechtspflege im neuen Staat: Vorrang der politischen Führung', *Kölnische Volkszeitung* (2 July 1933). Detailed article in *Westdeutscher Beobachter*, no. 154 (1 July 1933).

61 Carl Schmitt, 'Fünf Leitsätze für die Rechtspraxis' [Five guiding principles for legal practice], *Deutsches Recht* 3 (1933), pp. 201–2; here: p. 202.

62 Juridical hermeneutics as an instrument for coordination [Gleichschaltungsinstrument] formed a starting point for the early works of National Socialist jurisprudence. See Bernd Rüthers, *Die unbegrenzte Auslegung*, Tübingen, 1968. Michael Stolleis, *Gemeinwohlformeln im national-sozialistischen Recht*, Berlin, 1974.

63 Report of 4 August from the ministerial secretary Dr Müller to the Bavarian State Ministry (Bayerisches Hauptstaatsarchiv MK 69287).

64 Martin Tielke, *Der stille Bürgerkrieg: Ernst Jünger und Carl Schmitt im Dritten Reich*, Berlin, 2007, pp. 89ff.

65 Letter of 29 August 1933 from Hans Frank to Hermann Göring, enclosed in Frank's letter to Schmitt, dated 29 August 1933 (RW 265-4028/9).

66 Letter of 4 September 1933 from Schmitt to the ministerial secretary Achelis (RW 265-12760). See Koenen, *Der Fall Carl Schmitt*, pp. 449ff.

67 Stuckart to the Juridical Faculty, 7 September 1933 (Niedersächsische Staats- und Universitätsbibliothek Göttingen, Nachlass Rudolf Smend).

68 See Reinhard Mehring, '9. September 1933 im Kaiserhof? Martin Heidegger und Carl Schmitt in Berlin', *Merkur* 67/764 (2013), pp. 73–8.

69 Schmitt to the ministerial secretary Müller on 16 October 1933 (Bayerisches Hauptstaatsarchiv MK 69287).

70 See on this in detail, Anna-Maria Gräfin von Lösch, *Der nackte Geist: Die Juristische Fakultät der Berliner Universität im Umbruch von 1933*, Tübingen, 1999.

71 Letter of 11 September 1933 from Liebmann to Schmitt (RW 265-8758).

72 Invitation card and programme preserved in RW 265-20769.

73 Collection of photographs 'Der Preußische Staatsrat in Potsdam' [The Prussian State Council in Potsdam] from *Illustrierter Beobachter*, no. 39 (1933), pp. 1255–7, in RW 265-20083.

74 Using the critical case of Danzig as an example: Carl Schmitt, 'Die Verfassungsmäßigkeit der Einsetzung von Staatskommissaren' [Is the appointment of state commissars constitutional?], *Danziger Juristen-Zeitung* 13/11 (1934), pp. 113–16. See also Karl Maria Hettlage, *Das preußische vereinfachte Gemeindefinanzgesetz vom 15. Dezember 1933: Kommentar*, Berlin, 1934.

75 See the note in *Deutsche Juristen-Zeitung* 38 (1933), col. 678.

76 See Peter Landau, 'Die deutschen Juristen und der nationalsozialistische deutsche Juristentag in Leipzig 1933', *Zeitschrift für neuere Rechtsgeschichte* 16 (1994), pp. 373–90. Proceedings of the Jurists' Convention (without Schmitt's lecture) in *Deutsche Richterzeitung* 25 (1933), pp. 267–78. Programme for the convention in *Deutsche Juristen-Zeitung* 38 (1933), cols 1267–8. Report on the convention in *Deutsches Recht* 3 (1933), pp. 194–9.

77 Carl Schmitt, 'Der Neubau des Staats- und Verwaltungsrechts', in *Deutscher Juristentag 1933*, Berlin, 1933, pp. 242–52; here: p. 252. From the time of Alexander the Great, the notion of the monarch as the 'living law' (*nomos empsychos*) can be found again and again. See Henning Ottmann, *Geschichte des politischen Denkens*, vol. 1/2: *Die Griechen von Platon bis zum Hellenismus*, Stuttgart, 2001, pp. 269f.

78 Structure of the academy in *Deutsches Recht* 3 (1933), pp. 205–6. Further members of the Führer Council were the Prussian minister of justice Hanns Kerrl, State Secretary Roland Freisler, the Reich minister of justice Gürtner, Reich minister Ernst Röhm, the Prussian minister of finance Popitz, the minister of justice of Saxony Thierack, State Secretary Schlegelberger, the Reichsgeschäftsführer [executive director for the Reich] of the BNSDJ Wilhelm Heubner, SA-Obergruppenführer [senior group leader] Luetgebrune and the general director Wilhelm Ahrendts. Thus, Schmitt also met with prominent NS personalities in the Führer Council.

79 Published in *Mitteilungsblatt der Ortsgruppe Braunsfeld* (4 November 1933).

80 Nipperdey to Schmitt, 28 October 1933, and the letter of invitation of 28 October 1933, in Universitätsarchiv Köln, Fakultätsakten, Zugang 598/204.

81 Short summary in *Jahrbuch der Akademie für deutsches Recht* 1 (1933–4), pp. 63–4. Report on the first conference by State Councillor K. Meyer, 'Die Akademie für deutsches Recht', *Deutsche Juristen-Zeitung* 38 (1933), cols 1528–34.

82 In *Jahrbuch der Akademie für deutsches Recht* 1 (1933–4), pp. 207–11; here: pp. 208, 210.

83 Letter of 3 November 1933 and Schmitt's negative response of 11 November 1933, in Personalakte Carl Schmitt, Universitätsarchiv Köln, Zugang 17/5273, Bl. 72 and 74.

Notes to pp. 306–8

Directive no. 40 of 15 November 1933 (backdated to 1 November) from the Reich commissar for justice Hans Frank (RW 265-20895). See Schmitt's report in *Deutsches Recht* 4 (1934), p. 17.

85 Comprehensive statement of expenses in Schmitt's personnel file in the archive of Humboldt University: PA Carl Schmitt 159/a.

86 Letter of 14 January 1934 from Huber to Schmitt (BAK, N 1505-198).

87 Letter of 10 January 1934 from Huber to Schmitt (RW 265-6263).

88 Schmitt to Huber, 14 December 1933 (BAK, N 1505-198).

89 Hans Schneider, *Der preußische Staatsrat 1817–1918: Ein Beitrag zur Verfassungs- und Rechtsgeschichte Preußens*, Munich, 1952, p. 298; Joachim Lilla, *Der preußische Staatsrat 1921–1933*, Düsseldorf, 2005.

90 According to Carl Schmitt, 'Auf dem Weg zum neuen Reich (Besprechung einer Sammlung von Hans Gerber)' [On the way towards the new Reich (review of a collection of texts by Hans Gerber)], *Deutsche Juristen-Zeitung* 39 (1934), col. 1474.

91 Ernst Niekisch, 'Zum Begriff des Politischen', *Widerstand* 8 (1933), pp. 369–75. Niekisch spoke of his 'headaches' over this text and asked Schmitt whether they could have a conversation about it (letter from Niekisch to Schmitt, 25 September 1933: RW 265-10393). See Ernst Jünger's mitigating letter to Schmitt, dated 13 January 1934 (JS, pp. 22f.). The journal *Widerstand* was prohibited in 1934.

92 Waldemar Gurian (under the pseudonym Paul Müller), 'Entscheidung und Ordnung: Zu den Schriften von Carl Schmitt', *Schweizerische Rundschau* 34 (1934), pp. 566–76.

93 Letter of 6 December 1933 from Löwith to Leo Strauss, in Strauss, *Gesammelte Schriften*, vol. 3, Stuttgart, 2001, p. 641. In an earlier letter to Strauss (12 July 1933), Löwith told him that Werner Becker had been to his seminar and asked how Strauss was (ibid., p. 630; cf. p. 633). On 15 December 1933, Becker wrote extensively to Schmitt regarding Strauss's critique (WBCS, pp. 54f.). Cf. Karl Löwith (under the pseudonym Hugo Fiala), 'Politischer Dezisionismus', *Internationale Zeitschrift für Theorie des Rechts* 9 (1935), pp. 101–23. 'Well roared, Löwith!' [a pun on the German idiom 'Gut gebrüllt, Löwe!' = 'Well roared, lion!', which refers to a forceful, but appropriate, statement], Schmitt later noted in his personal copy (RW 265-28369). On the use of the criticism of Romanticism also against Schmitt, see Johannes Kirschweng, 'Der Romantiker Carl Schmitt', *Rhein-Mainische Volkszeitung*, no. 16 (21 January 1926). Schmitt would later indirectly comment on Löwith's interpretation, calling him someone who was 'initiated' into intellectual history but who, as far as Donoso Cortés was concerned, had missed the 'core of his [Cortés's] spiritual existence' (DC, p. 99).

94 Letter of 10 August 1933 from Huber to Schmitt (BAK, N 1505-198).

95 Letter of 19 August 1933 from Schmitt to Huber (BAK, N 1505-198).

96 Schmitt to Huber, 28 August 1933 (BAK, N 1505-198).

97 Letter of 12 November 1933 from Huber to Schmitt (BAK, N 1505-198). On the battles around and in journals at the time, see Lothar Becker, *'Schritte auf einer abschüssigen Bahn': Das Archiv des öffentlichen Rechts (AöR) und die deutsche Staatsrechtswissenschaft im dritten Reich*, Tübingen, 1999, pp. 98ff., 138ff.

98 Konrad Weiß, 'Justitia'. 'Cordially dedicated' to Carl Schmitt on 1 June 1933 (RW 265-19340). Weiß knew Schmitt from his time in Munich and had dedicated a poem – 'Die Muschel' [The seashell] – to him before, on 11 August 1921 (RW 265-19339). However, politically he probably did not quite agree

with Schmitt in 1933. Schmitt had in mind the text *Der christliche Epimetheus* (Berlin, 1933) and Weiß's religious attitude to history. In this text, Weiß referred to Schmitt as a 'Catholic teacher of jurisprudence' (p. 81). However, his Catholic perspective on the National Socialist seizure of power differed significantly from Schmitt's. To begin with, Weiß formulated 'concepts of a Catholic in the context of the Hindenburg election', in the form of diary-style notes, in which he took against Hitler and opted in favour of Hindenburg's 'non-partisan' [überparteilich] rule by presidential decree. He then discussed the further developments during 1932 under the heading of 'meaning off the centre' [Sinn außer der Mitte]. Weiß actualized his vision of history in extremely hermetic reflections and neologistic formulations in order to find 'Christian' meaning beyond the Zentrum party. In the course of his reflections, he marginalized 'General von Schleicher's practical and inter-party concept of the rule by presidential decree' (p. 91), so that he could hope for a non-partisan national revolution to emerge from the alliance between Hitler and Vice-Chancellor Papen. Schmitt did not share this view of the decision required by the situation in 1932; at best he shared a Christian trust that the events had a 'meaning' [Sinn]. Typescript and materials on Weiß: RW 265-19329/358.

99 See Thomas Marschler, *Kirchenrecht im Bannkreis Carl Schmitts: Hans Barion vor und nach 1945*, Bonn, 2004, pp. 23ff.

100 Karl Eschweiler to Schmitt, 23 August 1933 (RW 265-3372). Cf. also Eschweiler's article 'Kann ein Katholik Nationalsozialist sein? Der Weg aus dem Zwiespalt', *Sonntagmorgen: Die deutsche Wochenzeitschrift*, no. 32 (6 August 1932) (RW 265-19799). Further articles on the concordat and a type-script by Eschweiler in RW 265-20238/9.

101 Karl Eschweiler to Schmitt, 27 November 1933 (RW 265-3376).

102 Eschweiler to Schmitt, 4 October 1934 (RW 265-3382).

103 Barion to Schmitt, 20 December 1934 (RW 265-687).

104 See Werner Weber, 'Das Nihil Obstat: Beiträge zum Verhältnis von Staat und katholischer Kirche', *Zeitschrift für die gesamte Strafrechtswissenschaft* 99 (1938), pp. 193–244.

105 Letter of 3 November 1935 from Eschweiler to Schmitt (RW 265-3388).

106 Peterson to Schmitt, 31 May 1932 (RW 265-10924).

107 Peterson to Schmitt, 21 December 1932 (RW 265-10925).

108 Postcard to Schmitt, 27 February 1933 (RW 265-10926).

109 Erik Peterson, 'Kaiser Augustus im Urteil des antiken Christentums', *Hochland* 30 (1933), pp. 289–99.

110 On 2 November 1933, the publishing house suggested a new edition to Schmitt, who immediately requested a 'reprint without any changes, except for minor corrections' (Schmitt to Dr Geibel, 3 November 1933; Verlagsarchiv D & H, Mappe: Schmitt, Politische Theologie). On 17 November, Schmitt sent the shortened manuscript, and it was published in January 1934. The print run of 3,000 copies was sold out only in 1978. The most important cuts were on pp. 14–15, p. 20, pp. 26–8 and p. 37 in the first edition of 1922. The 'shortened' version, in which the discussions of Kaufmann are omitted, is the basis for all more recent editions and the one that is mostly read today.

111 See Heinrich Forsthoff, *Das Ende der humanistischen Illusion: Eine Untersuchung über die Voraussetzungen von Philosophie und Theologie*, Berlin, 1933; Friedrich Gogarten, *Politische Ethik*, Jena, 1932; Gogarten, 'Die Selbständigkeit der Kirche', *Deutsches Volkstum* 15 (1933), pp. 445–51. Cf. Hermann Lübbe, *Säkularisierung: Geschichte eines ideenpolitischen Begriffs*, Freiburg, 1965.

112 Erik Peterson, 'Monotheism as a Political Problem', in Peterson, *Theological Tractates*, Stanford, CA, 2011.

113 For instance Ferdinand Muralt, 'Politischer Katholizismus und politische Kultur in Deutschland', *Hochland* 30 (1933), pp. 233–51; Heinrich Getzung, 'Wie weit ist die politische Theologie des Reiches heute noch sinnvoll?', *Hochland* 30 (1933), pp. 556–8. Cf. also Karl T. Buddeberg, 'Gott und Souverän: Über die Führung des Staates im Zusammenhang rechtlichen und religiösen Denkens', *Archiv des öffentlichen Rechts* 28 (1936–7), pp. 257–325. The latter, a doctoral thesis written at Marburg University and read by Schmitt in draft form as early as 28 March 1928, was originally meant to be published in Schmitt's series, according to Lothar Becker, *'Schritte auf einer abschüssigen Bahn'*, pp. 201ff.

114 Erik Peterson, 'Die neueste Entwicklung der protestantischen Kirche in Deutschland', *Hochland* 31 (1933), pp. 65–79 and 144–60. Cf. Werner Löser, 'Inkulturation nicht um jeden Preis! Erik Petersons Auseinandersetzung mit der deutschen Evangelischen Kirche 1933', in Barbara Nichtweiß (ed.), *Vom Ende der Zeit: Geschichtstheologie und Eschatologie bei Erik Peterson*, Münster, 2001, pp. 254–64.

115 See Heiner Faulenbach, *Ein Weg durch die Kirche: Heinrich Josef Oberheid*, Cologne, 1992, pp. 71ff. On 5 October, Oberheid was appointed bishop of the Cologne-Aachen diocese.

116 According to Faulenbach, *Ein Weg durch die Kirche: Heinrich Josef Oberheid*, pp. 111, 117.

117 In his letter of 3 November 1933 (RW 265-18781) to the owner of the publishing house, Dr Geibel, Schmitt did not mention any plans for changing his publisher, but rather cited the book's low price as the reason for giving *The Concept of the Political* to the Hanseatische Verlagsanstalt. Duncker & Humblot later also wanted to bring out *Über die drei Arten des rechtswissenschaftlichen Denkens* [On the three types of juristic thought]: see Geibel to Schmitt, 26 February 1934, and Schmitt's agreement in principle of 7 March 1934 in a letter to Geibel (Verlagsarchiv D & H, Mappe: Schmitt, Allgemeines).

118 See Jörg Schmidt, *Otto Koellreutter 1883–1972: Sein Leben, sein Werk, seine Zeit*, Frankfurt, 1995, esp. pp. 81–6.

119 Otto Koellreutter, *Integrationslehre und Reichsreform*, Tübingen, 1929.

120 Otto Koellreutter, *Grundfragen des völkischen und staatlichen Lebens im deutschen Volksstaat*, Berlin, 1935; *Vom Sinn und Wesen der nationalen Revolution*, Tübingen, 1933, pp. 15, 27; *Volk und Staat in der Verfassungskrise: Zugleich eine Auseinandersetzung mit der Verfassungslehre Carl Schmitts*, Berlin, 1933; *Volk und Staat in der Weltanschauung des Nationalsozialismus*, Berlin, 1935; *Deutsches Verfassungsrecht: Ein Grundriss*, 2nd edn, Berlin, 1936, pp. 3f. On the 'case of "Koellreutter vs. Schmitt"' in detail, Andreas Koenen, *Der Fall Carl Schmitt*, pp. 527ff.

121 The polemic against Koellreutter can be found in an article written by Krauss, but published anonymously, in *Deutsches Recht* 4 (25 May 1934), pp. 241–3. This was followed by letters from Koellreutter to Frank (6 June 1934) and to Lammers (10 June 1934). The quotations are taken from the letter to Lammers (RW 579-674). A conversation with Koellreutter and Hans Frank took place on 15 June 1934 to clear the air.

122 According to Karl Lohmann, *Hitlers Staatsauffassung*, Berlin, 1933, preface: 'Above all, what must be avoided is the danger that a "programme" might be extracted, to which the Führer could then be "pinned down" with the help of cleverly arranged quotations from his speeches and his book.'

Chapter 21   The 'Year of Construction'?

1 See Gottfried Neeße, 'Verfassungsrechtliches Schrifttum', *Zeitschrift für die gesamte Straftrechtswissenschaft* 96 (1936), pp. 388–403; here: pp. 390–3. Neeße defended Schmitt against criticism from abroad. A more precise characterization of the role of the political 'movement' can be found in Neeße, *Partei und Staat*, Hamburg, 1936, esp. pp. 20ff. On this, see Günther Krauss, in *Deutsche Juristen-Zeitung* 41 (1936), cols 620–4. There was a very extensive correspondence between Neeße and Schmitt after 1945, which was initiated by Neeße. It does not contain any clear comments on National Socialism.

2 In retrospect: Carl Schmitt, 'Ein Jahr nationalsozialistischer Verfassungsstaat' [The first year of the National Socialist constitutional state], *Deutsches Recht* 4 (1934), pp. 27–30.

3 On 17 October, Schmitt had already sent the manuscript to the publisher (RW 265-13750), but then agreed a later publication date, sometime after 12 November, with Ziegler (request sent to Schmitt by Ziegler on 28 October 1933: RW 265-18526). The proofs were sent to Dr Fickel on 28 October 1933 (RW 265-13654). Schmitt must have asked for the text to be returned again. In 1935 an Italian translation by Delio Cantimore appeared. There were also plans for a translation of *The Concept of the Political* and *State Structure and Collapse*. Soon afterwards, William Guyedan de Roussel translated *Legality and Legitimacy* into French, as well as later *The Concept of the Political* (letter of 28 August 1941 from Gueydan de Roussel to Schmitt: RW 265-16544). Schmitt requested the translation rights from Duncker & Humblot on 27 November 1935 (Verlagsarchiv D & H, Mappe: Schmitt, Legalität). The numerous translations of the 1930s were the result not only of close contacts with foreign scholars but also of his representative position within National Socialism. The largest number of translations would soon be into Spanish. In the 1960s, Schmitt's daughter Anima also translated numerous works into Spanish.

4 Max Weber, *Parlament und Regierung im neugeordneten Deutschland* [Parliament and government in a reconstructed Germany], Munich, 1918.

5 Franz Blei, 'Der Fall Carl Schmitt: Von einem, der ihn kannte', *Der christliche Ständestaat* (25 December 1936), pp. 1217–20; here: 1219.

6 Roland Freisler, 'Rezension zu SBV', *Deutsche Justiz* 96 (1934), pp. 37–8 (RW 265-21401).

7 See, for instance, the letter of thanks from Papen to Schmitt, dated 10 January 1934 (RW 265-10851), and the letters from the state secretary of the interior, which include an invitation for a conversation on questions of state law (letters to Schmitt, dated 2 January 1934 and 12 April 1934: RW 265-11054/55).

8 Schmitt to Werner Sombart, 2 February 1934. See the inquiry of 24 March 1934 from the assistant Karl Schilling to the secretary of the association, Dr Broese, and further correspondence in Werner Sombart's posthumous papers.

9 Letter of 20 November 1933 from Georg Fickel of the HVA to Schmitt (RW 265-17048). There is an extensive correspondence with the HVA (RW 265-17044/121).

10 Typescript in RW 265-21752. It reached the publisher on 18 April 1934 (RW 265-17062).

11 See the vivid account of this tradition in Ewald Grothe, *Zwischen Geschichte und Recht: Deutsche Verfassungsgeschichtsschreibung 1900–1970*, Munich, 2005. Cf. also Hans-Christof Kraus, 'Verfassungslehre und Verfassungsgeschichte: Otto Hintze und Fritz Hartung als Kritiker Carl Schmitts', in *Staat –*

Souveränität – Verfassung: Festschrift für Helmut Quaritsch, Berlin, 2000, pp. 637–61. On the major discussion around the question of the 'legitimacy' of Wilhelminianism, which was begun by Huber, see Ernst-Wolfgang Böckenförde (ed.), *Moderne deutsche Verfassungsgeschichte (1815–1914)*, Königstein, 1971.

12 According to Dirk Blasius, 'Carl Schmitt und der "Heereskonflikt" des Dritten Reiches 1934', *Historische Zeitschrift* 281 (2005), pp. 659–82; here: pp. 673 and 682.

13 Letter of 31 May 1934 from Heckel to Schmitt (RW 265-5819). See also Johannes Heckel, 'Wehrpflicht und Verfassung', *Deutsche Verwaltungsblätter* 83 (1935), pp. 158–64; 'Heer und Staat', *Zeitschrift der Akademie für Deutsches Recht* 6 (1939), pp. 91–2.

14 Fritz Hartung, in *Historische Zeitschrift* 151 (1935), pp. 528–44. Otto Hintze expressed his approval in a letter of 4 April 1935 to Hartung, printed in *Otto Hintze und die moderne Geschichtswissenschaft*, ed. Otto Büsch and Michael Erbe, Berlin, 1983, pp. 55–6. At the end of 1935, the editorship moved to Karl Alexander von Müller: Müller, 'Zum Geleit', *Historische Zeitschrift* 153 (1935), pp. 1–5. Cf. the critical review by T. Brauer in March 1935, in *Der Gral* (RW 265-19503).

15 Carl Schmitt, 'Neubau von Staat und Reich', *Völkischer Beobachter* (31 January 1934), and 'Das neue Verfassungsgesetz', *Völkischer Beobachter* (1 February 1934), pp. 1–2. Reprinted in Wolfgang Schuller (ed.), *Carl Schmitt: Tagebücher 1930–1934*, Berlin, 2010, pp. 476–9.

16 Carl Schmitt, 'Die Logik der geistigen Unterwerfung', *Deutsches Recht* 4 (1934), pp. 225–9.

17 Contract with publisher: RW 265-21825. Letter of thanks from Huber to Schmitt, dated 8 May 1934 (BAK, N 1505-198).

18 See Huber's letters to Schmitt of 8 May 1934 (BAK, 1505-198 – 'The Hölderlin quotation on p. 17 and the Hegel quotation on p. 46 reminded me of our disagreement with regard to the Gestalt concept') and 12 May 1934 (BAK, N 1505-198). Schmitt's personal copy has some additional notes regarding classical philology (RW 265-27227).

19 See Roman Schnur (ed.), *Die Theorie der Institution und zwei andere Aufsätze*, Berlin, 1965.

20 Schmitt's examiner's reports on these doctoral theses, in *'Auf der gefahrenvollen Strasse des öffentlichen Rechts': Briefwechsel Carl Schmitt–Rudolf Smend 1921–1961*, ed. Reinhard Mehring, 2nd edn, Berlin, 2012, pp. 172–6. See also Günther Krauss, *Der Rechtsbegriff des Rechts: Eine Untersuchung des juristischen Rechtsbegriffs im besonderen Hinblick auf das rechtswissenschaftliche Denken Rudolph Sohms*, Hamburg, 1936; Albrecht Wagner, *Der Kampf der Justiz gegen die Verwaltung in Preußen: Dargelegt an der rechtsgeschichtlichen Entwicklung des Konfliktgesetzes von 1854*, Hamburg, 1936. See Huber's detailed review in *Zeitschrift für die gesamte Strafrechtswissenschaft* 97 (1937), pp. 367–71. Cf. also Josef Kölble, *Behördenfeindliche Verwaltungsjustiz*, Berlin, 1937. After 1945, Wagner presented the opposite perspective and wrote a critical history of the politicization of the judiciary: Albrecht Wagner, 'Die Umgestaltung der Gerichtsverfassung und des Verfahrens- und Richterrechts im national-sozialistischen Staat', in *Die deutsche Justiz und der Nationalsozialismus*, vol. 1, Stuttgart, 1968, pp. 191–369.

21 Georg Dahm hints at the flexibility of Schmitt's categories in his review in: *Zeitschrift für die gesamte Strafrechtswissenschaft* 95 (1935), pp. 181–8. Cf. also the letter of 28 August 1934 from Karl Larenz to Schmitt (RW 265-8646): 'On no account is the creation [Gestaltung] a new, independent moment

in addition to the order.' Further reviews: Karl Larenz, in *Zeitschrift für Deutsche Kulturphilosophie* 1 (1934), pp. 112–18; Reinhard Höhn, in *Jugend und Recht* 8 (1934), p. 71; Heinrich Lange, in *Juristische Wochenschrift* 63 (1934), p. 1896. On the National Socialist politicization of juridical hermeneutics, see Bernd Rüthers, *Entartetes Recht: Rechtslehren und Kronjuristen im Dritten Reich*, Munich, 1988; Oliver Lepsius, *Die gegensatzaufhebende Begriffsbildung: Methodenentwicklungen in der Weimarer Republik und ihr Verhältnis zur Ideologisierung der Rechtswissenschaft im Nationalsozialismus*, Munich, 1994.

22 Reports in *Deutsches Recht* 4 (1934), pp. 88–9, and in *Kölnische Zeitung*, no. 89 (18 February 1934). The speech was published in April.

23 Carl Schmitt, 'Nationalsozialismus und Rechtsstaat', *Juristische Wochenschrift* 63 (1934), pp. 713–18; here: p. 716. See Volker Epping, 'Die "lex van der Lubbe": Zugleich auch ein Beitrag zur Bedeutung des Grundsatzes "nullum crimen, nulla poena sine lege"', *Der Staat* 34 (1995), pp. 243–67.

24 Carl Schmitt, 'Nationalsozialistisches Rechtsdenken' [The juridical thought of National Socialism], *Deutsches Recht* 4 (1934), pp. 226–9.

25 Letter of 6 September 1934 from Fickel to Schmitt (RW 265-17070).

26 Fickel to Schmitt, 22 August 1935 (RW 265-17085).

27 See the letters of 21 January 1935 and 9 September 1935 from Fickel to Schmitt (RW 265-17074/88).

28 Letters of 11 September 1935 and 23 December 1935 from Ziegler to Schmitt (RW 265-18531/2). Sales figures for all titles in the series up to the end of 1936: RW 265-21825.

29 See the 'Übersicht über Urteile und Gutachten' [Survey of verdicts and legal opinions] which Schmitt had copied for his students' (RW 265-19216).

30 Letter of 26 October 1934 from the publisher Paul Juncker to Schmitt (RW 265-17150).

31 On 16 September 1934, Schmitt sent his corrections to the publisher Juncker & Dünnhaupt (RW 265-13671). Letters from the publisher Paul Juncker: RW 265-17147/54. The booklet was also meant to appear in Italian translation and as part of a collected edition, *Wesen und Aufbau des Dritten Reiches* [Nature and structure of the Third Reich] (on this, see Juncker to Schmitt, 9 December 1937: RW 265-17154).

32 List of addresses in Bung's letter to Schmitt, dated 3 October 1934. Further covering letters for the dispatch to National Socialist institutions (RW 265-2224).

33 Carbon copy of Schmitt's letter to the publisher Juncker & Dünnhaupt, dated 16 September 1934 (RW 265-13671). The publisher requested the 'blurb' in a letter dated 15 September 1934 (RW 265-1719).

34 See Carl Schmitt, 'Sowjet-Union und Genfer Völkerbund' [The Soviet Union and the League of Nations in Geneva] (1934), in FP, pp. 424–8.

35 Carl Schmitt, 'Paktsysteme als Kriegsrüstung – Eine völkerrechtliche Betrachtung' [Systems of pacts as a preparation for war – a reflection on international law] (FP, pp. 436–9); 'Über die innere Logik der Allgemeinpakte auf gegenseitigem Beistand' [On the internal logic of general pacts of mutual military assistance] (FP, pp. 447–51); 'Sprengung der Locarno-Gemeinschaft durch Einschaltung der Sowjets' [The breaking-up of the Locarno community throught the inclusion of the Soviets] (FP, pp. 456–9); 'Die siebte Wandlung des Genfer Völkerbundes' [The seventh transformation of the League of Nations in Geneva] (FP, pp. 469–72).

36 Report in *Deutsches Recht* 4 (1934), p. 238.

37 Carl Schmitt, 'Bildung eines Auschusses für Staats- und Verwaltungsrecht'

624 *Notes to pp. 320–2*

[Formation of a committee for state and administrative law], in *Jahrbuch der Akademie für Deutsches Recht* 1 (1933–4), pp. 207–11; here: p. 210. Report on the workshop in *Deutsche Juristen-Zeitung* 39 (1934), cols 795–6.

38 Numerous letters from his father, Johann, certificates, and certified documents, in Depositum Jürgen Becker.

39 Letter of 16 May 1934 from Huber to Schmitt (BAK, N 1505-198).

40 Letter of 24 May 1934 to Huber (BAK, N 1505-198).

41 Huber's congratulatory letter of 3 June 1934 (BAK, N 1505-198). The change of editor was explicitly justified in political terms in *Deutsches Recht* 4 (1934), p. 241.

42 See the calendar in which Schmitt kept his appointments (RW 265-19705).

43 This letter of early spring 1934 is quoted in Michael Stolleis, *Geschichte des öffentlichen Rechts*, vol. 3, p. 301(fn.). At the time, Friesenhahn also clarified his distance from National Socialism in the article 'Über den Eid des Beamten' [On the oath of civil servants], in Friesenhahn (ed.), *Festschrift zum 10 jährigen Bestehen der Mittelrheinischen Verwaltungs-Akademie Bonn–Koblenz–Trier*, Bonn, 1935, pp. 62–73. The article highlighted the shift from 'God' to 'people'. Friesenhahn left his post as an extraordinary assistant at the time, but was given the cover for a chair from the winter term 1935–6 (Universitätsarchiv Bonn, Personalakte Friesenhahn PA 2184). In a letter of 28 July 1938, he was appointed 'extraordinary professor not employed by the state'. In 1939 he became a civil servant. The correspondence between Friesenhahn and Schmitt ceased for decades. Only in 1976, upon the mediation of Josef Isensee, was there renewed contact. On 31 December 1976 (RW 265-4511) Friesenhahn wrote very reservedly: 'You did not directly do me any harm, but I cannot get over the fact that a man of your intellectual stature, someone who would not have needed to do that, entered into a pact with these criminals in such a fashion.' A last letter of 7 October 1983 (RW 265-4514), occasioned by Schmitt sending him the reprint of the *Leviathan*, also remained reserved.

44 After the discontinuation of the *Deutsche Juristen-Zeitung*, Lohmann took on the editorship of the *Zeitschrift der Akademie für Deutsches Recht* and of the *Deutsche Rechtswissenschaft*, which was in the hands of Eckhardt for three years and then had new editors from 1939. Detailed information in Lohmann's Personalakte PA 777, Universitätsarchiv Heidelberg.

45 Carl Schmitt, 'Der Weg des deutschen Juristen' [The path of the German jurist], *Deutsche Juristen-Zeitung* 39 (1934), cols 691–8. Cf. also Schmitt, 'Unsere geistige Gesamtlage und unsere juristische Aufgabe' [Our general intellectual situation and our juridical task], *Zeitschrift der Akademie für Deutshces Recht* 1 (1934), pp. 11–12.

46 Quoted in Heinrich Winkler, *The Long Road West*, vol. 2: *1933–1990*, Oxford, 2007, pp. 33f.

47 See Dieter Schenk's correction of Frank's account, in his *Hans Frank*, Frankfurt, 2006, pp. 103ff.

48 A fact emphasized by Lothar Gruchmann in his detailed account of the events, in *Justiz im Dritten Reich 1933–1940*, Munich, 1988, pp. 443ff.

49 Thomas Mann, diary entry of 8 July 1934, in *Tagebücher 1933–1934*, Frankfurt, 1977, p. 463 (the entry is omitted in the English edition of Mann's diaries).

50 According to Schmitt's retrospective interpretation in a late sketch titled 'Etappen der Legalen Revolution' [Stages of the legal revolution] (RW 265-21447). The speech by the Führer was printed verbatim in *Völkischer Beobachter*, no. 195 (Berlin edition of 14 July 1934). Schmitt's copy (RW 265-21449) contains important underlinings; cf. also his appointment calendar 1934 (RW 265-19705).

51 See also Carl Schmitt, 'Stellungnahme der Wissenschaftlichen Abteilung des NS Rechtswahrerbundes zum Entwurf einer Strafverfahrensordnung' [Statement by the academic section of the NS Association for the Protection of the Right on the draft of statutes for criminal persection], in Otto Rilk (ed.), *Neuordnung des Strafverfahrensrechts*, Berlin, 1937, pp. 81–112; here: p. 90 ('... that the Führer of the movement and of the German people is the supreme legal authority of the nation').

52 Carl Schmitt, 'Nationalsozialismus und Rechtsstaat', *Juristische Wochenschrift* 63 (1934), p. 717.

53 On the rejection of an 'agonal' conception of politics and on peace as the purpose, see Carl Schmitt, 'Politik' [Politics] (SGN, pp. 133–7; here: p. 137).

54 On this, in detail, Gruchmann, *Justiz im Dritten Reich 1933–1940*, pp. 445ff.

55 Including the Reich's minister of justice, Gürtner, in a conversation. The minister's son, Fritz Gürtner, had a conversation with Schmitt about this in spring 1968 in Plettenberg. As early as 20 March 1961, he had sought contact with Schmitt; however, a meeting took place only years later (see the letters dating from 20 March 1961 to 12 June 1968: RW 265-5434/5439).

56 Letter of 7 July to Huber (BAK, N 1505-198). After its publication, Schmitt thanked Huber a third time for the article (on 30 July 1934), because he considered it to be a parallel effort.

57 See letter of 19 October 1934 from Huber to Schmitt (BAK, N 1505-198).

58 Letter of 3 March 1935 to Huber (BAK, N 1505-198).

59 On the contemporary debate, see Stolleis, *Geschichte des öffentlichen Rechts in Deutschland*, vol. 3, pp. 330ff.

60 'Hindenburg zum Gedenken', *Deutsche Juristen-Zeitung* 39 (1934), cols 1009–10. The only conceivable alternative to Schmitt as the author would have been Lohmann. But such a 'memoriam' was a matter for the boss.

61 Letter of 6 August 1934 from Schmitt to the publisher de Gruyter (RW 265-13689).

62 Report in *Deutsche Juristen-Zeitung* 39 (1934), cols 1143–5.

63 Hans Frank's speech – 'Die Einwirkung des nationalsozialistischen Ideengutes auf das deutsche Rechtsleben' [The influence of National Socialist ideas on German legal life] – in *Deutsche Juristen-Zeitung* 39 (1934), cols 1169–74.

64 Postcard of 25 September 1934 from Schmitt to Huber (BAK, N 1505-198).

65 Report under the title 'Wandlungen des Rechtsempfindens' [Transformations of the sense of justice] in *Münchner Neueste Nachrichten* (16 October 1934) and in *Deutsche Juristen-Zeitung* 39 (1934), cols 1338–40.

66 The term used by Schmitt in a letter to Huber, dated 6 August 1935 (BAK, N 1505-198).

67 Carl Schmitt, 'Einleitung' [Introduction], in Günther Krauss and Otto von Schweinichen, *Disputation über den Rechtsstaat*, Hamburg, 1935, p. 8. The preparation of the text was delayed because the disputants wanted to elaborate on their presentations. Schmitt pushed for brevity, and it took him 'two full nights' (letter of 31 May 1935 to Krauss: RW 265-13199) to persuade the opponent, von Schweinichen. In order to avoid further delay, Schmitt wrote an 'Afterword', which took the place of the originally planned reply by Krauss. At the beginning of July, Schmitt received the proofs. The booklet appeared only in August.

68 Carl Schmitt, 'Nachwort' [Afterword], ibid., p. 87.

69 Bishop of Saxony to Schmitt, 3 September 1935 (RW 265-10889). See also Roland Freisler's confirmation of receipt of 2 September 1935 (RW 265-4060).

70 Letter of 16 September 1935 from Huber to Schmitt (BAK, N 1505-198).

71 Appointment calendar for 1934 (RW 265-19705).
72 Letter of 4 September 1934 from Huber to Schmitt (BAK, N 1505-198).
73 Letter of 19 October 1934 from Huber (BAK, N 1505-198).
74 Letter of 2 November 1934 from Huber to Schmitt (RW 265-6265).
75 Schmitt to Huber, 10 December 1934 (BAK, N 1505-198).
76 Schmitt to Huber, 1 December 1934 (BAK, N 1505-198).
77 See the circular letter no. 160/34 (RW 265-21497). Schmitt's notes on the conference: RW 265-21497. Conference programme in *Deutsche Juristen-Zeitung* 39 (1936), cols 1531–2, and in *Deutsches Recht* 4 (1934), p. 566. Report on the conference in *Deutsche Juristen-Zeitung* 40 (1936), cols 35–6. Carl Schmitt (ed.), *Berichte über die Lage und das Studium des öffentlichen Rechts* [Reports on the situation and the study of public law], Hamburg, 1935. Karl August Eckhardt, *Das Studium der Rechtswissenschaft*, Hamburg, 1935. Important material in RW 265-21497.
78 Report in *Deutsches Recht* 5 (1935), p. 21.
79 Circular letter no. 144/34 from Schmitt to all university teachers (RW 265-21502).
80 Karl August Eckhardt, 'Presentation of 21 December 1934', in Eckhardt, *Das Studium der Rechtswissenschaft*, Hamburg, 1935, p. 23. The guidelines for the study of jurisprudence were also published in *Deutsche Juristen-Zeitung* 40 (1935), cols 167–70.
81 Eckhardt, *Das Studium der Rechtswissenschaft*, pp. 24f.
82 The publication in two separate volumes of the series was decided in January 1935. On this, see Fickel's letter to Schmitt of 9 January 1935 (RW 265-17072). Schmitt wrote a 'concluding address' and a 'preliminary note'; on this, see Fickel's letter to Schmitt of 18 January 1935 (RW 265-17073). The last contributions arrived at the beginning of February. Schmitt's 'preliminary note' was published without the author's name (*Berichte über die Lage und das Studium des öffentlichen Rechts*, pp. 7–8); the 'concluding address' was left out of the publication.
83 Guiding principles for students issued by the minister of science [Wissenschaftsminister], in Eckhardt, *Das Studium der Rechtswissenschaft*, p. 9.
84 In the words of Michael Stolleis, *Geschichte des öffentlichen Rechts*, vol. 3, p. 342.
85 Schmitt to Huber, 27 December 1934 (BAK, N 1505-198).
86 Huber to Schmitt, 30 December 1934 (RW 265-6267).
87 Stolleis, *Geschichte des öffentlichen Rechts*, vol. 3, p. 349.

Chapter 22   Anti-Semitic Provision of Meaning

1 Ernst Rudolf Huber, *Vom Sinn der Verfassung*, Hamburg, 1935; *Wesen und Inhalt der politischen Verfassung*, Hamburg, 1935; *Verfassung*, Hamburg, 1937.
2 See Oliver Lepsius, 'Gibt es ein Staatsrecht im Nationalsozialismus?', *Zeitschrift für neuere Rechtsgeschichte* 26 (2004), pp. 102–16. On state theory's 'loss of object', cf. Horst Dreier, 'Die deutsche Staatsrechtslehre in der Zeit des Nationalsozialismus', *Veröffentlichungen der Vereinigung der Deutschen Staatsrechtslehrer* 60 (2001), pp. 10–72.
3 In his radio conversation with Dieter Groh and Klaus Figge, Schmitt said (transcription of the long version, p. 23) that he threw a 'large part' of the diaries into the fireplace 'after 30 June'. However, only the diaries between 1935 and about 1939 are missing. Thus, a potentially precarious situation for

Schmitt after 30 June 1934 was not the decisive reason for burning them. It is more likely that his *damnatio memoriae* was related to his collaboration with Hans Frank.

4 Helmut Quaritsch, *Positionen und Begriffe Carl Schmitts*, Berlin, 1989, p. 101.

5 Waldemar Gurian, 'Carl Schmitt, der Kronjurist des III. Reichs', in *Deutsche Briefe 1934–1938: Ein Blatt der katholischen Emigration*, vol. 1, Mainz, 1969, pp. 52–4; here: p. 54.

6 See Schmitt's texts listed in note 35 of the previous chapter.

7 Carl Schmitt, *Deutsche Juristen-Zeiting* 40 (1935), cols 107–9; 41 (1936), cols 181–2; 41 (1936), cols 624–5.

8 Carl Schmitt, 'Die Rechtswissenschaft im Führerstaat', *Zeitschrift der Akademie für Deutsches Recht* 2 (1935), pp. 435–40; here: p. 439.

9 On this, see the earlier 'Neue Leitsätze für die Rechtspraxis' [New guiding principles for legal practice], *Juristische Wochenschrift* 62 (1933), pp. 2793–4.

10 Carl Schmitt, 'Kodifikation oder Novelle? Über die Aufgabe und Methode der heutigen Gesetzgebung' [Codification or amendment? On the task and method of today's legislature], *Deutsche Juristen-Zeitung* 40 (1935), cols 919–25.

11 Schmitt suggested a Habilitation on this topic: Georg Daskalakis, *Das Gesetz als konkrete Seinsordnung und Planverwirklichung*, Berlin, 1938. Excerpts from the examiner's report in Christian Tilitzki, 'Carl Schmitt – Staatsrechtler in Berlin: Einblicke in seinen Wirkungskreis anhand der Fakultätsakten 1934–1944', in *Siebte Etappe*, ed. Heinz-Theo Homann, Bonn, 1991, pp. 62–117. For further legal-theoretical analysis, see also Gerhard Wacke, 'Staatsrechtliche Wandlung: Gedanken zur Verlängerung der Regierungsgesetzgebung', *Zeitschrift für die gesamte Staatswissenschaft* 104 (1945), pp. 273–303.

12 Schmitt's anti-Semitism was at no point entirely overlooked. With reference to the time of National Socialism, Hasso Hofmann spoke about a 'racist' conception in his work. With the publication of the *Glossarium* [Glossary] it lay in plain view; see Reinhard Mehring, 'Carl Schmitt Dämonologie – nach seinem Glossarium', *Rechtstheorie* 23 (1992), pp. 258–71. Despite serious shortcomings, it is the great achievement of Raphael Gross's study – *Carl Schmitt und die Juden: Eine deutsche Rechtslehre*, Frankfurt, 2000 – to have pointed out the continuous and central significance of anti-Semitism in Schmitt's life even before the publication of the diaries.

13 According to Tilitzki, 'Carl Schmitt – Staatsrechtler in Berlin: Einblicke in seinen Wirkungskreis anhand der Fakultätsakten 1934–1944'.

14 Letter of 18 May 1932 from Krauss to Schmitt (RW 265-8229). On Krauss's life, see Dirk van Laak, *Gespräche in der Sicherheit des Schweigens*, Berlin, 1993, pp. 246ff.

15 Günther Krauss, 'Erinnerungen an Carl Schmitt', in *Schmittiana* 2 (1990), pp. 73–101.

16 Günther Krauss, *Der Rechtsbegriff des Rechts: Eine Untersuchung des positivistischen Rechtsbegriffs im besonderen Hinblick auf das rechtswissenschaftliche Denken Rudolph Sohms*, Hamburg, 1936, pp. 88, 90. The invitation for the doctoral colloquium in RW 265-21495, Bl. 39. Schmitt first arranged the publication of the manuscript with Duncker & Humblot, but then gave it to 'the Hanseats' after all (Schmitt to Dr Geibel of D & H on 15 January 1936, in Verlagsarchiv D & H, Mappe: Schmitt, Legalität).

17 On the advice of Emge, von Schweinichen introduced himself to Schmitt in an extensive letter of 2 February 1934 (RW 265-15047). Von Schweinichen came from an 'estate in Styria' (letter of 5 July 1938 to Mrs Schmitt; RW 265-15052).

He studied philosophy, classical philology and jurisprudence, beginning his studies in the summer term 1930 in Berlin and then moving to Hans Leisegang in Jena for the winter term 1931–2. At Jena, he was also a member of Emge's seminar. He joined the NSDAP as early as 1 May 1931 and was also a member of the SA. He returned to Berlin for the winter term 1932–3, and in November 1933 he passed his juridical state examination. In the summer term 1934 he joined Schmitt's seminar. As a first example of his work, he sent Schmitt his ideas and excerpts on the concept of 'order' (on 26 May 1934; RW 265-15048). Von Schweinichen became Emge's assistant and (beginning with the February issue 1936) the editor of the *Archiv für Rechts- und Sozialphilosophie*. In his last letter to Schmitt, dated 5 July 1938, he thanked him for the invitation to the latter's fiftieth birthday (RW 265-15052). The last time he was a guest at the Schmitt home was 20 August 1938. On 28 August, he chose to take his life. Emge wrote an obituary (*Archiv für Rechts- und Sozialphilosophie* 32 [1938], pp. 1–4) and also published excerpts from his unfinished doctoral thesis (Otto von Schweinichen, 'Der Begriff der Rechtsnorm in der deutschen Philosophie der Gegenwart', *Archiv für Rechts- und Sozialphilosophie* 33 [1940], pp. 253–342). Von Schweinichen's successor as editor of the *Archiv für Rechts- und Sozialphilosophie* was Jürgen von Kempski.

18 Günther Krauss, 'Erinnerungen an Carl Schmitt: Nachträge', in *Schmittiana* 3 (1991), pp. 46–50; here: p. 49.
19 Bockhoff later became the legal advisor of the 'Anti-Komintern'. See Ernst H. Bockhoff, *Völker-Recht gegen Bolschewismus: Mit einem Geleitwort des Reichsrechtsführers Dr Hans Frank*, Berlin, 1937.
20 Schmitt's letter to Krauss, dated 2 August 1935. Cf. the letters to Krauss dated 6 April 1935 and 31 May 1935 (RW 265-13198/13200).
21 Letter of 4 January 1935 from Krauss to Schmitt (RW 265-8245).
22 Letter of 8 December 1935 from Krauss to Schmitt (RW 265-8280).
23 Letter of 27 December 1936 from Schmitt to Krauss (RW 265-13206).
24 Günther Krauss, 'Zum Neubau deutscher Staatslehre: Die Forschungen Carl Schmitts', *Jugend und Recht* 10 (1936), pp. 252–3.
25 Letter of 30 November 1936 from Krauss to Schmitt (RW 265-8291).
26 See Josef Kölble, 'Die Ausbildung des Rechtswahrernachwuchses: Bemerkungen zur veränderten Justizausbildungsordnung vom 4 Januar 1939', *Zeitschrift der Akademie für Deutsches Recht* 6 (1939), pp. 301–4; esp. p. 303. Very detailed: Lothar Gruchmann, *Justiz im Dritten Reich*, 3rd edn, Munich, 2001, pp. 299–319. Cf. also Folker Schmerbach, *Das 'Gemeinschaftslager Hanns Kerrl' in Jüterbog 1933–1939*, Tübingen, 2008.
27 According to Jens Banach, *Heydrichs Elite: Das Führerkorps der Sicherheitspolizei und des SD (1936–1945)*, Paderborn, 1998, pp. 236ff. On the 'flood of assessors' at the time, see, for instance, Dr Seidel, 'Zur Lage des juristischen Nachwuchses', *Deutsche Juristen-Zeitung* 38 (1933), pp. 950–3.
28 This may not be a fully exhaustive list.
29 Letter of 4 June 1934 from Schmitt to the director of the university administration (RW 265-13694). Approval dated 23 May 1934 (RW 265-17277).
30 See his retrospective pieces: Gustav von Schmoller, 'Neurath in Prag 1939 bis 1941', *Bohemia* 23 (1982), pp. 404–10; 'Heydrich im Protektorat Böhmen und Mähren', *Vierteljahreshefte für Zeitgeschichte* 27 (1979), pp. 626–45. Schmoller emphasizes Hans Frank's interest in substituting Heydrich for Neurath as well as the sharp oppositions between all those involved, but also Heydrich's administrative skills.

31 The account is based on the information given in a questionnaire of the Deutsche Studentenschaft and further documents in Universitätsarchiv der Humboldt-Universität Z-D I/338 Bl. 65. Letter from the dean, dated 18 November 1938 (RW 265-21496) Bl. 23). Letter of thanks from Gutjahr to Schmitt, dated 10 July 1939 (RW 265-5513). Biographical information on Gutjahr also based on his personnel file: BArch Berlin BDC, RS/5421 (thanks to Werner Treß for bringing the file to my attention).

32 Letter of 22 March 1934 from Bung to Schmitt (RW 265-2221). See, for instance, Bung's review in which he pulls Walter Jellinek's *Beamtenjahrbuch* to pieces, in *Deutsches Recht* 4 (1934), pp. 518–19, as well as his anti-Semitic elaborations in *Deutsches Recht* 5 (1935), p. 104.

33 Retrospective letter of 12 September 1978 from Bung to Schmitt (RW 265-2373). An impressive 'whitewash' or 'reference' for Schmitt by Bung, dated 8 April 1947 (RW 265-20377).

34 There are numerous letters by Mutius addressed to Schmitt, both before and after 1945 (RW 265-10085/123). Schmitt's later attestation of 10 November 1953 (RW 265-19394 Bl. 3 und 5).

35 According to Mutius's own declaration for the files of the 'Deutsche Studentenschaft', in Universtitätsarchiv der Humboldt-Universität ZB II 1321 Akte 23.

36 See Bernhard von Mutius, 'Die Entstehung des Rechtsstandes in England', *Deutsche Juristen-Zeitung* 41 (1936), cols 111–13.

37 Letter of 11 June 1943 from Mutius to Schmitt (RW 265-10094).

38 Letter of 28 December 1943 from Mutius to Schmitt (RW 265-10096).

39 Letter of 31 December 1936 from von Medem to Schmitt (RW 265-9319).

40 Letter of 7 December 1939 from von Medem to Schmitt (RW 265-9321).

41 Letters of 18 December 1939 and 5 March 1940 from von Medem to Schmitt (RW 265-9322/23).

42 Helmut Pfeiffer, *Der Versicherungsmakler*, Würzburg, 1932; *Das Generalgovernement und seine Wirtschaft*, Berlin, 1940.

43 See the note in *Deutsches Recht* 5 (1935), p. 166 (March 1935), and the note in *Deutsche Juristen-Zeitung* 41 (1936), col. 565. The Jurists' Convention was initially planned for the autumn of 1935 and was then, in May 1935, postponed to May 1936.

44 See Josef Kölble, *Die Rechtsprechung des Preußischen Oberverwaltungsgerichts zu §10 II 17 ALR bzw. §§14.41 PVG als Ausdruck verwaltungsfeindlichen Normdenkens*, Berlin, 1936. The theses for the disputation on 13 November 1936 (RW 265-7965). Kölble was born in Moscow and grew up in Berlin. Between the summer term 1931 and the winter term 1934–5 he studied in Berlin, and then took up his legal training. Schmitt remained in touch with Kölble, even after 1945.

45 See, for instance, the contributions in *Jugend und Recht* 11 (1937), pp. 197–209, and *Jugend und Recht* 12 (1938), pp. 193–6 and 212–15.

46 I was not able to locate the doctoral theses of Gutjahr, von Mutius and von Medem. Bung and Wasse completed their doctorates only after 1945.

47 Letter of 25 January 1935 from Schmitt to the minister, via the dean's office (RW 265-13221). Eckhardt signed the approval on 12 February 1935 on behalf of the minister (RW 265-8595; PA Carl Schmitt Universitätsarchiv der HUB 159/a Bl. 44).

48 Table listing Schmitt's lectures in Christian Tilitzki, 'Carl Schmitt's Auslandsreisen', in *Schmittiana* 6 (1998), pp. 252–9; here: p. 254. Report in *Deutsche Juristen-Zeitung* 40 (1935), col. 424.

49 Report in *Deutsches Recht* 5 (1935), p. 224. Eckhardt chaired the concluding discussion.
50 Schmitt to Huber, 6 April 1935 (BAK, N 1505-198).
51 Schmitt to Hartung, 9 April 1935 (RW 265-13069). Schmitt had arranged at his own expense for a copy to be sent to Hartung (letter of 23 May 1934 to the HVA – RW 265-16636).
52 Letter of 14 April 1935 from Huber to Schmitt (BAK, N 1505-198).
53 According to a report in *Deutsche Juristen-Zeitung* 38 (1934), col. 557.
54 Letter of 28 April 1935 sent from Zagreb by Schmitt to Huber (BAK, N 1505-198). Account also based on the pocket diary for 1935 (RW 265-19706).
55 Approval of the lecture tour given in a letter from the minister, dated 26 April 1935 (Tommissen RW 579-675). Presumably, Schmitt also sorted out question regarding Duška's 'Ariernachweis' [proof of Aryan descent] in Zagreb.
56 Report in *Deutsches Recht* 5 (1935), pp. 42–4.
57 Reports in *Jahrbuch der Akademie für Deutsches Recht* 2 (1935), pp. 168–70; *Deutsche Richterzeitung* 27 (1935), pp. 216–20. Thus, on this occasion, Schmitt presumably again had an opportunity to see Hitler at close quarters. Newspaper report: 'Die Akademie für Deutsches Recht tagt', *Münchner Neueste Nachrichten*, no. 174 (28 June 1935), p. 1.
58 In a letter of 25 September 1935, Fickel, of the HVA, encouraged Schmitt in that direction (RW 265-17090).
59 Schmitt to Huber, 6 August 1935 (BAK, N 1505-198).
60 Appointment diary 1935 (RW 265-19706).
61 Report: 'Vorrang des Rechts vor dem Gesetz', *Deutsche Allgemeine Zeitung*, 8 October 1935, and in *Deutsche Juristen-Zeitung* 40 (1935), cols 1233–4.
62 Report in *Deutsche Juristen-Zeitung* 40 (1935), cols 1294–6.
63 See Dr Kreß, 'Das Haus der Akademie für Deutsches Recht', in *Jahrbuch der Akademie für Deutsches Recht* 2 (1935), pp. 176–83.
64 Report in *Deutsche Juristen-Zeitung* 40 (1935), cols 1492–4. Another report: 'Zwischenstaatliches Recht: Dr Frank über die Bedingungen einer Mitarbeit Deutschlands', *Frankfurter Zeitung* (1 December 1935).
65 Letter of 21 August 1936 from Tula Huber-Simons to Schmitt. Huber let his wife send the negative reply.
66 Letter of 24 January 1938 from Huber to Schmitt (BAK, N 1505-198).
67 Schmitt's positive reference for Höhn (RW 265-21742). Schmitt tried to bring Johannes Heckel to Berlin at the time (see Heckel's letters to Schmitt, dated 22 October 1935 and 14 November 1935: RW 265-5821/2) and wrote a positive reference three pages long for Heckel's potential appointment, which is among the posthumous papers (RW 265-20235). In the winter term, Paul Koschaker also joined the faculty. Heinrich Triepel took retirement on account of his age, while Martin Wolff had to leave because of the new racial laws.
68 See the excellent study by Gideon Botsch, *'Politische Wissenschaft im Zweiten Weltkrieg': Die 'Deutschen Auslandswissenschaften' im Einsatz 1940–1945*, Paderborn, 2006.
69 See Shlomo Aronson, *Reinhard Heydrich und die Frühgeschichte von Gestapo und SD*, Stuttgart, 1971, pp. 195ff.; here: pp. 212ff. Michael Wildt (ed.), *Nachrichtendienst, politische Elite, Mordeinheit: Der Sicherheitsdienst des Reichsführers SS*, Hamburg, 2003. Carsten Dams and Michael Stolle, *Die Gestapo: Herrschaft und Terror im Dritten Reich*, Munich, 2008.
70 Reinhard Höhn, *Otto von Gierke*, Berlin, 1936. See also Höhn, *Otto von Gierkes Staatslehre und unsere Zeit*, Hamburg, 1936.

71 Von Medem sent a report to Schmitt on 21 January 1936 (RW 265-21745). In a retrospective documentation, Schmitt emphasized the connection between the conference and Eckhardt's protests. The extensive file also contains a copy of the SS dossier on Schmitt (RW 265-21745).

72 Letter of 18 January 1936 from Eckhardt to Schmitt (RW 265-3073). Detailed account of Schmitt's neutralization by Heydrich, Eckhardt, Höhn and the Reichssicherheitshauptamt in Andreas Koenen, *Der Fall Carl Schmitt: Sein Aufstieg zum 'Kronjuristen des Dritten Reiches'*, Darmstadt, 1995, pp. 651ff.

73 See Wilhelm Wolf, *Vom alten zum neuen Privatrecht: Das Konzept der norm-geschützten Kollektivierung in den zivilrechtlichen Arbeiten Heinrich Langes (1900–1977)*, Tübingen, 1998.

74 Letter of 24 January 1936 from Eckhardt to Raeke (RW 265-3071).

75 Reports in *Völkischer Beobachter*, no. 33 (2 February 1936); *Deutsche Juristen-Zeitung* 41 (1936), col. 246 (Frank, Gürtner and Raeke also were participants); *Mitteilungen des BNSDJ* of 15 February1936, pp. 46–7.

76 Letter of 3 February 1936 from Eckhardt to Hans Frank (RW 265-3070).

77 Calendar for 1936 (of the Hanseatische Verlagsanstalt) – RW 265-19707.

78 See the *Jahrbuch der Akademie für deutsches Recht* 3 (1936), pp. 225–7; *Mitteilungen des BNSDJ*, 15 March 1936, pp. 90–2.

79 See the apologetic memoir of Friedrich Berber, *Zwischen Macht und Gewissen*, Munich, 1986, pp. 72ff.

80 Note in *Deutsche Juristen-Zeitung* 41 (1936), cols 436–7.

81 Carl Schmitt, 'Die geschichtliche Lage der deutschen Rechtswissenschaft', *Deutsche Juristen-Zeitung* 41 (1936), cols 15–21; 'Aufgabe und Notwendigkeit des deutschen Rechtsstandes', *Deutsches Recht* 6 (1936), pp. 181ff.

82 Report in *Deutsche Juristen-Zeitung* 41 (1936), cols 500–1.

83 See Wolfgang Schieder, 'Carl Schmitt in Italien', *Vierteljahreshefte für Zeitgeschichte* 37 (1989), pp. 1–21. See also Schieder, 'Eine halbe Stunde bei dem Diktator', *Frankfurter Allgemeine Zeitung*, no. 2 (3 January 2007), N3; letter to the editor from Gerd Giesler, in *Frankfurter Allgemeine Zeitung*, no. 10 (11 January 2007), p. 9. An entry in Schmitt's appointment calendar confirms the meeting: 'Duce, Palazzo Venezia' (RW 265-19707).

84 Letters of 2 July 1938 and 27 January 1940 from the Italian embassy to Schmitt (RW 265-538/9).

85 Carl Schmitt, 'Faschistische und nationalsozialistische Rechtswissenschaft', *Deutsche Juristen-Zeitung* 41 (1936), cols 619–20; here: col. 620.

86 Carl Schmitt, 'Aufgabe und Notwendigkeit des deutschen Rechtsstandes', *Deutsches Recht* 6 (1936), pp. 181–5.

87 Announcement by Karl Lohmann, in *Deutsche Juristen-Zeitung* 41 (1936), cols 626–30. Programme in *Mitteilungen des BNSDJ* of 15 May 1936, pp. 121–2 (mentioning Pfeiffer as in charge of the organization). Report on the convention by Lohmann, 'Der Deutsche Juristentag 1936', *Deutsche Juristen-Zeitung* 41 (1936), pp. 684–8.

88 Meeting of the Reichsgruppe Hochschullehrer, in *Deutscher Juristentag 1936*, p. 367. *Mitteilungen des BNSDJ* of 15 June 1936, pp. 153–4.

89 Report in *Deutsche Juristen-Zeitung* 41 (1936), col. 695.

90 Report in *Berliner Börsen-Zeitung*, no. 331 (17 July 1936).

91 According to the *Mitteilungen des BNSDJ* of 15 May 1936, p. 132.

92 Report by an SS Sturmbannführer and director of the Zentralabteilung II 2 at the Reichssicherheitshauptamt, dated 28 August 1936 (RW 265-21745).

93 See Gruchmann, *Justiz im Dritten Reich 1933–1940*, pp. 768ff., 980ff., and esp. p. 1002 ('straight rejection').

94 Carl Schmitt, 'Können wir uns vor Justizirrtum schützen?' [Can we protect ourselves against legal errors?], *Der Angriff*, no. 204 (31 August 1936).

95 'Irrtum als Justizirrtum: Notwendige Klarstellung' [Error as legal error: a necessary clarification], *Der Angriff*, 5 September 1936 (RW 265-21317). Cf. Koenen, *Der Fall Carl Schmitt*, pp. 701f.

96 Carl Schmitt, 'Stellungnahme der Wissenschaftlichen Abteilung des NS-Rechtswahrerbundes zum Entwurf einer Strafverfahrensordnung' [Statement by the academic section of the NS Association of the Protectors of Right on the draft for a new code for criminal proceedings], in Otto Rilk (ed.), *Neuordnung des Strafverfahrensrechts*, Berlin, 1937, pp. 81–112. (The statement does not carry the name of an author; however, it is included in Benoist's bibliography of Schmitt's works, and was without a doubt written by Schmitt.)

97 Ibid., p. 97.

98 Ibid., p. 90.

99 Ibid., p. 105.

100 See Saul Friedländer, *Nazi Germany and the Jews*, 2 vols, New York, 1997–2007.

101 On the improvised drafting, see Uwe Dietrich Adam, *Judenpolitik im Dritten Reich*, Düsseldorf, 1972, pp. 125ff. Saul Friedländer, *Nazi Germany and the Jews: The Years of Persecution 1933–1939*, pp. 141–4. Dieter Gosewinkel, *Einbürgern und Ausschließen: Die Nationalisierung der Staatsangehörigkeit vom Deutschen Bund bis zur Bundesrepublik Deutschland*, Göttingen, 2001, pp. 383ff. Andreas Rethmeier, *'Nürnberger Rassegesetze' und Entrechtung der Juden im Zivilrecht*, Frankfurt, 1995.

102 Carl Schmitt, 'Die Verfassung der Freiheit', *Deutsche Juristen-Zeitung* 40 (1935), cols 1133–5; here: col. 1135.

103 On the 'warning addressed to the bureaucracy', see Adam, *Judenpolitik im Dritten Reich*, p. 129.

104 Stenographic lecture outline (RW 265-21439). See Adam, *Judenpolitik im Dritten Reich*, pp. 140ff.; Gosewinkel, *Einbürgern und Ausschließen*, p. 391.

105 On the workshop and meeting of the academy, see the reports in *Deutsche Richterzeitung* 27 (1935), pp. 347–8.

106 Carl Schmitt, 'Faschistisches und nationalsozialistisches Rechtsdenken', *Deutsche Juristen-Zeitung* 41 (1936), pp. 619–20; here: p. 620.

107 According to the testimony of Günter Blau, who attended the lectures: Blau, 'In Carl Schmitts Vorlesung', *Frankfurter Allgemeine Zeitung*, no. 197 (25 August 2000), p. 49.

108 Helmut Heiber, *Walter Frank und sein Rechtsinstitut für Geschichte des neuen Deutschlands*, Stuttgart, 1966.

109 Johannes Heckel, 'Der Einbruch des jüdischen Geistes in das deutsche Staats- und Kirchenrecht durch Friedrich Julius Stahl', *Historische Zeitschrift* 155 (1937), pp. 506–41. Cf. the lectures in the series 'Recht der Rasse' [The right of the race] at the German Jurists' Convention 1936 (pp. 83–169) or the contributions 'on the history of Jewish law in Germany' in Eckhardt's *Deutsche Rechtswissenschaft* 2 (1937), pp. 97–189.

110 Heinrich Lange, 'Das Judentum und die deutsche Rechtswissenschaft', *Deutsche Juristen-Zeitung* 41 (1936), cols 1129–33. Cf also Reinhard Höhn, 'Die Juden im Staatsrecht: Auseinandersetzung des Juden Jellinek mit Gierkes Staatslehre', *Jugend und Recht* 10 (1936), pp. 33–6.

111 Including the emigrant Valeriu Marcu, who belonged to the circle around Jünger: Marcu, *Die Vertreibung der Juden aus Spanien*, Amsterdam, 1934 (RW 265-22563).

112 This point is emphasized by Dirk Blasius, *Carl Schmitt: Preußischer Staatsrat in Hitlers Reich*, Göttingen, 2001, pp. 170ff.
113 Announcement and programme of the conference in *Deutsche Juristen-Zeitung* 41 (1936), cols 1019–20 and 1165. The connection between internal arguments and ideological attempts at saving himself is emphasized by Bernd Rüthers, *Entartetes Recht: Rechtslehren und Kronjuristen im Nationalsozialismus*, Munich, 1988; Rüthers, *Carl Schmitt im Dritten Reich: Wissenschaft als Zeitgeist-Verstärkung?*, Munich, 1989.
114 Report in *Berliner Tagebuch*, no. 469 (3 November 1936).
115 Late note by Schmitt (RW 265-21746, Bl. 22).
116 See Schmitt's remarks in a letter of 27 December 1976 to E.-W. Böckenförde (RWN 260-431) on Hitler's need at the time for a 'doctrine for a so-called new order', and also Schmitt's late draft for a letter (19 November 1981) to Hermann Cürten of the Wissenschaftliche Buchgesellschaft:

Dear Herr Cürten, the 'conference on the Jews' in the autumn/winter of 1936–37, at which I spoke for the NS Jurists' Assocation [NS-Juristenbund], was one of at least three important inner political discussions; in addition, there were the activities of the historian Walter Frank, and the new SS led by Heydrich, which consciously set out to establish itself as the new elite (whoever hasn't read the book by Heiber cannot join the discussion on this). It was the continuation of the civil war within the party, which Hitler did not manage to control.

Following his reading of Heiber, Schmitt also clarified the fronts [?] at the time for himself in private notes (RW 265-21746). The letter to Cürten was the negative response to a query regarding a partial publication (letters between 27 May 1981 and 18 May 1983: RW 265-17255/60).
117 See Hasso Hofmann, 'Die deutsche Rechtswissenschaft im Kampf gegen den jüdischen Geist', in Karlheinz Müller and Klaus Wittstadt (eds), *Geschichte und Kultur des Judentums*, Würzburg, 1988, pp. 228–40; here: p. 230. Christian Busse, '"Eine Maske ist gefallen": Die Berliner Tagung "Das Judentum und die Rechtswissenschaft" vom 3./4. Oktober 1936', *Kritische Justiz* 33 (2000), pp. 580–93. For a closer examination of Schmitt's concluding remarks, see Raphael Gross, *Carl Schmitt und die Juden: Eine deutsche Rechtslehre*, Frankfurt, 2000, pp. 120ff. The conference was already considered to be the climax of Schmitt's National Socialist ideologizing in the pioneering work by Horst Göppinger, *Die Verfolgung der Juristen jüdischer Abstammung durch den Nationalsozialismus*, Villingen, 1963. Report on the conference by H.G. (Herbert Gutjahr) in *Mitteilungen des BNSDJ* of 15 October 1936, pp. 200–2 and 215–16. Hubertus Bung, 'Judentum und Rechtswissenschaft', *Jugend und Recht* 10 (1936), pp. 253–4 (emphasis on the pioneering role as an 'intellectual police').
118 Hasso Hofmann, 'Die deutsche Rechtswissenschaft im Kampf gegen den jüdischen Geist', p. 237.
119 See Jacob Katz, *Richard Wagner: Vorbote des Antisemitismus*, Königstein, 1985. From the perspective of National Socialism: Richard Ganzer, *Richard Wagner und das Judentum*, Hamburg, 1938.
120 See Dina Porat, 'Richard Wagners Bedeutung für Adolf Hitler und die nationalsozialistische Führung', in Dieter Borchmeyer, Ami Maayani and Susanne Vill (eds), *Richard Wagner und die Juden*, Stuttgart, 2000, pp. 207–20.
121 See Jens Malte Fischer, *Richard Wagners 'Das Judentum in der Musik': Eine kritische Dokumentation als Beitrag zur Geschichte des Antisemitismus*, Frankfurt, 2000, pp. 62ff. In October 1938, Schmitt acquired a copy of Oskar

Goldberg, *Maimonides: Kritik der jüdischen Glaubenslehre*, Vienna, 1935 (RW 265-22560). Goldberg is usually seen as a 'Jewish fascist'. As is well known, Thomas Mann turned Goldberg's approach into a critical one.

122 Richard Wagner, *Judaism in Music: Being the Original Essay together with the Later Supplement. Translated from the German and Furnished with Explanatory Notes and Introduction* by Edwin Evans, London, 1910, p. 31 [trans. modified]; cf. Fischer, *Richard Wagners 'Das Judentum in der Musik'*, pp. 162f., 185.

123 See Udo Bermbach, 'Richard Wagners "Das Judentum in der Musik" im Kontext der Zürcher Kunstschriften', in Borchmeyer, Maayani and Vill (eds), *Richard Wagner und die Juden*, pp. 55–76.

124 See Dieter Borchmeyer, 'Heinrich Heine – Richard Wagner: Analyse einer Affinität', ibid., pp. 20–33.

125 Bruno Bauer, *Zur Judenfrage*, Braunschweig, 1843. On Schmitt's extensive study of Bauer and the history of German anti-Semitism after 1848, see Reinhard Mehring, '"Autor vor allem der 'Judenfrage' von 1843": Carl Schmitts Bruno Bauer', in Klaus-Michael Kodalle and Tilman Reitz (eds), *Bruno Bauer: Ein 'Partisan des Weltgeistes'?*, Würzburg, 2010, pp. 335–50.

126 On the Jewry as an 'elite of modernisation', see Helmuth Kiesel, *Geschichte der literarischen Moderne*, Munich, 2004, pp. 74ff.

127 Fischer, *Richard Wagners 'Das Judentum in der Musik'*, p. 196.

128 Ibid., p. 89.

129 Carl Schmitt (?), 'Preliminary Remarks', in *Die deutsche Rechtswissenschaft im Kampf gegen den jüdischen Geist*, vol. 1 of the series *Das Judentum in der Rechtswissenschaft*, Berlin, 1936, p. 5. List of participants in RW 265-21745.

130 Schmitt to Smend, 17 July 1936 (Niedersächsische Staats- und Universitätsbibliothek Göttingen, Cod Ms R. Smend A 759). For Smend's take on legal history and his critical view of Laband, see his 'Der Einfluß der deutschen Staats- und Verwaltungsrechtslehre des 19. Jahrhunderts auf das Leben in Verfassung und Verwaltung', *Deutsche Rechtswissenschaft* 4 (1939), pp. 25–39.

131 Letter of 4 October 1936 from Oberheid to Duška Schmitt (RW 265-10525).

132 The conference papers were published in nine volumes between 1936 and 1938 under the generic title *Das Judentum in der Rechtswissenschaft*. Carl Schmitt, 'Die deutsche Rechtswissenschaft im Kampf gegen den jüdischen Geist' [German jurisprudence and its battle against the Jewish spirit], in *Das Judentum in der Rechtswissenschaft*, vol. 1: *Die deutsche Rechtswissenschaft im Kampf gegen den jüdischen Geist*, Berlin, 1936, pp. 28–34, and also in *Deutsche Juristen-Zeitung* 41 (1936), cols 1193–9. Cf. also Schmitt's reference to Bodin's 'Jewish descent' in a review: *Deutsche Juristen-Zeitung* 41 (1936), cols 181–2.

133 From the summer term 1935 onwards, Ruttke had a teaching post for 'Rasse und Recht' [Race and right] at the University of Berlin; in 1940, he took the first chair for 'race and right' in Jena.

134 Vow of the conference participants, in *Die deutsche Rechtswissenschaft im Kampf gegen den jüdischen Geist*, p. 35.

135 'Eröffnung der wissenschaftlichen Vorträge durch den Reichsgruppenwalter Staatsrat Professor Dr. Carl Schmitt' [Introductory remarks to the academic papers by Reichsgruppenwalter Staatsrat Professor Dr Carl Schmitt'], in *Die deutsche Rechtswissenschaft im Kampf gegen den jüdischen Geist*, pp. 14–17; here: p. 16.

136 'Vorbemerkung' to Edgar Tatarin-Tarnheyden, 'Der Einfluss des Judentums in Staatsrecht und Staatslehre', in *Das Judentum in der Rechtswissenschaft*, vol. 5, Berlin, 1938, pp. 3–4. Schmitt's support for Tatarin-Tarnheyden was

meant to compensate for an earlier academic 'belittling', about which the latter had complained (in a letter of 27 December 1934 to Schmitt: RW 265-15945/1). Schmitt wanted to dispel this 'misunderstanding' straightaway (letter of 7 January 1935 from Schmitt to Tatarin-Tarnheyden: RW 265-13557/1). They remained in collegial contact after that. On the emergence of the concept of 'citizen', see the discussion by Albrecht Wagner, 'Zur Entstehung und Bedeutung des Begriffs "Staatsbürger"', *Deutsche Juristen-Zeitung* 40 (1935), cols 740–1, and Herbert Kier, 'Über die erste Verwendung des Ausdrucks "Staatsbürger" in der deutschen Gesetzessprache', *Deutsche Juristen-Zeitung* 41 (1936), cols 237–9, as well as, a little bit later, Heinrich Muth, 'Judenemanzipation und Staatsbürgerbegriff', *Jugend und Recht* 13/6 (1939), pp. 27–9.

137 'Vorbemerkung' to Tatarin-Tarnheyden, 'Der Einfluss des Judentums in Staatsrecht und Staatslehre', p. 3.

138 Schmitt, *Die deutsche Rechtswissenschaft im Kampf gegen den jüdischen Geist*, pp. 14 and 34. Also quoted before in Karl Lohmann, *Hitlers Weltanschauung*, Berlin, 1933, p. 30.

139 Hans Frank, 'Ansprache' [Address], in *Die deutsche Rechtswissenschaft im Kampf gegen den jüdischen Geist*, pp. 7–13; here: p. 10. The library of the academy began a 'register of Jewish-juridical authors' and removed books: Hans-Rainer Pichinot, *Die Akademie für deutsches Recht: Aufbau und Entwicklung einer öffentich-rechtlichen Körperschaft des Dritten Reiches*, Kiel, 1981, p. 88. A 'list of Jewish authors of juridical texts', printed by Kohlhammer, appeared as early as 1936 (RW 265-21745). Detailed discussion in Horst Göppinger, *Die Verfolgung der Juristen jüdischer Abstammung durch den Nationalsozialismus*, Villingen, 1963, pp. 59ff., 86ff.

140 Quoted in Busse, '"Eine Maske ist gefallen": Die Berliner Tagung "Das Judentum und die Rechtswissenschaft" vom 3./4. Oktober 1936', p. 591.

141 Referring to Hugo Sinzheimer (*Jüdische Klassiker der deutschen Rechtswissenschaft*, Amsterdam, 1938), Hasso Hofmann pointed out, against Schmitt, that 'Jewish jurists represented the most diverse positions and directions of thought, which they did not themselves invent' (p. 235). Schmitt's myth regarding the hostile 'founder' is wrong. A comprehensive edited volume from the 1990s also sets out to prove that 'Jewish' jurists cannot be identified as a homogeneous (not to mention 'hostile') group regarding the positions they take, not even with the help of the mythical figure of the originary 'founder': Helmut Heinrichs et al. (eds), *Deutsche Juristen jüdischer Herkunft*, Munich, 1993.

142 Waldemar Gurian, 'Carl Schmitt, der Kronjurist des III. Reiches', in *Deutsche Briefe 1934–1938: Ein Blatt der katholischen Emigration*, ed. Heinz Hürten, Mainz, 1969, vol. 1, pp. 52–4.

143 Gurian, letters of 12 October 1934 (vol. 1, p. 34) and 19 June 1936 (vol. 2, pp. 240–1).

144 See Gurian, letters of 15 February 1935 (vol. 1, p. 215), 19 July 1935 (vol. 1, pp. 465f.), and 13 March 1936 (vol. 2, pp. 107f.).

145 Gurian, letter of 7 June 1935 (vol. 1, pp. 403f.).

146 Gurian, letter of 13 December 1935 (vol. 2, pp. 716–17; here: p. 716).

147 Gurian, 'Carl Schmitt gegen Carl Schmitt', in letter of 22 May 1936 (vol. 2, pp. 204–5).

148 Gurian, 'Schwache Naturen', in letter of 5 June 1936 (vol. 2, pp. 222–3; here: p. 223).

149 Gurian, 'Staatsrat Carl Schmitt', in letter of 5 June 1936 (vol. 2, pp. 405–6).

150 Günther Krauss, 'Zum Neubau deutscher Staatslehre: Die Forschungen Carl Schmitts', *Jugend und Recht* 10 (1936), pp. 252–3.
151 'Eine peinliche Ehrenrettung', *Das Schwarze Korps*, no. 49 (3 December 1936), p. 14; 'Es wird immer noch peinlicher', *Das Schwarze Korps*, no. 50 (10 December 1936), p. 2. Report in *Jüdische Rundschau*, no. 100 (15 December 1936). See Mario Zeck, *Das Schwarze Korps: Geschichte und Gestalt des Organs der Reichsführung SS*, Tübingen, 2002, pp. 140ff., 246ff.
152 Appointment calendar 1936 (RW 265-19707).
153 Letter of 12 December 1936 from Gleispach to Schmitt (RW 265-5052). See Koenen, *Der Fall Carl Schmitt*, pp. 754ff.
154 Letter of 10 December 1936 from Palandt to Schmitt (RW 265-10788).
155 *Mitteilungen des BNSDJ* of 15 January 1937, pp. 9–10.
156 Dossier of 8 January 1937, in Tommissen (RW 579-675).
157 Anonymous letter, written in block capitals, no date (RW 265-16660).
158 Gurian, 'Der NS Kronjurist Carl Schmitt als Mohr...', 11 December 1936, in *Deutsche Briefe 1934–1938: Ein Blatt der katholischen Emigration* (vol. 2, pp. 489–91).
159 Gurian, 'Auf dem Wege in die Emigration oder ins Konzentrationslager?', 24 December 1936, ibid., p. 510.
160 Franz Blei, 'Der Fall Carl Schmitt: Von einem, der ihn kannte', *Der christliche Ständestaat* (25 December 1936), pp. 1217–20; here: p. 1220.
161 Gurian, 'Deutscher Geist in Gefahr', 9 July 1937, in *Deutsche Briefe 1934–1938*, vol. 2, p. 773.
162 Hans Frank to Gunter d'Alquen, 11 December 1936, quoted in Zeck, *Das Schwarze Korps*, p. 248.
163 Joseph Schmitt to Carl Schmitt, 16 December 1936 (RW 265-13835).

Chapter 23 A New Turn with Hobbes?

1 Franz Neumann, *Behemoth: The Structure and Practice of National Socialism*, New York, 1942.
2 Thomas Mann, *Diaries 1918–1939*, trans. Richard Winston and Clara Winston, London, 1983, p. 220, entry dated 29 July 1934. (The last sentence of the quoted passages is omitted in the English translation.)
3 Marcel Reich-Ranicki, *Mein Leben*, Stuttgart, 1999, p. 114.
4 Hermann Oncken, *Cromwell: Vier Essays über die Führung einer Nation*, Berlin, 1935.
5 Hans Freyer, *Machiavelli*, Leipzig, 1938.
6 René König, *Niccolo Machiavelli: Zur Krisenanalyse einer Zeitenwende*, Zurich, 1941.
7 Details in Reinhard Mehring, 'Friedrich Schillers "Demetrius": Ein später Baustein zu Carl Schmitts Hitler-Bild', *Weimarer Beiträge* 53 (2007), pp. 559–75. See also Mehring, 'Thomas Hobbes im konfessionellen Bürgerkrieg: Carl Schmitts Hobbes-Bild und seine Wirkung im Kreis der alten Bundesrepublik', *Leviathan: Zeitschrift für Sozialwissenschaft* 36 (2008), pp. 518–42.
8 Carl August Emge, 'Das Gedächtnis an René Descartes', *Archiv für Rechts- und Sozialphilosophie* 30 (1937), pp. 465–6; here: p. 465fn.
9 Dedication by Schmitt to Emge, Christmas 1937. Cf. Schmitt's letter of 19 April 1936, congratulating Emge on his fiftieth birthday. (I was kindly provided with copies of the letters from the private archive of his son Prof. Martinus Emge.)

10 Schmitt to Emge, 21 April 1938.
11 Winter term 1937–8, winter term 1939–40, first and third trimester of 1940.
12 Helmut Schelsky, 'Die Totalität des Staates bei Hobbes', *Archiv für Rechts- und Sozialphilosophie* 31 (1938), pp. 176–93. Schelsky wrote his later Habilitation, according to his retrospective view, because it offered the 'possibility of opposition' to Schmitt. See Schelsky, 'Vorwort' [preface] (1980) to his *Thomas Hobbes: Eine politische Lehre*, Berlin, 1981, p. 10.
13 As opposed to Ernst Cassirer, *The Myth of the State*, New Haven, CT, 1945.
14 Georg D. Daskalakis, 'Der totale Staat als Moment des Staates', *Archiv für Rechts- und Sozialphilosophie* 31 (1938), pp. 194–201.
15 Otto von Schweinichen to Schmitt, 9 November 1937, in RW 265-21317. In print: Review of Hans Krupa, 'Carl Schmitts Theorie des "Politischen"' (Leipzig, 1937), *Archiv des öffentlichen Rechts* 68 (1937–8), pp. 373–8.
16 Schmitt to Smend, 14 April 1938 (Niedersächsische Staats- und Universitätsbibliothek Göttingen, Cod Ms R. Smend A 759).
17 Pocket diary, month by month for 1938, in RW 265-19614. The birthday celebrations are entered, including the guests' seating order.
18 William Gueydan de Roussel, 'Der Staatsrat im Gesetzgebungs- und Verwaltungsstaat: Dargestellt an der Geschichte des französischen Staatsrats', *Zeitschrift der Akademie für Deutsches Recht* 5 (1938), pp. 505–8; 6 (1939), p. 534.
19 Carl Schmitt, 'Grußbotschaft an die Hobbes-Gesellschaft in Kiel' [Salutary message to the Hobbes Society in Kiel], in Baron Cay von Brockdorff (ed.), *Zum Gedächtnis des 350. Geburtstags von Hobbes*, Kiel, 1938, p. 15.
20 Report in *Flensburger Nachrichten* (29 April 1938), p. 3.
21 Invitation cards (RW 265-19963). See Christian Tilitzki, 'Der Mythos des Leviathan: Presseberichte und Anmerkungen zu Vorträgen Carl Schmitts in Leipzig und Kiel', in *Schmittiana* 6 (1998), pp. 167–81. On the lecture in Kiel, see the letters from the president of the Hobbes Society, von Brockdorff (RW 265-2084/2090).
22 Pocket diary 1938 (RW 265-19614). Postcard of 29 April 1938 from Carl to Duška Schmitt (RW 265-13458).
23 Confirmation of receipt from the publisher to Schmitt, dated 19 May 1938 (RW 265-17108). On 17 June the book went to press; at the beginning of July it was sent out by the publisher.
24 Report by Eberhard von Medem, 'Demokratie und Diktatur', *Deutsches Recht* 8 (1938), pp. 252–5.
25 Report by N.N. (Lohmann?) in *Zeitschrift der Akademie für Deutsches Recht* 5 (1938), pp. 457–60.
26 Universitätsarchiv der Humboldt-Universität R/S, Nr. 122 Blatt 59. Completion of the examination procedure on 8 August 1938. Report on the oral examination in RW 265-21499. Programme in RW 265-21433.
27 On the confirmation from the HVA that the copies had been dispatched, Schmitt noted as recipients (with the date added in each case): father Johann, Roßkopf, Evola, Gueydan de Roussel, Johann von Leers, Smend, Duška, Daskalakis, Beckerath, Lohmann, Marcks, A. Schmitz, Oberheid, Frau von Schnitzler, Krauss, Steinbömer, Emge, Medem, Mutius and Berber (RW 265-17111).
28 Negative reply from Smend, giving poor health as the reason, dated 3 July 1938 (RW 265-15225).
29 Rudolf Smend to Schmitt, 10 July 1938 (RW 265-15226). Also in *Schmittiana* 3 (1991), pp. 140–1.

30 Carl Schmitt, 'Eine Tischrede' [A dinner speech], in *Schmittiana* 5 (1996), pp. 10–11. On 20 August, Schmitt received the 'silberne Treudienst-Ehrenzeichen' [silver medal of honour for loyalty] for twenty-five years as a civil servant.

31 Hans Schneider was Werner Weber's assistant at the time. He remained one of the most important supporters of Schmitt, even after 1945. See Werner Weber, *Gerichtsherr und Spruchgericht*, Berlin, 1937; *Öffentliches Recht*, Leipzig, 1938; *Der preußische Staatsrat 1817–1918: Ein Beitrag zur Verfassungs- und Rechtsgeschichte Preußens*, Munich, 1952.

32 See Dr Pfeiffer's letter of congratulation to Schmitt, dated 10 July 1938 (RW 265-11045). Of Schmitt's pupils, among others, the following added a poem and signed the letter: Gutjahr, von Mutius, von Schweinichen, Kličković, Dr Ernst Bockhoff, Dr Josef Kölble and Manfred von Mackensen (RW 265-20127).

33 See Horst Bredekamp, *Thomas Hobbes' visuelle Strategien: Der Leviathan – Urbild des modernen Staates*, Berlin, 1998.

34 According to a letter of 18 July 1938 to one of the German Christians, Siegfried Leffler (RW 265-13228).

35 See the account in Josef Kölble, *Arbeitskraft schafft Wirtschaftsfreiheit: Rohstofffragen und Sozialprobleme der Gegenwart*, Leipzig, 1938, pp. 113–18. Between 1893 and 1936 there was no German whaling industry. In 1937–8, 1,800 sailors had already gone to sea whaling. As well as the Zeughaus museum in Berlin, a barge on the Spree, which served as a museum, displayed the large skeleton of a whale (Franz Hessel, *Spazieren in Berlin, 1929*, Munich, 1968, pp. 94ff.).

36 Postcard of 13 July 1938 from Peterson to Schmitt (RW 265-10931). Cf. Andreas Marxen's doctoral thesis in theology, supervised by Alois Dempf in Bonn, *Das Problem der Analogie zwischen den Seinsstrukturen, dargestellt im engeren Anschluss an die Schriften von Carl Schmitt und Erik Peterson*, Würzburg, 1937.

37 Steinbömer to Schmitt, 1 August 1938 (RW 265-15718).

38 Letter of 8 July 1938 from Herbert Meyer to Schmitt (RW 265-9445). Meyer had previously (19 June 1938) directed Schmitt to some literature, and Schmitt quoted him.

39 Scheuner to Schmitt, 10 July 1938 (RW 265-12434).

40 Albrecht Erich Günther, in *Deutsches Volkstum* 20 (1938), pp. 562–3; Wolff Heinrichsdorff, 'Das Symbol des Staates', in *Westfälische Landeszeitung* (20 November 1938); Horst Rüdiger, 'Der Leviathan', in *Rheinisch-Westfälische Zeitung*, no. 559 (5 November 1938); a very detailed, anonymous, review, 'Der Staat als Leviathan', in *Neue Züricher Zeitung* (11 September 1938); Alfred Verdross, in *Zeitschrift für öffentliches Recht* (1939), pp. 118–19; J. Gasse, in *Archiv des öffentliches Rechts* 30 (1939–40), pp. 249–51; Ernst Forsthoff, in *Zeitschrift für deutsche Kulturphilosophie* 7 (1941), pp. 206–14; Josef Saal, in *Rheinische Landeszeitung*, no. 343 (4 September 1938); Dr Geh., *Hallische Nachrichten*, no. 294 (15 December 1939). Schmitt collected all these articles, in RW 265-19966. See also Karl Anton Prinz Rohan, in *Vorarlberger Tageblatt* (17 December 1938), in RW 265-19965. Further reviews: Hans Welzel, in *Kritische Vierteljahresschrift für Gesetzgebung und Rechtswissenschaft* 30 (1939), pp. 337–40. Paul Kern (René König), 'Der Leviathan', in *Maß und Wert* 3 (1940), pp. 357–9.

41 On the reconstruction of canon law, see Werner Weber, *Die politische Klausel in den Konkordaten: Staat und Bischofsamt*, Hamburg, 1939.

42 Herfried Münkler, *Die Deutschen und ihre Mythen*, Berlin, 2009, p. 104; cf. p. 67.
43 Ernst Forsthoff, in *Zeitschrift für deutsche Kulturphilosophie* 7 (1941), pp. 206–14. Forsthoff ignores Schmitt's anti-Semitic stance and, following Reinhold Schneider and with reference to Prussia, indicates his reservations about Schmitt's critique of the liberal distinction between politics and morality.

Chapter 24　The Right to Power?

1 Schmitt to Smend, 16 July 1937 (Niedersächsische Staats- und Universitätsbibliothek Göttingen, Cod Ms R. Smend A 759).
2 Werner Weber to Duncker & Humblot, 28 January 1938, 2 February 1938 and 9 February 1938 (Verlagsarchiv D & H, Mappe: Schmitt, Bilfinger). Weber to Schmitt, 17 February 1938 (RW 265-17735). Cf. also *Zeitschrift der Akademie für Deutsches Recht* 5 (1938), p. 349. Weber urged the publisher to bring the book quickly to the printing stage, referring to the wishes of 'Herr Minister' Frank.
3 Letter of 25 May 1938 from Friedrich Kiener to Schmitt (RW 265-7582).
4 Letter of 29 June 1938 from Ribbentrop to Schmitt (RW 265-11609).
5 Transcript of a letter of 2 February 1938 from Eckhardt to Werner Weber (RW 265-17737).
6 Schmitt to Smend, 14 April 1938 (Niedersächsische Staats- und Universitätsbibliothek Göttingen, Cod Ms R. Smend A 759).
7 Carl Schmitt, 'Das neue vae neutris!' [The new *vae neutris*], in FP, pp. 612–15. Cf. also 'Völkerrechtliche Neutralität und völkische Totalität' [Neutrality in international law and the totality of a people], in FP, pp. 617–22.
8 Carl Schmitt, 'Inter pacem et bellum nihil medium' [There is no middle ground between peace and war], in FP, pp. 629–33.
9 See Herfried Münkler, *Die Deutschen und ihre Mythen*, Berlin, 2009.
10 See the comprehensive work by Helmut Heiber, *Walter Frank und sein Reichsinstitut für Geschichte des neuen Deutschlands*, Stuttgart, 1966, pp. 501–22. Steding's account was harshly criticized not only from a liberal perspective by, for instance, Theodor Heuss, but also by Alfred Baeumler, Ernst Krieck and others.
11 Ernst Rudolf Huber, *Heer und Staat*, Hamburg, 1938.
12 Ernst Forsthoff, *Deutsche Verfassungsgeschichte der Neuzeit*, Berlin, 1940. Forsthoff's account ends with 1918.
13 Carl Schmitt, 'Führung und Hegemonie' [Leadership and hegemony], in SGN, pp. 225–31.
14 Carl Schmitt, preface of March 1939, translated by Günter Maschke, in *Schmittiana* 3 (1991), p. 18.
15 Walz to Schmitt, 28 April 1939 (RW 265-17419).
16 Adolf Hitler, speech of 28 April 1939, quoted in SGN, p. 348. Schmitt underlined only this one sentence in his copy of *Der Führer antwortet Roosevelt: Reichstagsrede vom 28. April 1939*, Munich, 1939, p. 51 (RW 265-28535). Heinrich Winkler sees a direct connection in his *The Long Road West*, vol. 2: *1933–1990*, trans. A. J. Sager, Oxford, 2007, p. 64: 'The German or European "Monroe Doctrine" was not invented by Hitler, but by Carl Schmitt, who had referred to the American model in his speech in Kiel on 1 April 1939. Apparently, the "Führer" had learned about the idea via some high-ranking National Socialist jurists and since considered it to be his own creation' [my translation; Sager's translation differs significantly, mentioning that Hitler 'had

outlined a kind of "German Monroe doctrine" already in October 1930', and that his idea to extend it 'to cover all of Europe was inspired by Carl Schmitt's Kiel speech of 1 April 1939'.]

17 Beginning with the 2nd edition (Paul Rittersbusch (ed.), *Politische Wissenschaft*, Berlin, 1940, p. 28), Schmitt mentioned the publication 'in April' 1939 in a bibliographical preliminary note. The fact that the text went to press so fast matters because it means that Schmitt could not possibly have reacted to Hitler's speech of 28 April. A shortened version of the final chapter, 'Der Reichsbegriff im Völkerrecht' [The concept of the 'Reich' in international law], had already appeared in the issue of *Deutsches Recht* of 29 April 1939. The 'deed of the Führer' thus cannot refer to Hitler's answer to Roosevelt; it must refer to 'pan-German' expansion. The material added in the 1941 edition includes almost all of the introductory section 'Allgemeines' [General matters] (SGN, pp. 270–2), some further references (fn 8, 60, 62, 63) and a paragraph on the Hitler–Stalin pact (SGN, p. 295), as well as one on 'types of possible legal relations' (SGN, p. 305). The extensive expansion of the introductory section is the result of the incorporation of the later essay 'Raum und Großraum im Völkerrecht' [Space and Großraum in international law] (SGN, p. 235–7). Schmitt's personal copy with revisions and additions can be found in RW 265-20064. The conference presentations were published in 1940 in a volume titled *Politische Wissenschaft* [Political science]. Huber provided the introductory contribution, 'Der Volksgedanke in der Revolution von 1848' [The idea of the people in the revolution of 1848]. Gustav Adolf Walz spoke about 'Volksgruppenrecht' [The right of ethnic groups], Cezary Berezowski on 'Die Minderheiten als Rechtsproblem' [Minorities as a legal problem]. Thus, we can say that the volume looked at the notion of Großraum from the perspective of the 'idea of a people' [Volksgedanken], with Schmitt providing the fundamental legal concepts.

18 See Samuel Salzborn, *Ethnisierung der Politik: Theorie und Geschichte des Volksgruppenrechts in Europa*, Frankfurt, 2005.

19 Ernst Rudolf Huber, *Verfassungsrecht des Großdeutschen Reiches*, Hamburg, 1939.

20 Letter of 5 June 1939 to Pierre Linn (RW 265-13235). Schmitt continued to seek contact with Linn later, but then 'lost' him as a friend (Schmitt to Warnach, 27 October 1958; HAStK, Best. 1688).

21 Letter of 1 July 1939 from Schmitt to Ritter von Niedermayer (RW 265-13336).

22 Carl Schmitt, 'Großraum gegen Universalismus' [Großraum versus universalism], in PB, pp. 295–302. The text appeared in *Zeitschrift der Akademie für Deutsches Recht* on 7 May 1939.

23 On the key role of Schmitt's approach, see Lothar Gruchmann, *Nationalsozialistische Großraumordnung: Die Konstruktion einer deutschen Monroe-Doktrin*, Stuttgart, 1962. Matthias Schmoeckel, *Die Großraumtheorie: Ein Beitrag zur Geschichte der Völkerrechtswissenschaft im Dritten Reich, insbesondere der Kriegszeit*, Berlin, 1994. Jürgen Elvert, *Mitteleuropa! Deutsche Pläne zur europäischen Neuordnung (1918–1945)*, Stuttgart, 1999. Rüdiger Voigt (ed.), *Großraum-Denken: Carl Schmitts Kategorie der Großraumordnung*, Stuttgart, 2008.

24 Letters dating from the period 6 April 1939 to 7 November 1940 from the Deutscher Rechtsverlag to Schmitt (RW 265-16950/53).

25 Letters of 29 April 1939 (RW 265-6268) and 30 May 1939 (RW 265-6269) from Huber to Schmitt. Huber was also speaking in Kiel, and talked to Schmitt, but could not stay to attend his lecture.

26 Erich Wolgast, 'Großraum und Reich', *Zeitschrift für öffentliches Recht* 21 (1940), pp. 20–31. Herbert Krüger, *Der Raum als Gestalter der Innen- und Außenpolitik*, Darmstadt, 1941. Hermann Jahrreiß, 'Wandel der Weltordnung', *Zeitschrift für öffentliches Recht* 22 (1942), pp. 513–36. Reinhard Höhn, *Großraumordnung und völkisches Rechtsdenken*, Darmstadt, 1941; 'Reich–Großraum–Großmacht', *Reich–Volksordnung–Lebensraum* 2 (1942), pp. 97–226. Hans Spanner, 'Großraum und Reich', *Zeitschrift für öffentliches Recht* 22 (1943), pp. 28–58. Schmitt had these extensive discussions bound in one volume (RW 265-28282).
27 For instance, Werner Daitz, in letters to Schmitt dated 7 June 1939 and 5 October 1940 (RW 265-2739/40).
28 Werner Best, 'Völkische Großraumordnung', *Deutsches Recht* 10 (1940), pp. 1006–7. Reviews collected by Schmitt in RW 265-20067. Ulrich Herbert, *Best: Biographische Studien über Radikalismus, Weltanschauung und Vernunft*, 2nd edn, Bonn, 1996.
29 Letters of 31 March 1941 and 16 April 1941 from Hans Grimm to Schmitt (RW 265-5160/1).
30 Pocket diary (of the Hanseatische Verlagsanstalt) for 1939 (RW 265-19708).
31 Bernhard von Mutius to Schmitt, 29 October 1940, in *Schmittiana* 3 (1991), pp. 153f.; here: p. 154.
32 E.g., in Bremen (28 March 1940), Kiel (27 April 1940), Rostock (4 May 1940; lecture at the Verwaltungsakademie upon invitation by Tatarin-Tarnheyden. Report in *Rostocker Anzeiger*, no. 105 (6 May 1940): RW 265-19019 Bl. 7), Naumburg (26 June 1940), Cologne (27 June 1940), Halle (28 July 1940), Kiel (30 October 1940), Berlin (11 November 1940), Dortmund (25 January 1941), Nuremberg (8 February 1941), Bremen (26 March 1941), Bremen (19 March 1942), Budapest (6 May 1942), Brandenburg (15 October 1942) – this is an incomplete list of dates based on the list and lecture outlines in RW 265-20109.

Chapter 25   The Captain Held Hostage?

1 See Stefan Rückl (in cooperation with Karl-Heinz Noack), 'Studentischer Alltag an der Berliner Universität 1933 bis 1945', in *Die Berliner Universität in der NS-Zeit*, 2 vols, ed. Rüdiger vom Bruch and Christoph Jahr, Stuttgart, 2005, vol. 2, pp. 115–42.
2 Letter of 30 May 1934 from the chair of the examination office for politicial economists at Berlin University to Schmitt (RW 265-21545 Bl. 260).
3 Anna-Maria Gräfin von Lösch, *Der nackte Geist: Die Juristische Fakultät der Berliner Universität im Umbruch von 1933*, Tübingen, 1999. Letter of 29 September 1934 from Pallandt to Schmitt (RW 265-21545).
4 Letter of 15 March 1937 from the minister of justice to Schmitt (RW 265-21545 Bl. 98). The initial period of five years was extended beyond 1942 on 3 February 1942 (RW 265-21545 Bl. 2).
5 Extensive files in RW 265-21545.
6 According to the *curriculum vitae* of the legal trainee Horst Wolters (1913–?) in his doctoral thesis *Der Rechtsbegriff Soldat*, Berlin, 1938. Wolters mentions in his CV that his father works at the Volksgerichtshof [people's court], that he volunteered for the army, and that he currently works 'in the chancellery of the Führer'. Doctoral examination on 1 December 1938. First examiner's report: Schmitt (4 April 1938). Schmitt also took on the second report on the thesis of Höhn's pupil Justus Beyer, who, in 1941, was posted as an SS

Sturmbannführer 'to the NSDAP headquarters' (according to the CV in his doctoral thesis on *Die Ständeideologie der Systemzeit und ihre Überwindung*, Darmstadt, 1941).

7 The Siamese second lieutenant Pravis Sribibadhana, for instance, thanked the state councillor on a card sent from the 'joint Thai–German camp in Kiel'. Postcard with photos: RW 265-21420. Schmitt strongly rejected the suggestion of the retrospective award of a doctorate on 15 January 1940 (RW 265-21421). Sribibadhana visited Schmitt several times in the 1960s (letters: RW 265-15599/609). Other foreign students after 1936 were Wei Ren Feng (China), Cholam Reza Bahrami, Luciano Conti, Jaime Quijano Caballero, Hsi Ming-Wang, Dr Ancevicius (Lithuania) and Farhad Arasteh (Tehran). Short references for these in RW 265-21498.

8 Herwig Schäfer, *Juristische Lehre und Forschung an der Reichsuniversität Straßburg 1941–1944*, Tübingen, 1999, pp. 116ff.

9 Extensive stenographic outlines for lectures and other material relating to the years 1935 to 1941 in RWN 260-383/84. Herbert Franke's lecture notes on the course in international law (RWN 260-413).

10 Related documents in Universitätsarchiv der HUB PA Carl Schmitt, 159/a III Bl. 130/139. Approval by the ministry, dated 23 October 1936, in Universitätsarchiv der HUB PA Carl Schmitt, 159/a III Bl. 52. See also the letter of thanks of 30 October from the head of section [Fachgruppenleiter] Werner Weber to Schmitt (RW 265-17738).

11 See, for instance, Ewald Grothe, 'Verfassungsgeschichte als "politische Wissenschaft": Carl Schmitt "über die Aufgaben" und die Deutung der deutschen Verfassungsgeschichte im Nationalsozialismus', *Zeitschrift für neuere Rechtsgeschichte* 29 (2007), pp. 66–87.

12 See Carl Schmitt, 'Über die zwei großen "Dualismen" des heutigen Rechtssystems' [On the two major 'dualisms' in today's legal system] (PB, pp. 261–71).

13 First and third terms 1940, summer terms 1942, 1943 and 1944.

14 Letter of 12 September 1983 from Wolfgang Keilpflug to Schmitt (RW 265-7323).

15 I owe a survey of these to the unpublished juridical exam dissertation by Herbert Liebs, *Habilitationen in der Zeit des Nationalsozialismus: Eine Untersuchung der Verfahren an der juristischen Fakultät der Berliner Universität von 1933 bis 1945*, Berlin, 2008 (supervisor: Rainer Schröder).

16 Daskalakis is mentioned as a Greek lawyer in Georg D. Daskalakis, 'Die Verfassungsentwicklung Griechenlands', in *Jahrbuch des öffentlichen Rechts* 24 (1937), pp. 266–334.

17 Daskalakis to Schmitt, 16 July 1950 (RW 265-2776).

18 Schmitt to Warnach, 11 March 1959 (HAStK, Best. 1688).

19 Hans Franzen, *Gesetz und Richter: Eine Abgrenzung nach den Grundsätzen des nationalsozialistischen Staates*, Hamburg, 1935.

20 Hans Franzen, *Im Wandel des Zeitgeistes 1931–1991*, Munich, 1992, p. 68.

21 Hans Franzen, *Aus meinem Leben und meiner Zeit*, private imprint, no date, p. 70.

22 Longer excerpt in Franzen, *Im Wandel des Zeitgeistes 1931–1991*, pp. 77–9. Cf. also the biographical information in Hans Franzen, *Anwaltskunst: Faustregeln, Alternativen, Fälle*, Munich, 1989, p. 277. Letter of thanks of 19 January 1984 from Franzen to Schmitt (RW 265-4056). Letters to Schmitt, dated between 2 February 1937 and 1984 (RW 265-4039/57). Schmitt wrote to Franzen on 12 August 1938 (RW 579-469) expressing how delighted he was about the report Franzen had sent from Ireland.

23 Schmitt to Franzen, 14 January 1947, 16 August 1948 and 4 October 1948 (RW 579-469).

24 He had already attempted a Habilitation in Bonn in 1930. Files of the Juridical Faculty Bonn, Fach 4 Nr. 2 from [1918] to 2 February 1939 (Archive of the Juridical Faculty no. 45).

25 See Suthoff-Groß to Schmitt, 9 May 1939: he thanks for Schmitt for the invitation to join his seminar and announces the first part of his work (RW 265-15937). On 14 January 1941, Schmitt had already proposed the approval 'as a dissertation for the title of Dr habil.' to the dean (RW 265-12909). Report of 13 January 1941 and proofs of the review in RW 265-21486. Schmitt's review of Rudolf Suthoff-Groß, *Die Rechtstellung des Bürgermeisters in seinem Verhältnis zum Staat und zu den übrigen Beamten der Gemeinde*, Berlin, 1941, in *Zeitschrift für die gesamte Staatswissenschaft* 102 (1942–3), pp. 386–91. Schmitt now championed the old 'local administration', mentioned the 'extraordinary difficulties' of passing systematic legislation, which, he said, he knew from 'first-hand experience', and praised a cautious 'positivistic-pragmatic' way of proceeding as opposed to some 'booklets and articles from the period 1933 to 1937, which roamed around too much in issues of pure principle and pure ideology [im bloß Grundsätzlichen und bloß Weltanschaulichen].' Cf. also Höhn's review in *Zeitschrift der Akademie für Deutsches Recht* 11 (1944), p. 180.

26 Maiwald to Schmitt, 23 September 1939 (RW 265-8972).

27 Maiwald to Schmitt, 18 January 1944 (RW 265-8973). Maiwald to Schmitt, 8 December 1945 (RW 265-8975).

28 See the comprehensive list in Christian Tilitzki, 'Carl Schmitt – Staatsrechtslehrer in Berlin: Einblicke in seinen Wirkungskreis anhand der Fakultätsakten 1933–1944', in *Siebte Etappe*, Bonn, 1991, pp. 62–117. However, Tilitzki's list is incomplete, as there are further examiner's reports among the posthumous papers (esp. RW 265-21499 and RW 265-21485) In the following list, the names in italics are absent in Tilitzki: second examiner for Mladen Lorković (report dated 16 June 1935). Legal trainee Dr rer. pol. Harro Brenner (born in 1911, in South West Africa; school leaving certificate: 1930, Salem; in 1934, doctorate in political science, followed by a degree in jurisprudence), *Das Völkerbundsmandat, unter besonderer Berücksichtigung der Entstehungsgeschichte*, Berlin, 1937 (11 May 1936). Second examiner for Asche von Mandelsloh (1901–1937), *Politische Pakte und völkerrechtliche Ordnung*, Berlin, 1937 (31 May 1937). Second examiner for Eugen Ocklitz, *Die rechtliche Stellung des Gauleiters*, Berlin, 1939 (13 December 1937); Ocklitz mentions in his *curriculum vitae* that he joined the NSDAP in 1923, was a co-founder of the Hitler Youth and worked as an NS activist in the Gau headquarters at Posen; Höhn was the first examiner. Mihail Farcasanu (born in 1907 in Bucharest, in Berlin from November 1935), *Über die geistesgeschichtliche Entwicklung des Begriffs der Monarchie*, Würzburg, 1938 (12 February 1938). Hans Schmidt, *Entwicklung und Wesen des Begriffs 'mittelbarer Beamter'*; *magna cum laude*, Reppen, 1938 (examiner's report: 4 April 1938). Karl Schilling (born in 1910; according to his CV, 'specialist [Sachbearbeiter] in the Aviation Ministry' from 1937), *Ist das Königreich Jugoslawien mit dem früheren Königreich Serbien völkerrechtlich identisch?*, Berlin, 1939. Horst Kube (1914–?), *Die geistesgeschichtliche Entwicklung der Stellung des preußischen Oberpräsidenten*, Würzburg, 1939 (22 September 1938) – Kube's examination paper as a legal trainee was awarded a 'good' on 2 March 1936. Herbert Schwörbel, *Freiheit der Meere und Meistbegünstigung*, Leipzig, 1939 (17 November 1938). Franz

Johannes Schmidt-Dumont, *Vom Wesen der Führerordnung*, Berlin, 1942 (9 May 1939). Hermann Siebenhaar (born in 1902 in Hannover, school leaving certificate in 1924, then studied theology and became a priest; Siebenhaar left the clergy and studied jurisprudence in Berlin from the summer term 1936), *Der Begriff des politischen Delikts im Auslieferungsrecht*, Berlin, 1939 (19 June 1939). Heinrich Gremmels, *Das Problem der Ämterverbindung und Ämterunvereinbarkeit von Partei- und Staats- und Kommunalämtern*, Berlin, 1940 (22 September 1939; *summa cum laude*; RW 265-20248). Friedrich Karl, *Die Begriffsgeschichte des Ermessens seit Rudolf von Gneist*, 13 April 1940 and 13 January 1941 (RW 265-21485). Gholamreza Bahrami (born in 1915 in Tehran, the son of an army officer, German school leaving certificate 1934, changed his degree and studied jurisprudence in Berlin from the winter term 1936–7), *Kapitulationen: Ein Beitrag zur Lehre vom 'ius inter potestates'*; *cum laude*, Berlin, 1941 (5 June 1941). Adrian Güroff (1900–?), Bulgarian diplomat), *Der Balkanpakt von 1934 im System der Regionalverträge*; *cum laude* (13 November 1941). Gerd Autzen (born in 1917 in Silesia; school leaving certificate in 1936, then studied jurisprudence and took his first state examination in December 1939), *Die rechtliche Stellung der Reichsangehörigen nichtdeutscher Volkszugehörigkeit, aber deutschen oder artverwandten Blutes*; *cum laude*, Berlin, 1942 (2 January 1942). Günther Schwartz (24 November 1944).

29 Sava Kličković, 'Die Enteignung, ein dem Grundeigentum und der Bodenbeschaffung zugeordnetes Rechtsinstitut', *Deutsche Rechtswissenschaft* 3 (1940), pp. 137–53. See also Kličković, 'Das Rückerwerbsrecht bei der Enteignung', *Zeitschrift der Akademie für Deutsches Recht* 7 (1940), pp. 297–8. Some of the letters from 1935 onwards (RW 7709/7894) are addressed to Duška and written in Serbian.

30 Schmitt's examiner's report on the thesis, dated 5 February 1940, as well as further documents relating to the examination, in RW 265-20553.

31 Hans Peter Ipsen, *Politik und Justiz: Das Problem der justizfreien Hoheitsakte*, Hamburg, 1937.

32 Herbert Lemmel, *Die Volksgemeinschaft: Ihre Erfassung im werdenden Recht*, Stuttgart, 1941. Schmitt's examiner's report of 7 July 1939, in RW 265-19074.

33 Schmitt's examiner's report of 29 October 1942, sent to the dean in Tübingen (RW 265-21499).

34 Letter of 29 April from Dean Weigmann (RW 265-21496 Bl. 30). See the letter of 29 September 1943 from Werner Schulze-Thulin to Schmitt (RW 265-14791), in which he asked as faculty assistant to be assigned to Schmitt again. Schulze-Thulin was the son of a priest and a National Socialist. He did not complete his doctorate because of the war. After 1945, he worked as a lawyer and notary in Wilhelmshaven.

35 Letter of 12 April 1940 from Dean Gieseke (RW 265-21495 Bl. 46).

36 Detailed *curriculum vitae* for Lohmann, dated 26 February 1942, in PA 4868, Universitätsarchiv Heidelberg.

37 Information based on Lohmann's questionnaire for the German Lecturers' Association [Deutsche Dozentenschaft], in archive of Humboldt University, ZDI I/644. See Carl Bilfinger's letter to Schmitt, dated 4 June 1943, in which he reported extensively on the positive development Lohmann had taken in Heidelberg and about the completion of his Habilitation. From the first term 1941 Lohmann deputized in Heidelberg for Herbert Krüger. Bilfinger fostered Lohmann's career. However, Bilfinger and Engisch were not entirely uncritical of his Habilitation, after which Lohmann was drafted into the army. After the war (14 January 1947) Lohmann asked Walter Jellinek of Heidelberg

University for an exculpating letter and spoke of his Christian 'reservatio mentalis' against National Socialism. He later worked as an 'advisor' in the German Bundestag.

38 Letters by Erland Weber-Schumburg, written between 21 May 1943 and 24 May 1943 (RW 265-17800/05). Weber-Schumburg worked on a doctoral thesis on 'international inheritance law in Sweden' at the time and applied for his accreditation as a lawyer (letter of 23 October 1943 to Schmitt: RW 265-17804). In 1944 he passed his doctorate in Hamburg, and after 1945 worked as a lawyer.

39 Letter of 17 April 1943 from Schmitt to the dean (RW 265-21498).

40 Questionnaire of the Lecturers' Association [Dozentenschaft] and letter of approval as faculty assistant by Walter M. Schering, in archive of Humboldt University, Nr. 1862 Akte 14. Letter of 16 November 1943 from Dean Siebert regarding the allocation of assistants, RW 265-21432.

41 Letter of 29 October 1947 from Smend to Schmitt, inquiring about Wasse (RW 265-15230).

42 Wasse to Schmitt, 1 February 1983 (RW 265-17699). Some of Wasse's letters from the time after 5 October 1943 are preserved (RW 265-17693/79). Letter of 4 January 1948 from Wasse to Schmitt in RWN 260-375. Doctoral thesis: Günter Wasse, *Die Werke und Einrichtungen der evangelischen Kirche*, Göttingen, 1954 (Wasse thanks Weber and Smend, but not Schmitt).

43 According to a letter of 18 December 1972 from Winckelmann to Piet Tommissen (copy in RW 265-18203).

44 Winckelmann to Schmitt, 19 May 1941 (RW 265-18080).

45 Schmitt to Hans Franzen, 12 December 1942 (RW 579-469), referring to his circle of pupils in the 1930s.

46 See the letters from Friedensburg between 1941 and the end of the war (RW 265-4349/4368) and the remarks of his father in his *Lebenserinnerungen* (Frankfurt, 1969), pp. 301f. Cf. also the father's letters of 16 May 1944 and 25 February 1946 to Schmitt (RW 265-4366 and 4369).

47 Letter of 2 March 1944 from Friedensburg to Schmitt, sent from Freiburg (RW 265-4364).

48 Further names in RW 265-21498 and RW 265-21485. A project of the senior civil servant Helmut Roike failed because of Schmitt (letters to Schmitt, dated 7 October 1941 and 18 December 1942). The assessor Dietrich Scheid took care of 'real estate matters' for the Waffen SS and wanted to write a doctorate on expropriation! (letter of 10 July 1941 to Schmitt: RW 265-12369). Another problem is lost documentation: after decades, Rudolf Charlier, for instance, still asked Schmitt to confirm his participation in his examination (letters to Schmitt, dated 3 November 1969 and 18 December 1969: RW 265-2537/8).

49 Attendance lists for February 1944, in RW 265-21504 (Rüdiger Altmann was one of the participants).

50 Werner Haseroth, *Die treaty-making power und die Bedeutung der Ratifikation in der Sowjetunion*, 1942. See Tilitzki, 'Carl Schmitt –Staatsrechtler in Berlin', pp. 102f.

51 Letter of 17 November 1980 from Dr Werner Haseroth to Schmitt (RW 265-5756). Schmitt had sent Haseroth a confirmation of his doctoral examination on 10 November 1960 (RW 265-12787). Schmitt's examiner's report on the doctoral thesis, dated 13 April 1942 (RW 265-21436).

52 Letter of 25 September 1949 from Walter Golombek (RW 265-5067). See the letter of 15 April 1942, which Golombek sent from the front, and in which he

confirmed his wish to embark on a doctorate following the successful completion of his legal training.

53 Letter of 26 June 1940 from von Medem to Schmitt (RW 265-9326).

54 According to the succinct account of Roman Schnur, *Vive la République oder Vive la France: Zur Krise der Demokratie in Frankreich 1939/40*, Berlin, 1982.

55 Letter of 13 October 1940 from von Medem to Schmitt (RW 265-9327).

56 Letter of June 1940 from Schmitt to the university's trustee, in Universitätsarchiv der HUB PA Carl Schmitt 159/a Bl. 62.

57 Carl Schmitt, 'Die geschichtliche Lage der deutschen Rechtswissenschaft', *Deutsche Juristen-Zeitung* 41 (1936), cols 15–21.

58 Schmitt's 'Afterword' is longer than the separate publication as it discusses Stein's text in more detail in some of the closing passages. On the importance of Stein for 'modern thought on monarchism', see also the doctoral thesis (with Schmitt as the main supervisor and first examiner) by Mihail Farcasanu, *Über die geistesgeschichtliche Entwicklung des Begriffes der Monarchie*, Würzburg, 1938.

59 On the existence of a 'general law' below the level of state law, cf. Carl Schmitt, 'Über die zwei großen "Dualismen" des heutigen Rechtssystems' [On the two major 'dualisms' in today's legal system], in PB, pp. 261–71.

60 Körnchen to Schmitt, 9 October 1942 (RW 265-8059). The impressive letters from Hans Körnchen (1887–1944) to Carl Schmitt in Rolf Rieß, 'Eine Freundschaft im Dienste Bruno Bauers: Der Briefwechsel Carl Schmitt und Hans Körnchen', in Klaus-M. Kodalle and Tilman Reitz (eds), *Bruno Bauer (1809–1882): Ein 'Partisan des Weltgeists'?*, Würzburg, 2010, pp. 351–73. List of recipients of the offprint, which appeared at the end of August: RW 265-20927. Schmitt also sent offprints to scholars such as Gadamer, Meinecke, Otto Hintze and Koschaker, and to Ernst Jünger and Gottfried Benn.

61 Eugen Rosenstock, *Die europäischen Revolutionen: Volkscharaktere und Staatenbildung*, Jena, 1931.

62 Letter of 14 January 1942 from Schmitt to Smend on the occasion of Smend's sixtieth birthday (RW 265-13531; also in Niedersächsische Staats- und Landesbibliothek Göttingen, Cod Ms R. Smend A 759).

63 In addition to the published correspondence, we have numerous letters from Getha Jünger to Duška Schmitt, especially from the war years (RW 265-6914/6945).

64 On Jünger's participation in the war in Paris and the Caucasus, see Helmuth Kiesel, *Ernst Jünger. Die Biographie*, Berlin: 2007, pp. 497ff.

65 See David Clay Large, *Berlin*, New York, 2000, pp. 319ff. In 1940 there were 222 casualties and in 1941 there were 226. Because of their modest success, the English reduced the number of air raids. From the end of January 1943 the Americans carried out the attacks, and the number of casualties rose dramatically.

66 The distinction is made by Herfried Münckler, 'Clausewitz' Beschreibung und Analyse einer Schlacht: Borodino als Beispiel', in Münckler, *Der Wandel des Krieges: Von der Symmetrie zur Asymmetrie*, Weilerswist, 2006, pp. 75–102; here: pp. 96ff.

67 Ibid., p. 101.

68 See the annotated edition of Herman Melville's *Benito Cereno* by Marianne Kesting, Frankfurt, English edition: 'Benito Cereno', in Melville, *Billy Budd and Other Stories*, London, 1986, pp. 159–258.

69 Maria Hasbach to Schmitt, 4 October 1943 (RW 265-5738). Intense letters up

until 1968 evoke the memory of the common time in Bonn and Berlin together with her sister Dora (RW 265-5738/5742).

70 Letter of 10 July 1941 to Gretha Jünger: GJCS, p.45. There are numerous letters by Werner Gilles, in particular to Duška, dating from 1933 onwards (RW 265-5001/44). On 16 February 1936 (RW 265-5961) a support circle initiated by Alfred Heintzen sent out a round robin letter in order to secure financial support for Gilles. It was signed by, among others, Oberheid, Hans Frank, Popitz, Lilly von Schnitzler, Gerhard Marcks and Eta Harich-Schneider. The fact that Hans Frank appended his signature is particularly interesting. Schmitt owned a couple of paintings by Gilles, which were repeatedly requested for exhibitions. Schmitt also belonged to a support circle for Emil Nolde.

71 Letter of invitation of 20 September 1941 from Dr Klaen (RW 265-2852), referring to a letter of 17 July 1941, which had not reached Schmitt. Approval by express letter of 14 October 1941 from the Reich Ministry: Universitätsarchiv der HUB PA Carl Schmitt, 159/a Bl. II 23/24. See Eckhard Michels, *Das Deutsche Institut in Paris 1940–1944: Ein Beitrag zu den deutsch-französischen Kulturbeziehungen und zur auswärtigen Kulturpolitik des Dritten Reiches*, Stuttgart, 1993. Frank-Rutger Hausmann, *'Auch im Krieg schweigen die Musen nicht': Die Deutschen Wissenschaftlichen Institute im Zweiten Weltkrieg*, Göttingen, 2001. Information on Schmitt's meetings according to his appointment diary 1941 (RW 265-19710). Epting passed his Habilitation in 1943 at the Auslandswissenschaftlichen Fakultät [Faculty for Foreign Studies], which had opened in 1940 at the University of Berlin. See Gideon Botsch, *'Politische Wissenschaft im Zweiten Weltkrieg': Die 'Deutschen Auslandswissenschaften' im Einsatz 1940–1945*, Paderborn, 2006, p. 139.

72 Letter of thanks of 4 September 1941 from Grüninger (RW 265-5387). Around that time, Schmitt made the acquaintance of Hans Speidel, who kept loosely in touch throughout his life (RW 265-15553/76).

73 Ernst Jünger, *Strahlungen*, Tübingen, 1949, p.57 (entry for 21 October 1941).

74 Invitation of 7 October 1941 (RW 265-17975) and 30 November 1941 (RW 265-17973) from Franz Wieacker to Schmitt. Extensive lecture outlines and notes: RW 265-20011. Schmitt used Löwith's book *From Hegel to Nietzsche* (New York, 1991) for this lecture.

75 Jünger, *Strahlungen*, p.75 (entry for 24 December 1941).

76 Documented in Christian Tilitzki, 'Die Vortragsreisen Carl Schmitts während des Zweiten Weltkriegs', in *Schmittiana* 6 (1998), pp.191–270.

77 The journey is documented in Duška's pocket diary (RW 265-19741).

78 Invitation, dated 2 April 1942, from Freyer to Schmitt (RW 265-4317). See also the invitation from the dean of the university to Schmitt, dated 22 April 1942 (RW 265-16112).

79 From this time onwards, we again have Schmitt's stenographic diaries: diary May 1942 to March 1943 (RW 265-19602); diary July 1944 to April 1945 (RW 265-19601).

80 The occasion was an opening celebration of a lecture series of the Verwaltungs-Akademie Berlin, which began with the overture from *The Flying Dutchman* (material in RW 265-19878). Lecture outline: RW 265-20109 Bl. I.

81 Letter of 21 October 1942 from Benno Ziegler to Schmitt (RW 265-18535). Stapel had asked Schmitt 'for coffee in his apartment' before the celebration.

82 Schomerus to Schmitt, 30 December 1942 (RW 265-14493).

83 According to the report, dated 4 September 1942, sent to Duška Schmitt by the Berlin lodger M(aria) Hasb.(ach), who may have accompanied Schmitt (RW 265-16620). Also noted in the pocket diary (RW 265-19711).

84 Various letters relating to the talks from March 1942 onwards, in Universitätsarchiv der HUB PA Carl Schmitt, 159/a Bl. 25/32.

85 Jünger, *Strahlungen*, pp. 199f. (entries between 12 and 17 November 1942).

86 Letters from Fraenger between May 1943 and July 1951 (RW 265-3995/4007).

87 Wilhelm Fraenger, *Hieronymus Bosch: Das Tausendjährige Reich: Grundzüge einer Auslegung*, Coburg, 1947, p. 132. Fraenger interprets Bosch as the disciple of a 'grand master of free spirit'.

88 On 10 February, according to the pocket diary.

89 Veronica Runtze-Schrantz, 'Dr Franz Schranz und sein Siedlinghauser Kreis', in *Schmittiana* 3 (1991), pp. 63–88.

90 There are letters from Nay dating from the period between 1936 and 1948, some of which are addressed to Duška Schmitt (RW 265-10149/57).

91 After 1945, there were several reunions and an extensive correspondence with the internationally renowned musician (RW 265-5700/35). See also her memoirs: *Charaktere und Katastrophen*, Berlin, 1978.

92 See Antonescu's letter of thanks to Schmitt for a 'unique conversation', dated 8 April 1943 (RW 265-454). In 1944, Schmitt received a Romanian medal.

93 Tilitzki, 'Die Vortragsreisen Carl Schmitts während des Zweiten Weltkriegs', p. 215.

94 Outline in RW 265-2009 Bd. I.

95 Letter of 1 September 1943 from Gottfried Benn to Schmitt (RW 265-1231). Earlier, he gave his thanks following the receipt of *Land and Sea* on 28 March 1943 (RW 265-1230). The letters are reproduced in Piet Tommissen, 'Apropos des deux lettres inédites de Gottfried Benn', *Etudes Germaniques* 20 (1965), pp. 573–6. Benn sent a copy of *Kunst und Macht* (1934) to Schmitt on 3 April 1943. It contained the dedication: 'From the year 1934 – long long ago – ! To Herrn Prof. Dr Carl Schmitt with venerating greetings' ['long long ago' in English in the original].

96 A twenty-eight-page manuscript for a lecture in Spanish, written by Schmitt (RW 265-18923). Short note in *Frankfurter Zeitung*, no. 281/282 (4 June 1943).

97 Letter of 16 June 1944 to Gremmels, in *Schmittiana* 7 (2001), p. 56.

98 Tilitzki, 'Die Vortragsreisen Carl Schmitts während des Zweiten Weltkriegs', p. 238.

99 Letter of 22 October 1943 from the dean, Wolfgang Siebert (RW 265-15152), making reference to the personnel situation at the time: Ritterbusch and Peters were at the front.

100 Erland Weber-Schumburg to Schmitt, 21 May 1943 (RW 265-17802).

101 Erland Weber-Schumburg to Schmitt, 20 August 1943 (RW 265-17803).

102 Letters from Johannes Popitz, dated 4 October 1943, 22 October 1943, 1 November 1943, 6 December 1943 and 4 December 1943 (RW 265-11167/71).

103 Letter of 6 September 1943 from Oskar von Niedermayer to Schmitt (RW 265-10385). See Hans-Ulrich Seidt, *Berlin, Kabul, Moskau: Oskar Ritter von Niedermayer und Deutschlands Geopolitik*, Munich, 2002.

104 Hans Schneider to Schmitt, 29 December 1943 (RW 265-14024).

105 Günther Schwartz to Schmitt, 26 October 1943 (RW 265-15020). Letters from the period between 1941 and 1975 (RW 265-15016/22). Schmitt's examiner's report on the doctoral thesis, dated 24 November 1944, in RW 265-21499. Schwartz visited Schmitt in Plettenberg on 3 May 1975.

106 Certificate of the university's trustee, dated 8 November 1943 (RW 265-21268). Also in Universitätsarchiv der HUB PA Carl Schmitt, 159/a III Bl. 65/66.

107 Letter of invitation of 16 September 1943 from Hans Freyer to Schmitt (RW

265-2856), making reference to an agreement on the occasion of a former meeting in Berlin in July. Report by Schmitt, dated 2 December 1943, in Universitätsarchiv der HUB PA Carl Schmitt, 159/a III Bl. 74/75.

108 Letter of invitation and stenographic outline of the 'European Jurisprudence' talk in RW 265-21554.

109 Erland Weber-Schumburg to Schmitt, 23 October 1943 (RW 265-17804).

110 Werner Weber's wish for Schmitt in his letter of 25 November 1943 (RW 265-17743).

111 Popitz to Schmitt, 4 December 1943 (RW 265-11171).

112 Postcard of 1 December 1943 from André Steinlein to Schmitt (RW 265-16548).

113 Invitation of 20 November 1943 from Egmont Zechlin of the Berlin 'Reichsinstitut für Seegeltungsforschung' to Schmitt (RW 265-18460) [The institute was an organization which represented Germany's global maritime interests during the time of National Socialism].

114 Jünger, *Strahlungen*, p. 483 (entry for 29 February 1944). Schmitt also referred to a resistance book by Fritz Reck-Malleczewen, *Bockelson: Geschichte eines Massenwahns*, Berlin, 1937. Detailed discussion in Martin Tielke, *Der stille Bürgerkrieg: Ernst Jünger und Carl Schmitt im Dritten Reich*, Berlin, 2007, pp. 19ff.

115 Gremmels to Schmitt on 18 February 1944, in: *Schmittiana* 7 (2001), p. 55.

116 See the letters from the association dated 23 August 1943 and 16 October 1943 (RW 265-11331/333).

117 Letters of 28 March 1944 and 19 April 1944 from Gerhard von Steeg to Schmitt (RW 579-675).

118 Letter of 3 April 1944, sent by Schmoller from Prague, concerning a meeting (RW 265-676).

119 Letter of thanks from Sava Kličković to Schmitt, dated 16 December 1943 (RW 265-7805).

120 Schmitt's report in Tilitzki, 'Carl Schmitt – Staatsrechtslehrer in Berlin', p. 250. Extensive correspondence as well as the report on his travels also in Universitätsarchiv der HUB PA Carl Schmitt, 159/a III Bl. 57/72.

121 Albrecht Haushofer, 'Gefährten', in Haushofer, *Moabiter Sonnette*, Berlin, 1946, p. 31. Cf. also Winkler, *The Long Road West*, vol. 2: *1933–1990*, Oxford, 2007, [p. 105]: 'In front of Freisler's bench stood another Germany.'

122 Programme for the course, dated 22 July 1944, in RW 265-21496 Bl. 17.

123 Duška to Anima, 28 October 1944 (copy in the possession of Ernst Hüsmert).

124 Schmitt to Lohmann, 1 January 1945 (RW 579-490).

125 Letter of 2 January 1945 from Claußen to Schmitt (RW 579-676). Letter of thanks of 21 January 1945 from Peter Ipsen to Schmitt (RW 265-6393). Letter of 28 October 1947 from Rolf Stödters to Schmitt (RW 265-15791).

126 See Duška to Anima, 11 February (copy in the possession of Ernst Hüsmert) and the letter of 17 February 1945 from Joseph H. Kaiser to Schmitt (RW 265-7011). On the shift from the rights to the duties of the 'Volksgenosse' [compatriate], see the survey in Werner Weber, *Die Dienst- und Leistungspflichten der Deutschen*, Hamburg, 1943. In December 1944, Schmitt received a typescript, 'Über den deutschen Volkssturm', from the military academy in Potsdam (RW 265-19498).

127 Siebeck's medical note of 26 February 1945 (RW 265-21454).

128 Carl Schmitt, second examiner's report on the doctoral thesis of Erwin Rieckmann, typescript, dated 19 February 1945, p. 5. Schmitt awarded the thesis a '*cum laude*' (RW 265-18887).

129 Duška to Anima, 28 February 1945 (copy in the possession of Ernst Hüsmert).

130 On the programmatic distinction between 'liberal', 'democratic' and 'national' traditions of interpretation, see Ernst Rudolf Huber, *Vom Sinn der Verfassung*, Hamburg, 1935. On the nationalist interpretation of the bourgeois constitutional movement, see Huber, *Friedrich Christoph Dahlmann und die deutsche Verfassungsbewegung*, Hamburg, 1937, and *Verfassungkrisen des Zweiten Reiches*, Leipzig, 1940.

131 Schmitt to Huber, 28 May 1938 (BAK, N 1505-198).

132 Draft letter by Huber, no date (but before 11 July 1938).

133 Letter of 1 March 1939 from Huber to Schmitt; extensive excerpts made by Schmitt (RW 265-20927).

134 Letter of 30 May 1939 from Huber to Schmitt (RW 265-6269). See Schmitt's letter of 21 August 1942 (BAK, N 1505-198) and Huber's reply to Schmitt of 4 October 1942.

135 Letter of 30 May 1939 from Huber to Schmitt (RW 265-6269).

136 Ernst Rudolf Huber, *Verfassungsrecht des Großdeutschen Reiches*, Hamburg, 1939.

137 Letter of 21 February 1940 from Huber to Schmitt (RW 265-6270).

138 Letter of 4 May 1940 from Huber to Schmitt (BAK, N 1505-198). Cf. Schmitt's letter of 1 July 1940 to Huber and Schmitt's appointment calendar for 1940 (RW 265-19709).

139 Letter of 26 October 1940 from Schmitt to Huber (BAK, N 1505-198).

140 Letter of 2 November 1940 from Huber to Schmitt (BAK, N 1505-198). Letter of 4 November 1940 from Schmitt to Huber.

141 Ernst Rudolf Huber, '"Positionen und Begriffe": Eine Auseinandersetzung mit Carl Schmitt', *Zeitschrift für die gesamte Staatswissenschaft* 101 (1940–1), pp. 1–44; here: p. 22. Similar points were made by Carl Brinkmann ('Rezension', in *Schmollers Jahrbuch* 64 [1940], p. 495), who, however, judged 'the "constitutional" experiment of Prussia–Germany slightly differently and in more positive terms'. On the way Huber positioned himself at the time in relation, on the one hand, to Gerhard Ritter, see *Zeitschrift für die gesamte Staatswissenschaft* 102 (1941–2), pp. 168–76, and, on the other, to Reinhard Höhn, see *Zeitschrift für die gesamte Staatswissenschaft* 101 (1941), pp. 737–9; 103 (1942–3), pp. 546–58. On the discussion of Huber's approach, see Hans Gerber, 'Der politische Begriff des Volkes: Eine kritische Betrachtung zur Volkslehre E. R. Hubers', *Archiv des öffentlichen Rechts* 70 (1940), pp. 129–53.

142 Huber, '"Positionen und Begriffe"', p. 40.

143 Ibid., p. 42. Cf. also the letter of 4 December 1940 from Scheuner to Schmitt (RW 265-12436).

144 Huber to Schmitt, 23 December 1940 (RW 265-6271).

145 Under the leadership of Paul Ritterbusch, this campaign coordinated work by some 500 scholars in the humanities (Geisteswissenschaften) with the aim of preparing a new mental and spiritual order for a German-led Europe after the war. See Frank-Rutger Hausmann, *'Deutsche Geisteswissenschaften' im Zweiten Weltkrieg: Die 'Aktion Ritterbusch' (1940–1945)*, Dresden, 1998.

146 Letter of 15 September 1941 from Schmitt to Huber (BAK, N 1505-198).

147 Letter of 23 September 1941 from Huber to Schmitt (BAK, N 1505-198).

148 Huber to Schmitt, 1 May 1941 (RW 265-6272).

149 Letter of 7 October 1941 from Schmitt to Huber (BAK, N 1505-198).

150 Ernst Rudolf Huber, 'Vorwort' to vol. 1, in Huber, *Idee und Ordnung des Reiches*, Hamburg, 1941.

151 Ernst Rudolf Huber, 'Reichsgewalt und Reichsführung im Kriege', *Zeitschrift*

für die gesamte Staatswissenschaft 101 (1940–1), pp. 550–79. On Huber's Strasbourg works, see Herwig Schäfer, *Juristische Lehre und Forschung an der Reichuniversität Straßburg 1941–1944*, Tübingen, 1999, pp. 168–84.

152 Letter of 11 November 1941 from Huber to Schmitt (BAK, N 1505-198).

153 See the following publications by Ernst Rudolf Huber, *Aufstieg und Entfaltung des deutschen Volksbewusstseins*, Strasbourg, 1942; 'Der preußische Staatspatriotismus im Zeitalter Friedrich des Großen', *Zeitschrift für die gesamte Staatswissenschaft* 103 (1942–3), pp. 430–68; 'Adam Müller und der preußische Staat', *Zeitschrift für deutsche Geisteswissenschaft* 6 (1943–4), pp. 162–80; 'Lessing, Klopstock, Möser und die Wendung vom aufgeklärten zum historisch-individuellen Volksbegriff', *Zeitschrift für die gesamte Staatswissenschaft* 104 (1943–4), pp. 121–59. On Huber's situation at that time, see Ulf Morgenstern, 'Die riskante "Rückkehr in das gesegnete rheinische Land": Über Ernst Rudolf Hubers sächsische und elsässische Jahre und deren Darstellung in seinen "Straßburger Erinnerungen"', in Ronald Lambrecht and Ulf Morgenstern (eds), *Kräftig vorangetriebene Detailforschungen: Aufsätze für Ulrich von Hehl*, Leipzig, 2012, pp. 243–73.

154 Letter of 7 December 1941 from Huber to Schmitt (BAK, N 1505-198).

155 See the letter of 14 March 1943 from Huber to Schmitt (RW 265-6273).

156 Ernst Rudolf Huber, 'Reich, Volk und Staat in der Reichsrechtswissenschaft des 17. und 18. Jahrhunderts', *Zeitschrift für die gesamte Staatswissenschaft* 102 (1941–2), pp. 593–627.

157 Schmitt to Huber, 10 August 1942 (BAK, N 1505-198).

158 Schmitt owned a copy of Franz Grillparzer, *Ein Bruderzwist in Habsburg*, Leipzig, 1941.

159 Letter of 4 October 1942 from Huber to Schmitt (BAK, N 1505-198).

160 Ibid.

161 Letter of 14 March 1943 from Huber to Schmitt (RW 265-6273).

162 According to Schäfer, *Juristische Lehre und Forschung*, pp. 224–5.

163 Letter of 31 December 1943 from Huber to Schmitt (BAK, N 1505-198).

164 Ibid. The preface to the second edition is dated January 1943.

165 Letter of 6 April 1944 from Huber to Schmitt (BAK, N 1505-198).

166 Jünger, *Strahlungen*, pp. 454f. (entry for 14 December 1943).

Chapter 26 Last Writings under National Socialism

1 See Bernd Wegner, 'Hitler, der zweite Weltkrieg und die Choreographie des Untergangs', *Geschichte und Gesellschaft* 26 (2000), pp. 493–518. Herfried Münkler, *Die Deutschen und ihre Mythen*, Berlin, 2009, p. 107.

2 Frank-Rutger Hausmann, *Deutsche Geisteswissenschaften im Zweiten Weltkrieg: Die 'Aktion Ritterbusch'*, Dresden, 1998. A summary account: Hausmann, 'Der "Kriegseinsatz" der Deutschen Geisteswissenschaften im Zweiten Weltkrieg (1940–1945)', in *Deutsche Historiker im Nationalsozialismus*, ed. Winfried Schulze and Otto Gerhard Oexle, Frankfurt, 1999, pp. 63–86. Cf. also Hausmann (ed.), *'Vom Strudel der Ereignisse verschlungen'*, Göttingen, 2001.

3 Erik Wolf, 'Idee und Wirklichkeit des Reiches im deutschen Rechtsdenken des 16. und 17. Jahrhunderts', in Karl Larenz (ed.), *Reich und Recht in der deutschen Philosophie*, vol. 1, Stuttgart, 1943, pp. 33–168.

4 Schmitt added this 'against', as a late modification, in his personal copy (RW 265-28283).

5 According to Hans Freyer's review in *Deutsche Rechtswissenschaft* 5 (1940),

pp. 261–6; here: p. 265. Cf. also Carl Schmitt, 'Auf dem Wege ins Reich' [On the way to the Reich], *Deutsche Juristen-Zeitung* 39 (1934), col. 1474. Further reviews by, among others, Carl Brinkmann, in *Schmollers Jahrbuch* 64 (1940), pp. 493–5; Karl Lohmann, 'Rechtswissenschaft und Politik: Bemerkungen zu Carl Schmitts "Positionen und Begriffe"', *Zeitschrift der Akademie für Deutsches Recht* 7 (1940), pp. 108–10; Walter Mallmann, *Geistige Arbeit*, no. 24 (10 December 1940), pp. 11–12; Jürgen von Kempski, in *Zeitschrift für Politik* 31 (1941), pp. 258–9.

6 Wilhelm Grewe, 'Das "Reich" im Völkerrecht: Bemerkungen zu einem Buche von Carl Schmitt', *Frankfurter Zeitung*, 24 April 1940 (RW 265-28283).

7 As noted by Ulrich Scheuner: 'His contribution to the formation of new fundamental concepts for the National Socialist Reich does not [. . .appear] or [appears] only partly in the pages of this collection' ('Politische Grundfragen unserer Zeit', *Europäische Revue* 16 (1940), pp. 357–9; here: p. 358).

8 Sava Kličković to Schmitt, 21 April 1943 (RW 265-7720).

9 Carl Schmitt, 'Über das Verhältnis von Völkerrecht und staatlichem Recht' [On the relationship between international law and state law], in FP, pp. 624–8.

10 Carl Schmitt, 'Die Raumrevolution: Durch den totalen Krieg zu einem totalen Frieden' [The spatial revolution: total peace by way of total war], in SGN, pp. 388–91.

11 He collected quotations in a 'Jung-Deutschland-Tagebuch für Kolonie' [Young Germany diary for colony] (RW 265-19923).

12 Scheuner to Schmitt, 4 December 1940 (RW 265-12436).

13 Carl Schmitt, 'Raum und Großraum im Völkerrecht' [Space and Großraum in international law], in SGN, pp. 234–62; 'Die Auflösung der europäischen Ordnung im "International Law" (1890–1939)' [The dissolution of the European order in 'international law'], in SGN, pp. 372–83.

14 Letter of 27 February 1941 from Gerhard Ritter to Hermann Oncken, in *Gerhard Ritter: Ein politischer Historiker in seinen Briefen*, ed. Klaus Schwabe and Rolf Reichardt, Boppard, 1984, p. 363.

15 Gustav Steinböhmer to Schmitt, 15 October 1941 (RW 265-15719).

16 Wolgast to Schmitt, 18 August 1941 (RW 265-18403). Cf. NtE, pp. 172–3.

17 Carl Schmitt, 'Das Meer gegen das Land', in SGN, pp. 395–8.

18 Letter of 2 May 1941 from the Reclam publishing house to Schmitt (RW 265-11338). By the end of 1944, 38,911 copies of the brochure had been sold (statement sent from the publisher to Schmitt, dated 10 December 1944: RW 265-17190). A reprint of 20,000 copies was planned.

19 One source of inspiration was probably Charles Dickens's *A Children's History of England* (1852). See the letter of 14 January 1943 from Schmitt to Smend (Niedersächsische Staats- und Universitätsbibliothek Göttingen, Cod Ms R. Smend A 759).

20 Smend then wrote to Schmitt on 9 July 1943 (RW 265-15228), referring to an evening they had spent together. This may have been the last personal encounter between the two.

21 Thomas Mann, *Herr und Hund/Gesang vom Kindchen: Zwei Idyllen*, Berlin, 1919.

22 According to Saul Friedländer, *Nazi Germany and the Jews: The Years of Extermination 1939–1945*, London, 2007. For a different account, see Hans Mommsen, *Auschwitz, 17 July 1942: 20 Tage im 20, Jahrhundert: Der Weg zur europäischen 'Endlösung der Judenfrage'*, Munich, 2002.

23 Carl Schmitt, 'Die letzte globale Linie', in SGN, pp. 441–8. The common view of a 'turn from isolation to interventionism and universalism' was also held,

for instance, by Friedrich Berber, *Die amerikanische Neutralität im Kriege 1939–1941*, Essen, 1943.

24 Carl Schmitt, 'Behemoth, Leviathan und Greif: Vom Wandel der Herrschaftsformen' [Behemoth, Leviathan and griffin: on the transformation of forms of domination], *Deutsche Kolonialzeitung* 55 (1943), pp. 30–2.

25 Ernst Forsthoff, *Recht und Sprache: Prolegomena zu einer richterlichen Hermeneutik* [Right and language: prolegomena to a hermeneutics of the judge], Halle, 1940. Cf. also Forsthoff, 'Res sacrae', *Archiv des öffenlichen Rechts* 31 (1940), pp. 209–54.

26 Theodor Maunz, *Das Reich der spanischen Großmachtzeit*, Hamburg, 1944.

27 See Maunz's retrospection in his letter to Schmitt of 30 October 1948 (RW 265-9230).

28 Letter of thanks of 10 July 1953 from Maunz to Schmitt (RW 265-9232). Cf. also his letter to Schmitt of 17 December 1961 (RW 265-9239).

29 See the letter of 27 December 1941 from Maunz to Schmitt (RW 265-9228).

30 Maunz, *Das Reich der spanischen Großmachtzeit*, p. 41.

31 Ibid., p. 141.

32 See Friedrich Berber, *Der Mythos der Monroe-Doktrin*, Essen, 1942.

33 Hans Niedermayer, 'Aristoteles und der Begriff des Nomos bei Lykophron', in *Festschrift für Paul Koschaker zum 60. Geburtstag überreicht von seinen Fachgenossen*, Weimar, 1939, vol. 3, pp. 140–71.

34 Letter of 14 May 1939 from Schmitt to Niedermayer (RW 265-13337).

35 Reply from the Rechts- und Staatswissenschaftlichen Vereinigung of 23 August 1943 (RW 265-11331).

36 Personal copy of 11 November 1950 (RW 265-28259). At a later point, Schmitt wanted 'to place the corollaries, with some additional ones, at the end' (Schmitt to Broermann, 4 April 1961; Verlagsarchiv D & H, Mappe: Schmitt, Nomos der Erde).

37 Letter of thanks of 12 December 1941 from Grewe to Schmitt (RW 265-5151).

38 See the letter of 23 December 1943 from Grewe to Schmitt (RW 265-5152). Wilhelm Grewe, *Epochen der Völkerrechtsgeschichte*, Baden-Baden, 1984.

39 Letter of 3 March 1949 from Grewe to Schmitt (RW 265-5154).

40 Ludwig Dehio, *Gleichgewicht oder Hegemonie: Betrachtungen über ein Grundproblem der neueren Staatengeschichte*, Krefeld, 1948.

41 But see, e.g., the works by Schmitt's pupil Helmut Rumpf, *Die zweite Eroberung Ibero-Amerikas*, Essen, 1942, and *Westafrika: Geschichte einer Küste*, Berlin, 1943.

42 On this theme, inspired by Schmitt, Rüdiger Altmann, 'Die große Ent-Entung', in Rüdiger Altmann and Johannes Gross, *Die neue Gesellschaft: Bemerkungen zum Zeitbewusstsein*, Stuttgart, 1958, pp. 86–90.

43 Tilitzki ('Carl Schmitt – Staatsrechtslehrer in Berlin', pp. 77–80) mentions the extensive examiner's report on the doctoral thesis of Höhn's pupil Roger Diener, in which Schmitt emphasizes the 'idea of the katechon' as a 'spiritual [geistige] bridge from eschatological Christianity to the world-historical existence of the Franconian-German Reich' (p. 79).

44 See Armin von Bogdandy and Stephan Hinghofer-Szalkay, 'Das etwas unheimliche Ius Publicum Europaeum: Begriffsgeschichtliche Analysen im Spannungsfeld von europäischem Rechtsraum, droit public d'Europe und Carl Schmitt', *Zeitschrift für ausländisches öffentliches Recht und Völkerrecht* 73 (2013), pp. 209–48.

45 The French typescript in RW 265-20925.

46 Werner Weber to Schmitt, 28 April 1944 (RW 265-17747).

47 Weber to Schmitt, 6 July 1944 (RW 265-17748).
48 Weber to Schmitt, 22 December 1944 (RW 265-17749). On this particular 'myth' of academic freedom, see Rudolf Smend, *Die Göttinger Sieben*, Göttingen, 1951, and Smend's earlier 'Zum Gedenktag der Göttinger Sieben', *Zeitschrift der Akademie für Deutsches Recht* 4 (1937), p. 691.
49 See Franz Wieacker, *Vom römischen Recht*, Leipzig, 1944.
50 Weber to Schmitt, 28 May 1944 (RW 265-17747).
51 On 24 May 1950, Werner Weber confirmed to Walter Lewald that the text is identical with the pre-1945 version (carbon copy RW 265-17725). However, in particular towards the end, the printed version of 1950 deviates significantly from the typescript, which Schmitt sent to Smend on 9 January 1945. See Reinhard Mehring (ed.), *'Auf der gefahrenvollen Strasse des öffentlichen Rechts': Briefwechsel Carl Schmitt–Rudolf Smend 1921–1961*, 2nd edn, Berlin, 2012, pp. 113–15.
52 In 1942–3, Schmitt had repeated conversations on Bruno Bauer with Hans Körnchen (see Körnchen's letters: RW 265-8055/63). Schmitt's critique of Karl Löwith sets out from Löwith's views on Bauer. The correspondence between Schmitt and Körnchen was edited by Rolf Rieß, 'Eine Freundschaft im Dienste Bruno Bauers: Der Briefwechsel Carl Schmitt und Hans Körnchen', in Klaus-M. Kodalle and Tilman Reitz (eds), *Bruno Bauer (1809–1882): Ein 'Partisan des Weltgeists'?*, Würzburg, 2010, pp. 351–73.

Chapter 27   Detention and 'Asylum'

1 Saul Friedländer, *Nazi Germany and the Jews: The Years of Extermination 1939–1945*, London, 2007, p. 649.
2 Pocket calendar of Duška (RW 265-20827).
3 See David Clay Large, *Berlin*, New York, 2000, p. 357.
4 Diary, 1 March 1945 to 30 September 1945 (RW 265-19586).
5 Duška to Jacques Maritain, 11 January 1946 (RW 265-13763).
6 Identity card of the job centre in the Zehlendorf district, issued on 18 June 1945. The card states the holder's duty to report to the centre once a month (RW 265-21454).
7 Letter of 30 June 1945 from Spranger to the Academic Section [Amt Wissenschaft] at the former Reich Ministry (RW 579-676).
8 Schmitt received Spranger's statement on 24 January 1951 via Serge Maiwald. Cf. also Schmitt's materials on Spranger (RW 265-20832).
9 Hans Schneider to Schmitt, 29 June 1946 (RW 265-14026).
10 According to Markus Lang, *Karl Loewenstein: Transatlantisches Denken der Politik*, Stuttgart, 2007, pp. 249–51. Even more detailed: Joseph W. Bendersky, 'Carl Schmitt's Path to Nuremberg: A Sixty-Year Reassessment', *Telos* 139 (2007), pp. 6–43.
11 During the early years of the Federal Republic, Kaletsch, like Oberheid, was still part of the Düsseldorf circle that supported Schmitt (letters RW 265-7228/74). On their meetings in the summer of 1945, see the letter of 15 July 1948 (RW 265-7230) and the telegram of 11 July 1971 (RW 265-7261) from Kaletsch to Schmitt.
12 Carl Schmitt, 'Note as Conclusion of the Opinion of Prof. Dr Carl Schmitt' (RW 265-19372). Material and typescripts relating to the legal opinion (W 265-19547/55).
13 Confirmation by the personnel department: RW 265-21453.

14 Registered letter of 29 December 1945 from Rektor [Vice-Chancellor] Stroux (RW 265-15916). Also in Universitätsarchiv der HUB PA Carl Schmitt, 159/a III Bl. 73.

15 Among Schmitt's posthumous papers is an interesting letter of 1 September 1975 (RW 265-13185): 'Dear Mr Kohlbrecher, my judgement on Sade is probably still (after fifty years) influenced by Franz Blei. Blei considered Sade's books as pure pornography.' The use Peter Weiss made of Sade in his play *Marat/Sade* did not convince Schmitt either: 'Because Weiss represents a reality in which terror is no longer a criterion of the state of exception, and thus Sade and his cruelties, for Weiss, become a part of our terroristic reality.' In these remarks, Schmitt correlates sadistic conduct with the situation of the state of exception.

16 Carl Schmitt, 'Nationalsozialismus und Rechtsstaat' [National Socialism and the Rechtsstaat], *Juristische Wochenschrift* 63 (1934), pp. 713–18.

17 See the general account by Peter Reichel, *Vergangenheitsbewältigung in Deutschland: Die Auseinandersetzung mit der Diktatur von 1945 bis heute*, Munich, 2001.

18 Confiscation order of 16 October 1945 by the Office of the Director of Intelligence (RW 265-10602).

19 [English in the original.] Karl Löwenstein, 'Observations on Personality and Work of Professor Carl Schmitt' (14 November 1945), quoted in Bendersky, 'Carl Schmitt's Path to Nuremberg: A Sixty-Year Reassessment', p. 16.

20 Schmitt's camp diary (RW 265-19584). Letters from Carl to Duška and further pages from his diary in RW 265-19619. Dozens of long letters sent by Duška to Schmitt while he was in the camp also still exist.

21 Letter of 16 December 1945 from Anima, writing from Cloppenburg (RW 265-12626).

22 Letter of 10 October 1945 from Duška to Carl (RW 265-13772).

23 Entry in Duška's pocket calendar of 1945 (RW 265-20827).

24 Carbon copy of a letter of 20 December 1945 from Duška to Smend (RW 265-13823). Original in Niedersächsische Staats- und Universitätsbibliothek Göttingen, Cod Ms R. Smend A 759. Smend did not respond to the request that he might write to Schmitt.

25 Letter of 19 December 1945 from Duška to Carl (RW 265-13780).

26 Duška to Carl, 22 January 1946 (RW 265-13787).

27 Duška to Carl, 28 January 1946 (RW 265-13789).

28 Note by Schmitt added to the bundle of letters (RW 265-13466). Later letters are among the posthumous papers in the Tommissen collection.

29 Numerous letters by Duška dealing with organizational matters exist from that time (RW 265-13755/825).

30 Schmitt to Duška, January 1946 (RW 265-13469).

31 Carl to Duška, 8 February 1946 (RW 265-13741).

32 Carl Schmitt, 'Versuch eines Berichtes an P. Erich Przywara' [Attempt at a report for P. Erich Przywara] (RW 265-19389).

33 See Carl Schmitt, 'Leserbrief: Einen Druckfehler betreffend' [Letter to the editor: regarding a typographical error], *Frankfurter Allgemeine Zeitung*, no. 12 (15 January 1955).

34 Letter without date (February?) to Duška (RW 265-13470).

35 Koellreutter to Schmitt, 6 February 1946 (RW 265-8000).

36 Duška to Carl, 17 April 1946 (RW 265-13799).

37 Carl to Duška, 18 April 1946 (RW 265-13476).

38 Carl to Duška, 15 May 1946 (RW 265-13479).

39 Extensive details in the letters of 11 June 1946 and 13 June 1946 from Duška to Carl (RW 265-13806/7).
40 Duška to Carl, 20 June 1946 (RW 265-13808).
41 Ibid. Peters's report is dated 17 June 1946 (HUB, Archiv Jur Fak. Bl. 524). In it, Peters calls Schmitt a 'gravedigger of German state law theory' but emphasizes his 'great mental flexibility' and his distancing of himself from National Socialism after 1936. However, the report argues against allowing Schmitt to return to the university.
42 RWN 260-357: from, for instance, the priest Gebhardt, Erich F. Podach, Ferdinand Friedensburg, Corina Popitz and Frau Jessen.
43 Letter of 19 June 1946 from Duška to Carl (RW 265-13811).
44 Duška to Carl 13 August 1946 (RW 265-13813).
45 Duška to Carl, 4 September 1946 (RW 265-13814).
46 Duška to Carl, 31 September 1946 (RW 265-13817). Related material from Richard Siebeck and Kreuz: RW 265-21781.
47 The certificate of release of 10 October 1946 still exists: RW 265-21453.
48 Carl Schmitt, 'Prolog' [Prologue]; preface to the Spanish edition of *Ex captivitate salus* (RW 265-21479/21245). So far only a retranslation from the Spanish by Günter Maschke has been published, in *Schmittiana* 2 (1990), pp. 140–1.
49 Schmitt frequently visited Heinrich von Kleist's grave, for instance together with the painter Werner Heldt. Schmitt owned a drawing by him depicting Kleist's death. Schmitt was interested in the changes that were made to the inscription on the grave on 21 November 1941 on the occasion of the 130th anniversary of Kleist's death. On this see Josef Hadrich to Schmitt, 16 July 1964 (RW 265-5558).
50 Manuscript of the letter to Spranger in RW 579-676. Typescript of 'Zwei Gräber' [Two graves]: RW 265-20922.
51 For Spranger's view of the matter, see *Schmittiana* 5 (1996), p. 207. See also Schmitt's surprisingly unpolemical material in RW 265-20832.
52 Schmitt quotes from the lyrical poet Konrad Weiß. On the one hand, he has in mind his text *Der christliche Epimetheus* (1933), on the other, Weiß's religious perspective on history. On the rejuvenation of this perspective, see Schmitt's important letter to Walter Warnach, dated 20 February 1963 (HAStK, Best. 1688, Korrespondenz mit Carl Schmitt), in which he rejects Friedhelm Kemp's re-edition of the text as a 'neutralization'.
53 See Reinhard Mehring, 'Utopiker der Intellektuellenherrschaft: Karl Mannheim und Carl Schmitt', *Berliner Debatte Initial* 23 (2012), pp. 67–93.
54 Theodor Däubler, 'Sang an Palermo', in *Hymne an Italien*, 3rd edn, Leipzig, 1924, p. 65.
55 Certificate of Berlin magistrate of 18 March 1947 (Depositum Jürgen Becker).
56 Jupp Schmitt to Schmitt, 13 October 1946 (RW 265-13836).
57 Testament of Schmitt's father, Johann Schmitt, of 20 March 1941, in Depositum Jürgen Becker.
58 Telegram from Anna Schmitt, 2 May 1946 (RW 579-676).
59 Bernhard von Mutius to Schmitt, 9 January 1947 (RW 265-10097). In 1953, Mutius was arrested in the GDR and deported to a Russian camp. He returned at the end of 1955 and immediately published, under the pseudonym Bernhard Roeder, *Der Katorgan: Ein Traktat über die moderne Sklaverei*, Cologne, 1956.
60 Letter of 17 March 1947 from Flechtheim, member of the Counsel for War Crimes, to Schmitt (RW 265-3681).

61 Letter of 19 December 1965 to Margret Boveri (*Schmittiana* 7 (2001), p. 307). There is a highly detailed description of this journey by Schmitt's fellow traveller Heinz Schmid-Lossberg in a letter to Schmitt of 2 February 1976 (RW 265-12563).

62 Letter of 1 April 1947 from Duška to Jahrreiß (RW 265-13761). The letter explicitly mentions that it was not clear whether Schmitt was in Nuremberg 'as a witness or an accused'.

63 The record of this second interrogation has only recently been found in Kempner's posthumous papers, and it has been published in English translation by Joseph W. Bendersky, in *Telos* 139 (2007), pp. 39–43.

64 Carl from Nuremberg to Duška (RW 579-676).

65 Duška to Carl, 28 April 1947 (RW 265-13818).

66 Duška to Carl, 3 May 1947 (RW 265-13819).

67 Letter of transferral from the officer Donald E. Fawcett (RW 265-19370).

68 Herfried Münckler is therefore not quite correct; see his *Die Deutschen und ihre Mythen*, Berlin, 2009, pp. 130f.

69 Notebook 'Nuremberg 1947–1957' (RW 265-19203). Stenographic outlines of his answers in RW 19379/19383. Manuscripts and typescripts in RW 265-19374/19378.

70 Letter of 6 June 1947 from Barion to Schmitt (RW 265-691).

71 Letter of 30 December 1947 from Barion to Schmitt (RW 265-698).

72 Pocket diary for 1948 (RW 265-19624).

73 Gottfried Neeße to Schmitt (RW 265-10178/220).

74 Letter of 7 April 1947 from Bung to Duška Schmitt (RW 265-2227).

75 The grand piano was rented out and was to be sold in 1950 in order to pay for Duška's hospital expenses. It was put up at the home of the pianist Prof. Dr Adolf Steiner, who could not afford it and wanted to leave Berlin in the summer of 1950. There was some disgruntlement over the payment of the valuer. Duška did not want to sell it too cheaply and now rather wanted it for Anima in Plettenberg (letter of 14 July 1950 from Duška to Prof. Adolf Steiner; RW 579-677). The deal fell through, and in January 1951 the grand piano was still in commission in Berlin (letters from the period between 1 September 1950 and 8 January 1951from Claus Döll; RW 265-18627).

76 On 21 April 1954 (RW 265-11545) Dr Bürkle of the *Merian* editorial office requested a contribution at short notice. On 29 April (RW 265-11455) he thanked Schmitt for his positive reply: 'I would welcome it if you could write your contribution in a personal and literary style.' On 12 May the text arrived, and on 18 June (RW 265-11457) Bürkle wrote that he 'liked it very much' as an introductory article. On 30 August he sent Schmitt his author's copies.

77 Letter of 22 June 1947 from Peterson to Duška (RW 579-677) and of 5 April 1948 from Peterson to Carl Schmitt (RW 265-10933).

78 Thus, for instance, Theodor Nehen. See his striking letter to Schmitt, dated 25 November 1948 (RW 265-10222/3).

79 Letter of 2 June 1947 from Schmitt to Huber (BAK, N 1505-198).

80 Stödter to Schmitt, 28 October 1947 (RW 265-15791).

81 A recapitulation of the events leading up to their reunion in a letter of 7 July 1948 from Ipsen, sent on the occasion of Schmitt's sixtieth birthday (RW 265-6402).

82 Scheuner to Schmitt, 5 July 1948 (RW 265-12438).

83 Werner Weber to Schmitt, 3 July 1948 (RW 265-17754)

84 Wolfgang Siebert to Schmitt, 8 July 1948 (RW 265-15155). However, Siebert did not want any closer contact.

85 Letter of 3 September 1948 from Schmitt to Gremmels, in *Schmittiana* 7 (2001), p. 79. Cf. also BS, p. 35.
86 See Gustav von Schmoller, *Handbuch des Besatzungsrechts*, Tübingen, 1950–5.
87 See Schmoller's account: 'Die Affaire um einen Botschafter' (typescript: RW 265-19479).
88 Letter to Helmut Rumpf, 20 April 1948, in *Schmittiana* 7 (2001), pp. 369–70.
89 See Gerhard Nebel, *An der Mosel*, Wuppertal, 1948; *Unter Partisanen und Kreuzfahrern*, Stuttgart, 1948.
90 Cf. *Ernst Jünger/Gerhard Nebel: Briefe 1938–1974*, ed. Ulrich Fröschle and Michael Neumann, Stuttgart, 2003, pp. 144ff, 152f.
91 Nebel to Jünger, 23 April 1948, ibid., p. 198.
92 Nebel to Jünger, 8 October 1948, ibid., p. 240.
93 Schmitt to Gremmels, 10 October 1948, in *Schmittiana* 7 (2001), p. 83.
94 Nebel to Schmitt, 22 November 1948 (RW 265-10162).
95 Postcard of 29 November from Nebel and Ernst Jünger to Schmitt (RW 265-10176).
96 Nebel reported the completion of his work to Schmitt in a letter of 13 February 1949 (RW 265-10163). Cf. Gerhard Nebel, *Ernst Jünger und das Schicksal des Menschen*, Wuppertal, 1948; *Ernst Jünger: Abenteuer des Geistes*, Wuppertal, 1949 (in the preface, Nebel thanks Schmitt for conversations).
97 Nebel to Ernst Jünger, 30 March 1949, in *Briefe 1938–1974*, p. 295.
98 Hans Schneider to Schmitt, 5 December 1948 (RW 265-14030).
99 Schmitt soon afterwards started a notebook on 'Just War', in which he collected annotated newspaper articles (RW 265-19191).
100 Of biographical interest are also his remarks on Alsace–Lorraine (FP, pp. 756–8).
101 Hans Schneider to Schmitt, 7 July 1950 (RW 265-14033).
102 Hans Schneider to Schmitt, 27 March 1951 (RW 265-14035).
103 The diaries, not quite ordered, can be found in the posthumous papers under RW 265-19598/679.
104 Carl Schmitt, 'Amnestie oder die Kraft des Vergessens' [Amnesty or the force of forgetting] (SGN, pp. 218–19).
105 Wilhelm Grewe, 'Über das Völkerrecht des Nürnberger Prozesses', in *Nürnberg als Rechtsfrage: Eine Diskussion*, Stuttgart, 1947, pp. 7–48. Grewe sent Schmitt his article the following year, on 11 March 1948, together with an apologetic letter (RW 265-5153). On the wider context, see Annette Weinke, *Die Nürnberger Prozesse*, Munich, 2006.
106 Schmitt owned a copy of Theodor Fritsch (ed.), *Die zionistischen Protokolle: Das Programm der internationalen Geheimregierung*, Leipzig, 1924.
107 Erich Müller-Gangloff, *Vorläufer des Antichrist*, Berlin, 1948. Müller-Gangloff sees the history of Christianity accompanied by a history of precursors of the Antichrist, which is evident in particular in heretical movements. He discusses Rienzi, the Anabaptist Bockelson, Demetrius, Schiller's dramatic figure Wallenstein, and, with Sabbatai Zwi, also a Jewish-messianic case of the inversion of religiosity into the idea of an immanent redeemer. With Cagliostro, Robespierre and Napoleon, he then moves towards more recent precursors of the Antichrist. In the modern age, he argues, Don Juan and Faust have taken the place of the Antichrist. Hitler and National Socialism he describes as 'the presence of the Antichrist' and last 'precursors', which is why the end of history is not here yet. 'Vulgar idealism' has offered a 'substitute religion'. Prussianism and Wilhelminianism created further preconditions. Müller-Gangloff ends with Hitler's biography and the 'messianic delusion'

[Messiaswahn], 'Aryan delusion' and 'anti-Semitism' as the 'face of the Antichrist'. Such psychological and demonological reflections, based on solid historical knowledge, were common at the time. Parts of Schmitt's cryptic theology of history can be found in Müller-Gangloff.

108 Letters from 3 May 1949 onwards from Kemp to Schmitt (RW 265-7344/78). Over decades, Schmitt also kept in touch with the university chaplain – and an admirer of Weiß – Wilhelm Nyssen in Cologne (RW 265-10443/66).

109 Kemp sent his Däubler edition to Schmitt on 6 November 1951 (RW 265-7355). See also Friedhelm Kemp, 'Der Dichter Konrad Weiß', *Wort und Wahrheit* 4 (1949), pp. 180–292.

110 Letter of 14 August 1954 from Kemp to Schmitt (RW 265-7358).

111 At the time he was writing these lines, Schmitt, after decades, visited again Däubler's friend Ida Bienert, an old acquaintance of Schmitt from his time in Munich. On 25 November 1956, Kemp wrote to Schmitt (RW 265-7373), saying that Frau Bienert had 'told [him] enthusiastically about [Schmitt's] visit'. In 1961, Kemp sent a Weiß edition from the Kösel Verlag: letter of 12 December 1961 from Kemp to Schmitt (RW 265-7377).

Chapter 28   From Benito Cereno to Hamlet

1 The incomplete list of individuals, discussed in no particular chronological order in the following account, is based on 'Interview mit Anni Stand und Ernst Hüsmert zu Carl Schmitts Aufenthalt in Plettenberg v. 1947–1985', in *Verortung des Politischen: Carl Schmitt in Plettenberg*, ed. Ingeborg Villinger, Hagen, 1990, pp. 42–61.

2 The watercolours by Richter, with a dedication from Mohler, dated 1 September 1948, in RW 265-19101. On Mohler, see Helmuth Kiesel, *Ernst Jünger: Die Biographie*, Berlin, 2007, pp. 541, 544, 584 (Mohler was actually rejected by the Waffen SS and was interned).

3 Weber to Schmitt, 1 April 1949 (RW 265-17757).

4 Schmitt's carbon copy of a letter, dated 15 April 1950, to Javier Conde (RW 265-12874).

5 Winckelmann to Schmitt, 19 May 1941 (RW 265-18080).

6 Winckelmann to Schmitt, 3 January 1948 (RW 265-18085). Important information on their reunion: Freda Winckelmann to Schmitt, 31 December 1947 (RW 265-18044).

7 Winckelmann to Schmitt, 6 February 1948 (RW 265-18087).

8 Winckelmann to Schmitt, 11 July 1949 (RW 265-18111).

9 He described Schmitt's 'ingenious fishing of men' [geniale Menschenfischerei] in Henning Ritter, 'Mein Besuch bei Carl Schmitt', *Frankfurter Allgemeine Zeitung*, no. 287 (9 December 2006). Cf. Ritter, *Die Eroberer: Denker des 20. Jahrhunderts*, Munich, 2008, pp. 111–24.

10 Letters, dated between 1 December 1948 and 27 January 1949, from Stödter to Schmitt (RW 265-15800/5).

11 Agreement between the Phrix-Werke Aktiengesellschaft and Carl Schmitt, dated 15 February 1949, in Depositum Jürgen Becker. The contract on the provision of legal advice stipulates an 'annual fee for advice' of 6,000 Deutschmarks, to be paid by monthly instalments.

12 Schmitt made the acquaintance of the friend of Däubler and painter Wilhem Wessel on 5 January 1949 (Wessel to Schmitt, 7 July 1953: RW 265-17953). The plan for the conference, together with a letter of 24 January 1949 from Wessel

to Schmitt (RW 265-17945). Thank-you letter sent to Schmitt after the conference, dated 8 April 1949 (RW 265-17949).

13 Letter of 12 May 1949 from Kaiser to Schmitt (RW 265-7020).

14 Nebel to Jünger, 30 March 1949, in *Ernst Jünger/Gerhard Nebel: Briefe 1938–1974*, Stuttgart, 2003, p. 295.

15 Jünger to Nebel, 7 April 1949, ibid., p. 297.

16 Nicolaus Sombart to Schmitt, 6 March 1949 (RW 265-15366).

17 Schmitt to Gremmels, 27 June 1949, in *Schmittiana* 7 (2001), p. 99.

18 Sombart to Schmitt, 16 August 1949 (RW 265-15368).

19 Schmitt to Sombart, 21 August 1949.

20 Warnach to Schmitt, 12 September 1949 (RW 265-17443). Thank-you postcard of 14 September 1949 from Schmitt to Warnach, sent from Walberberg (HAStK, Best. 1688, Korrespondenz mit Carl Schmitt).

21 According to a letter of 23 July 1968 from Zierold to Schmitt (RW 265-18561) and a letter of 1 August 1958 to Schmitt (RW 265-18560). In 1968, Zierold remembered a visit to Plettenberg and emphasized: 'But all attempts at a meeting, be it in Plettenberg, be it even longer ago in Walberberg, were based on my initiative. After all, I had to respect your reserve.' Cf. Kurt Zierold, *Forschungsförderung in drei Epochen*, Wiesbaden, 1968.

22 Confirmation of receipt, dated 27 January 1950, sent from Zierold to Schmitt (RW 265-18557).

23 Letter of 7 October 1949 and postcard of 10 October 1949 from Nebel to Schmitt (RW 265-10170/1).

24 Ernst Forsthoff, *Lehrbuch des Verwaltungsrechts*, vol. 1: *Allgemeiner Teil*, Munich, 1950.

25 Jünger to Duška Schmitt, 22 October 1949 (RW 579-677).

26 The reference is to Friedrich August von der Heydte, 'Francisco de Vitoria und die Geschichte seines Ruhms: Eine Entgegnung', in *Die Friedens-Warte* 49 (1949), pp. 190–7. Cf. Heydte in *Hochland* (1951), pp. 288–94. On this, see Schmitt's letter to Gremmels, dated 1 November 1949, which very clearly reflects Schmitt's desperate mood, in *Schmittiana* 7 (2001), p. 103.

27 Schmitt to Gremmels, ibid.

28 Anima Schmitt to Duška, 7 November 1949 (RW 579-677). More details in Reinhard Mehring, 'Korrespondenz als Familiensache: Mikroanalyse der Entfremdung zwischen Carl Schmitt und Ernst Jünger – anhand unbekannter Briefe', *Zeitschrift für Germanistik*, NF (new series) 3 (2008), pp. 633–46. Anima's letter is now published in full, in *"Eine Tochter ist das ganz andere": Anima Schmitt de Otero (1931–1983)*, Plettenberger Miniaturen 5, Plettenberg, 2012. Reinhard Mehring, 'Don Capisco und sein Soldat: Carl Schmitt und Ernst Jünger', in Stephan Müller-Doohm and Thomas Jung (eds), *Prekäre Freundschaften: Über geistige Nähe und Distanz*, Munich, 2011, pp. 173–85.

29 Schmitt to Duška, 7 November 1949 (RW 579-556).

30 Ernst Jünger to Duška, 4 November 1949 (RW 579-677).

31 Schmitt to Duška, 24 November 1949 (RW 579-556).

32 Werner Weber to Schmitt, 12 December 1949 (RW 265-17759).

33 Zierold to Schmitt, 20 March 1950 (RW 265-18558). It is possible that the application was not even officially received by the DFG, as no personnel file on the process exists (information kindly provided by email on 28 January 2009 by Walter Pietrusziak of the DFG).

34 Jünger to Nebel, 21 January 1950, in *Ernst Jünger/Gerhard Nebel: Briefe 1938–1974*, p. 351, and Jünger to Nebel, 26 January 1950, ibid., pp. 357f.

35 Nebel to Jünger, 25 January 1950, ibid., p. 354.
36 See Nebel's letter of 18 October 1950 to Schmitt (RW 265-10173), as well as later attempts at reconciliation. Quoting from Goethe's *Faust*, Schmitt declared categorically on 28 October: 'Dear Gerhard Nebel, the information my informant gave talked not of a gap but of a grave.' ['Man spricht, wie man mir Nachricht gab / Von keinem Graben, doch vom Grab'; Goethe, *Faust Part II*, 11,557–8] (in *Ernst Jünger/Gerhard Nebel: Briefe 1938–1974*, p. 818.) A little later, Ernst Jünger would also break off any contact with Nebel for many years.
37 After 1933, Hettlage was the city treasurer of Berlin, held a personal chair and worked for Albert Speer. After 1945 he held a chair in Mainz, and from 1958 he was state secretary in the Ministry of Finance.
38 Letter of February and March 1950 from Stödter to Schmitt (RW 265-15811/15).
39 Nicolaus Sombart to Schmitt, 27 March 1950 (RW 265-15370).
40 See Freda Winckelmann to Schmitt, 25 March 1950 (RW 265-18047), and Johannes Winckelmann to Schmitt, 28 April 1950 (RW 265-18117).
41 On 24 August 1950, the physician in charge, Prof. Siebeck, spoke of a 'turning point' (RW 265-15140). Very many of Schmitt's letters to Duška in hospital are preserved (RW 579-677).
42 Letter of 8 September 1950 from Ernst Jünger to Duška (RW 579-677).
43 Nicolaus Sombart to Duška Schmitt, 20 September 1950 (RW 265-15429).
44 Siebeck to Schmitt, 6 October 1950 (RW 265-18813).
45 Schmitt's personal copy of 11 November 1950 has the dedication to Duška attached, but also a letter of protest from Fritz Pringsheim (RW 265-28259).
46 Corinna Sombart to Schmitt, 23 November 1950 (RW265-15341).
47 Weber to Schmitt, 13 October 1950 (RW 265-17766).
48 Postcard of 20 November 1950 from Ernst and Gretha Jünger (as well as Marguerite Meerschaum) to Duška Schmitt (RW 579-677).
49 Schmitt to Duška, 30 November 1950 (RW 579-557).
50 Eduard Rosenbaum, 'Carl Schmitt vor den Toren', *Rheinischer Merkur*, no. 48 (25 November 1950), pp. 18–19.
51 According to Barion in a letter of 8 December 1950 to Werner Weber's wife. Reproduced in Thomas Marschler, *Kirchenrecht im Bannkreis Carl Schmitts*, Bonn, 2004, pp. 491–3.
52 Nebel to Schmitt, 18 October 1950 (RW 265-10173).
53 Letter of 29 December 1950 from Grewe to Schmitt (RW 265-5155). Gisela Smend also sent a long letter of condolence, with personal memories (RW 265-15208). Numerous other letters of condolence from, among others, Carl Bilfinger, Wilhelm Neuß, Carl Brinkmann, Karl Lohmann, Erwin von Beckerath, Johannes Winckelmann, Joseph H. Kaiser, Arnold Schmitz, Gustav Steinbömer, Franz Josef Brecht and Wilhelm Stapel, in RW 260-360.
54 Erik Peterson to Schmitt, 11 December 1950 (RWN 260-360).
55 Heidi Hahn to Schmitt, 18 December 1950 (RWN 260-360).
56 Ernst Jünger's wife, Gretha von Jeinsen, wrote an obituary which emphasized Duška's courage and willingness to make sacrifices: Gretha von Jeinsen, 'Duška', in Jeinsen, *Silhouetten: Eigenwillige Betrachtungen*, Pfullingen, 1955, pp. 172–5.
57 Gerhard Günther in a letter to Schmitt of 10 May 1949, where the expression referred to a certain Dr von Wedel (RW 265-5424).
58 Notebook with list of recipients: RW 265-19600.
59 The social network of Schmitt's 'Plettenberg system' can be reconstructed

with great accuracy from this source. See Reinhard Mehring, 'Der esoterische Diskurspartisan: Carl Schmitt in der Bundesrepublik', in Thomas Kroll and Tilman Reitz (eds), *Intellektuelle in der Bundesrepublik Deutschland: Verschiebungen im politischen Feld der 1960er und 1970er Jahre*, Göttingen, 2013, pp. 232–48.

60 RW 265-19600 Bl. 7. Thus, Schmitt's 'Apocrypha' are today all known.

61 Welty to Schmitt, 26 September 1933 (RW 265-17911).

62 Letter of 22 December 1948 from Welty to Schmitt (RW 579-676). Cf. also Eberhard Welty, *Die Entscheidung in die Zukunft: Grundsätze und Hinweise zur Neuordnung im deutschen Lebensraum*, Heidelberg, 1946.

63 Letter of 22 January 1949 from Welty to Schmitt (RW 579-676). Letter of 22 December 1948 from Welty to Schmitt (RW 579-676). Cf. also Father Franziskus Stratmann, 'Carl Schmitts "Begriff des Politischen"', *Der Friedenskämpfer* 4 (1928), no. 5, pp. 1–7; no. 6, pp. 1–7.

64 Letter of 10 March 1949 from Schmitt to Gremmels, in *Schmittiana* 7 (2001), p. 93.

65 Friedrich August von der Heydte, 'Francesco di Vitoria und die Geschichte seines Ruhms: Eine Entgegnung', *Die Friedens-Warte* 49 (1949), pp. 190–7; here: pp. 192, 196f.

66 Letters of 20 October 1949 and 5 November 1949 from Welty to Schmitt (RW 265-17914/5). Typescript of a reply from the journal (RW 265-19385).

67 Welty to Schmitt, 15 December 1949 (RW 265-17916).

68 Letter of 10 December 1949 from Schmitt to Huber (BAK, N 1505-198).

69 Quoted from Wilhelm Schmitz, 'Zur Geschichte der Academia Moralis', in *Schmittiana* 4 (1994), pp. 119–56; here: p. 129.

70 Welty to Schmitt, 21 December 1949 (RW 265-17917).

71 Letter of 16 January 1950 from Welty to Schmitt (RW 579-676).

72 Letter of 13 May 1950 from Welty to Schmitt (RW 579-676).

73 On this in detail, see Dirk van Laak, *Gespräche in der Sicherheit des Schweigens*, Berlin, 1993, pp. 38–41.

74 Letter of 19 May 1952 from Welty to Schmitt (RW 265-17922).

75 Letter of 22 November 1958 from Welty to Schmitt (RW 265-17926).

76 Letter of 3 March 1946 from Maiwald to Schmitt (RW 265-8975/6).

77 Publication history documented in Piet Tommissen, 'Neue Bausteine zu einer Biographie Carl Schmitts', in *Schmittiana* 5 (1995), pp. 151–223; here: pp. 182–90. List of recipients of the article, dated 1 March (RW 265-18934): Forsthoff, Ipsen, Werner Weber, Arnold Schmitz, Bilfinger and Rothacker, among others. Huber is absent from the list. A long list of review copies sent to the international press (RW 265-17138).

78 Winckelmann to Schmitt, 28 April 1950 (RW 265-18117).

79 Winckelmann to Schmitt, 26 June 1950 (RW 265-18120).

80 J. Kaiser informed Schmitt in a letter dated 5 March 1952 (RW 265-7033). See the obituary in *Universitas* 7 (1952), pp. 427–8.

81 Letter of 16 October 1952 from Dr H. W. Bähr to Schmitt (RW 265-11488).

82 The head of the literary gazette was a former member of the SS, Günther Franz, and it was co-edited by Forsthoff. There are only formal letters from Franz to Schmitt (RW 265-4033/37).

83 See the letters of 10 July 1948 and 14 December 1949 from the publisher Philipp Reclam to Schmitt (RW 265-11339/41). The letters envisage a new edition of the small text, which had either sold out or had been destroyed by fire.

84 Ziegler to Schmitt, 27 July 1948 (RW 265-18538).

85 There are friendly expressions of interest from the HVA dating from the period between 26 October 1948 and 10 January 1949 (RW 265-17117). The HVA transferred an advance to Schmitt in order to signal the genuineness of their interest.

86 See Broermann to Schmitt, 7 January 1949 (RW 265-16948). Broermann was in charge of the publishing house from 1938.

87 Account of the relationship and reproduction of Schmitt's letter to Broermann, dated 22 May 1950, in Florian Simon, 'Legalität, Legitimität und das Politische – ein Briefwechsel', in *Theorie des Rechts und der Gesellschaft: Festschrift für Werner Krawietz zum 70. Geburtstag*, Berlin, 2003, pp. 83–98; here: pp. 97f.

88 Neske communicated his interest to Schmitt as early as January 1950 (RW 265-10230). Neske expected that the book on Cortés would certainly appear through his publishing house (letter of 22 August 1950: RW 265-10234) and was irritated and 'sad' that he 'came away empty-handed' (letter of 1 September 1950: RW 265-10236).

89 Dr Marcus of the Greven publishing house to Schmitt, 31 October 1949 (RW 265-17014).

90 Letter of 25 January 1950 from Epting to Schmitt (RW 265-3242). The progress with the production of Schmitt's works is clearly documented in the rich correspondence over the following months.

91 Schmitt to Marianne Greven, 14 December 1949 (RW 265-13041).

92 Schmitt to Georg Freund, 1 November 1950 (RW 265-13002).

93 Personal copy, dated 15 August 1950 (RW 265-27456). On 22 August 1950, a list of the review copies which had been distributed was sent to Schmitt (RW 265-3264). See Maiwald's review in *Universitas* 5 (1950), pp. 1221–4.

94 Protesting letter of 10 January 1951 from Barion to the publisher (RW 265-1079).

95 Letter of 10 October 1951 from Epting to Schmitt (RW 265-3289).

96 Sombart to Schmitt, 27 December 1951 (RW 265-15383).

97 Letter of 6 December 1951 from Epting to Schmitt (RW 265-3295).

98 Schmitt was informed of this by the publisher on 6 January 1953 (RW 265-17031; substantial number of letters from the publisher: RW 265-17013/43). Carbon copy of Schmitt's letter to Greven, dated 19 February 1953 (RW 265-13040). See also carbon copies of Schmitt's letters to Epting (RW 265-12938/947).

99 Letter of 25 December 1953 from Schmitt to Mrs Renner of Maiwald's Tübingen publishing house (RW 265-13413).

100 Letters of 5 February 1955 (RW 265-17039) and 12 February 1955 (RW 265-5149) from Greven to Schmitt.

101 See the numerous letters from Gisa-Alice von Renner d'Obrien, the wife of Serge Maiwald, to Schmitt (RW 265-11568/78) and Schmitt's letter of 16 May 1956 to Frau Renner (RW 265-13414).

102 Letter of 8 August 1960 from the publisher to Schmitt (RW 265-17040). More than 4,000 copies were bought for the price of 3,000 Deutschmarks.

103 Offer made by Schmitt to Broermann in a letter of 2 September 1960 (Verlagsarchiv D & H, Mappe: Carl Schmitt, Nomos der Erde). Further correspondence followed. At Easter 1961, the text appeared with a new binding.

104 On 6 April 1962, Otto Zeller approached Schmitt because he wanted to issue a new edition of the *Leviathan* book. However, Schmitt had political reservations. The two then considered a new edition of *The Guardian of the Constitution*, as well as an English translation of the *Leviathan* book (to be

done by Schwab). But Schmitt could not make up his mind about these plans, and thus the business relation remained limited to the distribution of the smaller texts (see especially the letters of 14 November 1962 and 10 May 1967 from Zeller to Schmitt: RW 265-18508 and RW 265-18517).

105 Letter of 9 April 1953 from Schmitt to Günter Neske (RW 265-13323).

106 Letter of 4 August to Neske (RW 265-13327). On 10 November 1960, Schmitt sent a telegram setting an ultimate deadline for a reply from Neske (RW 265-13328).

107 A letter of 9 October 1952 from the publisher to Schmitt (RW 265-17193) asked for a 'slight revision', which would remove anything 'that might erroneously be interpreted as anti-Semitic'. A clarifying meeting with Dr Nussbächer from the publishing house followed on 13 May 1953 (RW 265-13194). See the 'revision' Schmitt sent to Dr Nussbächer on 6 June 1953 (RW 265-13676). However, the slim volume appeared only in November 1954 (Nussbächer to Schmitt, 16 September 1954: RW 265-17200). The publisher forgot to print the table of contents (see Nussbächer to Schmitt, 27 July 1955: RW 265-17204).

108 Schmitt to Heinz Friedrich, 21 August 1976 (RW 265-13016). Schmitt made similar statements in a letter of 23 April 1973 to Sander (SSA, p. 267). In the case of Diederichs, the formulation certainly does not apply. Schmitt retracted *Hamlet or Hecuba* at the end of 1962, explicitly citing as the reason that Gräfin Dönhoff was an in-house author. That was company Schmitt did not want to keep (letters of 1 December 1962 and 8 December 1962 from Schmitt to Diederichs: RW 265-12920/21). The publisher was surprised by this: 'The expectation of an author only to be united in the same publishing house with authors that do not stand in any kind of opposition to him is, after all, entirely impractical and cannot be fulfilled' (Peter Diederichs to Schmitt, 5 December 1962: RW 265-2881).

109 See Dr Winkler's letters from the period between 12 October 1955 and 7 December 1955 (RW 265-16892/5).

110 Schmitt to the Scientia publishing house, 20 February 1967 (RW 265-13682). Schmitt 'no longer wanted anything to do' with Mohr (Siebeck), and thus also gave *The Guardian of the Constitution* to Duncker & Humblot (Schmitt to Broermann, 16 November 1967, Verlagsarchiv D & H, Mappe: Schmitt, Diktatur, 3. Aufl.).

111 The correspondence Schmitt–Bobbio, in Piet Tommissen, *In Sachen Carl Schmitt*, Vienna, 1997, pp. 113–55. Review of a Hobbes edition by Moncada, in *Universitas* 3 (1948), pp. 837–8, and of a book on Hobbes by Bobbio, in *Universitas* 4 (1949), p. 330.

112 Letter of 1 July 1949 from Paeschke to Schmitt (RW 265-10759).

113 Letter of 16 August 1949 from Paeschke to Schmitt (RW 265-10761).

114 Letter of 3 February 1950 from Paeschke to Schmitt (RW 265-10764).

115 Karl Löwith, *Meaning in History*, Chicago, 1949; German edn: *Weltgeschichte und Heilsgeschehen: Die theologischen Voraussetzungen der Geschichtsphilosophie*, Stuttgart, 1953. Cf. Löwith, 'Weltgeschichte und Heilsgeschichte', in *Anteile: Martin Heidegger zum 60. Geburtstag*, Frankfurt, 1950, pp. 106–53.

116 See Reinhard Mehring, 'Karl Löwith, Carl Schmitt, Jacob Taubes und das "Ende der Geschichte"', *Zeitschrift für Religions- und Geistesgeschichte* 48 (1996), pp. 231–48.

117 Hans Freyer, *Weltgeschichte Europas*, Wiesbaden, 1948.

118 See, for instance, Jacob Taubes, *Occidental Eschatology* (1947), Stanford, CA, 2009; 'The Issue Between Judaism and Christianity: Facing Up to the

Unresolvable Difference', in Taubes, *From Cult to Culture: Fragments Towards a Critique of Historical Reason*, Stanford, 2010, pp. 45–58.

119 Kesting to Schmitt, 22 September 1950 (RW 265-7467).

120 Else Hahn was in charge of organizing the publication. Schmitt knew her from his time in Berlin. Letters from Else Hahn from 8 July 1948 onwards; invitation to contribute to the commemorative publication, dated 25 August 1949 (RW 265-5650/56). In mid-1950, Schmitt submitted his contribution. The title refers to Homer (*Odysseus*, book 24, lines 80–4).

121 Stödter to Schmitt, 11 October 1950 (RW 265-15818).

122 Ernst Jünger to Duška, 22 August 1950 (RW 579-677).

123 Walter Lewald, 'Carl Schmitt redivivus?', *Neue Juristische Wochenschrift* 3 (1950), p. 377. Editorial note in *Frankfurter Hefte* 4 (1949), p. 985. Gotthard Montesi, 'Carl Schmitt redivivus', *Wort und Wahrheit* 6 (1951), pp. 221–4.

124 Letters from the period between 30 October 1950 and 19 February 1953 from Freund to Schmitt (RW 265-4292/99). Cf. Schmitt to Hans Franzen, 22 January 1958 (RW 579-469). Franzen avoided meeting Freund: 'But the resentment of the emigrants and those who return is unpredictable.'

125 Karl Korn, 'Der christliche Epimetheus', *Frankfurter Allgemeine Zeitung* (7 October 1950). Cf. also 'Der "authentische" Fall eines christlichen Epimetheus', *Neue Züricher Zeitung*, no. 156 (9 July 1951).

126 Karl Thieme, 'Carl Schmitts Apologie', *Deutsche Universitäts-Zeitung* (17 November 1950).

127 Eduard Rosenbaum, 'Carl Schmitt vor den Toren', *Rheinischer Merkur*, no. 48 (25 November 1950), pp. 18–19.

128 Schmitt to Günther Krauss, 3 December 1950, quoted in Tommissen, *In Sachen Carl Schmitt*, p. 53.

129 Franz Beyerle, in *Archiv des öffentlichen Rechts* 76 (1950), pp. 501–4; Jürgen von Kempski, in *Merkur* 5 (1951), pp. 491–5; Carl Brinkmann, in *Universitas* 6 (1951), pp. 907–9; Alfred Verdross, in *Zeitschrift für öffentliches Recht* 4 (1951), pp. 249–50; Hans Wehberg, in *Die Friedenswarte* 50 (1951), pp. 305–14; Rolf Stödter, in *Deutsches Verwaltungblatt* 67 (1952), p. 290; Theodor Schieder, in *Geschichte in Wissenschaft und Unterricht* 3 (1952), pp. 175–6.

130 His short review appeared with some delay in *Universitas* 7 (1952), pp. 299–300.

131 F. W. Koch, in *Mannheimer Morgen*, no. 262 (9 November 1950), p. 5 (RW 265-18935 Bl. 1).

132 Dr Brinkmann to the Greven publishing house, 9 October 1950 (RW 265-2080).

133 Golo Mann, 'Carl Schmitt und die schlechte Juristerei', in *Der Monat* 5 (1952), pp. 89–92.

134 Huber to Schmitt, 27 January 1947 (RW 265-6274).

135 Some years later, Schmitt would publish a short review of F. J. P. Veale, in which he referred to the Nuremberg trials against war criminals and also made reference to Raymond Aron, in *Das Historische Buch* 3 (1955), pp. 200–1. He then entered into closer and friendly contact with Veale (there are over a hundred letters from Veale, dating from the time between 12 June 1955 and 19 November 1974: RW 265-16740/856). Veale published numerous revisionist articles in the *Deutsche Soldaten- und Nationalzeitung*, and in other places, which Schmitt collected: RW 265-19916.

136 See Huber's typescript 'Idee und Realität eines Freideutschen Bundes' (RW 265-20250). Cf. Ewald Grothe, '"Strengste Zurückhaltung und unbedingter Takt": Der Verfassungshistoriker Ernst Rudolf Huber und die NS-Vergangenheit', in

Eva Schumann (ed.), *Kontinuitäten und Zäsuren: Rechtswissenschaft und Justiz im 'Dritten Reich' und in der Nachkriegszeit*, Göttingen, 2008, pp. 327–48.
137 Huber to Schmitt, 7 July 1948 (RW 265-6276).
138 Schmitt to Huber, 25 July 1948 (BAK, N 1507-198).
139 Schmitt to Huber, 25 August 1948 (BAK, N 1507-198). See Gerhard Ritter, *Carl Goerdeler und die deutsche Widerstandsbewegung*, Stuttgart, 1954. Cf. also Hans Rothfels, *Die deutsche Opposition gegen Hitler*, Krefeld, 1949.
140 Ernst Rudolf Huber, *Deutsche Verfassungsdokumente der Gegenwart*, Tübingen, 1951.
141 Huber to Schmitt, 7 February 1950 (RW 265-6280).
142 Schmitt to Huber, 24 March 1950 (BAK, N 1507-198). This old thesis, which had been formulated before – for example, by Helmut Kuhn – was later also confirmed by Reinhart Koselleck, 'Historik und Hermeneutik', in Koselleck, *Zeitgeschichten: Studien zur Historik*, Frankfurt, 2000, pp. 97–118, 'Sein zum Totschlagen' [Being towards beating to death].
143 Huber to Schmitt, 16 June 1950 (RW 265-6281). A similar argument was presented in great detail by Oskar von Niedermayer in a letter of 18 September 1948 sent to Schmitt from Göttingen (RW 265-10386).
144 Huber to Schmitt, 15 December 1950 (RW 265-6283).
145 Huber to Schmitt, 14 July 1963 (RW 265-6287).
146 Letter of 19 February 1978 from Huber to Schmitt (RW 265-6289).
147 Letter of 10 March 1978 from Schmitt to Huber (BAK, N 1505-198).
148 Huber to Schmitt, 8 July 1978 (RW 265-6290).
149 Ernst Rudolf Huber, 'Verfassungswirklichkeit und Verfassungswert im Staatsdenken der Weimarer Republik', in *Arbeiten zur Rechtsgeschichte: Festschrift Gustav Klemens Schmelzeisen*, Stuttgart, 1980, pp. 126–41.
150 Carl Schmitt, '1907 Berlin', in *Schmittiana* 1 (1988), pp. 13–21; here: p. 19.
151 Schmitt to Huber, 25 July 1948 (BAK, N 1505-198).
152 Hannah Arendt to Karl Jaspers, in *Hannah Arendt – Karl Jaspers: Correspondence 1926–1969*, ed. Lotte Köhler and Hans Saner, San Diego, New York and London, 1993, p. 142.
153 Invitation card from Tiedemann Ulrich Lemberg to a private house in Flottbek, Hamburg. Rolf Stödter chaired the ensuing discussion (RW 265-20107).
154 *Glossarium IV. Buch; 20 August 1951 to 6 October 1955* (RW 265-19610).
155 Letter of 16 February 1951 from Anima to Carl (RW 265-12631).
156 Winckelmann to Schmitt, 2 April 1951 (RW 265-18125). Letter of thanks 'for the nice evening', dated 17 April 1951 (RW 265-18126).
157 Letter of 19 May 1951 from Anima to Carl (RW 265-12633). Similar remarks in a letter of 25 May 1951 to Hüsmert (in private possession).
158 Mostly stenographic lecture outlines (RW 265-18294). Spanish lecture, handwritten by Schmitt (RW 265-18920), and typescript 'La unidad del mundo', with corrections added by hand (RW 265-18921/2).
159 Schmitt to Brinkmann, 13 August 1951 (RW 265-224/K9). Cf. Schmitt to Warnach, 17 June 1951 (HAStK, Best. 1688, Korrespondenz mit Carl Schmitt).
160 Editorial note by Maiwald, in *Universitas* 6 (1951), p. 1044.
161 Postcard of 29 May 1951 from Kathleen Murray to Schmitt (RW 265-10055). Years later, on 20 December 1960, she wrote again: 'Do you want to see me again in this life, Carl?'
162 Sombart to Schmitt, 28 June 1951 (RW 265-15379).
163 See Carl Schmitt's notebooks 'Irreale Bedingungssätze bei Historikern'

[Counterfactual conditional clauses in historical works] (RW 265-20800) and 'Reim-Übungen' [Rhyming exercises] (RW 265-20681).

164 Schmitt to Emge, 23 December 1951 (copy in the possession of Prof. Martinus Emge).

165 See letters of 17 October 1951, 22 December 1951 and 29 January 1952 from Vietta to Schmitt (RW 265-17312/14). Letters of 7 April 1952 and 11 July 1952 from the director Sellner to Schmitt (RW 265-15100/1).

166 Letter of 19 November 1951 from Schmitt to the Regierungspräsident of Arnsberg (RW 265-13403).

167 Heinrich Popitz, *Der entfremdete Mensch: Zeitkritik und Geschichtsphilosophie des jungen Marx*, Basel, 1953.

168 However, Popitz reacted positively to Schmitt's dedication of the VRA to his father (RW 265-11156).

169 The correspondence between Schmitt and Bobbio in Tommissen, *In Sachen Carl Schmitt*, pp. 113–55. Typescript of Schmitt's review of Bobbio's Hobbes edition, with a letter 15 April 1949 from Maiwald (RW 265-19000).

170 Passerin d'Entrèves to Schmitt, 6 February 1949 (RW 265-10862).

171 Letter of 1 August 1949 from the consul of Argentina Enrique C. Dubois to Schmitt (RW 265-3041). 'Permanent travel warrant' for Carl and Duška, dated 28 May 1949 (RW 265-19081).

172 Bernhard Wüst, the brother of Schmitt's old teacher Josef Wüst, told Schmitt that he had come across Schmitt being attacked as a National Socialist even in Argentina (letter of 4 August 1949 from Wüst to Schmitt; RW 265-18431).

173 See Dirk van Laak, *Gespräche in der Sicherheit des Schweigens: Carl Schmitt in der politischen Geistesgeschichte der frühen Bundesrepublik*, Berlin, 1993.

174 There were problems finding a date for the talk. See the letters between 1 July and 11 December 1950 from von der Groeben to Schmitt (RW 265-5163/72). At the talk, Schmitt saw his old pupil Karl Lohmann again (see Schmitt to Lohmann, 30 December 1950; RWN 260-438).

175 Letters from Schimpf regarding organizational matters (RW 265-12522/31).

176 Letter of invitation from Stödter, also in the name of his colleagues Ipsen and Hettlage, dated 8 December 1950; further letters from Stödter up until 26 February 1951 (RW 265-15819/26). The invitation was on Stödter's initiative, but he was then prevented from attending the talk. See the letter of 5 February 1951 from Karl M. Hettlage to Schmitt (RW 265-6031).

177 Handwritten outline (RW 265-18932). Guest list (RW 265-19600 Bl. 18).

178 Outline and typescript (RW 265-18961 Bl. 47/51; here: Bl. 50). Report in the *Süderländer Tageblatt*, no. 275 (22 November 1951).

179 Letter of invitation of 12 October 1951 from Lottmann to Schmitt (RW 265-930).

180 Letter of 14 July 1952, giving further details, from W. Volkmann, and Schmitt's acceptance of 12 September 1952 (RWN 260 1, 2-3). A contact with Dr Ehrenfried Schütte emerged. See the correspondence in RWN 260 1, Bl. 26-36 and RWN 260-417.

181 Letter of invitation of 30 June 1952 from the city councillor Dr Keller (RW 265-7334).

182 Schomerus to Schmitt, 12 and 19 March 1953 (RW 265-14494/5). Printed programmes: RW 265-19397. Forsthoff and Hans Freyer spoke at Bad Herrenalb.

183 Schmitt missed the figure of the katechon in Eric Voegelin's *The New Science of Politics*, although the figure appeared in Augustine's *City of God* (chapter XX.19), discussed by Voegelin (see Schmitt's draft letter of 30 April 1955 to Voegelin: RW 265-13706). In October 1955, Schmitt met Voegelin once

in Heidelberg (see Voegelin to Schmitt, 26 October 1955: RW 265-17337). However, Schmitt's prolonged efforts at establishing a lasting contact failed.

184 Letter of 4 May 1953 from the state secretary Walter Strauß to the bishop (RW 579-678).

185 Telegram of 5 May 1953 from Schomerus (RW 265-14496).

186 Letter of 5 May 1953 from Schomerus (RW 265-14497).

187 Schmitt was invited on 25 April 1953 (letter of 25 April 1953 from the Father Wilhelm Becker: RW 265-1160). He accepted the invitation, and Father Becker confirmed on 11 May 1953 (RW 265-1161): 'We are delighted that you will visit us and we'll be in touch with further details.' 'The further details were a cancellation', Schmitt noted in the margin of the letter. Over more than three decades, Schmitt also tried in vain to establish a contact with Hans Dombois of the Evangelische Forschungs-Akademie (RW 265-2994/3004).

188 Invitation note: RW 265-18961. Letter of invitation of 20 June 1953 from the Volkshochschule Iserlohn to Schmitt (RW 265-17372). Letter of 17 October 1953 from Harald Hasse of the Kaufmännischer Verein Iserlohn to Schmitt (RW 265-7301). Report 'Neue Deutung der modernen Technik' [A new interpretation of modern technology], in *Westfalenpost* (17 October 1953). Handwritten outline of the talk in RW 265-18962. List of recipients of an invitation in RW 265-19600 Bl. 27.

189 Walter Hallstein, who passed his Habilitation in Berlin in 1929 and soon became a professor in Rostock and Frankfurt. In 1951, Hallstein became state secretary in the Foreign Ministry and was very influential in shaping the Federal Republic's foreign policies. According to the so-called Hallstein doctrine, in force between 1955 and 1969, the recognition of the German Democratic Republic as an independent state by third-party countries was considered an 'unfriendly act' against the FRG. Its aim was to isolate the GDR internationally.

190 Schmitt to Brinkmann, 4 January 1954 (RW 265-224/K100). To Mohler, he wrote: 'But 4 x within a year it now has happened that I was formally invited and then the invitation was cancelled in an insulting manner: 2x Ev. Akademien, 1 x Darmstadt conversations, 1 x Mexico, German Industrial Fair' (BS, p. 151).

191 Lecture outline in RW 265-20109 Bl. 1.

192 Carl Schmitt, 'Die geschichtliche Struktur des Gegensatzes von Ost und West' [The historical structure of the opposition between East and West], in Armin Mohler (ed.), *Freundschaftliche Begegnungen: Festschrift für Ernst Jünger zum 60. Geburtstag*, Frankfurt, 1955, pp. 133–67. Reprinted in SGN.

193 Letters of April 1955 and 1 June 1955 from the Ministerialrat [undersecretary] Dr Nachtwey (RW 265-10125/6).

194 Invitation of 20 November 1954 from Dr Mager of the Volkshochschule. Thank-you letter of 18 February 1955 from Mager and agreement of Hamlet as topic on 11 March 1955 (RW 265-17356/72). Schmitt's detailed hand-written outline, making use of the contribution to the Jünger Festschrift, in RW 265-18963.

195 Mager to Schmitt, 3 February 1958 (RW 265-17371).

196 Letter of invitation of 12 November 1957 from Dr Küntzler (RW 265-20926).

197 Carl Schmitt, 'Ein- und Ausladungen' (RW 265-19395).

198 Letter of thanks of 21 October 1951 from Moras of *Der Merkur* (RW 265-9920). Letter of 24 October 1951 from Paeschke (RW 265-10773) and Paeschke's acceptance of the article, dated 6 December 1951 (RW 265-10774): 'The article will appear as the lead article in the January volume of the

"Merkur".' However, a further publication attempt with *Der Merkur* failed (letter of 9 July 1953 from Paeschke to Schmitt: RW 265-10779). After that, the contact ceased.

199 Letter of 8 March 1950 from Hanno Kesting to Schmitt (RW 265-7465). Kesting was drafted into the Wehrmacht in 1943 and soon wounded, lying in a field hospital for almost a year. While a prisoner of war with the British, he studied theology, belatedly took his school-leaving certificate, and then studied in Heidelberg from the summer term 1947.

200 See also the deviating German edition of a text by Carl Schmitt which was first published in Spanish: 'Die planetarische Spannung zwischen Ost und West und der Gegensatz von Land und Meer' [The planetary tension between East and West and the Opposition between land and sea], in *Schmittiana* 3 (1991), pp. 20–40.

201 Klostermann had already got in touch with Schmitt on 4 December 1948. When he had received the proofs he emphasized explicitly, on 9 February 1955 (RW 265-7906), 'how glad I am that my publisher has established contact with you'.

202 Ernst Jünger, *Der gordische Knoten*, Frankfurt, 1953.

203 Carl Schmitt, 'Die andere Hegel-Linie: Hans Freyer zum 70. Geburtstag' [The other line from Hegel: for Hans Freyer on his seventieth birthday], *Christ und Welt* (25 July 1957), p. 2. Schmitt's contacts with Freyer in Wiesbaden were also upheld by Schmitt's pupil Franzen (invitations: RW 265-19386). In his article Schmitt also used ideas of Johannes Winckelmann (*Gesellschaft und Staat in der verstehenden Soziologie Max Webers*, Berlin, 1957, p. 8), who – like Carl Schmitt – juxtaposed the great line Hegel–Marx–Nietzsche–Max Weber with the path 'from Hegel (1821) to Lorenz von Stein (1850) and Gustav Rümlin (1888) to Max Weber (1921)'.

204 Published in *Schmittiana* 6 (1998), pp. 100–24. Schmitt came across Kojève through the latter's conversation on tyranny with Leo Strauss, in which Strauss, it appeared to Schmitt, 'unfortunately now has become a thin-blooded academic' (letter of 30 November 1954 from Schmitt to Nicolaus Sombart: RW 265-13537).

205 On the publication process of this talk, see the correspondence with Dr Rudolf Hinder (from 7 September 1953) of the German national [deutschnationalen] journal *Gemeinschaft und Politik*. It came to differences over the question of payments for additional offprints (RW 265-6066/76).

206 Carl Brinkmann placed the title with an Italian journal (request by Brinkmann for some contribution from Schmitt, dated 19 May 1953: RW 265-2069). Then, on 26 May 1953, Brinkmann asked for the speedy completion of the manuscript. On 27 October 1953 (RW 265-224/K94), Schmitt suddenly wrote to Brinkmann indignantly that he had given the text to a German journal, because its appearance with the Italian journal had been delayed and the German audience should not be kept waiting. However, he agreed to an additional publication in Italian (letter of 3 November 1953 to Brinkmann: RW 265-178/K147). The German version appeared in December, with the Italian proofs arriving a little later.

207 On 25 February 1958 (RW 265-1186), Siegfried Behn, a former colleague from Bonn and the organizer of the Verwaltungsakademie in Koblenz, inquired with Schmitt as to a possible contribution to a commemorative publication for the theologian Erich Pryzwara, who was a Jesuit. While interned in 1946, Schmitt had approached him as a priest for spiritual assistance by sending him an 'intellectual-historical report on Benito Cereno' (RW 265-19864). In an article,

Przywara had recently called Schmitt a 'Rhenish Prussian of the spirit' and had put him in the tradition of 'another Prussia' – Przywara, 'Gegenwart', *Die Besinnung* 11 (1956), pp. 99–106; here: p. 105. On 10 March 1958, the editor Behn thanked Schmitt for his offer of a contribution (RW 265-1187), which Schmitt completed by September. Behn first thanked him for the good news and then for sending such a 'fascinating and monumental contribution' (Behn to Schmitt, 1 October 1958: RW 265-1189). By June 1959 the text was with the publisher. Minor changes could still be implemented, and shortly before Christmas the text appeared. It is possible that Schmitt's continual reflections on the concept of nomos were stimulated by Focke-Tannen Hinrichs, a student of ancient history with Hans Schaefer in Heidelberg. On 18 December 1953, Hinrichs had sent Schmitt extensive remarks on conceptual history, with further correspondence following (RW 265-6077/81). Important excerpts and preliminary ideas: RW 265-19201). Cf. also Winckelmann's 'remarks' on Schmitt's essay (RW 265-19199).

208 Letter of 7 February to Gustav Steinbömer.
209 Letter of 6 December 1951 from von Medem to Schmitt (RW 265-9332).
210 Letter of 29 August 1952 from Schmitt to the American officer G. B. Monroe (RW 265-13306).
211 In 1943–4, Ernst Schilly was Schmitt's neighbour in Schönerzeile (letters to Schmitt dating from the period between 11 January 1951 and 10 July 1978: RW 265-12514/21). Schilly brought Schmitt's *Constitutional Theory* to the attention of Schnur when the latter was preparing for his law examinations (Schnur to Schmitt, 5 July 1981: RW 265-14473).
212 Schnur to Schmitt, 22 October 1952 (RW 265-14220).
213 An attempt at mediating a deal by Karl M. Hettlage, who had moved to Mainz, failed. See Hettlage's letter to Schmitt of 16 May 1954 (RW 265-6037). Cf. also the letter of 23 January 1955 from Schmitt to Ernst Jünger (JS, pp. 267f.).
214 A catalogue of books, dated 18 August 1954, is among the posthumous papers: RW 265-21871.
215 Letter of 2 December 1954 from Schmitt to Lortz (RW 265-13245), as well as the latter's slightly irritated answer of 3 December 1954 (RW 265-8925). Schmitt later agreed to a contribution for a Festschrift for Lortz, but was then (letter of 7 November 1956 from Peter Mann to Schmitt: RW 265-8997) removed from the list of contributors because another author 'interpellated'. On a preliminary list of Festschrift contributors, Schmitt is still named, without a title (RW 265-19398). Lortz forcefully rejected a Habilitation by Günther Krauss: letter of 26 November 1952 from Lortz to Schmitt (RW 265-8923). Also negative: letter of 2 February from Scheuner to Krauss (RW 265-12442).
216 Patzig to Schmitt, 26 April 1965 (RW 265-10865).
217 Schmitt to Patzig, 29 April 1965 (RW 265-13357).
218 Letters from Rudolf Fischer between 1933 and 1957 (RW 265-3656/79).
219 Numerous letters from Fleig (RW 265-3682/729).
220 Giselher Wirsing, 'Carl Schmitt – zwischen gestern und morgen', *Christ und Welt* (24 January 1952). Approving letter to the editor by Joseph H. Kaiser, dated 20 February 1952 (RW 265-11351). Schmitt's review of *Maritime Weltpolitik* [Maritime world politics] was published on the initiative of Friedrich Vorwerk after a delay due to 'reasons of space and with some cuts', according to Vorwerk on 14 July 1949 after a visit to Schmitt (RW 265-17387). Letter of 8 October 1949 from the editorial office (Mehnert) to Schmitt (RW 265-9345).

221 Letter of 21 November 1949 from the editorial office (Mehnert) to Schmitt (RW 265-9347).
222 Carl Schmitt, 'Die andere Hegel-Linie: Hans Freyer zum 70. Geburtstag', *Christ und Welt* (25 July 1957), p. 2. Letter of 17 January 1959 from Wilhelm Westecker to Schmitt (RW 265-11355). Request of 17 January 1959 from Westecker regarding a readers' poll on books (RW 265-11356). Later request for a contribution to a series 'Recommended for Repeated Reading' on 'forgotten books' in a letter of 28 March 1963, sent by Barbara Klie to Schmitt (RW 265-11357). Inquiry by Klie of 4 September 1963 regarding a commemorative article on 1813 (RW 265-11359).
223 Letter of 15 August 1950 from Jürgen Eick to Schmitt (RW 265-11424).
224 Letters of 21 December and 29 December 1950 from Korn to Schmitt (RW 265-8118/9).
225 Letter of 29 October 1953 from Dr Dähnhardt to Schmitt (RW 265-11406).
226 Zehm to Schmitt, 20 July 1971 (RW 265-11412).
227 See Walter Petwaidic, *Die autoritäre Anarchie: Streiflichter des deutschen Zusammenbruchs*, Hamburg, 1946.
228 Carl Schmitt, 'Im Vorraum der Macht' [In the ante-chamber of power], *Die Zeit*, no. 30 (29 July 1954).
229 'Da werden Gräfinnen zu Hyänen' – an allusion to Friedrich Schiller's 'The Song of the Bell': Freedom! Equality! they shout; / the peaceful townsman grasps his arms. / Mobs stand the streets and halls about. / The place with bands of murderers swarms. / Into hyenas women grow / . . . '. In *The Poems of Schiller*, trans. Edgar Alfred Bowring ([1851] 2009), pp. 216–27.
230 Greiner to Schmitt, 2 July 1981 (RW 265-11417).
231 Copy of the *Deutsche Zeitung*, together with thanks for the 'advice', sent by Mathy on 3 May 1961 (RW 265-11394).
232 Letter of 18 July 1950 from Aloys Zimmer, a former pupil from Bonn and now Regierungspräsident [head of the regional government], Montabaur, to Schmitt (RW 579-677).
233 Sepp Schelz to Schmitt, 9 December 1959 (RW 265-11497).
234 Schmitt's typescript, dated 10 December 1959 (RW 265-11497). Schmitt sent it immediately to Schelz.
235 Augstein to Schmitt, 30 July 1952 (RW 265-544).
236 Augstein to Schmitt, 15 August 1952 (RW 265-545).
237 Augstein to Schmitt, 22 August 1956 (RW 265-552).
238 *Der Spiegel* 35 (28 August 1956). Letter of 7 August 1956 from Busse to Schmitt (RW 265-11375).
239 Letter of 9 November 1959 from Johannes Kayser, inviting Schmitt to contribute a piece (RW 265-11377).
240 Letter of 12 October 1982 from Harald Wieser to Schmitt (RW 265-11385).
241 Collection letter of 30 December 1950 (RW 579-677).
242 See, in detail, Dirk van Laak, *Gespräche in der Sicherheit des Schweigens*, Berlin, 1993, pp. 52ff.; Wilhelm Schmitz, 'Zur Geschichte der Academia Moralis', in *Schmittiana* 4 (1994), pp. 119–56.
243 Satzung des Vereins der Freunde Academia moralis e. V. [Statutes of the Association of Friends of the Academia Moralis, registered association] (RW 265-20380 Bl. 58/9).
244 On 1 December 1951, Ernst Forsthoff spoke at the Academia Moralis on 'Die Einheit der Justiz' [The unity of the judiciary]. Until 1954 there were further talks, by Hans Barion, Günther Krauss, Hubertus Bung, Tiesler, Oberheid,

Warnach, Werner Weber, Hans Schneider, Peter Scheibert, Helmut Schelsky and Joseph Plassmann.

245 Anima Schmitt, Peter Scheibert, Hanno Kesting and Heinrich Popitz, 'Einer bleibt übrig' (RW 265-19160), in *Schmittiana* 6 (1998), pp. 300–2.

246 According to Winckelmann in a letter to Schmitt, dated 13 July 1953 (RW 265-18137).

247 Warnach's exposition with questions, in RW 265-18936.

248 Letter of 15 September 1953 from Friedrich to Schmitt (RW 265-4432). On the text's history, see Gerd Giesler, 'Nachwort', in Carl Schmitt, *Gespräch über die Macht und den Zugang zum Machthaber*, Stuttgart, 2008, pp. 66–95.

249 Schmitt to Friedrich, 8 June 1954 (RW 26513013).

250 For a fascinating history of the genre of the philosophical dialogue, see Vittorio Hösle, *The Philosophical Dialogue: A Poetics and a Hermeneutics*, Chicago, 2013.

251 According to a letter of 30 June 1954 from Leo Faerber of the Hessischer Rundfunk to Schmitt (RW 265-11439), the speakers were Walter Hilsbecher and Walter-Andreas Schwartz, and the production was directed by Walter Grüntzig.

252 Schmitt to Warnach, 13 July 1954 (HAStK, Best. 1688, Korrespondenz mit Carl Schmitt).

253 Inquiry of 21 October 1954 from Irmengard Klewitz of Nordwestdeutscher Rundfunk (RW 265-11466). Text of the preamble in RW 265-20336.

254 Schmitt to the Abendstudio of Hessischer Rundfunk, 23 June 1954 (RW 265-13396).

255 Letter of 3 July 1954 from Neske to Schmitt (RW 265-10263). Cf. also Neske's earlier letter of 23 May 1954 (RW 265-10262). The reference is probably to Heidegger's text *Aus der Erfahrung des Denkens*, Pfullingen, 1954. Schmitt had met Neske in February while in Tübingen (BS, p. 150).

256 Note by Schmitt on the back of Neske's letter of 8 July 1954 (RW 265-10264).

257 Draft letter to Neske, dated 8 July 1954 (265-21591).

258 Contract, dated 24 July 1954, in RW 265-21590, together with invoices. 1,000 copies were printed to begin with. Schmitt's personal copy, dated September 1954, containing numerous corrections and a list of 'tests', or rather successes of the text (RW 265-27455). List of dedications (RW 265-21022). The contact with Neske ended in mid-1955. In 1960, Schmitt demanded the settlement of the account on the sold copies. On 1 January 1977, Neske attempted to establish contact again. Schmitt again demanded the settlement of the account, whereupon Neske told him that 1,762 copies had been sold by the end of December 1967. After that, there were no further sales, and the remaining copies were 'unfortunately silently scrapped without my knowledge' (RR 265-10282). Neske next planned an edition of Schmitt's 'conversations' (letter of 18 November 1977 to Schmitt: RW 265-10284). In April 1978 he again visited Schmitt in Plettenberg (letter of thanks of 24 April 1978 to Schmitt: RW 265-10286).

259 Friedrich to Schmitt, 29 July 1954 (RW 265-11440).

260 Friedrich to Schmitt, 8 August 1954 (RW 265-4445).

261 Friedrich to Schmitt, 4 March 1955 (RW 265-4450). See also the letter of 11 March 1955 to Schmitt from the Kröner publishing house (RW 265-16885). On 6 May 1955, the publisher's reader Walter Kohrs came to Plettenberg suggesting a popular 'general state theory' (letter of 28 April 1955 to Schmitt: RW 265-14886).

262 Typescript in RW 265-21788. Friedrich to Schmitt, 16 March 1955 (RW

265-4451). Cf. Schmitt to Warnach, 22 March 1955 (HAStK, Best. 1688, Korrespondenz mit Carl Schmitt).

263 Wirsing to Schmitt, 12 May 1955 (RW 265-18339), and BS, p. 200.

264 See Herbert Nette's letter to Schmitt, dated 16 June 1955, which positively confirms the willingness to publish the piece (RW 265-10308), and the letter of 28 June 1955 (RW 265-10309), which expresses concern over the shortness of the text.

265 Typescript: Nicolaus Sombart, 'Benito Cereno oder der Mythos Europas: Eine Plauderei am Kamin Selbstdritt' [Benito Cereno, or the myth of Europe: a chat in front of the fireplace self-threesome] (RW 265-20445). See Schmitt's lists of conversations on Benito Cereno (RW 265-20447).

266 Letter of 14 April 1959 from Gert H. Theunissen to Schmitt (RW 265-11500).

267 Theunissen to Schmitt, 8 July 1959 (RW 265-11502).

268 Schmitt to Karl Lohmann, 21 July 1950 (RW 579-490).

269 According to a letter of 28 August 1952 from Theodor Schieder to Schmitt (RW 265-12480). In 1941, Schieder heard Schmitt talk at the annual meeting of the historians in Nuremberg. Schieder's pupils (Wolfgang Mommsen, Hans-Ulrich Wehler and many more) dominated historical scholarship in the Federal Republic from the 1960s.

270 Conference programme in RW 265-20348. Schmitt to Dr Giere on 1 November 1952 (RW 265-13031). See letters of 29 October 1952 and 11 November 1952 from Giere to Schmitt (RW 265-4744/4745) and Giere's typescript on *The Merchant of Venice* (RW 265-21089).

271 Carl Schmitt, preface to the German edition of Lilian Winstanley, *Hamlet, Sohn der Maria Stuart*, Pfullingen, 1952, pp. 7–25. Typescript: RWN 260-382.

272 Carl Schmitt, preface to the German edition of Lilian Winstanley, p. 12.

273 Steinbömer to Schmitt, 23 December 1952 (RW 265-15727). Cf. Gustav Steinbömer, *Staat und Drama*, Berlin, 1932. Schmitt's erroneous 'historicism' is also criticized by Hans-Georg Gadamer in *Truth and Method*, London and New York, 2013, pp. 519–20. Detailed praise came from, for instance, Gerhard Günther in a letter to Schmitt dated 18 December 1952 (RW 265-5425).

274 Neske to Schmitt, 22 December 1952 (RW 265-10254). Cf. the review by Hermann Heuer in *Shakespeare-Jahrbuch* 59 (1953), pp. 235–8.

275 Schmitt forcefully suggested to Walter Warnach that he should attend the talk in a letter of 13 October 1955 (HAStK, Best. 1688, Korrespondenz mit Carl Schmitt).

276 Schmitt to Winckelmann, 15 December 1955 (Archiv der bayerischen Akademie der Wissenschaften, Nachlass Winckelmann, XIX. Korrespondenz Nr. 436).

277 See letters of 24 December 1954 and 5 April 1955 from Nette to Schmitt (RW 265-10304/06). First, Schmitt thought of 'Three-Way Conversation' in connection with Diederichs. However, compared to this short text, the one on Shakespeare was more suitable. At the same time, a republication of *Land and Sea* was under consideration. Letter of 17 December 1955 from Nette to Schmitt (RW 265-10311). Letter to Schmitt regarding details of the layout, dated 29 December 1955 (RW 265-10312).

278 Letters of 6 February 1956 and 23 February 1956 from Peter Diederichs to Schmitt (RW 265-2872/73). See also letters of 8 February 1956 and 21 February 1956 from Nette to Schmitt (RW 265-10313/4).

279 Walter Benjamin, *The Origin of German Tragic Drama*, London and New York, 2009. Schmitt's personal copy of the first edition of the book of 1928 is dated 10 December 1930. The numerous notes all date from later times

(RW 265-29012). In a second personal copy of the 'revised edition' of 1963, in a paperback reprint of 1969 and listed as purchased on 27 July 1972 (RW 265-26567), Schmitt checked in particular the changes made by the editor Tiedemann. For more detailed information on Schmitt's personal copy, see Reinhard Mehring, in *Benjamin-Studien* 2 (2011), pp. 239–56.

280 See Diederichs's positive reply to Schmitt, dated 2 June 1956 (RW 265-16998), after the latter had suggested the talk in a telephone conversation. Diederichs expected an audience of forty to fifty. Numerous reviews and materials are collected in RW 265-20351.

281 See Carl Schmitt, 'Was habe ich getan? (1957)', in *Schmittiana* 5 (1996), pp. 15–19 (cf. BS, pp. 221–4). A request from Tommissen, dated 22 August 1952, for a contribution to the journal *Dietsland-Europa* (RW 265-16162). Schmitt distributed more than a hundred copies of *Hamlet or Hecuba* and, equally, of the exposition almost a hundred copies. He also sent both texts to Jacob Taubes.

282 Invitation from the Außen-Institut [Institute for External Links] of the university, dated 8 October 1956 (RW 265-557; see also JS, p. 320). Arnold Gehlen was probably involved in the invitation. Presentation outline: RW 265-20313. Typescript and outline in RW 265-20311. Extensive excerpts and materials on Hamlet interpretations in RW 265-21087.

283 Raymond Aron, *The Opium of the Intellectuals*, London, 1957.

Chapter 29   Private Seminars in Plettenberg

1 See the not entirely conclusive letter of 18 September 1948 from Dr Haustein to Schmitt (RW 265-5783). Extensive correspondence until 1959.

2 Cf. Carl Schmitt (originally published under a pseudonym), 'Gegenwartsfragen der Verfassung (1949)' [Contemporary questions regarding the constitution (1949)]; 'Das Grundgesetz der Bundesrepublik Deutschland (1949/50)' [The Basic Law of the Federal Republic of Germany (1949–50)], both in *Carl Schmitt und die Liberalismuskritik*, ed. Klaus Hansen et al., Opladen, 1988, pp. 171–94.

3 According to the Frankfurt notary Heinz Wetzel, with whom Schmitt worked on the legal opinion, in a letter to Schmitt dated 5 April 1952 (RWN 260-354).

4 Schroer to Schmitt, 7 October 1954 (RW 265-18802) and 12 November 1956 (RW 265-18803).

5 Carl Schmitt, 'Reim-Übungen' (RW 265-20801).

6 Carl Schmitt, 'Gedichte: Carl Schmitt zum 11. Juli 1955 in Verehrung' (RW 265-21324).

7 The fact is documented in Ernst Forsthoff (ed.), *Rechtsstaatlichkeit und Sozialstaatlichkeit: Aufsätze und Essays*, Darmstadt, 1968.

8 Broermann mentioned his willingness to publish a new edition to Gustav von Schmoller on 19 February 1952. Schmitt was pleasantly 'surprised' by the offer (Schmitt to Broermann, 27 June 1953, Verlagsarchiv D & H, Mappe: Schmitt, Verfassungslehre).

9 Schmitt to Broermann, 19 April 1954 (Verlagsarchiv D & H, Mappe: Schmitt, Verfassungslehre).

10 Schmitt to Winckelmann, 15 December 1955 (Archiv der bayerischen Akademie der Wissenschaften, Nachlass Johannes Winckelmann, XIX. Korrespondenz Nr. 436).

11 Ulrich Scheuner, 'Carl Schmitt heute', *Neue politische Literatur* 1 (1956), pp. 181–8. Cf. Scheuner, in *Das Historisch-politische Buch* 4 (1955), pp. 103–4. Cf. also Friedrich Giese, in *Deutsches Verwaltungsblatt* 70 (1955), p. 408.

12 Anima to Schmitt, 2 April 1957 (RW 265-12642).
13 See the letter of 20 December 1957 from Corina Sombart to Schmitt (RW 265-15353); previously, their contact had ended almost completely.
14 According to Roman Schnur, 'Dankrede', in Schnur, *Die Ermächtigungsgesetze von Berlin 1933 und Vichy 1940 im Vergleich: Abschiedsvorlesung*, Tübingen, 1993, p. 53.
15 Winckelmann to Schmitt, 3 March 1952 (RW 265-18131).
16 Winckelmann to Schmitt, 13 December 1952 (RW 265-18135).
17 Winckelmann to Schmitt, 10 April 1953 (RW 265-18136).
18 Winckelmann to Schmitt, 30 July 1953 (RW 265-18139).
19 Carl Schmitt's review of Winckelmann's edition of Max Weber's *Economy and Society* in *Das Historisch-politische Buch* 4 (1956), pp. 195–6. The review of Winckelmann's monograph *Gesellschaft und Staat in der verstehenden Soziologie Max Webers*, Berlin, 1957, in *Das Historisch-politische Buch* 6 (1958), p. 102. The review of Winckelmann's edition of Weber's *Gesammelte politische Schriften* in *Das Historisch-politische Buch* 7 (1959), p. 53. See Winckelmann's letters of thanks to Schmitt, dated 1 August 1956 (RW 265-18170), 30 January 1957 (RW 265-18174) and 5 April 1959 (RW 265-18183).
20 Winckelmann to Schmitt, 12 June 1956 (RW 265-18165).
21 Schmitt to Winckelmann, 9 June 1956 (Archiv der bayerischen Akademie der Wissenschaften, Nachlass Johannes Winckelmann, XIX. Korrespondenz Nr. 437).
22 Postcard of 4 September 1950 from Sombart to Schmitt (RW 265-15371).
23 On Kesting's difficulties with his doctoral work, see Franz-Josef Brecht to Schmitt, 4 June 1952 (RW 265-2006).
24 Tommissen to Schmitt, 9 August 1950 (RW 265-16139).
25 Tommissen to Schmitt, 18 January 1952 (RW 265-16147). For the bibliography, Tommissen received a fee of 1,000 Deutschmarks from Academia Moralis (RW 265-20380 Bl. 29).
26 Schnur to Schmitt, 25 September 1951 (RW 265-14196). Cf. Roman Schnur, *Der Rheinbund von 1658 in der deutschen Verfassungsgeschichte*, Bonn, 1955.
27 Schnur to Schmitt, 29 September 1952 (RW 265-14216).
28 Schnur to Schmitt, 10 October 1952 (RW 265-14218).
29 Schnur to Schmitt, 6 May 1955 (RW 265-14252).
30 Schnur to Schmitt, 16 November 1955 (RW 265-14261).
31 Koselleck to Schmitt, 21 January 1953 (RW 265-8131/2).
32 Koselleck to Schmitt, 14 February 1954 (RW 265-8135). Cf. Reinhart Koselleck, *Critique and Crisis: Enlightenment and the Pathogenesis of Modern Society*, Cambridge, MA, 1988 (original dissertation, Heidelberg, 1954). On Koselleck's reception of Schmitt in general, see Reinhard Mehring, 'Begriffsgeschichte mit Carl Schmitt', in Hans Joas and Peter Vogt (eds), *Begriffene Geschichte: Beiträge zum Werk Reinhart Kosellecks*, Frankfurt, 2010, pp. 138–68.
33 Reinhart Koselleck, 'Rezension zu Herbert Butterfield', *Archiv für Rechts- und Sozialphilosophie* 41 (1955), pp. 591–9; here: pp. 594f.
34 Koselleck to Schmitt, January 1955 (RWN 260-1 Bl. 19).
35 Nicolaus Sombart to Schmitt on 5 February 1957 (RW 265-15403).
36 Nicolaus Sombart, *Rendezvous mit dem Weltgeist: Heidelberger Reminiszenzen 1945–1951*, Frankfurt, 2000, p. 266; cf. pp. 193–216.
37 Ottmar Ballweg, *Zu einer Lehre von der Natur der Sache*, Basel, 1960. Letters from Ballweg to Schmitt from the time between 1953 and 1970 (RW 265-610/637).
38 Further visitors were, among others, D. Köllen (RW 265-7980/94), Arndt Morkel

Notes to pp. 477–8

(BS, p. 180), Hans Buchheim (in 1955: RW 265-2136/40), Heinz Sladeczek (from 1955: RWN 260-1 Bl. 44-77; RWN 260-332: *Über das Widerstandsrecht: Versuch einer Darstellung seiner Problematik angesichts seines Wiederauflebens in einigen deutschen Nachkriegsverfassungen*, dissertation, Leipzig, 1950; Sladeczek, 'Zum konstitutionellen Problem des Widerstands', *Archiv für Rechts und Sozialphilosophie* 43 (1957), pp. 367–98), Martin Bullinger (from 1958: RW 265-2163/66), Reinhard Mußgnug (from 1958: RW 265-10067/75), Winfried Dallmayr (from 1954: RW 265-2741/56), Alexander Friedrich (from 1954: RW 265-4400/17), Wilhelm Henke (correspondence between 1956 and 1965 on *Die verfassungsgebende Gewalt des Volkes*: RW 265-5889/903), Karl-Heinz Ilting (correspondence between 1956 and 1981: RW 265-6348/76). Later: Ion Contiades (RW 265-2613/51; further material in RW 265-20076).

39 Werner Böckenförde to Schmitt, 15 March 1953 (RW 265-1911).
40 Ernst-Wolfgang Böckenförde to Schmitt, 10 April 1953 (RW 265-1591).
41 Ernst-Wolfgang Böckenförde to Schmitt, 28 January 1955 (RW 265-1593); see Schmitt's stenographic outline: RW 265-19131.
42 Ernst-Wolfgang Böckenförde to Schmitt, 22 February 1955 (RW 265-1595).
43 Letter of June/July 1955 from Peter Mantkes to Schmitt (RW 265-8998/9001). Outline of the lecture in RW 265-20109.
44 Joachim Ritter to Schmitt, 7 January 1956 (RW 265-11644).
45 Schmitt to Winckelmann, January 1956 (Archiv der bayerischen Akademie der Wissenschaften, Nachlass Johannes Winckelmann, XIX. Korrespondenz Nr. 436).
46 Letters of 18 January 1956 and 3 February 1956 from the 'Historisches Colloquium' to Schmitt (RW 265-6131/32).
47 Spaemann was in correspondence with Schmitt from 1951, but only through Böckenförde did their contact become more intense, from 1959 onwards. On 29 December 1959 (RW 265-15459) Spaemann thanked Schmitt for his reaction to his doctoral thesis on Bonald (*Der Ursprung der Soziologie aus dem Geist der Restauration: Studien über L. G. A. Bonald*, Munich, 1959).
48 Ernst-Wolfgang Böckenförde to Schmitt, 14 March 1957 (RW 265-1611). Schmitt recommended the manuscript to his publisher (Schmitt to Broermann, 30 April 1957: Verlagsarchiv D & H, Mappe: Schmitt, Verfassungslehre).
49 Ernst-Wolfgang Böckenförde to Schmitt, 20 January 1958 (RW 265-1629); Böckenförde, *Gesetz und gesetzgebende Gewalt: Von den Anfängen der deutschen Staatsrechtslehre bis zur Höhe des staatsrechtlichen Positivismus*, Berlin, 1958.
50 Schmitt to Ernst-Wolfgang Böckenförde, 24 January 1958 (RWN 260-431).
51 Ritter to Winckelmann, 23 June 1956 (Archiv der bayerischen Akademie der Wissenschaften, Nachlass Johannes Winckelmann, XIX. Korrespondenz Nr. 437).
52 Ritter to Schmitt, 6 January 1957 (RW 265-11647). Copies of their correspondence also in RWN 260-434. See Ritter's letter, from friend to friend, to Winckelmann, dated 7 January 1956 (Archiv der bayerischen Akademie der Wissenschaften, Nachlass Johannes Winckelmann, XIX. Korrespondenz Nr. 436).
53 Winckelmann to Schmitt, 12 January 1957 (RW 265-18173).
54 Schmitt to Winckelmann, 12 January 1957 (Archiv der bayerischen Akademie der Wissenschaften, Nachlass Johannes Winckelmann, XIX. Korrespondenz Nr. 438).
55 Related correspondence and the text of the lecture in *Schmittiana* 6 (1998), pp. 100–43. Cf. the official letters from the Club (RW 265-11596/608) and the letter expressing approval from Dr Justus Koch to Schmitt, dated 21 December

1956 (RW 265-7940). List of invitations and Schmitt's stenographic notes for the lecture in RW 265-20341).

56 Schmitt to Warnach, 7 March 1957 (HAStK, Best. 1688, Korrespondenz mit Carl Schmitt).

57 See Kesting to Schmitt, 12 February 1957 (RW 265-7482). Cf. Hanno Kesting, *Geschichtsphilosophie und Weltbürgerkrieg: Deutungen der Geschichte von der Französischen Revolution bis zum Ost–West-Konflikt*, Heidelberg, 1959.

58 Detailed hand-written outline in RW 265-19232.

59 See Winckelmann's retrospection in his letter of 31 March 1957 to Schmitt (RW 265-18175). Typescript of his 'remarks in discussion' (RW 265-19255). Publication, reviewed by Schmitt, as a part of Johannes Winckelmann, *Gesellschaft und Staat in der verstehenden Soziologie Max Webers*, Berlin, 1957.

60 Enthusiastic letter from Schmitt to Walter Warnach, dated 12 March 1957 (HAStK, Best. 1688, Korrespondenz mit Carl Schmitt), in which he particularly emphasized Spaemann's contributions. Marquard thanked Schmitt by letter (13 April 1957: RW 265-9059). The ballad was first published on 9 June 1955 in the journal *Civis*. Publication in the New Year's edition of *Münchner Merkur* in 1956, as envisaged by Armin Eichholz, fell through (letters of 19 December 1956 and 8 March 1957 from Eichholz to Schmitt: RW 265-3083/84).

61 Ritter to Schmitt, 1 April 1957 (RWN 260-434).

62 See the letter of invitation, signed by Martin Schürer, dated 3 April 1957 (RW 265-14676).

63 Some lists of participants at the Ebrach seminars (RW 265-20898 and RW 265-19770).

64 Presentation outline and notes from the conference (RW 265-19806).

65 Martin Schürer to Schmitt, 21 October 1957 (RW 265-146719).

66 Ernst Wolfgang Böckenförde to Schmitt, 23 May 1957 (RW 265-1614).

67 Schwab first made contact with Schmitt on 26 October 1956 (RW 265-14813). On 22 January 1957 he informed Schmitt of his wish to visit him. On 16 February he confirmed his plan, and at the end of April he arrived in Plettenberg.

68 Schwab to Schmitt, 25 March 1959 (RW 265-14825).

69 Von Mutius to Schmitt, 18 September 1957 (RW 265-10110).

70 See Schmitt to Broermann, 25 May 1957 (Verlagsarchiv D & H, Mappe: Schmitt, Verfassungsrechtliche Aufsätze).

71 RW 265-19600 Bl. 41.

72 Hans J. Wolff to Schmitt, 9 March 1958 (RW 265-18391).

73 Broermann to Schmitt, 22 March 1958 (RW 265-16972). Texts in RW 265-20929.

74 Schmitt to Broermann, 26 March 1958 (Verlagsarchiv D & H, Mappe: Schmitt, Verfassungsrechtliche Aufsätze).

75 Forsthoff, review, in *Das Historisch-politische Buch* 6 (1958), p. 246.

76 Ernst-Wolfgang Böckenförde to Schmitt, 12 January 1958 (RW 265-1628).

77 Schmitt to Huber, 10 March 1958 (BAK, N 1505-198).

78 Schmitt to Broermann, 13 July 1957 (Verlagsarchiv D & H, Mappe: Schmitt, Verfassungsrechtliche Aufsätze).

79 Kurt Sontheimer, 'Carl Schmitt: Seine "Loyalität" gegenüber der Weimarer Verfassung', *Neue politische Literatur* 3 (1958), pp. 758–70.

80 Winckelmann to Schmitt, 18 December 1959 (RW 265-18185).

81 Ernst-Wolfgang Böckenförde to Schmitt, 11 July 1958 (RW 265-1637).

82 'Der Umstrittene: Carl Schmitt wird siebzig Jahre alt' [The controversial one: Carl Schmitt will be seventy], *Frankfurter Allgemeine Zeitung*, no. 156 (10

July 1958). Cf. also Sepp Schelz, 'Carl Schmitt: Zu seinem 70. Geburtstag', *Westdeutsche Rundschau*, no. 157 (11 July 1958); Roman Schnur, 'Carl Schmitt und die Staatslehre', *Wirkendes Wort* 11 (1958), pp. 725–6.

83 Ernst Forsthoff, 'Der Staatsrechtler im Bürgerkrieg – Carl Schmitt zum 70. Geburtstag', *Christ und Welt*, no. 29 (17 July 1958).

84 Erich Kaufmann, 'Carl Schmitt und seine Schule: Offener Brief an Ernst Forsthoff', *Deutsche Rundschau* 84 (1958), pp. 1013–15. Informative on the relationships between the parties concerned is a report about a visit to Kaufmann on 13 April 1950 by Dr Haustein (RW 265-5785).

85 Letter of 8 December 1959 from Oberheid to Schmitt (RW 265-10492). Invitations went out to the editors of the Festschrift (see note 87) – Weber, Forsthoff and Barion – as well as to those who had made donations for it.

86 Tommissen to Schmitt, 11 March 1959 (RW 265-16169).

87 Hans Barion, Ernst Forsthoff and Werner Weber (eds), *Festschrift für Carl Schmitt: Zum 70. Geburtstag dargebracht von Freunden und Schülern*, Berlin, 1959. Letter of thanks of 14 July 1959 from Schmitt to the publisher Broermann (Verlagsarchiv D & H, Mappe: Festschrift für Carl Schmitt).

88 Ernst Wolfgang Böckenförde to Schmitt, 1 February 1959 (RW 265-1642). Ritter, in turn, wrote enthusiastically about Böckenförde in a letter to Schmitt, dated 22 January 1959 (RWN 260-434).

89 Ernst Wolfgang Böckenförde to Schmitt, 12 March 1959 (RW 265-1644). Schmitt met with Böckenförde, Spaemann and Marquard (Schmitt to Warnach, 11 March 1959; HAStK, Best. 1688, Korrespondenz mit Carl Schmitt).

90 Gerhard Henze to Schmitt, 16 March 1959 (RW 265-5969).

91 See Schmitt's notes in RW 265-19805. In the following years, Schmitt kept separate notebooks for the Ebrach meetings, in which he made stenographic notes on the presentations and discussions; notebooks for 1959 and 1960 (RW 265-19803/4), 1962 (RW 265-19802), 1964 (RW 265-19801), 1965 (RW 265-19807), 1966 (RW 265-19809), and 1967 (RW 265-19810).

92 Ernst Wolfgang Böckenförde to Schmitt, 29 October 1959 (RW 265-1657).

93 On *The Concept of the Political* within the context of the history of ideas, see Carl Schmitt, 'Der Gegensatz von Gemeinschaft und Gesellschaft als Beispiel einer zweigliedrigen Unterscheidung: Betrachtungen zur Struktur und zum Schicksal solcher Antithesen' [The opposition between community and society as an example of a dichotomous distinction. reflections on the structure and fate of such antitheses], in *Estudios juridico-sociales: homenaje al Professor Luís Legaz y Lacambra*, Zaragoza, 1960, vol. 1, pp. 165–76. Schmitt was asked to contribute to this Festschrift on 8 July 1959 by José de Frutos (RW 265-18830).

94 Winckelmann to Schmitt, 18 January 1960 (RW 265-18187) and 3 February 1960 (RW 265-18188).

95 Kriele to Schmitt, 29 March 1961 (RW 265-8455).

96 Quaritsch to Schmitt, 24 December 1961 (RW 265-11237).

97 Karl Engisch to Schmitt, 7 April 1960 (RW 265-3233).

98 Carl Schmitt, poem: 'In Karlsruhe wächst', written in April 1961 (RW 265-19507).

Chapter 30   The Partisan in Conversation

1 Martin Kriele to Schmitt, 22 October, 3 November and 2 December 1959 (RW 265-8452/54).

2 Wilms to Schmitt, 21 March 1960 (RW 265-18001). In June he visited Schmitt in Plettenberg (see Wilms's letter of 6 December 1960: RW 265-18003).
3 Enthusiastic report to Warnach, dated 1 October 1959 (HAStK, Best. 1688, Korrespondenz mit Carl Schmitt).
4 Schmitt to Julien Freund, 15 April 1960 (RWN 260-401).
5 List of participants and other material on this Ebrach seminar, in RW 265-19811. Among the participants were, for instance, the philosopher Lorenz Krüger and the daughter of Helmut Kuhn, Annette Kuhn. She was working on a historical dissertation on German Catholics during the time of early socialism, who 'have received little attention as they were hidden by the battles of the Hegel school' (Kuhn to Schmitt, 15 August 1960: RW 265-8543). Schmitt sent her his Cortès studies and later his 'Hobbes crystal' [see footnote on p. 495]. His sending of these materials was also an indirect response to Helmut Kuhn.
6 There are only a few letters of substance, especially from the years 1960–1 (RW 265-8937/44). Marquard did not have a close relationship with Schmitt either (see Marquard's letter to Schmitt dated 11 July 1978: RW 265-9061). Böckenförde and Koselleck are far more important points of reference. Throughout the 1960s, Schmitt also had closer contacts with Karlfried Gründer (RW 265-5350/71).
7 Roman Schnur, *Die französischen Juristen im konfessionellen Bürgerkrieg des 16. Jahrhunderts: Ein Beitrag zur Entstehungsgeschichte des modernen Staates*, Berlin, 1962; *Individualismus und Absolutismus: Zur politischen Theorie vor Thomas Hobbes (1600–1640)*, Berlin, 1963.
8 Schnur to Schmitt, 23 August 1959 (RW 265-14303), as well as 30 October 1961 (RW 265-14343).
9 Schnur to Schmitt, 7 September 1959 (RW 265-14304).
10 See Stephan Schlak, *Wilhelm Hennis: Szenen einer Ideengeschichte der Bundesrepublik*, Munich, 2008.
11 Schnur to Schmitt, 10 January 1961 (RW 265-14326). Andreas Anter (ed.), *Wilhelm Hennis' Politische Wissenschaft: Fragestellungen und Diagnosen*, Tübingen, 2013.
12 Schnur to Schmitt, 18 February 1961 (RW 265-14332).
13 Detailed report in a letter of 16 November 1961 from Schnur to Schmitt (265-14346).
14 The editors Gerhard Oestreich, Werner Weber and Hans J. Wolff, 'Zum Geleit', *Der Staat* 1 (1962), pp. 1–2; here: p. 1.
15 According to Michael Stolleis, 'Staatsbild und Staatswirklichkeit in Westdeutschland (1945–1960)', *Zeitschrift der Savigny-Stiftung für Rechtsgeschichte: Germanistische Abteilung* 124 (2007), pp. 223–45; here: p. 235. Stolleis, *Geschichte des öffentlichen Rechts*, vol. 4, Munich, 2012.
16 Schnur to Schmitt, 10 October 1962, writing from the 'Staatsrechtslehrervereinigung' [Meeting of the Association of State Theorists] (RW 265-14357).
17 Jürgen Habermas, 'Zur Kritik der Geschichtsphilosophie' (1960), in Habermas, *Politisch-Philosophische Profile*, Frankfurt, 1981, pp. 435–44.
18 Rudolf Smend, 'Zur Geschichte der Berliner Juristenfakultät im 20. Jahrhundert' (1960), in Smend, *Staatsrechtliche Abhandlungen*, 2nd expanded edn, Berlin, 1968, pp. 527–47, here: p. 542.
19 See Schmitt's friendly letter severing his ties with Smend, dated 13 January 1961 (Niedersächsische Staats- und Universitätsbibliothek Göttingen, Cod. Ms R. Smend A 759). Yet, later the same year, Smend still congratulated Schmitt on his birthday: letter of 9 July 1961 (RW 265-15246).

20 Dolf Sternberger, 'Begriff des Politischen', in Sternberger, *Staatsfreundschaft*, Frankfurt, 1980, pp. 295–321; here: p. 305. Cf. also Sternberger, *Die Politik und der Friede*, Frankfurt, 1986.

21 Letter of thanks from Morsey to Schmitt, dated 19 November 1960 (RW 265-9934). Cf. Rudolf Morsey, *Die deutsche Zentrumspartei 1917–1923*, Düsseldorf, 1966.

22 Rolf Schroers, *Der Partisan: Ein Beitrag zur politischen Anthropologie*, Cologne, 1961. Cf. also Carl Schmitt, 'Dem wahren Johann Jakob Rousseau', *Zürcher Woche*, no. 26 (29 June 1962).

23 Schroers to Schmitt, 15 June 1961 (RW 265-14586).

24 Schroers to Schmitt, 8 October 1961 (RW 265-14591).

25 Schroers to Schmitt, 19 October 1961 (RW 265-14592).

26 Francis Rosenstiel, *Supranationalität: Eine Politik des Unpolitischen*, Cologne, 1964. Schmitt's corrections: RW 265-20999. A twelve-page typescript by Schmitt, in RW 265-20090). Schmitt first contacted Duncker & Humblot regarding publication of the book (Schmitt to Broermann, 20 October 1961, Verlagsarchiv D & H, file without title). But it was then published with Kiepenheuer & Witsch, with Rolf Schroers being the point of contact there.

27 Schmitt to Giesler, 7 April 1962 (RWN 260-370).

28 Letter of 19 June 1962 from Hadrich to Schmitt (RW 265-5532). Extensive correspondence between January 1953 and 1980 (RW 265-5522/605).

29 For instance: H. F. Pfenninger, 'Carl Schmitt und der "Partisan" Rousseau', *Neue Zürcher Woche* (27 July 1962). G. v. R. [= Dr. Erwin Jaeckle], 'Hitlers Hofjurist in der "Zürcher Woche"', *Die Tat*, no. 174 (30 July 1962). Numerous other articles collected in RW 265-20071/73.

30 Some of Steinlein's letters from the period between 1957 and 1964 still exist (RW 265-15315/15325). After 1945, Steinlein initially avoided contact with Schmitt. On this, see the letter from Uncle André Steinlein to Schmitt, dated 15 November 1950 (RWN 260-360). The uncle was a notary in Vic-sur-Seille, between Metz and Nancy.

31 Manfred Hildermeier, *Geschichte der Sowjetunion 1917–1991*, Munich, 1998, p. 658. On the mobilization of the 'army of the fatherland' for terrorist purposes, see ibid., pp. 601ff., 617ff., as well as Jörg Baberowski, *Der rote Terror: Die Geschichte des Stalinismus*, Frankfurt, 2007, pp. 227ff.

32 Staedtke to Schmitt, 5 March 1964 (RW 265-15634). Letter of thanks from Staedtke to Schmitt, dated 16 May 1964 (RW 265-15638).

33 Correspondence with the Hanser publishing house between 20 August 1969 and delivery of the book on 25 May 1970 (RW 265-16900/3).

34 Ernst-Wolfgang Böckenförde, *Die deutsche verfassungsgeschichtliche Forschung im 19. Jahrhundert: Zeitgebundene Fragestellung und Leitbilder*, Berlin, 1961.

35 Ernst-Wolfgang Böckenförde, 'Die Historische Rechtsschule und das Problem der Geschichtlichkeit des Rechts', in Böckenförde, *Staat, Gesellschaft, Freiheit: Studien zur Staatstheorie und zum Verfassungsrecht*, Frankfurt, 1976, pp. 9–41; *Geschichte der Rechts- und Staatsphilosophie: Antike und Mittelalter*, Tübingen, 2002.

36 Schmitt to Ernst-Wolfgang Böckenförde, 7 May 1962 (RWN 260-431).

37 As Schmitt wrote to Julien Freund as early as 6 November 1960 (RWN 260-401).

38 Ernst-Wolfgang Böckenförde to Schmitt on 8 March 1963 (RW 265-1711).

39 On this, see Ernst-Wolfgang Böckenförde, 'Was kennzeichnet das Politische und was ist sein Grund? Bemerkungen zu einer Kommentierung von Carl Schmitts "Der Begriff des Politischen"', *Der Staat* 44 (2005), pp. 595–609.

40 Ernst-Wolfgang Böckenförde to Schmitt, 16 March 1963 (RW 265-1713).

41 Helmut Quaritsch, *Das parlamentslose Parlamentsgesetz*, 2nd edn, Hamburg, 1961. Quaritsch introduced himself on 27 September 1961 (RW 265-11235) as an acquaintance of Schnur and admitted some hesitation about getting in touch with an author whom he reads as canonical. Schmitt immediately replied on 1 October 1961 (RWN 260-410). On 8 October (RW 265-11236) Quaritsch thanked Schmitt for sending the VRA and expressed his wish to visit him; he 'would like to put the "Verfassungsrechtliche Aufsätze" in front of [him] and ask [him] to sign them. I have never collected autographs before, but in the case of this book and this author things are different.' Quaritsch submitted his Habilitation on 20 January 1964. However, the first version was 'disapproved', so Quaritsch revised it and submitted it again in June 1964. The examination process was quick (report to Schmitt, dated 28 August 1964: RW 265-11250). In 1966, Quaritsch was appointed to a chair in Bochum, and then in 1968 moved to the Free University of Berlin. From there he took refuge in Speyer in 1972. He gave his inaugural paper at the Staatsrechtslehrervereinigung [Assocation of the State Law Theorists] on 'Organisation und Führung der Streitkräfte als vollziehende Gewalt' [Organization and command of the armed forces as executive power], calling it a 'victory of the civil servant over the soldier'; letters of 20 December 1966 (RW 265-11254) and 28 January 1964 (RW 265-11246).

42 Schmitt to Quaritsch, 20 May 1963 (RWN 260-410).

43 Eberhard von Medem, Hans Schneider and Werner Böckenförde were in charge of the correspondence.

44 Letter of 17 April 1963 from Schmitt to Eberhard von Medem and further correspondence, in RW 260-407.

45 Cf. Hasso Hofmann, 'Feindschaft – Grundbegriff des Politischen?', *Zeitschrift für Politik* 12 (1965), pp. 17–39; Jürgen Fijalkowski, 'Das politische Problem der Feindschaft', *Politische Vierteljahresschrift* 6 (1965), pp. 105–11; Mathias Schmitz, *Die Freund–Feind-Theorie Carl Schmitts: Entwurf und Entfaltung*, Cologne, 1965; Helmut Ridder, 'Schmittiana II – Die Freund–Feind-Doktrin, der Begriff des Politischen, Theorie des Partisanen', *Neue Politische Literatur* 12 (1967), pp. 137–45; Ridder, 'Ex oblivion malum: Randnoten zum deutschen Partisanenprogress', *Gesellschaft, Recht und Politik: Wolfgang Abendroth zum 60. Geburtstag*, Neuwied, 1968, pp. 305–32.

46 Spaemann, on behalf of the dictionary's editors, to Schmitt, 9 July 1966 (RW 265-15465).

47 Schmitt's letter to Norbert Bobbio, dated 21 May 1949, in Piet Tommissen (ed.), *In Sachen Carl Schmitt*, Vienna, 1997, p. 125.

48 Postcard of 26 March 1964 from Schmitt to Gerd Giesler (RWN 260-370). Numerous long letters from Braun to Schmitt dating from the time between 5 October 1963 and 19 December 1966 (RW 265-1985/2001).

49 Review of Francis Campbell Hood, *The Divine Politics of Thomas Hobbes*, Oxford, 1964, in *Das Historisch-politische Buch* 12 (1964), p. 202 (see Schmitt's letter to Hood, dated 24 May 1965). Cf. also Schmitt's review of Peter Cornelius Mayer-Tasch, *Thomas Hobbes und das Widerstandsrecht*, Tübingen, 1965, in *Das Historisch-politische Buch* 13 (1965), p. 202.

50 See also Wilhelm Hennis, 'Zum Problem der deutschen Staatsanschauung', *Vierteljahreshefte für Zeitgeschichte* 7 (1959), pp. 1–12. Hennis's letter to Schmitt, dated 28 February 1959, in which he defends Mommsen (RW 265-5948).

51 Carl Schmitt, review of Wolfgang Mommsen, *Max Weber und die deutsche*

Politik 1890–1920, Tübingen, 1959, in *Das Historisch-politische Buch* 8 (1961), pp. 180–1. Karl Löwenstein, *Max Webers staatspolitische Auffassungen in der Sicht unserer Zeit*, Frankfurt, 1965. Karl Löwith, 'Max Weber und Carl Schmitt', *Frankfurter Allgemeine Zeitung*, no. 146 (27 June 1964). See Mohler's letter to the editor, opposing Löwith's article, in the *Frankfurter Allgemeine Zeitung* of 2 July 1964, in RW 265-20013. [English edn of Mommsen: *Max Weber and German Politics, 1890–1920*, Chicago, 1984.]

52 Winckelmann to Schmitt, 18 December 1959 (RW 265-18185).

53 Winckelmann to Schmitt, 3 February 1960 (RW 265-18188).

54 Winckelmann to Piet Tommissen, 18 December 1972 (RW 265-18203).

55 Carl Schmitt, review of Andreas Bühler, *Kirche und Staat bei Rudolph Sohm*, Zurich, 1965, in *Das Historisch-politische Buch* 14 (1966), p. 306.

56 Schmitt's carbon copy of a letter to Prof. Bolgiani in Turin, dated 14 January 1964 (RW 265-12830).

57 Dietrich Braun to Schmitt, 28 May 1964 (RW 265-1987).

58 However, Braun felt 'misunderstood' by Schmitt on this point (letter of 10 March 1965 from Braun to Schmitt: RW 265-1990). Braun cancelled a long-planned visit to Plettenberg at short notice by telegram on 21 September 1965. But at the beginning of November, a positive meeting of the two took place in Plettenberg: 'an altogether unusually educated, scholarly trained and person-ally sympathetic young theologian', Schmitt wrote to Giesler on 10 November 1965 (RWN 260-370).

59 Letters of 24 June 1964 and 8 August 1964 from Ilting to Schmitt (RW 265-6368/9).

60 Willms to Schmitt, 7 January 1965 (RW 265-18011).

61 Ilting to Schmitt, 6 March 1965 (RW 265-6371).

62 Specht to Schmitt, 12 September 1965 (RW 265-15526). On the hermetic char-acter of the text, see Schmitt to Warnach, 6 April 1965 (HAStK, Best. 1688, Korrespondenz mit Carl Schmitt).

63 Carl Schmitt, 'Losungen 1965' (RW 265-19587). The books of watchwords for 1976 and 1978 are shelved under RW 265-20966/7. 'Frottage' and 'Grattage' are the names of artistic techniques used by, for instance, Max Ernst.

64 Tommissen to Schmitt, 7 September 1965 (RW 265-16235).

65 Will of 24 November 1965, attested by a notary (RW 265-20376). Hubertus Bung was at first given as the executor of the will. On 13 April 1972 the will was amended and Anima Schmitt became the executor.

66 An interpretation he repeated again only very recently: Ernst-Wolfgang Böckenförde, *Der säkularisierte Staat: Sein Charakter, seine Rechtfertigung und seine Probleme im 21. Jahrhundert*, Munich, 2007.

67 Personal copy of Leo Strauss, *Hobbes' politische Wissenschaft*, Neuwied, 1965 (RW 265-22368) [Leo Strauss, *The Political Philosophy of Hobbes*, Chicago, 1963; originally published in 1936]. The following participants, among others, signed their names: Klaus-Michael Kodalle, Wolfgang Neusüß, Adalbert Podlech, Jon Contiades, Bernard Willms and Rainer Wahl. Schmitt's note on Ebrach: RW 265-19807.

68 Specht to Schmitt, 1 Feburary 1964 (RW 265-15519). Blumenberg's examiner's report was positive. Cf. Rainer Specht, *Commercium mentis de corporis: Über Kausalvorstellungen im Cartesianismus*, Stuttgart, 1966; *Descartes*, Reinbek, 1966.

69 Luís Díez del Corral, *Doktrinärer Liberalismus*, Neuwied, 1965.

70 Reinhart Koselleck, *Preußen zwischen Reform und Revolution*, Stuttgart, 1967.

71 Ernst-Wolfgang Böckenförde, *Die Organisationsgewalt im Bereich der*

Regierung: Eine Untersuchung zum Staatsrecht der Bundesrepublik Deutschland
[Organizational power in the sphere of government: an inquiry into the state
law of the Federal Republic of Germany], Berlin, 1964.
72 Helmut Quaritsch, *Staat und Souveränität*, vol. 1: *Die Grundlagen*, Frankfurt,
1970.
73 According to a letter, dated 14 December 1964, from Schmitt to E.-W.
Böckenförde (RWN 260-431), on the occasion of the latter sending his
Habilitation and being appointed to a chair in Heidelberg.
74 Christian Meier, *Res publica amissa: Eine Studie zur Verfassung und Geschichte
der späten römischen Republik*, Wiesbaden, 1966.
75 Vividly described by Christian Meier in conversation with Gerd Giesler,
'Besuche bei Carl Schmitt in Plettenberg', in Gerd Giesler and Ernst Hüsmert
(eds), *Carl Schmitt und Plettenberg: Der 90. Geburtstag*, Plettenberg, 2008,
pp. 6–16.
76 Notebooks on Ebrach 1966 in RW 265-19810.
77 Volkmar Hoffmann, 'Thomas Dehlers Worte wirkten wie ein Orkan',
Frankfurter Rundschau (16 December 1966). Claus Dreher, 'Thomas Dehler
hadert mit der ganzen Welt', *Weltspiegel* (17 December 1966).
78 'Kiesingers braune Berater', *Das Neue Deutschland* (17 December 1966).
Schmitt had heard Kiesinger talk at the Rhein-Ruhr Club in January 1952.
Announcement of the talk with stenographic notes (RW 265-18931 Bl. 3).
Schmitt did not talk to Kiesinger after that event. On the GDR perspective,
see Roland Meister, 'Mittler faschistischen Staatsdenkens: Carl Schmitt',
Staat und Recht 16 (1967), pp. 942–62.
79 Inquiry by Ansgar Skrivers, dated 8 December 1966 (RW 265-15189). In
addition to the WDR journalists Skriver and Rexin, Rolf Schroers took part.
As agreed, Schmitt received the transcript and made some 'cuts' (Skriver to
Schmitt, 30 December 1966: RW 265-15192).
80 Ernst-Wolfgang Böckenförde to Schmitt, 22 January 1967 (RW 265-1769).
81 Werner Böckenförde, *Das Rechtsverständnis der neueren Kanonistik und die
Kritik Rudolph Sohms: Eine ante-kanonistische Studie zum Verhältnis von
Kirche und Kirchenrecht* [The conception of right in more recent canon law and
the critique of Rudolph Sohm: an ante-canonical study on the relationship
between Church and Church law], Münster, 1969.
82 Schmitt to E.-W. Böckenförde, 27 January 1967 (RWN 260-431).
83 Ernst-Wolfgang Böckenförde to Schmitt, 29 March 1967 (RW 265-1762).
84 Schmitt sent his *Theory of the Partisan* to the historian Hahlweg in Münster
(letters of 16 February 1963 and 12 December 1963 from Hahlweg to Schmitt:
RW 265-5637/39). Schmitt also wrote a two-page 'résumé' of his treatise (RW
265-19423).
85 Ernst-Wolfgang Böckenförde to Schmitt, 6 March 1966 (RW 265-1750).
86 Schmitt to E.-W. Böckenförde, 12 April 1966, with the preliminary remark
enclosed (RWN 260-431).
87 Ernst-Wolfgang Böckenförde to Schmitt, 2 August 1966 (RW 265-1754).
Schmitt received the proofs of his contribution from the publisher on 16 June
1967 (RW 265-17242).
88 Notebooks on Ebrach 1967 in RW 265-19809.
89 In the words of Ernst-Wolfgang Böckenförde in a letter to Schmitt dated 4
August 1967 (RW 265-1769).
90 Schmitt to Ernst-Wolfgang Böckenförde, 22 October 1967 (RWN 260-431).
91 Ernst-Wolfgang Böckenförde to Schmitt, 22 November 1967 (RW 265-1772).
92 Schmitt to E.-W. Böckenförde, 24 January 1968 (RWN 260-431).

93 Ernst-Wolfgang Böckenförde to Schmitt, 5 February 1968 (RW 265-1774).

94 Oberheid, using his contact with Konrad Kaletsch, again organized a subsidy from the Flick Group (RW 265-3733). The largest donation was made by the Industrie- und Handelstag [Association of Chambers of Industry and Commerce] (complete list of donors in RW 265-19887). The intended submission date was 30 October 1967 (circular letter to the authors, dated 27 July 1967).

95 See Schmitt's draft for a preface (RW 265-19888) and extensive notes and materials in RW 265-19887.

96 Ernst-Wolfgang Böckenförde's birthday letter to Schmitt, dated 28 June 1968 (RW 265-1778).

97 Hans Barion, Ernst-Wolfgang Böckenförde, Ernst Forsthoff and Werner Weber (eds), *Epirrhosis: Festgabe für Carl Schmitt zum 80. Geburtstag*, 2 vols, Berlin, 1968.

98 Barion reporting about the celebration to Gustav Steinbömer, printed in Thomas Marschler, *Kirchenrecht im Bannkreis Carl Schmitt's*, Bonn, 2004, pp. 494–7. Among others, the following attended the celebration: Frau von Schnitzler, Hubertus Bung, Barion, Oberheid, Tommissen, Prince Rohan, Ernst-Wolfgang Böckenförde, Julien Freund, Walter Warnach, Rüdiger Altmann.

99 Barion to Schmitt, 2 July 1968 (RW 265-1012).

100 Ernst-Wolfgang Böckenförde to Schmitt, 10 November 1968 (RW 265-1779).

101 Schmitt to E.-W. Böckenförde, 30 October 1968 (RWN 260-431).

102 'Losungen 1968' (RW 265-19590).

103 See Schmitt to Marianne Kesting, 15 January 1969, and Kesting's reply (RWN 260-396).

104 Maunz to Schmitt, 29 December 1967 (RW 265-9246).

105 Quarisch to Schmitt, 9 July 1969 (RW 265-11275).

106 Specht to Schmitt, 15 December 1968 (RW 265-15536).

107 Schickel wrote to Schmitt on 16 January 1969 in his capacity as radio producer (RW 265-12451). The conversation took place on 23 and 24 April 1969 in Plettenberg and was broadcast by NDR 3 on 22 May 1969 (letter of 17 May 1969 from Schickel to Schmitt: RW 265-12455). It was later repeated on the Bayerischer Rundfunk (letter of 2 December 1969 from Schickel to Schmitt: RW 265-12462). Schickel arranged a transcript of the conversation (because he initially thought of a publication in *Der Merkur*), which he sent to Schmitt. He immediately envisaged another radio conversation on Hugo Ball. However, it then became the 'core element' of a book edited by Schickel (Schickel to Schmitt, 26 July 1969: RW 265-12458). On 10 August, Schickel sent the text to Schmitt, asking him for 'suggestions for corrections'. On 22 August 1969, Schickel accepted Schmitt's 'corrections' (RW 265-12460). On 2 December 1969 he thanked Schmitt for agreeing to a conversation on Hugo Ball.

108 See the letters from Hans-Martin Saß between 1967 and 1973 (RW 265-12246/62).

109 Letters from Friedrich Kabermann, as well as visits to Plettenberg between 1969 and 1981 (RW 265-6963). Friedrich Kabermann, *Widerstand und Entscheidung eines deutschen Revolutionärs: Leben und Denken Ernst Niekischs*, Cologne, 1973. Schmitt collected reviews of the book: RW 265-19308.

110 Schmitt's letters to Arndt from 1955 onwards, in RWN 260-405.

111 Arndt to Schmitt, 14 August 1961 (RW 265-489).

112 Schmitt's reference of 24 June 1959, in RW 265-20236. Letter of thanks from Friedrich, dated 6 July 1959 (RW 265-4429).

113 Arndt to Schmitt, 17 June 1977 (RW 265-510).

114 Bernard Willms, *Revolution und Protest oder Glanz und Elend des bürgerlichen Subjekts*, Stuttgart, 1969. Schmitt's notes on Willms's letter to Schmitt, dated 8 February 1971 (RW 265-18020).

115 Willms to Schmitt on the first advent of 1977 (RW 265-18023). In 1978, Willms did visit Schmitt.

116 Arndt to Schmitt, 17 November 1978 (RW 265-513). Cf. Hans-Joachim Arndt, *Die Besiegten von 1945: Versuch einer Politologie für Deutsche samt Würdigung der Politikwissenschaft in der Bundesrepublik Deutschland*, Berlin, 1978; Arndt (ed.), *Inferiorität als Staatsräson: 6 Aufsätze zur Legitimität der Bundesrepublik*, Krefeld, 1985.

117 Hans-Dietrich Sander, *Marxistische Ideologie und allgemeine Kunsttheorie*, Tübingen, 1970; here: p. 173 (fn), 2nd expanded edn, 1975; *Geschichte der schönen Literatur in der DDR: Ein Grundriss*, Freiburg, 1972.

118 Hans-Dietrich Sander, *Der nationale Imperativ: Ideengänge und Werkstücke zur Wiederherstellung Deutschlands*, Krefeld, 1980; see especially the 'Afterword on the author' (pp. 168–74).

119 'Auseinandersetzungen mit Carl Schmitt' (RW 265-28377/82). It contains texts by Hugo Ball, Werner Becker, Leo Strauss, Clemens Lang (Günther Krauss), Otto Kirchheimer, Ernst Niekisch, Kurt Wilk, Huizinga, Julius Evola, Hans Krupa, Ernst Rudolf Huber and Hans Freyer.

120 According to Moritz Julius Bonn, *So macht man Geschichte: Bilanz eines Lebens* [Thus history is made: the sum of a life], Munich, 1953. Schmitt modified the title in his personal copy (RW 265-25938) to 'So verwertet man Geschichte: Verkaufs-Bilanz eines Lebens' [Thus history is used: sales figures of a life]. Ernst Niekisch, *Das Reich der niederen Dämonen*, Berlin, 1957, pp. 330–7; *Gewagtes Leben: Begegnungen und Ergebnisse*, Cologne, 1958, pp. 241–5. Theodor Heuss, *Erinnerungen 1905–1933*, Tübingen, 1963. Edgar Salin, 'Grußwort', in *System und Methode in den Wirtschafts- und Sozialwissenschaften: Erwin von Beckerath zum 75. Geburtstag*, Tübingen, 1964, pp. 16–17.

121 Karl Schultes, *Der Niedergang des staatsrechtlichen Denkens im Faschismus: Die Lehren des Herrn Professor Carl Schmitt, Kronjurist der Gegenrevolution*, Weimar, 1947.

122 Carbon copy of Schmitt's letter to Werner Weber, dated 27 January 1954 (RW 265-13717).

123 Peter Schneider, *Ausnahmezustand und Norm: Eine Untersuchung zur Rechtslehre von Carl Schmitt*, Stuttgart, 1957. Schneider to Schmitt on 2 May 1957 (RW 265-18794). Personal copy (RW 265-28041), mostly unread.

124 Letter of 28 May 1957 from Hans Schneider (RW 265-13493). See Schmitt's letters to Mohler, dated 19 March 1957 and 31 May 1957 (BS, pp. 234, 238f.).

125 Schmitt to Warnach, 20 February 1963 (HAStK, Best. 1688, Korrespondenz mit Carl Schmitt).

126 Christian von Krockow, *Die Entscheidung: Eine Untersuchung über Ernst Jünger, Carl Schmitt und Martin Heidegger*, Stuttgart, 1958 (RW 265-28050).

127 Jürgen Fijalkowski, *Die Wendung zum Führerstaat: Ideologische Komponenten in der politischen Philosophie Carl Schmitts*, Cologne, 1958.

128 Peter Paul Pattloch, *Recht als Einheit von Ordnung und Ortung*, Aschaffenburg, 1961.

129 Heinz Laufer, *Das Kriterium politischen Handelns*, Munich, 1962.

130 Mathias Schmitz, *Die Freund–Feind-Theorie Carl Schmitts: Entwurf und Entfaltung*, Cologne, 1965.

131 Heinrich Wohlgemuth, *Das Wesen des Politischen in der heutigen neoroman-tischen Staatslehre*, Emmendingen, 1933 (Schmitt's personal copy: RW 265-28443).
132 Carbon copy of a letter from Schmitt to Prof. Wenzel, dated 4 June 1953 (RW 265-13726).
133 Schmitt to Pattloch, 13 September 1961 (RW 265-13356). Reply to material sent by Pattloch, dated 11 September 1961: RW 265-10864. Pattloch wrote his dissertation with von der Heydte and was related to Carl Muth (BS, p. 309).
134 Schwab to Schmitt, 11 June 1960 (RW 265-14832).
135 Schwab to Schmitt, 23 May 1961 (RW 265-14842).
136 Detailed report from Schwab to Schmitt, dated 11 March 1962 (RW 265-14851).
137 Schwab to Schmitt, 9 February 1965 (RW 265-14878).
138 Schmitt to Broermann, 5 September 1967 (Verlagsarchiv D & H, Mappe: Schmitt, Verfassungslehre), and 16 November 1967 (Verlagsarchiv D & H, Mappe: Schmitt, Diktatur, 3. Aufl.). Schwab to Schmitt, 26 November 1967 (RW 265-14898). Renewed request for publication in a letter from Schmitt to Broermann, dated 14 April 1969 (Verlagsarchiv D & H, Mappe: Schmitt, Hüter der Verfassung).
139 Schmitt to Prof. Abraham Schwartz, 2 November 1970 (RW 265-12869). George Schwab, *The Challenge of the Exception: An Introduction to the Political Ideas of Carl Schmitt between 1921 and 1936*, Berlin, 1970.
140 Schwab to Schmitt, 1 December 1970 (RW 265-14927).
141 Facsimile in Martin Tielke, *Der stille Bürgerkrieg*, Berlin, 2007, p. 68. Schwab was in Plettenberg at the end of July 1980 (see his letter of 8 July 1980: RW 265-14991).
142 Hasso Hofmann, *Legitimität gegen Legalität: Der Weg der politischen Philosophie Carl Schmitts*, Neuwied, 1964.
143 See Hasso Hofmann's retrospective piece 'Was ist uns Carl Schmitt?', in *Politik, Philosophie, Praxis: Festschrift für Wilhelm Hennis*, Stuttgart, 1988, pp. 545–55; Reinhard Mehring, 'Der menschenrechtliche Einwand: Hasso Hofmanns Antwort auf Carl Schmitt', *Der Staat* 47 (2008), pp. 241–57.
144 Copy of letter of 8 January 1963 from Hofmann to Piet Tommissen (RW 265-6191).
145 A copy of Hofmann's letter to Benseler granting permission, dated 4 April 1963, is among Schmitt's posthumous papers (RW 265-6189).
146 Benseler to Schmitt, 3 July 1963 (RW 265-1247).
147 See the reviews by Piet Tommissen in *Archiv für Rechts und Sozialphilosophie* 20 (1967), pp. 668–90, by Joseph Kaiser in *Das Historisch-politische Buch* 14 (1966), pp. 165–7, and by Böckenförde in *Die Öffentliche Verwaltung* 20 (1967), pp. 688–90.
148 Theodor Maunz to Schmitt, 11 March 1965 (RW 265-9243).
149 At least according to Schmitt, in a letter to Giesler dated 10 November 1965 (RWN 260-370).
150 Prospectus notes: RW 265-19075.
151 At the time, the Scientia publishing house was interested in taking on various of Schmitt's works (letters between 22 February 1967 and 14 June 1968: RW 265-17218/21). Schmitt was also considering a new edition of *Wert des Staates* [Value of the state]; letter of 3 March 1967 to Scientia publishing house (RW 265-13683). However, as the successor to Otto Liebmann, the Beck publishing house held the rights and, on 17 June 1968, inquired about a new edition (RW 265-16925). Schmitt wanted to reprint the book 'as a document without

any changes' (Beck publishing house to Schmitt, 3 September 1968: RW 265-16926), but then wrote a preliminary remark after all, which the publisher received in November (editor Hoeller to Schmitt, 6 November 1968: RW 265-16928). List of recipients of the new edition in Schmitt's personal copy (RW 265-28443). Parts of the *Three Types of Juristic Thought* were then published with Schmitt's permission by Suhrkamp (RW 265-17228/9).

152 Bernd Rüthers, *Die unbegrenzte Auslegung: Zum Wandel der Privatrechtsordnung im Nationalsozialismus*, Tübingen, 1968.
153 Jürgen Seifert to Schmitt, 14 October 1958 (RW 265-15078).
154 Schmitt to Seifert on 16 October 1958, and further letters from Schmitt to Seifert, in RWN 260-435.
155 Seifert to Schmitt, 11 June 1963 (RW 265-15085). Cf. Jürgen Seifert, 'Unterwegs zur Ebene über dem Gegensatz', in *Schmittiana* 5 (1996), pp. 109–27.
156 Schmitt to Seifert, 11 March 1968 (RWN 260-435).
157 Seifert to Schmitt, 10 September 1968 (RW 265-15088).
158 Schmitt to Jürgen Seifert, 30 August 1968 (RW 265-13522). Schmitt's response was written after discussing it with Schwab. See Schwab's letter to Schmitt dated 21 September 1968 (RW 265-14908).
159 Michael Stolleis, *Gemeinwohlformeln im nationalsozialistischen Recht*, Berlin, 1974.
160 Heinrich Muth, 'Carl Schmitt in der deutschen Innenpolitik des Jahres 1971', *Historische Zeitschrift* supplement 1971, pp. 75–147.
161 Lutz-Arwed Bentin: *Johannes Popitz und Carl Schmitt: Zur wirtschaftlichen Theorie des totalen Staates in Deutschland*, Munich, 1972. Letters from Bentin to Schmitt, dated between 31 December 1968 and 22 August 1973 (RW 265-1250/54). 'No reply!', Schmitt noted in his diary on 29 August 1973 (RW 265-19595). The dedicated copy sent by Bentin is unread (RW 265-28287).
162 Ingeborg Maus, 'Zur "Zäsur" von 1933 in der Theorie Carl Schmitts', *Kritische Justiz* 2 (1969), pp. 113–24. See Reinhard Mehring, 'Kant gegen Schmitt: Ingeborg Maus *Über Volkssouveränität*', *Der Staat* 52 (2013), pp. 435–54.
163 Maus to Schmitt, 11 February 1971 (RW 265-9287). Schmitt's letters to Maus in RWN 260-416).
164 According to Schnur in a letter to Schmitt, dated 12 September 1976 (RW 265-1443).
165 Maus to Schmitt, 16 March 1975 (RW 265-9292) and 30 June 1976 (RW 265-9293).
166 Ingeborg Maus, *Bürgerliche Rechtstheorie und Faschismus: Zur sozialen Funktion und aktuellen Wirkung Carl Schmitts*, Munich, 1976. See the review by Helmut Rumpf, 'Carl Schmitt und der Faschismus', *Der Staat* 17 (1978), p. 233–43.
167 Schmitt to Maus, 10 September 1981 (RWN 260-416).
168 Klaus-Michael Kodalle, *Politik als Macht und Mythos: Carl Schmitts 'Politische Theologie'*, Stuttgart, 1973. See the letters from Kodalle to Schmitt, dated between 14 June 1973 and 10 July 1973 (RW 265-7959/61). Schmitt to Warnach, 4 July 1973 (HAStK, Best. 1688, Korrespondenz mit Carl Schmitt).
169 Ruth Groh had written 'admiring' lines to Schmitt as early as 12 January 1959 (RW 265-18653). See Ruth Groh, *Arbeit an der Heillosigkeit der Welt: Zur politisch-theologischen Mythologie und Anthropologie Carl Schmitts*, Frankfurt, 1998.
170 Schmitt in his letter of recommendation to Helmut Rumpf, dated 23 November 1972 (RWN 260-390).
171 Bendersky to Schmitt, 10 October 1980 (RW 265-1221). On the events at the

conference, see Schwab's letter to Schmitt dated 9 September 1980 (RW 265-14993).
172 Joseph W. Bendersky, *Carl Schmitt: Theorist for the Reich*, Princeton, NJ, 1983. Schmitt's personal copy: RW 265-28289.
173 Letters from Kennedy to Schmitt, dated between 13 June 1979 and 5 May 1982 (RW 265-7382/97). Further material (RW 265-21092).

Chapter 31 Past Eighty

1 Böckenförde's request for a contribution from Schmitt, dated 29 June 1969.
2 Werner Böckenförde quotes this epigram in his report, in Hans Barion, *Kirche und Kirchenrecht: Gesammelte Aufsätze*, ed. Werner Böckenförde, Paderborn, 1984, p. 532. On Barion's sharp criticism of the Church, which he understood to be the 'deconstruction of its deconstructors', see Thomas Marschler, *Kirchenrecht im Bannkreis Carl Schmitts: Hans Barion vor und nach 1945*, Bonn, 2004, pp. 442ff.
3 Hans Barion, '"Weltgeschichtliche Machtform"? Eine Studie zur Politischen Theologie des II. Vatikanischen Konzils', in *Gesammelte Aufsätze*, Paderborn, 1984, p. 605. See also Theodor Maunz to Schmitt, 7 April 1971 (RW 265-9252): 'The official Church seems to be losing its own centuries-old consciousness.' See Wolfgang Spindler, *'Humanistisches Appeasement'? Hans Barions Kritik an der Staats- und Soziallehre des Zweiten Vatikanischen Konzils*, Berlin, 2011.
4 Hans Barion, '"Weltgeschichtliche Machtform"?' p. 640.
5 Schmitt to E.-W. Böckenförde, 4 July 1969 (RWN 260-431).
6 'Losungen 1969', p. 91 (RW 265-15951).
7 Inquiry by Schmitt to Giesler, dated 14 August 1969 (RWN 260-370). Letter of 17 August 1969 from Giesler to Schmitt (RW 265-4856). Giesler also sent Schmitt reviews by Löwith and Gadamer and spoke with him about his own manuscript (letter of 10 January 1970 from Giesler to Schmitt: RW 265-4862). On 17 September 1969 the priest Karl Tiesler sent Schmitt Peterson's lecture 'Was ist Theologie?' (RW 265-16067). Tiesler was a friend of Oberheid, who, as the faculty chair, had once been involved in initiating Peterson's lecture. See Tiesler's retrospective letter to Schmitt, dated 9 July 1978 (RW 26516087).
8 Schmitt to Giesler, 22 August 1969 (RWN 260-370).
9 Schmitt to Koselleck, 21 April 1970 (RWN 260-386).
10 Emphatic letters of thanks to Koselleck, dated 13 May and 16 July 1970 (RWN 260-386).
11 Schmitt to Broermann, 20 May 1970 (Verlagsarchiv Duncker & Humblot, Mappe: Schmitt, Politische Theologie II). On 25 May, he sent the typescript, which was immediately passed on to production.
12 List of recipients: RW 265-19989 Bl. 30.
13 On the title page of his personal copy, dated 3 October 1970 (RW 265-28245).
14 Erik Peterson, *Der Monotheismus als politisches Problem: Ein Beitrag zur Geschichte der politischen Theologie im Imperium Romanum*, Leipzig, 1935.
15 Oswald von Nell-Breuning, in *Theologie und Philosophie* 46 (1971), p. 314.
16 Gustav E. Kafka, 'Wer erledigt wen? Zu Carl Schmitts Politischer Theologie II', *Hochland* 63 (1971), pp. 475–82.
17 See Erik Peterson, *Theologische Traktate: Ausgewählte Schriften*, vol. 1, ed. Barbara Nichtweiß, Würzburg, 1994.
18 Excerpts published in Gerhard Ruhbach (ed.), *Die Kirche angesichts der Konstantinischen Wende*, Darmstadt, 1975, pp. 68–88.

19 Hans Blumenberg, *The Legitimacy of the Modern Age*, Cambridge, MA, 1983.
20 Koselleck to Schmitt, 2 August 1971 (RW 265-8166/2).
21 Letter of 12 May 1970 from Oberheid to Schmitt (RW 265-10514).
22 Postcard to Schmitt, dated 24 May 1970 (RW 265-10515), signed by, among others, Oberheid, Barion, Forsthoff, Werner Weber, Hans Schneider and Joseph Kaiser. Steinbömer gave a laudatory speech on Barion. The Festschrift was printed by the Brockhaus Verlag as a private publication. Barion had contributed to the Brockhaus *Konversationslexikon* [encyclopaedia] after the war.
23 Barion to Schmitt, 8 October 1970 (RW 265-1054).
24 Seminar programme (RW 265-19985).
25 Bung to Schmitt, 30 October 1973 (RW 265-2358).
26 See Schmitt to Warnach, 1 December 1970 (HAStK, Best. 1688, Korrespondenz mit Carl Schmitt). In communications with Warnach, Schmitt repeatedly distanced himself from Friedhelm Kemp from the 1960s onwards, though he wanted to hold on to their shared interest in Weiß.
27 Schickel came to Plettenberg on 9 February. 'Tomorrow conversation', Schmitt noted in his diary (RW 265-19592). Interesting material on the conversation in RW 265-21750. Schmitt's renewed interest in Hugo Ball was caused not least by his reading of Ball's early book *Tenderenda der Phantast*, which Giesler sent him in December 1967. See Schmitt to Giesler, 22 December 1967 (RWN 260-370). On 30 January 1970, Schmitt asked Giesler for Ball's *Folgen der Reformation* (RWN 260-370), whereupon Giesler sent Schmitt literature in preparation for the conversation (letters of 31 January 1970 and 4 February 1970 from Giesler to Schmitt: RW 265-4864/66). Schickel thanked Schmitt on 13 February 1970 and suggested further conversations 'on Benjamin or on Melville', or 'perhaps, and that seems more important, . . . on C. S. himself' (Schickel to Schmitt, 13 February 1970: RW 265-12467). However, the autobiographical conversation, which was planned for October 1970, had to be postponed because Schickel went on a trip to China (Schickel to Schmitt, 30 September 1970: RW 265-12472).
28 Schmitt to Giesler, 15 February 1970 (RWN 260-370).
29 Schmitt, in RW 265-21750, Bl. 44.
30 Marianne Kesting, 'Begegnung mit Carl Schmitt', in *Schmittiana* 4 (1994), pp. 93–118; here: p. 101. Kesting gives February 1971 as the time of the conversation. However, on 26 December 1970, Schmitt had already noted in his 'Losungen': 'Marianne Kesting on Peterson in Rome' (RW 265-19592).
31 Schmitt to Kesting, 2 July 1972 (RWN 260-396).
32 Later, Schmitt also discussed the role of the Church and Heinrich Oberheid in correspondence with Klaus Scholder: letters, dated between 12 December 1977 and 6 September 1982, from Scholder to Schmitt (RW 265-14488/91). In his last letter, Scholder asked Schmitt for a conversation on Oberheid in Plettenberg.
33 Kriele to Schmitt, 26 October 1970 (RW 265-8459).
34 For the television interview on the NDR, which was also broadcast by other regional television stations, Schmitt received a fee of 2,500 Deutschmarks. The broadcast caused Käthe Jessen, Schmitt's old acquaintance from Berlin, to visit him. See Käthe Jessen to Schmitt, 22 June 1970 (RW 265-6556), and her son Uwe Jessen to Schmitt, 29 April 1971 (RW 265-6557).
35 Carl Schmitt, 'Von der TV-Demokratie: Die Aggressivität des Fortschritts' [On TV-democracy: the aggression of progress], *Deutsches Allgemeines Sonntagsblatt*, no. 26 (28 June 1970), p. 8. List of recipients of the article: RW 265-21324. Schmitt also sent the text to Mohler.

36 Oberheid to Schmitt, 11 July 1970 (RW 265-10517).
37 Sombart to Schmitt, 24 February 1976 (RW 265-15416).
38 Nicolaus Sombart, 'Gruppenbild mit zwei Damen: Zum Verhältnis von Wissenschaft, Politik und Eros im Wilhelminischen Zeitalter', *Merkur* 30 (1976), pp. 972–90.
39 Sombart to Schmitt, 8 September and 17 September 1976 (RW 265-15419/20).
40 Schnur to Schmitt, 24 April 1977 (RW 265-14446).
41 Sombart to Schmitt, 28 July 1978 (RW 265-15424).
42 Sombart to Schmitt, 23 August 1979 (RW 265-15428).
43 Nicolaus Sombart, *Die deutschen Männer und ihre Feinde: Carl Schmitt – ein deutsches Schicksal zwischen Männerbund und Matriarchatsmythos*, Munich, 1991. Even more radical: Sombart, *Rendezvous mit dem Weltgeist*, Munich, 2000.
44 Schmitt in a letter to Koselleck, dated 30 January 1974 (RWN 260-386).
45 Böckenförde to Schmitt, 22 November 1970 (RW 265-1797).
46 Schmitt revised the relevant entries: see his diary for the period between 31 December 1932 and 30 January 1933 (RW 265-21637). After 1945, Schmitt met with Brüning at least once, in February 1955, and also exchanged letters with him on Brüning's memoirs (see Brüning to Schmitt, 8 December 1955: RW 265-2102). On 15 January 1973, Ansgar Skriver of the WDR came to visit one more time for another radio interview, on 30 January 1973 (letters from Skriver to Schmitt, dated 3 January 1973 and 16 January 1973: RW 265-15194/5); 'wonderful refreshment in my senile nervousness, nice radio recordings', Schmitt noted in his diary ('Losungen 1973': RW 265-19595). The conversation was broadcast on 30 January 1973 by WDR. Afterwards, the publishing house Jahr wanted a short version for a collected volume, to which Schmitt agreed (letters from Norbert Mezels to Schmitt, dated 14 August 1973 and 23 August 1973: RW 265-17144/5) Typescript by Carl Schmitt, 'Erinnerungen an den 30. Januar 1933' [Reminiscences of 30 January 1933] (RW 265-18784). Longer drafts and important materials in RW 265-21526.
47 Letter of 8 January 1971 from Ernst Hüsmert to Joachim Schickel (RW 265-6320).
48 Schmitt, 'Losungen 1971' (RW 265-19593). Schickel to Schmitt, 13 January 1971 (RW 265-12474). The contact with Schickel was broken off for many years. Only in June 1980 did Schickel visit Schmitt again in Plettenberg and produce an improvised conversation for NDR (Schickel to Schmitt, 14 June 1980: RW 265-12478), which was broadcast on 6 January 1981 by NDR 3.
49 Letter of 5 February 1971 from Hans Maier to Böckenförde (copy in RW 265-8968).
50 Christian Meier to Schmitt, 7 July 1971 and 25 October 1971 (RW 265-9371/2). Schmitt's postcard to Meier, dated 7 October 1971 (RWN 260-409).
51 Konrad Hesse, *Grundzüge des Verfassungsrechts der Bundesrepublik Deutschland*, Karlsruhe (1967), 20th edn, 1999.
52 Gerd Giesler's report on the seminar in a letter to Schmitt, dated 5 October 1971 (RW 265-4894).
53 Letter of 9 September 1969 from Johannes Gross to Schmitt (RW 265-5237). Joachim Fest to Schmitt, 28 October 1970 (RW 265-3462). Gross advised Schmitt to prepare such an edition (letter of 5 May 1971: RW 265-5316).
54 See the letters of 14 April 1971 and 26 August 1971 from Wolf Jobst Siedler to Schmitt (RW 265-15166/7).
55 Dieter Groh, *Russland und das Selbstverständnis Europas*, Neuwied, 1961.
56 Letter of 1 September 1971 from Dieter Groh to Schmitt (RW 265-5200).

57 Groh to Schmitt, 21 December 1971 (RW 265-5204).
58 The text of the conversation was recently published: Frank Hertweck and Dimitrios Kisoudis (eds), *'Solange das Imperium da ist': Carl Schmitt im Gespräch mit Klaus Figge und Dieter Groh 1971*, Berlin, 2010.
59 Schmitt, 'Losungen 1972', entry on 5 March (RW 265-19594).
60 'Carl Schmitt im Gespräch mit Dieter Groh und Klaus Figge', 1971, in Piet Tommissen (ed.), *Over en in zake Carl Schmitt*, Brussels, 1975, pp. 89–109; here: p. 101. Groh belonged to the wider circle of Schmitt's pupils; Figge was employed by Südwestfunk. The tape recording was later transcribed. See the letters of 24 February 1972 and 20 March 1972 from Klaus Figge to Schmitt (RW 265-3532 and 265-3524). Typescript, revised by Schmitt, in RW 265-19891. Schmitt's preparatory notes and material in RW 265-21410.
61 Typescript in RW 265-21505. Typescript sent by letter to Schmitt on 15 September 1971 (RW 265-6114). Publication of the original German version: Carl Schmitt, 'Der Begriff des Politischen: Vorwort von 1971 zur italienischen Ausgabe', in *Complexio Oppositorum: Über Carl Schmitt*, ed. Helmut Quaritsch, Berlin, 1988, pp. 269–73.
62 Marie-Luise Steinhauser was given the job of translating *Der Begriff des Politischen* and *Die Theorie des Partisanen* by Julien Freund. On 27 December 1970 she sent her first questions to Schmitt; on 28 August she thanked him for the days in Plettenberg (RW 265-15743/68).
63 According to the entries for May 1972, 'Losungen' (RW 265-19594).
64 Schmitt to Koselleck, 29 September 1973 (RWN 260-386).
65 See the investigations into this motto by Rüdiger Vollhardt in his letter to Schmitt, dated 5 May 1957 (RW 265-17354). Cf. also Eduard Spranger, 'Nemo contra Deum nisi Deus ipse', *Jahrbuch der Goethe-Gesellschaft*, NF (new series) 2 (1950), pp. 58–87.
66 Carl Schmitt, 'Ent-Arcanisierung: Entwurf eines Vortrags über den Katechon nach 2. Thess. 2,6 vom Winter 1974/75' [De-arcanization: draft, written in winter 1974–5, for a lecture on the katechon according to 2 Thess. 2:6] (RW 265-20023; cf. also the older material on the topic in RW 265-20026).
67 Schmitt copied these passages of the letter and, on 10 May 1976, sent them to Böckenförde (RWN 260-431).
68 Hans Blumenberg, 'Der Sturz des Protophilosophen: Zur Komik der reinen Theorie' [The fall of the proto-philosopher: on the comical aspect of pure theory], in *Das Komische*, ed. Wolfgang Preisendanz and Rainer Warning, Munich, 1976, pp. 11–64. See Blumenberg's later *Das Lachen der Thrakerin: Eine Urgeschichte der Theorie*, Frankfurt, 1987. See also *Hans Blumenberg – Carl Schmitt: Briefwechsel 1971–1978*, ed. Alexander Schmitz and Marcel Lepper, Frankfurt, 2007.
69 Hans-Dietrich Sander, 'Im Zentrum des Taifuns: Carl Schmitt redivivus – Gedanken zu seinem 85. Geburtstag', *Die Welt* (11 July 1973). Articles collected by Schmitt: RW 265-21273.
70 Friedrich Karl Fromme, 'Der Mann, der den lebenden Parlamentarismus sezierte: Carl Schmitt wird 85', *Frankfurter Allgemeine Zeitung* (11 July 1973).
71 Gerhard Leibholz, 'Die Haltung Carl Schmitts', letter to the editor, *Frankfurter Allgemeine Zeitung*, no. 169 (24 July 1973), p. 9.
72 Ernst J. Cohn, letter to the editor, *Frankfurter Allgemeine Zeitung* (17 July 1973).
73 Carola Braune to Schmitt, 11 July 1973 (RW 265-2002).
74 Grewe's telegram to Schmitt, sent on 11 July 1973 (RW 265-5156).
75 Arnold Schmitz to Schmitt, 7 July 1973 (RW 265-13879).

76 See Schmitt's letter to Broermann, dated 25 September 1973, in which he is positive about the project (Verlagsarchiv D & H, Mappe: Schmitt, Verfassungsrechtliche Aufsätze).

77 Schmitt to Broermann, 29 January 1974 (Verlagsarchiv D & H, Mappe: Schmitt, Nomos der Erde).

78 Schmitt to Broermann, 21 August 1974 (Verlagsarchiv D & H, Mappe: Schmitt, Verfassungsrechtliche Aufsätze).

79 Böckenförde to Schmitt, 18 December 1973 (RW 265-1814).

80 Schmitt knew Perroux (1903–1987) from his time in Berlin.

81 Quaritsch to Schmitt, 3 April 1975 (RW 265-11259). Tommissen produced a first translation in January 1975, which, however, was not satisfactory (two letters from Tommissen to Schmitt, sent in January: RW 265-16336/7).

82 Manuscript 'Weltrevolutionäre Legalität', dated 28 October 1975 (RW 265-19384).

83 Böckenförde to Schmitt, 26 May 1977 (RW 265-1836). This version, cautiously revised by Böckenförde, together with other versions, in RW 265-21588.

84 Schmitt prepared a third edition of *Dictatorship* at the time, which contains a short preface, dated February 1978. He also wanted new editions of *The Theory of the Partisan* and *The Crisis of Parliamentary Democracy*, without any changes, because of their 'value as documents'. See Schmitt to Broermann, 18 May 1978 (Verlagsarchiv D & H, Mappe: Schmitt, Diktatur, 3. Aufl.).

85 Böckenförde to Schmitt, 24 November 1977 (RW 265-1842).

86 Böckenförde to Schmitt, 20 December 1977 (RW 265-1843).

87 Böckenförde to Schmitt, 8 February 1978 (RW 265-1846).

88 Schmitt to E.-W. Böckenförde, 26 December 1978 (RWN 260-431).

89 Ernst-Wolfgang Böckenförde, 'Der verdrängte Ausnahmezustand: Zum Handeln der Staatsgewalt in außergewöhnlichen Lagen', *Neue Juristische Wochenschrift* 31 (1978), pp. 1881–90. On 14 December 1978, Böckenförde also published a letter to the editor of the *Frankfurter Allgemeine Zeitung*, in which he referred to Schmitt.

90 Letter of 16 September 1978 from Böckenförde to Schmitt (RW 265-1853).

91 Many of the presentations from the seminar are among Schmitt's posthumous papers (RW 265-21900/3). The seminar was also attended by Heinrich Meier, who would later publish important monographs on Schmitt. Even before the seminar, Meier had established contact with Schmitt, on 7 July 1976. Thereupon, Schmitt made an inquiry about him to Wilhelm Hennis, who replied on 21 February 1977 (RW 265-5949): an 'altogether unusually intelligent student'. Meier had a fairly extensive correspondence on Rousseau and Leo Strauss with Schmitt, and also visited him once in the autumn of 1978 in Plettenberg (letters from Meier to Schmitt: RW 265-9389/408 and RW 265-18732/5). The seminar in Freiburg was continued in a private context in Kassel, and Meier reported to Schmitt about this. Meier congratulated him on his ninety-fifth birthday, already mentioning his later study on Schmitt and Strauss (Meier to Schmitt, 9 July 1983: RW 265-18735).

92 In 1948, Ipsen established closer contact with Schmitt, and for several years he provided him with news from the academic world of jurisprudence. However, from the 1960s onwards their correspondence is limited mostly to birthday greetings (RW 265-6393/443). The last postcard is dated 8 July 1982 (RW 265-6443). Their correspondence did not touch on matters of European law.

93 Carl Schmitt, 'Der Begiff des Politischen: Vorwort von 1971 zur italienischen Ausgabe', in *Complexio Oppositorum: Über Carl Schmitt*, ed. Helmut Quaritsch, Berlin, 1988, pp. 269–73; here: p. 269.

94 See Ulrich Scheuner's in-depth letter to Schmitt on this, dated 9 December 1978 (RW 265-12449).
95 See Schmitt to Broermann, 3 February 1967 (Verlagsarchiv D & H, Mappe: Schmitt, Verfassungslehre).
96 Schmitt had already wanted to sell further parts of his library during the 1960s. See letter to Schmitt from the director of the library at the Hochschule für Verwaltungswissenschaften [Academy for Administrative Science] in Speyer, dated 24 November 1961 (RW 265-9304); letter to Schmitt from von Medem, dated 6 April 1966 (RW 265-9342), referring to the possibility of selling the library to the newly founded University of Bielefeld, and Schmitt's hesitant reply to von Medem, dated 20 May 1966 (RW 260-407).
97 Janssen to Schmitt, 20 January 1975 (RW 265-10433).
98 Schmitt welcomed the civil servants from the archive at midday with a glass of wine. He mentioned thematic keywords for individual packs, which were then entered on the boxes. In this way, he wanted to make sure that the focal points of his work would also be preserved in the order of the posthumous papers. It was also important to him that the rules for the use of the papers were strictly followed. However, there can be no mention of a fixed thematic order, given the successive fashion in which the papers were handed over. Initially, Dr Rolf Nagel corresponded with Schmitt, and he also picked up the first boxes (information kindly provided by Dr Nagel in a telephone conversation on 1 September 2007). Then, on 23 March, 23 June and 14 October 1977, Dr Dieter Weber fetched the bulk of the papers from Plettenberg. Practical questions regarding the use of the material were not discussed on these occasions. The rough ordering of the papers, which were then catalogued by Ingeborg Villinger and Dirk van Lark, was later revised in pragmatic fashion. The letters were collected from the various boxes and ordered according to addressee or sender (information kindly provided by Dr Dieter Weber in a telephone conversation on 13 August 2007). Later, Rainer Stahlschmidt of the archive drove to Plettenberg once more in order to pick up the library; he dealt only with Anni Stand, however (information kindly provided by Rainer Stahlschmidt in a telephone conversation on 16 August 2007).
99 Carl Schmitt, 'Testament' of 10 October 1975 (RW 265-1824).
100 Letter of 12 July 1976 from Nagel to Schmitt (RW 265-10437).
101 Nagel to Schmitt, 13 December 1976 (RW 265-10438).
102 History of the library in RW 265-21871.
103 See Nagel's letter to Schmitt, dated 13 December 1976 (RW 265-10438).
104 Folder 'Tu quis es?' (RW 265-21635).
105 Ibid., Bl. 84.
106 Ibid., Bl. 86.
107 Ernst Bloch, 'Die sogenannte Judenfrage', in Bloch, *Literarische Aufsätze* (*Gesammelte Werke*, vol. 9), Frankfurt, 1965, pp. 549–54; here: p. 552.
108 Carl Schmitt, notebooks on 'The So-Called Jewish Question' (RW 265-19333/5).
109 Ernst Bloch, *Thomas Münzer als Theologe der Revolution* (1921), Frankfurt, 1962.
110 Schmitt noted this down on an invitation card from the Rhein-Ruhr Club (RW 265-19533) in connection with the conversation about Ball on 9 February 1970. At the beginning of March, he then also copied it into his 'Losungsheft' [watchword book] (RW 265-19592).
111 Carl Schmitt, 'Gross-Verwerter' [Hyper-exploiter] (RW 265-19959/60). See Reinhard Mehring, 'Der "Groß-Verwerter": Carl Schmitts Geburtstagsmappe

für Thomas Mann', in Mehring, *Das 'Problem der Humanität': Thomas Manns politische Philosophie*, Paderborn, 2003, pp. 119–30.

112 Carl Schmitt, index of names for diaries (RW 265-20952).
113 See Kaiser's letters to Schmitt, dated 27 July and 27 December 1978 (RW 265-7168/70). Text of the speech as well as numerous articles on his birthday in RW 265-21267. The *Süderländer Tageblatt* had a special page with an appreciation by Ernst Hüsmert. Rüdiger Altmann published an article in the *Frankfurter Allgemeine Zeitung* (8 July 1978), whereupon Herbert Matschke sent a critical letter to the editor (published 25 July 1978).
114 Piet Tommissen and Julien Freund (eds), *Miroir de Carl Schmitt*, Geneva, 1978. See the retrospection that Tommissen sent to Schmitt on 3 August 1978 (RW 265-16358).
115 Heinz Baberg, 'Ansprache des Bürgermeisters', in *Carl Schmitt und Plettenberg: Der 90. Geburtstag*, ed. Gerd Giesler and Ernst Hüsmert, Plettenberg, 2008, pp. 22–5; here: p. 24. This volume also contains the speeches by Jünger and Kaiser. Report on the event in *Süderländer Tageblatt* (12 July 1978).
116 Gustav von Schmoller to Schmitt, 4 July 1978 (RW 265-13996), and letter of thanks to Schmitt dated 27 July 1978 (RW 265-13997).
117 The photograph is also printed and described in *Carl Schmitt und Plettenberg*, pp. 28f.
118 According to Christian Meier, 'Besuche bei Carl Schmitt in Plettenberg', ibid., pp. 6–16; here: p. 15.
119 A typical example: On 10 July 1978, the divorce lawyer Ilse Dormagen wrote: 'Of course, my name does not mean anything to you. As a student, my name back then was still Ilse Doenhardt. I was one of those who sat at your feet, and of course I also adored you and I doted on you. Nevertheless, or maybe because of that, I learned a lot from you in Bonn, because the inimitable way in which you led us half-baked youngsters to scholarly thinking, and how you made it possible to take something away from your lectures, deeply impressed me even back then' (RW 265-3025). Further letters of thanks, for instance from Hans Dichgans, who still kept in touch after 1945 (letter of 12 July 1978 – correspondence stretching from 1952 to 1978; letters from students in Bonn in 1927–8: RW 265-2860/68). Letter from Dr Karl du Mont, who had been examined by Schmitt in July 1925 in Cologne (RW 265-9911).
120 See Isensee's detailed letter to Schmitt dated 21 January 1977 (RW 265-6448), in which he tells him about Friesenhahn's late 'avowal' of Schmitt at a faculty celebration.
121 Letters of 10 July 1978 and 15 September 1978 from Karl Lohmann to Schmitt (RW 265-8910/11). Letter of thanks from Schmitt to Lohmann dated 30 August 1978 (RW 579-490).
122 Maunz to Schmitt, 8 July 1978 (RW 265-9259).
123 Scheuner to Schmitt, 8 July 1978 (RW 265-12448).
124 Schmitt wrote down his reply of 30 September 1978 at the end of Scheuner's letter (RW 265-12448).
125 Letter of 11 July 1978 from the Heimatkreis Plettenberg to Schmitt (RW 265-5842).
126 Taubes to Schmitt, 2 August 1955 (RW 265-15959).
127 Taubes to Schmitt, 17 November 1977 (RW 265-15960).
128 Schmitt to Taubes, 29 November 1977, in Herbert Kopp-Oberstebrink et al. (eds), *Jacob Taubes – Carl Schmitt*, Munich, 2012, p. 37.
129 Alfred Schindler (ed.), *Monotheismus als politisches Problem? Erik Peterson und die Kritik der politischen Theologie*, Gütersloh, 1978.

130 Schmitt had a collegiate relationship with Schindler throughout the 1930s (letters from Schindler from the period between 1930 and 1938: RW 265-12542/48).
131 Letters from Schindler to Schmitt, dating from the period between 10 November 1974 and 3 September 1976 (RW 265-12533/41).
132 See Karl Tiesler to Schmitt, 26 November 1974 (RW 265-16082).
133 See Schmitt's draft for a letter to Schindler, dated 22 January 1976 (RW 265-19981), as well as some cutting remarks in letters to Böckenförde, 5 April 1978 and 24 April 1978 (RWN 260-431).
134 Schmitt to Taubes, 10 February 1978. See Herbert Kopp-Oberstebrink, Thorsten Palzhoff and Martin Treml, *Jacob Taubes – Carl Schmitt: Briefwechsel mit Materialien*, Munich, 2012. Herbert Kopp-Oberstebrink and Martin Treml, *Hans Blumenberg – Jacob Taubes: Briefwechsel 1961–1981 und weitere Materialien*, Berlin, 2013.
135 Schmitt to Taubes, 24 February 1978, in Kopp-Oberstebrink et al., *Jacob Taubes – Carl Schmitt*, p. 50.
136 Taubes to Schmitt, 2 March 1978 (RW 265-15963).
137 Taubes to Schmitt, 18 September 1978 (RW 265-15965).
138 At least this was Taube's impression, as expressed in his letter to Schmitt dated 16 October 1978 (RW 265-15966).
139 Taubes to Schmitt on 'All Souls Day' 1978 (RW 265-15968).
140 Taubes to Schmitt, 24 November 1978 and 29 November 1978 (RW 265-15971/2). Schmitt's draft for a letter to Böckenförde, dated 14 December 1979 (RW 265-21652).
141 Schmitt to Taubes, 24 November 1978.
142 Schmitt to Taubes, 19 February 1979, in Kopp-Oberstebrink et al., *Jacob Taubes – Carl Schmitt*, p. 87.
143 Telegram from Taubes to Schmitt for his birthday, dated 11 July 1979 (RW 265-15978).
144 Unseld to Schmitt, 15 August 1979 and 14 November 1979 (RW 265-16703/4).
145 Schmitt to Taubes, 3 November 1979, in Kopp-Oberstebrink et al., *Jacob Taubes – Carl Schmitt*, p. 98.
146 Taubes's letter of thanks to Schmitt, dated 7 February 1980 (RW 265-15982). Schmitt's letter to Martin Kriele, dated 11 February 1980 (RWN 260-395).
147 Schmitt to Taubes, 12 March 1980, in Kopp-Oberstebrink et al., *Jacob Taubes – Carl Schmitt*, p. 106.
148 See Jacob Taubes, *Ad Carl Schmitt: Gegenstrebige Fügung*, Berlin, 1987.
149 Send by the publisher, Schöningh, to Schmitt on 21 October 1983 (RW 265-14482). Personal copy (RW 265-27210).
150 Jacob Taubes, *Die politische Theologie des Paulus*, ed. Aleida Assmann and Jan Assmann, Munich, 1993. In a telephone conversation with me on 1 September 2007, Norbert Bolz, Taubes's last assistant, emphasized the central role of theological questions and of Carl Schmitt for Taubes. The political-revolutionary appearance he had put on had, by contrast, been something of a camouflage. The Marxist circles at the Freie Universität did 'not even ignore' Taubes's theological interests. Taubes, he said, took Schmitt seriously as a Catholic, and he also studied anti-Semitism as a 'mental formation' [geistige Formation]. Despite their substance, the collected volumes, co-edited by Bolz, did not fully express the theoretical heritage of Taubes. Taubes, he suspected, did not find his Plato. Bolz applied Taubes's motifs in particular in his Habilitation: *Auszug aus der entzauberten Welt: Philosophischer Extremismus zwischen den Weltkriegen*, Munich, 1989.

151 Hans-Dietrich Sander, *Die Auflösung aller Dinge: Zur geschichtlichen Lage des Judentums in den Metamorphosen der Moderne*, Munich, 1988. Sander presents his epigonal treatise in the introduction as a 'refutation' of Taubes at the 'level' of Schmitt (pp. 18, 10).
152 Kličković to Schmitt, 13 June 1979 (RW 265-7799).
153 Gross to Schmitt, 20 November 1979 (RW 265-5341).
154 Schmitt to E.-W. Böckenförde, 26 October 1979 (RWN 260-431).
155 Draft of a letter from Schmitt to Böckenförde, dated 26 October 1979 (RW 265-12826).
156 Böckenförde to Schmitt, 21 November 1979 (RW 265-12826).
157 The negotiations were probably initiated by Dr Haller on 26 November 1980. Schmitt indicated his interest in having a conversation and possibly wanted to discuss various points only for tactical reasons. The letter of 6 May 1982 from Dr Haller to Schmitt conclusively rules out Münster as an option (RW 265-5666/73).
158 According to Schelz's formulation in his letter to Schmitt, dated 31 August 1979 (RW 265-12410). Schmitt received a fee of 1,000 Deutschmarks. On 16 August 1979, Schelz sent his text to Schmitt (RW 265-12409).
159 According to Taubes, in his letter to Schmitt dated 30 October 1979 (RW 265-15980).
160 Eberhard Jüngel, 'Wertlose Wahrheit: Christliche Wahrheitserfahrung im Streit gegen die Tyrannei der Werte', in Carl Schmitt, Eberhard Jüngel and Sepp Schelz, *Die Tyrannei der Werte*, ed. Sepp Schelz, Hamburg, 1979, pp. 45–75; here: p. 60.
161 Carl Schmitt, 'Rat für Pankraz' [Advice for Pankratz], *Die Welt* (25 April 1980). This was Schmitt's response to an article by Günther Zehm (Pankratz), 'Carl Schmitt und das "crisis management"', *Die Welt*, no. 87 (14 April 1980), p. 19 (in RW 265-21652).
162 Maschke to Schmitt, 28 December 1979 (RW 265-9150). Cf. Gerd Giesler, in *Liber Amicorum: Festschrift für Günter Maschke*, Murcia, 2008, pp. 187–94.
163 Schmitt to Maschke, 20 January 1980 (RWN 260-408).
164 Maschke to Schmitt, 26 June 1980 (RW 265-9158).
165 List of recipients in RW 265-20945.
166 Roman Schnur found the engraving in the Kupferstichkabinett Berlin [Berlin Gallery of Copper Engravings] and sent it to Schmitt on 18 February 1980 (RW 265-14466). Schmitt collected representations of the Leviathan (in RW 265-20698). Fifteen author copies were sent to Schmitt on 28 September 1981 by the Hohenheim publishing house (RW 265-17132). List of recipients in Schmitt's personal copy (RW 265-27464).
167 Letter of 4 December 1981 from Böckenförde to Schmitt (RW 265-1866).
168 Annie Kraus to Schmitt, 11 April 1983 (RW 265-8197). In 1963, Georg Eisler had married the painter Charlotte Johanna Eisler (1917–1979).
169 Wasse to Schmitt, 25 March 1983 (RW 265-17700). Letter of thanks regarding 11 July 1983, in RWN 260-358). Wasse was Schmitt's assistant in 1942.
170 Koselleck to Schmitt, 20 November 1983 (RW 265-18713).
171 Collected in RWN 260-358.
172 *Westfälische Rundschau* (11 July 1982): Bedeutender Plettenberger: Carl Schmitt wird heute 95'.
173 Walter Dirks, 'Ein Vordenker: Zum 95. Geburtstag des Staatstheoretikers Carl Schmitt', *Badische Zeitung* (10 July 1983).
174 Charles W. Wahl to Schmitt, 17 July 1983 (RW 265-17416). Wahl passed his doctorate on 25 July 1932 with a dissertation on 'Die rechtmäßige

Beobachtung von Lagerbewegung und Lagerbestand'. In his *curriculum vitae*, Wahl thanked his teachers, including Schmitt.

175 Medical certificate by the family doctor, Dr Cramer, dated 12 September 1982 (RW 579-68).

176 Letter of thanks from Christian Meier to Schmitt, dated 17 October 1983 (RW 265-9388).

177 Letter of 14 October 1983 from Böckenförde to Schmitt (RW 265-1872).

178 Annie Kraus to Schmitt, 25 November 1983 (RW 265-8198). Postscript July 2009: In the meantime, further biographical information has been extracted from the compensation file, inventory 351, 11 Georg Eisler [Wiedergutmachungsakte Bestand 351, 11 Georg Eisler], in the Staatsarchiv Hamburg. At the beginning of 1934, Georg Eisler emigrated with his three biological children and the two adopted children of his deceased sister Julie (1895–1920), first to London and in 1940 to New York. In 1937 his mother Ida Ernestine followed them; she died in London in 1939. Eisler continued to work as a publisher. However, in New York he was not particularly successful professionally. This was part of the reason why, in 1948, he returned to Hamburg for the first time. His company was handed back to him, and throughout the 1950s he shuttled back and forth between New York and Hamburg, where he was now also active again as a publisher. Divorced from his wife Käthe and then married to Charlotte Johanna in 1963, he started again to live exclusively in Hamburg from the early 1960s onwards. His story is documented in more detail in Themenheft 2 [special issue 2] of the *Plettenberger Miniaturen* on *Die Hamburger Verlegerfamilie Eisler und Carl Schmitt* [The Hamburg family of publishers Eisler and Carl Schmitt].

179 Ernst Hüsmert, 'Die letzten Jahre von Carl Schmitt', in *Schmittiana* 1 (1988), pp. 40–54; here: p. 52.

180 Letter from Kaiser thanking Schmitt for the 'wonderful conversations', dated 30 December 1983 (RW 265-7213).

181 Carl Schmitt, 'Testament' of 1 February 1984 (RW 579-680).

182 Kaiser died in 1998, and his pupil Jürgen Becker is in charge of his posthumous papers, and has been very helpful in his response to inquiries.

183 Franzen to Schmitt, 27 February 1984 (RW 265-4057).

184 Letter of 7 August 1984 from von Medem to Schmitt (RW 265-9343).

185 Niklas Frank, *Der Vater: Eine Abrechnung*, Munich, 1993, pp. 19f. Ernst Hüsmert followed this up and inquired whether the coffin had been opened in the chapel. An employee at the cemetery had, indeed, opened the coffin.

Afterword to the English Edition

1 See the – sometimes polemical – reviews by Stephan Schlak, in *Süddeutsche Zeitung*, no. 216 (19–20 September 2009); Patrick Bahners, in *Frankfurter Allgemeine Zeitung*, no. 239 (12 October 2009); Alf Christophersen, in *Neue Züricher Zeitung*, no. 236 (12 October 2009); Nicolaus German, in *Das Parlament*, no. 49 (30 November 2009); Micha Brumlik, in *Frankfurter Rundschau* (8 December 2009); Christian Meier, *Idee: Zeitschrift für Ideengeschichte*, 4/3 (2010), pp. 115–21; Hans-Cristof Kraus, in *Die Öffentliche Verwaltung* 63 (2010), pp. 1021–3; Alfons Söllner, in *Jahrbuch Extremismus & Demokratie* 22 (2010), pp. 357–60; Günter Frankenberg, in *Der Staat* 50 (2011), pp. 156–60.

2 *Jacob Taubes – Carl Schmitt: Briefwechsel*, ed. Herbert Kopp-Oberstebrink, Munich, 2012 (see my review of this in *Zeitschrift für Religions- und Geistesgeschichte* 64 (2012), pp. 204–7); *'Auf der gefahrenvollen Straße des*

öffentlichen Rechts': Briefwechsel Carl Schmitt – Rudolf Smend 1921–1961, ed. Reinhard Mehring, 2nd rev. edn, Berlin, 2012; *Schmittiana*, NF (new series) 1 (2011), Berlin, 2011; *Carl Schmitt, Tagebücher 1930 bis 1934*, ed. Wolfgang Schuller, Berlin, 2010; *'Solange das Imperium noch da ist': Carl Schmitt im Gespräch mit Klaus Figge und Dieter Groh 1971*, ed. Frank Hertweck and Dimitrios Kisoudis, Berlin, 2010.

3 See my review essay 'Rekonstruktion und Historisierung: Zur neueren Carl Schmitt-Forschung', *Zeitschrift für Geschichtswissenschaft* 49 (2001), pp. 1000–11.

4 Stefan Breuer, *Carl Schmitt im Kontext: Intellektuellenpolitik in der Weimarer Republik*, Berlin, 2012.

5 Michael Stolleis, *Geschichte des öffentlichen Rechts in Deutschland*, vol. 4: *Staats- und Verwaltungsrechtswissenschaft in West und Ost 1945–1990*, Munich, 2012. Cf. also Axel-Johannes Korb, *Kelsens Kritiker: Ein Beitrag zur Geschichte der Rechts- und Staatstheorie (1911–1934)*, Tübingen, 2010; Florian Meinel, *Der Jurist in der industriellen Gesellschaft: Ernst Forsthoff und seine Zeit*, Berlin, 2011.

6 www.carl-schmitt.de/neueste_veroeffentlichungen.php.

7 Reinhard Mehring, *Carl Schmitt zur Einführung*, 1992, 4th rev. edn, Hamburg, 2011.

8 Reinhard Mehring, 'Ein "katholischer Laie deutscher Staats- und Volkszugehörigkeit"? Carl Schmitts Konfession', in Hugo Eduardo Herrera (ed.), *Carl Schmitt: Análisis Crítico*, Valparaiso, 2012, pp. 387–409.

9 Correspondence with philosophers, in *Schmittiana*, NF (new series) 2 (2014).

10 Reinhard Mehring, '"Die Austreibung des Heidelberger Geistes": Carl Schmitt und der Heidelberger Rechtspositivismus', in Manfred Gangl (ed.), *Die Weimarer Staatsdebatte: Diskurs- und Rezeptionsstrategien*, Baden-Baden, 2011, pp. 127–57.

11 Reinhard Mehring, 'Die "Ehre Preußens" in der "legalen Revolution": Carl Schmitt im Frühjahr 1933', in Christoph Kopke and Werner Treß (eds), *Der Tag von Potsdam: Der 21. März 1933 und die Errichtung der nationalsozialistischen Diktatur*, Berlin, 2013, pp. 113–33. Review of Carl Schmitt, *Tagebücher 1930–1934*, Berlin, 2010, and *Carl Schmitt im Gespräch mit Klaus Figge und Dieter Groh 1971*, Berlin, 2010, in *Göttinger Gelehrte Anzeiger* 263 (2011), pp. 57–72.

12 Reinhard Mehring, 'Carl Schmitt in Köln: Sinnwandel eines Semesters: Vom Agon mit Kelsen zum Probelauf des "Kronjuristen"', in Steffen Augsberg and Andreas Funke (eds), *Kölner Juristen im 20. Jahrhundert*, Tübingen, 2013, pp. 137–61.

13 Reinhard Mehring, *Die Hamburger Verlegerfamilie Eisler und Carl Schmitt*, Plettenberg, 2009.

14 Reinhard Mehring, *"Eine Tochter ist das ganz andere": Anima Schmitt de Otero (1931–1983)*, Plettenberg, 2012.

15 Reinhard Mehring, 'Vordenker der souveränen Diktatur? Das antiliberale Rousseau-Bild und Carl Schmitt', in *Politisches Denken: Jahrbuch*, Berlin, 2012, pp. 129–44.

16 Reinhard Mehring, '"Autor vor allem der 'Judenfrage' von 1843": Carl Schmitts Bruno Bauer', in Klaus-Michael Kodalle and Tilman Reitz (eds), *Bruno Bauer: Ein 'Partisan des Weltgeistes'?*, Würzburg, 2010, pp. 335–50.

17 Reinhard Mehring, 'Politische Theologie des Anarchismus: Fritz Mauthner und Gustav Landauer im Visier Carl Schmitts', in Gerald Hartung (ed.), *An den Grenzen der Sprachkritik: Fritz Mauthners Beiträge zur Sprach- und Kulturtheorie*, Würzburg, 2013, pp. 85–111.

18 Reinhard Mehring, *Carl Schmitt – Rudolf Smend: Briefwechsel*, Berlin, 2010 (2nd edn, 2012).

19 Reinhard Mehring and Ellen Thümmler (eds), '"Machen Sie mir die Freude und erwähnen Sie die Negerplastik": Waldemar Gurian – Carl Schmitt: Briefwechsel 1924–1932', in *Schmittiana*, NF (new series) 1 (2011), pp. 59–111.

20 Reinhard Mehring, '"Ein typischer Fall jugendlicher Produktivität": Otto Kirchheimers Bonner Promotionsakte', www.forhistiur.de/zitat/1001mehring. htm; expanded version in Robert Christian von Ooyen and Frank Schale (eds), *Kritische Verfassungspolitologie: Das Staatsverständnis von Otto Kirchheimer*, Baden-Baden, 2011, pp. 19–34.

21 Reinhard Mehring, 'Utopiker der Intellektuellenherrschaft: Karl Mannheim und Carl Schmitt', *Berliner Debatte Initial* 23 (2012), pp. 67–93.

22 Reinhard Mehring, 'Carl Schmitt und die Weimarer Universitätsphilosophie', forthcoming in *Plessner-Jahrbuch*.

23 'Briefwechsel Walter Jellinek – Carl Schmitt 1926–1933', in *Schmittiana*, NF (new series) 2 (2014), pp. 87–117.

24 Reinhard Mehring, '9. September 1933 im Kaiserhof? Martin Heidegger und Carl Schmitt in Berlin: Nach neuer Quellenlage', *Merkur* 67/764 (2013), pp. 73–8.

25 Reinhard Mehring, '"Geist ist das Vermögen, Diktatur auszuüben": Carl Schmitts Marginalien zu Walter Benjamin', in Daniel Weidner (ed.), *Benjamin-Studien II*, Munich, 2011, pp. 239–56.

26 Reinhard Mehring, 'Don Capisco und sein Soldat: Carl Schmitt und Ernst Jünger', in Stephan Müller-Doohm and Thomas Jung (eds), *Prekäre Freundschaften: Über geistige Nähe und Distanz*, Munich, 2011, pp. 173–85.

27 Forthcoming in Kathleen Kanthner (ed.), *Gehlen*, Baden-Baden.

28 Reinhard Mehring, 'Der esoterische Diskurspartisan: Carl Schmitt in der Bundesrepublik', in Thomas Kroll and Tilman Reitz (eds), *Intellektuelle in der Bundesrepublik Deutschland: Verschiebungen im politischen Feld der 1960er und 1970er Jahre*, Göttingen, 2013, pp. 232–48.

29 See my forthcoming: 'Nemo contra theologum nisi theologum ipse: Carl Schmitt's Antwort auf Erik Peterson', in Michael Mayer-Blanck (ed.), *Erik Peterson* (in press).

30 Reinhard Mehring, 'Begriffsgeschichte mit Carl Schmitt', in Hans Joas and Peter Vogt (eds), *Begriffene Geschichte: Beiträge zum Werk Reinhart Kosellecks*, Frankfurt, 2010, pp. 138–68.

31 Reinhard Mehring and Rolf Riess (eds), *Ludwig Feuchtwanger: Auf der Suche nach dem Wesen des Judentums: Beiträge zur Grundlegung der jüdischen Geschichte*, Berlin, 2011; Reinhard Mehring and Rolf Rieß (eds), *Ludwig Feuchtwanger: Der Gang der Juden durch die Weltgeschichte*, Berlin, 2013 [unpublished typescript from the period 1935 to 1938, edited from Feuchtwanger's posthumous papers, together with supplementary material].

32 Reinhard Mehring, '"Die Waffen sind das Wesen der Kämpfer selbst": Form und Sinn des Krieges nach Carl Schmitt', in Thomas Jäger and Rasmus Beckmann (eds), *Handbuch Kriegstheorien*, Wiesbaden, 2011, pp. 248–55; Reinhard Mehring, 'Zur Aktualität Carl Schmitts: Sondierung eines globalen Phänomens', in Maurizio Bach (ed.), *Der entmachtete Leviathan: Löst sich der souveräne Staat auf?*, Baden-Baden, 2013, pp. 263–79.

33 Kathleen Murray, *Taine und die englische Romantik*, Munich and Leipzig, 1924.

34 Reinhard Mehring, 'Das Lachen der Besiegten: Carl Schmitt und Gelimer', *Idee: Zeitschrift für Ideengeschichte*, 6/1 (2012), pp. 32–45.

Bibliography

Agamben, Giorgio, *Ausnahmezustand*, Frankfurt, 2004.

Arendt, Hannah, *Die verborgene Tradition: Essays*, Frankfurt, 2000.

Arendt, Hannah, *Men in Dark Times*, New York, 1955.

Assmann, Jan, *Herrschaft und Heil: Politische Theologie in Altägypten, Israel und Europa*, Munich, 2000.

Balakrishnan, Gopal, *The Enemy: An Intellectual Portrait of Carl Schmitt*, London, 2000.

Balke, Friedrich, *Der Staat nach seinem Ende: Die Versuchung Carl Schmitts*, Munich, 1996.

Ball, Hugo, 'Carl Schmitts Politische Theologie', *Hochland* 21 (1924), pp. 263–86.

Ball, Hugo, *Flight out of Time: A Dada Diary*, ed. and intro. John Elderfield, trans. Ann Raimes, Berkeley and London, 1996.

Barion, Hans, *Kirche und Kirchenrecht: Gesammelte Aufsätze*, ed. Werner Böckenförde, Paderborn, 1984.

Barion, Hans, Böckenförde, Ernst-Wolfgang, Forsthoff, Ernst, and Weber, Werner (eds), *Epirrhosis:Festgabe für Carl Schmitt zum 80. Geburtstag*, 2 vols, Berlin, 1968.

Barion, Hans, Forsthoff, Ernst, and Weber, Werner (eds), *Festschrift für Carl Schmitt: Zum 70. Geburtstag dargebracht von Freunden und Schülern*, Berlin, 1959.

Beaud, Olivier, *Les derniers jours de Weimar: Carl Schmitt face à l'avènement du nazisme*, Paris, 1997.

Becker, Lothar, *'Schritte auf einer abschüssigen Bahn': Das Archiv des öffentlichen Rechts (AöR) und die deutsche Staatsrechtswissenschaft im dritten Reich*, Tübingen, 1999.

Bendersky, Joseph W., *Carl Schmitt: Theorist for the Reich*, Princeton, NJ, 1983.

Bendersky, Joseph W., 'Carl Schmitt's Path to Nuremberg: A Sixty-Year Reassessment, *Telos* no. 239 (2007), pp. 6–43.

Benoist, Alain de, *Carl Schmitt: Bibliographie seiner Schriften und Korrespondenzen*, Berlin, 2003.

Bentin, Lutz-Arwed, *Johannes Popitz und Carl Schmitt: Zur wirtschaftlichen Theorie des totalen Staates in Deutschland*, Munich, 1972.

Berend, Alice, *Der Glückspilz: Roman*, Munich, 1919.

Berthold, Lutz, *Carl Schmitt und der Staatsnotstandsplan am Ende der Weimarer Republik*, Berlin, 1999.

Bielefeldt, Heiner, *Kampf und Entscheidung: Politischer Existentialismus bei Carl Schmitt, Helmuth Plessner und Karl Jaspers*, Würzburg, 1994.

Blasius, Dirk, *Carl Schmitt: Preußischer Staatsrat in Hitlers Reich*, Göttingen, 2001.

Blasius, Dirk, 'Carl Schmitt und der "Heereskonflikt" des Dritten Reiches 1934', *Historische Zeitschrift* 281 (2005), pp. 659–82.

Bleek, Wilhelm, *Geschichte der Politikwissenschaft in Deutschland*, Munich, 2001.

Blei, Franz, 'Carl Schmitt', in Blei, *Zeitgenössische Bildnisse*, Amsterdam, 1940, pp. 21–9.

Blei, Franz, *Erzählung eines Lebens*, Leipzig, 1930.

Blei, Franz, *Menschliche Betrachtungen zur Politik*, 3rd edn, Berlin, 1916.

Blumenberg, Hans, *Die Legitimität der Neuzeit*, Frankfurt, 1966.

Böckenförde, Ernst-Wolfgang, *Die deutsche verfassungsgeschichtliche Forschung im 19. Jahrhundert: Zeitgebundene Fragestellungen und Leitbilder*, Berlin, 1961.

Böckenförde, Ernst-Wolfgang, *Die Organisationsgewalt im Bereich der Regierung: Eine Untersuchung zum Staatsrecht der Bundesrepublik Deutschland*, Berlin, 1964.

Böckenförde, Ernst-Wolfgang, *Geschichte der Rechts- und Staatsphilosophie: Antike und Mittelalter*, Tübingen, 2002.

Böckenförde, Ernst-Wolfgang, *Gesetz und gesetzgebende Gewalt: Von den Anfängen der deutschen Staatsrechtslehre bis zur Höhe des staatsrechtlichen Positivismus*, Berlin, 1958.

Böckenförde, Ernst-Wolfgang, *Recht, Staat, Freiheit: Studien zur Rechtsphilosophie, Staatstheorie und zur Verfassungsgeschichte*, enlarged edn, Frankfurt, 2006.

Böckenförde, Ernst-Wolfgang, *Schriften zu Staat – Gesellschaft – Kirche*, 3 vols, Freiburg, 1988–90.

Böckenförde, Ernst-Wolfgang, *Staat, Nation, Europa: Studien zur Staatslehre, Verfassungstheorie und Rechtsphilosophie*, Frankfurt, 1999.

Böckenförde, Ernst-Wolfgang, *Staat, Verfassung, Demokratie: Studien zur Verfassungstheorie und zum Verfassungsrecht*, Frankfurt, 1991.

Böhm, Helmut, *Von der Selbstverwaltung zum Führerprinzip: Die Universität Munich in den ersten Jahren des Dritten Reiches (1933–1936)*, Berlin, 1995.

Bohrer, Karl-Heinz, *Die Kritik der Romantik: Der Verdacht der Philosophie gegen die literarische Moderne*, Frankfurt, 1989.

Boldt, Hans, *Einführung in die Verfassungsgeschichte*, Düsseldorf, 1984.

Bolz, Norbert, *Auszug aus der entzauberten Welt: Philosophischer Extremismus zwischen den Weltkriegen*, Munich, 1989.

Bonn, Moritz Julius, *So macht man Geschichte: Bilanz eines Lebens*, Munich, 1953.

Borchmeyer, Dieter, *Richard Wagner: Ahasvers Wandlungen*, Frankfurt, 2002.

Borchmeyer, Dieter, Maayani, Ami, and Vill, Susanne (eds), *Richard Wagner und die Juden*, Stuttgart, 2000.

Botsch, Gideon, *'Politische Wissenschaft im Zweiten Weltkrieg': Die 'Deutschen Auslandswissenschaften' im Einsatz 1940–1945*, Paderborn, 2006.

Bracher, Karl Dietrich, *Die Auflösung der Weimarer Republik: Eine Studie zum Problem des Machtverfalls in der Demokratie*, Villingen, 1955.

Bracher, Karl Dietrich, *Die deutsche Diktatur: Entstehung, Struktur, Folgen des Nationalsozialismus*, Cologne 1969.

Bracher, Karl Dietrich, *Zeit der Ideologien: Eine Geschichte politischen Denkens im 20. Jahrhundert*, Stuttgart, 1982.

Brand, Gregor, 'Non ignobili stirpe procreatum: Carl Schmitt und seine Herkunft', in *Schmittiana* 5 (1996), pp. 225–98.

Braun, Matthias, and Pesch, Volker, 'Die Umstände der Berufung Carl Schmitts nach Greifswald', in *Schmittiana* 7 (2001), pp. 195–206.

Calker, Fritz van, *Einführung in die Politik*, Munich, 1927.

Calker, Fritz van, *Grundriß des Strafrechts*, Munich, 1916.

Cassirer, Ernst, *Vom Mythos des Staates*, Zurich, 1949.

Cristi, Renato, *Carl Schmitt and Authoritarian Liberalism: Strong State, Free Economy*, Cardiff, 1998.

Curtius, Ernst Robert, *Maurice Barrès und die geistigen Grundlagen des französischen Nationalismus*, Bonn, 1921.

Dahlheimer, Manfred, *Carl Schmitt und der deutsche Katholizismus 1888–1936*, Paderborn, 1998.

Däubler, Theodor, *Im Kampf um die moderne Kunst und andere Schriften*, ed. Friedhelm Kemp and Friedrich Pfäfflin, Darmstadt, 1988.

Deutsche Briefe 1934–1938: Ein Blatt der katholischen Emigration, ed. Heinz Hürten, 2 vols, Mainz, 1969.

Doremus, André, *Introduction à la pensée de Carl Schmitt*, Paris, 1981.

Dubnow, Simon, *Weltgeschichte des jüdischen Volkes*, vol. 3, Jerusalem, 1938.

Duso, Giuseppe, *Die moderne politische Repräsentation: Entstehung und Krise des Begriffs*, Berlin, 2006.

Dyzenhaus, David, *Legality and Legitimacy: Carl Schmitt, Hans Kelsen and Hermann Heller in Weimar*, Stanford, CA, 2005.

Eberl, Matthias, *Die Legitimität der Moderne: Kulturkritik und Herrschaftskonzeption bei Max Weber und Carl Schmitt*, Marburg, 1994.

Eckhardt, Karl August, *Das Studium der Rechtswissenschaft*, Hamburg, 1934.

Eichhorn, Mathias, *'Es wird regiert!' Der Staat im Denken Karl Barths und Carl Schmitts in den Jahren 1919 bis 1938*, Berlin, 1994.

Eisler, Fritz, *Rechtsgut und Erfolg bei Beleidigung und Kreditgefährdung*, Breslau, 1911.

Eulenberg, Herbert, *Schattenbilder*, Berlin, 1912.

Faulenbach, Heiner, *Ein Weg durch die Kirche: Heinrich Josef Oberheid*, Cologne, 1992.

Feuchtwanger, Lion, *Die Geschwister Oppenheim: Roman*, Amsterdam, 1933.

Feuchtwanger, Ludwig, *Gesammelte Aufsätze zur jüdischen Geschichte*, ed. Rolf Rieß, Berlin, 2003.

Fijalkowski, Jürgen, *Die Wendung zum Führerstaat: Ideologische Komponenten in der politischen Philosophie Carl Schmitts*, Cologne, 1958.

Fischer, Jens Malte, *Richard Wagners 'Das Judentum in der Musik': Eine kritische Dokumentation als Beitrag zur Geschichte des Antisemitismus*, Frankfurt, 2000.

Forsthoff, Ernst, *Der Staat der Industriegesellschaft: Dargestellt am Beispiel der Bundesrepublik Deutschland*, Munich, 1971.

Forsthoff, Ernst (ed.), *Deutsche Geschichte seit 1918 in Dokumenten*, 2nd edn, Stuttgart, 1938.

Forsthoff, Ernst, *Rechtsstaat im Wandel: Verfassungsrechtliche Abhandlungen 1954–1973*, 2nd edn, Munich, 1976.

Forsthoff, Heinrich, *Das Ende der humanistischen Illusion: Eine Untersuchung über die Voraussetzungen von Philosophie und Theologie*, Berlin, 1933.

Fraenger, Wilhelm, *Hieronymus Bosch: Das Tausendjährige Reich: Grundzüge einer Auslegung*, Coburg, 1947.

Fraenkel, Ernst, *Der Doppelstaat*, Frankfurt, 1974.

Fraenkel, Ernst, *Deutschland und die westlichen Demokratien*, Stuttgart, 1964.

Frank, Hans, *Im Angesicht des Galgens: Deutung Hitlers und seiner Zeit aufgrund eigener Erlebnisse und Erkenntnisse*, Munich, 1953.

Frank, Niklas, *Der Vater: Eine Abrechnung*, Munich, 1993.

Franzen, Hans, *Im Wandel des Zeitgeistes 1931–1991*, Munich, 1992.

Freyer, Hans, *Machiavelli*, Leipzig, 1938.

Freyer, Hans, *Weltgeschichte Europas*, 2 vols, Wiesbaden, 1948.

Friedländer, Saul, *Nazi Germany and the Jews*, vol. 1: *The Years of Persecution 1933–39*, London, 1997.

Friedländer, Saul, *Nazi Germany and the Jews*, vol. 2: *The Years of Extermination 1939–1945*, London, 2008.

Friedrich, Manfred, *Geschichte der deutschen Staatsrechtswissenschaft*, Berlin, 1997.

Friesenhahn, Ernst, 'Juristen an der Universität Bonn', in *Alma Mater: Beiträge zur Geschichte der Universität Bonn*, Bonn, 1970, pp. 21–48.

Fromme, Friedrich Karl, *Von der Weimarer Verfassung zum Bonner Grundgesetz*, Tübingen, 1960.

Galli, Carlo, *Genealogia della politica: Carl Schmitt e la crisi del pensiero politico moderno*, Bologna, 1996.

Gerhardt, Volker, *Partizipation: Das Prinzip der Politik*, Munich, 2007.

Giesler, Gerd, and Hüsmert, Ernst (eds), *Carl Schmitt und Plettenberg: Der 90. Geburtstag*, Plettenberg, 2008.

Golczewski, Frank, *Kölner Universitätslehrer und der Nationalsozialismus*, Cologne, 1988.

Göppinger, Horst, *Die Verfolgung der Juristen jüdischer Abstammung durch den Nationalsozialismus*, Villingen, 1963.

Gosewinkel, Dieter, *Einbürgern und Ausschließen: Die Nationalisierung der Staatsangehörigkeit vom Deutschen Bund bis zur Bundesrepublik Deutschland*, Göttingen, 2001.

Grewe, Wilhelm, *Epochen der Völkerrechtsgeschichte*, Baden-Baden, 1984.

Grewe, Wilhelm, 'Über das Völkerrecht des Nürnberger Prozesses', in Grewe, *Nürnberg als Rechtsfrage: Eine Diskussion*, Stuttgart, 1947, pp. 7–48.

Groh, Ruth, *Arbeit an der Heillosigkeit der Welt: Zur politisch-theologischen Mythologie und Anthropologie Carl Schmitts*, Frankfurt, 1998.

Gross, Raphael, *Carl Schmitt und die Juden: Eine deutsche Rechtslehre*, Frankfurt, 2000; Eng. trans. as *Carl Schmitt and the Jews: The 'Jewish Question', the Holocaust, and German Legal Theory*, trans. Joel Golb, Madison, WI, 2007.

Grossheutschi, Felix, *Carl Schmitt und die Lehre vom Katechon*, Berlin, 1996.

Grothe, Ewald, '"Strengste Zurückhaltung und unbedingter Takt": Der Verfassungshistoriker Ernst Rudolf Huber und die NS-Vergangenheit', in Eva Schumann (ed.), *Kontinuitäten und Zäsuren: Rechtswissenschaft und Justiz im 'Dritten Reich' und in der Nachkriegszeit*, Göttingen, 2008, pp. 327–48.

Grothe, Ewald, *Zwischen Geschichte und Recht: Deutsche Verfassungs-geschichtsschreibung 1900–1970*, Munich, 2005.

Gruchmann, Lothar, *Justiz im Dritten Reich: Anpassung und Unterwerfung in der Ära Gürtner*, 3rd edn, Munich, 2001.

Gruchmann, Lothar, *Nationalsozialistische Großraumordnung: Die Konstruktion einer deutschen Monroe-Doktrin*, Stuttgart, 1962.

Günther, Frieder, *Denken vom Staat her: Die bundesdeutsche Staatsrechtslehre zwischen Dezision und Integration 1949–1970*, Munich, 2004.

Günther, Gerhard, *Der Antichrist: Der staufische Ludus de Antichristo*, Hamburg, 1970.

Gurian, Waldemar, *Der katholische Publizist*, Augsburg, 1931.

Gurian, Waldemar (Paul Müller), 'Entscheidung und Ordnung: Zu den Schriften von Carl Schmitt', *Schweizerische Rundschau* 34 (1934), pp. 566–76.

Habermas, Jürgen, *Der gespaltene Westen*, in *Kleine politische Schriften*, vol. 10, Frankfurt, 2004.

Habermas, Jürgen, *Die Einbeziehung des Anderen: Studien zur politischen Theorie*, Frankfurt, 1996.

Haecker, Theodor, *Satire und Polemik 1914–1920*, Innsbruck, 1922.

Haecker, Theodor, *Was ist der Mensch?*, 3rd edn, Leipzig, 1935.
Hansen, Klaus, et al. (eds), *Carl Schmitt und die Liberalismuskritik*, Opladen, 1988.
Harnack, Adolf von, *Marcion: Das Evangelium vom fremden Gott: Eine Monographie zur Geschichte der Grundlegung der katholischen Kirche*, Leipzig, 1921.
Hausenstein, Wilhelm, *Die Welt um München*, Munich, 1929.
Hausmann, Frank-Rutger, *'Auch im Krieg schweigen die Musen nicht': Die Deutschen Wissenschaftlichen Institute im Zweiten Weltkrieg*, Göttingen, 2001.
Hausmann, Frank-Rutger, *'Deutsche Geisteswissenschaft' im Zweiten Weltkrieg: Die 'Aktion Ritterbusch' (1940–1945)*, Dresden, 1998.
Heiber, Helmut, *Walter Frank und das Reichsinstitut für Geschichte des neuen Deutschlands*, Stuttgart, 1966.
Heidegger, Martin, *Gesamtausgabe*, vol. 16, Frankfurt, 2000.
Heil, Susanne, *'Gefährliche Beziehungen': Walter Benjamin und Carl Schmitt*, Stuttgart, 1996.
Heinrichs, Helmut, et al. (eds), *Deutsche Juristen jüdischer Herkunft*, Munich, 1993.
Heller, Hermann, *Die politischen Ideenkreise der Gegenwart*, Breslau, 1926.
Heller, Hermann, *Europa und der Fascismus*, Berlin, 1929.
Heller, Hermann, *Staatslehre*, Leiden, 1934.
Hennis, Wilhelm, *Politikwissenschaftliche Abhandlungen*, vol. 1: *Regieren im modernen Staat*, Tübingen, 2000.
Hennis, Wilhelm, *Politikwissenschaftliche Abhandlungen*, vol. 2: *Politikwissenschaft und politisches Denken*, Tübingen, 2000.
Herbert, Ulrich, *Best: Biographische Studien über Radikalismus, Weltanschauung und Vernunft*, 2nd edn, Bonn, 1996.
Herbst, Ludolf, *Das nationalsozialistische Deutschland 1933–1945: Die Entfesselung der Gewalt: Rassismus und Krieg*, Frankfurt, 1996.
Hofmann, Hasso, 'Die deutsche Rechtswissenschaft im Kampf gegen den jüdischen Geist', in Karlheinz Müller and Klaus Wittstadt (eds), *Geschichte und Kultur des Judentums*, Würzburg, 1988, pp. 228–40.
Hofmann, Hasso, *Legalität gegen Legitimität: Der Weg der politischen Philosophie Carl Schmitts*, 4th edn, Berlin, 2002.
Hofmann, Hasso, 'Was ist uns Carl Schmitt?', in Hans Maier et al. (eds), *Politik, Philosophie, Praxis: Festschrift für Wilhelm Hennis zum 65. Geburtstag*, Stuttgart, 1988, pp. 545–55.
Holstein, Günther, 'Von Aufgaben und Zielen heutiger Staatsrechtswissenschaft', *Archiv des öffentlichen Rechts* 50 (1926), pp. 1–40.
Hösle, Vittorio, 'Carl Schmitts Kritik an der Selbstaufhebung einer wertneutralen Verfassung', *Deutsche Vierteljahrsschrift für Literaturwissenschaft und Geistesgeschichte* 61 (1987), pp. 1–34.
Huber, Ernst Rudolf (ed.), *Bau und Gefüge des Reiches*, Hamburg, 1941.
Huber, Ernst Rudolf, *Bewahrung und Wandlung: Studien zur deutschen Staatstheorie und Verfassungsgeschichte*, Berlin, 1975.
Huber, Ernst Rudolf, 'Carl Schmitt in der Reichskrise der Weimarer Endzeit', in Helmut Quaritsch (ed.), *Complexio Oppositorum: Über Carl Schmitt*, Berlin, 1988, pp. 33–70.
Huber, Ernst Rudolf, *Deutsche Verfassungsgeschichte seit 1789*, vol. 4: *Struktur und Krisen des Kaiserreichs*, Stuttgart, 1969.
Huber, Ernst Rudolf, *Deutsche Verfassungsgeschichte seit 1789*, vol. 5: *Weltkrieg, Revolution und Reichserneuerung 1914–1919*, Stuttgart, 1978.
Huber, Ernst Rudolf, *Deutsche Verfassungsgeschichte seit 1789*, vol. 6: *Die Weimarer Reichsverfassung*, Stuttgart, 1981.

Huber, Ernst Rudolf, *Deutsche Verfassungsgeschichte seit 1789*, vol. 7: *Ausbau, Schutz und Untergang der Weimarer Republik*, Stuttgart, 1984.

Huber, Ernst Rudolf, *Heer und Staat in der deutschen Geschichte*, Hamburg, 1938.

Huber, Ernst Rudolf, *Nationalstaat und Verfassungsstaat: Studien zur Geschichte der modernen Staatsidee*, Stuttgart, 1965.

Huber, Ernst Rudolf, '"Positionen und Begriffe": Eine Auseinandersetzung mit Carl Schmitt', *Zeitschrift für die gesamte Strafrechtswissenschaft* 101 (1940–1), pp. 1–44.

Huber, Ernst Rudolf, *Reichsgewalt und Staatsgerichtshof*, Oldenburg, 1932.

Hürten, Heinz, *Waldemar Gurian: Ein Zeuge der Krise unserer Welt in der ersten Hälfte des 20. Jahrhunderts*, Mainz, 1972.

Hüsmert, Ernst, 'Die letzten Jahre von Carl Schmitt', in *Schmittiana* 1 (1988), pp. 40–54.

Ishida, Yugi, *Jungkonservative in der Weimarer Republik: Der Ring-Kreis 1928–1933*, Frankfurt, 1988.

Jescheck, Hans-Heinrich, *Die juristische Ausbildung in Preußen und im Reich: Vergangenheit und Gegenwart*, Berlin, 1939.

Jünger, Ernst, *Strahlungen*, Tübingen, 1949.

Jünger, Ernst, and Nebel, Gerhard, *Briefe 1938–1974*, ed. Ulrich Fröschle and Michael Neumann, Stuttgart, 2003.

Kabermann, Friedrich, *Widerstand und Entscheidung eines deutschen Revolutionärs: Leben und Denken von Ernst Niekisch*, Cologne, 1973.

Kandora, Peter, 'Carl Schmitts Attendorner Schulzeit 1900–1907', in *Schmittiana* 8 (2003), pp. 261–73.

Karlauf, Thomas, *Stefan George: Die Entdeckung des Charisma*, Munich, 2007.

Kaufmann, Erich, *Kritik der neukantischen Rechtsphilosophie: Eine Betrachtung über die Beziehung zwischen Philosophie und Rechtswissenschaft*, Tübingen, 1921.

Kaufmann, Matthias, *Recht ohne Regel? Die philosophischen Prinzipien in Carl Schmitts Staats- und Rechtslehre*, Freiburg, 1988.

Kelsen, Hans, 'Gott und Staat', *Logos* 11 (1922–3), pp. 261–84.

Kelsen, Hans, *Reine Rechtslehre*, Leipzig, 1934.

Kelsen, Hans, *Staatsform und Weltanschauung*, Tübingen, 1933.

Kelsen, Hans, *Vom Wesen und Wert der Demokratie*, 2nd edn, Tübingen, 1929.

Kelsen, Hans, *Wer soll der Hüter der Verfassung sein?*, Berlin, 1931.

Kemp, Friedhelm, 'Der Dichter Konrad Weiß', *Wort und Wahrheit* 4 (1949), pp. 180–292.

Kennedy, Ellen, *Constitutional Failure: Carl Schmitt in Weimar*, Durham, NC, 2004.

Kershaw, Ian, *Hitler, 1889–1936: Hubris*, London, 1998.

Kershaw, Ian, *Hitler, 1936–1945: Nemesis*, London, 2000.

Kervégan, Jean-François, *Hegel, Carl Schmitt: La politique entre spéculation et positivité*, Paris, 2005.

Kessler, Heinrich, *Wilhelm Stapel als politischer Publizist: Ein Beitrag zur Geschichte des konservativen Nationalismus zwischen beiden Weltkriegen*, Nuremberg, 1967.

Kesting, Marianne (ed.), *Melville, Benito Cereno*, Frankfurt, 1972.

Kiesel, Helmuth, *Ernst Jünger: Die Biographie*, Munich, 2007.

Kodalle, Klaus-Michael, *Politik als Macht und Mythos: Carl Schmitts 'Politische Theologie'*, Stuttgart, 1973.

Koellreutter, Otto, *Volk und Staat in der Verfassungskrise: Zugleich eine Auseinandersetzung mit der Verfassungslehre Carl Schmitts*, Berlin, 1933.

Koenen, Andreas, *Der Fall Carl Schmitt: Sein Aufstieg zum 'Kronjuristen des Dritten Reiches'*, Darmstadt, 1995.

König, René, *Niccolò Machiavelli: Zur Krisenanalyse einer Zeitenwende*, Zurich, 1941.

Kopp-Oberstebrink, Herbert, Palzhoff, Thorsten, and Treml, Martin (eds), *Jacob Taubes – Carl Schmitt: Briefwechsel mit Materialen*, Munich, 2012.

Koselleck, Reinhart, *Kritik und Krise: Eine Studie zur Pathogenese der bürgerlichen Welt*, Freiburg, 1959.

Koselleck, Reinhart, *Vergangene Zukunft: Zur Semantik geschichtlicher Zeiten*, Frankfurt, 1979.

Koselleck, Reinhart, *Zeitschichten: Studien zur Historik*, Frankfurt, 2000.

Koselleck, Reinhart, and Schnur, Roman (eds), *Hobbes-Forschungen*, Berlin, 1967.

Kraus, Annie, *Über die Dummheit*, Frankfurt, 1948.

Krauss, Günther, 'Zum Neubau deutscher Staatslehre: Die Forschungen Carl Schmitts', *Jugend und Recht* 10 (1936), pp. 252–3.

Krockow, Christian von, *Die Entscheidung: Eine Untersuchung über Ernst Jünger, Carl Schmitt und Martin Heidegger*, Stuttgart, 1958.

Krupa, Hans, *Carl Schmitts Theorie des 'Politischen'*, Leipzig, 1937.

Kuhn, Helmut, 'Carl Schmitt, Der Begriff des Politischen', *Kantstudien* 38 (1933), pp. 190–6.

Kuhn, Helmut, *Sokrates: Ein Versuch über den Ursprung der Metaphysik*, Berlin, 1934.

Laak, Dirk van, *Gespräche in der Sicherheit des Schweigens: Carl Schmitt in der politischen Geistesgeschichte der frühen Bundesrepublik*, Berlin, 1993.

Landau, Peter, 'Die deutschen Juristen und der nationalsozialistische deutsche Juristentag in Leipzig 1933', *Zeitschrift für neuere Rechtsgeschichte* 16 (1994), pp. 373–90.

Landau, Peter, and Rieß, Rolf (eds), *Recht und Politik in Bayern zwischen Prinzregentenzeit und Nationalsozialismus: Die Erinnerungen von Philipp Loewenfeld*, Ebelsbach, 2004.

Larenz, Karl, *Rechts- und Staatsphilosophie der Gegenwart*, 2nd edn, Berlin, 1935.

Large, David Clay, *Berlin: Biographie einer Stadt*, Munich, 2002.

Leibholz, Gerhard, *Das Wesen der Repräsentation unter besonderer Berücksichtigung des Repräsentativsystems: Ein Beitrag zur allgemeinen Staats- und Verfassungslehre*, Berlin, 1929.

Leibholz, Gerhard, *Die Auflösung der liberalen Demokratie in Deutschland und das autoritäre Staatsbild*, Munich, 1933.

Lepsius, Oliver, *Die gegensatzaufhebende Begriffsbildung: Methodenentwicklungen in der Weimarer Republik und ihr Verhältnis zur Ideologisierung der Rechtswissenschaft im Nationalsozialismus*, Munich, 1994.

Lepsius, Oliver, 'Gibt es ein Staatsrecht im Nationalsozialismus?', *Zeitschrift für neuere Rechtsgeschichte* 26 (2004), pp. 102–16.

Linder, Christian, *Der Bahnhof von Finnentrop: Eine Reise ins Carl Schmitt Land*, Berlin, 2008.

Lösch, Anna-Maria, Gräfin von, *Der nackte Geist: Die Juristische Fakultät der Berliner Universität im Umbruch von 1933*, Tübingen, 1999.

Lokatis, Siegfried, *Hanseatische Verlagsanstalt: Politisches Buchmarketing im Dritten Reich*, Frankfurt, 1992.

Lokatis, Siegfried (ed.), 'Wilhelm Stapel und Carl Schmitt: Ein Briefwechsel', in *Schmittiana* 5 (1996), pp. 27–108.

Löwith, Karl (Hugo Fiala), 'Politischer Dezisionismus', *Internationale Zeitschrift für Theorie des Rechts* 9 (1935), pp. 101–23.

Löwith, Karl, *Weltgeschichte und Heilsgeschehen: Die theologischen Voraussetzungen der Geschichtsphilosophie*, Stuttgart, 1953.

Lübbe, Hermann, 'Carl Schmitt liberal rezipiert', in Helmut Quaritsch (ed.), *Complexio Oppositorum: Über Carl Schmitt*, Berlin, 1988, pp. 427–46.

Lübbe, Hermann, 'Politische Theologie als Theologie repolitisierter Religion', in Jacob Taubes (ed.), *Der Fürst dieser Welt: Carl Schmitt und die Folgen*, Munich, 1983, pp. 45–56.

Lukács, Georg, *Die Theorie des Romans: Ein geschichtsphilosophischer Versuch über die Formen der großen Epik*, Berlin, 1920.

McCormick, John P., *Carl Schmitt's Critique of Liberalism against Politics as Technology*, Cambridge, 1997.

Manemann, Jürgen, *Carl Schmitt und die Politische Theologie: Politischer Anti-Monotheismus*, Münster, 2002.

Mann, Thomas, *Diaries 1918–1939*, ed. Hermann Kesten, trans. Richard and Clara Winston, London, 1983.

Mann, Thomas, *Ein Briefwechsel*, Zurich, 1937.

Marschler, Thomas, *Kirchenrecht im Bannkreis Carl Schmitts: Hans Barion vor und nach 1945*, Bonn, 2004.

Maunz, Theodor, *Das Reich der spanischen Großmachtzeit*, Hamburg, 1944.

Maus, Ingeborg, *Bürgerliche Rechtstheorie und Faschismus: Zur sozialen Funktion und aktuellen Wirkung Carl Schmitts*, Munich, 1976.

Maus, Ingeborg, *Rechtstheorie und politische Theorie im Industriekapitalismus*, Munich, 1986.

Mehring, Reinhard (ed.), *Carl Schmitt: Der Begriff des Politischen: Ein kooperativer Kommentar*, Berlin, 2003.

Mehring, Reinhard, *Carl Schmitt zur Einführung*, 3rd edn, Hamburg, 2006.

Mehring, Reinhard, *Das 'Problem der Humanität': Thomas Manns politische Philosophie*, Paderborn, 2003.

Mehring, Reinhard, *Heideggers Überlieferungsgeschick: Eine dionysische Selbstinszenierung*, Würzburg, 1992.

Mehring, Reinhard, *Politische Philosophie*, Leipzig, 2005.

Mehring, Reinhard, *Thomas Mann: Künstler und Philosoph*, Munich, 2001.

Meier, Christian, *Die Entstehung des Politischen bei den Griechen*, Frankfurt, 1980.

Meier, Heinrich, *Carl Schmitt, Leo Strauss und 'Der Begriff des Politischen': Zu einem Dialog unter Abwesenden*, enlarged edn, Stuttgart, 1998.

Meier, Heinrich, *Die Lehre Carl Schmitts: Vier Kapitel zur Unterscheidung Politischer Theologie und Politischer Philosophie*, 3rd edn, Stuttgart, 2009.

Meyer, Martin, *Ende der Geschichte?*, Munich, 1993.

Michels, Eckard, *Das Deutsche Institut in Paris 1940–1944: Ein Beitrag zu den deutschfranzösischen Kulturbeziehungen und zur auswärtigen Kulturpolitik des Dritten Reiches*, Stuttgart, 1993.

Möllers, Christoph, *Der vermisste Leviathan: Staatstheorie in der Bundesrepublik*, Frankfurt, 2008.

Mommsen, Wolfgang, *Max Weber und die deutsche Politik 1890–1920*, Tübingen, 1959.

Montherlant, Henry de, *Erbarmen mit den Frauen*, Darmstadt, 1959.

Mouffe, Chantal (ed.), *The Challenge of Carl Schmitt*, London, 1999.

Mouffe, Chantal, *Über das Politische: Wider die kosmopolitische Illusion*, Frankfurt, 2007.

Müller, Jan Werner, *Ein gefährlicher Geist: Carl Schmitts Wirkung in Europa*, Darmstadt, 2007.

Müller-Gangloff, Erich, *Vorläufer des Antichrist*, Berlin, 1948.

Münkler, Herfried, *Der Wandel des Krieges: Von der Symmetrie zur Asymmetrie*, Weilerswist, 2006.

Münkler, Herfried, *Die Deutschen und ihre Mythen*, Berlin, 2009.

Münkler, Herfried, *Über den Krieg: Stationen der Kriegsgeschichte im Spiegel ihrer theoretischen Reflexion*, Weilerswist, 2002.

Murray, Kathleen, *Taine und die englische Romantik*, Munich, 1924.

Nachlass Carl Schmitt: Verzeichnis des Bestandes im Nordrhein-Westfälischen Hauptstaatsarchiv, ed. Dirk van Laak and Ingeborg Villinger, Siegburg, 1993.

Nagel, Rolf (ed.), 'Briefe von Ernst Robert Curtius an Carl Schmitt', *Archiv für das Studium der Neueren Sprachen und Literatur* 133 (1981), pp. 1–15.

Neumann, Franz, *Behemoth: The Structure and Practice of National Socialism*, New York, 1942.

Neumann, Volker, *Der Staat im Bürgerkrieg: Kontinuität und Wandlung des Staatsbegriffs in der politischen Theorie Carl Schmitts*, Frankfurt, 1980.

Neumann, Volker, 'Theologie als staatsrechtswissenschaftliches Argument: Hans Kelsen und Carl Schmitt', *Der Staat* 47 (2008), pp. 163–86.

Neuß, Wilhelm, *Die Anfänge des Christentums im Rheinlande*, Bonn, 1923.

Neuß, Wilhelm, *Die Kunst der alten Christen*, Augsburg, 1926.

Nichtweiß, Barbara, *Erik Peterson: Neue Sicht auf Leben und Werk*, Freiburg, 1992.

Nicoletti, Michele, *Trascendenza e potere: la teologia politica di Carl Schmitt*, Brescia, 1990.

Niekisch, Ernst, *Das Reich der niederen Dämonen*, Berlin, 1957.

Noack, Paul, *Carl Schmitt: Eine Biographie*, Berlin, 1993.

Nolte, Ernst, *Der Faschismus in seiner Epoche*, Munich, 1963.

Norden, Eduard, *Die Geburt des Kindes: Geschichte einer religiösen Idee*, Berlin, 1924.

Ottmann, Henning, *Geschichte des politischen Denkens*, Stuttgart, 2000–.

Ottmann, Henning, 'Politische Theologie als Herrschaftskritik und Herrschafts-relativierung', in Walther, Manfred (ed.), *Religion und Politik: Zu Theorie und Praxis des theologisch-politischen Komplexes*, Baden-Baden, 2004, pp. 73–83.

Otto, Martin, *Von der Eigenkirche zum Volkseigenen Betrieb: Erwin Jacobi (1884–1965)*, Tübingen, 2008.

Peterson, Erik, *Der Monotheismus als politisches Problem: Ein Beitrag zur Geschichte der politischen Theologie im Imperium Romanum*, Leipzig, 1935.

Peterson, Erik, 'Kaiser Augustus im Urteil des antiken Christentums', *Hochland* 30 (1933), pp. 289–99.

Peterson, Erik, *Theological Tractates*, ed. and trans. Michael J. Hollerich, Stanford, CA, 2011.

Peterson, Erik, *Theologische Traktate* (*Ausgewählte Schriften*, vol. 1), Würzburg, 1994.

Pichinot, Hans Rainer, *Die Akademie für Deutsches Recht: Aufbau und Entwicklung einer öffentlich-rechtlichen Körperschaft des Dritten Reiches*, Kiel, 1981.

Pinter, Stefan K., *Zwischen Anhängerschaft und Kritik: Der Rechtsphilosoph C. A. Emge im Nationalsozialismus*, Berlin, 1996.

Portinaro, Pier Paolo, *La crisi dello jus publicum Europaeum: saggio su Carl Schmitt*, Milan, 1982.

Preuß, Ulrich K., 'Vater der Verfassungsväter? Carl Schmitts Verfassungslehre und die verfassungspolitische Diskussion der Gegenwart', in *Politisches Denken: Jahrbuch 1993*, pp. 117–33.

Pringsheim, Fritz, 'Die Haltung der Freiburger Studenten in den Jahren 1933–1935', *Die Sammlung* 15 (1960), pp. 532–8.

Pyta, Wolfram, and Seiberth, Gabriel, 'Die Staatskrise der Weimarer Republik im Spiegel des Tagebuchs von Carl Schmitt', *Der Staat* 38 (1999), pp. 423–48, 594–610.

Quaritsch, Helmut (ed.), *Complexio Oppositorum: Über Carl Schmitt*, Berlin, 1988.

Quaritsch, Helmut, *Positionen und Begriffe Carl Schmitts*, Berlin, 1989.

Rauschning, Hermann, *Die Revolution des Nihilismus: Kulisse und Wirklichkeit im Dritten Reich*, Zurich, 1938.

Reck-Malleczewen, Fritz, *Bockelson: Geschichte eines Massenwahns*, Berlin, 1937.

Reichel, Peter, *Vergangenheitsbewältigung in Deutschland: Die Auseinandersetzung mit der Diktatur von 1945 bis heute*, Munich, 2001.

Renier, Ekkehart, and Waldhoff, Christian, 'Zu Leben und Werk Albert Hensels (1895–1933)', in *Albert Hensel, System des Familiensteuerrechts und andere Schriften*, Cologne, 2000, pp. 1–124.

Ritter, Gerhard, *Europa und die deutsche Frage: Betrachtungen über die geschichtliche Eigenart des deutschen Staatsdenkens*, Munich, 1948.

Ritter, Henning, *Die Eroberer: Denker des 20. Jahrhunderts*, Munich, 2008.

Rommen, Heinrich, *Die ewige Wiederkehr des Naturrechts*, Leipzig, 1936.

Rosenbaum, Eduard, *Das Gesicht Hamburgs*, Hamburg, 1927.

Rosenbaum, Eduard, *Der Vertrag von Versailles: Inhalt und Wirkung*, Leipzig, 1920.

Rosenstock, Eugen, *Die Europäischen Revolutionen: Volkscharaktere und Staatenbildung*, Jena 1931.

Rumpf, Helmut, *Carl Schmitt und Thomas Hobbes: Ideelle Beziehungen und aktuelle Bedeutung*, Berlin, 1972.

Runze-Schranz, Veronica, 'Dr. Franz Schranz und sein Siedlinghauser Kreis', in *Schmittiana* 3 (1991), pp. 63–88.

Rüthers, Bernd, *Carl Schmitt im Dritten Reich: Wissenschaft als Zeitgeist-Verstärkung?*, Munich, 1989.

Rüthers, Bernd, *Die unbegrenzte Auslegung: Zum Wandel der Privatrechtsordnung im Nationalsozialismus*, Tübingen, 1968.

Rüthers, Bernd, *Entartetes Recht: Rechtslehren und Kronjuristen im Dritten Reich*, Munich, 1988.

Schäfer, Herwig, *Juristische Lehre und Forschung an der Reichsuniversität Straßburg 1941–1944*, Tübingen, 1999.

Schenk, Dieter, *Hans Frank: Hitlers Kronjurist und Generalgouverneur*, Frankfurt, 2006.

Scheuerman, William, *Carl Schmitt: The End of Law*, Lanham, MD, 1999.

Scheuner, Ulrich, 'Die Vereinigung der Deutschen Staatsrechtslehrer in der Zeit der Weimarer Republik', *Archiv des öffentlichen Rechts* 97 (1972), pp. 349–74.

Scheuner, Ulrich, *Staatstheorie und Staatsrecht: Gesammelte Schriften*, Berlin, 1978.

Schickel, Joachim, *Gespräche mit Carl Schmitt*, Berlin, 1993.

Schieder, Wolfgang, 'Das italienische Experiment: Der Faschismus als Vorbild in der Krise der Weimarer Republik', *Historische Zeitschrift* 262 (1996), pp. 73–125.

Schindler, Alfred (ed.), *Monotheismus als politisches Problem? Erik Peterson und die Kritik der politischen Theologie*, Gütersloh, 1978.

Schlüter, Bernd, *Reichswissenschaft: Staatsrechtslehre, Staatstheorie und Wissenschaftspolitik im Deutschen Kaiserreich am Beispiel der Reichsuniversität Straßburg*, Frankfurt, 2004.

Schmidt, Jörg, *Otto Koellreutter 1883–1972: Sein Leben, sein Werk, seine Zeit*, Frankfurt, 1995.

Schmitt, Carl, '1907 Berlin', in *Schmittiana* 1 (1988), pp. 13–21.

Schmitt, Carl (ed.), *Berichte über die Lage und das Studium des öffentlichen Rechts*, Hamburg, 1935.

Schmitt, Carl, 'Der Schatten Gottes: Tolle Wirklichkeit und was ihr wollt' (provisional transcription) [diary entry, 30 April 1923; forthcoming publication 2014].

Schmitt, Carl, 'Der treue Zigeuner', in *Schmittiana* 7 (2001), pp. 20–7.

Schmitt, Carl, 'Gespräch mit Dieter Groh und Klaus Figge', in Piet Tommissen (ed.), *Over en in zake Carl Schmitt*, Brussels, 1975, pp. 89–109.

Schmitt, Carl, 'Gespräch mit Dieter Groh und Klaus Figge, 1971', von Dimitrios Kisoudis vorläufig transkribierte Langfassung des Radiogesprächs von 1971.

Schmitz, Arnold, *Das romantische Beethovenbild: Darstellung und Kritik*, Berlin, 1927.

Schmitz, Mathias, *Die Freund–Feind-Theorie Carl Schmitts: Entwurf und Entfaltung*, Cologne, 1965.

Schmoeckel, Mathias, *Die Großraumtheorie: Ein Beitrag zur Geschichte der Völkerrechtswissenschaft im Dritten Reich, insbesondere der Kriegszeit*, Berlin, 1994.

Schmoeckel, Mathias (ed.), *Die Juristen der Universität Bonn im 'Dritten Reich'*, Cologne, 2004.

Schneider, Hans, *Das Ermächtigungsgesetz vom 24. März 1933: Bericht über das Zustandekommen und die Anwendung des Gesetzes*, Bonn, 1961.

Schneider, Peter, *Ausnahmezustand und Norm: Eine Studie zur Rechtslehre von Carl Schmitt*, Stuttgart, 1957.

Schnur, Roman, *Die Ermächtigungsgesetze von Berlin 1933 und Vichy 1940 im Vergleich*, Tübingen, 1993.

Schnur, Roman, *Die französischen Juristen im konfessionellen Bürgerkrieg des 16. Jahrhunderts: Ein Beitrag zur Entstehungsgeschichte des modernen Staates*, Berlin, 1962.

Schnur, Roman, *Individualismus und Absolutismus: Zur politischen Theorie vor Thomas Hobbes (1600–1640)*, Berlin, 1963.

Schnur, Roman, *Vive la République oder Vive la France: Zur Krise der Demokratie in Frankreich 1939/1940*, Berlin, 1982.

Schollen, Franz (ed.), *Aus der Werkstatt der Justiz: Blätter zur Erinnerung an das 25 jährige Bestehen des Oberlandesgerichts Düsseldorf*, Anrath, 1931.

Schönberger, Christoph, *Das Parlament im Anstaltsstaat: Zur Theorie parlamentarischer Repräsentation in der Staatsrechtslehre des Kaiserreichs (1871–1918)*, Frankfurt, 1997.

Schönberger, Christoph, 'Die Verfassungsgerichtsbarkeit bei Carl Schmitt und Hans Kelsen: Gemeinsamkeiten und Schwachstellen', in Olivier Beaud and Pasquale Pasquino (eds), *Der Weimarer Streit um den Hüter der Verfassungsgerichtsbarkeit: Kelsen gegen Schmitt*, Paris, 2007, pp. 177–95.

Schroers, Rolf, *Der Partisan: Ein Beitrag zur politischen Anthropologie*, Cologne, 1961.

Schudnagies, Christian, *Hans Frank: Aufstieg und Fall des NS-Juristen und Generalgouverneurs*, Frankfurt, 1988.

Schütte, Christian, *Progressive Verwaltungsrechtswissenschaft auf konservativer Grundlage: Zur Verwaltungsrechtslehre Ernst Forsthoffs*, Berlin, 2006.

Schwab, George, *The Challenge of the Exception: An Introduction to the Political Ideas of Carl Schmitt between 1921 and 1936*, Berlin, 1970.

Seiberth, Gabriel, *Anwalt des Reiches: Carl Schmitt und der Prozess 'Preußen contra Reich' vor dem Staatsgerichtshof*, Berlin, 2001.

Sieg, Ulrich, *Jüdische Intellektuelle im Ersten Weltkrieg: Kriegserfahrungen, weltanschauliche Debatten und kulturelle Neuentwürfe*, Berlin, 2001.

Sinzheimer, Hugo, *Jüdische Klassiker der deutschen Rechtswissenschaft*, Amsterdam, 1938.

Smend, Rudolf, 'Die Vereinigung der deutschen Staatsrechtslehrer und der Richtungsstreit', in *Festschrift für Ulrich Scheuner zum 70. Geburtstag*, Berlin, 1973, pp. 575–89.

Smend, Rudolf, *Staatsrechtliche Abhandlungen und andere Aufsätze*, Berlin, 1955.

Sohm, Rudolph, *Kirchenrecht*, vol. 2: *Katholisches Kirchenrecht*, ed. Erwin Jacobi and Otto Mayer, Munich, 1923.

Söllner, Alfons, *Fluchtpunkte: Studien zur politischen Ideengeschichte des 20. Jahrhunderts*, Baden-Baden, 2006.

Sombart, Nicolaus, *Die deutschen Männer und ihre Feinde: Carl Schmitt – ein deutsches Schicksal zwischen Männerbund und Matriarchatsmythos*, Munich, 1991.

Sombart, Nicolaus, *Rendezvous mit dem Weltgeist: Heidelberger Reminiszenzen 1945–1951*, Frankfurt, 2000.

Sontheimer, Kurt, 'Carl Schmitt: Seine "Loyalität" gegenüber der Weimarer Verfassung', *Neue Politische Literatur* 3 (1958), pp. 758–70.

Staff, Ilse, *Staatsdenken im Italien des 20. Jahrhunderts: Ein Beitrag zur Carl Schmitt-Rezeption*, Baden-Baden, 1991.

Stammler, Rudolf, *The Theory of Justice*, trans. Isaac Husik, New York, 1969.

Stapel, Wilhelm, *Der christliche Staatsmann: Eine Theologie des Nationalismus*, Hamburg, 1932.

Steinbömer, Gustav, *Staat und Drama*, Berlin, 1932.

Steinlein, Andreas, *Die Form der Kriegserklärung: Eine völkerrechtliche Untersuchung*, Munich, 1917.

Sternberger, Dolf, *Die Politik und der Friede*, Frankfurt, 1986.

Sternberger, Dolf, *Drei Wurzeln der Politik*, Frankfurt, 1978.

Stier-Somlo, Fritz, 'Die zweite Tagung der Vereinigung der deutschen Staatsrechtslehrer', *Archiv des öffentlichen Rechts* 46 (1924), pp. 88–105.

Stolleis, Michael, *Der Methodenstreit der Weimarer Staatsrechtslehre – ein abgeschlossenes Kapitel der Wissenschaftsgeschichte?*, Stuttgart, 2001.

Stolleis, Michael, *Gemeinwohlformeln im nationalsozialistischen Recht*, Berlin, 1974.

Stolleis, Michael, *Geschichte des öffentlichen Rechts in Deutschland*, 3 vols, Munich, 1988–99.

Stolleis, Michael, *Recht im Unrecht: Studien zur Rechtsgeschichte des Nationalsozialismus*, Frankfurt, 1994.

Stolleis, Michael, 'Staatsbild und Staatswirklichkeit in Westdeutschland (1945–1960)', *Zeitschrift der Savigny-Stiftung für Rechtsgeschichte: Germanistische Abteilung* 124 (2007), pp. 223–45.

Taubes, Jacob, *Abendländische Eschatologie*, Zurich, 1947.

Taubes, Jacob, *Ad Carl Schmitt: Gegenstrebige Fügung*, Berlin, 1987.

Taubes, Jacob (ed.), *Der Fürst dieser Welt: Carl Schmitt und die Folgen*, Munich, 1983.

Taubes, Jacob, *Die Politische Theologie des Paulus*, ed. Aleida Assmann and Jan Assmann, Munich, 1993.

Taubes, Jacob, *Vom Kult zur Kultur: Bausteine zu einer Kritik der historischen Vernunft*, ed. Aleida Assmann and Jan Assmann, Munich, 1996.

Thiele, Ulrich, *Advokatorische Volkssouveränität: Carl Schmitts Konstruktion einer 'demokratischen' Diktaturtheorie im Kontext der Interpretation politischer Theorien der Aufklärung*, Berlin, 2003.

Tielke, Martin, *Der stille Bürgerkrieg: Ernst Jünger und Carl Schmitt im Dritten Reich*, Berlin, 2007.

Tilitzki, Christian, 'Carl Schmitt an der Handels-Hochschule Berlin 1928–1933', in *Schmittiana* 4 (1994), pp. 157–202.

Tilitzki, Christian, 'Carl Schmitt – Staatsrechtler in Berlin: Einblicke in seinen Wirkungskreis anhand der Fakultätsakten 1934–1944', in *Siebte Etappe*, ed. Heinz-Theo Homann, Bonn, 1991, pp. 62–117.

Tilitzki, Christian, *Die deutsche Universitätsphilosophie in der Weimarer Republik und im Dritten Reich*, Berlin, 2002.

Tilitzki, Christian, 'Vortragsreisen Carl Schmitts während des Zweiten Weltkriegs', in *Schmittiana* 6 (1998), pp. 191–270.

Tommissen, Piet, *In Sachen Carl Schmitt*, Vienna, 1987.

Tommissen, Piet (ed.), *Over en in zake Carl Schmitt*, Brussels, 1975.

Tommissen, Piet (ed.), *Schmittiana*, 8 vols, Brussels and Berlin, 1988–2003.

Ule, Carl Hermann, 'Zum Begriff des Kronjuristen', *Deutsches Verwaltungsblatt* 108 (1993), pp. 77–82.

Vesting, Thomas, *Politische Einheitsbildung und technische Realisation: Über die Expansion der Technik und die Grenzen der Demokratie*, Baden-Baden, 1990.

Viesel, Hansjörg (ed.), *Jawohl, der Schmitt: Zehn Briefe aus Plettenberg*, Berlin, 1988.

Villinger, Ingeborg, *Carl Schmitts Kulturkritik der Moderne: Text, Kommentar und Analyse der 'Schattenrisse' des Johannes Negelinus*, Berlin, 1995.

Villinger, Ingeborg (ed.), *Verortung des Politischen: Carl Schmitt in Plettenberg*, Hagen, 1990.

Voigt, Rüdiger (ed.), *Der Staat des Dezisionismus: Carl Schmitt in der internationalen Debatte*, Baden-Baden, 2007.

Voigt, Rüdiger (ed.), *Großraum-Denken: Carl Schmitts Kategorie der Großraumordnung*, Stuttgart, 2008.

Voigt, Rüdiger (ed.), *Mythos Staat: Carl Schmitts Staatsverständnis*, Baden-Baden, 2001.

Wacker, Bernd (ed.), *Die eigentlich katholische Verschärfung : Konfession, Theologie und Politik im Werk Carl Schmitts*, Munich, 1994.

Warnach, Walter (ed.), *Georges Bernanos, Vorhut der Christenheit: Eine Auswahl aus den polemischen Schriften*, Düsseldorf, 1950.

Weber, Max, *Gesammelte Aufsätze zur Religionssoziologie*, 3 vols, Tübingen 1920–1.

Weber, Max, *Gesammelte politische Schriften*, Munich, 1921.

Weber, Max, *The Vocation Lectures* ('Science as a Vocation', 'Politics as a Vocation'), trans. Rodney Livingstone, Indianapolis and Cambridge, 2004.

Weininger, Otto, *Geschlecht und Charakter: Eine prinzipielle Untersuchung*, 26th edn, Vienna, 1925.

Weiß, Konrad, *Der christliche Epimetheus*, Berlin, 1933.

Winckelmann, Johannes, *Gesellschaft und Staat in der verstehenden Soziologie Max Webers*, Berlin, 1957.

Winkler, Heinrich August, *Auf ewig in Hitlers Schatten? Über die Deutschen und ihre Geschichte*, Munich, 2007.

Winkler, Heinrich August, *Der lange Weg nach Westen: Deutsche Geschichte vom Ende des Alten Reiches bis zur Wiedervereinigung*, 2 vols, Munich, 2000; Eng. trans. as *Germany: The Long Road West*, trans. Alexander J. Sager, vol. 1: *1789–1933*, Oxford, 2006, vol. 2: *1933–1990*, Oxford, 2007.

Winkler, Heinrich August, *Streitfragen der deutschen Geschichte: Essays zum 19. und 20. Jahrhundert*, Munich, 1997.

Winkler, Heinrich August, *Weimar 1918–1933: Die Geschichte der ersten deutschen Demokratie*, Munich, 1993.

Wohlgemuth, Heinrich, *Das Wesen des Politischen in der heutigen neoromantischen Staatslehre*, Emmendingen, 1933.

Zander, Herbert, *Gründung der Handelshochschulen im deutschen Kaiserreich (1898–1919)*, Cologne, 2004.

Zeck, Mario, *Das Schwarze Korps: Geschichte und Gestalt des Organs der Reichsführung SS*, Tübingen, 2002.

Zschaler, Frank, *Vom Heilig-Geist-Spital zur Wirtschaftswissenschaftlichen Fakultät: 110 Jahre Staatswissenschaftlich-Statistisches Seminar an der vormals königlichen Friedrich-Wilhelms-Universität: 90 Jahre Handels-Hochschule Berlin*, Berlin, 1997.

Photographic Acknowledgements

Akg-images – Archiv für Kunst und Geschichte, Berlin: p. 85 (photographer: Abraham Pisarek), p. 151
Bildarchiv Preußischer Kulturbesitz, Berlin: p. 64 (Archive Heinrich Hoffmann)
Bundesarchiv, Berlin: p. 337 (SSO, Höhn, R. Dr.; 29.07.1904), p. 387 (BA – formerly BDC – NSDAP-Zentralkartei [central register of the NSDAP]
Bundesarchiv, Koblenz: p. 382 (Bild [photograph] 183-H27728 – Fotograf [photographer]: Schäfer, 1934)
Goethe University Frankfurt am Main – Universitätsarchiv: p. 264 (UAF Abt. 854, no. 552)
Humboldt University zu Berlin, Universitätsbibliothek, Berlin: pp. 124, 327
Landesarchiv Nordrhein-Westfalen, Abteilung Rheinland, Standort Düsseldorf: pp. 304, 415
Barbara Nichtweiß, Mainz: p. 161 (reproduction of privately owned photograph)
Ronald Pfaff: Attendorn: p. 534
Carl Schmitt-Förderverein Plettenberg e.V., in the Stadtarchiv, Plettenberg: pp. 4(a), 10, 52, 150, 277, 451, 484, 502; 4(b), 8, 205, 453, 536 (Archiv Ernst Hüsmert); p. 530 (Privatarchiv Gerd Giesler)
Stiftung Deutsches Historisches Museum, Berlin: p. 384
ullstein bild, Berlin: pp. 13, 36, 79 (photographer: Emil Bieber), pp. 122, 267, 281, 298

All other illustrations were taken from the following books and newspapers:
Briefwechsel Gretha Jünger/Carl Schmitt (1934–1953), ed. Ingeborg Villinger and Alexander Jaser, Berlin: Akademie Verlag, 2007, pp. 242, 378
Der Ring: Konservative Wochenschrift, vol. 12, Berlin (12 March 1934): p. 178
Die Korporation der Kaufmannschaft von Berlin: Festschrift zum hundertjährigen Jubiläum am 2. März 1920, Berlin, 1920: p. 202
Richard Hamann (ed.), *Das Straßburger Münster und seine Bildwerke*, 3rd edn, Berlin: Deutscher Kunstverlag, 1942: p. 16
Hamburger Woche, vol. 9 (15 October 1914): p. 15
Sydney Morning Herald (12 June 1922): p. 113

Index

Note: Works by Carl Schmitt (CS) appear directly under their title. Page numbers in *italic* refer to illustrations.